THE BRITISH YEAR BOOK OF INTERNATIONAL LAW

THE BRITISH YEAR BOOK OF INTERNATIONAL LAW

2009

EIGHTIETH YEAR OF ISSUE

OXFORD
AT THE CLARENDON PRESS
2010

This book has been printed digitally and produced in a standard specification in order to ensure its continuing availability

OXFORD
UNIVERSITY PRESS

Great Clarendon Street, Oxford OX2 6DP
United Kingdom

Oxford University Press is a department of the University of Oxford. It furthers the University's objective of excellence in research, scholarship, and education by publishing worldwide. Oxford is a registered trade mark of Oxford University Press in the UK and in certain other countries

First published 2010
Reprinted 2012

British Library Cataloguing in Publication Data
Data available

Library of Congress Cataloging in Publication Data
Data available

ISBN 978-0-19-959702-4

Editorial Communications should be addressed as follows:

Articles and Notes:

PROFESSOR JAMES CRAWFORD
Lauterpacht Centre for International Law,
5 Cranmer Road, Cambridge, CB3 9BL.
JRC1000@cam.ac.uk

Books for Review:

PROFESSOR J. CRAIG BARKER
Sussex Law School, University of Sussex,
Brighton, East Sussex BN1 9QQ.
J.C.Barker@sussex.ac.uk

The Editors and members of the Editorial Committee do not make themselves in any way responsible for the views expressed by contributors.

The British Year Book of International Law is indexed in *Current Law Index*, published by Information Access Company, and in *Legal Journals Index*, published by Legal Information Resources Limited.

Sir Ian Brownlie

As this volume was going to press, news came of the death of Professor Sir Ian Brownlie CBE, QC, FBA (1932–2010), Chichele Professor of Public International Law, University of Oxford (1980–1999) and co-editor of this Year Book from 1974 (vol. 47) to 1998 (vol. 69). A notice of his contribution to international law will appear in the next volume.

CONTENTS

LIST OF ABBREVIATIONS

AC	Appellate Court
AIDS	Acquired Immune Deficiency Syndrome
AIHRC	Afghan Independent Human Rights Commission
AMISOM	African Union Mission in Somalia
ASEAN	Association of South East Asian Nations
ASI	Agreement on Succession Issues
AU	African Union
AVR	Assisted Voluntary Return
BAS	British Antarctic Survey
BBC	British Broadcasting Company
BCG	British Coal Gasification
BCLC	Butterworths' Company Law Cases
BEE	Black Economic Empowerment
BG	British Gas
BGTW	British Gibraltar Territorial Waters
BIOT	British Indian Ocean Territory
BIT	Bilateral Investment Treaty
BTWC	Biological and Toxin Weapons Convention
BYIL	*British Year Book of International Law*
CAT	Convention against Torture
CBE	Commander of the Order of the British Empire
CBMs	Confidence Building Measures
CCAMLR	Commission for the Conservation of Antarctic Marine Living Resources
CDM	Clean Development Mechanism
CEDAW	Convention on the Elimination of All Forms of Discrimination against Women
CFATF	Caribbean Financial Action Task Force
CFSP	Common Foreign and Security Policy
CHOGM	Commonwealth Heads of Government Meeting
CITES	Convention on International Trade in Endangered Species of Wild Fauna and Flora
CJ	Chief Justice
CJA	Criminal Justice Act
CLC	Civil Law Cases
CLCS	Commission on the Limits of the Continental Shelf
CMAG	Commonwealth Ministerial Action Group
COP	Conference of the Parties
CPA	Coalition Provisional Authority (Iraq)
CPA	Comprehensive Peace Agreement (Sudan)

CPR	Civil Procedure Rules
CPS	Crown Prosecution Service
CR	Court Recordings
CSDP	Common Security and Defence Policy
CTBT	Comprehensive Nuclear Test Ban Treaty
CWC	Chemical Weapons Convention
DCF	Discounted Cash Flow
DDA	Disability Discrimination Act
DEA	*diplôme d'études approfondies*
DECC	Department of Energy and Climate Change
DEFRA	Department for Environmental, Food and Rural Affairs
DFID	Department for International Development
DPO	Disabled Peoples Organisation
DPP	Director of Public Prosecutions
DPRK	Democratic People's Republic of Korea
DWP	Department for Work and Pensions
EC	European Community
ECO	Export Control Organisation
ECHR	European Convention on Human Rights
ECRA	European Community Readmission Agreements
ECJ	European Court of Justice
ECOSOC	United Nations Economic and Social Council
ECT	Energy Charter Treaty
ECtHR	European Court of Human Rights
EEA	European Economic Area
EEC	European Economic Community
EEZ	Exclusive Economic Zone
EFTA	European Free Trade Association
EHRR	European Human Rights Reports
EIA	Environmental Impact Assessment
EITI	Extractive Industry Transparency Initiative
ELR	Exceptional Leave to Remain
EPA	Economic Partnership Agreement
ETS	European Treaty Series
EU	European Union
EUECJ	Court of Justice of the European Communities
EWCA	England and Wales Court of Appeal
EWHC	England and Wales High Court
FAC	Foreign Affairs Committee
FARDC	*Forces Armées de la République Démocratique du Congo*
FATF	Financial Action Task Force
FBA	Fellow of the British Academy
FCO	Foreign and Commonwealth Office
FDI	Foreign Direct Investment
FIC	Foreign Investment Commission

FLR	Family Law Reports
FRY	Federal Republic of Yugoslavia
FSA	Financial Services Authority
FTA	Free Trade Agreement
G8	Group of Eight (France, Germany, Italy, Japan, UK, US, Canada, Russia)
GA	General Assembly (of the United Nations)
GATT	General Agreement on Tariffs and Trade
GHG	Greenhouse Gas
GNI	Gross National Income
GSGSSI	Government of South Georgia and the South Sandwich Islands
GSP	Generalised System of Preferences
HC	High Court
HC	House of Commons
HIV	Human Immunodeficiency Virus
HL	House of Lords
HM	Her Majesty
HMG	Her Majesty's Government
HMS	Her Majesty's Ship
HRA	Human Rights Act
HRC	Human Rights Committee
IACtHR	Inter-American Court of Human Rights
IAEA	International Atomic Energy Agency
ICAO	International Civil Aviation Organization
ICC	International Chamber of Commerce
ICC	International Criminal Court
ICCAT	International Commission for the Conservation of Atlantic Tuna
ICCPR	International Covenant on Civil and Political Rights
ICED	International Convention for the Protection of All Persons from Enforced Disappearance
ICESCR	International Covenant on Economic, Social and Cultural Rights
ICJ	International Court of Justice
ICRC	International Committee of the Red Cross
ICRW	International Convention for the Regulation of Whaling
ICSID	International Centre for the Settlement of Investment Disputes
ICTR	International Criminal Tribunal for Rwanda
ICTY	International Criminal Tribunal for former Yugoslavia
IDP	Internally Displaced Person
IEC	Israel Electricity Company
IEHC	The High Court of Ireland
IFC	International Financial Corporation

IFCAs	In-shore Fishery and Conservation Areas
IGN	Institut géographique national
IHT	Iraqi High Tribunal
ILC	International Law Commission
ILM	International Legal Materials
ILO	International Labour Organization
ILR	International Law Reports
IMF	International Monetary Fund
INGO	International Non-Governmental Organization
IOM	International Organization for Migration
IPCC	Intergovernmental Panel on Climate Change
IRA	Irish Republican Army
IRGC	Iranian Revolutionary Guards Corps
ISAF	International Security Assistance Force
ISC	Intelligence and Security Committee
IT	International Tribunal
IT	Information Technology
ITLOS	International Tribunal for the Law of the Sea
IWC	International Whaling Commission
JCHR	Joint Committee on Human Rights
JHA	Justice and Home Affairs
KB	King's Bench
KCMG	Knight Commander of the Order of St Michael and St George
LCIA	London Court of International Arbitration
LTTE	Liberation of Tigers Tamil Eelam
LJ	Lord Justice
LJJ	Lords Justices
LLB	Bachelor of Laws
LLD	Doctor of Laws
LLM	Master of Laws
LLP	Limited Liability Partnership
LMCLQ	Lloyd's Maritime and Commercial Law Quarterly
LN	League of Nations
LNOJ	League of Nations Official Journal
LRTAP	Long-Range Transboundary Air Pollution
LSE	London School of Economics and Political Science
MANPADS	Man portable air defence systems
MARPOL	International Convention for the Prevention of Pollution from Ships
MDGs	Millennium Development Goals
MEK	Mujahedin-e Khalq
MFN	Most Favoured Nation
MLA	Mutual Legal Assistance
MLC	*Mouvement de Libération du Congo*

MNF	Multi-National Force
MNF-I	Multi-National Force Iraq
MoD	Ministry of Defence
MoI	Ministry of Interior (Iraq)
MoJ	Ministry of Justice (Iraq)
MOHC	Met Office Hadley Centre
MONUC	United Nations Organization Mission in the Democratic Republic of the Congo
MoU	Memorandum of Understanding
MP	Member of Parliament
MR	Master of the Rolls
MTBE	Methyl Tertiary-Butyl Ether
MTCR	Missile Technology Control Regime
NAFTA	North American Free Trade Agreement
NATO	North Atlantic Treaty Organization
NCPs	National Contact Points
NGO	Non-Governmental Organization
NHS	National Health Service
NL	The Netherlands
NPT	Treaty on the Non-Proliferation of Nuclear Weapons
NSG	Nuclear Suppliers Group
NSIDC	National Snow and Ice Data Centre
NSWLR	New South Wales Law Reports
OAS	Organization of American States
OAU	Organization of African Unity
OECD	Organization for Economic Co-operation and Development
OJ	Official Journal
OPCAT	Optional Protocol to the United Nations Convention Against Torture
OPCW	Organization for the Prohibition of Chemical Weapons
OPT	Occupied Palestinian Territories
OSCE	Organization for Security and Co-operation in Europe
OSPAR	Oslo and Paris Conventions for the Protection of the Marine Environment of the North-East Atlantic
OT	Overseas Territories
OUP	Oxford University Press
PACE	Police and Criminal Evidence (Act)
PCA	Permanent Court of Arbitration
PCIJ	Permanent Court of International Justice
PII	Public Interest Immunity
PKK	Kurdistan Workers Party
PMSCs	Private Military and Security Companies
PMRA	Pesticide Management Regulatory Agency
POMI	People's Mujahideen of Iran

PTA	Prisoner Transfer Agreement
QB	Queen's Bench
QBD	Queen's Bench Division
QC	Queen's Counsel
QF	Qods Force
R2P	Responsibility to Protect
RAF	Royal Air Force
RIAA	Reports of International Arbitral Awards
SBIRS	Space-Based Infrared System
SC	Security Council (of the United Nations)
SCC	Stockholm Chamber of Commerce
SCE	Stop Child Executions
SCR	Security Council Resolution
SFRY	Socialist Federal Republic of Yugoslavia
SI	Statutory Instrument
SIA	State Immunity Act
SIAC	Special Immigration Appeals Commission
SOFA	Status of Forces Agreement
SRSG	Special Representative of the Secretary-General
SUA	Suppression of Unlawful Acts Against the Safety of Maritime Navigation Protocol
TAC	Total Allowable Catch
TCI	Turks and Caicos Islands
TFG	Transitional Federal Government
TRNC	Turkish Republic of Northern Cyprus
UPDF	Uganda Peoples' Defence Force
UPR	Universal Periodic Review
UK	United Kingdom
UKHL	United Kingdom House of Lords
UKMIL	United Kingdom Materials on International Law
UKSC	United Kingdom Supreme Court
UKSIAC	United Kingdom Special Immigration Appeals Commission
UKTS	United Kingdom Treaty Series
UN	United Nations
UNAMID	African Union—United Nations Mission in Darfur
UNCAT	United Nations Convention against Torture
UNCIO	United Nations Conference on International Organization Official Records
UNCITRAL	United Nations Commission on International Trade Law
UNCLOS	United Nations Convention on the Law of the Sea
UNEPFI	United Nations Environmental Programme Finance Initiative

UNESCO	United Nations Educational, Scientific and Cultural Organization
UNFCCC	United Nations Framework Convention on Climate Change
UNGA	United Nations General Assembly
UNHCR	United Nations High Commissioner for Refugees
UNICEF	United Nations Children's Fund
UNIFIL	United Nations Interim Force in Lebanon
UNOMIG	UN Observer Mission in Georgia
UKPC	United Kingdom Privy Council
UNRIAA	United Nations Reports of International Arbitral Awards
UNSCOM	United Nations Special Commission
UNSCR	United Nations Security Council Resolution
UNTS	United Nations Treaty Series
US	United States
USA	United States of America
VCLT	Vienna Convention on the Law of Treaties
VERTIC	Verification Research, Training and Information Centre
VRS	*Vojska Republike Srpske* (the army of the Republika Srpska)
W	Written Answers
WH	Westminster Hall
WHA	World Health Assembly
WHO	World Health Organization
WMD	Weapon of Mass Destruction
WLR	Weekly Law Reports
WPC	Woman Police Constable
WS	Written Statements
WTO	World Trade Organization

Derek William Bowett was born on 20 April 1927 and was brought up near Manchester. He became a chorister at Manchester Cathedral, where the Choir School taught him to sing but—he said—little else. His career as Head Foundationer was cut short, first by evacuation of the Choir School after war broke out, then, after the School's return to base, by the bombing of the Cathedral in December 1940. He then went to William Hulme's School, paying his fees out of his head chorister's earnings.

Anticipating his 18th birthday, he chose the Navy as the only branch in which—given the imminent defeat of Germany—he was likely to see any action. Japan having been bombed into early submission, he never went to the Far East but spent the next few years in mine clearance work in the North Sea and the Mediterranean. In October 1946 the destroyers *Saumarez* and *Volage* were severely damaged by mines while transiting the North Corfu Channel. Derek Bowett was on board one of the ships charged with towing them to Malta for repairs; during the passage the *Saumarez* had to be sunk. The mining led to the first case before the new International Court of Justice, bringing together two areas of law—use of force and law of the sea—on which he was to become a leading authority.[4] It is worth stressing that Bowett was among the last generation of international lawyers to have experienced the impact of and seen active service in (or in his case, just after) a general war. For us now, wars are *local* difficulties (albeit sometimes large ones)—what is more, they are distant and impersonal difficulties.

After demobilization, he went up to Downing College, Cambridge, to read law under the accelerated post-war system. He got a first, but later claimed to have done so only because no one had told him just how much he needed to do to get a safe second—information rarely withheld from students these days. But this first brought him to the attention of Hersch Lauterpacht, the seventh Whewell Professor of International Law. It was Hersch Lauterpacht who suggested that Bowett stay on for a further year's graduate study in what was then the LLB, now the LLM. There he won the Whewell Scholarship, this time (the Scholarship being worth £150) by deliberate design.[5] While at Downing he represented the University against Oxford at lacrosse.

His first job was a university lectureship in law at Manchester University. There he shared a house with three young women, including a statuesque blonde with a sharp sense of humour. Derek and Betty were married in 1953.

He wrote his PhD while holding the lectureship and helping to bring up a young family—a good example of his capacity for organizing his time. The thesis was published under the title *Self-defence in International*

[4] See *Corfu Channel case (United Kingdom v Albania)*, [1949] ICJ Rep 1949, 4.

[5] The Prize was awarded for strong performance in three international law subjects plus a special paper. It still exists: *Statutes and Ordinances of the University of Cambridge 2009*, 945.

Law by Manchester University Press in 1958. It was almost wholly unsupervised. He says he saw his supervisor once, and gaining nothing from their interchange saw no need for further meetings. The book is still cited on the vexed subject of self-defence, anticipatory and other: he saw self-defence as a broad inherent right of States, a right having strong continuity with pre-Charter international law.[6] That view was opposed in 1963 by a young Oxford don, Ian Brownlie, who saw the Charter much more as a new beginning to this old problem.[7] Bowett and Brownlie, having started by sharing opposed theses, would come to work opposite each other as international law professors of the two Universities, as opponents before the International Court, and as co-editors of this Year Book, that far from titular burden of the two titular chairs. But in 1958 that was some time away.

Bowett's time at Manchester was interrupted by two years in the UN Codification Division in New York. There he worked as a staff lawyer for the International Law Commission, of which he would 30 years later become a member. The wheels of international codification grind, if not fine then exceedingly slow: several of the topics on the Commission's agenda in 1958 were still there when he was elected a member in 1992. It was a sort of *Bleak House* of codification!

In 1960 he returned to Cambridge as a University Lecturer, becoming a fellow of Queens' College. Here he maintained an active interest in sport, playing for the College rugby team on occasion.

In 1964 he was asked by the newly-independent Government of Somalia to advise it on its territorial disputes with Ethiopia and Kenya. This was his first international law brief. On arrival in Mogadishu he was immediately asked to draft a diplomatic note closing the British Embassy: this on the basis that HMG were refusing to give effect to a plebiscite in the Northern Frontier District of Kenya, which had voted by a large majority to reunite with Somalia. Lacking experience in rupturing diplomatic relations, he asked to see the standard work, *Satow's Guide to Diplomatic Practice*. But the Somali Foreign Ministry had no books of any kind, and he was told to borrow it from the British Embassy. The book was duly returned, with a note of thanks and another, more formal, note giving the Ambassador four days to leave. It seems to have been a case of *persona non grata sed liber gratus*.

As at Manchester so at Cambridge, his career was punctuated by a further period of international public service. He spent two years, from 1966 to 1968, in Beirut as Legal Adviser to the United Nations Relief and Works Agency for Palestinian Refugees (UNRWA). There he experienced, from a distance, the Six Day War and, much more directly, its effects in

[6] D Bowett, *Self-Defense in International Law* (University of Manchester Press, Manchester, 1958) 182–200.

[7] I Brownlie, *International Law and the Use of Force by States* (Clarendon Press, Oxford, 1963) 107–123.

terms of the great increase in the number of refugees falling under UNRWA's remit. It coloured his attitude to the Middle East conflict thereafter: his rooms at Queens' had on the walls photos of some of those refugees. In later years he successfully represented Egypt against Israel in a significant territorial dispute, the only time Israel has appeared before an international tribunal.[8]

When Sir Arthur Armitage left for Manchester in 1970, Bowett was elected, at the age of 43, to succeed him as President of Queens'—an office in those days tenable until the retiring age. He proved a popular choice. He, Betty and their still young family enjoyed living in the Lodge and did much entertaining of fellows, students and visitors. A dedicated fisherman, he could sometimes be found in the early morning casting his line into the Cam from the river steps of the Lodge, or even, conveniently, from the kitchen window. In the manner of the *Compleat Angler* he claims to have caught roach, pike, perch and bream; though Lady Bowett does not recall that he caught anything.

The Presidency came to him perhaps too soon for his own convenience; he was immediately involved in the time-consuming problems of a new building (the Cripps Building) and the accompanying college appeal. The words 'appeal' and 'Cripps Building' are not uniformly linked in Cambridge lore—but the appeal was a success, the building was built, and it incorporates the Bowett Room, appropriately.

In 1981, the eighth Whewell Professor, Robert Jennings, retired and was forthwith elected to the International Court. In his place, Bowett took the Whewell Chair. But he found it increasingly difficult to combine his academic and professional activities with the Presidency of Queens', and in 1982 he stepped down after 12 years as President. He held the Whewell Chair until taking early retirement from that too, in 1991.

During these years he gained a distinguished reputation as an international lawyer, and managed to combine academic study with considerable practical experience. Apart from *Self-Defense in International Law* (1958), another pioneer piece of research appeared in a large volume on *United Nations Forces*, published in 1964. Though ostensibly produced by a committee with Bowett as reporter, it was, as Lord McNair made clear in his Introduction, almost entirely Bowett's work.[9] His text on international organizations was first published in 1962: it was the first general book in English in the field and made this subject a distinct field of international law. He took it through four editions; two further editions have since appeared, edited by Philippe Sands and Pierre Klein.[10] Though the

[8] *Boundary Dispute Concerning the Taba Area (Israel/Egypt)*, Award of 29 September 1988, (1988) 27 ILM 1421; cf also D Bowett, 'The Taba Award of 29 September 1988', (1989) 23 *Israel Law Review* 429.

[9] D Bowett, G Barton, H Carnegie, A McNair, *United Nations Forces: A Legal Study of United Nations Practice* (Stevens & Sons, London, 1964) v–xiii.

[10] D Bowett, P Sands & P Klein, *Bowett's Law of International Institutions* (6th edn, Sweet & Maxwell, London, 2009).

subject is vastly bigger and the coverage correspondingly enlarged, in their editions one can still see the structure and descriptive and analytical focus of the original book. He became, through practice, an expert in the law of the sea and published a number of pieces, including a book on *The Legal Regime of Islands in International Law*, still a vexed issue.[11]

His teaching was characterised by clear, direct and systematic exposition. He was of course one of a group of significant teachers at Cambridge—including Robert Jennings, Clive Parry, Elihu Lauterpacht, and later Philip Allott, Christopher Greenwood, Vaughan Lowe, John Collier, John and Cherry Hopkins, Geoffrey Marston... His humour and lack of self-importance—characterized by one former student as being reflected in a permanently mischievous twinkle of the eye—made him a popular teacher. He was a careful and much appreciated doctoral supervisor—especially so by foreign students to whom he devoted much time. For those he became close to, he inspired a lifelong loyalty.

But in latter years he was above all a forceful, utterly lucid advocate in international law cases, both in arbitrations and before the International Court, where he appeared on numerous occasions.[12] He had the great advocate's ability to simplify and distil without distorting, reducing the case to carefully chosen essentials. But he also had a strong strategic sense—and a capacity to improvise, as when he fought a series of major expropriation cases, basing himself entirely on documents produced by the expropriated Claimants; his own client, the Islamic Republic of Iran, could produce no documents whatever. He belonged to the generation of international lawyers—not a large group—who saw an often speculative, peripheral subject transformed and greatly enlarged, and made to apply to new problems—a subject to an increasing extent influenced by case-law and precedent. By contrast, when Henry Maine, the second Whewell Professor, published his Tripos lectures on international law in 1888, he cited only two cases-both, in his view, wrongly decided![13] Unwittingly perhaps, Bowett played a leading role among the generation that brought international law to a wider audience.

He served a term as British member of the International Law Commission from 1991 to 1996. There his interventions combined wit, brevity and experience to a degree unknown in that august and often verbose body. A sample Bowett intervention will give the flavour. After two lengthy speeches in French expounding and praising the problematic notion of international crimes of States, Bowett is reported, in the third person of the Commission's Yearbook, as follows:

[11] D Bowett, *The Legal Regime of Islands in International Law* (Dobbs Ferry, Oceana Publications, 1979).

[12] A list of his major cases appears at <http://www.squire.law.cam.ac.uk/eminent_scholars/derek_bowett_international_litigation.php>(last accessed 26 August 2010).

[13] H Maine, *International Law* (2nd edn, John Murray, London, 1915) 39 (*R. v Keyn*), 216 (*Alabama Claims*).

> The problem of international crimes fell into three parts . . . He was apprehensive that the [Commission] might be proposing to go straight to the third of these parts without dealing with the first or second. He had little enthusiasm for dealing with the consequences of a concept that could be neither defined nor applied.[14]

It took less than two minutes but negated all that had gone before.

On stepping down from the Commission he was knighted for service to international law. The citation might have added—for commendable brevity of words—in that service.

To his regret he was not nominated to succeed Sir Robert Jennings as British judge on the International Court. But he had a real influence on the Court, not only through his advocacy but also through his teaching. Even today, despite the much greater diffusion of international law teaching around the world, five of the 15 current judges of the Court studied in Cambridge. He was influential in some of his criticisms of the Court's procedure, participating with Arthur Watts and others in a 1995 study which irritated some members of the Court but which (perhaps for that reason) helped pave the way for significant later reforms.[15]

He saw international law as essentially a practical subject, a profession as much as a discipline, an extension of ordinary legal technique into a domain of human activity that needed it. With his professional involvement, several States were brought in from the cold. He was not at all a theorist—he referred to a long theoretical essay by a colleague as 'a sure cure for insomnia'. But on his own terrain he was a master, grasping the legal field as a whole and contributing to the development of many departments of it.

In his last years he suffered from a long and debilitating illness. But we should remember him in his pomp—though 'pomp' is hardly the word for such a down-to-earth, practical and unaffected man. I remember him, white hair flowing, in pursuit of a point of law or fact, crisp sentences making his case and at the same time destroying his opponent's. Above all, there was his laugh, opening up his face, shedding light on the subject under discussion but also putting it into perspective.

JAMES CRAWFORD

[14] 2348th mtg, 2 June 1994: *Yearbook of the International Law Commission* 1994 Vol I, 137 (para 39). Cf D W Bowett, 'Crimes of State and the 1996 Report of the International Law Commission on State Responsibility', (1998) 9 *European Journal of International Law* 163.

[15] D Bowett & others in J P Gardner and Ch Wickramasinghe (eds), *The International Court of Justice: Process, Practice and Procedure* (British Institute of International and Comparative Law, London, 1997) 1–20.

Writings of D.W. Bowett

'Law Reform and Occupier's Liability' (1956) 19 *The Modern Law Review* 172–184
'International Law Opinions' (1957) 4 *Society of Public Teachers of Law* 36–40
Self-Defense in International Law (University of Manchester Press, Manchester, 1958)
'Decisions of British Courts during 1959–60 involving Questions of Public or Private International Law' (1960) 36 *BYIL* 398–408
'The Second United Nations Conference on the Law of the Sea' (1960) 9 *International and Comparative Law Quarterly* 415–435
'Decisions of British Courts during 1960–1 involving Questions of Public or Private International Law', (1961) 37 *BYIL* 413–557
'Decisions of British Courts during 1961–1962 involving Questions of Public or Private International law', (1962) 38 *BYIL* 472–483
'Decisions of British Courts during 1962–1963 involving Questions of Public or Private International Law', (1963) 39 *BYIL* 473–474
Law of International Institutions (1st–3rd edns, Stevens & Sons, London 1963; 4th edn Sweet & Maxwell, London, 1982) 431 pp
'Decisions of British Courts during 1963–1964 involving Questions of Public or Private International Law', (1964) 40 *BYIL* 372
United Nations Forces: A Legal Study of United Nations Practice (Stevens & Sons, London, 1964) 576 pp
The Law of the Sea (Manchester University Press, Manchester, 1967) 117 pp
The Search for Peace (Routledge & Kegan Paul, London, 1972) 236 pp
'The International Disarmament Organisation, the United Nations and the Veto: Some Observations on Problems of Relationship and Functioning' in *Essays in Honour of Lord McNair* (Stevens & Sons, London, 1972) 1–23
'Deep Sea-bed Resources: A Major Challenge' (1972) 31 *The Cambridge Law Journal* 50–66
'Reprisals involving Recourse to Armed Force' (1972) 66 *American Journal of International Law* 1–36
'Economic Coercion and Reprisals by States' (1972) 13 *Virginia Journal of International Law* 1–12
'The Interrelation of Theories of Intervention and Self-defense' in J Moore (ed), *Law and Civil War in the Modern World* (Johns Hopkins University Press, Baltimore, London, 1974) Chapter 2, 38–50
'The U.K./Icelandic Fisheries Cases' (1974) 33 *The Cambridge Law Journal* 179–181
'International Law and Economic Coercion' (1976) 16 *Virginia Journal of International Law* 245–259
'Reservations to Non-Restricted Multilateral Treaties' (1978) 49 *BYIL* 67–92
'The Arbitration between the United Kingdom and France concerning the Continental Shelf Boundary in the English Channel and South-Western Approaches, (1978) 49 *BYIL* 1–29
'The State Immunity Act of 1978' (1978) 37 *The Cambridge Law Journal* 193–196
The Legal Regime of Islands in International Law (Dobbs Ferry, Oceana Publications, 1979), 337 pp
'Preserving Order and Security' (1981) 75 *American Journal of International Law* 55–72
'Jurisdiction: Changing Patterns of Authority over Activities and Resources', (1982) 53 *BYIL* 1–26
'Tenure, Fixed term, Secondment from Governments: The United Nations Civil Service and the European Civil Service Compared' (1982) 14 *New York University Journal of International Law and Politics* 799–805
'Contemporary Developments in Legal Techniques in the Settlement of Disputes' (1983-II) 180 *Collected Courses of The Hague Academy of International Law* 177–235
'Claims between States and Private Entities: The Twilight Zone of International Law', (1986) 35 *Catholic University Law Review* 929–942

'The Use of Force for the Protection of Nationals Abroad' in A Cassese, *The Current Legal Regulation of the Use of Force: Legal Restraints on the Use of Force 40 Years after the U.N. Charter* (Nijhoff, Dordrecht, 1986) 39–55
Review of: *Encyclopaedia of Public International Law*, Vol 8, in (1986) 57 *BYIL* 376–377
Review of: A Grahl-Madsen, *Spirit of Uppsala: Proceedings of the Joint UNITAR—Uppsala University Seminar on International Law and Organisation for a New World Order* (1986), (1986) 57 *BYIL* 382–384
'Exploitation of Mineral Resources and the Continental Shelf' in U Leanza (ed), *Il Regime giuridico internazionale del Mare Mediterraneo. Atti del Convegno internazionale. Castelgandolfo, 18–19 ottobre 1985* (Giuffre, Milano, 1987) 21–31
Review of: R B Lillich (ed), *Valuation of Nationalised Property in International Law*, Vol 4 (1987), (1987) 58 *BYIL* 381–382
'International Incidents: New Genre or New Delusion', (1987) 12 *Yale Journal of International Law* 386–395
'The Economic Factor in Maritime Delimitation Cases' in *Essays in Honour of Roberto Ago*, Vol II (Giuffre, Milano, 1987) 45–63
'State Contracts with Aliens: Contemporary Developments on Compensation for Termination or Breach', (1988) 59 *BYIL* 49–74
Review of: E Luard, *Conflict and Peace in the Modern International System* (2nd edn, 1988), (1989) 60 *BYIL* 448–449
'The Taba Award of 29 September 1988', (1989) 23 *Israel Law Review* 429–442
Review of: M Evans, *Relevant Circumstances and Maritime Delimitation* (1989), (1989) 60 *BYIL* 442–443
Review of: M Spinedi (ed), *United Nations Codification of State Responsibility* (1987), (1989) 60 *BYIL* 456–457
Review of: V Gowlland-Debbas, *Collective Responses to Illegal Acts in International Law: UN Action in the Question of Southern Rhodesia* (1990), (1991) 62 *BYIL* 399–400
Review of: *Basic Documents on United Nations and related Peace-keeping Forces* (2nd edn, 1989), (1991) 62 *BYIL* 421
Review of: M Sornarajah, *International Commercial Arbitration* (1990), (1991) 62 *BYIL* 421–423
Review of: A Toth (ed) *Oxford Encyclopaedia of European Community law.* Vol 1. *Institutional Law* (1990), (1991) 62 *BYIL* 425
Review of: K Wellens (ed), *Resolutions and Statements of the United Nations Security Council (1946–1989): A Thematic Guide* (1990), (1991) 62 *BYIL* 427–428
'Vienna Convention on the Law of Treaties, 1969: Treaties and State Responsibility' in M Virally (ed), *Le droit international au service de la paix, de la justice et du développement. Mélanges* (Pedone, Paris, 1991) 137–145
'Islands, Rocks, Reefs, and Low-tide Elevations in Maritime Boundary Delimitations' in J Charney and L Alexander (eds), *International Maritime Boundaries* (Nijhoff, Dordrecht, 1991) 131–151
'The Canada-France Arbitration concerning the Delimitation of the Maritime Areas of St. Pierre et Miquelon' in M Perez Gonzalez et al (eds), *Hacia un nuevo orden internacional y europeo: estudios en homenaje al professor Don Manuel Diez de Velasco* (Editorial Tecnos, Madrid, 1993) 123–136
'Treaty Revision in the Light of the Evolution of Customary International Law', (1993) 5 *African Journal of International and Comparative Law* 84–96
Review of: E Raftopoulos, *The Inadequacy of the Contractual Analogy in the Law of Treaties* (1990), (1993) 64 *BYIL* 439
'The Impact of Security Council Decisions on Dispute Settlement Procedures' (1994) 5 *European Journal of International Law* 89–101
'The Dubai/Sharjah Boundary Arbitration of 1981', (1995) 65 *BYIL* 103–133
'Collective Security and Collective Self-defence: The Errors and Risks of Identification' in M Rama-Montaldo, *El decercho internacional en un mundo en transformacion* Vol 1 (FCU, Montevideo, 1995) 425–440

'*Res Judicata* and the Limits of Rectification of Decisions by International Tribunals', (1996) 5 *African Journal of International and Comparative Law* 577–591

'The Court's Role in Relation to International Organizations' in V Lowe and M Fitzmaurice (eds), *Fifty Years of the International Court of Justice* (Cambridge University Press, Cambridge, 1996) 181–192

'The Conduct of International Litigation', in J P Gardner and Ch Wickramasinghe (eds), *The International Court of Justice: Process, Practice and Procedure* (British Institute of International and Comparative Law, London, 1997) 1–20

'The Role of International Organizations in the Implementation of International Law' in *International Law on the Eve of the Twenty-First Century: Views from the International Law Commission* (United Nations, New York, 1997) 163–172

'Judicial and Political Functions of the Security Council and the International Court of Justice' in A Saab et al, *The Changing Constitution of the United Nations* (British Institute for International and Comparative Law, London, 1997) 73–88

'Crimes of State and the 1996 Report of the International Law Commission on State Responsibility', (1998) 9 *European Journal of International Law* 163–173

Review of: Nguyen Quoc Dinh, *Droit international public* (6th edn, LGDJ, Paris, 1999), (1999) 70 *BYIL* 268–270

The Law and Procedure of the International Court of Justice 1960–1989

SUPPLEMENT, 2009: PARTS SEVEN AND EIGHT

By Hugh Thirlway*

* Hugh Thirlway, 2009, Visiting Professor of International Law, Universities of Bristol (UK) and Leiden (NL), sometime Principal Legal Secretary, ICJ.

SIR DEREK BOWETT CBE, QC, FBA (1927–2009)

Derek Bowett was (with Ian Brownlie) editor of this Year Book for over a decade, from 1982 to 1993. He then served as Chairman of the Editorial Committee until 1999, when Brownlie took over that task on his own retirement from the Chichele Chair.

Derek had a multifaceted career as an international lawyer. He taught at Manchester and Cambridge and was simultaneously Whewell Professor and President of Queens' College, both posts held for a dozen or so years. He worked for the United Nations on secondment in New York and in the Middle East. He wrote important early works on use of force, international organizations, law of the sea and dispute settlement. He had an extensive practice at the international level, both before the International Court and in international arbitrations, appearing for a range of governments on all continents. He served as an influential member of the International Law Commission at a transitional period (1992–1996).

He remained throughout a realist and pragmatist, uninterested in theory but with nonetheless a clear view of international law as a significant aspect of the conduct of international relations in 'the search for peace'. His forthright view of the practicalities of the subject appears, for example, in the following passage from a late review:

> The time for analogies with private law contracts is past. This is certainly in part because it is now well recognised that treaties have a legislative role, to which such analogies are inapplicable, but also in part because the law, as reflected in State practice and judicial decisions, is now enriched sufficiently to make recourse to private law analogies unnecessary. Moreover, once it is demanded of any private law analogy that it reflects a "general principle of law", the private law rule has to be shorn of the particularities of any one legal system, to that the rule which emerges is of a very general, almost abstract, character. All too frequently, what a court needs is not an abstract principle but a refined and practical rule: so such analogies offer little help.[1]

The question is not—as his predecessor Hersch Lauterpacht had argued—whether private law analogies flow into international law by virtue of 'the principles of legal justice and of international progress',[2] but whether a given analogy is 'of any help'. If not, it should simply be discarded.[3]

* * *

[1] D W Bowett, Review of: E Raftopoulos, *The Inadequacy of the Contractual Analogy in the Law of Treaties* (1990), (1993) 64 *BYIL* 439.

[2] H Lauterpacht, *Private Law Sources and Analogies of International Law* (Longmans, London, 1927) xi.

[3] The following tribute is a lightly modified version of an address given at the Memorial Service for Sir Derek Bowett at Queens' College, Cambridge on 28 November 2009. See <http://www.squire.law.cam.ac.uk/eminent_scholars/derek_bowett_derek_bowett_memorial_service_address.php> (last accessed 26 August 2010). The writer has also drawn upon an unpublished autobiographical note by Bowett kindly made available by Lady Bowett.

Sir Derek Bowett
(1927–2009)

Preface

The present article is intended to be the penultimate in this series.

It is now 20 years since the author embarked on the task of completing and continuing the series of articles from the pen of Sir Gerald Fitzmaurice, commenting on the decisions of the International Court of Justice, which had been published in this *Year Book* between 1950 and 1959.[1] There was thus at the outset in 1989 a backlog of some 30 years' jurisprudence to be dealt with; and the author's first modest proposal was to examine this material so as to provide, with Sir Gerald's articles, a complete corpus of commentary for the period from the establishment of the Court to 1989. It rapidly became apparent that this could not be done in one year, nor in several; and over the years during which the first continuation series was written and published, the Court of course continued to deliver judgments and advisory opinions, many of which called for further comment. Consequently, the decision was taken, first by way of exception,[2] and subsequently on a regular but limited basis,[3] not merely to bring matters up to date as at 1989, but to examine also the subsequent decisions when their subject-matter brought them within the ambit of the discussion in each successive article.

In 2003 this first supplemental series was completed, but its coverage of the case-law was uneven: decisions from the years around the turn of the century were commented on so far as they dealt with subjects falling within the later part of the structure of the whole project (which followed so far as possible the structure of the original Fitzmaurice articles), but not insofar as they dealt with the questions (sometimes of greater importance) that had already been covered in the earlier parts. In 2005 therefore a further series was begun, intended in the first place to fill these gaps; but once again the production of decisions by the Court outstripped the efforts of the commentator to analyze them. The article here published, together with that planned for next year's *Year Book*, will, it is hoped, complete this second supplemental series.

Nevertheless, the coverage will still be incomplete, for the same reason as before: the impossibility of preparing and publishing commentary on the Court's decisions within the same time-frame as that within which the decisions themselves are handed down.[4] Furthermore, the rate of

[1] The reason why Sir Gerald left his survey uncompleted was that he was himself elected a Member of the Court in 1960; he did however find it not incompatible with his judicial position to write a further series of articles entitled 'Hersch Lauterpacht: The Scholar as Judge' between 1960 and 1963, which to some extent covered the ground that would have been covered by continuation of the original series.

[2] See (1993) 64 *BYIL* 3.

[3] See (1995) 66 *BYIL* 3.

[4] One compensating advantage should be mentioned: the delay between the delivery of a given decision, and the comment in this series made it possible to take some account of scholarly comment on the decision in other journals; but here too, the sheer amount of material continually becoming available increases the Sisyphean quality of the task.

production of such decisions, and even more strikingly the number and length of separate and dissenting opinions, have increased very considerably. The 1989 volume of the Court's *Reports* series ran to 221 pages and included only two substantive decisions: the *Elettronica Sicula* judgment, and the advisory opinion on *Applicability of Article VI, Section 22, of the Convention on the Privileges and Immunities of the United Nations* (the *Mazilu* case); attached to the first of these were two judges' separate or dissenting opinions, and to the second, three. By contrast, there are three volumes of the Court's *Reports* for 1996 and for 2004, running to a total of 913 and 1453 pages respectively; the 1996 volumes include no less than 42 separate and dissenting opinions.[5] Unless comment be restricted to the actual decision, and the opinions left on one side—which would be a major departure from the practice both of Fitzmaurice and as followed in previous articles—or the commentary offered be much less far-reaching than has been attempted hitherto, the amount of material to be covered is clearly tending towards the unmanageable. It has thus seemed both to the author and to the editors of the *Year Book* that the time has come to bring to an end the enterprise begun by Fitzmaurice; the *Year Book* will no doubt continue to publish comment on and analysis of the ICJ's decisions, but it is unlikely to be attempted in the same form as before.

The promise of a final article in the next *Year Book* has to be qualified as *Deo volente*; and in case it should fail to be fulfilled, the author would like to express at this stage his profound gratitude both to successive Editors of the *Year Book*, Ian Brownlie, Derek Bowett, James Crawford and Vaughan Lowe, for their support, understanding and (above all) criticisms, and to Assistant Editor Cherry Hopkins, who was of great assistance to a novice contributor in the early years.

[5] The 2004 volumes are atypical, in that they include the eight decisions on jurisdiction in the *Use of Force* cases, which are to a large extent identically worded, and therefore require less commentary than might at first appear.

In the case of *Maritime Delimitation and Territorial Questions between Qatar and Bahrain*, one of the questions before the Court was that of sovereignty over Zubarah, an area on the Qatar peninsula, but to which Bahrain laid claim. This claim was based upon an assertion of 'internationally recognized title... by reference to the international standard of contextually proportionate effective occupation' by the rulers of Bahrain from 1783 until 1937;[50] presumably it was alleged that the territory in 1783 had been *terra nullius*, though this aspect was not commented on specifically by the Court. Qatar's claim in response however amounted to a denial of such *terra nullius* status: it asserted that there had been a pre-existing local town owing allegiance to the 'local sheikhs', who had laid down conditions for the establishment of the Al-Utub tribes (through whom Bahrain was claiming).[51] The Court did not find it necessary to go back to the events of the 18th century in order to find that Qatar had sovereignty over Zubarah, relying first on events of 1868 and an Anglo-Ottoman Convention of 1913,[52] and secondly on the attitude of the British Government in 1937.[53]

In the *Nicaragua/Honduras (Caribbean Sea)* dispute, the first issue was the terminal point of the land boundary at the coast, and its impact on the maritime delimitation also requested from the Court, and the second the question of sovereignty over the various islands lying off the coast in the region. In respect of this latter question, the situation was that either the islands (or each of them individually) had appertained to one of the Spanish administrative divisions during the colonial period, in which case they passed under the sovereignty of the State that succeeded to that division, or that they had never been effectively part of the Spanish Empire in Latin America, and were thus, at least at the date of decolonisation, true *terra nullius*. The Court noted that the *uti possidetis juris* principle could apply to offshore possessions, and that 'a key aspect of the principle [of *uti possidetis juris*] is the denial of any possibility of *terra nullius*', following on these points the decision of the Chamber in the *Land, Island and Maritime Frontier Dispute*.[54] The parties were agreed in excluding the possibility of *terra nullius*; but this did not bind the Court, which pointed out that 'the mere invocation of the principle of *uti possidetis juris* does not of itself provide a clear answer as to sovereignty over the disputed islands... [*U*]*ti possidetis juris* presupposes the existence of a delimitation of territory between the colonial provinces concerned having been effected by the central colonial authorities.'[55]

[50] Quoted by the Court at [2001] ICJ Rep 64, para 72.

[51] Ibid, 65, para 77. Qatar's claim was reinforced by reference to events of the 19th century, when, according to Qatar, the then Ruler of Bahrain admitted to the British Government that he had no sovereignty over Zubarah (ibid, para 78).

[52] Ibid, 67–68, paras 86–91.

[53] Ibid, 68–69, paras 92–96.

[54] [1992] ICJ Rep 558, para 333; 589, para 386; 387, para 42; quoted in [2007-II] ICJ Rep 708–709, paras 155, 156.

[55] Judgment of [2007-II] ICJ Rep 708–709, para 158.

As the Court recalled, the same question had arisen in the earlier case before the Chamber, which had observed:

The attribution of individual islands to the territorial administrative divisions of the Spanish colonial system, for the purposes of their allocation to the one or the other newly-independent State, may well have been a matter of some doubt and difficulty, judging by the evidence and information submitted. It should be recalled that when the principle of the *uti possidetis juris* is involved, the *jus* referred to is not international law but the constitutional or administrative law of the pre-independence sovereign, in this case Spanish colonial law; and it is perfectly possible that that law itself gave no clear and definitive answer to the appurtenance of marginal areas, or sparsely populated areas of minimal economic significance.[56]

The Court's conclusion, on the basis of such historical record as was available, was in fact that

[n]otwithstanding the historical and continuing importance of the *uti possidetis juris* principle, so closely associated with Latin American decolonization, it cannot in this case be said that the application of this principle to these small islands, located considerably offshore and not obviously adjacent to the mainland coast of Nicaragua or Honduras, would settle the issue of sovereignty over them.[57]

The apologetic tone is striking; the Court appears to have been reluctant not only to appear to underrate the value of the *uti possidetis* principle, but to reject the view of the legal situation shared by both parties—a view which would have required the Court to make bricks without straw.

The Court was also unable to discern any significant *effectivités* during the colonial period, or to draw any assistance from an asserted principle of adjacency.[58] The Court therefore based its decision on post-colonial *effectivités*, on the basis (though this was not emphasized) that the islands had in effect been *terra nullius*. The case will be commented on further below (Section 3).

In the case of *Pedra Branca* (Malaysia/Singapore), Singapore had argued that the disputed island had been *terra nullius* in 1847–1851 when the United Kingdom (Singapore's predecessor in title) had constructed a lighthouse upon it, and had thereby acquired sovereignty over it.[59] The Court however did not accept this contention, since it held on the facts that at that time the Sultan of Johor had already an original title to the island.[60]

[56] *Land, Island and Maritime Frontier Dispute* [1992] ICJ Rep 558–559, para 333, cited in [2007-II] ICJ Rep 708–709, para 160.

[57] Ibid, para 163.

[58] Ibid, paras 164–166.

[59] Judgment of 23 May 2008, paras 39–41, 49.

[60] Ibid, para 69.

2. Acquisitive Prescription

The very existence of acquisitive prescription as a means of acquiring title to territory in international law has long been doubted;[61] and the *Right of Passage* case, discussed in the previous article on this subject,[62] is, as was there indicated, ambiguous in its implications. It might perhaps have been expected that claims of acquisitive prescription would not continue to be made in the twenty-first century, now that the land territories of the world are so clearly mapped out and subjected to surveillance by the State claiming sovereignty over them. It should not be overlooked that prescription implies the existence of a prior title, extinguished by inaction over a lengthy period of time; acquisition of *terra nullius* by occupation is a separate concept, and has been dealt with as such above. Nevertheless, in one modern case (*Kasikili/Sedudu Island*) a claim has been advanced based on prescription, but decided on other grounds; in another (*Cameroon/Nigeria*) a claim based on 'historical consolidation of title' amounted in effect to a claim of prescription, or something very like one; and in a third (*Sovereignty over Pedra Branca/Pulau Batu Puteh, Middle Rocks and South Ledge*) the doctrine of prescription was clearly present in the background, and could in the view of some observers had governed the decision, even though the State that could have invoked it chose not to do so.

Reserving for the present the question whether acquisitive prescription actually exists in international law, how is it to be defined? It would seem to be a process by which sovereignty over territory is transferred from one State to another, without a formal act of cession, and without the consent of the former sovereign (except to the extent that the acts and events form which acquisitive prescription is deduced may be seen as implied consent through failure to protest). So far as it may be derived from, or analogous, to an institution of national law, it may be equated with acquisitive prescription in the civil law, for example in French law. While in English law title to land may be based on continuous possession for a sufficient length of time, this is strictly an aspect of limitation of actions; prescription operates only in the acquisition, by time and usage, of rights over another's land (easements), not the acquisition of title.[63] This, coupled with the

[61] See, for example, Brownlie, above n 38, 145, who also suggests that acquiescence and estoppels may establish rights, and 'consequently an independent doctrine of 'prescription' has no function to fulfill'; ibid, 147; Nguyen Quoc Dinh, Patrick Daillier, Alain Pellet, *Droit international public* (5[e] edition, LGDJ, Paris, 1994) §354, 3°. In the *Land, Island and Maritime Frontier* case, Judge *ad hoc* Torres Bernárdez referred to the doctrine as 'a highly controversial concept which, for my part, I have the greatest difficulty in accepting as an established institution of international law': [1992] ICJ Rep 678, para 99.

[62] (1995) *BYIL* 1, 12–15.

[63] '[Limitation] simply extinguishes a former owner's right to recover possession of the land, leaving some other person with a title based on adverse possession. Prescription operates positively, like a conveyance; limitation operates negatively, by eliminating the claim of a person having a superior title.' R E Megarry and H W R Wade, *The Law of Real Property* (Stevens, London, 1957) 890.

nature of international relations, signifies that territory may be acquired by acquisitive prescription in more complex circumstances, but the acquisition is subject to less rigid requirements than would be the case for the establishment in English law of a title by limitation. It is therefore convenient, if no more, to look to French law for the incidents of acquisitive prescription, while bearing in mind that they are not necessarily transferable *en bloc* into international law.[64]

Le *temps* est l'élément commun à la préscription acquisitive et à la préscription extinctive.... Pour la prescription acquisitive, c'est sans doute l'inaction du véritable propriétaire, mais c'est aussi et surtout la possession de celui qui va préscrire, acquérir par préscription.[65]

For a definition of the requirements of international law, we may take, at least as a starting point, the claim based on prescription advanced by Namibia[66] in the case of *Kasikili/Sedudu Island*, in which the Court noted that '[t]he Parties [Namibia and Botswana] agree between themselves that acquisitive prescription is recognized in international law and they further agree on the conditions under which title may be acquired by prescription'.[67] Those conditions had been defined by Namibia as follows:

1. The possession of the... state must be exercised *à titre de souverain*.
2. The possession must be peaceful and uninterrupted.
3. The possession must be public.
4. The possession must endure for a certain length of time.[68]

As regards the first condition, in his Dissenting Opinion, Judge Fleischhauer added the interesting gloss that possession as holder of a League of Nations Mandate, which had been the status of South Africa in relation to the territory that became Namibia, is not equivalent to possession *à titre de souverain*.[69] The Court was however somewhat guarded in its treatment of the issue of prescription; it took the view that, for purposes of the case, it

[64] One may speculate that the source of acquisitive prescription may be a combination of custom with treatment of a 'general principle of law' observed in domestic systems; though the distinction, peculiar to English law, between limitation and prescription throws doubt on this.

[65] Jean Carbonnier, *Droit civil*, II (4ᵉ édition, Presses Universitaires de France, Paris, 1964) §62, 205–206.

[66] A claim however advanced in the alternative, its main claim being based, like that of Botswana, on the interpretation of an 1890 Anglo-German Treaty.

[67] [1999-II] ICJ Rep 1105, para 96.

[68] Ibid, 1103, para 94. A similar enumeration is given by Judges Simma and Abraham in paragraph 17 of their dissenting opinion in the *Pedra Branca* case (Malaysia/Singapore). In the *Cameroon/Nigeria* case, counsel for Cameroon added that the acts must not be with the permission (*nec precario*) of the territorial sovereign, and that there must not have been protest: [2002] ICJ Rep 413, para 219.

[69] [1999-II] ICJ Rep 1206–1207. Judge Rezek considered that the requirement of possession *à titre de souverain* was not part of international law, occupation by private persons being capable of being sufficient: ibid, 1236, para 13.

need not concern itself with the status of acquisitive prescription in international law or with the conditions for acquiring title to territory by prescription. It considers, for the reasons set out below, that the conditions cited by Namibia itself are not satisfied in this case and that Namibia's argument on acquisitive prescription therefore cannot be accepted.[70]

In other words, it reserved judgment on the question of the existence of acquisitive prescription in general international law, thereby strongly implying that it had doubts on the matter, even though the two parties before it considered that the concept was recognized in law, and had pleaded on that basis.[71] Writing before the case was decided, Jennings and Watts had already concluded that 'prescription is not so much now a singular mode of acquisition, or loss, of territorial sovereignty, as a convenient term for one group of elements which go together to make or break a title.'[72]

Mention of the issue was also made in argument in the *Land and Maritime Boundary* case between Cameroon and Nigeria.[73] Nigeria claimed title to the Bakassi Peninsula on three grounds, one of which was 'long occupation... constituting an historical consolidation of title' (the title of the 'Kings and Chiefs of Old Calabar', already referred to above[74]), and a second was 'peaceful possession by Nigeria, acting as sovereign, and an absence of protest by Cameroon'.[75] Cameroon suggested that what Nigeria was really claiming was title by acquisitive prescription, and pointed out that the acts to establish such title must meet the requirement of *nec vi, nec clam, nec precario*,[76] as had in Cameroon's view been recognized in the *Kasikili/Sedudu Island* case. As was observed in the earlier article in this series,[77] the circumstances of the *Right of Passage* case throw some doubt on the point whether these requirements, generally recognized in municipal legal systems, also form part of the international law of acquisitive prescription. In its 2002 Judgment, the Court emphasized that '[t]he legal question whether *effectivités* suggest that the title lies with one country rather than another[78] is not the same legal question as whether such *effectivités* can serve to displace an established treaty title'; and 'the

[70] [1999-II] ICJ Rep 1105, para 97.

[71] An interesting question, also not explored, was whether the shared recognition of the doctrine could have been held to constitute evidence of the existence of a rule of special or local customary law, as in the *Asylum* case.

[72] *Oppenheim's International Law*, Vol. I, above n 42, 708, §270.

[73] Generally on this case, see M Mendelson, 'The *Cameroon/Nigeria* case in the International Court of Justice: some sovereignty and boundary delimitation issues' (2004) *BYIL* 223–247.

[74] Text and n 6 above.

[75] Quoted in [2002] ICJ Rep 412, para 218.

[76] Ibid, 413, para 219.

[77] (1995) *BYIL* 1, 14.

[78] Which had been the question, as the Court found, in the previous decisions relied on by Nigeria, namely *Minquiers and Ecrehos, Western Sahara*, the *Rann of Kutch* arbitration and the *Beagle Channel* arbitration: [2002] ICJ Rep 415, paras 222–223.

more relevant legal question in this case is whether the conduct of Cameroon, as the title holder, can be viewed as an acquiescence in the loss of the treaty title that it inherited upon independence.'[79] The possible period for such acquiescence to have taken place was limited since, as the Court found, Nigeria had recognized Cameroon's title by the Maroua Declaration in 1975; accordingly,

> The Court considers that the foregoing shows that Nigeria could not have been acting *à titre de souverain* before the late 1970s, as it did not consider itself to have title over Bakassi; and in the ensuing period the evidence does not indicate an acquiescence by Cameroon in the abandonment of its title in favour of Nigeria.[80]

These cases would seem to go some way to support the view that the true rule of law in this connection is simply one of the effects of acquiescence, and that no distinct doctrine of prescription is necessary. In the *Land, Island and Maritime Frontier* case, the Chamber found that there were no pre-independence *effectivités* to be relied on; it therefore turned first to post-decolonization *effectivités,* but also to 'the conduct of the Parties in more recent years as possibly constituting acquiescence'.[81] Even the *Kasikili/Sedudu* judgment does not however go so far as to state this expressly, but in a more recent case the Court conspicuously declined to base on prescription a decision which, it seems, might have been fully supportable on that ground.

A key element in the case of *Sovereignty over Pedra Branca/Pulau Batu Puteh, Middle Rocks and South Ledge*, between Malaysia and Singapore, was the question of acquisition of territory not previously *terra nullius*, in that another State had an established title thereto. In 1844, as the Court found, the island known as Pedra Branca or Pulau Batu Puteh[82] was under the sovereignty of the Sultan of Johor, and the Court also indicated that in that respect Malaysia was the successor of the Sultan. Nevertheless the Court found that Singapore had obtained sovereignty over the island as a result of events subsequent to that date. The Court attributed this result to 'a convergent evolution of the positions of the Parties regarding title' to the island; and concluded,

> especially by reference to the conduct of Singapore and its predecessors *à titre de souverain*, taken together with the conduct of Malaysia and its predecessors including their failure to respond to the conduct of Singapore and its predecessors, that by 1980 sovereignty over Pedra Branca/Pulau Batu Puteh had passed to Singapore.[83]

[79] [2002] ICJ Rep 415, para 223.
[80] Ibid, 416, para 224.
[81] [1992] ICJ Rep 562, para 341.
[82] To avoid repeating the lengthy bilingual denomination which the Court was careful to use, Pedra Branca/Pulau Batu Puteh will here be referred to simply as 'the island'.
[83] Judgment of 23 May 2008, para 276.

A principal ground of criticism expressed by the dissenting judges was that the basis for this finding, in terms of traditional and established concepts of international law, was very difficult to grasp. As Judge *ad hoc* Dugard observed:

The Judgment is premised on the finding that the conduct of both Parties has resulted in the passing of sovereignty over Pedra Branca/Pulau Batu Puteh from Malaysia (previously Johor) to Singapore. While considerations of acquiescence, abandonment of title and tacit agreement or understanding feature prominently in the Court's reasoning no attempt is made to justify or explain the passing of sovereignty in terms of accepted principles governing the acquisition of territorial title....

Notions of conduct, acquiescence, tacit agreement and abandonment of title feature in the Court's explanation for its decision...However, the Court fails to explain how sovereignty over Pedra Branca/Pulau Batu Puteh passed from Johor/Malaysia to Singapore in terms of traditional or accepted rules governing the acquisition of territorial title.[84]

Judges Simma and Abraham analyze the paragraph quoted above from the Judgment as follows:

La Cour décrit ce processus comme témoignant d'une «évolution convergente des positions» des Parties, au fil du temps, concernant la souveraineté sur l'île...De cette «évolution convergente» l'on pourrait déduire soit qu'un «accord tacite» portant sur le transfert de souveraineté se serait formé entre les Parties, soit que le Johor aurait acquiescé à ce transfert par un comportement ayant donné naissance à des droits irréversibles au profit de Singapour. Entre le terrain juridique de l'«accord tacite» et celui de l'«acquiescement», . . . , la Cour s'abstient de choisir, se bornant à constater, *in fine*, que l'ensemble du comportement des Parties sur la période considérée—au total plus d'un siècle et demi—a changé le titulaire de la souveraineté.[85]

The Court thus exercised its function of settlement of disputes, providing an answer to the question of sovereignty, based on extensive reasoning; but for the theorist of law, and indeed for any State involved in dispute over territory or sovereignty that raises questions of the effect of the conduct of the States concerned, the judgment is perhaps less helpful than it might have been.

As regards prescription in particular, it was thus noted by the dissenting judges that the Court had, apparently deliberately, avoided using this term; and that in doing so it had followed the lead offered by Singapore which, it was suggested, could have effectively based its claims on that doctrine, but chose not to do so.[86] This can hardly be the reason for the

[84] Dissenting Opinion, paras 2, 30.

[85] Joint Dissenting Opinion, para 3; English translation not yet published.

[86] See Dissenting Opinion of Judge Dugard, paras 30–32; Joint Dissenting Opinion of Judges Simma and Abraham (who also suggest a tactical reason why Singapore chose not to invoke prescription), paras 11–12.

Court's approach, however; the principle of *jura novit curia* would not merely have permitted but required the Court, if it thought that the facts showed the existence of a valid claim on that basis, to have so stated, and upheld the claim.[87] Attention may however be drawn here to some observations and findings of the Court that may suggest the approach to such matters that it was endorsing; and for this purpose a more detailed account of the facts and examination of the decision will be required.

(1) The facts of the Pedra Branca/Pulau Batu Puteh *case*

The historical facts are not simple, and the Court had to devote no less than 159 paragraphs of its Judgment to their statement and elucidation. Some brief indication of their nature will be necessary here to explain the problems, and the Court's findings. The Court made two major temporal divisions of the factual record. It first established that in the 1840s the island was part of the possessions, and under the sovereignty, of the Sultan of Johor; if there had been no change in the legal situation, Malaysia would in the view of the Court have a valid claim on the basis of succession. Singapore was also claiming as a successor, its predecessor being the United Kingdom.[88] The Court then examined the events and activities brought to its attention during the subsequent period, up to the critical date[89] in order to ascertain whether there had been any change in the legal situation. As we shall see (Section 2 below), this apparently judicious way of proceedings in fact rests on a concealed ambiguity.

In the 1840s, when the island was (as the Court had thus found) under the sovereignty of the Sultan of Johor, there was a proposal by the United Kingdom (involving the Government of India), which then had sovereignty over Singapore, to build a lighthouse in the region, and the island was selected as its site. Initially however an island known as Peak Rock,[90] also under the sovereignty of Johor, had been chosen, and on that basis the Sultan and the Temenggong (a potentate with, apparently, co-terminous powers with the Sultan) of Johor were consulted. On 25 November 1844 both the Sultan and the Temenggong wrote letters of consent: the Temenggong indicated specifically that 'the [East India] Company are at full liberty to put up a Light House there [i.e., on Peak Rock], or any spot deemed eligible.'[91] For various reasons, it was later decided by the British authorities that Peak Rock was not suitable, and plans were prepared to build the lighthouse instead on the island that was to become the subject of the ICJ proceedings. Neither the Sultan nor the Temenggong was

[87] Judge *ad hoc* Dugard drew attention to this point, and regretted that the Court had not invited the parties to address the question: Dissenting Opinion, para 45.

[88] Though the situation was confused by the fact that Singapore under British sovereignty had been administered by the East India Company, as part of the Straits Settlements: Judgment of 23 May 2008, paras 21 and 24.

[89] See Chapter IV, Section 2, below.

[90] Also known as Romania Point.

[91] Quoted in the Judgment of 23 May 2008, para 128.

however consulted again, or (so far as the record showed) even informed of the change of plan. The Temenggong's letter (which was taken to reflect equally the views of the Sultan) was evidently capable of two possible constructions: that of a cession, an assignment of sovereignty, over what ever island might be used for the lighthouse; or as the grant of a licence to construct and operate a lighthouse, on territory retained by Johor. On that issue, the Court stated simply that 'on the basis of the case file, [it] is not in a position to reach a conclusion.'[92]

The lighthouse was built and commissioned in 1850–1851; the Court heard a number of arguments as to the possible significance of events involved in this, but finally '[did] not draw any conclusions about sovereignty based on the construction of the lighthouse.' However, it added mysteriously that 'Rather it sees those events as bearing on the issue of the evolving views of the authorities in Johor and Singapore about sovereignty over' the island.[93]

The Court next turned to 'activities undertaken by' the parties and their predecessors in title 'between 1852 and 1980, and indeed beyond'; for reasons of convenience the Court divided this period into two parts: up to 1953, and subsequently.[94] There were first British legislative acts relating to the lighthouse, which Singapore suggested demonstrated British sovereignty over the island, a claim which the Court did not accept;[95] nor did the Court uphold Malaysia's contentions based on British legislation.[96] The parties brought to the Court's attention the constitutional changes by which Singapore became independent, and later became for a short time part of the Federation of Malaysia, but these too did not, in the Court's view, help resolve the question of sovereignty over the island;[97] nor did facts concerning the regulation of fisheries by Johor in the 1860s.[98]

More relevant in the Court's view was an exchange of correspondence in 1953. In brief, the authorities of Singapore asked those of Johor for information about the island, in order to determine the extent of the territorial waters of Singapore, and cited an 1844 despatch from the Governor of Singapore to the British authorities (discussed earlier in the Court's Judgment), which had stated that the island was 'part of a territory of the Rajah of Johore who... has willingly consented to cede it gratuitously to the East India Company', i.e. to Great Britain.[99] Also mentioned was an

[92] Ibid, para 148. The hypothesis of an assignment of sovereignty over 'any spot deemed eligible' seems prima facie less probable than the grant of a licence to construct on such a 'spot'.

[93] Ibid, para 162.

[94] Ibid, para 164.

[95] Ibid, para 172.

[96] Ibid, para. 177.

[97] Ibid, para 186.

[98] Ibid, para 191.

[99] This proved to be a misreading of the 1844 situation, but no consequences were drawn from this circumstance.

entry in the Johor Register of Deeds showing that a part of another island (Pulau Pisang) had been formally granted to the British by the Sultan for the purpose of building a lighthouse (which in fact was never built); this deed had made it clear that 'there was no abrogation of the sovereignty of Johore.'[100] In reply to the 1953 request of Singapore for information, the Johor Government stated that 'the Johore Government does not claim ownership' of the island.[101]

The Court did not regard the 1953 letter sent by Singapore as suggesting that the views of that Government were that it had no rights over the island, but rather as showing that 'the Singapore authorities were not clear about events occurring over a century earlier and that they were not sure that their records were complete, a caution which is understandable in the circumstances.'[102] Turning to the letter from Johor, having satisfied itself that its author (the Acting State Secretary) had authority to send it[103] (i.e., to commit his Government), the Court ruled that it 'shows that as of 1953 Johor understood[104] that it did not have sovereignty over [the island]', and that '[i]n the light of Johor's reply, the authorities in Singapore had no reason to doubt that the United Kingdom had sovereignty over the island.'[105]

What exactly was the legal nature of the 1953 exchange as regards sovereignty over the island? The Court was offered (by counsel for Singapore) three alternative lines of legal reasoning by way of interpretation of the Johor letter: that it was a formal or express disclaimer of title; that it gave rise to an estoppel; and that it was a binding unilateral undertaking. The Court rejected all three possibilities, and simply maintained that these findings 'did not affect' the conclusions quoted above.[106]

That was not however the end of the matter; the Court then examined the conduct of the parties after 1953, including investigation by Singapore of shipwrecks in the waters around the island;[107] visits to the island by officials from Singapore, and visits from Malaysian officials to conduct scientific surveys, after obtaining permits from Singapore;[108] naval patrols in the area by vessels of both parties;[109] the flying of

[100] Judgment of 23 May 2008, para 192. [101] Ibid, para 196.

[102] Ibid, para 209. [103] Ibid, para 220.

[104] 'Understood' is a curious word to choose: it could be read as meaning 'had grasped that that was the true position'; but it is probable that the French text, 'considérait', more accurately reflects the Court's meaning.

[105] Judgment of 23 May 2008, para 223. The Court did not overlook that the 1953 letter made no mention of sovereignty, but stated that Johor '[did] not claim *ownership* of Pedra Branca' (emphasis added). It observed that '[i]n international litigation "ownership" over territory has sometimes been used as equivalent to "sovereignty"', and it referred to passages in the decision in the case of *Territorial Sovereignty and Scope of the Dispute, Eritrea/Yemen* (1998) 22 *UNRIAA*, 209, 219, para 19, and 317–318, para 474. It took the view that the letter 'is clear in its meaning', and that in its context 'it becomes evident that the letter addresses the issue of sovereignty over the island': Judgment of 23 May 2008, paras 222–223.

[106] Judgment of 23 May 2008, para 230.

[107] Ibid, paras 231–234. [108] Ibid, paras 235–239. [109] Ibid, paras 240–243.

British and Singapore ensigns on the island;[110] the installation by Singapore of military communications equipment on the island in 1977;[111] a proposal by Singapore early in the 1970s to carry out a land reclamation project in the area round the island;[112] and some other activities. It also considered the relevance of various official maps produced by either party.

(2) The Court's legal analysis

At the outset of its treatment of the post-1844 developments, the Court observed that

[a]ny passing of sovereignty might be by way of agreement between the two States in question. Such an agreement might take the form of a treaty...The agreement might instead be tacit and arise from the conduct of the Parties. International law does not, in this matter, impose any particular form. Rather it places its emphasis on the parties' intentions (cf. e.g. *Temple of Preah Vihear (Cambodia v Thailand), I.C.J. Reports 1961*, pp. 17, 31).

Under certain circumstances, sovereignty over territory might pass as a result of the failure of the State which has sovereignty to respond to conduct *à titre de souverain* of the other State or, as Judge Huber put it in the *Island of Palmas* case, to concrete manifestations of the display of territorial sovereignty by the other State (*Island of Palmas Case (Netherlands/United States of America)*, Award of 4 April 1928, *RIAA*, Vol. II, p. 839). Such manifestations of the display of sovereignty may call for a response if they are not to be opposable to the State in question. The absence of reaction may well amount to acquiescence. The concept of acquiescence "is equivalent to tacit recognition manifested by unilateral conduct which the other party may interpret as consent..." (*Delimitation of the Maritime Boundary in the Gulf of Maine Area (Canada/United States of America), Judgment, I.C.J. Reports 1984*, p. 305, para 130). That is to say, silence may also speak, but only if the conduct of the other State calls for a response.[113]

At the end of its exhaustive statement and analysis of the historical facts, the Court indicated that the question to which it had to respond was

whether in the light of the principles and rules of international law it stated earlier and of the assessment it has undertaken of the relevant facts, particularly the

[110] Ibid, paras 244–246. It is apparently possible to fly even the national flag on a territory without necessarily thereby claiming sovereignty: cf the *Eritrea-Yemen Arbitration*, First Stage, para 150. Note also the Court's ruling, in the *Dispute regarding Navigational and Related Rights* between Costa Rica and Nicaragua, on the right of Nicaragua to require that its flag be flown by Costa Rican vessels navigating in Nicaraguan waters in the River San Juan: Judgment of 13 July 2009, paras 130–132.

[111] Judgment of 23 May 2008, paras 247–248.

[112] Ibid, paras 249–250.

[113] Ibid, paras 120, 121.

conduct of the Parties, sovereignty over Pedra Branca/Pulau Batu Puteh passed to the United Kingdom or Singapore.[114]

It recalled elements of the conduct of the United Kingdom and Singapore that were unrelated to operation of the lighthouse, and noted that 'Malaysia and its predecessors did not respond in any way to that conduct', of which, as the Court found, it had notice. Mention was made of Malaysia's official maps, and the Court then emphasized that both conduct mentioned and the maps were consistent with the 1953 statement by Johor 'that Johor did not claim ownership of' the island, a statement which for the Court had 'major significance'.[115]

Thus the Court's ultimate conclusion was as follows:

The Court is of the opinion that the relevant facts, including the conduct of the Parties, previously reviewed and summarized in the two preceding paragraphs, reflect a convergent evolution of the positions of the Parties regarding title to Pedra Branca/Pulau Batu Puteh. The Court concludes, especially by reference to the conduct of Singapore and its predecessors *à titre de souverain*, taken together with the conduct of Malaysia and its predecessors including their failure to respond to the conduct of Singapore and its predecessors, that by 1980 sovereignty over Pedra Branca/Pulau Batu Puteh had passed to Singapore.[116]

Taking first the Court's opening remarks on the nature of the process, it is clear that the time element is not the key;[117] what matters is the conduct, in the sense both of action and of inaction, of the two parties concerned.[118] This in turn suggests the predominant role of the concept of acquiescence. If a party agrees to a passing of sovereignty, such agreement may be a virtually instantaneous act (e.g., a treaty of cession); there seems no reason why an equally prompt passing may not be the result of a less formal agreement. The role of time is therefore more of an evidential nature: a series of ambiguous or non-committal actions may add up to indicating acquiescence, and a series of its nature implies the passage of time.

One sentence used by the Court is however difficult to follow: 'concrete manifestations of the display of territorial sovereignty' by the other claimant State 'may call for a response if they are not to be opposable to the

[114] Ibid, para 273. The reference to 'the United Kingdom or Singapore' shows that at this point the Court was giving no indication of the possible *date* at which the passing of sovereignty might have taken place; but it later indicated that it had occurred 'by 1980' (para 276).

[115] Ibid, paras 274–275.

[116] Ibid, para 276.

[117] Compare the finding in *Cameroon/Nigeria*, mentioned above, where it was not the shortness of the period during which Nigeria could have acted *à titre de souverain* that mattered, but that fact that there was no evidence during that period of acquiescence by Cameroon: [2002] ICJ Rep 416, para 224.

[118] This again suggests comparison with *préscription* in French law, rather than German *Verjährung* or English limitation.

State in question.'[119] It seems that what is meant is not that such manifestations without response may be *opposable* to the other State, but rather that they may be *effective* against it. The question whether the actions are opposable is rather the question whether they are such as to *call for* a response, i.e. primarily the question whether they are known to the State concerned.[120]

The central idea in the Court's treatment of the problem appears to be that of an 'evolution' in the attitudes of the rival claimants to the island. The weakness of this approach is that it involves the idea of a process, presenting some degree of continuity: the extent to which the one State considered that it had a claim of sovereignty, or endeavoured to express, maintain or defend such a claim, increased as compared with, and in proportion to, the degree to which the other State's claim was maintained or defended. The historical picture was however more one of a succession of isolated and more or less unrelated incidents,[121] as may in fact generally be the case. Furthermore, this approach is not very consistent with the underlying idea of acquiescence, of agreement. Agreement—strictly—either exists or does not exist, and therefore involves, at least in theory a moment of birth: theoretically at least, there was a moment at which Johor/Malaysia acquiesced in the takeover of sovereignty, and thus a moment at which sovereignty 'jumped' from the one State to the other: it could not slowly slide there. The Court in the case before it did not need to determine when that moment was, except by defining a *terminus ad quem* in 1980, but it is salutary for the commentator to consider what could have been identified as the turning point. The danger of the Court's approach is in allowing the effects of one individual incident to be assessed by reference to another individual incident, perhaps many decades later, on the basis that sovereignty was slipping away by slow degrees, when in fact those were truly isolated incidents.

A special difficulty was that the situation of the island was far from being typical of a territorial dispute, because of the undoubted fact that it was the site of a lighthouse constructed and maintained by, and belonging to, Singapore. In a classic territorial dispute, activities by one State in an area of territory claimed by another are either in breach of the sovereignty of the latter State, or assertions of sovereignty by the active State—or, indeed, both. Many day-to-day activities by Singapore related to the management and upkeep of the lighthouse were, in effect, carried out pursuant to the original consent by the Sultan of Johor. It was however

[119] Judgment of 23 May 2008, para 120, quoted above.

[120] See below as to the significance attached by the Court to the installation by Singapore of military communications equipment on the island (para 248 of the Judgment).

[121] Examples, perhaps, of saltationism rather than evolution? Cf Richard Goldschmidt, *The Material Basis of Evolution* (Yale University Press, New Haven CT, 1940). It is however probable that the Darwinian overtones of the term 'evolution' were not in any way intended by the Court. One may speculate that the relevant passages of the decision were drafted in French: *évolution* is more commonly used in that language to mean simply 'development'.

highly obscure whether that consent had amounted to a transfer of sovereignty or merely a licence to operate a lighthouse; and, as noted above, the Court declined to settle that point in its decision.[122] The activities actually carried on had therefore to be judged against a scale of permissibility, rather than the simple test of infringement of sovereignty. The Court thus invoked in this connection a number of acts on the part of Singapore which it did not view as 'conduct as operator of Horsburgh lighthouse', and which therefore were to be classified as acts *à titre de souverain*.[123]

The Court's decision to leave open the question of the legal effect of the grant by the Sultan of Johor in 1851 points up the fact that sovereignty is, at least in circumstances of this kind, not so much a legal fact as a psychological state or psychological relationship. Any assessment of the legal significance of the conduct of the parties after 1844 has to take into account what the parties did or did not do in the light of what they thought they were entitled to do; but, contrariwise, it is only possible to form a view on what a party thought it was entitled to do on the basis of evidence of what it in fact it did or refrained from doing. There is inevitably a certain circularity in the argument, unless one can begin from an objective legal fact, i.e. unless one can establish that at a certain date, prior to the activity under examination, sovereignty appertained to one State or the other. It would however make no sense to interpret the actions of the parties against the background of a finding that, although they didn't know it, sovereignty was legally vested in one or other of them all the time, or at least from the outset. For this reason, the starting point of the discussion in this part of the Court's judgment, that the Sultan of Johor had sovereignty over the island in 1844, needs also to be understood as a finding that *that was the case to the knowledge of both parties*. It is only on this basis that a true interpretation of the events can be reached. Fortunately, the Temenggong's letter of 25 November 1844, whether it was to be regarded as a cession of territory or as a grant of permission to erect a lighthouse, was clearly written on the basis that the authorities of Johor were in a position to make a cession or a grant, i.e. that the island was regarded as under Johor sovereignty; and the request of the Singapore authorities is only consistent with an understanding that that was the case.

On the other hand, having once permitted the erection and maintenance of a lighthouse on the island, on whatever terms, the authorities of Johor and its successors would have no particular reason subsequently to take any action in relation to the island; it does not seem to have served any useful purpose other than as a site for a lighthouse. If there had been no original intention to transfer sovereignty, then it might perhaps have been wise to take some occasional formal step by way of reminder of the

[122] Ibid, paras 131, 145. [123] Ibid, para 274.

retention of sovereignty; or, more particularly, to be observant and to check any action that might suggest a claim to sovereignty on the part of Singapore. The mere passage of time would not in itself seem to have any particular weight; yet the Court regarded its as a relevant consideration that 'the Johor authorities and their successors took no action at all on [the island] from June 1850 for the whole of the following century or more.'[124] The relevance of this can be checked by asking: when and why was there ever any need, or any occasion, for the Johor authorities to take any action in relation to the island?

It may be suggested, on the basis of these recent decisions of the Court, that the doctrine of prescription is unnecessary, and that even the most complex series of events in relation to a territory can be analysed as meeting, or failing to meet, the criteria for a tacit agreement for transfer of sovereignty, acquiescence, or 'evolution' of the parties' relationship.[125] If that is accepted, however, the corollary must surely be that the requirements for a transfer of sovereignty on one of these bases can not be less exigent than those traditionally associated with title by prescription, however understood. Can it be said with certainty that this was so in the *Singapore/Malaysia* case? Faced with an immensely complex case-file, incorporating a great number of incidents whose individual significance might be regarded as minimal, the Court's approach looks somewhat impressionistic.

The Court's decision may be read as authority for the view that sovereignty can be lost in, as it were, a sustained fit of absent-mindedness, provided that there is a competitor for the territory whose attitude is one of encroachment—perhaps equally absent-minded encroachment—beyond the powers and privileges (short of sovereignty) it already enjoys in respect of the territory. Must it then be said that the price of sovereignty is eternal vigilance?[126]

A matter closely related to that of acquisitive prescription, and which was of some relevance in the case discussed, is that of the 'critical date'. It will however be convenient to maintain the arrangement of subjects in the previous article in this series (an arrangement derived from Fitzmaurice's articles), and deal with this question separately (Chapter IV, Section 2, below).

(3) Acts à titre de souverain

Frequent reference is made in the *Malaysia/Singapore* case to the class of acts of a State *à titre de souverain*; it is these, and (it seems) these only, that

[124] Ibid, para 275.

[125] Cf the views of Brownlie, quoted in n 61 above.

[126] Roman law recognized the maxim *contra non volentem agere non currit praescriptio*, which raises the question whether prescription runs against a territory under mandate or trusteeship; cf the remarks of Judge Fleischhauer in his opinion in the *Kasikili/Sedudu Island* case (text and n 69 above).

are of relevance to a claim of sovereignty based on prescription or acquiescence. Where the claim is on the basis of colonial *effectivités* in relation to an alleged *terra nullius*, it appears that the test is different, or is at least expressed in different terms. In the *Territorial and Maritime Dispute between Nicaragua and Honduras in the Caribbean Sea*, the Court cited with approval the definition of colonial *effectivités* given by the Chamber in the *Frontier Dispute (Burkina Faso/Mali)*: 'the conduct of the administrative authorities as proof of the effective exercise of colonial jurisdiction in the region during the colonial period.'[127] In the *Frontier Dispute* between Benin and Niger, the Court rejected a contention by Benin that no effect should be given to the administration by Niger of one of the disputed islands in the river, as this was a 'temporary and practical arrangement', precluding the existence of an intention to act as sovereign.[128] The Court however considered that 'the concept of the intention and will to act as sovereign . . . is a concept of international law and cannot be transplanted purely and simply to colonial law.'[129]

The earlier sources discussing the concept of prescription tend to use very much the same sort of terminology as this.[130] This is hardly surprising, as the essential difference between prescription and acquiescence, on the one hand, and appropriation of a *terra nullius* on the basis of *effectivités*, on the other, is that in the former case acquisition by one State goes along with dispossession of another; and accordingly the essential differentiating element is not so much the nature of the acts performed as the relation between those acts and the soon-to-be-dispossessed State.[131] The acts themselves that are required to show an acquisition of sovereignty would seem to be of a single class, whether or not there is a rival claimant to the territory. This latter circumstance may have an impact on the nature of the acts as regards the question of the opportunity that that State should have had to be aware of them, and to react to them, but not otherwise.

The intellectual overlap between the concepts of *effectivités* in the ex-colonial context and of acts *à titre de souverain* in the context of

[127] [2007-II] ICJ Rep 710, para 165, citing [1986] ICJ Rep 586, para 63, and the *Frontier Dispute (Benin/Niger)* Judgment, [2005] ICJ Rep 120, para 47.

[128] [2005] ICJ Rep 132–133, para 101.

[129] Ibid, 133, para 102; regarded by one commentator as 'une formulation quelque peu maladroite': Anne-Thida Norodom, 'L'arrêt de la chambre de la cour internationale de justice dans l'affaire du *Différend frontalier* (Bénin/Niger) 12 juillet 2005' (2005) LI *Annuaire français de droit international* 185, 200.

[130] Rousseau for example defines 'la condition qu'il y ait eu d'une part silence du souverain et d'autre part exercice effectif, continu et sans lacune de la souveraineté territoriale (possession paisible)' *Droit international public,* Tome III (8e édition, Dalloz, Paris, 1976) 185. The original definition in *Oppenheim's International Law,* retained in the current edition, referred to 'the acquisition of sovereignty over a territory through continuous and undisturbed exercise of sovereignty over it during such a period as is necessary to create under the influence of historical development the general conviction that the present condition of things is in conformity with international order' (above n 42, 706).

[131] Thus in the *Western Sahara* case, the Court commented on the PCIJ's decision in the case of the *Legal Status of Eastern Greenland* that very little in the way of actual exercise of sovereign rights 'might be sufficient *in the absence of a competing claim*': [1975] ICJ Rep 43, para 92 (emphasis added), citing PCIJ Series A/B No 53, 46.

prescription is visible in the Court's judgment in two cases in which no question of prescription arose, the matter being one of acquisition of title to *terra nullius*: the case of *Sovereignty over Pulau Ligitan and Pulau Sipadan*, and the case of the *Territorial and Maritime Dispute between Nicaragua and Honduras in the Caribbean Sea*. Both when examining the reliance by Malaysia on its construction of a lighthouse on Pulau Sipadan, and the claim of Honduras that certain public works carried out on the islands disputed with Nicaragua amounted to relevant *effectivités*, the Court cited as a relevant precedent its decision in the *Qatar/Bahrain* case, described below, which specifically used the expression 'acts *à titre de souverain*'.[132]

It is in these more modern cases, and in relation to more ambiguous activities, that the term *à titre de souverain* seems to have come into use. What then is the distinguishing mark of an act *à titre de souverain*? What acts fall within, and what outside, the category? The expression, and the concept, could be interpreted subjectively, in the sense that the question would be, did the State when performing this act consider itself to be performing it, and to be entitled to perform it, as the sovereign of the territory? It could also be interpreted objectively, the question being, were the acts performed such that they would be (or perhaps, could only be) performed by the sovereign of the territory? Did they by their nature constitute notice to all the world that the State performing them considered itself to be sovereign there?

In the case of *Maritime Delimitation and Territorial Questions between Qatar and Bahrain*, the disputed territory was a feature known as Qit'at Jaradah; and the first problem was whether this was an island, and therefore subject to appropriation in sovereignty, or a mere low-tide elevation; the Court decided that it was 'an island which should as such be taken into consideration for the drawing of the equidistance line' required for delimiting the maritime spaces disputed between the parties.[133] The Court then went on to consider activities that had been performed by Bahrain and which it relied on to support a claim of sovereignty.

> Certain types of activities invoked by Bahrain such as the drilling of artesian wells would, taken by themselves, be considered controversial as acts performed *à titre de souverain*. The construction of navigational aids, on the other hand, can legally be relevant in the case of very small islands. In the present case, taking into account the size of Qit'at Jaradah, the activities carried out by Bahrain on that island must be considered sufficient to support Bahrain's claim that it has sovereignty over it.[134]

[132] [2002] ICJ Rep 684–685, para 146; [2007-II] ICJ Rep 720, para 206.

[133] [2001] ICJ Rep 99, para 195. Despite this cautious formulation, the Court did find categorically in the operative clause of its judgment that 'the State of Bahrain has sovereignty over the island of Qit'at Jaradah': ibid, 117, para 252 (3).

[134] Ibid, 99–100, para 197. It is not entirely clear whether the Court is basing its finding on the navigational aids alone, or on the navigational aids plus the artesian wells.

The reference to 'types of activity' suggests that it is an objective test that is here being applied: to drill an artesian well is not, or not indisputably, an act *à titre de souverain* even if the State performing it is convinced of its sovereign rights over the area drilled. If the construction of navigational aids '*can* legally be relevant', what is the criterion for deciding when they are and when they are not? Is it perhaps the intention of the State concerned? In the *Malaysia/Singapore* case, discussed above, the United Kingdom constructed a lighthouse on an island under the sovereignty of the Sultan of Johor, on the basis of an ambiguously worded consent by the Sultan. If that consent was, and was understood to be, a licence to construct rather than a cession of territory, then whatever the inherent sovereign-like nature of the act of construction, the United Kingdom could never have had the subjective conviction of acting *à titre de souverain.*

The claim of Namibia to *Kasikili/Sedudu Island* on the basis of prescription was not examined by the Court in its judgment in that case. In its pleadings, Namibia referred to the requirement of acts *à titre de souverain* but did not elaborate on the theory of this. It explained its argument on the basis of prescription in these terms:

> [T]here was peaceful occupation and use of the Island by the Masubia of Caprivi for the greater part of the period under consideration under the authority of their traditional leadership, responsible to the German, British (as administrators of the Mandate for South Africa) and South African authorities. There was no objection, let alone control, by the Bechuanaland authorities.[135]

The only State (*souverain*) element here seems to be the allegation that the tribal authorities were 'responsible to' the authorities of the colonizing State, and it was the link between the colonizing State and any activities on the island that was challenged by Botswana.[136]

Despite the fact that the decision in the *Malaysia/Singapore* case was not specifically based on prescription, which had not as such been pleaded,[137] the Court did in fact employ the expression 'acts *à titre de souverain*' in order to distinguish the acts which in that case were regarded as relevant to the passage of sovereignty from the one State to the other, from those which were not. The essential period examined is that posterior to 1953, when there was an exchange of letters that the Court regarded as significant; it does not appear that a letter claiming, contesting or repudiating sovereignty falls itself within the category of acts *à titre de souverain.*

Of the post-1953 incidents, the Court categorised as acts *à titre de souverain*: the investigation of wrecks; requiring visiting Malaysian officials to

[135] Reply of Namibia, para 86; see also the dispatch of 14 February 1949 cited in [1999] ICJ Rep 1080–1081, para 59.

[136] See also [1999] ICJ Rep 1104, para 95.

[137] See above, text and n 86.

obtain permits; installation of military communication equipment on the island; and proposed land reclamation works (not in the event proceeded with). As regards the investigation of wrecks, Singapore claimed that 'investigating and reporting on maritime hazards and shipwrecks within the island's territorial waters' was an exercise of sovereign authority;[138] the matter was complicated by Singapore's responsibility, apparently independently of sovereignty over the island, for the Horsburgh lighthouse,[139] but in itself this activity is consistent with an assertion of sovereignty over waters as territorial waters, and the Court noted that one incident in particular 'assists Singapore's contention that it was acting *à titre de souverain*'.[140] The question of permits granted to Malaysian officials to visit the island was again complicated by the rights and duties of Singapore in respect of the lighthouse. Singapore asserted that the grant of these permits were in the 'exercise of exclusive control'; Malaysia retorted that Singapore required similar permits to visit all the lighthouses that it operated, whether or not they were on its own sovereign territory.[141] The Court's finding was however categorical: 'This Singaporean conduct is to be seen as conduct *à titre de souverain*', which 'does give significant support to Singapore's claim to sovereignty'.[142]

However, when Singapore installed military communication equipment on the island in 1977, this was, according to Malaysia, done secretly, so that it was not aware of the action. The Court was unable to reach a conclusion on the question of Malaysia's knowledge of the activity,[143] but regarded it as significant 'that Singapore's action is an act *à titre de souverain*' as being 'inconsistent with Singapore recognizing any limit on its freedom of action'.[144] However, traditionally acts capable of defeating the sovereignty of the territorial State must be performed *nec vi, nec clam, nec precario*; if the act is such that the territorial State could not have been aware of it, it must be disregarded.[145] It is probably a legitimate deduction from the action of the Singapore authorities that they regarded themselves as sovereign; but it surely takes more than a conviction on one side of the possession of sovereignty to effect a transfer of it.[146] For an act *à titre de souverain* to be relevant to the process of prescription, it must be seen, or capable of being seen, as having that quality by the other State concerned, so as to call for some reaction.

The Court's ruling on the value of the installation of the military communications equipment can perhaps be seen as involving a question of burden of proof. It was accepted that such equipment was installed; if this was

[138] Judgment of 23 May 2008, para 231.
[139] A point taken by Malaysia: ibid, para 232.
[140] Ibid, para 233.
[141] Ibid, para 235.
[142] Ibid, para. 239.
[143] It is suggested that the burden of proof should lie on the State claiming prescription, to show that the acts supporting its claim were known, or ought to have been known, to the original sovereign; on that basis, the inability of the Court to resolve the point should have weighed against Singapore.
[144] Judgment of 23 May 2008, para 248.
[145] Cf the Joint Dissenting Opinion of Judges Simma and Abraham, para 17.
[146] A point well taken by Judge Dugard in his Dissenting Opinion (para 42).

in itself an act *à titre de souverain* (and in view of the sensitivity of the matter, this is a reasonable view), the Court may have considered that it was for Malaysia to demonstrate that the condition of lack of secrecy was not fulfilled. Even on this basis, however, the decision is not entirely satisfactory.

In 1978, as the Court found, the Port of Singapore Authority invited tenders for 'Reclamation and Shore Protection Work at Horsburgh Lighthouse'; and Singapore claimed that this was 'classic conduct *à titre de souverain*'.[147] There was some documentation concerning the proposal which was not known to Malaysia, but the advertisement 'was public and attracted replies'.[148] The reclamation was ultimately not proceeded with; however since, as Malaysia conceded, 'the proposed action did go beyond the maintenance and operation of the lighthouse', the Court considered that it 'supports Singapore's case'.

On the basis of the cases discussed, it seems that, despite the conceptual difference between acquisition of a *terra nullius* and acquisition by prescription against an established title, the acts that the acquiring State must demonstrate fall into a single category, even if different terminology is used to refer to them.

3. Succession and the Principle of *Uti Possidetis*[149]

During the period under review, the principle of *uti possidetis juris*[150] has been invoked in a number of cases: *Maritime Delimitation and Territorial Questions between Qatar and Bahrain* (2001); *Land and Maritime Boundary between Cameroon and Nigeria* (2002); *Frontier Dispute (Benin/Niger)* (2005); and *Territorial and Maritime Dispute between Nicaragua and Honduras in the Caribbean Sea* (2007). The previous case-law of the Court on the matter, commented on to some extent in the relevant earlier article

[147] Ibid, para 249. [148] Ibid, para 250.

[149] Succession of States is examined here solely in relation to disputed claims to territory. The Court has had to deal with questions of succession in other contexts during the period under review. In the *Gabcíkovo/Nagymaros Project* case, the separation of the Czech Republic and Slovakia raised questions of succession to the rights and obligations of Czechoslovakia in relation to the project agreement with Hungary, in particular the question to what extent the Vienna Convention on Succession of States in Respect of Treaties represented customary law: [1997] ICJ Rep 69 et seq, paras 117 et seq. In the *Application of the Genocide Convention* case between Bosnia and Herzegovina and Serbia and Montenegro, the separation of Montenegro from Serbia during the course of the proceedings raised the problem of the identification of the respondent party to the proceedings: [2007-II] ICJ Rep 73 et seq, paras 67 et seq.

[150] The separate concept of *uti possidetis* (no *juris*) as in effect equivalent to simple occupation, and thus unrelated to legal succession, advanced by Brazil in its negotiations with its neighbours in the 19th century, has not been invoked as such in the disputes with which the Court has been concerned, and appears to amount to a special or local custom alongside the general customary rule of *uti possidetis* asserted by the Chamber in the *Frontier Dispute* between Burkina Faso and Mali. For a thorough study of the Brazilian practice and analysis of the concept, see Julio Barberis, 'La conception brésilienne de l'*uti possidetis*', in Emile Yakpo and Taha Boumedra (eds), *Liber Amicorum Mohammed Bedjaoui* (Kluwer International, The Hague, 1999) 49.

in this series,[151] consisted of the judgment on the *Frontier Dispute* between Burkina Faso and Mali, and the *Land, Island and Maritime Frontier* case between El Salvador and Honduras.[152]

(1) Application of the principle

In the case of *Maritime Delimitation and Territorial Questions between Qatar and Bahrain*, Bahrain invoked the principle of *uti possidetis juris* in support of its claim to the Hawar Islands. Relying on the dictum of the Chamber of the Court in the *Frontier Dispute* case, discussed in the 1995 article in this series,[153] that *uti possidetis* is 'a general principle, which is logically connected with the phenomenon of the obtaining of independence, wherever it occurs',[154] Bahrain referred to what it regarded as having been 'the colonial heritage' when the two States, in 1971, began to enjoy the full attributes of sovereignty, after having been protectorates of Great Britain. Part of this heritage, in Bahrain's contention, was a decision of the British Government in 1939 that the Hawar Islands belonged to Bahrain.[155] The Court upheld Bahrain's claim to the islands, not on the basis of the 1939 British decision, but on the simpler ground that the two States had agreed at that time that the question should be decided authoritatively by the British Government; and even though the decision could not be equated with an arbitral award, it still had legal effect.[156]

The Court was therefore able to leave open the question of 'the applicability of the principle of *uti possidetis juris* to the present case'.[157] For the reasons indicated in the 1995 article in this series,[158] it is suggested that it must be doubtful whether the *uti possidetis* principle had any application where the attribution of the islands had not, during the period preceding full independence of the two States, been a matter of internal administrative boundaries of the 'colonial' power, but of allocation of the islands to one or other of two distinct State entities.

In the case of the *Land and Maritime Boundary between Cameroon and Nigeria*, the Court found it unnecessary to deal with the arguments, advanced by both parties, based on the *uti possidetis* principle.[159] The principle was however discussed in the separate opinion of Judge *ad hoc*

[151] (1995) *BYIL* 15–16.

[152] An interesting point arises when a tribunal is asked to determine the location of an existing but disputed boundary: is the tribunal limited by the submissions of the parties, on the basis of *ne ultra petita*, or should it award a party more than it claims if that appears to correspond to the true position of the boundary? See the discussion of this in Kaiyan Homi Kaikobad, 'The Quality of Justice: "Excès de Pouvoir" in the Adjudication and Arbitration of Territorial and Boundary Disputes', in Guy S Goodwin-Gill, Stefan A G Talmon (eds), *The Reality of International Law: Essays in Honour of Ian Brownlie* (Clarendon Press, Oxford, 1999) 293, 299–302.

[153] [1986] ICJ Rep 565, para 20, discussed in (1995) *BYIL* 1, 15–17.

[154] Ibid, quoted without attribution at [2001] ICJ Rep 72, para 103.

[155] [2001] ICJ Rep 72, para 103.

[156] Ibid, 83, para 139.

[157] Ibid, 85, para 148.

[158] See (1995) *BYIL* 15–16.

[159] [2002] ICJ Rep 412, para 217.

Mbaye, who drew attention to the particular dimension taken on by the principle in the African context. He recalled the OAU Cairo Resolution of 1964,[160] showing that the new States of Africa wanted '[a]t all costs . . . to avoid having the boundaries bequeathed by the colonial Powers (however absurd, illogical or badly drawn, and even where they divided ethnic groups or tribes) called into question.'[161] As the case of the *Land, Island and Maritime Frontier Dispute* between El Salvador and Honduras shows, in Latin America the problem was less the illogicality of pre-independence boundaries than the difficulty in establishing their precise situation, at a period (round 1812) when surveying and cartographic techniques were far less advanced than in the 20th century; and there was generally even less concern at that early date for respect for the tribal dimension.

Judge Mbaye however quoted with approval[162] the dictum of the Chamber of the Court in the *Frontier Dispute* case between Burkina Faso and Mali to the effect that the principle of *uti possidetis* established in the relations between the former Spanish colonies in South America is 'a general principle, which is logically connected with the phenomenon of the obtaining of independence, *wherever it occurs*'.[163] In the earlier article in this series devoted to territorial questions, the view was expressed that that statement may be regarded as of somewhat doubtful general validity.[164] In Africa, at least, it has received endorsement in the Constitution of the Organization of African Unity (Lomé, 11 July 2001). It continues to be quoted by the Court; but, exceptionally, the recent Judgment of a further Chamber of the Court in the *Frontier Dispute* between Benin and Niger, while repeating some of the observations of the earlier Chamber concerning the principle, does not repeat the broad assessment just quoted.[165]

The two *Frontier Dispute* cases, of 1986 and 2005, shared one feature which rendered the *uti possidetis* principle, in some form or another,

[160] AGH/Res. 16 (1), cited by Judge Mbaye at [2002] ICJ Rep 508, para 15, and 521–522, para 76; also recalled in the Burkina Faso/Mali Judgment, [1986] ICJ Rep 565, para 22.

[161] [2002] ICJ Rep 508, para 15. On the difficulties in establishing any firm territorial boundaries in parts of Africa inhabited by nomadic tribes, cf the Court's opinion in *Western Sahara*, [1975] ICJ Rep 66–67, paras 158–160.

[162] [2002] ICJ Rep 522, para 78.

[163] [1986] ICJ Rep 565, para 20, emphasis added. In Africa in particular the 1964 Cairo Resolution of the OAU suggests 'the possibility that *uti possidetis* was no more than a policy decision adopted to avoid conflicts during decolonization': E K M Yakpo, 'The African Concept of *Uti Possidetis*—Need for Change', in Yakpo and Boumedra (eds), above n 150, 273. This author does not however question the conclusion that '*uti possidetis* is an established rule of customary international law' (ibid).

[164] Georges Abi-Saab has argued that when the question arises between two newly independent States which were, prior to independence, colonial possessions of two different powers, so that there was a precedent *international* frontier, the principle of *uti possidetis* 'ne fait que refléter, et par consequent il se confond totalement avec les règles de succession d'États': 'Le principe de l'*uti possidetis*: son role et ses limites dans le contentieux territorial international', in Marcelo Kohen (ed) *Promoting Justice, Human Rights and Conflict Resolution through International Law* (Nijhoff, Leiden, 2007) 658. However, even in that situation, the *uti possidetis* principle will presumably apply to the extent that it will exclude any *terra nullius* in case of inconsistent versions of the colonial frontier: cf Abi-Saab, ibid, 669.

[165] [2005] ICJ Rep 108, para 23.

appropriate; they were both cases in which each of the two States concerned had formerly been a colony of the same State—France, as it happened. Just as in South America, it was therefore necessary (in the absence of any specific agreement as to frontiers made at the time of independence) to consider what had been the administrative boundaries established by the colonial power between the units which had become transformed into independent States. In the *Benin/Niger* case, Article 6 of the Special Agreement by which the Chamber was seised specified that the law to be applied should include 'le principe de la succession d'États aux frontières héritées de la colonisation, à savoir l'intangibilité des frontières'.[166] In the earlier case, the Chamber had been at some pains to point out that the effect of the colonial law was nothing more than a relevant fact, that it did not apply to the question *as law*.

> [I]nternational law does not effect any renvoi to the law established by the colonizing State, nor indeed to any legal rule unilaterally established by any State whatever; French law—especially legislation enacted by France for its colonies and *territoires d'outre-mer*—may play a role not in itself (as if there were a sort of *continuum juris*, a legal relay between such law and international law), but only as one factual element among others, or as evidence of what has been called the "colonial heritage", i.e. the "photograph of the territory" at the critical date.[167]

It was suggested in the previous article that this passage was inspired less by considerations of law than by concern 'to avoid anything that might be interpreted as a defence or approval or colonialism'.[168] Certainly it is rather odd to employ the phrase *uti possidetis juris*, i.e. 'so far as you are *legally* in possession' while denying that the law in force prior to independence has any legal force. Furthermore, the position of an administrative boundary is inevitably a matter of law, internal law, not a mere 'factual element'.[169]

The clearest statement that the *uti possidetis juris* is a reference to the pre-independence law *as law* is to be found in the decision of the Chamber in the *Land, Island and Maritime Frontier Dispute* between El Salvador and Honduras. Dealing with the law applicable to the dispute over the islands in the Gulf of Fonseca, the Chamber recalled that

166 [2005] ICJ Rep 96 and 108, para 23.

167 [1986] ICJ Rep 568, para 30. For criticism of this approach as involving a 'legal fiction', see Philippe Weckel, 'Les premières applications de l'article 290 de la Convention sur le droit de la mer relatif à la prescription de mesures conservatoires' (2005) 109 *Revue générale de Droit international public* 941.

168 (1995) *BYIL* 1, 17. There is a certain inconsistency in using the term 'colonial heritage' while denying that its operation is a matter of law, 'heritage' itself being a legal term.

169 More recently Judge Bennouna, no friend to colonialism, has observed that 'il est difficile de ne pas s'aventurer dans le droit colonial, ne serait ce que pour apprécier quelles étaient les limites tracées par les colonisateurs': Declaration appended to the Judgment of 23 May 2008 in *Sovereignty over Pedra Branca/Pulau Batu Puteh*, para 12.

when the principle of the *uti possidetis juris* is involved, the *jus* referred to is not international law but the constitutional or administrative law of the pre-independence sovereign, in this case Spanish colonial law...[170]

The Chamber in this case also recognized the limitations of the principle, in that the law in question might sometimes 'give no clear and definite answer' to the questions referred to it, as where it was a matter of the appurtenance to one administrative unit or another of 'marginal areas, or sparsely populated areas of minimal economic significance.'[171]

Nevertheless the Chamber in the Benin/Niger case cited, with approval, the passage quoted from the decision in the Burkina Faso/Mali case.[172] Further on in its decision it was faced with two questions that raised directly the problem of the nature of the national law as seen from the standpoint of international law. First, the Chamber had occasion to consider whether a particular concept of international law—that of the need for authorities of a State to be acting in relation to a territory with 'the intention and will to act as sovereign'[173]—was applicable to administrative acts carried out during the colonial period; it held that that concept 'is a concept of international law and cannot be transplanted purely and simply to *colonial law*.'[174] Secondly, the Chamber was faced with this conundrum: a French Decree of 2 March 1907 had defined the boundary between the two relevant colonial entities in a particular way, but a number of administrative instruments promulgated after 1927, concerning game reserves and national parks, had employed a quite different boundary, a river known as the Mekrou. The Chamber concluded

that the 1907 line no longer corresponded, at the critical date [that of independence], to the intercolonial boundary and that, on the contrary, at that date, it was the course of the Mekrou [river] which, in the view of all the competent authorities of the colonial administration, constituted the boundary between the adjacent colonies....[175]

There remained the problem, however, that 'the decree of 2 March 1907, which clearly defined a different boundary, was never expressly abrogated or amended, or indeed superseded by some other instrument of at least equal authority'.[176] According to colonial law, therefore, which line was the intercolonial boundary? The Chamber handled the problem in this way: first it indicated that

the *uti possidetis juris* principle requires not only that reliance be placed on existing legal titles, but also that account be taken of the manner in which those titles

170 [1992] ICJ Rep 559, para 333.

171 Ibid.

172 [2005] ICJ Rep 120, para 46.

173 See the discussion in Section 2(3) above.

174 [2005] ICJ Rep 133, para 102, emphasis added. Judge *ad hoc* Bennouna argued persuasively that the concept should be 'adapted to the situation of the colonial authority': ibid, 162, para 45.

175 Ibid, 148, para 139.

176 Ibid, para 140.

were interpreted and applied by the competent public authorities of the colonial Power, in particular in the exercise of their law-making power.[177]

It then noted that

the administrative instruments promulgated after 1927 were never the subject of any challenge before the competent courts, and ... there is no evidence that the colonial administration was ever criticized at the time for having improperly departed from the 1907 decree.

What conclusion could or should be drawn as to the status in French law of the two rival boundaries? This was the answer given by the Chamber:

It is not for the Chamber to substitute itself for a domestic court (in this case the French administrative courts) by carrying out its own review of the legality of the instruments in question in light of the 1907 decree, nor to speculate on what the French courts might have decided had they been seised of the matter. The fact is that they were not so seised and that there is nothing to suggest that, in the decisions taken by them after 1927, the administrative authorities either manifestly exceeded their powers or acted in manifest breach of the applicable rules.[178]

As a matter of international law, therefore, the Chamber found that

[i]t follows from all of the foregoing that, at least from 1927 onwards, the competent administrative authorities regarded the course of the Mekrou as the intercolonial boundary separating Dahomey from Niger, that those authorities reflected that boundary in the successive instruments promulgated by them after 1927, some of which expressly indicated that boundary, while others necessarily implied it, and that *this was the state of the law at the dates of independence in August 1960*.[179]

The reference to the 'state of the law' can only, it seems, be to the internal law of the French colonial administration; and this finding therefore indicates that it is unrealistic to pretend, as the earlier *Frontier Dispute* Chamber had done, that it is not the *law* of the colonial Power that has to be consulted, and consulted *as law*, in order to establish the boundary for the purposes of international law. The situation is one of *renvoi*: before decolonization, international law has nothing to say on the position and status of an administrative boundary, and if the question were to arise before independence, would have to refer to the law of the colonial Power. Similarly, when the post-independence law has to refer back in time to the pre-independence boundary, it must refer to the same domestic law. Furthermore, there is the question how the parties themselves saw the situation at the time of decolonisation: what territories did they then *think* they were getting?

If that domestic law is uncertain, how then is the international tribunal to proceed? The Chamber disowned any possibility of substituting itself

[177] Ibid. [178] Ibid. [179] Ibid, 148–149, para 141, emphasis added.

for a domestic court, or 'carrying out its own review of the instruments in question'; but it is arguable that in fact this is nevertheless what it did, and what it could not avoid doing. It was saying that, so long as no French court had been seised of the question, and had decided that the post-1927 instruments were invalid as in conflict with the 1907 Decree, those instruments had to be given effect. This was an extremely sensible approach, but it does involve a value-judgement of the kind that the French domestic court might have been called upon to make. The International Court gave precedence to the consistent modern actions of the administrative authorities over the rule, impliedly found to exist in French administrative law, of the hierarchy of law-creating instruments. That might or might not have been the solution arrived at by the French administrative courts; but the point is that it was a solution to a legal problem, and not 'one factual element among others', to use the terminology of the earlier *Frontier Dispute* decision. The actual decision of 2005 cannot be faulted; but it did, contrary to the Chamber's protestations, constitute a substitution of the Chamber for the French domestic court which, never having been seised, had never spoken.

In the case of the *Territorial and Maritime Dispute between Nicaragua and Honduras in the Caribbean Sea*, the problem was not that the domestic law was uncertain: on the contrary, the Court found that it was 'beyond doubt that the *uti possidetis juris* principle is applicable to the question of territorial delimitation between Nicaragua and Honduras, both former Spanish colonial provinces'.[180] Furthermore, effect had been given to the principle in the Gamez-Bonilla Treaty of 7 October 1894, endorsed by an arbitral award of the King of Spain, the validity of which in its turn had been confirmed by the Court itself in 1960.[181] The existence of the law was certain; what was uncertain was whether it applied to the islands in dispute, as it did to the mainland territories of the two parties.

The Court had, as it recalled, already found that '*uti possidetis juris* may, in principle, apply to offshore possessions and maritime spaces.'[182] Since, as the Court had again already found, 'a key aspect of the principle [of *uti possidetis juris*] is the denial of the possibility of *terra nullius*',[183] it would seem to follow that the *uti possidetis* principle had necessarily to be applied, and would necessarily give an answer to the question of sovereignty. However, the Court found itself faced with a contradiction. It found as a fact that during the period of Spanish rule:

Unlike the land territory where the administrative boundary between different provinces was more or less clearly demarcated, it is apparent that there was no

[180] [2007-II] ICJ Rep 706–707, para 154.

[181] *Arbitral Award made by the King of Spain on 23 December 1906*, [1960] ICJ Rep 192.

[182] [2007-II] ICJ Rep 707, para 156, citing *Land, Island and Maritime Frontier Dispute (El Salvador/Honduras)* [1992] ICJ Rep 558, para 333; 589, para 386.

[183] Ibid, para 157, citing *Land, Island and Maritime Frontier Dispute* [1992] ICJ Rep 387, para 42.

clear-cut demarcation with regard to islands in general. This seems all the more so with regard to the islands in question, since they must have been scarcely inhabited, if at all, and possessed no natural resources to speak of for exploitation, except for fishing in the surrounding maritime area.[184]

Accordingly,

Notwithstanding the historical and continuing importance of the *uti possidetis juris* principle, so closely associated with Latin American decolonization, it cannot in this case be said that the application of this principle to these small islands, located considerably offshore and not obviously adjacent to the mainland coast of Nicaragua or Honduras, would settle the issue of sovereignty over them.[185]

In an earlier paragraph, the Court had anticipated the problem, and dealt with it as follows: referring to the dictum as to the exclusion of *terra nullius*, it observed that:

However, that dictum cannot bring within the territory of successor States islands not shown to be subject to Spanish colonial rule, nor *ipso facto* render as "attributed", islands which have no connection with the mainland coast concerned. Even if both Parties in this case agree that there is no question of the islands concerned being *res nullius*, necessary legal questions remain to be answered.[186]

The obvious difficulty is that if an island was not 'subject to Spanish colonial rule', then it was *terra nullius*, whether or not it was in the general area subject to Spanish rule.

One may perhaps translate the Court's argument and conclusion as a finding that, while in principle there could be no *terra nullius* in mainland areas to which the *uti possidetis juris* principle applied, nor in islands of such a size and position that it would have been in the interest of the Spanish administration to allocate them to an administrative region, there could also be island territories which remained unallocated in fact, and which had to be regarded as unallocated in law for the purpose of *uti possidetis*. The exclusion of *terra nullius* which was the purpose of the principle would not be prejudiced, since by definition the islands would be such as to offer no inducement to a third State to take control of them—at least until the late 20th century when undersea petroleum exploitation gave a new interest to territories fronting on the sea.

(2) The role of effectivités

A concept which has been much employed in argument over boundary and territorial questions involving the *uti possidetis* principle, and which has featured in a number of decisions of the Court in that field, is that of

[184] [2007-II] ICJ Rep 709, para 162. [185] Ibid, para 163.
[186] [2007-II] ICJ Rep 707, para 157.

effectivités. The origin of the concept, at least so far as the jurisprudence of the Court is concerned, appears to be in the arguments of the parties in the first *Frontier Dispute* case in 1986, in the form of what were called 'colonial *effectivités*'. In the arguments of the parties and the decision of the Chamber, '*effectivités*' became the code-word for these considerations; they were defined as 'the conduct of the administrative authorities as proof of the effective exercise of territorial jurisdiction in the region during the colonial period.'[187] These were to be contrasted, or reconciled, with any written or cartographical title that might exist, including 'the text of a treaty' or some other 'legislative or conventional form'; the Chamber did not at the outset give a definition of 'title', but the meaning of the term can be deduced from its judgment, and it did subsequently, in the course of a discussion of the value of maps, refer to a 'territorial title' as 'a document endowed by international law with intrinsic legal force for the purpose of establishing territorial rights'.[188]

The 'basic document' in the *Frontier Dispute* between Burkina Faso and Mali was a French law of 4 September 1947 re-establishing the colony of Upper Volta, with the same boundaries as a former colony of the same name;[189] this was supplemented by a number of other 'legislative and regulatory texts' and 'relevant administrative documents', none of which however contained any complete description of the inter-colonial boundary that had become, with independence, the international boundary.

The Chamber in that case defined as follows the relationship between *effectivités* and titles:

[The Chamber] must . . . state forthwith, in general terms, what legal relationship exists between such acts and the titles on which the implementation of principle of *uti possidetis* is grounded. For this purpose, a distinction must be drawn among several eventualities. Where the act corresponds exactly to law, where effective administration is additional to the *uti possidetis juris*, the only role of *effectivité* is to confirm the exercise of the right derived from a legal title. Where the act does not correspond to the law, where the territory which is the subject of the dispute is effectively administered by a State other than the one possessing the legal title, preference should be given to the holder of the title. In the event that the *effectivité* does not co-exist with any legal title, it must invariably be taken into consideration. Finally, there are cases where the legal title is not capable of showing exactly the territorial expanse to which it relates. The *effectivités* can then play an essential role in showing how the title is interpreted in practice.[190]

The distinction prompts the question: what then is the status of maps, official and unofficial? The Chamber supplied a useful statement of

[187] [1986] ICJ Rep 586, para 63. [188] Ibid, 582, para 54.
[189] Ibid, 580, para 51. [190] Ibid, 586–587, para 63.

principle on this question also (to be discussed further in Section 1B below), emphasizing that in principle

maps merely constitute information which varies in accuracy from case to case; of themselves, and by virtue solely of their existence, they cannot constitute a territorial title, that is, a document endowed by international law with intrinsic legal force for the purpose of establishing territorial rights.[191]

As was mentioned in the previous article,[192] the Chamber commented on the meaning of the word 'titles' in this connection, and in relation to the distinction between 'delimitation disputes' and 'disputes as to attribution of territory'. It explained that the term 'legal title' did not refer to 'documentary evidence alone', but might comprehend 'both any evidence which may establish the existence of a right, and the actual source of the right'.[193] These findings were cited with approval by the Chamber in the second *Frontier Dispute* case (Benin/Niger).[194] The Chamber in that case was faced with a conflict within colonial law, in the form of French legislative acts on the one hand and subordinate legislation on the other; in that context it referred to maps as 'confirming and reinforcing the conclusions' based on this latter class of material.[195]

In the later case of the *Land, Island and Maritime Boundary Dispute* between El Salvador and Honduras, the expression 'the titles on which the implementation of principle of *uti possidetis* is grounded' referred to international titles such as a boundary treaty or a joint declaration, or to colonial titles such as legislation specifying the boundaries of a colony. In a later section of the judgment, however, the Chamber pointed out that

Spanish colonial divisions in Spanish America did not originally have any "original" or "historic" titles, as these concepts are understood in international law. The original title belonged exclusively to the Spanish Crown, not the internal subdivisions established by it; and it was equally the Spanish Crown which had sovereignty of the colonial territories.[196]

In this case, a further terminological complication was imported through the reliance of both parties on 'titles' in the form of grants of lands by the Spanish authorities to various communities on each side of the administrative boundary that was to become the frontier, and even on the so-called 'republican titles', similar grants made by the authorities of the two new States succeeding to the old administrative units.

Similar questions to those faced by the Chamber in the Burkina Faso/Mali *Frontier Dispute*, of title versus *effectivité,* had in fact arisen in the El Salvador/Honduras case. In that case, the parties were agreed that the essential consideration governing the determination of the land boundary

[191] Ibid, 582, para 54. [192] (1995) *BYIL* 1, 30.
[193] [1986] ICJ Rep 564, para 18. [194] [2005] ICJ Rep 119–120, para 44.
[195] Ibid, 147, para 138. [196] [1992] ICJ Rep 565, para 345.

was the principle of the *uti possidetis juris*, and this was provided for in the 1980 General Treaty of Peace on the basis of which the parties agreed ultimately to bring the case to a Chamber of the Court. The Joint Frontier Commission provided for in that Treaty was to take into account, along with the *uti possidetis juris* principle, 'other evidence and arguments of a legal, historical, human or any other kind, brought before it by the Parties and admitted under international law'.[197]

The qualification added by the last four words of this text was in effect applied to exclude certain categories of considerations urged upon it as being relevant *effectivités*. El Salvador mentioned demographic pressures creating a need for territory, both prior to and after independence, as compared with the relatively sparsely populated Honduras. The Chamber of the Court did not accept this as relevant:

> For the *uti possidetis juris*, the question is not whether the colonial province needed wide boundaries to accommodate its population, but where those boundaries actually were; and post-independence *effectivités*, where relevant, have to be assessed in terms of actual events, not their social origins.[198]

Both parties to the case also relied on *effectivités* in the sense of occupation of disputed areas by citizens of the one State or the other, the supply of public services, and the exercise of judicial, administrative and political competences and military jurisdiction.[199] Similarly both parties invoked the dicta of the *Frontier Dispute* Chamber on the relationship between titles and *effectivités*.

The extent to which *effectivités* were in fact found to have a role to play in the delimitation between El Salvador and Honduras was fairly limited. The Chamber was asked to delimit the land frontier in six sectors.[200] In the first, the Chamber was able to establish a line on the basis of the pre-independence land titles. It then considered 'material put forward by Honduras ... concerning settlement of Honduran nationals in the disputed area and the exercise there by Honduras of judicial and other functions'. The Chamber found however that, even assuming that the localities referred to fell on the 'wrong' side of the boundary it had drawn (a fact which it was unable to establish) the material offered did 'not appear sufficient by way of *effectivités* to be capable of affecting the decision'.[201] In the second section of the boundary, no question of *effectivités* was raised. In the third section, both sides offered evidence of settlements

[197] Article 26 of the General Treaty of Peace, cited in [1992] ICJ Rep 396, para 57.

[198] [1992] ICJ Rep 396, para 58.

[199] [1992] ICJ Rep 396–397, para 59 (El Salvador); 397–398, para 60 (Honduras).

[200] For the problems that have arisen in implementing this part of the decision, see Colter Paulson, 'Compliance with Final Judgments of the International Court of Justice since 1987' (2004) 48 *American Journal of International Law* 434, 437–439.

[201] [1992] ICJ Rep 422–423, para 102, referring to ibid, 597–398, para 60.

and of the exercise of various forms of State jurisdiction in the region, but the Chamber, having drawn a line on the basis of the titles produced, was not convinced that any of this evidence would 'justify the Chamber in doubting the validity of that boundary as representing the *uti possidetis juris* line'.[202] A similar finding, though expressed in different words, was reached on the claims based on *effectivités* in the fourth sector,[203] and in the fifth sector.[204] The dispute over the sixth sector turned entirely on the question of the course of a particular river, and no *effectivités* were relied on.

Turning to the dispute over the islands in the Gulf of Fonseca, the Chamber made it clear at the outset that it had 'no doubt that the starting-point for the determination of sovereignty over the islands must be the *uti possidetis juris* of 1821'.[205] Both parties also advanced arguments based on alleged pre-independence *effectivités*, but the Chamber came to the conclusion that the material available to it, 'whether presented as evidence of title...or of pre-independence *effectivités*, is too fragmentary and ambiguous to be sufficient for any firm conclusion to be based upon it.'[206] For this reason, the Chamber considered that it should proceed 'to consider the conduct of the parties in the period following independence, as indicative of what must have been the 1821 position'.[207] Citing as authority the provision of the General Treaty of Peace quoted above, the Chamber also indicated that

> [t]his may further be supplemented by considerations independent of the *uti possidetis* principle, in particular the possible significance of the same conduct, or the conduct of the Parties in more recent years, as possibly constituting acquiescence.[208]

The situation contemplated in the first *Frontier Dispute* case, in which the *effectivités* co-existed with, and contradicted, a legal title, also arose in the case of the *Land and Maritime Boundary between Cameroon and Nigeria*. In the area of Lake Chad, the Court found that the boundary had been defined by a number of international instruments dating from before the Second World War.[209] Between 1983 and 1991 the Lake Chad Basin Commission established by the neighbouring States was engaged in a process of demarcation based, as the Court found, on the pre-war delimitation, but this demarcation had not become binding on the two States before the Court. At the same time, however, there was a gradual process of settling of Nigerians in villages lying on the Cameroonian side of the delimitation line which was to be upheld by the Court, and organization

[202] Ibid, 471–472, para 181 and 470–471, para 179. [203] Ibid, 515–516, paras 264–266.
[204] Ibid, 542–543, paras 303–304. [205] Ibid, 558, para 333.
[206] Ibid, 563, para 341. [207] [1992] ICJ Rep 563, para 341. [208] Ibid.
[209] [2002] ICJ Rep 344, para 55. The instruments in question were the Milner-Simon Declaration of 1919; the Thomson-Marchand Declaration of 1929–1930, and the Henderson-Fleuriau Exchange of Notes of 1931.

by Nigeria of 'public health and education facilities, policing, [and] the administration of justice' in the areas of those villages, and the Court found that these 'could normally be considered as acts *à titre de souverain*'.[210] The Court however recalled the dictum of the 1986 *Frontier Dispute* judgment, quoted above, as to the situation where effective administration is conducted by a State other than that holding the legal title, and found that it was this eventuality that corresponded to the situation as between Cameroon and Nigeria.[211]

That was however not quite the end of the matter, as the Court pointed out that the conduct of Cameroon in the disputed area could still have pertinence 'for the question whether it acquiesced in the establishment of a change in treaty title', and the Court cited in this connection the decision in the *Land, Island and Maritime Frontier Dispute*.[212] The Court however found on the facts that 'there was no acquiescence by Cameroon in the abandonment of its title in the area in favour of Nigeria'; therefore, since 'the *effectivités* adduced by Nigeria did not correspond to the law... "preference should be given to the holder of the title"' as in the *Frontier Dispute* case.[213] The Court mentioned that Cameroon's protests at acts of administration were limited to a few specific incidents, but it did protest vigorously when Nigeria made an actual claim of sovereignty in a diplomatic note.[214]

In the *Frontier Dispute* between Benin and Niger, the Court examined what were advanced by the parties as colonial titles supportive of their claims as to the course of the boundary in the river Niger, but concluded that neither of them had 'succeeded in providing evidence of title on the basis of regulative or administrative acts during the colonial period', and therefore turned to an examination of 'the evidence furnished by the Parties with respect to *effectivités*'.[215] It recalled for this purpose its previous case-law to the effect that '[i]n the event that the *effectivité* does not co-exist with any legal title, it must inevitably be taken into consideration.'[216] The *effectivités* in question however remained limited to those prior to the critical date—the date of the parties' accession to independence in 1960. For the period from 1914 to 1954, it found that there had been a *modus vivendi* adopted by the French administrators of the colonial possessions on each side of the river, whereby the permanently navigable channel of the Niger was used as the boundary. It was presumably because of the provisional nature of

[210] [2002] ICJ Rep 353, para 67.

[211] Ibid, para 68.

[212] [2002] ICJ Rep 353–354, para 68, citing [1992] ICJ Rep 408–409, para 80.

[213] [2002] ICJ Rep 354–355, para 70, citing [1986] ICJ Rep 587, para 63. The expression 'did not correspond to the law' used both in 1986 and in 2002, is curious; the French text uses the word 'droit', and it seems that 'were not consistent with the legal title' is what is meant.

[214] [2002] ICJ Rep 354, para 69.

[215] [2005] ICJ Rep 127, paras 75–76.

[216] Ibid, para 77, citing [1986] ICJ Rep 587, para 63 and subsequent decisions.

this arrangement, and the fact that it was concluded at a low administrative level, that this did not rank as a title, but merely as an *effectivité*. During the period 1954–1960 there were some incidents and difficulties, but the Court was able to conclude that 'the terms of the *modus vivendi*...were in general respected and that, during this period, the main navigable channel of the river Niger was considered by both sides to be the boundary', and the islands to the left and to the right of that line were administered on that basis.[217] In short, it appears that 'ce n'est que le provisoire qui dure'!

However, Benin objected that since 'the *modus vivendi* was merely a temporary and practical arrangement, pending a definitive settlement of the boundary issue'; therefore, '[by] its very nature it precluded the existence of an intention to act "as of right" and these administrative acts cannot therefore be relied on as *effectivités*.'[218] The Chamber ruled that

> the concept of the intention and will to act as sovereign, as mentioned in the *Legal Status of Eastern Greenland (Denmark v Norway)* case (*1933, P.C.I.J. Series A/B, No. 53*, pp. 45–46) is a concept of international law and cannot be transplanted purely and simply to colonial law. The Chamber's sole task in applying the principle of *uti possidetis juris* is to ascertain whether it was the colony of Dahomey or that of Niger which effectively exercised authority over the areas which the Parties now claim as sovereign States.[219]

The response of the Chamber is not entirely convincing. One way in which an *effectivité* is of value is in indicating the consent of the parties to a particular boundary: thus in the *Land, Island and Maritime Frontier Dispute* between El Salvador and Honduras, the Chamber referred to 'the conduct of the Parties...as possibly constituting acquiescence';[220] and in the Cameroon/Nigeria case, the Court, as noted above, found that, in a conflict between titles and *effectivités*, the conduct of Cameroon had pertinence 'only for the question whether it acquiesced in the establishment of a change in treaty title'.[221] In the Benin/Niger Judgment itself, the Chamber had ruled that documents posterior to the critical date of independence could not lead to any modification of the 'photograph of the territory' at that date, 'unless, of course, such documents clearly express the parties' agreement to such a change'.[222] Any agreement constituted by the *modus vivendi* was, as that designation implies, only a provisional one, and did not express the informed will of the colonial authorities.[223] While

217 Ibid, 132, para 98.
218 Ibid, 132–133, para 101. This view was adopted by Judge *ad hoc* Bennouna: Dissenting Opinion, [2005] ICJ Rep 158, para 29.
219 Ibid, 133, para 102.
220 [1992] ICJ Rep 563, para 341.
221 [2002] ICJ Rep 353, para 68.
222 [2005] ICJ Rep 109, para 26.
223 Who had, apparently neither approved it nor officially disapproved it: cf Dissenting Opinion of Judge *ad hoc* Bennouna, [2005] ICJ Rep 158, para 20.

the distinction drawn by the Chamber between international law and colonial law[224] may well be sound, it does not really resolve the issue; on what basis is a provisional *effectivité*, adopted for convenience, determinative?

In the light in particular of the decision in the *Pedra Branca* case, the question thus nevertheless arises whether there is any distinction to be made between *effectivités* as contributing to establish sovereignty over either a *terra nullius* or a territory which is to be attributed on the basis of the *uti possidetis juris*, on the one hand, and acts *à titre de souverain* capable of contributing to the acquisition of a title by prescription, on the other. This question was raised directly by Judges Simma and Abraham in their dissenting opinion in *Pedra Branca*. They asked whether the activities of Singapore, which they found to be insufficient to establish sovereignty over the island, should be judged more indulgently (in the sense that less marked assertions of sovereignty would suffice) because the territory in question was a small island serving no purpose other than that of a lighthouse; they cited in this connection dicta in the cases of the *Legal Status of Eastern Greenland*[225] and *Pulau Ligitan and Pulau Sipadan.*[226]

Notre réponse est résolument négative. La tâche du juge, dans les deux affaires susmentionnées, consistait à attribuer la souveraineté sur un territoire déterminé sur la base des effectivités (le cas échéant, de la mise en balance des effectivités concurrentes), en l'absence d'un titre originaire de souveraineté. Ici, la question est tout autre: il existe un souverain originel—tout au moins d'après l'analyse de la Cour, à laquelle nous adhérons—et il s'agit de déterminer si le titre a été transféré à un autre souverain, sans que le premier ait expressément donné son accord. Dans un tel contexte, rien ne justifie que l'on abaisse le niveau d'exigence; car ce ne sont pas les effectivités en elles-mêmes que l'on recherche, c'est le consentement (ou l'acquiescement) du souverain d'origine, qui, à défaut d'avoir été exprimé, doit au moins pouvoir se déduire sans l'ombre d'un doute du comportement de celui-ci. Une telle conclusion, nous dira-t-on, sera très difficile à tirer dans le cas de petites portions de territoires inhabitées ou peu propices à l'activité humaine. Cela est sans doute vrai; mais il en résultera seulement que le maintien du titre originel de souveraineté, qui est présumé, constituera la solution juridiquement appropriée.[227]

[224] A distinction which, it has been suggested, is based on, or consistent with, the absence of a *continuum juris* between pre-independence colonial law and international law, referred to above text and n 167: Norodom, above n 129, 200. One may however also ask what is meant by 'colonial law'? The Chamber does not mention any investigation into what effect, if any, French colonial law may have attributed to the *modus vivendi*; it rather speaks of 'colonial law' as a general concept, like 'municipal law', which must however be tied to a particular legal system to acquire any effective content.

[225] PCIJ Rep Series A/B No 53, 45–46.

[226] [2002] ICJ Rep 682, para 134.

[227] Judgment of 23 May 2008, Dissenting Opinion of Judges Simma and Abraham, para 29; official English translation not yet available.

Whether one agrees with the Court's finding on the facts, or with the rejection of it by the two judges concerned, this is, it is suggested, an appropriate approach to the question.

CHAPTER III: LAND FRONTIERS

It is long established in legal theory that an international frontier divides the spatial extent of adjacent States *ab inferis ad coelum*, that is to say not merely on the earth's surface but below it, and above it so as to divide the airspace.[228] The Chamber of the Court seised of the *Frontier Dispute* between Benin and Niger had occasion to apply this principle in unusual circumstances, in order to determine sovereignty over jointly-owned bridges crossing a river that constituted an international boundary (see Section 4 below).

1. Fully Delimited Frontiers not Essential

As the Permanent Court recalled in its Advisory Opinion on *Interpretation of Article 3, paragraph 2, of the Treaty of Lausanne*, '[i]t often happens that, at the time of signature of a treaty establishing new frontiers, certain portions of these frontiers are not yet determined', in which case it may or may not be the case that, as with the treaty then under examination, 'the treaty provides certain measures for their determination'.[229] That does not however necessarily signify that there is an absence of frontier.

In the case of the *Land and Maritime Boundary between Cameroon and Nigeria*, there were in existence instruments dating from the colonial period, and the period of a League of Nations Mandate and a UN Trusteeship, dealing with the boundary that was to become the frontier between Cameroon and Nigeria. Nigeria however argued that the boundary in the area of Lake Chad had remained undetermined, so that it remained to be settled by agreement between the parties.[230] Apart from a reference to 'the mouth of the Ebeji [river]' which, it was suggested, was imprecise, the Mandate had provided that the boundary line of the territory of Cameroon as defined in an earlier instrument 'may, however, be slightly modified by mutual agreement [between Britain and France] where an examination of the localities shows that it is undesirable, either in the interests of the inhabitants or by reason of inaccuracies in the

[228] See the 1944 Chicago Convention on Civil Aviation, Article 1, recognizing that 'every State has complete and exclusive sovereignty over the airspace above its territory', and note the decision in the *Military and Paramilitary Activities* case as to the illegality of unauthorized US overflights of Nicaraguan territory: [1986] ICJ Rep 52–53, para 91; 147, para 292 (5).

[229] PCIJ Rep Series B No 12, 20. Note also the situation of Albania in 1914 referred to in the Permanent Court's Advisory Opinion on the *Monastery of Saint-Naoum*, PCIJ Rep Series B No 9, 10, referred to in the *North Sea Continental Shelf* case, [1969] ICJ Rep 32, para 46.

[230] [2002] ICJ Rep 341, para 51.

map' employed in the earlier instrument.[231] Even without recourse to the maxim *id certum est qui certi reddi potest*, it is clear that this provision did not prevent the establishment of an international boundary in the area.[232]

A related issue was one that arose in the case of *Sovereignty over Pulau Ligitan and Pulau Sipadan*, and provoked a vigorous dissent by Judge *ad hoc* Franck. One of the principal questions in dispute was the effect of an 1891 Convention between the Netherlands and Great Britain defining 'the boundaries between the Netherlands possessions in the Island of Borneo and the States in that island which [were] under British protection'. The text which provoked the dispute was Article IV. From a starting point on the east coast of Borneo, defined in terms of 4° 10' North latitude, a boundary line between Dutch and British possessions was to run 'eastward along that parallel, across the Island of Sebittik'. There were however also two insignificantly small islands, which became the subject of the litigation, further out to sea. If the line were to continue along the 4° 10' parallel, sovereignty over these would be determined, but the Convention did not indicate that the line was so to continue; but neither did it indicate that it was not to do so.

The Court interpreted the Convention, for reasons which are not here material, as meaning that the boundary line indicated was to divide up the island of Sebittik but not to run eastward out to sea beyond that island; thus the Convention did not determine sovereignty over Pulau Ligitan and Pulau Sipadan; that question was determined by the Court on the basis of later *effectivités*. Judge Franck considered that the Convention, correctly interpreted, had allocated sovereignty over the two small islands; he invoked the 'object and purpose' of the Convention as a guide to, if not determinative of, its interpretation. In addition, however, he appealed to the dictum of the Permanent Court in its Advisory Opinion on *Interpretation of Article 3, paragraph 2, of the Treaty of Lausanne*:

> It is . . . natural that any article designed to fix a frontier should, if possible, be so interpreted that the result of the application of its provisions in their entirety should be the establishment of a precise, complete and definitive frontier.[233]

He also recalled the separate opinion of Judge Shahabuddeen in the *Territorial Dispute* between Libya and Chad, stating that the Franco-Libyan boundary convention 'must . . . be construed so as to produce a

[231] Ibid, 339, para 49.

[232] Cf also the Contract between the Netherlands East Indies and the Sultan of Bulungan dated 12 November 1850, referred to in *Pulau Ligitan and Pulau Sipadan* case, which provided: 'This delimitation is established provisionally and shall be completely examined and determined again': [2002] ICJ Rep 638, para 18.

[233] [1925] PCIJ Rep Series B No 12, 20. This dictum had also been invoked by Indonesia: [2002] ICJ Rep 651, para 49.

comprehensive definition of the frontiers' unless there are 'compelling reasons' to the contrary.[234]

In the context of the present discussion, it is pertinent to ask whether these dicta imply that there is some special feature of treaties dealing with international frontiers; or whether they merely constitute the application to frontier treaties of unquestioned principles of treaty law. In the case of the Treaty of Lausanne, the treaty defined part of the frontier between Turkey and Iraq, and provided for determination of the other part by the Council of the League; the question before the Permanent Court was whether the treaty conferred on the Council the power to make a binding decision as to the course of the frontier. The Permanent Court was engaged in interpreting the treaty in the light of its object and purpose; having satisfied itself that that object was the establishment of a complete frontier, it deduced from this that the action by the Council contemplated by the treaty was necessarily a binding decision, in order that the treaty's object and purpose might be achieved.[235]

In the *Pulau Ligitan* case, the division of views between Judge Franck and his colleagues was not so much one of interpretation of the Convention as a divergence of views as to the object and purpose of the Convention. Taking into account the fact that the two uninhabited islets were more than 50 nautical miles to the East of, and well outside, the area of overlapping claims depicted at the time of the Convention, that they were of no foreseeable use or interest, and that they were, as the Court observed, 'little known at the time',[236] it is reasonable to suppose that the fact that the Convention did not expressly extend to their allocation meant that there was no intention to allocate them; and the Court interpreted the text of the Convention (and the inconsistent maps) on that basis. Judge Franck's view practically amounts to saying that a treaty dealing with frontiers enjoys a legal presumption of intended completeness; that interpretation should be based on a presumed intention to define a frontier wherever one needs to be defined between the parties—a rebuttable presumption, of course, but one which serves as guide in the shape of the 'object and purpose' of the treaty. The decision of the Court may therefore be taken as a rejection of any idea that special rules of this kind apply to a frontier treaty.

[234] [1994] ICJ Rep 44; but see next footnote.

[235] This is in fact the interpretation of the PCIJ decision accepted by Judge Shahabuddeen in the *Frontier Dispute*: [1994] ICJ Rep 46.

[236] [2002] ICJ Rep 652, para 51. The Court did not in this context mention the 'elephant in the room', namely the possible importance of the islands to support a claim to areas of continental shelf. Judge Oda however was at pains to point out, in a separate opinion, that the parties might have been deceiving themselves if they thought that modern maritime delimitation law would support a claim on that basis: [2002] ICJ Rep 687–690.

2. The Distinction between Terrestrial and Maritime Boundaries

The terminological question that vexed the Chamber in the *Gulf of Maine* case, referred to in the previous article,[237] has not arisen subsequently; the accepted terminology for a line dividing areas of continental shelf or EEZ between two States is generally *limite* or *ligne de délimitation* rather than *frontière*.[238] A dictum that may be noted here, though of an arbitral tribunal and not the ICJ, is the rejection by the *Eritrea/Yemen* arbitration tribunal of 'the proposition that the international law governing land territory and the international law governing maritime boundaries are not only different but also discrete, and bear no juridical relevance to each other'.[239]

Other decisions of the Court however confirm, if confirmation were needed, that the boundary between two States in a lake, or in the bed of a river, is a land frontier just as much as one drawn across land territory, and is governed by the same rules of law. This is clear from the case of the *Land and Maritime Boundary between Cameroon and Nigeria*, where part of the boundary lay in Lake Chad, and those of *Kasikili/Sedudu Island* and the *Frontier Dispute* between Benin and Niger, where the boundary ran along the bed of a river, the dispute being simply as to which side of a river island it passed; and the less common situation in the *Dispute regarding Navigational and Related Rights* between Costa Rica where the frontier ran along the Costa Rican bank of the river. In the Benin/Niger case, the Court had also to rule on the extent of sovereignty in relation to the bridges over the river, and found that in each case the boundary on the bridge was directly above the boundary line in the river.[240]

3. The *Erga Omnes* Character of a Territorial Frontier

The only case before the Court during the period under consideration in which a land frontier between two States also involved the interests of a third State was that of the *Land and Maritime Boundary between Cameroon and Nigeria*. The boundary between these two States ran from Lake Chad to the coast (the Bakassi Peninsula); its starting point in Lake Chad was a tripoint where the territories of the two parties met those of Chad, the exact location of which was disputed; Chad did not intervene or participate in the proceedings in any way. A third State (Equatorial Guinea) was also

[237] (1995) *BYIL* 1, 19–20.

[238] Contra, Prosper Weil, 'Délimitation maritime et délimitation terrestre', in Y Dinstein (ed), *International Law at a Time of Perplexity, Essays in Honour of Shabtai Rosenne* (Nijhoff, Dordrecht, 1989) 1021.

[239] 114 *ILR* 119, para 112.

[240] [2005] ICJ Rep 142, para 124.

involved in the delimitation of the maritime boundary, and had intervened in the proceedings for that purpose, but as indicated in previous articles in this series, the considerations relating to maritime boundaries between more than two States are different from those relating to land boundaries.

The factual circumstances of the case were markedly different from those of the Burkina Faso/Mali *Frontier Dispute*, discussed in the previous article on this subject.[241] In that case, the end-point of the frontier would be a tripoint with Niger, but there had never been an agreement with Niger as to its position, and even the extent of Niger's claims was unascertained. The Cameroon-Chad-Nigeria tripoint, on the other hand, had been fixed, if not with the accuracy possible with modern methods, by international agreements preceding the independence of the three States.

Originally, the frontiers in the area were regulated by bilateral agreements between three colonial States: France, Germany and Great Britain; but after the First World War Germany's colonies in Africa had been taken away and placed under League of Nations Mandates; thereafter only France and Great Britain were present in the area, either as territorial sovereigns or mandatory Powers. A bilateral declaration (the Milner-Simon Declaration) of 1919 provided that the frontier between the French and British mandated territories of the Cameroons should run from 'the meeting-point of the three old British, French and German frontiers situate in Lake Chad', with an indication of 'approximate' co-ordinates. The Declaration was approved and incorporated in a Franco-British Exchange of Notes (the Henderson-Fleuriau Exchange of Notes of 1931), and the Court found that these instruments in combination had 'the status of an international agreement', and 'provided for a delimitation that was sufficient in general for demarcation'. Accordingly, the Court's view was that 'certainly by 1931, the frontier in the Lake Chad area was indeed delimited and agreed by Great Britain and France.'[242] As such, the agreement was clearly binding on the three successor States.[243]

In its 2002 Judgment the Court however found it appropriate to redefine the exact position of the tripoint; and it thus did so in proceedings to which only two of the three States present at the tripoint were parties. This raises, at least in theory, the question of the position of Chad: there would be no effect of *res judicata* in relation to Chad, but insofar as the Court was defining the exact significance of an agreement concluded by Chad's predecessor in title, its conclusion might be said to be effective against Chad on the basis rather of *pacta sunt servanda*. There also remains however the 'presumption' referred to in the Burkina Faso/Mali case, and discussed in the previous article,[244] the effect of which is obscure.

Whatever the theoretical interest of these questions, there remains a third Latin tag applicable to the case: *de minimis non curat lex*. In the first

[241] (1995) *BYIL* 22–24. [242] [2002] ICJ Rep 341, paras 50, 52.

[243] There are in fact four States bordering Lake Chad, but Niger's boundaries meet those of Chad and Nigeria at a different tripoint, further North.

[244] See (1995) *BYIL* 23–24.

place, unlike the tripoint between Burkina Faso, Mali and Niger, the tripoint between Cameroon, Chad and Nigeria lies in the middle of a lake, so that only a difference of position substantial enough to affect, for example, fishing rights would have any real relevance. Secondly, the adjustment or refinement introduced by the Court was to substitute longitude 14°04'59"9999 East for the longitude stated 'approximately' in the international instruments mentioned above: 14°05'.[245] In the circumstances, it would have been out of all proportion for the Court to concern itself with the exact legal impact of its findings on Chad.[246]

4. The Intangibility of Land Frontiers

Under this heading, there are two consequences of the principle to be noted. First, as already noted in Section 1 above, the Court has found that an international agreement relating to a boundary is not incomplete merely because it contains provision for minor modification of the line indicated in the agreement. In the *Cameroon/Nigeria* case, a bilateral Declaration supplemented by an Exchange of Notes, had provided for a boundary, but had 'some technical imperfections' and 'certain details remained to be specified'; the Court however did not accept the argument of Nigeria that the frontier was as a result not fully delimited. The provisions as to 'the entitlement, by mutual agreement, to make modest alterations to the line... in no way suggest a frontier line that is not fully delimited.'[247]

The more important consequence is that a boundary established by treaty is in principle not affected by the subsequent termination of the treaty. The Court had occasion to refer to this principle in an unexpected context, when dealing with the preliminary objections of Colombia in the case concerning the *Territorial and Maritime Dispute* between Nicaragua and Colombia. The Court's jurisdiction was invoked on the basis of the 1948 Pact of Bogotá, which excluded from its scope 'matters already settled by arrangement between the parties... or which are governed by agreements or treaties in force on the date of the conclusion of the present Treaty'.[248] Colombia claimed that the issues brought before the Court had been settled by a 1928 bilateral treaty between itself and Nicaragua, and that they were thus excluded from the jurisdiction established by the Pact of Bogotá; Nicaragua responded that that treaty was invalid, or alternatively had been terminated by material breach by Colombia, from 1969

[245] The Court also adopted in this respect the (non-binding) conclusion of the Lake Chad Basin Commission, on which Chad was represented: [2002] ICJ Rep 332–333, para 36; 337, para 45; 345, para 57.

[246] The latitude of the tripoint was defined in the relevant instruments as 13°05' N. At 15° N latitude, one degree of arc (longitude) is equal to 110.649 kilometres; thus one second of arc is about 30 metres.

[247] [2002] ICJ Rep 340, para 49; see also ibid, 341, para 50.

[248] Article VI of the Pact, quoted in [2007-II] ICJ Rep 853, para 56.

onwards. For purposes of jurisdiction the latter contention was irrelevant, since the question was whether at the date of the Pact the issues had been 'settled', i.e. whether the 1928 treaty was in force in 1948.[249] Nevertheless the Court added, perhaps *ex abundanti cautela*:

Even if the Court were to find that the 1928 Treaty has been terminated, as claimed by Nicaragua, this would not affect the sovereignty of Colombia over the islands of San Andrés, Providencia and Santa Catalina. The Court recalls that it is a principle of international law that a territorial régime established by treaty "achieves a permanence which the treaty itself does not necessarily enjoy" and the continued existence of that régime is not dependent upon the continuing life of the treaty under which the régime is agreed (*Territorial Dispute (Libyan Arab Jamahiriya/Chad), Judgment, I.C.J. Reports 1994*, p. 37, paras. 72–73).[250]

It was observed in the previous article that this rule must yield to the contrary intention of the parties, i.e. that a treaty may be concluded to define a boundary but containing provisions for its future modification by the parties.[251] Could a repudiation of a boundary treaty by one party, coupled with a reaction on the part of the other party, be in such terms as to involve not merely a termination of the treaty but an abandonment of the boundary created by the treaty? The hypothesis is perhaps far-fetched; and the Court presumably did not consider there was any possibility of its being fulfilled in the circumstances of the case, since it was prepared to rule out such a situation by implication in a judgment of an interlocutory character. If however the repudiation took the form of a suggestion that the treaty was void *ab initio*, it would, if it were a treaty fixing a frontier, entail the contention that there was no agreed frontier; the Vienna Convention on the Law of Treaties states categorically that '[a] treaty the invalidity of which is established under the present Convention is void', and '[t]he provisions of a void treaty have no legal force.'[252] It was in fact contended by Nicaragua that the 1928 Treaty was invalid as inconsistent with the Nicaraguan Constitution (cf Article. 46 of the Vienna Convention); this was as basis for resisting Colombia's objection that the existence of the 1928 Treaty excluded jurisdiction under the Pact of Bogotá, but the same argument would presumably have been advanced at the merits stage if the Court had not rejected it at the interlocutory stage. Similar claims were made in the *Qatar/Bahrain* case and the *Cameroon/Nigeria* case: that there was no international agreement for unilateral seisin of the Court because the Bahraini Minister for Foreign Affairs had no competence to sign an agreement to that effect;[253] and that the

[249] As the Court noted: ibid, para 82.

[250] Ibid, para 89. For an acute criticism of the Court's inconsistency, see the Separate Opinion of Judge Abraham, paras 24–27.

[251] (1989) *BYIL* 1, 26–27.

[252] Article 89 (1); cited, in connection with the 1928 treaty in the *Nicaragua/Colombia* dispute, by Judge Abraham in his Separate Opinion, para 29.

[253] [1994] ICJ Rep 123, para 26.

1911 Anglo-German Agreement relied on by Cameroon as defining the boundary in the Bakassi Peninsula, was invalid as not having been approved by the German Parliament.[254]

5. International Rivers and River Boundaries

Three recent cases before the Court have involved boundaries running along the course of a river: the case of *Kasikili/Sedudu Island* between Botswana and Namibia;[255] the *Frontier Dispute* between Benin and Niger; and the case of the *Dispute regarding Navigational and Related Rights* between Costa Rica and Nicaragua.

In the first case, the Court was asked

> to determine, on the basis of the Anglo-German Treaty of 1 July 1890 and the rules and principles of international law, the boundary between Namibia and Botswana around Kasikili/Sedudu Island and the legal status of the island.[256]

The main role of the Court was therefore to interpret the 1890 Treaty, which provided that in the disputed area the boundary between British and German possessions (and hence between Botswana and Namibia as successor States) 'descends the centre of the main channel of [the] river [Chobe] to its junction with the Zambesi'.[257] There was no doubt therefore that the river served as the boundary, and could therefore be categorized as an 'international river';[258] the sole problem was the position of the 'main channel', and in particular whether it ran to the right or to the left of the disputed island. The Court was able to resolve the dispute on the basis of its interpretation of the text of the Treaty, in the light of (*inter alia*) subsequent practice. Taking into account the reference in the Special Agreement to 'the rules and principles of international law', the Court considered an argument advanced by Namibia on grounds of prescription, but considered that the necessary conditions for a prescriptive title were not satisfied.[259] The Court was not asked to apply any rules of general or special customary law relating to international watercourses. It did however note a certain treaty practice as regards agreed boundaries in rivers:

[254] [2002] ICJ Rep 400–401, paras 196–197.

[255] For a detailed study of this case, see Charalambos Apostolidis, 'L'affaire de l'île de Kasikili/Sedudu (Botswana/Namibie): l'arrêt de la CIJ du 13 décembre 1999' (1999) XLV *Annuaire français de droit international* 434.

[256] Special Agreement between Botswana and Namibia, 15 February 1996, cited at [1999] ICJ Rep 1049, para 2.

[257] Cited at ibid, 1060, para 21.

[258] The Court found that '[t]here are grounds for thinking that one of the reasons underlying' the choice by the parties to the 1890 Treaty of the 'centre of the main channel' as boundary was to preserve their respective rights of navigation down to the Zambesi: ibid, 1074, para 45.

[259] Ibid, 1105 para 97. See above, Chapter II, text and n 67.

Treaties or conventions which define boundaries in watercourses nowadays usually refer to the thalweg as the boundary when the watercourse is navigable and to the median line when it is not, although it cannot be said that the practice has been fully consistent.[260]

In the Benin/Niger case, the Chamber had to deal with two stretches of boundary following rivers, the river Niger, and one of its tributaries, the river Mekrou. As regards the Niger, Benin contended that the boundary ran along the left bank, thus leaving the river itself within the territory of Benin; this contention was based on Benin's interpretation of the colonial legislation. Niger however argued that during the colonial period 'an understanding... developed that the boundary was constituted by "the course of the river" and that this could only mean that the boundary was situated within the watercourse of the river';[261] specifically Niger identified the line of deepest soundings as the frontier. The Chamber examined the colonial history, and concluded that neither party had 'succeeded in providing evidence of title on the basis of regulative or administrative acts during the colonial period'.[262] On the basis of *effectivités*, the Court reached the conclusion that the boundary followed the main navigable channel.[263] This part of the judgment is therefore mainly of interest as regards the role of *effectivités* in post-colonial boundary determination rather than any aspect peculiar to rivers. However, in a pre-echo of the *Kasikili/Sedudu Island* case, an early administrative document relied on (*inter alia*) by the Court took care to specify that the line contemplated, as a boundary of administrative and judicial competences, should be 'not the widest channel, but the only channel navigable at low water'.[264]

As regards the river Mekrou, there was agreement that the boundary followed the river, not one of its banks, but there was little material, or argument, on which the Court could base a choice of a specific line. After quoting the dictum in the *Kasikili/Sedudu Island* Judgment quoted above,[265] the Court held that

in view of the circumstances, including the fact that the river is not navigable, a boundary following the median line of the Mekrou would more satisfactorily meet the requirement of legal security inherent in the determination of an international boundary.[266]

A particular feature of the boundary problem in the river Niger was that the parties had built two bridges across the river: what was to be the impact of the boundary determination on sovereignty over these?[267] The construction

[260] [1999-II] ICJ Rep 1062, para 24. [261] [2005] ICJ Rep 121, para 52.
[262] Ibid, 127, para 75. [263] Ibid, 132–133, paras 98–103.
[264] Ibid, 128, para 84. [265] Above, text and n 260.
[266] [2005] ICJ Rep 150, para 144.
[267] The point was not covered in the Special Agreement, and Benin suggested that the Court had therefore no jurisdiction to determine it, but the Court dismissed this objection: [2005] ICJ Rep 141, paras 119–120.

and maintenance of the bridges had been financed by the two States on an equal basis, and the structures were their joint property. The Chamber noted that 'neither of the Parties has contended that there is a rule of customary international law regarding territorial delimitation in the case of bridges over international watercourses', though some bilateral agreements covered the point.[268] The Chamber cut the Gordian knot thus:

> [T]he solution is to extend vertically the line of the boundary on the watercourse. This solution accords with the general theory that a boundary represents the line of separation between areas of State sovereignty, not only on the earth's surface but also in the subsoil and in the superjacent column of air.[269]

The Chamber added that this solution avoided 'the difficulties which could be engendered by having two different boundaries on geometrical planes situated in close proximity to one another'.[270]

In the case brought by Costa Rica against Nicaragua, however, the claim of the Applicant was that the Respondent was 'in breach of its international obligations ... in denying to Costa Rica the free exercise of its rights of navigation and associated rights on the San Juan River'. The boundary between the two States, so far as relevant, had been fixed at that river by a Treaty of 15 April 1858, but the boundary was not situated in the waters of the river, but on the Costa Rican bank, so that the whole of the river lay within Nicaraguan territory,[271] but certain rights were reserved to Costa Rica;[272] it was the exact extent of those rights and the manner of their exercise that was the subject of the dispute.

Costa Rica based its claims not only on the 1858 Treaty, however, but also on 'the rules of general international law that are applicable, even in the absence of treaty provisions, to navigation on "international rivers".' The San Juan was said to fall into this category, at least as regards the section whose course follows the border, 'with Costa Rica thus possessing a customary right of free navigation in its capacity as a riparian State'.[273] As the Court noted:

> According to Nicaragua, on the contrary, the San Juan is not an "international river", since it flows entirely within the territory of a single country by virtue of the provisions of the 1858 Treaty of Limits, which establish the border in such a way that no part of the river falls under the sovereignty of a State other than

[268] Ibid, para 124. [269] Ibid, 141–142, para 124. [270] Ibid.

[271] This arrangement is apparently not so unusual as might be thought: see the declaration of Judge *ad hoc* Guillaume appended to the Judgment, who cites (in para 6) seven international examples, and others from federal States.

[272] The text of the Treaty on this point read (in English translation): 'The Republic of Nicaragua shall have exclusive *dominium* and *imperium* over the waters of the San Juan river from its origin in the lake to its mouth at the Atlantic Ocean; the Republic of Costa Rica shall however have a perpetual right of free navigation on the said waters between the mouth of the river and a point located three English miles below Castillo Viejo'; there followed a phrase the meaning of which was disputed.

[273] Judgment of 13 July 2009, para 32.

Nicaragua. Moreover, Nicaragua challenges the existence of a general régime that might be applicable, under customary international law, to rivers whose course, or one of whose banks, constitutes the border between two States, and more widely to "international rivers".[274]

To the possible disappointment of commentators, the Court refused to go into this question at all, finding that the regime created by the Treaty was sufficient in itself to regulate the matters in dispute. All that it could be induced to say about a possible customary law of 'international rivers' was that, if and insofar as it existed, it was a matter of *jus dispositivum*:

Indeed, even if categorization as an "international river" would be legally relevant in respect of navigation, in that it would entail the application of rules of customary international law to that question, such rules could only be operative, at the very most, in the absence of any treaty provisions that had the effect of excluding them, in particular because those provisions were intended to define completely the régime applicable to navigation, by the riparian States on a specific river or a section of it.[275]

Judge *ad hoc* Guillaume, while agreeing with the Court's approach, indicated in a declaration that in his view there are in any event no such rules of customary law; in his view,

il n'existe en droit international coutumier aucune définition des «fleuves internationaux» et aucun régime gouvernant la navigation sur de tels fleuves. Certains d'entre eux sont par convention ouverts à la navigation des navires marchands de tous les Etats et parfois administrés par des commissions fluviales ayant des pouvoirs étendus. D'autres sont ouverts à la seule navigation des bateaux des Etats riverains avec ou sans constitution de commissions fluviales. D'autres enfin ne sont pas ouverts à la navigation internationale et relèvent de la seule souveraineté des Etats riverains. En outre, le statut de ces fleuves en ce qui concerne leur entretien, la pêche, la police de la navigation, la protection de l'environnement, la construction de barrages ou l'irrigation est extrêmement divers.[276]

The lacuna identified by Judge Guillaume would be unlikely to pose problems in practice, since it is highly improbable in this context that there would be a complete absence of treaty provision to determine the respective rights of two riparian States; but in the event of a treaty being rendered, or found to be, void, or incomplete, one would suppose that international law could furnish a solution. It is not unknown for the

[274] Ibid, para 33.

[275] Ibid, para 35. A curious feature of this finding is its placing at an early stage in the judgment, before the Court has examined the detailed provisions of the Treaty to ascertain whether any of these would 'have the effect of excluding' the rules of customary law.

[276] Declaration appended to Judgment of 13 July 2009, para 3, (English translation not yet available) citing Lucius Caflisch, «Règles générales du droit des cours d'eau internationaux» (1989) VII *Recueil des cours de l'académie de droit international de La Haye* 117, and the arbitral award in the *Faber* case, X *UNRIAA* 466.

Court, in particular, to find the existence of a custom on the basis of little evidence of practice.

CHAPTER IV: TERRITORIAL DISPUTES AND THE CRITICAL DATE

1. 'Frontier Disputes', 'Delimitation Disputes' and Attribution of Territory

The conclusion reached in the previous article in this series, on the basis of the case-law of the Court up to that date, was that these terms amounted to nothing more than 'labels, practically interchangeable, or at least lying at different positions along a spectrum so as to shade into one another, and thus usually without substantive or procedural significance'.[277] This view tends to be confirmed by a superficial glance at the titles chosen by the Court for the various more recent cases before it involving territorial claims: two cases relating to 'Sovereignty over . . . '[278]; one to 'Maritime Delimitation and Territorial Questions . . . ';[279] one 'Frontier Dispute';[280] two classified as 'Territorial and Maritime Dispute';[281] and one taking its title simply from the disputed territorial unit.[282]

A more useful classification may be that, already adverted to above, of disputes into categories according as they involve claims to territory allegedly *res nullius* at the appropriate moment, and thus (theoretically, at least) involving considerations of unilateral *effectivités*, or claims of transfer of title from one State to another on the basis of prescription, by whatever name called, and thus involving in principle both asserted activities and alleged responses.

1A. Delimitation and Demarcation

The two terms 'delimitation' and 'demarcation', applied to processes entailed in the establishment of a precise and definitive territorial frontier, were the subject of some discussion and argument in the case of the *Land and Maritime Boundary between Cameroon and Nigeria*. Earlier, in the case of the *Territorial Dispute* between Libya and Chad, the Court had occasion to interpret the minutes of a diplomatic proposal during the

[277] (1989) *BYIL* 1, 31.

[278] *Pulau Ligitan and Pulau Sipadan* (2002); *Pedra Branca/Pulau Batu Puteh* (2008).

[279] *Qatar/Bahrain* (2001).

[280] *Benin/Niger* (2005).

[281] *Nicaragua/Honduras (Caribbean)* (2007); *Nicaragua/Colombia* (Preliminary Objections, 2007).

[282] *Kasikili/Sedudu Island* (1999). Both this and the *Frontier Dispute* between Benin and Niger involved a frontier running along a river, and consequent determination of sovereignty over the river islands; the different titles of the case reflect differences of emphasis only.

negotiation of a 1955 Franco-Libyan Treaty of Friendship and Good Neighbourliness, referring to reaching 'an agreement on demarcation' of certain frontiers; it found that

Use of the term "demarcation" creates a presumption that the parties considered the definition of the frontiers as already effected, to be followed if necessary by a demarcation, the ways and means of which were defined in Annex 1 [to the 1955 treaty].[283]

The context of this finding was the disputed interpretation of the 1955 Treaty which, according to Chad, had defined the frontiers between Libya and the French colonial territory which subsequently became Chad; Libya contended that the Treaty had intended to recognize only *existing* frontiers between the two territories, not to establish them where they did not already exist, and that in the south of the country there was, in 1955, no frontier. The Court rejected the Libyan argument as a matter of construction of the Treaty, but it went to indicate that it found it 'possible by reference to the *travaux* [*préparatoires* of the Treaty] to confirm its reading of the text'.[284] The French term employed in the 1955 minutes was 'démarcation'; the Court does not appear to have thought worthy of remark that where Annex I to the 1955 Treaty was clearly intended to refer to the indication on the ground of a frontier already delimited by agreement, the French term employed was not 'démarcation' but 'abornement'.[285]

The meaning of the terms 'delimitation' and 'demarcation' was the subject of 'lengthy arguments' of the parties in the *Cameroon/Nigeria* case. The reason mentioned for this was that the parties were in disagreement over

the nature and extent of the role which the Court is called upon to play in relation to the sectors of the land boundary in respect of which there has been disagreement between the Parties at various stages of the proceedings, either on the ground that the relevant instruments of delimitation were claimed to be defective or because the interpretation of those instruments was disputed.[286]

Although the Court mentioned the terms of Cameroon's Application as defining the task referred to the Court by Cameroon,[287] the question was not really one of the powers of the Court under that instrument, as a matter of jurisdiction *ratione materiae*. The real point was that, while both parties recognized the existence of international instruments establishing a complete frontier from Lake Chad to the sea, which the Court was called

283 [1994] ICJ Rep 28, para 56.

284 Ibid, 27, para 55.

285 Translated (by the ICJ Registry) once as 'demarcation' and once as 'marking out'. See the text of Article 3 of Annex I to the 1955 Treaty set out at ibid, 21, para 40.

286 [2002] ICJ Rep 359, para 83.

287 Ibid, para 85.

upon to apply, they disagreed whether those instruments were sufficiently complete and had been sufficiently consistently applied for the process of establishment of the frontier to be no more than a confirmation by the Court of those instruments. Nigeria asked the Court

> to "clarify" the delimitation in the areas in which the delimitation instruments are defective and to correct the boundary line claimed by Cameroon in the areas where Nigeria maintains Cameroon is not observing the clear terms of these instruments.[288]

Neither party expected the Court to 'demarcate' the boundary, in the sense that the judges would visit the area armed with maps, theodolites and marker pegs; but Cameroon was understandably nervous about admitting that the Court might see its task as 'delimitation' if that meant re-thinking the boundary in the way in which Nigeria urged it to do.

The Court cited, or rather paraphrased, its earlier ruling in the *Libya/Chad* case, as stating that 'the delimitation of a boundary consists in its "*definition*", whereas the demarcation of a boundary, which presupposes its prior delimitation, consist of operations marking it out on the ground'.[289] This is hardly consistent with, for example, the terminology used in the *Temple of Preah Vihear* case, and the 1904 Treaty involved in that case. There the frontier, in the area that came to be disputed, was defined by that Treaty as following 'the watershed between the basins of the Nam Seng and the Mekong, on the one hand, and the Nam Moun, on the other hand', and the following Article of the treaty provided that there should be 'a delimitation of the frontiers' so defined.[290] This was to be carried out by a Mixed Commission, and the Court observed that it seemed clear 'that a frontier was surveyed and fixed';[291] it found that '[t]he final stage of the operation of delimitation was the preparation and publication of maps.'[292] It will be recalled that it was the conflict between the definition of the frontier as following the watershed, and the actual line drawn on the maps, that gave rise to the dispute brought before the Court.[293]

Another term often employed is that of 'determination' of a boundary. Judge *ad hoc* Mbaye in the *Cameroon/Nigeria* case explained that he used the word (or more precisely, *détermination* in French) 'in a general sense which encompasses the terms "delimitation", "demarcation" and "indication"

288 Ibid, 357, para 78.

289 [2002] ICJ Rep 359, para 85 (italics original). Similarly the Court refers in a different context to the work of the Lake Chad Boundary Commission as 'intended to lead to an overall demarcation of a frontier already delimited': ibid, 351, para 64.

290 See the texts in [1962] ICJ Rep 16.

291 Ibid, 18.

292 Ibid, 20.

293 This dispute is in fact still unsettled: it was reported on 7 November 2008 that UNESCO officials would begin 'demarcating' or 'marking out' the boundary after clashes had occurred between Thai and Cambodian forces (see <http://portal.unesco.org/en/ev.php-URL_ID=43713&URL_DO=DO_TOPIC&URL_SECTION=201.html>, accessed 21 April 2009).

...meaning here: to indicate with precision.'[294] In the *Frontier Dispute* between Benin and Niger, the Chamber mentioned that it had been asked, according to the authoritative French text of the judgment, to *déterminer le tracé de la frontière* on two bridges spanning the river that constituted the international boundary. This phrase is at one point translated 'to determine the frontier', and at another 'to determine where the boundary is located'.[295] The Court decided that the boundary on the bridges 'follows the course of the boundary in the river' beneath;[296] is this an operation of delimitation or demarcation? It is not easy to say.

Modern practice seems to be to use 'demarcation' to mean activities on the ground to give physical expression to an agreed boundary-line, and 'delimitation' to mean operations of a purely intellectual or documentary nature preceding those activities.[297] It appears that it is possible to be committed by agreement to a particular delimitation, yet not necessarily to the subsequent demarcation,[298] which implies that the demarcation process is not automatic, or dictated by the delimitation. Some further distinction however seems necessary within the earlier stages, and the term 'definition' suggests itself. This may be illustrated by the case of *Kasikili/Sedudu Island*. An Anglo-German Agreement of 1 July 1890 provided (*inter alia*) that the boundary between British and German spheres of influence in the region should 'descend the centre of the main channel' of the river Chobe to its junction with the Zambesi.[299] This was a definition of the frontier, but there remained the problem of determining what was the 'main channel' of the river in any region where it split into two or more channels. While this remained an intellectual activity, it was one which could only be carried out by inspection of the channels in question, at least;[300] it seems appropriate to term it an operation of delimitation.[301] 'Demarcation' in the traditional sense of setting up boundary posts or markers would seem

[294] Separate Opinion, [2002] ICJ Rep 510.

[295] [2005] ICJ Rep 141, paras 119, 120.

[296] Ibid, 142, para 124. Since the Court noted that neither party had contended that there was a rule of customary international law governing the question, the basis of the decision seems to be common sense and simplicity—almost, but not quite, *ex aequo et bono*!

[297] One analysis sees it as '[t]he process of actually determining the course of a given boundary in theory and quite often in practice includes three steps: allocation, delimitation and demarcation.' (Michael Bothe, 'Boundaries' in R Bernhardt *et al.* (eds), I *Encyclopedia of Public International Law* (Elsevier, Amsterdam, 1992) 446.) 'Delimitation means the actual description of a border in a written document. Demarcation means the actual marking on the ground.' (ibid).

[298] See the decision in *Land and Maritime Boundary between Cameroon and Nigeria*, [2002] ICJ Rep 351, para 64; and the confused situation in the case of the *Temple of Preah Vihear* where a 'delimitation' (in fact a demarcation) effected under an earlier treaty was tacitly adopted under a later one, even though the two treaties indicated different criteria for fixing the frontier: Separate Opinion of Sir Gerald Fitzmaurice, [1962] ICJ Rep 56.

[299] See text in [1999] ICJ Rep 1060, para 21.

[300] In fact in the *Kasikili/Sedudu Island* case, the Court was considerably assisted by flow measurements and aerial photographs: see for example the photograph reproduced at [1999] ICJ Rep 1069.

[301] '[N]atural features such as rivers or mountains usually need further definition in order to produce a precise boundary line': *Oppenheim's International Law*, above n 42, Vol I, 662; cited by Judge *ad hoc* Ajibola in *Cameroon/Nigeria*, [2002] ICJ Rep 555.

excluded by the nature of a river as boundary, though an indication on the ground that the one channel or the other constituted the boundary would seem both possible and convenient: this then would be a demarcation.[302]

Past inconsistency of terminology would however seem to throw some doubt on the Court's conclusion in the *Frontier Dispute* case that Libya's use of the term 'demarcation' constituted a recognition that only activities on the ground remained to be carried out, there being an agreed frontier at least as an intellectual concept. As noted above, however, this argument was not the sole ground of the Court's decision, but merely a supplementary consideration.

A similar question of terminology may have influenced the decision of the Court in the case of *Sovereignty over Pulau Ligitan and Pulau Sipadan*, between Indonesia and Malaysia. In issue was the interpretation and effect of a Convention of 1891 between the United Kingdom and the Netherlands, by which a boundary line was agreed across the Island of Borneo; the Convention provided that the line should be continued eastwards across the island of Sebittik. The islands of Pulau Ligitan and Pulau Sipadan lay still further to the east, and the essential question in dispute was whether sovereignty over them was also determined by the 1891 Convention, on the basis that the line was impliedly to be continued in order to complete the delimitation between the possessions of the two parties. Indonesia, which advanced this argument, referred to the line envisaged as an 'allocation line between [the] island possessions' of the parties.[303] In its judgment rejecting this contention, the Court mentioned two questions of terminology. First, it noted that 'a "boundary" in the ordinary meaning of the term, does not have the function that Indonesia attributes to the allocation line that was supposedly established' by the Convention; secondly, it considered that 'the object and purpose of the 1891 Convention was the delimitation of boundaries between the parties' possessions within the Island of Borneo itself . . . The Court does not find anything in the Convention to suggest that the parties intended to delimit the boundary between their possessions to the east of the islands of Borneo and Sebittik or to attribute sovereignty over any other islands.'[304]

1B. The Relevance of Maps

In the two *Frontier Dispute* cases, the parties relied on map evidence in support of their cases; in the first case, between Burkina Faso and Mali, the Chamber made a valuable general statement, already noted above, on

[302] For similar practical reasons, maritime areas are subject to delimitation, but normally not to demarcation, though in shallower waters a system of marker buoys would not be inconceivable. In these days of satellite navigation there is however no longer any excuse for infringement of a maritime area whose co-ordinates have been published.

[303] [2002] ICJ Rep 651, para 49.

[304] Ibid, 648, para 43 and 652, para 51.

the probative value of maps in boundary or territorial disputes, which was repeated and adopted in the later case between Benin and Niger:

Whether in frontier delimitations or in international territorial conflicts, maps merely constitute information which varies in accuracy from case to case; of themselves, and by virtue solely of their existence, they cannot constitute a territorial title, that is, a document endowed by international law with intrinsic legal force for the purpose of establishing territorial rights. Of course, in some cases maps may acquire such legal force, but where this is so the legal force does not arise solely from their intrinsic merits; it is because such maps fall into the category of physical expressions of the will of the State or States concerned. This is the case, for example, when maps are annexed to an official text of which they form an integral part.[305]

An example of this situation appeared in the case of the *Land and Maritime Boundary between Cameroon and Nigeria*, where an instrument having the status of an international agreement, the Milner-Simon Declaration of 1919, specifically stated that a particular map, 'the Moisel 1:300,000 map' was the map 'to which reference is made in the description of the frontier'.[306]

The Chamber in the *Frontier Dispute* case continued:

Except in this clearly defined case, maps are only extrinsic evidence of varying reliability or unreliability which may be used, along with other evidence of a circumstantial kind, to establish or reconstitute the real facts.[307]

The 'facts' referred to are presumably the physical facts on the ground, rather than any legally significant facts connecting the will of the parties to the map delineation.

A map which originally has no legal force may acquire it, not only by being annexed to a treaty, but by more informal processes. In the case of the *Temple of Preah Vihear*, the parties had agreed by treaty that their frontier should follow 'the watershed between the basins' of two named rivers;[308] a map was prepared showing what purported to be that watershed, but it proved later to be inaccurate, and placed the disputed Temple on the wrong side of the line. In that case, the Court distinguished between the fact that the map was 'invested with an official standing' and 'had its own inherent technical authority', and the fact that 'at its inception, and at the moment of its production, it had no binding character'.[309] The decision in the case turned on the question whether the parties had

[305] [1986] ICJ Rep 582, para 54, quoted in [2005] ICJ Rep 119, para 44.
[306] [2002] ICJ Rep 339, para 48.
[307] [1986] ICJ Rep 582, para 54, cited in [2005] ICJ Rep 119, para 44.
[308] Article 1 of the Treaty of 13 February 1904 between France and Siam, quoted at [1962] ICJ Rep 16.
[309] [1962] ICJ Rep 21. The 'official standing' resulted from the fact that it was 'produced by French Government topographical experts in response to a request made by the Siamese authorities'.

accepted the map as defining their frontier, even though—unknown to them at the relevant time—it did not correctly implement their treaty, and thus had in effect made it part, and an over-riding part, of their treaty. In the light of all the circumstances, the Court held that that was the situation.[310] In the later case of the *Territorial Dispute* between Libya and Chad, the Court cited this precedent when ruling that

[t]he fixing of a frontier depends on the will of the sovereign States directly concerned. There is nothing to prevent the parties from deciding by mutual agreement to consider a certain line as a frontier, whatever the previous status of that line. If it was already a territorial boundary, it is confirmed purely and simply. If it was not previously a territorial boundary, the agreement of the parties to "recognize" it as such invests it with a legal force which it had previously lacked.[311]

In the case of the *Land, Island and Maritime Frontier Dispute*, the Chamber seised of the case had to deal with, *inter alia*, documents 'referred to collectively as "titles" (*titulos*), concern[ing] grants of land in the area concerned by the Spanish Crown',[312] in particular concerning the land of Indian settlements called *ejidos*. No reliable contemporary maps were made of these, but in some cases the lands were resurveyed in the 19th or 20th centuries, and maps drawn up.[313] Such maps had, in accordance with the principle stated in the first *Frontier Dispute* case, no authority of themselves; but they were relevant insofar as the Chamber worked with a presumption that such grants would at least not straddle an administrative boundary.[314] It did not find it necessary to make any general observation as to the value of maps.

In the first *Frontier Dispute*, the Chamber added a further explanation, also adopted as its own by the Chamber in the second (Benin/Niger) case:

[E]xcept when the maps are in the category of a physical expression of the will of the State, they cannot in themselves alone be treated as evidence of a frontier, since in that event they would form an irrebuttable presumption, tantamount in fact to legal title. The only value they possess is as evidence of an auxiliary or confirmatory kind, and this also means that they cannot be given the character of a rebuttable or *juris tantum* presumption such as effect a reversal of the onus of proof.[315]

[310] Ibid, 33–35. Sir Gerald Fitzmaurice, while agreeing, observed that there had been cases where a map had been expressly made part of a treaty settlement, and had yet been found to yield, in a conflict with the text, to that text, as a matter of interpretation of the treaty as a whole: ibid, 65–66.

[311] [1994] ICJ Rep 23, para 45.

[312] [1986] ICJ Rep 388, para 44.

[313] For an example, see ibid, 411, para 85.

[314] Ibid, 394, para. 54.

[315] Ibid, 583, para 56. The logic here is hard to follow: if a contemporary map is discovered, purporting to show an agreed frontier, then a question of onus of proof arises: should the party relying on it have to prove its connection with the agreement it appears to reflect, or should the other party have to show that it is incorrect, unreliable, or unconnected with what was agreed? Either solution is reasonable, but the Chamber's reasoning does not seem to support its conclusion on the point.

As to the actual use of, or effect given to, maps in these two cases, in the first, the Chamber noted the 'curious fact' that whenever a relevant legal text referred to a map, it was that map that had somehow gone missing since the text was drawn up;[316] the Chamber therefore did not derive much assistance from what might be termed official maps. There was however a map drawn up by a neutral authority, the French Institut géographique national (IGN); the Chamber considered that 'although it does not posses the status of a legal title, [it] is a visual portrayal both of the available texts and of information obtained on the ground.' Accordingly, 'where all other evidence is lacking, or is not sufficient to show an exact line, the probative value of the IGN map becomes decisive.'[317] In the later case, since the boundary followed the river Niger, and (as the Chamber found) the 'main navigable channel' of the river, the maps that were of assistance were those made during surveys of the river, valuable to settle the technical question of the whereabouts of that channel rather than as showing what frontier line had been agreed between the two States.[318]

The maps invoked by the parties in the case of *Kasikili/Sedudu Island* included a map which, though not attached to the treaty which fell to be interpreted, was contemporary with it and expressly associated with it. Article III, paragraph 2 of the Anglo-German Treaty of 1890 stated that '[t]he course of the... boundary is traced *in general accordance with* a Map officially prepared for the British Government in 1889' (emphasis added). There was no dispute that this map was one which had been identified as such in the British archives, but it did not in fact indicate any boundary line.[319] The Court therefore dismissed the idea that this map was in any way authoritative:

> The Court notes that there was no map appended to the 1890 Treaty officially expressing the intentions of Germany and Great Britain with regard to the course of the boundary between their respective possessions in the area.[320]

The Court therefore considered what maps might be of value as constituting 'subsequent practice' of the parties. A number of maps had been published that did show a boundary, in the south channel, but there was evidence showing, first that this placing was probably influenced by the fact that a local tribe from the north side was using the island (a fact which, for reasons not here relevant, the Court did not regard as amounting to evidence of subsequent practice), and secondly that local officials on each side had been convinced that these maps were wrong in this respect, and had so reported to their superiors. The Court concluded that

[316] [1986] ICJ Rep 584, para 58.
[317] Ibid, 586, para 62.
[318] [2005] ICJ Rep 134, para 107.
[319] [1999] ICJ Rep 1098–1099, para 84. Hertslet's *Map of Africa by Treaty* had also included a version of it, but this too was of no assistance (ibid).
[320] Ibid, 1099, para 84.

once the disagreement over the boundary had arisen and had 'hardened', 'the parties largely ignored the maps, which they regarded as either accurate or inaccurate according to their respective positions on the course of the boundary.'[321]

After reviewing post-independence cartographic material, the Court summed up its findings as follows:

In view of the absence of any map officially reflecting the intentions of the parties to the 1890 Treaty and of any express or tacit agreement between them or their successors concerning the validity of the boundary depicted in a map (cf. *Temple of Preah Vihear, Judgment, Merits, I.C.J. Reports 1962*, pp. 33–35), and in the light of the uncertainty and inconsistency of the cartographic material submitted to it, the Court considers itself unable to draw conclusions from the map evidence produced in this case. That evidence cannot therefore "endors[e] a conclusion at which a court has arrived by other means unconnected with the maps" *(Frontier Dispute (Burkina Faso/Republic of Mali), I.C.J. Reports 1986*, p. 583, para 56), nor can it alter the results of the Court's textual interpretation of the 1890 Treaty.[322]

2. The 'Critical Date' in Territorial Disputes

In the case concerning the *Territorial and Maritime Dispute between Nicaragua and Honduras in the Caribbean Sea*, one of the disputed issues between the parties was that of the 'critical date', and the Court took the opportunity to give a definition of the concept.

In the context of a maritime delimitation dispute or of a dispute related to sovereignty over land, the significance of a critical date lies in distinguishing between those acts performed *à titre de souverain* which are in principle relevant for the purpose of assessing and validating *effectivités*, and those acts occurring after such critical date, which are in general meaningless for that purpose, having been carried out by a State which, already having claims to assert in a legal dispute, could have taken those actions strictly with the aim of buttressing those claims. Thus a critical date will be the dividing line after which the Parties' acts become irrelevant for the purposes of assessing the value of *effectivités*.[323]

The Court cited a further explanatory passage from its decision in the case of *Sovereignty over Pulau Ligitan and Pulau Sipadan*:

[The Court] cannot take into consideration acts having taken place after the date on which the dispute between the Parties crystallized unless such acts are a normal continuation of prior acts and are not undertaken for the purpose of improving the legal position of the Party which relies on them.[324]

[321] Ibid, 1099, para 85.
[322] Ibid, 1100, para 87.
[323] [2007-II] ICJ Rep 868, para 117.
[324] [2002] ICJ Rep 682, para 135, quoted ibid.

Both these dicta were cited in the subsequent case of *Sovereignty over Pedra Branca/Pulau Batu Puteh* between Malaysia and Singapore.[325]

The critical date in this sense is not the date at which the situation concerning the disputed territory is claimed to have become established, but the date at which it became evident that there was a dispute in existence over the territory, so that acts otherwise explicable as *effectivités* became suspect as possibly merely intended to improve one State's position.[326] There is however another sense in which the term is used, in the context of a territorial dispute between two States that emerged from a colonial situation. In the previous article in this series, attention was drawn to a dictum of the Chamber in the *Land, Island and Maritime Frontier Dispute*, equating the critical date with the date of independence of the two States, the date at which the Chamber had been asked to determine the territorial claims.[327]

It is against this background that one must interpret the use of the term in the Judgment on the *Frontier Dispute* between Benin and Niger. The Chamber noted that 'the period between 1 and 3 August 1960', that is to say between the dates on which the two States acceded successively to independence, 'can be considered as the critical date'.[328] Some pages later in its decision, the Chamber considered 'the various activities prior to 1954, presented as *effectivités* by the Parties',[329] and subsequently to 'the *effectivités* in the period from 1954 until the critical date in 1960'.[330] These are thus what the Chamber in the *Frontier Dispute (Burkina Faso/Mali)* referred to as 'colonial *effectivités*', that is to say 'the conduct of the administrative authorities as proof of the effective exercise of territorial jurisdiction in the region during the colonial period'.[331] The date of independence was, in this respect, the critical date in the sense that after that date the colonial authorities were *functus officio*, and no act of theirs could affect the issue; it is perhaps also in this sense that the Chamber used the expression. Unless there was a dispute between the *colonial* authorities as to the limits of their respective jurisdictions, no critical date could arise before the independence of the parties to a

[325] Judgment of 23 May 2008, para 32.

[326] The underlying idea would seem to be that 'no action taken *pendente lite* by a State engaged in a dispute before the Court "can have any effect whatever as regards the legal situation which the Court is called upon to define"...and such action cannot improve its legal position vis-à-vis that other State': *Passage through the Great Belt*, [1991] ICJ Rep 19, para 32, citing *Legal Status of the South-Eastern territory of Greenland*, PCIJ Rep Series A/B No 48, 287. In the *Great Belt* case however the Court was guarding against any attempt by a State to establish a *de facto* situation so as to then argue that damages, rather than a modification of the situation, would be a sufficient remedy; cf the Separate Opinion of Judge Oda, ibid, 75, and the Separate Opinion of Judge *ad hoc* Broms, ibid, 38.

[327] [1992] ICJ Rep 401, para 67, quoted in (1995) *BYIL* 1, 37. In his Separate Opinion Judge *ad hoc* Torres Bernárdez referred to dates on which certain aspects of the dispute crystallized as being distinct from the 1821 'critical date': see ibid, 677–678, para 98 and 707, para 164.

[328] [2005] ICJ Rep 120, para 46.

[329] Ibid, 128, para 82.

[330] Ibid, 130, para 89.

[331] [1986] ICJ Rep 586, para 63; cited in *Land, Island and Maritime Frontier Dispute*, [1992] ICJ Rep 389, para 45.

dispute before the Court; but there seems no reason why the date of independence should be treated as critical unless it was then that the dispute between the nascent States already came into the open, which does not appear to have been the case. The Chamber does not in fact mention any acts or events after 1960 which were asserted by a party to be relevant. It also noted that one party relied on documents and maps prepared after that date 'not only to demonstrate current physical realities, but also to establish the situation in the colonial era'.[332]

The distinction between acts occurring before the critical date, and thus *in tempore non suspecto*, and acts occurring after it, is well recognized, but its significance is worth examining. Does the distinction relate to the motive underlying the acts; or to the position of the other State involved in the dispute, and to the reaction that might be made, or ought to be made, to the acts? Where a claimant State relies, by way of *effectivités*, solely on acts performed after the dispute has crystallized, they may be *à titre de souverain* by their nature, as acts of administration, but be inspired, not by a conviction of possessing sovereignty, but by a desire to bolster a shaky claim. Where however there is a continuous sequence of acts technically *à titre de souverain*, or ranking as *effectivités*, both before and after the critical date, there is no reason to suppose that the psychological motivation alters radically at the moment of the critical date, that the State is any less convinced of its rights after that date than it was before. If on the other hand what matters most is the reaction of the other State to an action relied on as an *effectivité*, any negligence in protest may be the more significant after the critical date, since the State that should have reacted can hardly claim to be unaware of the implications of the asserted *effectivité*.

Since it is of the essence of a dispute that it is (at least) two-sided, it follows that the dispute must have 'crystallized' at the same moment for each of the parties to it; but they may nevertheless not agree on the identification of that moment. The problem is similar to that of the determination of the date on which a dispute 'arose' for purposes of interpretation of a temporal limitation in a clause conferring jurisdiction on the Court.[333]

CHAPTER V: TERRITORY AND JURISDICTION

The preceding chapters have above all been concerned with the extent and limits of national territory, and how these are to be determined in cases of dispute; they have not been concerned with what the State sovereign may do or has done within that territory (except to the extent that

[332] [2005] ICJ Rep 109, para 26. This may be regarded as a derogation form the *uti possidetis* (in this sense, Norodom, above n 129), or simply as a transfer of sovereignty subsequent to, and independent of, the accession to independence.

[333] See the earlier article in this series (1999) *BYIL* 1, 17–20.

actes à titre de souverain may be relevant in disputed claims).[334] A few words may however be added on the extent to which State jurisdiction may be exercised within the territory in relation to acts committed outside the territory, in the light of the decision in the *Yerodia* case,[335] which initially raised the problem of 'universal jurisdiction'. As a result of the choice of the parties to the case ultimately not to ask the Court to deal with that issue, the Judgment leaves it aside, but a number of judges commented on it in their separate or dissenting opinions.

The question as originally presented to the Court was whether the issue of an arrest warrant by a Belgian judge against M. Yerodia, who was at the time of issue the Minister for Foreign Affairs of the DRC, was a breach of international law involving the responsibility of Belgium, so that Belgium should be directed to have it withdrawn. The warrant was issued pursuant to the Belgian Law of 16 June 1993 (as amended by the Law of 10 February 1999), which gave the Belgian courts jurisdiction over genocide, crimes against humanity, and war crimes, irrespective of where, by whom and against whom the crime was committed (universal jurisdiction), and even irrespective of the presence of the alleged perpetrator on Belgian territory (i.e. universal jurisdiction *in absentia*, unconditional or absolute universal jurisdiction). The DRC claimed at first that the Belgian judge had no jurisdiction to issue the warrant, thereby rejecting the assertion of universal jurisdiction made by Belgium by adopting the Laws of 16 June 1993 and 10 February 1999. At a later stage in the proceedings it concentrated its arguments on the claim that the warrant violated the immunity from jurisdiction of its Minister for Foreign Affairs, and the Court found that the challenge to universal jurisdiction was 'only a secondary consideration' in the Congolese argument, and accepted Belgium's contention that 'the Court consequently cannot rule on the issue of universal jurisdiction in any decision it renders on the merits of the case', by application of the *ne ultra petita* rule.[336] Such limitation did not, in the Court's view, exclude the Court from dealing 'with certain aspects of that question in the reasoning of its Judgment, should it deem this necessary or desirable'.[337] It does not however appear to have done so.[338]

The statements by judges in their separate or dissenting opinions show that views were divided. For President Guillaume, the position was clear:

[334] See also the study of 'Responsibility flowing from Control of a Territory', Division C, Chapter I, section 2, below.

[335] *Arrest Warrant of 11 April 2000 (Democratic Republic of the Congo v Belgium)*, [2002] ICJ Rep 3.

[336] [2002] ICJ Rep 18–19, paras 41–43, citing the *Asylum* case, [1950] ICJ Rep 402.

[337] Ibid, 19, para 43 *in fine*.

[338] Judge Rezek indicates in his opinion that 'no majority could be found to address the crucial aspect of the problem before the Court', i.e. the question of universal jurisdiction: ibid, 91, para 1 of the Opinion. It is legitimate for commentators to criticise the Court's application of the *ne ultra petita* rule, but it is hardly fair to say that the decision 'fails to reflect important developments that have taken place in international (criminal) law during the last decades' (Jan Wouters, 'The Judgment of the ICJ in the *Arrest Warrant* case: Some Critical Remarks' (2003) 16 *Leiden Journal of International Law* 253)—those developments were simply *ultra petita*.

'Universal jurisdiction *in absentia* is unknown to international conventional law', i.e. treaty law; as regards customary law, President Guillaume reviewed the national legislation cited by Belgium,[339] and concluded by citing with approval the words of Lord Slynn of Hadley in the *Pinochet* case:

"It does not seem... that it has been shown that there is any State practice or general consensus let alone a widely supported convention that all crimes against international law should be justiciable in National Courts on the basis of the universality of jurisdiction.... That international law crimes should be tried before international tribunals or in the perpetrator's own state is one thing; that they should be impleaded without regard to a long established customary international law rule in the Courts of other states is another.... The fact even that an act is recognised as a crime under international law does not mean that the Courts of all States have jurisdiction to try it.... There is no universality of jurisdiction for crimes against international law...."[340]

An important joint separate opinion was appended by Judges Higgins, Kooijmans and Buergenthal. These judges expressed the view that 'a State may choose to exercise a universal criminal jurisdiction *in absentia*', provided that it ensures that 'certain safeguards are in place' which are 'absolutely essential to prevent abuse and to ensure that the rejection of impunity[341] does not jeopardize stable relations between States'.[342] These safeguards include respect for recognized immunities; a previous invitation to the national State of the prospective accused to take action; and independence of the prosecutor from the government of the State.[343] Nor should universal jurisdiction be available except for a limited range of particularly serious crimes: the classic example of piracy, and war crimes and crimes against humanity.

Judge Rezek took a restricted view of the matter; he considered that 'domestic criminal jurisdiction based solely on the principle of universal justice' existed but was 'necessarily subsidiary in nature', i.e. that the courts of the *locus delicti* were best equipped to try the delinquent. He recognized the existence of exceptions to the principle of territoriality,

339 Examples mentioned: France: article 689-1 of the *Code de procedure pénale*; Germany: *Strafgesetzbuch*, Section 6, paras 1 and 9, and Section 7, para 2; Netherlands: decision of the *Hoge Raad* in the *Bouterse* case; with Israel's legislation as the exception that proved the rule.

340 House of Lords, 25 November 1998, *R. v Bartle, ex parte Pinochet*, cited in the Separate Opinion of President Guillaume, [2002] ICJ Rep 42.

341 In a different context, the Court was careful to emphasize that the *immunity* of a diplomat or Foreign Minister from jurisdiction 'does not mean that they enjoy *impunity* in respect of any crimes they might have committed, irrespective of their gravity': ibid, 25, para 60. The three judges are however using 'impunity' to refer to the situation whereby persons (whether or not entitled to immunities) guilty of grave crimes may not be (or are not) pursued in the territories where they could be arrested, and cannot be reached through the exercise by some other State of universal jurisdiction.

342 Ibid, 80, para 59 of the Opinion.

343 Ibid.

justified by the 'principle of the *defence of certain legal interests* to which the State attaches particular value';[344] otherwise, jurisdiction on the basis of active or passive nationality existed, provided that the crimes have not been pursued in a more appropriate forum, and provided the accused is present within the territory of the forum.[345] He entirely rejected Belgium's contention that it was entitled—even 'obliged'—to initiate the proceedings against M. Yerodia on a universal jurisdiction basis.

The Belgian judge *ad hoc*, Judge van den Wyngaert, observed that there was 'no generally accepted definition of universal jurisdiction in conventional or customary international law', and that '[m]any views exist as to its legal meaning and its legal status under international law.'[346] She confined her remarks to the question whether Belgium was 'under international law entitled to assert *extraterritorial* jurisdiction against Mr. Yerodia (apart from the question of immunity)'.[347] She further emphasized the distinction between prescriptive jurisdiction and enforcement jurisdiction, in the light of the Permanent Court's decision in the case of *S.S. Lotus*.[348] The essence of the dispute in her view was whether Belgium was seeking to exercise enforcement jurisdiction; on the facts, Judge van den Wyngaert held that it was not. However, taking the directly opposite view to President Guillaume, she held that '[t]here is no rule of *conventional international law* that universal jurisdiction *in absentia* is prohibited', and that '[t]here is no customary international law to this effect either'.[349]

The distinction between prescriptive and enforcement jurisdiction found an echo in the Dissenting Opinion of Judge Oda. While he supported the Court's decision to refrain from deciding the issue, he voted against all provisions of the operative part of the Judgment. He pointed out that in practice the issue of an arrest warrant was one thing, but its enforcement in the territory of another States was another: 'The crucial point in this regard is *not* the issuance or international circulation of an arrest warrant but the response of the State receiving it.'[350] Certainly any customary rule that upheld the validity of the assertion of universal jurisdiction *in absentia*, of the kind exemplified in the Belgian legislation, would remain ineffective unless coupled with a customary-law duty of other States to recognize and enforce warrants issued in this way—except of course if international conventions for reciprocal enforcement of warrants were to be interpreted as extending to the new warrants of this kind. The first question is however whether there is a customary law prohibition of exercise of universal jurisdiction *in absentia*, including the issue and circulation of a warrant, so that the national State of the defendant[351] could, as

[344] Ibid, 92, para 4, emphasis original. [345] Ibid, para 5.

[346] Ibid, 165, 166, paras 44–45. [347] Ibid, 167, para 47.

[348] Ibid, 167–168, citing PCIJ Judgment No 9, 1927, Rep Series A No 10, 19.

[349] Ibid, 170, paras 54 and 55. [350] Ibid, 52.

[351] Or, possibly, any State that would have had jurisdiction on the basis of, e.g. being the *locus delicti*.

the DRC did, complain of a breach of its rights under international law. The second question is, assuming that no such prohibition exists, whether there is any duty on other States to co-operate in implementing the warrant, so as to render the act of universal jurisdiction effective.

The decision, and in particular the opinions, in the *Yerodia* case have left the question of the existence in customary law of universal jurisdiction *in absentia* perhaps more obscure than before the case was brought. However, Judge Oda's comments in particular may serve to remind us that the creation of a custom is a two-sided process: if an increasing number of States confer on their courts a universal jurisdiction going beyond what is generally accepted, this in itself does not prove the development of a customary rule.[352] The attitude of other States whose courts might have jurisdiction under classical rules, or whose nationals are threatened with the exercise of universal jurisdiction over them, is at least as significant; the absence of objection from this quarter, and *a fortiori* co-operation in the enforcement of a warrant, are certainly significant as indicating the establishment of a custom.

Division C: State Responsibility and International Claims

CHAPTER I: THE 'ACT OF THE STATE' UNDER INTERNATIONAL LAW

I do not know the method of drawing up an indictment against a whole people.

Edmund Burke (1729–1797), Speech on the Conciliation of America, May 1775, *Speeches*, Vol. II, p. 136.

1. Imputability in General

At the outset, it may be noted that it is of course not only in the context of State responsibility that it may be necessary to consider whether or not an act attributed to a State was in fact, and as a matter of law, performed by an entity empowered for that purpose to represent the State internationally. Where responsibility is invoked on the basis of an 'organ' of the State, as contemplated by Article 4 of the ILC Articles on State Responsibility, it will be necessary to show that the act was that of a person having the

[352] There is here the thorny problem of finding an *opinio juris sive necessitatis* underlying a positive act rather than a reaction to another State's act: see the present writer's *International Customary Law and Codification* (Sijthoff, Leiden,1972), 48–49. In the case of universal jurisdiction, however, this may be eased by the general sentiment in favour of effective protection of human rights.

status of an 'organ', and acting in that capacity, to establish imputability in face of denial by the respondent State. But contrariwise, a State may assert the status and authority of one of its organs to establish that an act performed by that organ was effectively an act of the State, and to claim it as such. In the case of *Applicability of the Genocide Convention*, it was objected by the Federal Republic of Yugoslavia (FRY) that the proceedings brought against it by Bosnia and Herzegovina were not effectively instituted because the authorization to institute them was granted by a person who was not the Head of State of the Applicant. The objection was however dismissed by the Court on the facts, and also as a matter of law, citing Article 7, paragraph 2 *(a)* of the Vienna Convention on the Law of Treaties.[353] In either case, what is at stake is the link between the State and a particular act, whether the matter is one of imputability or of authority.

The request for the indication of provisional measures in the context of the *Request for Interpretation of the Judgment of 31 March 2004* in the *Avena* case gave rise to a delicate distinction between the responsibility of a State for the acts of its organs or component entities, and the attributability of the views of such organs or components to the State as expressing the view of the State itself. The question before the Court was whether or not there existed a 'dispute' between the United States and Mexico 'as to the meaning and scope' of the Judgment given in the *Avena* case. The United States denied that any such dispute existed, even though, for constitutional reasons, it had not up to then been able to ensure the 'review and reconsideration' of the convictions of the Mexican nationals concerned; it fully recognized its obligations, and agreed with Mexico that these were obligations of result. Mexico however relied on the attitude of the authorities of Texas, who did not recognize that the decision of the Court was binding upon them. There was no doubt that the actions of the authorities of Texas, if in conflict with the international obligations of the United States, would engage the responsibility of the United States. But did the attitude of Texas have the effect of giving rise to, or evidencing, a dispute between Mexico and the United States as to the 'meaning and scope' of the Court's Judgment?

At the stage of the Order on the Request for the Indication of Provisional Measures, the majority of the Court held that there was such a dispute, inasmuch as

> while it seems both Parties regard paragraph 153 (9) of the *Avena* Judgment as an international obligation of result, the Parties nonetheless apparently hold different views as to the meaning and scope of that obligation of result, namely, whether that understanding is shared by all United States federal and state authorities and whether that obligation falls upon those authorities;[354]

[353] [1996] ICJ Rep 621–622, para 44. Cf also the treatment by the Chamber in the *Gulf of Maine* case of the 'Hoffman letter', [1984] ICJ Rep 305–308, paras 132–139.

[354] Order of 16 July 2008, para 55.

In a powerful dissent, Judge Burgenthal argued that there was in fact no such dispute; but he also considered that the Court's conclusion was based on an error of law. He pointed out that the Court had in effect ruled

> that the views of Texas, a state of the United States which does not and cannot speak for the United States on the international plane, are relevant in determining whether there exists a dispute between the United States and Mexico within the meaning of Article 60 [of the Statute]. The latter conclusion has no basis in international law and appears to establish a novel and dangerous precedent regarding the legal consequences of positions espoused by local governmental entities that conflict with the views of national authorities concerning the nation's international obligations and policies.[355]

The point was also clearly made in the Joint Dissenting Opinion of Judges Owada, Tomka and Keith:

> The proposition of law on which Mexico relies . . . helps to determine the existence or not of the international responsibility of a State for a breach of international law when the breach is committed by an organ exercising public functions, whatever position that organ holds in the organization of the State. Undoubtedly, as the United States accepts, if the Texas authorities go ahead and put Mr. Medellín to death before the required review and reconsideration is carried out, the United States will be in breach of its international obligations. But it does not follow that Mexico and the United States are in dispute about the meaning or scope of the *Avena* judgment simply because the Texas authorities have so far not given effect to the obligation of the United States under the 2004 Judgment.[356]

It is suggested, with great respect, that the majority view may have been influenced by concern to delay the threatened execution, and that *in law* the view of the dissenters is clearly correct. A dispute can be seen as a failure to agree; and the only entities whose attitude is relevant are those empowered to enter into an agreement on behalf of a State of the kind and in the field under consideration.

The decision cited was of course merely an interlocutory one. When the Court dealt with the merits of the request for interpretation of its 2004 Judgment, it devoted a lengthy section of its decision to the question whether or not there was a dispute between the parties as to the meaning or scope of that Judgment; but finally it left that question open, and rejected the request for interpretation on a different ground.[357] The discussion of

355 Dissenting Opinion of Judge Buergenthal, para 24, [2008] ICJ Rep 340.

356 Joint Dissenting Opinion of Judges Owada, Tomka and Keith, para 16, ibid, 346.

357 The Court held that 'The Parties'' different stated perspectives on the existence of a dispute reveal also different contentions as to whether paragraph 153 (9) of the *Avena* Judgment envisages that a direct effect is to be given to the obligation contained therein' (Judgment of 10 January 2009. para 43). This however was a question that was 'not decided in the Court's original Judgment and thus cannot be submitted to it for interpretation under Article 60 of the Statute' (ibid, para 44).

the alleged existence of a dispute does not throw any further light on the question whether, in the Court's view, the attitude of the Texan authorities could or should be relevant in determining that point.[358] The Order of July 2008 therefore stands unconfirmed, and the criticisms of the dissenters on that occasion unrefuted.

2. Responsibility Flowing from Control of a Territory

In the previous article in this series, the cases discussed under this heading involved questions of attribution of responsibility to a State for actions not shown to have been performed by it or on its behalf, but which occurred on territory over which it had sovereignty or control.

In the period now under consideration, the Court had to consider in detail the obligations resting upon Israel as a consequence of its occupation of Palestinian territory. Those obligations however derived from specific international instruments binding upon Israel, and did not derive form the simple fact of its control over what happened in the territory.[359] Injury to another State resulting from events occurring in the Occupied Palestinian Territory would potentially involve the responsibility of Israel to the same extent as comparable events occurring on the territory of Israel itself; but that was not the question before the Court.

3. Attribution of Conduct to a State

(1) *Action by agents or organs of the State*[360]

As the Court observed in the advisory case of *Difference relating to Immunity from Legal Process of a Special Rapporteur of the Commission on Human Rights*, [1999] ICJ Rep 87, para 62: 'According to a well-established rule of international law, the conduct of any organ of a State must be regarded as an act of the State.'[361] The most evident example must be that of the military forces of a State; and in the case concerning *Armed Activities on the Territory of the Congo (DRC v Uganda)*, the answer to 'the question as to whether the acts and omissions of the UPDF [Uganda

[358] Judge Koroma, in a separate opinion, suggested that the Court could have found Mexico's request for interpretation admissible and examined 'the relatively narrow question of whether paragraph 153 (9) of *Avena* creates a direct obligation on state and local officials in the United States to provide review and reconsideration, or whether it creates an international obligation which is subject to domestic implementation in the United States according to United States law' (Separate Opinion, para 7).

[359] See [2004] ICJ Rep 171–181, paras 86–113.

[360] Not dealt with here are problems concerning consent allegedly given by an organ of the State on its behalf, which are more appropriately examined in the context of the law of treaties: see, for example, the earlier article at (2006) *BYIL* 5–7.

[361] [1999] ICJ Rep 87, para 62.

Peoples' Defence Force] and its officers and soldiers are attributable to Uganda' was predictable; and the Court duly found that '[t] the conduct of individual soldiers and officers of the UPDF is to be considered the conduct of a State organ', that is to say, of Uganda.[362] The Court went on to add, in an equally classic dictum, that '[i]t is... irrelevant for the attribution of their conduct to Uganda whether the UPDF personnel acted contrary to the instructions given or exceeded their authority.'[363]

Other activities of which the DRC complained, and for which it attributed responsibility to Uganda, were those of the *Mouvement de Libération du Congo* (MLC). The Court examined in a single paragraph the ways in which the relationship between Uganda and this movement might have involved Uganda's responsibility for some or all of its activities. It began as follows:

> The Court concludes that there is no credible evidence to suggest that Uganda created the MLC. Uganda has acknowledged giving training and military support and there is evidence to that effect. The Court has not received probative evidence that Uganda controlled, or could control, the manner in which Mr. Bemba [the leader of the MLC] put such assistance to use. In the view of the Court, the conduct of the MLC was not that of "an organ" of Uganda (Article 4, International Law Commission Draft Articles on Responsibility of States for internationally wrongful acts, 2001), nor that of an entity exercising elements of governmental authority on its behalf (Article 5).[364]

The creation of the MLC, taken in isolation, would not appear necessarily to involve responsibility for its activities, though such creation would be a suggestive circumstance if it were argued that the MLC was nevertheless wholly independent of Uganda. The MLC was clearly not *formally* an organ of the Government of Uganda, but the Court considers that it might still fall within the ambit of Article 4 of the ILC Articles on State Responsibility as what was called, in the subsequent case concerning the *Application of the Genocide Convention*, an organ *de facto*. At the end of the paragraph quoted, the Court in fact quotes the *Military and Paramilitary Activities* case, in which, as explained below, the Court dealt with the concept of *de facto* organs; it does so however in connection with the possibility of a group being not even a *de facto* organ, but nevertheless under the direction and control of Uganda.

In the *Genocide Convention* case between Bosnia and the FRY (Serbia), the problem of imputability was more complex. The Court found that genocide had been committed at Srebrenica in July 1995, and then turned to

[362] [2005] ICJ Rep 242, para 213; see also para 243.
[363] Ibid, para 214, citing Article 3 of the 1907 Fourth Hague Convention respecting the Laws and Customs of War on Land, and Article 91 of Protocol I additional to the 1949 Geneva Convention.
[364] [2005] ICJ Rep 226, para 160.

the question whether the FRY could be held responsible in international law for the commission of such genocide. The first question posed was whether it could be attributed to the respondent on the basis of the conduct of its organs.[365] The Court began by citing afresh

the well-established rule, one of the cornerstones of the law of State responsibility, that the conduct of any State organ is to be considered an act of the State under international law, and therefore gives rise to the responsibility of the State if it constitutes a breach of an international obligation of the State[366]

and quoting Article 4 of the ILC Articles on State Responsibility as reflecting this rule. On that basis, the Court noted that it was required to determine whether the genocide at Srebrenica was committed by 'persons or entities' (the expression used by the ILC) having the status of organs of the FRY under its internal law as then in force; and concluded that

there is nothing which could justify an affirmative response to this question. It has not been shown that the FRY army took part in the massacres, nor that the political leaders of the FRY had a hand in preparing, planning or in any way carrying out the massacres... Further, neither the Republika Srpska, nor the VRS [the army of the Republika Srpska] were *de jure* organs of the FRY, since none of them had the status of organ of that State under its internal law.[367]

The Applicant had however seized on an aspect of the relationship between the FRY and the Republika Srpska, and claimed that, since all officers in the VRS 'remained under FRY military administration, and... their salaries were paid from Belgrade', therefore these officers 'were *de jure* organs of [the FRY], intended by their superiors to serve in Bosnia and Herzegovina with the VRS'.[368] The Court's ruled as follows on this contention:

The Court notes first that no evidence has been presented that either General Mladić or any of the other officers whose affairs were handled by the 30th Personnel Centre were, according to the internal law of the Respondent, officers of the army of the Respondent—a *de jure* organ of the Respondent.... There is no doubt that the FRY was providing substantial support, *inter alia*, financial support, to the Republika Srpska..., and that one of the forms that support took was payment of salaries and other benefits to some officers of the VRS, but this did not automatically make them organs of the FRY. Those officers were appointed to their commands by the President of the Republika Srpska, and were subordinated to the political leadership of the Republika Srpska. In the absence of evidence to the contrary, those officers must be taken

365 [2007-II] ICJ Rep 202–206, paras 385–395.
366 Ibid, para 385. No reference was made to the *Armed Activities* case.
367 Ibid, para 386.
368 Ibid, para 387.

to have received their orders from the Republika Srpska or the VRS, not from the FRY. The expression "State organ", as used in customary international law and in Article 4 of the ILC Articles, applies to one or other of the individual or collective entities which make up the organization of the State and act on its behalf (cf. ILC Commentary to Article 4, para (1)). The functions of the VRS officers, including General Mladić, were however to act on behalf of the Bosnian Serb authorities, in particular the Republika Srpska, not on behalf of the FRY; they exercised elements of the public authority of the Republika Srpska.[369]

While open to conviction by evidence to the contrary, the Court took a formalistic approach to the question of the identification of an 'organ' for the purposes of responsibility.

The use by the Court in the *Genocide* case of the expression '*de jure* organs' suggests the existence of another class of organs; and indeed the Court did not consider merely whether those responsible for the Srebrenica genocide could be so categorized. The Applicant had also argued they had to be regarded as '*de facto* organs', so that their acts 'must be considered attributable to the FRY, just as if they had been organs of that State under its internal law; reality must prevail over appearances.'[370] This concept of a *de facto* organ, without a formal place in the State's administrative structure, was advanced in the *Military and Paramilitary Activities* case, where it was suggested that

the relationship of the *contras* to the United States Government was so much of dependence on the one side and control on the other that it would be right to equate the *contras*, for legal purposes, with an organ of the United States Government, or as acting on behalf of that Government.[371]

The concept found its place in the Articles on State Responsibility of the International Law Commission, but in a form that avoided the expression '*de facto* organs':

The conduct of a person or persons shall be considered an act of a State under international law if the person or group of persons is in fact acting on the instructions of, or under the direction or control of, that State in carrying out the conduct.

In the Bosnia/Serbia case, the Court invoked the earlier decision[372] in support of the view that

it is possible in principle to attribute to a State conduct of persons—or groups of persons—who, while they do not have the legal status of State organs, in fact act

[369] Ibid, para 388; see also the discussion of the status of the force known as the 'Scorpions', ibid, para 389.
[370] Ibid, para 390.
[371] [1986] ICJ Rep 62, para 109, discussed in the previous article, (1995) *BYIL* 41–43.
[372] Specifically, paras 109–110 of the Judgment in that case, [1986] ICJ Rep 62–63.

under such strict control by the State that they must be treated as its organs for purposes of the necessary attribution leading to the State's responsibility for an internationally wrongful act.[373]

The decision in the *Nicaragua* case had indicated, in the Court's view, that

persons, groups of persons or entities may, for purposes of international responsibility, be equated with State organs even if that status does not follow from internal law, provided that in fact the persons, groups or entities act in "complete dependence" on the State, of which they are ultimately merely the instrument. In such a case, it is appropriate to look beyond legal status alone, in order to grasp the reality of the relationship between the person taking action, and the State to which he is so closely attached as to appear to be nothing more than its agent: any other solution would allow States to escape their international responsibility by choosing to act through persons or entities whose supposed independence would be purely fictitious.[374]

Emphasizing the need for 'complete dependence', the Court found that 'neither the Republika Srpska nor the VRS could be regarded as mere instruments through which the FRY was acting, and as lacking any real autonomy'.[375] In this connection, it also followed the view taken in the decision in the *Military and Paramilitary Activities* case that, for purposes of State responsibility, he who paid the piper cannot necessarily be presumed to have called the tune. In that case, the Court noted the dependence of the *contras* on United States finance and supplies, but considered that whether the United States could be held responsible for the acts of the *contras* 'depend[ed] on the extent to which the United States made use of the potential for control inherent in that dependence.'[376] The very important support given by the FRY to the Republika Srpska did not, in the Court's view, signify 'a total dependence' of the one upon the other.[377]

These considerations did not exhaust the question of the possible responsibility of the FRY for the Srebrenica genocide; and the Court proceeded to indulge in a somewhat didactic disquisition on the different possible grounds of imputability of wrongful acts to a State. It indicated that it was turning to a question that was

different from the question whether the persons who committed the acts of genocide had the status of organs of the Respondent under its internal law; nor however, and despite some appearance to the contrary, is it the same as the question whether those persons should be equated with State organs *de facto*, even

[373] Ibid, para 391. [374] Ibid, para 392. [375] Ibid, para 394.

[376] [1986] ICJ Rep 62, para 110; see the discussion in the earlier article in this series, (1995) *BYIL* 41–43.

[377] The Court had more difficulty with the facts regarding the possible *de facto* status of the 'Scorpions', which was currently in issue before the ICTY, but explained that it could only form its opinion on the material available at the time of its decision: ibid, para 395.

though not enjoying that status under internal law. The answer to the latter question depends, as previously explained, on whether those persons were in a relationship of such complete dependence on the State that they cannot be considered otherwise than as organs of the State, so that all their actions performed in such capacity would be attributable to the State for purposes of international responsibility. Having answered that question in the negative, the Court now addresses a completely separate issue: whether, in the specific circumstances surrounding the events at Srebrenica the perpetrators of genocide were acting on the Respondent's instructions, or under its direction or control. An affirmative answer to this question would in no way imply that the perpetrators should be characterized as organs of the FRY, or equated with such organs. It would merely mean that the FRY's international responsibility would be incurred owing to the conduct of those of its own organs which gave the instructions or exercised the control resulting in the commission of acts in breach of its international obligations. In other words, it is no longer a question of ascertaining whether the persons who directly committed the genocide were acting as organs of the FRY, or could be equated with those organs—this question having already been answered in the negative. What must be determined is whether FRY organs—incontestably having that status under the FRY's internal law—originated the genocide by issuing instructions to the perpetrators or exercising direction or control, and whether, as a result, the conduct of organs of the Respondent, having been the cause of the commission of acts in breach of its international obligations, constituted a violation of those obligations.[378]

The findings of the Court on this aspect of the case will be considered in Section 4, below; in the meantime however, we may note a controversy provoked by one particular sentence in this passage. The Court states that if it should find the Srebrenica genocide attributable to the Respondent on the basis that its perpetrators 'were acting on the Respondent's instructions, or under its direction and control', this 'would in no way imply that the perpetrators should be characterized as organs of the FRY, or equated with such organs.' Then follows this sentence:

It would merely mean that the FRY's international responsibility would be incurred owing to the conduct of those of its own organs which gave the instructions or exercised the control resulting in the commission of acts in breach of its international obligations.

It has been objected that this formulation 'entirely stripped Article 8 of the ILC Articles of its character as an attribution rule'.[379] The authors read the Judgment as expressing the view that 'the responsibility incurred

[378] [2007-II] ICJ Rep 207, para 397.

[379] Jörn Griebel and Milan Plücken, 'New Developments Regarding the Rules of Attribution? The International Court of Justice's Decision in *Bosnia v Serbia*' (2008) 21 *Leiden Journal of International Law* 607.

by the state under Article 8 of the ILC Articles flows from the conduct of the state's organs in giving the instructions or exercising the control in question, as opposed to the action of the instructed or controlled entities.'[380] However, Article 8 provides that

[t]he conduct of a person or group of persons shall be considered an act of a State under international law if the person or group of persons is in fact acting on the instructions of, or under the direction or control of, that State in carrying out the conduct.

It is difficult to see how the person or group can be acting on the instructions of the State unless those instructions are conveyed to it by an organ of that State. Some organ of the State must therefore intervene or have intervened at some stage in the process for Article 8 to come into operation at all; it is simply this evident truth that is expressed in the sentence quoted from the Judgment. The responsibility incurred by the State does not however flow simply from those instructions; they may in fact never be carried out. It flows from the linking of the acts of the person or group concerned to the State as an entity through the normal channel of an organ of the State.[381] As regards 'direction or control', this is presumably to be taken as signifying direction and control *in respect of the internationally wrongful act*; if a person or group is continuously under such direction and control, then must it not fall into the category of *de facto* organs?[382]

(2) Inaction by agents of organs of the State

In the previous article, it was noted that, particularly in the case of obligations imposed by a convention, there will frequently rest upon parties to the convention both positive obligations to take action and negative obligations to refrain from certain action, and that often the one will be implicit in the other.[383] In the case of *Application of the Genocide Convention* between Bosnia and Serbia a central issue was whether, in addition to the obligations specifically stated in the Convention, parties thereto were under 'an obligation, by virtue of the Convention, not to commit genocide themselves', despite the fact that 'such an obligation is not expressly imposed by the actual terms of the Convention'.[384] One of the reasons for holding that there was such a negative obligation was deduced by the Court from the existence in the Convention of a positive obligation: the obligation not to commit genocide, the Court considered,

[380] Ibid.

[381] The article of Griebel and Plücken has been the subject of a detailed refutation by Marko Milanović in a subsequent issue of the same journal: 'State Responsibility for Acts of Non-State Actors: A Comment on Griebel and Plücken' (2009) 22 *Leiden Journal of International Law* 307. The present writer is wholly in agreement with the views of Milanović on this question.

[383] (1995) *BYIL* 43–45.

[384] [2007-II] ICJ Rep 113, para 166.

'follows from the expressly stated obligation to prevent the commission of acts of genocide'.[385]

It would seem at first sight that this is not a necessary interpretation of the Convention. If genocide is committed on the territory of a State, then *prima facie* it has failed in its duty to prevent it; and whether the genocide was committed by persons whose actions engage the responsibility of the State, or by others (revolutionary elements, perhaps), whose actions the State could have prevented, would not seem to affect the issue. For a State actively to commit genocide, as a matter of government policy, may be morally more heinous, but that is another matter. However, responsibility for failing to prevent implies the possibility of prevention, whereas responsibility for acts of, for example, the forces of a State rests on the simple connection between the forces and the State. If a detached military unit in a remote province committed acts of genocide which had not been foreseeable, and were completed before the central government was aware of what was happening, there would be a strong case for saying that there had been no breach of an obligation to prevent; but the responsibility of the State would, according to the Court's finding, still be involved on the basis of the general imputability to it of the acts of its armed forces.

Where an obligation to prevent is found to exist, the problem of imputability is of course considerably simplified. If the event that was to be prevented has in fact occurred, the question which of the State organs had the duty of implementing the obligation is irrelevant; it may indeed have been because no such organ existed that the event occurred. The task of the Court on a request for provisional measures is also made easier if the obligation is one of prevention. At the provisional measures stage of the case of *Application of the Genocide Convention*, the Court was able to indicate measures on the basis that

> in the circumstances brought to its attention . . . in which there is a grave risk of genocide being committed, Yugoslavia and Bosnia-Herzegovina, whether or not any such acts in the past may be legally imputable to them, are under a clear obligation to do all in their power to prevent the commission of any such acts in the future . . .[386]

(3) Possible conditions of a positive obligation

In the previous article in this series, attention was drawn to the indication given by the Court in the case of *United States Diplomatic and Consular Staff in Tehran* of the elements adding up to the commission by the Iranian authorities of a breach of their international obligations, an indication amounting to an enumeration of the conditions of establishment of responsibility. Among these was the fact that the Iranian authorities 'were fully aware . . . of the urgent need for action on their part'; it was noted that the ILC Draft Articles, as they then stood, made no express

[385] Ibid. [386] [1993] ICJ Rep 22, para 45.

mention of the question of knowledge of a need to act. This is still the case; but the ILC's authoritative commentary on the Articles mentions that '[w]hether there has been a breach of a rule [of international law] may depend on the intention *or knowledge* of relevant State organs or agents and in that sense may be "subjective".'[387]

In the case of *Application of the Genocide Convention* between Bosnia and Serbia, the Court discussed the requirements for establishing the breach by a State party to the Convention of its obligation of non-complicity in genocide. After noting that a breach of this obligation always requires that some positive action should have been taken by the State, the Court continued:

> [T]here cannot be a finding of complicity against a State unless at the least its organs were aware that genocide was about to be committed or was under way, and if the aid and assistance supplied, from the moment they became so aware onwards, to the perpetrators of the criminal acts or to those who were on the point of committing them, enabled or facilitated the commission of the acts. In other words, an accomplice must have given support in perpetrating the genocide with full knowledge of the facts.[388]

A violation of the obligation to prevent genocide, the Court had noted, did not necessarily result from positive action, but rather from 'failure to adopt and implement suitable measures to prevent genocide from being committed'.[389] As regards this obligation, the Court saw a distinction:

> By contrast, a State may be found to have violated its obligation to prevent even though it had no certainty, at the time when it should have acted, but failed to do so, that genocide was about to be committed or was under way; for it to incur responsibility on this basis it is enough that the State was aware, or should normally have been aware, of the serious danger that acts of genocide would be committed.[390]

The distinction is thus not between being aware or unaware of a situation demanding action; it is between being aware of imminent or actual genocide, as a fact—necessary for the establishment of the status of accomplice—and being aware of a 'serious danger' giving rise to an obligation to endeavour to prevent that danger being realized.

(4) Actions by persons or groups other than organs of the State[391]

The Court's analysis, in its decision in the case concerning *Armed Activities on the Territory of the Congo*, of the various ways in which it might be

[387] James Crawford, *The International Law Commission's Articles on State Responsibility* (Cambridge University Press, Cambridge, 2002) 81–82, *sub* Article 2, para (3).

[388] [2007-II] ICJ Rep 223, para 432.

[389] Ibid.

[390] Ibid.

[391] In the previous article, reference was made to 'agents' of the State, but the necessary distinction emerges better from the terminology employed by the International Law Commission: 'organs'.

considered that the activities of the liberation movement known as the MLC were attributable to Uganda, has already been quoted above insofar as it concerned the possible categorization of the MLC as an 'organ' of Uganda. The Court continued:

> The Court has considered whether the MLC's conduct was "on the instructions of, or under the direction or control of" Uganda (Article 8) and finds that there is no probative evidence by reference to which it has been persuaded that this was the case. Accordingly, no issue arises in the present case as to whether the requisite tests are met for sufficiency of control of paramilitaries (see *Military and Paramilitary Activities in and against Nicaragua (Nicaragua v United States of America), Merits, Judgment, I.C.J. Reports 1986*, pp. 62–65, paras. 109–115).[392]

The preamble to the Court's examination of this question in the case concerning *Application of the Genocide Convention* has already been quoted in Section 2 above, together with a note of the academic controversy it has provoked. After that introduction, the Court cited Article 8 of the ILC Articles on State Responsibility:

> The conduct of a person or group of persons shall be considered an act of a State under international law if the person or group of persons is in fact acting on the instructions of, or under the direction or control of, that State in carrying out the conduct.

This had, the Court observed, to be understood in the light, in particular of the *Military and Paramilitary Activites* case, with its test of 'effective control'. The Court proceeded again to dot the i's and cross the t's in that pronouncement:

> The test thus formulated differs in two respects from the test—described above—to determine whether a person or entity may be equated with a State organ even if not having that status under internal law. First, in this context it is not necessary to show that the persons who performed the acts alleged to have violated international law were in general in a relationship of "complete dependence" on the respondent State; it has to be proved that they acted in accordance with that State's instructions or under its "effective control". It must however be shown that this "effective control" was exercised, or that the State's instructions were given, in respect of each operation in which the alleged violations occurred, not generally in respect of the overall actions taken by the persons or groups of persons having committed the violations.[393]

It can of course be contemplated that the operations in question formed part of a series to such an extent that the 'effective control' demonstrated in respect of some of them gave rise to a presumption, if no more, of a continuing 'effective control'; though at some point the question might arise whether the persons carrying out the operations had thus become, *pro tanto*, organs *de jure* of the controlling State. At all events, in the special circumstances of

[392] [2005] ICJ Rep 226, para 160. [393] Ibid, para 400.

the case the Applicant attributed this effect to a particular feature of the crime of genocide: that 'it may be composed of a considerable number of specific acts separate, to a greater or lesser extent, in time and space.'[394] This is correct in the sense that, in order to establish genocidal intent, a certain pattern of activity may have to be shown; but it is suggested that this is not always an inherent feature of the crime. A single act of killing, if carried out with proven genocidal intent, might be sufficient.[395] Turning to the situation in the Balkans, it would be perfectly possible for persons to be directed by a higher authority to carry out a specific genocidal mission on one occasion, and to then proceed to other such missions on their own initiative; the very nature of genocide is such that it is likely to be committed by those having very specific personal convictions. In such case the State would presumably be responsible for all genocidal acts so committed.

At all events, the Court was not convinced on this point: it took the view that 'the particular characteristics of genocide do not justify the Court in departing from the criterion elaborated in' the *Military and Paramilitary Activities* case. However it was faced with a jurisprudential conflict: the ICTY in the *Tadič* case[396] had held that

> the appropriate criterion, applicable in its view both to the characterization of the armed conflict in Bosnia and Herzegovina as international, and to imputing the acts committed by Bosnian Serbs to the FRY under the law of State responsibility, was that of the "overall control" exercised over the Bosnian Serbs by the FRY; and further that that criterion was satisfied in the case...[397]

With some tact,[398] the Court extricated itself from this apparent contradiction. It pointed out that the jurisdiction of the ICTY is criminal, and 'extends over persons only'; it is not called upon to rule on questions of State responsibility.[399] The 'overall control' test adopted by the ICTY

[394] Ibid, para 401.

[395] It is true that the Genocide Convention defines the crime as, *inter alia*, 'killing members'—in the plural—of the targeted group; but if, for example, a racist attack on a group were to be successful in killing only a single member of it, would the attack be less genocidal? Similarly, the intention of destroying the group 'in whole or in part' (Convention, Article II *(c)*) would not appear to exclude destroying a significant individual; cf the *Krstić* case referred to in the Bosnia/Serbia judgment, para 200.

[396] IT-94-1-A, Judgment, 15 July 1999. A similar approach had been adopted by the ECHR in the *Loizidou* case: *Loizidou v Turkey* (preliminary objections), 23 March 1995, ECHR Series A no 310.

[397] [2007-II] ICJ Rep 209, para 402.

[398] The Court's response has been described as 'fairly measured': Richard J Goldstone and Rebecca J Hamilton, 'Bosnia v Serbia: Lessons from the Encounter of the ICJ with the ICTY' (2008) 21 *Leiden Journal of International Law* 95, 101.

[399] On the conflict between the ICJ and the ICTY in this respect see Jörn Griebel, *Die Zurechnungskategorie der de-facto-Organe in Recht der Staatenverantwortlichkeit* (Lit Verlag, Köln, 2004) 170 et seq; Astrid Epiney, 'Zur Rechtsfigur des *de-facto*-Organe im Recht der Staatenverantwortlichkeit', in A Fischer-Lescano et al (eds), *Frieden in Freiheit, Festschrift für Michael Bothe* (Dike, Zürich 2008) 883. It has been suggested that this is no more than an example of a normal healthy relationship between different tribunals: Benedetto Conforti, 'Unité et fragmentation du droit international: "Glissez, mortels, n'appuyez pas!"' (2007) 111 *Revue générale de droit international public*, 5, 10–12.

might (though the Court left the point open) well be suitable for the purpose of determining whether a conflict was national or international, 'the sole question which the [ICTY] Appeals Chamber was called upon to decide'.[400] Accordingly, the finding in the *Tadić* case had been unnecessary for the Tribunal's decision on its jurisdiction, and was, in short, to that extent an *obiter dictum*.

The Court however did not leave it there. It emphasized the difference between the 'two issues, which are very different in nature' of State responsibility and the international character of a conflict.[401] More profoundly, the Court stated as follows:

> It must next be noted that the "overall control" test has the major drawback of broadening the scope of State responsibility well beyond the fundamental principle governing the law of international responsibility: a State is responsible only for its own conduct, that is to say the conduct of persons acting, on whatever basis, on its behalf. That is true of acts carried out by its official organs, and also by persons or entities which are not formally recognized as official organs under internal law but which must nevertheless be equated with State organs because they are in a relationship of complete dependence on the State. Apart from these cases, a State's responsibility can be incurred for acts committed by persons or groups of persons—neither State organs nor to be equated with such organs—only if, assuming those acts to be internationally wrongful, they are attributable to it under the rule of customary international law reflected in Article 8 [ILC Articles]...This is so where an organ of the State gave the instructions or provided the direction pursuant to which the perpetrators of the wrongful act acted or where it exercised effective control over the action during which the wrong was committed. In this regard the "overall control" test is unsuitable, for it stretches too far, almost to breaking point, the connection which must exist between the conduct of a State's organs and its international responsibility.[402]

In other words, the conduct of a State organ must enter the picture somewhere: if the wrongful act complained of is not carried out by an organ, whether *de jure* or *de facto*, those who did carry it out must have been linked in some way with such an organ if the State is to be held responsible. This is clearly right. However, it is less clear why the link between the organ and the perpetrators must be that of 'direction and control', as in Article 8 and following *Military and Paramilitary Activities*, and may not be one of 'overall control', as suggested by the ICTY. The underlying thought may however be that the 'overall control' test blurs the distinction between a *de facto* organ and an independent perpetrator linked *pro hac vice* with a recognized organ.[403] The last

[400] [2007-II] ICJ Rep 210, para 404. [401] Ibid, para 405. [402] Ibid, para 406.

[403] This indeed seems to be the objection of Griebel and Plücken, New Developments, above n 380; see also Griebel's *Die Zurechnungskategorie der de facto-Organe im Recht der Staatenverantwortlichkeit* above n 399 et seq.

sentence quoted seems to be saying that the 'overall control' test would, in practice, mean that the State would be held responsible for acts going beyond either its wishes and intentions or its power to prevent; this seems already to be the case where an otherwise independent entity is classified as a *de jure* organ.[404]

In a powerful dissent, Vice-President Al-Khasawneh urged that the Court should have adopted the same approach as that of the ICTY in the *Tadič* case, and pointed out that, rightly or wrongly, the ICTY had in fact 'framed the question as one of international responsibility.'[405] He also distinguished the *Military and Paramilitary Activities* decision, essentially on the basis that, unlike in that case, 'in the present case there was a unity of goals, unity of ethnicity, and a common ideology, such that effective control over non-State actors would not be necessary.'[406] The theoretical point is a good one; but its application requires a slide from a purpose of ethnic cleansing, shared by the Serbian government and those responsible for Srebrenica, to a common purpose of genocide, which is difficult to demonstrate from the facts available.[407]

(5) *Responsibility for acts of another State*

Article 28 of the 1996 Draft Articles of the International Law Commission, referred to in this connection in the previous article,[408] now takes the form of Chapter IV of the final Articles, consisting of Articles 16–19. The Court has not however had occasion to consider or apply these provisions. Whatever the role played by the 'Republika Srpska' in the events in Bosnia underlying the case of *Application of the Genocide Convention*, it was not at any time recognized as a State. A question that was raised in the *Legality of the Use of Force* cases, but remained unresolved when the Court disclaimed jurisdiction, was that of responsibility of States members of an international organization (NATO) for acts of that organization;[409] the ILC Articles specifically reserve this question (Article 57).

404 As in the hypothetical example (already quoted in the previous article: (1995) *BYIL* 48) of an unauthorized and spontaneous attack by the occupiers of the US Embassy in Tehran on another embassy in the neighbourhood.

405 Dissenting Opinion, [2007-II] ICJ Rep 256, para 38.

406 Ibid, 255, para 36.

407 Vice President Al-Khasawneh in fact rejected this as an 'artificial distinction' (ibid, para 41); on the facts, he was more ready than was the majority of the Court to draw conclusions adverse to the FRY from the fact that portions of relevant documents had been kept from the Court ('redacted'): ibid, para 35.

408 (1995) *BYIL* 1, 49.

409 See Ian Brownlie, 'The Responsibility of States for the Acts of International Organizations' in Maurizio Ragazzi (ed), *International Responsibility Today, Essays in Memory of Oscar Schachter* (Nijhoff, Leiden, 2005) 355, and Rosalyn Higgins, 'The International Court of Justice: Selected Issues of State Responsibility', ibid, 273–274, with comments on the work of the *Institut de droit international* on the question.

CHAPTER II: THE BREACH OF AN INTERNATIONAL OBLIGATION

1. Inter-State Obligations

In the previous article on this subject, note was taken of the rejection by the Court in the *Military and Paramilitary Activities* case of the argument by the United States that its actions in relation to Nicaragua might have been justified by breaches by Nicaragua of obligations owed, not to the United States, but to the OAS. The Court observed that only the OAS, as the entity to which the obligation was owed, was 'empowered to monitor its implementation';[410] similarly, only the beneficiary of an obligation (setting aside obligations *erga omnes*, dealt with below) is entitled to assert the existence of State responsibility in respect of an alleged breach of such obligation.

At the merits stage of the case concerning *Application of the Genocide Convention* between Bosnia and Serbia, the Court made something of a general statement that is significant in this connection. When dealing with the breach by Serbia of its obligation under the Convention to prevent genocide, the Court stated that its decision did not 'purport to find whether, apart from the texts applicable to specific fields, there is a general obligation on States to prevent the commission by other persons or entities of acts contrary to certain norms of general international law.'[411] Does the term 'entities' include other States? An obligation on a State to prevent another State from acting in a certain way would, if it existed, imply the existence of a right to endeavour to prevent such action; and the corollary of such a right would seem to be the existence of an obligation on the other State, not to take such action, owed to the State asserting the right to prevent it. All that the Court said was that its decision should not be generalized, but the dictum is nevertheless welcome when the temptation is widely felt, and not always resisted, to consider that if an international obligation is important enough it is necessarily an obligation on everybody and owed to everybody. Such obligations may certainly exist, but they have to be established by recognized international law processes.

2. Obligations *Erga Omnes*

In the previous article in this series, it was noted that up to that date (1995) there had 'not yet been a case before the Court in which responsibility has been found to exist on the basis of an obligation of this type, let alone a case in which the applicant State had not itself suffered direct injury as a result of the act' complained of.[412] This is still the position; but in addition

[410] [1986] ICJ Rep 132, para 262.
[411] [2007-II] ICJ Rep 220, para 429.
[412] (1995) *BYIL* 58.

to certain *dicta* in other cases, the Court in its Advisory Opinion *Legal Consequences of the Construction of a Wall in the Occupied Palestinian Territory* expressed the view that Israel was in breach of certain obligations which were 'essentially of an *erga omnes* character'.[413] Furthermore, in the case of *Application of the Genocide Convention* between Bosnia and Serbia, the Court did draw a conclusion from the status of the prohibition of genocide as an international obligation *erga omnes*.

The Court's handling of the matter in the *Wall* case was discussed at some length in an earlier article in this series.[414] Here it may be recalled that the Court continued to maintain the confusion noted in the *East Timor* case, and commented on in an earlier article,[415] between a right *erga omnes* and an obligation *erga omnes*.[416] The fact that a right is maintainable against all the world, *erga omnes*, does not necessarily mean that anyone other than the beneficiary of the right can enforce it, that the obligation to respect the right is owed to all other States, *erga omnes*.

In its Advisory Opinion, the Court, after citing its celebrated dictum in the *Barcelona Traction* case,[417] observed that

> The obligations *erga omnes* violated by Israel are the obligation to respect the right of the Palestinian people to self-determination, and certain of its obligations under international humanitarian law

and continued:

> As regards the first of these, the Court has already observed . . . that in the *East Timor* case, it described as "irreproachable" the assertion that "the right of peoples to self-determination, as it evolved from the Charter and from United Nations practice, has an *erga omnes* character".[418]

It buttressed this by reference to General Assembly resolution 2625 (XXV)—not itself a source of law—which declared: 'Every State has the duty to promote, through joint and separate action, realization of the principle of equal rights and self-determination of peoples', which adds up to rather less than a recognition of a right *erga omnes*. The further step consisting in the deduction from the *erga omnes* character of the right to the *erga omnes* character of the obligation to respect it, is conspicuously absent: the Court next turns to obligations of international humanitarian law. The argument on this is a simple *non sequitur*:

> With regard to international humanitarian law, the Court recalls that in its Advisory Opinion on the *Legality of the Threat or Use of Nuclear Weapons* it stated

[413] [2004] ICJ Rep 199, paras 155 and 157.

[414] (2005) *BYIL* 42–59.

[415] (1995) *BYIL* 59, n 205.

[416] In this sense, James Crawford and Simon Olleson, 'The Nature and Forms of International Responsibility' in Malcolm Evans (ed), *International Law* (2nd edn, Oxford University Press, Oxford, 2006) 459. This passage is not repeated in the 3rd edition (2010).

[417] [1970] ICJ Rep 32, para 33.

[418] [2004] ICJ Rep 199, paras 155–156, citing [1995] ICJ Rep 102, para 29.

that "a great many rules of humanitarian law applicable in armed conflict are so fundamental to the respect of the human person and 'elementary considerations of humanity' . . . ", that they are "to be observed by all States whether or not they have ratified the conventions that contain them, because they constitute intransgressible principles of international customary law" (*I.C.J. Reports 1996 (I) p.* 257, para 79). In the Court's view, these rules incorporate obligations which are essentially of an *erga omnes* character.[419]

The first finding goes no further than establishing that the rules are rules of customary law, binding independently of treaty obligation (or lack of it); the term 'intransgressible' seems to have no independent meaning, unless it is another way of referring to *jus cogens*.[420] The last sentence quoted therefore stands on its own, unsupported by what has gone before. The Court then observes that it

would also emphasize that Article 1 of the Fourth Geneva Convention, a provision common to the four Geneva Conventions, provides that "[t]he High Contracting Parties undertake to respect and to ensure respect for the present Convention in all circumstances." It follows from that provision that every State party to that Convention, whether or not it is a party to a specific conflict, is under an obligation to ensure that the requirements of the instruments in question are complied with.[421]

One must however ask: under an obligation to whom? Since this is a provision of a convention, the obligation is owed to all other parties to the convention; even when the convention has received such quasi-universal adoption as the Fourth Geneva Convention, such an obligation is nevertheless difference in essence from an obligation *erga omnes* of general law, of the kind contemplated in the *Barcelona Traction* Judgment.

In the case concerning *Application of the Genocide Convention*, Yugoslavia had submitted a preliminary objection to the jurisdiction allegedly based on Article IX of the Genocide Convention; as one of the grounds of this objection Yugoslavia

contests the existence in this case of an "international dispute" within the meaning of the Convention, basing itself on two propositions: first, that the conflict occurring in certain parts of the Applicant's territory was of a domestic nature, Yugoslavia was not party to it and did not exercise jurisdiction over that territory at the time in question;[422]

[419] [2004] ICJ Rep 199, para 157.

[420] The concept of an 'intransgressible' rule was discussed in an earlier article, and it was there noted that in the *Palestine Wall* Advisory Opinion the Court left open the question of the possible *jus cogens* character of such rules, thereby indicating that 'intransgressible' means something other than *jus cogens*: (2005) *BYIL* 59–62.

[421] [2004] ICJ Rep 199–200, para 158.

[422] [1996] ICJ Rep 615, para 30.

In this respect, the Court first pointed out that the only provision of the Convention directly relevant to the question of territorial scope was Article VI, conferring jurisdiction to try offenders on the courts of the State in the territory of which the act was committed. The relevance of this observation is not evident, and the Court did not pursue it. It then recalled 'its understanding of the object and purpose of the Convention, as set out in' its 1951 Advisory Opinion on *Reservations to the Genocide Convention*, and in particular its finding as to 'the universal character both of the condemnation of genocide and of the co-operation required "in order to liberate mankind from such an odious scourge" (Preamble to the Convention).'[423] The Court deduced two bold propositions from this finding:

> It follows that the rights and obligations enshrined by the Convention are rights and obligations *erga omnes*. The Court notes that the obligation each State thus has to prevent and to punish the crime of genocide is not territorially limited by the Convention.[424]

Since the question under examination was whether or not the Court had jurisdiction to examine a claim of breach of the Convention allegedly constituted by acts not committed on the territory of the defendant State, the *erga omnes* status of the obligation not to commit genocide is apparently advanced as a reason why the Court did posses such jurisdiction. This is not the same as the question whether a State commits a breach of the Convention by making itself in some way responsible for acts of genocide committed outside its territory; and even this proposition does not seem necessarily to follow from the classification of the Convention rights and obligations as *erga omnes*. This is not to say that the Court's conclusion as to non-territorial responsibility is wrong, but the reasoning in support is somewhat tenuous.

A more convincing reasoning, possibly underlying the passage quoted, is that the obligation to prevent and punish in the Genocide Convention must have been intended by the parties to be co-extensive with the power to prevent and punish. On its own territory a State is sovereign, and therefore necessarily has that power; but if it has some analogous power outside its territory, resulting from control of its nationals or otherwise, it is an interpretation consistent with the advancement of the object and purpose of the Convention to understand the obligation to prevent and punish as equally applicable.

A parallel question arose in the case concerning the *Legal Consequences of the Construction of a Wall in the Occupied Palestinian Territory*, in relation to the applicability of the International Covenant on Civil and Political Rights and the International Covenant on Economic, Social and Cultural Rights. Israel denied that either of these instruments applied to

[423] [1951] ICJ Rep 23. [424] [1996] ICJ Rep 616, para 31.

the occupied Palestinian Territory; it distinguished them from, for example, the Fourth Geneva Convention, inasmuch as 'humanitarian law is the protection granted in a conflict situation . . . whereas human rights treaties were intended for the protection of citizens from their own Government in times of peace.'[425] The Court first observed that 'the protection offered by human rights conventions does not cease in case of armed conflict.'[426]

The International Covenant on Civil and Political Rights provided that '[e]ach State Party to the present Covenant undertakes to respect and to ensure to all individuals within its territory and subject to its jurisdiction the rights recognized in the present Covenant, without distinction of any kind'. The Court noted that these words could be read conjunctively, or disjunctively so as to apply to individuals outside the State's territory but subject to its jurisdiction.[427] It decided in favour of the latter interpretation, on the basis first of all that it would be consistent with the object and purpose of the Covenant for States parties to be bound to comply with it when exercising jurisdiction outside of the national territory.[428] The Court also relied on 'the constant practice of the United Nations Human Rights Committee', and on the *travaux préparatoires*.[429] As to the International Covenant on Economic, Social and Cultural Rights, the Court recognized that the absence of any provision as to scope of application 'may be explicable by the fact that this Covenant guarantees rights that are essentially territorial'.[430] Nevertheless, citing Article 14 of the Covenant,[431] it held that 'it is not to be excluded that it applies both to territories over which a State party has sovereignty and to those over which that State exercises territorial jurisdiction.'[432] It treated Israel's interpretation as based solely on the distinction between humanitarian conventions and human rights conventions, already mentioned, and therefore felt able to reject it.

[425] Quoted in [2004] ICJ Rep 177, para 102. Since Israel did not appear in the proceedings, and confined its Written Statement to reasons why the Court should not give effect to the request for opinion, its arguments on the merits of the matter were available to the Court only in the form of a summary supplied by the Secretary-General in an Annex to his Report to the General Assembly prepared pursuant to Resolution ES-10/13 (A-ES-10/248, 20 November 2003). The information in the summary was stated to be derived in part from material supplied by Israel, and in part from publicly available sources; it is no doubt accurate, but may not entirely reflect some nuances in Israel's position.

[426] [2004] ICJ Rep 178, para 106. It is not clear from the summary (see previous note) that Israel was arguing the contrary, or whether it was contending simply that humanitarian law was the primary protection during hostilities.

[427] Ibid, 179, para 108.

[428] Ibid, para 109.

[429] These showed, in the view of the Court, that 'the drafters of the Covenant did not intend to allow States to escape from their obligations when they exercise jurisdiction outside their national territory. They only intended to prevent persons residing abroad from asserting, vis-à-vis their State of origin, rights that do not fall within the competence of that State, but of that of the State of residence.': ibid.

[430] Ibid, 180, para 112.

[431] Which refers to transitional measures concerning education, and mentions a State's 'metropolitan territory *or other territories under its jurisdiction*'.

[432] [2004] ICJ Rep 180, para 112.

The position of Israel in relation to the occupied Palestinian territory is one which is at present, though perhaps decreasingly, exceptional. A wider question is that which had already arisen in the *Genocide Convention* case, of the responsibility of States for breaches of an international treaty obligation committed in a territory over which the State party to the relevant convention had, at the time, neither sovereignty nor jurisdiction. This was again the issue in the recent Order on the request of Georgia for the indication of provisional measures in the proceedings brought against Russia concerning *Application of the International Convention on the Elimination of all Forms of Racial Discrimination.* Georgia was claiming that acts attributable to Russia committed in Georgia's territory, 'and in particular in Abkhazia and South Ossetia', were breaches of the Convention (CERD); Russia argued that 'the provisions of CERD cannot be applied extraterritorially and that in particular Articles 2 and 3 of CERD cannot govern a State's conduct outside its own borders.'[433] The Court's ruling (given, it should be recalled, in the context of the summary examination of the case required for provisional measures), was:

> Whereas the Court observes that there is no restriction of a general nature in CERD relating to its territorial application; whereas it further notes that, in particular, neither Article 2 nor Article 5 of CERD, alleged violations of which are invoked by Georgia, contain a specific territorial limitation; and whereas the Court consequently finds that these provisions of CERD generally appear to apply, like other provisions of instruments of that nature, to the actions of a State party when it acts beyond its territory;[434]

It is striking that there is here no appeal, whether express or implied, to the nature of the specific Convention, or to its object and purpose; the Court is content to suppose (apparently) that every international convention commits the parties to it to compliance within and without their respective territories unless a contrary intention is expressed. Russia urged that this is inconsistent with the general rule stated in Article 29 of the Vienna Convention on the Law of Treaties: 'Unless a different interpretation appears from the treaty or is otherwise established, a treaty is binding upon each party in respect of its entire territory.' The Court did not comment on this argument, but the reference to the 'entire' territory shows that the intended meaning is simply that no part of the territory of a State is excluded from the application of a treaty concluded by that State in the absence of express provision. It does not address whether or not a treaty may impose obligations on a State as to its conduct outside its territory.

A decision on a request for provisional measures cannot however be regarded as the Court's last word on a question of law arising in that context; and it is to be hoped that in its eventual decision on the merits the

[433] Order of 15 October 2008, para 108. [434] Ibid, para 109.

Court will give a clearer and more fully reasoned determination. In particular, the arguments of Russia that the nature of the specific obligations invoked, under Articles 2 and 5 of the CERD, are such as to imply an intention to limit their scope to the territory of (or at most territory controlled by) a party, deserve further consideration.

In the case concerning *Armed Activities on the Territory of the Congo (Congo v Uganda)*, one of Uganda's counterclaims concerned alleged violations of international humanitarian law committed against 17 private persons at Ndjili International Airport in August 1998. The Court found that this claim was based on the international minimum standard relating to the treatment of foreign nationals, not on direct injury to Uganda, and that the preconditions for a claim by Uganda to exercise diplomatic protection in this respect were not satisfied: it was not shown that the persons in question were Ugandan nationals, and their nationality remained undetermined.[435] Judge Simma however, in a separate opinion, considered that the Court should not have confined itself to this finding. In his view, breaches had been shown both of humanitarian law, namely Article 75 of Protocol I Additional to the 1949 Geneva Conventions, and of human rights law, namely the International Covenant on Civil and Political Rights of 19 December 1966, the African Charter on Human and Peoples' Rights of 27 June 1981, and the Convention against Torture and Other Cruel, Inhuman or Degrading Treatment or Punishment of 10 December 1984, to all of which both the DRC and Uganda were parties.

Judge Simma did not consider that the absence of a link of nationality precluded Uganda from presenting a claim against the Congo for breaches of these instruments. As regards international humanitarian law, he cited the Court's finding in the *Palestine Wall* case, quoted above.[436] He invoked Article 48 of the International Law Commission's Articles on State Responsibility, which recognizes the right of '[a]ny State other than the injured State' to invoke the responsibility of another State if the obligation breached is either 'owed to a group of States including that State, and is established for the protection of a collective interest of the group', or 'owed to the international community as a whole'.[437] In his view, the obligations deriving from the human rights treaties that he had cited fell into the former category, as 'instances *par excellence* of obligations that are owed to a group of States including Uganda, and are established for the protection of a collective interest of the States parties to the Covenant'.[438] The Judgment of the Court does not go into these possibilities; as Judge Simma recognized, the claim had not been presented to

[435] [2005] ICJ Rep 276 para 333.

[436] Text and n 419; separate Opinion of Judge Simma, [2005] ICJ Rep 346–347, para 33.

[437] Ibid, 347–348, para 35.

[438] Ibid, 348. Judge Simma thus regarded the obligation as one *erga omnes partes* rather than *erga omnes* in the fuller sense.

it with the professional competence that might have made it more convincing.[439]

3. Relationship between State Responsibility and Municipal Law

The *Fisheries Jurisdiction* case between Spain and Canada involved some examination of the relationship between the Canadian legislation, the enforcement of which on the high seas formed the subject of Spain's complaint, and concepts of international law. The question before the Court was limited to the effect of Canada's reservation to its acceptance of jurisdiction under Article 36, paragraph 2, of the Statute. Canada had adopted legislation to provide for control of fisheries in an area known as the 'NAFO Regulatory Area';[440] the Court found (and the point was not disputed) that this area was part of the high seas,[441] and thus outside Canada's EEZ. In anticipation of its legislation, or action taken on that basis, being challenged before the Court, Canada added to its declaration an exclusion of 'disputes arising out of or concerning conservation and management measures taken by Canada with respect to vessels fishing in the NAFO Regulatory Area . . . and the enforcement of such measures'[442] When a Spanish vessel, the *Estai,* was arrested by the Canadian authorities while fishing in this area, Spain brought a claim before the Court, and was met by a plea of lack of jurisdiction.

Spain's complaint on the merits was essentially that Canada's actions in the implementation of the legislation, if not the legislation itself, were contrary to international law; and this clearly involved the application of the principle that a State cannot rely on its own internal law to justify a breach of international law. However, at the first and only stage that the proceedings reached, the Canadian fisheries legislation was not directly relevant, since the task of the Court was to interpret the reservation, i.e., to say whether or not the dispute arose out of or concerned 'conservation and management measures taken by Canada'. Spain argued, *inter alia,* that the measures taken by Canada, and referred to in its declaration, were not 'conservation and management measures' as understood in general international law, because they went beyond the conservation and management of fishery resources under the control of the enacting State. This contention of course concerned the interpretation of the declaration, not of the underlying Canadian legislation. However, the Court, having found that the intention of Canada had been to use the expression

[439] Ibid, 339, para 18.

[440] Defined in the 1978 Convention on Future Multilateral Co-operation in the Northwest Atlantic Fisheries.

[441] [1998] ICJ Rep 463, para 74.

[442] Ibid, 439, para 14.

in its declaration in the sense 'generally accepted in international law and practice', went on to observe that 'any other interpretation of that expression would deprive the reservation of its intended effect';[443] and it defined the intended effect by reference to the Canadian legislation.

A further argument employed by Spain was that the use of force (as had allegedly occurred on the arrest of the *Estai*), being unlawful as a matter of general international law, fell outside the reservation; the Court rejected this, and then turned to a subsidiary contention of Spain that the Canadian legislation 'constitute[d] measures of penal law other than enforcement of fisheries conservation measures, and thus [fell] outside of the reservation'.[444] The Court considered the Canadian legislation referred to, and noted that 'the purpose of these enactments appears to have been to control and limit any authorized use of force, thus bringing it within the general category of measures in enforcement of fisheries conservation.'[445] Accordingly,

> the use of force authorized by the Canadian legislation and regulations falls within the ambit of what is commonly understood as enforcement of conservation and management measures and thus falls under the provisions of paragraph 2 (d) of Canada's declaration. This is so notwithstanding that the reservation does not in terms mention the use of force. Boarding, inspection, arrest and minimum use of force for those purposes are all contained within the concept of enforcement of conservation and management measures according to a "natural and reasonable" interpretation of this concept.[446]

The question of the relationship between municipal law and responsibility under international law arose in an unusual way in the case of *Certain Questions of Mutual Assistance in Criminal Matters*. Djibouti claimed that France was in breach of a 1986 bilateral Convention on Mutual Assistance in Criminal Matters, which provided that 'the requested State shall execute in accordance with its law any letters rogatory relating to a criminal matter and addressed to it by the judicial authorities of the requesting State…'. France had refused to execute a letter rogatory issued by the prosecuting authorities in Djibouti, relying on a provision in the Convention whereby assistance of this kind might be refused, *inter alia*, 'if the requested State [i.e., France] considers that the execution of the request is likely to prejudice its sovereignty, its security, its *ordre public* or others of its essential interests'.[447] The decision to refuse had been taken, specifically by reference to this text, and citing considerations of national security, on 8 February 2005 by an investigating judge at the Paris *Tribunal de grande instance*.[448] France had informed Djibouti of this by a letter of 31 May 2005 addressed to the Embassy in Paris.[449] Djibouti suggested that this

[443] Ibid, 462, para 71. [444] Ibid, 466, para 83. [445] Ibid. [446] Ibid, para 84.

[447] Article 2 *(c)* of the 1986 Convention.

[448] See paras 23–24 of the Judgment of 4 June 2008.

[449] The letter appeared to have gone astray and never reached the Embassy; but in response to an enquiry by Djibouti the French Ambassador there informed the relevant Minister on 6 June 2005 that the request constituted by the letter rogatory had been refused; ibid, para 144.

was insufficient because 'under French law, matters relating to security and *ordre public* could not fall for determination by the judiciary alone';[450] that 'this type of assessment, concerning a possible risk to the sovereignty, security, *ordre public* or other essential interests of a State, must by its nature lie with the highest organs of that State.'[451] The question had however in fact been raised before a higher French judicial authority, the *Chambre de l'instruction* of the Paris Court of Appeal, which had held that the application of Article 2 of the Convention 'is a matter solely for the investigating judge (who will have available information from the relevant government departments)', and that such a decision was 'a decision in law, and not an advice to the executive'.[452] The International Court therefore simply stated that '[i]t is not for this Court to do other than accept the findings of the Paris Court of Appeal on this point.'[453]

In the case of the *Request for Interpretation of the Judgment of 31 March 2004* in the *Avena* case, mentioned above,[454] the domestic law of the United States presented an obstacle to the fulfilment by the United States of its international obligations as declared by the Court's earlier judgment. The US was required not to execute the Mexican nationals mentioned in the Judgment without their being afforded review and reconsideration of their sentences, which had been imposed following application of the 'procedural default' rule. Such review and reconsideration was however a matter for the courts of the individual states concerned, not for the federal courts or authorities, and the question of execution, postponement or reprieve was a matter for the state authorities. As a result of the intransigence of the authorities of (in particular) Texas, the federal authorities found themselves unable (otherwise than by new legislation, which would take time) to prevent an execution which would be a breach of the international obligations of the United States.

Mexico sought to establish the existence of a dispute between the two governments which would justify a request for interpretation (which, in turn, would serve as a basis for a request for fresh provisional measures). It argued that the Judgment had imposed an obligation of result, and that the United States was disputing this, contending that the obligation was one of means; since the US government stated clearly that it agreed with Mexico that the obligation was one of result, Mexico was obliged to argue that the actions of the authorities at state level were contradicting this position. The President of the United States had issued a memorandum directing state courts to give effect to the ICJ Judgment in the *Avena* case; but in an appeal involving one of the Mexican nationals, the US Supreme Court had ruled that this was unconstitutional and thus ineffective.[455]

450 Ibid, para 146. 451 Ibid, para 131. 452 Ibid, para 146. 453 Ibid.
454 See above Chapter I, Section 1; also section 4 of the present Chapter, below.
455 *Request for Interpretation of the Judgment of 31 March 2004*, Order of 16 July 2008, paras 3–4.

For present purposes, the significance of the case is simply that it was accepted on all sides that even if the United States had done everything in its power to ensure compliance with the *Avena* Judgment, so that failure to comply was due to obstacles presented by the internal law of the United States, there would still be a breach of an international obligation of result, on the basis of the recognized 'fundamental principle of international law that international law prevails over domestic law'.[456]

3A. Relationship between State Responsibility and International Criminal Law

Nothing in international law could be more definitively and authoritatively stated than the declaration in Article I of the Genocide Convention that 'genocide is a crime under international law.' This formulation conveyed that criminal responsibility of individuals for genocidal acts would not be dependent on the prohibition of genocide under the criminal *lex loci*, but would be created by the Convention itself. The implications of the Convention for State responsibility were however only specifically spelled out to the extent that the parties to the Convention undertook the obligation to prevent and punish genocide, and incitement or conspiracy to commit genocide, and complicity, were also declared criminal. Until the decision in the case concerning *Application of the Genocide Convention* between Bosnia and Serbia, the question whether and in what way genocide could be sanctioned through the mechanism of State responsibility, and in what way the 'criminal' character of the offence might be legally material in that context, had not arisen for judicial settlement.

It is, and was in 2007, difficult to look at the problem with a mind freed of the implications of the term 'crime' as handled in the work of the International Law Commission, leading to the celebrated (or infamous) draft Article 19, particularly since the international crimes as defined by that Article mentioned genocide as part of the definition: 'a serious breach on a widespread scale of an international obligation of essential importance for safeguarding the human being, such as those prohibiting slavery, genocide and *apartheid*.'[457] By 2007, Article 19 had however come and gone;[458] and all that remained of it was the references to obligations *erga omnes*[459] and to *jus cogens*,[460] matters which had also been mentioned by the Court in its

[456] *Applicability of the Obligation to Arbitrate under Section 21 of the UN Headquarters Agreement*, [1988] ICJ Rep 34, para 57. The fundamental nature of this principle is related to the fact that perhaps the majority of international legal obligations, or at least of those of customary law, are obligations of result.

[457] Article 19, para 3 *(c)*.

[458] For a threnody on its passing, see Georges Abi-Saab, 'What happened to Article 19?' in Fischer-Lescano et al (eds), above n 399, 821.

[459] ILC Articles, Article 48 (1).

[460] Ibid, Article 40 (1); Vienna Convention on the Law of Treaties, Article 53.

decisions;[461] and in an earlier stage of the *Genocide Convention* case, the Court had itself linked obligations *erga omnes* with the concept of international crimes.[462] It would nevertheless have been possible in the *Genocide Convention* case to put aside the complexities of Article 19 and to start from the basic idea of a crime:[463] a breach of legal provisions sanctioned, in view of its importance to society, by action taken on behalf of the community as a whole, distinct from, though possibly additional to, the remedies available to the direct victim of the act.[464] In this respect, the Genocide Convention was ahead of its time, there being no mechanism for judging and penalizing on behalf of the community of States; hence Article VI contemplated the creation of an 'international penal tribunal'. By the time the ICJ came to judge the *Genocide Convention* case, the ICTY and the ICC had been created to fill that need; but legal thinking remained influenced by an Article 19-oriented philosophy, which may be crudely summed up as to the effect that an international crime involves a sort of outlawry, that its presence suspends or modifies other limitative rules.

In the *Genocide Convention* case, one of the reasons why the Court held that 'the effect of Article I is to prohibit States from themselves committing genocide' (despite the fact that it did not specifically say so), and that accordingly the responsibility of a State could be engaged on that basis, was that 'such a prohibition follows... from the fact that the Article categorizes genocide as "a crime under international law".'[465] In connection with the other acts enumerated in Article III of the Convention (conspiracy, incitement, attempt, complicity), the Court observed that 'the international responsibility of a State' is 'quite different in nature from criminal responsibility', but could nevertheless be engaged through these acts, i.e., by acts classified as international crimes.[466] What then is the significance of this difference? Does the categorization of these acts as criminal have any impact on the general regime of State responsibility when invoked in respect of such an act? The Court did not make any specific statement on the point.

The relation between the two fields of responsibility in fact remained a delicate point for a number of issues in the case, including even at the

[461] On obligations *erga omnes*, see *Barcelona Traction*, [1970] ICJ Rep 32, para 33.

[462] *Application of the Genocide Convention (Preliminary Objections)* [1996–II] ICJ Rep 616, para 31. This decision was commented on, and the extent to which the subject of international crimes has been bedevilled by the confusions introduced by Article 19 was discussed, in the writer's previous article on this subject: (2005) *BYIL* 52–62.

[463] This would be the more justified in that, according to an informed and influential observer, the word 'crime' in what was to become Article 19 was 'devoid of any penal connection': Alain Pellet, 'The New Draft Articles of the ILC on the Responsibility of States for Internationally Wrongful Acts: A Requiem for States' Crime?' (2001) 32 *Netherlands Yearbook of International Law* 55, 58.

[464] It is the lack of mechanism for indicting and judging a State that held international law back from arriving at a workable concept of State crime, rather than the notion that a corporate body like a State cannot commit a crime - a notion long exploded in municipal law in relation to corporations: cf François Rigaux, 'Le crime d'État' in *International Law at the Time of its Codification (Mélanges Ago)* (Giuffrè, Milan 1987, Vol IV) 321.

[465] [2007–II] ICJ Rep 113, para 166.

[466] Ibid, 114, para 167.

level of proof and the Court's powers to call for evidence.[467] A more serious issue appears to lie behind the following paragraph of the decision:

> The Respondent has raised the question whether it is necessary, as a matter of law, for the Court to be able to uphold a claim of the responsibility of a State for an act of genocide, or any other act enumerated in Article III, that there should have been a finding of genocide by a court or tribunal exercising criminal jurisdiction. According to the Respondent, the condition *sine qua non* for establishing State responsibility is the prior establishment, according to the rules of criminal law, of the individual responsibility of a perpetrator engaging the State's responsibility.[468]

The Court does not indicate the reasoning advanced by the Respondent to support this contention, and it seems that such reasoning probably did not go as far as is here suggested.[469] The Court's ruling on the question, as it had itself posed it, was as follows:

> [The Respondent's] interpretation could entail that there would be no legal recourse available under the Convention in some readily conceivable circumstances: genocide has allegedly been committed within a State by its leaders but they have not been brought to trial because, for instance, they are still very much in control of the powers of the State including the police, prosecution services and the courts and there is no international penal tribunal able to exercise jurisdiction over the alleged crimes; or the responsible State may have acknowledged the breach. The Court accordingly concludes that State responsibility can arise under the Convention for genocide and complicity, without an individual being convicted of the crime or an associated one.[470]

The argument of the Respondent is certainly not a very convincing one, but the response it evoked from the Court is not entirely satisfying either.[471] The matter is one of interpretation of a treaty; and it is, generally speaking, not sufficient to show that a particular interpretation of a

[467] See the problem of the redacted Serbian documents, dealt with in paras 204–206 of the Judgment, and the criticism of (e.g.) Goldstone and Hamilton, above n 398, 107–108.

[468] [2007–II] ICJ Rep 119, para 180.

[469] In a passage that may have been contemplated by the Court when making this finding, counsel for the FRY argued that 'il semble nécessaire d'établir préalablement comme la condition *sine qua non* de la responsabilité de l'Etat, la responsabilité de l'auteur individuel pouvant engager la responsabilité de l'Etat. La responsabilité de l'Etat sera gouvernée par les règles de la responsabilité générale applicables à la responsabilité internationale de l'Etat, mais tout d'abord et préalablement le crime de génocide doit être établi conformément aux règles du droit pénal et l'auteur individuel du crime doit être identifié (CR 2006/43, 47 (Fauveau-Ivanović)).' However counsel did not specifically mention the need for a judgment of a criminal court, whether a municipal court or another tribunal such as the ICTY, and continued by arguing simply that the genocidal *intent* of the individual had to be established; the expression 'conformément aux règles du droit pénal' may thus simply refer to the constituent elements of the crime, and not to any need for such a prior judgment.

[470] [2007–II] ICJ Rep 119–120, para 182.

[471] Though it receives the endorsement of a former ICTY Prosecutor: see Goldstone and Hamilton, above n 398, 103.

treaty would lead to undesirable consequences; the question is what did the parties intend: what is the object and purpose of the treaty?[472] The Court also, while dealing with the point as a matter of 'recourse under the Convention', implies that if there is no recourse under the Convention, then there is no recourse in international law *at all*.[473] Further, inasmuch as the Court rests its argument on hypothetical practical considerations, it may be pointed out that there are practical problems involved in the Court arriving at a satisfactory conclusion on criminal guilt without the assistance of a criminal tribunal, as is shown by the extent to which, in the Bosnia/Serbia case, it did in fact rely on the findings of the ICTY.[474]

The passage may however perhaps be seen not so much as a reply to the arguments of the Respondent, as a response to those advanced in the declaration of Judge Skotnikov, in particular the following:

> The Court simply cannot establish individual responsibility for the crime of genocide by persons capable of engaging a State's responsibility since it lacks criminal jurisdiction.
>
> In particular, by reason of the lack of criminal jurisdiction, the Court cannot establish the existence or absence of genocidal intent, since nothing in the Genocide Convention indicates that it deals with genocidal intent in any other sense than it being a requisite part, a mental element, of the crime of genocide.
>
> What the Court can and must do is to make a finding as to whether it has been sufficiently determined that genocide was committed.
>
> To make this determination, it would have been sufficient for the Court in this case to rely on the findings of the International Criminal Tribunal for the former Yugoslavia (the ICTY), to the extent they are in conformity with the Genocide Convention, which is the sole basis for jurisdiction in these proceedings.[475]

The position of Judge Skotnikov also requires a deeper analysis than the passage quoted from the majority judgment. His opinion links this

[472] As was observed by Judge Shahabuddeen in the *Qatar/Bahrain* case, 'the fact that a treaty has a discernible object does not mean that it has to be interpreted so as to accomplish that object at all costs. A treaty must of course be interpreted "in the light of its object and purpose"; but it is not for the Court to make it more effective for achieving its apparent purpose than the parties themselves saw fit to do': [1995] ICJ Rep 59.

[473] There is of course no jurisdiction under the Convention in respect of a breach of the customary law prohibition of genocide, so that *in fact* the situation sketched by the Court might remain unremedied. The Court has however never accepted that it has jurisdiction over a particular matter merely because it is desirable that it should have such jurisdiction; if the decision in the *Genocide Convention* case shows a lack of firmness on this point, it may be evidence of the influence of the 'outlaw' approach to an international 'crime', mentioned above.

[474] It also relied on 'negative evidence', in the shape of decisions of the Prosecutor *not* to lay a charge of genocide ([2007–II] ICJ Rep 197–198, para 374), an approach criticized by former Prosecutor Goldstone: see the article of Goldstone and Hamilton, above n 398, 106–107.

[475] Declaration of Judge Skotnikov [2007–II] ICJ Rep 373.

question of criminal jurisdiction with the problem whether the Genocide Convention imposed an obligation (not specifically stated in the Convention) of States parties not themselves to commit genocide. The majority relied on (*inter alia*) Article IX of the Convention, which included among the disputes that might be referred to the Court 'those relating to the responsibility of a State for genocide or any of the other acts enumerated in Article III'. For Judge Skotnikov, 'nothing in Article IX suggests that the Court is empowered . . . to actually conduct an enquiry and make a determination whether or not the crime of genocide was committed.'[476]

He was apparently supported by Judge Tomka, who also dissented from the Court's finding that the Genocide Convention imposed an obligation on States parties not to commit genocide themselves, and explained:

> My understanding of the intention of the States when they elaborated and adopted the Genocide Convention is different. In my view, they intended to achieve the above-mentioned noble aim as set forth in the Preamble by imposing an absolute duty on States parties to hold criminally liable individuals who commit such an odious act and to punish them "whether they are constitutionally responsible rulers, public officials or private individuals" (Article IV of the Convention). A State as an abstract entity cannot act without a concrete person undertaking an act. Subjecting individuals, including those who exercise governmental authority, to international criminal responsibility is arguably an effective way of achieving the goal of the Convention because a State can only act through the conduct of individuals. This exposure to criminal prosecution makes it less likely that such individuals would disregard the obligations of the Genocide Convention, particularly since they may not assert an "act of State" defence to such violations . . .[477]

For this and the other reasons set out in his opinion, his conclusion is 'that genocide in Article I of the Convention is conceived as a crime of individuals, and not of a State. The States parties have the obligation to prevent the commission of such crime and, if it was committed, to punish the perpetrators.'[478]

Our present concern is with the secondary obligations of the law of State responsibility rather than with the detailed requirements for, or even the existence of, specific primary obligations imposed by international law (using these terms in the sense in which they are employed by the International Law Commission). However, the Court's finding that there was a primary obligation on States parties to the Genocide Convention not themselves to commit genocide is linked with a particular approach to the question of the relationship between the law of State responsibility and criminal law.

[476] Ibid. [477] [2007–II] ICJ Rep 334, para 42. [478] Ibid, 335, para 45.

The starting point for any discussion would seem to be that genocide, a crime requiring the coupling of specific acts with an equally specific intent, is in the first instance at least committed by men, not by institutions. Thus if the Court is asked to find that a State has incurred responsibility for a breach of the Genocide Convention, by having committed, permitted, or failed to punish genocide, then somewhere at some time someone must have had a genocidal intent and put it into effect. To establish judicially that an act capable of constituting genocide has been performed may be difficult in practice, but presents no particular problems of theory. When Judge Skotnikov states that the Court 'cannot establish individual responsibility for the crime of genocide by persons capable of engaging a State's responsibility since it lacks criminal jurisdiction', it does not seem to be this element that he has in mind; the Court possesses jurisdiction to enquire into 'the establishment of any fact which, if established, would constitute a breach of an international obligation'.[479] As Judge Skotnikov explains, 'by reason of the lack of criminal jurisdiction, the Court cannot establish the existence or absence of genocidal intent.' Again, however, there seems in principle to be no reason why the Court should not base its findings in a case on a particular interpretation of the intentions of a State—and thus of the individual empowered to make decisions.[480] The essence of the problem then is the nature of a *criminal* finding, a finding that an individual had a criminal intent. Here perhaps is the distinction: where it is appropriate to establish the intention of a State, it is what went on in the mind of one or more individuals that is the key, and that intention can without distortion be attributed to the State. The question then is, can a State have a criminal mind? Or to put the matter in terms of interpretation of the Genocide Convention, was it in the minds of the drafters of the Convention that a State might have a criminal mind? The absence of a provision for commission of the crime by a State suggests otherwise.[481]

Thus Judge Skotnikov's doubts, which appear to be merely on a procedural point, prove to go to the main issue in his declaration: the correctness or otherwise of the majority's analysis of the Convention. For Judges Skotnikov and Tomka, the system of the Convention is coherent: to establish whether genocide has been committed, the *mens rea* must be established in individuals, according to criminal processes. If it is thus established that the crime has been committed a State may be found, by the international 'civil' court, as it were, to have failed to prevent it, failed

[479] Statute, Article 36, para 2 *(c)*.

[480] For example, in the *Qatar/Bahrain* case, the Court rejected the explanation given by the Minister for Foreign Affairs of Bahrain of his state of mind when affixing his signature to a joint minute: [1994] ICJ Rep 121–122, paras 26–27.

[481] A striking historical circumstance is that the Convention, with its marked absence of express provision for the possibility of commission of genocide by the State itself, was adopted only three years after the fall of the one regime in recent history that could most convincingly be accused of having *itself* committed genocide.

to punish it, been complicit,[482] or attempted it; but not to have itself committed it.

On the central point of the interpretation of the Genocide Convention, it must apparently be accepted that *Roma locuta, causa finita*: the majority has spoken, and its finding is much more in tune with the current *Zeitgeist* than the minority judges' view, whatever the merits of that view as a legal and historical approach. The dissension is however of interest as indicating the difficulties in reconciling the traditional concepts of State responsibility with the innovation effected by the Convention.

4. Obligations of Means and Obligations of Result

Article 12 of the Articles on State Responsibility prepared by the International Law Commission states that '[t]here is a breach of an international obligation by a State when an act of that State is not in conformity with what is required of it by that obligation, regardless of its origin or character.' The last phrase amounted to a reversal of the approach adopted earlier in the work of the Commission, in particular in the Reports prepared by Professor Roberto Ago, of including in the Articles a distinction between obligations of conduct, obligations of result and obligations of prevention.[483] The provisions in question were deleted by the Commission on second reading, essentially because, for purposes of the Articles, no consequences followed from the distinction, which was regarded as over-complex for most purposes.[484] There was however no intention to deny that such distinctions could be made, and might be useful for some purposes; and the International Court has subsequently referred to or made use of them in a number of decisions.

In the case of the *Gabčíkovo/Nagymaros Project*, the Court had determined that the 1977 Treaty providing for the carrying-out of the Project, despite having been breached by both parties, remained in force and continued to govern the relationship between the parties.[485] It was on that basis that, as the Court found, it had to determine 'what the *future*

[482] It might be suggested that idea of criminal *mens rea*, driven out of the door by the exclusion of State responsibility *for* genocide, creeps back in through the window insofar as the Convention recognizes that a State may be guilty of complicity in genocide. Does complicity, in the case of genocide, postulate that the accomplice State must have shared the genocidal intent? The ILC Articles on State Responsibility require, for a State which aids or assists another State in the commission of an internationally wrongful act to be equally responsible, that it should have acted 'with knowledge of the circumstances of the internationally wrongful act' (Art. 16 (a)). James Crawford explains that this means 'the circumstances making the conduct of the assisted State internationally wrongful' (above n 387, 149, *sub* Article 16, para (4)). If this is a correct statement of the law also as regards complicity in genocide, then knowledge of this kind would be sufficient, and there would be no need to require State *mens rea*.

[483] See Articles 20, 21 and 23 of the draft in *ILC Yearbook 1997–II(2)*, 11–18, 18–30 and 81–86.

[484] See the explanation in Crawford, above n 387, [383], 20–23.

[485] [1997] ICJ Rep 76, para 132.

conduct of the Parties should be'.[486] The Court indicated what, in its opinion, the objectives of the 1977 Treaty had been, and noted that '[n]one of these objectives has been given absolute priority over the other[s]' and '[n]one of them has lost its importance.' It continued: 'In order to achieve these objectives the parties accepted [in the 1977 Treaty] obligations of conduct, obligations of performance and obligations of result.'[487] However, the Court does not indicate which treaty obligations were to be regarded as falling within each category (except that 'part of the obligations of performance... related to the construction of the System of Locks'[488]), nor does it draw any conclusions from the categorisation. Later decisions suggest that each of the first two is to be regarded as an obligation of means, the distinction between them being that the one is directed to behaving in a particular way in relation to a given situation,[489] and the other to taking certain steps in relation to such a situation, without however being held to achieve a particular result by doing so; but the distinction is necessarily a narrow one.

More attention was paid to the distinction in the judgment of the Court on the merits in the case concerning *Application of the Genocide Convention* between Bosnia and Serbia. The Court first examined the question whether Serbia was responsible for the genocide committed at Srebrenica on the basis that the acts concerned were committed by its organs or other persons engaging its responsibility, and the question whether, alternatively, Serbia was guilty of complicity in genocide. In this context it did not discuss the nature of the obligation in relation to the categories mentioned in the earlier Reports of the ILC, and in the judgment in *Gabčíkovo/Nagymaros*. At a later stage in the decision, however, the Court noted that

> while complicity results from commission, violation of the obligation to prevent results from omission; this is merely the reflection of the notion that the ban on genocide and the other acts listed in Article III, including complicity, places States under a negative obligation, the obligation not to commit the prohibited acts, while the duty to prevent places States under positive obligations, to do their best to ensure that such acts do not occur.[490]

Having concluded in the negative on these issues,[491] the Court turned to the question of possible responsibility for breach of the obligation under

[486] Ibid, 75–76, para 131 (emphasis original).

[487] Ibid, 77, para 135.

[488] Ibid, 77, para 136.

[489] In the decision in the case of *Certain Questions of Mutual Assistance in Criminal Matters*, the Court referred to obligations under a particular treaty as being 'obligations of law, articulated as obligations of conduct, or, in this case, of co-operation, of a broad and general nature'. Judgment of 4 June 2008, para 104.

[490] [2007–II] ICJ Rep 223, para 432.

[491] Ibid, paras 413–415 and 424.

the Convention to prevent and punish genocide, and offered a number of 'introductory remarks and clarifications',[492] including the following:

[I]t is clear that the obligation in question is one of conduct and not one of result, in the sense that a State cannot be under an obligation to succeed, whatever the circumstances, in preventing the commission of genocide: the obligation of States parties is rather to employ all means reasonably available to them, so as to prevent genocide so far as possible. A State does not incur responsibility simply because the desired result is not achieved; responsibility is however incurred if the State manifestly failed to take all measures to prevent genocide which were within its power, and which might have contributed to preventing the genocide. In this area the notion of "due diligence", which calls for an assessment *in concreto*, is of critical importance.[493]

The reference to the concept of due diligence suggests that the Court had in mind the possibility that the degree of diligence to be expected and required of the State might not be absolute, in the sense that such degree would not be the same for all, but tailored to the individual circumstances of the State concerned. The Judgment in fact continues:

Various parameters operate when assessing whether a State has duly discharged the obligation concerned. The first, which varies greatly from one State to another, is clearly the capacity to influence effectively the action of persons likely to commit, or already committing, genocide. This capacity itself depends, among other things, on the geographical distance of the State concerned from the scene of the events, and on the strength of the political links, as well as links of all other kinds, between the authorities of that State and the main actors in the events. The State's capacity to influence must also be assessed by legal criteria, since it is clear that every State may only act within the limits permitted by international law; seen thus, a State's capacity to influence may vary depending on its particular legal position vis-à-vis the situations and persons facing the danger, or the reality, of genocide.[494]

This ruling is in line with the classical approach to obligations of means, formulated for example by Max Huber,[495] who assessed the obligation as *diligentia quam in suis*, i.e. the degree of diligence that a State would apply to protection of its own interests in the same circumstances.

Recognition that the means available to a State to prevent the commission of an internationally unlawful act may vary according to the circumstances involves the possibility that in a given situation the State in

[492] Ibid, para 428. [493] Ibid, 221, para 430. [494] Ibid.

[495] *Affaire des Réclamations britanniques dans le Zone espagnol du Maroc*, II *UNRIAA*, 644. The case concerned the depredations of brigands, and the extent to which the State could be held responsible for damage caused by them. Koskenniemi suggests that a similar philosophy of contextual determinants underlies variation in assessment of the legal obligations of, for example, industrialized or developing States (*From Apology to Utopia: The Structure of International Legal Argument* (Lakimiesliiton Kustannus, Helsinki, 1989) 345). Cf Principle 23 of the 1972 Stockholm Declaration of the UN Conference on the Human Environment.

question could not have prevented it by using such means as were available to it, but in fact did not even exercise those means (whether from a conviction that they would be ineffective, or otherwise).[496] The Court commented on this hypothesis, too:

On the other hand, it is irrelevant whether the State whose responsibility is in issue claims, or even proves, that even if it had employed all means reasonably at its disposal, they would not have sufficed to prevent the commission of genocide. As well as being generally difficult to prove, this is irrelevant to the breach of the obligation of conduct in question, the more so since the possibility remains that the combined efforts of several States, each complying with its obligation to prevent, might have achieved the result—averting the commission of genocide—which the efforts of only one State were insufficient to produce.[497]

The final phrase is evidently appropriate to genocide as a matter of more than bilateral international concern; but the Court is apparently here intending to make a statement of general applicability.[498] Furthermore, genocide being *malum in se*, it can hardly be argued that standing by and failing to attempt to prevent genocide is not a breach of an international obligation, whether or not the attempt would have averted the genocide. However, the Court recognizes the relevance of geographical constraints: if a State were to learn that an incursion into a remote region of its territory was in progress, with a limited—but genocidal—objective, would it be obliged to send troops, knowing that the operation would have been completed, and the participants would have withdrawn, by the time the troops arrived? More difficult still might be cases in which damage to the injured State, such as to render it an injured State, would be a necessary component of the existence of the internationally unlawful act. Could the necessary link be made between the inaction of the defendant State and the damage suffered, if it were shown that that damage could not have been prevented by any means in the power of the defendant State?

The Court did not examine the question whether the obligation to punish genocide is also an obligation of conduct. The matter is governed, as the Court found, by Article VI of the Convention, which requires that persons charged with genocide be 'tried by a competent tribunal of the State in the territory of which the act was committed', or by an international tribunal, *in casu* the ICTY. Since the genocide alleged was not committed on Serbian territory, the Court concluded that Serbia 'cannot be charged with not having tried before its own courts those accused of having participated in the Srebrenica genocide', and therefore turned to the

[496] This aspect is discussed in more detail below, Chapter V, Section 1.

[497] [2007-II] ICJ Rep 221, para 430 *in fine*.

[498] Note the introductory words 'the more so since'. In the previous paragraph, the Court has however disclaimed any intention of 'establish[ing] a general jurisprudence applicable to all cases where a treaty instrument, or other binding legal norm, includes an obligation for States to prevent certain acts': ibid, para 429.

question of co-operation with the ICTY. This would seem to leave open the question whether a State whose legislation provides for jurisdiction over genocide on a non-territorial basis (e.g., the nationality of the accused), or claiming so-called 'universal jurisdiction', may be under a wider duty of prosecution and punishment under the broad terms of Article I of the Convention; or whether in the case of punishment, but not of prevention, the scope of that Article is limited by Article VI.

The distinction between obligations of result and obligations of means was raised by Malaysia in the case concerning *Immunity from Legal Process of a Special Rapporteur of the Commission of Human Rights* (the *Cumaraswamy* case). Proceedings for slander had been brought against Mr. Cumaraswamy in the Malaysian courts for words spoken by him and quoted in an interview published in the press; the Secretary-General had determined that in making these remarks, Mr. Cumaraswamy had been acting in the course of the performance of his mission as Special Rapporteur of the Human Rights Commission, so that in that respect he was immune from legal process of every kind under Article VI, Section 22 *(b)*, of the General Convention on Immunities and Privileges of the United Nations. The Court found that the Secretary-General's determination was correct, and then turned, in accordance with the resolution of the Economic and Social Council requesting an advisory opinion, to the question of 'the legal obligations of Malaysia in this case'.[499] Malaysia argued however that it was premature to deal with this question. At the time of the Court's Opinion, the proceedings instituted against Mr. Cumaraswamy in the Malaysian courts were still in progress; those courts, despite being informed of the question of immunities, had not passed on that question *in limine litis,* but held that they had jurisdiction to hear the cases on the merits, 'including making a determination of whether Mr. Cumaraswamy was entitled to any immunity'.[500] In the meantime, substantial orders for costs had been made against Mr. Cumaraswamy.[501]

The grounds of Malaysia's contentions were that

> the obligation to ensure that the requirements of Section 22 of the Convention are met is an obligation of result and not of means to be employed in achieving that result.... Malaysia has complied with its obligation under Section 34 of the General Convention, which provides that a party to the Convention must be "in a position under its own law to give effect to [its] terms", by enacting the necessary legislation; finally it contends that the Malaysian courts have not yet reached a final decision as to Mr. Cumaraswamy's entitlement to immunity from legal process.[502]

The Court's response on this point is somewhat Delphic.

[499] [1999-I] ICJ Rep 86, paras 56–57. [500] Ibid, 72, para 17.
[501] Ibid, 68, citing para 8 of the Secretary-General's Note, E/1998/94.
[502] Ibid, 86, para 58.

The Court wishes to point out that the request for an advisory opinion refers to "the legal obligations of Malaysia in this case". The difference which has arisen between the United Nations and Malaysia originated in the Government of Malaysia not having informed the competent Malaysian judicial authorities of the Secretary-General's finding that Mr. Cumaraswamy had spoken the words at issue in the course of the performance of his mission and was, therefore, entitled to immunity from legal process.... It is as from the time of this omission that the question before the Court must be answered.[503]

Only Judge Koroma and (apparently) Judge Oda were prepared to agree with Malaysia in this respect;[504] but there is perhaps more to the point than the Court was prepared to recognize.

The Court in effect concentrates on the question put by ECOSOC, and reads it as meaning that what the Council wanted to know was whether Malaysia, by not notifying its Court of the Secretary-General's ruling, was in breach of its obligations under Article VII, Section 22, of the General Convention. It therefore assumed, without deciding, that a correct legal answer to that question was possible at the time that the Court gave its Opinion, and on the basis of the facts as they then stood. However, a convention may impose an obligation on a State to ensure a certain result, 'by means of its own choosing',[505] and in the event of a dispute over whether the convention has been complied with it may be that compliance or non-compliance can only be determined *ex post facto*, and that during the currency of the dispute it cannot (yet) be said that a State is in breach of its obligations. Whether Malaysia was justified in claiming that this was the case for the application of the General Convention is more doubtful: for example, the failure to deal with the question of immunities *in limine litis* could itself be regarded as a breach of immunities, so that there would already be an obligation to remedy this. The Court might however have usefully clarified its thinking on the operation of the distinction between an obligation of result and an obligation of means, which does appear to have been significant in the case before it.

In the case of *Certain Questions of Mutual Assistance in Criminal Matters* Djibouti claimed that France had failed to comply with Article 3 of a 1986 Convention between the two States concerning judicial assistance, which provided that '[t]he requested State shall execute in accordance with its law any letters rogatory relating to a criminal matter and addressed to it by the judicial authorities of the requesting State' France based its refusal on an exception of a kind recognized by Article 2 of the Convention, for matters of national security, according to its own law. An issue in dispute was the significance of the words 'in accordance with its

[503] Ibid, 86–87, para 59.

[504] Dissenting Opinion of Judge Koroma, [1999-I] ICJ Rep 121–122, para 28; Separate Opinion of Judge Oda, ibid, 107–108, paras 23–26.

[505] The formula used in *Avena*, [2004] ICJ Rep 72, para 153 (9).

law': for Djibouti, this was merely 'an indication of the procedure to be followed in performing the obligation', that obligation remaining 'an obligation of result'.[506] The Court observed that

> the obligation to execute international letters rogatory laid down in Article 3 of the 1986 Convention is to be realized in accordance with the procedural law of the requested State. Thus, the ultimate treatment of a request for mutual assistance in criminal matters clearly depends on the decision by the competent national authorities, following the procedure established in the law of the requested State. While it must of course ensure that the procedure is put in motion, the State does not thereby guarantee the outcome, in the sense of the transmission of the file requested in the letter rogatory.[507]

The Court took into account other provisions of the Convention, particularly the fact that Article 2 described situations in which assistance might be refused, and concluded that

> those who are empowered to address these matters will do so by applying the provisions of Article 2 or of other Articles in the Convention that may lead to the rejection of the requesting State's demarche[508]

i.e., that the obligation was no more than an obligation of means.

The appeal made to the concept of obligations of result made by Mexico in the case of the *Request for Interpretation of the Judgment of 31 March 2004*, in the *Avena* case, has already been mentioned above.[509] The issue there was however perhaps less whether or not the Court's 2004 Judgment in the *Avena* case had imposed an obligation of result on the United States, than whether or not the two parties each considered that that Judgment had imposed such an obligation, since Mexico needed to establish the existence of a 'dispute as to the meaning or scope' of the Judgment, in order to found its request for interpretation.[510] Since the official attitude of the United States Government was to recognize that the *Avena* Judgment had imposed (or declared) an obligation of result, Mexico had to argue that the actions of the State and federal authorities, in relation to the protected Mexican nationals, not only constituted breaches of an obligation of result, but also showed that the obligation was not in practice being recognized as an obligation of that nature. The Court noted:

> According to Mexico, the United States, by word and deed, has contradicted its avowed acceptance of review and reconsideration as an obligation of result. Reference is made to the choice of the United States Government not to appear at the Supreme Court hearings on Mr. Medellín's petition for a stay of execution. Mexico also points to the very tardy attempts to engage Congress in ensuring that all constituent elements do indeed act upon this obligation.

[506] Judgment of 4 June 2008, paras 120–121. [507] Ibid, para 123.

[508] Ibid. [509] Above, Chapter 1, section 1.

[510] The true object of which was, as mentioned above, to provide a vehicle for a fresh request for provisional measures to prevent the execution of Mexican nationals.

...Further, Mexico contends that the [US] Supreme Court found that the obligation within paragraph 153 (9) [of the *Avena* Judgment] could not be directly enforced by the judiciary on the basis of a Presidential memorandum nor otherwise without intervention of the legislature. In Mexico's view, this necessarily means that the obligation is not really regarded as one of result—a viewpoint not shared by the United States.[511]

Since the Court did not even decide whether or not there was a dispute between the parties on the question of the nature of the obligation, it did not need to rule on that question, and indicate what in its view would be the distinguishing marks of an obligation of result. It is however worth noting the significance of the irreversibility of the carrying out of a death sentence. As was argued by Ago in his Sixth Report on State Responsibility:

[W]here international law defines the obligation it lays on the State by a simple indication of the result to be achieved, the discretion it gives the State as to the means of achieving this result usually goes beyond mere initial freedom of choice. So long as the required result has not become finally unattainable by reason only of the fact that the initial conduct of the State failed to achieve it, international law does not usually preclude a State, one of whose organs has created a situation incompatible with the result required by an international obligation, from still achieving this result through a new course of conduct by State organs, which eliminates the existing situation and replaces it by another that will *ab initio* be in conformity with the required result.[512]

Clearly if any of the Mexican nationals were executed without being afforded the measures of review and reconsideration of their sentences called for by the Court's Judgment, the required result would indeed have become 'finally unattainable'. But the significance of this is simply that there would, at that moment, have been a breach of the obligation of result, and the respondent State could no longer point to the existence of other legal and administrative methods of reaching the required result; it does not mean that the obligation is to be classified as one simply of means, or of conduct, still less that, without more, it indicates a view by that State that the obligation is one of conduct.

5. The Impact of the State Act: The Relevance of Damage

In this section of the previous article, note was taken of the development in the work of the International Law Commission on State Responsibility towards a definition of the internationally wrongful act as complete

[511] Judgment of 19 January 2009, paras 33–34.
[512] Sixth Report by Professor Ago on State Responsibility, A/CN.4/302, para 41.

without any requirement that damage or prejudice be caused by that act.[513] This is also the final position adopted by the Commission; as explained by Crawford in his authoritative study of the Commission's Articles:

> It is sometimes said that international responsibility is not engaged by conduct of a State in disregard of its obligations unless some further element exists, in particular, "damage" to another State. But whether such elements are required depends on the content of the primary obligation, and there is no general rule in this respect.[514]

One example of a primary international obligation in respect of which damage is, it seems, required for responsibility to attach is the obligation, found by the Court to exist under the Genocide Convention alongside its existence in customary law, not to commit genocide. Since genocide by definition involves killing, damage to individuals at least is of the essence of the internationally wrongful act. The Court in fact stated in its judgment in the case of *Application of the Genocide Convention* between Bosnia and Serbia that 'if a State is to be responsible because it has breached its obligation not to commit genocide, it must be shown that genocide as defined in the Convention has been committed. That will also be the case with conspiracy under Article III, paragraph *(b)*, and complicity under Article III, paragraph *(e)*.'[515]

As the Court also noted, the same applies when what is alleged is a breach of the obligation to prevent the commission of genocide.[516] In its judgment in the same case, the Court stated specifically that 'a State can be held responsible for breaching the obligation to prevent genocide only if genocide was actually committed.' It indicated that 'a State's obligation to prevent, and the corresponding duty to act, arise at the instant that the State learns of, or should normally have learned of, the existence of a serious risk that genocide will be committed', but that

> if neither genocide nor any of the other acts listed in Article III of the Convention are ultimately carried out, then a State that omitted to act when it could have

[513] (1995) *BYIL* 65–70.

[514] Crawford, above n 387, 84, para (9); see also ibid, 12. This solution escapes from the controversy raised by, in particular, the work of Ago as ILC Rapporteur, concisely summarized by Prosper Weil, 'Le droit international en quête de son identité' (1992-VI) 237 *Recueil des Cours* 339–347. As the present writer has pointed out elsewhere, the reasoning of the ILC was directed to primary obligations arising from treaty commitments; in the case of obligations of customary law, it remains at least arguable that damage is a condition for responsibility to be occurred: see H W A Thirlway, 'Concepts, Principles, Rules and Analogies: International and Municipal Legal Reasoning' (2002) 294 *Recueil des Cours* 325–326.

[515] [2007-II] ICJ Rep 119, para 180. The observation was made as introduction to the Court's consideration of the question whether it was necessary, for the Court to be able to find that a State had committed genocide, that some individual had been found guilty of genocide by a competent court (the Court ruled that this was not required).

[516] Ibid; this is under Article 1 of the Convention, but here too the obligation no doubt exists as a matter of customary law also.

done so cannot be held responsible *a posteriori*, since the event did not happen which, under the rule set out above, must occur for there to be a violation of the obligation to prevent.[517]

It is noticeable that the Court consistently puts the matter in terms of holding the State 'responsible', rather than in terms of the question whether an internationally wrongful act has been committed. If a State deliberately failed to take action to prevent an imminent act of genocide, which was however unexpectedly averted by, shall we say, the intervention of another State, it would be difficult not to feel that the inaction was at least morally reprehensible. Ultimately however it is, as the ILC recognized, a matter of interpretation of the primary obligation: under the Convention at least, States parties undertake 'to prevent' genocide and not, for example, to take all action within their power to prevent the commission of genocide.

Despite the Court's statement quoted above, the situation is less clear regarding the obligation not to be involved in conspiracy to commit genocide, and to avoid complicity in genocide, under Article III, paragraphs *(b)* and *(e)* of the Convention. It is arguable that conspiracy was intended to be an international crime in itself, even if the conspiracy was frustrated before fruition;[518] but the point did not arise in the case, and may be left aside. Complicity was indeed dealt with in the judgment in the Bosnia/Serbia case, but the question here under examination was not discussed; the Court found on the facts that, while the genocide at Srebrenica was 'committed, at least in part, with the resources which the perpetrators' had obtained from the authorities of the FRY (Serbia), it was not established that at the relevant time those authorities 'were clearly aware that genocide was about to take place or was under way.'[519] What would have been the position if the resources had been made available with every intention that they be used for acts of genocide, but no genocide subsequently occurred?

As the Court noted, the concept of 'complicity' is one of those employed in the Convention that 'refer to well known categories of criminal law',[520] and 'is not a notion which exists in the current terminology of the law of international responsibility'; but it assimilated the concept to that of 'aid

[517] Ibid, para 431 (and see also para 180). For the apparent distinction between the general obligation assumed by virtue of becoming party to the Convention, and the specific obligation which the Court saw as arising as soon as a State party was 'on notice' of an imminent risk of genocide, see the next following section, below.

[518] Cf Rome Statute of the International Criminal Court, art. 25 (3) *(f)*. There is an underlying difference in approach between the continental and the common law systems on the question whether or not the offence of conspiracy requires that a crime be actually committed by the principal offender: see William A Schabas, *An Introduction to the International Criminal Court* (Cambridge University Press, Cambridge, 2001) 82–83.

[519] [2007-II] ICJ Rep 218, para 422. The Court left aside the question whether complicity requires that the accomplice share the genocidal intent of the perpetrator, but considered that at least he must be aware of that intent: ibid, para 421.

[520] Ibid, 114, para 167.

or assistance' furnished for the commission of a wrongful act, dealt with in Article 16 of the ILC Articles on State Responsibility.[521] In this connection, it has been authoritatively stated that, for the responsibility of the State furnishing assistance to be engaged, 'the aid or assistance must be given with a view to facilitating the commission of the wrongful act, and must actually do so', and no responsibility is incurred on this head unless 'the internationally wrongful conduct [contemplated] is actually committed by the aided of assisted State.'[522] It is consistent with this that the Court in the *Application of the Genocide Convention* case, when examining the question of complicity, limited its attention to the events at Srebrenica, where (as it found) genocide was demonstrably committed, and did not find it necessary to consider whether aid and assistance might have been furnished, with genocidal intent, on other occasions; however, too much weight should of course not be attached to this observation.

A theoretical case frequently mentioned in this context is that of an international obligation which may be breached by the adoption, or retention, of legislation contravening the obligation, even before any implementation of the legislation causes injury to another State. A slightly more complex situation arose in the *LaGrand* case, where what was at stake was compliance by the United States with the requirements of Article 36 of the Vienna Convention on Consular Relations, concerning notification to the relevant consulate, and to the defendant, when a foreign national is arrested.[523] Appropriate legislative provision existed in the United States; but in the case referred to the International Court (and, it was said, in numerous other cases), the notifications were not in fact given when they should have been; and the situation of the defendant was rendered incapable of remedy by the existence of a rule of United States criminal procedure called the 'procedural default' rule, which severely limited the possibilities of raising the breach of the Convention as a ground of appeal. The Court took care to make clear that

> a distinction must be drawn between [the] rule as such and its specific application in the present case. In itself, the rule does not violate Article 36 of the Vienna Convention. The problem arises when the procedural default rule does not allow the detained individual to challenge a conviction and sentence by claiming, in reliance on Article 36, paragraph 1, of the Convention, that the competent national authorities failed to comply with their obligation to provide the requisite

[521] Ibid, paras 419–420.

[522] Crawford, above n 387, 149, *sub* Article 16, para (5).

[523] Paragraph (1)*(b)* of Article 36, reads as follows: 'if he so requests, the competent authorities of the receiving State shall, without delay. inform the consular post of the sending State if, within its consular district, a national of that State is arrested or committed to prison or to custody pending trial or is detained in any other manner. Any communication addressed to the consular post by the person arrested, in prison, custody or detention shall be forwarded by the said authorities without delay. The said authorities shall inform the person concerned without delay of his rights under this subparagraph.' The text of the whole Article is set out in n 648 below.

consular information "without delay", thus preventing the person from seeking and obtaining consular assistance from the sending State.[524]

The same point is referred to later in the Judgment, when the Court is examining the request by Germany for assurances of non-repetition:

The Court observes in this regard that it can determine the existence of a violation of an international obligation. If necessary, it can also hold that a domestic law has been the cause of this violation. In the present case the Court has made its findings of violations of the obligations under Article 36 of the Vienna Convention when it dealt with the first and the second submission of Germany. But it has not found that a United States law, whether substantive or procedural in character, is inherently inconsistent with the obligations undertaken by the United States in the Vienna Convention. In the present case the violation of Article 36, paragraph 2, was caused by the circumstances in which the procedural default rule was applied, and not by the rule as such.[525]

A finding of the kind contemplated, that 'a domestic law has been the cause of this violation' may of course simply mean that the violation was constituted by the *implementation* of the legislation; but if the Court were to find that a particular law was, as the Court puts it, 'inherently inconsistent' with the international obligations of the State, this would presumably signify that there was a breach of obligation even before implementation of the law had led to damage to another State.

Something of a half-way house within the hypothetical antithesis between the adoption of legislation inconsistent with an international obligation, and its implementation to the detriment of a foreign State, may be seen in the circumstances of the case concerning the *Arrest Warrant of 11 April 2000*. A Belgian judge had issued a warrant for the arrest of a Congolese national, at the time Foreign Minister of the Democratic Republic of the Congo, who was not present in Belgium. The DRC brought proceedings claiming that this was an infringement of the immunities in international law of incumbent foreign ministers. Belgium contended that the warrant, 'in its effects, was national in character', and that outside Belgium 'the warrant does not create any obligation for the authorities of any other State to arrest Mr. Yerodia in the absence of any further step by Belgium'.[526] Belgium argued therefore that 'the character of the arrest warrant of 11 April 2000 is such that it neither infringes the sovereignty of, nor creates any obligations for, the DRC.'[527]

The Court held as follows:

The Court notes that the *issuance*, as such, of the disputed arrest warrant represents an act by the Belgian judicial authorities intended to enable the arrest on

[524] [2001] ICJ Rep 497, para 90. [525] Ibid, 513, para 125.

[526] [2002] ICJ Rep 27, paras 65–66. *Quaere* whether a foreign State, while not required to arrest Mr Yerodia, might be enabled by its own law, in combination with the Belgian warrant, to arrest him if it chose.

[527] First conclusion on the Merits, Counter-Memorial of Belgium, para 10.3.

Belgian territory of an incumbent Minister for Foreign Affairs on charges of war crimes and crimes against humanity. The fact that the warrant is enforceable is clearly apparent from the order given to "all bailiffs and agents of public authority . . . to execute this arrest warrant" . . . and from the assertion in the warrant that "the position of Minister for Foreign Affairs currently held by the accused does not entail immunity from jurisdiction and enforcement". The Court notes that the warrant did admittedly make an exception for the case of an official visit by Mr. Yerodia to Belgium, and that Mr. Yerodia never suffered arrest in Belgium. The Court is bound, however, to find that, given the nature and purpose of the warrant, its mere issue violated the immunity which Mr. Yerodia enjoyed as the Congo's incumbent Minister for Foreign Affairs. The Court accordingly concludes that the issue of the warrant constituted a violation of an obligation of Belgium towards the Congo, in that it failed to respect the immunity of that Minister and, more particularly, infringed the immunity from criminal jurisdiction and the inviolability then enjoyed by him under international law.[528]

Here the existence of the warrant constituted a threat of the same kind as legislation which might later give rise to damage to the foreign State, but a threat which was at once both more personal and direct, and yet less assured of application, in view of the exception for official visits.

6. The Time Element[529]

The International Law Commission found it appropriate to devote three of its Articles on State Responsibility (Articles 13, 14 and 15) to the question of the 'Extension in time of the breach of an international obligation.' This is the title of Article 14; Article 13 contains the basic rule that '[a]n act of a State does not constitute a breach of an international obligation unless the State is bound by the obligation in question at the time the act occurs', and Article 15 deals with 'composite acts'.

Article 13 at first sight might have been drafted by M de la Palisse, but was clearly a necessary starting point for the further qualifications stated in the subsequent articles. An act which would be a breach of a treaty obligation, for example, is no such breach if the treaty was not in force at the relevant time. That does not of course settle the question whether an obligation originally created by treaty may in some circumstances, or even as a general rule, survive the formal termination of the

[528] [2002] ICJ Rep 29, para 70. The Court then proceeded to examine the implications of the fact that the warrant was circulated internationally, and held that this also was a violation of the obligation of Belgium to respect the immunity of the Foreign Minister of the DRC: ibid, 29–30, para 71.

[529] Similar problems to those discussed in this section frequently arise in the context of the Court's jurisdiction, when the question is, for example, whether an acceptance of jurisdiction limited to 'disputes arising' before or after a specified date does or does not apply to a particular claim. These however are better examined in the context of the Court's jurisdiction; cf the previous article in (1999) *BYIL* 30–32.

treaty: in particular, it is clear that if a breach of the treaty is committed while it is in force, the consequent claim to reparation continues to exist even if the treaty itself comes to an end.[530]

Where the wrongful act complained of is one which is not in itself instantaneous, and is also a stage in a continuing process, moving from legality to illegality, the principles as to the operation of the time element remain the same, but difficult questions may arise on the facts. In the *Gabčíkovo/Nagymaros* case, the Court referred to the work of the International Law Commission on a slightly different point: the distinction between 'the actual commission of a wrongful act (whether instantaneous or continuous) and the conduct prior to that act which is of a preparatory character and which "does not qualify as a wrongful act."'[531] The question was at what stage in the implementation by Czechoslovakia of 'Variant C', its unilateral version of the Project, adopted after Hungary had withdrawn from it, that operation constituted a breach of its obligations toward Hungary.

Article 14, paragraph 3, of the ILC Articles was quoted by the Court in its judgment in the case of *Application of the Genocide Convention* between Bosnia and Serbia, in the context of the obligation to prevent genocide imposed by Article I of the Convention. The Court began its examination of Bosnia's claims in this respect with a number of 'introductory remarks and clarifications.'[532] One of these began 'a State can be held responsible for breaching the obligation to prevent genocide only if genocide was actually committed', and '[i]t is at the time when commission of the prohibited act . . . begins that the breach of the obligation of prevention occurs.'[533] The Court then referred to the 'general rule of State responsibility', stated in Article 14, paragraph 3, and continued:

This obviously does not mean that the obligation to prevent genocide only comes into being when perpetration of genocide commences; that would be absurd, since the whole point of the obligation is to prevent, or attempt to prevent, the occurrence of the act. In fact, a State's obligation to prevent, and the corresponding duty to act, arise at the instant that the State learns of, or should normally have learned of, the existence of a serious risk that genocide will be committed. From that moment onwards, if the State has available to it means likely to have a deterrent effect on those suspected of preparing genocide, or reasonably suspected of harbouring specific intent *(dolus specialis)*, it is under a duty to make such use of these means as the circumstances permit. However, if neither genocide nor any of the other acts listed in Article III of the Convention

[530] As the Court indicated in the *Northern Cameroons* case, [1963] ICJ Rep 35; cf also the *Rainbow Warrior* arbitration, XX *UNRIAA* 265–266.

[531] [1997] ICJ Rep 54, para 79. The quotation is from the ILC Commentary to what was then Article 41 of the Draft Articles, later absorbed into Article 30: see (1993-II) ILC *Yearbook* 57, para 14.

[532] [2007-II] ICJ Rep 220, para 428.

[533] Ibid, 221–222, para 431.

are ultimately carried out, then a State that omitted to act when it could have done so cannot be held responsible *a posteriori*, since the event did not happen which, under the rule set out above, must occur for there to be a violation of the obligation to prevent.[534]

The need for this somewhat didactic passage in the Judgment is not evident, and some doubts of a theoretical nature may be felt. Despite the introductory material, and the reference to Article 14 of the ILC's Articles on State Responsibility, the point is probably not really one of time at all. The essential practical point being made is that an obligation to prevent something implies being alert to the possibility of it happening; it is not sufficient to wait until it does happen before taking action. It is not a question of when the obligation to prevent arises, but of the interpretation of what an 'obligation to prevent' means. The Court seems to be making a curious, and perhaps artificial, distinction between the general obligation assumed by Serbia as a party to the Convention, to prevent genocide, whenever and wherever, and an obligation of Serbia to prevent certain specific threatened acts of genocide, an obligation that only comes into existence when a 'serious risk that genocide will be committed' becomes apparent. All that matters to a Court called upon *ex post facto* to determine whether there has been breach of an obligation is whether the act alleged to constitute the breach occurred at a time when the obligation was in force; though it is of course true that the mere fact of genocide having been committed, coupled with Serbia's obligation under the Convention to prevent genocide, does not add up to a breach by Serbia of that obligation; it must be shown that the genocide was committed on Serbia's watch, so to speak.

The paragraph cited from the judgment in the *Genocide Convention* case leads up to the following conclusion:

In consequence, in the present case the Court will have to consider the Respondent's conduct, in the light of its duty to prevent, solely in connection with the massacres at Srebrenica, because these are the only acts in respect of which the Court has concluded in this case that genocide was committed.[535]

The obligation to prevent *specific* genocide which has been conjured into existence by the Court thus takes us no further than the general obligation under the Convention: no genocide, no responsibility.

It is of course not only compliance with an obligation of prevention that may be triggered by facts coming to the notice of the State upon

[534] Ibid, 222.

[535] Ibid. A large number of other atrocities had been cited and attributed to Serbia, or persons engaging Serbia's responsibility; but the Court's finding on the facts had been 'that—save in the case of Srebrenica—the Applicant has not established that any of the widespread and serious atrocities, complained of as constituting violations of Article II, paragraphs *(a)* to *(e)*, of the Genocide Convention, were accompanied by the necessary specific intent *(dolus specialis)* on the part of the perpetrators': ibid, para 376.

which the obligation rests. In the cases involving the responsibilities of the United States under the Vienna Convention on Consular Relations, the *LaGrand* and *Avena* cases, the obligations of notification to a consulate, and informing the criminal defendant of his rights, became applicable only if the defendant was in fact a non-US national; and would be implemented only once the United States authorities became aware that he was such. In the latter case, the Court found that

> the duty upon the detaining authorities to give the Article 36, paragraph 1 *(b)*, [of the Vienna Convention] information to the individual arises once it is realized that the person is a foreign national, or once there are grounds to think that the person is probably a foreign national. Precisely when this may occur will vary with circumstances.[536]

Here the Court refers to the specific duty, or perhaps the duty in relation to the specific foreign national, as *arising* when the authorities become aware of the nationality of the defendant, with the implication that, although the general Convention obligation was pre-existing and continuous, the obligation in relation to that specific instance was not pre-existing. This is a different analysis from that quoted above in the *Genocide* case.

CHAPTER III: CIRCUMSTANCES PRECLUDING WRONGFULNESS

1. Preliminary

In the previous article on this subject,[537] attention was drawn to cases in which a consideration closely allied to one or other of the circumstances identified by the ILC as precluding unlawfulness might operate as one of the elements going to make up the internationally wrongful act itself. Citing the *Right of Passage* and *Electronica Sicula* cases, it was suggested that to establish the existence of a wrongful act might require, for example, the absence of a consideration of necessity, because of the definition and nature of the obligation concerned, so that unless the condition of 'non-necessity' were met, the disputed act would not be wrongful at all, rather than being wrongful but excused, as it were. Another example, suggested by the *Gabčikovo/Nagymaros Project* case, would be the case of a treaty providing that if one party committed a breach of provision A, the other party would no longer be required to perform its obligations under provision B; if these clauses were implemented, there would be no need to analyse the action taken contrary to provision B as

[536] [2004] ICJ Rep 43, para 63. The Court noted the very considerable difficulties encountered by the United States authorities in ascertaining whether persons arrested were entitled to rights under the Convention, and the steps taken in this respect by some of the state jurisdictions.

[537] (1995) *BYIL* 70–73.

a counter-measure to the breach of provision A, since it would, according to the terms of the treaty, be no infringement of provision B, and thus not an unlawful act at all.[538]

It was however there recognized that there is 'a very fine dividing line' between these two analyses of such a legal situation.[539] There does not appear to be any further case during the period now under review which could be viewed in this light; and now that the ILC Articles on State Responsibility are available as the touchstone, it appears unlikely that the alternative analysis discussed in the previous article will be called on as a tool of intellectual or forensic debate.

2. Consent

In the case of *Armed Activities on the Territory of the Congo (DRC v Uganda)*, the question of consent as precluding the wrongfulness of an otherwise unlawful act arose at two stages. The DRC complained of the presence of Ugandan forces on its territory; however, it was accepted that initially those forces were present there with the consent of the Government of the Congo. The Court had however to decide, first whether and at what date that consent had been withdrawn; and thereafter, on the basis that it had been withdrawn, whether the conclusion of a Ceasefire Agreement to which the two States were parties indicated that the troops either had been, or at least were from then on, on the territory with consent.

When a continuing act which would otherwise be an infringement of the rights of another State, and thus an internationally unlawful act, has been consented to by that State, the modalities of a withdrawal of the consent may be defined specifically, or have to be deduced from the nature of the arrangement. In the *DRC v Uganda* case, the Court found on the facts that 'no particular formalities would have been required for the DRC to withdraw its consent to the presence of Ugandan troops on its soil'.[540] The Congo relied before the Court on an official statement by its President dated 28 July 1998, addressed to the people of the Congo, announcing the termination of the *Rwandan* military presence; the final sentence of the statement read 'This marks the end of the presence of all foreign military forces in the Congo.'[541] The Congo explained that Ugandan forces were not mentioned because they were very few in number, and not to be treated in the same way as the Rwandan forces, but nevertheless that the phrase quoted 'indicated that consent was withdrawn for Ugandan as well as Rwandan troops'.[542]

[538] This was of course not the situation that arose in the *Gabčikovo/Nagymaros Project* case, where breaches of the relevant Treaty were committed on both sides, and the Treaty contained no provisions of the kind here imagined.

[539] (1995) *BYIL* 72.

[540] [2005] ICJ Rep 198, para 51.

[541] Ibid, para 49.

[542] Ibid.

The Court did not expressly accept this argument; it went on to find that there was an unambiguous withdrawal of consent at the Victoria Falls Summit meeting, which terminated on 8 August 1998,[543] and then noted that the Congo's claim began with an alleged aggression on 2 August 1998. The implication seems to be that it therefore did not matter whether the consent was withdrawn on 23 July by the President's announcement, or at the Victoria Falls Summit in August.[544]

It does not seem that the President's announcement would have been sufficient. If consent is given to an otherwise unlawful act, the operation is in essence of a treaty nature, even if it appears to be unilateral. The unilateral element in fact resides in the possibility of termination; the agreement may be presumed (if it is not specifically stated) to be terminable at the will of the State consenting to the infringement of its rights.[545] Some communication addressed by the one State to the other, preferably through official channels, would seem to be appropriate, rather than the latter State being expected to draw conclusions from an ambiguous announcement made to a different addressee. The act which the Court viewed as an undoubted withdrawal of consent was an accusation made by the Congo, at the Victoria Falls Summit, of invasion of its territory by Rwanda and Uganda—an accusation made directly in a diplomatic context.

Further on in the Judgment, the Court considered activities by Uganda on Congolese territory near to the common border from 2 August 1998 onwards, and found that the nature of these activities was such that '[t]he issue of when any consent [to the presence of troops] may have terminated is irrelevant when the actions concerned are so clearly beyond co-operation 'in order to ensure peace and security along the common border'.[546]

At a later stage in the conflict, however, arrangements were made for a cease-fire and the withdrawal of foreign troops from Congolese territory.

[543] Ibid, 199, para 53.

[544] The construction of the Judgment is confusing on the point. Having left open the question of the effect of the President's announcement, the Court later examined the allegation of aggression committed on 2 August, i.e. before the Victoria Falls Summit (the Kitona incident) and found that 'on the basis of the evidence before it', it had not been established to the Court's satisfaction that Uganda participated in the attack': [2005] ICJ Rep 205, para 71. The Court noted that, according to Uganda, its troops did not participate, but were present elsewhere on the territory 'with the consent of the Congolese authorities', but it did not comment on this assertion: ibid, 202, para 73. The other cases of alleged aggression having occurred after the Victoria Falls Summit, the finding of withdrawal of consent on that occasion covered them all.

[545] Cf Vienna Convention on the Law of Treaties, Art 54. A Aust gives an example of a typical provision for termination of a bilateral treaty, requiring 'written notice to the other party', which takes effect only after six months (*Modern Treaty Law and Practice* (Cambridge University Press, Cambridge, 2000) 225). This is not of course to say that the State benefiting from the consent given to infringement of the other State's rights may not terminate the arrangement, but the other State can be presumed to have no objection to such termination.

[546] [2005] ICJ Rep 215, para 111. The quotation is from the Protocol of 27 April 1998 agreed between the two parties (see ibid, 197, para 46).

The Lusaka Agreement, signed by the Heads of State of the two parties and of other African States on 18 April 1999[547] was presented by Uganda before the Court as constituting (*inter alia*) consent by the Congo to the presence of Ugandan troops on Congolese territory until their withdrawal in accordance with the Agreement. Specifically, Uganda claimed that that Agreement, which provided for the withdrawal to be completed 180 days after its signature, 'constituted consent by the DRC to the presence of Ugandan forces for at least 180 days from 10 July 1999'.[548] The Court considered that

> this conclusion cannot be drawn. The Agreement took as its starting point the realities on the ground. Among those realities were the major Ugandan military deployment across vast areas of the DRC and the massive loss of life over the preceding months. The arrangements made at Lusaka, to progress towards withdrawal of foreign forces and an eventual peace, with security for all concerned, were directed at these factors on the ground and at the realities of the unstable political and security situation. The provisions of the Lusaka Agreement thus represented an agreed *modus operandi* for the parties. They stipulated how the parties should move forward. They did not purport to qualify the Ugandan military presence in legal terms. In accepting this *modus operandi* the DRC did not "consent" to the presence of Ugandan troops. It simply concurred that there should be a process to end that reality in an orderly fashion. The DRC was willing to proceed from the situation on the ground as it existed and in the manner agreed as most likely to secure the result of a withdrawal of foreign troops in a stable environment. But it did not thereby recognize the situation on the ground as legal, either before the Lusaka Agreement or in the period that would pass until the fulfilment of its terms.[549]

The finding that the Lusaka Agreement did not recognize the situation on the ground immediately preceding the conclusion of the Agreement as 'legal', in the sense of 'not an infringement of the rights of the territorial sovereign' is unproblematic. However, what is the significance of the finding that the parties to the Agreement 'did not purport to qualify the Ugandan military presence in legal terms'? At one level, this seems to mean merely that the Agreement did not contain any explicit statement bearing on the legal situation of the Ugandan troops; but that did not mean that their situation was not governed by international law. If there was no consent by the Congolese Government, however unwilling and limited a consent, to the troops continuing in their places until the agreed withdrawal was complete, it would follow, first that the presence of those troops was unlawful,[550] and secondly that the Congolese

[547] See [2005] ICJ Rep 193, para 33.
[548] [2005] ICJ Rep 210–211, para 98.
[549] Ibid, 211, para 99.
[550] In this sense, Phoebe Okowa, 'Congo's War: The Legal Dimension of a Protracted Conflict' (2006) *BYIL* 203, 236–237.

Government could require them to leave even before the time stipulated in the Lusaka Agreement, thus rendering the Agreement so far a nullity: *quod est absurdum*.[551] As was pointed out by Judge Parra-Aranguren in his separate opinion, on the basis of the Court's reasoning Uganda would be in breach of international law whether it complied with the Lusaka Agreement or did not.[552] In short, like Byron's heroine, the Congo, 'whispering I will ne'er consent—consented',[553] and the Court, swearing it could find no consent, could not exclude such consent.

In August 1988, Ugandan troops carried out operations on Congolese territory in close proximity to the border between the two States, on the basis that consent had been given by President Kabila. The Court however found that the operations in question went far beyond co-operation 'in order to ensure peace and security along the common border', the terms in which the consent had allegedly been given; accordingly, the issue which had also been raised of when any consent might have terminated became 'irrelevant'.[554]

3. Self-Defence

(1) The condition of the existence of an armed attack

A central question examined by the Court in the *Oil Platforms* case was,[555] in view of the reliance by the United States on self-defence as excluding the unlawfulness of its attacks on Iranian oil platforms, whether or not an 'armed attack' had been made by Iran on the United States. In that context one useful clarification was the Court's finding that an attack on a ship is to be treated as an attack on the State whose flag the ship flies; the ownership of the ship is not the relevant factor.[556] The United States made two attacks on the Iranian platforms, and on each occasion it gave notice to the Security Council under Article 51 of

[551] It is far from clear why the point was of any importance in the Judgment. The submissions of the Congo asserted breaches of international law by Uganda *inter alia* 'by occupying its territory', but the only finding in the Judgment concerning occupation referred to 'occupying Ituri': [2005] ICJ Rep 280, para 345 (1), and this involved a finding of *belligerent* occupation involving application of the 1907 Hague Regulations (see ibid, 230–231). The Congo does not appear ever to have asked the Court to find specifically that the mere continued presence of the Ugandan troops after the Lusaka Agreement was an infringement of its sovereignty.

[552] [2005] ICJ Rep 294, para 8.

[553] George Gordon, Lord Byron, *Don Juan*, Canto I, cxvii.

[554] [2005] ICJ Rep 215, para 111.

[555] Though one which, according to one view, it need not have, and perhaps should not have, examined: see David H Small, 'The *Oil Platforms* case: Jurisdiction through the Closed Eye of the Needle' (2004) 3 *The Law and Practice of International Courts and Tribunals*, 113–124.

[556] '[T]he *Texaco Caribbean*, whatever its ownership, was not flying a United States flag, so that an attack on the vessel is not in itself to be equated with an attack on that State': [2003] ICJ Rep 191, para 64. The phrase 'in itself' suggests that, for example, a sustained campaign of attacks singling out vessels owned by the nationals of a particular State might conceivably be regarded as an attack on the State.

the Charter.[557] While the failure to do so was a negative element in the assessment of the United States' actions in the *Military and Paramilitary Activities* case,[558] and was apparently to be similarly treated in the *Congo/Uganda* case, discussed below, the giving of the notice only indicated that the United States regarded itself as having acted in self-defence (and wished others to share that view), but carried no weight for the Court's determination whether the conditions for self-defence were in fact satisfied.

In general, apart from the general weakness of the evidence adduced by the United States to show that armed attacks had been made on it, and that they had been made by Iran, the general pattern of events in the Gulf was clearly of hostilities primarily between Iran and Iraq having effects generally on seaborne traffic, either because of incidental hostile action against perceived allies or sympathisers of the other side, or simply because of side effects, for example, when mines laid by the one side of the other were encountered by neutral vessels, mines being no respecters of national flags.[559] In these circumstances, while United States interests undoubtedly suffered from the hostilities, the necessary intent to make an armed attack on any specific State was extremely difficult to establish. The Court was ready to consider a whole series of incidents to judge whether in combination they could be regarded as adding up to an armed attack;[560] but concluded that they did not 'constitute an armed attack on the United States, of the kind that the Court, in the case concerning *Military and Paramilitary Activities in and against Nicaragua,* qualified as a "most grave" form of the use of force.'[561] It was also prepared to consider that in some circumstances 'the mining of a single vessel might be sufficient to bring into play' the right of self-defence,[562] though in the case before it that was not so.

In the case concerning *Legal Consequences of the Construction of a Wall in the Occupied Palestinian Territory*, the essential reason why the Court did not accept the contention that Israel's action in building the wall was justified on the basis of self–defence was that 'Article 51 of the Charter . . . recognizes the existence of an inherent right of self-defence in the case of an armed attack *by one State against another State*'; and the

[557] The notifications are reproduced at [2003] ICJ Rep 185, para 48, and 193–194, para 67. The justification adduced was essentially the same; it has been observed that 'there is now a tendency to over-report claims to individual self-defence', and that 'when there is a prolonged conflict the states parties tend not simply to make their claims to self-defence at the start of the conflict, but often to report each episode separately' (Christine Gray, *International Law and the Use of Force* (Oxford University Press, Oxford, 2008) 91). The United States was however not a State directly party to the Iran/Iraq conflict.

[558] [1986] ICJ Rep 121–122, para 235.

[559] See [2003] ICJ Rep 183, para 44 (in connection with the US claim to be protecting legitimate security interests).

[560] [1986] ICJ Rep 121–122, para 235.

[561] Ibid, 192, para 64, citing [1986] ICJ Rep 101, para 191.

[562] Ibid, 195, para 72.

Court noted that 'Israel does not claim that the attacks against it are imputable to a foreign State.'[563] The text of Article 51[564] gives no indication of any condition as to the entity responsible for an armed attack; nor did the Court give any attention to the question whether, even if such a condition was an implied part of the Charter provision, the right of self-defence in customary law might not necessarily be subject to the same limitation.[565] Judge Higgins drew attention to the silence of Article 51 on the point, and suggested the sole authority for the view that only an armed attack from or by another State could justify action in self-defence was the Court's decision in *Military and Paramilitary Activities in and against Nicaragua*,[566] a decision which Judge Higgins had criticized in an academic capacity.[567] In her separate opinion in the *Wall* case, Judge Higgins rejected the majority's view that, in effect, 'an occupying Power loses the right to defend its own civilian citizens at home if the attacks emanate from the occupied territory – a territory which [the Court] has found not to have been annexed and is certainly "other than" Israel.'[568] Judge Kooijmans considered that the limitation which the Court saw in Article 51, a view which he considered to be correct on the basis of 'the generally accepted interpretation' of that Article 'for more than 50 years', was however no longer relevant:

> [Security Council] Resolutions 1368 (2001) and 1373 (2001) recognize the inherent right of individual or collective self-defence without making any reference to an armed attack by a State. The Security Council called acts of international terrorism, without any further qualification, a threat to international peace and security which authorizes it to act under Chapter VII of the Charter. And it actually did so in resolution 1373 (2001) without ascribing these acts of terrorism to a particular State. This is the completely new element in these resolutions.[569]

Judge Kooijmans nevertheless held that, even on the basis of these resolutions, the argument based on self-defence must fail, because

> The right of self-defence as contained in the Charter is a rule of international law and thus relates to international phenomena. Resolutions 1368 (2001) and 1373 (2001) refer to acts of *international* terrorism as constituting a threat to *international* peace and security; they therefore have no immediate bearing on terrorist acts originating within a territory which is under control of the State which is

[563] [2004] ICJ Rep 194, para 139.

[564] 'Nothing in the present Charter shall impair the inherent right of individual or collective self-defence if an armed attack occurs against a Member of the United Nations, until the Security Council has taken measures necessary to maintain international peace and security.'

[565] As was, in effect, the view of Judge Kooijmans: see below.

[566] [2004-I] ICJ Rep 215, para 33, referring to [1986] ICJ Rep 103–104, para 195.

[567] Rosalyn Higgins, *Problems and Process: International Law and How We Use It* (Clarendon Press, Oxford, 1994), 248–251.

[568] [2004] ICJ Rep 215, para 34.

[569] Ibid, 230, para 35.

also the victim of these acts. And Israel does not claim that these acts have their origin elsewhere.[570]

Self-defence as a circumstance precluding wrongfulness was asserted by all the States involved in the hostilities that came before the Court in the complicated circumstances of the cases concerning *Armed Activities on the Territory of the Congo*. In 1999 the Democratic Republic of the Congo brought proceedings against Burundi, Rwanda and Uganda (*Armed Activities on the Territory of the Congo*), and a fresh action against Rwanda in 2002; of these, only the case against Uganda has proceeded to trial and judgment. The cases against Burundi and Rwanda were discontinued (Orders of 30 January 2001); the new application against Rwanda led to an Order on a request for provisional measures (10 July 2002), but by a Judgment of 3 February 2006 the Court found that it had no jurisdiction.

The Court examined in particular[571] a claim by Uganda relating primarily to operations carried out by its forces on the territory of the Congo under the operational title of 'Safe Haven', the basis for which, as the Court found, was a document of the Ugandan High Command dated 11 September 1998, reproduced *in extenso* in the Court's Judgment.[572] In respect of earlier operations, Uganda was relying on the circumstance of alleged consent by the Congo, but the Court rejected this contention, and considered that these earlier operations also could only be justified, if at all, on the basis of self-defence.[573]

The Court's ruling was essentially that the operations did not qualify as self-defence because any 'armed attack' to which they were intended to respond did not come from the DRC (the Congo), but from the ADF (the Allied Democratic Forces), rebellious forces whose actions did not engage the responsibility of the Congo as a State. The point is however expressed in the Judgment in a rather indirect way. The Court first observed, presumably as a consideration relevant to assessment of the plea of self-defence, that 'in August and early September 1998 Uganda did not report to the Security Council events that it had regarded as requiring it to act in self-defence.'[574] This is a curious wording, since what Article 51 of the Charter requires to be reported to the Security Council is '[m]easures taken by members in the exercise of th[e] right of self-defence'. When reporting such measures the State concerned will no doubt also indicate

[570] Ibid, para 36.

[571] Cf Phoebe Okowa, 'Congo's War: The Legal Dimension of a Protracted Conflict' (2006) *BYIL* 203, 238–239, who notes a contention by the DRC that, once its consent to the presence of foreign troops on its territory had been withdrawn, the continued presence of such troops 'could be regarded as an act of aggression' which 'triggered its entitlement to rely on a right of self-defence under the terms of the Charter': ibid, 240. The Court did not find it necessary to examine the question of self-defence in this context.

[572] [2005] ICJ Rep 213–214, para 109.

[573] Ibid, 222, para 144.

[574] Ibid. para 145.

what were the events to which it felt obliged to respond in self-defence; but there is, for example, no obligation to report the existence of an armed attack by another State *before* responding to it in self-defence. Furthermore, 'it is clear that the reporting requirement is merely procedural; failure to comply does not of itself invalidate a claim to self-defence.'[575]

The Court continued:

> It is further to be noted that, while Uganda claimed to have acted in self-defence, it did not ever claim that it had been subjected to an armed attack by the armed forces of the DRC. The "armed attacks" to which reference was made came rather from the ADF. The Court has found above . . . that there is no satisfactory proof of the involvement in these attacks, direct or indirect, of the Government of the DRC. The attacks did not emanate from armed bands or irregulars sent by the DRC or on behalf of the DRC, within the sense of Article 3 *(g)* of General Assembly resolution 3314 (XXIX) on the definition of aggression, adopted on 14 December 1974. The Court is of the view that, on the evidence before it, even if this series of deplorable attacks could be regarded as cumulative in character, they still remained non-attributable to the DRC.[576]

The Court here followed the decision in the *Armed Activities* case, where it relied on the Definition of Aggression to elucidate the meaning of 'armed attack' for the purposes of determining the legitimacy of actions in purported self-defence.[577] The definition in Article 3 *(g)* extends not merely to the sending of armed bands, but also to the 'substantial involvement therein' of the State in question, 'therein' referring apparently to the act of 'sending'; it is for this reason that the Court excluded 'involvement . . . direct or indirect' of the DRC. The final sentence of the passage is clearly correct in context: but there could be circumstances in which armed attacks by independent forces were of such degree and frequency as to suggest that they could only have been carried on with the covert involvement of the territorial sovereign.

On the basis of the General Assembly resolution quoted, and of the decision in the *Nicaragua* case discussed in the previous article, which was and is consistent with general State practice,[578] it is difficult to fault this finding on the basis of the facts as found by the Court. *De lege ferenda*, however, one may consider that there is a problem which has been addressed by commentators[579] but not yet resolved. If attacks on State A are made from the territory of State B, but by military or paramilitary units for whose acts the Government of State B is not responsible, the only appropriate response by State A may nevertheless involve cross-border

[575] Gray, above n 557, 91, citing D W Greig, 'Self-Defence and the Security Council: What does Article 51 require?' (1991) 40 *International and Comparative Law Quarterly* 366.

[576] [2005] ICJ Rep 222–223, paras 145–146.

[577] See the discussion in the previous article, (1995) *BYIL* 1, 74 et seq.

[578] Gray, above n 557, 98.

[579] See the extensive discussion in ibid, 99–105.

action encroaching on the territory of State B.[580] Obviously the consent of State B may be sought, but may not be easily or rapidly forthcoming. In the view of some scholars,

For the purpose of responding to an "armed attack", the State acting in self-defence is allowed to trespass on foreign territory, even when the attack cannot be attributed to the State from whose territory it is proceeding. It does not follow from the fact that the right of self-defence pursuant to Article 51 [of the Charter] is restricted to the case of an "armed attack" that defensive measures my only affect the attacker.[581]

There was an assertion in the *DRC v Uganda* case that appeal might in these circumstances be made to the doctrine of necessity, and the Court commented on this in its decision (see the next following section).

The Court was careful to express no view on the equally difficult question whether and to what extent the use of force may be used against an anticipated attack. It noted that the parties to the *Nicaragua* case had not raised the issue of 'the lawfulness of a response to the imminent threat of an armed attack', and that it had therefore expressed no view on the issue in that case.[582] While following this example, the Court did however 'feel constrained to observe' that the key document produced before it 'makes no reference whatever to attacks that have already occurred', and was so worded as to deal with 'specified security needs' that were 'essentially preventative'.[583] It is slightly disturbing to note that, while this reference therefore appears wholly supererogatory, the subsequent paragraph summing up the Court's conclusions on this part of the case begins 'For all these reasons'.[584] Was the Court influenced, despite its disclaimer, by the possibility that Uganda had in fact been engaging in anticipatory self-defence?

(2) Necessity and proportionality of measures

While the ILC Articles on State Responsibility reflect the distinction in customary international law between self-defence (Article 21) and

[580] It was because Uganda was, or considered itself to be, in this situation that it was obliged to claim that it was acting in self-defence while not claiming that it was the victim of an armed attack by the DRC, an inconsistency to which the Court drew attention (see the passage quoted above).

[581] A Randelzhofer in B Simma (ed) *The Charter of the United Nations: A Commentary* (2nd edn), 51:29. Cf however the attitude of the USA and the UK to incursions by Turkey into Iraq from April 2000 onwards in response to attacks by the PKK from Iraqi territory. 'This failure to rely on any doctrine of self-defence against non-state terrorist actors operating from outside Turkey is an indication that this doctrine was by no means well-established before September 11, and that even states like the USA and the UK were reluctant to resort to it in this case': Christine Gray and Simon Olleson, 'The Limits of the Law of the Use of Force: Turkey, Iraq and the Kurds' (2001) *XII Finnish Yearbook of International Law* 355, 407.

[582] [2005] ICJ Rep 222, para 143, citing *Military and Paramilitary Activities*, [1986] ICJ Rep 103, para 194. In the case of nuclear weapons, the Court in 1996 was similarly disinclined to express any opinion on 'the practice known as the "policy of deterrence"': *Legality of the Threat or Use of Nuclear Weapons*, [1996] ICJ Rep 254, para 67.

[583] [2005] ICJ Rep 222, para 143.

[584] Ibid, 223, para. 147.

necessity (Article 25) as circumstances precluding wrongfulness, the former Article is expressed to apply only to 'a lawful measure of self-defence taken in conformity with the Charter', and it was explained that the term 'lawful' implies, *inter alia*, 'compliance with the requirements of proportionality and of necessity inherent in the notion of self-defence'.[585] Where the potentially wrongful act complained of is a use of force, this condition usually renders otiose any consideration whether the act could have been justified on the grounds of necessity *simpliciter*; in the case of the *Legal Consequences of the Construction of a Wall in the Occupied Palestine Territory*, however, the Court decided in the same breath that 'Israel cannot rely on a right of self-defence or on a state of necessity in order to preclude the wrongfulness of the construction of the wall.'[586]

In the *Oil Platforms* case it was argued, in connection with the interpretation of a treaty contemplating the taking of 'measures necessary to protect [the] essential security interests' of a party, that it was sufficient that the measures were deemed necessary in good faith by the party concerned, and that '[a] measure of discretion should be afforded to a party's good faith application' of such measures. The Court dismissed this contention, and also took the opportunity to note that, in general law,

> the requirement of international law that measures taken avowedly in self-defence must have been necessary for that purpose is strict and objective, leaving no room for any "measure of discretion".[587]

It endorsed the statement in the *Military and Paramilitary Activities* case that in customary law the lawfulness of the response to an armed attack depends on 'observance of the criteria of the necessity and proportionality of the measures taken'.[588] A relevant consideration was the nature of the target of the retaliatory attacks: the Court was not satisfied that the United States had proved military presence and activity on the oil platforms that were attacked, and noted that one of them had not been originally specified as 'an appropriate military target', but had been attacked as a 'target of opportunity'.[589] The argument of the United States was certainly over-bold on the facts; but does to say that the test is 'strict and objective' mean that the degree of necessity is to be legally assessed on calm consideration by a dispassionate observer (or judge) *ex post facto*? There should, it is suggested, be some allowance to be made for a good faith snap judgment in circumstances which by definition would probably require instant or rapid reaction. The difficulty is that self-defence has

[585] Crawford, above n 387, 167, para (6).
[586] [2004] ICJ Rep 195, para 142.
[587] [2003] ICJ Rep 196, para 73.
[588] [1986] ICJ Rep 103, para 194, cited in [2003] ICJ Rep 196, para 74; see also ibid, 198, para 76.
[589] [2003] ICJ Rep 198, para 76.

been recognized as 'precluding wrongfulness', i.e. an absolute rather than a mitigating factor.[590]

As regards the requirement of proportionality, the Court noted that the attacks on the platforms, the sole subject of Iran's complaint before the Court, had been part of a larger operation ('Operation Praying Mantis'). It held that, although the other components of that operation were outside the Court's jurisdiction, it

> cannot assess in isolation the proportionality of that action to the attack to which it was said to be a response; it cannot close its eyes to the scale of the whole operation, which involved, inter alia, the destruction of two Iranian frigates and a number of other naval vessels and aircraft. As a response to the mining, by an unidentified agency, of a single United States warship, which was severely damaged but not sunk, and without loss of life, neither "Operation Praying Mantis" as a whole, nor even that part of it that destroyed the Salman and Nasr platforms, can be regarded, in the circumstances of this case, as a proportionate use of force in self-defence.[591]

As to the *Congo/Uganda* Judgment, the paragraph referred to above, summing up the Court's conclusions on the self-defence issue, reads in full as follows:

> For all these reasons, the Court finds that the legal and factual circumstances for the exercise of a right of self-defence by Uganda against the DRC were not present. Accordingly, the Court has no need to respond to the contentions of the Parties as to whether and under what conditions contemporary international law provides for a right of self-defence against large-scale attacks by irregular forces. Equally, since the preconditions for the exercise of self-defence do not exist in the circumstances of the present case, the Court has no need to enquire whether such an entitlement to self-defence was in fact exercised in circumstances of necessity and in a manner that was proportionate. The Court cannot fail to observe, however, that the taking of airports and towns many hundreds of kilometres from Uganda's border would not seem proportionate to the series of transborder attacks it claimed had given rise to the right of self-defence, nor to be necessary to that end.[592]

Again the Court departs somewhat from the minimum findings necessary to reach a conclusion on the point (if the attacks were in any event not justified as self-defence, whether they would, had they been so justified, nevertheless have to be condemned as excessive is immaterial).[593]

[590] On the relationship between, on the one hand, the primary norm excluding the use of force, which contains within it the exception for self-defence, which in turn is subject to the requirement of necessity, and on the other hand the general doctrine of necessity as a circumstance excluding wrongfulness, cf n 586 above, and see Crawford, n 387 above, *sub* Article 25, para (21).

[591] [2003] ICJ Rep 198, para 77.

[592] [2005] ICJ Rep 223, para 147.

[593] On the same lines, in the *Oil Platforms* case, the Court took the various questions raised in an order which seems to have been dictated less by logic than by the desire to make a specific finding which could, and *semble* should, have been unnecessary.

3A. Necessity

Whether it be attributed to Saint-Augustine, to Seneca the Elder or some other of the ancient philosophers, the maxim 'Necessity knows no law'[594] or 'Nécessité n'a pas de loi' is of respectable antiquity, both as a philosophical maxim and, in some sense as a contradiction, as part of law itself.[595] It was however not discussed in the previous article in this series, as it was only in the 1997 decision in the *Gabčíkovo/Nagymaros Project* case that the Court first had to deal with the contention that responsibility for a breach by a State of an international obligation was precluded by considerations of necessity.[596] Hungary relied on the doctrine as one of the grounds justifying its suspension and abandonment of the works on the Project to which it was committed by its treaty obligations toward Czechoslovakia. In essence its contention was that completion of the Project as originally planned in the 1977 Treaty between the parties, would, in the light of information and studies not available at the time the treaty was concluded, have disastrous effects on the environment and the water supply, so that a 'state of ecological necessity' could be said to exist.[597]

The parties each recognized, and the Court agreed, that 'the existence of a state of necessity must be evaluated in the light of the criteria laid down by the International Law Commission' in the text which became Article 25 of the Articles on State Responsibility.[598] The Court also noted, with apparent approval, the definition given by the ILC of a 'state of necessity':

594 This formulation led to a 20th-century member of the British judiciary being privately known to the Bar as 'Old Necessity'.

595 See the introductory Report by Theodore Christakis to the 2007 Grenoble Colloquium of the *Société francaise pour le droit international*, 'La Nécessité en Droit international', Proceedings of the Colloquium, 11 et seq. For a very full survey of the subject, see Maria Agius, 'The Invocation of Necessity in International Law' (2009) *LVI Netherlands International Law Review* 95.

596 The ILC noted that the question of necessity had been raised before the PCIJ in the *Oscar Chinn* case (and discussed by Judge Anzilotti in his separate opinion), and something akin to necessity had been argued in the case of *Rights of US Nationals in Morocco*, but in neither case had the Court found it necessary to rule on the matter: see Report of the ILC on the Work of the 33rd Session, A/35/10, 41–42, paras 19–20. In the dispute between Belgium and Greece underlying the *Société commerciale de Belgique* case, Greece had claimed that it was 'materially impossible' for it to pay the sums found by an arbitration to be due to the Belgian company, which appears to amount to a plea of necessity (PCIJ Rep Series A/B No 78, 176). The Court however found that this question was 'outside the scope of the proceedings before the Court' (ibid, 177).

597 [1997] ICJ Rep 35–36, para 40. For a detailed study of the problem by one of the counsel engaged in the case, see Pierre-Marie Dupuy, 'L'invention de l'état de nécessité écologique' in the 2007 Grenoble Colloquium of the *Société française pour le droit international*, 'La Nécessité en Droit international', Proceedings of the Colloquium, 223–246.

598 Then Article 33 of the Draft Articles: [1997] ICJ Rep 39, para 49. Article 25 reads as follows:
Necessity

1. Necessity may not be invoked by a State as a ground for precluding the wrongfulness of an act not in conformity with an international obligation of that State unless the act:
   (a) Is the only way for the State to safeguard an essential interest against a grave and imminent peril; and
   (b) Does not seriously impair an essential interest of the State or States towards which the obligation exists, or of the international community as a whole.

"the situation of a State whose sole means of safeguarding an essential interest threatened by a grave and imminent peril is to adopt conduct not in conformity with what is required of it by an international obligation to another State"

and the ILC's view that '"the notion of state of necessity is... deeply rooted in general legal thinking"'[599] The controversies which formerly existed, and continued during the work of the ILC, as to whether the plea of necessity existed, or should be permitted to exist, as part of customary international law, must thus now be regarded as closed.[600]

Again following the ILC, the Court emphasized that as a ground for precluding wrongfulness necessity 'can only be accepted on an exceptional basis'. But what does that mean in practical terms? The Court quoted the ILC as saying that the such a justification would be 'even more rarely admissible than is the case with other circumstances precluding wrongfulness';[601] but to suggest that circumstances will only rarely, thus exceptionally, arise in which a plea of necessity would be justified is unhelpful for ascertaining whether in a particular case it would be so justified. The Court went on to cite the ILC as considering that 'the state of necessity can only be invoked under certain strictly defined conditions which must be cumulatively satisfied; and the State concerned is not the sole judge of whether those conditions have been met';[602] but the latter observation is surely applicable to all grounds of precluding wrongfulness, and the former to most of them. Perhaps a more satisfactory explanation of the significance of the 'exceptional' quality of the plea is that of Crawford:

[Necessity] arises when there is an irreconcilable conflict, between an essential interest on the one hand and an obligation of the State invoking necessity on the other. These special features mean that necessity will only rarely be available to excuse non-performance of an obligation and that it is subject to strict limitations to guard against possible abuse.[603]

It thus appears that to say that necessity as an exceptional case of preclusion of wrongfulness is no more than a prediction that, as a matter of fact, the conditions which must be satisfied for such a plea will rarely be met; it does not add anything to those conditions.

The Court first examined the question whether Hungary had shown a threat to an 'essential interest', and concluded that Hungary's concerns for the impact of the Project on its natural environment did relate to an

2. In any case, necessity may not be invoked by a State as a ground for precluding wrongfulness if:

(a) The international obligation in question excludes the possibility of invoking necessity; or
(b) The State has contributed to the situation of necessity.

599 *Yearbook of the ILC*, 1980, II, part 2, p.34, quoted in [1997] ICJ Rep 40, para 50.

600 The decision in the *Gabčikovo/Nagymaros* case was quoted with approval by the International Tribunal for the Law of the Sea in the case of the *M/V Saiga (No. 2)*, paras 133–134.

601 [1997] ICJ Rep 40, para 51.

602 Ibid.

603 Crawford, above n 387, 178.

'essential interest'; that such an interest did not have to be, for example, one related to the existence of the State concerned.[604] Was there then a 'grave and imminent peril' to that interest? The Court endeavoured to define, in the abstract, what is signified by the word 'peril':

The word "peril" certainly evokes the idea of "risk": that is precisely what distinguishes "peril" from material damage. But a state of necessity could not exist without a "peril" duly established at the relevant point in time: the mere apprehension of a possible "peril" could not suffice in that respect. It could moreover hardly be otherwise, when the "peril" constituting the state of necessity has at the same time to be "grave" and "imminent". "Imminence" is synonymous with "immediacy" or "proximity" and goes far beyond the concept of "possibility". As the International Law Commission emphasized in its commentary, the "extremely grave and imminent" peril must "have been a threat to the interest at the actual time" (*Yearbook of the International Law Commission,* 1980, Vol. II, Part 2, p. 49, para 33). That does not exclude, in the view of the Court, that a "peril" appearing in the long term might be held to be "imminent" as soon as it is established, at the relevant point in time, that the realization of that peril, however far off it might be, is not thereby any less certain and inevitable.[605]

Another way of putting the point might be that, for an action to be justified on the ground of necessity, it must be possible, at the moment the action is taken, to point to something deleterious that *will* happen (not merely *may* happen) if the action is not taken, even if that something will only happen after the lapse of a period—perhaps a considerable period—of time.[606] The longer the expected time-lag, however, the more difficult it will be to establish that nothing that could be done in the meantime (other than the injurious action contemplated) will, by averting the anticipated event, render that action unnecessary. In the nature of things, it will also often be difficult in such circumstances to show that action must be taken *now*, that there is no room for a wait-and-see policy.

In the *Gabčíkovo/Nagymaros* case Hungary was also in the difficulty that it was pleading necessity as a justification, not for action, but for inaction, or rather for refusal to co-operate in action, namely the carrying out of the Project. To justify that refusal at the moment that it was made, Hungary therefore had, in theory at least, to show that the 'grave and imminent peril' would inevitably be realized if it took one more step to comply with its obligations under the Project. This was an almost impossible task. The Court found, for example, that the realization of

[604] [1997] ICJ Rep 41, para 53. [605] Ibid, 42, para 54.

[606] The Hungarian judge, Herczegh, took a slightly different view: 'The expression "grave peril" refers to the existence of *a strong likelihood* that detrimental effects and very extensive damage will occur': Dissenting Opinion, [1997] ICJ Rep 184 (emphasis added). It has been argued, in the context of an analysis concluding that necessity, as a circumstance excluding responsibility, is not part of customary international law, that it is necessarily impossible to point to an event that *will* happen, and is not merely likely to happen: see Sarah Heathcote, 'Est-ce que l'état de nécessité est un principe de droit international coutumier?' (2007) 40 *Revue belge de droit international*, 53, 58.

one specified peril depended on the modalities of the operation of an aspect of the project, which were as yet undetermined.[607] In respect of another potential peril, Hungary, as the Court found, had other means of averting it, even if these might prove more costly;[608] this marks the evident point that the risk that something is going to be more difficult or more costly cannot rank as a peril to an essential interest. As observed by Judge Anzilotti in the *Oscar Chinn* case, 'the plea of necessity . . . by definition, implies the impossibility of proceeding by any other method than the one contrary to law'.[609]

The Court observed in respect of one peril that it 'had . . . already materialized to a large extent for a number of years, so that it could not, in 1989, represent a peril arising *entirely* out of the project'.[610] This was not presented as a ground for rejecting the plea of necessity, so the Court does not explain further. It would however seem that if the threat to an essential interest results from two factors in combination, neither of them sufficing in itself to constitute a peril, action taken to disarm one of the factors must be justifiable on the basis of necessity. What the Court may have meant was that suspension of the Project would not have averted the peril, because it was caused by factors independent of, and antedating, the Project, even if the Project contributed to the impact.

The overall conclusion of the Court on the question of necessity was as follows:

The Court concludes from the foregoing that, with respect to both Nagymaros and Gabčíkovo, the perils invoked by Hungary, without prejudging their possible gravity, were not sufficiently established in 1989, nor were they "imminent"; and that Hungary had available to it at that time means of responding to these perceived perils other than the suspension and abandonment of works with which it had been entrusted. What is more, negotiations were under way which might have led to a review of the Project and the extension of some of its time-limits, without there being need to abandon it. The Court infers from this that the respect by Hungary, in 1989, of its obligations under the terms of the 1977 Treaty would not have resulted in a situation "characterized so aptly by the maxim *summum jus summa injuria*" (*Yearbook of the International Law Commission,* 1980, Vol. II, Part 2, p. 49, para 31).[611]

A provision in the ILC Articles, endorsed by the Court, which may possibly have constituted an innovation was the requirement of Article 33 (2) *(b)* that 'necessity may not be invoked by a State as a ground for precluding

607 [1997] ICJ Rep 43, para 55 (operation of the Nagymaros portion of the Project).

608 Ibid. (lowering of the riverbed downstream of the Nagymaros Dam).

609 PCIJ Rep Series A/B No 63, 114.

610 [1997] ICJ Rep 43, para 55, emphasis added.

611 Ibid, 45, para 57; see now A/35/10, 39, para 31. The Latin tag was quoted by the ILC in the context of the debate whether, in view of the dangers of abuse, necessity should be recognized at all as a 'circumstance precluding wrongfulness'. It is doubtful whether the Court meant to imply here that only cases of the utmost injustice (*summa injuria*) would justify accepting a plea of necessity: grave peril to an essential interest is not an identical concept.

wrongfulness if . . . [t]he State has contributed to the situation of necessity.'[612] In the *Gabčíkovo/Nagymaros* case, the Court considered the information available to Hungary when it concluded the 1977 Treaty, and its vacillating and inconsistent conduct in relation to the Project between 1983 and 1989, and concluded that

> in the present case, even if it had been established that there was in 1989, a state of necessity linked to the performance of the 1977 Treaty, Hungary would not have been permitted to rely upon that state of necessity in order to justify its failure to comply with its treaty obligations, as it had helped, by act or omission to bring it about.[613]

A final reflection prompted by the *Gabčíkovo/Nagymaros* case concerns the relationship between the plea of necessity and the system of judicial settlement of disputes. If, at the moment when Hungary came to the conclusion that the Project involved a grave and imminent peril to its essential interests, there had been in force unconditional acceptances of the Court's jurisdiction by the two States concerned, would it have been open to the Hungary to bring proceedings to protect its interests; and what form should such proceedings take? Could it have asked the Court to declare that the 1977 Treaty was invalid insofar as it would bring about a result which could otherwise only be averted by a refusal of compliance based on a plea of necessity? On such a basis, it could presumably have asked for provisional measures to protect its interests.[614] If such a course had been possible, would it also have been obligatory? As indicated in the ILC's Article 25 (1) *(a)*, if an act is to be justified on the basis of necessity it must be the *only* way in which an essential interest can be safeguarded; thus if recourse to the Court for provisional measures would be an effective preventative action, no other action could be justified on the ground of necessity. The present international judicial system is however probably too weak as regards enforcement of decisions for such a view to be maintainable.

In the case of the *Construction of a Wall in the Occupied Palestinian Territory*, the Court indicated that it had 'considered whether Israel could rely on a state of necessity which would preclude the wrongfulness of the construction of the wall'. It continued:

[612] The ILC simply stated this as though it were self-evident, without citing previous instances in State practice or judicial/arbitral precedent: Report of the ILC on the Work of the 33rd Session, A/35/10, 50, para 34.

[613] [1997] ICJ Rep 46, para 57.

[614] Note the observation of the ILC that only the imperilled State itself 'can decide whether [the justifying] conditions exist; it does not really have time in its situation of imminent peril to refer the matter to any other instance. But this does not mean that the determination of the existence of the conditions that permit the State to act out of a state of necessity will be left for good to the unilateral discretion of the State that relies on those conditions. The State affected by the conduct alleged to have been adopted in a state of necessity may very well object that the necessary conditions did not exist. This will give rise to a dispute, which will need to be settled by one of the peaceful means specified in Article 33 of the Charter.': Report of the ILC on the Work of its 33rd Session, A/10/35, 50, para 36.

> In this regard the Court is bound to note that some of the conventions at issue in the present instance include qualifying clauses of the rights guaranteed or provisions for derogation.... Since those treaties already address considerations of this kind within their own provisions, it might be asked whether a state of necessity as recognized in customary international law could be invoked with regard to those treaties as a ground for precluding the wrongfulness of the measures or decisions being challenged. However, the Court will not need to consider that question.[615]

The qualifying clauses that the Court had in mind were Articles 49, paragraph 2, and 53 of the Fourth Geneva Convention, and some provisions of the International Covenant on Civil and Political Rights and of the International Covenant on Economic, Social and Cultural Rights.

The reason why the Court left the point open was because in any event it was 'not convinced that the construction of the wall along the route chosen was the only means to safeguard the interests of Israel against the peril which it has invoked as justification for that construction'.[616] In this respect the Court cited the requirement of Article 25 of the ILC Articles that the act challenged be 'the only way for the State to safeguard an essential interest against a grave and imminent peril'.

In both the decided cases involving a plea of necessity the Court has proceeded on the basis that the gravity and imminence of the peril, and the question whether the means taken to avert it were the only such means available, was for the Court to judge *ex post facto*. It did not consider, or at least not explicitly, whether the State concerned might in good faith have concluded that its intended action was justified on grounds of necessity. This is consistent with the approach of the ILC, that the peril has to be 'objectively established';[617] in effect, a claim of necessity, even made in the utmost good faith, is made at the claimant State's own risk.

4. Counter-Measures

In the original series of articles, aspects of this matter were discussed under two separate headings: 'The limits of reaction to unlawful conduct',[618] and 'Counter-measures';[619] in this supplementary series it is more convenient to deal with it solely under the present heading.

[615] [2004] ICJ Rep 194–195, para 140. This formulation also seems to leave open the question whether it could have been held that the construction of a wall *somewhere* where it would, in the absence of a circumstance precluding wrongfulness, be unlawful, *was* a matter of justifiable necessity, but that the specific route chosen was not the only one, nor the most appropriate. Could there have been a finding of partial necessity, or had the wall to be declared either entirely lawful, or entirely unlawful?

[616] Ibid, 195.

[617] Crawford, above n 387, 183, *sub* Article 25, para (15). A more flexible approach has in the past been adopted in cases of *military* necessity: see, e.g., *In Re Wilhelm List and Others*, US Tribunal at Nuremberg, VIII UN War Crimes Commission Reports 34–92.

[618] (1989) *BYIL* 107–113; (2005) *BYIL* 62 (title reference only).

[619] (1995) *BYIL* 79–80.

The concept of counter-measures as a circumstance precluding unlawfulness was invoked in the case of the *Gabčíkovo/Nagymaros Project*. The act which it was sought to justify as a legitimate counter-measure was the putting into operation by Czechoslovakia of a modified version ('Variant C') of a portion, involving its own territory, of the agreed works on the Danube contemplated by the Project; the Court had concluded that this constituted an internationally wrongful act vis-à-vis Hungary, its partner in the Project. However Hungary had also, in the contention of Czechoslovakia, failed to comply with its treaty obligations under the Project, and Variant C was, it was suggested, legitimate as a counter-measure.[620]

The Court first noted that '[i]n order to be justifiable, a countermeasure must meet certain conditions,'[621] and cited its decision in the *Military and Paramilitary Activities* case.[622] At the time, the ILC Articles on State Responsibility were in the form of a draft adopted on first reading: the Court took note of them also, as well as the *Air Services Agreement* case.[623] It continued:

> In the first place it must be taken in response to a previous international wrongful act of another State and must be directed against that State. Although not primarily presented as a countermeasure, it is clear that Variant C was a response to Hungary's suspension and abandonment of works and that it was directed against that State; and it is equally clear, in the Court's view, that Hungary's actions were internationally wrongful.

The reference to the Variant having been 'not primarily presented as a countermeasure' appears to mean that Czechoslovakia did not, when putting Variant C into operation, announce that this was by way of countermeasure. On the basis that the only permitted purpose of countermeasures is 'to induce [the other] State to comply with its obligations'[624] one would expect that countermeasures should be announced clearly as such, so that the State against which they are directed would be aware of what it should do to gave them brought to an end. The Court in fact indicated as a necessary condition of the lawfulness of a countermeasure that 'the injured State must have called upon the State committing the wrongful act to discontinue its wrongful conduct or to make reparation for it.'[625] This condition was complied with, as the Court found, in that it was 'clear from the facts of the case . . . that Czechoslovakia requested Hungary to resume the performance of its treaty obligations on many occasions'.[626]

The Court however did not say that it was made clear to Hungary that Variant C was linked with the non-performance by Hungary of its treaty

[620] It appears that Czechoslovakia only advanced this as an 'alternative legal argument', and did not develop it fully: see Dissenting Opinion of Judge Vereshchetin, [1997] ICJ Rep 219.

[621] [1997] ICJ Rep 55, para 83.

[622] [1986] ICJ Rep 127, para 249.

[623] *Arbitral Award of 9 December 1978 in the case concerning the Air Service Agreement of 27 March 1946 between the United States of America and France*, XVII *UNRIAA* 443 et seq. James Crawford indicates also the '*Naulilaa*' case, II *UNRIAA* 1025–1026 and the '*Cysne*' case, ibid, 1035, 1052: above n 387, 168.

[624] ILC Articles, Art. 49 (1).

[625] [1997] ICJ Rep 56, para 84.

[626] Ibid.

obligations in the full sense of a countermeasure, i.e. on the lines of 'we are going to infringe your rights in this way until you comply with your obligations.' The matter is perhaps one of good faith: presumably a wrongful act which was hastily attributed by its author, *ex post facto*, to an intention to react by way of countermeasure to some newly discovered wrong would not be legitimate. The circumstances of the *Gabčíkovo* case were however such that Hungary could be in no doubt as to the relationship between Variant C, the original Project, and Hungary's abandonment of it, even if Czechoslovakia did not formally invoke the law on countermeasures.

Variant C still fits awkwardly into the framework of the law on countermeasures as expounded by the Court, since a countermeasure must apparently in principle be terminable or revocable by the party resorting to it. In terms of the ILC Articles on State Responsibility, 'Countermeasures are limited to the non-performance *for the time being*' of the State's obligations.[627] If pressure is brought to induce the other State to cease and desist from a wrongful act, or to make reparation, it must be possible for the pressure to be turned off, as it were, once the intended result has been achieved. It is not at all clear that, in the complicated circumstances resulting from the abandonment of the Project half-way by Hungary, and Czechoslovakia's self-help, that anything as simple as a compliance by Hungary and a reversal of its acts by Czechoslovakia could be achieved. The Court did not examine this aspect in its Judgment, but Judge Vereshchetin discussed it in his dissenting opinion, and held that 'at least at the time of the damming of the Danube, variant C was a reversible measure';[628] the qualification suggests that the judge would concede that at some point the measure became effectively irreversible.

In any event, however, the Court did not uphold Czechoslovakia's reliance on countermeasures, for a different reason. In the view of the Court, 'an important consideration is that the effects of a countermeasure must be commensurate with the injury suffered, taking account of the rights in question',[629] and it held that 'the diversion of the Danube carried out by Czechoslovakia was not a lawful countermeasure because it was not proportionate.'[630] It cited the decision of the Permanent Court in the *River Oder* case regarding the 'perfect equality of all riparian States in the user of the whole course of the river',[631] and found that

> Czechoslovakia, by unilaterally assuming control of a shared resource, and thereby depriving Hungary of its right to an equitable and reasonable share of the natural resources of the Danube . . . failed to respect the proportionality which is required by international law.[632]

[627] Article 49 (2), emphasis added.
[628] [1997] ICJ Rep 222.
[629] [1997] ICJ Rep 56, para 85.
[630] Ibid, para 87.
[631] *Territorial Jurisdiction of the International Commission of the River Oder, Judgment No. 8, 1929*, PCIJ Rep Series A No 23, 27.
[632] [1997] ICJ Rep 56, para 85.

Judge Vereshchetin, dissenting, thought that this was too superficial an approach, and argued for a more detailed point-by-point comparison of the effects of Hungary's breach of the treaty provisions and those of the countermeasures.[633]

A matter which was not specifically mentioned in the Judgment is whether it would have been possible for Czechoslovakia to adopt a different variant of the original Project which would have respected this requirement of riparian proportionality. In view of the technical complication of the case, it may have been impossible to determine this point; but it is suggested that it is one that could in principle be relevant.

One other possible condition for the adoption of countermeasures is mentioned in passing in the Dissenting Opinion of Judge Vereshchetin: that the countermeasure should have been 'the only means available in the circumstances'. As Judge Vereshchetin notes, this was regarded by the International Law Commission as a condition of invocation of a state of necessity;[634] he does not commit himself on the question whether it is also a condition of valid countermeasures, but considered that in the case before the Court there was in fact no other option open to Czechoslovakia.

CHAPTER IV: THE RULE OF EXHAUSTION OF LOCAL REMEDIES

1. A Rule of Substance or of Procedure?

Before comment is made on decisions of the Court in this field handed down since the publication of the previous article in this series,[635] it may be noted that during that period the International Law Commission has completed its Articles on State Responsibility, Article 44 of which refers to the question of the exhaustion of local remedies as a bar to an international claim. It does so however merely by recording that '[t]he responsibility of a State may not be invoked if: . . . (b) the claim is one to which the rule of exhaustion of local remedies applies and any available and effective local remedy has not been exhausted.' In the context of its work on State Responsibility, the ILC ultimately did not see the need to go further into the matter,[636] which was being treated separately in the context of its work on Diplomatic Protection. Commenting on Article 44, the ILC cites

[633] [1997] ICJ Rep 224–225.

[634] Ibid, 220; cf Article 25 (1) *(a)* of the Articles on State Responsibility.

[635] (1995) *BYIL* 80–93.

[636] As noted in the previous article (ibid, 81), Professor Ago as Rapporteur took the view that the rule is substantive, no international legal responsibility arising until remedies have been exhausted without success. However, the draft article he presented giving effect to this view (which was ultimately not retained) was clearly influenced by his theoretical distinction between obligations of conduct and obligations of result, which also did not survive into the final text (see Dugard in A/CN.4/514, 20, para 42; 28, para 54, quoting Borchard; 32, para 66).

the decision in the *ELSI* case (discussed in the previous article in this series), and suggests that the Chamber's definition of the rule of exhaustion of local remedies implied that it viewed that matter as 'being distinct, in principle, from "the merits of the case"',[637] i.e., as a procedural principle. What is clear is that the rule has never been regarded as applicable to direct claims, where the claimant State alleges solely a breach by the respondent State of the claimant State's own rights, as distinct from injury to an individual national of the claimant State.

The Draft Articles on Diplomatic Protection deal with the exhaustion of local remedies in Articles 14 and 15 in terms which again do not specifically resolve the problem of the substantive or procedural nature of the rule. Rapporteur Dugard however examined it in his Second Report, in which he distinguished between cases in which the wrongful act is merely a breach of local law, and contrary to the rules on treatment of aliens, and cases in which the wrongful act is a breach both of local and international law; he included a draft article specifically stating that in the latter case the rule is merely procedural.[638] This article did not however survive into the final text.[639]

The principal reason why the distinction between a procedural rule and a substantive rule in this context may be of more than theoretical interest is its implications for the intertemporal law. As Dugard pointed out in his ILC Report,

> If the rule is substantive, international responsibility will arise only after all local remedies have been exhausted, whereas international responsibility is incurred immediately on the commission of an internationally wrongful act if the rule is procedural.[640]

In the previous article, the present writer noted this point, and commented (in the light of an observation made by the Chamber in the *Elettronica Sicula* case) that, where the matter is one of breach of treaty, a procedural objection could of course be waived by the interested party, but that there might be doubt whether parties could agree in advance to waive a substantive rule.[641]

In the case concerning the *Arrest Warrant of 11 April 2000*, the Democratic Republic of the Congo asserted that the issue and circulation

[637] Crawford, above n 387, 265 (*sub* Article 44, para (4)).

[638] 'The requirement that local remedies must be exhausted is a procedural precondition that must be complied with before a State may bring an international claim based on injury to a national arising out of an internationally wrongful act committed against the national where the act complained of is a breach of both local law and international law.' Draft article 12, A/CN.4/514, 15.

[639] '[W]hile some implications might follow from the adoption of one or another of the theories, and that the question whether such remedies were substantive or procedural in nature was, to some extent, inescapable in special circumstances..., they were not of primary importance and did not justify inclusion of the draft articles in question.' ILC, Report of the 54th Session (2002) A/57/10, 134, para 164.

[640] A/CN.4/514, 16, para 33.

[641] (1995) *BYIL* 84–85, citing C F Amerasinghe, *Local Remedies in International Law*, Cambridge University Press, 1990, 133–137.

by a Belgian judge of a warrant for the arrest of Mr. Yerodia, at the time Foreign Minister of the DRC, was a breach of the customary law rules of the immunity of incumbent foreign ministers. One of the preliminary objections raised by Belgium was that, Mr. Yerodia having subsequently ceased to be Foreign Minister, 'the case has assumed the character of an action of diplomatic protection but one in which the individual being protected has failed to exhaust local remedies'; from this Belgium deduced either lack of jurisdiction or inadmissibility of the claim.[642] In response, the Court considered first that the character of the case, as one concerning a warrant issued against an incumbent foreign minister, had not changed; and secondly, citing the *Interhandel*[643] and *Elettronica Sicula*[644] cases, it recalled that such an objection relates to the admissibility of the application, and 'the critical date for determining the admissibility of an application is the date on which it was filed.'[645] However, since Belgium accepted that on the date of filing of the application 'the Congo had a direct legal interest in the matter, and was asserting a claim in its own name', the rejection of the objection does not seem to support either the procedural or the substantive interpretation.

Two other recent cases[646] before the Court have raised the question of the exhaustion of local remedies in the context of alleged breaches by the United States authorities of the provisions of Article 36 of the Vienna Convention on Consular Relations.[647] Both these cases were of the kind often referred to as 'mixed' cases in which the applicant State claims both by way of diplomatic protection of its national and for alleged direct State-to-State injury; it was cases of this type that would have been the subject of Dugard's draft article defining the rule as procedural. A curiosity of these cases was that at the moment the initial breach of treaty was committed, the national affected was unaware that any wrong had been done, and therefore

[642] [2002] ICJ Rep 16–17, para 37.

[643] [1959] ICJ Rep 26.

[644] [1989] ICJ Rep 42, para 49.

[645] [2002] ICJ Rep 17–18, para 40, second part, citing the *Lockerbie* cases: *Questions of Interpretation and Application of the 1971 Montreal Convention arising from the Aerial Incident at Lockerbie*, [1998] ICJ Rep 25–26, paras 43–44 and 130–131, paras 42–43. The Court does not however mention the decision in the case of *Border and Transborder Armed Actions* between Nicaragua and Honduras, in which the Court stated this rule, but went on to add that 'subsequent events may render an application without object, or even take such a course as to preclude the filing of a later application in similar terms': [1988] ICJ Rep 95, para 96.

[646] A similar case had been brought by Paraguay: case concerning the *Vienna Convention on Consular Relations*, which was discontinued after an Order had been applied for and granted indicating provisional measures: [1998] ICJ Rep 248, 426. In the case of *Certain Property (Liechtenstein v Germany)* non-exhaustion of local remedies was presented as a preliminary objection, and some interesting arguments were presented in the pleadings; but the Court dismissed the case on a different preliminary issue.

[647] Although the problem which gave rise to these cases apparently continues to arise in the United States courts, no further cases are likely to come to the International Court in this connection, as the United States has now withdrawn from the system of compulsory jurisdiction linked to the Vienna Convention: Notification to the UN Secretary-General of 11 March 2005, UN ref. C.N.186.2005. TREATIES-1 (Depositary Notification). See also *Sanchez-Llamas v Oregon*, 548 U.S. 331 (2006).

in no position to seek local remedies: it was the very fact that he was not notified of his rights that constituted the international wrong.

The text at the centre of these disputes was, as noted above, Article 36, paragraph 1, of the Vienna Convention of 1963.[648] The facts of the individual cases differed in details, but essentially the complaint was that the defendants in the US criminal proceedings had not been informed of their rights, nor had the relevant consuls been informed of the criminal proceedings, or not until the criminal process had reached an advanced stage. Breaches had therefore been committed of the Vienna Convention, giving rise to the responsibility of the United States vis-à-vis the governments of the individual defendants, but also (as the Court found) vis-à-vis these defendants themselves.

In the *LaGrand* case, Germany was claiming against the United States both on the basis of the injury done to its nationals and for the direct injury to itself constituted by the breach of the Vienna Convention: the United States had 'violated its international legal obligations to Germany, in its own right and in its right of diplomatic protection of its nationals'.[649] The United States presented a number of preliminary objections, one of which was that

> Germany's first submission, as far as it concerns its right to exercise diplomatic protection with respect to its nationals, is inadmissible on the ground that the LaGrands did not exhaust local remedies. The United States maintains that the alleged breach concerned the duty to inform the LaGrands of their right to consular access, and that such a breach could have been remedied at the trial stage, provided it was raised in a timely fashion.[650]

The key words are these last, since the problem lay in a rule of United States criminal procedure known as the 'procedural default rule', which meant that, broadly stated, a criminal defendant who had not raised an issue in a state court was debarred from raising it later in appeal

[648] 'With a view to facilitating the exercise of consular functions relating to nationals of the sending State:

(a) consular officers shall be free to communicate with nationals of the sending State and to have access to them. Nationals of the sending State shall have the same freedom with respect to communication with and access to consular officers of the sending State;
(b) if he so requests, the competent authorities of the receiving State shall, without delay, inform the consular post of the sending State if, within its consular district, a national of that State is arrested or committed to prison or to custody pending trial or is detained in any other manner. Any communication addressed to the consular post by the person arrested, in prison, custody or detention shall be forwarded by the said authorities without delay. The said authorities shall inform the person concerned without delay of his rights under this subparagraph;
(c) consular officers shall have the right to visit a national of the sending State who is in prison, custody or detention, to converse and correspond with him and to arrange for his legal representation. They shall also have the right to visit any national of the sending State who is in prison, custody or detention in their district in pursuance of a judgement. Nevertheless, consular officers shall refrain from taking action on behalf of a national who is in prison, custody or detention if he expressly opposes such action.'

[649] Final submission (1) of Germany, [2001] ICJ Rep 473–474, para 12.

[650] [2001] ICJ Rep 487, para 58.

proceedings before a federal court,[651] even in a case involving the death penalty. By the time defendants had discovered the possibility of invoking consular assistance, it was too late.

The Court's ruling on the preliminary objection was as follows:

> The Court notes that it is not disputed that the LaGrands sought to plead the Vienna Convention in United States courts after they learned in 1992 of their rights under the Convention; it is also not disputed that by that date the procedural default rule barred the LaGrands from obtaining any remedy in respect of the violation of those rights. Counsel assigned to the LaGrands failed to raise this point earlier in a timely fashion. However, the United States may not now rely before this Court on this fact in order to preclude the admissibility of Germany's first submission, as it was the United States itself which had failed to carry out its obligation under the Convention to inform the LaGrand brothers.[652]

It was apparently taken for granted that the rule of exhaustion of local remedies would not have applied if the applicant State had been asserting solely a breach of its own rights;[653] the point was made clearly in the subsequent *Avena* case (see below). It is however noteworthy that the Court dealt with, and dismissed, the objection based on failure to exhaust local remedies at a stage in its judgment before it had decided whether or not Germany's claim based on diplomatic protection of its nationals was maintainable under the Vienna Convention; the United States had argued that 'rights of consular notification and access under the Vienna Convention are rights of States and not of individuals'.[654] Had this argument been upheld by the Court, the local remedies rule would presumably in any event have had no application unless that rule could also apply to a claim of direct State-to-State injury.

In the second, the case of *Avena and Other Mexican Nationals*, the Court appears to have taken the view that the local remedies rule is one of substance. It was alleged that in a number of criminal cases before the United States courts involving defendants of Mexican nationality, the authorities had failed to comply with the obligation imposed by that Article to inform the defendant of his right to consular assistance and to

[651] For the explanation of the rule given to the Court by the US Government, see [2001] ICJ Rep 477, para 23.

[652] [2001] ICJ Rep 488, para 60. The logic of the last sentence is unclear: presumably what is meant is that since, through the fault of the United States, the brothers did not know that they could have consular assistance, they cannot be blamed for failing to raise the matter timeously. If so, it does not seem to resolve the question whether they (or their counsel) should have acted more promptly once they *were* aware of their rights, or whether the application of the procedural default rule either constituted a separate breach of obligation by the United States, or at least signified the exhaustion of available remedies.

[653] Counsel for the US did recognize that 'diplomatic protection and any individual rights are indeed subject to the exhaustion of local remedies', without referring to direct claims: CR 2000/31, 16, para 3.7.

[654] [2001] ICJ Rep 493, para 76.

notify the relevant consulate. The Court began its consideration of the point as follows:

The Court would first observe that the individual rights of Mexican nationals under paragraph 1 *(b)* of Article 36 or the Vienna Convention are rights which are to be asserted, at any rate in the first place, within the domestic legal system of the United States. Only when that process is completed and local remedies are exhausted would Mexico be entitled to espouse the individual claims of its nationals through the procedure of diplomatic protection.[655]

The indication in the second sentence that there is no *entitlement*, as a matter of international law, to exercise diplomatic protection, appears to point to the rule being more than one of procedure. The Court however continued:

In the present case Mexico does not, however, claim to be acting solely on that basis. It also asserts its own claims, basing them on the injury which it contends that *it has itself suffered, directly and through its national*s a result of the violation by the United States of the obligations incumbent upon it under Article 36, paragraph 1 *(a)*, *(b)* and *(c)*. The Court would recall that, in the *LaGrand* case, it recognized that "Article 36, paragraph 1 [of the Vienna Convention], creates individual rights [for the national concerned], which . . . may be invoked in this Court by the national State of the detained person" (*I.C.J. Reports 2001, p.* 494, para 77). It would further observe that violations of the rights of the individual under Article 36 may entail a violation of the rights of the sending State, and that violations of the rights of the latter may entail a violation of the rights of the individual. In these special circumstances of interdependence of the rights of the State and of individual rights, Mexico may, in submitting a claim in its own name, request the Court to rule on the violation of rights which it claims to have suffered both directly and through the violation of individual rights conferred on Mexican nationals under Article 36, paragraph 1 *(b)*. The duty to exhaust local remedies does not apply to such a request.[656]

Since in the Court's view the two heads of claim were so intertwined that it did 'not find it necessary to deal with Mexico's claims of violation under a distinct heading of diplomatic protection', the objection to admissibility could simply be dismissed.[657] Thus the Court did not find, in what appeared to be a characteristic 'mixed' claim,[658] that the local remedies rule applied as a mere procedural rule; it apparently did not apply at all.

655 [2004] ICJ Rep 35, para 40.

656 [2004] ICJ Rep 35–36, para 40 (emphasis original).

657 Ibid.

658 Whether a claim is direct State-to-State, diplomatic protection, or 'mixed' may not always be a simple question. In the *Certain Property* case (Liechtenstein *v* Germany), Liechtenstein contended that its claim was purely for breach of neutrality and of its sovereignty (Liechtenstein Memorial, para 7.20), but Germany advanced the local remedies rule as an objection, on the basis that the claim was, at least partly, an exercise of diplomatic protection. The Court found it unnecessary to determine the point: Judge *ad hoc* Berman seems to have read it as a State-to-State case (Dissenting Opinion, [2005] ICJ Rep 71, para 4), while Judge Kooijmans was clear that it was a 'mixed' case (Dissenting Opinion, ibid, 39, para 41).

The problem however arose in these recent cases in slightly unusual contexts. The classic pattern is that the national of a complainant State has allegedly been injured by the defendant State, has suffered some physical or financial damage; and the claim on his behalf is then met with the response that relief was available to him in the courts (or by administrative remedies), and he has not availed himself of these possibilities of redress. In the *Arrest Warrant* case, the question of local remedies was something of a red herring: the fact that Mr. Yerodia might have been able to have the warrant set aside (for example, on the ground that he was not present in Belgium)[659] had nothing to do with the complaint before the Court, which was that no warrant should have been issued against an incumbent foreign minister; and that was not something that could be cured by local remedies, since the complaint invoking the status of foreign minister was not one of diplomatic protection, so that the local remedies rule had no application.[660] The Court correctly noted that the fact that Mr. Yerodia had ceased to be Foreign Minister did not change the character of the dispute as a State-to-State dispute,[661] so that the local remedies rule did not apply; by then raising the intertemporal point, as explained above, it merely confused this issue.

In the cases concerning the Vienna Convention on Diplomatic Relations, the Court noted that the Convention itself conferred on the nationals of a State party to it the rights stipulated in Article 35; and these were thus not mere rights of domestic law—in fact, they might not be recognized in domestic law, but their infringement would still be a breach of international law. In response to an objection by the United States that 'rights of consular notification and access under the Vienna Convention are rights of States, and not of individuals',[662] the Court noted that Article 36, paragraph 1 *(b)*, provided for notification 'without delay' to the consular post of the sending State of the fact of detention of the national and transmission of any communication from him to the consular post. It continued:

> Significantly, this subparagraph ends with the following language: "The said authorities shall inform the person concerned without delay of *his rights* under this subparagraph" (emphasis added). Moreover, under Article 36, paragraph 1 *(c)*, the sending State's right to provide consular assistance to the detained person may not be exercised "if he expressly opposes such action". The clarity of these provisions, viewed in their context, admits of no doubt. It follows, as has been held on a number of occasions, that the Court must apply these as they stand [references omitted]. Based on the text of these provisions, the Court concludes that Article

[659] See the discussion in the Belgian Counter-Memorial, paras 2.64–2.71.

[660] When Bulgaria invoked non-exhaustion of local remedies in the case of the *Aerial Incident of 27 July 1955*, counsel for Israel (Rosenne) pointed out that this implied that, for Bulgaria, shooting down a foreign aircraft was not itself a violation of international law: *ICJ Pleadings*, 521.

[661] [2002] ICJ Rep 17, para 40 (first part).

[662] [2001] ICJ Rep 493, para 76.

36, paragraph 1, creates individual rights, which, by virtue of Article 1 of the Optional Protocol, may be invoked in this Court by the national State of the detained person. These rights were violated in the present case.[663]

The rights violated were thus rights conferred by treaty, not on the State as party to the treaty, but on its nationals. The 'classic' cases of diplomatic protection, however, involve responsibility of the respondent State under the heading of customary international law referred to as the treatment of aliens.[664] This field includes such matters as denial of justice and expropriation, but does not constitute an orderly system of customary rules: in this respect '[i]nternational law is not a system replete with nominate torts or delicts, but the rules are specialized in certain respects.'[665] In this context, it is of course well established that 'by taking up the case of one of its subjects and by resorting to diplomatic action or international judicial proceedings on his behalf, a State is in reality asserting its own rights—its right to ensure, in the person of its subjects, respect for the rules of international law.'[666]

The exact nature of the right or interest vested in the national who is being protected, viewed from the level of international law, is therefore obscure: since, at least in the classic period, he was unable to implement or enforce his right at the international level except through the intervention of his national State, the point was academic. In the leading case of the *Mavrommatis Palestine Concessions*, the Permanent Court noted that since a State undertaking diplomatic protection is exercising its own right, it is irrelevant that the dispute 'originates in an injury to a private interest'—not 'a private right'—and adds that this 'in point of fact is the case in many international disputes'.[667] Recent cases before the Court have however apparently demonstrated that the national injured may in fact be recognized by international law as enjoying a right of his own, conferred by a treaty.[668]

[663] Ibid, 494, para 77. The argument based on the term 'his rights' was put forward by counsel for Germany: CR 2000/26, 57, para 3 (Simma). The contention of Germany was however that the right of the individual under Article 36 was, or had developed into, a human right (ibid, 59, para 7 et seq); the Court found it unnecessary to consider this argument; [2001] ICJ Rep 494, para 78.

[664] Cf the commentary to the ILC Draft Articles on Diplomatic Protection, explaining that the primary rules in that field are not the subject of the Articles, those being confined to the secondary rules: (2006) *Report of the Commission of the 58th Session*, A/61/10, 22–23.

[665] Brownlie, above n 38, 506. In 1995 the same author was of the view that '[i]n strict analytical terms, it still cannot be said that the individual *per se* is a subject of international law': 'International Law at the Fiftieth Anniversary of the United Nations' (1995) 255 *Recueil des Cours* 62.

[666] *Mavrommatis Palestine Concessions,* PCIJ Rep Series A No 2, 12. This doctrine has been condemned as 'insufficiently penetrating' and as 'a survival of the nineteenth century thesis of a world composed of absolute sovereignties unwilling to limit their freedom of action except in their own interests': D P O'Connell, *International Law* (Stevens, London 1970), Vol. II, 1030.

[667] *Mavrommatis Palestine Concessions,* PCIJ Rep Series A No 2, 12. This characteristic is particularly marked in the *Mavrommatis* case, because (as explained by the British judge Lord Finlay in his dissenting opinion) there was no real dispute between the two Governments, the Greek Government obligingly taking up the claim at a very late stage so that it could be submitted to the Court: ibid, 40.

[668] Treaties of this kind, or which may have this effect, are increasingly common in modern international relations: cf *Oppenheim's International Law*, above n 42, 909–910.

This is of course not a wholly new phenomenon. In the *Chorzów Factory* case, the beneficiaries of the claim before the Permanent Court were nationals of the claimant State, but that claim was not expressed as one of diplomatic protection, but as one of breach of treaty.[669] It was however, in that case, the that Permanent Court made the well-known observation that

[t]he rules of law governing the reparation are the rules of international law in force between the two States concerned, and not the law governing relations between the State which has committed an unlawful act and the individual who has suffered damage. Rights or interests of an individual the violation of which rights causes damage are always in a different plane to rights belonging to a State, which rights may also be infringed by the same act. The damage suffered by an individual is never therefore identical in kind with that which will be suffered by a State; it can only afford a convenient scale for the calculation of the reparation due to the State.[670]

The Court therefore recognized that the individuals had, or could have, 'rights', but does not spell out whether these were rights under national law, but which could be protected internationally, or rights conferred by international law but which could only be enforced by State action. They were rights created by treaty; yet in the case of *Jurisdiction of the Courts of Danzig*, the Court stated as 'a well established principle of international law' that the instrument before it, 'being an international agreement, cannot, as such, create direct rights and obligations for private individuals',[671] which rather points to the latter analysis.

A tentative conclusion which may perhaps be drawn is that a 'mixed' claim will arise, or at least is highly likely to arise, when the injury to the national is not constituted simply by a breach of the customary law rules concerning treatment of aliens, but by a breach of a treaty that recognizes the individual national as holder of a right susceptible of being prejudiced by action of another State. In such a situation, the national State of the person injured will almost certainly be injured in its own rights under the treaty; it is difficult to see how it could be otherwise. Since the act causing injury is one and the same, the rule of exhaustion of local remedies cannot be applied in respect of the one claim but not of the other.

[669] Article 6 of the Geneva Convention of 15 May 1922 between Germany and Poland provided that Poland was entitled to carry out certain expropriations in Polish Upper Silesia, but that subject thereto, 'the property, rights and interests of German nationals or of companies controlled by German nationals may not be liquidated in Polish Upper Silesia': PCIJ Rep Series A No 6, 16.

[670] PCIJ Rep Series A No 17, 28; cited by Judge Lauterpacht in his opinion in the *Interhandel* case, [1959] ICJ Rep 120.

[671] PCIJ Rep Series B No 15, 17. For an analysis of the breach made in this principle by the development of human rights law, cf Prosper Weil, 'Le droit international en quête de son identité' (1992-VI) 237 *Recueil des cours* 118 et seq.

2. The Case of an Alleged Breach of State Rights

This heading is maintained primarily for consistency with the earlier article in this series, the matters then discussed under it having been examined above in section 1. It is however a convenient point to note the implications of the Court's decision, in the case of *Armed Activities on the Territory of the Congo*, to apply the requirement of exhaustion of local remedies to part of Uganda's claim arising out of the incidents at Ndjili International Airport in August 1998. Uganda claimed that members of its diplomatic staff had been maltreated both when its Embassy was attacked and subsequently when they were at the Airport endeavouring to leave the country. On both occasions persons without diplomatic status (and whose nationality was not proved) were also mishandled by Congolese troops. The DRC invoked the rule of exhaustion of local remedies as barring these claims. So far as the diplomats were concerned, the Court held that it had no application, since this was a claim of breach of Article 29 of the Vienna Convention on Diplomatic Relations, and Uganda was 'not exercising diplomatic protection on behalf of the victims but vindicating its own rights' under that Convention.[672] Similarly, as regards the non-diplomats caught up in the attack on the Embassy, this claim fell 'within the ambit of Article 22 of the Vienna Convention', so that it was not excluded by the local remedies rule. There remained the case of the non-diplomats caught up in the attack at the Airport; the Court regarded this as a claim to diplomatic protection, thus involving 'the requirement of Ugandan nationality of the claimants and the prior exhaustion of local remedies'.[673] The concept of a mixed claim can apparently not be carried so far as to enable a diplomatic protection claim simply to ride on the back of a direct claim, so to speak, so as to exclude the local remedies rule, even when the injury was caused on the same occasion by the same persons and as part of the same pattern of events.[674]

3. The Nature of the Municipal Claim and the Burden of Proof

Under this heading in the previous article in this series[675] the question examined was primarily one that arose in the *Elettronica Sicula* case: does the rule of exhaustion of local remedies require the injured national not merely to employ such remedies as are afforded by municipal law but also to invoke

[672] [2005] ICJ Rep 275–276, para 330.

[673] Ibid, 276, para 333. It seems unlikely that the existence of any appropriate remedies could have been shown, but the nationality point was determinative. For the criticism of this finding by Judge Simma in his separate opinion, see above, Chapter II, section 2, text and nn 436–439.

[674] Contrast the fate of the two non-diplomats present in the United States Embassy at the time of the attack by militants giving rise to the case of *United States Diplomatic and Consular Staff in Tehran*. The United States claim in respect of these individuals was accepted, both as a matter of substantive law and for jurisdictional purposes, on the basis of a Treaty of Amity between the two States: [1980] ICJ Rep 36, para 77.

[675] (1995) *BYIL* 91–93.

such provisions of international law as may have the potential to afford relief? The question arose in relation to provisions of the treaties in force between Italy and the United States which had allegedly been breached by the treatment given to the Elettronica Sicula company. In the *LaGrand* and *Avena* cases, the parallel would have been if the German or Mexican nationals had invoked, or could be expected to have invoked, the provisions of the Vienna Convention before the United States courts, not merely as conferring the rights to consular notification and assistance but as justifying non-application of the 'procedural default' rule. The point was not in fact argued directly in either case; in the *LaGrand* case, the question whether US law would have permitted reliance on the Convention itself at the municipal level was not raised. In the *Avena* case, Mexico explained that

> the courts of the United States have never granted a judicial remedy to any foreign national for a violation of Article 36. The United States courts hold either that Article 36 does not create an individual right, or that a foreign national who has been denied his Article 36 rights but given his constitutional and statutory rights, cannot establish prejudice and therefore cannot get relief.[676]

The Court observed in this respect that

> the individual rights of Mexican nationals under paragraph 1 *(b)* of Article 36 of the Vienna Convention are rights which are to be asserted, at any rate in the first place, within the domestic legal system of the United States.[677]

This finding is not specific on the question whether 'within the domestic legal system' is merely a procedural indication, or a reference to the law to be invoked. However, Mexico also claimed that 'the United States violated its obligations under Article 36 (2) of the Vienna Convention by failing to provide meaningful and effective review and reconsideration of convictions and sentences impaired by a violation of Article 36 (1)'.[678] In this connection, the Court found that

> [i]t...remains the case that the procedural default rule may continue to prevent courts from attaching legal significance to the fact, *inter alia,* that the violation of the rights set forth in Article 36, paragraph 1, prevented Mexico, in a timely fashion, from retaining private counsel for certain nationals and otherwise assisting in their defence. In such cases, application of the procedural default rule would have the effect of preventing "full effect [from being] given to the purposes for which the rights accorded under this article are intended", and thus violate paragraph 2 of Article 36.[679]

The situation would appear to be thus that there was no possibility for the arrested national to invoke the Vienna Convention itself as a justification for asking the United States courts to waive or set aside the 'procedural default' rule.

676 [2004] ICJ Rep 35, para 39. 677 Ibid, para 40.
678 Ibid, 55, para 107. 679 Ibid, 57, para 113.

It may also be observed that in each of the cases discussed above concerning the Vienna Convention on Consular Relations, the claim was both that the individual criminal defendant had not been informed of his rights, and that the local consular post had not been informed. The second of these breaches would appear to be a direct infringement of the rights of the sending State, even though it adversely affected the rights of the individual national; probably therefore the local remedies rule would not apply to this breach of the Convention taken in isolation. If one concentrates on the rights of the defendants to be informed of their rights, and sets aside (as irrelevant in the context of the local remedies rule) the right of their national State to be informed through its consular post, a simpler approach, based on an alternative analysis of the legal situation, might be as follows. The injury to the German/Mexican nationals was the failure by the United States authorities to inform them of their right to consular assistance, i.e. a breach of the last sentence of Article 36 (1) *(b)*. It is difficult to see what remedy could, at that stage, have been available in this respect. If a wrongful act were committed by the authorities of a State against a foreign national without his knowledge—if, say, his property were expropriated without his having been notified—administrative or judicial remedies might well exist that he could use, provided, or so soon as, he became aware of their existence. But how could a remedy exist against a failure to inform the foreign national of his rights, unless he were, at that time, somehow aware that he had not been made aware of them? The argument of the United States was addressed to the question of remedies in respect of a failure to *make available* consular assistance, in effect a breach of Article 36 (1) *(c)*. In relation to the original failure of notification these are not in point: no remedy could exist for the failure to notify, and therefore there could be no failure to exhaust such a remedy. On this basis, the Court's invocation, as a basis for rejection of the argument that remedies were not exhausted, of the failure of the United States to inform the defendants of their rights, begins to resemble something of a circular argument.

CHAPTER V: REPARATION AND RESTITUTION

1. The Causal Relationship Required for Reparation

In two recent cases, that of the *Gabčikovo-Nagymaros Project* and that of *Application of the Genocide Convention* between Bosnia and Herzegovina and the FRY (Serbia), the Court had occasion to consider closely the question of the relationship between an internationally wrongful act and the appropriate means of reparation for that act,[680] and in the second of

[680] In this connection see also Chapter II, Sections 4 and 5, above.

those cases for the first time against the background of the definitive Articles on State Responsibility prepared by the International Law Commission. As the Court noted in the *LaGrand* and *Avena* cases, 'where jurisdiction exists over a dispute on a particular matter, no separate basis for jurisdiction is required by the Court in order to consider the remedies a party has requested for breach of the obligation.'[681] In many recent cases however either no question of responsibility and of reparation arose at all (for example, in the numerous cases of maritime delimitation), or the claim was dismissed on the merits or on a preliminary objection, or the question of reparation was reserved for a later stage of the proceedings, either at the instance of the successful Applicant, or by decision of the Court,[682] and that stage was not in fact reached. In some cases, a finding of responsibility was itself treated as sufficient reparation.[683] As for the *LaGrand* and *Avena* cases, the reparation found appropriate fell within the broad category of cessation of wrongful conduct and guarantees of non-repetition, dealt with below.

In addition, in the context of advisory proceedings in which the Court was asked to state the 'legal consequences' of a particular action by a State, the Court, having found that that action was unlawful and engaged the responsibility of the State, proceeded to indicate its views as to reparation.[684]

The Special Agreement in the case of the *Gabčíkovo-Nagymaros Project* did not request the Court to deal with reparation as such, but to determine the 'legal consequences, including the rights and obligations of the Parties, arising from its Judgment' on the questions referred to it,[685] which were questions of the legality, or legal effects, of actions taken by each of the parties in relation to the Project. The Court in fact found that each of the parties had committed, in relation to the 1977 Treaty concerning the Project, internationally wrongful acts against the other, and on the basis of this provision in the Special Agreement it considered the 'legal consequences' of those acts.[686] The Court began its examination of the question of reparation with a general restatement of 'the principle governing the determination of reparation for an internationally wrongful act... as stated by the Permanent Court of International Justice in the *Factory at Chorzów* case: "reparation must, so far as possible, wipe out all the consequences of the illegal act and reestablish the situation which would, in all

[681] [2001] ICJ Rep 485; [2004] ICJ Rep 33.

[682] E.g. *Military and Paramilitary Activities in and against Nicaragua* [1986] ICJ Rep 143, para 285 and 149, para 292 (14) and (15); *Armed Activities on the Territory of the Congo (Congo v Uganda)* [2005] ICJ Rep 279, para 344, and 282, para 345 (13) and (14).

[683] E.g. *Certain Questions of Mutual Assistance in Criminal Matters*, Judgment of 4 June 2008, paras 203–204 and 205 (2) *(a)*.

[684] *Legal Consequences of the Construction of a Wall in the Occupied Palestinian Territory*, [2004] ICJ Rep 197–198, paras 149–153.

[685] See [1997] ICJ Rep 11–12 (Article 2 of the Special Agreement).

[686] [1997] ICJ Rep 80, para 148.

probability, have existed if that act had not been committed."'[687] The background to the Court's findings in this respect was that it had held, contrary to the contentions of both parties, that the 1977 Treaty establishing the Project was still in force, despite breaches on both sides, and that it was for the parties rather than the Court to negotiate on that basis and work out their destiny in this respect.[688] However, while, as the Court noted, it had not been asked to determine the quantum of damages due on either side, it had been asked 'by both Parties to determine the consequences of the Judgment as they bear upon the payment of damages'.[689] The Court did not however offer much guidance beyond re-stating the principle that 'an injured State is entitled to obtain compensation from the State which has committed an internationally wrongful act for the damage caused by it', and identifying acts on each side that had caused damage to the other party.[690] It directed that the compensation be paid by each State to the other 'unless the Parties otherwise agree'.[691] Earlier in the judgment it had however observed that,

> [g]iven the fact that there have been intersecting wrongs by both Parties, ... the issue of compensation could satisfactorily be resolved in the framework of an overall settlement if each of the Parties were to renounce or cancel all financial claims and counter-claims.[692]

In the first *Genocide Convention* case, the Court's decisions on the various heads of claim involved the possibility of ordering reparation on only three grounds: on the basis of the finding that Serbia had violated the obligation to prevent genocide; on the basis of the finding that Serbia had violated its obligations under the Genocide Convention by having failed to transfer Ratko Mladić to the ICTY; and on the basis of the finding of failure to comply with the provisional measures ordered by the Court. As in the *Gabčikovo-Nagymaros* case, the Court began by citing the *Factory at Chorzów* case, and referred also to Article 31 of the ILC's Articles on State Responsibility.[693] There is however a difficulty in applying the *Chorzów* dictum to the situation where the act in question was negative, was a failure to act rather than the taking of action, *in casu* a failure to prevent an act of genocide. The Court had explained at an earlier stage of its judgment that the obligation under the Convention to prevent genocide

> is one of conduct and not one of result, in the sense that a State cannot be under an obligation to succeed, whatever the circumstances, in preventing the commission of genocide: the obligation of States parties is rather to employ all means

[687] PCIJ Rep Series A No 17, 47, quoted at ibid, paras 149–150.
[688] [1997] ICJ Rep 78, para 14.
[689] Ibid, 81, para 151.
[690] Ibid, para 152.
[691] Ibid, 83, para 155 (2) D (operative part).
[692] Ibid, 81, para 153.
[693] [2007-II] ICJ Rep 232–233, para 460.

reasonably available to them, so as to prevent genocide so far as possible. A State does not incur responsibility simply because the desired result is not achieved; responsibility is however incurred if the State manifestly failed to take all measures to prevent genocide which were within its power, and which might have contributed to preventing the genocide. In this area the notion of "due diligence", which calls for an assessment *in concreto*, is of critical importance.[694]

Since what is involved is a failure to act, the dictum of the Permanent Court must apparently be read by inversion: reparation should reestablish the situation if the respondent State had acted when it should have done. But what if it is shown that, even if the State had acted when it should have done, and in the way that it should have done, the same factual outcome would have resulted? This was what Serbia contended on the facts. To put the matter simply: is reparation owed for a result which the respondent State could not have prevented, whatever it did? On the other hand, should a State escape liability for reparation for a breach of an obligation to act merely because, although it did not and could not know it in advance, its action would not have prevented the injury? The Court distinguished, correctly, it is submitted, between the elements constituting the wrongful act and the liability to make reparation.

[I]t is irrelevant whether the State whose responsibility is in issue claims, or even proves, that even if it had employed all means reasonably at its disposal, they would not have sufficed to prevent the commission of genocide. As well as being generally difficult to prove, this is irrelevant to the breach of the obligation of conduct in question, the more so since the possibility remains that the combined efforts of several States, each complying with its obligation to prevent, might have achieved the result—averting the commission of genocide—which the efforts of only one State were insufficient to produce.[695]

Serbia was therefore in breach of its obligation in this respect; but was it bound to make restitution? The injury suffered was of a kind where restitution in the strict sense was simply not possible: no-one could bring back to life the victims of the genocide committed. There remained however the possibility of reparation or compensation.

In the circumstances of this case, as the Applicant recognizes, it is inappropriate to ask the Court to find that the Respondent is under an obligation of *restitutio in integrum*. Insofar as restitution is not possible, as the Court stated in the case of the *Gabčíkovo-Nagymaros Project (Hungary/Slovakia)*, "[i]t is a well-established rule of international law that an injured State is entitled to obtain compensation from the State which has committed an internationally wrongful act for the damage caused by it" (*I.C.J. Reports 1997*, p. 81, para 152; cf. *Legal Consequences of the Construction of a Wall in the Occupied Palestinian Territory, Advisory Opinion,*

[694] Ibid, 221, para 430. [695] Ibid.

I.C.J. Reports 2004, p. 198, paras. 152–153; see also Article 36 of the ILC's Articles on State Responsibility). It is therefore appropriate to consider what were the consequences of the failure of the Respondent to comply with its obligations under the Genocide Convention to prevent and punish the crime of genocide, committed in Bosnia and Herzegovina, and what damage can be said to have been caused thereby.[696]

There was still the problem of causality: if the genocide would have taken place anyway, whether or not the Serbian authorities had acted as they were required to do, was the damage suffered the result of their inaction? The Court considered that it was not called upon to ascertain whether this link of causality had been established.

The obligation to prevent the commission of the crime of genocide is imposed by the Genocide Convention on any State party which, in a given situation, has it in its power to contribute to restraining in any degree the commission of genocide. To make this finding, the Court did not have to decide whether the acts of genocide committed at Srebrenica would have occurred anyway even if the Respondent had done as it should have and employed the means available to it. This is because, as explained above, the obligation to prevent genocide places a State under a duty to act which is not dependent on the certainty that the action to be taken will succeed in preventing the commission of acts of genocide, or even on the likelihood of that outcome. It therefore does not follow from the Court's reasoning above in finding a violation by the Respondent of its obligation of prevention that the atrocious suffering caused by the genocide committed at Srebrenica would not have occurred had the violation not taken place.[697]

At this point, therefore, the Court appears to be moving towards a finding that since the inaction by the Serbian authorities had contributed to the commission of genocide, Serbia had not only committed a breach of its legal obligations, but was bound to make full reparation for the injury suffered, even though it could not be excluded that even if it had taken all measures in its power the tragic outcome would have been the same. The Court however did not consider that it could 'leave it at that':

Since it now has to rule on the claim for reparation, it must ascertain whether, and to what extent, the injury asserted by the Applicant is the consequence of wrongful conduct by the Respondent with the consequence that the Respondent should be required to make reparation for it, in accordance with the principle of customary international law stated above. In this context, the question just mentioned, whether the genocide at Srebrenica would have taken place even if the Respondent had attempted to prevent it by employing all means in its possession, becomes directly relevant, for the definition of the extent of the obligation of reparation borne by the Respondent as a result of its wrongful conduct. The question is

[696] [2007-II] ICJ Rep 232–233, para 460.
[697] Ibid, para 461.

whether there is a sufficiently direct and certain causal nexus between the wrongful act, the Respondent's breach of the obligation to prevent genocide, and the injury suffered by the Applicant, consisting of all damage of any type, material or moral, caused by the acts of genocide. Such a nexus could be considered established only if the Court were able to conclude from the case as a whole and with a sufficient degree of certainty that the genocide at Srebrenica would in fact have been averted if the Respondent had acted in compliance with its legal obligations.[698]

The causal nexus is of course an essential element of the system of the ILC's Articles on State Responsibility, Article 31 (1) of which states that '[t]he responsible State is under an obligation to make full reparation for the injury *caused by* the wrongful act.'

The Court therefore returns to the question which it had, at the earlier stage, left open: would the action required of Serbia by its legal obligations, if it had been carried out, have been effective in preventing the genocide (or minimizing its impact)? It held that it could not reach this conclusion.

As noted above, the Respondent did have significant means of influencing the Bosnian Serb military and political authorities which it could, and therefore should, have employed in an attempt to prevent the atrocities, but it has not been shown that, in the specific context of these events, those means would have sufficed to achieve the result which the Respondent should have sought. Since the Court cannot therefore regard as proven a causal nexus between the Respondent's violation of its obligation of prevention and the damage resulting from the genocide at Srebrenica, financial compensation is not the appropriate form of reparation for the breach of the obligation to prevent genocide.[699]

This did not mean that Bosnia was left without any satisfaction whatsoever:

It is however clear that the Applicant is entitled to reparation in the form of satisfaction, and this may take the most appropriate form, as the Applicant itself suggested, of a declaration in the present Judgment that the Respondent has failed to comply with the obligation imposed by the Convention to prevent the crime of genocide.[700]

Attention is drawn to the careful finding by the Court, not that action by the Serbian authorities *would not* have made any difference, but that it had not been proved that it would. It is a well-known saying that 'What has hit is history; what had missed is mystery': it is always possible in theory that urgent representations from Belgrade might have tipped the scale, but in the absence of evidence no conclusion could be reached, and the maxim as to the onus of proof operated to enable the Court to make a decision.

The Court did not find that there had been no injury to Bosnia (since such a conclusion would have been absurd), but it found that there was no causal nexus between the internationally wrongful act of Serbia and the

[698] Ibid, para 462. [699] Ibid.
[700] Ibid, para 463, citing the *Corfu Channel* case, [1949] ICJ Rep 35–36.

injury suffered. The decision might thus be read as signifying that, at least as regards the specific obligation to prevent genocide, damage—in the sense of damage attributable to the wrongful act—is not a prerequisite for categorizing the act as unlawful. There is, it seems, no general rule in international law determining whether *iniuria* can exist without *damnum* (though *damnum sine iniuria* would seem to be recognized). The general approach of the ILC has of course been that, in respect of the application of any particular primary rule of conduct, whether damage suffered is a condition for establishing breach of the obligation imposed by the rule is a question to be determined by that primary rule.[701] There is here something of a paradox, however: there is presumably no breach of an obligation to prevent something happening if that something does not in fact happen, so in that sense, the existence of an injury is relevant to the determination of responsibility.

The request to the Court to indicate the *Legal Consequences of the Construction of a Wall in the Occupied Palestinian Territory* being a request for an Advisory Opinion, the Court was not required to consider the particular claim of a party for reparation. It found that

> [s]ince the Court has concluded that the construction of the wall in the Occupied Palestinian Territory, including in and around East Jerusalem, and its associated régime, are contrary to various of Israel's international obligations, it follows that the responsibility of that State is engaged under international law[702]

but did not at that stage consider in relation to whom such responsibility was engaged. It next dealt with the 'obligation to respect the rights of the Palestinian people to self-determination' and Israel's 'obligations under international humanitarian law and international human rights law',[703] before turning to more concrete matters.

> [G]iven that the construction of the wall in the Occupied Palestinian Territory has, *inter alia,* entailed the requisition and destruction of homes, businesses and agricultural holdings, the Court finds further that Israel has the obligation to make reparation for the damage caused to all the natural or legal persons concerned.[704]

Israel is accordingly under an obligation to return the land, orchards, olive groves and other immovable property seized from any natural or legal person for purposes of construction of the wall in the Occupied Palestinian Territory. In the event that such restitution should prove to be materially impossible, Israel has an obligation to compensate the persons in question for the damage suffered. The Court considers that Israel also has an obligation to compensate, in accordance

[701] This resolved the controversial question whether the mere enactment of legislation in conflict with the State's international obligations would amount to a breach of those obligations, or whether only the implementation of the legislation, to the detriment of another State or of its citizens, would have that effect. See Crawford, above n 387, 12–13, 84, 203.

[702] [2004] ICJ Rep 197, para 149.

[703] Ibid, para 150.

[704] [2004] ICJ Rep 198, para 152.

with the applicable rules of international law, all natural or legal persons having suffered any form of material damage as a result of the wall's construction.[705]

Which are, however, 'the applicable rules of international law'? The Court quotes the dictum in the *Factory at Chorzów* case[706] in support of its finding; in that case however it was made clear in the Court's judgment that the compensation ordered was due, not to the German companies injured, but to the German Government, both in view of the principle that an international tribunal, 'in principle has cognizance only of interstate relations', and because the claim was based on alleged breaches of an international convention.[707] Since in the *Palestine Wall* case the finding was not made in response to the claim of a party, the Court did not examine at this point the question of the precise nature and beneficiary of the obligation breached, and of the duty of reparation. Is this a case impliedly of diplomatic protection, whereby Palestine might claim on behalf of its nationals? In an earlier paragraph the Court had indicated that

it appears that the construction of the wall has led to the destruction or requisition of properties under conditions which contravene the requirements of Articles 46 and 52 of the Hague Regulations of 1907 and of Article 53 of the Fourth Geneva Convention.[708]

Does a breach of these international instruments open a direct right for the individuals dispossessed to compensation? Later in the Opinion it stated that

[t]he wall, along the route chosen, and its associated régime gravely infringe a number of rights of Palestinians residing in the territory occupied by Israel, and the infringements resulting from that route cannot be justified by military exigencies or by the requirements of national security or public order. The construction of such a wall accordingly constitutes breaches by Israel of various of its obligations under the applicable international humanitarian law and human rights instruments.[709]

Was the Court then finding that the compensation for lost immovable property was based on breaches of human rights conventions? It is difficult to arrive at a clear picture of the Court's thinking in this part of its Opinion; but it is evident that the approach adopted is, as one commentator has tactfully observed, 'far from classical'.[710]

[705] Ibid, para 153. In his Dissenting Opinion, Judge Buergenthal pointed out that Israel's contention had been that there had been 'no change in ownership of the land', and that compensation was available for use of land and for damage; this contention had, Judge Buergenthal suggested, been ignored by the Court ([2004] ICJ Rep 244, para 8), a course of action which would have been less likely in contentious proceedings.

[706] PCIJ Rep Series A No 17, 47.

[707] Ibid, 27.

[708] [2004] ICJ Rep 189, para 132.

[709] Ibid, para 137.

[710] Pierre d'Argent, 'The Wall Advisory Opinion of the ICJ', in P-M Dupuy (ed), *Völkerrecht als Weltordnung, Festschrift für Christian Tomuschat* (Kehl, Engel, 2006) 463, 473, drawing attention to a survey of practice in A Randelzhofer and C Tomuschat, *State Responsibility and the Individual: Reparation in Instances of Grave Violations of Human Rights* (1999).

2. Restitution or Compensation: Has the Wrongdoer a Choice?

The ILC Articles on State Responsibility indicate restitution as the first-named form of reparation for injury resulting from an unlawful act. At an earlier stage of the work of the ILC, it was presented specifically as the primary form of reparation, and the text was so worded as to suggest that the choice between restitution and compensation was open solely to the claimant State.[711] Thus it may be asked whether, if the breach of an international obligation is established, it is open to the peccant State to avoid specific reparation in the form of *restitutio in integrum*, simply by the payment of adequate financial compensation?[712] In principle, it would seem that it should not be open to a respondent State, without the consent of the injured State, to buy an entitlement to infringe the rights of that State. This view is supported by the approach of the Court in its Order on the request for provisional measures in the case of *Passage through the Great Belt*.

Finland had asked the Court to indicate measures to suspend the construction by Denmark of a bridge over the Great Belt which, it was claimed, would interfere with the right of Finland to passage through that waterway for, in particular, oil rigs. One of the arguments employed by Denmark to justify refusal of measures was that

> if the Court ruled in favour of Finland on the merits, any claim by Finland could not be dealt with by an order for restitution, but could only be satisfied by damages inasmuch as restitution in kind would be excessively onerous. . . .[713]

The Court emphasized that at that stage it was not 'called upon to determine the character of any decision which it might make on the merits', but added that

> in principle however if it is established that the construction of works involves an infringement of a legal right, the possibility cannot and should not be excluded *a priori* of a judicial finding that such works must not be continued or must be modified or dismantled. . . .[714]

The argument of Denmark was however not so brazen as it may appear. It was linked to the requirement, recognized in the Court's case-law, that

[711] See the criticisms of Christine Gray, 'The Choice between Restitution and Compensation' (1999) 10 *European Journal of International Law* 413.

[712] A similar problem may arise in the context of the rule of exhaustion of local remedies: must a remedy that would only furnish monetary compensation be exhausted, or are the only 'effective' remedies those that involve restitution? Cf Fausto Pocar, 'Épuisement des recours internes et réparation en nature ou par équivalent', *International Law at the Time of its Codification (Mélanges Ago)* III, above n 464, 291.

[713] [1991] ICJ Rep 19, para 31.

[714] Ibid. See also the comments in the same sense of Judge Oda, ibid, 25 and Judge *ad hoc* Broms, ibid, 38.

for provisional measures to be indicated on the basis of a *prima facie* case which may later turn out to be unfounded,[715] the possibility (at least) must be shown that *irreparable* prejudice will result if no measures are indicated.[716] Denmark was not insisting that it should be permitted to buy the right to infringe Finland's interests; it was suggesting that at the interlocutory stage it could not be assumed that the prejudice would necessarily be irreparable.[717] However, if monetary compensation could never be regarded as constituting reparation, then all damage would necessarily be irreparable, and this condition for granting or refusing measures would be meaningless. 'Irreparable damage' in the context of provisional measures must therefore mean damage that once done could never be repaired, only compensated; loss of life, for example, as in the cases involving capital punishment,[718] and those of *US Diplomatic and Consular Staff in Tehran* and *Military and Paramilitary Activities in and against Nicaragua*. It was into this category that, in Denmark's submission, the *Great Belt* case fell.

The case was ultimately withdrawn when the parties came to an agreement, which reportedly involved compensation by Denmark for the expense incurred by Finland in partially dismantling oil rigs so as to pass under the new bridge. This does not however weaken the force of the Court's enunciation of the principle. It might be that, in an extreme case, where the injured State was unreasonably insisting on *restitutio in integrum* at vast expense,[719] rather than monetary compensation for a small infringement of its rights, such a demand would be rejected by a court: essentially, that was what Denmark was suggesting. The idea was later taken up by the International Law Commission: in Article 35 of the Articles on State Responsibility it was recognized that the obligation 'to make restitution, that is, to re-establish the situation which existed before the wrongful act was committed' does not exist if restitution would 'involve a burden out of all proportion to the benefit deriving from restitution instead of compensation'.[720] While this is eminently reasonable, there do not seem to be any reported cases in which an order for restitution has been refused on this ground.[721]

[715] This is a consideration which has become the more relevant since the Court's decision in the *LaGrand* case that provisional measures are binding on the State or States to whom they are addressed: see the previous article in this series, (2001) *BYIL* 111–126.

[716] See the previous article, (2001) *BYIL* 91–99.

[717] See in particular the argument of Professor Bowett, CR 91/12, 10–11.

[718] *Vienna Convention on Consular Relations (Paraguay v USA). Order of 9 April 1998*, [1998] ICJ Rep 248; *LaGrand (Germany v USA), Order of 3 March 1999*, [1999] ICJ Rep 9; *Avena and other Mexican Nationals (Mexico v USA)*, Order of 5 February 2003, [2003] ICJ Rep 77.

[719] It was asserted by Denmark at the hearings that even a three-year suspension of the works would cost Denmark around US$ 500 million: CR 91/11, (Magid).

[720] The article also excludes the case where restitution, in this sense, would be impossible; *quaere* whether it is primarily anticipation of this situation arising which is the only real justification for provisional measures.

[721] A question that appears not yet to have been resolved is that of the impact (if any) of the existence of insurance which would recompense the claimant State for pecuniary loss caused by an inter-

The approach adopted in the *Great Belt* case is based on the assumption that if the respondent State proceeds with the allegedly unlawful enterprise, an order can be made at the merits stage of the proceedings directing it to undo what has been done. A different situation arises if the action contemplated is such that *restitutio in integrum* would effectively be impossible,[722] the obvious example being, as already mentioned above, the death penalty cases. The ruling in the *LaGrand* case that an order indicating provisional measures creates a binding obligation in international law upon the State to whom the measures are addressed, and the finding in the *Avena (Request for Interpretation)* case suggesting that this is so even if the Court subsequently finds that it lacks jurisdiction on the merits, may together constitute a powerful incentive to comply; but the fact remains that a State is always free to choose not to comply with even a final decision of the Court, if it is prepared to accept the consequences of doing so. In domestic systems these consequences may involve penal damages, or intervention of the public power (e.g. demolition of works illegally constructed that the defendant has been directed to demolish, but has failed to do so). These remedies remain however unavailable in the international judicial system (reserving of course the question of enforcement action in the case of breach of the peace, under Chapter VII of the UN Charter).

It has also been suggested that, particularly when necessity is invoked as a circumstance precluding wrongfulness, it may be admitted not on that basis, but rather as a mitigating circumstance,[723] thus going rather to the question of quantum of damage. In this connection reference has been made to Article 27 *(b)* of the ILC Articles on State Responsibility, providing for compensation for material loss suffered by the State affected, even where the plea of necessity is successful.[724] This would be distinct from the general rule that in the event that restitution for breach of an international obligation 'should prove to be materially impossible', there is an obligation of the wrongdoer to compensate for the damage suffered.[725]

nationally wrongful act of another State. Cf *Aerial Incident of 27 July 1955*, where Bulgaria argued that the injury was covered in this way, and Israel pointed out that the insurance contracts were *res inter alios acta*: *Pleadings*, 132, 159, 524.

[722] On the distinction between irreparability in law and irreparability in fact, see Yoshiyuki Iwamoto, 'The Protection of Human Life through Provisional Measures Indicated by the International Court of Justice' (2002) 15 *Leiden Journal of International Law* 345.

[723] See for example Christian Tomuschat, 'Conclusions générales', 2007 Grenoble Colloquium of the *Société française pour le droit international*, 'La Nécessité en Droit international' 380.

[724] See Crawford, above n 387, 190 (*sub* Article 27), para (4).

[725] *Legal Consequences of the Construction of a Wall in the Occupied Palestinian Territory*, [2004] ICJ Rep 198, para 153.

3. Cessation of Wrongful Conduct and Guarantees of Non-Repetition

As expressed in the ILC Articles on State Responsibility, the State responsible for an internationally wrongful act is under an obligation 'to cease the act, if it is continuing' (Article 30 *(a)*), and 'to offer appropriate assurances and guarantees of non-repetition, if circumstances so require'. Such an obligation is something which can be declared by the Court in a judgment as a consequence of a finding that an internationally wrongful act has been committed. In the *LaGrand* case, both parties appear to have accepted that the ILC Articles had codified an existing rule of customary law.[726] The United States accepted that the Court had jurisdiction to order cessation, but contended that it had no jurisdiction to order the provision of guarantees of non-repetition, since this would be 'to impose... obligations that are additional to or differ in character from those' accepted by the United States as party to the Vienna Convention on Consular Relations, the text allegedly breached by the United States. The Court rejected this objection to jurisdiction on the rather general ground that

> [w]here jurisdiction exists over a dispute on a particular matter, no separate basis for jurisdiction is required by the Court to consider the remedies a party has requested for the breach of the obligation *(Factory at Chorzów, P. C. I. J., Series A*, No. 9, p. 22).[727]

The case of the *United States Diplomatic and Consular Staff in Tehran* afforded perhaps the most flagrant example of conduct in breach of an international obligation which was continuing at the time of the Court's judgment, namely the continued occupation of the United States Embassy and consulates, and the detention of the staff. In its decision the Court decided accordingly that Iran 'must immediately take all steps to redress the situation resulting from' the seizure of the Embassy and consulates, and specifically that the hostages were to be released and enabled to leave Iran, and the premises, property and archives of the Embassy

[726] Cf Giuseppe Palmisano, 'Les garanties de non-répétition entre codification et réalisation juridictionnelle du droit: à propos de l'affaire *LaGrand*' (2002) 106 *Revue générale de Droit international public* 753.

[727] [2001] ICJ Rep 485, para 48. The *Chorzów Factory* decision of course concerned the interpretation of a different compromissory clause, but the Permanent Court did state (on the page preceding that to which the later decision refers) that '[d]ifferences relating to reparations, which may be due by reason of failure to apply a convention are... differences relating to its application'. Whether a guarantee of non-repetition can be regarded as included in the concept of 'reparations' is another matter; it has been suggested that, in view of the distinction drawn by the ILC between cessation and restitution (see Crawford, above n 387, 197, *sub* Article 30, para (7)), the ICJ was wrong to assimilate them here: see Franck Laity, 'La CIJ face aux tiraillements du droit international: les arrêts dans les affaires des *Activités armées sur le territoire du Congo*' (2005) *Annuaire français* 222, citing Myriam Benlolo-Carabot, 'L'arrêt de la CIJ dans l'affaire *Avena et autres Ressortissants mexicains*' (2004) *Annuaire français* 288–289, and Laurence Dubin, 'Les garanties de non-répétition à l'aune des affaires *LaGrand* et *Avena*: La révolution n'aura pas lieu' (2005) 109 *Revue générale de droit international public* 859–887.

and consulate to be placed in the hands of the Protecting Power under Article 45 of the Vienna Convention on Diplomatic Relations.[728]

In the *Military and Paramilitary Activities* case, the decision of the Court was less specific: the United States was required 'immediately to cease and refrain from all such acts as may constitute breaches of' the obligations that the Court had found to exist and to have been violated.[729] At the same time, it emphasized the obligation of the parties to the case 'to seek a solution to their disputes by peaceful means in accordance with international law',[730] and in this context took note of the negotiations known as the Contadora Process.[731] Against this background, the Court may have felt it inappropriate to try to ascertain which, if any, of the acts of the United States mentioned in the judgment were still continuing.

In the cases brought against the United States arising out of the Vienna Convention on Consular Relations, the treatment by the Court of an obligation of cessation was less clearly consistent. The breach by the United States authorities of the provisions of the Convention was, in both cases, in the past, even though its effects continued subsequently in the shape of procedural disadvantages in the criminal appeal process, and at least in the later of the two cases, that of *Avena and Other Mexican Nationals*, those effects were continuing, as regards some of the individuals concerned, up to and after the date of the judgment. In this latter case the Court appears to have taken the view that inasmuch as the case concerned named individuals, it was only possible continuation of breaches of international obligations in relation to those individuals that would justify a finding and order by the Court for cessation. The Court held that 'Mexico has not established a continuing violation of Article 36 of the Vienna Convention with respect to the 52 individuals referred to in the final submissions; it cannot therefore uphold Mexico's claim seeking cessation.'[732] Mexico had however based its request on 'its contention that beyond these 52 cases there is a "regular and continuing" pattern of breaches by the United States of Article 36'; and it was in fact a matter of public knowledge that this was so, despite the efforts of the federal government to ensure respect for the Convention by the authorities of the states. The Court however limited itself to 'the evidence properly before it', and found that there was none 'that would establish a general pattern.'[733] One would have thought that the 52 cases in themselves would go some way to establish a 'general pattern', since they appeared to be typical of a nationwide problem,[734] and the criterion for their selection appears to have been

[728] [1980] ICJ Rep 44–45, para 95 (3).
[729] [1986] ICJ Rep 149, para 292 (12).
[730] Ibid, para 292 (16).
[731] Ibid, 145, para 291.
[732] [2004] ICJ Rep 68, para 148. To some extent, the Court seems to have regarded the United States obligation of ensuring 'review and reconsideration' of the cases as equivalent to an order for cessation: ibid.
[733] Ibid, para 149.
[734] They were not confined to one state, but came from ten different US states.

simply that they all involved the death penalty.[735] It is interesting to speculate whether the solution might have been different if the case had been pleaded more as a general allegation of continued non-observance, with the 52 cases as illustrative examples.

In the earlier case of *LaGrand*, which concerned a single individual, who had been executed while the proceedings were still in progress,[736] an order directing cessation would have had no meaning, but Germany did ask for a direction that the United States should provide 'an assurance that it will not repeat its unlawful acts' and that in future comparable criminal cases, it would 'ensure in law and practice the effective exercise of the rights under Article 36' of the Vienna Convention.[737] The United States presented objections both to the Court's jurisdiction in respect of this request, and to its admissibility, which were rejected by the Court on grounds not here relevant; it did not raise the question whether, in proceedings relating to a specific German national, it would be appropriate for the Court to direct the respondent State not to treat German nationals in that way in the future. As was noted in the later *Avena* case, there seems to have been no evidence submitted of a consistent pattern of conduct, even though no-one doubted that such existed; but the United States did provide the Court with information on the programme it had put in place to improve compliance by state authorities with the requirements of the Vienna Convention, thereby in effect conceding its relevance, and therefore the Court's power to make a general directive as to compliance.

In the case of *Armed Activities on the Territory of the Congo*, the Court found that Uganda had committed various breaches of international obligations vis-à-vis the DRC, including military incursions into its territory, violations of human rights, looting and plundering; it did not however find Uganda responsible for the actions of the irregular force known as the *Mouvement de Libération du Congo* (MLC). The DRC claimed that in a number of respects Uganda was under an obligation to 'cease forthwith all continuing internationally wrongful acts', including occupation of Congolese territory, support for irregular forces, detention of Congolese nationals, and exploitation of the Congo's natural resources.[738] The Court however noted that it had 'not been presented with evidence to support allegations with regard to the period after 2 June 2003', and that in particular there was no evidence of continuing Ugandan support for irregular forces, or involvement in exploitation of natural resources; it therefore concluded that the request for an order directing cessation 'cannot be upheld'.[739] It does not appear to have considered the possibility, in face of

[735] The background to the series of cases on the Vienna Convention (*Breard*, *LaGrand*, *Avena*) in fact involved movements opposed to capital punishment.

[736] And in defiance of the terms of the Court's Order, prepared at the last minute with commendable despatch, indicating provisional measures: Order of 3 March 1999, [1999] ICJ Rep 15, para 26.

[737] [2001] ICJ Rep 508–509, para 117.

[738] [2005] ICJ Rep 254, para 253.

[739] Ibid, 255, para 254.

the confused situation on the ground, of indicating that, if any such activities should be in fact continuing, they were to cease.[740]

In the case of the *Land and Maritime Boundary between Cameroon and Nigeria*, the decision of the Court as to the position of the land boundary signified that Nigerian armed forces and administrators found themselves in territory adjudged to be Cameroonian. The Court recalled that a similar situation had arisen in the case of the *Temple of Preah Vihear,* and it had there found that Thailand was under an obligation to withdraw its military or police forces.[741] It confined itself to 'noting' that 'Nigeria is under an obligation in the present case expeditiously and without condition to withdraw its administration and its military and police forces' from the area in question.[742] In these cases, the occupation of the territory had however been under a claim of right later found to have been unjustified, not a deliberate encroachment, and accordingly it was not appropriate to add provision for guarantees of non-repetition.

In its most recent decision in a case in which the issue of cessation and guarantees of non-repetition was raised, the Court adopted a fairly restrictive approach to these issues, and indeed to the question of compensation. In the *Dispute regarding Navigational and Related Rights* between Costa Rica and Nicaragua, the Court found in favour of Costa Rica's claims that Nicaragua had been in breach of certain of its obligations toward Costa Rica under the 1858 Treaty that regulated questions of navigation on the river San Juan. Costa Rica asked the Court to give a declaration as to the existence of those obligations, and that Nicaragua had been in breach of them, which request was granted. Costa Rica however also asked the Court 'to order Nicaragua to cease all the breaches of its obligations which have a continuing character', to find that Nicaragua should make reparation, and to find that Nicaragua should 'give assurances and guarantees that it will not repeat its unlawful conduct'.[743] The Court ruled as follows:

As far as the first of these three submissions is concerned, it should be recalled that when the Court has found that the conduct of a State is of a wrongful nature, and in the event that this conduct persists on the date of the judgment, the State concerned is obliged to cease it immediately. This obligation to cease wrongful conduct derives both from the general obligation of each State to conduct itself

[740] Something of the sort was done in the case of the *Temple of Preah Vihear*, in connection with the claim of Cambodia for return by Thailand of objects removed from the temple. The Court found there was no evidence that any such objects had in fact been removed, but felt able to make 'a finding of principle in favour of Cambodia, without relating it to any particular objects': [1962] ICJ Rep 36–37. It did however note as relevant that 'Thailand has not so much denied the allegation as contended that it is irreceivable' (ibid).

[741] [1962] ICJ Rep 37. The Court also recalled that in the *Territorial Dispute* between Chad and Libya, the two States had concluded an agreement for evacuation by Libyan administrators and forces of the territories found by the Court to be under the sovereignty of Chad: [2002] ICJ Rep 451, para 313.

[742] Ibid, para 314.

[743] Judgment of 13 July 2009, para 147.

in accordance with international law and from the specific obligation upon States parties to disputes before the Court to comply with its judgments, pursuant to Article 59 of its Statute.

It is not necessary, and it serves no useful purpose as a general rule, for the Court to recall the existence of this obligation in the operative paragraphs of the judgments it renders: the obligation incumbent on the State concerned to cease such conduct derives by operation of law from the very fact that the Court establishes the existence of a violation of a continuing character.

The Court may consider it appropriate, in special circumstances, to mention that obligation expressly in the operative part of its judgment. It sees no particular reason to do so in the present case.[744]

The precedent of the *US Diplomatic and Consular Staff in Tehran* was thus shown to be a special case, in which the plight of the hostages certainly constituted a 'special circumstance' justifying the Court in specifically requiring Iran to release them. As regards compensation, the Court simply noted that Costa Rica had 'not submitted any evidence capable of demonstrating that it has suffered a financially assessable injury'.[745] On the question of guarantees of non-repetition, the Court again announced a restrictive policy:

Finally, while the Court may order, as it has done in the past, a State responsible for internationally wrongful conduct to provide the injured State with assurances and guarantees of non-repetition, it will only do so if the circumstances so warrant, which it is for the Court to assess.

As a general rule, there is no reason to suppose that a State whose act or conduct has been declared wrongful by the Court will repeat that act or conduct in the future, since its good faith must be presumed (see *Factory at Chorzów, Merits, Judgment No. 13, 1928, P.C.I.J., Series A, No. 17*, p. 63; *Nuclear Tests (Australia v France), Judgment, I.C.J. Reports 1974*, p. 272, para 60; *Nuclear Tests (New Zealand v France), Judgment, I.C.J. Reports 1974*, p. 477, para 63; and *Military and Paramilitary Activities in and against Nicaragua (Nicaragua* v *United States of America), Jurisdiction and Admissibility, Judgment, I.C.J. Reports 1984*, p. 437, para 101). There is thus no reason, except in special circumstances of which the Court is not aware in the present case, to order a measure such as that requested by Costa Rica.[746]

4. Non-Material Damage

Finally mention may be made of cases in which the Court makes a finding that a State has infringed a rule of law or legal obligation, but on the question of reparation confines itself to declaring that the finding in

[744] Ibid, para 148. [745] Ibid, para 149. [746] Ibid, para 150.

itself 'constitutes appropriate satisfaction'. Satisfaction is a concept defined in Article 37 of the ILC's Articles on State Responsibility as a remedy which may be given or offered by the State that has offended; the Court's formula amounts to a judicially established equivalent. From one angle, the formula, which can be traced back to, e.g., the *I'm Alone* case,[747] may be regarded as a sort of fallback, or residual, remedy: thus in the case of *Application of the Genocide Convention (Bosnia and Herzegovina v Serbia and Montenegro)*, the Court found that Serbia had violated its obligation to prevent genocide, and had also failed to comply with the provisional measures that the Court had earlier indicated;[748] as regards these breaches it however went on to find that its findings in that respect 'constitute appropriate satisfaction, and that the case is not one in which an order for payment of compensation, or . . . a direction to provide assurances and guarantees of non-repetition, would be appropriate'.[749] This case was unusual in that the findings referred to in the last-quoted paragraph were already expressed as earlier paragraphs of the operative clause; it is more common for this formula to be used in relation to a point established in the reasoning part of the decision. There may be more to the formula than a fallback however: in a more positive sense, the inclusion of such a text in the operative part may, even where the reasoning of the decision adds up to a clear and definite finding, add an element of *res judicata* to the legal situation.[750] This is so even though the same decision in the *Genocide* case found that the force of *res judicata* attached to a finding in an earlier judgment which was not only not part of the operative clause, but was not even stated in explicit terms in the text of the judgment at all![751]

The most recent decision in which such a declaration has been made is that of *Certain Questions of Mutual Assistance in Criminal Matters* brought by Djibouti against France, which has prompted a valuable academic study of this aspect of the law of reparation.[752] The facts of that case were complicated, but for present purposes may be stated in a very simplified

[747] III *UNRIAA*, 1618.

[748] [2007] ICJ Rep 238, para 471 (5) and (7).

[749] Ibid, para 471 (9). No similar declaration endorsed the finding of a breach of provisional measures in the case of *Armed Activities on the Territory of the Congo (DRC v Uganda)*: see [2005] ICJ Rep 281, para 345 (7), probably since that breach involved material damage, even though the finding that Uganda owed reparation precedes in the operative clause the finding of breach of provisional measures.

[750] Another view of the matter is that of Elena Fasoli, 'Declaratory Judgments and Official Apologies as Forms of Reparation for the Non-Material Damage Suffered by the State: the Djibouti-France Case' (2008) 7 *Law and Practice of International Courts and Tribunals* 177: 'Such a declaration, in line with legal literature and considerable international case law, can be seen as a reparatory result for the non-material injury inherent in any breach of the law (i.e. legal damage). It pursues the fundamental aim of avoiding the weakening of the obligation—and of the corresponding right—which has been breached. In this regard, the function of the declaratory judgment is precisely that to confirm the legally binding force of the international rule violated.'

[751] [2007] ICJ Rep 100, para 136.

[752] Fasoli, above n 750, 177–192.

form as follows.[753] Following the mysterious death of a French lawyer, Judge Bernard Borrel, in Djibouti in 1995, legal investigations were commenced both in Djibouti and in a French court, in the latter case with the widow and children of the deceased as *parties civiles*. In the course of these proceedings, which were still uncompleted when the case was brought to the ICJ, a number of procedural steps were taken in each country involving the transmission by the one State to the other of requests, summonses or invitations to appear. Before the Court, Djibouti complained on the one hand of non-co-operation by France, contrary, it was said, to its obligations under a 1986 Convention on Mutual Assistance in Criminal Matters, and on the other of infringements of the immunities, honour and dignity of the President and other high officials of Djibouti, through the issue and making public of witness summonses.

In respect of the first head of claim, the Court found only that that France had 'failed to comply with its international obligations' under Article 17 of the 1986 Convention,[754] which provides that '[r]easons shall be given for any refusal of mutual assistance'.[755] From the reasoning of the judgment, we learn that this breach of France's obligations resulted from a refusal to give reasons for declining to execute a letter rogatory presented by Djibouti in November 2004; and the Court continued by ruling 'that its finding of this violation constitutes appropriate satisfaction'.[756] By the time the Court gave its decision, these reasons had become publicly known; accordingly the Court indicated that it would 'not order the publication of the reasons underlying the decision...to refuse the request for mutual assistance,' as Djibouti had requested, 'these having in the meantime passed into the public domain'.[757] One interpretation of this would be that it is possible for material damage to be transformed into non-material damage; the fact that the information became available to Djibouti (even if only along with the public at large) made its request *sans objet*; but the failure to supply it at the proper time—and in the proper way—remained wrongful and therefore appropriately covered by the Court's finding of a violation of obligation.

On the second head of claim, in the operative clause of the judgment the Court rejected all the submissions of Djibouti. However, in the course of its reasoning it examined the circumstances in which a witness summons had been addressed to the President of Djibouti by the French investigating magistrate; it noted that this had not been done in accordance with the relevant provisions of French criminal procedure. It considered that, as a result, the French judge 'failed to act in accordance with the courtesies due to a foreign Head of State', and noted that 'French law

753 A fuller account will be found in the article of Fasoli (previous footnote); or in the Press Release issued by the ICJ Registry at the time of the judgment.

754 Judgment of 4 June 2008, para 205 (2) *(a)*.

755 Ibid, para 149. It is unfortunate that neither this text, nor that of Article 2 *(c)*, invoked by France as the justification for its refusal, is quoted in full in the Judgment. Article 2 is set out in full in the Declaration of Judge Keith.

756 Ibid, para 205 (2) *(a)*.

757 Ibid.

itself takes account of the demands of international courtesy' by laying down special procedures for such a case.[758] It was 'regrettable' that the proper procedures were not complied with, and that no apologies were offered at an appropriate moment. Having taken note of 'all the formal defects under French law surrounding the summons', the Court considered that 'these do not in themselves constitute a violation by France of its international obligations regarding the immunity from criminal jurisdiction and the inviolability of foreign Heads of State', but added that '[n]evertheless ... an apology would have been due from France.'[759] Judge Koroma, in a separate opinion, regretted that these findings were not expressed in the operative clause; and at first sight it is not evident why the operative clause did not follow the formula of a statement of them coupled with an indication that 'constitutes appropriate satisfaction'. It may be, however, that the Court did not accept Koroma's view that 'the actions complained of [were] not merely matters of courtesy, they concerned the obligation implied in' the inviolability and immunity of a Head of State.[760] We may recall the distinction, noted, for example in the *North Sea Continental Shelf* cases, between acts which are performed in recognition of a legal obligation, and those 'which are motivated only by considerations of courtesy, convenience or tradition, and not by any sense of legal duty'.[761] The latter do not give rise to, or form part of, customary law; and therefore failure to perform them, not being an internationally wrongful act, would not involve even non-material damage, and thus would not properly fall within the ambit of the operative part of a judgment.

Division D: International Organizations

Introduction

The previous article on this subject[762] departed, for the reasons there indicated, from the pattern set by Sir Gerald Fitzmaurice in his treatment of the subject.[763] The case-law of the Court over the period since the publication of that earlier article has centred round issues rather different from those treated either by Sir Gerald or in the last article; to preserve the analytical structure of that article would therefore involve some Procrustean re-arrangements, and leave a number of sections with no more than a title and a note that no recent decision has any relevance to them. Particularly since this will be the last occasion on which matters of international organization will be dealt with,[764] it is therefore simpler to include only such headings as have an actual content, and to make some

[758] Ibid, para 172. [759] Ibid, para 173.
[760] Separate Opinion of Judge Koroma, paras 13–14.
[761] [1969] ICJ Rep 44, para 77. [762] Part Eight, (1996) 67 *BYIL* 1.
[763] (1952) 29 *BYIL* 1–37; 34 (1958) 1–5. [764] See the Preface to this article.

re-arrangement of the order in which they are treated. In particular, since the great majority of the case-law has related to the United Nations, the division of the material into a first chapter on international organizations in general, and a second on the UN, is now unnecessary.

1. The Legal Personality of International Organizations

The question of the legal personality of an international organization arises most frequently in relation to its ability to exercise rights, but it may also arise when the question is whether certain liabilities may attach to it for its acts, which of the nature of things will mean the acts of its organs. Such liability of course includes responsibility of organizations under international law (in the same sense as the international responsibility of States), the question at present under study by the International Law Commission.[765] If however an international organization has legal personality recognized by the internal law of its member States, it can in that capacity incur responsibility at the national level, for infringement of the rights of other subjects of law recognized by that legal system, including individuals and bodies having legal personality.[766]

In the case of the *Difference Relating to Immunity from Legal Process of a Special Rapporteur of the Commission on Human Rights*, the Special Rapporteur had allegedly made defamatory remarks about certain commercial companies in Malaysia, resulting in claims for damages amounting to several million dollars.[767] The question before the Court was whether the Secretary-General had correctly determined that the Rapporteur had been acting in performance of his mission, so that he enjoyed immunity from suit in Malaysia by virtue of the General Convention on the Privileges and Immunities of the United Nations. The Court held that the determination was correct, and that the Rapporteur was therefore immune from suit in Malaysia. However, the Court included in its Advisory Opinion the following final paragraph:

> Finally, the Court wishes to point out that the question of immunity from legal process is distinct from the issue of compensation for any damages incurred as a result of acts performed by the United Nations or by its agents acting in their official capacity.
>
> The United Nations may be required to bear responsibility for the damage arising from such acts. However, as is clear from Article VIII, Section 29, of the

[765] See ILC Report of the Fifty-Seventh Session, 2005, A/60/10, Chapter VI.

[766] The International Law Commission took notice of practice in this domain as relevant to the question of the *international* responsibility of international organizations when it stated or applied a concept relevant to attribution of conduct to such an organization: ILC Report of the Fifty-Ninth Session, A/59/9, para 72 (7).

[767] For fuller details of the case, see Section 5, below.

General Convention, any such claims against the United Nations shall not be dealt with by national courts but shall be settled in accordance with the appropriate modes of settlement that "[t]he United Nations shall make provisions for" pursuant to Section 29.[768]

Section 29 (b) applies to, *inter alia*, 'disputes involving any official of the United Nations who by reason of his official position enjoys immunity, if immunity has not been waived by the Secretary-General.'

The Court was apparently anxious to indicate that its decision did not imply that the plaintiffs in the Malaysian proceedings were necessarily deprived of all remedy; if a tortious act is committed by an agent of the Organization in circumstances involving his immunity, it still remains a tort, and one committed by an identifiable entity, even if it is excluded from the jurisdiction of any national court. Section 1 of the General Convention provides that

[t]he United Nations shall possess juridical personality. It shall have the capacity: (a) to contract; (b) to acquire and dispose of immovable and movable property; (c) to institute legal proceedings.

Only positive powers are here mentioned, but juridical personality necessarily entails the possibility of incurring liability, both contractual (necessarily involved in capacity to contract) and tortious. In the *Reparation for Injuries* case, the Court indicated that the Organization possessed 'international legal personality . . . together with the capacity to bring international claims';[769] it would be a strange personality that was at the same time exempt from claims made against it. The Court also said that '[w]hereas a State possesses the totality of rights and duties recognized by international law, the rights *and duties* of an entity such as the Organization must depend upon its purposes and functions as specified or implied in its constituent documents and developed in practice.'[770] The duty to make reparation for injury must however be taken to be one that is universal, and not dependent on the nature and functions of the organization. It is recognized that, as the ILC Draft Articles on Responsibility of International Organizations state, '[e]very internationally wrongful act of an international organization entails the international responsibility of the international organization';[771] the same must in principle apply to wrongful acts so characterized by *national* law, entailing responsibility under that system. Questions will arise as to attributability of conduct to an international organization as they do when responsibility for an act is attributed to any legal *persona*. In this respect, the Draft Articles provide that

[t]he conduct of an organ or agent of an international organization in the performance of functions of that organ or agent shall be considered as an act of that

[768] [1999-I] ICJ Rep 88–89, para 66.

[769] [1949] ICJ Rep 185.

[770] Ibid, 180 (emphasis added).

[771] Article 3 of the Draft Articles on the Responsibility of International Organizations, Report of the ILC on its Sixty-First Session, A/64/10, 52.

organization under international law whatever position the organ or agent holds in respect of the organization[772]

and add that for this purpose, 'the term "agent" includes officials and other persons or entities through whom the organization acts.'[773] Whether this includes an expert on mission may not always be clear.[774] The ILC however had taken note of the Court's decision in the *Cumaraswamy* case when drafting the text above, and explained that the term 'agents' was 'intended to refer not only to officials but also to other persons acting for the United Nations on the basis of functions conferred by an organ of the organization.'[775]

The legal personality of an international organization is of course a well-established concept; is it possible however for an individual organ of such an organization to have a distinct legal personality of its own, at least for some purposes? The question of action that may be *ultra vires* arises in relation to an organ of an international organization as much as, or even to a greater extent than, in relation to the organization itself.[776] However, there may be wider questions of the status of such an organ. In his dissenting opinion in the *Lockerbie* cases, Judge Schwebel noted that the Security Council cannot be a party to proceedings before the Court, and thus:

For the Court to adjudge the legality of the Council's decisions in proceedings brought by one State against another would be for the Court to adjudicate the Council's rights without giving the Council a hearing.[777]

The notion of the Council as an entity having rights of its own, distinct from the Organization as a whole, and distinct also from the States comprising either the Council, or the Organization (at a date that might have to be determined), is rhetorically effective but legally dubious.

[772] Ibid, Article 4 (1).

[773] Ibid, para (2).

[774] The Special Rapporteur noted that some authors regard the essential criterion as one of 'control' (see A/CN4/541, 9–10, n 28, citing in particular P Klein, *La responsabilité des organisations internationales dans les ordres juridiques internes et en droit des gens*).

[775] ILC Report on the Fifty-Ninth Session, A/59/10, 106, commentary to Article 4, para (3). A problem not apparently considered, but which is more likely to arise in the context of responsibility under national law, is that of determining when the agent is acting in pursuance of his mission and when he is, in the vivid language of the UK courts, 'on a frolic of his own' (a phrase originated in 1843 by Baron Parke in *Joel v Morrison*, 6 C. & P., 503, and regularly used since). This however is presumably an issue that is primarily for the relevant system of national law to determine.

[776] See Section 4 (1) below.

[777] [1998] ICJ Rep 80–81. The Statute and Rules provide a means of meeting this problem as regards the United Nations as a whole, in Article 34, paragraph 2, of the Statute: 'The Court, subject to and in conformity with its Rules, may request of public international organizations information relevant to cases before it, and shall receive such information presented by such organizations on their own initiative'; see also Rules, Article 69. This would seem sufficient, without raising the theoretical issue of the Security Council as a party in its own right.

2. Attributes of International Personality

One privilege that does not of course automatically go along with the possession of international personality is access to the International Court itself, as distinct from the power to submit information to the Court, in view of the provisions of Article 34, paragraph 1, of the Statute.[778] In the cases concerning the *Legality of the Use of Force*, it was argued, on the basis of the principle laid down in the *Monetary Gold* case,[779] that the Court was precluded from exercising any jurisdiction it might have in the cases because this would necessarily involve ruling on the rights and interests of international organizations, and specifically NATO, that were not and could not be parties to the cases.[780] Since the Court held that it did not have jurisdiction, or more precisely that the Applicant, Serbia and Montenegro, did not have access to the Court under Article 35 of the Statute, it did not proceed to consider this aspect of the case.

The case concerning *Legality of the Use by a State of Nuclear Weapons in Armed Conflict* was dealt with by the Court as a question of its own jurisdiction to give an advisory opinion, but it is also possible, and perhaps instructive, to view it as one relating to the powers of the WHO and the possibility of action *ultra vires*—*ultra vires* not merely the organ concerned, the World Health Assembly, but *ultra vires* the organization. The Assembly had decided to request an advisory opinion of the Court on the question whether the use by a State of nuclear weapons in armed conflict would be 'a breach of its obligations under international law including the WHO Constitution'.[781] The Court began its examination of the request by observing that

> three conditions must be satisfied in order to found the jurisdiction of the Court when a request for an advisory opinion is submitted to it by a specialized agency: the agency requesting the opinion must be duly authorized, under the Charter, to request opinions from the Court; the opinion requested must be on a legal question; and this question must be one arising within the scope of the activities of the requesting agency. . . .[782]

The Court had no difficulty in finding that the first two conditions were met; its decision to refuse an opinion was based simply on a negative finding in respect of the third. The Court took a narrower view of the 'scope of the activities' of the WHO than had been taken by the Assembly when

[778] Contrast, for example, the International Tribunal for the Law of the Sea, where in certain circumstances the International Seabed Authority and certain 'other entities' may be parties to proceedings (ITLOS Statute, Arts. 20 (1) and 34; Convention, Part XI, Section 5).

[779] [1954] ICJ Rep 33.

[780] See the Preliminary Objections of France in the case of *Legality of the Use of Force (Yugoslavia v France)*, paras 29–47.

[781] Resolution WHA 46.40, reproduced in [1996] ICJ Rep 67–68.

[782] Ibid, 71–72, para 10, citing *Application for Review of Judgment No. 273 of the United Nations Administrative Tribunal*, [1982] ICJ Rep 333–334.

adopting the resolution, and concluded that 'an essential condition of founding [the Court's] jurisdiction in the present case is absent and that it cannot, accordingly, give the opinion requested'.[783] It therefore treated the matter as essentially one of the limits of its own jurisdiction, rather than as a question of the possible *ultra vires* nature of the resolution requesting the opinion.[784] Nevertheless, in effect this amounts to a finding that the request was one *ultra vires* the agency, this being in fact the reason why the Court would lack jurisdiction. It may be objected that the request might be regarded as perfectly valid in itself, assuming (as appeared to be the case) that it was not itself in conflict with the WHO Constitution, but as a request that could not be accepted or complied with by the Court, for reasons connected with the *vires* of the Court rather than those of the agency. If however it had been the second aspect of the first of the Court's three conditions that was not met, if a request had been made to the Court by a specialized agency that could have been authorized by the UN General Assembly under Article 96, paragraph 2, of the Charter, but had not, the request would surely have to be regarded as having been *ultra vires* the agency (though possible valid internally, for what that might be worth); is there any essential difference for this purpose between the two situations?

This approach is also alluded to or implied in three of the individual opinions of judges. Judge Oda, who also had other reasons for considering that the Court should not reply to the request, stated as one of his conclusions that 'the WHO lack[s] the competence to submit a request for advisory opinion to the Court on the above-mentioned question'.[785] Judge Shahabuddeen defined as one of the questions to be resolved that of 'the competence of the WHO to ask for an advisory opinion as to whether some unspecified conduct of a member State... would breach its obligation under the Constitution of the WHO'.[786] Judge Weeramantry went furthest in this direction: in his dissenting opinion he disagreed (*inter alia*) with the expression of the Court's finding as one of lack of jurisdiction:

783 Ibid, 84, para 31.

784 It is possible that the Court had in mind the fact that, as pointed out by Judge Koroma in his dissent (ibid, 218–219), the Court had previously held that an organ of an international organization is entitled to determine its own competence; a similar point is made by Judge Ranjeva (ibid, 299). However, the principal authority for this is the decision in the *Certain Expenses* case, in which the Court indicated that 'each organ must, *in the first place at least*, determine its own jurisdiction': [1962] ICJ Rep 168, emphasis added. The Court appears therefore to have contemplated that it might *ex post facto* reject such determination.

785 Ibid, 96, para 16.

786 Ibid, 98. He pointed out that the Court, by finding that the WHO had no competence to ask for an advisory opinion on this question, was impliedly stating that, 'under the Constitution of the WHO, a member State has no obligation not to use... nuclear weapons... for if a member State had such an obligation, the WHO would have had some competence to address a question of the legality of a use of weapons which might have occurred in breach of that constitutional obligation'; consequently the Court, by declining to answer the question, the Court was answering it! (ibid, 99). For a different approach to this point see the Dissenting Opinion of Judge Weeramantry, ibid, 339.

I do not think this is a case of lack of jurisdiction. The dismissal is based not upon any incapacity of the Court, for constitutional reasons, to consider the request, but rather upon the Court's view that WHO, in requesting this opinion, is traversing outside the proper area of its legitimate authority. The Court has held that WHO has no status to make this enquiry. It is for this reason that the application is refused.[787]

The Court itself did indeed examine the question of the powers of the Organization, but not directly in respect of its power to request an advisory opinion: it saw the point as situated at one remove from this aspect. In order to determine whether the question on which the opinion was requested was or was not one arising 'within the scope of the activities' of the WHO, the Court set out to 'delimit the field of activity or the area of competence' of the Organization, and to do so it referred to 'the relevant rules' of the Organization, 'and, in the first place, to its constitution'.[788] The Court was able to interpret the WHO Constitution as 'authorizing the Organization to deal with the effects on health of the use of nuclear weapons . . . and to take preventive measures aimed at protecting the health of populations'; but whatever the health effects might be, 'the competence of the WHO to deal with them is not dependent on the legality of the acts which caused them.'[789] As a matter of interpretation of the Constitution, therefore, the question laid before the Court had not arisen 'in the scope of the activities' of the WHO.

Highly relevant to the question of *vires* is the Court's statement of the 'principle of speciality'.

The Court need hardly point out that international organizations are subjects of international law which do not, unlike States, possess a general competence. International organizations are governed by the "principle of speciality", that is to say, they are invested by the States which create them with powers, the limits of which are a function of the common interests whose promotion those States entrust to them.[790]

After citing the PCIJ decision in the *European Commission of the Danube* case,[791] the Court continued:

The powers conferred on international organizations are normally the subject of an express statement in their constituent instruments. Nevertheless, the necessities of international life may point to the need for organizations, in order to achieve their objectives, to possess subsidiary powers which are not expressly provided for in the basic instruments which govern their activities. It is generally accepted that international organizations can exercise such powers, known as "implied" powers.[792]

787 Ibid, 168.
788 Ibid, 74, para 19.
789 Ibid, 76, para 21.
790 Ibid, 78, para 25.
791 PCIJ Rep Series B No 14, 64.
792 [1996] ICJ Rep 79, para 25.

Citing the *Reparation for Injuries* and *Effect of Awards* cases,[793] the Court emphasized that these must have been conferred on the organization 'by necessary implication as being essential to the performance of its duties.' Such implied powers would therefore not, in the Court's view, justify the WHO's request for advisory opinion, since

> to ascribe to the WHO the competence to address the legality of the use of nuclear weapons—even in view of their health and environmental effects - would be tantamount to disregarding the principle of speciality; for such competence could not be deemed a necessary implication of the Constitution of the Organization in the light of the purposes assigned to it by its member States.[794]

The Court supplemented this finding with an analysis of the position of the WHO within the United Nations system.

In the case before it, the Court thus did not consider that the legality of nuclear weapons fell within either the constitutional powers or the implied powers of the WHO. It was however only concerned with the point in order to assess the effect of the request for opinion, which, as indicated above, it treated as a matter of its own jurisdiction. The question whether interference by the WHO in matters of the legality of nuclear weapons, in general, would be *ultra vires,* and if so whether acts or decisions constituting such interference might be void, did not arise. The conclusion as to the powers of the Organization was the basis for placing the request for opinion in a category which made it impossible for the Court to respond to it, whether as a jurisdictional question or a question of capacity.

Approaching the matter in the light of the powers of the WHO and its organs, rather than that of the jurisdiction of the Court to give advisory opinions, the applicable texts, as the Court noted, are, first, Article 96, paragraph 2, of the Charter, whereby 'specialized agencies, which may at any time be so authorized by the General Assembly, may . . . request advisory opinions of the Court on legal questions arising within the scope of their activities'; second, Article 76 of the WHO Constitution authorizing the Organization to request opinions '[u]pon authorization by the General Assembly of the United Nations'; and third, paragraph 2 of Article X of an Agreement of 10 July 1948 between the UN and the WHO, whereby the General Assembly authorized the WHO to request opinions 'within the scope of its competence'.[795] If a request had been made for opinion before 10 July 1948, the situation would be as suggested above, and the request would have been *ultra vires*. If a request was made that was clearly and undisputedly outside the 'scope of the

[793] *Reparation for Injuries Suffered in the Service of the United Nations, Advisory Opinion,* [1949] ICJ Rep 182–183 and *Effect of Awards of Compensation Made by the United Nations Administrative Tribunal, Advisory Opinion,* [1954] ICJ Rep 57.

[794] [1996] ICJ Rep 79, para 25.

[795] Texts quoted in ibid, 71–72, paras 10–11.

competence' or the 'scope of the activities' of the WHO, this too surely would be *ultra vires*. The problem arises when it is not clear upon the face of a resolution requesting an opinion whether it is within this 'scope'; it is only *ex post facto* when the request has been rejected by the Court that it becomes clear that the request was not backed up by the governing texts.[796] In such case, it is suggested that Judge Weeramantry's analysis is to be preferred, assimilating the situation to that of an application to a domestic court by an applicant who lacks capacity to make it (for example by reason of minority): 'the want or shortcoming is not in the powers of the court but in the status of the applicant.'[797]

In the previous article in this series, consideration was given to the distinction between acts of an international organization which are *ultra vires* the organization itself, and acts which are within the powers of the organization but which were performed by an organ, or in such a way, as to be capable of being regarded as *ultra vires* the organ.[798] The case-law appeared somewhat ambiguous: dicta in the decision in the *Certain Expenses* case seemed to support the view that

> a third party [is] concerned to enquire whether an action affecting him was or was not within the *vires* of the organization, but entitled to disregard questions of distribution of powers within the organization, and to treat as valid a decision taken by the wrong organ, or a decision preceded by procedural irregularities. . . .[799]

At the same time, other dicta of the Court, even in the same case, seemed to vary, in particular depending on whether the question was commitment of the organization toward 'third parties', or the effect of a decision for dissident member States.

It is the latter category that embraces the question examined in the Advisory Opinion on the *Legal Consequences of the Construction of a Wall in the Occupied Palestinian Territory*, concerning compliance with Article 12, paragraph 1, of the Charter. There was no question but that the United Nations as an organization had power to examine the 'situation'; the matter was one of distribution of powers between two of the principal organs, and specifically the conditions under which the General Assembly, rather than the Security Council was empowered to adopt resolutions. Israel, as in this respect a 'dissident member State', questioned whether

[796] Until then, the situation is that a request has been made, and may or may not prove to have been *intra vires*. Compare the dialogue between Glendower and Hotspur in *Henry IV, Part I* (Act III, Sc. 1): when Glendower boasts 'I can call spirits from the vasty deep', Hotspur retorts 'But will they come when you do call for them?'

[797] [1996] ICJ Rep 168.

[798] Cf the distinction made in the judgment on preliminary objections in the *Military and Paramilitary Activities* case, where the Court noted that it was 'not asked to say that the Security Council was wrong in its decision, nor that there was anything inconsistent with law in the way in which members of the Council employed their right to vote': [1984] ICJ Rep 436, para 98.

[799] (1999) *BYIL* 35.

Article 12, paragraph 1, had been respected; and it was not open to the Court simply to say, as it had in the case of *Jurisdiction of the ICAO Council*, that the right conclusion remained the right conclusion even though it had been reached in the wrong way.[800]

The Court had for this purpose to consider the effect of what it referred to as 'the accepted practice of the General Assembly' in relation to a question which could be regarded as one of distribution of competences within the Organization, or as one of interpretation of the Charter. Article 12, paragraph 1, of the Charter provides:

> While the Security Council is exercising in respect of any dispute or situation the functions assigned to it in the present Charter, the General Assembly shall not make any recommendation with regard to that dispute or situation unless the Security Council so requests.

On the basis of this text, it was argued that

> given the active engagement of the Security Council with the situation in the Middle East, including the Palestinian question, the General Assembly acted *ultra vires* under the Charter when it requested an advisory opinion on the legal consequences of the construction of the wall in the Occupied Palestinian Territory.[801]

The ruling given in this respect is of interest not only as regards the question of the validity of acts allegedly *ultra vires* the organ concerned, but also as regards the significance of the practice of that organ, and the possibility that a change in practice may signal a change in the legal position.

The Court noted that the competence of the Security Council to deal with the maintenance of international peace and security was 'primary, but not necessarily exclusive'.[802] Apparently as a basis for interpreting the Charter, the Court examined 'the practice of the United Nations', that is to say how Article 12, paragraph 1, was interpreted and applied by the Security Council and the General Assembly. It noted that there had in this respect been a change in practice.[803] 'Both the General Assembly and the Security Council initially interpreted and applied Article 12 to the effect that the Assembly could not make a recommendation concerning the maintenance of international peace and security while the matter remained on the Council's agenda', even if the Council was not actively seised of it. 'However,' the Court noted, 'this interpretation of Article 12 has evolved subsequently'; there had been 'an increasing tendency over time' for the two organs 'to deal in parallel with the same matter concern-

[800] [1972] ICJ Rep 69–70, para 45; and see (1996) *BYIL* 34–35.

[801] [2004] ICJ Rep 148, para 24.

[802] Ibid, para 26, citing the Opinion in the *Certain Expenses* case, [1962] ICJ Rep 163.

[803] This had been noted by informed observers: see B Simma (ed), *The Charter of the United Nations: A Commentary*, above n 581, Article 12, 295:31.

ing the maintenance of international peace and security.'[804] The Court's conclusion was that 'the accepted practice of the General Assembly, as it has evolved, is consistent with Article 12, paragraph 1, of the Charter',[805] and accordingly the request for advisory opinion was not contrary to that provision. This presumably means that *both* practices were consistent with the Charter, rather than that the new practice had replaced a mistaken interpretation.

Where the practice of parties to a treaty is first consistent with one interpretation of it, and later consistent with a different interpretation, there is no problem in reconciling this with the integrity of the treaty: the new practice can be regarded as an implicit variation by agreement. In order to reconcile the principle of the consensual nature of a treaty, and therefore of its modification, with action by the organs of an international organization created by the treaty, some subtlety of analysis is required, particularly if the organ (or one of the organs) concerned is not fully representative of the membership—even leaving aside the problem of consistency between the present-day will of the members and the intentions of the founders of the organization, responsible for the original drafting of the treaty.[806]

One of the most interesting discussions of the basis of the powers of international organizations or organs is to be found in a judge's opinion dissenting from a practice of the Court itself which has, despite the force of that dissent, since become a standard practice. In the case of the *Land, Island and Maritime Frontier* between El Salvador and Honduras, the Court had, at the request of the parties, formed a Chamber to deal with the case, and following the precedent set in the *Gulf of Maine* case,[807] had elected to the Chamber the Members of the Court discreetly indicated by the parties to the Court as those whom they wished to see appointed.[808] In 1989 Nicaragua applied for permission to intervene in the case, and the question arose whether that application should be dealt with by the Chamber or by the full Court; the Court ruled that it should be decided by the Chamber.[809] Judge Shahabuddeen, who had not been a Member of the Court in 1987, dissented, and wrote a powerful dissent indicating (*inter alia*) why he considered that the practice of allowing the

[804] [1972] ICJ Rep 149, para 27.

[805] Ibid, 150, para 28.

[806] Cf B Simma, above n 581, s.v. Interpretation, 27–28:27, referring to 'a dynamic consensus of interpretation based on the original consensus', and citing E Klein, 'Vertragsauslegung und 'spätere Praxis' internationaler Organisationen' in *Die Dynamiek des Europäischen Gemeinschaftsrechts* (1987).

[807] Order of 20 January 1982 [1982] ICJ Rep 3; see the discussion in a previous article, (2001) *BYIL* 48–49.

[808] Order of 8 May 1987, [1987] ICJ Rep 10. The Order does not mention this aspect, but it is evident from the declaration of Judge Oda attached to the Order (ibid, 13).

[809] Order of 28 February 1990, [1990] ICJ Rep 3.

parties to determine the composition of a Chamber was contrary to the Statute.[810]

Judge Shahabuddeen's essential contention was that

[t]he whole nature of the Court, as a court of justice, constitutes a prohibition, no less clear for being implied, against giving the parties any say in the selection of judges to hear a case, whether through the Rules of Court or otherwise, and whether in whole or in part, except in the case of *ad hoc* judges... This implied prohibition is not neutralized by approaching the matter from the point of view of the doctrine of implied powers. True, the fact that specific powers are conferred on a body does not necessarily imply the non-existence of others. But the latter do not float around at large. In the last analysis, all the powers of a body must be conferred by its constituent instrument, whether expressly or impliedly.[811]

After citing the Opinion in the *Reparation for Injuries* case, and Judge Hackworth's dissent in the *Effect of Awards* case,[812] Judge Shahabuddeen continued:

However elastic may be the test to be applied in determining the existence and extent of implied powers—and undue rigidity is surely to be avoided—it seems in any event clear that a constituent instrument cannot be read as implying the existence of powers which contradict the essential nature of the organization which it creates to exercise them. Powers of that kind could not be described as "required" or "essential"... to enable the organization effectively to discharge the functions laid on it by its organic text.[813]

On the substance of the question, whether the Court should permit the parties to dictate the composition of a Chamber, Judge Shahabuddeen's view has not prevailed.[814] This may be because other judges have been less convinced that, as he argued, the judicial power includes 'the power to decide what particular members of the court shall hear and determine any particular case'.[815] The force of his general propositions as to implied powers of an international body remains, it is suggested, unabated.

Another phenomenon which, it has been suggested, may be regarded as action by the Court going beyond its powers under the Charter and Statute, is the practice in recent decisions of including recommendations to the parties.[816] In the case of *Armed Activities on the Territory of the*

[810] Discussed, in the context of the constitution of the Court for a particular case, in the previous article at (2001) *BYIL* 47–50.

[811] [1989] ICJ Rep 40–41.

[812] [1949] ICJ Rep 179; [1954] ICJ Rep 80.

[813] [1989] ICJ Rep 41–42.

[814] The practice of forming a Chamber as desired by the parties has been followed in all the subsequent cases: see for example *Frontier Dispute (Benin/Niger), Formation of Chamber, Order of 27 November 2002*, [2002] ICJ Rep 613.

[815] [1989] ICJ Rep 42.

[816] See Jean d'Aspremont, 'The Recommendations Made by the International Court of Justice' (2007) 56 *International and Comparative Law Quarterly* 185, and the present author's response, 'The Recommendations Made by the International Court of Justice: A Sceptical View' (2009) 58 ibid, 1.

Congo (Congo v Rwanda); New Application, one Member of the Court was moved to object to the inclusion of such recommendations in an Order rejecting a request for provisional measures. The Court had mentioned the duties of States under the Charter, and a number of Security Council resolutions, and had indicated *inter alia* that it

> wishe[d] to stress the necessity for the Parties to these proceedings to use their influence to prevent the repeated grave violations of human rights and international humanitarian law which have been observed even recently in the region.[817]

Judge Buergenthal took the view that such recommendations, in an Order on a request for provisional measures by which the Court had found that it had no jurisdiction to order such measures, were not proper.

> My purpose in appending this declaration to the instant Order is to express my disagreement with the inclusion in the Court's Order of the language found in paragraphs 54–56 and 93. My objection to these paragraphs is not to the high-minded propositions they express. Instead, I consider that they deal with matters the Court has no jurisdiction to address once it has ruled that it lacks prima facie jurisdiction to issue the requested provisional measures. ... The Court's function is to pronounce itself on matters within its jurisdiction and not to voice personal sentiments or to make comments, general or specific, which, despite their admittedly "feel-good" qualities, have no legitimate place in this Order.[818]

3. Problems of Membership of an International Organization[819]

A complicated question of membership in the United Nations was presented to the Court in the litigation involving the Federal Republic of Yugoslavia (FRY), one of the entities emerging from the break-up of the Socialist Federal Republic of Yugoslavia (SFRY) in the period 1990–1993.[820] Proceedings were brought against it as respondent in the two cases concerning *Application of the Genocide Convention*, brought by Bosnia and Herzegovina and by Croatia; and it instituted proceedings itself as applicant

[817] Order of 10 July 2002, [2002] ICJ Rep 249–250, para 93.

[818] Dissenting Opinion of Judge Buergenthal, ibid, 257–258, paras 2, 4.

[819] It is only in relation to the United Nations that a question of this kind has arisen before the Court, and it is perhaps improbable that such a question will present itself in relation to another organization; this section may however have wider implications. The previous article in this series (1996 *BYIL* 1 et seq) did not deal with questions of UN membership, as no such question had arisen in the cases resolved by the Court during the period under examination. Unlike other articles in the series, the plan of the 1996 article was not modelled on an article by Sir Gerald Fitzmaurice, since the questions concerning international organizations that he had dealt with were different from those that had arisen up to 1996. For Sir Gerald's comments on questions of UN membership see (1952) *BYIL* 22 et seq (Collected Edition, Vol I, 81 et seq).

[820] The question is the subject of a fuller examination in the article by Shabtai Rosenne, 'Capacity to Litigate in the International Court of Justice: Reflections on Yugoslavia in the Court', this *Year Book*.

against the member States of NATO in the cases concerning *Use of Force*. In the first two cases, the question was raised whether the FRY was at the relevant time a party to the Genocide Convention so as to be bound by its terms (and in particular by its jurisdictional clause); such status involved a question of successorship to the SFRY;[821] there was also—though this at first passed almost unobserved—a more radical problem of the status of the FRY as a party to the Statute on the basis that it had succeeded to the SFRY's membership of the United Nations. In the NATO cases, the issue was directly whether at the relevant time the FRY was a party to the Statute of the Court in right of United Nations membership, and it was thus that it became belatedly apparent that this issue had also been present in the *Genocide Convention* cases, but had perhaps been swept under the carpet.

The factual background was reasonably clear; its legal implications less so. The FRY claimed, from the time that it emerged from the break-up of the SFRY, to be the continuation of the SFRY and as such entitled to United Nations membership; this claim was rejected by the Security Council by resolution 777 (1992), by which it also recommended to the General Assembly to decide that the FRY should apply for membership 'and that it shall not participate in the work of the General Assembly'.[822] The General Assembly followed this lead by resolution 47/1, expressed in substantially the same terms.[823] On 29 September 1992, however, the UN Legal Counsel wrote a letter to the Permanent Representatives of Bosnia and Croatia, in which he stated that the 'considered view of the United Nations Secretariat' was to interpret the decision of the General Assembly in this way:

> [T]he only practical consequence that the resolution draws is that the Federal Republic of Yugoslavia (Serbia and Montenegro) shall not *participate* in the work of the General Assembly. It is clear, therefore, that representatives of the Federal Republic of Yugoslavia (Serbia and Montenegro) can no longer *participate* in the work of the General Assembly, its subsidiary organs, nor conferences and meetings convened by it. On the other hand, the resolution neither terminates nor suspends Yugoslavia's *membership* in the Organization ... The resolution does not take away the right of Yugoslavia to participate in the work of organs other than Assembly bodies. The admission to the United Nations of a new Yugoslavia under Article 4 of the Charter will terminate the situation created by resolution 47/1.[824]

[821] The status of party to the Genocide Convention was not dependent on UN membership, nor a matter for determination by the United Nations (though the Secretary-General was the depositary, and his recognition of the FRY as a successor State to the Convention was noted by the Court); but that of United Nations membership was eminently within the domain of the Security Council and the General Assembly (Charter, art 4).

[822] Quoted in full in [2004] ICJ Rep 303, para 59. (The reference is to the judgment in the proceedings brought against Belgium, which will be used here for simplicity; the judgments in the other cases may be taken to be identical so far as here relevant.)

[823] Ibid, 303–304, para 60.

[824] UN doc A/47/485, quoted at ibid, 304, para 62.

To the uninformed observer, this does not seem a very evident interpretation of the resolutions of the two principal organs: if Yugoslavia's membership had been neither terminated nor suspended, why should it—and how could it—apply for membership *de* novo?[825] The situation created on this basis was *sui generis*: the Court referred to it as 'highly complex', 'ambiguous' and 'open to different interpretations.'[826] The Secretariat, consistently with this document, continued to 'keep up the practice of the *status quo ante*';[827] it was presumably hoped and expected that the FRY would give in and apply for membership fairly soon. In fact however the 'rather confused and complex state of affairs' so created (as the Court called it[828]) continued unchanged up to 2000, the FRY continuing to insist that it was a UN member as successor to the SFRY, and the General Assembly continuing to refuse to accept this. Finally, on 24 September 2000, following 'fundamental democratic changes' in the FRY, a formal request was made by it for admission 'in light of the implementation of Security Council resolution 777 (1992)'; and on 1 November 2000 the General Assembly, acting on the recommendation of the Security Council, admitted the FRY to membership.[829]

The proceedings in the case of *Application of the Genocide Convention* were instituted against the FRY by Bosnia and Herzegovina on 20 March 1993, and by Croatia on 2 July 1999; the proceedings against the NATO States in the *Use of Force* cases were instituted by the FRY on 29 April 1999. These procedural steps were thus taken during the period in which the position of the FRY vis-à-vis the United Nations was 'ambiguous'. For purposes of application of Article 93, paragraph 1, of the Charter, was the FRY a member of the United Nations, and thus '*ipso facto*' a party to the Statute, on these dates? If it was not, the Court was not 'open' to it under Article 35 of the Statute (subject to the possibility of application of paragraph 2 of that Article, which may be left aside in the present discussion).

When on 8 April 1993, thus during the 'ambiguous' period, the Court made an order on the request of Bosnia for provisional measures in the *Genocide Convention* case, the Court noted the position in the United Nations, and observed that 'while the solution adopted [by the Legal Counsel's letter] is not free from legal difficulties', the question of UN membership was 'one which the Court does not need to determine

825 As Judge *ad hoc* Dimitrijević noted in 2003, there were conflicting views in the Security Council when resolution 797 (1992) was adopted: Russia and China, for example, did not consider that Yugoslavia was excluded from the UN: Dissenting Opinion in the *Application for Revision* case concerning the *Genocide Convention*, [2003] ICJ Rep 61–62, para 35.

826 [2004] ICJ Rep 305, para 64.

827 Ibid, 307, para 71.

828 Ibid, 308, para 73.

829 Ibid, 309–310, paras 75–76.

definitively at the present stage of the proceedings'.[830] On 11 July 1996, thus still in the ambiguous period, the Court gave judgment on the preliminary objections brought by the FRY in the case brought by Bosnia and Herzegovina, in which the FRY did not raise the issue;[831] in that judgment the point was not touched on.

After its admission as a UN member in 2002, the FRY saw the opportunity to re-open the question in the *Genocide Convention* case, and filed an application for revision of the 1996 Judgment on the basis of a 'new fact', under Article 61 of the Statute. It must have seemed clear that there was here a 'fact of such a nature as to be a decisive factor', since the admission in 2000 implied, in the view of the FRY, that it had not been a party to the Statute since 1993. However, the confused situation between 1993 and 2000 made it difficult to specify precisely what was the *new* fact which was, 'when the judgment was given, unknown to the Court, and also to the party claiming revision,' as required by Article 61, paragraph 1. The Court was able to dismiss the request for revision without doing violence to the terms of Article 61; but the situation could hardly be called satisfactory in legal terms.

The problem finally came to a head in the *Use of Force* cases; once the FRY had indisputably become a United Nations member, the respondent States filed preliminary objections contending that it could not therefore have been such a member, and thus a party to the Statute, at the time that it had instituted the proceedings in those cases. The Court was thus at last faced squarely with the problem: had the FRY been a member of the United Nations between 1993 and 2000, if one with very limited rights; or had resolution 777 (1992), contrary to the gloss put on it by the Secretary-General and the Legal Counsel, terminated the membership of the SFRY and, by rejecting the claim of the FRY to be the successor to that membership, put an end, from that time until to 2000, to any presence of a 'Yugoslavia' in the organization? The Court, while making much of the 'legal difficulties' and the 'amorphous state of affairs' and '*sui generis* position' of the FRY during the period, arrived at a firm conclusion.

In the view of the Court, the significance of this new development in 2000 is that it has clarified the thus far amorphous legal situation concerning the status of the

[830] [1993] ICJ Rep 14, para 18. This would probably have been sufficient at that stage, but the Court also referred to the possibility of jurisdiction under Article 35, paragraph 2, of the Statute, which indicates that 'the conditions under which the Court shall be open to other States shall, subject to the special provisions contained in treaties in force, be laid down by the Security Council...' The Court in 1993 was prepared to consider that Article IX of the Genocide Convention might itself qualify as a 'treaty in force' for this purpose: the point was not mentioned again in the *Genocide Convention* case. The Court however took an opposite view when it examined the point fully in the *Use of Force* cases: see for example [2004] ICJ Rep 318 et seq, para 99 et seq.

[831] It is evident that for the FRY to have asserted in The Hague that it was *not* a UN Member would have undermined its position in New York, where it was continuing to maintain that it *was*.

Federal Republic of Yugoslavia vis-à-vis the United Nations. It is in that sense that the situation that the Court now faces in relation to Serbia and Montenegro is manifestly different from that which it faced in 1999. If, at that time, the Court had had to determine definitively the status of the Applicant vis-à-vis the United Nations, its task of giving such a determination would have been complicated by the legal situation, which was shrouded in uncertainties relating to that status. However, from the vantage point from which the Court now looks at the legal situation, and in light of the legal consequences of the new development since 1 November 2000, the Court is led to the conclusion that Serbia and Montenegro was not a Member of the United Nations, and in that capacity a State party to the Statute of the International Court of Justice, at the time of filing its Application to institute the present proceedings before the Court on 29 April 1999.[832]

In the second sentence quoted the Court recognized the difficulty that there would have been in defining the legal situation vis-à-vis the United Nations of the FRY during the period 1993–2000; but it seems to follow from its eventual conclusion that a finding during that period that the FRY *was* a UN member would have been legally erroneous. What then of the 1996 decision on the preliminary objections in the *Application of the Genocide* case? The judgment in that case made no mention of the problem; but if at that time the FRY was not a party to the Statute, the whole proceedings were without legal basis, and there would have been no point in examining the specific preliminary objections made on other grounds.

It is understandable thus that the FRY re-opened the matter in the context of the *Genocide* case, by unusual procedural means the details of which are not here relevant.[833] At the stage of the merits in this case, the Court found itself faced with an objection by the FRY that

when the present proceedings were instituted . . . it was not . . . a party to the Statute of the Court by virtue of membership in the United Nations; and that, not being such a party, it did not have access to the Court, with the consequence that the Court had no jurisdiction *ratione personae* over it.[834]

The Court's ruling in response to this was essentially simple: the 1996 Judgment possessed the force of *res judicata*; a judgment with this status could only be re-opened by revision under Article 61 of the Statute; and that

[s]ubject only to this possibility of revision, the applicable principle is *res judicata pro veritate habetur*, that is to say that the findings of a judgment are, for the purposes of the case and between the parties, to be taken as correct, and may not

[832] [2004] ICJ Rep 310–311, para 79.

[833] On 4 May 2001, the FRY submitted a document entitled 'Initiative to the Court to Reconsider *ex officio* Jurisdiction over Yugoslavia' ([2007-II] ICJ Rep 54, para 26), and the Court decided in June 2003 that the FRY could submit argument on the jurisdictional point during the oral proceedings on the merits (ibid, para 35).

[834] [2007-II] ICJ Rep 77, para 80. The FRY also contended that it had similarly been established *ex post facto* that it had not succeeded to the status of party to the Genocide Convention, and that for this reason also there was no jurisdiction.

be reopened on the basis of claims that doubt has been thrown on them by subsequent events.[835]

Since the Court had already in 2003 rejected the FRY's application for revision, 'the principle of *res judicata* precludes any reopening of the decision embodied in the 1996 Judgment.'[836]

The FRY drew attention to the fact that the 1996 judgment had not dealt specifically with the question of the status of the FRY as a party to the Statute, and the Court recognized this. It explained that

> [s]ince, as observed above, the question of a State's capacity to be a party to proceedings is a matter which precedes that of jurisdiction *ratione materiae*, and one which the Court must, if necessary, raise ex officio... this finding must as a matter of construction be understood, by necessary implication, to mean that the Court at that time perceived the Respondent as being in a position to participate in cases before the Court. On that basis, it proceeded to make a finding on jurisdiction which would have the force of *res judicata*. The Court does not need, for the purpose of the present proceedings, to go behind that finding and consider on what basis the Court was able to satisfy itself on the point.[837]

This ingenious argument enables the Court to reach a defensible conclusion on the question of jurisdiction, but it leaves unsatisfied the quest for a logical explanation of how the FRY could apparently be, at one and the same time, a member of the United Nations for the purposes of the application of the Statute in one case, and not a member of the United Nations for exactly the same purpose in another case. The commentator however, unlike the Court, need have no scruples in saying bluntly that the 1996 judgment was based on an unspoken false premise, an assumption deliberately (presumably) left unexamined; that the principle of *res judicata* subsequently gave permanency to an incorrect judgment; and that the correct legal view (if that expression means anything in the context) must be that the FRY was never a United Nations member until its admission in 2000,[838] and that the Secretary-General and the Legal Counsel were mistaken to suggest otherwise. It must however be conceded that these officials were acquainted not only with the statements made in the Security Council at the time of adoption of resolution 777 (1992), indicating that in the view of some States voting for the resolution did not signify the exclusion of Yugoslavia from the organization, but also with the interpre-

[835] Ibid, 93, para 120.

[836] Ibid, 101, para 140.

[837] Ibid, 98–99, para 132.

[838] This does of course involve, as Judge Kooijmans pointed out in the *Use of Force* cases, treating retrospectively as wholly ineffective the undertakings given by Yugoslavia in 1992, to 'fulfil all the rights conferred on, and obligations assumed by,' the SFRY: [2004-III] ICJ Rep 926–927. However, there can be no question, in relation to an organization like the UN, of a sort of 'baptism of desire', of the unilateral acquisition by a State of the rights and status (and duties) of a member.

tation that was no doubt given to the resolution by delegations in less formal ways.

In its decision in 2008 on the preliminary objections in the case, also concerning *Application of the Genocide Convention* brought by Croatia against the FRY, the Court noted that its decisions in the case brought by Bosnia and Herzegovina had no force of *res judicata* for the later case, but observed that

> they may be of relevance in the present instance, as, first, they address the legal position of the Respondent in the present case during a period—from 1992 to 2000—covering the date of filing of the Application on which the Court must rule, and second . . . the Court departs from settled jurisprudence only if it is of the opinion that there are very particular reasons to do so.[839]

It apparently followed, though the Court seems to have been reluctant to say so explicitly, that at the date (2 July 1999) that Croatia instituted proceedings, the FRY was not a UN Member, and thus not a State to which the Court was open. The Court however found, for reasons not here material, that the relevant date was not 2 July 1999, but 1 March 2001, the date on which Croatia filed its Memorial, by which date the FRY had indisputably become a UN Member.

4. Organs of the United Nations

(1) Consideration by the Court of the powers of the other principal organs

As was observed in the previous article on this subject, questions of this kind may arise before the Court in one of two ways: either by anticipation of conflict, when it is argued that the Court 'should not decide a particular case because to do so would encroach on the functions' of another principal organ, primarily the Security Council, or *ex post facto* if 'it is contended that a decision already taken by a principal organ of the United Nations cannot be reviewed by the Court.'[840]

It was noted above that questions of *vires* may arise for the Court itself, not merely in terms of the extent of its jurisdiction in a specific case, but in terms of the limits of its powers (to form Chambers, or to make recommendations at the same time as declining jurisdiction).[841] There is of course no other organ empowered to examine such matters, but commentators are free to advert to them!

(a) Separation of functions

In the case of the *Legality of the Use of Nuclear Weapons in Armed Conflict*, the Court, as noted above, took the view that for the WHO to involve itself

[839] Judgment of 18 November 2008, para 76.

[840] (1996) *BYIL* 40. In that article, however, the discussion was framed in terms of the 'Relationship between the Court and the other principal organs'.

[841] See above, Section 2.

in the question of the legality of the use of nuclear weapons, to the extent of asking for an advisory opinion on the matter, was contrary to the general principle of speciality, governing the extent of the powers of international organizations. It pursued the matter, however, in terms of the particular constitutional position of the WHO in relation to the UN system, and the distribution of competences in that system. Examining Articles 57 and 63 of the Charter, it found that these provisions demonstrated that

the Charter of the United Nations laid the basis of a "system" designed to organize international co-operation in a coherent fashion by bringing the United Nations, invested with powers of general scope, into relationship with various autonomous and complementary organizations, invested with sectorial powers.[842]

After citing the Agreement of 10 July 1948 between the UN and the WHO, by which the latter was recognized as 'the specialized agency responsible for taking such action as may be appropriate under its Constitution for the accomplishment of the objectives set forth therein', the Court concluded that

the WHO Constitution can only be interpreted, as far as the powers conferred upon that Organization are concerned, by taking due account not only of the general principle of speciality, but also of the logic of the overall system contemplated by the Charter. If, according to the rules on which that system is based, the WHO has, by virtue of Article 57 of the Charter, "wide international responsibilities", those responsibilities are necessarily restricted to the sphere of public "health" and cannot encroach on the responsibilities of other parts of the United Nations system. And there is no doubt that questions concerning the use of force, the regulation of armaments and disarmament are within the competence of the United Nations and lie outside that of the specialized agencies.[843]

The unspoken premise of the argument, particularly of the last sentence quoted, appears to be that there can be no overlap of functions, or at least that any such overlap could only consist in the UN, as the body with wide general functions, being able to concern itself with matters within the scope of a specialized agency, not the other way round. Seen in this light, the question is not so much whether disarmament is the fief of the UN as whether disarmament can in any way be brought within the ambit of 'public health'; the WHO Assembly endeavoured to achieve this, but the Court held that the attempt failed.

It appears to be established that the principle of separation of functions does not of itself preclude the Court from considering questions already under examination by the General Assembly or the Security Council. There seems to have been some hint of a different view in the

842 [1996] ICJ Rep 80, para 26.
843 Ibid.

suggestion in the case of the *Legality of the Threat or Use of Nuclear Weapons* that the Court would be examining issues 'which are the subject of consideration . . . within other bodies of the United Nations which have an express mandate to address these matters', but the thrust of the objection was rather that 'an opinion by the Court . . . would provide no practical assistance to the General Assembly in carrying out its functions.'[844]

(b) Review by the Court of the decisions of political organs

The views expressed on this question in the previous article in this series,[845] on the basis of the Court's case-law up to 1996, may be summed up in the following propositions:

(1) The Court has no power of 'review' entitling it to call in and examine the validity of a decision of another UN organ, either of its own motion or at the request of a State.
(2) It is however open to a political organ, entitled to seek advisory opinions, to use this means to ask the Court what are the legal consequences of a decision of its own, or of another political organ; and the Court may give effect to this request. In doing so, it may thus be led to examine the legal validity of the decision in question.
(3) If the validity or effect of the decision of a political argument constitutes a link in the necessary chain of reasoning that the Court has to follow in order to decide a disputed question in a contentious case, the Court is not debarred from examining such validity or effect on the grounds of any asserted 'non-reviewability' of the decision.

The last proposition in particular was essential to the twin cases of *Interpretation and Application of the 1971 Montreal Convention arising from the Aerial Incident at Lockerbie*; in the previous article the Court's Orders on the requests for the indication of provisional measures in those cases were examined from this angle. To recall briefly the facts: criminal charges were brought in Scotland against two Libyan nationals in connection with the destruction on 21 December 1988 of Pan Am flight 103, by means of explosives placed on board. Thereupon the British and US governments issued a joint declaration calling upon the Libyan government, *inter alia*, to surrender for trial those charged with the crime.[846] On 21 January 1992 the Security Council considered the subject of the declaration and adopted resolution 731 (1992), which in operative paragraph 3 '[urged] the Libyan Government immediately to provide a full and effective response' to the requests of the UK and the US. On 3 March 1992 Libya filed with the

[844] Quotation from the Written Statement of the United States, reproduced in the advisory opinion, [1996] ICJ Rep 236, para 15.

[845] (1996) *BYIL* 45–55.

[846] [1992] ICJ Rep 11, para 28.

Court applications instituting proceedings against each of those States, claiming (to summarize) that they were interfering with Libya's jurisdiction under the Montreal Convention for the Suppression of Unlawful Acts against the Safety of Civil Aviation of 23 September 1971. On the same day Libya filed a request for provisional measures. On 31 March 1992 the Security Council, '[a]cting under Chapter VII of the Charter', adopted resolution 748 (1992), which expressly '[d]ecide[d] that the Libyan Government must now comply without any further delay with paragraph 3 of resolution 731 (1992) regarding the requests' for surrender of the suspects made by the UK and the US. The Court rejected the request for provisional measures by an Order of 14 April 1992, indicating that

> the Court, while thus not at this stage called upon to determine definitively the legal effect of Security Council resolution 748 (1992), considers that, whatever the situation previous to the adoption of that resolution, the rights claimed by Libya under the Montreal Convention cannot now be regarded as appropriate for protection by the indication of provisional measures;[847]

Since then the Court has given judgments on the preliminary objections of the UK and the US; but following the transfer of the two alleged authors of the bombing to the Netherlands for trial by a Scottish court, the proceedings in the case were first suspended[848] and then discontinued 'with prejudice' by agreement between the parties.[849] It had been expected that the decision of the Court on the preliminary objections would contribute much to the debate on the issue of the treatment to be given by the Court to decisions of the Security Council; but the Court found reasons for not dealing with this issue as a preliminary one and reserved it for the proceedings on the merits which, in the event, never took place. However, some of the opinions of judges appended to the Judgment on preliminary objections dealt at some length with the point.

The most emphatic and extensively reasoned rejection of any power of judicial review that the Court might be thought to possess over Security Council resolutions is to be found in the Dissenting Opinion of President Schwebel.[850] The reader of this Opinion however has for much of the time the impression that the author is, at least at the outset, pushing at an open door; as long ago as 1962, as Schwebel notes, the Court had made it clear that the Charter system contains nothing analogous to the various procedures in domestic systems for review of legislative or governmental acts.[851] It is only toward the end of the Opinion that the real point of the *Lockerbie* case is touched on:

[847] [1992] ICJ Rep 15, para 40.
[848] Orders of 29 June 1999, [1999] ICJ Rep 975 and 979.
[849] Orders of 10 September 2003, [2003] ICJ Rep 149, 152.
[850] [1998] ICJ Rep 73–81.
[851] *Certain Expenses of the United Nations* [1962] ICJ Rep 168, cited by Judge Schwebel in his dissenting opinion in [1998] ICJ Rep 74.

> The conclusion that the Court cannot judicially review or revise the resolutions of the Security Council is buttressed by the fact that only States may be parties in cases before the Court. The Security Council cannot be a party. For the Court to adjudge the legality of the Council's decisions in a proceeding brought by one State against another would be for the Court to adjudicate the Council's rights without giving the Council a hearing, which would run counter to fundamental judicial principles. It would run counter as well to the jurisprudence of the Court. (Cf. *East Timor (Portugal v Australia), Judgment, I.C.J. Reports 1995*, pp. 100–105; *Monetary Gold Removed from Rome in 1943, Judgment, I.C.J. Reports 1954*, pp. 32–33.) Any such judgment could not bind the Council, because, by the terms of Article 59 of the Statute, the decision of the Court has no binding force except between the parties and in respect of that particular case.[852]

On the first point, attention has been drawn above[853] to Article 34, paragraph 2, of the Statute, which would enable the Court to seek or receive any observations that the Security Council might wish to make; but in any event, the assimilation of the case to the situation in the *Monetary Gold* case is not entirely convincing. On the second point, the question is not whether the Security Council would be bound by the Court's decision, but whether the parties to the case are bound by a resolution of the Council which the Court has ruled to be invalid or ineffective. President Schwebel continues:

> At the same time, a judgment of the Court which held resolutions of the Security Council adopted under Chapter VII of the Charter not to bind or to be "opposable" to a State, despite the terms of Article 25 of the Charter, would seriously prejudice the effectiveness of the Council's resolutions and subvert the integrity of the Charter. Such a holding would be tantamount to a judgment that the resolutions of the Security Council were *ultra vires*, at any rate in relation to that State. That could set the stage for an extraordinary confrontation between the Court and the Security Council. It could give rise to the question, is a holding by the Court that the Council has acted *ultra vires* a holding which of itself is *ultra vires?*[854]

The situation contemplated would certainly be an unfortunate one; but the alternative is a power of decision vested in the Security Council not merely totally unfettered by judicial review, but also capable of creating legal truth, or something which *pro veritate habetur*, for (at least) all UN Members. Nor has the Court held back in the past from contemplating such a possibility: as in the *Namibia* case where, despite declaring that '[a]

852 [1998] ICJ Rep 80–81.

853 Section 1 above, n 777.

854 Ibid, 81. The question in the last sentence is presumably rhetorical: the Court, by deciding that the Council had acted *ultra vires*, would be asserting its own *vires*.

resolution of a properly constituted organ of the United Nations which is passed in accordance with that organ's rules of procedure... must be presumed to have been validly adopted', the Court went on to consider on their merits objections made to that validity.[855]

The opinion of Judge Sir Robert Jennings[856] is more subtly expressed, and seems at first sight to recognize a distinction between judicial review and the possibility of questioning the validity of a resolution for the purposes of correctly declaring the law as between parties to a dispute. He too noted that 'there is no power of judicial review of Security Council decisions under Chapter VII of the Charter', and added that this was so

> not merely because of the dictum of the Court in the *Namibia* case. The position is established by the provisions of the Charter itself. Moreover it is evident from the records of San Francisco that a power of judicial review was proposed and rejected by the drafting conference. The Court is not a revising body, it may not substitute its own discretion for that of the Security Council; nor would it in my view be a suitable body for doing that; nor is the forensic adversarial system suited to the making of political decisions.[857]

However, he had earlier indicated the difference between organs of political and judicial competence, and stated that the relationship between them, and their respective decisions, was to be ordered in this way:

> In a society governed by the rule of law this relationship is to be resolved according to the relevant principles and rules of constitutional and administrative law. It is precisely the lot of a court of justice to apply those principles and rules; as indeed has happened in this case. So, the task of the Court in this case, as I see the matter, is simply to apply international law.
>
> The first principle of the applicable law is this: that all discretionary powers of lawful decision-making are necessarily derived from the law, and are therefore governed and qualified by the law. This must be so if only because the sole authority of such decisions flows itself from the law. It is not logically possible to claim to represent the power and authority of the law and, at the same time, claim to be above the law.[858]

Specifically, this was applicable to the powers of the Security Council, so that the decisions and actions of that body were not immune from scrutiny.

[855] [1971] ICJ Rep 22, para 20. The Court explained that this was because 'the objections concern the competence of the Court' (ibid), but it is not apparent why a resolution which allegedly was in conflict with general legal rules or subsisting legal rights should be intangible, while a resolution allegedly conflicting with the rules of the Court's jurisdiction should not be so.

[856] Sitting as judge *ad hoc* appointed by the UK, in view of the disqualification of Judge Higgins on the grounds of previous participation in the case as counsel.

[857] [1998] ICJ Rep 111. The last observation is evidently true, but perhaps beside the point. Whether an organ that has made a decision of a political character (that is to say, on the basis of political considerations) was acting within the scope of its powers as *legally* defined is itself a legal question. Judge Jennings does, it seems, go on to recognise this (see next quotation).

[858] Ibid, 109–110.

The practical significance of this for Judge Jennings was however as follows:

When, therefore, as in the present case, the Security Council, exercising the discretionary competence given to it by Article 39 of the Charter, has decided that there exists a "threat to the peace", it is not for the principal judicial organ of the United Nations to question that decision, much less to substitute a decision of its own, but to state the plain meaning and intention of Article 39, and to *protect* the Security Council's exercise of that body's power and duty conferred upon it by the law; and to protect the exercise of the discretion of the Security Council to "decide what measures not involving the use of armed force are to be employed to give effect to its decisions".[859]

It is difficult to see how the finding that the UK and the US asked the Court to make would be tantamount to contradicting the Council's finding of the existence of a 'threat to the peace'. Be that as it may, however, what does 'protect' mean in this context? If the relevant decision of the Security Council is, in the view of the Court, legally valid, it has no need of 'protection'; if it is not, the question arises whether the Court has power to find that the rights of the parties to a case before it are governed by international law into which that decision does not fit; and this question cannot be conjured out of existence by the mere device of talking of 'protection' of the decision—unless indeed Judge Jennings is in fact sharing the view of President Schwebel that such decisions must be sacrosanct, lest worse befall.

The approach of Judge Rezek was similar to that of Judge Jennings, but he was prepared to contemplate, as Judge Jennings apparently was not, the possibility that the Court might tell the Security Council that it was wrong.

[T]he Court is the definitive interpreter of the Charter of the United Nations. It is the Court's responsibility to determine the meaning of each of its provisions and of the text as a whole, and this responsibility becomes particularly serious when the Court finds itself faced with a challenge to decisions taken by one of the Organization's two principal political organs. Ensuring the primacy of the Charter in its true and full meaning is one of the most eminent of the tasks which fall to the Court, and the Court, as of right and out of duty, acts to that end whenever the occasion arises, even if this may in theory result in criticism of another organ of the United Nations, or rather in disavowal of that organ's analysis of the Charter.[860]

In the *Lockerbie* case, the decision of the Security Council was clear, and it was possible to say that it was legally binding, and on that basis determine the rights of the parties to the case. A more delicate situation, already discussed above,[861] was presented to the Court in the litigation involving the Federal Republic of Yugoslavia (FRY), one of the entities emerging from the break-up of the Socialist Federal Republic of Yugoslavia (SFRY) in the period 1990–1993. Proceedings were brought against it as respondent

[859] Ibid, 110. [860] Ibid, 61.
[861] See Division C, Chapter I, and Division D, Section 3, above.

in the two cases concerning *Application of the Genocide Convention*, brought by Bosnia and Herzegovina and by Croatia; and it instituted proceedings itself as applicant against the member States of NATO in the cases concerning *Use of Force*. There was no question in those cases but that the admission of new members to the Organization, and generally questions of membership, were primarily matters for the Security Council and the General Assembly; the problem arose from the drafting of Security Council resolution 777 (1992), which decided that the FRY had not succeeded to the membership of the SFRY, but then went on to add that the FRY could not participate in the work of the General Assembly. General Assembly resolution 47/1 was in the same terms. If however the FRY was not a UN member, this went without saying.

The UN Legal Counsel (followed by the Secretary-General) seemingly deduced that the second part of the resolution was not superfluity; it was 'the only practical consequence' drawn by the resolution from the fact of non-succession, and that accordingly

> the resolution neither terminates nor suspends Yugoslavia's *membership* in the Organization.... The resolution does not take away the right of Yugoslavia to participate in the work of organs other than Assembly bodies.[862]

For the Court, the question of the status of the FRY as Member or non-Member of the United Nations arose as soon as proceedings were instituted before the Court against that State; under Article 35, paragraph 1, the Court is 'open to the States parties to the present Statute', and under Article 93, paragraph 1 of the Charter, 'All Members of the United Nations are *ipso facto* parties to the Statute'. Unless the FRY qualified for access under paragraph 2 of Article 35,[863] if it was to be brought before the Court it could only be in the quality of UN Member. At the outset of the proceedings brought by Bosnia and Herzegovina, the Court had to determine whether it had sufficient *prima facie* jurisdiction to deal with a request for the indication of provisional measures. It postponed any definitive ruling: noting that the solution adopted in New York was 'not free from legal difficulties', it indicated that the question was 'one which the Court does not need to determine definitively at the present stage of the proceedings'.[864]

When the Court examined the preliminary objections submitted by the FRY, which did not include an objection that the FRY, as a non-member of the UN, could not be a party, the Court could (and, it is suggested, should) have raised this point *ex officio*; if it had done so, it would have had to determine what resolution 777 (1992) meant, and possibly whether it constituted a proper exercise of the powers of the Security Council.

[862] UN Doc A/47/485, quoted in the case of *Use of Force (FRY v Belgium)* [2004] ICJ Rep 304, para 62.

[863] A jurisdictional question unrelated to Membership in the United Nations, or the powers of the principal organs: see n 821 above.

[864] Order of 8 April 1993, [1993] ICJ Rep 14, para 18. The Court, with some inconsistency, also found that the compromissory clause relied on (Article IX of the Genocide Convention) could 'be

(2) Decisions of United Nations principal organs: effect for Member States

(a) Decisions of the Security Council

The decisions on the preliminary objections submitted in the two cases concerning *Questions of Interpretation and Application of the 1971 Montreal Convention arising from the Aerial Incident at Lockerbie* involved consideration of the effect of three resolutions of the Security Council in relation to the operation of the provisions of the Montreal Convention. The two judgments[865] helpfully cite the relevant provisions of the Montreal Convention, but do not outline the facts of the dispute, and do not quote the Security Council resolutions involved; some explanation has been given in Section 4 (1) (b) above.[866] At the stage of preliminary objections, the central issue was again the relationship between Libya's rights and obligations under the Montreal Convention and its obligations under the Security Council's resolutions.[867] The matter was raised in different ways by the United Kingdom in its objections.

It was first contended that there was no dispute, on the basis that under Articles 25 and 103 of the Charter, resolutions 748 (1992) and 883 (1993) had 'priority over all rights and obligations arising out of the Montreal Convention', and that 'because of the adoption of these resolutions, the only dispute which existed from that point on was between Libya and the Security Council...'[868] The Court summarily rejected this objection on a *ratione temporis* basis, since the two resolutions mentioned were both adopted after the Court had been seised of the case. Resolution 731 (1992) was not mentioned in this context: the Respondent apparently recognized that this resolution, not expressed to

regarded *prima facie*' as meeting the conditions of paragraph 2 of Article 35 of the Statute: ibid, para 19. It should be recalled that at this date the Court had never committed itself to a ruling on the question whether provisional measures impose legally binding obligation on the State to which they were addressed. Since the ruling in the *LaGrand* case that they do have such an effect, it may be less defensible for the Court to leave open such a vital point. In its decision on the merits in the *Genocide Convention* case, the Court in effect treated the *LaGrand* ruling as retroactive, since it found the FRY responsible for breaches of the Order made in 1993: [2007-II] ICJ Rep 236–237, paras 467–470. The Court had however found earlier in the Judgment that it did have jurisdiction over the FRY; if it had come to the contrary conclusion, would the measures have been binding nevertheless? The decision in the case of Mexico's request for interpretation of the *Avena* Judgment suggests that it would (see Judgment of 19 January 2009, para 51); but since the principal jurisdiction in the interpretation proceedings was statutory (Article 60 of the Court's Statute) rather than consensual, the ruling may perhaps not be transferable from interpretation proceedings to a contentious case. This is however not a question requiring examination here.

865 UK case: [1998] ICJ Rep 9; US case, ibid, 115. For convenience, the judgment in the UK case will be quoted and discussed here; the judgment in the US case, which is to a great extent identical except for the paragraph and page numbers, will be referred to only if it contains a passage departing from the UK decision.

866 Most of the relevant material is contained in the earlier Orders on the Libyan requests for the indication of provisional measures in the two cases: [1992] ICJ Rep 3 and 113.

867 A further resolution, resolution 883 (1993) had been adopted by the Council in the meantime, reaffirming its earlier resolutions, and '[a]cting under Chapter VII of the Charter', by which it '[d]emand[ed] once again that the Libyan Government comply without any further delay with' those resolutions.

868 [1998] ICJ Rep 23, para 37.

have been adopted under Chapter VII of the Charter, and lacking the verb 'decides', did not rank as a 'decision' for purposes of Article 25.[869] For the same temporal reason the Court rejected an objection to the admissibility of the Application, based on the view that the two resolutions were 'legally binding and create legal obligations for Libya and the United Kingdom which are determinative of any dispute over which the Court might have jurisdiction'.[870] Following its own case-law, the Court pointed out that admissibility had to be determined at the date of the institution of proceedings.[871]

The third basis of objection was not open to refutation on this ground: it was that 'the intervening resolutions of the Security Council have rendered the Libyan claims without object'; and the Court had in the past decided that 'events subsequent to the filing of an application may "render an application without object".'[872] The Court however held that the objection did not have 'an exclusively preliminary character' within the meaning of Article 79, paragraph 7, of the Rules of Court, but had 'the character of a defence on the merits'.[873] The result of this ruling was that the objection was reserved to be decided along with the merits at a later stage of the proceedings. In 2003 the cases were withdrawn, so the point remained undecided. It is however to be noted that in the course of its reasoning, the Court stated that the United Kingdom was in effect asking for two decisions 'which the decision not to proceed to judgment on the merits would necessarily postulate', namely

> on the one hand a decision establishing that the rights claimed by Libya under the Montreal Convention are incompatible with its obligations under the Security Council resolutions; and, on the other hand, a decision that those obligations prevail over those rights by virtue of Articles 25 and 103 of the Charter.[874]

This is of course correct as an analysis of the argument, but it is striking nevertheless that the Court appears to treat as arguable the thesis that the Security Council decisions did *not* prevail over the Convention obligations. What may underlie the passage is an issue not mentioned in the judgment, but discussed in the dissenting opinions of President Schwebel and Judge Jennings: 'the question whether the Court is empowered to exercise judicial review of the decisions of the Security Council';[875] this has been discussed above.[876]

[869] Judge Herczegh, dissenting, was apparently prepared to link this resolution with the two later ones, so that '[i]t should all the more be taken into consideration', but it is unclear quite what this signified: ibid, 51–52.

[870] Ibid, 24, para 41, quoting the UK argument.

[871] Ibid, 25–26, paras 43–44. In this context mention was made of the Libyan argument that resolution 731 (1992) 'was not adopted under Chapter VII of the United Nations Charter and was only a mere recommendation'.

[872] Ibid, 26, para 46, citing in particular the *Border and Transborder Armed Actions* case, [1988] ICJ Rep 95, para 66.

[873] Ibid, 29, para 50. This is not equivalent to a finding in favour of jurisdiction: the objection remains as a jurisdictional point, but is to be settled at the merits stage. This misunderstanding appears in, for example, Said Hamdauni, 'A propos de l'arrêt de la CIJ relative aux exceptions préliminaires de l'incident aérien de Lockerbie' (2000) XXXI (1) *Etudes internationales* 91.

[874] Ibid. [875] Schwebel, Dissenting Opinion, ibid, 73. [876] Chapter II, Section 1 (2) (b).

Judge Kooijmans was apparently sympathetic to the argument of the UK and the US that

that the case should... be terminated at the present stage as any judgment on the merits would be without practical effect since the relief sought by Libya cannot be provided by the Court because of the overriding legal effects of the mandatory resolutions of the Security Council.[877]

He noted the principle laid down in the *Northern Cameroons* case that the Court should not give a judgment incapable of effective application, but distinguished that case on the ground that

[r]esolutions of the Security Council taken under Chapter VII of the Charter may have far-reaching legal effects, but they are not irrevocable or unalterable. In the exercise of its function the Security Council is free to confirm, revoke or amend them and consequently they cannot be called "final" even if during their lifetime they may be dispositive of the rights and obligations of member States, overriding rights and obligations these States may have under other treaties.[878]

This is undoubtedly correct; its relevance for him was that it justified the decision of the Court to find that the objection did not have 'an exclusively preliminary character' and postpone a ruling on it.[879] Presumably in such a situation, one might apply by analogy the rule stated in Article 70, paragraph 1 *(b)* of the Vienna Convention on the Law of Treaties, that the revocation of a binding resolution 'does not affect any right, obligation or legal situation... created through the execution' of the obligations under the resolution 'prior to its termination'.[880]

(b) Decisions of the General Assembly

When the Court was asked for an advisory opinion on the *Legality of the Threat or Use of Nuclear Weapons*, its attention was drawn to 'the important series of General Assembly resolutions, beginning with resolution 1653 (XVI) of 24 November 1961, that deal with nuclear weapons and that affirm, with consistent regularity, the illegality of nuclear weapons'.[881] It was not however contended that these resolutions had in themselves imposed any obligations on member States; the parties that considered that such weapons were unlawful argued that

[877] Kooijmans, Dissenting Opinion, ibid, 58.

[878] Ibid, 59, para 17.

[879] The argument is not wholly convincing: at the merits stage the resolutions, if still standing unamended, would have to be applied even though at that stage also they could be amended or withdrawn subsequently.

[880] This would be particularly appropriate since the ultimate force of an obligation under a binding Security Council resolution is acceptance by the State concerned of the Charter, i.e. the obligation is of a treaty-law character. For the possible application by analogy of the Vienna Convention on the Law of Treaties to the interpretation of such resolutions, see Michael C Wood, 'The Interpretation of Security Council Resolutions' (1998) 2 *Max Planck Yearbook of United Nations Law* 73, 85 et seq.

[881] [1996] ICJ Rep 254, para 68.

the resolutions in question did no more than apply to nuclear weapons the existing rules of international law applicable in armed conflict; they were no more than the "envelope" or *instrumentum* containing certain pre-existing customary rules of international law.[882]

The question was thus not of the *effect* of the resolutions, but rather of their *significance*, and this has been examined in an earlier article.[883]

(c) Decisions of the Secretary-General

The Secretary-General has of course a vital role to play in the operation of the United Nations, but he is not himself an organ;[884] the relevant section of the Charter (Chapter XV) is devoted to the Secretariat, which under Article 7 constitutes a principal organ of the Organization. The Court has previously had to consider decisions of the Secretary-General in staff matters; and in the case of *Application of the Genocide Convention,* the Court was ready to attach some weight to the view of the Secretary-General as depositary of the Convention that a succession of States had taken place in relation to that Convention.[885] However, in 1999 the question was raised before the Court of the authority of a decision of the Secretary-General as possibly determinative for and, in effect binding upon, a member State. In the case of the *Difference relating to Immunity from Legal Process of a Special Rapporteur of the Commission on Human Rights* (the *Cumaraswamy* case), the Secretary-General had decided that words spoken by the Rapporteur which had been made the subject of slander proceedings in the Malaysian courts had been so spoken in the course of his mission, and that he was therefore entitled to 'immunity from legal process of every kind' in that respect, in accordance with Article VI, Section 22, of the General Convention on the Privileges and Immunities of the United Nations.[886] The Court was asked for an advisory opinion 'on the legal question of the applicability' of that text;[887] and it was suggested by Malaysia before the Court that the 'existing difference between the United Nations and Malaysia' in this connection was whether the Secretary-General 'has the exclusive authority to determine whether the acts of an expert...were performed in the course of his or her mission.'[888]

[882] Ibid, para 69. [883] (2006) *BYIL*, 97–100.

[884] Which is the reason why it does not appear possible for him to be given the right to request advisory opinions from the Court: *contra*, Stephen M Schwebel, 'Authorizing the Secretary-General of the United Nations to request Advisory Opinions of the International Court of Justice' (1984) 78 *American Journal of International Law* 869.

[885] [1996] ICJ Rep 611, para 20 (see also [1993] ICJ Rep 16, para 25).

[886] This point had not arisen in the earlier case of *Applicability of Article VI, section 22, of the Convention on the Privileges and Immunities of the United Nations* (the *Mazilu* case), where the question was whether Mr. Mazilu was entitled to privileges and Immunities as a Special Rapporteur of the Sub-Commission on Prevention of Discrimination and Protection of Minorities, or had ceased to hold that position; the Court relied on the recorded decisions of the Sub-Commission rather than any certificate by the Secretary-General: [1989] ICJ Rep 197–198, para 57 (see also the discussion in the previous article (1996) *BYIL* 37–39).

[887] See ECOSOC decision 1998/297, reproduced in [1999-I] ICJ Rep 63–64.

[888] [1999-I] ICJ Rep 79, para 32.

In the Advisory Opinion, the Court does not directly pose and answer this question. It first defined its own understanding of what was required of it by the request for advisory opinion as being 'whether . . . the Secretary-General's finding that the Special Rapporteur acted in the course of his mission is correct',[889] and concluded that it was.[890] However it then went on to the second part of the question put to it, namely 'the legal obligations of Malaysia in this case'. Those obligations derived from its position as a party to the General Convention, Article 34 of which provides that a party must be 'in a position under its own law to give effect to the terms' of the Convention.[891] The key point here was whether Malaysia should have communicated the Secretary-General's finding to its own domestic courts. The Court's ruling was as follows:

[T]he Secretary-General, as the chief administrative officer of the Organization, has the primary responsibility to safeguard the interests of the Organization; to that end, it is up to him [*il lui incombe*] to assess whether its agents acted within the scope of their functions and, where he so concludes, to protect these agents, including experts on mission, by asserting their immunity. This means that the Secretary-General has the authority and responsibility to inform the Government of a member State of his finding and, where appropriate, to request it to act accordingly and, in particular, to request it to bring his finding to the knowledge of the local courts if acts of an agent have given or may give rise to court proceedings.

When national courts are seised of a case in which the immunity of a United Nations agent is in issue, they should immediately be notified of any finding by the Secretary-General concerning that immunity. That finding, and its documentary expression, creates a presumption which can only be set aside for the most compelling reasons and is thus to be given the greatest weight by national courts.[892]

The Court seems here to be tip-toeing round the question of the exact authority of a finding by the Secretary-General for a member State. Does the expression 'it is up to him to assess' simply mean that he is the person (rather than any other) to make the assessment, or that he is empowered to make a binding assessment?[893] The passage has also to be read against the background of the ruling by the Court earlier in the decision that in the instant case the Secretary-General's finding was legally correct; that ruling had of course not been made at the time that Malaysia should have communicated the view of the Secretary-General to its own courts, and Malaysia was presumably entitled, at that time, to contend that the Secretary-General

[889] Ibid, 84, para 49. [890] Ibid, 86, para 56. [891] See ibid, 86, para 58.

[892] Ibid, 87, paras 60–61. As the High Court of Malaysia was later to comment, it seemed inappropriate 'for the ICJ to hold that the question of immunity ought to be decided as a preliminary issue and then to take upon itself the right to decide that the defendant enjoyed such immunity. What then is the purpose of holding that the Malaysian courts ought to deal with the question of immunity as a preliminary issue?' *Insas Bhd v Cumaraswamy*, [2000] 4 AMR 4947; accessed 14 August 2009 at <http://www.ipsofactoj.com/highcourt/2001/Part1/hct2001(1)-004.htm>.

[893] To the present outside observer, the choice of 'it is up to him' rather than 'for him' in the English text rather points to the former reading.

was wrong. Must not a State which does communicate to its own courts the view of the Secretary-General as to the existence of immunities, as the Court's ruling requires, still be free to argue before those courts, by whatever procedural mechanism may be available to it, that the Secretary-General is wrong?[894]

Judge Weeramantry, in a separate opinion, was prepared to be a little more definite as to the authority of the Secretary-General's decision: he noted that the Secretary-General was much better informed than any external authority of the circumstances of any particular case, and that in practice his determinations in cases of this kind were treated as conclusive; he therefore found that such a determination was to be treated as binding on a domestic tribunal 'unless compelling reasons can be established for displacing that weighty presumption'.[895] Judge Oda, on the other hand, thought that the point was not in fact 'directly at issue' in the case before the Court.[896]

The Court was perhaps wise to avoid committing itself to any definite finding either that the Secretary-General's ruling is final and binding (since it is difficult to point to Charter authority for this), or that it is simply provisional (which would gravely weaken the protection of the Privileges and Immunities Convention).

Mention may be made here of the role of the UN Legal Counsel, on whose advice the Secretary-General presumably acts in taking decisions of this kind. In two cases the view of the Legal Adviser of an international organization have assumed some individual significance in a case before the Court: the view of the WHO Legal Counsel in the case of *Legality of the Use by a State of Nuclear Weapons in Armed Conflict*, and the view of the UN Legal Counsel on the consequences of the break-up of Yugoslavia for purposes of the membership of that State and its successor States in the Organization. In the first case, when the World Health Assembly adopted the resolution requesting an advisory opinion from the Court, it did so in face of clearly expressed advice from the Legal Counsel that the matter was one within the mandate of the UN General Assembly, not that of the WHO. Judge Oda, in his separate opinion in the case, set out at length the successive stages at which the Legal Counsel had expressed this view, and concluded 'We cannot shut our eyes to interpretations [apparently, of the WHO Constitution] given by the competent officials of the Organization.'[897] He does not however make clear what weight should be given to these views, as such, though clearly they are significant as showing that the Assembly acted in full awareness of the existence of, at least, a controversial legal point.

The views of the UN Legal Counsel on the consequences of the break-up of the former Yugoslavia, and the effect of Security Council resolutions 757 (1992) and 777 (1992) and General Assembly resolution 47/1 have been

[894] Jan Klabbers, for example, interprets the Opinion as indicating that the Secretary-General's decision creates no more than a presumption, which like all presumptions may be rebutted: 'The Life and Times of the Law of International Organizations' (2001) 70 *Nordic Journal of International Law* 315.

[895] [1999-I] ICJ Rep 97.

[896] Ibid, 101–102, paras 7–10.

[897] [1996] ICJ Rep 96.

referred to earlier in the present article.[898] The Court characterized the situation of the FRY in relation to the UN over the ensuing years, until 2001, as 'highly complex' and 'ambiguous and open to different assessments'.[899] It did not indicate whether the opinion of the Legal Counsel was to blame for this state of affairs, as having complicated, perhaps needlessly, the situation as stated in the resolutions of the Council and the Assembly, though this is a view that may well be taken by an outside observer.[900]

5. Privileges and Immunities of International Organizations and their Staff[901]

The question of the privileges and immunities of 'experts on mission', dealt with in the earlier *Mazilu* case in 1989,[902] was again before the Court as a result of the request for advisory opinion made by the United Nations Economic and Social Council concerning the *Difference Relating to Immunity from Legal Process of a Special Rapporteur of the Commission on Human Rights*. The problem was, as in the *Mazilu* case, whether the relevant privileges and immunities of an 'expert on mission', deriving from the 1946 General Convention on the Privileges and Immunities of the United Nations, were being respected by the national State of the person concerned. A Malaysian jurist, Dato' Param Cumaraswamy, had been appointed by the Commission on Human Rights as its Special Rapporteur on the Independence of Judges and Lawyers. In an interview with a magazine he commented, in perhaps incautious terms, on certain litigation carried on in the Malaysian courts. Two commercial companies brought proceedings for defamation against him, claiming enormous damages. The UN Legal Counsel, on behalf of the Secretary-General 'determined' that Mr. Cumaraswamy was interviewed in his official capacity as Special Rapporteur, and requested the Government of Malaysia 'to promptly advise the Malaysian courts of the Special Rapporteur's immunity from legal process'.[903] Mr. Cumaraswamy himself applied to the Malaysian court for the action to be set aside on this ground; his application was refused and the Federal Court of Malaysia took the view that he had no immunity, being merely 'an unpaid, part-time provider of information' to the UN.[904] At the

[898] Above, Division D, Section 3.

[899] *Legality of Use of Force (FRY v Belgium)*, [2004] ICJ Rep 305, para 64 (and similarly in the other judgments in this set of cases).

[900] There can be little doubt that there were political pressures and considerations in the background which immensely complicated the task of the Legal Counsel.

[901] The period under review has also seen an interesting decision of the Supreme Court of the Netherlands concerning the privileges and immunities of the Registrar of the International Court in respect of taxation of pensions, and by implication those of the members of the Court: see *Hoge Raad,* Decision 07/12243, 16 January 2009. The decision is in line with an earlier decision of the French *Conseil d'État,* arrêt du 6 juin 1997, no 148683.

[902] *Applicability of Article VI, Section 22, of the Convention on the Privileges and Immunities of the United Nations*, [1989] ICJ Rep 177, discussed in the previous article at (1996) *BYIL* 37–39.

[903] [1999-I] ICJ Rep 67, para 6. [904] Ibid, 70, para 13.

time that the Court examined the case, Mr. Cumaraswamy was faced with orders for costs against him amounting to over $200,000.[905]

Before the Court, Malaysia recognized that Mr. Cumaraswamy had the status of expert on mission, 'and that such experts enjoy the privileges and immunities provided for under the General Convention in their relations with States parties, including those of which they are nationals or in the territory of which they reside'.[906] The central question was therefore 'whether the immunity provided for in Section 22 *(b)* [of the General Convention] applies to Mr. Cumaraswamy in the specific circumstances of the case; namely whether the words used by him in the interview . . . were spoken in the course of the performance of his mission, and whether he was therefore immune from legal process with respect to these words'.[907] The Court put the matter in terms of an examination of the Secretary-General's determination of the point, and was able to find that 'the Secretary-General correctly found' that Mr. Cumaraswamy had been acting in the course of performance of his mission.[908] This approach was consistent with the view taken by the Court, noted above,[909] that the Secretary-General had authority to make such a determination which would apparently be conclusive.

The question that the Secretary-General had had to resolve was a question of interpretation of a treaty, the General Convention. The Court noted that 'the Secretary-General was "reinforced in his view" that Mr. Cumaraswamy had been acting in the performance of his mission "by the fact that it has become standard practice of Special Rapporteurs to have contact with the media."'[910] This may appear to be practice invoked for purposes of interpreting the word 'mission' in the General Convention, but it is rather an argument in support of a particular definition of the extent of the specific mission entrusted to Mr. Cumaraswamy. In effect, the point is that even if Mr. Cumaraswamy was not instructed, as part of his mission, to have regular contact with the media, he was given a mission which, according to the general practice of the Organization, would involve such contact; and therefore such contact would be part of the 'performance of his mission'. Does this however signify that anything said in the course of such an interview would necessarily be protected by immunities? Mr. Cumaraswamy's remarks were capable of being defamatory; they were however closely linked with the specific mission entrusted to him, of examining the independence of judges and lawyers, and therefore fell within his mandate. In a different context, such remarks, while part of an interview properly regarded as part of a mission, might themselves be out of place and improper; should they then be covered by immunity?

An aspect of the problem not in fact discussed in the Advisory Opinion is the principle of the functional necessity of immunities. The General Convention is supplemental to Article 105 of the Charter, which refers to enjoyment by the Organization of 'such privileges and immunities as are

[905] Ibid, 73–74, para 19.
[906] Ibid, 83–84, para 45.
[907] Ibid, 84, para 47.
[908] Ibid, 86, para 56.
[909] Section 4 *(c)* above.
[910] [1997-I] ICJ Rep 85, para 53.

necessary for the fulfilment of its purposes'. At the level of a special rapporteur, this would mean that his role should be covered by the mantle of the purposes of the Charter (and this should be assumed to be the case in anything but an extremely exceptional situation), and the acts complained of should be in the fulfilment of the mission entrusted to him for the furthering of those purposes.

The Court also cited in support of the Secretary-General's findings the fact that the Human Rights Commission 'took note of the Special Rapporteur's reports and of his methods of work', and that '[i]n 1997, it extended his mandate for another three years', adding that '[t]he Commission presumably would not have so acted if it had been of the opinion that Mr. Cumaraswamy had gone beyond his mandate and had given the interview...outside the course of his functions.'[911] This is a less convincing argument. A special rapporteur might act in a way that was not part of the performance of his mission, for purposes of the General Convention, without necessarily thereby contravening the terms of his mission so as to justify sanctions by the Commission. Furthermore, by 1997 negotiations were in progress between the Secretary-General and the Malaysian Government, and the Commission might well have felt it should back up its Special Rapporteur, even if it had doubts whether he might have been indiscreet.

6. Regional Agencies (Article 52 of the UN Charter)

In two cases, the Court has had occasion to consider the nature and role of bodies alleged to constitute 'regional arrangements or agencies for dealing with such matters relating to the maintenance of international peace and security as are appropriate for regional action', as contemplated by Article 52, paragraph 1, of the United Nations Charter.

In the case of *Armed Activities in and against Nicaragua*, it was contended by the United States that the 'Contadora Process' constituted an arrangement of this kind.[912] The relevance of this contention lay in two of the objections made by the United States to the admissibility of the Nicaraguan Application. The first objection was that Nicaragua's 'single fundamental claim' was that the United States was engaged in an unlawful use of armed force, or aggression, and that that was 'a matter which is committed by the Charter and by practice to the competence of other organs', including regional agencies and arrangements, *in casu* the Contadora Process.[913] The

[911] [1999-I] ICJ Rep 86, para 55.

[912] The Court's judgment does not explain the nature of the process. It was in fact a negotiating process initiated in January 1983 at a meeting of the foreign ministers of Mexico, Venezuela, Colombia and Panama on Contadora Island in the Gulf of Panama, based on the idea of a purely Latin-American diplomatic effort to stabilize the Central American situation and prevent either military confrontation between neighbouring states or direct military intervention by the United States.

[913] [1984] ICJ Rep 431–432, para 89.

second relevant objection was to some extent a repetition: it was that 'Nicaragua has failed to exhaust the established processes for the resolution of the conflicts occurring in Central America', and was 'obliged to make every effort to achieve a solution to the security problems of Central America through the Contadora Process'.[914] The Court rejected both objections; central to its position was the distinction between the role of the Court and that of the Security Council.[915] It observed that 'even the existence of active negotiations in which both parties might be involved should not prevent both the Security Council and the Court from exercising their separate functions'.[916] The United States' contention was in effect that the Contadora Process was more than just a negotiation: it was the Security Council operating through a regional agency; but the principle of the distinction between the role of the political and judicial organs of the Organization entailed, in the Court's view, the possibility of their simultaneous operation in relation to the same matter.[917] On that basis, the question whether the Contadora Process was legally to be treated as a 'regional arrangement' or 'regional agency' might appear to become moot;[918] but the Court nevertheless indicated that it did not 'consider that the Contadora Process, whatever its merits, can properly be regarded as a "regional arrangement" for the purposes of Chapter VIII of the Charter of the United Nations'.[919] Unfortunately it did not elaborate on the reasons for this finding. The fact that the process was instituted and carried on entirely independently of any supervision or assistance from the UN, and without any other link with the organization, would seem to exclude the concept of a 'regional agency'; but the Charter itself contemplates that the initiative in establishing regional arrangements may come from 'the States concerned', with the 'encouragement' of the Security Council presumably following after.[920]

The second case in which the Court had to consider the Charter provisions on regional agencies and arrangements was that of the *Land and Maritime Boundary between Cameroon and Nigeria*, the entity concerned being the Lake Chad Basin Commission. This had been created by agreement between Cameroon, Chad, Niger and Nigeria, the States each of whose territories included parts of the Lake. Nigeria had submitted a preliminary objection to the request submitted by Cameroon for a delimitation by the Court of the boundary between the two States in the region of the Lake; it contended that 'the settlement of boundary disputes within the Lake Chad region is subject to the exclusive competence of the Lake

914 Ibid, 438, para 102.

915 Ibid, 439–440, para 105.

916 Ibid, 440, para 106.

917 Ibid, 439–440, para 105.

918 The more so in that the Court invoked Article 103 of the Charter, apparently to suggest that the existence of other dispute settlement arrangements could never serve as a ground for excluding the competence of the Security Council or of the Court.

919 Ibid, 440, para 107.

920 Charter, Article 52, para 3.

Chad Basin Commission.'[921] Nigeria argued, *inter alia*, that '"the role and Statute of the Commission" must be understood "in the framework of regional agencies" referred to in Article 52 of the United Nations Charter.'[922] What is not clear from the judgment is why, in Nigeria's contention, it would follow from this that the Commission would have 'exclusive competence' over boundary disputes in the region.[923] Be that as it may, the Court did not accept the contention; after quoting Article 52, paragraphs 1 and 2, it noted that

> the Lake Chad Basin Commission is an international organization exercising its powers within a specific geographical area; . . . it does not however have as its purpose the settlement at a regional level of matters relating to the maintenance of international peace and security and thus does not fall under Chapter VIII of the Charter.[924]

The Court however also followed the *Nicaragua* precedent in finding that even if the Commission were a regional arrangement, the objection to jurisdiction must fail: 'Whatever their nature, the existence of procedures for regional negotiation cannot prevent the Court from exercising the functions conferred upon it by the Charter and the Statute.'[925] This must perhaps be regarded as the true *ratio decidendi* of the earlier case, since the Contadora process, unlike the Lake Chad Basin Commission, did 'have as its purpose the settlement at a regional level of matters relating to the maintenance of international peace and security', and it is not clear why it did not therefore qualify as a 'regional arrangement.'

[921] [1998] ICJ Rep 304, para 61.

[922] Ibid, 306, para 66.

[923] Nigeria also argued that the Commission was a 'tribunal' for the purposes of Article 95 of the Charter, and that a pronouncement on Cameroon's submission would therefore be 'in breach of the principle of the autonomy of jurisdictional competence' and the exercise of 'an appellate jurisdiction': ibid, 307, para 69.

[924] Ibid, 307, para 67. Judge *ad hoc* Ajibola dissented on this point: he considered that since the Commission was empowered by its Statute to 'examine complaints, promote settlement of disputes and resolve differences', '[t]he maintenance of international peace and security, as stipulated in Article 52 (1) of the Charter, is in accord with the assignments conferred on the Commission by this regional group of States': ibid, 406.

[925] Ibid, para 68.

Capacity to Litigate in the International Court of Justice: Reflections on Yugoslavia in the Court

By Shabtai Rosenne*

Article 34 (1) of the Statute of the International Court of Justice regulates capacity to be a party in contentious litigation in that Court. By that provision, 'Only States may be parties in cases before the Court' [*Seuls les Etats ont qualité pour se présenter devant la Cour*]. That is the sole provision in the Statute to govern the type of international personality having capacity to be a party in a contentious case in the Court. It was the only provision of Article 34 of the Statute of the Permanent Court of International Justice. The remainder of current Article 34, added at the United Nations Conference on International Organization, the San Francisco Conference of 1945, addresses a different matter altogether, the possible role of public international organizations in contentious litigation between States. Article 35, the principal statutory provision dealing with the Court's jurisdiction *ratione personae*, refines this. It sets out the States that can access the Court. It distinguishes between States that are parties to the Statute, a community of States which today, by virtue of Article 93 of the United Nations Charter, includes all members of the United Nations *ipso facto* (para 1), and 'other States'. By Article 93 (2) of the Charter:

> A State which is not a Member of the United Nations may become a party to the Statute of the International Court of Justice on conditions to be determined in each case by the General Assembly upon the recommendation of the Security Council.

Article 35 (2) of the Statute addresses the access to the Court of other States which are not parties to the Statute:

> The conditions under which the Court shall be open to other states shall, subject to the special provisions contained in treaties in force, be laid down by the Security Council, but in no case shall such conditions place the parties in a position of inequality before the Court.

* Honorary member, Institute of International Law. In this article cases in the International Court of Justice that have not yet been printed in the Court's Reports are indicated by their full date of issuance. They are available at the Court's website, <www.icj-cij.org>. This article was completed in December 2009.

The Security Council set out the relevant conditions for participation in litigation of a State that is not a party to the Statute in its resolution 9 (1946), 15 October 1946.

Article 36 (1) gives the rule for the Court's substantive or material jurisdiction (jurisdiction *ratione materiae*):

> The jurisdiction of the Court comprises all cases which the parties refer to it and all matters specially provided for in the Charter of the United Nations or in treaties and conventions in force.

In this paradigm, the consent of the States involved in the litigation is the condition for the International Court's entertaining any contentious case brought before it, with the precondition that each State involved as a party or otherwise (as in the exceptional case of what the Court denominates as the 'non-party intervener') in a contentious case is qualified to have access to the Court. According to this precondition, the Court must be 'open' to each such State (under Article 35); that is to say, each one of those States must have what the Court has identified as 'capacity to be a party to the proceedings',[1] before the Court should consider hearing the case brought before it. However, there is no provision in the Statute laying down precisely when this precondition has to be met: this is a matter that the Statute leaves to the Court which, by virtue of Article 36 (6) of its Statute, has jurisdiction to decide the matter of any dispute as to whether it has jurisdiction. What is certain is that the precondition of capacity (as distinct from any matter of jurisdiction) has to be met when the Court delivers its judgment in a particular phase. If not, the Court will decline to entertain the case. The Court's silence on this matter in a given decision indicates that for the purposes of that decision the precondition is met.

The complicated litigation following the dissolution of the Socialist Federal Republic of Yugoslavia (SFRY)[2] in 1992 led to a series of cases involving the capacity of Yugoslavia or what is called its 'continuator state', by virtue of membership in the United Nations, to be a party in contentious litigation in the International Court of Justice, whether as applicant or as respondent. This article examines various aspects of that litigation-capacity brought out by those cases.

[1] *Case Concerning Application of the Convention on the Prevention and Punishment of the Crime of Genocide* (*Croatia v Serbia*), Judgment of 18 November 2008 on Preliminary Objections (para 57) (hereafter '*Genocide, Croatia*' case).

[2] The various name-changes of the different States concerned are a cause of difficulty. In this article the term 'Yugoslavia' means as a start the country included among the founder members of the United Nations, originally under the name of Democratic Federal Yugoslavia, and since 1963 known as the Socialist Federal Republic of Yugoslavia (SFRY). Under various names reflecting internal constitutional developments the continuator State of the SFRY, known at one time as the Federal Republic of Yugoslavia (FRY), is now a member of the United Nations under the name of Serbia. See on this the section on the identification of the respondent party in the judgment on the merits of the *Application of the Convention on the Prevention and Punishment of the Crime of Genocide (Bosnia and Herzegovina v Serbia and Montenegro)* case (hereafter '*Genocide, Bosnia*' case), [2007] ICJ Rep 43, 73 (paras 67–79).

All the cases considered here involved 'Yugoslavia' as the SFRY disintegrated. In this context, major importance attaches to two resolutions of the United Nations General Assembly, both adopted on the recommendation of the Security Council. The first is resolution 47/1, 22 September 1992. Here the General Assembly, following Security Council resolution 777 (1992), 19 September 1992 which had noted that the State formerly known as the SFRY had ceased to exist, '[c]onsider[ed] that the Federal Republic of Yugoslavia (Serbia and Montenegro) [FRY] cannot continue automatically the membership of the former [SFRY] in the United Nations; and therefore decide[d] that the [FRY] (Serbia and Montenegro) should apply for membership in the United Nations and that it [should] not participate in the work of the General Assembly'. This was to lead to the question whether the FRY was the continuator State of the SFRY.

This resolution, which the FRY did not accept at the time, was the subject of an important interpretation by the Under-Secretary-General and Legal Counsel of the United Nations on 29 September 1992. The main burthen of that interpretation was that resolution 47/1 'neither terminates nor suspends Yugoslavia's *membership* in the Organization' and 'does not take away the right of Yugoslavia to participate in the work of organs other than Assembly bodies.... The admission...of a new Yugoslavia under Article 4...will terminate the situation created by resolution 47/1'.[3]

The second relevant resolution concerns the FRY's request, contained in a letter of 27 October 2000, for admission to the United Nations 'in light of the implementation of Security Council resolution 777 (1992)'. On the recommendation of the Security Council in resolution 1326, 31 October 2000, the General Assembly adopted resolution 55/12, 1 November 2000, admitting the Federal Republic of Yugoslavia to membership in the United Nations. This terminated the situation created by resolution 47/1. The Yugoslavia cases considered here were instituted unilaterally between those two dates by the filing of an application. They related to Yugoslavia both as respondent and as applicant.

While, obviously, all parties in contentious litigation must have the capacity to be a party in a case in the International Court under Article 35 of the Statute and must have consented to the exercise of its jurisdiction over the specific case under Article 36, there is possibly a difference as to the time at which that capacity and that consent have to exist on the part of the applicant and on the part of the respondent. In the Yugoslavia litigation both the question of capacity and the question of consent arose,

[3] UN Doc. A/47/485, emphasis in original. The document makes no mention of suspension of Yugoslavia's rights under Articles 4, 8, 12, 14, 33 and 69 of the Court's Statute which, by Article 92 of the Charter, 'forms an integral part' of the Charter. In resolution 47/229, 29 April 1993, the General Assembly, again on the recommendation of the Security Council, decided that the FRY (Serbia and Montenegro) should not participate in the work of the Economic and Social Council. In March 1994 the FRY was excluded from participating in meetings of States Parties to the International Covenant on Civil and Political Rights, 999 UNTS 171, 1057 UNTS 407.

always in a form that related to the precise status of the FRY as a party to the Statute through membership in the United Nations after the dissolution of the SRFY and its replacement by initially the FRY (Serbia and Montenegro) and later, after further disintegration, by Serbia alone. This article is concerned only with the question of capacity, which is distinct from the issue of consent in any specific case.

*

On the question of the capacity of the respondent, the first relevant case was *Genocide, Bosnia*.[4] This was probably the most complex case, procedurally, ever to have come before either the Permanent Court of International Justice or the present International Court of Justice.[5]

A State named the Republic of Bosnia and Herzegovina (hereafter 'Bosnia-Herzegovina') filed an application instituting proceedings against the FRY (Serbia and Montenegro) on 20 March 1993, basing jurisdiction on Article IX of the Convention on the Prevention and Punishment of the Crime of Genocide of 9 December 1948.[6] At the same time the applicant filed a request for the indication of provisional measures under Article 41 of the Statute of the Court. In paras 21–26 of the Order on Provisional Measures of 8 April 1993[7] the Court discussed the status of the parties in litigation in relation to the Genocide Convention, as at the date of those provisional measures proceedings, that is to say, as a matter of jurisdiction *ratione personae*. The Court found that the Convention could constitute a basis on which its jurisdiction might be founded, and

[4] For this complicated case see [1993] ICJ Rep 3 (Provisional Measures) and 325 (Further Provisional Measures); [1996] 595 (Preliminary Objections); [1997] 243 (Counter-Claims); [2001] 572 (Withdrawal of Counter-Claims); [2003] 7 (Application for Revision of Judgment of 11 July 1996 in the *Case concerning Application of the Convention on the Prevention and Punishment of the Crime of Genocide (Bosnia and Herzegovina v Yugoslavia)* (Preliminary Objections), and [2007] 43 (*Bosnia and Herzegovina v Serbia and Montenegro*) (Merits). The judicial discussion in these (and other) cases was confused.

[5] Other issues that arose in these cases, but equally beyond the scope of this article, include the scope of the principle of *res judicata* maintained in Article 59 of the Statute; the Court's adaptation of the continental principle of *la jurisprudence constante*—the common law doctrine of the binding force of judicial precedents (*stare decisis*) was deliberately excluded from the Statute by the opening words of Article 38, para 1 d, of the Statute—; and questions of State succession such as what entity was the 'continuator' of the SFRY.

[6] 58 UNTS 277. Article IX—the compromissory clause—provides: 'Disputes between the Contracting Parties relating to the interpretation, application or fulfilment of the present Convention, including those relating to the responsibility of a State for genocide or any of the other acts enumerated in Article III, shall be submitted to the International Court of Justice at the request of any of the parties to the dispute.' See also H Abtahi and P Webb, *The Genocide Convention: The* Travaux Préparatoires (Martinus Nijhoff, Leiden/Boston, 2008). Article XI of the Convention—the participation clause—provides that the Convention could be signed (and later ratified) on behalf of any member of the United Nations 'and of any other State to which an invitation to sign has been addressed by the General Assembly [of the United Nations]'. Any non-member to have received such an invitation could accede to the Convention. Membership in the United Nations was nowhere made a condition of participation in this Convention.

[7] [1993] ICJ Rep 3.

that this was sufficient to enable it to deal with a request for the indication of provisional measures. Although the FRY as respondent raised a question about the 'legitimacy of the Applicant' which the Court dismissed (Order, paras 12 and 13), the Court found that the question whether or not Yugoslavia was a member of the United Nations and as such a party to the Statute of the Court was 'one which the Court [did] not need to determine definitively at the present stage of the proceedings' (para 18). The order continued with a discussion of Article 35 (2) of the Statute and concluded that both parties in the litigation were parties to the Genocide Convention, within the Court's jurisdiction *ratione personae* (para 19). In the second Order on Provisional Measures of 13 September 1993,[8] FRY repeated that contention, which the Court simply rejected (para 23). In the course of those second provisional measures proceedings, the FRY, on 9 August 1993, filed a request to indicate a provisional measure to be observed by Bosnia-Herzegovina.[9] The operative clause of this order indicated provisional measures which both parties were to apply, thus meeting the FRY's request.

In due course, after the memorial had been filed, the FRY lodged a series of preliminary objections, but none of those objections directly raised the capacity of either party to participate in these proceedings. The objections concerning Bosnia-Herzegovina remained within the compass of Article 35 (2) of the Statute, contending that on the date of the filing of the application instituting these proceedings Bosnia-Herzegovina was not a party to the Genocide Convention by virtue of any rule of State succession. The Court rejected that argument. In its 1996 Judgment on the Preliminary Objections the Court had recourse to what is frequently called the *Mavrommatis* doctrine.[10] The Court said:

> It is the case that the jurisdiction of the Court must normally be assessed on the date of the filing of the act instituting proceedings. However, the Court, like its predecessor, the Permanent Court of International Justice, has always had recourse to the principle according to which it should not penalize a defect in a procedural act that the applicant could easily remedy.... Bosnia and Herzegovina

[8] Ibid, 325.

[9] FRY's request, apparently made without adequate legal advice, was to have an effect on later proceedings, as showing that in the relevant period between the two resolutions FRY had held itself out as having the capacity to introduce proceedings in the Court. This request is mentioned at 27, para 58, of the 2003 Judgment on Revision of the Preliminary Objections Judgment of 1996 (above n 4), at 50, para 8 of the Merits Judgment of 2007 (above n 4), and at para 114 of the 2008 Judgment in the *Genocide, Croatia* Preliminary Objections case (above n 1).

[10] For *Mavrommatis Palestine Concessions* (*Greece v Great Britain*), see PCIJ Rep Series A No 2. Jurisdiction in that case was said to rest on the compromissory clause of the Mandate for Palestine (article 26) and Protocol XII annexed to the Lausanne Treaty of Peace with Turkey, 28 LNTS 11. Greece filed the application instituting these proceedings on 15 May 1924. On that date the necessary ratifications to bring the Treaty of Lausanne into force had not yet been deposited but the process was completed on 6 August 1924. The Permanent Court delivered its judgment on preliminary objections on 30 August 1924. The Court said: 'Since the Treaty [of Lausanne] is now in force and Protocol XII has become applicable... it is not necessary to consider what the legal position would have been if the Treaty had not been ratified *at the time of the Court's judgment*.' (emphasis added).

might at any time file a new application identical to the present one, which would be unassailable in this respect.[11]

On 29 April 1999, during the so-called 'Kosovo War', the FRY filed ten separate applications instituting proceedings against Belgium and nine other NATO members in a series of cases entitled *Legality of Use of Force* cases.[12] We will discuss those cases later, when dealing with the capacity issue as regards the FRY as applicant.

As stated, after a change of government, the FRY applied for and was admitted to membership in the United Nations by General Assembly resolution 55/12, 1 November 2000. This led to a change in its policy regarding the proceedings in the International Court of Justice.

On 24 April 2001 the FRY filed an application for the revision of the preliminary objections judgment in the *Genocide, Bosnia* case, on the basis of Article 61 of the Statute. The principal contention was that the admission of the FRY to the United Nations in November 2000 was a 'new fact' of such a nature as to be a decisive factor regarding the question of jurisdiction *ratione personae* over the FRY, justifying revision under Article 61. In its 2003 Judgment dismissing the application for revision, the Court pointed out that resolution 47/1 'did not *inter alia* affect the FRY's right to appear before the Court or to be a party to a dispute before the Court under the conditions laid down by the Statute'.[13]

While those proceedings were pending, on 4 May 2001, the Respondent raised the capacity issue of that judgment in an unusual procedure entitled 'Initiative to the Court to consider *ex officio* jurisdiction over Yugoslavia'. At the time the Court took no action on that Initiative, to which it referred at p. 30 (para 64) of its 2003 Judgment on the revision issue. On 12 June 2003 the Court decided not to take any decision on that Initiative at that stage, but to allow the Respondent to present further

[11] Judgment on Preliminary Objections (above n 4) para 26.

[12] Cases against Belgium, [1999] ICJ Rep 124; Canada, 259; France, 363; Germany, 422; Italy, 481; the Netherlands, 542; Portugal, 656; Spain, 761; United Kingdom, 826; USA, 916 (Provisional Measures). The Court ordered the cases against Spain and the USA to be removed from the List since the Court 'manifestly' lacked jurisdiction and could not indicate any provisional measure whatsoever (*Case against Spain*, 761, 773, para 35; *Case against the United States,* 916, 925, para 29, On the remaining cases, see the cases against Belgium, [2004] ICJ Rep 279; Canada, 429; France, 575; Germany, 720; Italy, 865; the Netherlands, 1011; Portugal, 1160; United Kingdom, 1307. The Court upheld the preliminary objections and put an end to those cases. In this article citations are to the case against Belgium unless otherwise stated. In the provisional measures phase the Court sat with 14 of its then members, Judge Rezek not participating, together with Yugoslav appointed Judge ad hoc Kreča, and judges ad hoc appointed by Belgium, Canada, Italy, and Spain (Portugal did not a appoint a judge ad hoc). Partial elections of five members of the Court took place in 1999 and in 2002. For the preliminary objections phase the Court decided that the judges ad hoc should not sit (Judgment in the Case against Belgium, [2004] ICJ Rep 279, 287, para 18). In that phase Judge Simma, elected to the Court in 2002, informed the Court that he considered that he should not take part in the decision in these cases (ibid, 286, para 16).

[13] [2003] ICJ Rep 7, 31, para 70. By Article 61 (1), 'An application for revision of a judgment may be made only when it is based upon the discovery of some fact of such a nature as to be a decisive factor, which fact was, when the judgment was given, unknown to the Court and also to the party claiming revision, always provided that such ignorance was not due to negligence'.

arguments on jurisdictional questions during the oral proceedings on the merits.[14]

In its final submissions at the oral proceedings on the merits the Respondent pleaded that the Court had no jurisdiction 'because the Respondent had no access to the Court at the relevant moment'.[15] The parties argued the issue in terms of whether at the time of the institution of the proceedings the Respondent was or was not the 'continuator' of the SFRY, and a party not only to the Genocide Convention but also to the Statute of the Court by virtue of membership in the United Nations on that date.

Part III, pp. 76–102 (paras 80–141) of the Court's 2007 Judgment on the merits deals with the Court's jurisdiction in this case. It is divided into seven sub-sections: (1) introduction; the jurisdictional objections of Serbia and Montenegro (paras 80–87); (2) history of the status of the FRY with regard to the United Nations (paras 88–99); (3) the response of Bosnia and Herzegovina (paras 100–104); (4) relevant past decisions of the Court (paras 105–113); (5) the principle of *res judicata* (paras 114–120); (6) application of the principle of *res judicata* to the 1996 judgment [on preliminary objections] (paras 121–139); (7) conclusion: jurisdiction confirmed (paras 140–141). The Court, in the first operative clause of the judgment at p. 237 (para 471 (1)) '*rejects* the objections contained in the final submissions made by the Respondent to the effect that the Court has no jurisdiction; and *affirms* that it has jurisdiction, on the basis of Article IX of the Convention on the Prevention and Punishment of the Crime of Genocide, to adjudicate upon the dispute brought before it on 20 March 1993 by the Republic of Bosnia and Herzegovina'.

Subsection (1) of this part of the Judgment commences with the following statement:

> Notwithstanding the fact that in this case the stage of oral proceedings on the merits has been reached, and the fact that in 1996 the Court gave a judgment on preliminary objections to its jurisdiction..., an important issue of a jurisdictional character has been raised by the Initiative, and the Court has been asked to rule upon it....The basis of jurisdiction asserted by the Applicant, and found applicable by the Court in the 1996 judgment, is Article IX of the Genocide Convention. The [SFRY] became a party to that Convention on 29 August 1950. In substance, the central question now raised by the Respondent is whether at the time of the filing of the Application instituting the present proceedings the Respondent was or was not the continuator of the SFRY. The Respondent now contends that it was not a continuator State, and that therefore not only was it not a party to the Genocide Convention when the present proceedings were instituted, but it was not then a party to the Statute of the Court by virtue of membership in the United Nations; and that, not being such a party, it did not have

[14] Judgment on the Merits, [2007] ICJ Rep 43 at 56, para 35.

[15] Ibid, 70, para 66.

access to the Court, with the consequence that the Court had no jurisdiction *ratione personae* over it.[16]

On the capacity issue, the Court observed:

Nothing was stated in the 1996 Judgment about the status of the FRY in relation to the United Nations, or the question whether it could participate in proceedings before the Court; for the reasons already mentioned above (paragraph 106), both Parties had chosen to refrain from asking for a decision on those matters. The Court however considers it necessary to emphasize that the question whether a State may properly come before the Court, on the basis of the provisions of the Statute, whether it be classified as a matter of capacity to be a party to the proceedings or as an aspect of jurisdiction *ratione personae*, is a matter which precedes that of jurisdiction *ratione materiae*, that is, whether that State has consented to the settlement by the Court of the specific dispute brought before it. The question is in fact one that the Court is bound to raise and examine, if necessary, ex officio, and if appropriate after notification to the parties. Thus if the Court considers that, in a particular case, the conditions concerning the capacity of the parties to appear before it are not satisfied, while the conditions of its jurisdiction *ratione materiae* are, it should, even if the question has not been raised by the parties, find that the former conditions are not met, and conclude that, for that reason, it could not have jurisdiction to decide the merits.

The operative part of a judgment possesses the force of *res judicata*. The operative part of the 1996 judgment stated . . . that the Court had found "that [. . .] it has jurisdiction to decide upon the dispute". That jurisdiction is thus established with the full weight of the Court's judicial authority.[17]

This passage serves to introduce the Court's complicated reasoning about the effect as *res judicata* of the 1996 Judgment dismissing the preliminary objections and upholding its jurisdiction under the Genocide Convention.[18] For the purposes of this article it is not necessary to enter into the details of the Court's discussion of this matter. One passage from this part of the Judgment suffices:

The finding [French—*conclusion*] [of jurisdiction] must as a matter of construction be understood, by necessary implication, to mean that the Court at that time perceived the Respondent as being in a position to participate in cases before the Court. On that basis, it proceeded to make a finding on jurisdiction which would have the force of *res judicata*. The Court does not need, for the purposes of the present proceedings, to go behind that finding and consider on what basis the Court was able to satisfy itself on the point. Whether the Parties classify the matter as one of "access to the Court" or of "jurisdiction *ratione personae*", the fact remains that the Court could not have proceeded to determine the merits unless

[16] Ibid, 76, para 80. [17] Ibid, 94 (paras 122–123).

[18] On this issue see my 'Article 59 of the Statute of the International Court of Justice Revisited', in *Essays on International Law and Practice* (Martinus Nijhoff, Leiden/Boston, 2007) 129, particularly137 (hereafter *Essays*).

the Respondent had had the capacity under the Statute to be a party to proceedings before the Court.[19]

The Court continued this part of the Judgment with the observation that it considered that the 1996 Judgment contained a finding, whether it be regarded as one of jurisdiction *ratione personae*, or as one anterior to questions of jurisdiction, which was necessary as a matter of logical construction, and related to the question of the FRY's capacity to appear before the Court under the Statute.[20]

The Court went on to deal with Respondent's contention that in the circumstances, reliance on the *res judicata* principle would justify the Court's *ultra vires* exercise of its judicial functions contrary to the mandatory requirements of the Statute. Answering this, the Court said:

[T]he operation of the "mandatory requirements of the Statute" falls to be determined by the Court in each case before it; and once the Court has determined, with the force of *res judicata*, that it has jurisdiction, then for the purposes of that case no question of *ultra vires* action can arise, the Court having sole competence to determine such matters under the Statute. For the Court *res judicata pro veritate habetur* and the judicial truth within the context of a case is as the Court has determined it, subject only to the provision in the Statute for revision of judgments. This result is required by the nature of the judicial function, and the universally recognized need for stability of legal relations.[21]

The Court finished this part of the Judgment with the remark that there had been some reference in the parties' arguments to the question whether Article 35, paras (1) and (2), of the Statute applied equally to applicants and to respondents. 'This matter, being one of interpretation of the Statute, would be one for the Court to determine.' It was not necessary for the Court to do this in the present case (para 141). The Court adopted its decision on jurisdiction by ten votes against five.

The next case—and the final one to date in this series relating to the capacity of Yugoslavia as respondent—is the *Genocide, Croatia* case that is still pending on the merits at the time of writing.[22] On 2 July 1999 the Republic of Croatia filed an application against the FRY in respect of a dispute concerning alleged violations of the Genocide Convention, again invoking Article IX of that Convention as the title of jurisdiction. After the memorial had been filed, on 11 September 2002, the FRY raised preliminary objections. The FRY's first preliminary objection was simply to ask the Court to declare that it lacked jurisdiction over Croatia's claims. There had been some interlocutory exchanges with the parties and these had involved decisions by the Court. On 6 May 2008 the Court asked the parties during the hearings on the preliminary objections to address 'the issue of the capacity of the Respondent to

[19] [2007] ICJ Rep 43, 99, para 132. [20] Ibid, 100, para 136.
[21] Ibid, 101, para 139. [22] Judgment on Preliminary Objections, 18 November 2008.

participate in proceedings before the Court *at the time of filing of the Application*, given the fact that the issue had not been addressed as such in the written pleadings'.[23] At the hearings the Respondent's final submission was simply 'that the Court lacks jurisdiction'. The Applicant's final submission requested the Court to reject the preliminary objections and declare that the Court had jurisdiction to adjudicate upon Croatia's application.

The Court's 2008 Judgment is its first full examination of the issue of capacity as distinct from any issue of jurisdiction.[24] On the preliminary objections to the jurisdiction of the Court, the Court first examined 'Issues of capacity to be a party to the proceedings' (paras 57–92).[25] The Court found that 'central to the . . . proceedings [wa]s the question of the status and position of the State known at the time of the filing of the Application as the FRY, in relation to the Statute of the Court and the Genocide Convention'.[26] After describing the circumstances which gave rise to the issue of Serbia's capacity to participate in these proceedings, the Court explained:

> It should first be observed that the question whether or not a State meets the conditions of Article 35 of the Statute can be regarded either as an issue relating to the Court's jurisdiction *ratione personae* or as an issue preliminary to the examination of jurisdiction. The Court sees no need to settle this debate, any more than it felt obliged to do so in its earlier decisions [here the Court referred to para 126 of its 2007 Judgment, noted above]. Where the conditions of Article 35 are not met, the Court is without jurisdiction to adjudicate the dispute *on the merits* [italics supplied]. From this standpoint, a Respondent raising an objection on the basis that the conditions of Article 35 have not been met must be deemed to be making a jurisdictional objection and, if the Court sustains the argument, its judgment will be a finding of lack of jurisdiction. Thus, Serbia is here asking the Court to decide, drawing on its arguments relating to its first preliminary objection, that it is without jurisdiction in the case.
>
> Secondly, the issue arises whether the Court, if presented with both an objection based on one party's lack of access to the Court and an objection based on lack of jurisdiction *ratione personae*,—or indeed, which comes to the same thing, an objection to the jurisdiction advancing both of these grounds—must necessarily examine the two questions in a prescribed order, so that it could not consider the second (jurisdiction *ratione personae*) until after it has answered the first (access to the Court) in the affirmative.[27]

The Court had addressed the latter issue in its 2004 Judgments in the *Legality of Use of Force* cases. The 2008 Judgment continues:

[23] 2008 Judgment, para 16. Emphasis added.

[24] It should be noted that Article 79(1) of the Rules of Court as revised in 1978 refers to three types of objection: an objection by the respondent to the jurisdiction of the Court, or to the admissibility of the application, *or other objection the decision upon which is requested before any further proceedings on the merits* (emphasis supplied).

[25] 2008 Judgment, para 57.

[26] Ibid, para 52.

[27] Ibid, para 66.

After pointing out that, as a general rule, it remained free to select the ground on which to base its judgment where several grounds were capable of leading to the same conclusion, and it therefore remained free to decide the order in which to deal with these questions, the Court determined that the position was otherwise in the matter before it. It stated that where the applicant's right to access to the Court had been challenged—as it had been—this "fundamental question" had to be decided before any other, because, if the applicant was not a party to the Statute, the Court was not open to it and accordingly it could not seise . . . the Court, whatever title of jurisdiction it might . . . invoke.

The Court therefore found it necessary in those cases first to examine the question of Serbia and Montenegro's access to the Court, so as to determine whether the Court could 'exercise its judicial function' in respect of that State, observing that it could then examine the issues involving jurisdiction *ratione personae* and any other jurisdictional issues "[o]nly if the answer to that [first] question is in the affirmative".

In the present case, even though no question arises as to seisin so far as the Applicant is concerned, the Court considers that here also it is appropriate first to examine the issues relating to the application of Article 35 of the Statute.[28]

Thirdly, the Court recalls that, as it pointed out in its [2007 Judgment in the *Genocide, Bosnia* case], the question whether a State may properly appear before the Court, on the basis of the Statute, is "one which the Court is to raise and examine, if necessary, ex officio, and if appropriate after notification to the parties (para 122)".[29]

The Court then referred to the consequence which it had drawn from this in paragraph 132 of the 2007 Judgment and continued:

Obviously, it does not however follow that the Court is under an obligation to treat the question expressly in the reasoning in any judgment in which it rules on a preliminary objection to jurisdiction. If neither party has raised the issue and the Court finds that the conditions of Articles 34 and 35 are satisfied in the case, it may well choose to omit from the reasoning in its judgment any specific discussion of the point and to confine itself to responding to the arguments raised by the parties. It may also choose, if it finds appropriate, to deal with the point expressly in its reasoning.

If however the Court in a judgment on preliminary objections to jurisdiction rejects them, and upholds its jurisdiction, without saying anything on the question of access to the Court, the conclusion may be drawn that the Court has perceived the conditions on access to have been satisfied.[30]

The Court again referred to paragraph 132 of its 2007 Judgment and continued that the Respondent in 1996 and in 2007 had been the same State as was Respondent in the present case. The Court observed that in the present case no implicit finding that Serbia had the necessary capacity to participate in the proceedings could be inferred from any previous judgment of the Court. The 1996 Judgment, to which the Court gave

[28] Ibid, para 67. [29] Ibid, para 68. [30] Ibid.

effect as *res judicata* in its 2007 Judgment on the merits in the same case, did not of itself have any authority as *res judicata* in the present case. The question of the Respondent's capacity would therefore have to be examined *de novo,* in the context of the dispute now before the Court. The Court recalled that the Respondent had not raised the capacity issue but the Court had informed the parties of its wish to hear this issue addressed in the hearings.[31] The Court also pointed out that in the *Legality of Use of Force* cases in 2004 the Court had concluded that the words 'treaties in force' for purposes of Article 35 (2) of the Statute related to treaties in force at the entry into force of the Statute (24 October 1945) and thus did not cover the Genocide Convention.[32]

Concerning the order in which the Court would examine the various questions arising out of the application of Article 35 of the Statute in the present case, the Court deemed it appropriate to examine the question of Serbia's access to the Court on the basis of Article 35 (1) before any examination on the basis of paragraph (2). Only if the Court were to find that Serbia was not a party to the Statute 'at the relevant time—to be determined below'—and that as a result it did not satisfy the condition of paragraph 1, should the Court address the question of Serbia's capacity to participate on the basis of 'special provisions contained in treaties in force' within the meaning of Article 35 (2).[33]

The Court made two observations to serve as the starting point for the reasoning on this issue.

The first observation related to the 2004 judgments in which the Court had determined the legal status of the FRY (Serbia) in the period from the dissolution of the SFRY to the admission of the FRY to the United Nations. While those judgments did not have the force of *res judicata* for the purposes of the present case, it was

> equally certain that they may be of relevance in the present instance, as, first, they address the legal position of the Respondent . . . during a period—from 1992 to 2000—covering the date of the filing of the Application on which the Court must rule, and second . . . the Court departs from settled jurisprudence only if it is of the opinion that there are very particular reasons to do so.[34]

The second point was that from 1 November 2000 up to the date of the 2008 Judgment the Respondent was a party to the Statute by virtue of its membership in the United Nations. It was thus indisputable that at the date of the Judgment both parties had access to the Court, in the words of the Court, on the basis of Article 35 (1) of the Statute. Had the application been filed on 2 November 2000 instead of 2 July 1999, 'no objection to jurisdiction could have been based on lack of access to the Court within the meaning of Article 35 of the Statute'. This brought the Court to address an issue of particular importance in the present case, namely, whether fulfilment of the conditions laid down in Article

[31] Ibid, para 69. [32] Ibid, para 71. [33] Ibid, para 72. [34] Ibid, paras 76–85.

35 of the Statute must be assessed as at the date of the filing of the application, or whether it can be assessed, 'at least under the special circumstances of the present case, at a subsequent date, more precisely at a date after 1 November 2000'. The Court recalled the 'general rule which it applies in this regard', namely 'the jurisdiction of the Court must normally be assessed at the date of the filing of an act instituting proceedings' (para 79). After explaining and justifying this rule (para 80), the Court went on to say that like the Permanent Court, it 'had also shown realism and flexibility in certain situations in which the conditions governing the Court's jurisdiction were not fully satisfied when proceedings were initiated but were subsequently satisfied, before the Court ruled on its jurisdiction' (para 81).[35] After surveying the parties' arguments, the Court continued:

[G]iven the logic underlying the cited jurisprudence of the Court deriving from the 1924 Judgment in the *Mavrommatis Palestine Concessions* case, it does not matter whether it is the applicant or the respondent that does not fulfil the conditions for the Court's jurisdiction, or both of them—as is the situation where the compromissory clause invoked as the basis for jurisdiction only enters into force after the proceedings have been instituted. The Court sees no convincing reason why an applicant's deficiency might be overcome in the course of proceedings, while that of a respondent may not. What matters is that, at the latest by the date when the Court decides on its jurisdiction, the applicant must be entitled, if it so wishes, to bring fresh proceedings in which the initially unmet condition would be fulfilled. In such a situation, it is not in the interests of the sound administration of justice to compel the applicant to begin the proceedings anew—or to initiate fresh proceedings—and it is preferable, except in special circumstances, to conclude that the condition has, from that point on, been fulfilled.[36]

Based on a contention that would distinguish the present case from the cited earlier cases, the Judgment went on to say:

[I]t is true that all of the cited precedents concern cases where the initially unfulfilled condition related to jurisdiction *ratione materiae* or *ratione personae* in the narrow sense and not to the question of access to the Court, which has to do with a party's capacity to participate in any proceedings whatever before the Court. Nevertheless, the Court cannot endorse the radical interpretation advanced by Serbia, namely that whenever it is seised by a State which does not fulfil the conditions of access under Article 35, or seised of a case brought against a State which does not fulfil those conditions, the Court does not even have the *compétence de la compétence,* the competence to decide whether or not it has jurisdiction. Nothing of the sort is to be found in the 2004 Judgments . . . In

[35] Here the Court relied on a series of previous decisions, including the *Mavrommatis Palestine Concessions* case (above n 10), *Certain German Interests in Polish Upper Silesia*, PCIJ Rep Series A No 6, *Northern Cameroons*, [1963] ICJ Rep 68, *Military and Paramilitary Activities in and against Nicaragua*, [1984] ICJ Rep 428, para 83, and finally the 1996 Judgment in the *Genocide, Bosnia* case, above n 4.

[36] 2008 Judgment, para 85.

those Judgments, the Court did no more than indicate that the question of access to the Court was a "fundamental one" which needed to be examined before the others, and that if the Applicant did not fulfil the Article 35 conditions the Court had to deduce from that fact that it had not been "properly seised". Not being "properly seised" does not mean that the Court lacks the competence necessary to decide on its own jurisdiction, in other words to decide whether it has been properly seised and whether the conditions necessary to allow it to hear a case on the merits have been satisfied. That is true whether it is the applicant which ... does not fulfil the conditions for access to the Court. It is true *a fortiori* when it is the respondent which allegedly does not meet those conditions since in such circumstances the act of seising the Court, performed by a State which does have access to the Court, is not at issue; that is the case in the present proceedings. The Court always possesses the *compétence de la compétence* (see Article 36, paragraph 6, of the Statute). In any event, the Court notes that Serbia asks it in its principal submission to decide by a judgment that it lacked jurisdiction to entertain Croatia's Application.[37]

The Court then turned to another Serbian argument, to the effect that when the defect is that one party does not have access to the Court, it is so fatal that it can in no case be cured by a subsequent event in the course of the proceedings. On this the Court said:

As stated ... the question of access is clearly distinct from those relating to the examination of jurisdiction in the narrow sense. But it is nevertheless closely related to jurisdiction, inasmuch as the consequence is exactly the same whether it is the conditions of access or the conditions of jurisdiction *ratione materiae* or *ratione temporis* which are unmet; the Court lacks jurisdiction to entertain the case. It is always within the context of an objection to jurisdiction, as in the present case, that arguments will be raised before the Court regarding the parties' capacity to participate in the proceedings.

That being so, it is not apparent why the arguments based on the sound administration of justice which underpin the *Mavrommatis* case jurisprudence cannot also have a bearing in a case such as the present one. It would not be in the interests of justice to oblige the Applicant, if it wishes to pursue its claims, to initiate fresh proceedings. In this respect it is of no importance which condition was unmet at the date the proceedings were instituted, and thereby prevented the Court at that time from exercising jurisdiction once it had been fulfilled subsequently.[38]

The Court pointed out that it was true that in its 2004 judgments in the *Legality of Use of Force* cases the Court had apparently not taken account of the fact that Serbia and Montenegro had by that date become a party to the Statute. There the Court had found that it lacked jurisdiction on the sole ground that the Applicant [Serbia and Montenegro] did not have access to the Court when the application was filed, without taking its reasoning any further. The Court continued:

[37] Ibid, para 86. [38] Ibid, para 87.

But if the Court abided in those cases strictly by the general rule that its jurisdiction is to be assessed at the date of the filing of the act instituting proceedings without adopting the more flexible approach following the other decisions cited . . . , that is justified by particular considerations relevant to those cases.[39]

The Court went on to explain at some length that in those cases Serbia and Montenegro did not intend to pursue the claims by way of new applications. In those particular circumstances there would have been no justification for the Court to disregard the applicant's initial incapacity to seise the Court on the ground that the defect had been cured in the course of the proceedings.[40]

The Court then brought two additional considerations which lent weight to the conclusion that there was reason, in the present case, to look beyond the situation prevailing at the date of the application. Recalling an earlier remark that a State filing an application should normally be expected to demonstrate sufficient care to avoid doing so prematurely, the applicant in this case could not be said to have shown any careless approach in this regard. In April 1999 the Respondent had filed the applications instituting the proceedings in the *Legality of Force* cases and the Applicant could feel entitled to seise the Court on what at first sight seemed to be an appropriate basis of jurisdiction. The Court also pointed out that while the application, a short text of some ten pages, was filed before the admission of the FRY to the United Nations, the memorial on the merits, a document of some 414 pages, was submitted on 1 March 2001, after that date. The Court observed:

Although it is not possible to equate the filing of a memorial with that of an instrument initiating proceedings, since by definition a memorial concerns proceedings which are already under way, it should be noted that the Memorial is of considerable importance, not just because it expands the Applicant's arguments, but also because it specifies the submissions. While this cannot be considered a decisive element, it cannot be entirely ignored; if Croatia had submitted the substance of its Memorial on 1 March 2001, in the form of a new application, as it could have done, no question with respect to Article 35 of the Statute would have arisen.[41]

The Court accordingly reached the conclusion that on 1 November 2000 'the Court was open to the FRY' (para 91). In the operative clause of this judgment, therefore, the Court, by ten votes to seven, rejected the first preliminary objection in relation to capacity to participate in the proceedings instituted by Croatia's application (para 146 (1)).

This concludes the survey of the cases relating to the capacity of Yugoslavia as respondent to participate in contentious proceedings in the Court.

*

[39] Ibid, para 89. [40] Ibid. [41] Ibid, para 90.

We now turn to the situation where the capacity of Yugoslavia as applicant to institute contentious proceedings is in question.[42] This issue arose in 1999, as stated, when the FRY initiated ten separate proceedings against members of NATO 'for violation of the obligation not to use force'. In each one of the cases, the FRY invoked Article IX of the Genocide Convention as a basis of jurisdiction. In addition, in the cases against Belgium, Canada, the Netherlands, Portugal, Spain and the United Kingdom it relied on compulsory jurisdiction under Article 36 (2) of the Statute. In the cases against France, Germany, Italy and the United States of America, the FRY invoked Article 38 (5) of the Rules of Court[43]—the *forum prorogatum* provision.

On the same date the FRY filed requests for the indication of provisional measures in each case. In the hearings in common on those requests each respondent, in its own way, submitted that the Court had no jurisdiction to decide on provisional measures, or even to decide upon the application as a whole. In its Orders of 2 June 1999 the Court rejected the requests for provisional measures. Its reasoning began:

> [T]he Court, under its Statute, does not automatically have jurisdiction over legal disputes between States that are parties to that Statute or between other States to whom access to the Court has been granted;...and whereas the Court can...exercise jurisdiction only between States parties to a dispute who not only have access to the Court but also have accepted the jurisdiction of the Court, either in general form or for the individual dispute concerned.[44]

The Court found that in the absence of reciprocity *ratione temporis*, a condition found in the declarations accepting the compulsory jurisdiction, the Court could not, on the basis of the declarations, establish its prima facie jurisdiction to indicate provisional measures. The Court decided in light of this finding that it did not need to consider the question of the FRY's capacity.[45]

The Court then turned to the Genocide Convention. It reached the conclusion that at that stage of the proceedings it was not in a position to find that the impugned acts were 'capable of coming within the provisions

[42] On 22 July 1997 the FRY filed its counter-memorial in the *Genocide, Bosnia* case, including counter-claims. Bosnia-Herzegovina objected to the counter-claims and contended that they should not be joined to the original proceedings. After an exchange of written observations, on 17 December 1997 the Court found the counter-claims to be admissible as such and to form part of the original proceedings (see above n 4). No question of the FRY's capacity arose in this interlocutory phase; obviously it was to no party's interest to raise such a question at that stage of those proceedings. The counter-claims were later withdrawn.

[43] By that provision, 'When the applicant State proposes to found the jurisdiction of the Court upon a consent thereto yet to be given or manifested by the State against which such application is made, the application shall be transmitted to that State. It shall not however be entered in the General List, nor any action be taken in the proceedings, unless and until the State against which such application is made consents to the Court's jurisdiction for the purposes of the case.' Not one of the Respondents against which such application was made accepted the jurisdiction, and the Court found that 'it is quite clear that...the Court cannot exercise jurisdiction in the present case, even prima facie'. (*Case against Spain*, [1999] ICJ Rep 761, 773, para 34).

[44] [1999] ICJ Rep 124, 132, para 20.

[45] Ibid, 135, paras 30–33.

of the Genocide Convention', which accordingly could not 'constitute a basis on which the jurisdiction of the Court could prima facie be founded in this case'.[46] The Court thus rejected the requests for provisional measures in all ten cases.

In the cases against Spain and the United States, the Court went further and ordered the removal of the cases from the General List, arguing that it manifestly lacked jurisdiction and that 'within a system of consensual jurisdiction, to maintain on the General List a case upon which it appears certain that the Court will not be able to adjudicate on the merits would most assuredly not contribute to the sound administration of justice.'[47] The removal of the case against the United States, the principal member of NATO at that time, probably rendered continuation of the remaining cases of little real value, although this is not mentioned in the subsequent judgments on preliminary objections.

In due course each of the remaining respondents filed preliminary objections. The final submissions of the respondents requested the Court to remove each case from the General List, and in the alternative, to rule that the Court lacked jurisdiction and/or that the case was inadmissible. The Applicant's final submission requested the Court to adjudge and declare on its jurisdiction *ratione personae*; to dismiss the remaining preliminary objections and to order proceedings on the merits if it found that it had jurisdiction.

While the written pleadings in these ten cases were in progress, the FRY, on 24 April 2001, filed an application instituting proceedings in revision of the Judgment on Preliminary Objections of 11 July 1996. In its Judgment of 3 February 2003 the Court rejected the request for revision on ground of non-compliance with Article 61 of the Statute. This required an examination of the position of the FRY as a member of the United Nations before and after resolution 55/12 and the admission of the FRY to the United Nations. The Court pointed out that resolution 47/1 'did not *inter alia* affect the FRY's right to appear before the Court or to be a party to a dispute before the Court under the conditions laid down in the Statute'. Resolution 55/12 could not have changed retroactively the *sui generis* position in which the FRY found itself vis-à-vis the United Nations over the period 1992 to 2000, or its position in relation to the Statute of the Court.[48]

On 15 December 2004, the Court rendered its Judgments on the objections raised in the *Legality of the Use of Force* cases. The Judgments are complicated, and in some respects read like a patchwork of at least two separate approaches to the main question posed by the final submissions. The operative clause, in which the Court found that it had no jurisdiction to entertain the claims, was adopted unanimously, by all the fifteen judges who sat in that phase. However, an annexed Joint Declaration by seven of the judges indicates that they voted in favour of the *dispositif* of the

[46] Ibid, 136, paras 34–41.

[47] Ibid, 761, 773, para 35, Spain; 916, 925, para 29, USA.

[48] 2008 Judgment, paras 70–71.

Judgment while profoundly disagreeing with the reasoning upon which the Judgment rested, in particular the ground upon which the Court found that it had no jurisdiction. This suggests that on this issue the presence on the Court of Judge ad hoc Kreča was decisive in avoiding a deadlock that would have required the president (Judge Shi) to exercise his casting vote.

For present purposes it is sufficient to limit our survey to the Court's pronouncements on the issue of capacity.

One of the Respondents' arguments had been that since the Applicant was not a party to the Statute, there was no dispute over which the Court had jurisdiction. On this the Court said:

> [I]t is the view of the Court that a distinction has to be made between a question of jurisdiction that relates to the consent of a party and the question of the right of a party to appear before the Court under the requirements of the Statute, which is not a matter of consent. The question is whether *as a matter of law* Serbia and Montenegro was entitled to seise the Court as a party to the Statute at the time when it instituted the proceedings in these cases. Since that question is independent of the views or wishes of the Parties, even if they were now to have arrived at a shared view on the point, the Court would not have to accept that view as necessarily the correct one. The function of the Court to enquire into the matter and reach its own conclusion is thus mandatory upon the Court irrespective of the consent of the parties and is in no way incompatible with the principle that the jurisdiction of the Court depends on consent.[49]

After examining various contentions concerning the possibility of a simple removal of the cases from the General List (paras 37–44), the Court approached the issue of capacity. Following some preliminary remarks not relevant here (para 45), the Court turned to the principal aspect. The question whether the Applicant was or was not a party to the Statute at the time of the institution of the proceedings was 'fundamental', for if it were not such a party, the Court would not be open to it under Article 35 (1) of the Statute and the Applicant, subject to any application of Article 35 (2), could not have 'properly seised' the Court, whatever title of jurisdiction it might have invoked, 'for the simple reason that Serbia and Montenegro did not have the right to appear before the Court'. 'The Court can exercise its judicial function only in respect of those States which have access to it under Article 35 of the Statute. And only those States which have access to the Court can confer jurisdiction upon it'. On that basis the Court indicated that it was incumbent upon it to examine first of all the question whether the Applicant met the conditions laid down in Articles 34 and 35 of the Statute and whether the Court was thus open to it. 'Only if the answer to that question is in the affirmative will the Court have to deal with the issues relating to the conditions laid down in Articles 36 and 37 of the Statute of the Court'.[50]

The Court proceeded to review the provisional measures proceedings (paras 48–50) before turning to the first preliminary objection. It noted

[49] [2004] ICJ Rep 2004, 279, 295, para 36. Emphasis supplied.

[50] Ibid, 299, para 46.

(para 52) that it had always been common ground between the parties that Serbia and Montenegro had not claimed to have become a party to the Statute on any other basis than by membership in the United Nations. The Court then recapitulated the sequence of events relating to the Applicant's legal position vis-à-vis the United Nations (paras 64–72). It summarized that examination as testifying to the 'rather confused and complex state of affairs' within the United Nations surrounding the legal status of the FRY during the period ending with resolution 55/12 of 1 November 2000, which the Court qualified as being 'the *sui generis* position in which the FRY found itself during that period' (para 73). That expression was merely descriptive of that amorphous state of affairs. The Court drew no final and definitive conclusion from this descriptive term. The Court did not commit itself to a definitive position on the issue of the FRY's legal status in relation to the Charter and the Statute 'in its pronouncements in incidental proceedings' (para 74). The eventual admission of the FRY was a 'new development' which 'effectively put an end to the *sui generis* position of the FRY within the United Nations'. Nevertheless it became clear that the *sui generis* position of the applicant could not have amounted to its membership in the Organization (para 78), a statement that is not consistent with the Legal Counsel's understanding of resolution 47/1 quoted above.[51] The Court concluded this part of the Judgment with the following observation:

> [T]he significance of this new development in 2000 is that it has clarified the thus far amorphous legal situation concerning the status of the Federal Republic of Yugoslavia vis-à-vis the United Nations. It is in that sense that the situation that the Court now faces in relation to Serbia and Montenegro is manifestly different from that which it faced in 1999. If, at that time, the Court had had to determine definitively the status of the Applicant vis-à-vis the United Nations, its task of giving such a determination would have been complicated by the legal situation which was shrouded in uncertainties relating to that status. However, from the vantage point from which the Court now looks at the legal situation, and in light of the legal consequences of the new development since 1 November 2000, the Court is led to the conclusion that Serbia and Montenegro was not a Member of the United Nations, and in that capacity a State party to the Statute of the International Court of Justice, at the time of filing its Application to institute the present proceedings before the Court on 29 April 1999.[52]

A further point which the Court then considered was the relevance of the *Revision* proceedings in connection with the *Genocide, Bosnia* case (paras 80–89). Given the specific characteristics of the revision procedure under Article 61 of the Statute, there was no reason to treat the 2003 Judgment in that case

> as having pronounced upon the issue of the legal status of Serbia and Montenegro vis-à-vis the United Nations. Nor does the Judgment pronounce upon the status of Serbia and Montenegro in relation to the Statute of the Court.[53]

[51] Above n 3. [52] [2004] ICJ Rep 2004, 310, para 79. [53] Ibid, 314, para 90.

The Court's final words on the capacity issue follow:

> For all these reasons, the Court concludes that, at the time of filing of its Application to institute the present proceedings before the Court on 29 April 1999, the Applicant in the present case, Serbia and Montenegro, was not a Member of the United Nations, and, consequently, was not, on that basis, a State party to the Statute of the International Court of Justice. It follows that the Court was not open to Serbia and Montenegro under Article 25, paragraph 1, of the Statute.[54]

The operative clause of this Judgment, adopted unanimously, contains a single sentence, that the Court finds 'that it has no jurisdiction to entertain the claims made in the Application filed by Serbia and Montenegro on 29 April 1999'. Nevertheless, as stated, there was a strong joint dissent by seven members of the 15-member Court that determined this case—Vice-President Ranjeva, Judges Guillaume, Higgins, Kooijmans, Al-Khasawneh, Buergenthal and Elaraby. They review the Court's jurisprudence to date on the sole issue of capacity of Yugoslavia, as a member of the United Nations, to participate as applicant or as respondent in contentious litigation before the International Court of Justice. This jurisprudence has no direct relation to participation in any other capacity in contentious litigation, although it may be presumed to be applicable to the specific case of intervention under either Article 62 or Article 63 of the Statute. It has no relevance for participation in advisory proceedings, where indeed the present court has shown some flexibility in allowing participation of non-State entities.[55]

* * *

What does this show us?

In the period between the two General Assembly resolutions 47/1 and 55/12 the FRY was applicant or, in interlocutory matters, the initiator or cross-claimant in 15 mainline cases (the *Revision* case, ten *Legality of Use of Force* cases, and preliminary objections in the two *Genocide* cases, cross-claimant in the second provisional measures case of 1993 and counter-claimant in the same case) and respondent in two mainline cases (*Genocide, Bosnia* and *Genocide, Croatia*). The jurisprudence shows that there is a difference in the Court's treatment of the capacity issue according to whether the issue arose in relation to the applicant or in relation to the respondent.

[54] Ibid, para 91.

[55] Thus, in the *Legal Consequences of the Construction of a Wall in Occupied Palestinian Territory*, the Court authorized the participation of 'Palestine' in both the written and the oral proceedings of the Advisory Opinion, [2003] ICJ Rep 428. In the Advisory Opinion *Accordance with International Law of the Unilateral Declaration of Independence by the Provisional Institutions of Self-Government of Kosovo* the Court has authorized those Institutions to participate in the proceedings (Order of 17 October 2008).

The Charter of the United Nations regulates participation in the Statute by virtue of membership in the United Nations. Chapter II (Articles 3–6), entitled 'Membership', governs membership in the United Nations. Article 3 indicates the original members, of which Yugoslavia, then named the SFRY, was one. Article 4 regulates the admission of new members, of which the current Serbia, previously the FRY, admitted on 1 November 2000, is one. Admission of a new member is effected by a decision of the General Assembly upon the recommendation of the Security Council. Article 5 permits the suspension of the rights and privileges of membership by a decision of the General Assembly on the recommendation of the Security Council. Article 6 provides for the expulsion from membership of a member which has persistently violated the principles contained in the Charter, again by the General Assembly upon recommendation of the Security Council. By virtue of the San Francisco declaration on the interpretation of the Charter (not mentioned in any of the judicial pronouncements considered here), the International Court of Justice is entitled to make its own interpretation of those parts of the Charter that are applicable to its particular functions.[56] It follows that the interpretation of the General Assembly resolutions by the Legal Counsel and adopted by the General Assembly does not necessarily bind the Court, which is entitled to make its own interpretation of those resolutions, in light of its Statute and its functions as a principal organ and the principal judicial organ of the United Nations. In the case of Yugoslavia, the Court followed the General Assembly's understanding of Yugoslavia's position as being *sui generis* until the FRY's admission in 2000. The Court also faced a question which did not arise in the same form in the United Nations, namely, the effect on Yugoslavia's *sui generis* position of the FRY's admission to the United Nations in 2000, insofar as concerns the functioning of the Court.

The capacity issue in all these cases was whether Yugoslavia, now named the FRY and admitted to the United Nations under Article 4 of the Charter—a new member—was the continuator State of the SFRY as a member of the United Nations, at all events for United Nations purposes. The Court was able to avoid deciding on this issue in all these cases except the last two, the merits of the *Genocide, Bosnia* case and the *Genocide, Croatia* preliminary objections case. The decisive change in Yugoslavia's *sui generis* position occurred on 27 September 2000 when the newly elected president of the FRY requested admission of the FRY to the United Nations, effectively terminating that *sui generis* position. In the *Legality of Use of Force* cases the Court explained this:

[56] 13 United Nations Conference on International Organization Official Records (UNCIO) 703.

> The Applicant thus has the status of membership in the United Nations as from 1 November 2000. However, its admission to the United Nations did not have, and could not have had the effect of dating back to the time when the [SFRY] broke up and disappeared; there was in 2000 no question of restoring the membership rights of the [SFRY] for the benefit of the [FRY]. At the same time, it became clear that the *sui generis* position of the Applicant could not have amounted to its membership in the Organization.[57]

The Court explained the significance of this 'new development' as clarifying the thus far amorphous legal situation concerning the status of the FRY vis-à-vis the United Nations, and it was in that sense that the situation facing the Court was 'manifestly different' from that which it faced in 1999.[58]

The first thing to notice is that a major consideration running through the Court's decisions is the formal interpretation of resolution 47/1 given by the Legal Counsel of the United Nations[59] which had gone unchallenged in the General Assembly. In all the instances that arose before resolution 55/12 and the admission of the FRY to the United Nations the Court was able to reach its decision on the precise issue then before it without prejudicing Yugoslavia's *sui generis* position in the United Nations. From that it followed that during that period, for the Court's purposes Yugoslavia remained a party to the Statute, notwithstanding that it was unable to participate in any of the activities which the Statute requires the General Assembly to perform. To maintain this *sui generis* position, the Court adopted several other considerations, arriving at most of them through a process of interpretation, and some with a basis in previous decisions.

The first, and in this instance perhaps the most important, is the strictly limited effect given to the principle of *res judicata*, especially in relation to interlocutory or other procedural decisions involving the Court's jurisdiction made before the formal decision embodied in an operative clause of a judgment addressing a question of jurisdiction. As a matter of principle, the concept of *res judicata* applies only to the *dispositif*, the operative provisions of a judgment, not to its reasoning.[60] In these cases the reasoning always reflected Yugoslavia's then current position in the United Nations. As seen from the text of General Assembly resolution 47/1, reflecting the Security Council's decision embodied in resolution 777 (1992), that *sui generis* position contained a built-in provision for eventual change; it indicated how the FRY could terminate that unusual situation. The Court was careful not in any way to prejudice that eventuality, which would depend on a political decision to be taken by the FRY in due course. When the FRY changed its political position

[57] [2004] ICJ Rep 279, 310, para 78. [58] Ibid, para 79. [59] Above n 3.

[60] See above text to n 17. And cf R Bernhardt on Article 59 in A Zimmermann *et al*, *The Statute of the International Court of Justice: A Commentary* (Oxford, Oxford University Press, 2006) 1231, 1242.

and acted in accordance with resolution 47/1, the Court responded accordingly.

In this subtle and complex process, the Court based itself on a combination of three factors: (1) at what point of time is the decision on capacity to be made; (2) the temporal extent of the jurisdiction-competence (*compétence de la compétence*) embodied in Article 36 (6) of the Statute; and (3) the relativity of procedural decisions embodied in the *Mavrommatis* principle. These now require consideration.

On the first of these issues, precisely when the decision on capacity should be made, it is of course a truism that normally the Court should determine this kind of issue by reference to the time when the proceedings were instituted. For the mainline or principal case, Article 40 of the Statute together with Articles 38 (application instituting proceedings) and 39 (notification of special agreement) are the governing texts. Once the Court is properly seised of the case and the case has been duly entered in the Court's General List,[61] all further correspondence is conducted between the agents and the Registrar, and a communication is effective as from the time of receipt (during working hours at the place of receipt). Interlocutory proceedings are introduced by an appropriate communication addressed to the Registrar. The Statute contains provisions governing certain types of interlocutory proceedings, amplified in the Rules, as will be seen hereafter. However, the Court has indicated in its Judgment on the Preliminary Objections in the *Genocide, Bosnia* case[62] that in a contentious case circumstances may justify a later date for determining the Court's mainline jurisdiction. The Court repeatedly found that cases involving Yugoslavia instituted in the period 1992–2000 justified applying a later time for determining the mainline jurisdiction. That time is at the latest when the Court delivers its decision on the merits if the case proceeds that far, or its decision disseising itself of the case if objections to the jurisdiction or admissibility are sustained. This has had the effect of overriding all interlocutory and other incidental decisions or decisions in derivative cases, leaving the Court quite free to deal with the capacity issue in its decision on the case as a whole. It is on that basis that the Court was able to deal with requests for the indication of provisional measures in the *Genocide, Bosnia* and *Legality of Use of Force* cases, with the admission of counter-claims in the *Genocide, Bosnia* case, and with the admission of a request for revision of a judgment, technically a new case and not part of the original case, in that same *Genocide, Bosnia* case. In requests for the indication of provisional measures, the Court requires to be satisfied only that it has prima facie jurisdiction over the merits, and has no need to probe into

[61] See my 'The General List of the International Court of Justice', *Essays* (above n 18) 197.
[62] Above n 4 and n 7.

jurisdictional issues any further. In the case of a decision to open proceedings to review a judgment, the Statute requires a judgment making a specific finding, so again there was no need for the Court to examine jurisdictional issues any further.[63]

It is in this context that the question of the temporal extent of Article 36 (6) of the Statute—the provision giving the Court the jurisdiction-competence—has arisen. In the series of cases being considered here, the Court has twice given new approaches to questions of its own jurisdiction. In *Genocide, Croatia* it took the initiative in requesting the parties, in the hearings on preliminary objections, to address the capacity issue which had not been addressed in the pleadings to date; and in other respects it gave to Article 36 (6) a temporal scope that commenced with the initiation of the case and continued until the disposal of all jurisdictional issues. This meant that the existence of a capacity issue does not impair the seisin of the Court if prima facie the dispute comes within the scope of the title of jurisdiction that the applicant has invoked. The Court's competence-jurisdiction is broad enough to enable the Court to deal with the capacity issue at a convenient moment, without prejudice to its powers under other provisions of the Statute, such as under Article 41 regarding provisional measures of protection, or under Article 61 (2) requiring proceedings in revision to be opened by a judgment. As stated, in the case of Yugoslavia the capacity issue deriving from its *sui generis* position in the United Nations was not a permanency. By postponing decision on the issue for as long as possible the Court kept open Yugoslavia's option to bring about a change.

This leads to the relativity of the procedural decisions and reliance on the doctrine of the *Mavrommatis* case. An interlocutory or a procedural decision, whether embodied in a judgment or a formal order, or in some less formal pronouncement of the Court, settles the immediate question that gave rise to it, but is without substantive effect on the Court's mainline jurisdiction to deal with the case as set forth in the act introducing the proceedings and the pleadings that followed it. Every judgment produces a *res judicata* and comes within the scope of Article 60 of the Statute—it is final and without appeal (subject to revision and to interpretation). That status attends the *dispositif*, not the reasoning, which, in the nature of things, is limited to the issue that led to the interlocutory

[63] In the *Case concerning the Request for Interpretation of the Judgment of 31 March 2004 in the Case concerning Avena and other Mexican Nationals (Mexico v United States of America)* (Provisional Measures), Order of 16 July 2008, the Court explained that its jurisdiction under Article 60 of the Statute (on the interpretation of a judgment) is not preconditioned by the existence of any other basis of jurisdiction as between the parties to the original case (para 44). It appears that the Court applies this principle whenever it exercises a jurisdiction for which the Statute makes specific provision—here called 'statutory jurisdiction'. The Court confirmed this in para 15 of its Judgment of 19 January 2009 dismissing Mexico's request for interpretation.

or procedural matter requiring judicial determination. In Yugoslavia's case, any change in the *sui generis* position required initiative to be taken by the FRY itself.

The accumulated case-law above brings out that the International Court exercises two kinds of jurisdiction, each independent of the other. The mainline jurisdiction has a personal element (jurisdiction *ratione personae*) and a substantive or material element (jurisdiction *ratione materiae*), and the scope of both can be further defined by reference to time (*ratione temporis*) and space (*ratione loci*).[64] In addition the Statute gives the Court jurisdiction over several distinct procedures and prescribes the conditions for its exercise. This includes the competence-jurisdiction under Article 36 (6), the power to indicate provisional measures under Article 41, the power to make orders for the conduct of a case under Article 48 and generally to control the oral proceedings under Article 54 (1), and the power to open proceedings for revision of a judgment under Article 61 (2). This statutory jurisdiction is independent of the mainline jurisdiction and depends on the showing in the act introducing the proceedings of a prima facie possibility that the asserted title of jurisdiction could constitute a basis on which the Court's jurisdiction over the matter might be founded. In all cases, a decision by the Court on the issue then before it carries the implication that the condition of capacity is met.[65] In particular, the fact that the competence-jurisdiction can be exercised at any time after the filing of the act introducing the proceedings and is independent *per se* of the capacity issue ensures that the judicial process can always proceed within the limits of the Court's Statute. Only if the absence of mainline jurisdiction is manifest will the Court decline to take any action at all on a document purporting to be an act introducing the case. This aspect of the rules on jurisdiction is what enabled the Court to face up to the different challenges posed by the procedural and political complexities of this series of cases.

It is here that the inherent relativity of the *Mavrommatis* jurisprudence comes into play with regard to the capacity issue. If the precondition of capacity is unmet for reasons that the party concerned can control, as for instance in the *forum prorogatum* cases brought under Article 38 (5) of the Rules of Court, the party's action can regularize the situation, and the Court will not allow technical considerations to hinder that by a premature decision disseising itself of the case. The *Mavrommatis* line of cases applies where the lack of capacity follows from a situation that is not the

[64] The scope of jurisdiction *ratione loci* has only recently been identified. See the Order on the Request for the Indication of Provisional Measures of 15 October 2008 in the *Case concerning the Application of the International Convention on the Elimination of All Forms of Racial Discrimination (Georgia v Russian Federation)*.

[65] Cf the passage cited above in n 30 in para 68 of the Court's Judgments in the *Legality of Use of Force* cases with regard to decisions on preliminary objections. The logic of that passage is equally applicable to all other decisions of the Court, relative to the issue that was decided.

making of the party concerned, in that case the absence of the quorum required to bring into force the multilateral treaty invoked as the basis for jurisdiction, when it was clear that the required quorum would be reached, possibly within a short space of time. The Yugoslav series of cases carries this further, to the situation where the *sui generis* position of the party concerned was created by an external body, there the General Assembly of the United Nations, but can be rectified at will by the party concerned. The Yugoslav jurisprudence shows how the Court will not allow purely technical considerations of the moment to stand in the way of eventual removal of the obstacle to mainline jurisdiction should the State party concerned be prepared to take the political action required to unmake its *sui generis* position.

* * *

As has been repeatedly stressed throughout this series of cases, following resolution 47/1 Yugoslavia has been in a '*sui generis* position' in the General Assembly. Yugoslavia was prevented from taking part in the work of the General Assembly, and later of ECOSOC, but not of any other principal organ of the United Nations, the Security Council and the International Court of Justice. The procedure of the Security Council is sufficiently relaxed that accommodation was found for Yugoslavia whenever necessary, the various items that were on the Council's agenda when resolution 47/1 was adopted remaining unchanged. As far as the Court was concerned, there was no relevant case involving Yugoslavia on the General List when the General Assembly adopted that resolution. The Court had to face the problem created by that resolution in light of all the relevant circumstances before it whenever it was essential for the Court to take a decision on the matter. This put the Court in a *sui generis* position, in its quality of a principal organ of the United Nations, governed by the integrated Charter and Statute. Consequently, all the Court's decisions on this matter are coloured by the *sui generis* quality of each decision. That *sui generis* position contained its own built-in provision for its termination, leading to a return of Yugoslavia to normalcy as a member of the United Nations and hence as a party to the Statute of the Court. It is unlikely that the *sui generis* position of Yugoslavia—and hence of the Court—will be repeated in precisely the same terms. It is more likely that the requirements of diplomacy will find new forms of *sui generis* quasi-membership positions within the United Nations context, and should international litigation arise while such a position exists, the deciding organ will face a situation similar to that which the International Court of Justice faced in cases in which Yugoslavia, partly suspended in the exercise of its rights as a member of the Organization, was involved. Such situations have no precedent in traditional international inter-State litigation, whether before a standing international judicial or quasi-judicial body or an ad hoc body. The value as precedent of the Yugoslav experience, here as in other matters occurring in the last decade of the twentieth century, is how it demonstrates the inherent adaptability of today's international judicial institutions and procedures to meet the challenges of the unexpected and unprecedented, brought on by the ever-changing requirements of modern multilateral international diplomacy.[66]

[66] We might note that the disintegration of Yugoslavia—itself something of a *sui generis* creation of the 1919 Peace Settlement following the break-up of the great Empires existing across the European continent in 1914—produced more and varied types of international litigation than any other single incident of the twentieth century. See, for instance, the *Kosovo* case (above n 18) and (a case not directly involving Yugoslavia) the *Case concerning the Implementation of Article 11, Paragraph 1 of the Interim Accord of 13 September 1995 (Former Yugoslav Republic of Macedonia* v *Greece*) (pending). See also my 'A Role for the International Court of Justice in Crisis Management?' *Essays* (above n 18), 35.

Foreign Investment and the Environment in International Law: An Ambiguous Relationship

By Jorge E Viñuales*

* PhD (Institut d'Etudes Politiques de Paris), LLM (Harvard), DEA (HEI). Jorge E. Viñuales is the Pictet Chair in International Environmental Law and an Assistant Professor of International Law at the Graduate Institute of International and Development Studies, in Geneva. He is also Counsel with the law firm Lévy Kaufmann-Kohler, in Geneva, where he specialises in international investment law, as well as the Executive Director of the Latin-American Society of International Law. The opinions expressed in this study are personal and do not reflect those of any of the organizations with which the author is affiliated. The study takes into account developments until 6 August 2010. The author is grateful to Professor James Crawford for his comments on an earlier draft of this article. Any mistakes that the text may contain are the author's exclusive responsibility.

I. Introduction

The purpose of this study is to analyse the interactions between two thriving fields of current international law, namely international investment law and international environmental law. Since their modern inception back in the 1960s,[1] the historical development of these two bodies of

[1] Although the protection of foreign investors in international law can be traced back to the nineteenth century, and perhaps even earlier, its development in the last decades (particularly since the 1990s) has been totally unprecedented. For a survey of the new dawn of international investment law, see P Juillard, 'L'évolution des sources du droit des investissements', (1994) 250 *Recueil des cours* 9. Regarding international environmental law, again, despite the existence of some international practice relating to the protection of particular species or the distribution of shared resources, the development of modern international environmental law started only in the 1960s and particularly from the 1970s onwards, after the United Nations Conference on the Human Environment, of June 1972. For a survey of the historical development of international environmental law see M A Fitzmaurice, 'International Protection of the Environment', (2001) 293 *Recueil des cours* 27.

law has been characterised by a remarkable transformation from loosely-defined arrays of standards and principles, often controversial and with limited legal impact, to sophisticated legal fields, of considerable importance from both the policy and business perspectives. This transformation has also changed the relations between investment and environmental regulation.

For several decades, both international investment law and international environmental law evolved in relative autarchy, as specialised fields of international law.[2] Such relative autarchy explains why the interactions between the two fields remained limited. Indeed, so long as the norms informing these fields remained vague, conflicts were less likely to materialise. Moreover, the possibility of such conflicts was largely overshadowed by the apparent solution that the concept of 'sustainable development' offered to the trade-off between protecting the environment and promoting growth and development.[3] Yet, the 'environment-development equation' proved to be a resilient beast, lurking in the shadows of most major environmental negotiations.[4] And even in those cases where conflicts between the two terms of the equation were singled out, the attention tended to focus mostly on trade restrictions based on environmental considerations.[5]

However, with the increasing reach and sophistication of both international investment law and international environmental law, the possibility that foreign investment protection may encroach on environmental protection and vice versa has started to receive more attention from legal commentators. The unifying concept of sustainable development is indeed no longer perceived as a sufficient tool to manage the possibility of conflicts between these two bodies of law. As one commentator has noted, sustainable development is a multilevel concept, with different meanings at different levels.[6] At a superficial level, sustainable development can be defined,

[2] Both international investment law and international environmental law have often been regarded as 'special regimes' in the meaning of paragraphs 11 and 12 (third paragraph) of the Conclusions of the work of the Study Group on the Fragmentation of International Law: Difficulties arising from the Diversification and Expansion of International Law, *Yearbook of the International Law Commission, 2006*, vol. II, Part Two (Conclusions-Fragmentation). On the scope and limits of this concept see, particularly, paragraphs 8 and 123–194 of the Analytical Study prepared by this Group, Document A/CN4/L.682 and Corr.1. (Report-Fragmentation).

[3] On this concept see D Barstow Magraw, L D Hawke, 'Sustainable Development' in D Bodansky, J Brunnée, E Hey (eds), *The Oxford Handbook of International Environmental Law* (Oxford University Press, Oxford, 2007) 613–638.

[4] The modest results achieved in the fifteenth Conference of the Parties to the United Nations Framework Convention on Climate Change (UNFCCC), in December 2009, can be largely explained by the trade-off between environmental protection and development. Developing countries, especially emerging economies, are extremely reluctant to compromise their development effort by undertaking genuine emission commitments. Industrialized countries refuse in turn to adopt or expand, as the case may be, their emissions commitments unless emerging countries are also subject to some significant restraint. See L Rajamani, 'From Berlin to Bali and Beyond: Killing Kyoto Softly?' (2008) 57 *International & Comparative Law Quarterly* 909.

[5] For an updated overview see P Birnie, A Boyle, C Redgwell, *International Law and the Environment* (Oxford University Press, Oxford, 2009) 766 et seq.

[6] See A Dobson, *Fairness and Futurity: Essays on Environmental Sustainability and Social Justice* (Oxford University Press, Oxford, 1999) 23–30.

along the lines of the well known Brundtland Report, as development that meets the needs of the present without compromising the needs of future generations.[7] Such a broad definition is admittedly helpful in gathering consensus from different constituencies in an international negotiation. But it provides little or no guidance on how the two terms of the environment-development equation should be reconciled in case of conflict.[8] It is only when one's attention moves onto a deeper level, in search of a more rigorous definition of sustainable development, that the extent to which the contents of this concept are unsettled can be fully appreciated.

The emerging legal literature on the interactions between investment and environmental regulation seeks to capture different dimensions of this interface, focusing on issues such as the environmental responsibility of multinational corporations,[9] the scope of investment protection clauses,[10] the role of non-disputing parties,[11] the operation of emergency or necessity clauses,[12] or the treatment given in foreign investment disputes

[7] *Report of the World Commission on Environment and Development*, '*Our Common Future*', UNGA Res A/42/427, Annex, Chapter II, 54 (para 1).

[8] See *Gabčíkovo-Nagymaros Project (Hungary/Slovakia)*, [1997] ICJ Rep 7 ('*Gabčíkovo-Nagymaros*'), paras 140–141 (referring to the need for the parties to find an 'agreed solution'); *Iron Rhine ('IJzeren Rijn') Railway Arbitration (Belgium/Netherlands)*, RIAA vol. XXVII, 25 ('*Iron Rhine Arbitration*'), paras 59–60 (noting that '[t]he mere invocation of such matters [the principle of sustainable development] does not, of course, provide the answers in this arbitration to what may or may not be done, where, by whom and at whose costs'); *Case concerning Pulp Mills in the River Uruguay (Argentina v Uruguay)*, Judgment of 20 April 2010, General List No 135 ('*Pulp Mills* case'), paras 75–77 (referring to the duty of co-operation) and 177 (stating that sustainable development requires a balance between the use of the waters and the protection of rivers).

[9] See P Muchlinsky, *Multinational Enterprises and the Law* (Oxford University Press, Oxford, 2007), chapter 14; E Morgera, *Corporate Accountability in International Environmental Law* (Oxford University Press, Oxford, 2009); B J Richardson, 'Climate Finance and its Governance: Moving to a Low Carbon Economy through Socially Responsible Financing?' (2009) 58 *International & Comparative Law Quarterly* 597; B J Richardson, 'Financing Sustainability: The New Transnational Governance of Socially Responsible Investment' (2006) 17 *Yearbook of International Environmental Law* 73; D M Ong, 'The Contribution of State-Multinational Corporation "Transnational" Investment Agreements to International Environmental Law' (2006) 17 *Yearbook of International Environmental Law* 168.

[10] See O K Fauchald, 'International Investment Law and Environmental Protection' (2006) 17 *Yearbook of International Environmental Law* 3; S Robert-Cuendet, *Protection de l'environnement et investissement étranger: Les règles applicables à la dépossession du fait de la réglementation environnementale*, thèse, Université de Paris I; J Waincymer, 'Balancing Property Rights and Human Rights in Expropriation' in P-M Dupuy, F Francioni, E U Petersmann (eds), *Human Rights in International Investment Law and Arbitration* (Oxford University Press, Oxford, 2009, hereafter referred to as 'Dupuy et al') 275; I Knoll-Tudor, 'The Fair and Equitable Treatment Standard and Human Rights Norms' in Dupuy et al, 310; F Ortino, 'Non-Discriminatory Treatment in Investment Disputes' in Dupuy et al, 344.

[11] See B Stern, 'Civil Society's Voice in the Settlement of International Economic Disputes' (2007) 22 *ICSID Review* 280; F Grisel, J E Viñuales, L'*amicus curiae* dans l'arbitrage d'investissement' (2007) 22 *ICSID Review* 380; E Triantafilou, 'Amicus Submissions in Investor-State Arbitration after Suez v Argentina' (2008) 24 *Arbitration International* 571; S Menétrey, L'amicus curiae, *vers un principe de droit international procédural?*, PhD dissertation (Université Panthéon-Assas, Paris—Université Laval, Québec), December 2008.

[12] See D Dobos, 'The Necessity of Precaution: The Future of Ecological Necessity and the Precautionary Principle' (2002) 13 *Fordham Environmental Law Journal* 375; J Neuman, E Turk, 'Necessity Revisited: Proportionality in World Trade Organization Law after Korea-Beef, EC-Asbestos and EC-Sardines' (2003) 37 *Journal of World Trade* 199; P-M Dupuy, 'L'invocation de l'état de nécessité

to some particular environmental question.[13] Despite the importance of this research, the overall picture that emerges from these contributions remains difficult to appraise, mostly as a result of the specific nature of the issues and perspectives selected.

In this context, the purpose of the present study is to build on this emerging literature in order to present a broader assessment of the current state of international law on this topic. In the first section, the study provides a conceptual framework to facilitate the analysis of both mutually supportive and conflicting interactions between foreign investment and environmental protection and their international legal regimes (II). This is followed by an analysis of the most significant questions posed by such interactions in the light of the relevant investment-related decisions from international courts and tribunals. The analysis is structured into two sections dealing with issues arising, respectively, in the conduct of arbitration proceedings (jurisdiction, applicable law, procedural issues) (III) and in the assessment of the merits of investment claims (normative and legitimacy conflicts, compensation) (IV). The last section is devoted to some reflections on the future interactions between international investment law and international environmental law (V).

II. Conceptualising Interactions

In order to frame the discussion of the relations between international investment law and international environmental law, it is useful to look first at how the two underlying realities regulated by these bodies of law interact in practice (A). Our aim is not to characterise foreign investment or environmental degradation as socio-economic phenomena in general, but only to provide the foundations for an analysis of how international law deals with their interactions, either as mutually supportive (B) or as potentially conflicting realities (C).

A. Foreign Investment and the Environment

Foreign investment in developing countries[14] can constitute both a vector of sustainable development, most notably through financial and

écologique. Les enseignements tirés d'une étude de cas' in Société française pour le droit international, *La nécessité en droit international* (Pedone, Paris, 2007) 223; J E Viñuales, 'Las Cuestiones Medioambientales y el Concepto de Estado de Necesidad' (2009) 119 *Universitas. Revista de derecho* 223.

[13] See P Thielbörger, 'The Human Right to Water versus Investor Rights: Double Dilemma or Pseudo Conflict?' in Dupuy et al, above n 10, 487; J E Viñuales, 'Access to Water in Foreign Investment Disputes' (2009) 21 *Georgetown International Environmental Law Review* 733; R Pavoni, 'Environmental Rights, Sustainable Development, and Investor-State Case Law: A Critical Appraisal' in Dupuy et al, above n 10, 525; L Liberti, 'The Relevance of Non-Investment Treaty Obligations in Assessing Compensation' in Dupuy et al, above n 10, 557.

[14] In 2009, for the first time ever, emerging markets received more inflows of foreign direct investment than developed countries. See L Kekic, 'The Global Economic Crisis and FDI Flows to Emerging Markets' (October 2009) *Columbia FDI Perspectives* no 15.

technology transfers, and a threat to the environment, when its production processes and methods are risky or harmful. In practice, both dimensions are often combined.

One interesting illustration of this latter point is offered by the so-called race-to-the-bottom argument. The basic idea is that States wishing to attract foreign investment to further their development will have an incentive to lower their environmental protection standards.[15] In such a situation, other States may be led to do the same in order to avoid a competitive disadvantage, with a resulting overall decline of environmental protection. This would be a problem for both developed and developing countries, although for different reasons. Whereas the former fear the delocalisation of firms driven by the adoption of relatively less costly environmental regulations abroad, the latter have expressed concern over the environmental damage that may result from the activities of foreign investors located in their territory. A prominent example of such risks is given by the Bhopal tragedy, on 3 December 1984, when the accidental release of approximately 42 tonnes of toxic methyl isocyanate (MIC) gas from a Union Carbide pesticide plant located in the Indian city of Bhopal killed and injured several thousand people. The link between the accident and poor (or poorly enforced) regulation is difficult to establish, as were the exact circumstances that led to the release of the gas. The Bhopal tragedy has nevertheless become a common reference in discussions of the risks associated with the transfer of dangerous activities to developing countries.[16]

The perception of the desirability of foreign investment may also change throughout the life of an investment. Numerous illustrations of this phenomenon can be provided. For instance, if one looks at cases of water and sewerage concessions, the initial perception of foreign investors is often positive, as a necessary contribution to the modernisation of the water distribution infrastructure. However, after some time, this initially positive perception may evolve towards a negative one, for a variety of justified or unjustified reasons, ranging from the imposition of high or simply unpopular tariffs to the occurrence of a crisis or to a sudden change in the government of the host country, to name but a few. Such changes have given rise to foreign investment disputes in a number of cases.[17] Another example of perception shifts concerns waste disposal/treatment

[15] This argument has received particular attention in the context of environmental regulatory competition within the United States. See among others R L Revesz, 'Rehabilitating Interstate Competition: Rethinking the Race-to-the-Bottom Rationale for Federal Environmental Regulation' (1992) 67 *New York University Law Review* 1210; K H Engel, 'State Environmental Standard-Setting: Is There a Race and Is It to the Bottom' (1996–1997) 48 *Hastings Law Journal* 271.

[16] See S Jasanoff (ed), *Learning from Disaster: Risk Management after Bhopal* (University of Pennsylvania Press, Philadelphia PA, 1994).

[17] See, for instance *Aguas del Tunari S.A. v Republic of Bolivia*, ICSID Case No. ARB/02/3, Decision on Objections to Jurisdiction of 21 October 2005 ('*Aguas del Tunari*') (later settled); *Biwater Gauff (Tanz.) Ltd. v United Republic of Tanzania*, ICSID Case No. ARB/05/22, Award of 24 July 2008 ('*Biwater v Tanzania*'); *Compañía de Aguas del Aconquija S.A. and Vivendi Universal S.A. v Argentine Republic*, ICSID Case No. ARB/97/3, Award of 20 August 2007 ('*Vivendi II*').

facilities or related services operated by foreign investors. A number of developing countries or of their political subdivisions have outsourced such activities to foreign investors, often because investors can more easily mobilise the necessary capital and technology to set up such facilities or provide such services. But, again, throughout the life of the investment, the perception may change from a positive to a negative one and give rise to an investment dispute.[18]

As the foregoing examples suggest, the relations between foreign investment and environmental protection are complex and raise a number of difficult issues. It is, for instance, unclear what would happen with investments in environmentally-sensitive sectors, such as energy production, water distribution, waste treatment or chemical safety, if the host State's environmental regulations were to become more stringent during the life of the investment. In other cases international investment law could be used to protect the environment, for instance, by requiring a State to respect its own environmental laws upon which an investment is based.[19] Overall, what these examples show is that the relation between international investment law and international environmental law has two dimensions, one in which the two terms appear as mutually supportive and another in which they seem to conflict with each other. The emerging international regulation reflects the dual nature of this relation.

B. *Mutual Supportiveness*

The mutually supportive dimension of foreign investment and environmental protection is at the heart of the concept of sustainable development. When considered from this perspective, however, sustainable development appears mainly as a policy goal, the operational contours of which are circumscribed in political declarations, recommendations and soft-law instruments.[20] Although such policy considerations are not the

[18] See, for instance, *Metalclad Corp. v United Mexican States*, ICSID Case No. ARB(AF)/97/1, Award of 25 August 2000 ('*Metalclad v Mexico*'); *Técnicas Medioambientales Tecmed S.A. v United Mexican States*, ICSID Case No. ARB(AF)/00/2, Award of 29 May 2003 ('*Tecmed v Mexico*'); *Abengoa, S.A. y COFIDES, S.A. v United Mexican States*, ICSID Case No. ARB(AF)/09/2 ('*Abengoa v Mexico*') (pending).

[19] See, for instance, the case brought by a Canadian investor against Barbados for failure to enforce its own environmental law (adopted in accordance with international environmental law) in connection with the protection of a natural ecosystem. The investor, who acquired 34.25 acres of natural wetlands and subsequently developed it into an ecotourism facility, claims that, through its acts and omissions, Barbados has *inter alia* failed (a) to prevent the repeated discharge of raw sewage into wetlands, (b) to investigate or prosecute sources of runoff of grease, oil, pesticides, and herbicides from neighbouring areas, and poachers that have threatened the wildlife within the ecosystem. The text of the notice of arbitration is available at <http://graemehall.com/legal/papers/BIT-Complaint.pdf> (last accessed on 16 February 2010). Irrespective of whether this claim prospers, its interest lies in the way it has been formulated, which illustrates a novel form of complementariness between international investment law and international environmental law.

[20] For an overview of the main political documents characterizing sustainable development see N Schrijver, 'The Evolution of Sustainable Development in International Law: Inception, Meaning and Status', (2008) 329 *Recueil des cours* chapters 1–3.

object of this study, it may be useful to provide a brief survey of the overall framework for environmental investment.

The main addressees of the international policy instruments dealing with sustainable development are States. Instruments such as Agenda 21, adopted in the 1992 Earth Summit,[21] or the Plan of Implementation adopted in the 2002 World Summit on Sustainable Development,[22] provide policy guidance to foster sustainable development. However, these instruments also provide some guidance to private and non-state actors.[23] In addition to these two instruments, numerous other 'guidelines', 'recommendations', 'principles' and 'codes' have been developed by either international organizations, non-governmental organizations or industry groups to regulate the environmental dimensions of foreign investment.[24] Generally speaking, one may distinguish two types of instruments,[25] those focusing directly on the activities of multinational corporations, and those affecting such activities indirectly, by targeting the main sources of project finance.

The most prominent illustrations of the first category are perhaps the OECD Guidelines for Multinational Enterprises[26] and the UN Global Compact.[27] Both instruments operate as normative frameworks that seek to influence the behaviour of multinational corporations in a number of areas, including environmental protection. The OECD Guidelines, adopted in 1976 and subsequently revised, contain eight recommendations focusing on environmental matters. Interestingly, States adhering to the guidelines agree to establish 'national contact points' (NCPs), the function of which is *inter alia* to receive complaints relating to the implementation of the guidelines by multinational corporations. Many com-

[21] See Report of the United Nations Conference on Environment and Development, A/CONF.151/26/Rev.l (Vol. l), Resolution 1, Annex 2: Agenda 21 ('Agenda 21').

[22] See Report of the World Summit on Sustainable Development, A/CONF.199/20, Part I, item 2: Plan of Implementation of the World Summit on Sustainable Development ('Plan of Implementation').

[23] See, for instance, chapter 30 of Agenda 21, which contains a statement of the role of business and industry in pursuing sustainable development. This chapter focuses on promoting cleaner production and responsible entrepreneurship. As to the Plan of Implementation, it develops the idea of multi-stakeholder partnerships as a tool to pursue sustainable development. See, for instance, paragraphs 7(j), 9(g), 20(t), 25(g), 43(a) or 49.

[24] See Morgera, above n 9.

[25] See Richardson, above n 9 (Financing Sustainability), 74.

[26] See Organisation for Economic Co-operation and Development (OECD), Guidelines for Multinational Enterprises, 2000 ('OECD Guidelines'); E Morgera, 'An Environmental Outlook on the OECD Guidelines for Multinational Enterprises: Comparative Advantage, Legitimacy, and Outstanding Questions in the Lead Up to the 2006 Review' (2006) 18 *Georgetown International Environmental Law Review* 751; S Tully, 'The 2000 Review of the OECD Guidelines for Multinational Enterprises' (2001) 50 *International & Comparative Law Quarterly* 394.

[27] See UN Global Compact, at <http://www.globalcompact.org> (last accessed on 25 April 2010). On the operation of the Global Compact see UN Global Compact Office, *United Nations Guide to the Global Compact: A Practical Understanding of the Vision and the Nine Principles*; B King, 'The UN Global Compact: Responsibility for Human Rights, Labour Relations, and the Environment in Developing Nations' (2001) 34 *Cornell International Law Journal* 481.

plaints were brought before NCPs in connection with the exploitation of natural resources in the Democratic Republic of Congo,[28] which in turn triggered the establishment, in 2000, of a 'Panel of Experts on the Illegal Exploitation of Natural Resources and Other Forms of Wealth of the Democratic Republic of the Congo' by the United Nations Security Council.[29] The Panel issued its first 'final' report in 2002, finding that 85 named enterprises were in violation of the guidelines.[30] Eventually, however, the follow-up of these cases was mostly[31] left to the NCPs of the relevant home countries, and very few cases were actually continued, allegedly for lack of sufficiently detailed information.[32] As to the Global Compact, it is a UN-led initiative, launched in July 2000, addressing four areas potentially affected by the activities of businesses, namely human rights, labour standards, environment (principles 7 to 9) and corruption. The Global Compact is structured as a public-private-partnership and operates essentially as a policy network with more than 7700 participants worldwide, including some 5300 businesses. It was established as a tool to channel the activities of the private sector towards the accomplishment of the Millennium Development Goals (MDGs) adopted by the United Nations General Assembly in 2000.[33]

The second category encompasses a number of principles and policy instruments aimed at regulating the activities of financial intermediaries, including the World Bank's International Finance Corporation (IFC) and private financial institutions (commercial banks, investment banks, insurance companies and pension funds).[34] Among the numerous instruments falling under this category, one may mention the IFC's Performance Standards on Social and Environmental Sustainability,[35] the Equator Principles,[36] the UNEPFI-led Statement by Financial

[28] See Fauchald, above n 10, 43 et seq. [29] See UN Doc S/PRST/2000/20.

[30] See Final Report (1) of the Panel of Experts on the Illegal Exploitation of Natural Resources and Other Forms of Wealth of the Democratic Republic of the Congo, S/2002/1146 (2002), paras 170–8 and Annex III, referred to by Fauchald, above n 10, 43.

[31] The UN Security Council followed up on those cases where the illegal resource exploitation was closely linked to illegal import of arms into the Congo. See UN Doc S/RES/1533 (2004) establishing a Committee to examine such cases. This committee took a number of measures, but none of the multinational enterprises subject to the OECD Guidelines seems to have been targeted. See ibid, 44 n 180.

[32] Fauchald, above n 10, 44–45.

[33] See United Nations Millennium Declaration, UN Doc A/RES/55/2 Millennium (18 September 2000).

[34] See generally Richardson, above n 9 (Financing Sustainability).

[35] See International Finance Corporation (IFC), *Performance Standards on Social and Environmental Sustainability*, adopted on 21 February 2006, available at <http://www.ifc.org/sustainability> (last accessed on 25 April 2010). On the operation of the Standards see E Morgera, 'Significant Trends in Corporate Environmental Accountability: The New Performance Standards of the International Financial Corporation' (2007) 18 *Colorado Journal of International Law and Policy* 151.

[36] See Equator Principles, available at <http://www.equator-principles.com> (last accessed on 25 April 2010). On the operation of these principles see B J Richardson, 'The Equator Principles: The Voluntary Approach to Environmentally Sustainable Finance' (2005) 14 *European Environmental Law Review* 280.

Institutions on the Environment and Sustainable Development,[37] the UN Principles of Responsible Investment,[38] and many others. Despite some variation from one instrument to another, they all operate by setting social and environmental standards for project financing by public, institutional or private financiers. Thus, access to funding by promoters of infrastructure or other projects with significant implications for the environment is subject to the respect of a number of environmental standards.

In addition to the policy initiatives mentioned so far, there are many other forms of fostering mutual supportiveness between foreign investment and environmental protection. Two major examples are the project-based flexibility mechanisms established, respectively, in Articles 6 (joint-implementation mechanism) and 12 (clean development mechanism) of the Kyoto Protocol.[39] States having undertaken quantified emission reduction commitments under Article 3.1 and Annex B of the Kyoto Protocol can earn emission credits by conducting certain projects that reduce emissions in other countries. By providing such possibility, these mechanisms induce 'green' investment in transitional and/or developing countries, thereby constituting an additional vector of sustainable development.

The instruments surveyed in the foregoing paragraphs provide apposite illustrations of the potential convergence between foreign investment and environmental protection. While such instruments suggest that foreign investment and environmental protection are not antagonistic terms, one must not underestimate the potential for conflicts to arise between the two. The remainder of this article focuses on such conflicts from the perspective of international law.

C. Potential Conflicts

The potentially conflicting dimension of the relations between investment and environmental protection calls for a variety of legal techniques through which conflicts can be managed.

To analyse these techniques, it is useful to introduce a distinction between two fundamental types of conflicts arising from the interactions

[37] See UNEP Finance Initiative, *Statement by Financial Institutions on the Environment and Sustainable Development*, available at <http://www.unepfi.org/signatories/statements/fi/index.html> (last accessed on 23 April 2010).

[38] See United Nations Principles of Responsible Investment, available at <www.unpri.org/principles> (last accessed on 25 April 2010).

[39] See Kyoto Protocol to the United Nations Framework Convention on Climate Change, Kyoto, 11 December 1997, 2303 UNTS 148 (entered into force on 16 February 2005), arts 6 and 12. See also M Wara, 'Measuring the Clean Development Mechanism's Performance and Potential' (2008) 55 *UCLA Law Review* 1759; J E Viñuales, 'El régimen jurídico internacional relativo al cambio climático: Perspectivas y prospectivas' in Organization of American States (OAS)/Inter-American Juridical Committee, *Annual Course on International Law. Universalism and Regionalism at the Beginning of the 21st Century* (2010) 36, section III.

between foreign investment and environmental regulation. On the one hand, conflicts may arise between one international obligation stemming from international investment law and another international obligation stemming from international environmental law. Such scenario shall be referred to as a 'normative conflict'. On the other hand, conflicts may arise between norms or measures stemming from different legal systems. Although many scenarios are possible, in the context of foreign investment disputes the most common one is that of a measure/regulation adopted by the host State for environmental reasons adversely affecting the interests of a foreign investor, who claims that the measure/regulation is in breach of an international investment obligation of the host State. This type of conflict shall be referred to as a 'legitimacy conflict' between investment protection and environmental considerations.

An environmental measure/regulation adopted by a State may also be based on a norm (be it an obligation or other type of norm) of international environmental law. However, such a hypothesis will be treated as a normative conflict only when the argument is clearly formulated as a conflict between two or more international obligations. The distinction between normative and legitimacy conflicts is, as discussed in section IV below, both analytically useful and legally relevant, because the rules applicable to the resolution of each of these types of conflict are different.

Before undertaking the analysis of these rules, it is necessary to discuss a number of issues that may arise in the course of an investment proceeding as a result of the environmental ramifications of a dispute.

III. Investment Proceedings

This section is devoted to a number of issues that arbitral tribunals must determine in the conduct of investment proceedings before they move onto (or as they proceed to) the assessment of the merits of the claims. The selection of these issues is based on the practice of investment tribunals as well as on the emerging literature referred to in the introduction. They can be organised under three main rubrics, namely jurisdictional matters (A), matters pertaining to the applicable law (B), and procedural matters (C).

A. Jurisdictional Matters

There are two main hypotheses under which environmental considerations may have an impact on jurisdictional matters, namely (1) in connection with the claims that may be heard by an investment tribunal, and (2) in connection with the scope of protected investments under a given investment treaty.

1. Environmental claims

(i) Environmental claims as investment claims

An investment protection standard may be breached as a result of conduct of the host State in violation of an environmental norm, either domestic or international. This could be the case where the investment heavily depends upon the host State's implementation of environmental law.

An example is provided by the notice of arbitration filed by a Canadian national, Peter A Allard, against Barbados,[40] for failure to enforce[41] applicable international and domestic environmental law in connection with the protection of a natural wetlands ecosystem. According to the investor, the profitability of its investment (an ecotourism facility) was reduced as a result *inter alia* of 'Barbados' actions and omissions' which 'have severely damaged the natural ecosystem that [the investor's facility] relies upon to attract visitors'.[42] These and other actions and omissions would allegedly amount to a breach of the fair and equitable treatment, full protection and security, and expropriation clauses of the Canada-Barbados BIT.[43]

Other potential illustrations are the two *Unglaube v Costa Rica* cases brought before ICSID.[44] According to the information publicly available, the investors claimed mistreatment by the State of parcels of land contained in a 33 hectare oceanfront resort community development in Costa Rica. Reportedly, the claims arose from certain measures taken by Costa Rica in order to create a preserve for endangered leatherback turtles. The investors disagree with Costa Rica regarding the appropriate means for safeguarding turtle breeding sites.[45]

Still another example would be a situation where the uneven enforcement of environmental standards to different foreign and/or domestic investors would fall foul of the most-favoured-nation and/or national treatment clauses contained in an investment treaty. For instance, one could think of a case where mandatory emissions targets for companies in the electricity generation are unevenly enforced. In this hypothesis, the

[40] See *Peter A Allard v Government of Barbados*, Notice of Dispute ('*Allard v Barbados*'), above n 19.

[41] A more difficult hypothesis would be a claim based on the absence of enactment of a domestic law or measure as required by treaty. Such a hypothesis could arise in the context of investments made in reasonable anticipation of an action required from the host State by a norm of international environmental law, and that has not been taken. Depending on the facts, issues relating to the self-executing character of the international norm at stake or of analogical reasoning with the implementation of European Community directives could arise.

[42] See *Allard v Barbados*, above n 19, para 16.

[43] Ibid, paras 14–21, referring to the Agreement between the Government of Canada and the Government of Barbados for the Promotion and Reciprocal Protection of Investments (Canada-Barbados BIT), Articles II(2), and VIII(1).

[44] See *Reinhard Hans Unglaube v Republic of Costa Rica*, ICSID Case No. ARB/09/20 (pending); *Marion Unglaube v Republic of Costa Rica*, ICSID Case No. ARB/08/1 (pending).

[45] See 'Another Investor in Costa-Rican Resort Development filed BIT Claim', *Investment ArbitrationReporter*, 13November2009, availableat<http://www.iareporter.com/articles/20091124_21> (last accessed on 26 February 2010).

affected investor could bring a claim for breach of investment protection standards arguing that the host State is not enforcing its environmental laws upon the investor's competitors. This is of course not to say that such claim would be justified, a question that will depend upon the circumstances of each case.

For the purpose of establishing jurisdiction, this type of claims does not present any significant specificity and must therefore be treated as a regular investment claim. A number of issues may arise, however, with respect to applicable law, as it will be discussed later.

(ii) Environmental claims as independent heads of claim

The situation is different when an environmental claim is brought as an independent head of claim, i.e. when the investor claims that the conduct of the host State is in breach of an environmental norm, irrespective of any breach of an investment protection standard.

In *Biloune v Ghana*,[46] the claimant had asked an investment tribunal organised under the UNCITRAL Arbitration Rules to examine a claim for violation of international human rights law by the host State. The tribunal considered that it did not have jurisdiction to examine such issues as an independent head of claim but only within the context of specific investment claims:

> This Tribunal's competence is limited to commercial disputes arising under a contract entered into in the context of Ghana's Investment Code. As noted, the Government agreed to arbitrate only disputes "in respect of" the foreign investment. Thus, other matters—however compelling the claim or wrongful the alleged act—are outside this Tribunal's jurisdiction. Under the facts of this case it must be concluded that, while the acts alleged to violate the international human rights of Mr Biloune may be relevant in considering the investment dispute under arbitration, this Tribunal lacks jurisdiction to address, as an independent cause of action, a claim of violation of human rights.[47]

The decision of the tribunal suggests that, as a rule, an investment tribunal would not have jurisdiction over a claim brought solely for breach of an environmental norm, irrespective of any breach of an investment protection clause.

This conclusion seems consistent with the approach followed by some treaties according to which the availability of arbitration is limited to certain causes of action. For instance, Article 1116(1) of the North-American Free Trade Agreement (NAFTA)[48] provides that '[a]n investor of a Party

[46] See *Antoine Biloune v Ghana Investment Centre*, UNCITRAL, Award on Jurisdiction and Liability of 27 October 1989, 95 ILR 183 ('*Biloune v Ghana*').

[47] Ibid, paras 202–203.

[48] See *North American Free Trade Agreement*, US-Canada-Mexico, 17 December 1992, 32 ILM 296 (entered into force on 1 January 1994) ('NAFTA').

may submit to arbitration under this Section a claim that another Party *has breached an obligation under . . . Section A*.'[49] Section A of Chapter 11 of NAFTA provides for the usual investment protection standards. Similarly, Article 26(1)-(2) of the Energy Charter Treaty (ECT)[50] limits the availability of arbitration to '[d]isputes between a Contracting Party and an Investor of another Contracting Party relating to an Investment of the latter in the Area of the former, which concern an *alleged breach of an obligation of the former under Part III*.'[51] Part III of the ECT provides for the usual investment protection standards.

The foregoing examples also suggest that the question whether an investment tribunal may assert jurisdiction over an environmental claim brought as an independent head of claim depends upon the scope of the arbitration clause and the substantive provisions contained in the applicable treaty. The conjunction of these two elements was discussed by the ICJ in the *Pulp Mills* case. Argentina argued that the jurisdictional clause contained in Article 60 of the 1975 Statute of the River Uruguay, read in the light of Articles 1 and 41 of said statute, which Argentina characterized as 'referral clauses', gave the Court jurisdiction over breaches of obligations arising from multilateral environmental treaties and general international law. The Court rejected this argument on the grounds that Articles 1 and 41 of said statute could not operate as referral clauses.[52] However, the reasoning of the Court suggests *a contrario* that, under a relatively broad jurisdictional treaty clause, an investor could bring an independent environmental claim if the treaty in question contains a referral clause. As it will be discussed in section IV of this study, bilateral investment treaties ('BITs') and free trade agreements ('FTAs') may incorporate environmental protection standards either in their text or in parallel agreements. However, if an investor were to bring a claim under such circumstances, the claim would operate as an investment claim, much in the same way as a claim for breach of a fair and equitable treatment clause imported from another treaty through a most-favoured-nation clause in the applicable treaty is technically based on this latter clause.

2. *Investments in accordance with (environmental) law*

The relevance of environmental considerations in determining the existence of a protected investment can take at least two forms. First, the specific contours of what the claimant asserts as an investment may not be covered by an investment treaty (i). Second, an otherwise covered

[49] Emphasis added.

[50] Energy Charter Treaty, 17 December 1994, 2080 UNTS 95 (entered into force on 16 April 1998) ('ECT').

[51] Emphasis added. Both the NAFTA and the ECT are mentioned C Reiner, C Schreuer, 'Human Rights and International Investment Arbitration' in Dupuy et al, above n 10, 83.

[52] See *Pulp Mills case*, above n 8, paras 48–63.

investment may be contrary to domestic environmental laws and therefore excluded from the protection of a treaty (ii).

(i) Environmental rights as investments

The first scenario can be illustrated by reference to *Bayview v Mexico*,[53] where the US based claimants argued that the diversion by Mexico of the waters of the Rio Grande River amounted to a breach of NAFTA Chapter 11. This argument supposed that water rights held by the US claimants in the US territory could constitute a protected investment under NAFTA. However, in a submission made before the tribunal on the basis of Article 1128 of NAFTA,[54] the United States government itself argued against this proposition.[55] Eventually, the tribunal concluded that such water rights were not protected under Article 1101 of NAFTA. The tribunal noted, in this regard, that:

> [I]n order to be an "investor" within the meaning of NAFTA Art. 1101(a), an enterprise must make an investment in another NAFTA State, and not in its own. Adopting the terminology of the *Methanex v United States* Tribunal, it is necessary that the measures of which complaint is made should affect an investment that has a "legally significant connection" with the State creating and applying those measures. The simple fact that an enterprise in a NAFTA State is affected by measures taken in another NAFTA State is not sufficient to establish the right of that enterprise to protection under NAFTA Chapter Eleven: it is the relationship, the legally significant connection, with the State taking those measures that establishes the right to protection, not the bare fact that the enterprise is affected by the measures.[56]

The reasoning of the tribunal on this point may be of relevance for potential cases brought as a result of long-arm environmental statutes, which strongly affect investments made in either Canada or Mexico, but whose main market is in the United States.

(ii) Investments contrary to environmental law

The second scenario has more often been argued in investment cases, although not in connection with violations of domestic environmental

[53] See *Bayview Irrigation District v United Mexican States*, ICSID Case No. ARB(AF)/05/1, Award of 19 June 2007 ('*Bayview v Mexico*').

[54] Article 1128 of NAFTA provides: 'On written notice to the disputing parties, a Party may make submissions to a Tribunal on a question of interpretation of this Agreement.'

[55] The United States Article 1128 Submission states that '[a]ll three NAFTA Parties thus agree that the scope and coverage of NAFTA Chapter Eleven is restricted to investors of a NAFTA Party that are seeking to make, are making or have made investments in the territory of another NAFTA Party', *Bayview v Mexico*, Submission of the United States of America, 27 November 2006, para 14, <http://www.naftaclaims.com/Disputes/Mexico/Texas/TexasClaimsMexico-USA_1128-Jurisdiction.pdf> (last accessed on 17 February 2010).

[56] See *Bayview v Mexico*, above n 53, para 101.

laws.[57] A number of investment treaties subject the definition of protected investments to their conformity with the laws of the host State.[58] As a result, domestic environmental laws may have an impact on whether an investment is protected.[59] Such characterization may, under some circumstances, be relevant for the determination of a tribunal's jurisdiction.

Most tribunals have considered that such a reference to the host State's laws concerns the validity of an investment and not the definition of the term investment itself. As noted by the tribunal in *Salini v Morocco*, the provisions in BITs requiring the conformity of the investments with the host State's laws refer 'to the validity of the investment and not to its definition. More specifically, [such provisions seek] to prevent the Bilateral Treaty from protecting investments that should not be protected because they would be illegal.'[60] However, in at least two cases, the legality of an investment was considered as a jurisdictional obstacle.

In *Inceysa v El Salvador*,[61] the respondent argued that it had not consented to the protection of investments procured by fraud, forgery or corruption.[62] The applicable BIT did not qualify the definition of investment in the provision defining this term but contained a reference to compliance with national laws in the provisions dealing with admission and protection. The tribunal concluded that, under the circumstances, it did not have jurisdiction over the claim brought by the investor, as the respondent had not consented to extend the protections of the treaty or those of its domestic code to an investment made in an openly illegal manner.[63]

A similar conclusion was reached in *Fraport v Philippines*.[64] The respondent had argued, in essence, that 'the protections afforded by the

[57] The question has arisen most notably in connection with European Community law, particularly on State aid. For a discussion of the so-called 'intra-EU BITs' see H Wehland, 'Intra-EU Investment Agreements and Arbitration: Is European Community Law an Obstacle?' (2009) 58 *International & Comparative Law Quarterly* 297; M Burgstaller, 'European Law and Investment Treaties' (2009) 26 *Journal of International Arbitration* 181.

[58] For instance, the Egypt—Pakistan BIT (2000), provides in Article 1(1) that '[t]he term investment means every kind of assets . . . invested by investors of a Contracting Party in the territory of the other Contracting Party in accordance with the laws and regulations of that Party.' Another example is given by the Bahrain—Thailand BIT (2002), which provides, in Article 2 that '[t]he benefits of this Agreement shall apply to the investments by the investors of one Contracting Party in the territory of the other Contracting Party which is specifically approved in writing by the competent authority in accordance with the laws and regulations of the latter Contracting Party.' Both examples are quoted from A Joubin-Bret, 'Admission and Establishment in the Context of Investment Protection' in A Reinisch (ed) *Standards of Investment Protection* (Oxford University Press, Oxford, 2008) 17.

[59] See ibid, 19.

[60] *Salini Costruttori v Morocco*, Decision on Jurisdiction, 23 July 2003, 42, para 46, reproduced in R Dolzer, C Schreuer, *Principles of International Investment Law* (Oxford University Press, Oxford, 2008) 113 and decisions cited therein.

[61] *Inceysa Vallisoletane, SL v El Salvador*, ICSID No ARB/03/26, Award of 2 August 2006 ('*Inceysa v El Salvador*').

[62] Ibid, para 45.

[63] Ibid, paras 257, 264.

[64] *Fraport AG Frankfurt Airport Services Worldwide v Republic of the Philippines*, ICSID Case No. ARB/03/25, Award, 16 August 2007 ('*Fraport v Philippines*').

BIT at issue [did] not extend to investments made in violation of Philippine law' and that such conclusion applied even once an investment had been admitted if the investment was 'implemented in a manner that materially violates the host State's laws that directly regulate the investment or the investment activities'.[65] The domestic laws at issue restricted foreign ownership and control of corporations engaging in certain activities. In its analysis, the tribunal distinguished between initial and subsequent illegality, considering that, whereas the latter could only operate as a substantive defence, the former could potentially limit jurisdiction.[66] This was so irrespective of whether the investment had been accompanied by some explicit agreement with or communication from the host State,[67] as even where the host State had issued an authorisation, a potential estoppel argument could be dismissed if the arrangements making an investment illegal were covert.[68] That was, as a matter of fact, the conclusion of the tribunal in this case.[69]

The significance of the *Inceysa* and *Fraport* decisions for the relations between foreign investment and environmental protection should not be underestimated. One could imagine, for instance, a case where a landfill or a chemical production plant has been established in a developing country in violation of local laws requiring the conduct of an environmental impact assessment, especially if the investor has resorted to corruption or other unacceptable means prohibited by international public policy or *ordre public international*.[70] Even if establishing such facts could be difficult

[65] Ibid, paras 285–286, 344.

[66] The tribunal reasoned that '[a]though this contention [jurisdictional limits arising from subsequent illegality] is not relevant to the analysis of the problem which the Tribunal has before it, namely the *entry* of the investment and not the way it was subsequently conducted, the Tribunal would note that this part of the Respondent's interpretation appears to be a forced construction of the pertinent provisions in the context of the entire Treaty. The language of both Articles 1 and 2 of the BIT emphasizes the *initiation* of the investment. Moreover the effective operation of the BIT regime would appear to require that jurisdictional compliance be limited to the initiation of the investment. If, at the time of the initiation of the investment, there has been compliance with the law of the host state, allegations by the host state of violations of its law in the course of the investment, as a justification for state action with respect to the investment, might be a defense to claimed *substantive* violations of the BIT, but could not deprive a tribunal acting under the authority of the BIT of its jurisdiction', ibid, para 345 (italics original).

[67] Ibid, para 343.

[68] Ibid, paras 346–347. Such conclusion is exceptional. Where the actions of the host State's own authorities were themselves illegal, an objection to jurisdiction based on the non-conformity of the investment with laws of the host State would normally fail. See *Ioannis Kardassopoulos v Georgia*, ICSID Case No. ARB/05/18, Decision on Jurisdiction, 6 July 2007, para 182.

[69] *Fraport v Philippines*, above n 64, para 404, stating that '[c]ompliance with the host state's laws is an explicit and hardly unreasonable requirement in the Treaty and its accompanying Protocol. Fraport's ostensible purchase of shares in the Terminal 3 project, which concealed a different type of unlawful investment, is not an "investment" which is covered by the BIT. As the BIT is the basis of jurisdiction of this Tribunal, Fraport's claim must be rejected for lack of jurisdiction ratione materiae.'

[70] In *Inceysa v El Salvador*, the tribunal considered that Inceysa's investment was contrary to international public policy and that asserting jurisdiction over such investment would also constitute a violation of international public policy. See above n 61, paras 245–252.

in practice, treating this issue at the jurisdictional phase instead of waiting until the merits phase would increase the efficiency of investment arbitration proceedings, saving some of the scarce resources that developing countries can devote to such proceedings.

B. Applicable Law

The question of the law applicable to investment disputes is different from, although related to, the question of the scope of jurisdiction.[71] Even in cases where an independent human rights or environmental claim has been deemed to be outside the scope of jurisdiction of the tribunal, human rights or environmental rules may remain relevant for the consideration of an investment claim.[72] The potential confusion between jurisdiction and applicable law stems *inter alia* from the diversity of the provisions from which the applicable law can be determined, and the fact that, in some treaties, the same provision deals with both jurisdiction and governing law.[73]

The legal framework potentially applicable to an investment consists of three main layers, namely contractual provisions (if the investment has been made through a contract with the host State or its instrumentalities), domestic law (of the host State or, potentially, of another State), and international law (treaty law or customary international law). Environmental considerations may be included in a clause of the investment contract (and/or of a related agreement, such as a credit facility agreement), in domestic regulations or in the applicable investment treaty. Environmental protection standards may also arise from an applicable environmental treaty or, exceptionally, from general international law.[74] The specific body of norms (contractual, domestic, international) which will be applicable for the determination of a given dispute as well as the precise articulation of such norms will depend upon (1) the law possibly chosen by the parties or indicated by other means (mainly a default clause), and (2) the relevance of potentially applicable norms in the light of the scope of the dispute. These two aspects must not be considered as a sequential test but merely as two questions that help organise the process of determining the applicable law.

1. Choice of law and other indications

Concerning the first issue, indications as to the applicable law may appear in different forms including (i) in a choice of law clause contained in an

[71] See *Pulp Mills case*, above n 8, para 66.

[72] See *Biloune v Ghana*, above n 46, paras 202–203.

[73] See, for instance, Article 26 of the Energy Charter Treaty, which defines both the scope of jurisdiction of (paragraphs 1 and 2) and the law applicable by (paragraph 6) arbitral tribunals constituted under paragraph 4.

[74] See *Legality of the Threat or Use of Nuclear Weapons*, [1996] ICJ Rep 226 ('*Legality of Nuclear Weapons*'), para 29 (affirming the prevention principle); *Pulp Mills case*, above n 8, para 204 (asserting a requirement of prior environmental impact assessment).

investment contract between a foreign investor and the host State, (ii) in a choice of law provision contained in an investment treaty between the host State and the investor's home State (choice that the investor accepts in availing itself of the treaty's arbitration clause), (iii) in an 'indirect' reference to the applicable law in the form of a provision in a treaty or in an investment code specifying that only investments made in accordance with the host State's laws are protected, or (iv) in a default clause contained in the rules governing the arbitration proceedings.

(i) Choice of law clause in an investment agreement

When there is a choice of law, the applicable law is quite often that of the host State, although it may also be that of the investor's home State, that of a third State or another body of law such as international law.[75]

The place occupied by environmental laws in this choice raises a number of questions. The most basic one is whether environmental laws are included in the scope of the choice. Whereas the answer will normally be affirmative when the parties have chosen the laws of the host State, the situation is less clear when the laws chosen are those of the investor's home State or of a third State, to the extent that environmental law could take the form of either private or public law and that there are limitations in the application of a foreign public law.[76]

Where the parties have chosen a foreign law to govern contractual matters, an argument could be made in favour of applying the environmental laws of the host State if and to the extent that they can be considered as *lois de police*.[77] The application of the environmental laws of the investor's home State or of a potentially affected third State is much more difficult to assess.[78] In practice, the overriding character of *lois de police* and their application by arbitral tribunals seem to be in decline. As a result, the application of foreign (or even local) *lois de police* will often turn on the specificities of the case.[79]

[75] For examples see Dolzer, Schreuer, above n 60, 265 et seq; D Bishop, J Crawford, M Reisman, *Foreign Investment Disputes* (Kluwer International, The Hague, 2005) 255 et seq.

[76] See H Batiffol, P Lagarde, *Droit international privé, vol. I* (6th edn, LGDJ, Paris, 1974) paras 245–246; G Van Hecke, 'Droit public et conflit des lois', in *Travaux du Comité français de droit international privé* (1982–1984) 228; Institut de Droit International, 'The Application of Foreign Public Law', Session of Wiesbaden, 1975.

[77] On the concept of *lois de police* see Ph Franceskakis, 'Quelques précisions sur les lois d'application immédiate et leurs rapports avec les règles de conflit de lois' (1966) 55 *Revue critique de droit international privé* 1; T Guedi, 'The Theory of the Lois de Police—A Functional Trend in Continental Private International Law—A Comparative Analysis with Modern American Theories' (1991) 39 *American Journal of Comparative Law* 661; T C Hartley, 'Mandatory Rules in International Contracts: The Common Law Approach', (1997) 266 *Recueil des cours* 337; A Bonomi, *Le norme imperative nel diritto internazionale privato* (Publications of the Swiss Institute of Comparative Law, Zurich, 1998).

[78] On the conceptual aspects of the extraterritorial application of such laws see B Stern, 'Une élucidation du concept d'application extraterritoriale du droit', (1986) 3 *Revue québécoise de droit international* 49–78.

[79] See L Radicati di Brozolo, 'Arbitrage commercial international et lois de police. Considérations sur les conflits de juridictions dans le commerce international', (2005) 315 *Recueil des cours* 402.

(ii) Choice of law provision in an investment treaty

The inclusion of a choice of law provision in an investment treaty is frequent in practice. Indeed, multilateral and bilateral investment treaties often include provisions specifying the law applicable for the resolution of disputes. For instance, Article 1131(1) of NAFTA states: 'A Tribunal established under this Section shall decide the issues in dispute in accordance with this Agreement and applicable rules of international law.'[80] Similarly, Article 26(6) of the Energy Charter Treaty states: 'A tribunal established under paragraph (4) [arbitral tribunal] shall decide the issues in dispute in accordance with this Treaty and applicable rules and principles of international law.'[81] Turning to bilateral investment treaties, one may mention, among many others, the Canadian Model BIT 2004, which states in Article 40(1): 'A Tribunal established under this Section shall decide the issues in dispute in accordance with this Agreement and applicable rules of international law.' Similarly, the Chinese Model BIT 2003 states in Article 9(3) that 'the arbitration award [of the investment tribunal] shall be based on the law of the Contracting Party to the dispute including its rules on the conflict of laws, the provisions of this Agreement as well as the universally accepted principles of international law.'[82] Still another example is provided by Article 30 of the United States Model BIT 2004, which is much more detailed than most other BITs:

1. Subject to paragraph 3, when a claim is submitted under Article 24(1)(a)(i)(A) or Article 24(1)(b)(i)(A) [claims for breach of an investment protection brought, respectively, by a foreign entity or by a local entity under foreign control], the tribunal shall decide the issues in dispute in accordance with this Treaty and applicable rules of international law.
2. Subject to paragraph 3 and the other terms of this Section, when a claim is submitted under Article 24(1)(a)(i)(B) or (C), or Article 24(1)(b)(i)(B) or (C) [idem before except for the cause of action, which is, respectively, breach of an investment authorization or an investment agreement], the tribunal shall apply:

   (a) the rules of law specified in the pertinent investment authorization or investment agreement, or as the disputing parties may otherwise agree; or
   (b) if the rules of law have not been specified or otherwise agreed:
      (i) the law of the respondent, including its laws on the conflict of laws; and
      (ii) such rules of international law as may be applicable.

3. A joint decision of the Parties, each acting through its representative designated for purposes of this Article, declaring their interpretation of a provision of this Treaty shall be binding on a tribunal, and any decision or award issued by a tribunal must be consistent with that joint decision.[83]

[80] NAFTA, above n 48, art 1131(1). [81] ECT, above n 50, Art 26(6).
[82] Chinese Model BIT 2003, reproduced in Dolzer, Schreuer, above n 60, 352 et seq.
[83] United States Model BIT 2004, reproduced in ibid, 385 et seq.

In all these examples, some room is left for the potential application of environmental norms stemming from both domestic and international law. As noted by two commentators with respect to the potential application of human rights law, 'human rights [and also by analogy environmental] provisions are applicable to the extent to which they are included in the parties' choice of law.'[84]

One potentially important issue arising from the scope of the choice-of-law clause in a BIT relates to the possibility for a State to bring a counterclaim against an investor for breach of the domestic environmental laws. The admissibility of such type of counterclaims will depend on a variety of factors, including the scope of the jurisdictional and the choice-of-law clauses as well as the facts of the case. Assuming *ratio arguendi* that neither the jurisdictional clause nor the facts preclude such possibility, an independent environmental counterclaim could be brought only if the applicable treaty directs the arbitral tribunal to apply domestic (environmental) law. This hypothesis would be similar to a case where a treaty with a broad jurisdictional clause directs the tribunal to apply the provisions of investment contracts. In both cases, the investor would be subject to substantive obligations (arising, respectively, from the host State's law or from a contract) capable of founding a State counterclaim. Such substantive obligations would not be present if the applicable law is limited to the provisions of the treaty and/or international law, as private investors have no obligations under either treaties or customary international law.[85] In practice, instead of bringing a counterclaim, States will more likely bring claims against investors before State courts. A State may nevertheless decide to bring a counterclaim within an investment proceeding to facilitate the set-off of the opposing claims or to benefit from the more sophisticated international regime for the recognition and enforcement of arbitral awards.[86]

(iii) References to the validity of an investment

This hypothesis has already been discussed in some detail in connection with jurisdictional matters. In essence, the reference in an investment treaty to investments made 'in accordance with the laws' of the host State is, as a rule, considered through the lens of the 'validity' theory. Thus, where the operation of an investment is (or becomes) in breach of the host State's environmental laws, investment tribunals tend to recognise

[84] See Reiner, Schreuer, above n 51, 84.

[85] On claims and counterclaims by host States see J Crawford, 'Treaty and Contract in Investment Arbitration' (2008) 24 *Arbitration International* 351; H E Veenstra-Kjos, 'Counter-claims by Host States in Investment Dispute Arbitration "without Privity"' in P Kahn, T Waelde (eds), *New Aspects of International Investment Law* (Martinus Nijhoff Publishers, Leiden, 2007) chapter 14; G Laborde, 'The Case for Host State Claims in Investment Arbitration' (2010) 1 *Journal of International Dispute Settlement* 97.

[86] See Convention on the Recognition and Enforcement of Foreign Arbitral Awards, 10 June 1958, 330 UNTS 38 ('New York Convention') (entered into force on 7 June 1959).

that the host State could avail itself of this circumstance in the form of a substantive defence.[87] The technical operation of such a defence is not entirely clear and could be spelled out in at least three manners, depending on the circumstances of the case.

Let us assume, for the purposes of the analysis, that, as a result of an investor's breach of the domestic environmental regulations, a State adopts a measure adversely affecting the interests of such investor. Let us also assume that this latter brings only treaty claims under a treaty providing that the dispute will be decided solely on the basis of its provisions and other relevant rules of international law. In this first situation, the non-conformity of the investment with local environmental regulations would be a mere fact relevant to assess whether the adverse measures were justified or not, which is in turn important for determining whether an investment protection clause in the treaty has been breached or not.

A second situation would arise where the treaty does not contain a provision excluding the applicability of domestic law[88] or where the choice of law provision expressly mentions the applicability of the host State's domestic laws. In such a hypothesis, the domestic environmental laws could be applied as law instead of as facts. In *Maffezini v Spain*,[89] the choice of law clause in the Argentina–Spain BIT expressly mentioned the applicability of the 'the law of the Contracting Party in whose territory the investment was made'.[90] Maffezini argued that the Spanish authorities had forced him to proceed with the construction of a chemical plant even before the implications of the environmental impact assessment (EIA) conducted as part of the process were known, and that they had then asked for additional information in this connection. Spain replied that Maffezini was well aware of the standards for the conduct of an EIA under Spanish and European law and had nevertheless decided to start the construction works before the conclusion of the EIA. After reviewing the arguments of the parties, the tribunal concluded that the Spanish authorities had strictly abided by the applicable domestic and European environmental laws on this point.[91]

The third situation would arise where the violation of the domestic laws by the investor is so glaring that it brings into operation the rules on inter-

[87] See above section III.A(2)(ii).

[88] Although this is not a choice of law *stricto sensu*, the initiation of arbitration proceedings by an investor based on the arbitration clause in a treaty containing such a reference to the validity of investments can arguably amount to consent by the investor to the application of the relevant domestic laws.

[89] See *Emilio Agustín Maffezini v Kingdom of Spain*, ICSID Case No. ARB/97/7, Award of 13 November 2000 ('*Maffezini v Spain—Award*').

[90] See *Emilio Agustín Maffezini v Kingdom of Spain*, ICSID Case No. ARB/97/7, Decision on Jurisdiction of 25 January 2000 ('*Maffezini v Spain—Jurisdiction*'), para 19.

[91] The tribunal reasoned that '[t]he Kingdom of Spain and SODIGA have done no more in this respect than insist on the strict observance of the EEC and Spanish law applicable to the industry in question. It follows that Spain cannot be held responsible for the decisions taken by the Claimant with regard to the EIA. Furthermore, the Kingdom of Spain's action is fully consistent with Article 2(1) of the Argentine-Spain Bilateral Investment Treaty, which calls for the promotion of investment in compliance with national legislation.', *Maffezini v Spain—Award*, above n 89, para 71.

national public policy or *ordre public international.*[92] Of course, it is unclear whether certain environmental norms are or could be part of international public policy. However, this is by no means impossible, in light of the increasing environmental conscience in the population of many countries as well as of the morally unacceptable effects that a violation of certain environmental norms, such the prohibition of indiscriminate disposal of radioactive or other highly toxic waste, could have on the local population.

(iv) Default rules

The arbitration rules most frequently used in investment proceedings, namely the ICSID[93] and UNCITRAL[94] Arbitration Rules, as well as other rules increasingly in use, such as those of the LCIA,[95] the ICC,[96] the PCA[97] or the Stockholm Chamber of Commerce,[98] contain provisions indicating how the applicable law must be determined in the absence of a choice of law by the parties. Article 42(1) of the ICSID Convention goes a step further because, unlike the other provisions mentioned, it expressly identifies the applicable law:

> The Tribunal shall decide a dispute in accordance with such rules of law as may be agreed by the parties. In the absence of such agreement, the Tribunal shall apply the law of the Contracting State party to the dispute (including its rules on the conflict of laws) and such rules of international law as may be applicable.

Thus, in the absence of a choice of law clause, the laws of the host State and the rules of international law will be applicable. There has been some discussion as to the meaning of the term 'and' in Article 42(1).[99] This

[92] On this concept see P Lalive, 'Ordre public transnational (ou réellement international) et arbitrage international' (1986) *Revue de l'arbitrage* 329; L Matray, 'Arbitrage et ordre public transnational' in J C Schultsz, A-J van den Berg (eds), *The Art of Arbitration—Essays on International Arbitration Liber Amicorum Pieter Sanders* (Kluwer Law and Taxation Publishers: Deventer, 1967) 241.

[93] See Convention on the Settlement of Investment Disputes between States and Nationals of other States, 18 March 1965, 575 UNTS 159 (entered into force on 14 October 1966) ('ICSID Convention'), art 42(1).

[94] United Nations Commission on International Trade Law (UNCITRAL), Arbitration Rules, 1976 ('UNCITRAL Rules'), Article 33(1).

[95] See London Court of International Arbitration (LCIA), Arbitration Rules ('LCIA Rules'), art 22.3.

[96] See International Chamber of Commerce (ICC), Arbitration Rules (January 2009) ('ICC Rules'), art 17(1)-(2).

[97] See Permanent Court of Arbitration (PCA), Optional Rules for Arbitrating Disputes between two Parties of which only one is a State ('PCA Rules'), art 33(1).

[98] See Stockholm Chamber of Commerce (SCC), Arbitration Rules 2010, art 22(1).

[99] See M Reisman, 'The Regime for Lacunae in the ICSID Choice of Law Provision and the Question of Threshold' (2000) 15 *ICSID Review* 362; C Schreuer, 'Failure to Apply the Governing Law in International Investment Arbitration' (2002) 7 *Austrian Review of International and European Law* 147; E Gaillard, Y Banifatemi, 'The Meaning of "and" in Article 42(1), second sentence, of the Washington Convention: The Role of International Law in the ICSID Choice of Law Process' (2003) 18 *ICSID Review* 375; O Spiermann, 'Applicable Law' in P Muchlinsky, F Ortino, C Schreuer (eds) *The Oxford Handbook of International Investment Law* (Oxford University Press, Oxford, 2008) 89.

answer heavily depends upon the specific legal question at issue. Three basic scenarios can be identified.

First, the two bodies of law may have to be 'separately' applied, for instance, when the investor has brought both contract claims, which will then be governed by the contract and the host State's laws, and treaty claims, which will be decided on the basis of the treaty as well as of other relevant rules of international law. As noted by the ad hoc committee in *Vivendi v Argentina*:

> [W]hether there has been a breach of the BIT and whether there has been a breach of contract are different questions. Each of these claims will be determined by reference to its own proper or applicable law—in the case of the BIT, by international law; in the case of the Concession Contract, by the proper law of the contract, in other words, the law of Tucumán [a territorial subdivision of Argentina]. For example, in the case of a claim based on a treaty, international law rules of attribution apply, with the result that the state of Argentina is internationally responsible for the acts of its provincial authorities.[100]

In this first scenario, international environmental law may be applicable to assess a treaty claim (e.g. whether the conduct of a State allegedly in breach of an investment protection standard was required by an international obligation of that State pursuant to an environmental treaty), whereas domestic environmental law may apply to assess a contract claim (e.g. whether termination of an investment contract by the host State was justified by the investor's violation of domestic environmental law).

Second, in deciding treaty claims (whether or not they have been brought together with contract claims), the tribunal may have to consider the operation of domestic laws. Domestic environmental laws may then be indirectly relevant to decide a treaty claim. For instance, in *Azurix v Argentina*, the claimant had brought treaty claims in connection with a water concession contract. As part of its defence, Argentina argued that, in the absence of a choice of law by the parties, Argentine law was applicable to the dispute. The application of Argentine law was relevant *inter alia* in connection with the standards of quality of the water distributed by the investor. In its award, the tribunal noted that domestic law was relevant for the assessment of the treaty claims, but only as 'an element of the inquiry':

> Azurix's claim has been advanced under the BIT and, as stated by the Annulment Committee in Vivendi II, the Tribunal's inquiry is governed by the ICSID Convention, by the BIT and by applicable international law. While the

[100] *Compañía de Aguas del Aconquija S.A. and Vivendi Universal S.A. v Argentine Republic*, ICSID Case No. ARB/97/03, Decision on Annulment of 3 July 2002 ('*Vivendi v Argentina—Annulment*'), para 96. See further Z Douglas, *The International Law of Investment Claims* (Cambridge University Press, Cambridge, 2009) 41 et seq.

Tribunal's inquiry will be guided by this statement, this does not mean that the law of Argentina should be disregarded. On the contrary, the law of Argentina should be helpful in the carrying out of the Tribunal's inquiry into the alleged breaches of the Concession Agreement to which Argentina's law applies, but it is only an element of the inquiry because of the treaty nature of the claims under consideration.[101]

As this passage suggests, there is some ambiguity as to the precise status of domestic law. Traditionally, international law views domestic laws as facts, although quite particular ones, in that they may be necessary for the operation of international law. For instance, in the *Pulp Mills* case, after concluding that the requirement to conduct an environmental impact assessment prior to the execution of a project is part of general international law, the ICJ added that general international law does not specify the scope and content of an environmental impact assessment and, for this reason, in the absence of a treaty clause to such effect, 'it is for each State to determine in its domestic legislation or in the authorization process for the project, the specific content of the environmental impact assessment required in each case'.[102] An alternative view is that tribunals select a given set of norms from both domestic and international law and then apply such set as a distinct body of law. This is how the tribunal in *CMS v Argentina* seems to have proceeded when it circumscribed the applicable law as follows: 'there is a close interaction between the legislation and the regulations governing the gas privatization, the License and international law, as embodied both in the Treaty and in customary international law. All of these rules are inseparable and will, to the extent justified, be applied by the Tribunal'.[103]

Third, in those cases where the same legal question is regulated by both domestic and international law, it may be necessary to determine the relative hierarchy of each body of law[104] or even of different norms within the same body of law.[105] Such conflicts will be analysed in section IV of this study, when discussing the legal techniques available to address them.

2. *Relevance*

Let us now turn to the issue of relevance. The scope of the dispute imposes 'relevance boundaries' on the selection of the applicable norms.

[101] See *Azurix Corp. v The Argentine Republic*, ICSID Case No. ARB/01/12, Award of 14 July 2006 ('*Azurix v Argentina*'), para 67.

[102] *Pulp Mills case*, above n 8, para 205.

[103] *CMS Gas Transmission Company v Argentine Republic*, ICSID Case No. ARB/01/08, Award, 12 May 2005 ('*CMS v Argentina—Award*'), para 117. For a theoretical account of this approach see F Grisel, *L'arbitrage international ou le droit contre l'ordre juridique*, thèse Paris I, Pantheon-Sorbonne, 2010.

[104] See *Compañía del Desarrollo de Santa Elena S.A. v Republic of Costa Rica*, ICSID Case No. ARB/96/1, Award, 17 February 2000 ('*CDSE v Costa Rica*'), paras 64–65.

[105] See *S.D. Myers Inc. v Canada, NAFTA Arbitration* (UNCITRAL Rules), Partial Award, 13 November 2000 ('*S.D. Myers v Canada*'), paras 214–215 (italics original) and 255–256.

The fact that a provision in an investment contract or in a BIT or a default rule contained in the rules governing the arbitration may point to international law as the applicable law does not mean that any rule of international law will be relevant for the determination of the case. Relevance is a complex concept, as there are different ways to characterise it and there may also be different degrees of relevance. Arbitral tribunals, as other international jurisdictions, have wide discretion in determining whether and to what extent a given norm is relevant.[106] In conducting such analysis they are guided by several considerations. Let us mention three of them, namely the boundaries of the dispute (i), the pleas of the parties (ii), and some specific uses of environmental norms (iii).

(i) Boundaries of the dispute

The starting-point for determining the boundaries of relevance is the definition of the dispute over which a tribunal has asserted jurisdiction. For instance, if the parties have brought treaty (as opposed to contract) claims,[107] the relevance of the contractual layer as well as of the domestic norms governing the contract will be lower. As noted by the tribunal in *Bayindir v Pakistan*:

> As a threshold matter, the Tribunal recalls that its jurisdiction covers treaty and not contract claims. This does not mean that it cannot consider contract matters. It can and must do so to the extent necessary to rule on the treaty claims. It takes contract matters, including the contract's governing municipal law, into account as facts as far as they are relevant to the outcome of the treaty claims. Doing so, it exercises treaty not contract jurisdiction.[108]

This point has already been discussed above in the sub-sections devoted to choice-of-law clauses and default rules, particularly in connection with the *Azurix v Argentina* case.

(ii) The pleas of the parties

Another indication of the relevance of a given (set of) norm(s) is provided, quite obviously, by the pleadings of the parties. For instance, in *Chemtura v Canada*,[109] the respondent specifically referred to the provisions of the Aarhus Protocol to the Convention on Long-Range

[106] This is a consequence of the *jura novit curia* principle. See Spiermann, above n 99, 90–92, and the case-law cited therein.

[107] On the relations between treaty and contract claims see generally Crawford, above n 85.

[108] See *Bayindir Insaat Turizm Ticaret ve Sanayi A Ş v Pakistan*, ICSID Case No ARB/03/29, Award, 27 August 2009 ('*Bayindir v Pakistan*'), para 135. The tribunal in *Bayindir v. Pakistan* relied on the reasoning of the tribunal in *Vivendi II*, above n 17, para 7.3.9.

[109] *Chemtura Corporation (formerly Crompton Corporation) v Government of Canada*, UNCITRAL, Award, 2 August 2010 ('*Chemtura v Canada*').

Transboundary Air Pollution ('LRTAP Convention')[110] to justify the launching of a special review of lindane, which eventually led to the suspension of the registration of certain lindane-based products manufactured by the claimant.[111] In its award, the tribunal accepted the argument of the respondent, considering that the Aarhus Protocol had indeed been at the origin of the special review process.[112]

Beyond this basic hypothesis, the effect of the parties' pleadings on the tribunal's room for manoeuvre is difficult to determine conceptually. In *Klöckner v Cameroon*, the ad hoc committee established a distinction between arguments that are within the 'legal framework established by the Claimant and Respondent' and those that are 'beyond':

> As for the Tribunal itself [the one that had issued the award under review], when in the course of its deliberations it reached the provisional conclusion that the true legal basis for its decision could well be different from either of the parties' respective arguments, it was not, subject to what will be said below, in principle prohibited from choosing its own argument. Whether to reopen the proceeding before reaching a decision and allow the parties to put forward their views on the arbitrators' "new" thesis is rather a question of expedience. The real question is whether, by formulating its own theory and argument, the Tribunal goes beyond the 'legal framework' established by the Claimant and Respondent.[113]

The tribunal gave an example of this '*hors sujet*' by referring to a hypothetical case in which the tribunal would have 'rendered its decision on the basis of tort while the pleas of the parties were based on contract'.[114] Aside from such extreme cases, the tribunal considered that 'arbitrators must be free to rely on arguments which strike them as the best ones, even if those arguments were not developed by the parties (although they could have been).'[115]

Thus, a tribunal would have some freedom to introduce environmental questions even if the parties have not focused on such questions in their pleadings. Conversely, when such questions have been raised and

[110] Protocol on Persistent Organic Pollutants to the UNECE Convention on Long-Range Transboundary Air Pollution, of 24 June 1998 ('Aarhus Protocol').

[111] See *Chemtura v Canada*, above n 109, para 131.

[112] Ibid, paras 139–141.

[113] *Klöckner Industrie-Anlagen GmbH and others v United Republic of Cameroon and Société Camerounaise des Engrais*, ICSID Case No. ARB/81/2, Decision on Annulment, 3 May 1985 ('*Klöckner v Cameroon*'), para 91.

[114] Ibid.

[115] Ibid. However, the tribunal added a caveat: 'Even if it is generally desirable for arbitrators to avoid basing their decision on an argument that has not been discussed by the parties, it obviously does not follow that they therefore commit a "serious departure from a fundamental rule of procedure". Any other solution would expose arbitrators to having to do the work of the parties' counsel for them and would risk slowing down or even paralyzing the arbitral solution to disputes... [b]earing in mind what was said above regarding jurisdiction, it is impossible to hold that the Tribunal failed to respect the principle of due process' or the equality of the parties', ibid, paras 91–92.

the tribunal does not deem them relevant for the resolution of the case, it would also have some leeway to leave them aside. In practice, however, a tribunal would be well advised to give the parties an opportunity to comment on such issues and/or to explain why it does not consider certain arguments relevant.

This latter issue can be illustrated by reference to the decision of the tribunal in *Glamis v United States*.[116] The case concerned an open-pit gold mining project, the development of which was prevented on the basis of environmental and human rights reasons.[117] Several groups sought to intervene invoking domestic and international environmental and other norms.[118] These arguments were to some extent echoed in the respondent's briefs.[119] It was therefore understandable that, until the very moment when the tribunal issued its award, some commentators referred to the potential of such decision for clarifying the relations between foreign investment and the environment.[120] For those groups and commentators, it came as a disappointment to see the tribunal's explanations as to why it preferred not to decide many of the most controversial issues pertaining to the environmental and human rights dimensions of the dispute. The tribunal gave the following explanation for proceeding as it did:

> First, a tribunal should confine its decision to the issues presented by the dispute before it. The Tribunal is aware that the decision in this proceeding has been awaited by private and public entities concerned with environmental regulation, the interests of indigenous peoples, and the tension sometimes seen between private rights in property and the need of the State to regulate the use of property. These issues were extensively argued in this case and considered by the Tribunal. However, given the Tribunal's holdings, the Tribunal is not required to decide many of the most controversial issues raised in this proceeding. The Tribunal observes that a few awards have made statements not required by the case before it. The Tribunal does not agree with this tendency; it believes that its case-specific mandate and the respect demanded for the difficult task faced

[116] *Glamis Gold Ltd. v The United States of America*, NAFTA Arbitration (UNCITRAL), Award of 16 May 2009 ('*Glamis v United States*').

[117] See C Knight, 'A Regulatory Minefield: Can the Department of Interior say "No" to a Hardrock Mine?' (2002) 73 *University of Colorado Law Review* 619.

[118] See Quechan Indian Nation Amicus Application & Submission, 19 August 2004; Friends of the Earth Amicus Application, 30 September 2005; Friends of the Earth Amicus Submission, 30 September 2005; Sierra Club & Earthworks Application for Leave to File a Non-Party Submission, 16 October 2006; Submission of Non-Disputing Parties Sierra Club & Earthworks, 16 October 2006; Quechan Indian Nation Application for Leave to File Supplementary Non-Party Submission, 16 October 2006; Supplemental Submission of Non-Disputing Party Quechan Indian Nation, 16 October 2006, all available at <http://www.naftaclaims.com> (last accessed on 26 April 2010).

[119] See Respondent's Counter-Memorial, of 19 September 2006, 33 et seq, available at <http://www.naftaclaims.com> (last accessed on 26 April 2010).

[120] See J Cantegreil, 'Implementing Human Rights in the NAFTA Regime—The Potential of a Pending Case: Glamis Corp v USA' in Dupuy et al, above n 10, 367.

squarely by some future tribunal instead argues for it to confine its decision to the issues presented.[121]

An alternative way to handle considerations that the tribunal deems of limited relevance would be to mention them without, however, integrating them in the analysis.[122]

(iii) Specific uses of environmental norms

A given norm may be relevant for different purposes, including (a) as the norm governing a particular conduct, (b) as an interpretation tool, or (c) as mere inspirational guidance.

An illustration of (a) is provided by the *SPP v Egypt* case, where the tribunal considered that the UNESCO World Heritage Convention[123] governed the respondent's conduct. The tribunal noted, in this regard, that there was no question that 'the UNESCO Convention [was] relevant: the Claimants themselves acknowledged during the proceedings before the French *Cour d'Appel* that the Convention obligated the Respondent to abstain from acts or contracts contrary to the Convention'.[124] Also, in *Chemtura v Canada*, the tribunal considered that the Aarhus Protocol, and more specifically the undertaking to reassess the restricted uses of lindane contemplated in Annex II to this protocol, governed the conduct of Canada.[125]

Regarding (b), environmental norms may also be relevant for the purpose of interpreting the scope of an investment protection clause. For instance, in *Parkerings v Lithuania*, the tribunal interpreted the most-favoured-nation clause of the applicable bilateral investment treaty in the light of UNESCO World Heritage Convention to conclude that two foreign investors were not in a like position.[126] In a similar vein, in the *Pulp Mills* case, the ICJ excluded the application, as such, of the multilateral environmental agreements and principles of general international law invoked by Argentina, while stressing that such agreements and principles remained relevant to interpret the provisions of the Statute of the River Uruguay.[127]

Finally, environmental or human rights law may be relevant as an inspirational source (c). An example would be the *Tecmed v Mexico* case, where the tribunal turned to the case-law of the European Court of Human Rights (ECtHR), despite the fact that Mexico was not a party to the

[121] *Glamis v United States*, above n 116, para 8.

[122] This path was arguably followed in a water-related case, *Biwater v Tanzania*, above n 17, para 392.

[123] See *Southern Pacific Properties (Middle East) Limited (SPP) v Arab Republic of Egypt*, ICSID Case No. ARB/84/3, Award of 20 May 1992 ('*SPP v Egypt*').

[124] Ibid, para 78.

[125] See *Chemtura v Canada*, above n 109, paras 139–141.

[126] See *Parkerings-Compagniet AS v Republic of Lithuania*, ICSID Case No. ARB/05/8, Award, 11 September 2007 ('*Parkerings v Lithuania*'), para 392.

[127] See *Pulp Mills case*, above n 8, paras 64–66.

European Convention on Human Rights (ECHR), for intellectual guidance in applying the expropriation clause of the applicable BIT.[128]

C. Procedural Matters

The range of procedural issues potentially influenced by the incorporation of environmental matters in international proceedings is broad enough to have raised the question of the need for an international environmental court,[129] as well as to have justified, in the 1990s, the creation of a special chamber of the ICJ focusing on environmental matters[130] or the adoption by the PCA, in 2001, of a specific set of arbitration rules for natural resource and environmental disputes.[131] In this sub-section, the analysis focuses on two main procedural issues, namely (1) the role of non-disputing parties, and (2) the challenges posed by environmental matters in terms of evidentiary procedures.

1. Role of non-disputing parties

It is useful first to look at how environmental considerations can be introduced into a foreign investment dispute (i) before assessing the reasons explaining the intervention of non-disputing parties in investment proceedings (ii) and the legal framework applicable to such intervention (iii).

(i) Raising environmental issues

How can environmental considerations be introduced into a foreign investment dispute? The first part of the answer to this question is quite obvious.

[128] See *Tecmed v Mexico*, above n 18, para 122. Unless the approach of the ECtHR were to be considered as a reflection of international customary law or of general principles of law, the reasoning of the tribunal could not be deemed to be an application of Article 31(3)(c) of the Vienna Convention on the Law of Treaties, 23 May 1969, 1155 UNTS 331 (entered into force on 27 January 1980) ('VCLT'). The ECtHR's role is therefore merely inspirational.

[129] See E Hey, *Reflections on an International Environmental Court* (Kluwer, The Hague, 2000).

[130] The Chamber for Environmental Matters was established in July 1993, pursuant to Article 26(1) of the ICJ Statute, which entitles the Court to 'form one or more chambers, composed of three or more judges as the Court may determine, for dealing with particular categories of cases; for example labour cases and cases relating to transit and communications', Statute of the International Court of Justice, 26 June 1945, Art. 26(1). See Press Release 93/20, Constitution of a Chamber of the Court for Environmental Matters, 19 July 1993, <http://www.icj-cij.org/presscom/files/7/10307.pdf> (last accessed on 20 February 2010). However, this chamber was never put to use and, in 2006, after thirteen years, it was eventually decided that it would not be reconstituted. On this issue See E Valencia Ospina, 'The Use of Chambers of the International Court of Justice', in V Lowe, M Fitzmaurice (eds), *Fifty Years of the International Court of Justice: Essays in Honour of Sir Robert Jennings* (Cambridge University Press, Cambridge, 1996) 503; J E Viñuales, 'The Contribution of the International Court of Justice to the Development of International Environmental Law: A Contemporary Assessment' (2008) 32 *Fordham International Law Journal* 232–233.

[131] See Permanent Court of Arbitration Optional Rules for Arbitration of Disputes relating to Natural Resources and/or the Environment ('PCA Environment Rules'), <http://www.pca-cpa.org/upload/files/ENVIRONMENTAL(3).pdf> (last accessed on 20 February 2010). On the PCA Environment Rules see D P Ratliff, 'The PCA Optional Rules for Arbitration of Disputes Relating to Natural Resources and/or the Environment' (2001) 14 *Leiden Journal of International Law* 887.

It is the prerogative of the parties to a dispute to refer to all those considerations that they deem relevant in support of their case. Despite the fact that, in practice, host States will be the ones most likely finding support for their argumentation in environmental considerations,[132] such considerations may also serve to buttress the legal case of an investor. As already mentioned, in *Allard v Barbados* the investor refers, in support of its investment claims, to both domestic and international environmental law, including the Ramsar Wetlands Convention[133] and the Convention on Biological Diversity.[134]

Second, environmental considerations could be introduced by the tribunal itself. This point has been discussed in some detail in the preceding sub-section, in the context of issues relating to the applicable law.

The third and remaining procedural access point is the submission of a non-disputing party.[135] Such submissions have significantly increased in the last years in both investment[136] and other international proceedings.[137] As noted above, our analysis will focus on only two aspects relevant to understand the role of such non-disputing parties in environment-related disputes, namely the reasons for and the emerging legal framework applicable to such intervention.

(ii) Reasons for third-party intervention

The reasons underlying third-party intervention can be better understood by reference to the historical roots of this phenomenon, which can be traced back to the early history of the English legal system.[138] This

[132] See Viñuales, above n 13; Reiner, Schreuer, above n 51, 88–90.

[133] See Convention on Wetlands of International Importance especially as Waterfowl Habitat, of 2 February 1971, 996 UNTS 245 (entered into force on 21 December 1975) ('Ramsar Convention').

[134] See Convention on Biological Diversity, of 5 June 1992, 1760 UNTS 79 (entered into force on 29 December 1993).

[135] See above n 11.

[136] In the context of investment disputes conducted under the aegis of ICSID, the following cases have triggered environment-related interventions by non-disputing parties: *Piero Foresti, Laura de Carli and others v Republic of South Africa*, ICSID Case No. ARB(AF)/07/1 ('*Foresti v South Africa*'); *Suez, Sociedad General de Aguas de Barcelona, S.A. and Vivendi Universal, S.A. v The Argentine Republic*, ICSID Case No. ARB/03/19 ('*Suez v Argentina—03/19*'); *Suez, Sociedad General de Aguas de Barcelona S.A. and InterAguas Servicios Integrales del Agua S.A. v The Argentine Republic*, ICSID Case No. ARB/03/17 ('*Suez v Argentina—03/17*'); *Biwater v Tanzania*, above n 17; *Aguas del Tunari v Bolivia*, above n 17. In the context of investment disputes concerning the application of NAFTA, the following cases have triggered environment-related interventions by non-disputing parties: *Methanex Corporation v United States of America*, NAFTA (UNCITRAL), Award of 3 August 2005 ('*Methanex v United States*'); *Glamis v United States*, above n 116.

[137] Even limiting the analysis to *amicus curiae* intervention, the examples of such interventions are numerous. See D Shelton, 'The Participation of Nongovernmental Organizations in International Judicial Proceedings' (1994) 88 *American Journal of International Law* 611; H Ruiz Fabri, J-M Sorel (eds), *Le tiers à l'instance devant les juridictions internationals* (Pedone, Paris, 2005); L Boisson de Chazournes, M Mbengue, 'L'Amicus Curiae devant l'organe de règlement des différends de l'OMC' in S Maljean-Dubois (ed), *Droit de l'Organisation Mondiale du Commerce et protection de l'environnement* (Bruylant/CERIC, Brussels, 2003) 400.

[138] On this early practice see the note on *Amici Curiae* in (1921) 34 *Harvard Law Review* 773 ('Harvard Note'); E Angell, 'The Amicus Curiae: American Development of English Institutions' (1967) 16 *International & Comparative Law Quarterly* 1017.

affiliation has two interesting implications for the understanding of the role of this institution.

First, *amicus* intervention provided an avenue to bring points of law or fact to the attention of courts in an epoch characterised by considerable uncertainty as to the contents of the law.[139] Nowadays, the centre of gravity of such function would be instead on points of fact (e.g. informing the tribunal on the specific environmental consequences of a given project) or, to a lesser extent, on legal questions requiring specific knowledge (e.g. the application of certain environmental conventions to the issues under consideration). One difficulty with such function stems, however, from the potential inclination of *amici curiae* to forgo objectivity in favour of advocating a broader cause.[140]

The second and related implication of the origins of *amicus* intervention concerns its potential contribution to the legitimacy of courts' decisions. To the extent that, in the common law tradition, certain decisions had force of law and, as a result, could potentially modify the legal situation of third parties, *amicus* intervention served to give a voice to such third parties.[141] In the modern law of foreign investment, this function could be illustrated by reference to Article 1128 of NAFTA, which allows NAFTA member States to intervene in investment proceedings against one of them,[142] or to *Foresti v South Africa*,[143] where the tribunal took pains to give civil society groups the opportunity to express their views, and even requested feedback from such groups on the adequacy of the intervention framework.[144]

(iii) Applicable framework

The discussion of *Foresti v South Africa* takes us to the analysis of the legal framework for *amicus* intervention. The dispute arose from a mining

[139] In Abbott's *Dictionary of Terms and Phrases* an *amicus* is defined as: 'A friend of the court. A term applied to a bystander, who without having an interest in the cause, of his own knowledge makes suggestion on a point of law or of fact for the information of the presiding judge'. Holthouse's *Law Dictionary* stresses the contribution of *amicus* intervention to the correct application of the law: 'When a judge is doubtful or mistaken in matter of law, a bystander may inform the court thereof as *amicus curiae*. Counsel in court frequently act in this capacity when they happen to be in possession of a case which the judge has not seen or does not at the moment remember'. Both dictionaries are quoted in S Krislov, 'The Amicus Curiae Brief: From Friendship to Advocacy' (1963) 72 *Yale Law Journal* 694–695.

[140] See F V Harper, E D Etherington, 'Lobbysts before the Court' (1953) 101 *University of Pennsylvania Law Review* 1172; J D Kearney, T W Merrill, 'The Influence of Amicus Curiae Briefs on the Supreme Court' (2000) 148 *University of Pennsylvania Law Review* 743; B Stern, 'L'entrée de la société civile dans l'arbitrage entre État et investisseur' (2002) *Revue de l'arbitrage* 334.

[141] See S Krislov, *The Amicus Curiae Brief*: From Friendship to Advocacy, above n 139, 698.

[142] Article 1128 of NAFTA provides: 'On written notice to the disputing parties, a Party may make submissions to a Tribunal on a question of interpretation of this Agreement.'

[143] *Foresti v South Africa*, above n 136.

[144] *Foresti v South Africa*, above n 136, Letter of 5 October 2009 from the Secretary of the Tribunal, <http://www.investmenttreatynews.org/cms/news/archive/2009/10/10/an-icsid-tribunal-introduces-innovative-steps-into-non-disputing-party-procedure.aspx>) (last accessed on 26 April 2010) ('*Foresti—Letter from Tribunal*').

investment made by Italian nationals, who claimed *inter alia* that they had been expropriated by South Africa as a result of measures adopted by this latter in the context of Black Economic Empowerment (BEE) policies to eliminate the consequences of the apartheid regime. Given the public ramifications of the dispute, the tribunal anticipated that several civil society groups would likely seek to intervene. It therefore prepared, in agreement with the parties, a short summary of the dispute as well as rules governing *amicus* intervention.[145]

Despite its technical rooting in Rule 41(3) of the ICSID's Additional Facility Arbitration Rules,[146] the document prepared by the tribunal can arguably be seen as a current statement of the basic requirements for the submission of *amicus* briefs:

Non-disputing parties seeking to make a written submission should file a petition with the Tribunal for leave to file a written submission and such petition should include the following information:

- the identity and background of the petitioner, the nature of its membership if it is an organization, and the nature of its relationships, if any, to the Parties to the dispute;
- the nature of the petitioner's interest in the case;
- whether the petitioner has received financial or other material support from any of the Parties or from any person connected with the Parties in this case; and
- the reasons why the Tribunal should accept the petitioner's written submission.[147]

Thereafter, two petitions were submitted, one from the International Commission of Jurists, a human rights organization,[148] and another from a group of four non-governmental organisations ('NGOs'), including two focusing on environmental protection.[149]

In its decision granting leave for intervention,[150] the tribunal authorized the petitioners not only to submit written briefs, but also to access

[145] See *Foresti v South Africa*, Agreed text for potential non-disputing parties ('*Foresti v South Africa—Intervention Instructions*').

[146] Article 41(3), Arbitration (Additional Facility) Rules, available at <http://icsid.worldbank.org/ICSID/StaticFiles/facility/iii.htm> (last accessed on 26 April 2010).

[147] *Foresti v South Africa, Intervention Instructions*, above n 145, 2.

[148] See Petition for participation as Non-disputing party pursuant to Article 41(3) of the ICSID Arbitration (Additional Facility) Rules, presented by the International Commission of Jurists, available at <http://www.icj.org/IMG/ICJ_Petition_Foresti_v_RSA_19_Aug2009.pdf> (last accessed on 26 April 2010).

[149] See Petition for Limited Participation as Non-Disputing Parties in Terms of Articles 41(3), 27, 39, and 35 of the Additional Facility Rules, presented by the Centre for Applied Legal Studies (CALS), the Center for International Environmental Law (CIEL), the International Centre for the Legal Protection of Human Rights (INTERIGHTS), and the Legal Resources Centre (LRC), available at <http://www.interights.org/view-document/index.htm?id=543> (last accessed on 26 April 2010).

[150] See *Foresti—Letter from Tribunal*, above n 144.

redacted versions of documents of the case file, and it even left open the possibility of granting them access to the hearing.[151] Even more interesting was the system established by the tribunal to receive feedback from the *amici curiae*:

In view of the novelty of the NDP procedure, after all submissions, written and oral, have been made the Tribunal will invite the Parties and the NDPs to offer brief comments on the fairness and effectiveness of the procedures adopted for NDP participation in this case. The Tribunal will then include a section in the award, recording views (both concordant and divergent) on the fairness and efficacy of NDP participation in this case and on any lessons learned from it.[152]

The introduction by the tribunal of this additional step was in all likelihood due to the exceptionally sensitive context of the case, in which procedural openness could no doubt add legitimacy to any future decision made by the tribunal on the merits of the dispute.[153] It must be noted, in addition, that the procedure established by the tribunal was not exactly novel. Although neither the access to the file nor the potential access to the hearing had been previously granted to non-governmental organizations acting as *amici curiae*, the requirements set out by the tribunal for *amicus* intervention are fundamentally the same as those established by both previous tribunals and international instruments.[154]

In essence, *amicus* intervention is allowed if the petitioner can make a substantive (points of law or fact) and procedural (enhancing legitimacy)

[151] The tribunal stated, in this regard: 'Accordingly, the Tribunal has taken the view that the NDPs must be allowed access to those papers submitted to the Tribunal by the Parties that are necessary to enable the NDPs to focus their submissions upon the issues arising in the case and to see what positions the Parties have taken on those issues. The NDPs must also be given adequate opportunity to prepare and deliver their submissions in sufficient time before the hearing for the Parties to be able to respond to those submissions. The Tribunal does not at this stage envisage that the NDPs will be permitted to attend or to make oral submissions at the hearing. A final decision on those questions will be taken after March 12, 2010, by which date the Parties will have responded to the NDP submissions', ibid, 1–2.

[152] Ibid, 2 *in fine*.

[153] However, thereafter, the claimant requested the discontinuance of the proceedings. The respondent opposed such request and asked, in turn, for a default award. Beginning of August 2010, the tribunal rendered a discontinuance award ordering the claimants to pay part of the respondent's costs. See *Foresti v South Africa*, above n 136, Award of 4 August 2010 ('*Foresti v South Africa—Award*').

[154] See the remarks of the tribunals in *Suez v Argentina - 03/19*, above n 136, Order in Response to a Petition for Transparency and Participation as Amicus Curiae, 19 May 2005 (Order I), paras 17–29; *Suez v Argentina—03/19*, above n 136, Order in Response to a Petition by Five Non-Governmental Organizations for Permission to Make an Amicus Curiae, 12 February 2007 (Order II), para 15; *Suez v Argentina—03/17*, above n 136, Order in Response to a Petition for Participation as Amicus Curiae, 17 March 2006 (Order), paras 17–34; *Biwater v Tanzania*, above n 17, Procedural Order No. 5 (Order 5), paras 46–61. See also ICSID Arbitration Rules (2006), Article 37(2). In *Suez v Argentina—03/19*, the tribunal took position on the conditions that it had set, prior to the entry into force of the new Article 37(2) of the ICSID Arbitration Rules, for the admission of *amicus* briefs and found them to be in accordance with the new rules, Order II, para 15. For a survey of codification efforts regarding *amicus* intervention See Grisel, Viñuales, above n 11, 402–413.

contribution to the proceedings,[155] without severely encroaching on the parties due process and confidentiality rights (proportionality). Whereas the first two requirements are the same for the three types of requests (written intervention, access to document, access to the hearing) usually made by *amici curiae*, the third requirement is more demanding with respect to two of these requests (access to documents and to the hearing).[156]

Environment-related disputes, such as those concerning water services, natural resources extraction, waste treatment facilities, or regulated substances are particularly prone to present broader public considerations,[157] which a tribunal should take into account in reaching a decision. An important function of *amicus* intervention in this context is therefore to assist the tribunal in understanding such broader public repercussions as well as to enhance the legitimacy of arbitration proceedings by presenting the perspective of civil society. In order to perform such function, however, *amici curiae* must be both competent and representative of relevant constituencies. Representativeness further supposes the absence of bias arising from any relevant relation with one of the parties, especially financial relations. Such are the conceptual underpinnings of the requirements set for *amicus* intervention.

2. *Evidentiary issues*

Environment-related disputes present some specific challenges in terms of evidence as a result of both the highly technical nature and the considerable scientific uncertainty often associated with environmental issues. In order to deliberate the merits of an investment dispute with environmental components, tribunals must not only understand in some detail complex environmental processes but may also have to take position on a scientific debate where the views of the experts presented by the parties are often at odds. This can be challenging for judges or arbitrators who, as a rule, do not have a sufficient scientific background to understand the intricacies of such complex processes.[158] In order to respond to such challenge, international courts and tribunals could follow four main approaches,[159] namely (i) to downplay the need for an explicit decision on

[155] The tribunal in *Biwater v Tanzania* seemed to imply that either one of these two conditions (substantive contribution and legitimacy enhancement) would be sufficient, Order 5, above n 154, para 54.

[156] See ICSID Arbitration Rules (2006), Article 32(2); *Suez v Argentina—03/19*, Order I, above n 154, para 6; *Suez v Argentina—03/17*, Order, above n 154, para 7.

[157] On the public dimensions of investment arbitration see G van Harten, *Investment Arbitration and Public Law* (Oxford University Press, Oxford, 2007).

[158] This point was underlined in the Joint-Dissenting Opinion of Judges Al-Khasawneh and Simma in the *Pulp Mills* case, above n 8, para 2 (stating that 'the Court has evaluated the scientific evidence brought before it by the Parties in ways that we consider flawed methodologically').

[159] On these and other techniques see J E Viñuales, 'Legal Techniques for Dealing with Scientific Uncertainty in Environmental Law' (2010) 43 *Vanderbilt Journal of Transnational Law* 437; L Savadogo, 'Le recours des jurisdictions internationales à des experts' (2004) 50 *Annuaire français de droit international* 231; M Orellana, 'The Role of Science in Investment Arbitrations Concerning Public Health and the Environment' (2006) 17 *Yearbook of International Environmental Law* 48.

the scientific merits of each position, (ii) to appoint an independent expert to assist the tribunal, (iii) to adjust the burden or the standard of proof, or (iv) to defer to the scientific assessment made by specialized agencies. Here, we will focus on the first three avenues, leaving the fourth for our discussion of the margin of appreciation doctrine in section IV below.[160]

(i) Downplaying the role of science

The first approach can be illustrated by reference to a number of international proceedings where the adjudicators were asked by the parties, either explicitly or (more often) implicitly, to take position on a scientific debate.

In *Gabčíkovo-Nagymaros*,[161] Hungary argued, to justify its non performance of a treaty with Slovakia for the construction of a system of dams, that if it had conducted the works as planned 'the environment—and in particular the drinking water resources—in the area would have been exposed to serious dangers'.[162] In the course of the proceedings, both Hungary and Slovakia presented what the Court itself qualified as an impressive amount of scientific material to buttress their respective argumentations. In its decision, however, the Court considered that 'it [was] not necessary in order to respond to the questions put to it in the Special Agreement for it to determine which of those points of view is scientifically better founded.'[163]

This may appear as an exceptional solution to the extent that the Court was able to decide the issue for which the scientific evidence had been adduced on the basis of different legal grounds. But such a way of proceeding is not uncommon.[164] To take another example, the panel established by the WTO to decide the *EC Asbestos* case noted, in the same vein:

> In relation to the scientific information submitted by the parties and the experts, the Panel feels bound to point out that it is not its function to settle a scientific debate, not being composed of experts in the field or the possible human health risks posed by asbestos. Consequently, the Panel does not intend to set itself up as arbiter of the opinions expressed by the scientific community.[165]

It seems reasonable not to require international adjudicators to take a position in an unsettled or at least arguable scientific debate. But the problem with this solution is that it is sometimes impossible to decide a legal dispute without forming a general opinion on the scientific debate underlying it, and that adjudicators do in practice form such an opinion,

[160] See below section IV(C)(2)(iii). [161] See *Gabčíkovo-Nagymaros*, above n 8.
[162] Ibid, para 55. [163] Ibid. [164] See below section IV(C)(2)(iii).
[165] European Communities—Measures Affecting Asbestos and Asbestos-Containing Products, Panel Report, Doc. WT/DS135/R, 18 September 2000, para 8.181. See also *Continental Shelf (Libya v Malta)*, [1985] ICJ Rep 36, para 41; *Southern Bluefin Tuna Cases (New Zealand v Japan; Australia v Japan)*, Provisional Measures, ITLOS Nos. 3 and 4, 1999 ('*Bluefin Tuna—ITLOS*'), paras 40, 65, all quoted in Orellana, above n 159, 52–53.

whether or not it is spelled out in the final decision. An alternative way of proceeding would consist of providing adjudicators with the assistance they need to reach a reasonable and informed opinion on the science underlying the law.

(ii) Scientific assistance

A number of arbitration and procedural rules contain specific provisions allowing the tribunal to appoint its own expert. For instance, Article 27(1) of the UNCITRAL Arbitration Rules states:

> The arbitral tribunal may appoint one or more experts to report to it, in writing, on specific issues to be determined by the tribunal. A copy of the expert's terms of reference, established by the arbitral tribunal, shall be communicated to the parties.[166]

Similarly, the IBA Rules on the Taking of Evidence in International Commercial Arbitration, frequently used in investment cases, provide in Article 6(1):

> The Arbitral Tribunal, after having consulted with the Parties, may appoint one or more independent Tribunal-Appointed Experts to report to it on specific issues designated by the Arbitral Tribunal. The Arbitral Tribunal shall establish the terms of reference for any Tribunal-Appointed Expert report after having consulted with the Parties. A copy of the final terms of reference shall be sent by the Arbitral Tribunal to the Parties.[167]

Still another illustration of this possibility is provided by Article 27(1) of the PCA Environment Rules:

> After having obtained the views of the parties, the arbitral tribunal may upon notice to the parties appoint one or more experts to report to it, in writing, on specific issues to be determined by the tribunal. A copy of the expert's terms of reference, established by the arbitral tribunal, shall be communicated to the parties.[168]

The PCA Environment Rules also provide an alternative method to assist tribunals, namely the possibility to ask the parties to provide it with non technical summaries or explanations of the scientific or technological

[166] UNCITRAL Arbitration Rules, above n 94, art 27(1).

[167] International Bar Association, Rules on the Taking of Evidence in International Commercial Arbitration ('IBA Evidence Rules'), art 6(1).

[168] PCA Environment Rules, above n 131, art 27(1). Other examples of this type of provision include the following: ICJ Statute, art 50; WTO Understanding on Rules and Procedures Governing the Settlement of Disputes, art 13(2); United Nations Convention on the Law of the Sea, of 10 December 1982, 1833 UNTS 3 (entered into force on 16 November 1994) ('UNCLOS'), art 289; NAFTA, art 1133. In their Joint Dissenting Opinion in the *Pulp Mills* case, judges Al-Khasawneh and Simma regretted, in particular, that the Court did not resort to the possibility offered by Article 50 of the Court's Statute, above n 158, para 8.

issues relevant to assess the merits of the dispute.[169] Although such possibility is not expressly mentioned in other arbitration and procedural rules, it is arguably encompassed by the tribunals' general procedural powers.[170]

(iii) Adjustments to evidentiary standards

This approach is more controversial, as deviations from the basic rules governing the burden and the standard of proof in international adjudication[171] should be admitted only under particular circumstances.[172] The difficulties involved in establishing environmental risk or harm in international proceedings[173] may, however, justify some adjustment of those basic rules. In this regard, two main avenues could be followed.

The first possibility would be to shift the burden of proof from the claimant to the respondent by means of a treaty provision. For instance, under the London Dumping Convention, as amended by the 1996 Protocol, it is for the party dumping industrial waste at sea to prove that such dumping does not harm the environment.[174] A conventional shift of the burden of proof has also been proposed by the European Community within the context of the Doha round in connection with the relations between trade restrictions in multilateral environmental agreements and the general exceptions clause in Article XX of the GATT.[175] According to this proposal, a trade restriction based on a multilateral environmental agreement would be presumed to fall within the general exceptions clause in Article XX unless otherwise established by the party affected by the measure.[176] Such solution can be seen as an application of one of the

[169] Article 24(4) of the PCA Environment Rules provides: 'The arbitral tribunal may request the parties jointly or separately to provide a nontechnical document summarizing and explaining the background to any scientific, technical or other specialized information which the arbitral tribunal considers to be necessary to understand fully the matters in dispute'.

[170] See L Creig, W W Park, J Paulsson, *International Chamber of Commerce Arbitration* (3rd edn, Oceana/Oxford University Press, New York, 2000), 300 et seq; D Caron, L M Caplan, M Pellonpaa, *The UNCITRAL Arbitration Rules. A Commentary* (Oxford University Press, New York, 2006), 25 et seq; C Schreuer, L Malintoppi, A Reinisch, A Sinclair, *The ICSID Convention. A Commentary* (2nd edn, Cambridge University Press, Cambridge, 2009), 672 et seq.

[171] On these two concepts see C Santulli, *Droit du contentieux international* (Montchrestien, Paris, 2005) paras 846–868. See also PCA Environment Rules, Article 24(1): 'Each party shall have the burden of proving the facts relied on to support its claim or defense'; UNCITRAL Arbitration Rules, Article 24(1), with identical language; *Bayindir v Pakistan*, above n 108, paras 140–143; *Pulp Mills case*, above n 8, para 162.

[172] See the reasoning of the ICJ in the Corfu Channel Case with respect to the use of circumstantial evidence: *Corfu Channel Case (UK v Albania)*, [1949] ICJ Rep 4, 18.

[173] See E Truilhé-Marengo, 'Les règles relatives à la preuve: quelle place pour l'incertitude scientifique?' in Maljean-Dubois, above n 137, 443.

[174] See Birnie, Boyle, Redgwell, above n 5, 158–159, referring to the 1996 Protocol to the London Convention.

[175] See General Agreement on Tariffs and Trade, 1947, incorporated into the General Agreement on Tariffs and Trade, of 15 April 1994 ('GATT'), Article XX(b) and (g), <http://www.wto.org/english/docs_e/legal_e/legal_e.htm> (last accessed on 26 April 2010).

[176] See Committee on Trade and Environment, Resolving the Relationship Between the WTO Rules and Multilateral Environmental Agreements, communication by the European Communities of 19 October 2000, WT/CTE/W/170, paras 10, 15.

formulations of the precautionary principle.[177] In the absence of an agreement along the lines of the foregoing examples, a shift of the burden of proof seems unlikely in the present state of international law. In the *Pulp Mills* case, Argentina argued that the Statute of the River Uruguay implicitly adopted a precautionary approach whereby the burden of proving that the mills would not cause significant damage to the environment was on Uruguay.[178] The ICJ rejected this argument stating that 'while a precautionary approach may be relevant in the interpretation and application of the provisions of the Statute, it does not follow that it operates as a reversal of the burden of proof'.[179]

The second possibility would be to maintain the burden of proof on the party alleging a fact while relaxing the standard for proving such fact. For instance, in the *EC—Hormones* case,[180] the WTO Appellate Body confirmed that, under the SPS Agreement,[181] the claimant only needs to make a prima facie showing that the respondent is in breach of its obligations, after which the burden of proving an exception shifts to the respondent.[182] The International Tribunal on the Law of the Sea (ITLOS) has followed an arguably similar approach in the *Southern Bluefin Tuna* cases, in that it seems to apply precautionary reasoning to somewhat compensate for the absence of conclusive indications on a fact alleged by the petitioner.[183] However, this approach has not been followed consistently.[184]

* * *

[177] See D Bodansky, Deconstructing the Precautionary Principle' in D Caron, H N Scheiber (eds), Bringing New Ocean Waters (Brill, The Hague, 2004) 381.

[178] See *Pulp Mills* case, above n 8, para 160.

[179] Ibid, para 164.

[180] See *EC Measures concerning meat and meat products (hormones)*, 16 January 1998, WT/DS26/AB/R, WT/DS48/AB/R ('*EC—Hormones*').

[181] See Agreement on Sanitary and Phytosanitary Measures, of 15 April 1994 ('SPS Agreement'), available at: available at: <http://www.wto.org/english/docs_e/legal_e/legal_e.htm> (last accessed on 26 April 2010).

[182] See *EC—Hormones*, para 109, stating: 'In accordance with our ruling in *United States—Shirts and Blouses*, the Panel should have begun the analysis of each legal provision by examining whether the United States and Canada had presented evidence and legal arguments sufficient to demonstrate that the EC measures were inconsistent with the obligations assumed by the European Communities under each Article of the *SPS Agreement* addressed by the Panel, i.e., Articles 3.1, 3.3, 5.1 and 5.5. Only after such a *prima facie* determination had been made by the Panel may the onus be shifted to the European Communities to bring forward evidence and arguments to disprove the complaining party's claim.'

[183] The standard of proof applied seems to be lower than the one applicable for provisional measures. See *Bluefin Tuna—ITLOS*, above n 165, noting the following in paras 79–80: 'Considering that there is scientific uncertainty regarding measures to be taken to conserve the stock of southern bluefin tuna and that there is no agreement among the parties as to whether the conservation measures taken so far have led to the improvement in the stock of southern bluefin tuna... Considering that, although the Tribunal cannot conclusively assess the scientific evidence presented by the parties, it finds that measures should be taken as a matter of urgency to preserve the rights of the parties and to avert further deterioration of the southern bluefin tuna stock.' See also *Case concerning Land Reclamation by Singapore in and around the Straits of Johor (Malaysia v Singapore)*, Provisional Measures, ITLOS Case No. 12, Order, 8 October 2003 ('*Land Reclamation—ITLOS*'), paras 93–96.

[184] See *The MOX Plant Case (Ireland v United Kingdom)*, Provisional Measures, ITLOS Case No. 10, Order, 3 December 2001 ('*MOX Plant—ITLOS*'), paras 69–81.

The foregoing analysis of the issues that may arise in investment proceedings in connection with the environmental components of a dispute leads to the following conclusions: (1) environmental claims may be brought before an investment tribunal (i) in the form of an investment claim or (ii) potentially also as an independent head of claim, under a broadly formulated jurisdictional clause, for breach of either the host State's environmental laws or of international environmental law, if the applicable treaty contains a referral clause; (2) references in the applicable investment treaties to investments made 'in accordance with the laws' of the host State bring to bearing domestic (and potentially international) environmental laws in defining the scope of protected investments for jurisdictional purposes in cases where, for instance, an investment has been initially made in wilful, albeit covert, violation of such laws; (3) domestic and/or international environmental laws may be applicable to an investment dispute (i) through a choice of law clause contained in an investment contract or in an investment treaty, (ii) through an indirect reference in a treaty or a domestic investment code limiting the scope of protection to investments made 'in accordance with the laws' of the host State, or (iii) through a default clause in the rules governing the arbitration proceedings; (4) whether environmental law is relevant for the resolution of an investment dispute will depend *inter alia* on (i) the scope of the dispute over which the tribunal asserts jurisdiction, (ii) the norms invoked by the parties in their pleas or identified by the tribunal *ex officio* or, still, by a submission of a non-disputing party, and (iii) such norms may be relevant in different forms, including as a primary norm governing the conduct of the host State, an interpretation tool or a mere inspirational guide; (5) the usefulness of non-disputing parties' intervention in environment-related investment disputes is conditioned upon their ability to make a contribution in terms of substance and legitimacy, and subject to a proportionality test; (6) the environmental components of an investment dispute may pose specific challenges in terms of evidentiary procedures, which in practice could be handled *inter alia* by (i) downplaying the need for an explicit decision on the merits of the scientific debate underlying the dispute, (ii) appointing an independent expert to assist the tribunal, or (iii) adjusting the burden or the standard of proof.

IV. Investment Claims

The issues analysed in this section all concern the assessment of the merits of environment-related investment disputes. International law provides a number of legal techniques to determine which norm(s) prevail(s) in a case where conduct potentially in breach of international investment law is adopted to fulfil an obligation arising from international environmental law. It also provides conflict rules for cases in which a domestic law or a measure taken for environmental reasons conflicts with an investment protection standard. The techniques applicable in the case of 'normative conflicts' (B) are not the same as those applied to deal with 'legitimacy conflicts' (C). In order to understand the respective scopes of these 'conflict rules', it is necessary to look first at the conceptual aspects of the distinction between these two types of conflicts (A). Finally, environmental considerations may have an impact on the assessment of compensation (D).

A. Normative conflicts v legitimacy conflicts

In order for a 'normative conflict' to exist, an international environmental norm must require a State to adopt certain conduct. In other words, it must be a sufficiently precise international obligation. There are different degrees in which an international environmental norm may 'require' the adoption of certain conduct. Let us elaborate on this point in the light of those environmental norms that have been or could likely be invoked in the context of investment disputes.

First, the norm in question may clearly command the adoption of certain conduct. For instance, pursuant to Article 4(5) of the Basle Convention on the Control of Transboundary Movements of Hazardous Wastes and their Disposal ('Basle Convention') '[a] Party shall not permit hazardous wastes or other wastes to be exported to a non-Party or to be imported from a non-Party.'[185] Were a host State to enact regulations preventing such exports to non-parties, such behaviour could squarely be characterised as an application of an international environmental obligation.[186] In a similar vein, a provision such as the one contained in Annex II of the Aarhus Protocol clearly requires the conduct of a reassessment of certain uses of lindane, although such reassessment may also be triggered by domestic health and environmental considerations.[187]

However, many environmental conventions contain less commanding requirements. For instance, Article 3(1) of the Kyoto Protocol provides:

> The Parties included in Annex I shall, individually or jointly, ensure that their aggregate anthropogenic carbon dioxide equivalent emissions of the greenhouse gases listed in Annex A do not exceed their assigned amounts, calculated pursuant to their quantified emission limitation and reduction commitments inscribed in Annex B and in accordance with the provisions of this Article, with a view to

[185] Article 4(5), Basle Convention on the Control of Transboundary Movements of Hazardous Wastes and their Disposal, of 22 March 1989, 1673 UNTS 57 (entered into force 5 May 1992) ('Basle Convention').

[186] In *S.D. Myers v Canada*, above n 105, the respondent argued that it had acted in accordance with Article 4(5) of the Basle Convention. See Counter-Memorial, of 5 October 1999, para 106, <http://www.naftaclaims.com> (last accessed on 26 April 2010).

[187] See *Chemtura v Canada*, above n 109, paras 131 and 137–142.

reducing their overall emissions of such gases by at least 5 per cent below 1990 levels in the commitment period 2008 to 2012.[188]

In this case, although there is a specific emissions objective for States having undertaken quantified targets, the means to achieve those objectives are left to each State. It would therefore be less clear whether a specific measure adopted by a State in furtherance of its obligations under the Kyoto Protocol could be characterised as strictly required by an international environmental obligation.

A somewhat less stringent variant of this type of requirement appears in a number of international treaties dealing with the protection of habitats and biological diversity. For instance, paragraphs 1 and 4 of Article 2 of the Ramsar Convention require States to designate (at least) one or more suitable wetland(s) within their territory for inclusion in the list of wetlands of international importance.[189] A number of consequences follow from the voluntary act of designation, including the formulation and implementation of plans to promote the conservation of listed wetlands[190] or the creation of nature reserves on wetlands.[191] Whereas the designation of one wetland in its territory is mandatory under the Convention, the State has considerable discretion in the selection of particular zones as protected wetlands as well as in the specific measures to be adopted for their protection. Were a State to select a zone near the location of an industrial plant owned by a foreign investor and thereafter adopt stringent regulations restricting the activities of such investor, it would be unclear whether such conduct is commanded by international environmental law.[192] Conversely, if a State failed to adopt or implement stringent environmental regulations, or established only a limited protection framework, it would be unclear whether such conduct would be in breach of international environmental law.

Even less stringent are the requirements established by the Convention on Biological Diversity or by the Western Hemisphere Convention. Article 6 of the Convention on Biological Diversity states:

Each Contracting Party shall, in accordance with its particular conditions and capabilities:

(a) Develop national strategies, plans or programmes for the conservation and sustainable use of biological diversity or adapt for this purpose existing

[188] Kyoto Protocol, above n 39, art 3(1). [189] Ramsar Convention, above n 133, art 2(1) and (4).
[190] Ibid, art 3(1). [191] Ibid, art 4(1).
[192] This issue arose in *Empresa Lucchetti v Peru*, in connection with the construction and operation of a pasta factory near a protected wetland (Pantanos de Villa). However, the tribunal found that it lacked jurisdiction over the dispute, a decision that was confirmed on annulment. See *Empresa Lucchetti S.A. and Lucchetti Peru S.A. v Republic of Peru*, ICSID Case No. ARB/03/4, Decision of 7 February 2005 ('*Lucchetti v Peru—Jurisdiction*'); *Industria Nacional de Alimentos S.A. and Indalsa Perú S.A. v Republic of Peru*, ICSID Case No. ARB/03/4, Decision on Annulment of 7 February 2005 ('*Lucchetti v Peru—Annulment*'). A similar issue arose in *SPP v Egypt*, above n 123, para 154, in connection with a site protected under the UNESCO World Heritage Convention, see below IV.C(2)(i).

strategies, plans or programmes which shall reflect, inter alia, the measures set out in this Convention relevant to the Contracting Party concerned; and

(b) Integrate, as far as possible and as appropriate, the conservation and sustainable use of biological diversity into relevant sectoral or cross-sectoral plans, programmes and policies.[193]

The Western Hemisphere Convention is even less precise as to the specific obligations undertaken by the States parties:

The Contracting Governments will explore at once the possibility of establishing in their territories national parks, national reserves, nature monuments, and strict wilderness reserves as defined in the preceding article. In all cases where such establishment is feasible, the creation thereof shall be begun as soon as possible after the effective date of the present Convention . . . [t]he Contracting Governments agree to adopt, or to propose such adoption to their respective appropriate law-making bodies, suitable laws and regulations for the protection and preservation of flora and fauna within their national boundaries but not included in the national parks, national reserves, nature monuments, or strict wilderness reserves to in Article II hereof. Such regulations shall contain proper provisions for the taking of the specimens of flora and fauna for scientific study and investigation by properly accredited individuals and agencies.[194]

Thus formulated, these provisions leave such a broad discretion to States that measures taken under their umbrella could be reasonably considered, depending on the perspective that one adopts, either as conduct required by an international obligation or, conversely, as an essentially domestic initiative.

A similar analysis could also be conducted with respect to investment protection standards. From the specific provisions on direct expropriation or on performance requirements, to the less precise protections such as the national treatment and most-favoured-nation clauses, to the broad provisions on full protection and security or fair and equitable treatment, the requirements of investment protection are increasingly open to debate, and they would have largely remained so if it had not been for the contribution of the case-law arising from investment disputes.[195]

[193] Convention on Biological Diversity, above n 134, art 6.

[194] Convention on Nature Protection and Wild Life Preservation in the Western Hemisphere, of 12 October 1940, 56 Stat. 1354, TS 981 (entered into force on 1 May 1942) ('Western Hemisphere Convention'), arts II(1) and V(1).

[195] For overviews of the foreign investment case-law see E Gaillard, *La jurisprudence du CIRDI*, vols I—II (Pedone, Paris, 2004–2010); T Weiler (ed) *International Investment Law and Arbitration: Leading Cases from the ICSID, NAFTA, Bilateral Treaties and Customary International Law* (Cameron May, London, 2005); J Fouret, D Khayat, *Recueil des commentaries des decisions du CIRDI* (Bruylant, Brussels, 2009); R Happ, N Rubins, *Digest of ICSID Awards and Decisions 2003–2007* (Oxford University Press, Oxford, 2009).

The preceding observations are useful to understand more fully the distinction between normative and legitimacy conflicts. As a result of the varying degree of precision with which different environmental norms are formulated, as illustrated by the abovementioned examples, normative and legitimacy conflicts may enter into subtle interactions. For instance, the conflict arising in a situation where a State has adopted an adverse environmental measure based on Article 6 of the Convention on Biological Diversity would in practice be very similar to one in which the environmental measure makes no reference to such article or, still, to one in which the host State is not a party to that convention. In the same vein, the conflict arising where a measure has been adopted pursuant to Annex II of the Aarhus Protocol would also be very similar, despite the more specific content of Annex II, to a conflict where the measure has been adopted on the basis of domestic environmental and health considerations. At the margin, the distinction between normative and legitimacy conflicts turns on whether an international environmental norm can reasonably be invoked as a norm governing the conduct of the host State, as opposed to a mere source of inspiration.[196] In this latter case, international environmental law would not be directly applicable and the conflict would be one of legitimacy. The boundary between normative and legitimacy conflicts is even thinner if an international environmental norm is invoked as an interpretation tool, as in this case it would be intervening as applicable law and not simply as policy. Indeed, Article 31(3)(c) of the VCLT refers to 'any relevant rules of international law applicable in the relations between the parties'[197] as a tool for systemic integration.[198]

Despite the thin boundary between normative and legitimacy conflicts, the distinction remains important because the rules applicable to solving normative conflicts are different from those applicable to solving legitimacy conflicts. The former set of rules consists, essentially, of specific conflict rules contained in treaties and general conflict rules arising from general international law.[199] These rules are technically not applicable to legitimacy conflicts, in which the opponents are an international instrument (most often an investment treaty) and a national instrument (most often environment-related domestic law or measures).[200] Legitimacy

[196] See above section III.B.(2)(iii) of our analysis of the relevance of an environmental norm (i) as a primary rule governing the conduct of the host State, (ii) an interpretation tool, or (iii) as a mere source of inspiration.

[197] VCLT, above n 128, art 31(3)(c).

[198] See below section IV.B(2)(v).

[199] See Report-Fragmentation, above n 2, para 18.

[200] It must be noted, however, that the international law component of a legitimacy conflict could also stem from international environmental law. For instance, an investment made in reliance of the legal framework of an internationally protected area could be adversely affected by a more liberal investment code or another investment-related measure that lowers the level of environmental protection on which the profitability of the initial investment is based. A potential example would be provided by the *Allard v Barbados* case, above n 19. Other examples could be derived from investment-related cases before regional human rights courts. For instance, in the *Awas Tigni* case, the

conflicts call for a more composite set of conflict rules, including specific conflict rules in treaties, rules governing the relations between international and domestic laws, rules of conflicts of laws stricto sensu (private international law), rules governing the hierarchy of norms within a domestic legal system, or rules defining the scope of the State's regulatory powers.

B. *Normative conflicts*

The approaches available to solving normative conflicts can be either (1) specific, focusing explicitly on the relations between investment and environmental protection, or (2) general, i.e. applicable to any potential conflict of international obligations.

1. *Specific conflict rules*

As the interactions between foreign investment and environmental protection became better understood, negotiators and policy-makers were minded to take such interactions specifically into account in the drafting of agreements.[201] As it will be discussed in the context of legitimacy conflicts, the environmental provisions contained in investment and free trade agreements focus mainly on the scope for domestic environmental regulation. There are, however, some investment and free trade agreements which contain specific language on the relations between international investment law and international environmental law.

Among the first treaties to include such language, one must mention the NAFTA. Article 104 of NAFTA states that:

1. In the event of any inconsistency between this Agreement and the specific trade obligations set out in:
   a) the Convention on International Trade in Endangered Species of Wild Fauna and Flora, done at Washington, March 3, 1973, as amended June 22, 1979,
   b) the Montreal Protocol on Substances that Deplete the Ozone Layer, done at Montreal, September 16, 1987, as amended June 29, 1990,

Inter-American Court of Human Rights upheld the customary right to property of an indigenous community over its ancestral land against the right of property of an investor, to whom Nicaragua had granted a concession over the same lands. See *Mayagna (Sumo) Awas Tingni Community v Nicaragua*, IACHR, 31 August 2001, Series C No. 79, para 164. On the case-law of regional human rights courts relating to investment see De Sena, 'Economic and Non-Economic Values in the Case Law of the European Court of Human Rights' in Dupuy et al, above n 10, 208; U Kriebaum, 'Is the European Court of Human Rights an Alternative to Investor-State Arbitration?' in Dupuy et al, above n 10, 219; P Nikken, 'Balancing of Human Rights and Investment Law in the Inter-American System of Human Rights' in Dupuy et al, above n 10, 246.

[201] The following discussion is based on a survey by the Organisation of Economic Cooperation and Development (OECD) focusing on a sample of 269 investment and free trade agreements concluded by the 30 OECD members (as well as the 9 non-member adherents): OECD, *International Investment Law: Understanding Concepts and Tracking Innovation*, 2008 ('OECD 2008 Study').

c) the Basel Convention on the Control of Transboundary Movements of Hazardous Wastes and Their Disposal, done at Basel, March 22, 1989, on its entry into force for Canada, Mexico and the United States, or
d) the agreements set out in Annex 104.1,

such obligations shall prevail to the extent of the inconsistency, provided that where a Party has a choice among equally effective and reasonably available means of complying with such obligations, the Party chooses the alternative that is the least inconsistent with the other provisions of this Agreement.

2. The Parties may agree in writing to modify Annex 104.1 to include any amendment to an agreement referred to in paragraph 1, and any other environmental or conservation agreement.[202]

The annex to which this provision refers guided the reasoning of the tribunal in *S.D. Myers v Canada* with respect to the relations between the Basle Convention and the NAFTA. The tribunal noted in this regard:

The drafters of the NAFTA evidentially considered which earlier environmental treaties would prevail over the specific rules of the NAFTA in case of conflict. Annex 104 provided that the Basel Convention would have priority if and when it was ratified by the NAFTA Parties... Even if the Basel Convention were to have been ratified by the NAFTA Parties, it should not be presumed that CANADA would have been able to use it to justify the breach of a specific NAFTA provision because... *where a party has a choice among equally effective and reasonably available alternatives for complying... with a Basel Convention obligation, it is obliged to choose the alternative that is... least inconsistent... with the NAFTA*. If one such alternative were to involve no inconsistency with the Basel Convention, clearly this should be followed.[203]

The NAFTA also contains other references potentially relevant for the relations between international investment law and international environmental law. Its preamble expressly refers to the need to act 'in a manner consistent with environmental protection and conservation', to 'promote sustainable development' and to 'strengthen the development and enforcement of environmental laws and regulations'.[204] Moreover, the States parties to the NAFTA concluded a side agreement focusing specifically on environmental cooperation,[205] which will be discussed below in connection with legitimacy conflicts.

Another provision addressing a potential conflict between international investment law and international environmental law is Article 72(c) of the

[202] NAFTA, above n 48, art 104.
[203] *S.D. Myers Inc. v Canada*, above n 105, paras 214–215 (italics original) and 255–256.
[204] NAFTA, above n 48, preamble.
[205] North American Agreement on Environmental Cooperation, of 17 December 1992, 32 ILM 1519 (entered into force on 1 January 1994) ('NAAEC').

CARIFORUM—European Union Economic Partnership Agreement (EPA) signed on 15 October 2008,[206] which states, in relevant part:

Investors do not manage or operate their investments in a manner that circumvents international environmental or labour obligations arising from agreements to which the EC Party and the Signatory CARIFORUM States are parties.

This provision is somewhat less clear than Article 104 of NAFTA, because it does not state that the environmental instruments identified prevail over the obligations of the State parties regarding economic co-operation. Rather, it stresses the importance of certain environmental treaties in connection with the activities contemplated in the Partnership Agreement. A similar, albeit slightly less assertive, approach is followed in Article 69 of the EU-Russia Agreement on Partnership and Cooperation, which states, in relevant part:

1. Bearing in mind the European Energy Charter and the Declaration of the Lucerne Conference of 1993, the Parties shall develop and strengthen their co-operation on environment and human health.
2. Co-operation shall aim at combating the deterioration of the environment and in particular:...

   - waste reduction, recycling and safe disposal, implementation of the Basle Convention;
   - implementation of the Espoo Convention on Environmental Impact Assessment in a transboundary context.[207]

Again, the focus of this provision is on the implementation of environmental treaties and not on solving conflicts between international investment law and international environmental law. A similar focus appears in Article 5(3) of the Belgian/Luxembourg model BIT, which reads as follows:

The Contracting Parties reaffirm their commitments under the international environmental agreements, which they have accepted. They shall strive to ensure that such commitments are fully recognised and implemented by their domestic legislation.[208]

This approach is not limited to the treaty practice of the European Union or of some European States. It also seems to characterize the practice of

[206] Economic Partnership Agreement between the Cariforum States and the European Community and its Member States, of 15 October 2008.

[207] Agreement on partnership and cooperation establishing a partnership between the European Communities and their Member States, of one part, and the Russian Federation, of the other part, of 26 June 1994, reproduced in *OECD 2008 Study*, above n 201, 223–224.

[208] Belgian/Luxembourg model BIT, Article 5(3), quoted in *OECD 2008 Study*, above n 201, 177. The same language appears in the BIT between Belgium and the Democratic Republic of Congo, ibid.

the United States regarding the conclusion of free trade agreements (FTAs).

Indeed, several FTAs concluded by the United States such as the so-called CAFTA-DR[209] or those with Australia, Chile, Morocco, Oman, Peru or Singapore, contain a specific provision on 'Relationship to Environmental Agreements'. With some variation in wording from one treaty to the other, this provision essentially stresses the importance of environmental agreements and the need to enhance the mutual supportiveness between environmental and trade agreements. For instance, Article 17.12.1 of CAFTA-DR states:

> The Parties recognise that multilateral environmental agreements to which they are all party play an important role in protecting the environment globally and domestically and that their respective implementation of these agreements is critical to achieving the environmental objectives of these agreements. The Parties further recognise that this Chapter and the ECA [side environmental agreement] can contribute to realising the goals of those agreements. Accordingly, the Parties shall continue to seek means to enhance the mutual supportiveness of multilateral environmental agreements to which they are all party.[210]

In the same vein, Article 18.8 of the US-Singapore provides that:

> The Parties recognise the critical role of multilateral environmental agreements in addressing some environmental challenges, including through the use of carefully tailored trade measures to achieve specific environmental goals and objectives. Recognising that WTO Members have agreed in paragraph 31 of the Ministerial Declaration adopted on 14 November 2001 in Doha to negotiations on the relationship between existing WTO rules and specific trade obligations set out in multilateral environmental agreements, the Parties shall consult on the extent to which the outcome of those negotiations applies to this Agreement.[211]

Other FTAs concluded by the United States contain similar provisions, with some minor variations of wording.[212]

Without minimizing the normative significance of such provisions, upon closer examination, most of them appear to be insufficient to solve potential conflicts between international investment law and international environmental law. If their scope is evaluated in the light of the criteria set by the ILC Group on Fragmentation for the elaboration of conflict

[209] Dominican Republic—Central America—United States Free Trade Agreement, of 5 August 2004 (initially concluded on 28 May 2004, by and between the United States, Costa Rica, El Salvador, Guatemala, Honduras and Nicaragua, later joined the Dominican Republic), 43 ILM 514 ('CAFTA-DR').

[210] CAFTA-DR, reproduced in *OECD 2008 Study*, above n 201, 214.

[211] US-Singapore FTA, reproduced in ibid, 212.

[212] See US-Australia FTA, art 19.8; US-Chile FTA, art 19.9; US-Morocco FTA, art 17.7; US-Oman FTA, art 17.9; US-Peru FTA, art 18.12, reproduced in ibid, 206–212.

clauses,[213] arguably none of the aforementioned provisions would reach the bar, except perhaps for Article 104 of NAFTA. In order to supplement the operation of such conflict rules, tribunals may turn to more general conflict rules.

2. General conflict rules

There are several approaches in general international law to solving conflicts between two or more international obligations. Such approaches may be based on the following considerations: (i) the order in which norms grounded on different sources are applied in practice, (ii) the relative substantive hierarchy of different norms, (iii) priority by reason of the degree of specificity of different norms, (iv) priority by reason of the temporal relations between norms, and (v) systemic integration techniques.

(i) Sequential application

The first approach concerns the relations between norms grounded on different formal sources of international law. Whereas it is generally admitted in public international law that there is no hierarchy among formal sources,[214] the application of norms arising from different sources follows certain logic.[215]

According to this logic, both treaty and customary law are considered to be principal sources of international law, whereas general principles of law are treated as subsidiary sources.[216] Despite their great importance in practice, especially in the investment field,[217] judicial decisions and the teachings of the most highly qualified publicists are only auxiliary sources, in that they help identify the contents of norms founded on formal sources.[218] Finally, the possibility for a tribunal to judge *ex aequo et bono* should be seen an alternative formal source of international law, based on the consent of the parties to a dispute.[219]

Thus, in practice, it would be highly unlikely, although theoretically possible, that a normative conflict between a rule arising from a treaty and

[213] Paragraph 30 of the Conclusions-Fragmentation, notes in connection with conflict clauses: 'When States enter into a treaty that might conflict with other treaties, they should aim to settle the relationship between such treaties by adopting appropriate conflict clauses. When adopting such clauses, it should be borne in mind that: (a) They may not affect the rights of third parties; (b) They should be as clear and specific as possible. In particular, they should be directed to specific provisions of the treaty and they should not undermine the object and purpose of the treaty; (c) They should, as appropriate, be linked with means of dispute settlement', above n 2.

[214] For a discussion of this question see M Akehurst, 'The Hierarchy of the Sources in International Law' (1974–1975) 47 *British Yearbook of International Law* 273.

[215] See Conclusions-Fragmentation, above n 2, para 31; G Abi-Saab, 'Les sources du droit international: essai de deconstruction' in R Rama Montaldo (dir.), *Le droit international dans un monde en mutation. Liber Amicorum en hommage au Professeur Eduardo Jiménez de Aréchaga, vol. I* (Montevideo, 1994) 29.

[216] Abi-Saab, above n 215, 33.

[217] See G Kaufmann-Kohler, 'Arbitral Precedent: Dream, Necessity or Excuse?' (2007) 23 *Arbitration International* 357.

[218] Abi-Saab, above n 215, 34. [219] Ibid, 35.

one arising from general principles of law be solved in favour of the latter. Normative conflicts will, as a rule, arise between either two treaty (or customary) norms or between a treaty norm and a norm of customary international law. Such more specific normative conflicts could be solved by reference to the different substantive hierarchy of the norms involved, to their relative degree of specificity or to their temporal relations.[220]

(ii) Lex superior

In contemporary international law, the existence of hierarchical relations between norms depends upon the contents of such norms.[221] A norm is in a hierarchical relation in respect of another if it (or a specific conflict rule) expressly states so or if it possesses a given character that as such carries hierarchical effect.

For instance, a norm will be hierarchically inferior to another if it (or a specific conflict rule) expressly states so. This hypothesis has been studied in connection with specific conflict rules, which in some cases give priority to environmental norms over investment protection clauses. Conversely, a norm (or a specific conflict rule referring to such norm) may assert priority over another with an ensuing hierarchical effect. An example where such assertion of hierarchy has been widely recognised is Article 103 of the Charter of the United Nations,[222] which confers material hierarchy to any obligation arising from the Charter over any obligation arising from other agreements. Certain norms, referred to as peremptory norms or *jus cogens*, possess a particular character that excludes any derogation from them, except for potential derogations stemming from a norm with the same character.[223]

[220] See Report-Fragmentation, above n 2, para 18.

[221] On this topic see J H Weiler, A L Paulus, 'The Structure of Change in International Law or is there a Hierarchy of Norms in International Law?' (1997) 8 *European Journal of International Law* 545; M Koskenniemi, 'Hierarchy in International Law: A Sketch' (1997) 8 *European Journal of International Law* 566; D Shelton, 'Normative Hierarchy in International Law' (2006) 100 *American Journal of International Law* 291.

[222] Article 103 of the United Nations Charter states: 'In the event of a conflict between the obligations of the Members of the United Nations under the present Charter and their obligations under any other international agreement, their obligations under the present Charter shall prevail.' On this provision, see Conclusions-Fragmentation, above n 2, paras 34–36 et 40–41; Report-Fragmentation, above n 2, paras 328–360; Ch Cadoux, 'La supériorité du droit des Nations Unies sur le droit des Etats Membres', (1959) *Revue Générale de Droit International Public* 649; R Bernhardt, Article 103', in B Simma (ed), *The Charter of the United Nations: A Commentary* (Oxford University Press, New York, 2002) 1293. See, however, the decision of the European Court of Justice in Joined Cases C-402/05 P & C-415/05 P, *Kadi & Al Barakaat v Council of the European Union*, 3 CMLR 41 (2008).

[223] This characterization is provided in Article 53 of the VCLT, above n 128. On the concept of *jus cogens* see Conclusions-Fragmentation, above n 3, paras 32–33, 38, 40–41; Report-Fragmentation, above n 3, paras 361–379; A Verdross, '*Jus dispositivum* and *jus cogens* in International Law' (1966) 60 *American Journal of International Law* 55; G Gaja, 'Jus cogens beyond the Vienna Convention', *Recueil des cours* 172 (1981) 271; G M Danilenko, 'International *jus cogens*. Issues of Law-Making' (1991) 2 *European Journal of International Law* 42; R Kolb, *Théorie du Ius Cogens international: Essai de relecture du concept* (PUF/IUHEI, Paris/Geneva, 2001); A Orakhelashvili, *Peremptory Norms in International* Law (Oxford University Press, Oxford, 2006).

There has been some discussion as to whether at least some international environmental norms are of a peremptory nature.[224] However, there does not seem to be sufficient evidence to conclude that in the current state of international law this is the case; most of the arguments advanced to support *jus cogens* status are purely theoretical or have been disproved by subsequent developments.[225] This is not to say that environmental norms cannot display some hierarchical effects through other channels.

For instance, environmental norms can help characterise certain interests as essential, which in turn would open the way for the invocation of necessity or public emergency clauses. In the *Gabčíkovo-Nagymaros* case, the ICJ preferred not to discuss the question of whether a peremptory norm had arisen that commanded the protection of the environment.[226] Yet, it considered that the protection of the environment amounted to an essential interest. To justify this latter conclusion, the ICJ referred to its Advisory Opinion in *Legality of Nuclear Weapons*, issued the previous year, where the Court had asserted the customary nature of States' obligation to ensure that activities within their jurisdiction and control respect the environment of other States or of areas beyond national control.[227]

The importance attached to certain interests, and specifically to the protection of the environment, is also relevant in connection with the interpretation of certain treaty clauses to accommodate environmental or human rights considerations. In the *Gabčíkovo-Nagymaros* case, the ICJ discussed this point by reference to Articles 15, 19 and 20 of the treaty in question, which contemplated the possibility to adapt the project to take into account emerging norms of international law.[228] However, the Court asserted the need for adaptation of treaty clauses in stronger and more general terms when it stated that:

> Throughout the ages, mankind has, for economic and other reasons, constantly interfered with nature. In the past, this was often done without consideration of the effects upon the environment. Owing to new scientific insights and to a growing awareness of the risks for mankind—for present and future generations—of pursuit of such interventions at an unconsidered and unabated pace, new norms and standards have been developed, set forth in a great number of instruments during the last two decades. Such new norms have to be taken into consideration,

[224] See E Kornicker, *Ius cogens und Umweltvölkerrecht. Kriterien, Quellen und Rechtsforgen zwingender Völkerrechtsnormen und deren Anwendung auf das Umweltvölkerrecht* (Schriftenreihe für Internationales Recht, bund 78, 1997); E Kornicker, 'State Community Interests, jus cogens and Protection of the Global Environment: Developing Criteria for Peremptory Norms', (1998–1999) 11 *Georgetown International Environmental Law Review* 101; Orakhelashvili, above n 223, 65.

[225] See Fitzmaurice, above n 1, 132 et seq; J E Viñuales, 'La protección del medio ambiente y su jerarquía normativa en derecho internacional' (2008) 13 *International Law. Revista Colombiana de Derecho Internacional* 11.

[226] *Gabčíkovo-Nagymaros*, above n 8, para 112.

[227] Ibid, para 53, referring to *Legality of Nuclear Weapons*, above n 74, para 29.

[228] *Gabčíkovo-Nagymaros*, above n 8, para 112.

> and such new standards given proper weight, not only when States contemplate new activities but also when continuing with activities begun in the past. This need to reconcile economic development with protection of the environment is aptly expressed in the concept of sustainable development.[229]

Vice-president Weeramantry further developed this passage in his Separate Opinion. He noted that what he called the 'principle of contemporaneity in the application of environmental norms' was important to 'all treaties dealing with projects impacting on the environment', and that such need was insufficiently taken into account by Article 31(3)(c) of the VCLT.[230] This principle has been used by the ICJ in the *Pulp Mills* case in connection with the interpretation of the Statute of the River Uruguay.[231] In the practice of investment tribunals, a similar question has arisen in some water-related disputes where the human right to water appeared relevant for assessing the scope of the investment protection clauses invoked by the investors or the necessity defence.[232] These issues will be further discussed in subsequent sections.

Despite the possibility of such hierarchical effects, as a rule, absent an amendment to the UN Charter introducing environmental obligations or the emergence of a peremptory environmental norm, normative conflicts will most likely be solved by reference to either a specific conflict rule or some other general methods discussed next.

(iii) Lex specialis

Another frequently used approach is to compare the degree of specificity of the norms potentially applicable to the same situation, an approach often referred to as the principle *lex specialis derogat legi generalis*.[233] This principle rests on the idea that

> special law, being more concrete, often takes better account of the particular features of the context in which it is to be applied than any applicable general law.

[229] Ibid, para 140. [230] Ibid, Weeramanty—Separate Opinion, 114.

[231] See *Pulp Mills case*, above n 8, paras 66, 194, 197 and 204. This latter paragraph refers to a passage of the *Dispute Regarding Navigational and Related Rights (Costa Rica v Nicaragua)*, Judgment of 13 July 2009, para 64, where the Court stated that 'there are situations in which the parties' intent upon conclusion of the treaty was, *or may be presumed to have been*, to give the terms used—or some of them—a meaning or content capable of evolving, not one fixed once and for all, so as to make allowance for, among other things, developments in international law.' (emphasis added).

[232] See *Suez, Sociedad General de Aguas de Barcelona, S.A., and Vivendi Universal S.A. v Argentine Republic*, ICSID Case No. ARB/03/19, Amicus Curiae Submission, 4 April 2007 ('*Suez—Amicus Submission*'), <http://www.ciel.org/Publications/SUEZ_Amicus_English_4Apr07.pdf> (last accessed on 27 February 2010). In their submission, the *amici* noted, with reference to the decision of the tribunal in *LG&E v Argentina*, that: a state of necessity is identified by those conditions in which a State is threatened by a serious danger ... to the possibility of maintaining its essential services in operation', Suez—Amicus Submission, paras 27–28. See Viñuales, above n 13, 750–752.

[233] See Conclusions-Fragmentation, above n 2, paras 5–16; Report-Fragmentation, above n 2, paras 46–222.

Its application may also often create a more equitable result and it may often better reflect the intent of the legal subjects.[234]

Thus, the rationale for justifying the prevalence of a special rule over a general one is that special rules are assumed to be better adapted to a specific situation than rules governing a much broader range of situations. The level of specialty or generality of a norm may however be difficult to assess.

For instance, Article 15(5) of the Convention on Biological Diversity provides that '[a]ccess to genetic resources shall be subject to prior informed consent of the Contracting Party providing such resources, unless otherwise determined by that Party.'[235] This norm could conflict with an investment protection standard in a BIT such as a clause providing for fair and equitable treatment of foreign investors. Indeed, a situation could arise in which an investor having established a laboratory in a developing country with the consent of the host State suddenly sees its operation license revoked on the grounds that such consent was not sufficiently informed. In such a situation, it would be difficult to reach a conclusion on the basis of the *lex specialis* principle.

If we look at the rationale of this principle, it would not be unreasonable to argue that Article 15(5) is more specifically adapted than any investment protection accorded in general terms for any type of investment. And yet, depending on the facts of the dispute, one could also make a persuasive case in favour of protecting the investment based on good faith or proportionality considerations. Moreover, as noted in the section relating to the applicable law, the fact that the dispute is heard by an investment tribunal does not exclude the potential application of international environmental law, nor does it preclude the admissibility of an environmental claim. International investment law may be argued to be a highly specialized field,[236] but this is not a reason to exclude environmental matters from the consideration of investment tribunals. In other terms, the fact that international investment law may be considered as a specialized regime does not mean that investment protection standards must be treated as *lex specialis* in case of a normative conflict. This is but one illustration of the potential problems in resorting to the principle of *lex specialis* to solve potential conflicts between branches of international law that, until recently, had evolved in relative autarchy, paying little or no attention to each other.

(iv) Lex posterior

Another potentially relevant approach is to focus on the temporal dimension of norms. According to this approach, commonly referred to as *lex*

[234] See Conclusions-Fragmentation, above n 2, para 7.

[235] Convention on Biological Diversity, above n 134, art 15(5).

[236] See *Case Concerning Ahmadou Sadio Diallo (Republic of Guinea v Democratic Republic of the Congo)*, Preliminary Objections, Judgment of 24 May 2007, General List No. 103 ('*Diallo case*'), paras 88, 90.

posterior derogat legi priori, later norms should in principle supersede earlier law.[237] The impact of this approach is conditioned by three main considerations.

As noted by the ILC Group on Fragmentation, it cannot be 'automatically extended to the case where the parties to the subsequent treaty are not identical to the parties of the earlier treaty'.[238] The Group further noted:

> In case of conflicts or overlaps between treaties in different regimes, the question of which of them is later in time would not necessarily express any presumption of priority between them. Instead, States bound by the treaty obligations should try to implement them as far as possible with the view of mutual accommodation and in accordance with the principle of harmonization.[239]

Furthermore, where the conflict arises between provisions in treaties that belong to different regimes 'special attention should be given to the independence of the means of settlement chosen'.[240]

The two latter considerations seem relevant in connection with the potential formal or informal bias of international courts and tribunals created under the aegis of a field-specific treaty or system of treaties, such as regional human rights courts or the WTO dispute settlement body, in favour of their own regime.[241] They may also be relevant for the investment context, where tribunals are often constituted on the basis of an investment treaty (as well as, as the case may be, the ICSID Convention) for the purpose of deciding a specific investment dispute. We are, however, not aware of any investment or other case specifically applying the *lex posterior* principle in order to establish priority between an investment protection standard and a norm of international environmental law.

(v) Systemic integration

Interpretation techniques may operate not only in conflict solving but also, and more importantly, in conflict characterization. As noted by the ILC Group on Fragmentation:

[237] See VCLT, above n 128, art 30; Conclusions-Fragmentation, above n 2, paras 24–30; Report-Fragmentation, above n 2, paras 223–323.

[238] Conclusions-Fragmentation, above n 2, para 25.

[239] Ibid, para 26.

[240] Ibid, para 28.

[241] The Group on Fragmentation refers, in this regard, to a case before the ECtHR, *Slivenko and others v Latvia* (Decision as to the admissibility of 23 January 2002) ECHR 2002-II, 482–483, paras 60–61, where the Court concluded that the ECHR prevailed over a previous treaty between Latvia and Russia: It follows from the text of Article 57(1) of the [ECHR], read in conjunction with Article 1, that ratification of the Convention by a State presupposes that any law then in force in its territory should be in conformity with the Convention... In the Court's opinion, the same principles must apply as regards any provisions of international treaties which a Contracting State has concluded prior to the ratification of the Convention and which might be at variance with certain of its provisions', Conclusions-Fragmentation, above n 2, para 25, note 17.

> Whether there is a conflict and what can be done with prima facie conflicts depends on the way the relevant rules are interpreted... Interpretation does not intervene only once it has already been ascertained that there is conflict. Rules appear to be compatible or in conflict as a result of interpretation.[242]

In the context of investment disputes with environmental components, the use of interpretative techniques at the conflict characterization phase is important because it allows tribunals to avoid in some measure making controversial statements on the relative weight of investment and environmental protection.[243] In fact, some of the approaches already discussed (or that will be discussed later) in connection with conflict rules can also be seen as involving interpretative techniques to the extent that they seek to circumscribe the contours of investment protection standards so as to carve out some space for environmental regulation.

In a number of international instruments, the concept of mutual supportiveness has been used as a tool for avoiding conflicts between trade and environmental requirements. The so-called 'principle of mutual supportiveness' seeks to articulate multilateral environmental agreements with international trade agreements through a harmonising interpretation.[244] The concept of mutual supportiveness can be seen as a specific application of a general interpretation technique that is receiving increasing attention from legal commentators,[245] namely the so-called principle of 'systemic integration', provided for in Article 31(3)(c) of the VCLT. This provision states: 'There shall be taken into account, together with the context: ... (c) any relevant rules of international law applicable in the relations between the parties.'[246] The underlying rationale of this principle is explained by the ILC Group on Fragmentation as follows:

> All treaty provisions receive their force and validity from general law, and set up rights and obligations that exist alongside rights and obligations established by the other treaty provisions and rules of customary international law. None of such rights or obligations has any intrinsic priority against the others.[247]

[242] Fragmentation-Report, above n 2, para 412.

[243] See J E Viñuales, 'Conflit de normes en droit international: normes environnementales vs. protection des investissements', in Société française pour le droit international, *Le droit international face aux enjeux environnementaux* (Pedone, Paris, 2010) 407.

[244] See L Boisson de Chazournes, M Mbengue, 'A propos du principe du soutien mutuel. Les relations entre le Protocole de Cartagena et les Accords de l'OMC' (2007) 111 *Revue Générale de Droit International Public* 829. Mutual supportiveness has attracted renewed attention as a result of a much commented case brought before the WTO dispute settlement body: *European Communities—Measures Affecting the Approval and Marketing of Biotech Products*, WT/DS291/R, WT/DS292/R, WT/DS293/R, 29 September 2006.

[245] Such renewed attention stems primarily from some observations made by the ICJ in the *Oil Platforms case (Islamic Republic of Iran v United States of America)*, [2003] ICJ Rep 161, para 41. See C McLachlan, 'The Principle of Systemic Integration and Article 31 3) c) of the Vienna Convention' (2005) 54 *International & Comparative Law Quarterly* 279.

[246] VCLT, above n 128, art 31(3)(c).

[247] Report-Fragmentation, above n 2, para 414.

The Group further notes that, sometimes, there will be no need to go beyond the framework of the treaty itself for purposes of its interpretation, and adds that: 'Article 31(3)(c) deals with the case where material sources external to the treaty are relevant in its interpretation. These may include other treaties, customary rules or general principles of law.'[248] This latter observation seems important in the light of a number of investment disputes where systemic integration appeared relevant.[249] The following disputes illustrate this point.

One early reference to systemic integration in connection with international environmental law appears in the *Gabčíkovo-Nagymaros* case and, more specifically, in the Separate Opinion of vice-president Weeramantry. As already noted when discussing hierarchical effects among different norms of international law, the ICJ stressed the importance of taking into account new environmental norms in interpreting existing treaties. In his opinion, Judge Weeramantry referred expressly to Article 31(3)(c) of the VCLT as a vector for the 'principle of contemporaneity in the application of environmental norms'. In the *Pulp Mills* case, the Court also referred to this provision in connection with the interpretation of the Statute of the River Uruguay. Implying that the interpretation of treaties in the light of 'any relevant rules of international law applicable in the relations between the parties' was a rule of customary international law, the Court stressed that consideration of such other rules for interpretation purposes had no bearing on the scope of its jurisdiction.[250]

In some investment cases, tribunals have deployed systemic integration reasoning[251] to assess allegations of discrimination against foreign investors. In *S.D. Myers v Canada*, the tribunal interpreted the term 'like circumstances' in Article 1102 of NAFTA (national treatment) by reference to its 'legal context', which, according to the tribunal, included:

> [T]he various provisions of the NAFTA, its companion agreement the NAAEC and principles that are affirmed by the NAAEC (including those of the Rio declaration). The principles that emerge from that context, to repeat, are as follows... states have the right to establish high levels of environmental protection. They are not obliged to compromise their standards merely to satisfy the political or economic interests of other states... states should avoid creating distortions to

[248] Conclusions-Fragmentation, above n 2, para 18.

[249] For a discussion of the use of Article 31(3)(c) in other international courts and tribunals see Report-Fragmentation, above n 2, paras 433–460; McLachlan, above n 245, 293–309.

[250] See *Pulp Mills case*, above n 8, paras 65–66.

[251] The fact that in most cases tribunals do not refer explicitly to Article 31(3)(c) of the VCLT is secondary. As noted by the Group on Fragmentation: 'it is really immaterial whether or not a tribunal expressly chooses to invoke article 31(3)(c). These general rules and principles are applicable as a function of their mere "generality" and their validity is based on nothing grander than their having passed what Thomas Franck calls the "but of course test"—a more or less unstable "common sense of the international community (Governments, judges, scholars)"', Report-Fragmentation, above n 2, para 468.

trade... environmental protection and economic development can and should be mutually supportive.[252]

The NAAEC, which stands for North-American Agreement on Environmental Cooperation, is a parallel though separate agreement concluded by the three members of NAFTA.[253] The preamble of the NAAEC reaffirms 'the Stockholm Declaration on the Human Environment of 1972 and the Rio Declaration on Environment and Development of 1992'.[254] Some parts of these declarations, most notably Principles 21 of the Stockholm Declaration and 2 of the Rio Declaration, are declaratory of customary international law.[255] Thus, the tribunal also included in the legal context of Article 1102 of NAFTA principles of customary international law. Eventually, the tribunal concluded that the export ban affecting the investor was nevertheless a breach of Article 1102.[256]

Another illustration is given by *Parkerings v Lithuania*, where the tribunal interpreted the most-favoured-nation clause of the applicable investment treaty in the light of different considerations, including the fact that the projects of the two investors did not have the same consequences for a UNESCO protected site. The tribunal noted:

[T]he fact that the [Claimant's] MSCP [multi-storey car park] project in Gedimino extended significantly more into the Old Town as defined by the UNESCO, is decisive. Indeed, the record shows that the opposition raised against the [Claimant's] projected MSCP were important and contributed to the Municipality decision to refuse such a controversial project. The historical and archaeological preservation and environmental protection could be and in this case were a justification for the refusal of the project. The potential negative impact of the [Claimant's] project in the Old Town was increased by its considerable size and its proximity with the culturally sensitive area of the Cathedral. Consequently, [Claimant's] MSCP in Gedimino was not similar with the MSCP constructed by [the other investor].[257]

The interpretation provided by the tribunal thus carved out some space for the incorporation of environmental considerations in assessing the scope of the MFN (but also the national treatment) clause. After noting the similarities between the MFN and the national treatment clauses, as well as of other discrimination standards, the tribunal set out the following test for assessing whether two investors are in like-circumstances:

In order to determine whether Parkerings was in *like circumstances* with Pinus Proprius, and thus whether the MFN standard has been violated, the Arbitral Tribunal considers that three conditions should be met:

[252] *S.D. Myers v Canada*, above n 105, para 247. [253] NAAEC, above n 205.
[254] Ibid, preamble. [255] See *Legality of Nuclear Weapons*, above n 74.
[256] *S.D. Myers v Canada*, above n 105, paras 255–256.
[257] *Parkerings v Lithuania*, above n 126, para 392.

(i) Pinus Proprius must be a foreign investor;
(ii) Pinus Proprius and Parkerings must be in the same economic or business sector;
(iii) The two investors must be treated differently. The difference of treatment must be due to a measure taken by the State. No policy or purpose behind the said measure must apply to the investment that justifies the different treatments accorded. *A contrario*, a less favourable treatment is acceptable if a State's legitimate objective justifies such different treatment in relation to the specificity of the investment.[258]

Thus, reference to recognised environmental objectives identified in international environmental instruments, such as the UNESCO World Heritage Convention, could potentially justify differentiated treatment.

Systemic integration could also be a useful tool for redefining the boundaries of expropriation clauses in investment treaties, particularly with respect to its relations with environmental regulation.[259] This issue will be further discussed in connection with the police powers doctrine.[260]

Finally, reference to systemic integration has also been made in the context of some water-related disputes. In the *amicus* brief presented in *Suez v Argentina*, the *amici* exhorted the tribunal to follow this interpretive approach:

> In application of this principle of systemic interpretation, human rights law can add color and texture to the standards of treatment included in a BIT. In addition, systemic interpretation is particularly apt when the terms of a treaty are by their nature open-textured, such as the fair and equitable treatment standard. A contextual interpretation of language in a BIT is also necessary because investment and human rights law seem to encounter frictions at the level of regimes, particularly in regards to quantitative policy space available for social development. Indeed, the "regulatory chill" that may result from certain interpretations of investment disciplines could reduce the capabilities of States to fulfill their human rights obligations, including their duty to regulate. In that sense, a contextual interpretation leads to normative dialogue, accommodation, and mutual supportiveness among human rights and investment law.[261]

Interestingly, and no doubt aware of the realities of investment arbitration, the *amici curiae* contemplated the possibility of a conflict of norms between human rights (including the right to water) and investment protection standards, but advocated rather for a harmonized reading of the

[258] Ibid, para 371.
[259] These relations have received considerable attention from legal commentators. For an up-to-date legal analysis and review of the legal literature see Robert-Cuendet, above n 10.
[260] See below section IV.C(2)(iii).
[261] *Suez—Amicus Submission*, above n 232, 15.

applicable treaty in the light of human rights.[262] This observation is quite perceptive, given the general reluctance of investment tribunals openly to decide potential conflicts between investment protection and public policy objectives. Argentina had instead argued that the application of investment protection standards was trumped by the human right to water. In its decision on liability, the tribunal avoided making a determination on the relevant hierarchy of investment protection standards and the international norms relating to the human right to water. In the view of the tribunal 'Argentina [was] subject to both international obligations, i.e. human rights *and* treaty obligations, and [had to] respect both of them equally. Under the circumstances of these cases, Argentina's human rights obligations and its investment treaty obligations [were] not inconsistent, contradictory, or mutually exclusive'.[263]

C. Legitimacy conflicts

The rules applicable to solve legitimacy conflicts are diverse in nature, reflecting the diversity of forms that such conflicts can take. However, for the purposes of their analysis, one can make a distinction between (1) specific conflict rules and (2) general conflict rules.

1. Specific conflict rules

As noted above when discussing normative conflicts, environmental considerations are increasingly being taken into account in the drafting of agreements. The OECD's survey of 269 investment and free trade agreements found indeed that FTAs tend to include express language on environmental issues, whereas such reference is rather exceptional in BITs.[264] Such language mostly concerns the scope for domestic environmental regulation in three main forms, namely the assertion of a right to adopt environmental regulations, the statement that it is inappropriate for States to lower environmental regulations to attract foreign investment, and certain environmental exceptions either general or specific (in connection with some investment protection clauses, such as those on expropriation or on performance requirements).

One of the earliest manifestations of this trend towards the introduction of environmental considerations in trade and investment treaties appears in the text of NAFTA. Chapter 11 of NAFTA contains the three

262 Ibid, 17, stating that 'a question that arises under the particular factual circumstances of the case is whether strict compliance with every term of the concession contract was at all compatible with the human rights obligations of the State. This question may involve a conflict of norms situation, addressed further below. This conflict of norms issue need not arise, however, if the F&ET standard is interpreted under a human rights lens.'

263 *Suez v Argentina—03/19*, above n 136, para 262 (italics original); see also *Suez v Argentina—03/17—Liability*, above n 136, para 240.

264 See *OECD 2008 Study*, above n 201, 141 et seq.

types of environmental clauses identified above. Article 1114 reads as follows:

1. Nothing in this Chapter shall be construed to prevent a Party from adopting, maintaining or enforcing any measure otherwise consistent with this Chapter that it considers appropriate to ensure that investment activity in its territory is undertaken in a manner sensitive to environmental concerns.
2. The Parties recognize that it is inappropriate to encourage investment by relaxing domestic health, safety or environmental measures. Accordingly, a Party should not waive or otherwise derogate from, or offer to waive or otherwise derogate from, such measures as an encouragement for the establishment, acquisition, expansion or retention in its territory of an investment of an investor. If a Party considers that another Party has offered such an encouragement, it may request consultations with the other Party and the two Parties shall consult with a view to avoiding any such encouragement.

This provision circumscribes the boundaries of environmental regulation of foreign investment. An exercise of regulatory power which unreasonably interferes with foreign investment would not be 'consistent' with Chapter 11. Conversely, regulatory competition by relaxing environmental standards would be 'inappropriate'. This latter component is strengthened by the mechanisms established in the NAAEC,[265] which contemplates both non-compliance and individual complaint procedures in case a State party does not respect its own environmental regulations.[266] Chapter 11 of NAFTA also contains specific environmental exceptions to the prohibition of performance requirements. Article 1106(2) provides, in relevant part, that '[a] measure that requires an investment to use technology to meet generally applicable health, safety or environmental requirements shall not be construed to be inconsistent with paragraph 1(f) [protection against forced transfer of technology]'. In addition, Article 1106(6) provides for a more general exception to the prohibition of performance requirements:

Provided that such measures are not applied in an arbitrary or unjustifiable manner, or do not constitute a disguised restriction on international trade or investment, nothing in paragraph 1b) or c) or 3a) or b) shall be construed to prevent any Party from adopting or maintaining measures, including environmental measures: a) necessary to secure compliance with laws and regulations that are not inconsistent with the provisions of this Agreement; b) necessary to protect human, animal or plant life or health; or c) necessary for the conservation of living or non-living exhaustible natural resources.

Another early manifestation of the same trend appears in the Energy Charter Treaty, concluded around the same time as NAFTA, which also addresses the relations between environment and investment, albeit with

[265] See NAAEC, above n 205. [266] Ibid, art 14.

a somewhat different accent. Indeed, Article 19(1) of the ECT emphasizes that the protection of the environment should not be pursued through economically inefficient measures:

In pursuit of sustainable development and taking into account its obligations under those international agreements concerning the environment to which it is party, each Contracting Party shall strive to minimize in an economically efficient manner harmful Environmental Impacts occurring either within or outside its Area from all operations within the Energy Cycle in its Area, taking proper account of safety.[267]

These provisions suggest that by the early 1990s environmental protection had gained considerable strength, not only politically but also legally.

Later generations of BITs or FTAs have further developed this approach expressly addressing the relations between foreign investment and environmental protection. For instance, the investment chapter of CAFTA-DR[268] contains specific provisions on issues such as performance requirements,[269] the adoption, maintenance and enforcement of environmental regulations[270] and the scope of indirect expropriation.[271] In a similar vein, several model BITs have also incorporated express references to the relations between foreign investment and environmental protection. Examples include the 2004 model BIT of the United States[272] and Canada,[273] as well as the current model BIT of Belgium/Luxembourg,[274] Finland,[275] the Netherlands[276] and Sweden.[277]

The potential effect of some of these clauses must not be underestimated, especially when they are formulated as exceptions to specific investment protection clauses. The impact of more broadly formulated clauses, such as Article 1114 of NAFTA or Article 19(1) of the ECT, is more difficult to assess. Such treaty clauses would, for instance, provide limited assurance to a State contemplating the adoption of domestic environmental regulations with potentially adverse effects on foreign investors established in its territory. To take one example, the implementation of the international climate change regime may increasingly require countries to

[267] See ECT, above n 50. The requirements of Article 19 of the ECT are further developed by the Energy Charter Protocol on Energy Efficiency and Related Environmental Aspects (PEEREA), negotiated, opened for signature and entered into force at the same time as the ECT, on 17 December 1994, 2081 UNTS 3.

[268] See CAFTA-DR, above n 209.

[269] See ibid, art 10.9(3).

[270] See ibid, art 10.11.

[271] See ibid, Annex 10-B, Section 4(b).

[272] See Canada's 2004 Model BIT, arts10 and 11, reproduced in *OECD 2008 Study*, above n 201, 178–179.

[273] See United States' 2004 Model BIT, preamble, arts 8, 12 and 32, and Annex B (expropriation), reproduced in ibid, 183–185.

[274] See Belgium/Luxembourg's Model BIT, preamble, reproduced in ibid, 180.

[275] See Finland's 2004 Model BIT, art 5, reproduced in ibid, 176–177.

[276] See The Netherlands' 2004 Model BIT, preamble, reproduced in ibid, 182.

[277] See Sweden's 2003 Model BIT, preamble, reproduced in idem.

adopt far-reaching environmental measures to curb emissions. Such measures may in turn affect the profitability of foreign investments made prior to their adoption. But not every type of measure will entail the same litigation risk. Some measures may appear more compatible than others with the obligations assumed by a State in connection with the protection of foreign investment, and therefore present a lower litigation risk. Given the substantial amounts often at stake in foreign investment proceedings, a State may be well advised to undertake an assessment of potential litigation risks, and provisions like those referred to above would be of little help in conducting such an assessment. Similarly, on the assumption that the host State would take an adverse environmental measure, such provisions would provide limited guidance to a foreign firm (or its legal counsel) in assessing the probability of recovering an investment made in an environmentally sensitive sector. Such provisions would be of limited use even for arbitral tribunals tasked with solving an investment dispute with environmental dimensions, particularly when the dispute has a significant public dimension and the tribunal is, as is often the case, reluctant to make an open pronouncement on the relative hierarchy between investment protection and environmental considerations.[278] For these reasons, it is important to discuss which additional approaches could be used to deal with potential conflicts between investment and environmental protection.

2. *General conflict rules*

There are different approaches to solving legitimacy conflicts. In this sub-section, the analysis focuses on the following: (i) rules governing the relations between international and domestic law, (ii) rules governing conflicts of laws belonging to different domestic legal systems or within one domestic system, (iii) rules governing the scope of the State's regulatory powers including in case of necessity.

(i) Relations between domestic and international law

The relation between international and domestic law is a traditional subject of study by international law scholars.[279] The purpose of the

[278] See Viñuales, above n 243.

[279] See Ch Rousseau, *Droit international public* (9th edn, Dalloz, Paris, 1979) 3–16; A Cassese, *International Law* (Oxford University Press, Oxford, 2001) 162–171; H Triepel, *Völkerrecht und Landesrecht* (Hirschfeld, Leipzig, 1899); H Triepel, 'Les rapports entre le droit interne et le droit international', *Recueil des cours* 1 (1923) 77; D Anzilotti, 'Il diritto internazionale nei giudizi interni', in *Scritti di diritto internazionale pubblico*, vol. 1, (Cedam, Padova, 1956 [1905]); D. Anzilotti, *Cours de droit international* (Sirey, Paris, 1929) 49; H Kelsen, 'Les rapports de système entre le droit interne et le droit international', *Recueil des cours* 14 (1926) 231; H Kelsen, 'La transformation du droit international en droit interne' (1936) *Revue Générale de Droit International Public* 5. Regarding this question from the perspective of international investment law, see M Sasson, *Substantive Law in Investment Treaty Arbitration. The Unsettled Relationship between International Law and Municipal Law* (Kluwer, The Hague, 2010).

following remarks is limited to an assessment of this relation's relevance in the context of legitimacy conflicts between investment and environmental protection. As noted when discussing the law applicable to investment disputes, there is some controversy as to the specific relations between international and domestic law. But such divergence of views does not affect one fundamental point, namely that when there is inconsistency between domestic and international law, international courts and tribunals give priority to the latter.

An apposite illustration is provided by the decision of the tribunal in *SPP v Egypt*.[280] In this case, brought under the aegis of ICSID, the investor claimed that it had been expropriated in breach of a domestic law and an investment agreement of 1974. The parties disagreed as to the law applicable to the dispute. The respondent argued that the parties had implicitly agreed to apply Egyptian law and, therefore, under Article 42(1) first sentence of the ICSID Convention, the dispute was to be exclusively governed by Egyptian law. The respondent further argued that international law could apply only to the extent it had been incorporated in Egyptian law, as was the case of the UNESCO World Heritage Convention.[281] The claimants argued, for their part, that there was no such implicit choice of law and, as a result, international law was applicable in accordance with Article 42(1) second sentence of the ICSID Convention.[282] The tribunal considered that both Egyptian law and international law, including the UNESCO World Heritage Convention, were applicable to the dispute.[283] It further stated:

> When municipal law contains a lacuna, or international law is violated by the exclusive application of municipal law, the Tribunal is bound in accordance with Article 42 of the Washington Convention to apply directly the relevant principles and rules of international law.[284]

This position, which ascribes a supplemental and corrective role to international law over domestic law, has received considerable support in the investment case-law.[285] Under the specific circumstances of the *SPP v Egypt* case, the application of international law was important because the host State had argued *inter alia* that the allegedly expropriatory acts had been taken pursuant to its obligations under the UNESCO World Heritage Convention.[286] Egypt had ratified this latter convention in 1975,

[280] *SPP v Egypt*, above n 123. [281] Ibid, paras 75–76. [282] Ibid, para 77.

[283] Ibid, paras 78–80. [284] Ibid, para 84. [285] See Dolzer, Schreuer, above n 60, 269–270.

[286] Pursuant to Article 4 of the UNESCO Convention '[e]ach State Party to this Convention recognizes that the duty of ensuring the identification, protection, conservation, presentation and transmission to future generations of the cultural and natural heritage referred to in Articles 1 and 2 and situated on its territory, belongs primarily to that State. It will do all it can to this end, to the utmost of its own resources and, where appropriate, with any international assistance and co-operation, in particular, financial, artistic, scientific and technical, which it may be able to obtain.' Article 5(d) of the Convention further states that '[t]o ensure that effective and active measures are taken for the protection, conservation and presentation of the cultural and natural heritage situated on its territory, each State Party to this Convention shall endeavour, in so far as possible, and as appropriate for each

i.e. some three years before the adoption of the measures challenged, in 1978. However, the World Heritage Committee had not registered the sites proposed by Egypt for the Committee's list of protected sites until 1979. Based on this latter fact, the tribunal considered that the obligation to protect the site had not arisen until 1979, i.e. after the date of the expropriatory acts. Thus, these acts could not be justified as conduct required by the provisions of the UNESCO World Heritage Convention.[287] More importantly for our purpose, the tribunal considered that from 1979 onwards the obligations of Egypt under the Convention prevailed over the protections granted to investors. As a result, the compensation due to the investor could not take into account gains that would have accrued after the emergence of the obligation under the Convention.[288] The priority of international environmental law over domestic investment disciplines was implied in this conclusion.

The corrective role of international law was also discussed in *CDSE v Costa Rica*, a dispute concerning the expropriation of a biodiversity-rich land for purposes of its protection. At stake were the different approaches to the valuation of the property expropriated arising, respectively, from the laws of Costa Rica and from international law. The tribunal applied

country . . . to take the appropriate legal, scientific, technical, administrative and financial measures necessary for the identification, protection, conservation, presentation and rehabilitation of this heritage'. These protection obligations are effected through a listing system whereby States propose sites to be included in a list managed by the World Heritage Committee. According to Article 11(1)–(2) '[e]very State Party to this Convention shall, in so far as possible, submit to the World Heritage Committee an inventory of property forming part of the cultural and natural heritage, situated in its territory and suitable for inclusion in the list provided for in paragraph 2 of this Article. This inventory, which shall not be considered exhaustive, shall include documentation about the location of the property in question and its significance . . . On the basis of the inventories submitted by States in accordance with paragraph 1, the Committee shall establish, keep up to date and publish, under the title of "World Heritage List", a list of properties forming part of the cultural heritage and natural heritage, as defined in Articles 1 and 2 of this Convention, which it considers as having outstanding universal value in terms of such criteria as it shall have established. An updated list shall be distributed at least every two years', Convention for the Protection of the World Cultural and Natural Heritage, of 16 November 1972, 1037 UNTS 151 (entered into force on 17 December 1975) ('UNESCO Convention').

[287] The tribunal noted, in this regard, that '[i]n the Tribunal's view, the UNESCO Convention by itself does not justify the measures taken by the Respondent to cancel the project, nor does it exclude the Claimants' right to compensation. According to the system of the Convention, as acknowledged by the Respondent, 'le classement est finalement le fait des autorités internationales de l'Unesco (Comité).' Thus, the choice of sites to be protected is not imposed externally, but results instead from the State's own voluntary nomination. Consequently, the date on which the Convention entered into force with respect to the Respondent is not the date on which the Respondent became obligated by the Convention to protect and conserve antiquities on the Pyramids Plateau. It was only in 1979, after the Respondent nominated 'the pyramid fields' and the World Heritage Committee accepted that nomination, that the relevant international obligations emanating from the Convention became binding on the Respondent. Consequently, it was only from the date on which the Respondent's nomination of the 'pyramid fields' was accepted for inclusion in the inventory of property to be protected in the UNESCO Convention in 1979 that a hypothetical continuation of the Claimants' activities interfering with antiquities in the area could be considered as unlawful from the international point of view', see *SPP v Egypt*, above n 123, para 154.

[288] See ibid, para 191.

the second sentence of Article 42(1) of the ICSID Convention and concluded that international investment law was controlling:

This leaves the Tribunal in a position in which it must rest on the second sentence of Article 42(1) ("In the absence of such agreement...") and thus apply the law of Costa Rica and such rules of international law as may be applicable. No difficulty arises in this connection. The Tribunal is satisfied that the rules and principles of Costa Rican law which it must take into account, relating to the appraisal and valuation of expropriated property, are generally consistent with the accepted principles of public international law on the same subject. To the extent that there may be any inconsistency between the two bodies of law, the rules of public international law must prevail. Were this not so in relation to takings of property, the protection of international law would be denied to the foreign investor and the purpose of the ICSID Convention would, in this respect, be frustrated... [t]he parties' divergent positions lead, in substance, to the same conclusion, namely, that, in the end, international law is controlling. The Tribunal is satisfied that, under the second sentence of Article 42(1), the arbitration is governed by international law.[289]

Although the tribunal referred to the rules on 'appraisal and valuation of expropriated property', which have apparently nothing to do with environmental matters, it is important to note that the respondent's arguments on quantum were partly based on its domestic environmental laws. According to the respondent, such laws restricted and even prohibited the commercial development of the expropriated site, with obvious consequences for the estimation of the fair market value of the property.[290] Moreover, we know from an article published by counsel for Costa Rica that the respondent had invoked a number of environmental treaties as part of its argumentation on quantum,[291] which were dismissed rather hastily by the tribunal in a footnote to the award.[292] The tribunal's conclusion in this case would suggest that an act of expropriation for environmental purposes is subject to the rules on compensation arising from international investment law, irrespective of whether domestic valuation and environmental laws would lead to a different result.

[289] *CDSE v Costa Rica*, above n 104, paras 64–65. [290] Ibid, paras 34–35.

[291] See Ch Brower, J Wong, 'General Valuation Principles: The Case of Santa Elena', in Weiler, above n 195, 764.

[292] The tribunal stated, in the body of the award, that '[w]hile an expropriation or taking for environmental reasons may be classified as a taking for a public purpose, and thus may be legitimate, the fact that the Property was taken for this reason does not affect either the nature or the measure of the compensation to be paid for the taking. That is, the purpose of protecting the environment for which the Property was taken does not alter the legal character of the taking for which adequate compensation must be paid.[32] The international source of the obligation to protect the environment makes no difference' (para 71). Footnote 32 to this paragraph added: 'For this reason, the Tribunal does not analyse the detailed evidence submitted regarding what Respondent refers to as its international legal obligation to preserve the unique ecological site that is the Santa Elena Property', *CDSE v Costa Rica*, above n 104, para 71.

A different conclusion as to the relations between international investment law and domestic (and European) environmental law was reached by the tribunal in *Maffezini v Spain*.[293] In this case, the tribunal seemed to give priority to the standards for the conduct of environmental impact assessments emanating from both Spanish and European law. The reasoning of the tribunal suggests that, to the extent that they abided by the applicable environmental laws, the Spanish authorities were not in breach of the applicable bilateral investment treaty.[294]

(ii) Conflicts of (domestic) laws

Legitimacy conflicts may also arise between norms stemming from different domestic systems or within a domestic system. There are essentially two methods to determine the applicable law in such cases.

First, the traditional conflict of laws or private international law methods will be applicable to assess whether and to what extent a foreign law (or the law of a territorial subdivision, in some federal States like the United States) is applicable to the substance of the dispute. As was discussed in the section devoted to applicable law, the main arbitration rules give tribunals some discretion in the selection of the applicable law *inter alia* by allowing tribunals to use the conflict of laws rules that they deem appropriate.[295]

Second, domestic norms may be applicable as a result of their higher substantive hierarchy, as is the case, for instance, of *lois de police* or other overriding norms. Again, arbitration tribunals have considerable leeway in deciding whether or not the *lois de police* of the host State or of other States may be applicable.[296] The limits of such discretion are basically the causes of annulment of the award set out, as the case may be, in Article 52 of the ICSID Convention,[297] in Article V of the New York Convention,[298] or in the relevant provisions of the arbitration laws of the State where the legal seat of the arbitration proceedings has been situated.

(iii) State regulatory powers

Reference to the State's regulatory powers has emerged in recent years as one of the most important techniques for solving conflicts between investment protection standards and environmental, health or human rights considerations. Although the doctrine of regulatory powers is not as such a conflict rule, it may operate as one to the extent that it shields certain

[293] *Maffezini v Spain—Award*, above n 89, paras 65–71.

[294] Ibid, para 71. However, the reasoning of the tribunal seems to depend much more on the factual record (the absence of pressure from the Spanish authorities for Maffezini to start the construction of the contemplated chemical plant before having presented a satisfactory EIA) and, potentially, on the grounding in international law of the need to conduct an EIA prior to any project with potential environmental consequences. See on this latter point *Pulp Mills* case, above n 8, para 204.

[295] See above n 94 to 98.

[296] See Radicati di Brozolo, above n 79.

[297] ICSID Convention, above n 93, art 52.

[298] New York Convention, above n 86, art V.

measures taken by the State from being considered as a breach of investment protections.

The scope of the State's regulatory powers is difficult to determine precisely. Commentators and tribunals have often sought to circumscribe this doctrine by reference to more specific formulations of the underlying concept. In what follows, the analysis focuses on three of these formulations, namely the police powers doctrine, the margin of appreciation doctrine, and emergency and necessity clauses.

The police powers doctrine—The police powers doctrine as it is applied in international investment law seems to have developed from two main sources, one rooted in North-American scholarship and practice,[299] and the other in general international law.[300] In both cases it has mostly been discussed and applied in connection with non-compensable expropriations.[301] However, its effect is not to exclude compensation but, more drastically, to exclude a qualification of expropriation, which justifies its treatment as a sort of conflict rule. Moreover, this doctrine has increasingly permeated the drafting of model investment treaties in the last years[302] and has also been discussed and applied in the specific context of environmental regulations adverse to the interests of foreign investors. One may refer in this regard to the general observation made by the

[299] On the North-American source see S Friedman, *Expropriation in International Law* (Stevens, London, 1953) 51; American Law Institute (ALI), *Restatement (Second) of the Law of Foreign Relations of the United States*, 1965, section 197(1)(a); ALI, *Restatement (Third) of the Law of Foreign Relations of the United States*, 1986, section 712, commentary, letter (g); L B Sohn, R R Baxter, 'Draft Convention on the International Legal Responsibility of States for Injuries to Aliens' (1961) 55 *American Journal of International Law* 545 (Harvard Draft 1961) art 10(5). This source has influenced the case-law of the Iran-United States Claims Tribunal and of arbitral tribunals constituted under NAFTA Chapter Eleven. See G H Aldrich, 'What Constitutes a Compensable Taking of Property? The Decisions of the Iran-United States Claims Tribunal' (1994) 88 *American Journal of International Law* 585, referring to the following cases: *Too v Greater Modesto Insurance Associates*, Award 460–880–2, 29 December 1989, Iran-US Cl Trib Rep, vol. 23, 378, *Sedco Inc. v National Iranian Oil Co.*, ITL 55–129–3, 28 October 1985, Iran-US Cl Trib Rep, vol. 9, 248, see also *Sea-Land Services v Iran*, Award 135–33–1, 22 June 1984, Iran-US Cl Trib Rep vol. 6, 149; M Kinnear, A K Bjorklund, J F G Hannaford, *Investment Disputes under NAFTA. An Annotated Guide to NAFTA Chapter 11* (Kluwer Law International, The Hague, 2006), commentary ad Article 1110, 49–55, referring to the following cases: *Pope & Talbot Inc. v Canada*, NAFTA (UNCITRAL), Interim Merits Award, 26 June 2000, para 99; *S.D. Myers v Canada*, NAFTA (UNCITRAL), Partial Award, 13 November 2000, paras 287–288; *Marvin Roy Feldman Karpa v Mexico*, ICSID Case No. ARB(AF)/99/1, Award, 16 December 2002, paras 101–105, 110–114; *Methanex v United States*, NAFTA (UNCITRAL), Award, 3 August 2005, part. IV, D, para 7; *International Thunderbird Gaming Corp. v Mexico,* NAFTA (UNCITRAL), Award, 26 January 2006, para 127. See also *Fireman's Fund Insurance Company v Mexico*, ICSID Case No. ARB(AF)/02/1, Award, 14 July 2006, para 176(j).

[300] See Friedman, above n 299; G C Christie, 'What Constitutes a Taking of Property under International Law' (1962) 38 *BYIL* 307 et seq; I Brownlie, *Principles of Public International Law* (Oxford University Press, Oxford, 2008) 535–536; A Newcombe, 'The Boundaries of Regulatory Expropriation in International Law' (2005) 20 *ICSID Review* 1.

[301] See, for instance, Friedman, above n 299, 50–51; Christie, above n 300, 331; Brownlie, above n 300, 536.

[302] See, for instance, US Model BIT 2004, above n 273, Annex B; Canada Model BIT 2004, above n 272, Annex B 13(1). See also our discussion in section IV.C(1) above.

tribunal in *S.D. Myers v Canada*,[303] in connection with the distinction between expropriation and regulation (in this case, the adoption of administrative orders preventing the export of toxic waste across the border between Canada and the United States):

The general body of precedent does not treat regulatory action as amounting to expropriation. Regulatory conduct by public authorities is unlikely to be the subject of legitimate complaint under Article 1110 [expropriation] of the NAFTA, although the Tribunal does not rule out that possibility... Expropriations tend to involve the deprivation of ownership rights; regulations a lesser interference. The distinction between expropriation and regulation screens out most potential cases of complaints concerning economic intervention by a state and reduces the risk that governments will be subject to claims as they go about their business of managing public affairs.[304]

In a subsequent environment-related case, *Methanex v United States*,[305] this distinction was confirmed and nuanced. The claimant argued that it had been expropriated as a result of a measure adopted by the Californian authorities banning a fuel additive, methyl tertiary-butyl ether (MTBE), which had been found to be a groundwater pollutant. The claimant was not a producer of MTBE but rather of a feedstock, methanol, used in the production of MTBE.[306] The tribunal rejected the claim on the basis that the Californian regulations had been adopted in the use of the State's police powers, and made the following statement:

[A]s a matter of general international law, a non-discriminatory regulation for a public purpose, which is enacted in accordance with due process and, which affects, inter alios, a foreign investor or investment is not deemed expropriatory and compensable unless specific commitments had been given by the regulating government to the then putative foreign investor contemplating investment that the government would refrain from such regulation.[307]

This statement has been subsequently confirmed in another investment dispute, albeit not related to environmental regulation, where the tribunal considered, by reference to the *Methanex* award, that:

the principle that a State does not commit an expropriation and is thus not liable to pay compensation to a dispossessed alien investor when it adopts general regulations that are "commonly accepted as within the police powers of States" forms part of customary law today.[308]

In turn, this latter award was used as authority in a paragraph of the award in *Chemtura v Canada*, which provides the clearest formulation of

[303] *S.D. Myers v Canada*, above n 105. [304] Ibid, paras 281–282.
[305] *Methanex v United States*, above n 136. [306] Ibid, part IV, ch. D, para 1. [307] Ibid, para 7.
[308] See *Saluka Investments B.V. v The Czech Republic*, UNCITRAL, Partial Award, 17 March 2006 ('*Saluka v Czech Republic*'), para 262.

the police powers doctrine in the context of environmental regulation so far:

[T]he Tribunal considers in any event that the measures challenged by the Claimant constituted a valid exercise of the Respondent's police powers. As discussed in detail in connection with Article 1105 of NAFTA, the PMRA took measures within its mandate, in a non-discriminatory manner, motivated by the increasing awareness of the dangers presented by lindane for human health and the environment. A measure adopted under such circumstances is a valid exercise of the State's police powers and, as a result, does not constitute an expropriation.[309]

This strong statement leaves no doubt as to the effects of the police powers doctrine. Interestingly, it is also an implicit acknowledgement of the formulation of the police powers doctrine contained in the Harvard Draft of 1961, although another contemporary decision has nuanced this conclusion.[310] Summarizing, in principle, where a legitimacy conflict arises between a domestic environmental measure and an investment protection clause in a treaty, the former would 'prevail' if it is not *ultra vires*, pursues a public purpose and is not discriminatory, unless the host State has given specific assurances to the investor that such regulation would not be adopted.

With respect to this latter condition, the *Methanex* tribunal referred *inter alia* to another environment-related dispute, namely *Waste Management v Mexico*,[311] where the tribunal considered that in assessing a potential breach of Article 1105 of NAFTA 'it is relevant that the treatment is in breach of representations made by the host State which were reasonably relied on by the claimant'.[312] The same reasoning appears in the *Metalclad v Mexico* case,[313] in connection with the refusal by the local Mexican authorities to issue a construction permit on environmental grounds. The tribunal considered that such refusal was *ultra vires* and contrary to the previous assurances received by the investor from the federal Mexican authorities.[314] However, upon application by Mexico, the award was partially set aside by the Supreme Court of British Columbia on the grounds that the tribunal had exceeded its powers by introducing

[309] *Chemtura v Canada*, above n 109, para 266, referring to paragraph 262 of *Saluka v Czech Republic*.

[310] In *Suez v Argentina—03/17*, above n 136, Decision on Liability, 31 August 2010 ('*Suez v Argentina—03/17—Liability*'), the tribunal analysed Argentina's police powers defence in the light of the Harvard Draft. In this regard, the tribunal made a nuanced statement which is, however, not inconsistent with the position taken by the tribunal in *Chemtura v Canada*: 'While this Tribunal does not pronounce on the legal authority of the [Harvard] Draft, it does acknowledge that States have a legitimate right to exercise their police powers to protect the public interest and that the doctrine of police powers, as the above-quoted excerpt from the Draft clearly states, has been particularly pertinent in cases of expropriation where tribunals have had to balance an investor's property rights with the legitimate and reasonable need for the State to regulate', para 147.

[311] See *Waste Management Inc. v Mexico*, ICSID Case No. ARB(AF)/00/3, Award, 30 April 2004 ('*Waste Management II*').

[312] Ibid, para 98. [313] *Metalclad v Mexico*, above n 18. [314] Ibid, paras 79–101.

an obligation of transparency in Article 1105 of NAFTA and deciding the dispute on such basis.[315]

Another case addressing the impact of specific assurances is *MTD v Chile*[316] where the tribunal concluded that Chile had breached the fair and equitable treatment standard of the applicable BIT by reason of the incoherent behaviour of its authorities. Whereas the Chilean Foreign Investment Commission (FIC) had approved the investment plan of the investor, the Minister of Urban Development rejected the application made by MTD for the necessary zoning changes on the grounds that the project fell foul of the urban development policy of the Santiago area. Significantly, the investor had not conducted a due diligence inquiry into the feasibility of its project from the perspective of zoning. In its argumentation, the respondent heavily relied on a meeting where, allegedly, the investor had been made aware of the fact that the project was contrary to planning regulations. The tribunal did not resolve this factual issue. Instead, it focused on the assurances given by the FIC, which it found decisive to allocate regulatory risk between the investor and the host State. It thus concluded that Chile had breached the applicable BIT:

> [T]he Tribunal agrees that it is the responsibility of the investor to assure itself that it is properly advised, particularly when investing abroad in an unfamiliar environment. However, in the case before us, Chile is not a passive party and the coherent action of the various officials through which Chile acts is the responsibility of Chile, not of the investor. Whether the Claimants acted responsibly or diligently in reaching a decision to invest in Chile is another question... Chile claims that it had no obligation to inform the Claimants and that the Claimants should have found out by themselves what the regulations and policies of the country were. The Tribunal agrees with this statement as a matter of principle, but Chile also has an obligation to act coherently and apply its policies consistently, independently of how diligent an investor is. Under international law (the law that this Tribunal has to apply to a dispute under the BIT), the State of Chile needs to be considered by the Tribunal as a unit.[317]

Chile sought annulment of the award arguing, *inter alia*, that the tribunal had confused attribution and breach. The ad hoc committee agreed that 'to mix up attribution and breach would require explanation and would indicate confusion' but rejected Chile's argument that the tribunal had committed an annullable error.[318]

[315] See *United Mexican States v Metalclad*, 2001 BCSC 664, Supreme Court of British Columbia, Reasons for the Judgment (2 May 2001), paras 67–77.

[316] *MTD Equity Sdn Bhd and MTD Chile SA v Republic of Chile*, ICSID Case No. ARB/01/7, Award of 25 May 2004 ('*MTD v Chile—Award*').

[317] Ibid, paras 164–165.

[318] *MTD Equity Sdn Bhd and MTD Chile SA v Chile*, ICSID Case No ARB/01/7, Decision on Annulment of 16 February 2007 ('*MTD v Chile—Annulment*'), para 89.

These three cases stress the importance of specific assurances given to a foreign investor, even when the State authorities act *ultra vires* or when the investor does not exercise due diligence. One may wonder, however, how far such reasoning can go and, particularly, whether such assurances would suffice to uphold investment protection clauses over environmental measures even in those cases where the assurances have been given by a former government in conscious disregard of environmental considerations. In such a situation, two competing values would be at stake, namely the legitimate need to protect the environment and the reasonable expectations of the investors when making the investment. Although the reasoning of the tribunals in *Metalclad v Mexico*, *MTD v Chile* and *Methanex v United States* would seem to prioritize the latter, some remarks appearing in these awards tend to nuance this conclusion, by pointing to the legitimate environmental concerns of the host State[319] as well as to the need, for the investor, reasonably to anticipate the evolution of environmental regulation.[320] In other words, not any specific assurance could be reasonably relied upon by an investor who, at the same time, should be aware of the growing demands of environmental protection.[321] This would suggest that real environmental threats may sometimes prevail over any specific assurances.[322]

Aside from this specific hypothesis, a more general question arises as to the conditions under which certain environmental objectives could trump specific assurances given to foreign investors. Admittedly, this is a fact-sensitive assessment that cannot be settled once and for all. As a rule of thumb, one may, however, introduce a distinction based on the type of environmental purpose. Thus, when an environmental regulation is adopted as a result of a new scientific understanding of a given substance

[319] Indeed, in *Metalclad v Mexico*, the tribunal noted that its conclusion was 'not affected by NAFTA Article 1114, which permits a Party to ensure that investment activity is undertaken in a manner sensitive to environmental concerns. The conclusion of the Convenio and the issuance of the federal permits show clearly that Mexico was satisfied that this project was consistent with, and sensitive to, its environmental concerns', *Metalclad v Mexico*, above n 18, para 98.

[320] In *Methanex v United States*, the tribunal noted, in connection with the question of whether Methanex had received specific assurances that '[n]o such commitments were given to Methanex. Methanex entered a political economy in which it was widely known, if not notorious, that governmental environmental and health protection institutions at the federal and state level, operating under the vigilant eyes of the media, interested corporations, non-governmental organizations and a politically active electorate, continuously monitored the use and impact of chemical compounds and commonly prohibited or restricted the use of some of those compounds for environmental and/or health reasons... Methanex entered the United States market aware of and actively participating in the process. It did not enter the United States market because of special representations made to it', *Methanex v United States*, above n 136, part IV, ch. D, paras 9–10.

[321] In *Bayindir v Pakistan*, the tribunal noted that some specific assurances could not be relied upon when it is clear that the political volatility of a country places such assurances under a high risk of being frustrated, above n 108, paras 193–194.

[322] For a policy analysis of the impact of unilateral commitments to investment protection see K Tienhaara, 'Unilateral Commitments to Investment Protection: Does the Promise of Stability Restrict Environmental Policy Development?' (2006) 17 *Yearbook of International Environmental Law* 139.

in order to protect human health, either directly or indirectly (by protecting the proximate human environment), environmental regulation should have more chances to prevail. Conversely, when an environmental regulation is adopted mostly for efficiency purposes, i.e. to manage a known environmental threat with more cost-effective means, previous assurances given to investors would be likely to prevail. Between these two extremes, the balance between environmental protection and legal certainty would be more difficult to strike.

The margin of appreciation doctrine—Another expression of the doctrine of regulatory powers is the so-called margin of appreciation doctrine, developed by the ECtHR[323] on the basis of the practice of several European civil law jurisdictions,[324] and subsequently adopted by other human rights as well as other bodies.[325] This doctrine was initially formulated in the context of derogations from human rights standards in accordance with Article 15 of the ECHR,[326] and it was later used in the context of Articles 6 (due process) and 8 (right to private and family life, extended to cover environmental aspects) of the Convention, and Article 1 (right to private property) of the First Protocol. In the *Handyside case*, the Court formulated the underlying rationale of this doctrine as follows:

> [I]t is not possible to find in the domestic law of the various Contracting States a uniform European conception of morals. The view taken by their respective laws of the requirements of morals varies from time to time and from place to place, especially in our era which is characterised by a rapid and far-reaching evolution of opinions on the subject. By reason of their direct and continuous contact with the vital forces of their countries, State authorities are in principle in a better position than the international judge to give an opinion on the exact content of these requirements as well as on the "necessity" of a "restriction" or "penalty" intended to meet them . . . This margin is given both to the domestic legislator ('prescribed by law') and to the bodies, judicial amongst others, that are called upon to interpret and apply the laws in force.[327]

Thus, the margin of appreciation is, in essence, a standard of deference given to the national authorities to assess a situation because of their better

[323] See Y Arai-Takahashi, *The Margin of Appreciation Doctrine and the Principle of Proportionality in the Jurisprudence of the ECHR* (Intersentia, Antwerp, 2002); M Hutchinson, 'The Margin of Appreciation Doctrine in the European Court of Human Rights' (1999) 48 *International & Comparative Law Quarterly* 638.

[324] See Arai-Takahashi, above n 323, 2–3, referring to the theories of '*marge d'appréciation*' applied by the French *Conseil d'Etat* and of '*Ermessensspielraum*' applied by German courts.

[325] In particular, the Inter-American Court of Human Rights and the United Nations Human Rights Committee, see ibid, 4.

[326] See *Ireland v United Kingdom*, ECHR, Judgment of 18 January 1978, A 25, para 207, quoted in ibid, 5.

[327] See *Handyside v United Kingdom*, ECHR, Judgment of 7 December 1976, A 24, para 48, quoted in ibid, 7–8.

position to understand it. This is particularly important for environment-related disputes where a regulatory agency focusing on health or environmental protection takes measures that are subsequently challenged by the investor as being in breach of international investment law.

Three main questions arise in this connection. The first is whether such doctrine is applicable in the context of investment disputes. This seems to be the case, if one judges by the reasoning of the tribunals in *Methanex*[328] and *Glamis Gold*.[329] Indeed, both tribunals seem to have considered that their role was not to judge the scientific conclusions on which the measures challenged by the investors were based, but only the acceptability of the process followed to reach such conclusions. The tribunal in *Chemtura v Canada* also followed this approach.[330] However, it took a more nuanced position as regards the question of whether its scope of review was limited by a margin of appreciation doctrine,[331] which takes me to the second question.

The second question concerns, indeed, the tribunal's scope of review regarding the assessments conducted by such specialized agencies. Part of the answer to this second question has already been given in connection with the first question. Tribunals must not focus on the science but on the process. However, the articulation between science and process is not entirely clear.[332] Moreover, focusing only on process may sometimes lead to unsatisfactory solutions as, under some circumstances, it could be unreasonable to penalize a State which took a decision based on sound science but through a procedurally inefficient process. Assuming the result of the regulatory process to be the same, mere procedural breaches would be relevant only where and to the extent that they have imposed an unnecessarily heavy burden on the claimant. In other terms, the articulation between science and process must leave some room to accommodate proportionality considerations. For instance, in *Chemtura v Canada*, the tribunal considered that the delays in the registration process of a lindane-free replacement pesticide submitted by the claimant did not amount to a violation of the Article 1105 of NAFTA.[333]

The third question concerns the differences between the margin of appreciation doctrine and the police powers doctrine. Although the concepts underlying these two doctrines overlap to some extent, some

[328] See *Methanex v United States*, above n 136, part III, ch. A, para 101.

[329] See *Glamis v United States*, above n 116, para 779.

[330] See *Chemtura v Canada*, above n 109, paras 133–134.

[331] Ibid, para 123, noting that '[i]n assessing whether the treatment afforded to the Claimant's investment was in accordance with the international minimum standard, the Tribunal must take into account all the circumstances, including the fact that certain agencies manage highly specialized domains involving scientific and public policy determinations. This is not an abstract assessment circumscribed by a legal doctrine about the margin of appreciation of specialized regulatory agencies. It is an assessment that must be conducted *in concreto*.'

[332] In *Methanex v United States*, the tribunal made explicit what it gathered from the discussion of scientific evidence. See *Methanex v United States*, above n 136, part III, ch. A, para 102.

[333] See *Chemtura v Canada*, above n 109, paras 217–220.

differences of accent can be identified. One such difference has been identified by the tribunal in *Suez v Argentina—03/17*, according to which the police powers doctrine would be relevant only in connection with expropriation because the same considerations underlying this doctrine are already taken into account in the definition and scope of other standards of investment protection, such as fair and equitable treatment.[334] Another difference rests on the reason for deferring to State authorities. Whereas the police powers doctrine is based on the deference due by tribunals to the policy choices made by State authorities, including the level of environmental or health protection, the margin of appreciation doctrine, as applied in the investment context,[335] seeks rather to avoid second guessing the assessment of the relevant material made by a specialized agency.[336] Still another difference is that, as it has already been noted, the police powers doctrine concerns liability, whereas the margin of appreciation doctrine concerns factual analysis. Indeed, if the police powers doctrine is found to shield a given measure, the result is that such measure is not in breach of investment protection standards (expropriation). By contrast, the deference to a scientific assessment conducted by State authorities is only a finding of fact, which may or may not lead to liability. An additional difference, that flows from the one just mentioned, concerns the room for proportionality reasoning within the two doctrines, which seems to be larger within the margin of appreciation doctrine. Thus, in a case where a measure has been adopted for environmental reasons, the

[334] See *Suez v Argentina—03/17—Liability*, above n 136, stating in paragraph 148 that 'the application of the police powers doctrine as an explicit, affirmative defense to treaty claims *other* than for expropriation is inappropriate, because in judging those claims and applying such principles as full protection and security and fair and equitable treatment, both of which are considered in subsequent sections of this Decision, a tribunal must take account of a State's reasonable right to regulate. Thus, if a tribunal finds that a State has violated treaty standards of fair and equitable treatment and full protection and security, it must of necessity have determined that such State has exceeded its reasonable right to regulate. Consequently, for that same tribunal to make a subsequent inquiry as to whether that same State has exceeded its legitimate police powers would require that tribunal to engage in an inquiry it has already made. In short, a decision on the application of the police powers doctrine in such circumstance would be duplicative and therefore inappropriate.'

[335] In the context of the ECtHR, the doctrine serves much broader purposes, including the adaptation of the European Convention standards to the cultural and political specificities of each State party to the Convention. See above n 324.

[336] To understand this distinction a useful, albeit not entirely accurate, analogy could be made to the different roles in United States federal law of, on one hand, the act of State doctrine and, on the other, of judicial deference to statutory interpretation by specialized agencies. This analogy must be nuanced in a number of ways, including the fact that the Act of State doctrine accounts for the respect due by the organs of one State vis-à-vis the organs of another State, and that administrative statutory interpretation belongs to the province of legal, as opposed to factual reasoning. On the Act of State doctrine see L Henkin, 'Act of State Today: Recollections in Tranquility' (1967) 6 *Columbia Journal of Transnational Law* 175; F L Kirgis, 'Understanding the Act of State Doctrine's Effect' (1988) 82 *American Journal of International Law* 58. On administrative statutory interpretation see *Chevron U.S.A. Inc v National Resources Defence Council Inc.*, 467 U.S. 867 (1984). For a discussion of the standards laid out in this case see A Scalia, 'Judicial Deference to Administrative Interpretation of Law' (1989) *Duke Law Journal* 511; R J Krotoszynsky, 'Why Deference?: Implied Delegations, Agency Expertise, and the Misplaced Legacy of Skidmore' (2002) 54 *Administrative Law Review* 735.

application of the police powers doctrine would tend to be more favourable to the host State, as it would in principle exempt it from liability. By contrast, the application of the margin of appreciation doctrine may allow a tribunal to defer to the environmental assessment conducted by the State authorities while considering that the measures taken on that basis were not proportional. In *Tecmed v Mexico*,[337] the tribunal analyzed the refusal by the local authorities to renew a license for the operation of a landfill facility in the light of both the police powers and margin of appreciation doctrines. The tribunal subjected the characterisation of a measure as legitimate under the police powers doctrine to domestic instead of to international law.[338] This preliminary (and debatable) step allowed the tribunal to make some additional room for assessing the conformity of the measures with the applicable investment treaty, without reviewing the reasons and motivations that led to the adoption of the measure challenged.[339] Thus, it placed itself under the margin of appreciation doctrine. In fact, the tribunal recognised that even those regulations that have a legitimate public purpose, such as environmental protection, could fall under the expropriation clause of the treaty.[340] It then proceeded to a proportionality analysis, borrowed from the case-law of the ECtHR:

> [A]fter establishing that regulatory actions and measures will not be initially excluded from the definition of expropriatory acts, in addition to the negative financial impact of such actions or measures, the Arbitral Tribunal will consider, in order to determine if they are to be characterized as expropriatory, whether such actions or measures are proportional to the public interest presumably protected thereby and to the protection legally granted to investments, taking into account that the significance of such impact has a key role upon deciding the proportionality. *Although the analysis starts at the due deference owing to the State when defining the issues that affect its public policy or the interests of society as a whole, as well as the actions that will be implemented to protect such values, such situation does not prevent the Arbitral Tribunal, without thereby questioning such due deference, from examining the actions of the State in light of Article 5(1) of the Agreement to determine whether such measures are reasonable with respect to their goals, the deprivation of economic rights and the legitimate expectations of who suffered such deprivation.* There must be a reasonable relationship of proportionality between the charge or weight imposed to the foreign investor and the aim sought to be realized by any expropriatory measure. To value such charge or weight, it is very important to measure the size of the ownership deprivation caused by the actions of the state and whether such deprivation was compensated or not.[341]

[337] *Tecmed v Mexico*, above n 18. [338] Ibid, para 119. [339] Ibid, para 120.
[340] Ibid, para 121, referring to a controversial conclusion in *CDSE v Costa Rica*.
[341] *Tecmed v Mexico*, above n 18, para 122 (emphasis added), referring to the decision of ECtHR *In the case of James and Others*, Judgment of 21 February 1986, 63, 24.

This paragraph suggests that, under the margin of appreciation doctrine, the link between deference and exemption of liability is mediated by the concept of proportionality whereas, under the police powers doctrine, proportionality plays a part only with respect to whether the doctrine is applicable or not. Once applied, the police powers doctrine excludes liability. This difference has also some bearing in connection with issues of compensation, as it will be discussed later.

Emergency and necessity clauses—Still another expression of the State regulatory powers is provided by emergency and necessity clauses. There is some overlap between such clauses and the two doctrines discussed above. Indeed, some of the traditional hypotheses covered by both the police powers and the margin of appreciation doctrines were situations of public emergency.[342] Here, the analysis focuses instead on the relevance of public emergency clauses in investment treaties as well as of the customary international rule governing the necessity defence for the protection of environmental interests.

The potential application of the necessity defence for the protection of environmental interests was recognised for the first time in the *Gabčíkovo-Nagymaros* case, before the International Court of Justice.[343] In this case, the Court expressly admitted that

> the concerns expressed by Hungary for its natural environment in the region affected by the Gabčíkovo-Nagymaros Project related to an "essential interest" of that State, within the meaning given to that expression in Article 33 of the Draft of the International Law Commission.[344]

In this particular case, Hungary had raised concerns relating *inter alia* to the potential effects of the construction projects contemplated in a treaty of 1977 on the aquifer providing Budapest with freshwater. Despite recognising the importance of environmental protection, the ICJ rejected Hungary's argument on the grounds that some of the conditions for the admissibility of the customary necessity defence were not met.

Public emergency clauses and the necessity defence have also been invoked in the context of a series of investment disputes relating to the Argentine crisis of 2001–2003.[345] Although these cases do not focus on

[342] See above nn 299, 301, 326.

[343] See *Gabčíkovo-Nagymaros*, above n 8. On the so-called 'ecological necessity' see above n 12.

[344] *Gabčíkovo-Nagymaros*, above n 8, para 53.

[345] See *Continental Casualty v Argentine Republic*, ICSID Case No. ARB/03/9, Award of 5 September 2008 ('*Continental Casualty v Argentina*'); *Metalpar c. Argentine Republic*, ICSID Case No. ARB/03/5, Award of 6 June 2008 ('*Metalpar v Argentina*'); *Sempra Energy v Argentine Republic*, ICSID Case No. ARB/02/16, Award of 28 September 2007 ('*Sempra v Argentina—Award*'), Decision on Annulment of 29 June 2010 ('*Sempra v Argentina—Annulment*'); *Enron and Ponderosa Assets v Argentine Republic*, ICSID Case No. ARB/01/3, Award of 22 May 2007 ('*Enron v Argentina—Award*'), Decision on Annulment of 30 July 2010 ('*Enron v Argentina—Annulment*'); *LG&E v Argentine Republic*, ICSID Case No. ARB/02/1, Decision on liability of 13 October 2006 ('*LG&E—Liability*'), Award of 25 July 2007 ('*LG&E—Award*'); *CMS v Argentina—Award*, above n 103, *CMS Gas Transmission Company v Argentine Republic*, ICSID Case No. ARB/01/08, Decision on

environmental issues, they remain relevant to assess the potential operation of emergency and necessity clauses in connection with such issues. The first case in which the tribunal admitted an argument of necessity to justify the breach of an investment treaty is *LG&E v Argentina*.[346] The respondent had argued that the measures challenged by the investor were justified under both Article XI of the Argentina—United States BIT[347] and the customary rule on necessity codified in Article 25 of the ILC Articles on State Responsibility.[348] Article XI of the applicable BIT could in fact be considered as a public emergency rather than as a necessity clause. It provides the following:

This Treaty shall not preclude the application by either Party of measures necessary for the maintenance of public order, the fulfilment of its obligations with respect to the maintenance or restoration of international peace or security or the protection of its own essential security interests.[349]

The tribunal in LG&E found that such clause was applicable under the specific circumstances that prevailed in Argentina from 2001 to 2003:

While unemployment, poverty and indigency rates gradually increased from the beginning of 1998, they reached intolerable levels by December 2001. Unemployment reached almost 25%, and almost half of the Argentine population was living below poverty. The entire healthcare system teetered on the brink of collapse. Prices of pharmaceuticals soared as the country plunged deeper into the deflationary period, becoming unavailable for low-income people. Hospitals suffered a severe shortage of basic supplies. Investments in infrastructure and equipment for public hospitals declined as never before. These conditions prompted the Government to declare the nationwide health emergency to ensure the population's access to basic health care goods and services. At the time, one quarter of the population could not afford the minimum amount of food required to ensure their subsistence. Given the level of poverty and lack of access to healthcare and proper nutrition, disease followed. Facing increased pressure to provide social services and security to the masses of indigent and poor people, the Government was forced to decrease its per capita spending on social services

Annulment, 25 September 2007 ('*CMS v Argentina—Annulment*'). For a discussion of these awards see Ch Leben, 'L'état de nécessité dans le droit international de l'investissement' (2005) 3 *Les Cahiers de l'arbitrage* 47; J E Viñuales, 'State of Necessity and Peremptory Norms in International Investment Law' (2008) 14 *NAFTA: Law and Business Review of the Americas* 79; J Fouret, 'CMS c/ LG&E ou l'état de nécessité en question' (2007) *Revue de l'arbitrage* 249; A Reinisch, 'Necessity in International Investment Arbitration: An Unnecessary Split of Opinions in Recent ICSID Cases?' (2007) 8 *Journal of World Investment & Trade* 191.

[346] *LG&E v Argentina—Liability*, above n 345.

[347] Treaty between the United States of America and the Argentine Republic concerning the Reciprocal Encouragement and Protection of Investment, 14 November 1991, 31 ILM 124 ('Argentina-US BIT').

[348] Responsibility of States for Internationally Wrongful Acts, G.A. Res. 56/83, U.N. Doc A/RES/56/83, 12 December 2001 ('ILC Articles'), art 25.

[349] Argentina-US BIT, above n 347, art XI.

by 74%... By December 2001, there was widespread fear among the population that the Government would default on its debt and seize bank deposits to prevent the bankruptcy of the banking system. Faced with a possible run on banks, the Government issued on 1 December 2001 Decree of Necessity and Emergency No. 1570/01. The law triggered widespread social discontent. Widespread violent demonstrations and protests brought the economy to a halt, including effectively shutting down transportation systems. Looting and rioting followed in which tens of people were killed as the conditions in the country approached anarchy. A curfew was imposed to curb lootings... By 20 December 2001, President De la Rúa resigned. His presidency was followed by a succession of presidents over the next days, until Mr. Eduardo Duhalde took office on 1 January 2002, charged with the mandate to bring the country back to normal conditions... All of these devastating conditions—economic, political, social—in the aggregate triggered the protections afforded under Article XI of the Treaty to maintain order and control the civil unrest.[350]

It then confirmed its reasoning by reference to the customary rule on necessity, but without technically applying it.[351]

The second case in which a necessity argument was admitted in the context of the Argentine crisis is *Continental Casualty v Argentina*.[352] Although both the customary and the treaty-based defence were invoked by Argentina, the decision of the tribunal on admitting the defence was, again, based on Article XI of the Argentina-US BIT, and not on the requirements for the admissibility of the customary necessity defence.[353] The tribunal clearly spelled out how the operation of Article XI would simply exclude the existence of a breach instead of excusing an existing breach, as would arguably be the case of the customary necessity defence.[354]

[350] *LG&E v Argentina—Liability*, above n 345, paras 234–237.

[351] The tribunal reasoned as follows: 'While the Tribunal considers that the protections afforded by Article XI have been triggered in this case, and are sufficient to excuse Argentina's liability, the Tribunal recognizes that satisfaction of the state of necessity standard as it exists in international law (reflected in Article 25 of the ILC's Draft Articles on State Responsibility) supports the Tribunal's conclusion', ibid, para 245. This *modus operandi* is important because it contrasts with the reasoning of the tribunal in *CMS v Argentina*, which applied both the treaty provision and the customary requirements for the admissibility of necessity together (see *CMS v Argentina—Award*, above n 103, paras 357–358). On annulment, the CMS tribunal was severely criticized for having proceeded in this manner. According to the Ad Hoc Committee: 'Those two texts having different operation and content, it was necessary for the Tribunal to take a position on their relationship and to decide whether they were both applicable in the present case. The Tribunal did not enter into such an analysis, simply assuming that Article XI and Article 25 are on the same footing... In doing so the Tribunal made another error of law. One could wonder whether state of necessity in international law goes to the issue of wrongfulness or that of responsibility. But in any case, the excuse based on customary international law could only be subsidiary to the exclusion based on Article XI', *CMS v Argentina—Annulment*, above n 345, paras 131–132.

[352] See *Continental Casualty v Argentina*, above n 345.

[353] See ibid, para 162.

[354] Ibid, para 164. See also V Lowe, 'Precluding Wrongfulness or Responsibility: A Plea for Excuses' (1999) 10 *European Journal of International Law* 405.

More specifically, the tribunal described Article XI as a safeguard, in the meaning usually given to this term in the international trade context, which in fact limits the scope of the substantive investment disciplines.[355] This had the important consequence of making the availability of such emergency clause less exceptional than the customary necessity defence. As noted by the tribunal:

> [I]n view of these differences between the situation regulated under Art. 25 ILC Articles and that addressed by Art. XI of the BIT, the conditions of application are not the same. The strict conditions to which the ILC text subjects the invocation of the defence of necessity by a State is explained by the fact that it can be invoked in any context against any international obligation. Therefore 'it can only be accepted on an exceptional basis.' This is not necessarily the case under Art. XI according to its language and purpose under the BIT. This leads the Tribunal to the conclusion that invocation of Art. XI under this BIT, as a specific provision limiting the general investment protection obligations (of a 'primary' nature) bilaterally agreed by the Contracting Parties, is not necessarily subject to the same conditions of application as the plea of necessity under general international law.[356]

Moreover, in interpreting the scope of the term 'essential security interests' used in Article XI, the tribunal retained a fairly broad characterization encompassing the protection of the environment, an element which could be used in future investment cases.[357] Thus, the protection of environmental interests would be technically possible under both the customary necessity defence and at least some public emergency clauses.

This latter point has been confirmed in the two *Suez v Argentina* cases with respect to the protection of what can be seen as environment-related interests, namely access to water. The customary necessity defence was discussed in connection with the right to water by both the respondent and the *amici curiae*. The *Amicus* Brief referred *inter alia* to the observation of the LG&E tribunal that 'a state of necessity is identified by those conditions in which a State is threatened by a serious danger . . . to the possibility of maintaining its essential services in operation'.[358] However,

[355] See *Continental Casualty v Argentina*, above n 345, para 164. [356] Ibid, para 167.

[357] The tribunal noted the following in this regard: 'As to "essential security interests," it is necessary to recall that international law is not blind to the requirement that States should be able to exercise their sovereignty in the interest of their population free from internal as well as external threats to their security and the maintenance of a peaceful domestic order. It is well known that the concept of international security of States in the Post World War II international order was intended to cover not only political and military security but also the economic security of States and of their population. The Preamble to the Charter of the United Nations and, even more relevant for the present case, that of the International Monetary Fund support this approach. As noted by the International Law Commission, States have invoked necessity "to protect a wide variety of interests, including safeguarding the environment, preserving the very existence of the State and its people in time of public emergency, or ensuring the safety of a civilian population"', ibid, para 175.

[358] See Suez—Amicus Submission, above n 232, 27–28.

whereas the necessity defence was well articulated by the respondent, its application seems to have been excluded by the *amici curiae*. This point is noteworthy because it underlines the ambiguities of the distinction between primary and secondary norms in the law of State responsibility, particularly in the context of circumstances precluding wrongfulness.[359] Indeed, the *amici* stressed the fact that 'the state of necessity does not apply to human rights treaties that provide guarantees to human rights in times of national emergency'[360] such as the American Convention on Human Rights. The purpose of this assertion is not entirely clear. First, the *Amicus* brief itself referred to provisions encompassing the right to water in instruments that do not impose such limitations on their relevant primary norms.[361] Second, even in those instruments that do impose limitations on their primary norms, not every primary norm can be limited in a public emergency. For instance, Article 6(1) of the International Covenant on Civil and Political Rights, also referred to by the *amici* as encompassing the right to water,[362] is one of the provisions from which it cannot be derogated on grounds of public emergency. Third, irrespective of whether the scope of primary norms is limited or not, such norms may entertain a more subtle relationship with the necessity defence, for instance, by attaching importance to an interest to facilitate its characterization as an essential interest.[363] Primary norms[364] have already played such role in connection with the crystallization of environmental protection as an essential interest in the meaning of the customary rule codified by Article 25 of the ILC Articles. In any event, the necessity defence was rejected in the two *Suez v Argentina* cases, although the tribunals acknowledged that '[t]he provision of water and sewage services ... certainly was vital to the health and well-being of [the population] and was therefore an essential interest of the Argentine State'.[365]

The rejection of the necessity defence in two other cases[366] has been considered as a ground for annulment by the ad hoc committees formed

[359] See E David, 'Primary and Secondary Rules', in J Crawford, A Pellet, S Olleson (eds) *The Law of International Responsibility* (Oxford University Press, Oxford, 2010) 29 et seq.

[360] *Suez—Amicus Submission*, above n 232, 28.

[361] Ibid, 4, referring *inter alia* to arts 11(1) and 12 of the International Covenant on Economic, Social and Cultural Rights, of 16 December 1966, 993 UNTS 3 (entered into force on 3 January 1976) ('ICESCR'), which does not impose such limitations.

[362] See *Suez—Amicus Submission*, above n 232, 7, referring *inter alia* to Article 6(1) of the International Covenant on Civil and Political Rights, of 16 December 1966, 999 UNTS 171 (entered into force on 23 March 1976) ('ICCPR'). Article 4(2) of the ICCPR expressly prohibits derogations, even in times of public emergencies, from Article 6.

[363] See above section IV.B(2)(ii). We have discussed this point more generally in Viñuales, above n 345.

[364] We refer here to the customary principles codified in Principle 21 of the Stockholm Declaration on the Human Environment and in Principle 2 of the Rio Declaration on Environment and Development, see Viñuales, above n 130, 248–249.

[365] See *Suez v Argentina—03/17—Liability*, above n 136, para 238; *Suez v Argentina—03/19—Liability*, above n 136, para 260.

[366] See *Sempra v Argentina—Award*, above n 345, paras 344–354, 364–391; *Enron v Argentina—Award*, above n 345, paras 303–313, 331–342.

in these cases.[367] The reasoning of the ad hoc committees on this point is debatable but, in any case, it does not undermine the proposition that a threat to an environmental interest may potentially trigger the customary necessity defence or a public emergency clause.

D. Issues of Compensation

The question of whether a taking based on environmental (or human rights) reasons should be compensated or not has attracted some attention from legal commentators.[368] Broadly speaking, there are two opposite approaches with regard to compensation for environment-related takings. One considers environmental justifications as irrelevant (1); the other holds that takings for environmental reasons are non-compensable (2). Between these two stances, one may identify some middle-ground positions followed in some cases (3).

1. The irrelevance thesis

The first approach focuses on the sole effects of a deprivation of property. It holds that such taking must be compensated irrespective of its reasons. The awards in *CDSE v Costa Rica*[369] and *Metalclad v Mexico* illustrate this first stance. The dispute in *CDSE v Costa Rica* concerned the amount due for the direct expropriation of a land that the claimant had acquired in order to build a resort. The respondent had invoked a number of domestic and international environmental instruments to challenge the calculation of the amount of compensation. The tribunal held the following view:

> While an expropriation or taking for environmental reasons may be classified as a taking for a public purpose, and thus may be legitimate, the fact that the property was taken for this reason does not affect either the nature or the measure of compensation to be paid for the taking. That is, the purpose of protecting the environment for which the property was taken does not alter the legal character of the taking for which adequate compensation must be paid. The international source of the obligation to protect the environment makes no difference.[370]

This stance was confirmed in *Metalclad v Mexico*,[371] this time with respect to a regulatory taking. The claimant argued that Mexico had breached Articles 1105 (minimum standard of treatment) and 1110 (expropriation) as a result of the acts and omissions of the municipal authorities in

[367] See *Sempra v Argentina—Annulment*, above n 345, paras 186–219 (ground: manifest excess of powers for not applying Article XI of the Argentina-US BIT); *Enron v Argentina—Annulment*, above n 345, paras 355–395 (grounds: failure to state reasons and manifest excess of powers in connection with the application of the customary necessity defence), paras 400–405 (ground: manifest excess of powers for not applying Article XI of the Argentina-US BIT).

[368] See above n 259. [369] *CDSE v Costa Rica*, above n 104. [370] Ibid, para 71.

[371] *Metalclad v Mexico*, above n 18.

connection with the construction of a waste disposal landfill. Indeed, whereas the federal government had granted a permit for the project and represented that no further permits were required, the local authorities declined to grant a second construction permit and subsequently declared the area to be an ecological preserve. The tribunal held that, irrespective of the environmental reasons invoked by Mexico, the measures amounted to both a breach of the minimum standard of treatment and a compensable expropriation:

Although not strictly necessary for its conclusion, the Tribunal also identifies as a further ground for a finding of expropriation the Ecological Decree issued by the Governor of SLP on September 20, 1997. This Decree covers an area of 188,758 hectares within the 'Real de Guadalcazar' that includes the landfill site, and created therein an ecological preserve. This Decree had the effect of barring forever the operation of the landfill . . . The Tribunal is not persuaded by Mexico's representation to the contrary. The Ninth Article, for instance, forbids any work inconsistent with the Ecological Decree's management program. The management program is defined by the Fifth Article as one of diagnosing the ecological problems of the cacti reserve and of ensuring its ecological preservation. In addition, the Fourteenth Article of the Decree forbids any conduct that might involve the discharge of polluting agents on the reserve soil, subsoil, running water or water deposits and prohibits the undertaking of any potentially polluting activities. The Fifteenth Article of the Ecological Decree also forbids any activity requiring permits or licenses unless such activity is related to the exploration, extraction or utilization of natural resources . . . The Tribunal need not decide or consider the motivation or intent of the adoption of the Ecological Decree. Indeed, a finding of expropriation on the basis of the Ecological Decree is not essential to the Tribunal's finding of a violation of NAFTA Article 1110. However, the Tribunal considers that the implementation of the Ecological Decree would, in and of itself, constitute an act tantamount to expropriation.[372]

These cases would suggest that international obligations (or related considerations) other than those provided for in investment treaties are simply not relevant for the assessment of compensation for expropriation. However, other tribunals have followed an entirely different approach.

2. *The police powers thesis*

Indeed, as pointed out when discussing the police powers doctrine, some tribunals have held that deprivations of property resulting from environmental regulations are not compensable or, more precisely, that they do not even constitute an expropriation.

[372] Ibid, paras 109–111.

Perhaps the clearest formulation of this stance appears in the decision of the tribunal in a dispute without environmental dimensions, namely *Saluka v Czech Republic*,[373] where the tribunal made the following statement:

> In the opinion of the Tribunal, the principle that a State does not commit an expropriation and is thus not liable to pay compensation to a dispossessed alien investor when it adopts general regulations that are "commonly accepted as within the police powers of States" forms part of customary law today.[374]

One may consider, of course, that the doctrine of police powers focuses only on liability and not on compensation. Although we agree with this view, this is not to say that environmental considerations may not as such exclude compensation, even in cases where there has been an expropriation. In *SPP v Egypt*,[375] the tribunal concluded that Egypt had expropriated the investors. However, in assessing compensation, the tribunal excluded the amounts of damages corresponding to the period after the emergence of Egypt's obligations of protection in accordance with the UNESCO World Heritage Convention. The tribunal reasoned as follows:

> Even if the Tribunal were disposed to accept the validity of the Claimant's DCF calculations, it could only award lucrum cessans until 1979, when the obligations resulting from the UNESCO Convention with respect to the Pyramids Plateau became binding on the Respondent. From that date forward, the Claimant's activities on the Pyramids Plateau would have been in conflict with the Convention and therefore in violation of international law, and any profits that might have resulted from such activities are consequently non-compensable.[376]

This is a clear statement in favour of incorporating environmental considerations in the calculation of compensation. The question then becomes how exactly such incorporation should be operated.

3. *Middle grounds*

A number of tribunals have followed approaches that can be situated between the two preceding stances. The reasoning of the tribunals in *Methanex v United States*,[377] *MTD v Chile*[378] and *Tecmed v Mexico*[379] in

[373] *Saluka v Czech Republic*, above n 308. [374] Ibid, para 262. [375] *SPP v Egypt*, above n 123.

[376] Ibid, para 191. The tribunal specifically noted that its reasoning applied to the calculation of compensation: 'The next factor invoked by the Respondent to mitigate the amount of compensation in the present case is the fact that the reclassification of the land on the Pyramids Plateau was a lawful act. This factor, however, has already been taken into consideration in the Tribunal's decision not to award compensation based on profits that might have accrued to the Claimants after the date on which areas on the Plateau were registered with the World Heritage Committee', ibid, para 250. See the analysis of L Liberti, 'The Relevance of Non-Investment Treaty Obligations in Assessing Compensation' in Dupuy et al, above n 10, 557.

[377] *Methanex v United States*, above n 136.

[378] *MTD v Chile*, above n 316. [379] *Tecmed v Mexico*, above n 18.

connection with the police powers and margin of appreciation doctrines has already been discussed. Here, the analysis will therefore focus on those aspects of these decisions that could assist in clarifying the impact of environmental considerations on the assessment of damage.

In *Methanex v United States*,[380] the tribunal took a stance that, in essence, corresponds to the police powers thesis. It concluded indeed that the measures adopted by the Californian authorities banning MTBE fell within the scope of the State's police powers and, as a result, were not an expropriation in the meaning of Article 1110 of NAFTA. What is interesting for the issue of compensation is the caveat introduced by the tribunal regarding situations where the host State has given specific assurances that an adverse regulation will not be adopted. A situation could arise where the State has given such specific assurances to an investor on the basis of its contemporaneous scientific understanding of an environmental question. We could think, for instance, of topics on which the scientific community is divided, or of fields where a major scientific or technological breakthrough permits the replacement of a lesser evil (i.e. a very important product with some undesirable consequences but with no serious substitute)[381] with a new healthier product. After new developments in the scientific understanding of the question, the State decides, despite its previous assurances, to adopt a measure that makes the investor's business unviable. The question would then be how to balance environmental and investment protection. Admittedly, the solution will heavily depend on the specific facts of the case as well as on the ability of counsel to mobilise such facts in support of a claim. But broadly speaking, there are two possible solutions.

One would be to bring the situation under the umbrella of the police powers doctrine and conclude that the measures are not an expropriation.[382] A similar reasoning could also intervene *mutatis mutandis* in connection with a claim for breach of fair and equitable treatment if the possibility of a change in the scientific understanding of a product was reasonably predictable, as it may be the case for heavily regulated products.

The other alternative would be to conclude that, as a result of the assurances given to the investor, the measures are not covered by the police powers doctrine and constitute an expropriation. What is unclear is whether the amount of compensation could be adjusted to take into account the specific circumstances in which the expropriation intervened.

380 *Methanex v United States*, above n 136.

381 An example is the continuing use of DDT, one of the most widely known persistent organic pollutants, in some developing countries, as an effective way to fight malaria. See WHO gives indoor use of DDT a clean bill of health for controlling malaria, press release of 15 September 2006, <http://www.who.int/mediacentre/news/releases/2006/pr50/en/print.html> (last accessed on 21 April 2010).

382 See above section IV.C(2)(iii).

There are different ways to incorporate such considerations in the assessment of compensation.

One approach would be to reduce the amount of compensation to take into account the degree of diligence or reasonableness of the investor. In *MTD v Chile*, the tribunal considered that the investor, which had acted negligently in assessing regulatory risks, had to bear part of the damages that it had suffered. The tribunal considered, indeed, that such damage was attributable to business risk because the investor could have mitigated it if it had deployed better business judgment.[383]

Another approach, in the context of the hypothetical situation described above, would be to assess the value of the expropriated asset as a going concern and/or of the *lucrum cessans* resulting from the expropriation by reference to a shorter time horizon. The time horizon may be limited by reference to international legal developments, as in *SPP v Egypt*,[384] or by the specific characteristics of some markets.[385] Markets in highly regulated products or activities sometimes face fast-moving scientific and technological environments, which may limit their lifespan. Indeed, specific assurances are not insurances against all odds. It may also happen that the investor knew, at the time it invested, that a market was still profitable in some countries but not in others, as a result of different perceptions of a health or an environmental risk. An apposite illustration would be tobacco-related investments made in emerging markets based on specific assurances of the host State.[386] In such cases, the reasoning of the tribunal in *Tecmed v Mexico*, which distinguished environmental risks from the socio-political reaction attached to their perception by the population,[387] would be problematic. A risk may indeed exist despite the fact that the affected population is not actively aware of it. Moreover, the

[383] *MTD v Chile—Award*, above n 316, paras 242–243. The damages assessment of the tribunal withstood an annulment challenge, see *MTD v Chile—Decision on Annulment*, above n 318, para 101.

[384] *SPP v Egypt*, above n 123, para 191. Interestingly, the *SPP v Egypt* decision also leaves open the possibility of adjusting compensation on the basis of other factors, such as the potential benefits (monetary or other) derived by one of the parties. The existence of such benefits was invoked by the respondent as a mitigation factor but eventually rejected by the tribunal. See ibid, paras 245–249.

[385] In assessing other potential mitigating factors, the tribunal in *SPP v Egypt* made the following comment, which could by analogy illuminate the situation of regulated markets: '[T]he Respondent contends that the project was located in an area where the Claimants should have known there was a risk that antiquities would be discovered. Again, this is a factor that is already reflected in the method used by the Tribunal to value the Claimants' loss, and particularly in the Tribunal's decision and not to base compensation on profits that might have been earned after the Plateau areas were registered with UNESCO', ibid, para 251.

[386] We are not aware of a case presenting the particular features of our hypothetical. Tobacco (or tobacco-related) regulation has however been discussed in at least two investment cases: *Marvin Roy Feldman Karpa v Mexico*, ICSID Case No. ARB(AF)/99/1, Award, 16 December 2002; *Grand River Enterprises Six Nations Ltd and others v United States*, NAFTA (UNCITRAL), Decision on Objections to Jurisdiction, 20 July 2006 (currently pending). See V S Vadi, 'Reconciling Public Health and Investor Rights: The Case of Tobacco' in Dupuy et al, above n 10, 452.

[387] *Tecmed v Mexico*, above n 18, paras 132–151.

perception of the relevant population, irrespective of whether the environmental risk is high or low, is an important factor in assessing the value of an investment, to the extent that such perception affects the current and future demand for an investor's product. An example could be provided by investments relating to genetically modified organisms, which are negatively perceived in some countries, despite the fact that their environmental and health implications are still difficult to determine.

Thus, environmental considerations could indeed affect the reasoning of a tribunal regarding the assessment of compensation. Technically, tribunals have considerable room for manoeuvre in selecting the appropriate standard of compensation and even when they retain the fair-market-value approach, either for expropriation or for other breaches, they still have considerable leeway in deciding which valuation techniques are the most appropriate to calculate such value.[388]

* * *

This analysis of the substantive issues that may arise in environment-related investment proceedings suggests the following conclusions: (1) a distinction may be drawn between normative conflicts—involving two or more international obligations arising respectively from international environmental law and international investment law—and legitimacy conflicts—involving an international and a domestic component—on the basis of the nature of the conflicting norms and of the rules applicable to solve such conflicts; (2) normative conflicts may be handled either (i) through specific conflict rules addressing the relations between investment and environmental protection or (ii) through general approaches, including those relating to the relations between sources (sequential application) as well as between norms (*lex superior*, *lex specialis*, *lex posterior*, systemic integration); (3) legitimacy conflicts may also be addressed through (i) specific conflict rules or (ii) through general approaches, including the rules governing the relations between domestic and international law or between different domestic legal systems, or through the different expressions of a State's regulatory powers (the police powers doctrine, the margin of appreciation doctrine and emergency/necessity clauses); (4) the extent to which environmental considerations may be relevant for the assessment of compensation is not settled in the case-law, with (i) some tribunals depriving such considerations of any relevance for compensation, (ii) other tribunals applying such considerations to limit or even exclude compensation, and (iii) still other tribunals suggesting a middle ground approach.

[388] See P-Y Tschanz, J E Viñuales, 'Compensation for Non-Expropriatory Breaches of International Investment Law. The Contribution of the Argentine Awards' (2009) 6 *Journal of International Arbitration* 729; I Marboe, 'Compensation and Damages in International Law. The Limits of "Fair Market Value"' (2006) 7 *Journal of World Investment and Trade* 723.

V. Future Trends

The purpose of this concluding section is to draw upon the foregoing analysis of the main points of contact between international investment law and international environmental law in order to identify the axis along which the interactions between these two bodies of law will unfold in the future. In conducting this inquiry, one must take into account several trends, as well as the main features of the mechanisms available to manage their potentially conflicting consequences.

Regarding the first aspect of the inquiry, two main trends affecting the relations between foreign investment and environmental protection can be discerned. The first trend concerns the nature of environmental regulation, which is becoming increasingly precise and demanding, with significant consequences for the conduct of business operations abroad. This trend can be observed in the development of environmental regulation both at the international and domestic levels, as well as in the growing number of disputes, brought before investment tribunals or other international judicial or quasi-judicial bodies, involving an environmental component.[389] The second trend concerns the nature of foreign investment, which increasingly flows to developing countries[390] and is in part driven by environment-related concerns or by opportunities in environment-related sectors. This second trend seems to reflect the attractiveness of major emerging economies such as China, India, Brazil and others, as well as the capital exports from these countries to other regions, such as Chinese investments in Africa. Some of these investments concern sectors, such as energy or agriculture, with important consequences for environmental regulation. Moreover, the expected increase in the transfer of resources from developed to developing countries as part of strategies to mitigate and adapt to climate change, the mounting fears over the availability of freshwater resources in many developing countries, and the high costs associated with waste treatment in developed countries, may also channel foreign investment towards developing countries. These two trends combined are likely to place increasing pressure on the legal mechanisms governing the relations between foreign investment and the environment. One may therefore ask how adapted these mechanisms are to manage such pressure.

[389] For a concise overview see T Stephens, *International Courts and Environmental Protection* (Cambridge University Press, Cambridge, 2009); S Maljean-Dubois (ed), *Le droit de l'environnement comme exemple de la mondialisation des concepts juridiques: place et role des juridictions internationals et constitutionnelles*, Rapport final de recherche, May 2008, <http://www.gip-recherche-justice.fr/IMG/pdf/170-RF_Maljean-Dubois_Droit_Environ.pdf> (last accessed on 22 February 2010). The most complete collection of domestic and international decisions (although it does not cover investment decisions) remains the series of five volumes published by Cambridge University Press: *International Environmental Law Reports* (vol. 1–3, edited by Cairo A R Robb; vol. 4, edited by Alice Palmer and Cairo A R Robb; vol. 5, edited by Karen Lee).

[390] Foreign investment in developing countries seems to be growing relatively to that in developed countries, see Kekic, above n 14.

In order to answer this question, it is necessary to assess the main features of such mechanisms. For the purposes of this inquiry, two features are particularly relevant. The first feature concerns the increasing availability and use of international adjudication mechanisms. Investment arbitration is one major illustration of this trend, with numerous cases brought and decided each year.[391] However, not every area of international law has been equally affected by this trend, and one of the most conspicuous illustrations of this fact is precisely international environmental law. Lacking a specialised body, international environmental adjudication has unfolded in a variety of 'borrowed forums', including the International Court of Justice, the International Tribunal on the Law of the Sea, the WTO Dispute Settlement Body or the different bodies and courts established to hear human rights cases.[392] This imbalance could be explained by the fact that international adjudication is ill-suited to solve environmental disputes, which would be better handled by other mechanisms, such as the so-called 'non-compliance procedures' (NCPs). While there may be some truth in this argument, one cannot overlook the limited results achieved by NCPs so far.[393] Moreover, the lack of an environmental court is not due to the absence of initiatives in this regard.[394] One could therefore wonder whether the environmental dimensions of foreign investment could be adequately taken into account by other adjudication mechanisms, and above all by investment tribunals. This takes us to the second feature, namely the resilience of the investment arbitration regime. Indeed, despite some criticism from both scholars and States, it appears unlikely that the investment arbitration regime will be fundamentally modified in the next few years. As a result, the environmental dimensions of investment disputes that may arise in the next decade will arguable have to be handled with the means currently available to international lawyers. This is partly because, despite attempts at including specific language in investment treaties and free trade agreements, the practical impact of such language remains limited and, in all events, does not modify the foundations of the international investment regime. For this reason, the analysis conducted in this study was aimed at exploring the scope and limits of the existing institutions in accommodating environmental considerations.

The overall conclusion that can be derived from this analysis is rather optimistic. The investment arbitration regime provides several entry points for environmental considerations. This conclusion is suggested by a number of developments, which have been analysed in some detail in

[391] See above n 195. [392] See above n 389.

[393] For an overview of these mechanisms including up-to-date case-studies and comparative analysis see T Treves, L Pineschi, A Tanzi, C Pitea, C Ragni, F Romanin Jacur (eds) *Non-Compliance Procedures and Mechanisms and the Effectiveness of International Environmental Agreements* (T M C Asser Press, The Hague, 2009).

[394] See above nn 129 and 130.

the preceding pages, including: (i) the increasing role of environmental protection groups as non-disputing parties in investment proceedings, (ii) the growing part played by environmental arguments in the argumentations of the parties and in the awards, (iii) the relative openness of some tribunals to the use of environmental law either to interpret investment disciplines or to delimitate the boundaries between such disciplines and the State's regulatory powers, (iv) the increasing incorporation of specific conflict, emergency or necessity clauses in investment treaties and free-trade agreements, and (v) the possibility of introducing environmental components within investment claims. These developments present some interest not only to carve out a role for environmental considerations in foreign investment disputes but also, and perhaps more importantly, to make investors aware of the need to take such considerations seriously in planning and conducting their activities in other countries.

* * *

Gaps, the *Nuclear Weapons* Advisory Opinion and the Structure of International Legal Argument between Theory and Practice

By Jörg Kammerhofer*

A gap in the law or *lacuna* is the absence of something that arguably ought to be there.[1] Gaps are a negative quantity; they depend for their 'existence' on the 'other' that surrounds them.[2] The question whether there are putative additional characteristics in order to make non-existing norms into 'gaps' is one of the central problems of legal theory. The question whether there is a benchmark makes defining 'gaps in the law' difficult. There is too little law in relation to what, exactly, one might ask. *Lacunae* as negative entities are difficult to prove, because one has to prove the absence of norms, not their 'validity', in the sense of 'existence'.[3] While questions of proof will not be discussed in this article, the formulation of the question does point to the question of where norms 'end'.

The problem of gaps is well recognised in international legal scholarship and it is not generally disputed that they can exist. In the present paper, the issue will be tackled in four steps. We will begin by analysing the important debate between Julius Stone and Hersch Lauterpacht that started with articles on *non liquet* in international law (Section I). Forming an important background to both writers' arguments are Hans Kelsen's views on the completeness of the law, which will then be outlined (Section II). In a case study, we will look at the nearest international tribunals have come to pronouncing a *non liquet* to-date—the International Court of Justice (ICJ) in its *Nuclear Weapons* advisory opinion of 8 July 1996[4] (Section III).

* Senior Research Fellow at the Hans Kelsen Research Group, University of Erlangen-Nuremberg, Germany.

[1] E.g. Claus-Wilhelm Canaris, Die Feststellung von Lücken im Gesetz: Eine methodologische Studie über Voraussetzungen und Grenzen der richterlichen Rechtsfortbildung praeter legem (Duncker und Humblot, Berlin, 1964) 16.

[2] Ulrich Fastenrath, *Lücken im Völkerrecht. Zu Rechtscharakter, Quellen, Systemzusammenhang, Methodenlehre und Funktionen des Völkerrechts* (Duncker und Humblot, Berlin, 1991) 15–18.

[3] In the Pure Theory of Law's ontology, validity is the specific form of existence of norms—their analogous form of 'Being'. See Hans Kelsen, *Allgemeine Theorie der Normen* (Manz, Vienna, 1979) 4.

[4] *Legality of the Threat or Use of Nuclear Weapons*, advisory opinion of 8 July 1996, [1996] ICJ Rep 226. The ICJ's *Accordance with International Law of the Unilateral Declaration of Independence in Respect of Kosovo*, advisory opinion of 22 July 2010, has given rise to similar questions. The Opinion was delivered after this article had been finalised, but references have been added where appropriate.

A concluding section will consolidate the arguments, developing a distinctly *neo*-Kelsenian view on the matter—in apparent contradiction, but affinity to Kelsen's theory (Section IV).

I. The Lauterpacht-Stone Debate on Non Liquet

The late 1950s to early 1970s saw a renewed[5] interest in the related problems of *lacunae* and *non liquet* in international legal scholarship. A vivid exchange of articles ensued, in particular between Hersch Lauterpacht and Julius Stone.[6] This exchange forms the basis of most of what is written on the topic today. In this contribution only one particular strain of the debate will be extracted, namely the views on *gaps*. The participants' focus on *non liquet* is to some extent misdirected, because they fail to distinguish that concept from the concept of gaps.[7] Nonetheless, we can learn some things from the arguments proposed in the *non liquet* debate.

The connection between gaps and *non liquet* lies in the definition of the latter. A *non liquet* occurs when a tribunal 'decline[s] to give a decision on the ground of the absence of an applicable rule of law'.[8] Where there is no law, there is a gap, and only if there is a gap can the question of a *non liquet* arise.[9] Hersch Lauterpacht was not the only, but by far the best-known of those who argued that international tribunals are prohibited from declaring *non liquet*. Unlike Kelsen, however, he acknowledged the possibility of gaps in the law.[10] If there are gaps in international law—'in

[5] There had been earlier writings in municipal law, e.g. Ernst Zitelmann, *Lücken im Recht* (Duncker und Humblot, Leipzig, 1903).

[6] Gerald G Fitzmaurice, 'The Problem of Non-liquet: Prolegomena to a Restatement' in *Mélanges offerts à Charles Rousseau: La communauté internationale* (Pedone, Paris, 1974) 89; L F E Goldie, 'Legal Pluralism and "No Law" Sectors' (1958) 32 *Australian Law Journal* 220; Hersch Lauterpacht, *The Function of Law in the International Community* (Clarendon Press, Oxford, 1933) 51–134; Hersch Lauterpacht, 'Some Observations on the Prohibition of "Non Liquet" and the Completeness of the Law' in *Symbolae Verzijl. Présentées au Professeur J.H.W. Verzijl à l'occasion de son LXX-ième anniversaire* (Martinus Nijhoff, The Hague, 1958) 196; Hersch Lauterpacht, 'International Law—The General Part' in Elihu Lauterpacht (ed) *International Law. Being the collected papers of Hersch Lauterpacht*, Vol 1, (Cambridge University Press, Cambridge 1970) 94; Lucien Siorat, *Le problème des lacunes en droit international: Contribution a l'étude des sources du droit et de la fonction judiciaire* (Librairie Générale de Droit et de Jurisprudence, Paris, 1958); Julius Stone, *Legal Controls of International Conflict. A Treatise on the Dynamics of Disputes and War-Law* (Stevens, London, 1954) 153–64; Julius Stone, '*Non Liquet* and the Function of Law in the International Community' (1959) 35 *BYIL* 124; Julius Stone, '*Non liquet* and the International Judicial Function' in Chaim Perelman (ed) *Le problème des lacunes en droit* (Bruylant, Brussels, 1968) 305; Illmar Tammelo, 'On the Logical Openness of Legal Orders: A Modal Analysis of Law with Special Reference to the Logical Status of *Non Liquet* in International Law (1959) 8 *American Journal of Comparative Law* 187; Illmar Tammelo, 'Logical Aspects of the Non-Liquet Controversy in International Law (1974) 5 *Rechtstheorie* 1.

[7] See also *Kosovo* (2010) above n 4, declaration Simma, para 9.

[8] Lauterpacht (1958) above n 6, 200.

[9] Tammelo (1959) above n 6, 200.

[10] Lauterpacht (1958) above n 6, 204.

a sense, they are the rule rather than the exception',[11] writes Lauterpacht—why would *non liquet* not be possible, avoidable (or at least be prohibited)? As to the second option, Gerald Fitzmaurice warns us, that 'the ability of a tribunal to avoid a *non-liquet* in no way involves that the legal order is necessarily "gapless", and comprises no silences'.[12] Are the two notions at the same time connected and independent—gaps do not necessitate *non liquet*, but without gaps there is no *non liquet*?

In 1958 Lauterpacht wanted to found the prohibition of *non liquet* on a positive norm of international law, but this prohibition also creates (or means) the necessary completeness of the legal system. Unlike Hans Kelsen, he does not argue that completeness is achieved because there are no gaps. How did Lauterpacht make his argument work? Two strands of argument are developed: first, the 'adversarial principle' allows a decision in every case;[13] second, recourse to the 'general principles of law recognized by civilized States' make 'certain that there would always be at hand, if necessary, a legal rule or principle for the legal solution of any controversy'.[14] The ICJ Statute contains these 'general principles' as sources of international law in Article 38(1)(c).[15]

Lauterpacht's first argument is intimately connected with the debate on gaps proper. The 'adversarial principle' is only an expression of the logic of tribunals which are bound by previously enacted norms and cannot make up norms 'on the spot'. If no norm can be found to obligate the respondent or defendant, for instance, if the public prosecutor cannot prove that the defendant's actions violated a section of the penal code, the prosecutor's case against the respondent or defendant fails. The tribunal needs a legal basis for its decision against the passive party. If none can be found, the active party fails by default. Thus 'a legal tribunal is—and must always be—in the position to determine whether a claim is justified in law'.[16]

There are grounds for disputing that the 'adversarial principle' is a matter of logic. In advisory proceedings there is no-one to fill the roles of applicant or respondent and consequently no-one will 'lose by default'. The General Assembly, for example, may ask the International Court of Justice 'any legal question' (Article 96(1) UN Charter). The problem will also arise where the tribunal is asked to give a declaratory judgment or where a case submitted by *compromis* asks, with Fitzmaurice, ' "which" of the parties is in the right...or which is entitled to exercise certain

[11] Ibid.

[12] Fitzmaurice (1974) above n 6, 102.

[13] Lauterpacht (1958) above n 6, 199.

[14] Ibid, 205.

[15] The existence of such 'general principles' as formal source of international law outside the purview of the applicable law clause in Article 38 ICJ Statute is disputed. See Kelsen (1979) above n 3, 99, 266.

[16] Lauterpacht (1958) above n 6, 199.

rights...—and the answer may well be "neither".'[17] A tribunal, when faced with an alternative, rather than a claim and a defence, has not got before it a 'natural' or 'logical' preference for the legal basis of one of the cases, but has two equal cases to choose from. Lauterpacht counters Fitzmaurice's arguments by presuming that every request, even for a declaratory judgment, may be couched in the form of a claim.[18] This may be so, but tribunals have to face the questions and requests they were asked, not those they could have been asked.[19] Julius Stone questions how the court ascertains whether there is law on the point. He argues that the decision that the claimant's case is unfounded is already a decision, rather than the mere application of the 'adversarial principle', for 'a rule covering the precise circumstances of the instant case'[20] does not exist before the court's decision.

Does the possibility of *non liquet* depend on the 'state' of the law, then? No, and this is because gaps and *non liquet* are different concepts. While *non liquet* is a matter for the procedural rule of a given tribunal, determining gaps is a matter for an ontology of norms.[21] A tribunal may be authorised by the law to 'fill gaps' or to decide *ex aequo et bono*,[22] whereas it may also be prohibited from declaring that there is no law even when there is none. For instance, according to the Napoleonic *Code Civil*, '[t]he judge who shall refuse to judge under pretext of the silence, obscurity, or insufficiency of the law, shall be liable to be proceeded against as guilty of a refusal of justice.'[23]

Having set the concept of *non liquet* aside, we will proceed to the notion of the 'completeness of the law'. This concept has been understood in various ways. For Lauterpacht, completeness stems from the connection between the procedural and the substantive elements of the legal order. He acknowledges that there can be substantive incompleteness of the law, that 'a *lacuna* properly so-called' exists in 'cases in which there is no clear rule of international law in existence'.[24] But in his view a normative order which includes gaps can be called complete as long as tribunals may 'fill' them: 'the principle affirming the completeness of the international legal order...is the positive formulation of the prohibition of *non liquet*'.[25]

[17] Fitzmaurice (1974) above n 6, 106.

[18] Lauterpacht (1958) above n 6, 199 (n 2).

[19] We will return to the issue of the question asked and the answer given in the discussion of *Nuclear Weapons* (Section III); this article is not concerned with *ne ultra petita*.

[20] Stone (1960) above n 6, 134–5.

[21] If norms find an analogous state of Being in validity to entities existing in reality (above n 3), the ontology of norms is concerned with discussing valid ('existing') norms and where no norm covers a situation. On this problem, see further below, Section IV.

[22] ICJ Statute, art 38 (2).

[23] 'Le juge qui refusera de juger, sous prétexte du silence, de l'obscurité ou de l'insuffisance de la loi, pourra être poursuivi comme coupable de déni de justice.' Article 4 Code Civil des Français (Code Napoléon) 1804.

[24] Lauterpacht (1958) above n 6, 198, 204.

[25] Ibid, 199.

Substantive completeness and the negation of the idea of 'gaps' comes from what has been called the 'residual negative principle': what is not expressly prohibited is permitted by law. This maxim is much older than the Lauterpacht–Stone debate; the Permanent Court of International Justice in 1927 pronounced a variant of it in *Lotus*.[26] The implications of such a 'residual' principle are clear. As Stone has argued:

> The 'residual negative principle'... would directly provide such a substantive rule in contentious cases.... [A]ny absence of a legal prohibition would under this principle constitute the *presence of a legal permission*. The 'no-law's land' of *non liquet* would be occupied by *permissive legal rules*.[27]

All the authors discussed in this section—Lauterpacht, Stone, Tammelo and Fitzmaurice—doubt that such a 'residual principle' exists, or at least exists in international law.[28] Are they rallying against the *Lotus dictum* or against Kelsen's position (as discussed in Section II)? The 'residual negative principle' largely remains their undefined enemy.[29]

However, the arguments against the principle depend on its definition. What exactly is the 'residual negative principle'? Is it a norm of international law; is it an implication from positive regulation or even an assumption of legal theory? If it is one of the latter two alternatives, all normative orders would contain this principle and there could be no normative order that did not have it. If it is part of positive international law, its validity as a norm of the relevant normative order must be proved. In this sense, Gerald Fitzmaurice is right when he argues that in a decision arrived at 'on a presumptive or residual basis... the presumptions and residualities involved are still presumptions or residualities *of law*'.[30] Despite the importance of the question, legal literature has remained silent on the character of the residual principle.[31]

The argument that what is not prohibited is necessarily permitted, and that there therefore can be no gaps, is based on a logically bivalent view of normative modality: either prohibition or permission. However, the argument falters because 'the law' simply does not concern itself with all forms of behaviour, in other words, there is 'space devoid of law' (*rechtsfreier Raum*).[32] The sharpening of a pencil, for example, is most likely not directly

[26] *The Case of the S.S. 'Lotus' (France v Turkey)*, Judgment of 7 September 1927, PCIJ Rep Series A No 10, 18. See, however: *Lotus* (1927) ibid, dissenting opinion Loder, 34 and dissenting opinion Nyholm, 60.

[27] Stone (1960) above n 6, 136 (emphasis added).

[28] Eg Lauterpacht (1958) above n 6, 207–8; Stone (1960) above n 6, 129.

[29] Tammelo (1974) above n 6, 2.

[30] Fitzmaurice (1974) above n 6, 101 (emphasis added).

[31] Ilmar Tammelo argues that any such principle will either be a positive norm or has to be interpreted as natural law (Tammelo (1974) above n 6, 8). He finds no evidence in positive international law (Tammelo (1959) above n 6, 201).

[32] Karl Engisch, 'Der rechtsfreie Raum' (1952) 108 *Zeitschrift für die gesamte Staatswissenschaft* 385; Tammelo (1959) above n 6; Heinrich Comes, *Der rechtsfreie Raum. Zur Frage der normativen Grenzen des Rechts* (Duncker und Humblot, Berlin, 1976).

the *actus reus* of any law. Should we now assume, in order to close the legal system, that therefore this behaviour is somehow permitted *by law*? This may sound like unnecessary theoretisation in order to achieve a predetermined outcome, but it is not. In fact, this argument assumes that 'permitted' means the same thing for all authors discussed, which may not be the case.

For Ilmar Tammelo[33] and Julius Stone, the fundamental distinction underpinning the 'residual negative principle' is that between 'open' and 'closed' legal orders. Tammelo first described this important distinction: 'This is the distinction based on the question whether there can be under the particular legal order an absence of law on any matter which can be posed for legal solution.'[34] While this formulation suggests a possibility of *non liquet* or of 'gaps in the law', this possibility in fact depends on whether the system is open or closed. The difference is expressed in terms of 'a judgment in favour of the respondent on the ground that no applicable rule of law... supports the applicant's contention' as against 'a judgment in favour of the respondent on the more positive ground that no rule of law *prohibits* the latter's conduct'.[35] Whereas in the first case the substantive question remains open and does not imply that the respondent's conduct was permitted, in the second case the judgment actually validates his behaviour and closes the substantive issue.[36]

Through a logical deduction of deontic modalities, Tammelo dispenses with the bivalence. He identifies five deontic modes—'obligatory', 'prohibitory', 'licensory', 'permissory' and 'legally neutral'—and establishes their logical relationship.[37] The category of 'legally neutral' is most relevant to the question of gaps. It allows us to distinguish between, for example, being permitted to own a firearm despite a general prohibition of ownership, and being 'permitted' to sharpen a pencil. Tammelo explains the category of 'legally neutral' as follows:

> Where a legal order does not contain any norm specifying how to qualify legally the behavior about which the law in question is silent, obscure, or self-contradictory, one can say that *it has left such matters completely at large*. It has neither "willed"... nor has it "willed not to will" their regulation.[38]

Here is the crux of the matter and here lies the difference between open and closed systems: a legal system that excludes 'legally neutral behaviour' is closed; one that admits it is an open system. In a later paper,

[33] In many ways, Tammelo's argumentation is more sophisticated than that of many others. He follows one of the pioneers of deontic logic (concerned with the effort to apply logic to norms or at least to normative statements), Georg Henrik von Wright. Von Wright, in turn, also stirred Kelsen, in his late phase in thinking, into action about the role of logic in norms. Ultimately, however, Kelsen's approach is fundamentally different from von Wright's or Ota Weinberger's.

[34] Tammelo (1959) above n 6, 188.

[35] Fitzmaurice (1974) above n 6, 108.

[36] Ibid, 108.

[37] Tammelo (1959) above n 6, 194–200.

[38] Ibid, 194 (emphasis added). See also *Kosovo* (2010) above n 4, separate opinion Simma, para 9.

which expands the deontic functors to six (not including 'legally neutral'), Tammelo defines the distinction in slightly different terms. (*a*) In closed systems the relationship between 'obligatory' and 'dispensory' (the right to refrain from doing something), on the one hand, and 'prohibitory' and 'permissory', on the other hand is a dichotomic exclusion (contravalence or alternation: '#'). Thus, behaviour is, for example, either prohibited or permitted, but cannot be anything else; this constitutes the 'residual negative principle' or 'hermeneutic normative principle'. (*b*) In open legal systems, the above relations are one of simple exclusion (contrajunction or disjunction: '∨'). That means that while an obligation to do something and a right not to do something contradict, it is not the case that there must exist either the obligation or the right. A third possibility can exist only in an open system: the behaviour can be 'normatively neutral', which is the conjunction of the negation of obligation (O) and the negation of prohibition (H) of a given behaviour p: $(\neg Op \wedge \neg Hp)$. It is also a negated alternation of the right to do something (P) and the right to refrain from doing something (D) of the behaviour p: $\neg(Pp \# Dp)$.[39] This is Tammelo's attempt to couch the 'non-willed' in logical terms. Stone puts it in more traditional terms:

> [T]here may be conduct which does not fall within any of the modalities which characterise a closed system, that is, which may be neither prohibited *by a norm*, nor made obligatory *by a norm*, nor permitted *by a norm*. There may be, in short, the category of conduct . . . which is *neither* prohibited, *nor* required, *nor* permitted by the norms. There may be conduct, that is, about which the norms say nothing at all.[40]

This description of the issue helps, first, better to discern the character of gaps and, second, to detect an essential error in the idea of gaps *in law*, namely the supposition of a normatively neutral deontic mode.

The four or six deontic modes which Tammelo describes are willed, which makes them, in his terms, 'deontic actualities or, in other words, the field of positive law'.[41] Kelsen saw positive norms as the 'sense of an act of will',[42] and Tammelo admits that if only 'deontic actualities' are accepted, the legal order is closed. In an open order, the legally neutral behaviour is a 'deontic mere-possibility'. In other words it is not the sense of an act of will—not a positive, but a fictional norm—a charge that can be levelled against Kelsen's negative legal regulation as well (Section II). There cannot be absence of norms *within* a normative order, because a normative order can consist only of norms. Only if a further normative order (natural law?) is superimposed upon the positive order can we

[39] Tammelo (1974) above n 6, 7–8.
[40] Stone (1968) above n 6, 308–9.
[41] Tammelo (1959) above n 6, 200.
[42] Kelsen (1979) above n 3, 4.

classify *lacunae* as relating to 'situations which this legal order *ought to govern*'.[43] We can refer to any behaviour that could be made the object of norms, and has not been made the object of norms, as gaps—and that means that any behaviour not so governed is a gap (like the sharpening of a pencil), yet it cannot be called a gap *within* the legal order.

II. Kelsen's Negative Legal Regulation

The discussion above has repercussions for our reading of Kelsen's arguments. Kelsen's name is associated with the 'residual negative principle', even though he did not support it. Critics tend to mention but do not engage with Kelsen's ideas on this point, which may be the cause of the confusion as to how to read 'Kelsen on Gaps'. This section will elaborate on his view of gaps in order to lay the foundation for a slightly different solution (Section IV).

There is no evidence, however, that Hans Kelsen—unlike Lauterpacht or any of the participants in the debate set out above—saw normative orders as necessarily and substantially complete. As early as 1934, he denied the existence of gaps in the law:

> Real gaps do not exist in the sense that it would [somehow] not be possible to solve a legal dispute in accordance with the valid norms, because the law . . . cannot not be applied due to a lack of rules.[44]

While it may seem that Kelsen here confuses the adversarial principle[45] and the substantial completeness of the law, his argument in fact goes beyond the adversarial principle. We can argue that even if the adversarial principle were eliminated from Kelsenian theory, the law would still necessarily be complete. The following discussion will proceed on the assumption that the adversarial principle is not relevant for our purposes.

The crucial concept of Kelsen's argument is 'negative legal regulation' ('negative rechtliche Regelung'). In his *Allgemeine Theorie der Normen* (1979) Kelsen explains:

[43] Tammelo (1959) above n 6, 192. regarding *non liquet* see also: Daniel Bodansky, '*Non liquet* and the Incompleteness of International Law' in Laurence Boisson de Charzournes and Phillipe Sands (eds) *International Law, the International Court of Justice and Nuclear Weapons* (Cambridge University Press, Cambridge, 1999) 153, 157.

[44] '[E]chte Lücken in dem Sinne, daß ein Rechtsstreit gemäß den geltenden Normen nicht entscheidbar wäre, weil das Gesetz . . . mangels einer auf diesen Fall beziehbaren Vorschrift nicht angewendet werden kann, gibt es nicht.' Hans Kelsen, 'Zur Theorie der Interpretation' (1934) 8 *Revue internationale de la théorie de droit* 9, reprinted in Hans Klecatsky, René Marcić and Herbert Schambeck (eds) *Die Wiener rechtstheoretische Schule. Ausgewählte Schriften von Hans Kelsen, Adolf Julius Merkl, Alfred Verdross* (Europa, Vienna, 1968) 1363, 1369. All translations are by the present author. The original versions are given in the footnotes and translations in the main text.

[45] Clear support for the adversarial principle can be found *inter alia* in: Kelsen (1934b) above n 44, 1369–70 and Hans Kelsen, *Reine Rechtslehre* (2nd edn, Franz Deuticke, Vienna, 1960) 251.

The preceding discussion named "prescription", "positive permission" and "empowerment" of a certain behaviour as functions of a legal norm. We did not mention behaviour which is negatively permitted. This behaviour is not the object of a legal norm, because a legal norm neither obligates nor prohibits it. Yet such a negatively permitted behaviour can be regarded as *legal regulation*.... By thus distinguishing positive and negative legal regulation of human behaviour by the legal order, any behaviour of a human subject to a legal order can be regarded as... "legally regulated". Thus in this sense we can speak of the *completeness of the legal order*. There can be no "gaps" in the law, if "gaps" are understood in the sense that a certain human behaviour is not legally regulated and that the law cannot be applied to that behaviour.[46]

Even though Kelsen argues that there can be no 'gaps' in the law, he does not construct a bivalent theory of *tertium non datur*, at least not in a certain sense, for his 'negative legal regulation' is close to Stone's concept. Behaviour which is 'not the object of a legal norm'[47] sounds very much like Tammelo's 'legally neutral behaviour', though differences remain. Kelsen's 'negative legal regulation' is also different from Stone's 'residual negative principle'. (Differences between orthodox interpretations of the *Lotus dictum*[48] and Kelsen's own are also caused by the application of the concept of 'residual negative principle'.) For Stone, the residual principle is like a (hierarchically superior) norm that creates positive legal permission in instances where no positive legal prohibition can be found. Kelsen's negative legal regulation, however, is neither a positive norm of a given legal system[49] nor does it convert a legal non-entity into a positive permission.

When it comes to fleshing out Kelsen's negative legal regulation, we can read his work in two ways. On the first reading, Kelsen's theory goes further than a mere *a contrario* argument. Some of Kelsen's writings support this reading. For instance, in *Principles of International Law* (1952) Kelsen states that there exists a 'fundamental principle that what is not legally forbidden to the subjects of the law is legally permitted to

[46] 'Im Vorhergehenden wurden als normative Rechtsfunktionen: Gebieten, positives Erlauben und Ermächtigen eines bestimmten Verhaltens, nicht aber negatives Erlauben eines Verhaltens bezeichnet, das keinen Gegenstand einer Rechtsnorm, weil von einer Rechtsnorm weder geboten noch verboten ist. Unterscheidet man in diesem Sinne eine positive und eine negative Regelung menschlichen Verhaltens durch die Rechtsordnung, ist jedes Verhalten eines Menschen, der unter einer Rechtsordnung steht...rechtlich geregelt. Dann kann man—in diesem Sinne—von einer *Geschlossenheit der Rechtsordnung* sprechen. Dann kann es keine 'Lücken' im Recht geben, sofern man darunter versteht, daß ein bestimmtes menschliches Verhalten rechtlich nicht geregelt ist und daher das geltende Recht nicht auf dieses Verhalten angewendet werden kann.' Kelsen (1979) above n 3, 106.

[47] 'Gegenstand keiner Rechtsnorm' Kelsen (1979) above n 3, 106.

[48] See also *Kosovo* (2010) above n 4, declaration Simma, para 8: 'The Court's reading of the General Assembly's question and its reasoning, leaping as it does straight from the lack of a prohibition to permissibility, is a straightforward application of the so-called *Lotus* principle.'

[49] Law-makers are free to specifically create such a norm in a particular legal order.

them'.[50] In the second edition of his *Reine Rechtslehre* (1960), Kelsen opines unambiguously that certain behaviour is 'regulated in such a way that... that behaviour is legally not prohibited and thus permitted',[51] which is an equation of 'not prohibited' and 'permitted'. This passage accords with L F E Goldie's interpretation of a bivalent Kelsenian theory.[52] Elsewhere, Kelsen writes that the freedom that comes from behaviour not being the object of a legal norm means that we are in this case is '*legally* free'.[53] As to the ontological status of this notion, he argues that '[t]he legal order not only contains a norm that one ought to behave in a certain way, but also the norm: whatever one is not under a duty, one is free to do or omit to do.'[54] On this first reading Kelsen implies a *norm* of freedom of action and all behaviour that is not a matter for positive regulation is inherently for 'negative regulation'. This means that somehow (for instance by way of a logical deduction) the freedom has already been enacted and permission can be implied from the absence of prohibition. This implies, however, that positive normative orders also consist of things other than positive norms. It is unlikely that Hans Kelsen would contradict the positivism of the Pure Theory of Law and accept non-positive norms within a positive normative order (except for the *Grundnorm*, which serves a very specific purpose as condition for the possibility of cognition).

On a second rating, however, we are only drawing inferences from a given architecture of positive regulation. Using the analogy of a fisherman's net, Kelsen argues that the net defines the holes, and that holes constitute 'non-net', rather than the net being 'non-hole'. 'When a human being is free,... it is *free only within the limits set by legal norms*,... which constitute a positive regulation of its behaviour.'[55] 'Negative freedom' is the absence of norms as defined by the sum-total of positive norms, not the creation of positive freedom (as permission) because of the absence of positive norms of prohibition or obligation. This train of thought is also evident in the following passage: '*By obligating humans* to behave in a certain way, *the legal order ensures freedom* beyond legal obligations.'[56]

[50] Hans Kelsen, *Principles of international law* (Rinehart & Company, New York, 1952) 306.

[51] 'dadurch geregelt, daß... dieses Verhalten rechtlich nicht verboten und in diesem Sinne erlaubt ist' Kelsen (1960) above n 45, 251.

[52] Goldie (1958) above n 6, 224.

[53] '*von Rechts wegen* frei' Kelsen (1979) above n 3, 106.

[54] 'Die Rechtsordnung enthält nicht nur den Satz, daß man zu einem bestimmten Verhalten verpflichtet ist..., sondern auch den Satz: wozu man nicht verpflichtet ist, das zu tun oder zu lassen ist man frei.' Kelsen (1934b) above n 44, 1269–70.

[55] 'Wenn ein Mensch frei ist,... ist er *frei nur innerhalb der Grenzen, die ihm durch Rechtsnormen gezogen sind*,... die also sein Verhalten positiv regeln.' Kelsen (1979) above n 3, 106 (emphasis added).

[56] 'Denn *indem* [*die Rechtsordnung*] die Menschen zu einem ganz bestimmten Verhalten *verpflichtet, gewährleistet sie* jenseits dieser Rechtspflichten *die Freiheit*.' Kelsen (1934b) above n 44, 1369 (emphasis added).

The Permanent Court may have meant no more than this when it held in *Lotus* that, '[r]estrictions upon the independence of States cannot therefore be presumed.'[57] Judge Nyholm saw this sentence in the conventional light—that 'over and above positive international law, there is a kind of international law'[58] constituting the 'residual negative principle'. But strip away the knee-jerk reaction upon hearing the phrase 'independence of states', look at the final sentence in the light of the whole paragraph—what do we get? We have a restatement of the very idea of positive law: that only positive law is positive law and that we simply cannot presume law ('restrictions') to be valid if their validity cannot be proven by regress to its sources. 'Restrictions' are only applicable if they are positive law of the normative system 'international law'. If there is no law, there is no law. No more than this was meant.[59] The second reading of Kelsen's theory seems the preferable one because it is more consistent with his concept of a Pure Theory of Law and because, on account of its emphasis on 'existence' (validity) of positive norms, we do not have to invent regulation where there is none.

Finally, the 'technical gap' presents its own unique problems. What happens if the absence of regulation renders the law useless and inapplicable?[60] Kelsen gives the following example:

> A statute prescribes *inter alia* that a collegiate organ, in order to function, needs to be convened by its chairman, but also prescribes that it has to elect its chairman. If this rule cannot be read to mean that the organ may convene through any arbitrary procedure in case there is no chairman, but only that even in this case the collegiate organ may be convened only by its chairman, then the collegiate organ cannot function lawfully, that is in accordance with its statute.[61]

[57] *Lotus* (1927) above n 26, 18.

[58] Ibid, dissenting opinion Nyholm, 63.

[59] Cf Jörg Kammerhofer, 'Uncertainty in the Formal Sources of International Law: Customary International Law and Some of its Problems' (2004) 15 *European Journal of International Law* 523, 550–1. Ole Spierman has pointed out that there are two conjunct items in the *dictum*. Not only is there a presumption of proof of the non-existence of 'rules', but the 'residual principle' is the consequence of this presumption: if there are no rules, freedom of action ensues (Ole Spiermann, '*Lotus* and the Double Structure of International Legal Argument' in Laurence Boisson de Charzournes and Phillipe Sands (eds) *International Law, the International Court of Justice and Nuclear Weapons* (Cambridge University Press, Cambridge, 1999) 131, 132–4). While one may question a contingent connection between 'no rule' and 'freedom', which Kelsen has also made, Spierman makes an important point regarding the phenomenon of uncertainty—the question of proof of the 'existence' (validity) of a norm is not the same as the question of the 'existence' of a norm.

[60] According to Ernst Zitelmann only these are the 'real gaps'. Zitelmann (1903) above n 5, 27.

[61] 'Ein Gesetz bestimmt unter anderem, daß ein Kollegium, um tätig zu sein, durch seinen Vorsitzenden einberufen werden muß, zugleich aber, daß es seinen Vorsitzenden selbst zu wählen hat. Läßt sich dieser Norm nicht der Sinn abgewinnen, daß, falls kein Vorsitzender vorhanden ist, jede beliebige Art des Zusammentritts gesetzmäßig ist, sondern nur der Sinn, daß auch in diesem Falle das Kollegium von seinem Vorsitzenden einberufen werden soll, dann kann dieses Kollegium auf gesetzmäßige Weise, das heißt: in Anwendung des Gesetzes, nicht funktionieren.' Kelsen (1934b) above n 44, 1371.

Consistency can require tough decisions, as Kelsen's demonstrates when he continues the example:

> Even this does not constitute a 'gap'. The statute wants the collegiate organ to be convened by its chairman, even if it does not have one.... The statute requires something that is simply nonsensical. But since statutes are man-made, this possibility is not to be ruled out. A norm can also have a nonsensical content.[62]

This line of reasoning leads Kelsen in the end to deny the existence of any sort of 'gaps' and even to claim their theoretical impossibility. Christoph Kletzer is correct to point out that for Kelsen (on a legal view), there can be no 'space devoid of law' *within law*.[63] The legal view means looking at the law only. To use the analogy of the net again, as legal scholars we must look at only the net and ignore the holes in-between, because these are not the object of our study. Just as the fisherman must concentrate on mending the net, rather than admire the view of the sea-front through the holes in the mesh, legal scholars must study the norms that actually make up the legal system, not the behaviour that could be—but is not—the object of legal norms. A perspective that focuses on the law as body of norms unmasks those who attempt to fill gaps as law-makers who super-ordinate external norms (for instance personal value preferences) on positive norms. A norm is only a claim to be observed and no claim is *a priori* better than the other; no value is absolute. Claims to the contrary are but another level of claims. Kletzer is right in arguing that for Kelsen 'not gaps are the problem of legal scholarship but the *concept* of "gaps"' is.[64]

III. *Nuclear Weapons* and the Applied Theory of Gaps

The 8 July 1996 advisory opinion in *Legality of the Threat or Use of Nuclear Weapons* and the judges' individual opinions[65] serve as a case study for testing the arguments of legal theory and international legal scholarship on the problem of gaps, understood as a 'missing' part of the

[62] 'Aber auch hier liegt keine "Lücke" vor. Denn das Gesetz will ja, daß das Kollegium, auch wenn es keinen Vorsitzenden hat, von diesem einberufen werden soll.... Das Gesetz bestimmt hier eben etwas unsinniges. Das ist, da Gesetze Menschenwerk sind, nicht ausgeschlossen. Eine Norm kann auch einen sinnlosen Inhalt haben.' Ibid, 1371–2.

[63] Christoph Kletzer, 'Das Goldene Zeitalter der Sicherheit: Hersch Lauterpacht und der Modernismus' in Robert Walter, Clemens Jabloner and Klaus Zeleny (eds) *Hans Kelsen und das Völkerrecht. Ergebnisse eines internationalen Symposiums in Wien (1.–2. April 2004)* (Manz, Vienna, 2004) 223, 228.

[64] 'nicht die Lücke ist das Problem der Rechtswissenschaft, sondern der *Begriff der Lücke*.' Ibid, 229.

[65] *Nuclear Weapons* (1996) above n 4.

totality of norms within a normative order. We will seek to extract specific information as to how the Court and the individual judges argued about the nature of 'gaps'. The subject-matter of the question asked of the Court—the legality of the threat or use of nuclear weapons—will not be the focus of this section. The case study confronts us, again, with a mistaken focus on *non liquet*, which was not the real problem that the Court faced. However, in *Nuclear Weapons* the focus on *non liquet* as the 'procedural' side of the problem of gaps is more understandable than in scholarly debate (Section I), where a predilection for the judicial function could be criticised as losing its way in procedure, rather than staying with the substance. Moreover, the discussion of *non liquet* can, again, be instructive for understanding the issue of gaps.

A. What did the opinion return as answer?

What exactly did the Opinion of 8 July 1996 say? Did the Court really pronounce a *non liquet*? Did it really find a *lacuna* in the substantive law?

(*a*) The Court was asked the following question by the General Assembly: 'Is the threat or use of nuclear weapons in any circumstance permitted under international law?'[66] The Court was faced with *this* question—and the very framing of the question not only gave rise to debates in the proceedings, but naturally also influenced what the Court said in the *dispositif*. The Assembly asked whether the threat or use of this type of weapon was *permitted* under international law, not whether it was *prohibited*. The Court held that the framing of the question was irrelevant and proceeded to tackle a different problem: it set out 'to determine the legality or illegality of the threat or use of nuclear weapons'.[67]

Why is there a difference between the General Assembly's question and the task the Court set itself? If we believe that norms can have differing normative functions (as mentioned above, for instance prohibition, permission or derogation),[68] the Court would have had to prove, had it simply answered the question given to it, the validity of a norm of international law *permitting* the use of nuclear weapons, hence a positive permission, rather than the absence of a positive norm, hence a 'negative' or 'weak' permission. No *non liquet* could have resulted from an answer to this question, because if the Court had not found such a positive norm, it would have answered 'no', irrespective of whether there was a positive prohibition or a gap.

[66] A/RES/49/75 (Section K).

[67] *Nuclear Weapons* (1996) above n 4, 238 (para 20).

[68] Dekker and Werner mention Atienza and Manero's reductionism, where all other normative functions are reducible to prohibitions. Ige F Dekker and Wouter G Werner, 'The Completeness of International Law and Hamlet's Dilemma: Non Liquet, the Nuclear Weapons Case and Legal Theory' (1999) 68 *Nordic Journal of International Law* 225, 238; citing: Manuel Atienza, Juan Ruiz Manero, *A Theory of Legal Sentences* (Kluwer, Dordrecht, 1998).

As it was, the Court set itself a different question, namely to determine the 'legality or illegality' of the issue under consideration. This was an ambiguous task. On the one hand, the Court could have argued that it had a bivalent choice of proving a positive permission ('legality') or a positive prohibition or contrary obligation ('illegality'). In that case, finding an absence of norms would mean that it could not answer the question and its only finding would be '*non liquet*'! On the other hand, the Court could have argued (and this would have been more convincing) that it had to find that 'threat or use of nuclear weapons' either violates a norm of international law (a prohibition or contrary obligation) or that it does not—because it is expressly permitted despite a prohibition,[69] or because the *actus reus* is not the object of a norm (negative permission). Had it adopted the latter approach, the Court could always have returned an answer, always providing, of course, that it had no problems in cognising international law.[70]

In the *Kosovo* case it was also argued before the Court that the question—'Is the unilateral declaration of independence by the Provisional Institutions of Self-Government of Kosovo in accordance with international law?'[71]—skirted the real issue, namely the legal status of Kosovo. The Court recalled, unlike in *Nuclear Weapons*, its consideration in *WHO–Egypt* that it was entitled to 'ascertain what are the legal questions really in issue in questions formulated in a request'.[72] However, the Court, somewhat surprisingly, did not see a 'reason to reformulate the scope of the question'[73] to include, for example, the legal status of Kosovo after the declaration of independence.[74] Yet—as in *Nuclear Weapons*—the ICJ had no compunction to reverse the deontic modality (perhaps due to the Court's orthodox reading of the *Lotus dictum*):

> [T]he General Assembly has asked whether the declaration of independence was "*in accordance with*" international law. The answer to that question turns on whether or not the applicable international law *prohibited* the declaration of independence.[75]

(*b*) The formulation of the question indirectly influences an assessment of the Opinion in another respect. In *Nuclear Weapons*, the Court distinguished between an 'as such' prohibition (or permission) of 'threat or use of nuclear weapons' and what one could call a 'material prohibition' in a preliminary approximation. In paragraphs 51–73 it purported to look for

[69] Dekker (1999) above n 68, 238.

[70] Bodansky (1999) above n 43, 154.

[71] A/RES/63/3.

[72] *Interpretation of the Agreement of 25 March 1951 between the WHO and Egypt*, advisory opinion of 20 December 1980, [1980] ICJ Rep 73, 88 (para 35).

[73] *Kosovo* (2010) above n 4, para 51.

[74] Ibid, para 56.

[75] Ibid (emphasis added).

an 'as such' prohibition in conventional or customary international law, whereas the rest of the *motifs* deal with finding a 'material prohibition'. As the *dispositif* concluded in paragraph 105(2)(A) and (B), the search for an 'as such' prohibition is fruitless:

There is in neither customary nor conventional international law *any specific authorization* of the threat or use of nuclear weapons;... There is in neither customary nor conventional international law *any comprehensive and universal prohibition* of the threat or use of nuclear weapons as such;...[76]

The difference between the first and second types of prohibition is categorical. The 'as such' prohibition is one where the relevant behaviour (in our case: 'threat or use of nuclear weapons') is made the *actus reus* (*Tatbestand*) of a prohibition. The behaviour itself is prohibited (as such), irrespective of the consequences of the behaviour. In a 'material prohibition' the behaviour in this case can be subsumed to a prohibition of a certain result. The Court focussed on the norms of international humanitarian law in an attempt to ascertain whether the factual occurrence 'threat or use of nuclear weapons' would, for example, violate the prohibition of 'unnecessary suffering' or the obligation to limit attacks to military objectives.[77]

The Court's distinction is also between the prohibition of a specific type of behaviour and the prohibition of certain consequences or results (*Verhaltensunrecht* and *Erfolgsunrecht*). Taking an example from municipal law, road traffic acts typically prohibit exceeding the speed limit irrespective of the consequences. Even if driving 70 kph in a built-up area in Austria harms no-one (has no consequences), the driver has still violated s. 20(2) of the Austrian Road Traffic Act,[78] because its *actus reus* is 'driving faster than 50 kph'. Penal codes, on the other hand, may punish 'reckless endangerment' by specifying that a set of consequences like 'endangerment of the public' is prohibited.[79] All acts that endanger the public qualify; theoretically, even the sharpening a pencil could be 'reckless endangerment'. In this case, a certain behaviour is a factual occurrence that may create the prohibited consequence.

(*c*) The Court chose to include both kinds of prohibition, because the General Assembly had asked whether a specific conduct is permitted 'in any circumstance'. Had the Court found an 'as such' prohibition, the factual occurrence of 'threat or use of nuclear weapons' would by definition have fulfilled the prohibition of 'threat or use of nuclear weapons'. However, in answering the question by reference to whether a specific set

[76] *Nuclear Weapons* (1996) above n 4, 266 (para 105(2)(A),(B)) (emphasis added).

[77] Stefan Oeter, 'Methods and Means of Combat' in Dieter Fleck (ed) *The Handbook of Humanitarian Law in Armed Conflicts* (Oxford University Press, Oxford, 1995) 105, 153.

[78] § 20 Abs 2 Straßenverkehrsordnung 1960, BGBl 1960/159 idF BGBl I 2005/52.

[79] Eg § 177 Strafgesetzbuch 1975, BGBl 1974/69 [Austrian Penal Code 1975].

of circumstances is covered by any sort of prohibition in international law, the Court had a far greater problem. The Court cannot go through every possible set of facts that could be called 'threat or use of nuclear weapons'. It complained 'that none of the States advocating the legality of the use of nuclear weapons under certain circumstances... ha[d] indicated what... would be the precise circumstances justifying such use'.[80] Just as the discharge of a firearm may be legal at one time and place, but 'reckless endangerment' at another time and place, the Court considered that it could not determine *a priori* when the threat or use of nuclear weapons would be legal or illegal. Such research would result in an infinite list of possible circumstances.[81] The ICJ could not have written an advisory opinion that reflects all possible combinations. Even if, as the Court points out, the threat or use of nuclear weapons 'in fact seems scarcely reconcilable with respect for'[82] the requirements of humanitarian law, this is a categorically different statement than that the use of nuclear weapons 'could never be compatible with the principles and rules of humanitarian law'.[83] Against this background, the Court's answer, in paragraph 105(2)(E), is clear:

> It follows from the above-mentioned requirements that the threat or use of nuclear weapons *would generally be contrary* to the rules of international law applicable in armed conflict, and in particular the principles and rules of humanitarian law;... However, in view of the current state of international law, and of the elements of fact at its disposal, the Court *cannot conclude definitively* whether the threat or use of nuclear weapons would be lawful or unlawful [*in certain circumstances*].[84]

(*d*) What is, then, the combined return of subparagraphs A, B and E of paragraph 105(2)? Is it a *non liquet*? Does the International Court of Justice believe that there can be gaps in international law or that there is a gap relative to the behaviour specified in the Assembly's question? Insofar as the Court denied the existence of a certain norm referring to a certain type of behaviour we must conclude—at least as regards general norms—that the combined force of paragraph 105(2)(A) and (B) is that it believes there can be gaps. With respect to the 'as such' prohibition, the Court denied the existence of either a positive prohibition or a positive permission to use nuclear weapons. To the extent that there is a gap when the behaviour in question does not form the *actus reus* of a norm, the Court thus found a gap: the legal system 'international law' does not contain such a norm. Had the question to the Court—as posed by the General

[80] *Nuclear Weapons* (1996) above n 4, 262 (para 94).
[81] Ibid, dissenting opinion Schwebel, 321–2. Bodansky (1999) above n 43, 153.
[82] Ibid, 263 (para 96).
[83] Ibid, 262 (para 92).
[84] Ibid, 266 (para 105(2)(E)) (emphasis added).

Assembly or as it posed itself—indeed merely been whether international law contained a norm on the 'threat or use of nuclear weapons', the Court would have been justified in finding this 'gap' and pronouncing a *non liquet*.

However, the question the Assembly asked, and the task the ICJ set itself, was wider. The question was whether the behaviour 'threat or use of nuclear weapons' was 'permitted' (GA) or 'legal or illegal' (ICJ) under 'international law'. This is a question of matching the factual behaviour to a wide variety of norms of international law (this matching is hereinafter referred to as 'subsumption'), including the UN Charter, international environmental law, human rights law and humanitarian law. Subsuming a given set of facts under a variety of norms is a different matter from finding an 'as such' norm in international law. There is plenty of law, applicable norms are not lacking, only the form of reference to the behaviour is changed. The Court did not think there was a gap and it expressly acknowledged the applicability of humanitarian law to the use of nuclear weapons—'the principles and rules of humanitarian law apply to nuclear weapons'.[85] The Court's finding of 'indeterminacy'[86] in paragraph 105(2)(E) (and in paragraph 97) is not the admission of a gap in the totality of norms. The Court only admits to the epistemological problems of fully cognising valid law. If such an admission of the impossibility of conducting a final subsumption in light of the infinity of possible circumstances is a *non liquet*, then the Court did pronounce a *non liquet*. However, it did not do so for a lack of norms and it did not do so because of a 'gap in the law'. The references of commentators to the 'residual negative principle'[87] are misguided at least in respect to paragraph 105(2)(E), because epistemological uncertainty is not the same as the creation or implication of a permission.

B. *Individual opinions and gaps*

True to tradition, the Court in its Opinion kept its theoretical cards close to its chest. Its function is to decide a case or answer a question put to it, not to engage in scholarly arguments, which is a reasonable interpretation of the judicial function. We will have to extract the Court's theoretical presuppositions from hints in the text of the judgments or opinions, which is a form of interpretation that runs the risks of speculation.

This is different, however, for the individual opinions appended; they pay for their freedom to engage in scholarly debate by not being part of the individual norm that is the judgment, in the case of an advisory opinion by not being considered part of the answer to the (United Nations)

[85] Ibid, 260 (para 87).
[86] Spiermann (1999) above n 59, 135.
[87] Ibid, 135–6.

organ. But theirs is a privileged position nonetheless. These judges are the first and best-placed commentators upon the Court's decisions, their opinions may help explain what the Court argued. However, their opinions are also personal opinions of members of a collective organ and therefore have the potential to be highly destructive of that organ's efforts.[88]

This section will look at how the individual judges saw the issue of 'gaps'. While the majority of the judges' efforts were quite understandably directed towards the specific subject-matter of the opinion—nuclear weapons—and while many of the arguments deal with our, more general, topic in the specific environment the General Assembly's question provides, we can extract some additional arguments.

(*a*) *Distinguishing* Lotus? Judge Guillaume expressly affirmed the relevance of *Lotus* for the present case, where—he argued—the Court itself had recognised the existence of the same principle.[89] '[T]he illegality of the use of certain weapons as such does not result from an absence of authorization but, on the contrary, is formulated in terms of prohibition.'[90] President Bedjaoui and Judges Shahabuddeen and Weeramantry, however, distinguished the *Lotus dictum*[91] from the present case.[92] Bedjaoui argued that the judgment in the *Lotus* case reflected '*l'air du temps*' and was an expression of a less developed international society 'governed by an international law of strict coexistence.'[93] For Shahabuddeen, *Lotus* can be distinguished on the basis that the discussion of 'act[s] which could bring civilization to an end and annihilate mankind' meant that the *Lotus dictum* is in effect reversed for *Nuclear Weapons*: states have 'no right to do such an act unless the act is one which is authorized under international law'.[94] Contrary to these historical, categorical and moralist distinctions, Weeramatry held that *Lotus* was decided on the basis of a different *lex specialis*. 'This', he stated, referring to the collision of 2 August 1926, 'was a situation far removed from that to which the humanitarian laws of war apply.'[95] For him the distinction between 'law of peace' and 'law of war' (as then commonly used) was translated into a distinction between 'ordinary' international law and international humanitarian law. For him the 'Martens clause' is the crucial distinction in law, because it 'expressly provides that its humanitarian principles would apply "in

[88] See Jörg Kammerhofer, 'Oil's Well That Ends Well? Critical Comments on the Merits Judgment in the *Oil Platforms* Case' (2004) 17 *Leiden Journal of International Law* 695, 716.

[89] *Nuclear Weapons* (1996) above n 4, separate opinion Guillaume, 288 (para 3), 292 (para 11).

[90] Ibid, 247 (para 52).

[91] 'Restrictions upon the independence of States cannot therefore be presumed.' *Lotus* (1927) above n 26, 18; see Section I.

[92] *Nuclear Weapons* (1996) above n 4, declaration Bedjaoui, 270–1 (paras 12–14), dissenting opinion Shahabuddeen, 394–7, dissenting opinion Weeramantry, 495–6.

[93] Ibid, declaration Bedjaoui, 270 (para 12).

[94] Ibid, dissenting opinion Shahabuddeen, 394.

[95] Ibid, dissenting opinion Weeramantry, 495.

cases not included in the Regulations adopted by them"'.[96] Again, the result is a reversal of the presumptive freedom of states, for 'beyond the domain of express prohibitions, there lies the domain of the general principles of humanitarian law',[97] which seem to provide non-explicit prohibitions.

But the question remains whether *Lotus* can be distinguished at all. It certainly cannot be distinguished in the technical sense employed by common lawyers, for international law is not common law and the International Court of Justice is not bound by its previous decisions (much less by the decisions of other tribunals). It can, however, also not be distinguished in a more substantive sense. In distinguishing, Bedjadoui and others assumed that the principle stated in the *Lotus dictum* is a norm of international law. But that is the question, because for some the Permanent Court stated nothing else than the 'residual negative principle'.

(*b*) *Debating* Lotus. What did the judges think the *Lotus dictum* represented and how did they evaluate the construct? As has been argued above, the crucial distinction is whether 'whatever is not prohibited is permitted' is seen as a positive norm or as a necessary conclusion of the construction of any normative order.[98] In contrast, Ole Spiermann distinguishes between 'residual principles' and 'presumptions'. Residual principles 'attach consequences to the non-existence of rules or principles of international law in a given matter',[99] while 'a presumption is the action of supposing something to exist or to be true.'[100] While residual principles require an ontological absence to be proven, presumptions overcome epistemological uncertainty regarding the 'existence' of norms by presupposing their validity. In this respect, Spiermann's distinction fits in with Daniel Bodansky's distinction between ontological and epistemological insufficiency in the law.[101] One might ask, however, whether the 'non-existence of rules or principles' would not necessarily include Spiermann's 'residual principle'. In other words, would the existence of the 'residual principle'—as norm—not by definition mean that there was always one 'rule or principle' in existence, namely the 'residual principle' itself and that it could not apply because of a logical circle?

The judges generally did not justify their standpoint on the existence of some sort of 'residual negative principle'. Legal scholars have ascribed Judge Guillaume's acceptance of such a principle to the principle's 'necessary truth',[102] but a better view may be to see it as a logical extension of his

96 Ibid.
97 Ibid, 493.
98 Similarly: Bodansky (1999) above n 43, 162.
99 Spiermann (1999) above n 59, 132.
100 Ibid, 133.
101 Bodansky (1999) above n 43, 154.
102 Ibid, 162.

support for the orthodox interpretation of the *Lotus dictum*, thus not prejudging the character of the 'residual negative principle'.[103] For Vice-President Schwebel the matter was so clear that he relegated to the introduction his observation that, 'the practice of States does not debar, *and to that extent supports*, the legality of the threat or use of nuclear weapons in certain circumstances.'[104] As with Guillaume's acceptance, Bedjaoui's rejection of the principle is consistent with his distinction of *Lotus*.[105] Where the *Lotus dictum* is not 'applicable law', there is no need to justify its rejection.

The matter is even more complicated with the dissents of Judges Shahabuddeen, Weeramantry and Koroma, although their discussions are for theoretical purposes not significantly more fruitful. While Shahabuddeen's arguments were clear, he did not, *pace* Dekker and Werner, construct a residual principle along the lines of 'what is not expressly authorised is prohibited'.[106] All three judges were in opposition to the Court's perceived finding of no law and thus of an application of the *Lotus dictum*. Their positions were ultimately based on their opinion that positive law contains some form of general prohibition of the threat or use of nuclear weapons (even if not 'as such'). Hence they advocated a specific positive norm, rather than some form of 'reverse-*Lotus* principle'.[107] However, Shahabudeen and Weeramantry seemed not to have based their position on natural law either, for if that were not the case they would have found it more difficult to come to the same conclusions. Holding that '[b]lack-letter formulations have their value, but by no stretch of the imagination can they represent the totality of the law'[108]—and thus having that 'totality' transcend the positive law—will mean fewer problems in proving a point of law, because one will be in a position to transform that 'totality' simply by presupposing fictional law in addition to positive law.

In the 2010 *Kosovo* opinion, Judge Simma delivered a remarkable declaration in which he denounced the Court's decision as reflecting 'an old, tired view of international law ... famously expressed in the "*Lotus*" Judgment',[109] which 'equate[s] the absence of a prohibition with the existence of a permissive rule'.[110] Simma correctly identified the orthodox reading as 'extremely consensualist'[111] and as 'redolent of nineteenth-century positivism'[112]—but did not contemplate a more differentiated

[103] This is apparent when one takes into account the whole argumentation. *Nuclear Weapons* (1996) above n 4, separate opinion Guillaume, 291–2 (paras 9–11).

[104] *Nuclear Weapons* (1996) above n 4, dissenting opinion Schwebel, 311 (emphasis added).

[105] Ibid, declaration Bedjaoui, 270–2 (paras 11–18).

[106] Dekker (1999) above n 68, 244–5.

[107] *Nuclear Weapons* (1996) above n 4, dissenting opinion Shahabuddeen, 397–414, dissenting opinion Weeramantry at 493, dissenting opinion Koroma, 575.

[108] Ibid, dissenting opinion Weeramantry, 494.

[109] *Kosovo* (2010) above n 4, declaration Simma, para 2.

[110] Ibid, para 3.

[111] Ibid.

[112] Ibid, para 8.

reading of the *Lotus dictum* (Section I) which modern and more theoretically informed forms of positivism might favour. In contradistinction to the judges in *Nuclear Weapons* and in a manner reminiscent of the line of argument developed by Tammelo and adopted in Section IV, Simma envisaged 'the possibility that international law can be neutral or deliberately silent on the international lawfulness of certain acts...possible degrees of non-prohibition, ranging from "tolerated" to "permissible" to "desirable".'[113]

(*c*) *Views on gaps*. What did the judges in *Nuclear Weapons* opine on the possibility of gaps in international law? The opinions on the 'residual negative principle' will inform, but not determine the views on gaps. Judge Higgins, for example, did not discuss the residual principle, yet in the discussion of the role of *non liquet* in the Court's jurisprudence, she implied that the reason why there can be no *non liquet* is because there can be no 'deficiencies in the law'.[114]

It would have been interesting to find the judges' position on gaps in their individual opinions, but it seems that most judges saw the issue determined by the 'residual negative principle'. They seemed reluctant to consider matters outside the conventional line of arguments, including deontic logic, such as exemplified in Tammelo's 'legally neutral behaviour'.[115] Judges Guillaume and Shahabuddeen derived their conclusion that gaps cannot exist in law from the existence of a closing rule:

> It follows that, so far as this case at any rate is concerned, the principle on which the Court acts, be it one of prohibition or one of authorization, leaves no room unoccupied by law and consequently no space available to be filled by the *non liquet* doctrine or by arguments traceable to it.[116]

Guillaume went even further. Arguing that 'if the law is silent in this case, States remain free to act as they intend'[117] he admitted both that law can be silent and that states are free to act. He was adamant about supporting the *Lotus dictum* as commonly understood. However, the absence (silence) of law is qualitatively different to the presence of a default permission. President Bedjaoui's position on gaps is equally a function of the rejection of the 'residual negative principle'. Gaps are possible if the Court cannot 'find the threat or use of nuclear weapons to be either legal or illegal'.[118] Gaps are inevitable if it is possible that the Court neither shows a 'red light'

[113] Ibid, paras 3, 8.

[114] *Nuclear Weapons* (1996) above n 4, dissenting opinion Higgins, 591 (para 37) (citing: Shabtai Rosenne, *The Law and Practice of the International Court* (2nd edn, Martinus Nijhoff, Dordrecht, 1985) 100).

[115] Tammelo (1959) above n 6, 194–200. See above, Section I and *Kosovo* (2010) above n 4, declaration Simma, para 3, 8.

[116] *Nuclear Weapons* (1996) above n 4, dissenting opinion Shahabuddeen, 389. Spiermann (1999) above n 59, 141; Dekker (1999) above n 68, 244.

[117] *Nuclear Weapons* (1996) above n 4, separate opinion Guillaume, 291 (para 9).

[118] Ibid, declaration Bedjaoui, 271 (para 14).

nor a 'green light', that is when it can turn off the traffic-lights. Judges Vereshschetin and Fleischhauer merely implied that gaps are possible, but did not provide a legal justification for this position.[119] Vice-President Schwebel and Judge Herczegh based their rejection of gaps on the powers of the 'general principles of law' (Article 38(1)(c) ICJ Statute), arguing:

> [T]he application of the general principles of law makes it possible to regulate the behaviour of subjects of the international legal order, obliging or authorizing them, as the case may be, to act or refrain from acting in one way or another.[120]

However, if general principles—as norms—can always deliver positive law to the judge there can by definition be no gap. What would Schwebel and Herczegh do if no general principles could be found? Or is the term 'general principles' to be understood as shorthand for 'natural law' or 'unfettered law-creation by judges'?[121]

IV. Synthesis: Gaps and the Normative Environment

A. The points of reference

This article has argued that the key question in defining 'gaps' is not what gaps are, but on what we are measuring whether there are gaps. If we are to be able to speak of 'gaps in the law' as a distinct entity, we need to give a point of reference against which to measure the absence. Defining the problem in this manner helps us in clarifying the theoretical choice of reference-system and the question of the 'externality' vis-à-vis the normative system in question. In contrast (taking an example from domestic debates on legal theory) German writers seem agreed that one can avoid both making an awkward choice and choosing an external element simply by using an immanent reference.[122] In an early work, Claus-Wilhelm Canaris describes 'proper' gaps thus:

> A gap is an a-systematic insufficiency within positive law…measured *by reference to the entirety of the valid legal order*….A gap occurs, when neither statutes…nor customary law contain a regulation *even though the legal order in its entirety* [or totality] *demands it*.[123]

[119] Ibid, declaration Vereshschetin, 280, separate opinion Fleischhauer, 310 (para 6).

[120] Ibid, declaration Herczegh, 275, dissenting opinion Schwebel, 323.

[121] Kelsen (1979) above n 3, 99.

[122] Fastenrath (1991) above n 2, 220.

[123] 'Eine Lücke ist eine planwidrige Unvollständigkeit innerhalb des positiven Rechts…gemessen *am Maßstab der gesamten geltenden Rechtsordnung*….Eine Lücke liegt vor, wenn das Gesetz…und das Gewohnheitsrecht eine Regelung nicht enthalten, *obwohl die Rechtsordnung in ihrer Gesamtheit eine solche fordert*.' Canaris (1964) above n 1, 39 (original emphasis removed, emphasis added); Zitelmann (1903) above n 5, 9.

It seems that in this domestic tradition, the emphasis lies on distinguishing 'gaps' from a 'space devoid of law' (*rechtsfreier Raum*), because judges have the competence to close gaps but must respect a space devoid of law.[124] Indeed on some accounts the state is prohibited from enacting any law with respect to the space devoid of law.[125] The emphasis thus lies on finding an immanent point of reference.

Yet strictly speaking the concept of an immanent reference-point is a *contradictio in adiecto*. By definition a point of origin, *datum* or reference-point is external to the entity to be evaluated by reference to that *datum*. If this were not so, no difference could ever be found, because there is nothing that it could be measured against. The *datum* and the entity would be identical; after all, the reference-point is imminent. If the law as a whole is the measuring-stick for the law, then absence of a particular law is part of the law, hence part of the *datum*.

The explanation for the adoption of the distinction between gaps proper and 'space devoid of law' is not logic, but the ideology of natural-law scholarship. It is concealed by the notion of finding the 'missing law' within the legal system and is intended to placate those fearing for the rule of law. But as comforting as this thought may be, a consistently positivist analysis shows that the demand for wholeness that Canaris ascribes to the legal order in its entirety,[126] does not originate from the legal order. The distinction of the reference point from within *Recht*, yet outside *Gesetz* (positive law) means transcending positive law for an extra-positive value-judgment. The 'demand' is in effect created by legal scholars, who put their personal views of what the law should be in place of what the law is (with all its 'imperfections'). Consistently, Wilhelm Sauer points out that '[t]he problem of "gaps" presupposes a value-judgment on positive legal norms'.[127] Thus is the 'quasi-immanent' standard unmasked as an external standard; a different norm is superimposed on positive law and the problem of 'externality' remains.

The problem of externality is weighty because of the idea that An Other judges and thus defines the entity in question. With respect to norms this is a particularly tough problem. This is so, first, because norms are no more than a claim to be observed; second, because no claim is *a priori* better than the other and third, because *a posteriori* or empirical differences, such as effectiveness of a norm, belong to the world of Is and cannot influence an Ought. If externality is thus abandoned the difference

[124] Canaris (1964) above n 1, 40–4.
[125] Comes (1976) above n 32, 99.
[126] Canaris (1964) above n 1, 39.
[127] '[d]as Problem der Lücke setzt daher ein Werturteil über die positiven Rechtsnormen voraus' Wilhelm Sauer, *Juristische Methodenlehre. Zugleich eine Einleitung in die Methodik der Geisteswissenschaften* (F Enke, Stuttgart, 1940) 281.

between 'gaps' and 'non law' falls away.[128] The importation of an external reference-point such as morals, political ideology or a scholar's personal value-preferences is not impossible, but it would mean attempting to change law by ineligible means.

If we declare that there is a gap just because we think the absence of a norm is immoral (as might be the case for the theft of electricity where a penal code speaks only of 'things' the taking of which is a criminal offence and not of energy)[129]—if thus the notion of 'gaps' is ethically charged and if thus the possibility of closing gaps by any means is implied, positive law would be transcended. This is no problem for natural lawyers, but a theory that restricts the scope of law to positive law, such as the Pure Theory of Law, would not be able to adopt such a solution. On the one hand, one normative order is *a priori* not higher than another: morals are not above law, nor is law above morals. On the other hand, the dichotomy of Is and Ought means that facts alone (such as efficacy or the behaviour of the subjects of law) cannot create norms. Since we cannot distinguish gaps from a 'space devoid of law', this distinction has no consequences and we cannot 'close gaps' while leaving non-law untouched.

B. The residual negative principle resolved

This section and the next one review the results of the two preceding debates as building blocks for a synthesis. The first such debate was on the character of the residual negative principle. It was argued that we must finally do away with this confusing notion. As it is commonly understood—that in the absence of a prohibition there is a permission—it cannot be a necessary feature of normative orders. If it is understood as implying or creating a norm of freedom, Ulrich Fastenrath's conclusion is apt, for positivists leave their positivistic creed behind if they join Kant in asserting every human being's 'originary freedom'.[130] A residual negative principle as Stone understands it[131] would have to be a positive norm of international law. However, it is doubtful whether such a general norm exists in international law. The Martens clause could, however, be seen as serving a similar, but reverse function in humanitarian law.[132]

However, in the shape of Hans Kelsen's 'negative legal regulation' along the lines of the second interpretation (Section II), the matter is much less problematic and more consistent with both the normativist

[128] Fastenrath (1991) above n 2, 17, 213.
[129] Kelsen (1960) above n 45, 252.
[130] Fastenrath (1991) above n 2, 241.
[131] Stone (1960) above n 6, 135.
[132] *Nuclear Weapons* (1996) above n 4, dissenting opinion Shahabuddeen, 408, dissenting opinion Weeramantry, 493.

and the positivist arguments of the Vienna School of Jurisprudence. Kelsen, while undoubtedly influenced by Kant, never joined the philosopher in his moral philosophy and was also influenced by logical and legal positivism. Fastenrath's conclusion makes the best case for the second interpretation of Kelsen's theory. This second interpretation sees non-law defined by the law, nothing more. The 'freedom' to act is merely factual and since there are no norms, the law itself is silent. In other words, the concept of 'negative legal regulation' is not a norm of the normative order—not even a 'negative' or implied norm—but only a statement of the *fact* that positive norms are absent where they are not present. Where there are norms, there are norms; where there are no norms, there are no norms. That is how the *Lotus dictum* should have been understood as well, and that is what makes it a necessary element of the cognition of normative orders.

C. *Prohibition and permission*

The other debate concerns the alleged bivalence between 'prohibition' and 'permission' as normative modalities which leads some to assume a 'residual negative principle'. As Section I has shown, there is a way out using the concept of 'negative' (Kelsen) or 'weak' (Wright) permission. Hans Kelsen sees 'negative permission' in the sense of a third way beyond deontic bivalence; thus the second interpretation of Kelsen's theory on gaps is confirmed once more.

> The statement "certain behaviour is permitted" can mean that no norm has this behaviour as its object... In this sense "being permitted" has a *negative* connotation only. Certain behaviour being "permitted" in this sense means that there is *no* valid norm which would obligate, prohibit, positively permit or authorise this behaviour.... "Permission" in this negative sense is not the function [mode] of a norm; there is only *Being-permitted* as property of behaviour which is the object of *no* norm.[133]

Because permission in a negative sense is not a norm, 'no conclusions can be drawn with respect to the existence of permission in the strong sense.'[134] If there is 'legally neutral' behaviour, however, such as the one described as 'negative permission', one may rightly ask whether legal neutrality can be described as 'legal' at all.

[133] 'Die Aussage: "ein bestimmtes Verhalten ist erlaubt", kann bedeuten, daß überhaupt keine Norm dieses Verhalten zum Gegenstand hat... In diesem Sinne hat 'Erlaubt-sein' eine bloß *negative* Bedeutung. Daß ein bestimmtes Verhalten in diesem Sinn "erlaubt" ist, besagt, daß *keine* Norm gilt, die dieses Verhalten gebietet oder verbietet, positiv erlaubt oder ermächtigt.... Es gibt kein "Erlauben" in diesem negativen Sinne als Funktion einer Norm; es gibt nur ein *Erlaubt-sein* als Eigenschaft eines Verhaltens, das den Gegenstand *keiner* Norm bildet.' Kelsen (1979) above n 3, 78.

[134] Dekker (1999) above n 68, 236.

D. The internal and external views

Once we admit the possibility of a third way beyond normative modalities we must ask what standpoint we hold in relation to the normative system in question. Tammelo's dichotomy between open and closed legal orders calls this distinction by a different name. Do we perceive only law from the view-point of law, or do we perceive law in relation to behaviour, for example in relation to 'the case'? The view-point decides whether there can be such a thing as 'gaps'.

On the one hand—on the external view—it can be argued that there *is* legally neutral behaviour and that such a phenomenon is obviously true. Nobody will claim that English law regulates the sharpening of pencils at all. It is highly unlikely that 'pencil sharpening' is the content of any norm of the English legal order. The same can be said for the colour of paper used at international conferences. It is highly unlikely that international law prescribes, proscribes or even positively permits using red, white or blue paper. When certain behaviour is not regulated one is neither free nor not free to behave in this manner; one neither 'may' nor 'may not' do this; one cannot have a 'right' or 'freedom' to do this, because all these formulations already imply that the behaviour is regulated (is the content of a norm). Behaviour of this sort is legally irrelevant and it simply does not figure from a legal point of view. Only the decision to admix law and fact, Is and Ought, could lead Judge Shahabuddeen to argue:

> If international law has nothing to say on the subject of the use of nuclear weapons, this necessarily means that international law does not include a rule authorising such use. Absent such authorisation, States do not have a right to use nuclear weapons.[135]

On the external view normative orders do not necessarily regulate all possible behaviour, because negative regulation is precisely not part of the legal order—not even by implication—and remains outside. Gaps exist only in relation to a given case[136] or behaviour. International law most likely 'does not regulate certain conduct at all',[137] but this has no consequences for law. States are not acting contrary to international law if they behave in a way international law does not regulate. 'Gaps' still cannot be closed absent positive norms that authorise someone to create law.

On the other hand—on the internal view—the law is necessarily complete, even without a 'residual negative principle' creating law from thin air. It is complete simply because there is nothing to measure the law against.[138]

[135] *Nuclear Weapons* (1996) above n 4, dissenting opinion Shahabuddeen, 390.
[136] Dekker (1999) above n 68, 228.
[137] Ibid, 237.
[138] Adolf Julius Merkl, *Die Lehre von der Rechtskraft, entwickelt aus dem Rechtsbegriff. Eine rechtstheoretische Untersuchung* (Deuticke, Vienna, 1923) 234.

Hence, any architecture of norms is complete in the sense that from a legal point of view nothing is missing. All other points of view, including moral, sociological, factual, political or natural-legal, are external to the legal view. Therefore they are irrelevant and cannot change the law, not only because external norms are not hierarchically higher than the legal system under consideration, but also because legal scholars have only law as their object of study. This does not mean that the legal system is better than other norms, but it means that no normative order is by definition higher than any other and that Is and Ought are separate and do not directly create each other. Law is complete *in itself*, but not in relation to all possible forms of behaviour. Possible forms of behaviour might be a measuring-stick for the law, but it is not a measuring-stick on a strictly legal view-point.

V. Conclusion

The seemingly contradictory synthesis to the whole debate about 'gaps in the law' is that the law is at the same time complete and incomplete. There may be 'non-norm-governed behaviour',[139] but non-norm-governed behaviour does not constitute a gap in any sense of a 'flaw' that needs to be 'rectified'. We cannot speak of 'gaps' in the sense that the law *itself contains its gaps*. That would indeed be a paradox. As soon as a norm that regulates certain behaviour for one reason or another no longer does so (loses its validity), 'the law' is reduced by that norm and the behaviour formerly regulated by the norm falls outside 'the law'. Gaps and the 'space devoid of law' (as mentioned above, they are one and the same) are always 'zones' devoid of law, in other words, zones where norms are absent. Gaps *in law* are impossible; gaps *of prescription in behaviour* are common. Christoph Kletzer's argument is apposite:

> From a Kelsenian position one can agree with Lauterpacht insofar as there cannot be a space devoid of law from the view-point of law.... because legal cognition always means *legalisation*. In a different but comparable context Kelsen says: "In this respect law resembles King Midas. Just as everything he touched turned into gold, everything the law refers to turns into law."[140]

[139] Dekker (1999) above n 68 at 245.

[140] 'Darin ist Lauterpacht auch von kelsenianischer Seite insofern zuzustimmen, als es vom Standpunkt des Rechtes aus betrachtet keinen rechtsfreien Raum geben kann.... da rechtliche Betrachtung immer schon *Verrechtlichung* ist. In einem anderen, aber vergleichbaren Zusammenhang sagt Kelsen: "In dieser Hinsicht gleicht das Recht dem König Midas. So wie alles, was dieser berührte, sich in Gold verwandelte, so nimmt alles, worauf sich das Recht bezieht, Rechtscharakter an."' Kletzer (2004a) above n 63, 228 (emphasis on scholars' names removed); citing Kelsen (1960) above n 45, 282.

Gaps are factors of uncertainty in international law. They are 'missing' pieces of the 'totality' of norms in a normative order and 'exist' irrespective of our problems in cognising international law.[141] The normative 'existence' is missing in respect to factual, pragmatic problems, but then 'uncertainty' is always a pragmatic factor of the interaction of real human beings with the ideal idea[142] that is norms.

[141] Contra: Bodansky (1999) above n 43, 154; Fitzmaurice (1974) above n 6, 102.
[142] Philip Allott, *Eunomia. New Order for a New World* (paperback edn, Oxford University Press, Oxford, 2001) xxii.

On Disillusionment and its Limits: Images of the Interwar Legal Project in International Relations and International Law

By Kristian Wohlström*

I. Introduction

In 1946 Hersch Lauterpacht wrote in this Year Book about the 'Grotian tradition' in international law. No doubt his purpose was to uphold a progressive tradition of international law even, or perhaps especially, in the hardest of times, in the aftermath of what might still be called its defining crisis. It is perhaps not surprising, given the surrounding circumstances, that the 'tercentenary of the death of Grotius' in 1945 had 'passed almost unnoticed in the literature of international law', as Lauterpacht observed regretfully at the beginning of his essay. But his point was to supply a long-term perspective against the short-term immediacy of World War II and its immediate aftermath. Regarding the work of Grotius and the times, he wrote: 'At no time was it therefore more necessary than after the Second World War to sustain hope by drawing inspiration from works in which principle has asserted itself against makeshifts.'[1]

In the same year, Martin Wight concluded his pamphlet *Power Politics* with the observation:

> The outstanding contrast between the mood of 1945 and the mood of 1918, which is reflected in the contrast between the United Nations Charter and the League Covenant, is the absence of optimism, the greater realism. Realism can be a very good thing: it all depends whether it means the abandonment of high ideals or of foolish expectations.[2]

In hindsight, Wight's comment was just about all that needed to be said in summing up the spiritual heritage of the interwar era. This was not to be the case, of course. In much international theory, the 'turn to realism' and the associated view of the interwar years as an extended Utopian folly

* LLM, LLD candidate, Faculty of Law, University of Helsinki. I wish to thank the Editors for many valuable comments on a previous draft, and Tuuli Heinonen for numerous illuminating conversations and comments during the writing of this article.

[1] Hersch Lauterpacht, 'The Grotian Tradition in International Law' (1946) 23 *BYIL*; 1, 1.

[2] Martin Wight, *Power Politics, 'Looking forward' Pamphlets, No. 8* (Royal Institute of International Affairs, London, 1946) 68.

have been extraordinarily resilient,[3] and one corollary has been the widespread dismissal of international law especially in the discipline of international relations.

In this essay I propose to question these conceptions of the interwar experience and to assess the influence they have had on thinking about international law in later international theory. My argument is that while this may not always have seemed the case—only fairly recent times have seen the proliferation of calls for interdisciplinarity and 'joining' the disciplines[4]—international law and international relations theory have in fact been intimately connected from the outset. This is because the latter has been constructed on a specific interpretation of the interwar legal project; law has provided the 'mirror' for later theoretical developments, international relations as that which law was not, as it were. Recent discussions on the 'realist challenge'[5] and related interdisciplinary ambitions have failed to take this connection into account.

While for the realist challengers the interwar project was behind the problems the world faced *then*, Martti Koskenniemi has recently portrayed Lauterpacht's work, and the interwar legal project more generally, as the reason for the problems the international legal project is facing *today*.[6] While Koskenniemi's position is intended as a reply to the 'international relations challenge', it is founded on a theoretical 'platform' that shares many key assumptions with the realist approach. His critical approach, I shall argue, suffers from grave deficiencies at its core. These deficiencies not only undermine Koskenniemi's theoretical position as such; they also render it unable to provide a convincing answer to the widespread dismissal of law in discussions on international affairs.

This contribution proceeds in a more or less chronological order. The next section looks at the beginnings of 'international relations' at Aberystwyth and the discipline's formative phases during the interwar years. The third section discusses Koskenniemi's interpretation of Lauterpacht as representative of the modern legal project. The fourth section looks at the realist critiques of the interwar effort through the work of the two central figures of the period, E H Carr and Hans Morgenthau. The fifth section continues where Morgenthau left the field, by looking at

[3] Only very recently have there been real attempts at a more comprehensive understanding of the interwar 'effort'. See Zara Steiner, *The Lights that Failed: European International History 1919–1933* (Oxford University Press, Oxford, 2005). In this volume, to be followed by a sequel, *Triumph of the Dark*, on the later interwar years until 1939, Steiner examines the 1920s not as a 'frustrated prelude' to another war but 'as a fascinating decade in its own right, when politicians and diplomats strove to reassemble a viable European order'. See also David Long and Peter Wilson (eds), *Thinkers of the Twenty Years' Crisis: Inter-war Idealism Reassessed* (Oxford University Press, Oxford, 1995).

[4] See Anne-Marie Slaughter, Andrew S Tulumello and Stepan Wood, 'International Law and International Relations Theory: A New Generation of Interdisciplinary Scholarship' (1998) 92 *American Journal of International Law* 367 and Anne-Marie Slaughter Burley, 'International Law and International Relations Theory: A Dual Agenda' (1993) 87 *American Journal of International Law* 205.

[5] See Slaughter Burley, above n 4, 207–209.

[6] Martti Koskenniemi, 'The Fate of Public International Law: Between Technique and Politics' (2007) 70 *Modern Law Review* 1, 27–30.

the heritage of the realist critiques and the image of the interwar legal project in later international relations theory, and its consequences for the later identities of the discipline. Finally, the sixth section concerns international lawyers' reactions to the 'interwar heritage' in international relations theory, with a concluding discussion as to the meaning of the interwar legal project for the future course of international law.

Three interconnected stories thus come together in this essay: the story of the historical development of international relations theory, the story of interdisciplinarity between international law and international relations and the story of the history and theory of international law. In order finally to overcome the disillusionment associated with the interwar experience—and to give proper credit to the efforts of Lauterpacht and his contemporaries—we need to understand the ways in which historical and theoretical understandings have become intertwined in the disciplinary and interdisciplinary debates on international law and international relations.

II. The Beginnings of Academic 'International Relations' During the Interwar Era

A. *Aberystwyth, 1919: 'A new discipline for peace'?*

It is often implied that the origins of international relations as an academic discipline in its own right are located in the founding of the first Chair in the field of International Politics at the University College of Wales, Aberystwyth, in 1919. The Woodrow Wilson Chair, as it was named in 1922 in order to honour Mr Wilson's activities on behalf of the League of Nations, was established through a donation received from a Mr David Davies (1880–1944, from 1932 Lord Davies) and his two sisters, Gwendoline and Margaret Davies. Mr Davies, a Welsh Liberal MP, was the driving force behind the establishment of the Chair, an enterprise that from his point of view was but one aspect of a much wider venture aimed at nothing less than guaranteeing world peace for future generations.[7]

The explicit purpose of this Chair was the promotion of peace and the League of Nations (which, Mr Davies later bitterly observed, all the holders of the Chair had failed to do).[8] Mr Davies has been described as

[7] Brian Porter, 'David Davies and the Enforcement of Peace', in Long and Wilson, above n 3, 58–59. The somewhat unlikely location is explained by the fact that Mr Davies and his sisters were also in other ways great benefactors of their local university, and Davies was also 'passionately keen to associate Wales with the cause of internationalism and to see that it enjoyed a worldwide reputation as a nation committed to peace', ibid, 60. From the College's point of view this was an excellent arrangement: it expected the new Chair to 'do more than anything else to give international rank to the College', and to be useful in the attempt to 'introduce a new department of Social Science and Public Administration'. E L Ellis, *The University College of Wales, Aberystwyth, 1872–1972* (University of Wales Press, Cardiff, 1972) 188.

[8] The Chair was originally founded 'in memory of the fallen students of our University for the study of those related problems of law and politics, of ethics and economics, which are raised by the

'a man of action', an intense personality who had 'inherited his father's formidable personal energy', and the cause of peace had come to form a central aspect of his character and self-understanding.[9] The First World War had been a traumatic experience; he had raised and commanded a volunteer battalion on the Western Front before Lloyd George enlisted him, in 1916, to serve as his Parliamentary Private Secretary.[10] The war had made him see that nothing similar should ever be allowed to happen again, and this outlook characterised the greater part of his later activities; he for instance actively advocated an international police force.[11] But he was no academic and his understanding of the nature of academic work had its limitations, as is made evident by his stance on any research or activity that did not seem to suit his immediate purposes.[12]

So, in spite of the fact that the idea was very well received in the academic world and that similar Chairs were founded soon afterwards in the London School of Economics (1923), Oxford (1930) and elsewhere, there was in fact no 'properly academic' concern behind the founding of this Chair. Indeed from the point of view of the development of international theory, the year 1919 was probably not very significant. These events might be better read as just one aspect of a wider movement of promoting education and awareness concerning international issues following the Great War. The effects of the War were of course in many ways devastating. As Zara Steiner observes in the opening line of her history of the interwar years: 'The Great War was like a terrible volcanic eruption that left immeasurable destruction in its wake.' The metaphor of a natural disaster is telling, not only for all the death and destruction the Great War caused, but also because, at the time, it was considered a 'natural' event rather than 'an end of an epoch', as E H Carr once observed.[13]

Crucially, the War could still be explained as something external to human nature, and largely for this reason it did not do away with public

prospect of a League of Nations and for the truer understanding of civilizations other than our own'. In a new Trust Deed made in 1922 the duties of the Professor were set out as 'giving lectures and instruction in International Politics, travelling in foreign countries and studying foreign political systems, reading publications relating to International Politics, and writing books and pamphlets on the subject'. The field of International Politics was defined as 'political science in its application to international relations, with special reference to the best means of promoting peace between nations'. Ieuan John, Moorhead Wright and John Garnett, 'International Politics at Aberystwyth, 1919–1969', in Brian Porter (ed) *The Aberystwyth Papers: International Politics 1919–1969* (Oxford University Press, Oxford, 1972) 86–87.

[9] Porter, above n 7, 58.

[10] Ibid, 59.

[11] His plan for an international police force was set out in his 800-page pamphlet, *The Problem of the Twentieth Century: A Study in International Relationships* (Benn, London, 1930) 360–705.

[12] Davies gradually became convinced that founding the Chair had been a mistake, since in his opinion all its holders had worked only to undermine his own plans. Davies unsuccessfully fought a fierce battle against the nomination of E H Carr to the Chair in 1936. See Brian Porter, 'E. H. Carr—the Aberystwyth Years, 1936–47', in Michael Cox (ed), *E. H. Carr: A Critical Appraisal* (Palgrave, Basingstoke, 2000) 39–60.

[13] Michael Cox, 'Introduction', in E H Carr, *The Twenty Years' Crisis*, with a new introduction by Michael Cox (Palgrave, Basingstoke, 2001) xiv. Looking at international law in nineteenth-century

optimism regarding the possibilities of progress and reason in human existence. This was now a fertile ground for a project of informing the public about international affairs, law and the practice of diplomacy. An example of this kind of work is D P Heatley's *Diplomacy and the Study of International Relations*, published in 1919.[14] This was an attempt 'to portray diplomacy and the conduct of foreign policy from the standpoint of history'.[15] It consisted of an introductory text going through different facets of the management of diplomacy—the actual conduct of which 'must be left to the hands of the few'—and chapters on various aspects of helpful international literature: 'juristic literature', texts on treaties and recent (British) diplomacy, maps and 'literature of international ethics'. Heatley clearly had a feeling that international law was more important than was perhaps generally perceived: 'No apology should be needed for the attention given in this book to works on International Law and on the History of International Law.' He continued:

> The history of international relations has fruit for each age in treaties, which the international lawyer interprets as expressions of movement of thought, and in the developing of conventions and standards that are recognised in the Society of Nations. In the history of International Law is shown a large part of the fruit of the intercourse of nations. The two studies have, of late, been too much severed in this country.[16]

This kind of attitude among thinkers on international affairs was not new. Heatley was drawing on a text he had written three years earlier in 1916, 'a very few pages intended to help towards the study of international relations'.[17] A much better known example, Norman Angell's *The Great Illusion*, originally published in 1909, had demonstrated a similar effort and mindset a decade earlier.[18]

Activities of a more practical nature were taking place in the same spirit. Both before and during the war new organizations had been founded, for instance the American Society of International Law in 1906 and the Grotius Society in 1915. After the war, Woodrow Wilson with his 'Fourteen Points' and the founding of the League of Nations provided excitement and a positive sense of urgency to discussions on what to do

Britain, Casper Sylvest summarizes that '[t]he Great War of 1914 to 1918 questioned and contradicted many of the magnanimous formulations of pre-war international legal argument and, as a consequence, this intellectual discourse was transformed. But it was not changed beyond recognition.... Insofar as international law in late-nineteenth-century Britain was informed by a liberal and internationalist ethos, ... this ethos proved not only ideologically malleable but also remarkably resilient.' Casper Sylvest, 'International Law in Nineteeth-Century Britain' (2004) 75 *BYIL* 9–69.

[14] D P Heatley, *Diplomacy and the Study of International Relations* (Clarendon Press, Oxford, 1919).

[15] Ibid, v.

[16] Ibid, vii–viii.

[17] Ibid, ix.

[18] Norman Angell, *The Great Illusion: A Study of the Relation of Military Power in Nations to their Economic and Social Advantage* (William Heinemann, London, 1911).

with 'the international'. Against such a background it is not difficult to understand that Davies's contribution to Aberystwyth was already, without any perceived need for the construction of disciplinary histories, regarded as a 'brilliant academic innovation'.[19] But, notwithstanding the obvious merits in the endeavour, was it really that?

Up to 1919 'international thought' had not been a specific discipline. It had been seen as but a part of general philosophy or of political theory, as well as (international) law and (diplomatic) history. A recent collection entitled *International Relations in Political Thought: Texts from the Ancient Greeks to the First World War* presents thinkers on 'the classical theory of international relations', from Thucydides to Plato, from Dante Alighieri and Martin Luther to Thomas Aquinas and Francisco de Vitoria, from Niccolo Machiavelli to Edmund Burke, from Hugo Grotius to Thomas Hobbes, Samuel Pufendorf and Emmerich de Vattel, from the Abbé de Saint-Pierre and Montesquieu to David Hume, Jean-Jacques Rousseau and Immanuel Kant, from Hegel to von Treitschke and from Adam Smith to Karl Marx and Friedrich Engels.[20] All these authors had views on the state of the world, but they were certainly not, in their own times, part of an 'international relations' discipline.

So how then, in 1919, did this new discipline distinguish itself? It has been said that 'the question of separateness from other disciplines' was 'solved at Aberystwyth', because unlike in some other early instances, the Wilson Chair was explicitly dedicated to International Politics.[21] In fact, however, the whole idea of a discipline is a later invention. Aberystwyth did not signal a decisive shift in any new direction, international politics continued to be a point of view instead of a discipline.[22] E H Carr's later claim that he had established the foundations for a 'science' of international relations was met with widespread scepticism.[23] Mr Davies for his part did not intend to found an academic discipline or a scientifically consistent body of thought. When it appeared that he to some extent had done so, he regretted its negative impact on his own efforts. His wish was not for a discipline, but for World Peace.

B. Interwar international studies: Activism in disguise?

Discussing the work of Alfred Zimmern, this section reviews the prevailing criticism of interwar international relations scholarship as a specifically

[19] Porter, above n 7, 59.

[20] Chris Brown, Terry Nardin and Nicholas Rengger (eds), *International Relations in Political Thought: Texts from the Ancient Greeks to the First World War* (Cambridge University Press, Cambridge, 2002).

[21] William Olson and Nicholas Onuf, 'The Growth of a Discipline: Reviewed', in Steve Smith (ed), *International Relations: British and American Perspectives* (Blackwell, Oxford and New York, 1985) 3.

[22] Ellis, above n 7, 218.

[23] Peter Wilson, 'Carr and his Early Critics: Responses to *The Twenty Years' Crisis*, 1939–46', in Cox, above n 12, 165, 177–181.

Utopian type of academic work. Zimmern was the first person selected to the Wilson Chair in 1919. He came to hold the Aberystwyth Chair for only a short period, as he was forced to resign in 1921. (The Aberystwyth of the time did not tolerate his marriage to the ex-wife of the Professor in French.) He then had a temporary teaching post at Cornell before he was appointed as the first Montague Burton Professor of International Relations at Oxford in 1930. He also worked as deputy director of the League of Nations International Committee for Intellectual Cooperation (ICIC), the forerunner of UNESCO, in Paris.[24] Partly through this last assignment, one of Zimmern's specialisations became international education, or education in internationalism: for Zimmern 'international relations' was an important part of an educational endeavour.

Zimmern had started his career as a classics scholar and was an eminent historian. In 1911 he had published *The Greek Commonwealth*, which in his own words was 'the result of an attempt to make clear to myself what fifth-century Athens was really like'.[25] But the book also revealed, according to Paul Rich, the 'emotional attachment that many classicists had in the high noon of British imperialism with the ideals of Hellenic Greece', as '[t]hese ideals were seen as providing an ethical yardstick by which to evaluate the civilizing goals of British imperial policy.'[26] Zimmern had a soft spot for the British Commonwealth, which he considered a model for internationalism and a pioneer of the League—a 'smaller and more intimate League'—as it was able to contain what he saw as the most powerful causes of war: interracial and economic relations and nationality.[27]

Zimmern's most important publication, *The League of Nations and the Rule of Law*[28] has been characterised as 'the most polished work of the interwar idealists' and Zimmern's approach in general as 'cautious idealism':[29] cautious presumably because he was actually rather well aware of the surrounding situation and idealist since he was not obsessed with the concept of power, from any perspective. Indeed it has been suggested that the 'interplay of ethics and politics' in Zimmern's work might be of increasing relevance for contemporary international relations scholarship.[30]

The book itself is a study of various aspects of the League and its functioning, for instance the elements of the Covenant, the history of the League from its founding until 1935 and the functioning of its organs. The book does not include, Zimmern points out, analysis of the political,

[24] Paul Rich, 'Alfred Zimmern's Cautious Idealism: The League of Nations, International Education, and the Commonwealth', in Long and Wilson, above n 3, 81.

[25] Alfred Zimmern, *The Greek Commonwealth: Politics and Economics in Fifth-Century Athens* (Clarendon Press, Oxford, 1911).

[26] Rich, above n 24, 89.

[27] Rich, above n 24, 87–91.

[28] Alfred Zimmern, *The League of Nations and the Rule of Law 1918–1935* (Macmillan, London, 1936).

[29] Rich, above n 24.

[30] Rich, above n 24, 95–96.

economic, social or psychological problems 'which have formed the stuff and substance of international politics during the period under review', in part because it was still completely unclear 'whether or not, in some form or another, the rule of law . . . is to be established in the sphere of international relations'. As to this, Zimmern noted:

At the moment of writing, this question still awaits an answer. At times indeed, in penning these pages, I have been in doubt whether to employ the past or the present tense, whether I was writing a history of an experiment that had reached its conclusion or describing the early phases of a living and developing institution. If in this matter of style I have erred on the side of optimism, I trust that the reader will not feel that I have allowed it to colour the substance of the book or to affect the impartiality of the analysis.[31]

'Erred on the side of optimism'. The nature of the interwar era as a period of dangerous and unfounded optimism has largely come to be defined from E H Carr 'backwards', as it was really only from Carr onwards that the self-understanding of 'international relations' as a discipline eventually started to take shape. Indeed much of the 'interwar effort' did not take the shape of academic studies but of various forms of internationalist activism. Carr 'produced' the category of idealism as a part of the later discipline by writing both his critique of 'failed' idealist/utopian approaches (of an ultimately largely practical orientation) *and* a proposal for a more 'scientific', 'realist' international relations in the same lucid package. Carr mostly criticised efforts that were not intended as 'studies' of international politics, such as the project of the League. In *The League*, the most 'polished' of interwar books, Zimmern openly stated his normative aspiration—'erring on the side of optimism'—and did not disguise it as 'objective' science.

Carr's writings suggest that the (mostly unnamed) interwar Utopians were either few in number or strictly uniform in their outlook, but they were in fact neither.[32] The interwar effort in favour of peace understandably had to take *some* direction: something had to be done. That things did not work out the way they could have is only in a very small part attributable to the efforts of these various sorts of activists. Carr himself had resolved the question of what ought to be done by advocating appeasement. Without the benefit of hindsight, it may be difficult to know the right direction for political action. At the time, as Chris Brown points out, many observers did not know whether to praise Chamberlain for his peaceful orientation or criticise him for cowardly appeasement, and as a consequence they 'resolved this dilemma by doing both'.[33]

[31] Zimmern, above n 28, vii–viii.
[32] Peter Wilson, 'Introduction', in Long and Wilson, above n 3, 1, 15.
[33] Chris Brown, *Understanding International Relations* (Palgrave, Basingstoke, 2001) 27.

III. Hersch Lauterpacht as Representative of the Interwar Legal Project

When Lauterpacht wrote about Grotius in 1946, he discussed the various elements of what he wanted to call to a 'Grotian tradition' in international law, among them 'the subjection of the totality of international relations to the rule of law', 'the fundamental rights and freedoms of the individual', 'the idea of peace' and 'the tradition of idealism and progress'.[34] More recently, Martti Koskenniemi has written about elements of a 'Victorian tradition' in international law, represented by Lauterpacht.[35] While Lauterpacht, after having discussed the many defects of *De Jure Belli ac Pacis*, ultimately wished to appreciate the enduring values in the work of Grotius, Koskenniemi ultimately regards Lauterpacht as a Utopian—sympathetic as such but hopelessly out of date, his work the reason for today's problems—and consigns him to the archives of history with other things 'Victorian'.

For Koskenniemi, Lauterpacht's work and the interwar legal project of developing international law in general were about 'the effort of becoming technical', and he suspects that this is largely to blame for the current managerialist culture in contemporary international life. This interpretation is problematic because it is based on theoretical premises that, I shall argue, prevent us from appreciating the proper meaning of Lauterpacht's and his contemporaries' work. Before discussing Koskenniemi's interpretation of Lauterpacht's work in more detail, I shall first take a brief look at the background—the state of international law in Britain as an academic and practical phenomenon by the beginning of the twentieth century.

International law in nineteenth century England, writes James Crawford, was 'a developed system of practice for dealing with certain classes of relations beyond the state, a practical system with an accompanying literary tradition, whose local focus was the Foreign Office and the embassies and lawyers' chambers in London rather than the universities'.[36] International law as such was a 'developed study' in England already in the nineteenth century, but, in Crawford's estimation, this had 'relatively little to do with the universities, and it was based on no new theoretical underpinnings or insights'.[37] Indeed, he notes, '[i]t is significant that many of the textbooks of international law written in English during the nineteenth century came

[34] Lauterpacht, above n 1.

[35] Martti Koskenniemi, *The Gentle Civilizer of Nations: The Rise and Fall of International Law 1870–1960* (Cambridge University Press, Cambridge, 2002) 353–412. See also Koskenniemi, 'Hersch Lauterpacht (1897–1960)' in Jack Beatson and Reinhard Zimmermann (eds) *Jurists Uprooted: German-speaking Émigré Lawyers in Twentieth-century Britain* (Oxford University Press, Oxford, 2004) 601.

[36] James Crawford, 'Public International Law in Twentieth-century England', in Beatson and Zimmermann, above n 35, 681, 691–92.

[37] Ibid, 691.

from writers who did not hold chairs, or indeed any secure teaching positions, in international law at any of the universities.'[38] 'The notable British contribution to the development of international law occurred through public life rather than scholarly work, so to speak.'[39]

At the time, there was in fact not much of a tradition of studying or teaching law in general. Crawford describes the situation as follows: 'The major British legal scholars of the second half of the century . . . had that tradition to create.'[40] In the field of international law the creation of the Chichele Chair in Oxford in 1859 and the Whewell Chair—to which Lauterpacht was elected in 1935—in Cambridge in 1867, along with the reform of university legal education in general, provided a better platform for the development of teaching and scholarship, but, Crawford notes, 'th[is] opportunity was taken only to a limited degree'.[41]

The situation in the universities had not greatly improved by the early twentieth century. Koskenniemi refers to a critical review of the state of international law in Britain published by E A Whittuck (1844–1924) in 1917. There were on the whole only a few teaching posts in the subject, and none of the professorships in the field were located in London, where teaching in the subject was given only in the London School of Economics and Political Science (LSE). The lecturer's salaries were often poor; Koskenniemi notes: 'though some additional teaching was arranged through the Council of Legal Education at the Inns of Court, Foreign Office, and the Admiralty at Portsmouth and Devonport, this may have contributed to the lecturer's standard of living but hardly compensated for the weakness of university instruction'.[42]

Against such a background, it is not surprising that in Crawford's estimation, the influence of the international law academy on international law developments also remained fairly limited during the first half of the twentieth century. He writes: 'The professional tradition of international law in Britain remained both alive and essentially distinct from scholarly initiatives.'[43] The influence of academics on legal developments, he notes, would have been of a long-term rather than a short-term variety.[44]

Koskenniemi's essay on Lauterpacht opens with the following remark: 'The way we think about international law today is the effect of the imagination of a small number of academic and practising lawyers during the "twenty-years' crisis" of 1919–1939.' For Koskenniemi, the different aspects and phases of Lauterpacht's work—first as an academic at the LSE and in Cambridge, later as participant in Nuremberg and member of the ILC and finally as a Judge at the ICJ—when brought together, serve to

[38] Ibid, 689. [39] Ibid, 692.

[40] Ibid, 689. Crawford mentions Dicey, Maitland, Pollock and Westlake.

[41] Ibid, 692.

[42] Koskenniemi, *Lauterpacht*, above n 35, 609–611. Koskenniemi refers to E A Whittuck, 'International Law Teaching' (1918), 3 *Transactions of the Grotius Society* 44–46.

[43] Crawford, above n 36, 692–695. [44] Ibid, 695–696.

illustrate the step-by-step emergence of a specifically 'modern' understanding of international law. He notes: 'So close is the parallel between the emergence of modern international law and the stages of Lauterpacht's life that one loses track of which is reality and which metaphor.'[45]

Koskenniemi characterises Lauterpacht as representative of a 'Victorian tradition' in international law, this tradition consisting of four basic elements, namely rationalism, individualism, cosmopolitanism and sentimentalism.[46] Koskenniemi argues that these elements 'combine into a sensibility about international matters' that can also be used to characterise the profession at later times. Since Lauterpacht is the most important representative of this sensibility, 'an account of his life provides a particularly illuminating genealogy of modern international law'.[47] For Koskenniemi, Lauterpacht's consistent emphasis on unity, solidarity, the rule of law and an ultimate harmony of interests even at hard times—such as in the depths of the war in 1941—constitutes the best expression of this Victorianism. But it also gives us reason to 'wonder about the political wisdom of a mindset so determined to insist on human goodness during one of the darkest moments of European history, or about its psychological costs for the speaker himself.'[48]

Crawford for his part takes a notably reserved attitude regarding Lauterpacht's 'Victorianism': 'To what extent the overworked adjective "Victorian" is useful in describing someone who came to England two decades after the Queen's death, and to a transformed domestic and international scene, may be doubted. But there is no doubting Lauterpacht's combination of high seriousness, moral vision and capacity for seizing the main chance.'[49] From the point of view of the present work, the question that needs to be asked is the following: what sort of 'genealogy of modern international law' would Koskenniemi's interpretation be? A project of modern international law whose very essence would entail 'psychological costs' for its practitioners?

Koskenniemi has characterised the interwar effort of attacking sovereignty and positivism as a 'strategy' rather than a 'view': 'In [the contemporary] stream of anti-sovereignty scholarship and practice, Lauterpacht's technique was to read the law as an emanation of the general principles—

[45] Koskenniemi, *Lauterpacht*, above n 35, 601–603. [46] Ibid, 603. [47] Ibid, 603–4.

[48] Ibid, 602. Koskenniemi quotes Lauterpacht's speech as follows: 'The disunity of the modern world is a fact; but so, in a truer sense, is its unity. Th[e] essential and manifold solidarity, coupled with the necessity of securing the rule of law and the elimination of war, constitutes a harmony of interests which has a basis more real and tangible than the illusions of the sentimentalist or the hypocrisy of those satisfied with the existing *status quo*. The ultimate harmony of interests which within the State finds expression in the elimination of private violence is not a misleading invention of nineteenth century liberalism.' Hersch Lauterpacht, 'The Reality of the Law of Nations', in Hersch Lauterpacht, *International Law: Being the Collected Papers of Hersch Lauterpacht*, volume 2, edited by Elihu Lauterpacht (Cambridge University Press, Cambridge, 1975) 22, 26.

[49] Crawford, above n 36, 682. The wonderful irony about 'Victorian' as an adjective is of course just that it can be used to describe something that one wishes to portray as something to be admired but that is also completely outdated and inevitably belongs to the past.

that is to say, ultimately principles of morality—that animated it and provided the profession with its normative direction.'[50] Koskenniemi observes that Lauterpacht's aim was to demonstrate that there was

> no fundamental difference between international law and forms of private law. On the contrary, analogous and sometimes even identical arguments prevailed. The fact that international law had to do with states did not make it an altogether different type of legal order.[51]

This seems consistent with Lauterpacht's ambitions, but one wonders whether it is the case, as in Koskenniemi's view, that Lauterpacht's first book, *Private Law Sources and Analogies of International Law*, 'spoke to domestic lawyers in their own language: international order was not an effect of state policies but of familiar legal arguments carried out in courts and tribunals'.[52] Is this not stretching the point about Lauterpacht's strategic ambitions a little too far?

Analogies was published in 1927. This was an examination of the different ways private-law thinking influenced the practice of States and the reasoning of international tribunals. In the book Lauterpacht points out that while private law analogies would at the time have been mostly viewed with suspicion, this had historically not always been the case:

> It is the modern positivist doctrine which is chiefly responsible for the acceptance of the prevalent iconoclastic view. A true offspring of the doctrine of sovereignty, it could not countenance the intrusion, into the field of binding rules of international law, of notions and principles not directly derived from the will of the States. The same doctrine of sovereignty, with its conception of eternal and inalienable interests protected by the State and of their public and absolute character, was bound to reject any recourse to private law as concerned with interests deemed to be of an economic and lower order.[53]

Lauterpacht emphasised that the book's focus was specifically on international law, writing: 'It will be observed that the subject of this book is in no way connected with questions of international private law or with the relation between international and municipal law. It deals with problems of international public law only and exclusively.'[54] However, the book's chief aim was to reinforce the connections between international law and legal thought more generally, in order to move beyond the idea of the international legal system and the different national legal systems as separate 'black boxes':

[50] Koskenniemi, 'Epilogue', in Koskenniemi, *From Apology to Utopia. The Structure of International Legal Argument. Reissue with new epilogue* (Cambridge University Press, Cambridge, 2005) 605.

[51] Koskenniemi, *Lauterpacht*, above n 35, 618–19.

[52] Ibid, 618–19.

[53] Hersch Lauterpacht, *Private Law Sources and Analogies of International Law* (Archon, 1970, originally Longmans, Green & Co. Ltd., 1927) ix.

[54] Ibid, xi.

Law must be based on facts—sociological, historical and others—and it must take facts into account. But it can never be a mere reflection of them. As there is in law a perpetual conflict between the element of stability and the element of change, between the traditional form of law and the substance of social life, so there is also in every legal community, and especially in the international community, a conflict between the idea of right and justice and the immediate powerful interests shaping the law. *There were, and are, many factors which combined in order to create, to maintain and to develop in international law those elements of stability, of the generally accepted conception of law, and of the ideals of right and justice* as against the crude reality of an unorganised community where every change, however lawless and discretionary, tends to become a legal rule, where every aspect of international life, however wanton and repugnant, claims to set a legal standard, and where every predominant interest asserts itself as law. *This monograph shows that private law was and is one of these factors.*[55]

Among the book's aims was thus the legal contextualisation of the doctrine of sovereignty, as to which Lauterpacht observes:

It would have been an easy task, therefore, to criticise the current repudiation of private law from the point of view of the now so popular rejection of the doctrine of sovereignty. The author, however, decided not to avail himself of this method of approach. The international lawyer, if he wishes to assist in the searching investigation which is now taking place on the subject of external sovereignty, will be well employed if he confines himself to the examination of the question whether the doctrine of sovereignty is in accordance both with the practice of States as expressed in customary and conventional international law, and with a rational and consistent system of international law as developed by international publicists, positivist and non-positivist. If he succeeds in showing that certain widely spread notions, directly and demonstrably resulting from the doctrine of sovereignty, run counter to the practice of States and to the conception of international law as taught by the general body of writers, he has done his share. The doctrine of sovereignty as a legal conception cannot be shattered by well-meaning publicists and pacifists who denounce it as mischievous and out of date. It will only disappear when notions usually associated with it are shown to be inconsistent both with the practice of States and with the science of international law in its individual branches.[56]

As for the 'doctrine of positivism', Lauterpacht explained:

It is necessary to point out at this stage that when referring here and elsewhere in this book to modern positivism, the author in no way alludes to that legitimate aspiration of the science of international law which regards custom and treaties as the primary sources, whose authority, so far as existing law is concerned, is higher than

[55] Ibid, 304–5, emphasis added. The notion of 'black boxes' has been used by William Twining to describe theories that 'treat nation states or geographically bounded "societies" or legal systems as discrete entities that can be studied in isolation either internally or at the international level'. Twining, *Globalisation & Legal Theory* (Butterworths, London, 2000) 8.

[56] Lauterpacht, above n 53, ix–x.

any conflicting rule of natural law or morality. What he has in mind is the uncompromising tendency which isolates international law from any outside influence, which obstructs the task of interpretation and the attempts at consciously developing international law, and which not infrequently goes the length of disregarding the practice of States if the latter happens to run counter to positivist formulas.[57]

Lauterpacht's next book, *The Function of Law in the International Community*,[58] published in 1933, grew out of his article 'The Doctrine of Non-Justiciable Disputes in International Law', published in this *Year Book* in 1928. Lauterpacht notes that the book eventually became 'no longer a plea in support of a definite doctrine or an argument against a particular theory', but 'an attempt at an exposition, by reference to the problem of the international judicial function, of what are believed to be the principal issues of the philosophy of international law'.[59] Here Lauterpacht wished to see international law as a 'general jurisprudence', for the 'specific character of international law has revealed itself as the negation of the idea of law':

It is better that international law should be regarded as incomplete, and in a state of transition to the finite and attainable ideal of a society of States under the binding rule of law, as generally recognised and practised by civilized communities within their borders, than that, as the result of the well-meant desire to raise its formal authority qua law, it should be treated as the perfect and immutable species of a comprehensively diluted *genus proximum*.[60]

As in *Analogies*, this was the long-term perspective, and a call in favour of the progressive development of international law as a 'general jurisprudence', based on the fruits, or 'best practices', of universal juristic thought in general. Lauterpacht called for the 'vindication of the dignity of the science of international law', which would consist of two tasks: first, it was of 'imperative necessity' to abandon the distinction between justiciable and non-justiciable, or legal and political, disputes, while the second task had to do with method and approach:

Just as positivism in the domain of international law has become unscientific by being driven, through its own exaggerations, to disregard the very practice of States which it professes to regard as the only source of law, so the desire of generations of international lawyers to confine their activity to a registration of the practice of States has discouraged any determined attempt at relating it to higher legal principle, or to the conception of international law as a whole. The latter function can—effectively, it is submitted—be performed by means of the legitimate methods of juridical criticism and analysis.[61]

As to the question of justiciable and non-justiciable disputes, Koskenniemi observes:

[57] Ibid, ix–x.

[58] Hersch Lauterpacht, *The Function of Law in the International Community* (Oxford University Press, Oxford, 1933).

[59] Ibid, viii. [60] Ibid, 432. [61] Ibid, 434–38.

Like Hans Morgenthau a few years earlier, Lauterpacht showed that it was impossible to draw the distinction between the political and the legal by a determinate rule. Because anything can, from some perspective, be labelled "political", the doctrine of non-justiciable disputes will always leave it open for a state to opt out of the law's constraint by insisting on the "political" nature of the case. Like Morgenthau—the paradigmatic realist—Lauterpacht thought that the legal/political (justiciable/non-justiciable) distinction, together with the principle that its application was dependent on the state's own view, led international law beyond the vanishing point of jurisprudence. But where Morgenthau concluded that the absence of a delimiting rule meant that everything was *politics*, Lauterpacht drew the contrary conclusion. For him: "...all international disputes are, irrespective of their gravity, disputes of a legal character in the sense that, so long as the rule of law is recognised, they are capable of an answer by the application of legal rules".[62]

But in *which sense* was this the contrary conclusion? Perhaps in the sense of casting law and facts, or 'idealism' and 'realism', as contrary positions that however 'depend' on viewpoints in each other:

In the continuing idealist—realist debates, each side has been caricaturing its opponent and unwilling to recognise to what extent one's own position was dependent on aspects in that of the adversary. Lauterpacht was rightly critical of the monopolization of the word "realism" for his adversaries' cause—something he felt a dishonest debating strategy. Today we may suspect that the "idealism" and "realism" of a doctrine may lie in the eye of the beholder. Lauterpacht is important not because of his "idealism" or "realism", but because he embodies, in a strikingly obvious way, the elements that have made the profession of international law—and thus international law—what it is.[63]

I agree that Lauterpacht's importance is neither his idealism nor his realism. But I am inclined to think that Lauterpacht did not view realism as just a dishonest debating strategy; it was more (or less) than that. Indeed to portray the idealist-realist 'debate' as a debate between two opposing poles that ultimately 'depend' on viewpoints in each other is just pure realism, the very viewpoint which for Lauterpacht constituted a position that was 'intellectually faulty':

These, then, are the features of the current realistic attitude in international affairs. In the first instance, the realist sees mainly the obvious and the conspicuous. It is for that reason that he magnifies the phenomena of conflict of interest and the immorality of States. Secondly, he is pessimistic about human nature and its capacity for improvement. He has no faith in the power of the human will to shape the fate of men. He is distrustful of principle. He is attracted by immediate advantage. He is a moral relativist. All these features of realism are, like its very name, superficially attractive. They appeal to men almost as much as their opposites; they are very plausible; and they are in practice easier to follow. They have been widely followed in the last quarter of the century. While the sombre events in the international

[62] Koskenniemi, *Lauterpacht,* above n 35, 620–21. [63] Ibid, 603.

sphere of that era may be explained by a variety of causes, it is my conviction that they have been powerfully influenced, for evil, by the temper of realism.

To return to the initial theme, I believe that when conceived as an argument in itself—and it is so often used either in good or in bad faith—the appeal to realism is intellectually faulty. It assumes at the very outset a quality of wisdom and soundness which it denies to the opponent. What then, shall we do when confronted with that kind of argument? Shall we steal the thunder from our opponent, get in first and call *ourselves* realists and *him* a Utopian? I have occasionally, in this matter, advised undergraduates as follows:

"If in the future, in argumentative zeal, you call yourselves realists, you should blush for very shame. For realism, properly conceived, is a quality which we must concede to our opponent in the same measure as we claim it for ourselves. Neither ought we to meet the egregious claim half-way by calling ourselves 'realistic idealists' or 'idealistic realists'. Let us distrust labels. If you ask me whether, apart from *calling* ourselves realists, it is not a good thing that we *should* be realists, my answer is that I am not certain what exactly a realist is. If it is the kind of realism which I have been describing, and which has been very real in recent years, my answer can be surmised from my questions. If it is the kind of realism which often goes by that name and which has been identified with the temporary successes of wilful men in history—the Borgias, the Frederick the Greats, the Napoleons, the Bismarcks, the Hitlers, the Mussolinis—the realism of lawlessness, opportunism, and denial of sanctity of man—then no answer is necessary. By all means let us see and learn to see things as they are—this is the main reason why you are in the University—but to know things does not mean to be content with them. Certainly, let us respect power, but let us not identify it with physical force, and let us not worship it unless as an instrument of right. Guns are propelled by ideas. Except in military language, there are no self-propelling guns. By all means let us acknowledge the authority of facts. But we need not think of facts in terms of narrow realism. In the realm of human action ideas are facts. Revolt against injustice and prejudice is a fact. Projects of improvement are a fact. As such they must assuredly play a part—not as an infinite ideal, but in our time. Let us study them, all of them, whether they be projects of world federation, or of the constitution of the world, or of the revision of the Charter. Let us treat with serenity the gibe that we are engaged in producing perfectionist blueprints. If we must be realists, let us have a realism which does not merely register experience in a mood of pessimism or resignation, but which learns from experience and which is impatient of its defects as seen by reason. Nowhere are these defects more glaring or more destructive of the good life than in the external relations of States which are, mostly, civilized except in their mutual relations. If we are realists in that sense, perhaps we shall be forgiven if, in the heat of argument, we fall into the trap and resort to the little trick of calling ourselves so."

This is the advice which I have occasionally ventured to give to undergraduates. If pressed hard I might make so bold as to impart it to others. But I would not be inclined to exaggerate its importance. For it is possible that the matter is not one of substance, but of method of argument.[64]

In Koskenniemi's view, Lauterpacht was unable to answer the realists because he was 'never willing to face political issues directly', and for this reason these were critiques to which he 'could add nothing'. For Koskenniemi, Lauterpacht's work

heralds the end of jurisprudence and grand theory in the same way legal hermeneutics does, by focusing on the interpretative practices of the legal profession. Simultaneously, however, it remains hostage to and is limited by the conventions and ambitions of that profession. In this sense, *Function* is the last book on international theory—the theory of non-theory, the sophisticated face of legal pragmatism.[65]

For Koskenniemi, then, the 'unanswered [realist] critiques reveal the limits of Lauterpacht's moral pragmatism, and those of the late nineteenth-century liberal cosmopolitanism that animated them':

Lauterpacht's pragmatic cosmopolitanism failed to open the horizon for more wide-ranging change in the international society than what was possible through work—even enlightened work—in international courts. Some such horizon would have been needed for international law to develop from its relative isolation as an aspect of official diplomacy into a representative of the aspirations of progress and international justice that Lauterpacht, too, saw as its proper task.[66]

I am not convinced it was difficult for Lauterpacht to understand what the realists were saying; Lauterpacht's answer is evident from the above quotation. Lauterpacht's emphasis on human goodness and the progressive development of international law in the Kantian vein was not an accident or a 'psychological expense' but a deliberate answer to the question: what ought to be done with the world? A long-term approach, with an emphasis on legal reason as an 'element of stability', *was* Lauterpacht's 'politics'.

Koskenniemi rightly notes the difference between the short and the long term.[67] But, as the philosopher Georg Henrik von Wright has observed, trying to answer the question whether 'progress' in the human condition is possible eventually leads one to succumb either to the myth of progress or the myth of retrogression.[68] The problem with all idealism/realism–inspired discussions regarding, for example, the nature of the modern legal project, is that they end up trying to answer precisely this question. Elsewhere Koskenniemi quotes Kant approvingly on essentially this same

[64] Hersch Lauterpacht, 'On Realism, especially in International Relations', in Lauterpacht, above n 48, 52, 65–66.

[65] Koskenniemi, *Lauterpacht*, above n 35, 623.

[66] Ibid, 661. Emphasis added.

[67] Ibid, 647 n 221.

[68] Georg Henrik von Wright, 'Edistyksen myytti' [trans.: The Myth of Progress] in Von Wright, *Minervan pöllö* [trans.: The Owl of Minerva] (Otava, Helsinki, 1992) 171.

point: 'Even if the complete realization of [perpetual peace] always remains a pious wish, we still are not deceiving ourselves in adopting the maxim of working incessantly towards it.'[69]

Ultimately, it is not possible to eliminate modern law's character as a project. Law is and remains a tool. The question is: a tool for what? Neil MacCormick frames his answer to the charge of legal science being necessarily connected with values, and thus in this sense indeed 'ideological', as follows:

> [H]uman artefacts and contrivances, including any rules by which people try to live, or get others to live, have to be understood functionally. What is their point, what is the final cause to which they are oriented? They perform well or ill, are in good shape or bad, to the extent that they can be seen to work towards these essential ends with a minimum of regrettable side-effects. It is undoubtedly controversial what functions should be ascribed to law in general or to particular laws or any other human production. Failure to confront and account openly for values involved, and to defend one's own proposals as to what the relevant values are, may confer on work about law an apparently greater objectivity than if a proper openness were practised. But it is this concealment of value-orientation, not its open avowal, that is ideological in a sinister sense. Honest interpretation that is open about the values it presupposes and that is as alert to system-failures and system-successes judged against those values is the best objectivity that is available to the human sciences, jurisprudence included.[70]

I see no reason to doubt that Lauterpacht managed to communicate his values in an open and honest manner. His purpose was to advance peace and the rule of law in the international context through the 'legitimate methods of juridical criticism and analysis'. Koskenniemi, however, sums up Lauterpacht's historical significance for the profession of international law as follows:

> Lauterpacht was a Victorian liberal in a time when the dialectic of the enlightenment is only slowly asserting itself. That he had no doubt about the intrinsically beneficent character of legal reason defines him as an historical agent whose defense of legal reason maps out for us a large field of our shared professional past.[71]

We may mostly agree with Koskenniemi's historical description of Lauterpacht's life and professional activities, and, with some reservations, with the appraisal of Lauterpacht's significance in the development of international law. But his portrayal of Lauterpacht as a historical agent working energetically in various roles at the surface level of the law but lacking a 'horizon', and thus being unable to answer the realists, is unsatisfactory.

[69] In Koskenniemi's words, what is at stake is 'the struggle for freedom in conditions where the critique of theoretical reason has done its work'. Koskenniemi, 'Formalism, Fragmentation, Freedom: Kantian Themes in Today's International Law', (2007) 4 *No Foundations* 7, 23 n 30.

[70] Neil MacCormick, *Institutions of Law* (Oxford University Press, Oxford, 2007) 305.

[71] Koskenniemi, *Civilizer*, above n 35, 412.

When one's long-term project is met with disbelief that is based on a short-term critique of the present situation and a pessimistic conception of human nature, one can only reaffirm, again, one's point of view. Trying to defend one's position as anything other than the political project it is would make it precisely what MacCormick calls 'ideology in a sinister sense'. For Lauterpacht's was the 'Kantian project', the defence of legal reason in international life. Through all the 'Victorian' and other ages, the work of Kant and his contemporaries has been there. Lauterpacht, too, had a copy of *The Metaphysics of Morals*.

The problem with Koskenniemi's interpretation is that it is based on his 'critical' perspective on law. This theoretical position was originally presented in his *From Apology to Utopia,* published in 1989.[72] The book presented a 'structuralist' analysis of law and put forth the thesis of 'indeterminacy' in international law. As Koskenniemi points out, 'this image of the law remained rather static',[73] and he explains that the origins of his work on Lauterpacht lie in an attempt to 'move away from the cool structuralism'. But here, too, 'apology' and 'utopia' remain the ultimate point of departure for historical analysis.[74] A historical analysis of legal thought based on this critical approach—'all law as politics'—is unable to appreciate the most important aspect of Lauterpacht's professional activities. I return to this topic at the end of the essay, but I doubt whether a 'morality of pragmatism' is to be found in Lauterpacht's activities any more than in the most 'enlightened' work of the present international law profession.

IV. The 'Realist' Critiques of the Interwar Effort

If it might have been possible to characterise the First World War with a metaphor of a natural disaster, this was for obvious reasons not possible in the case of the Second. This War was not a 'volcanic eruption'; it was Auschwitz and the 'banality of evil'. The problem of evil, Hannah Arendt proclaimed in 1945, was to become the central problem for the intellectual life of the later twentieth century.[75]

The turn from idealism to realism in the study of international relations has generally been referred to as the first 'great debate' in later disciplinary histories, even though the 'debate' was limited, as Steve Smith notes, to a 'series of statements of faith'[76] The turn in the discipline consisted of a shift in the prevailing arguments and a more general 'end of optimism'. The work of two men, E H Carr and Hans Morgenthau, has profoundly contributed to the image in later discussion on international relations of a radical departure from the interwar legal project.

[72] Koskenniemi, above n 50. [73] Koskenniemi, *Civilizer*, above n 35, 1. [74] Ibid, 5–6.

[75] Hannah Arendt, *Essays in Understanding* (Harcourt, New York, 1994) 134.

[76] Steve Smith, 'The Self-Images of a Discipline: A Genealogy of International Relations Theory', in Ken Booth and Steve Smith (eds), *International Relations Theory Today* (Polity, Cambridge, 1995) 1, 13–17.

A. E H Carr

E H Carr's *The Twenty Years' Crisis* continues to be regarded in the field of international relations as somehow an unusually 'complex' and 'nuanced' work, even though, as Paul Rich observes, it 'can ultimately be read as a simple polemic'.[77] Carr himself did not have much sympathy for the field. He begins his classic with the statement that 'the science of international politics is in its infancy'. His later assessments of the field were even more critical—he was adamant that it could never become a true science. For him international relations was a 'rag-bag into which one was entitled to put anything one pleases', and attempts to 'turn it into some sort of organized self-contained subject had ended in fiasco'.[78] In a letter to Stanley Hoffmann in 1977 Carr wrote that there was no such thing as a science of international relations, and that the study of the subject in the English-speaking world was 'simply a study of the best way to run the world from positions of strength'.[79] By that time Carr himself had long since abandoned the field. He did not consider *The Twenty Years' Crisis* as particularly important: by the end of the war, he said it 'was already a period piece and such it remains'.[80]

Carr was born in 1892 into a suburban middle-class household in north London; his 'early world was marked by certainty and security', 'security not only in family relations but in a sense scarcely imaginable today', he later noted. He also 'grew up in an entirely sheltered environment of public school, Cambridge and the Foreign Office'. Surrounded by solidity and stability, Carr had been a 'committed liberal' in his early years, but gradually became disillusioned and set out to find an alternative way of understanding the world. The First World War had been a shock, albeit not a fundamental one. But Carr was, like Keynes, disappointed with the Versailles Peace Treaty as economically senseless, and this was one reason for his growing disillusionment. Carr was not anti-American, but he was anti-Woodrow Wilson, whose 'brand of crusading politics raised serious doubts in his mind about both liberalism as a doctrine and Wilsonianism as a guide to international politics'.[81]

But the greatest blow to Carr's liberalism was the economic collapse after 1929. For Carr, England and the world were adrift and in need of a new faith if there was to be hope for the future. Carr found his faith in social reform and economic planning. He thought a social revolution from below was necessary, a new programme of radical change, a 'new society based on new social and economic foundations', full employment, equality and social justice. Carr developed an interest in what was happening in

[77] Paul Rich, 'E.H. Carr and the Quest for Moral Revolution in International Relations' in Cox, above n 12, 198, 205.

[78] Cox, 'Introduction', above n 13 xii.

[79] Cox, 'Introduction', above n 12, 2 n 5.

[80] Carr, above n 13, ciii.

[81] Cox, above n 13, xiv–xvii.

the Soviet Union, as part of his 'growing love affair with Russian culture more generally'. Cox comments: '[A]s an increasingly unsettled intellectual, Carr was bound to be influenced by new ideas, and as one set of truths collapsed he logically began to look around for another with which to make sense of a world in crisis'. He became interested in Marx and Marxism, and he was also 'impressed by certain writers who had been influenced by Marx without necessarily being Marxist themselves', especially Karl Mannheim and Reinhold Niebuhr, both of whom came to have an important influence on *The Twenty Years' Crisis*.[82]

In Jonathan Haslam's characterisation, *The Twenty Years' Crisis* was a 'product of bitter disillusion'.[83] The originally intended title for the book was 'Utopia and Reality', revealing Carr's reasons for writing it as well as its argument. Carr was 'anxious that the title would not accurately reflect what was in the book itself', for, he stressed, it was not a new history but rather about 'international relations in general'.

Behind his original idea for the title was Mannheim's *Ideology and Utopia*. Charles Jones writes: 'In *The Twenty Years' Crisis*, Carr adopted the main argument of *Ideology and Utopia* but twisted its rhetorical structure almost out of recognition.'[84] Carr renamed as utopianism that which Mannheim had called ideology. Carr's realism, on the other hand, was not what Mannheim had called 'Utopia', but the critical technique of the sociology of knowledge itself. This twist then allowed Carr to 'set up, and then discredit for their extremism, two positions misleadingly labelled Left and Right in the early chapters of the book'.[85] Carr's aim in this was to 'position his own substantive policy positions in the later chapters as moderate compromises'.[86] Jones observes: 'In sliding from an account of the *Realpolitik* tradition to one of the sociology of knowledge, and bringing both under the term 'realism', Carr departs from the symmetry of Mannheim.'[87] According to Jones, Carr managed to get away with this by using repeated dichotomies—such as the primacy of fact versus the primacy of value—that provided for two extremes between which one would conveniently compromise with the aid of Carr's new science.[88]

This strategy laid the foundations for the later idealism/realism dichotomy in international relations, where indeed the (realist) strategy has since then remained the same. The question of the ultimate primacy of idealism or realism, law or facts, and the presentation of these alternatives in the form of a dichotomy, shaped the image of law in international relations. Lauterpacht pointed to inconsistencies in some of Carr's arguments regarding the character of international society:

[82] Ibid, xvii–xix.

[83] Jonathan Haslam, 'E.H. Carr's Search for Meaning, 1892–1982', in Cox, above n 12, 21, 27.

[84] Charles Jones, *E.H. Carr and International Relations. A Duty to Lie* (Cambridge University Press, Cambridge, 1998) 127.

[85] Ibid, 128. [86] Ibid, 128.

[87] Ibid, 130. [88] Ibid, 130.

Undoubtedly the very action of enlightened self-interest implies the necessity of secondary sacrifices for the sake of the ultimate good, but the supreme problem is to make such sacrifices effective and rational within the scheme of an organized life. This Professor Carr rejects, and the reader to his astonishment (and to his utter confusion) is presented with the demand for sacrifice on the part of States as the principal basis of international ethics and of an international community and with the mocking description of those holding to the identity of national and international interests as indistinguishable from those asserting the overriding supremacy of national interest. The result is astonishing and confusing in its suddenness because one of the principal features of Professor Carr's scepticism about international morality is that nations, unlike individuals, cannot easily manifest and are not expected to manifest feelings of sacrifice and generosity. The result is sudden and astonishing because, after having reduced the possibilities of international morality to next to nothing, Professor Carr finishes by basing it on the rigid and exacting test of sacrificial obligation as distinguished from interest.

The result is astonishing but only so long as we are not conscious of the underlying purpose of the book. That purpose is to supply a justification for the policy of negation towards effective international organization which characterised the conduct of the principal Governments in power in Europe since 1920. The best way of proving this is to show that the ideal of international organization, conceived often as the effective rule of a supra-national authority, or, in the absence of such authority, as the collective enforcement of peace, is unsound and Utopian. The principal theme in that negative proof is that there is in fact no common interest in the preservation of peace because, owing to the disparity between the "haves" and "have nots", peace, conceived as an effective rule of law, works only in the interest of those in possession. The primary factor in international relations is not harmony but conflicts of interests. Those who advocate the political integration of the international society are merely the deliberate or unconscious advocates of the preservation of the *status quo*. Conflicts of interest—impervious to any regulative scheme of legal organization—are the basic elements. A harmony of interests expressed in the postulate of an international community, securing under the reign of law the full development of its members and the progressive levelling of removable injustices, is a dream of Utopians as distinguished from realists. (Nine-tenths of the book are devoted to attacking the Utopian position, although Professor Carr, in order to render the assault more effective, affects an intermediate position between realists, whom he occasionally attacks *pour mieux sauter*, and Utopians.) These conflicts, in his view, are a perennial feature of international life. He gives reasons why they cannot be solved or kept within bounds by any scheme of international law or organization. For in the absence of international legislature, international law is static because it has no machinery for effecting changes in the *status quo* so as to bring about a just solution to conflicts. The problem of peaceful change is thus the central problem of international society. But unlike within the State it is not a problem capable of solution by way of the establishment of a supra-national authority decreeing changes in the existing law. Change must remain a function of power. But, and this is the comfort which Professor Carr offers, it need not remain exclusively a function of power. States may show that enlightened spirit of sacrifice, generosity and morality (which we are told elsewhere they ought not, and cannot be expected, to show) which may render the use of power on the other side unnecessary. But power—not the organized and important power of the community, rather the power of each interested party—is, and must remain the *ultima ratio* of the central problem of international relations.[89]

This commentary was not published at the time, possibly due to its uncharacteristically polemical tone,[90] but it seems that Lauterpacht would have shared Jones's analysis of Carr's strategy of dichotomization and structure of argumentation. Perhaps it is the inability of *The Twenty Years' Crisis* to take into account differences in long-term and short-term points of view, and the consequences thereof on the direction of political action, that convinced Carr himself at a rather early stage that it was only a 'period piece'. As for Carr's later views on international society, Tim Dunne notes that we can see how 'reason and progress, the two utopian scourges which Carr sought to banish in the early chapters of *The Twenty Years' Crisis*, are returning to provide for the foundations for a new and more inclusive social order'.[91]

There were, and are, many who wish to see *The Twenty Years' Crisis* as containing some sort of a much-sought-after, longer-term wisdom. On this level, the ageless elements were about raising awareness as to the need to balance utopia with reality; the conclusion would thus be that there would be no point in not being an 'idealist realist'. But, as many have pointed out, this is a logically meaningless position.

Carr's critique was ultimately not a critique of any research but rather of the *Zeitgeist*. This explains the great receptiveness to Carr's work of an understandably disillusioned post-Second World War audience. Many of the ideas and projects of the 'interwar idealists' are, however, still applicable today, and even at the time, the Utopians were not that devastated by Carr's attack.[92]

B. Hans Morgenthau

While E H Carr abandoned the topic of international relations and moved on to write his monumental *History of Soviet Russia*, Hans Morgenthau for his part 'abandoned' international law and went on to build on Carr's and others' contributions, ending up in formulating the basis for what

[89] Hersch Lauterpacht, 'Professor Carr on International Morality', in Lauterpacht, above n 48, 67, 90–92.

[90] Elihu Lauterpacht comments in his editorial note that the text was 'uncharacteristic because of its polemical tone and its relatively unrestrained style... Lauterpacht normally avoided the public pursuit of controversy, which doubtless explains why he put aside this piece without even correcting the typescript.' Ibid, 67.

[91] Tim Dunne, 'Theories as Weapons', in Cox, above n 12, 217, 228.

[92] For a survey of responses to Carr, see Peter Wilson, 'Carr and his Early Critics: Responses to *The Twenty Years' Crisis*, 1939–46', in Cox, above n 12, 165.

was to become the new discipline of international relations on realist principles. Morgenthau had been 'deeply influenced' by *The Twenty Years' Crisis*,[93] but came to think that ultimately Carr had 'surrendered to the immanence of power':

There can be no doubt that Mr. Carr's work constitutes a contribution to political thought of the first order. No contemporary thinker, with the exception of Reinhold Niebuhr, has seen more clearly and exposed with more acute brilliance the essential defects of Western political thought. Even in so monumental a failure as *The Soviet Impact on the Western World*—a failure because it confronts Soviet ideology with democratic practice—there is much critical analysis which Western thinkers might well ponder. Yet, as we have seen, it was Mr. Carr's purpose not only to give a critical analysis of the Western tradition of political thought but also to replace the old and obsolete with a new synthesis of realism and utopianism, theory and practice, ethics and politics; and the main bulk of Mr. Carr's work is dedicated to that purpose. In view of this purpose the over-all impression of Mr. Carr's work is one of failure. What are the reasons for the failure of a work undertaken with so singular an equipment of mind, learning and honest purpose?

The fundamental reason is philosophic. Mr. Carr sets out to discover a new morality in the political world without a clear notion of what morality is. The philosophically untenable equation of utopia, theory and morality, which is at the foundation of *The Twenty Years' Crisis*, leads of necessity to a relativistic, instrumentalist conception of morality. Morality, then, becomes "an escape from the logical consequences of realism, which, once it is achieved, must once more be attacked with instruments of realism".... In another contribution to the problem, "The Moral Foundations for World Order," Mr. Carr has nothing better to offer than a "compromise between morality and power," and throughout his work he relies heavily upon Niebuhr's *Moral Man and Immoral Society*, unaware that Mr. Niebuhr has long since given up the juxtaposition which the title indicates.

Consequently, Mr. Carr has no transcendent point of view from which to survey the political scene and to appraise the phenomenon of power. Thus the political moralist transforms himself into a utopian of power. Whoever holds seeming superiority of power becomes of necessity the repository of superior morality as well. Power thus corrupts, not only the actor on the political scene, but even the observer, unfortified by a transcendent standard of ethics. This is the lesson taught by the fate of the political romantics of whom the outstanding representatives are Adam Müller and Carl Schmitt. It is a dangerous thing to be a Machiavelli. It is a disastrous thing to be a Machiavelli without *virtù*.[94]

[93] Francis Boyle, *World Politics and International Law* (Duke University Press, Durham, NC, 1985) 12 n 37.

[94] Hans Morgenthau, 'The Surrender to the Immanence of Power: E.H. Carr', in Hans Morgenthau, *Dilemmas of Politics* (The University of Chicago Press, Chicago, 1958), 350, 356–57.

This was of course the virtue of the individual statesman that Morgenthau later developed as the focal point of his own thinking. In recent years there has been rising interest in the European intellectual roots of the American scholar that Morgenthau is usually considered to represent. The influence in particular of Carl Schmitt on the development of Morgenthau's thought has received a lot of attention.[95] Morgenthau's 1929 dissertation *Die Internationale Rechtspflege: Ihr Wesen und ihre Grenzen*[96] was in part a 'friendly critique' of Schmitt's *Der Begriff des Politischen,* which had been published two years earlier.[97] In *Der Begriff* Schmitt had defined the political as its own sphere of human activity—distinct, for example, from those of morality or economics—in which the central issue was the contrast between 'friend' and 'enemy'. Morgenthau's argument was that the 'political' ought instead to be defined in terms of the 'intensity' of the conflict in question, as the genuinely political issues among those found in the other spheres—for instance, morality, aesthetics, economics—in fact were the ones with the highest degree of intensity. This idea of the concept of politics defined through intensity found its way into the second edition of Schmitt's *Der Begriff des Politischen*, with no recognition however of Morgenthau's contribution.[98]

On the basis of their varying degrees of intensity, disagreements between States could be divided into those that could be solved by legal means and those that were so obviously political that they could not be so solved. This conceptual academic play closely resembles the way Schmitt employed conceptual strategies to advance his positions.[99] In Koskenniemi's view the two men had shared five elements: they both thought that the 'European era' had come to an end, both shared a central focus on power, both saw international law as a part of a 'liberal strategy of depoliticization', both argued that 'moralizing' and 'legalistic' language intensified international conflicts, and, finally, their 'critiques of legal and moral principles shifted attention to the decisions in which they received meaning in the context of political struggle'.[100]

Koskenniemi observes that '[t]hough Morgenthau shared Schmitt's rule-skepticism, he still retained the ideal of the rule of law in a domestic context.' But Morgenthau thought this could not work in the international realm

[95] See e.g. Koskenniemi, *Civilizer*, above n 35, 413–509. See also Chris Brown, 'The Twilight of International Morality'? Hans J Morgenthau and Carl Schmitt on the end of the *Jus Publicum Europaeum*', and William E Scheuerman, 'Carl Schmitt and Hans Morgenthau: Realism and Beyond', in Michael C Williams (ed) *Realism Reconsidered. The Legacy of Hans J. Morgenthau in International Relations* (Oxford University Press, Oxford, 2007) 42 and 62, respectively.

[96] Hans Morgenthau, *Die Internationale Rechtspflege. Ihr Wesen und ihre Grenzen* (Noske, Leipzig, 1929).

[97] Brown, above n 95, 42.

[98] Scheuerman, above n 95, 62–63.

[99] Kaarlo Tuori, *Oikeuden Ratio ja Voluntas* [transl.: Ratio and Voluntas in Law] (WSOYPro, Helsinki, 2007) 167–182. Tuori describes the way in which Schmitt used legal concepts as rhetorical tools in order to legitimise totalitarian tendencies. One example would be his use of the concept of the 'total state due to its weakness' (*totaler Staat aus Schwäche*) to criticize the Weimar Republic. Schmitt advocated instead in favour of a future post-Weimar 'total state due to its strength' (*totaler Staat aus Stärke)*.

[100] Koskenniemi, *Civilizer*, above n 35, 460–465.

where, unlike in the domestic context, situations were unique in their nature. Thus Morgenthau's arguments—through the paradox of an individualized rule of law—in fact led him to adopt Schmitt's decisionism.[101] 'Like Schmitt', Koskenniemi continues, 'Morgenthau saw the international as a context where strategically placed individuals made choices' and here the relevant question for the statesman making these decisions was not 'between legality and illegality but between political wisdom and political stupidity'.[102]

Morgenthau had also been influenced by Kelsen, but only on a rather selective basis. Koskenniemi notes that Morgenthau's 1934 *Habilitationsschrift* in Geneva, titled *La réalité des normes: En particulier des normes du droit international*, 'was heavily influenced by Kelsen, though his attitude towards formalism remained unrepentantly Schmittian'. For Morgenthau, 'Neokantianism was "the faithful expression of the decadence of philosophical thought at German universities at the end of the last century"'. What Morgenthau adopted from Kelsen was a stress on the idea of 'validity' as central for legal analysis, but, Koskenniemi notes, 'Morgenthau's views of human nature and motivation left no space for a law that would be anything but an instrument of causality whereby one will determines the content of another will'.[103] In practice Morgenthau's conception of law was thus based on first embracing but then rejecting Kelsen's doctrine.

Morgenthau's last legal contribution was his 1940 article *Positivism, Functionalism, and International Law,* which was a critique of 'positivism' in international law and a call for a more context-sensitive and 'functional' jurisprudence.[104] But Morgenthau never developed such a jurisprudence—this has been characterised by Scheuerman as a 'theoretical missed opportunity'.[105] Instead, he stopped writing about international law and concentrated, as he in a way had always done, on the 'genuinely political'. As to Morgenthau's new undertaking, Koskenniemi observes:

> Morgenthau's influence as the founder of international relations follows from his conscious departure from legal formalism, on the one hand, but, crucially, of his steadfast refusal to collapse the field into mainstream sociology or ethics, on the other. He did not found the discipline *despite* the contradiction between idealism and realism in *Politics among Nations*. He founded it *on* that contradiction.[106]

Morgenthau founded the discipline on the contradiction between realism and idealism because he believed in the existence of such a contradiction. In his first edition of *Politics among Nations*, published in 1948, Morgenthau defined international politics as a struggle for power, before

[101] Ibid, 463. [102] Ibid, 463. [103] Ibid, 455.

[104] Morgenthau, 'Positivism, Functionalism and International Law' (1940) 34 *American Journal of International Law* 260.

[105] Scheuerman, 'A Theoretical Missed Opportunity? Hans J. Morgenthau as Critical Realist', in Duncan Bell (ed), *Political Thought and International Relations. Variations on a Realist Theme* (Oxford University Press, Oxford, 2009) 41.

[106] Koskenniemi, *Civilizer*, above n 35, 465.

discussing the doctrine of the balance of power, international morality, world public opinion and international law as limitations on national power.[107] As to international law, Morgenthau emphasised that 'the conception of a divisible sovereignty is contrary to logic and politically unfeasible'.[108]

In spite of its 'logical' orientation, the book was not intended as a theory of international politics in the strictly scientific sense, as Oliver Jütersonke points out, but was rather intended to serve what Morgenthau himself described as a 'polemic purpose'. In Jütersonke's conclusion, the book is 'a work on the practical limitations to the use of law in the international realm'.[109] Morgenthau appealed to diplomacy as an alternative way forward:

> The way toward international peace which we have shown cannot compete in inspirational qualities with the simple and fascinating formulae which for a century and a half have fired the imagination of a war-weary humanity. There is something spectacular in the radical simplicity of a formula which with one sweep seems to dispose of the problem of war once and for all. This has been the promise of such solutions as free trade, arbitration, disarmament, collective security, universal socialism, international government, and the world state. There is nothing spectacular, fascinating, or inspiring in the business of diplomacy.[110]

It is understandable that Morgenthau was impatient with all the other methods, but it is hard to see how his call for diplomacy could even at the time have formed a new opening. Moreover, Morgenthau is rather selective in his use of 'logic'. His logic seems to require treating sovereignty as conceptually indivisible, but does not inhibit lumping together free trade, disarmament and universal socialism and dismissing the whole collection as 'simplistic', compared with the supposedly more complex everyday boredom of diplomacy.

In the second edition of *Politics among Nations*, published in 1954, Morgenthau added a chapter titled 'A Realist Theory of International Politics', which contained his *Six Principles of Political Realism*. He argues that 'politics, like society in general, is governed by objective laws that have their roots in human nature'; that 'human nature has not changed since the classical philosophies of China, India and Greece endeavoured to discover these laws'; and that 'the concept of interest defined in terms of power … provides the link between reason trying to understand international politics and the facts to be understood'. The argument continues that 'the idea of interest defined as power … is unaffected by the circumstances of time and

[107] Hans Morgenthau, *Politics among Nations. The Struggle for Power and Peace* (Knopf, New York, 1948).

[108] Ibid, 258–59.

[109] Oliver Jütersonke, 'Hans J. Morgenthau on the Limits of Justiciability in International Law' (2006) 8 *Journal of the History of International Law* 181, 209–210.

[110] Morgenthau, above n 107, 443–44.

space'; that '[r]ealism considers prudence—the weighing of the consequences of alternative political actions—to be the supreme virtue in politics'; that '[p]olitical realism refuses to identify the moral aspirations of a particular nation with the moral laws that govern the universe'; and that 'it is exactly the concept of interest defined as power that saves us from both moral excess and political folly' of not understanding that '[t]here is a world of difference between the belief that all nations stand under the judgment of God, inscrutable to the human mind, and the blasphemous conviction that God is always on one's side and that what one wills oneself cannot fail to be willed by God also'. Finally, we learn that while the 'political realist is not unaware of the existence and relevance of standards of thought other than the political one[, a]s political realist, he cannot but subordinate these other standards to the political one'.[111]

Here, then, was the 'Bible' for later disciplinary developments in international relations, in all its sophistication. Perhaps Morgenthau did not intend to develop a theory of international politics in the scientific sense, as he was in the end more focused on providing 'advice of prudence' to the continually more enlightened statesman. Subsequent generations, however, have accepted Morgenthau's positions as theory. Further, Morgenthau probably belongs to the category of scholars that are 'more cited than read'.[112] Against this background the problem of Morgenthau's theoretical position may appear to be his reductionist view of the phenomenon of politics, and the solution a wider understanding of politics.

However, the problem with this way of approaching Morgenthau—to the extent that it is useful to approach him at all—is the very question 'what shall I take into account as relevant?' *Principles & Problems of International Politics: Selected Readings*, published in 1950, is an answer to precisely this question. The volume consists of chapters on diplomacy, the foreign policies of different countries and on national power. In stark contrast to Heatley's emphasis in his similar volume in 1919,[113] international law is discussed in only one of the 66 chapters. By this time it was clear what was relevant for international politics 'thus conceived', and what was not.[114] This fundamental bias has remained a problem at the core of international relations ever since. With these assumptions, international relations theory has remained a theory of the 'limits of international law' instead of a theory explaining social phenomena.

Morgenthau was not able to take Lauterpacht's and others' projects seriously because he had been disillusioned by their failure in a particular historical context. Morgenthau's conception of law, his simultaneous embrace and rejection of Kelsen's formalism led to an inescapably reductionist

[111] Hans Morgenthau, *Politics among Nations* (2nd edn, Knopf, New York, 1954) 4–11.

[112] As Michael Williams notes in his *The Realist Tradition and the Limits of International Relations* (Cambridge University Press, Cambridge, 2005) 82.

[113] Above, text to n 14.

[114] Hans Morgenthau and Kenneth Thompson (eds), *Principles & Problems of International Politics: Selected Readings* (Knopf, New York, 1950).

image which he combined with a Schmittian understanding of politics as struggle, as well as a spirit of nihilism regarding the possibilities of progress in the human condition. These elements led him to the 'paradox of individualised rule of law' and, as noted, a Schmittian decisionism. Scheuerman concludes that it is 'unlikely that any normatively desirable cosmopolitan vision will be able to borrow much if anything from the political thought of Carl Schmitt; Morgenthau's own failures stem at least in part from his unwieldy Schmittian intellectual baggage'.[115]

Like Carr, Morgenthau had difficulty in recognising differences in the short and long term because he took his disillusioned critical point of view too seriously and refused to see its limits. Georg Henrik von Wright has stressed the need for a proper contextualization for critique to be constructive:

> In the history of thought there are times when the best thing a philosopher can do is destroy (Wittgenstein), or deconstruct (Derrida) or "philosophise with a sledgehammer" (Nietzsche)—in the hope that when everything has been demolished, there will be revealed a soil in which can be grown something essentially new and fresh. I am inclined to believe that we live in this kind of age.[116]

It seems that both E H Carr and Hans Morgenthau understood this in the end.[117] But how well has it been understood in the collective effort of building on the heritage left by the two men?

V. The 'Interwar Heritage' in Later International Relations Theory

How the interwar project has been, indeed continues to be, interpreted has had a significant influence on discussions on international matters right up to the present day. The critiques of the interwar effort set the scene for theoretical discussion in international relations by cementing the position of realism as the one approach to which every other way of 'seeing the world' has had to relate, in one way or another. That the English school is called the English school is a testament to the influence and enduring appeal of these arguments.[118]

As a discipline, international relations was not born in Aberystwyth or even with Morgenthau, but only gradually in the decades after him and through reactions mainly to his thought. In this sense Morgenthau, even as he had little sympathy with the whole endeavour, might be called the

[115] Scheuerman, above n 95, 86.

[116] Georg Henrik von Wright, 'Arvot ja tarpeet' (1986), cited in *Trains of Thought* (The National Library of Finland, Gallery Publications 6, Helsinki, 2004) 142.

[117] Boyle, above n 93, 70–71.

[118] In the field of international relations the 'international society approach' has come to be known as the 'English school'. See e.g. Alex J Bellamy (ed), *International Society and its Critics* (Oxford University Press, Oxford, 2005).

reluctant father of the discipline. But then with this logic we might also credit Zimmern and, perhaps even more so, Lauterpacht, for they were among the prime targets of the realists' own thinking.

Morgenthau's own work may not have been 'theory' in the sense that the term has later been understood. But the construction of all subsequent international relations theory as a reaction to his position, together with the 'scramble to become a science', has cemented the foundations of the international relations edifice firmly upon Morgenthau's *Six Principles*. Morgenthau's was a deeply reductionist image, but perhaps more of law than of politics. This reductionist view has since then been partially 'deconstructed', but from the wrong end, so to speak. The concept of the political has been expanded to cover ever new aspects of the issues—society, legitimacy and the like—the original view excluded. But the reductionist image of law, inherited from critiques of the interwar effort, has not been deconstructed, although the whole theoretical construction rests on it. Instead, the resulting theoretical options have been organised into a disciplinary history in the form of successive 'paradigmatic' periods separated by 'great debates'.

The urge for interdisciplinary collaboration has recently resulted in a new period of détente between international law and international relations. The topic 'international law and international relations' has received increasing attention, to the extent that it now seems international law actually works, even if still only through a rational choice framework.[119] International relations is also (re)discovering ties with political thought in a wider sense, apparently searching for something missing inside the field.[120]

Still today, however, the two main disciplinary trends remain. Realism in its various forms proclaims we are forever lost in the conceptual mirror maze of power, interests and sovereignty, while the competition is in perennial search for that theoretical gap in which to put some sort of community or society, anarchical or otherwise. Two recent contributions, both, incidentally, written by faculty at the Aberystwyth Department, nicely illustrate the present state of international relations as a discipline. Ian Clark's twin contribution, *Legitimacy in International Society* and *International Legitimacy and World Society*, represents the English school in its attempt to dig up responsible topics from the disciplinary graveyard in the best traditions of the 'international society approach'.[121] The contribution 'Realism Reconsidered', on the other hand, reengages yet again with the all-important question 'what does it mean to be a realist?'[122]

[119] See Andrew T Guzman, *How International Law Works: A Rational Choice Theory* (Oxford University Press, New York, 2008).

[120] See e.g., David Boucher, *Political Theories of International Relations: From Thucydides to the Present* (Oxford University Press, Oxford, 1998) and Chris Brown, Terry Nardin and Nicholas Rengger (eds) *International Relations in Political Thought: Texts from the Ancient Greeks to the First World War* (Cambridge University Press, Cambridge, 2002).

[121] Ian Clark, *Legitimacy in International Society, International Legitimacy and World Society* (Oxford University Press, Oxford, 2005 and 2007, respectively).

[122] Williams, above n 95.

Meanwhile, the discipline's search for foundations continues. In recent scholarship it has been suspected that such 'foundations' might really be vampires—that is, 'philosophical undead'[123]—but the problem and the point with foundations is that there are none. Indeed there cannot be. As Jan Klabbers notes, 'international relations, as a discipline, does not exist and cannot exist, and ... its most enlightened practitioners are fully aware of this (without of course, understandably, telling anyone)'.[124] He continues:

> It has become increasingly clear that social and economic processes, and indeed political processes ... do not stop at national boundaries. This is where it becomes clear that there is a big void (call it a black hole, if you will) at the very heart of the discipline of international relations that plagues the discipline and makes its value as a source of information and understanding about what is happening in the world rather limited, and it is this black hole that renders the discipline subject to a multitude of methodological squabbles.[125]

Now, the existence of theories is not usually legitimated—a discipline needs them and that is that—but a refreshing exception in this regard is found in the basic introductory text in international relations by Baylis and Smith.[126] There is certainly a commendable pedagogic aim here, interesting just because it seems the authors have felt compelled to explain to their students the very existence of these theories that they themselves probably do not regard as very useful. Many in the discipline have grown wary of the whole theoretical apparatus, and some have argued in favour of transforming the field into the study of 'world politics', or taken a somewhat sarcastic distance to theories, describing them as mere 'belief systems'.

In their widely-used textbook Baylis and Smith present international relations theories as 'sunglasses' through which one brings order to the millions of facts that one is forced to observe in the world and which when combined would otherwise make no sense at all. They argue that theories are compulsory and either explicit or implicit. In a sense this is of course true. But from the (pedagogical) assertion that a theory ought to be made explicit it does not follow that the theory ought to be of any particular type. Implicit theories may often be contradictory and complex, notably more so than many theories of a more explicit nature. Introducing 'complex interdependence' to an international finance professional would probably not give much insight in terms of professional development; it would

[123] See Nuno Monteiro and Keven Ruby, 'IR and the False Promise of Philosophical Foundations' (2009) 1 *International Theory* 15, 42–43.

[124] Jan Klabbers, 'The Relative Autonomy of International Law or the Forgotten Politics of Interdisciplinarity' (2005) 1 *Journal of International Law and International Relations* 35, 42.

[125] Ibid, 43.

[126] John Baylis & Steve Smith (eds) *The Globalization of World Politics: An Introduction to International Relations*, (2nd edn Oxford University Press, Oxford, 2001). The latest edition is by Baylis, Smith & Owens (Oxford University Press, Oxford, 2007).

remain an essentially academic story, only understandable in the light of the discipline's own lack of theoretical sophistication.

This argument about the millions of facts is what Carr must have meant by characterising the discipline as a 'rag-bag'. The discipline is plagued by a lack of focus and thus the theoretical approaches—sunglasses—it has on offer for the student to choose from and observe the world through suffer from what it would be tempting to call a 'level-of-complexity' problem. There is no overarching way to limit the facts in the abstract; the limitation will follow from the discovery of a meaningful focus and subfocuses of inquiry. It will be possible to comment on international affairs in an informed and responsible manner only by giving up such sunglasses. For when there is a meaningful focus, these theories or visions become entirely meaningless to the effort of analysing the topics in question. In his recent study *War in Human Civilization* Azar Gat discusses the use of international relations theories in his topic, observing:

> Attempts made to find the root cause of war in the nature of the individual, the state, or the international system are fundamentally misplaced. In all these "levels" there are necessary but insufficient causes for war, and the whole cannot be broken into pieces.[127]

International relations scholars have discovered that 'balance-of-power' theory does not necessarily work any better:

> We know now that balance-of-power theory simply does not deserve pride of place in international relations theorizing. Balancing is not the main thing states do. Hegemony, we now know, is a normal condition of the international system, but no more so than diversity or balance. Which direction an international system moves depends simply on the relative strength of forces pushing it in each direction.[128]

In analysing the international system we should thus focus on the 'relative strength of forces pushing it in each direction'. In addition to such classical topics as balance of power, one area where international relations theory has been of very little use is (European) integration. Marlene Wind observes that the problem is not only about substance:

> It is also about method. In one of his well-known critiques of conventional IR theory, Gaddis notes that in general IR scholars have been so eager to boil everything down to a few variables that they have ended up saying nothing of interest to anyone outside their own narrow circle. Gaddis is also to the point when it comes to the manner in which we conceptualize the EU. One of the most glaring examples is the problem that many theorists have making sense of the—somewhat contradictory—simultaneous process of disintegration and federalisation.

[127] Azar Gat, *War in Human Civilization* (Oxford University Press, Oxford, 2006) 669.

[128] Stuart Kaufman, Richard Little and William Wohlforth, 'Conclusion: Theoretical Insights from the Study of World History' in Stuart Kaufman, Richard Little and William Wohlforth (eds) *The Balance of Power in World History* (Palgrave Macmillan, Basingstoke, 2007) 228, 246.

This sometimes confusing picture does not fit well into abstract models moulded around just a few variables.[129]

One of the variables usually left out is law. For example, in his *Ethics, Liberalism and Realism in International Relations*, Mark D Gismondi argues in favour of a 'covenantal future'. While for Gismondi prime examples of such covenants are the Universal Declaration of Human Rights, the International Covenant on Civil and Political Rights and the International Covenant on Economic, Social and Cultural Rights, international law is discussed only in passing.[130] Granted, the third edition of that international relations textbook included a new chapter on the basics of international law under the heading 'Structures and processes'. But then this is a development that is taking place more in spite of theory than because of it.[131]

As it remains unclear whether theories like these ultimately have any explanatory force, it would seem necessary to have some disciplinary reflexivity that would go beyond 'explanation and understanding', for what remains is the normative force of these theories, taken as a whole. Where Carr perhaps gave the impression that the interwar activities had been too much biased in favour of law, this 'new normative approach' has taken things to the other end of the spectrum, in the sense that all meaningful discussion on law is effectively suffocated. Chris Brown observes that the scepticism concerning the possibilities of international institutional reform 'was built into the discourse of international relations at its foundation and has informed—perhaps "disabled" would be a better word—IR theory ever since'.[132] As concerns the topic of international justice, he concludes that 'the need now is to pick up the story where the interwar reformers were forced to let it drop'.[133]

But the reformers were not 'forced to let it drop'. We cannot pretend that nothing has been achieved since the interwar era, however tempting this analysis for some might seem. But there is a need in the discipline of

[129] Marlene Wind, *Sovereignty and European Integration: Towards a Post-Hobbesian Order* (Palgrave, Basingstoke, 2001) 4. The reference to Gaddis is to his 'International Relations Theory, and the End of the Cold War' (1992) 17 *International Security* 5. Teija Tiilikainen and Teemu Palosaari (eds) *Integraation teoria* [trans.: The Theory of Integration] (Gaudeamus Helsinki University Press, Helsinki, 2007) conclude that explaining or indeed meaningfully discussing the issue of European integration is not assisted in any sense by the current body of international relations theory.

[130] Mark Gismondi, *Ethics, Liberalism and Realism in International Relations* (Routledge, Abingdon, 2008).

[131] Baylis & Smith, above n 126. The chapter on international law has been written by Christian Reus-Smit, whose theoretical contribution is a 'constructivist reinterpretation' of international law and politics, Christian Reus-Smit (ed) *The Politics of International Law* (Cambridge University Press, Cambridge, 2004). As such, this is a welcome addition to the earlier literature, as long as one bears in mind that the perspectives on offer are not really new, but reflect a process of erasing artificial limitations concerning conceptions of law.

[132] Chris Brown, 'Justice and International Order', in Tony Coates (ed) *International Justice* (Ashgate, Aldershot, 2000) 27, 28.

[133] Ibid, 42.

international relations to return to a pre-theoretical phase of its evolution—to 'overcome theory', as it were.

VI. The Interwar Era in Contemporary International Law

Finally, we can discern at least three ways in which international lawyers have related themselves to this heritage of the interwar era that is international relations theory. As Anne-Marie Slaughter observes in her impeccable if somewhat fatalistic logic: 'In the end, the excursion into another discipline brings us back to our own.'[134] Slaughter has advocated closer collaboration between international relations and international law, even proposing the construction of a 'joint discipline'. But the idea of a joint discipline remains, at best, vague, and a more interdisciplinary agenda first requires a genuine and meaningful dialogue in which international relations engages with international law as law.

The second approach is that of applying this law-derived theoretical apparatus as an explanation of the nature and functions of law, as Goldsmith and Posner have done in their much-discussed *The Limits of International Law*. This is a crude version of a rational choice framework the very premises of which include the dismissal of the possibility of a specifically legal reason.[135] Suffice it to say that here the only conceivable option as to the discovered nature or essence of the law is the one from which the analysis proceeds in the first place.

But by far the most sophisticated response in approaching this *problematique* is offered by Koskenniemi. He has condensed what he calls the present state of international managerialism into six steps: from institutions to regimes, from rules to regulation, from government to governance, from responsibility to compliance, from law to legitimacy and, finally, 'from lawyers to international relations experts', in which the discipline of international relations functions 'as Supreme Tribunal of a managerial world'.[136] For Koskenniemi this culture of managerialism and widespread dismissal of law as law is the result of the dark side of the interwar legal project, which is 'the effort of becoming technical'. He writes:

> The great achievement of Lauterpacht and his generation was to create space for progressive law outside the vocabularies of nationhood. That achievement came at a cost. Thinking of international law in apolitical and technical terms opened the door for expert rule and managerialism, not in competition with politics as in

[134] Anne-Marie Slaughter, 'International Law and International Relations' (2000) 285 *Collected Courses of the Hague Academy of International Law* 235.

[135] Jack Goldsmith and Eric Posner, *The Limits of International Law* (Oxford University Press, New York, 2005).

[136] Koskenniemi, above n 69, 12–18.

the domestic realm, but as a *substitute* for it.... Managerialism was the dark side of the inter-war project of imagining international law in technical terms.[137]

Koskenniemi observes that the '[l]aw is a whole', that '[h]ere is a battle European jurisprudence seems to have won': '[i]nternational law is a legal system'. 'But', he then asks, 'how useful is this victory?' For we are anyhow at a situation of a 'war of conflicting regimes', each of which comes with its own interests and 'structural bias(es)', with no overarching way of resolving conflicts between them.[138] To shed light on the current state of managerialism and the possibilities of contesting this 'governance', Koskenniemi looks at the opposition of Kant and Pufendorf: the latter as representative of a more instrumental conception of law, the former of a conception of international law founded on freedom. Koskenniemi writes that he wishes to 'examine the power of Kant's formalism, *formalism sans peur et sans reproche*, against the novel natural law of empirical political science, offered as an invitation to "international relations"'. In this connection he asks: 'Can formalism—the fidelity to law—and legal indeterminacy be reconcilable? Kant as critical legal studies?'[139]

While sharing Koskenniemi's objective of providing a more enlightened conception of law for discussion on international matters, I am unsure about the idea of 'Kant as critical legal studies' in this context. To begin with, Koskenniemi has himself taken a mostly lukewarm stance when philosophers such as Jürgen Habermas and Jacques Derrida have appealed in favour of the development of international law in a Kantian vein. The question that needs to be asked here is the following: in which way is this Kant in the end different from the Kant employed by, for instance, Habermas? For why *should* international relations scholars take a Kantian view as to the nature of the legal project seriously if Habermas and Derrida should not appeal to it but rather criticise it?[140]

Certainly the idea of a postmodern Kantianism as such is not as far-fetched as it might seem, as Ian Ward points out.[141] Koskenniemi begins with reading Kant's *Critique of Pure Reason*: since rules do not spell out the conditions of their application, judgment is needed.[142] Koskenniemi aims to affirm the indeterminacy aspect in Kant. However, Kant is not necessary to prove that judgement is needed in law; such 'indeterminacy' is an essential part of the tacit knowledge of the legal profession. 'Kant as critical legal studies' is also 'critical legal studies as Kant'. In the end this

[137] Koskenniemi, above n 6, 29.

[138] Ibid, 18 and Koskenniemi, above n 50, 606–607.

[139] Koskenniemi, above n 69, 7–10.

[140] Martti Koskenniemi, 'Book Review: Giovanna Borradori (ed) Philosophy in a Time of Terror: Dialogues with Jürgen Habermas and Jacques Derrida' (2003) 4 *German Law Journal* 1087, 1091.

[141] Ian Ward, *Kantianism, Postmodernism and Critical Legal Thought* (Kluwer, Dordrecht, 1997).

[142] Koskenniemi, above n 69, 9–10.

argumentation only serves to demonstrate the limits of what a post-modern version of the indeterminacy critique has to offer. Surely, invoking Kant is one of the most conservative moves in the field of legal theory.

But Koskenniemi's idea is also of a post-modern version of (a Kelsenian) legal formalism. Koskenniemi quotes Kelsen's most 'striking sentence' in the *Pure Theory*: 'There is no criterion on the basis of which one of the possibilities given within the frame of the norm to be applied could be favoured over the other possibilities.'[143] From this Koskenniemi goes on to ask: 'How is it that formalism as theory leads into a conception of legal practice that is thoroughly political?'[144] For Koskenniemi, Kant's work 'seems to suggest [that l]aw cannot be used as a technique of control', since 'everything will be left to the *judgement* by the law-applier'.[145] Koskenniemi notes that, as a Kantian, Kelsen would agree with this. But does this interpretation remain within the trajectory of Kelsen's thought?

Attempts to move on from a Kelsenian formalism have taken various shapes in the field of legal theory; mostly these attempts have in essence embraced the critique that Lauterpacht presented on Kelsen's theory in a speech at the LSE in 1932:

It may be that—as Kelsen assumes—the content of a positive legal order is only a compromise between conflicting group interests of which ultimately none is fully satisfied and none totally defeated, but if this is so it is because natural law and natural justice have consciously or subconsciously played their part. The positive legal order is not the result of a physical balance of forces. We may sympathize with Kelsen's insistence on the dignity of man—this is one of the philosophical reasons underlying his attitude to natural law—but, to say the least, we may doubt whether human dignity is involved at all. Affirmation of the autonomy of man need not necessarily result in ethical agnosticism. And frankly, it is not suggested that Kelsen aspires to or succeeds in maintaining his moral relativism. There is, throughout his writings, behind the dialectical and abstract form of the pure science of law, a prophetic pathos—from what other source could there have sprung an iconoclasm so powerful and so creative—which will remain an abiding source of inspiration and which suggests that his ethical relativism is in itself dictated by a moral idea. Kelsen insists that he has always kept his legal science apart from his moral *Weltanschauung*. But we doubt whether this is so as a matter of fact and whether it ought to be so as a matter of method.

I have dealt with this point at some length because there is a danger that this aspect of Kelsen's doctrine may deprive his teaching of the effectiveness to which it is entitled. Kelsen's criticism of the established doctrines is effective not because he has shown them to be natural law, but because he has proved that they are inconsistent with the admitted and necessary assumptions of law. This is the reason why he ought to be able to dispense with the doubtful weapon of the

[143] Ibid, 10. [144] Ibid. [145] Ibid, 9–10.

imputation of natural law to anything he disapproves. He finds himself in company which he may otherwise not find congenial. But a slight retreat would strengthen the position as a whole. He has only to admit—as every positivist lawyer ought to do in justice to himself—that positive law has always incorporated and does incorporate ideas of natural law and justice. There would, on our part, be no difficulty in admitting that natural law thus incorporated has ceased to be an independent system and has become part and parcel of positive law. We do not mind if natural law has served a good cause at the expense of its separate existence. But we will mind if a purely negative attitude towards the perennial source of legal justice succeeds in diminishing the effectiveness of a great contribution to the cause of law and—we may say this as Kelsen is not here to correct us—to the cause of justice.[146]

Whether in the form of a 'Critical Positivism'[147] or a 'post-positivism',[148] a large part of the endeavour has been the integration of values and morality into the theoretical framework. In a sense, the culture of formalism proposed by Koskenniemi is also an attempt to move on from Kelsen in the state of legal indeterminacy: 'Even if formalism may no longer be open as a jurisprudential doctrine of the black and white of legal validity (a position perhaps never represented by anyone), nothing has undermined formalism as a culture'.[149] 'There is room for a culture of formalism even after the critique of rules has done its work'.[150] For Koskenniemi, the question here is of 'the possibility of a non-imperialist universality'.[151] He explains that the 'culture of formalism is recognisable, or indeed has identity, only in terms of its opposition to something that it is not', 'it has no essence', it is 'constantly redefined':

As a *culture*, formalism is certainly not a substance or a theory, but straddles such frontiers as well as other dichotomies such as the social and the individual, constraint and freedom, even past and future. Although every (legal) decision is constitutive, and not just a reproduction of some underlying structure, each decision also acts as a kind of surface on which the horizon of universality becomes visible. Formalism's utopian moment lies in its resistance towards being reduced to structure (which is anyway indeterminate) or pure subjectivity (Schmitt's "decision"), and in its identifying itself as a practice of decision-making that persists in time and through which the aspirations of self-determining communities remain alive—even as (or perhaps precisely because) the universal they embody remains only a "horizon".[152]

Thus the culture of formalism can be understood as an approach, a way of relating to the world and one's professional role as a lawyer, a suggestion for a sensibility, a spirit, a mindset of approaching legal tasks. This is

[146] Hersch Lauterpacht, 'Kelsen's pure science of law', in Lauterpacht, above n 48, 404, 428–29.
[147] Kaarlo Tuori, *Critical Legal Positivism* (Ashgate, Aldershot, 2002).
[148] As Neil MacCormick describes his theoretical orientation, above n 70, v.
[149] Koskenniemi, *Civilizer*, above n 35, 500.
[150] Ibid, 503. [151] Ibid, 506. [152] Ibid, 507–8.

a point of view with which I am entirely in sympathy. But as an answer to the way law has been conceptualised in the field of international relations it remains only partial. For to understand it as in any way explaining the content or structure of the law would be seriously to misinterpret what it is about. It does not attempt to say anything as to the content of the law or legal discussion, it remains empty, indeed this is its very point. The difference between traditional legal formalism and formalism as a culture is ultimately not in the condition of their emptiness—for this, on a conceptual level, is what both are. The difference is rather that one is an attempt at a description of the law and the other the theoretically formulated requirement of how law needs to be approached if one is to avoid turning it into a tool for one's own pursuits at the expense of others' points of view.

This would seem more or less analogous to the category of 'an international lawyer's approach' developed by Ole Spiermann in his *International Legal Argument in the Permanent Court of International Justice: The Rise of the International Judiciary*.[153] Both the culture of formalism and the international lawyer's approach might be seen as pleas for taking the character of law as formal seriously so as to avoid its becoming only a façade for some specific interests. If the culture of formalism *were* applied as a way of thinking about—and not as relating to—the law, it would become what it was supposed to avoid; nothing would remain of law except the facade it would provide for all the enlightened subjective decisions made by people who had, or perhaps ought to have, embraced this culture. This in essence would be the same position as Morgenthau's 'paradox of [the] individualized rule of law'.

In order to resist the contemporary managerialist culture, Koskenniemi argues, international law 'must be redeemed as a political project'. He explains that there are two aspects to this. The first is the 'development of a professional sensibility that feels at home in all regimes, yet is imprisoned in none of them'. The second is the re-imagining of international law 'as the surface over which managerial governance may be challenged, the sole vocabulary with a horizon of transcendence', 'as the placeholder for the vocabularies of justice and goodness, solidarity, responsibility and—faith'.[154]

The first aspect mentioned by Koskenniemi is the essence of what the culture of formalism is meant to be about. The second aspect can have one of the following three meanings. It is either just a repetition of the first aspect, a way of approaching rather than describing law. Or it refers to law as an empty façade for individual decisions, but this would amount to precisely that (Schmittian) decisionism that the culture of formalism was to withstand. The only sensible reading of the second aspect is that

[153] Ole Spiermann, *International Legal Argument in the Permanent Court of International Justice. The Rise of the International Judiciary* (Cambridge University Press, Cambridge, 2005).

[154] Koskenniemi, above n 6, 30.

of the development of international law as advocated by Lauterpacht, namely as 'general jurisprudence' based on the values of justice and responsibility (though not necessarily as a 'faith'). However, Koskenniemi's whole point was to provide the 'horizon' that Lauterpacht was supposed to have lacked!

The underlying problem here is the over-emphasis on the critical point of view, as this line of thinking proceeds from the assumption that the critique of rules is correct. The critique of rules is indeed in its way correct, given its own starting points. Since Koskenniemi himself notes that his critical thesis had originally been 'inspired by a thorough-going frustration with the isolation of public international law from developments in legal theory and method',[155] a brief look at this topic is in order.

One need not accept as valid for legal analysis the philosophical innovation of an institutional fact. But an explanation is owed of such a dismissal before a theory can be considered as having general explanatory significance. Koskenniemi cites MacCormick and Weinberger on this topic, but only to reinforce his point about the ageless ideas/facts dilemma in philosophy and law.[156] For Koskenniemi, then, much of the work of Lauterpacht and his contemporaries was simply 'academic hubris'.[157] On the other hand, he writes that he is 'puzzled by the taking away of "law"' from contemporary instrumentalist legal analyses. But what is that law? If legal structures, thought and institutions will not do, what does this mean? For one thing, I do not think that ideas of faith or religion can form cogent answers as to why anyone ought to take the point about law as law seriously.

As a contemporary general analysis of law, the critical point of view is not able to capture all relevant aspects of a specifically legal discourse. As Koskenniemi himself observes regarding the critique of indeterminacy, 'little seems to depend on it'.[158] In order to make the critique stronger, he argues, an empirical argument is therefore needed. This empirical argument is the fact that 'irrespective of indeterminacy, *the system still de facto prefers some outcomes or distributive choices to other outcomes or choices*'.[159]

For Koskenniemi, this is a sign of a 'structural bias' in the institution, since the critique of indeterminacy is presumed to be correct. But it might

[155] Martti Koskenniemi, 'The Politics of International Law—20 Years Later' (2009) 20 *European Journal of International Law* 7, 7.

[156] Koskenniemi, above n 50, 519–520. The reference to MacCormick and Weinberger is to their *Institutional Theory of Law* (Reidel, Dordrecht, 1986). The idea of institutional facts has been developed by G E M Anscombe and John Searle, and in the legal field especially by Neil MacCormick and Ota Weinberger in their institutional theory of law. The point is to emphasise that in addition to sheer physical facts, there are also facts that exist on the basis of the institutional rules defining them, such as credit cards, money or marriage. This enables us to get beyond the ideas/facts dichotomy by understanding law as neither ideas nor facts but as institutional facts instead.

[157] Koskenniemi, *Civilizer*, above n 35, 504.

[158] Koskenniemi, above n 50, 600. Elsewhere he notes that '[c]ompetent lawyers know that the world of legal practice is actually quite predictable'. Koskenniemi, above n 155, 9.

[159] Koskenniemi, above n 50, 606–607. Emphasis in original.

also be argued that this empirical evidence, far from making the critical thesis stronger, in fact testifies against it, as it shows that in practice 'little seems to depend on it'. Is this not a typical case of 'making the facts fit the theory'? The empirical facts that speak against the theory—that '[v]ery little is fully random out there'[160]—are used, from the starting point that the theory anyhow is correct, as *further proof* of the point that the theory wishes to make. In effect this is about simultaneously accepting and denying the status of law as institutional fact.

In order to reinforce his point about structural bias, Koskenniemi refers to Susan Marks' recent point about 'false contingency': 'As Susan Marks has recently put it, alongside the demonstration of "false necessity"—by now a classical critical theme—what needs demonstration is "false contingency", the idea that because the argumentative structures are open anything goes in fact.'[161] But is this really what was originally intended by the concept? In her article Marks wishes to emphasise the point that while indeed men do make their own history, 'they do not make it just as they please in circumstances of their choosing but rather in circumstances they inherit', and that 'things can be, and quite frequently are, contingent without being random, accidental or arbitrary'.[162] She underlines that, in order to make visible the underlying systemic processes, the analysis of false necessity and false contingency need to be 'pursued in tandem', and that indeed 'enquiry into false necessity becomes itself necessitarian when false contingency is ignored'.[163]

Instead, Koskenniemi seems to follow a two-track approach. He first leaves his indeterminacy as it is, the 'argumentative structures open', untouched by Marks' argument. Then, in the resulting structural bias, he does take the point about false contingency in some way into account. But holding on to indeterminacy prevents us from appreciating that the formation of this bias/pattern of legal decision-making is not arbitrary, is subject to (historically constructed) systemic limits and constraints. As everything about the law is always both completely random (indeterminate) yet preordained (bias), this leaves little room for understanding what actually happens in legal decision-making. How is the bias/pattern of legal decision-making formed? How could one reach a different conclusion or argue in a different way? How could the court or 'regime' have decided otherwise? What is left out is, in short, an(y) understanding of how one could use one's legal imagination to change things in a progressive direction in concrete situations. As Marks puts it, '[t]he category of possibility—not just abstract possibility, but real, historical possibility—drops out of sight.'[164]

In his (re)assessment of this critical position Koskenniemi states that he is still 'as committed as ever' to his point about indeterminacy.[165] But

[160] Koskenniemi, above n 155, 9. [161] Ibid.
[162] Susan Marks, 'False Contingency' (2009) 62 *Current Legal Problems* 1, 1–2.
[163] Ibid, 10.
[164] Ibid, 20. [165] Koskenniemi, above n 155, 7.

one wonders whether commitment ought to be the point about theory. Overall, we are told logical connections unite the various constituent parts of this critical thesis into a (logically) coherent whole. Since all law is indeterminate, the content of law needs to be renamed as structural bias.[166] Then the point about everything being 'always already legalized' and the corresponding need to focus one's professional attention to 'political contestation' and thus pure 'decisions' not guided by legal constraints 'follows logically from the combination of the critique of indeterminacy and structural bias'.[167]

But nothing 'follows logically' from the already in itself fundamentally illogical combination of indeterminacy and structural bias. Instead, since the logical connections between the various parts of the thesis do not exist, or are better left in the dark, this critical position is really a collection of arguments. They are 'valid' as arguments that can be presented, but—as with Carr perhaps—rather than logic the uniting factor seems to be the use of repeated dichotomies in various parts of the theoretical edifice. The whole position is not an elaboration of the 'conditions of possibility' of the profession, or of international law. It is, as Koskenniemi seems to recognize, an exposition of the conditions of possibility for the construction of legal arguments from scratch, and it pays little attention to the quality (or lack of quality) of the arguments in question. There is an important difference here.

As Neil MacCormick notes in his *Legal Reasoning and Legal Theory*: 'Any study of legal reasoning is . . . an attempt to explicate and explain the criteria as to what constitutes a good or a bad, an acceptable or an unacceptable type of argument.'[168] But the question arises whether this is a study of legal reasoning at all. In his interesting critique of Koskenniemi's critical position, Kaarlo Tuori offers J L Austin's speech-act theory as a way into discussions with representatives of the critical position who tend to label critiques of their own position as merely a hegemonic manoeuvre. Speech-act theory makes an analytical distinction between locutionary, perlocutionary and illocutionary dimensions of speech acts. Tuori notes that this distinction also applies to legal speech acts, such as laws or judgments. The locutionary dimension concerns the meaning of a legal speech act. The perlocutionary dimension concerns its effects in the world. But the most important dimension from the legal point of view is the illocutionary: it concerns the conditions, as defined by legal regulation or legal culture, that give legal speech acts their character as legal speech acts. In this dimension, the normative validity claims of legal speech acts are tested, and it is this reciprocal testing of normative validity that links the various legal speech acts into a legal discourse.

[166] Koskenniemi, above n 50, 606–7.

[167] Ibid, 613–15.

[168] Neil MacCormick, *Legal Reasoning and Legal Theory* (Oxford University Press, Oxford, 1978) 12–13.

Tuori's point is that in his description of the law, Koskenniemi focuses solely on the strategic, perlocutionary dimension and reduces the significance of the locutionary and illocutionary dimensions to that of mere instruments in reaching the perlocutionary effects. Lacking an illocutionary dimension, one which separates good and competent legal arguments from bad and incompetent ones, Koskenniemi's critical 'grammar' is unable to characterize legal discourse as such.[169] The grammar is ultimately not a grammar for lawyers but for laymen, because it lacks that element that entitles arguments to be considered as legal arguments—beyond a mere skeleton of general notions that are hardly useful in a court of law (such as consent/justice, sovereignty/sources, etc.). The fact that the theory does not work in practice also means that the claim that for every 'ascending' argument there is an equally valid 'descending' argument does not work either: this validity is subject to legal evaluation; only after such an evaluation can we say whether the argument is competent or not. Koskenniemi's theory lacks this perspective of legal evaluation almost entirely.

Instead, his theory teaches us only that everything depends on interests and decisions, and that, if one doubts this, one is guilty of 'hubris'. As Tuori points out, this critical position is the adversarial position of an attorney, a point which Koskenniemi seems to admit.[170] Tuori observes that Koskenniemi in his analysis of law forces this adversarial perspective upon other lawyers, such as judges and scholars. The problem is that this cannot be the only view on law. It is the responsibility of the judge to evaluate the illocutionary dimensions of legal speech acts—the competence of the legal arguments presented (by the attorneys). An emphasis on only the strategic, perlocutionary dimension is not able to properly capture the nature of this activity.[171]

In the critical optic, the quality of legal arguments is evaluated only in the rather narrow gap 'between special interests and hubris'. Why then, Tuori asks, does Koskenniemi make the focus on interests such a totalizing one? One possible explanation, Tuori notes, might be Koskenniemi's background in international law, where political aspects are often seen to be more pronounced than in other areas of law.[172] But, he continues, the relative weakness of enforcement mechanisms in international law compared with national legal systems ought to be taken for what it is. International law has traditionally been the exceptional case in legal theory and to accept it instead as the paradigmatic model would in effect be to turn legal theory on its head, since the main rule would be subordinated to the exception.[173]

[169] Tuori, above n 99, 39–40.
[170] Ibid, 41. Koskenniemi, above n 50, 596–99.
[171] Tuori, above n 99, 41–42.
[172] Ibid, 42.
[173] Ibid.

In his assessment of Koskenniemi's thesis, Hannu Tapani Klami, Tuori's predecessor in the Chair of Jurisprudence at the University of Helsinki, has pointed out that the deep structure of specifically international law cannot be the reason for these inherent oppositions, since similar oppositions can also be found in national legal systems (which seem to function in a satisfactory manner). The difference between national and international law thus has to be located somewhere outside the level of linguistic deep structure.[174] Indeed, in line with his focus on interests and preferences, Koskenniemi argues that his indeterminacy is 'much stronger' than a mere linguistic version and has rather to do with 'contradictory premises'.[175] This truly is a theoretical position with many faces. It is at the same time a linguistic theory of indeterminacy that is not a theory about linguistic indeterminacy; a theory about the pervasive indeterminacy of legal practice but one that does not work in practice; a defence of valid law that excludes the possibility thereof; and an exposition of a legal grammar for the construction of competent legal arguments that says little about the legal competence or otherwise of the arguments in question.[176]

Ultimately, for all the erudition, there is no escaping the following logic: if (a) in order for something to be the case, it ought to be the case in practice, and (b) it is not the case in practice, then it simply is not the case. The original thesis was in large part a practical argument for indeterminacy—Koskenniemi himself notes that he wanted to keep methodological commitments 'below the surface so as to speak directly to the field'[177]—with extensive analysis of cases and materials, and the hugely popular message was: 'anything can be argued'. But, since in practice, even in international law, not anything can (successfully) be argued, what are the cases and materials then supposed to prove? What is the 'main political point' in the act of simply renaming law as 'bias'? A sort of 'theory we can believe in'? To quote Dworkin's discussion of Rorty:

> Rorty says that we must give up the idea that legal or moral or even scientific inquiry is an attempt to discover what is really so, what the law really is, what texts really mean, which institutions are really just, or what the universe is really like. We should give up the idea that one vocabulary of concepts, one collection of propositions, can be more faithful than another to some independently existing "reality". Instead, we should accept that the vocabulary we have is *just* the one we have, the one that seems to suit us, or be useful to us. We should also accept that when that vocabulary of ideas and propositions no longer seems to be

[174] Hannu Tapani Klami, 'Från apologi till utopi – och fantasi?' [transl.: From Apology to Utopia—and Fantasy?] (1989) 102 *Tidsskrift for rettsvitensskap* [Journal of Legal Science] 679.

[175] Koskenniemi, above n 50, 590.

[176] In his review of Koskenniemi's work Iain Scobbie notes that Koskenniemi has two separate projects that are not mutually compatible. Iain Scobbie, 'Towards the Elimination of International Law: Some Radical Scepticism about Sceptical Radicalism' (1990) 61 *BYIL* 339, 340.

[177] Koskenniemi, above n 155, 7.

useful—no longer seems to suit us—we can and should change it, to see "how we get on" with a different one. Inquiry, so understood, is experimental. We try out new ideas to see how they work out, to see which ideas or vocabularies prove to be useful or interesting.

This sounds exciting, but it is philosophically a dog's dinner, as many philosophers have by now pointed out. I quote a succinct restatement of the point by Bernard Williams summarizing Hilary Putnam's devastating critique. "[Rorty's views] simply tear themselves apart. If, as Rorty is fond of putting it, the correct description of the world (for us) is a matter of what we find it convenient to say, and if, as Rorty admits, we find it convenient to say that science discovers a world that is already there, there is simply no perspective from which Rorty can say, as he also does, that science does not really discover a world that is already there, but (more or less) invents it."[178]

At times Koskenniemi has noted that many of his intellectual opponents regard him as a 'cynic'. But this is entirely beside the point: one's commitment or cynicism or whatever is ultimately all the same; it is the logic of an argument, or the lack of it, that matters. I agree that in the current atmosphere of theoretical discussion on international matters, international law needs to be redeemed as a political project. But this cannot be done by turning it into an 'empty horizon of transcendence' that is never 'fixed' into any concrete structure or institution, for as a conception of law this results in a façade for the decisions of the dichotomy-straddling, enlightened individuals. Emphasising too much the importance of decisions as against legal reasoning or the structures of juristic thought guiding those decisions is to 'take the law out of law'. But, that being said, emphasising the role of the lawyer as a decision-maker within the legal framework of possible interpretations is certainly important, as Kelsen would also have agreed.

Instead of structural bias, then, we would see a structure of legal reason, a substantive legal system, as guiding the (legal) decisions in the direction of a particular, established (legal) interpretation. Crawford gives a contemporary international lawyer's description of the character of this legal 'project' vis-à-vis its individual, critical and other, constituents:

[178] Ronald Dworkin, *Justice in Robes* (Harvard University Press, Cambridge, 2006) 37. In a somewhat similar fashion, in his review of Koskenniemi's thesis, Iain Scobbie asks: 'If the indeterminacy of language is inevitable, "objectivity" lacking and meaning a mirage, then how are such texts privileged, in the sense that they are not meaningless or hopelessly indeterminate? On his own lights, how can we "understand" Mr Koskenniemi's book "if 'all' is interpretation" and "interpretation creates meaning rather than discovers it?"' Scobbie calls for the 'erasure', in a Derridean sense, of the word deconstruction in legal theory and asks Koskenniemi to recognize the importance of inter-subjective meaning. Scobbie, above n 176, 346–52. In Koskenniemi's view the 'sense' of Scobbie's critique is however that Koskenniemi's argument would have fallen 'on the side of the apologetic' by being too timid in advocating change. Koskenniemi, above n 50, 603 n 112.

All in all, this suggests in international legal scholarship a pattern beyond the merely biographical, which individuals may influence but hardly decisively. It suggests a pattern of practice and language rooted in a long history; one whose outcomes at any time, though expressed definitively in terms of current international law, are at the same time part of a process, and are to that extent provisional. This is an international law for sceptics as for believers, an international law for those who find Schwarzenberger's assumption of "objectivity" in the decisions of the World Court as misplaced as Lauterpacht's assumption of a gradual and progressive evolution to some form of political unity. Problematic international law no doubt is; but it is also a shared attempt at addressing and resolving the problematic of order in a diverse world. Rise and fall, rise and fall, that is its enduring significance.[179]

In order for (international) law to form a historically constructed pattern of legal reason, of 'practice and language', there has to be an identity for law beyond the enlightened mindset of the lawyer; an identity which needs to be concretely ascertainable and in this sense also, even if only temporarily, 'fixed'. This structure of juristic thought is the product of the efforts of jurists such as Lauterpacht. The critical argument that the main reason for the problems the project of international law faces in its present incarnation lies in these efforts fails to convince. Lauterpacht would have understood that in order to act as an effective surface of criticism, as a 'gentle civilizer', international law must be constructed, like other law, as a specifically legal discourse and must have a 'general jurisprudence' that shares a common background of juristic thought with other forms of law, with a (Kantian) 'horizon' underlying the legal activities and practices of different times.

At the end of his evaluation of Tuori's critique, after showing a willingness to distance himself from Tuori's portrayal of his critical position and laying out the opposition of 'conservative' (represented by Tuori) and 'critical' legal science in the form of a dichotomy, Koskenniemi ultimately downplays the differences between their respective views:

Thus also the dichotomy of "conservative" and "critical" legal science can be questioned: what ultimately is the significance of a difference that does not seem to lead to differing normative recommendations regarding legal policy? Seen from the inside, this dichotomy does renew the tradition we call "jurisprudence". But from the outside the question is of a purely scholastic nature and if it has significance, this is only due to the phenomenon defining our contemporary political culture in which the leftist worldview of middle-aged professors joins the resistance to change embedded in traditional conservatism.[180]

One answer is that differences of a theoretical character cannot be without significance if they could lead to divergent interpretations of history.

[179] Crawford, above n 36, 700–701.

[180] Koskenniemi, book review (2008) 106 *Lakimies* [Finnish Law Journal] 119, 127.

Here the interwar legal project is being interpreted in essentially the same way as (the early) Carr interpreted it. This seems due to similar theoretical underpinnings behind historical interpretations that however do not allow for a balanced view on the topic, as Carr perhaps already realised. What is completely missing from this understanding—since nothing of legal relevance ever really takes place, and established patterns of legal decision-making are merely 'biases' in 'regimes'—is any appreciation for the fact that, as Iain Scobbie has put it, 'the construction of a legal system is an historical process, [l]egal systems do not drop ready-made from the skies'.[181] And if this is so, there are also implications for evaluating what can be considered 'academic hubris', and what cannot. Since both international relations theory and international legal theory may affect this interpretation of history with a similar 'bias', a different, at the minimum complementary, reading of the interwar legal project seems called for.

VII. Epilogue

There is every reason today, in spite of all the associated problems, for upholding what Lauterpacht defined as the 'Grotian tradition', by that name or some other. In taking up the Whewell Chair in Cambridge in 1993, Crawford quoted Sir Robert Jennings' words from his inaugural lecture, held in 1958 and titled 'The Progress of International Law':

> It is obvious today that a community of rival sovereignties, which claim to be above the law or which, while professing submission to it, in fact refuse to recognize its supremacy, cannot escape self-destruction. The only mechanism by which a viable international society of States can be reached is through effective submission to a developing international law.[182]

'If that was obvious in 1958, it is even more obvious now', Crawford noted.[183] Fifteen or fifty years on, the reasons for upholding the rule of law in the international context have hardly disappeared or diminished. One way of doing this is 'by means of the legitimate methods of juridical criticism and analysis', as Lauterpacht defined that part of the 'task of the science of international law' that would be of use in relating observed practice to 'higher legal principle, or to the conception of international law as a whole'.[184] If this seems a rather practical orientation, then it might be pointed out that the perennial 'crisis' of international law usually seems to be one of theory; 'practice' is more seldom

[181] Scobbie, above n 176, 350.

[182] Robert Jennings, 'The Progress of International Law' (1958) 34 *BYIL* 334, 355, quoted in James Crawford, 'Democracy and International Law' (1993) 64 *BYIL* 113, 133.

[183] Crawford, above n 182, 133.

[184] Lauterpacht, above n 58, 438.

in crisis. Another way of 'upholding the tradition' could be to accord as unbiased and fair a hearing as possible to the efforts of those who have gone before.

I have discussed here two contemporary challenges to this tradition, one perhaps more external and one more internal to international law discourse. The international relations 'disciplinary culture' of dismissing the possibility of an international rule of law has its basis in an ultimately personal, sentimental disillusionment dressed up as theoretical reflection in a decades-long process that has, as is the way with such matters, taken on a 'life of its own'. This 'international relations challenge' certainly deserves a response; there is a need to finally overcome the interwar disappointment also as a matter of theoretical reflection. Since 1989 or thereabouts, however, sophisticated theoretical discussion in the field of international law has for the most part concentrated on elaborating the critical point of view, which remains insufficient for the reasons discussed above.

In conclusion, international law today is in need of being rescued both from international relations theorising and the totalisingly critical view in international legal theory. Much is going on in the world because of theories like these, and the phenomenon of 'logic going on holiday' ought to be taken as seriously as ever. Getting imprisoned for too long inside critiques that originated as a reaction to the Holocaust may lead to undesirable consequences. Waiting for the reappearance of evil in the image of the past—to be then curtailed the moment it would appear with all the wisdom our twentieth-century realist tradition could possibly muster—may lead to a different evil taking place elsewhere just because the eyes of the world are so keen on looking only in that one direction. In other words, Auschwitz may *explain* Abu Ghraib. Or, at the very least, the question needs to be asked: where *did* this whole culture of opposition to an international rule of law come from? Which factors or disciplines gave it direction? On whose teachings was it based, on which questions, assumptions and reductions?

As has been amply demonstrated in recent decades by 'critiques from within and without', thinking of international law exclusively as the guardian of the forces of light on earth will not do. But this observation is already made from the position of understanding that, more perhaps than many other efforts in various other walks of life, international law has the potential of being that, too. The profession of international relations scholars, as self-proclaimed 'citizens of the world',[185] might do

[185] Finnish philosopher Juha Sihvola writes about the theme of ethics in the context of the idea of 'world citizenship' in his *Maailmankansalaisen etiikka* [trans.: Ethics of the World Citizen] (Otava, Helsinki, 2004). In his critical review, written from a predominantly 'realist' standpoint, Koskenniemi would like Sihvola's philosophy, once again, to go and 'face' the 20th century realist tradition of, especially, Carr and Morgenthau, and observes that the failure of philosophy to take up this challenge serves to assure that 'philosophy remains on the [intellectual battle]field, if not as a winner then at least by itself'. Martti Koskenniemi, 'Kosmopoliitin tunteellinen rationalismi' [trans.: The Sentimental Rationalism of a Cosmopolitan] (2006) 50 *Niin & näin* [Finnish philosophical journal] 133–136.

better to understand the present state of international law as a 'platform' of juristic thought that enables continued work towards that potential. The international law we have today is the result of the work of previous generations of lawyers, philosophers, politicians and others. If an appreciation of the deeply path-dependent nature of law calls for a re-assessment of theoretical doctrines in our modern-day disciplines concerned with international theory, so much the worse for the doctrines. Surely the point of theory—even critical theory—is to make it easier and not more difficult for us to understand the world around us.

A point of view on law founded on its historical development and significance can of course be dismissed like any other. But its proper articulation will make this dismissal of law appear as the politics it is, making this move much more difficult to perform in the sinister way we have so often been confronted with during recent decades.

Reviews of Books

Human Dignity and the Foundations of International Law. By Patrick Capps, Oxford, Hart Publishing, 2009. 308 pp. £22.00.

Law at the Vanishing Point: A Philosophical Analysis of International Law. By Aaron Fichtelberg, Aldershot, Ashgate Publishing, 2008. 244 pp. £60.00.

Philosophy of International Law. By Anthony Carty, Edinburgh, Edinburgh University Press, 2007. 272 pp. £80.00.

The social performance of reviewing a book rests on a collusive illusion that should delude no one. It is a small and rare, but anxious, pleasure for the reviewer to be able to adopt, briefly, an olympian tone of voice in discussing and judging the published work of others. And yet it is, of course, impossible for a reviewer with a strongly developed intellectual worldview—a committed Marxist, say, or a Thomist, Nietzschean nihilist, American Pragmatist or, in the present case, passionately committed Social Idealist—simply to slough off that commitment for a while to dispense a measure of benign objectivity.

Also, there is an illusion in treating a particular book in relative isolation from its cultural background. A particular way of understanding the cultural background in question is a central feature of a particular reviewer's worldview. Ideology in, ideology out. Defying social convention, therefore, a particular reviewer may think that it is proper to acknowledge, at the outset and as sparely as possible, the cultural perspective and the intellectual prejudices that will warp his or her judgment.

Those who undertake to write about the philosophy of international law in the twenty-first century take on several seemingly hopeless challenges. Surely twentieth-century philosophy finally demonstrated the impossibility of philosophy in the perennial philosophical tradition, allowing the philosopher Martin Heidegger to announce (1964) 'the end of philosophy'. What he called 'thinking' would remain, until even that is taken over by machines, and the private minds of human individuals become peripherals of a universal cybernetic mind.

Surely the twentieth century finally demonstrated, intellectually and empirically, the impossibility of treating international law as law like any other kind of law, so long as an essential condition for the existence of law is not present, namely, a self-identifying and self-constituting society making and enforcing the law as an integral part of its self-identifying and self-constituting. Pending the improbable emergence of such a society at the global level, 'international law' would continue its strangely vigorous existence as a living and breathing contradiction in terms—the law of an anarchical society (to echo Hedley Bull).

Surely it is vain to suppose that anyone professionally involved in the international system—politicians, diplomats, government officials, judges, lawyers—would have any interest in, let alone allow their professional worldview to be radically altered by, the arcane musings of social or legal philosophers. They might see such things not merely as irrelevant but as a potential distraction or impediment in doing their difficult work. Law, like life and love, does not need theory to work effectively.

Those of us who, as social or legal philosophers, wantonly or valiantly take on these seemingly hopeless challenges do not underestimate them. We may see ourselves as traumatised refugees from the intellectual devastation of the twentieth century, but we know that we have saved at least one thing from the wreckage, something that, whether they know it or not, makes the practitioners of the international system, and of its national extensions, vulnerable to our intervention into their self-absorbed and complacent world. Like life and love, law needs good ideas to make it better.

As the spider spins a web out of its own substance, so the mind makes ideas—to borrow an image from Francis Bacon. We spin webs of ideas in our own minds. And we share ideas, mind to mind. We spin webs of shared ideas. And when the spiders leave, the cobwebs remain. A person, a nation, a state, a government, a religion, a philosophy, a science, a legal system all seem to be part of the furniture of the world—to borrow an image from Ludwig Wittgenstein. But they are all merely products of the infinitely fertile human mind.

Remarkably, we can even think about our own thinking. Francis Bacon called it the *radius reflexus*—the beam of light that the human mind focuses on its own activity. Such is the nature of philosophy in the perennial tradition. Philosophy is the mind thinking at the most general level about its own activity.

Remarkably also, the human mind can form ideas that are not merely generalisations from experience, not part of the furniture of the world. They are ideas produced in the mind—Locke's archetypal ideas, Kant's ideas of reason (*Vernunftideen*). Matter, mind, time, space, reason, order, law, obligation—and countless others—are structuring elements of our thinking, allowing us to construct an orderly picture of what we think of as reality, allowing us to participate with other minds in the making and re-making of that reality.

Philosophy is a form of life (to echo another of Wittgenstein's images). Mind is motion (to borrow an idea attributed to Anaxagoras). It is part of the ceaseless activity of the universe. Thinking is a form of energy which makes our *being* into a *becoming* (to invoke one of Aristotle's most fruitful ideas). Through philosophy the human mind may choose how to actualise human potentiality.

Among our universalising ideas are *ideal values*—justice, truth, beauty, the good, rationality, altruism, sociability, compassion, human dignity, human flourishing, the good life, happiness. They propel our becoming, as individuals and as societies, in a particular direction, towards a goal that is unreachable but which acts on our minds like a magnet. We translate our ideals into our *purposes*. Impelled by our ideal purposes we can make a better society, a better human world, a better humanity. And we can use law as an instrument for making our potentiality actual in everyday social life.

Law is not an absolute good. It is a contingent good. A knife can be a tool or a weapon. Law can be a maker of the common good, and it can be an instrument of oppression, exploitation, and public evil of all kinds. It is the quality of ideas transcending the law, ideas processed by the law, that determines whether law does good or evil. Good in, good out. Evil in, evil out.

From the ravages of the twentieth-century mind we have rescued the idea (emanating from Plato) that the human mind has a power to take power over all forms of social power, since all forms of social power are products of the human mind. A true believer in the wonderful capacity and necessity of *law*—its miraculous power to transform the human condition (echoing Rousseau)—could not deny the possibility and the necessity of international law. A true believer in the wonderful capacity and necessity of *philosophy*—guide of our lives, explorer of all that is good within us (echoing Cicero)—could not deny the possibility and the necessity of a philosophy of international law.

*

Facing the cultural situation of the twenty-first century and armed with a predisposing philosophical *a priori*, we approach three books that could not be more different in their response to the challenge of philosophising about international law.

In *Human Dignity and the Foundations of International Law*, Patrick Capps proposes an important and provocative interpretation of the nature of international law. It is important because its complex and sophisticated journey originates at an unusual starting-point, so far as the theoretical study of international law is concerned. The book builds a valuable bridge between well-established thought about the nature of international law and a particularly active field of general legal philosophy. It is provocative because it obliges us to consider carefully the merits of such an approach and, more or less enthusiastically, to respond to it substantively.

The starting-point is something called *legal science* or, something which may or may not be the same thing under another name, *analytical jurisprudence*. The term 'legal science' seems to be a distinct usage in the Anglo-American world of legal theory, distinct from its use in a well-established European-Continental, and especially German, tradition. The word 'analytical' seems to be used in an Aristotelian or Kantian sense, meaning a study that investigates the inner logic of a mental phenomenon in order to uncover something called its 'concept', without reference to its wider social and cultural and historical contexts. There is a latent analogy with Kantian 'critical' theory and Kelsenian 'pure' theory.

The word 'seems' is used in the previous paragraph to show that the enterprise in question is wholly alien to the mind of the present reviewer. The first half of Capps's study is a painstaking and fascinating examination of the extraordinarily busy world of 'legal science'. Capps is a good guide, sometimes identifying himself as a legal scientist, sometimes presenting himself as an interested observer. (The way in which the book has been organised means that there are repetitions and dissonances.) One travels with him feeling like a cultural anthropologist visiting a highly intelligent tribe living a vigorous life of the mind in their own sacred wood, surrounded by the dark world made by twentieth-century philosophy, in which words like 'science', 'analytical', 'pure' and 'theory' struggle to survive.

Capps structures the first half of his book around a discussion of 'method'—unfortunately, one might think, given that an obsessive effort to find an analytical (*a priori*) 'method' has been the chosen instrument of self-destruction of 'social science'. The first sentence of Chapter 3 is dramatic and explains a great deal. 'Hart's legal positivism, which is mainly set out in his book *The Concept of Law*, is currently the most popular and influential approach to legal philosophy in the Anglo-American tradition.' If this is empirically true, then it reveals a sad state of affairs. Hart's approach illuminates nothing and leads nowhere.

With luminous intelligence, Capps disentangles the *querelles de chapelle*, the narcissism of small academic differences in the world of legal science, sorting out 'us' from 'not-us' (to echo Freud). For an uneasy witness of it all, the unfolding of the laborious story is something of a negative adventure (to borrow a characteristically dispiriting formula from Henry James).

However, the patient social idealist becomes more cheerful when Capps, in the second half of his book, manages to produce from somewhere within the Hartian wasteland something which is unexpected and important. He finds that it is possible to have an analytic concept of law that contains a familiar and substantial ideal value.

A striking feature of pure theorists is that they seem to be haunted by nostalgia for the transcendental. Pure theorists cannot bear too much purity. Pure theorists cannot bear too little morality. Like Weber, whom Capps admires, they have to find a way of inserting *value*, in however vestigial and wraith-like a form, into a pure concept of law without destroying its 'essential' purity. In the case of legal scientists, this seems to involve an almost unspoken underlying assumption that law properly so called is intrinsically and necessarily *a good thing,* and that law may even have some intrinsic and necessary connection with something called 'morality' which, they also seem to assume, is intrinsically and necessarily *a good thing*. They seem to believe that Immanuel Kant is on their side in these assumptions. Others of us may think that Kant cannot be used in this way. And we may think that he certainly cannot be invoked uncritically, as if, in the meantime, Hegel and Schopenhauer and Marx and Nietzsche and Freud and Wittgenstein and Heidegger had not spoken about morality.

Capps does not approve of Tony Anghie's exposing of international law as an instrument of imperialism—and yet Anghie must be right, for the following reason. It is impossible to suppose that the ruling classes who construct general social structures, including law, would construct social structures that threaten their fundamental interests. The international system in its present structural form is the product of the collusive and competitive interaction of governments, some of whom have had to protect vast world-wide interests, using the charismatic and iconic thing called 'law' as a form of self-defence in depth.

At least from the point of view of method, Capps also does not approve of Thomas Franck's sidelining of the supposed theoretical problem of international law, in order to turn his and our attention to the question of how it, whatever it is, can be made to satisfy our highest human and social values.

The best of pure social theory (Hobbes, Locke, Vico, Jefferson-Hamilton-Madison, Bentham, Comte, Weber, Kelsen, Lauterpacht, Lasswell-McDougal—ideologically committed witnesses of some of the great hinge-periods of history) has been significantly impure, with add-ons conjured out of thin air: religion seen as prudential public policy; natural law seen as the ultimate form of self-interest; morality seen as a collective moral sense; human rights seen as practically reasonable, or as cultural universalism; high social values seen as supra-social. But, it should be noted, the best of pure theory has been intensely *practical* in its aim, designed to help to manage social change at times of dramatic social transformation, by a calculated appeal to something that shares in the spirit of, but is not to be identified with, ancient (and presumptively exploded) transcendentalisms.

The best of *pure* social theory is a bridge between *transcendental* theory which postulates the logical necessity of high social values and *practical* theory which adapts transcendental and pure theory to condition actual social reality. The best of pure social theory is intended to be a way of overcoming the extreme impurity of actual social reality.

Even John Austin, dark star in the Benthamite constellation and progenitor of Hartism, managed to catch the spirit of the age (a phrase then much in vogue) in postulating a *legislative* idea of law (*Province of Jurisprudence Determined*, 1832). It was a time when the old governing class and a new kind of middle class made a deal (Reform Act 1832) to prolong the life of the mysterious post-medieval tricephalous parliament (Crown, Lords, Commons) within a new kind of society, industrialising and urbanising itself with fierce energy and at terrible human cost, with workers and the unemployed treated like animals, and with rampant free-market capitalism destroying the very idea of morality.

The appalling 'condition of England', as it was called at the time, was of a nation of two nations, the rich and the poor (to echo Benjamin Disraeli, politician and polemical novelist, writing in 1845). Engels, also writing in 1845, approved a contemporary slogan to the effect that the condition of the masses in England amounted to 'social murder', with their living conditions destroying their health and shortening their lives. Mr Gradgrind's younger children were called Adam Smith and Malthus (Charles Dickens, *Hard Times*, 1853).

In Britain 'human dignity' was the great rallying cry of those (Coleridge, Godwin, Kingsley, Carlyle, Ruskin, Morris and others) whose fierce polemics helped to inspire a 'revolution by process of law' (*per* the Duke of Wellington, leader of the canny survivors of the old regime) mainly achieved through legislation. Engels said that the nineteenth-century British Parliament was the most revolutionary body in Europe.

It is interesting to find that Austin's name can still be invoked with respect among legal scientists. For Frederick Pollock, Austin was one of those who, knowing a little political philosophy, were able 'to impose the shallowest of dogmas upon lawyers who knew none'.

Within an analytical concept of international law, Capps finds immanent value in the ideal of human dignity. It is important to note that he is not, in the second part of the book, simply deserting legal science in favour of Lasswellian sociology, although he admires the policy-science school's (non-analytic) inclusion of high values (including human dignity) in the very structure of international law.

Capps's argument is that practical reasonableness compels us to see that a pure concept includes an idea of the concept's *purpose* (the *focal* nature of a concept), and, especially in the case of international law, that purpose cannot possibly be (cannot logically be, as it were) other than the flourishing of all human beings.

He finds that various *a priori* high social and moral values which he assembles under the portmanteau term 'human dignity' have been enacted in many international documents and decisions, from the United Nations Charter onwards. For Capps, we may now be able, at last, to regard international law as a conceptually coherent instance of an ameliorative concept of law in general.

His book will be welcomed as a deeply serious source of intellectual and moral support for those who believe that what seems to be a recent humanising of the constitutional principles of international law is a fundamental and permanent transformation of the international system. Others of us may, sadly, continue to believe that the new principles are little more than delusional social poetry, an ignoble lie, the self-interested de-transcendentalising of transcendental values by the masters of ultimate social power. The gross public evils flowing from the international system, and its national extensions, continue, and will continue, unabated.

The nineteenth-century 'condition of England' has been globalised to become the *human condition* of the twenty-first century, a human world of two worlds whose inhabitants might be inhabitants of different planets (to borrow the very words that Disraeli used to describe the two nations of England in 1845), with the world's poorest as victims of the *social murder* that Engels had diagnosed in the England of 1845. Both worlds are full of gross affronts, material and moral, to human dignity.

Could the ideal of human dignity be a rallying-cry of a new revolution by process of law, including the process of international law? Perhaps Patrick Capps's difficult and challenging and rewarding book could be used to help to make the masters of ultimate social power become even dimly aware of a strange idea: the idea that the essential purpose of law, including international law, might be seen to be human self-perfecting or, in other words, human happiness. We may catch the masters of ultimate social power in the silken webs of their pseudo-benevolence, our power over their power.

*

Philosophically, the United States of America is another country. From a European perspective, it is us and not-us, with small differences that are also large differences. A nation unlike any other, the United States developed its own national mind, a mind unlike any other. An important aspect of the American mind is its attitude to law. In Aaron Fichtelberg's *Law at the Vanishing Point: A Philosophical Analysis of International Law* we can witness an American mind at work on what some people have seen as the elusive phenomenon of international law. For Fichtelberg international law is not an elusive phenomenon. It is a fact.

His book is as American in its brisk intellectual certainties as Capps's book is European in its arduous complexity. Their books seem to be webs of ideas spun by spiders of different mental species. It is a contrast that demands an explanation which will take us far beyond international law and its problems. It is a contrast with profound real-world consequences.

For a non-American reader, Fichtelberg's book is an event. American Pragmatism meets International Law. Notwithstanding the book's title, it is better seen as embodying philosophy at the vanishing point. Its theoretical analysis is in the tradition of American Pragmatism, which might be considered as a state of mind rather than a philosophy. The book is designed as an answer to a number of different forms of scepticism about the 'reality' of international law. These forms of scepticism are not exclusively American, but it is their American projection and significance that it is the focus of the discussion. In this sense, the book is part of an American-American debate (to echo the useful French term *franco-français* for the corresponding phenomenon).

Fichtelberg identifies and names four forms of scepticism whose substance one might summarise in the following way: descriptive realism (international law *does not* play a decisive role in international decision-making; national interest is decisive); prescriptive realism (international law *should not* play a decisive role, given that the overriding duty of governments is to do what is in their country's national interest); Critical Legal Studies and New Stream theory (a sub-sub-Marxist dissecting of international law as a manipulative conspiracy (sub-sub-Marxist being, one may think, somewhat better than not-Marxist-at-all)); and postmodernism (international law as a collusive fantasy, generating wishful-thinking or cynicism, causing people to expect too much or too little of international law).

Fichtelberg devotes very few pages to the latter two forms of scepticism. His main targets are the two forms of 'realism'. He also does not devote any significant discussion to the vast mass of writing about the problem of the nature of international law extending over many centuries. He explains this using a delightfully ingenious pragmatist gambit. Writers about that problem are part of the problem, because they are participating in the making of what they are writing about. They are intellectual competitors, not expert witnesses. For those of us who do spend, or waste, a great deal of time on such matters, it would be a glorious release to be able to play this gambit.

However, this approach is part of a wider and important discussion by Fichtelberg about how law, and not merely international law, is made—the following summary being one reader's understanding of his discussion. Law is not a thing that sits there waiting to be applied. It is not (to echo Oliver Wendell Holmes Jr) a brooding omnipresence in the sky. Law is made *ambulando*, as it were, by the interaction of those who participate in its making. And they include not only the obvious people—legislators, judges, lawyers—but also those who debate the law and write commentaries, learned treatises and op-ed pieces.

But the argument goes further. Law in general, and international law in particular, are not metaphysical entities waiting for us to identify their 'true' nature. There are social sub-systems that people regard as legal systems, and there are phenomena within those systems that people refer to as law. But the class of such phenomena is open-ended and they may take any number of forms, and what people say about them may differ and may take any number of different forms. Law in general, and international law in particular, are what people, explicitly or as an inference from their behaviour, think they are. There is no point in searching for some abstract and universal meaning for 'the sources of international law' or 'the subjects of international law' or 'the binding-force of international law' or 'sovereignty' or 'legal personality'. Such things are simply what they *are* in practice, what they *do* in practice.

Fichtelberg suggests that this approach is related to philosophical nominalism. Nominalism, in the Western philosophical tradition, has been a permanent sceptical counterpoint, suggesting that most of the problems of philosophy are false problems caused by the tendency of philosophers to suppose that any idea which has a substantive name (truth, justice, law, evil, duty, matter, spirit, the soul, the self, and so on) can be discussed using the kind of language that we use to discuss things present in material (non-mind-made) reality, whereas the apparent substantiality of such ideas is nothing more than a mind-made linguistic illusion. The problem with nominalism is that such ideas *are* treated substantively, not merely by many philosophers, but by everyone else every minute of every day, as Wittgenstein II recognised.

Fichtelberg's general approach is, perhaps, better seen as an echo of American Legal Realism, with its decisive focus on what law does rather than what law is. We remember Karl Llewellyn, collaborating with the anthropologist Adamson Hoebel and concluding that law is a social institution doing a number of 'law-jobs' that all societies require to be done, including, above all, dispute settlement. The approach may also seem to echo the work of the Scandinavian Legal Realists (Hägerström, Olivecrona, Lundstedt, Ross) for whom it was nonsensical to search for some mystical thing called 'the binding-force of law', other than in the minds of those who feel bound by the law. For Alf Ross, law is a set of normative ideas interpreting the phenomena of law, ideas that are treated normatively because they are felt to be socially binding by those who have to apply the law. Karl Olivercrona said: 'I do not regard it as necessary to formulate a definition of law.'

However, Fichtelberg's approach reflects more than American Legal Realism and requires us to delve more deeply into the nature of the American mind.

Piety and pragmatism are the permanent pillars of American consciousness. The religious earnestness characteristic of people with a sense of liberation and exile took on a more rigid form in the mini-theocracies of the founding American settlements. The revival of religion in the eighteenth century (the Great Awakenings, led by the preaching of Edwards and Whitefield) brought to the United States something of the return to seriousness of European Pietism, Jansenism, and Methodism. And even the Transcendentalism of mid-nineteenth-century New England represented, for a narrow social class, a return to seriousness of a deistic kind. All these things established in American consciousness a generalised socio-moral spirit transcending or subtending all social thought and behaviour. It is a secular ethos of benevolence, generosity, optimism, social duty, and faith in progress which thoughtful foreign visitors have regularly observed and, if they are European, have often found puzzling.

In Virgil's Aeneid, Aeneas is described as *pius* on seventeen occasions (including twice by himself). The word seems to be referring not merely to religious piety but to a sense of respect for higher things, for honour, for established convention. But Aeneas, in his mission to found Rome, had also to do some less than pious things. American piety, not unlike that of Aeneas, co-exists with a pragmatism which is concerned with means rather than ends. A sort of social piety seems to lie behind even the most realist of American legal realists. Llewellyn and the others had in their intellectual background a keen concern with the social purposes which law should serve. One might even say that they saw themselves as puritan legal theorists, cleaning out the stables. American sociological jurisprudence was explicitly concerned with the function of law as a means of social transformation. Roscoe Pound saw law in the pragmatic service of what he called social interests, but he also spoke of a *positive natural law* embodying the universal principles that ultimately inspire the everyday activity of the law.

The permanent struggle between the spirit of piety and the spirit of pragmatism has formed the American soul. It is not merely a mental dialectic. It has large practical consequences. Nowhere is the struggle more apparent than in the oscillation of American foreign policy between idealism and realism. It is reflected also in American ambivalence about international law. Americans seem to be frustrated that international law cannot do two things at once—to serve important social ends, such as making a better world, and to act as an efficient means for pursuing essential material interests.

Fichtelberg does not have much time for general philosophy, or social or legal philosophy of the general kind. He refers to the notorious epistemological problem of the social sciences (the so-called problem of 'method'), but he confidently proposes his own method. In his book Patrick Capps has considered the epistemological problem, and is attracted by Weber's ingenious, but ultimately unsatisfactory, idea of the ideal-type (*Idealtypus*)—a matrix of generalised ideas in some way derived from observation of actual social and mental phenomena in the human world which is then applied heuristically to actual phenomena of the human world, to allow us to understand them better by measuring how far they conform to the ideal-type. (It is 'ideal' only in the sense that it is takes the form of ideas.)

Fichtelberg calls his own method for dealing with the sceptics 'empirical'. But we may be reminded of David Hume's claim in the title of the *Treatise on Human Nature* that he will be applying 'the experimental method'—which turns out to be, in the rest of the book, a method of worldly-wise observation and intelligent introspection. In Fichtelberg's case, we may see his method as essentially that of the American Pragmatists—a summons to a conversation among interested and well-informed people about puzzling social phenomena with the aim of constructing something that they might regard as the 'truth' of the matter.

The leading American Pragmatists (Peirce, W. James, Dewey) were never able to say, still less to agree, precisely what American Pragmatism is. (One commentator has said that the movement is largely James's misunderstanding of Peirce.) But this confusion should not tempt us to underestimate the movement's profound importance in the history of human thought. It is a withdrawal from the perennial and universal tradition of philosophy. It is an egalitarian repudiation of an idea of truth associated with an idea of wisdom. For Peirce, the opinion which is ultimately agreed upon by all who investigate something is what Pragmatists mean by truth; and 'the object represented by this opinion is real.' This claim sidelines, at a stroke, centuries, millennia even, of thought about truth and reality.

It corresponds well to Fichtelberg's method here. The intellectual atmosphere of his book is reminiscent of that of William James's investigation of the phenomena of religion (in his *Varieties of Religious Experience*, 1902), which patiently and calmly, entomologically even (to echo the French historian Hippolyte Taine), surveys the phenomena. In the central part of the book he surveys briefly various crucial instances in which international law seemed to play a significant part, in order to determine what role international law actually played, and how the actors in those cases treated international law (humanitarian intervention, Pinochet, Nicaragua).

William James concludes ironically with what he calls a pragmatist's view of religion, cool and benevolent. The often bizarre phenomena of human religiosity, taken together and made coherent, might lead us to think that 'the world of our present consciousness is only one out of many worlds of consciousness that exist'. One of Fichtelberg's conclusions (stated as such) is that international law is not as radically distinct from international politics as some theories have led us to believe. It is a force (among many) that influences the outcome of events on the global political landscape. For those whose thinking is determined by perennial philosophy, these uses of the word 'is' by James and Fichtelberg seem daring in the extreme.

Fichtelberg's conclusion *contra* the prescriptive realists, in their rejection of the normative claim of international law, is that they may have misunderstood the nature and mechanisms of international law. It is not a system containing underlying values. It has no underlying values. It is compatible with any values held by those who operate it. There is no deep normative structure to international law, showing why it ought to be followed. The existence of international law is real because it plays a real role in international affairs, which can be proved empirically, and any further argument is superfluous. International law is legitimate to the extent that the professional communities that use it acknowledge that it is legitimate in both their actions and their words. The search for 'the foundations of international law' might possibly be interesting and useful in deepening our understanding of the phenomenon. But it is not necessary. No mere theory will ever convince a committed sceptic of the value of international law. But the reality of international law speaks for itself and should be heard by the sceptic.

We may be tempted to hope that Fichtelberg's non-theory of international law, even if it seems to us to amount to rather a substantial theory, will be enough to convince a reasonably minded sceptic of the reality and the value of international law. We may want to welcome any affirmation of the potential reality and value of international law. But the method of this particular affirmation may also leave us with serious anxieties, anxieties which will be discussed further below. Pragmatism, in both senses of the word, theoretical and practical, may not be able to provide what piety, in its perennial American form, and self-interest urgently demand of the United States in the chaotic world of the twenty-first century.

*

To move from Fichtelberg to Carty is to cross more than one kind of ocean. Anthony Carty is one of those who have responded valiantly to the seemingly hopeless challenges of the twentieth-century intellectual inheritance described in the first part of the present review. His theoretical writings are filled with a tragic sense of international law (to echo Miguel de Unamuno). His ruling passion is a sense of loss, the loss of the international law that might have been, and never will be.

There is an undertone of irony, a Brechtian *Verfremdung*, in all of Carty's writing about international law, as if he knows that his range of cultural reference is a standing affront to the poverty of international law's intellectual ethos. It is almost as if his writing is in the tradition of satire, grinding the actual of human folly on the stone of human potentiality. Carty on international law might remind us of Swift on religion (*A Tale of a Tub*), Pope on the money culture of eighteenth-century England (*Epistle to Bathurst*), Voltaire on unreason (*Candide*), or Chekhov on the perversities of the Russian privileged classes (*The Cherry Orchard*).

Satire makes us smile when we should weep. Carty's irony goes further—towards the grim premonitions of *R.U.R.*, *The Trial*, *Animal Farm*, *Brave New World*—with an important difference. Carty is describing a world of the imagination that already exists, the inter-state world of diplomacy and war. In his writings, he offers a phenomenology, a symptomology, an ecology of this deranged world, the world of an intensely unsociable international unsociety, in which a sickly international law is among the strangest of its flora and fauna.

A satirical literary style is not appropriate in writing for the contemporary academy, however. In *Philosophy of International Law*, Carty writes, for the most part, about things that practitioners of international law know and care about, in a form and in a context which may, however, be less familiar to them.

How is it that the intellectual superstructure of international law (the 'philosophy' of international law) came to acquire its present miserably feeble state? Carty offers two answers—one large-scale, one small-scale, not mutually exclusive; perhaps mutually dependent. Under real-world pressures, international law came to be seen as the law of and by and for 'states'. Since 1945, legal practitioners have simply taken over, in an unopposed bid, the enterprise of international law.

Always and everywhere, law has been seen as part of things that transcend it, not least the social institutions that make it possible, and the social values that cause it to have the substance that it has at a particular time and in a particular place. Even the idea of a law between nations at one time shared in the prestige of big ideas—universal law as a particularisation of ancient Greek and Stoic ideas of the rational order of the universe (Cicero); the *ius gentium* as a universalised legal system reflecting the rationality and necessity of natural law (Ulpian); the law of nations as an integral part of the amalgamated natural reason and faith of established religion (Aquinas); a secular natural law constructed inductively from the best of all human experience, real and imagined (Grotius); a law between nations reflecting practical deductions from reason and a sense of justice (Wheaton); rules of conduct that civilised states recognise as binding on them as law-abiding citizens regard law in general as binding on them (Hall); the bare survival of basic ideas of decent behaviour amid the twentieth century's manifestations of very bad behaviour (Lauterpacht).

The rise of the mindless thing called the 'state' in the philosophy of the international system evacuated from international law the active presence of reason, faith, conscience, and personal responsibility, which are attributes of thinking human beings. A legal system whose subjects are not subjective subjects of the system but law-making, law-recognising, law-applying and law-enforcing robots is certainly a legal system unlike any other known in human history. Carty has labelled this 'the decay of international law'. In 1986 he published *The Decay of International Law? A Reappraisal of the Limits of Legal Imagination in International Affairs*.

Carty refers to David Johnson's admirably perceptive identification, in an article published in the *International and Comparative Law Quarterly* in 1962, of the take-over of international law by legal practitioners, as at last giving international law a tough no-nonsense image to impress specialists in other legal disciplines. The Hoebel-Llewellyn law-job of dispute settlement became the paradigm function of international law, because it became the primary place where the law is found and, more or less blatantly, made. Carty performs yet another biopsy or post-mortem of the *Nicaragua* and *Nuclear Weapons* decisions of the International Court.

For legal practitioners, the post-Vattelian system has the great advantage that it is easy to understand and easy to operate, whist rather than bridge. 'The American [practising] lawyer need not perplex his head with vexed questions of the law of nature, and the Roman law, as a source of International Law, nor need he worry himself about Mr John Austin and his ways.' (J. Scott Brown, writing in 1904; elsewhere he treated seriously the jurisprudential aspects of international law.)

Also, by evacuating higher ideas from the system, to the extent that that proved humanly possible, international law could preserve a spurious aura of universalism. It was even possible to suggest that international law-making is a technocratic activity, with an International Law Commission, containing government-appointed practitioners and fellow-travelling academics, somehow producing law out of the conjuror's hat of their own value-transcending intelligence. The International Court of Justice, a remarkable product of American piety, came to be little more than a voice of law rather than the voice of justice.

Also, by cynically appropriating from national social philosophy the idea of law based on 'consent', it was possible to regard the law-job of treaty-making as a law-making activity, and even to see customary international law as reflecting somebody's actual consent. The crass idea that *opinio iuris* requires a consideration of the actual (and non-existent) psychological attitudes of 'states' has displaced the subtle philosophy of customary law, familiar from the whole history of human society. Carty is not the first to expose this particular form of decay. Customary law is best understood as a phenomenon of a Kantian kind—the extraction of universal principles detectable as patterns of obligation within repetitive behaviour (see: an argument to this effect by the present reviewer in this *Yearbook* in 1971). There has been a corresponding decay in the philosophy of the Common Law, the customary-law system that underlies law in the Anglo-American legal tradition, if not, strictly speaking, effective legal systems in all legal traditions.

Because of the triumph of the *vita activa* over the *vita contemplativa* in international law, it has remained bizarrely possible to leave obscure the sense in which governments can justify their participation in the international system on the ground of some theory of their representation of the people, when the majority of governments practise no such theory within their own national systems. The crazy excess of international governmental and administrative institutions, and government-managed international courts and tribunals, is a measure of the absence of an international politics without which justifiable international law, and justifiable international government and administration, are not possible. (The European Union suffers from an analogous pathology.)

It may be suggested here that there is an underlying seven-layer schematic structure in Carty's phenomenology of the inter-statal world. Using it as a crucial example, he analyses at length an incident in 1957–8 when Britain intervened to assist the Sultan of Muscat and Oman to put down an insurrection in Oman. Carty reviews the internal Foreign Office documents of the time (made available to the public, under the general rule, thirty years later), apparently revealing the thinking of a government, but concealing the personal response of officials. Discussion (in the Office or with outsiders over lunch) is hidden behind lifeless official memoranda (the first and second layers of phenomena). The records then reveal discussion among officials about what to say in public to the media and at the United Nations (a third layer). This, in turn, generates comment and discussion by other governments (a fourth layer), presumably based on similar internal discussions. The whole thing then is used (a fifth layer) by legal commentators to discuss the significance of the events for the *law* of intervention and the use of force. All this then becomes fodder for historians and writers on international relations and international law (a sixth layer) about questions relating to the nature of the state (was Oman, or even Muscat and Oman, a state?), the nature of government decision-making, and the role of law at every level of discussion, with unverifiable and uninnocent speculation about the 'real' intentions of the governments involved, as meaningless a search as the search for their *opiniones iuris*.

Finally, the whole package gives rise to the broadest questions of social and legal philosophy. It is with this seventh layer that Carty is most concerned. His discussion of the imagining of the *state* draws attention to a whole spectrum of ideas that have been invoked, in theory and in practice, from the most Hobbesian to the most constructivist, including ideas that link the artificial reality of the state to the supposedly real reality of ethnicity. It is remarkable that deeply divergent views can be held by writers from backgrounds that are otherwise culturally so proximate.

The winner in practice is, of course, the wholly pragmatic view of the state purveyed by governments, arbitrarily commandeering this theoretical view or that to deal with colonial entities (not 'states', surely) and successor states to colonial entities, states in the process of decomposition, entities within states claiming independence, and so on and on. Carty focuses especially on the way governments find pragmatic resolutions of the impossible contradiction between the imperious need to protect the stability of the state-structure and the perennial appeal made in the name of self-determination.

Most interestingly, Carty shows that 'recognition', the term of art which international lawyers treat with puzzled respect, conceals the way in which the existing governments *create* the inter-statal system itself, using pragmatically, and as some particular occasion demands, all the constructive matrices of international law—customary international law, legal personality, intervention, use of force, state responsibility, state succession—to construct, develop and protect the state-structure of the international system. It is, in this sense, that one can say that the inter-statal system and the current form of international law are *facts*. An alternative global reality can only be an idea or an ideal. The mind-made ecology of the world of all-humanity, however unfit it may be, however poorly adapted to the human and environmental challenges that humanity has created for itself, nevertheless seems to have within it a paradoxical and tragic evolutionary capacity for survival.

The present reviewer is unable to comment usefully on Carty's painful chapters (painful for writer and reader) discussing Anglo-American strategic governmental thinking on the use of force, except to the extent that the withholding of comment is itself a comment. To respond to the views attributed to those governments to the effect that present and foreseeable threats to international peace and security render inappropriate or even obsolete existing international law on war (euphemistically referred to as 'the use of force') would require one to appear to treat dispassionately what passes for the existing law on the subject, law which is merely the cynical rationalising of monstrous human evil, a phenomenon far beyond the reach of irony or satire.

Thomas Hobbes is a brooding presence throughout Carty's book. We all owe a debt to Hobbes for being infinitely interpretable—*tot homines, tot sententii*—or a little more than *tot sententii*, given that some of us must admit to having had different views of him at different times. Where is the Hobbesian heart—in power or in order? Was he the friend of governments or the friend of the people? John Locke, his successor who, in the *Two Treatises*, kept rather quiet about his debt to Hobbes for public relations reasons (Hobbes being an unpopular brand in semi-revolutionary times), acquired the reputation of being the friend of the people, not least the American people. But (to echo J.S. Mill) is any corporatist view of society necessarily the friend of the people when it can be used to justify definitively the actual power of actual social institutions, even when that power is used excessively or abusively, even when it justifies a majoritarian tyranny?

Is the international system an exteriorisation of the Hobbesian state—'state' in the sense of a total integration of society, self-contained, self-explaining, self-justifying, self-preserving at all costs, with the organisation of social power being enforced through law backed by public violence (on one commonly held reading of Hobbes)? Is this kind of state turned inside out, as it were, in the international sociosphere in which the organisation of violence and law is produced by an *upward* movement of the 'sovereign' power of the states, acting through the peculiar social processes of war and diplomacy, and through the spasmodic and tactical mutual self-limiting known as international law?

Is the international system an anachronistic prolongation of such an idea of the state, long after revolutionary transformations have created a new idea of the state in its internal form, at least in liberal democratic societies? The survival of the anachronism leaves governments acting on the external stage more or less in the same way, and with the same assumptions, as their medieval and post-medieval predecessors behaved. The outcome is a two-realm view of the human world, both realms confusingly signified by the same signifier—'state'—but with a fundamental dichotomy between the realities of the two realms.

Carty identifies this most commonly held view of the international system, and deplores its consequences. Could there be room for an idea of an international sociosphere in which the organisation of violence and law is derived from a *downward* delegation to the constituent societies from a constitutional superstructure, as supposed by previous religious and humanist worldviews? Carty has an illuminating discussion of such a view, as postulated by Hans Kelsen and others.

In the last part of his book, Carty expands the contextual focus to consider international law in relation to macro-political perspectives of the twenty-first-century world. He discusses a strange collection of writings which purvey a fierce cultural pessimism, an apocalyptic vision of a world doomed to extrapolate the worst of the present into an even worse future. Some of these writings imagine an hegemony of the United States as a Mephistopheles whose dark arts are in the service of the final triumph of an American ideology of democratic-capitalist imperialism, making the world safe for the United States, its ideas, its values, and its interests. The nightmare is of a world in which an enlightened international law would be more or less unimaginable, and in which force and the absolute sovereignty of uncontrollable global systems would be the *ultima ratio* of all global social existence. These ideas seem to represent a movement from the End of Philosophy in the twentieth century to an End of Hope in the twenty-first century.

The present reviewer can offer no professional view on such an hysterical farrago of the psychology of decadence (to echo Thomas Mann's exploration of Nietzsche's ambivalence). Carty considers some possible theoretical responses, from within the American mind itself, including the approaches of John Rawls and Fernando Tesón, offering a more enlightened vision of the future of a law-governable world. It might be better simply to say that, in human affairs, the future is never simply an extrapolation of the past or of the present. The morphology of the human world changes unceasingly and dramatically. Already, the global configuration of power is not what it was a couple of years ago. We may be reminded of Frederic Maitland's view that to seek to tell a piece of history is to tear at a seamless web.

We must also remember that seemingly autonomic social systems, even dangerous and destructive social systems, have been made by the human mind, the same human mind that will make the human future. Carty's own preference is for a re-imagining of law and international law within its total anthropological context, the context of individual human beings and human society in general. Such an approach is one that any Social Idealist would be glad to discuss further.

*

All three books under review here may be seen as concerned with the *future* of international law. For Capps, it is possible to regard international law as truly law and, therefore, containing intrinsic core values. For Fichtelberg, it is possible to accept international law as capable of being and doing what law in general is and does. For Carty, recognising the structural anachronism of international law might allow us to begin to cure its substantive inadequacy.

The attitude of the American mind is of crucial importance. Before 1776, America was part of what this reviewer has elsewhere called a *genetic* nation—a Britain-in-exile, overseas British subjects sharing a complex cultural inheritance. After 1776, Americans set about turning themselves, with remarkable speed and clarity of purpose, into a *generic* nation, an invented nation, to use a term that Americans themselves have used, defined by a uniformity of ideas and ideals and way of life. It is the nation which Alexis de Tocqueville wrote about, already in the 1830s, an anthropologist exploring, with amazing clairvoyance, a strange New Atlantis, a nation which, with immigrants from all over the world, was able to turn itself into a *Weltstaat*, a world-state closely contained within the borders of the United States.

Seen from this city on a hill, transatlantic magic mountain, the rest of the world became an alien place, a place of existential threats and splendid opportunities, and tiresome entanglements. American Pragmatism explained and justified the way in which the United States talks to itself, in its own private conversation, its own *community of investigators* (Peirce), its own *communicative community* (Habermas), constructing collectively its own *reality* and *truth* and *law*, in the conscious and unconscious cerebration (to echo William Carpenter) of the unique American mind. But it is worth recalling that John Dewey, a leading American Pragmatist, was deeply troubled by the fact that transient ideas of 'the true' and 'the good', formed from random social consensus, proved to be cruelly inadequate in the face of the terrible worldwide social realities of the late-nineteenth and early-twentieth centuries.

Philosophyless law is only possible in a United States where law is a central feature of everyday social self-constituting within an intensely cohesive collective consciousness. The United States was separated from the social history of Europe, including the turbulent history of radically reformist socialism and applied Marxism, and from the turbulent philosophical history of Europe, phenomena that have affected the political and cultural development of very many non-European countries.

Philosophyless international law will not be possible in an international society formed from countless different philosophy-filled subordinate societies. It will be difficult to invent a new international law, to imagine a new world order for a globalised world, if the American mind cannot find a way to take part, as a fully committed participant, in a conversation with the not-insignificant minds of non-America, in the making of a true global politics, making possible a true international law. Before the door of the fullest possible expression of an international legal system there stands no gatekeeper, only the self-imposed limits of the human imagination.

PHILIP ALLOTT
UNIVERSITY OF CAMBRIDGE

Contemporary Issues in International Environmental Law. By MALGOSIA FITZMAURICE. Cheltenham, Edward Elgar, 2009. 228 pp. £59.95.

International Courts and Environmental Protection. By TIMOTHY STEPHENS. Cambridge, Cambridge University Press, 2009. 458 pp. £60.00.

Environmental Law and Justice in Context. By JONAS EBBESON AND PHOEBE OKOWA (eds). 496 pp. Cambridge, Cambridge University Press, 2009. £75.00.

There has been a tendency in some quarters to suggest that international environmental law scholarship suffers from a number of weaknesses. First, that it has failed to demarcate accurately that which is and that which ought to, or which might, be. Second, that it has hidden behind the relative early stage of the discipline (i.e. forever noting that the 'modern' era of international environmental law really only began at the 1972 Stockholm Conference on the Human Environment) to deflect criticism away from the challenges that are still to be overcome, preferring instead to focus on its achievements. Third, that it is almost evangelical about the significance of international environmental law and thus does not approach the topic with either sufficient rigour or detachment. And fourth, that international environmental law is overly-descriptive, and lacks either theoretical or analytical insight. Of course, categorising the criticisms in this way is, itself, an over-generalisation as it fails to reflect important nuances within the comments that have been levelled against environmental scholarship over the years. Moreover, it should not be viewed that such criticisms either are cumulative or, in fact, cover the majority of works on international environmental law, be that monographs, textbooks, journal articles, or other legal writings. Nevertheless, there is a reasonably firm view, held particularly amongst some general international lawyers, that international environmental legal writings—and thus, by default, international environmental lawyers—do not always approach their subject with the necessary rigour.

Professor Vaughan Lowe, for instance, has had occasion to talk of the 'faintly depressing wooliness that characterizes some of the writing on international environmental law'.[1] Indeed, even environmental lawyers themselves have recognised the issue. As noted in an article published in the *Journal of Environmental Law* in 2009, 'in international environmental law scholarship, overlaps and gaps are all too common, and scholars have, thus far, failed to develop effective mechanisms for facilitating coordination between distinct areas of international environmental law'.[2] Of course, the easiest, and most obvious, response to both criticisms is to reject them entirely; to suggest that the weaknesses identified in international environmental law scholarship are not weaknesses at all, but characteristic of the discipline. International environmental law, so the argument might go, though drawn from public international law, has now shown itself to be a sufficiently distinct body of law that the scholarship surrounding it invariably reflects this difference. In that regard, for instance, emphasis is inevitably placed as much on the importance of soft law as it is on those rules which are subject to formal ratification procedures. Indeed, one could go further and point to those issues on which international environmental law is forcing change in general international law; for instance, the evolution of putative rules of customary environmental law, primarily through the identification of *opinio juris* in declaratory texts, or the increasing elaboration of innovative treaty procedures, such as those on monitoring and reporting, tacit consent and non-compliance. Thus, one response to such criticism is to highlight how international environmental law differs from public international law, implicitly suggesting that this somehow affects the accompanying scholarship. However, this in truth provides no answer to the real criticism, which focuses less on the nature and structure of the (legal) discipline and concentrates rather more upon the cohesion and, indeed, stringency of the parallel (academic) one.

So, a self-referencing defence of international environmental law (i.e. that its speciality justifies its peculiarities) may work, at some levels and on some issues, but it is hardly a coherent defence overall. Moreover, many international environmental lawyers would not recognise the caricature of the discipline that I have just drawn; for most, international environmental law remains squarely within the systemic framework of public international law. True, developments in environmental law might help push the boundaries of

[1] V Lowe, *International Law* (Oxford University Press, Oxford, 2007) 243.

[2] E Fisher, B Lange, E Scotford, and C Carlarne, 'Maturity and Methodology: Starting a Debate about Environmental Law Scholarship' (2009) 21 *Journal of Environmental Law* 240.

how general international law functions, but it does so from within the established legal order, and certainly not from without. No; it is much better when responding to such criticism, to accept—at least in part—the comments made. In truth, as with all scholarship, there has been material published which may have been better served if it had been more carefully revised before publication. But that is entirely different from criticising a whole body of work. Thus, rather than seeking to defend international environmental law scholarship in blind faith (which merely serves to substantiate the claim of evangelism noted above) it is preferable to note the criticisms and to respond intelligently, critically—and with good grace! In short, it should prompt international environmental lawyers, for want of a better phrase, to want to raise their game.

Thus, in undertaking a review of these three particular books, this paper seeks to place them within the broader context of international environmental law scholarship. This is not to argue that these books are altogether representative in either content or tone of the current literature, but rather to suggest that *together* they provide a useful overview of the present state of the discipline. So while it is clearly not possible to provide a review of the entirety of recent scholarship simply by commenting on these books alone, these works do, nevertheless, allow us to reflect on the general quality of the debate. And in this regard, a number of discrete issues should be kept in mind, which I would suggest are characteristic—at least, in part—of a more sophisticated legal literature on international environmental law. First, does the literature take us beyond mere description of that which is 'expected', to provide new insight and level of analysis on those issues that are perhaps less well-explored and/or less well-understood? Second, does the literature self-reflect on the discipline's preconceived assumptions and perhaps its own biases, to analyse inherent tensions, and to consider how international environmental law (and writings thereon) might seek to correct such failings and ensure progress in the future? Third, does the literature place international environmental law within a broader context, for instance within wider debates on fragmentation, coherence or in terms of the opening up of the international system to a wider range of actors? Alternatively, does discussion on international environmental law not take place in a legal vacuum but recognise the equal importance of developments in other fields of international law, which may have an equally profound effect on nature conservation and environmental issues (for instance, the law of international investment). Fourth, does the literature engage with legal and/or political theory—not in a deferential or piecemeal way, but as an integral element thereof? And fifth, does the literature add anything to our understanding of the role and place of law with an increasingly complex global society?

Invariably not all literature—even the best literature—on international environmental law will be able to provide coherent answers to all five of these questions in the same piece of work. Indeed, there is, and always should be, still ample room in the literature for short positivist assessments of recent developments of the law. Without this type of literature, much of the rest could not be written. However, as a body of literature as a whole, one must also look for a rich supply of writings that also seek to challenge our understandings of the discipline from a diverse array of perspectives. It is thus, on this basis, that this review will now consider each of the selected books in turn. They cover a range of issues, including the increasingly vital role international judicial and arbitral bodies play in deciding difficult matters of environmental protection, a reassessment of some of the general principles on which international environmental law is premised and the significance and operationalisation of notions of fairness and justice within environmental law. At the end of the review, in a brief conclusion, some further thought will be given to the questions posed above and consider the extent to which much of the recent international environmental legal scholarship, far from being 'faintly depressing wooliness' is, in fact, dynamic and worthy of being studied not just by international environmental lawyers but the academic legal community, more generally.

*

Malgosia Fitzmaurice's *Contemporary Issues in International Environmental Law* is not—as she notes herself—'meant as a textbook or a comprehensive study... it is a collection of essays which analyse certain concepts... the legal character, normative content and practical application of which are questionable' (xvii). In truth, this is something of an understatement when one looks at the concepts in question, *viz.*, the precautionary principle, sustainable development, intergenerational equity, and the right to a clean environment. Indeed, one might rightly have an initial sense that as many, if not all, of these concepts have been the subject of so much critical analysis over many years that they could have been drained of nearly all useful comment. Is there much that can be usefully left to say? But this was perhaps Fitzmaurice's aim; to consider those foundational—but also fundamentally contested—principles, which underpin the discipline, and which many evangelically discuss but rarely consider in a sufficiently critical manner. Fitzmaurice shows, however, that the most appropriate approach to such issues is neither whole-hearted support nor overt suspicion, but rather dispassionate, grounded and scholarly analysis. In each of the chapters, she begins with an inevitable summary of the matter—its historical evolution, its principled contours and its usage in international law (thus far)—but then quickly proceeds to consider the invariable tensions that continue to surround the concept and assesses its continued utility as a meaningful contribution within the international environmental debate. For instance, Fitzmaurice discusses the polarised debate between those who view the precautionary principle as a legally-binding obligation, indeed perhaps even the foundational cornerstone of international environmental law, and those who remain deeply critical of its ambivalence and indeterminacy. Fitzmaurice steers a midpoint, noting both the central role it plays within international environmental law and the ongoing debates surrounding its ambiguity. More significantly, Fitzmaurice seeks to avoid the temptation of searching for a meta-understanding of the precautionary principle, preferring instead to emphasise the inevitable contextual nature in the way in which it is applied. As she notes, 'being mindful of its unclear legal status and the uncertainty of its practical application, as it stands at present, it perhaps would be a futile effort to attempt to define this principle in a general manner. The better approach appears to be to analyse it on a case-by-case basis' (65). This is no opt-out of a difficult discussion; in fact, quite the reverse. International environmental lawyers have arguably, in the past, been too eager to over-generalise—in particular, to find customary rules before they are fully substantiated—Fitzmaurice forcefully reminds us of the false security in such an endeavour. So, if one were looking for the answer to the conundrum as to whether the precautionary principle is a rule of international law; you won't find it here. But what it will tell you, is that you are probably asking the wrong question.

A second notable feature of this book is Fitzmaurice's continuing emphasis upon the importance that such principles be capable of being operationalised at the political and normative level. The chapter on sustainable development, for instance, scrutinises the current literature for its continuous repetition of dilemmas over definition and meaning, rather than the impact it is actually capable of having 'on-the-ground', in treaty law and in policy. One needs to move on and to accept that there is no one comprehensive and universal meaning; indeed, as she says, 'the efforts to identify such definition will be futile' (86). Such criticism is, in equal measure, directed towards international courts and tribunals, which have yet to address fully the legal implications of sustainable development.

Commenting on the use of the concept in its case-law so far, Fitzmaurice notes, for example, that the International Court of Justice has yet to 'bring any new dimensions into this notion' (106). As an alternate approach, on the other hand, Fitzmaurice explores the implication of sustainable development in a number of discrete areas, including recent developments in the Baltic Sea Area and as part of revisions to the Southern African Development Community in 2000. In both cases, she is able to discern a positive move away from generality and platitude towards the adoption and implementation of specific action plans and programmes. This should, she argues, be welcomed and, on this basis, '[t]he continuing reliance on clichéd and worn out definitions should be abandoned and the concept (or principle) of sustainable development must acquire a tangible and concrete content' (108). Though this statement is aimed, in particular, at this one concept, there is nevertheless a sense that it applies across the book more broadly. Never dogmatic, it is nevertheless apparent that Fitzmaurice is as impatient with the lack of progress of ideas within the literature, as she is with the lack of political movement on environmental issues.

A third feature of the book is the use of a range of interesting examples to exemplify the general principles perhaps better than any general discussion could ever do. These are not case studies in the traditional sense, but they do serve to illustrate some key points of the debate. Mention has already been made of the discussion of recent trends in legal and policy-making as regards the Baltic Sea, an area she also discusses in relation to the implementation of the precautionary principle. But perhaps more noticeable still is Fitzmaurice's detailed consideration of the legal framework surrounding the Republic of Marshall Islands' compact with the United States as an instance—as she sees it—of the application of intergenerational responsibility. For Fitzmaurice, the acceptance by the US of its responsibility for loss or damage caused by US nuclear testing in the area and, in particular, the establishment of a claims tribunal to resolve these claims is of 'paramount importance' (169) in the elaboration of intergenerational equity in international law; the idea that each generation must take responsibility for its acts for the benefit of future generations. Though Fitzmaurice's wording might prove too strong a sentiment for some readers in the absence of much in the way of express references to intergenerational responsibility[3]—thus leading some to wonder how far such a scheme truly exhibits an intergenerational character—Fitzmaurice is able to draw out the argument, not in a declaratory manner but cautiously and carefully to highlight both the essence of her thesis and the admittedly tentative nature of the concept. This is no 'normative peg' from which international environmental lawyers can lazily hang their endorsement of intergenerational equity, such as has been the case with the overly-used 1993 Supreme Court of The Philippines decision in *Minors Oposa v. Secretary of the Department of Environmental and Natural Resources* (1993).[4] However concurrently, this is no reason to ignore, or to marginalise, such developments either; as Fitzmaurice rightly notes, these legal processes are 'not a widely known fact' (153). Indeed, in a field where the global nature of the discipline is

[3] 1983 Agreement for the Implementation of Section 177 of the Compact of Free Association, preamble: 'to create and maintain, in perpetuity, a means of to address past, present and future consequences of the Nuclear Testing Program'.

[4] (1994) 33 *International Legal Materials* 185: 'This case... has a special and novel element. Petitioners minors assert that they represent their generation as well as generations yet unborn. We find no difficulty in ruling that they can, for themselves, for others of their generation and for the succeeding generations, file a class suit. Their personality to sue in behalf of the succeeding generations can only be based on the concept of intergenerational responsibility insofar as the right to a balanced and healthful ecology is concerned'. Cf D Gatmaytan, 'The Illusion of Intergenerational Equity: Oposa v. Factoran as Pyrrhic Victory' (2003) 15 *Georgetown International Environmental Law Review* 457–485.

often ironically missed, this is an instructive reminder as to the importance of seeking for the *universal* in State practice.

Thus, in conclusion, the Fitzmaurice book is highly recommended as a key contribution to the literature. It fulfils its title in being contemporaneous, but more than that it also provides a subtle critique of how many international environmental lawyers have approached their subject. It was clearly not the author's intention purposively to express herself as critiquing others, but rather it occurs through the scholarship of her own work. If there is a fault, it is with the 'book-ends' to the work; the introduction and conclusion are summary at best. Though Fitzmaurice was rightly concerned with the content of the individual chapters, some of the inter-weaving themes might have deserved a little more attention. Nevertheless, this book will be an essential read for anyone interested in the subject.

*

If the Fitzmaurice book has a particularly distinctive structure, the Stephens book is a much more classical monograph, reflecting a more single narrative. His thesis is surprisingly simple, but then sometimes the best often are; as he says 'international adjudication cannot be advocated as an institutional panacea; however, nor can its potential contribution in the effective functioning of international environmental law be dismissed' (365). This might, on first reading, seem almost trite, but it is, in fact, a balanced and measured response to the opportunities, challenges, strengths, and limitations of international adjudication in the field of environmental protection. Grounded firmly in public international law but also embedded, where appropriate, within legal and political theory, the book ranges widely to consider the diverse range of issues that affect the utility of adjudication as a means not only of dispute settlement but also, what Stephens terms, 'compliance control'. Nor does he ignore, though he does not over-labour the point, the influential role such adjudication can play in the development of the law, which has proved an important feature of environmental adjudication, thus far.

The book is structured into ten substantive chapters, divided into three parts. Part one, provides an analysis of not only the current tribunals mandated to adjudicate environmental disputes (including a short, but interesting, discussion of the arguments for and against what Stephens calls an 'International Court for the Environment') but also the relative merits of 'traditional approaches to compliance control' (i.e. adjudication, mediation, conciliation, fact-finding) vis-à-vis newer approaches to compliance, most notably the non-compliance procedures negotiated under an increasing range of multilateral environmental agreements. Part two then takes the analysis further through a discussion of the evolution of the case-law, including such renown disputes as the *Trail Smelter Arbitration* (1938 and 1941) (which is historically attributed as vocalising the international obligation against transboundary harm), the *Gabčíkovo-Nagymaros Project* case (1997) before the ICJ (which raised important issues not only of international environmental and watercourse law, but also of the law of treaties, as well as referencing sustainable development) and the various manifestations of the more recent *MOX Plant* dispute between the Republic of Ireland and the United Kingdom concerning the risks to the Irish Sea of radioactive discharges through the establishment of a new processing plant at the Sellafield nuclear installation. Each is looked at not only on its own merits, but also in terms of their contribution to the broader development of international environmental law. In particular, Stephens continually highlights the persistent tension an environmental dispute will often raise between general principle and environmental consideration. As he says of the role of the International Tribunal for the Law of the Sea (ITLOS)—and he presumably would include the other dispute adjudicatory mechanisms provided for in the 1982 UN Convention on the Law of the Sea—'ITLOS operates at the interface between the "traditional logic" of the law of the sea and the more "progressive ethic" of international environmental law' (243). This creative juxtaposition of the traditional paradigm and the need for a more nuanced approach to tackle the particularities of an environmental issue is one of a number of major themes that run throughout this book.

Despite the strengths in the first two-thirds of the book, it is perhaps the third part which is of most interest, namely a deeply scholarly evaluation of the challenges facing international environmental adjudication. These include the opportunities and difficulties in establishing public interest and public participation in international environmental litigation, ensuring jurisdictional coordination between competing proceedings, and the benefits and risks of environmental law being applied in a range of alternate judicial settings, primarily human rights bodies and the World Trade Organization. On this latter point, Stephens makes a strong case against complacency. For instance, instead of forever relying on the Appellate Body's decisions in the so-called *Shrimp Turtles* cases (1998 and 2001) as evidence that the WTO is now sufficiently receptive to environmental concerns, he rightly points out the reversible nature of the gains achieved; 'it is entirely possible that future decision-makers may be more sympathetic to the views of some WTO members from the global south that the WTO regime should not privilege environmental interests at the expense of trade-led developmental policies' (342). This is a salutary reminder to both trade and environmental lawyers that they must continuously be aware of the risks of normative divergence, as well as the hegemony that each side, in turn, possesses. But unlike previously when each approached the other as the 'opposing camp', arguments raised now must show a level of maturity and coherence that not only convince those who want to listen, but also the general legal community as a whole.

This brief review is unable to do justice to the full merits of this excellent book. It is packed with both detailed exposition and insightful analysis. Stephens has brought together material from a diverse array of sources and created a work which deserves to be widely and seriously read. It, of course, has its failings. Although a work of fewer than four hundred pages could never be comprehensive, one might have expected more on the increasingly controversial 'environmental' disputes arising under bilateral investment treaties and the investment clauses of regional trade agreements. But this is a relatively minor fault in light of its very obvious strengths. In short, though the role of international adjudication in international environmental law is a reasonably well-known story, and both its successes and its inherent weaknesses are integral to an understanding of the subdiscipline, it is rarely accurately and systematically told. This book fortunately does just that.

*

Environmental Law and Justice in Context is an edited collection, bringing some of the leading writers on international environmental law together with a range of other commentators. Moreover, this is not just a book about *international* environmental law, though admittedly that is its primary focus. Rather, the central theme of this book—as is evident from its title—is the place of justice and fairness within environmental discourse, both international and domestic. Of course, not all chapters appreciate fairness in the same way or, at least in one case, are necessarily supportive of the argument that one can (or should) understand environmental law from such a principled perspective. The chapter by Twining, in particular, sets out a number of qualifications to viewing environmental law from a justice approach. Nevertheless, the overarching theme of the collection is favourable towards the inclusion of a fairness dimension within environmental regulation.

Indeed, in the light of the severe pressures that are now imposed upon the global environment through human activity and, concurrently, the increasingly competing demands that are placed on being able to exploit its natural resources, it is certainly not unsurprising that debates on 'fairness', 'justice', even 'equity'—and there must be a valid discussion as to the meaning and inter-changeability of such terms (and concepts)—have become pertinent as to how the international community should seek to tackle environmental issues. Of course, fairness can be endorsed purely for the instrumental purpose of achieving more *effective* environmental law—effective in the sense of some form of demonstrable reduction in environmental harm or measurable improvement in environmental quality—but as various contributions to the collection make very clear, this is but one of a number of objectives that incorporating a 'fairness' perspective into law might ultimately secure. Other motivations might include seeking fairness as a basis for promoting greater universal participation within multilateral environmental agreements or as a means of enhancing one's own self-interest, be that individualist or altruistic. But as Shelton notes in her chapter, there is also a deeper justification for a fairer system of law; '[j]ustice and equity are important and, with their emphasis on fairness, are more attractive to many than economic efficiency or open conflict as a means of deciding how to allocate and sustain limited common resources' (72). An appreciation of environmental law premised upon justice thus can never merely be about its instrumental impact or making it more effective and inclusive, it is about ensuring that it is the right law; 'right' not only for the participants involved but also, for those prepared to endorse a more radical understanding, for the environment itself. In this sense, fairness raises some of the most profound questions surrounding modern environmental law. But one also needs to be careful to distinguish between fairness as an intrinsic element of *de lege ferenda* and the current state of the law. As Nollkaemper is quoted, writing more broadly about international justice, '[w]hile much has been done to promote development and the redistribution of resources, the international legal system as a whole remains pitted against a more equitable distribution' (258, note removed).

Of course, saying something must be fair or just does little to answer the seemingly impossible question of what this actually means within any particular context. In this short review, even a summary of this debate is impossible. But two particular features of many, though certainly not all, of the chapters are worth noting. First, many rely on the work of John Rawls to consider the relevance of fairness to environmental issues. And though this is certainly not without its problems—especially at the global level—his ideas on justice (either in their original form or as modified by subsequent theorists, including prominently by Thomas Pogge) are invariably attractive. Second, many of the contributions rely on the tripartite division of justice-*cum*-fairness into distributive justice, corrective justice and procedural fairness to consider its relevance in the environmental context. Significantly, though many contributors are able to highlight aspects of each which are visible in present-day international environmental law, the concepts remain deeply contested both in meaning and application. In particular, the link between maximising procedural guarantees so that all participants can take full advantage of open negotiations and achieving substantive fairness is rarely a mechanical process, in which the former will inevitably result in the latter. Indeed, in relation to the latter, when confronted with how to balance the demands of correcting historical wrongs with ensuring fair distribution on the basis of current and future needs, it is unsurprising that many contributors rightly only seek to raise the issues, rather than promulgate given solutions. As Ebbesson notes in the introduction. 'Justice considerations arise in just about any legal context involving health, the environment and natural resources, be it local, global or structural. The studies help clarifying essential issues in justice deliberations in the context of environmental law; not necessarily by telling what *is* just and fair, but rather by highlighting important factors and indicators of justice considerations' (34–35).

This gets possibly as close as any of the other chapters to an important truth, namely that searching for a predetermined form of justice is always likely to be something of a fool's errand. Rather, notions such as justice and fairness are not to be understood in absolute terms, but by degrees.

In some ways, the most noticeable thing about this edited collection is the introductory chapter by Ebbesson. Tightly written, deeply insightful and achieving that most difficult of tasks of balancing a review of the subsequent chapters with the identification of an editorial voice, the introduction sets out clearly, comprehensively and astutely the contours of the debate. Moreover, it sets the scene for an intensely rich collection of essays, and though some perhaps seek fairness and justice where others might see only law, it has forcefully introduced into the literature a topic that has always been there, but never as noticeable as it is now.

*

This review has already had occasion to quote from a paper published in 2009 in the *Journal of Environmental Law*, which concerned the general state of environmental scholarship. At another point in the same paper, the authors noted that '[a]ccording to environmental law scholars, environmental law as an academic discipline has spent the last 20 years coming of age. The maturing of it as a scholarly enterprise has been eagerly awaited and predicted but adulthood has never arrived. Environmental law scholars still perceive that the best is yet to come.'[5]

Is this comment still true for international environmental law scholarship? Without giving these three books unnecessary adulation, let me nevertheless suggest that this view is altogether too dismissive when confronted with the level of scholarship displayed in these books. Five questions were raised above. First, do these works display new insight and present an incisive level of analysis? Second, are these works self-reflective of discipline's preconceived assumptions and willing to analysis its inherent tensions and weaknesses? Third, do these works place international environmental law firmly within broader themes of general international law? Fourth, do these works engage meaningfully with theoretical insights? And finally, fifth, do these works contribute to our understanding of the role of law in a reordering global society? Each work, to a greater or lesser extent, answers many—if not most—of these issues in an intelligent, articulate and confident manner. Stephens in particular is to be credited for presenting an incisive analysis of a topic, which is generically understood but is, in fact, usually either misrepresented or over-simplified. Fitzmaurice, for her part, has reinvigorated some 'old' debates with fresh insight, whilst concurrently ensuring attention continues to be paid to the situation of environmental law within the wider framework of public international law. As she says, 'international environmental law is part and parcel of and plays a significant role in the development of international law' (207). This call for generality and, more particularly, ensuring a balance between this and the inevitable speciality that comes with the study of a 'sub-discipline' is something that international environmental lawyers must continuously

[5] Fisher *et al*, above n 2, 214 (note removed).

struggle to achieve. Finally, the edited collection by Ebbesson and Okowa has highlighted something particularly significant. As Ebbesson notes in the substantive introduction, there is a distinct 'value of critically appraising existing rules, principles, institutions and concepts of environmental law from a justice perspective, and the usefulness of such an approach to guide social change' (35–36). Environmental law cannot be assessed *just* on its own merits by reference exclusively to a worthy, but usually ill-defined, notion of 'environmental improvement'. This is, of course, supremely important, but it has never been the totality of what international environmental law is all about. As the Ebbesson and Okowa collection capably demonstrate, fairness, whether as an objective in its own right or as a consequence to be forever borne in mind, is—and arguably always has been—a key feature of environmental legal discourse. Perhaps even more revealing is the closing comment by Jutta Brunnée in her chapter on climate change, in which she remarks, '[i]f justice is to be pursued through the climate change regime, the hard work of international law has only just begun' (329). So returning to Fisher *et al*'s comment that '[e]nvironmental law scholars still perceive that the best is yet to come',[6] I would seek to defend those who inculcate a normative aspiration within their work, but would say that even better are those (such as to be found in all three of these books) who also include a critical analysis of the difficulties in actually getting there. International environmental law scholarship may not be the senior statesman of public international law, but nor is it—to stretch the analogy perhaps a little too far—the over-confident teenager, often found day-dreaming of a better world, occasionally wayward from the ways of its elders and naive enough to think that s/he is always right. International environmental law has, in the most part, grown up.

DUNCAN FRENCH
UNIVERSITY OF SHEFFIELD

Constituting Equality: Gender Equality and Comparative Constitutional Law. By SUSAN H WILLIAMS (ed). New York, Cambridge University Press, 2009. xv + 361 pp. £60.00.

The Gender of Reparations: Unsettling Sexual Hierarchies while Redressing Human Rights Violations. By RUTH RUBIO-MARIN (ed). New York, Cambridge University Press, 2009. xv + 416 pp. £65.00.

The Convention on the Elimination of All Forms of Discrimination Against Women is the second most ratified human rights instrument to date, and UN Resolution 1325 was passed unanimously just over 10 years ago. Both suggest a significant level of international agreement on the promotion of gender equality and the empowerment of women. Yet these two recently published books show that the reality of ensuring that gender is addressed in international and national processes is very different. Moreover they illustrate that much more discussion is needed on what it means to 'recognise gender' whether in constitution making or through a reparations process. Both volumes make valuable contributions to those discussions and tackle the difficult dichotomy of how to give formal recognition to women's lived experience without freezing dominant gender identities and precluding future change. Though these books appear to focus on women's human rights from very different perspectives, ultimately they share very similar concerns.

[6] Ibid.

Constitutions have the potential to be transformative—through the process of their formation and through their design. Yet the danger for women and other political minorities is that if insufficient attention is paid to 'difference' then constitution making can also freeze and legitimate existing power structures. Susan H Williams, W Foskett Professor of Law at Maurer Law School, Indiana University, has directed her edited collection, based on contributions given at a 2007 conference of the same name, to addressing the gender gap in mainstream literature on comparative constitutionalisation. Professor Williams felt this 'gap' acutely in 2003 when she became an advisor on constitutional drafting to the Women's League of Burma within the Burmese democracy movement. The volume sets out to address how one can design for gender equality in constitutional drafting. It consists of 13 chapters which move the discussion away from a narrow focus on the incorporation of equality clauses (Irving—'More than Rights'). It is usefully themed, dividing the chapters into five different sections reflecting aspects of constitutionalism: 'structure' (Drude Dahlerup & Lenita Fredenvall and Susan Williams); 'rights' (Helen Irving, Mary Anne Case, Joanna Erdman); 'culture/religion and gender equality' (Aili Mari Tripp, Pascale Fournier, Felicia Coleman and Beverley Baines), 'constitutions and international law' (Veronica Undurraga & Rebecca Cook and Christina Ochoa); and 'women in the process of constitution making' (Thin Thin Aung & Susan Williams and Adrien Wing & Hisham Kassim). Different perspectives on gender and constitutionalism and different strategies for constitutionalising gender are discussed and in general it provides a truly comparative analysis going beyond 'issues of gender equality within particular constitutional regimes,' (2) though many of the chapters use illustrations from a specific country or region (the African continent, and specifically Liberia, Burma, Palestine, Colombia, Guatemala, Canada, US, Germany, UK and France). The book rejects gender essentialism, asserts the complexity of gender analysis and opens up debate. For instance the chapters by Beverley Baines and Mary Ann Case, while focussing on completely different illustrations, respectively sex equality and religion & rights to abortion, both challenge received wisdom on the entrenchment of women's rights. Chapters by Undurraga and Cook and by Ochoa reflect on both the opportunities for, and the limits of, international law in constitutionalising women's rights. Dahlerup and Freidenvall in one chapter and Williams in another provide both qualitative and quantative assessments of a wide variety of quotas systems and turn attention back to a deeper analysis of the democratic system itself, in a refutation of the 'add women and stir' approach.

Williams gives the collection a clear and thoughtful introduction; a conclusion which pulled together the different issues and concerns raised in the introduction and the chapters would have been equally welcome. Vicki Jackson's excellent point, which was originally given as the keynote address at the start of the March 2007 conference, is part of the conclusion, but it would have been better employed as a first chapter, providing an overview and drawing further attention to the nuances of this field. Despite that, the quality of all the contributions, the introduction, detailed index and excellent overviews of the field make this a very useful and stimulating book and much more than a collection of disparate essays on gender and constitutionalisation.

Ruth Rubio-Marin is the chair in Comparative Public Law at the European University Institute in Florence, and also a Professor in Constitutional Law at the University of Seville. *The Gender of Reparations* was produced as a project through the International Center for Transitional Justice (ICTJ). The author notes that never before has this area 'received specific in-depth scholarly attention' (vii). The aim of the project is to bring together a basis for 'gender sensitive analysis of reparations programs' (3) with moves to engender transitional justice thus maximising 'the transformative potential of reparations programs' (3). Although social constructions of both men and women are addressed through the methodological framework the ultimate purpose of the project is to 'increase the effectiveness of redress for female victims and their families' (3). The first two chapters by Walker and Ruth Rubio-Marin provide a 'normative framework' for respectively identifying the gendered nature of harms to women and for how reparations might recognise those harms. Five further chapters focus on specific aspects and contexts of reparations. Colleen Duggan and Ruth Jacobson address sexual and reproductive violence against women. They note that the last decade has 'seen unprecedented progress in the construction of an international legal framework for criminalization and prosecution' (121) but argue that 'justice' in this context has to be seen more holistically. Dyan Maurana and Khristopher Carlson address the reparations in relation to crimes and grave rights violations against children and analyse 'how gender matters' in relation to the understanding of these harms and possible redress (163). In the chapter following this, titled 'Repairing Family Members', Ruth Rubio-Marin, Clara Sandoval and Catalina Diaz explore whether reparations programmes recognise that violations can harm dependents and relations of those directly harmed and thus produce a 'domino effect' (216, citing Ruth Rubio-Marin). A chapter on tort theory, microfinance and gender equality from Anita Bernstein assesses forms of pecuniary transfers to victims and considers the most appropriate forms to repair the 'effects of a crisis which has ravaged the whole nation' (291). Bernstein advocates micro-finance rather than micro-credit arrangements and transfers which are made directly to women. She also argues for transfers which make women shareholders of financial institutions. These transfers are not easily lost or alienated and recipients are invested with a lasting agency in the country's future. Brandon Hamber and Ingrid Palmary take a wide remit in relation to 'symbolic reparations' in a chapter which uses the examples of truth commissions, apologies and monuments and examines how these 'can be used to challenge dominant femininities and masculinities that are produced in times of armed conflict and in its aftermath'. They suggest ways that symbolic reparations can be made to 'make a more substantial contribution to promoting gender justice by incorporating... rich notions of masculinity and femininity' (327) and provide a series of policy recommendations.

At the start of the volume Rubio-Marin notes the 'underlying goals of reparations program... [as] recognition, civic trust, and social solidarity for men and women' (3). In the final chapter Rubio-Marin reflects further on the dual function of reparations: as repair for past wrongs and with the goal of rebuilding society. While reparations must actually reflect the real experiences of women and not just any 'new conception of a more emancipated woman in a more egalitarian society', approaches which focus too heavily on restoring victims to their position before atrocities are inadequate (398). Such approaches may not recognise the links between ordinary and extraordinary forms of gender violence or the peculiar relationship between the individual and collective effects of gender violence: 'gender violence results in harms to all women and not just victims of certain atrocities' (398). Moreover they miss the link between reparations and the attempt to achieve 'ever more inclusive democratic orders' (399). Elsewhere Rubio-Marin has written extensively about gender and constitutionalism and in these concluding reflections she draws on deliberative democracy theory to discuss 'the struggles for reparations... as an on-going struggle for recognition... contestation of hegemonic discourses and patterns of exclusion' (399). Rubio-Marin argues that women and other minorities can use the 'banner of reparations to contest the terms of their political association'(400). The question is how participation, processes, and rights can be used within a reparations dialogue to shape the whole society. This relates discussions and debate about reparations closely to concern about the constitutional order and in this way the Rubio-Marin and Williams volumes are usefully connected.

CHARLOTTE SKEET
UNIVERSITY OF SUSSEX

The Impact of Human Rights Law on General International Law. By MENNO T KAMMINGA AND MARTIN SCHEININ. Oxford, Oxford University Press, 2009. xxvii + 258pp. £70.00.

This book represents the conclusion of a four year study by the Committee on International Human Rights Law and Practice of the International Law Association (ILA), initiated at the ILA's Conference in Berlin in 2004. The book is edited by Menno Kamminga and Martin Scheinin, the Rapporteur and Chair respectively of the Committee. As the Committee is composed of human rights experts from some 30 countries nominated by their national ILA branches and representative of a broad range of legal scholarship in the relevant fields, it was believed that the Committee was the appropriate forum to undertake an examination of the impact of international human rights law on general international law. As the Preface makes clear, this subject matter had already been analysed by Bruno Simma in his 'International Human Rights and General International Law: A Comparative Analysis' (*Collected Courses of the Academy of European Law*, volume IV-2 Kluwer, Dordrecht 1993, 153–256) and Theodor Meron in *The Humanization of International Law* (Martinus Nijhoff, Leiden/Boston, 2006). However, it was felt that a more systematic and comprehensive treatment was justified. The book consists of a slightly edited version of the Final Report of the Committee as adopted by the 2008 ILA Conference at Rio de Janeiro together with ten chapters contributed by selected Committee members, who developed their original papers that had informed the Final Report. The contributions of the various Committee members developed through interaction with other Committee members at workshops held at the Maastricht Centre for Human Rights (2006) and the University of Siena (2007). An interim report was presented at the ILA's Toronto Conference in 2006.

The book offers an evaluation of the continuing development of the impact of human rights law on general international law and seeks to provide the first comprehensive analysis of such impact and trace the extent to which concepts from international human rights law are being applied in general international law by institutions such as the International Law Commission (ILC) and International Court of Justice (ICJ). This review highlights some of these most interesting contributions.

Chapter 3, by Jonas Christoffersen, deals with 'Impact on General Principles of Treaty Interpretation'. The author addresses the issue from the standpoint solely of the European Court of Human Rights at Strasbourg. He argues that it was not possible within the scope of the chapter to include the practice of other human rights instances, but claims that 'the answers provided would be similar'. This is a bold and sweeping claim for which he provides no evidence. The author examines first the 'General Doctrines of Treaty Interpretation', and after extensive review of the Strasbourg Court's approach, concludes that the Court's approach to interpretation is based on the traditional principles of interpretation established in general international law. The author then considers whether the Strasbourg Court's view that the European Convention on Human Rights (ECHR) must be interpreted in the light of its special character as a treaty for the collective enforcement of human rights is justified (the 'Special Doctrines of Human Rights Interpretation' as it is termed by the author). The author concludes that the 'special nature' claim cannot be based on the principle of effectiveness (*effet utile*); nor can it be based on the claimed 'law making' nature of the ECHR, the 'objective nature of human rights obligations' (and/or the attached enforcement systems), or the doctrine of 'dynamic interpretation'. However, the author concedes that the system of 'Subsidiary Review under the ECHR' (the principle of Subsidiarity or the Margin of Appreciation doctrine) in the Strasbourg Court's examination of the observance by Contracting States of their obligations 'is yet to be embraced by other branches of international law'. The author asserts that 'there is little, if any reason to think that the Court's method of review deviates substantially from that of other comparable international tribunals'. Once again, this is a tremendously wide statement to make without any evidence in support: certainly, the Human Rights Committee does not operate a 'margin of appreciation' doctrine. Thus, the author concludes that the principles governing the interpretation and application of human rights treaties are not special, and while conceding that the degree of dynamic interpretation may not be identical in different areas of international law', concludes that the general principles of treaty interpretation have a profound impact on human rights law. Whether this paper answers the question posed in the book's title is a moot point: very little of the argument in this chapter is addressed to the issue of the impact of human rights law on the techniques of interpretation in general international law.

Chapter 4 deals with the 'Impact on the Law of Treaty Reservations' authored by Dr Ineke Boerefijn. This chapter examines in depth the approach of the UN human rights treaty monitoring bodies (particularly the Human Rights Committee (HRC)) in relation to the practice of reservations and compares it with that of the ILC; at one point, reference is made also to the judgment of the ICJ in the case of *Armed Activities on the Territory of the Congo (Democratic Republic of the Congo v. Rwanda)* of 3 February 2006. Generally, the author discovers a considerable degree of congruence between the ILC and the practice of the treaty bodies, but difference too, particularly in their respective approaches to the consequences of invalid reservations. For example, the 'object and purpose' of the International Covenant on Civil and Political Rights (ICCPR) as articulated by the HRC in General Comment No. 24 is compared with the articulation by the ILC of the 'object and purpose' of general human rights treaties (such as the ICCPR) in ILC draft guideline 3.1.12; the author observes that both bodies accept that rights which are not qualified as non-derogable may be of such importance that they may not be subject to derogations; on the other hand, the ILC draft guideline refers to 'the gravity of the impact the reservation has' whereas the HRC's general comment does not distinguish between reservations which have a grave impact on a right and those that have a minor impact. Another example of a variance in views between the two sets of bodies is exemplified by their difference of approach to reservations affecting *jus cogens* norms: whereas the ILC states that 'a reservation cannot exclude or modify the legal effect of a treaty in a manner contrary to a peremptory norm of general international law' (draft guideline 3.1.9), the HRC maintains that such reservations are, as such, incompatible with the 'object and purpose' of the ICCPR; both bodies achieve the same result of invalidity, but by different routes. The author comments that 'it is difficult to establish what impact practice in international human rights organs has had on the formulation of this particular draft guideline, since hardly any reservations to *jus cogens* norms seem to exist'. Again, while the HRC has maintained that its monitoring role constitutes an essential element of the ICCPR, which is directed to securing the enjoyment of the protected rights and that accordingly, 'reservations that purport to evade that essential element in the design of the Covenant' are incompatible with the 'object and purpose' of the ICCPR (General Comment No. 24), the ILC in draft guideline 3.1.13 maintains that initially a reservation affecting the monitoring of the implementation of the treaty is not in itself incompatible with the 'object and purpose' of the treaty subject to several exceptions. On the other hand, the HRC has asserted its competence to determine whether a specific reservation is compatible with the 'object and purpose' of the ICCPR (General Comment No. 2) and the competence of the UN human rights treaty bodies to examine reservations was accepted by the ILC Special Rapporteur Alain Pellet (ILC Second Report on Reservations to Treaties by Alain Pellet, Special Rapporteur). In its 'Preliminary Conclusions on Reservations to Normative Multilateral Treaties, including Human Rights Treaties' the ILC accepted the competence of treaty monitoring bodies to pronounce on the admissibility of reservations. In addition, as Dr Boerefijn points out, the impact of the practice of human rights treaty bodies is clearly visible in a proposed sub-guideline by Professor Pellet in his Tenth Report: 'Where a treaty establishes a body to monitor application of the treaty, that body shall be competent, for the purpose of discharging the functions entrusted to it, to assess the validity of reservations formulated by a State'. The most serious disagreement between the HRC and the ILC concerns the consequences of an invalid reservation, with the HRC asserting that 'such a reservation will generally be severable, in the sense that the Covenant will be operative for the reserving party without benefit of the reservation' (General Comment No. 24). From the early part of his mandate, Special Rapporteur Pellet has maintained that the reserving State must decide whether an invalid reservation constitutes an essential element of its consent to be bound: it can decide to withdraw a reservation or modify it, or decide not to remain a party to the treaty—'no organ can take the place of the reserving State in determining the latter's intentions regarding the scope of the treaty obligations it is prepared to assume' (Pellet's Second Report). States such as the USA, UK and France had lodged critical observations on the HRC's position as reflected in General Comment No. 24. As far as the ILC is concerned, the position still awaits determination with members divided on the issue of whether the doctrine of 'severability' is the appropriate approach or whether it conflicts with the free will of the reserving State. This chapter on reservations is detailed and interesting. It draws many comparisons between the ILC and the HRC and illustrates the impact of human rights law on general international law. The thrust of the chapter, however, is on comparison rather than on impact. Impact is given only brief attention and little analysis.

Chapter 5, an admirably short, very clearly written and interesting paper, authored by one of the co-editors himself, Menno Kamminga, is an analysis of the 'Impact on State Succession in Respect of Treaties' and focuses on the contribution of the Strasbourg Court and the HRC, but also contains a brief comparison with the approach of the ICJ. The author demonstrates clearly that both the Strasbourg Court (in numerous individual cases against the Czech Republic and Slovakia) and the UN human rights treaty bodies, most especially the HRC (though the approach to be taken by the other treaty monitoring bodies will be virtually consistent: see the 1994 Joint Statement by the Chairpersons of UN Treaty Bodies), have decided that the protection afforded by such human rights treaties devolves with territory and is not affected by State succession (General Comment No. 26). Accordingly, successor States remain bound by human rights treaties from the date of independence and this is not dependent on any confirmation made by them. Kamminga surmises correctly that this regime represents another major exception to the general rule of non-continuity of treaty obligations to add to the pre-existing category of treaties establishing boundaries and other territorial regimes. Kamminga demonstrates that practice under the ECHR has been the most consistent and principled, though it is true that the precedents established relate only to the split of the Czech and Slovak Federal Republic into separate States on 1

January 1993. By contrast, Kamminga points out that the HRC has accepted that while successor States may accede rather than succeed to their treaties and that this may entail long delay on occasion, it insists that accession takes effect retrospectively to the date when the successor State became independent; the treaty bodies also welcome notifications of confirmation by successor States that they consider themselves bound by human rights treaties accepted by their predecessors. By the same token, successor States have not been held liable for breaches by their predecessors. On the other hand, the first reports submitted by such States are termed 'initial' reports. Thus, the HRC, and by emulation the other treaty bodies, have adopted a 'pragmatic approach'. Of course, it must be remembered that practice has centred on the collapse of the Union of Socialist Soviet Republics, Socialist Federal Republic of Yugoslavia and former Czechoslovakia in the 1990s. However, Kamminga remarks that it would be unduly restrictive to describe this as a regional European custom only, in view of its widespread acceptance by States and lack of opposition from successor States. Finally, it should be remembered that this doctrine of 'automatic succession' has not been accepted or rejected specifically by the ICJ in the *Bosnian Genocide* case, in which the Court declined to pass judgment on the matter. This chapter demonstrates that while human rights law has influenced general international law in this regard, there is no strong evidence that the doctrine of 'automatic succession' has passed into customary international law.

Chapter 9, by Christina Cerna, traces the fascinating history of the 'Impact on the Right to Consular Notification'. The whole range of cases at the ICJ (*Breard*, *LaGrand* (Provisional Measures and Merits) and *Avena* (Provisional Measures and Merits)) is examined in detail, as is the seminal *Advisory Opinion No. 6* of the Inter-American Court of Human Rights (IACtHR) and a number of domestic US cases. The author demonstrates how the landmark opinion of the IACtHR in the above mentioned case '*aggressively* created a "human right" in finding that whenever a foreign national is detained, he has the fundamental human right, recognized in the Vienna Convention, to be informed by the authorities that he may contact the consular agents of his own country, and that failure to do so, *even without a showing of prejudice* (since prejudice is presumed) constitutes a violation of the human right to due process sufficient to incur international responsibility and the duty to make reparation.'

Cerna also points out, however, that the ICJ in the *LaGrand* case was prepared to characterise such rights only as 'individual' rights (the closest approximation to finding that a human right of the LaGrand brothers had been violated was the Court's use of the expression 'but also to the rights of the detained individual' (para 89)) and in the *Avena* case laconically declared: 'Whether or not the Vienna Convention rights are human rights is not a matter that this Court need decide. The Court would, however, observe that neither the text nor the object and purpose of the Convention, nor any indication in the *travaux préparatoires*, support the conclusion that Mexico draws from its contention in that regard.' (para. 124)

Thus, in this respect the ICJ appears unwilling to follow the lead of the IACtHR. With respect to the IACtHR's view on the un-obligatory nature of the 'showing of prejudice', Cerna states that 'the ICJ dismissed the requirement of a finding of actual prejudice to the purported victim in the failure to provide consular notification and held that the failure to provide notification was sufficient to constitute a violation of the Convention'. However, Cerna remarks that in the later *Avena* case 'the ICJ stepped back from the position of assuming prejudice in the failure of notification to a requirement of showing actual notification'. So again, while influential, the IACtHR's view was not determinative of that of the ICJ. It should be observed that in the *LaGrand* (Merits) judgment, the ICJ declared that its provisional measures orders were binding. The author speculates whether this development was influenced by the IACtHR's conventional authority to issue legally binding provisional measures (article 63(2) of the American Convention). Subsequently, both the HRC (*Piandiong and others* v *The Philippines*) and the European Court of Human Rights (ECtHR) (*Mamatkulov and Askarov v Turkey*) have declared interim measures orders to be binding. All these consular access cases must be viewed in the context of a concerted attack by Latin American countries and some European countries on the imposition of the death penalty in the U.S.A. This chapter is remarkable in showing the extent to which human rights discourse has developed or 'humanised' general international law on consular relations.

Finally, reference will be made to chapter 11 on the 'Impact on State Responsibility' written by the leading scholar Robert McCorquodale. This chapter explores the extent to which general international law principles of state responsibility have been influenced by international human rights law, while focussing on two fundamental aspects of state responsibility: attribution to a State and the international obligations of a State. The author points out that the ILC itself considered that international human rights law was relevant to the development of the general provisions about state responsibility when it adopted its Articles on State Responsibility; indeed, as McCorquodale suggests, the ILC Commentary is replete with human rights examples and cases. McCorquodale demonstrates the connection between international human rights law and the general principles of state responsibility by the fact that international human rights treaty monitoring bodies often have occasion to apply the general law of state responsibility to cases litigated before them, either expressly, or more often implicitly. As far as the issue of attribution to a State is concerned, after a searching examination of the relevant case-law, McCorquodale reasons that: 'overall international human rights law has had minimal impact on the general international law of state responsibility in regard to attribution to the state. While its interpretations and practices have largely supported the development of the general international law of attribution, in the area of attribution through control by the state of the acts of non-State actors extraterritorially, its approach has been rejected by the ICJ as not applicable to the general rules on state responsibility.'

As far the issue of positive obligations in international human rights law is concerned, McCorquodale concludes that: 'international human rights law has interpreted the nature of a state's obligations and extended the scope and depth of those obligations. As a consequence, there could be some impact by international human rights law on the general international law of state responsibility.'

With respect to the converse situation of positive obligations in State responsibility, after a detailed examination, the author concludes that: 'it has become accepted within the general law of state responsibility that states have positive obligations. This position arises primarily from the practices and principles developed within international human rights law. In this way, international human rights law has had a significant, and potentially long-lasting, impact on the general law of state responsibility.'

In the section 'State Responsibility and the Individual', McCorquodale explains how the de-coupling of 'nationality' and human rights protection, marks a significant development in the understanding of the obligations to individuals for which state responsibility extends within international human rights law. As one would expect from a scholar of such distinction, the author provides a keen analysis with convincing argument and answers the question posed in the title to the book.

On the whole, this book represents a valuable and interesting collection of contributions, some of which have been highlighted in this review. All the essays are engaging, thoroughly researched and make a considerable contribution to the understanding of the interplay between international human rights law and general international law. However, in the opinion of the reviewer, only some of the essays address directly and in a detailed fashion the question posed by the title of the book. Kamminga's 'Final Report' does attempt to draw conclusions from the contributions, which justifies this compilation in a book. All international and international human rights lawyers will find something of interest.

SANDY GHANDI
UNIVERSITY OF READING

Terrorism, War and International Law: The Legality of the Use of Force against Afghanistan in 2001. By MYRA WILLIAMSON. Aldershot, Ashgate, 2009. xi + 227 pp. £57.00.

The core aim of this book is to 'demonstrate why the use of military force against Afghanistan, beginning on 7 October 2001, was unlawful' (233). It therefore takes a fresh look at a use of force that was, at the time, accepted relatively uncritically as being a lawful action of self-defence. That is not to say, of course, that all scholars saw the intervention as lawful in 2001,[7] but the contrary voices that did exist were, to a large extent, soon lost in the noise of the louder and more widespread legal objections to the use of force against Iraq in 2003. This reappraisal of the lawfulness of the Afghanistan intervention makes good use of eight years of hindsight.

Terrorism, War and International Law is a book steeped in history; it draws on historical accounts of terrorism and armed conflict, and state and scholarly reactions to these phenomena. It also, in its early sections, makes use of conflict data analysis to provide a qualitative statistical understanding of the changing nature of conflict. Similarly, when the book does turn to more conventional legal analysis (chapters four and five), it is strongly grounded in actual incidents of state practice to illustrate and establish positions taken regarding customary international law: a coalface approach to the subject that is regrettably absent from many works of international law scholarship. In other words, the book takes a 'wide angle lens' approach to its core question. For this reviewer, this is very much to the author's credit.

However, one could argue a little too much of the book is dedicated to the contextual background underpinning the central analysis: of the five substantive chapters here, only one (the final chapter) actually examines the 2001 conflict at all. This potentially makes the book slightly top heavy, with lots of background and comparatively little application. The trade off here, though, is a willingness to forgo a more streamlined approach to the question posed, in favour of as comprehensive an understanding of the wider context as possible. This approach ultimately gives the conclusions reached a greater weight than they may otherwise have had.

The first substantive section, Chapter Two, considers the changing nature of conflict, primarily through conflict data analysis. The data here is wisely drawn from a number of sources, primarily from various independent projects focused on 'patterns of conflict

[7] For an excellent example see J Quigley, 'The Afghanistan War and Self-Defence' (2002–2003) 37 *Valparaiso University Law Review* 541.

occurrence' (12). Based on this data it is convincingly argued that 9/11 did not represent a fundamental change in the nature of conflict or terrorist activity.

Chapter Three examines the notion of terrorism and its historical development. It particularly focuses on the problems associated with defining the concept, both for lawyers and political scientists. The main contribution to the book's central argument here is that such definitional problems have contributed to states traditionally viewing terrorist acts as criminal actions—to be dealt with through judicial mechanisms (international and domestic)—and not as acts of war. Indeed, it is argued that this is a desirable approach to responding to terrorist activity, as opposed to the use of military force (65–68). This feeds into later claims that the use of force against Afghanistan was a relatively unusual response to a terrorist attack. This chapter is worthwhile in and of itself and contributes well to the overall context of the 2001 intervention. Having said this, it is perhaps by human rights discourse questionable whether the arguable desirability or commonality of a criminal-law-based response to terrorism has a bearing on the *lawfulness* of an alternative approach involving the use of force.

Chapters Four and Five focus on the specifics of the law on the use of force. They are split chronologically, with Chapter Four examining the development of law on the use of force from 1919–1944, and Chapter Five covering the period from 1945–2008. As such, they essentially constitute one substantive chapter—in terms of content and contribution to the work—with the split presumably being one of convenience. This section of the book is probably its most successful aspect. Again, the topic is approached in a commendably comprehensive manner; these chapters essentially set out and critique the key elements of law on the use of force from 1945 to the present. That this is done in just a hundred pages without seeming superficial is noteworthy.

It must be admitted that nothing in these chapters is especially groundbreaking and it will offer no surprises for anyone who is relatively familiar with the international law on the use of force today. Equally, these chapters present the law in this area in a clear and concise manner; the analysis here is relatively uncontroversial and is suitable for both international lawyers and those unfamiliar with the discipline. This reviewer intends to prescribe these chapters as 'essential reading' for his final year LLB international law students studying the law on the use of force.

The crucial final chapter provides the book's central contention, that the 2001 Afghanistan intervention was unlawful. A number of arguments are set out to support this conclusion, some of which are more convincing than others. For example, the position that the intervention failed to meet the requirement of 'proportionality' is a difficult one to refute. Simply put: 'Regime change was a step too far' (213). Indeed, the consideration of proportionality—and how one calculates it in the context of self-defence—is particularly nuanced here.

A compelling argument is also made that it was not 'necessary' for there to be a military response in 2001. This is both because the attacks of 9/11 were over before any response took place and because non-forcible options were available to respond to any ongoing threat (206–210). As such, it is argued that the only way self-defence could have been invoked in 2001 was in its highly controversial 'pre-emptive' manifestation. Indeed, it would have had to have been pre-emptive self-defence of the 'non-imminent' variety, in that there was no sign of another imminent attack against the United States following 9/11 (218–221). This 'Bush doctrine' of non-imminent pre-emptive self-defence is then rejected: 'If all states were permitted to... employ force in "self-defence" whenever they identify a source of future attacks, the list of potential targets could be endless... the limitations on the use of force in self-defence would be undermined to such an extent that they would be rendered virtually meaningless' (221). Even in the post-Bush world, such contributions to the ongoing debate surrounding non-imminent pre-emptive self-defence remain important, given President Obama's apparent willingness to retain the doctrine.[8]

Not all of the analysis in the crucial final chapter is as compelling, however. For example, the much relied on argument that there was no 'armed attack' against the United States because 9/11 was perpetrated by non-state actors is far from as straightforward as is indicated. It is true, as the author points out (152–153), that the ICJ, both in 1986 (*Nicaragua* case) and in 2004 (*Israeli Wall* advisory opinion), has appeared to require a level of state involvement for an 'armed attack' to occur. However, there could have been more consideration of the counterargument that state practice is now shifting towards allowing self-defence actions in response to attacks perpetrated by non-state actors,[9] as well as of the objections raised by various ICJ judges to the Court's majority position on this issue (briefly noted in footnote 326, on page 153). The author also falls into the trap of assuming that the level of state involvement required by the ICJ for an armed attack necessarily equates to the state responsibility 'effective control' test (154–157 and 202–205). In fact these tests are, conceptually, different things: one relates to whether a state is responsible for a breach of international law and the other to whether an armed attack has occurred. There is nothing to be found in the jurisprudence of the ICJ, or elsewhere, to indicate that they are necessarily synonymous.[10]

When the arguments presented are taken cumulatively, the final chapter makes a convincing case that the 2001 intervention was unlawful. The outstanding issue is that a large number of states accepted the action as lawful. It is rightly pointed out that a failure to condemn the intervention may have its basis in the overwhelming culture of sympathy towards the United States following 9/11 (177 and 183). Moreover, it is also convincingly argued that a failure to condemn is not the same as accepting an action as being lawful (189–202). However, states did not merely fail to condemn the United States: many condoned the action and a significant number explicitly stated that it was lawful.[11] Support for the lawfulness of the use of force by states must surely be legally relevant, given how customary international law is made and altered. Whether the reactions of states here were *relevant enough* to counteract the application of the law as it stood prior to the intervention is another matter. This book convincingly demonstrates that such an application leads to a determination of unlawfulness. The question, then, is whether the law on the use of force could have been 'instantly' adapted by way of the acceptance of the intervention. This goes to the heart of customary international law theory and is perhaps beyond

[8] See C J Westra, 'Will the Bush Doctrine Survive Its Progenitor – An Assessment of *Jud Ad Bellum* Norms for the Post-Westphalian Age' (2009) 32 *Boston College International and Comparative Law Review* 399, particularly 399–401; and 'American Society of International Law Interview with Barack Obama' (2008), <http://www.asil.org/obama.cfm>, section on the 'Laws of War and the Use of Force', Q3.

[9] M Byers, 'Terrorism, the Use of Force and International Law After 11 September' (2002) 51 *International and Comparative Law Quarterly* 401, 407–409.

[10] This reviewer has written on this point in more detail elsewhere, see J A Green, *The International Court of Justice and Self-Defence in International Law* (Hart Publishing, Oxford, 2009) 44–51 and 156–159.

[11] For example, the European Union, Brazil and Chile all explicitly took the view that the intervention was lawful in the UN General Assembly, UN Doc. A/56.PV44, 37, 3–4, and 27 respectively. See Congressional Report Service, 'Operation Enduring Freedom: Foreign Pledges of Military & Intelligence Support' (2001) <http://fpc.state.gov/documents/organization/6207.pdf>; and House of Commons Research Paper, 'Operation *Enduring Freedom* and the Conflict in Afghanistan: An Update' (2001), 31, for lists of states that condoned the intervention and/or offered support. However, state support was admittedly not universal, see E P J Myjer and N D White, 'The Twin Towers Attack: An Unlimited Right to Self-Defence?' (2002) 7 *Journal of Conflict and Security Law* 5, 6–11.

the scope of the book under review. Nonetheless, the explicit acceptance of the action as being lawful, by states, probably needed to be considered in more detail.

Ultimately *Terrorism, War and International Law* offers a detailed analysis of the use of force against Afghanistan in 2001. It is a work of real scholarship that is most notable for two things: the clear, comprehensive and accurate summary of the development of the law on the use of force from 1945–2008 and the willingness of its author to engage in wider contextual analysis (historical development, conflict data and numerous instances of state practice) to underpin the legal arguments made. This book is undoubtedly a very important addition to the literature.

JAMES A GREEN
UNIVERSITY OF READING

The International Law of Belligerent Occupation. By YORAM DINSTEIN. Cambridge, Cambridge University Press, 2009. xxxii and 303 pp. £23.99.

As its title suggests this book deals with all of the major issues which one would expect to see covered under the topic of belligerent occupation. Given its length it is able to explore issues in much more depth than can be found in many other modern works which include the topic alongside others dealing with the whole range of the *ius in bello*. Professor Dinstein brings to the task his usual high standards of scholarship.

A substantial part of the book involves discussion of matters arising from the territories occupied by Israel in 1967. What Dinstein is able to show particularly effectively are the problems involved in applying the Hague Regulations 1907 and Geneva Convention IV, 1949 to an occupation which has been prolonged in time. These include transfers of individuals from the occupied territories, internment, the destruction of property (particularly of homes), settlements, the security barrier and the judicial system in occupied territory. With his trenchant criticism of the Advisory Opinion of the International Court of Justice in *Legal Consequences of the Construction of a Wall in the Occupied Palestinian Territory* (2004), in which he relies heavily on dissenting opinions in that case, it is, perhaps, no surprise to learn that 'Israel has largely ignored the Advisory Opinion on the *Wall*' (255).

There is very limited discussion in detail of issues arising from other modern instances of belligerent occupation such as in the Falkland Islands (1982), Kuwait (1990–91) and in Iraq (2003–04). It is not easy to see why this should be so given the title of the book. In their own way each of these short periods of belligerent occupation gave rise to the need to interpret provisions, particularly, of Geneva Convention IV 1949 in modern day settings. It may also be that short, rather than lengthy, periods of belligerent occupation will form the pattern of future occupation of territory.

Dinstein uses a large number of judgements of the Supreme Court of Israel to give substance to particular issues which have arisen in the territories occupied by Israel since 1967. Reliance on national decisions to show or to explain principles of international law can, however, be problematic. The relationship between national law and international law in Israel is similar to that in the United Kingdom. In particular, the Geneva Conventions 1949 have not been implemented into the national law of Israel and therefore do not form part of it unless particular norms are seen as customary international law (28). Israel does, however, recognise that the Hague Regulations 1907 reflect customary international law and, as such, are part of Israeli law.

The effect is that judges can ignore any part of the Geneva Convention IV, unless it is customary international law, if it conflicts with Israeli national law. This should not be seen as surprising since it is a consequence of the particular relationship between international and national law adopted by a number of States. Judges will, no doubt, try to interpret national law in a manner which is consistent with the State's international obligations or, indeed, rely on international law where there is a lacuna in national law. But where the norms clash the international law rule must remain silent. Dinstein sums up the position well when he writes that: 'given the construct that the Geneva Convention could not be applied directly by the Court...leading Judgments revolved exclusively around clauses of the Hague Regulations (as a faithful picture of customary international law)...the legal tactics of [an] indirect approach—challenging the legality of acts of the military government on the somewhat opaque rationale of property rights, in keeping with the Hague Regulations—actually proved to be quite productive in certain sets of circumstances.' (29)

This relatively simple solution to a constitutional difficulty can be seen in three distinct, but important, areas arising from the occupation since 1967, namely the question of Israeli settlements, that of deportation of individuals from occupied territory and the demolition or sealing off of houses.

In relation to settlements permitted by Israel as the occupying power Dinstein shows how the Supreme Court of Israel decided that the sixth paragraph of Art 49 of Geneva Convention IV ('the Occupying Power shall not...transfer parts of its own population into the territory it occupies') did not apply since it was not a part of customary international law. The Court was, however, prepared to consider the cases on the basis of the Hague Regulations 1907, Articles 46 and 52. The wording in the relevant Articles of the Hague Regulations is not, of course, the same as that which appears in Article 49 (sixth paragraph).

Deportations from occupied territory are prohibited by Article 49 (first paragraph) of Geneva Convention IV. Dinstein shows how the Supreme Court relied on national law—the Defence (Emergency) Regulations—which appeared to permit individual deportations and it argued that this was not, in any event, inconsistent with Article 49. To reach this conclusion the Court took the view that that Article prohibits only 'Nazi-style mass deportations, in contradistinction to ordinary individual deportations' (163).

The demolition or sealing off of houses by an occupying power, particularly those properties in which individuals lived prior to their acts as suicide bombers, appears to raise the issue of whether this could amount to 'collective penalties' prohibited by Article 33 of Geneva Convention IV. Once again, the Court was faced with the same national law which permitted demolition of houses and, although it may have taken into account the issue of proportionality, this was not the same as the Court having to address directly the issue of whether the actions of the Israeli authorities amounted to a collective penalty.

These examples should be sufficient to show the sometimes very limited value which national decisions can add to the debate at the international level. This is particularly so where the relationship between international law and national law is dualist and international law has not been incorporated into domestic law, and where the occupation of territory is prolonged. Thus, the dualist model can place national courts in a difficult position if faced with legislation which appears to be at odds with treaties to which the State is a party. It can lead to judges interpreting a relevant treaty provision so as to make it sit comfortably with national law but in doing so produce an interpretation which will not be accepted by international lawyers or international courts. It can also lead to national courts declining to consider a norm of treaty law on the basis that it would raise a non-justiciable issue. In addition, the rule of law within occupied territories can be greatly compromised by the dualist approach. The International Court of Justice, for example, can express its legal opinion on whether the settlements are in breach of Article 49 of

Geneva Convention IV (as a majority did in the *Wall* Case) but this will not avail those, who in occupied territory, make applications before a national court, which is not bound as a matter of national law to apply Article 49.

Dinstein puts these national decisions before the reader but does not shy away from scholarly criticism where he feels this is necessary. With the caveats expressed above these decisions can, however, show how the Israeli courts have dealt with the myriad of issues arising from prolonged occupation.

The relevance and importance of the applicability of human rights law during belligerent occupation is discussed well although concentration on the prolonged occupation by Israel has had the effect that issues which may arise during the course of the (normally) short term occupation of territory have not been given the same detailed treatment. A case in point is the occupation of Iraq in 2003–04 and whether the European Convention on Human Rights 1950 applied to the activities of British armed forces. There are a number of significant decisions of the European Court of Human Rights subsequent to the *Bankovic* Case (discussed at 71) on the reach of the Convention outside the territory of a State which raise real practical issues, particularly where civilians are killed, detained or are ill-treated by the armed forces of the occupying State. Where, for instance, would the *lex specialis* be seen as international humanitarian law and not (in this case) the European Convention on Human Rights? Would Article 66 (assuming it applied) of Geneva Convention IV (the 'occupying power may hand over the accused to its properly constituted, non-political, military courts') prevail over Article 6 of the European Convention or Article 78 of Geneva Convention IV over Article 5 of the European Convention?

Dinstein is, of course, quite correct in drawing a distinction between international humanitarian law and human rights law on the ground that derogations can be made from some of the rights given by a human rights treaty. The fact that a State may make a derogation is not the same as a derogation having been made. By way of example, the United Kingdom made no derogation as an occupying power in Iraq (including from the right to life for deaths resulting from lawful acts of war). Subject to a decision as to whether an individual comes within the jurisdiction of the United Kingdom under Article 1 of the European Convention, that Convention applies to give rights to the inhabitants of occupied territory, which, because the relevant parts of the European Convention had been implemented into English law by the Human Rights Act 1998, gives them also a right to pursue an action against the Government of the United Kingdom in the courts of England and Wales.

It is becoming clear, at least from experience in Iraq and from those territories occupied by Israel, that during the course of belligerent occupation the inhabitants need to be able to secure, where necessary, access to a judicial process in order to pursue their claims against the occupying power. No one would seriously argue that their legal rights should be placed in suspension during a period of occupation of their territory. The dualist model (discussed above) ill-serves such individuals where the 'rights' which they are told they possess (through international humanitarian law or through human rights law) cannot be applied by a judicial body for lack of their incorporation into domestic law. The decisions of the superior courts in Israel cannot take into account Geneva Convention IV (as discussed above). Neither can the courts in England (except for those areas specifically implemented by the Geneva Conventions Act 1957, as amended) but those courts can adjudicate claims brought under the Human Rights Act 1998. A number of such cases have been brought by Iraqi nationals who claim their rights have been infringed by the British armed forces in Iraq.

It would have been good to read Dinstein's view on the applicability of the ICRC's Interpretive Guidance on the Notion of Direct Participation in Hostilities under

International Humanitarian Law (2009) to occupied territory but it came too late for inclusion in this book.

In conclusion, Professor Dinstein has cast much scholarly light on an area of international humanitarian law which has resided in dim places since 1949.

PETER ROWE
LANCASTER UNIVERSITY

The Multilateralization of International Investment Law. By STEPHEN W SCHILL. Cambridge University Press, Cambridge, 2009. xxxvii + 451 pp. £65.

The exponential growth of the network of investment treaties and corresponding increase in cases brought before investor-state tribunals has not only changed the face of international investment law, but also spawned fragmentation, diversity and incoherence. Nonetheless, scholars remain optimistic about the evolution of international investment law into a homogeneous and effective instrument of good governance. In his contribution to this strand of scholarship, Stephan Schill proposes the paradigm of multilateralism to help understand contemporary investment treaty practice and jurisprudence, whilst also providing a normative basis for developing uniform approaches to the interpretation and application of investment treaty provisions.

Schill's theory of the multilateralisation of international investment law is grounded in a process of economic, cultural and political globalisation. Investment treaties are seen not as mere instruments of bilateral protection, but rather as a mechanism fostering the functioning of international markets in which 'capital flows in an increasingly liberal fashion between different national economies to wherever it is allocated most efficiently' (17). Analysing multilateralism in an historical context, Schill identifies the multilateral foundations of investment protection in customary international norms and early FCNs, which pursued, inter alia, engagement in international commerce without on a non-discriminatory basis (28–30). Despite acknowledging the many failures to agree multilaterally on the *substantive* protection of foreign investment, Schill concludes that the rise of BITs and regional economic integration instruments after WWII, together with the conclusion of the Washington and Multilateral Investment Guarantee Agency Conventions, exemplify 'genuine multilateralism' (44).

In Chapter 3, Schill rejects as unconvincing the 'hegemonic behaviour' and 'transaction cost benefits' explanations of the current convergence of investment treaties. This convergence is not coincidental but reflects the common interests of states in establishing universal rules for investment protection because such rules underpin global welfare (68). Yet, while admitting that the adoption of uniform standards of investment protection is rational and efficient, it is somewhat unconvincing that contracting states *intentionally* subscribe for the multilateral investment protection regime. Similarly contentious is Schill's reference to the dynamics of treaty negotiation to support his argument that the conclusion of bilateral treaties is embedded in multilateral processes (89). Even supposing that the similarity between bilateral solutions resulted in fact from a 'disguised' push for multilateralism, such reasoning is likely to rekindle debates about the legitimacy of international investment law. As the author admits, model treaties are usually drafted by a developed country and offered to a developing country for signature, with only minor changes incorporated into the final agreement (90–91). If a State imposes its view of the international law on foreign investment, striving to ensure its acceptance through the use of model texts and offering other contracting states little room to manoeuvre, one wonders how far the resulting homogeneity is truly multilateral, in the sense of reflecting the intentions of all the negotiating parties.

The focus of Chapter 4 is on most-favoured-nation treatment, which Schill views as a manifestation of multilateralism in a normative framework. Addressing the existing contention over the scope of MFN treatment, he emphasises the primacy of text and argues that MFN clauses should be understood broadly as multilateralising both substantive and procedural investor rights, including the investor's rights to benefit from the host state's consent to arbitration under a third party BIT (175). The chapter is very well argued, though one cannot help noticing that in highlighting the importance of text, Schill departs from his general inclination to gloss over the nuances in treaty formulations.

Chapter 5 deals with multilateralisation through corporate structuring. Indeed, a broad definition of 'investment' and 'investor' extends investment treaty protection to natural persons, corporations and indirect shareholdings, thus turning the nationality link into an increasingly 'drifting' requirement (199). The diversity of shareholder nationalities multiplies the number of potential claimants under various investment treaties, effectively transforming bilateral commitments into *erga omnes* obligations (219–220). However, Schill does not regard 'treaty shopping' as necessarily disruptive; instead he refers to practical difficulties in ascertaining the nationality link in the complex investment structures and the irrelevance of the origins of investments (235).

Enforcement is the third pillar of Schill's theory of multilateralism in international investment law. In Chapter 6, the mechanism of investor-state arbitration is presented as a depoliticised adjudicatory body which multilateralises international investment law through clarification, gap-filling and the creation of new norms. The emergence of a system of *de facto* precedent is further addressed in Chapter 7, which provides useful insights into cross-treaty interpretation, the use of model texts and teleological approaches to mitigate the inconsistencies and fragmentation in investment treaty law. Finally, in Chapter 8, Schill tackles the existing critiques of the capacity of investment arbitration to review public acts. He objects to establishing a standing judicial body, but endorses the need to define standards of review which would allow states to pursue legitimate policy goals. In line with global constitutional law approaches to investment arbitration, Schill suggests drawing analogies with domestic legal orders, including the adoption of the 'margin of appreciation' doctrine. Schill's book is an eloquent, boldly original and intellectually stimulating contribution to scholarship in international investment law by an ardent supporter of economic liberalism. It benefits from a flawless structure and a thoughtfully composed argument. Yet the author's inclination to gloss over the material differences in the existing framework of investment protection detracts from the strength of his descriptive claim for multilateralisation. His scepticism about the ability of states to influence arbitral rule-making through treaty amendment is also somewhat misplaced, notably in the light of recent trends in investment law-making. Finally, the 'constitutionalisation' perspective on international investment law would have benefited from a discussion of investors' responsibilities; indeed, good governance is a two-way street, and the evolution of investment treaty law into a truly multilateral global order would seem to call for universal enforcement not only of investors' rights but also their responsibilities.

MAVLUDA SATTOROVA
UNIVERSITY OF BIRMINGHAM

The United Nations Security Council and War. By VAUGHAN LOWE, ADAM ROBERTS, JENNIFER WELSH AND DOMINIK ZAUM (eds). Oxford, Oxford University Press, 2008. xxi + 640 pp and Appendices. £105.00.

This is a collection of essays written by international lawyers, diplomats, political scientists and practitioners, whose aim is to 'describe and evaluate the UN Security Council's part in addressing—and sometimes failing to address—the problem of war, both civil and international, in the years since 1945' (1). The collection is divided into four thematic parts: Part I provides the framework within which the Security Council (SC) operates; Part II explores the different roles of the SC; Part III analyses a number of indicative case studies; and Part IV reviews the transformation of the Security Council's role in view of the changing character of war. The chapters are preceded by an introduction and are followed by seven appendices which contain lists of cases or figures relating to the SC's practices in this area.

As far as individual chapters are concerned, Chapter 2 in Part I provides a historical account of the creation of the SC and subsequent attempts at reform, and concludes with a sobering note: that the SC remains 'undependable, unaccountable and unrepresentative', with little prospect of that changing. Chapter 3 presents the UN framework concerning the use of force and the challenges it is facing; whilst Chapter 4 discusses the proposals for a UN standing force, with the author remaining sceptical as to whether such a force would be able to address questions about the legitimacy or effectiveness of SC action. In Part II, Chapter 5 examines the relationship between the SC with the Great Powers, concluding that the relationship in that case is characterised by interdependence and mutual constraints; whilst Chapter 6 assesses the relationship between the Security Council and the General Assembly in peace and security, as formulated by the Uniting for Peace resolution, and contends that the role of the General Assembly in this respect has been less drastic than initially thought. Chapter 7 discusses the SC's role in peacekeeping and, after reviewing a number of cases which expose the political and material limitations facing the UN, claims that peacekeeping operations in the twenty-first century can still be political and multidimensional. The following chapter assesses the role of economic sanctions imposed by the SC, including the monitoring and implementation mechanisms. Chapter 9 examines the legal dimensions of the SC's authorisation of regional organisations to use force by focusing on NATO, whilst Chapter 10 considers the influence of national interests on SC action.

In Part III, Chapters 11–22, discuss certain indicative cases where the SC dealt with wars or conflicts; these include the Korean war, the Suez crisis, the Israeli-Arab wars, the Indian-Pakistani wars, East Timor, the Iran-Iraq war, the 1991 and 2003 Iraq wars, the wars of the Former Yugoslavia, the Bosnian Conflict, and the wars in western Africa, as well as cases where the Council refrained from getting involved in conflicts. These chapters are central to the book because they bring together issues raised in previous chapters and illuminate the book's main arguments. For example, the discussion of the SC's engagement with Iraq since 1991 demonstrates the limits of the SC's political and legal powers as well as the ambivalence of states' attitudes towards the SC; particularly that of the US. Chapter 23, in Part IV, identifies three main functions of the SC with respect to humanitarian law; executive, adjudicatory and legislative. Chapter 24 assesses the SC practice with regard to humanitarian crises by focusing on those cases where the SC has authorised states to take action for humanitarian purposes, whilst Chapter 25 discusses the role of the SC in military operations and its power to engage in 'transformative occupations'. The next chapter provides an overview of the SC's involvement in the fight against terrorism, and finally Chapter 27 deals with the SC's attitude towards the use of private force, contending that the General Assembly's moralising tone about the use of private force has constrained the SC.

Overall, the book contains an insightful analysis of the way the SC has been addressing the issue of war. What is not so evident is a narrative of the normative context within which the SC operates. For example, it is all very well to speak of the role of the SC in humanitarian crises or in occupation; but its evolving and often inconsistent practices can be better explained or understood if the normative premises and priorities of the international system and any subsequent changes thereto are also explained. Questions about the extent to which the concepts of democracy or human dignity have become political and/or legal principles that guide international governance or SC action are pertinent in this regard. Whilst individual chapters often deal with such issues, this does not happen evenly throughout the book and the links are not always apparent. On the other hand, the book, particularly the Introduction, provides an excellent exposition of the political and legal parameters—often translated as constraints—within which the SC operates, and assesses their impact on the SC's action in an un-emotive but perceptive manner.

The present reviewer agrees with many of the contentions made in this book; for example, that the UN system is not a pure collective security system or a world government. On the other hand, it should be added that such ambivalence may also be its strength, because it allows the Organisation to adapt, evolve or even contract when necessary. Moreover, it allows its diverse membership to vow their support to the Organisation or to the SC for different reasons. The current international security system may indeed resemble a tapestry of actors: the UN is not the only actor or even the most important one, but one with particular strengths and particular weaknesses amongst many other actors. This book thus succeeds in presenting 'a realistic and multi-dimensional picture of the Organisation and its capabilities'(18).

Nikolaos Tsagourias
University of Bristol

Ethics in Action—The Ethical Challenges of International Human Rights Nongovernmental Organizations. By Daniel A Bell and Jean-Marc Coicaud (eds). Cambridge, Cambridge University Press, 2007. 334 pp. £24.99.

Bell and Coicaud have put together a fascinating collection of papers which reveal the complex and sometimes highly contentious ethical dilemmas that international non-governmental organisations (INGOs) face, not only in relation to their priorities and responsibilities but also in terms of their relationship with international organisations such as the UN, home and host governments and other (I)NGOs. Contributions to the book are from representatives of well-established INGOs such as Amnesty International, Human Rights Watch and Oxfam as well as from human rights theorists, all of whom were brought together in a unique multiyear international project.

The focus of the project was on those INGOs that are working predominantly in the field of human rights, rather than, for example, in providing humanitarian assistance. The focus reflects the development in the 1990s of INGOs utilising human rights as their normative framework. The challenges this development has created constitute a recurring theme throughout the book, not just in the third section were the debate focuses on the division between civil and political (CP) rights as against economic, social and cultural (ESC) rights. Contributors raise ideological debates covering issues such as the universalism of human rights and political dimensions of human rights, for example in relation to the confrontation between the United States and China.

The book is well structured. It divides the ethical challenges into three different topics. The first section entitled 'Northern INGOs and Southern Aid Recipients: The Challenge of Unequal Power' looks firstly at issues relating to funding. Betty Plewes and Ricky Stuart reveal the dilemma faced in the choice of images used in INGO fundraising campaigns. Whilst images of starving children are a particularly effective way of raising funds, they perpetuate a view of people in developing countries as victims. A similar observation is made by Bonny Ibhawoh who states that communities in developing countries are represented 'as needy, incapable of self-government, and in need of long-term external assistance'. (87)

Mona Younis's chapter discusses, on the basis of experiences of the Mertz Gilmore Foundation, dilemmas concerning the selection of projects for funding. Specific issues addressed in her chapter include whether funding should be provided to northern or southern human rights groups; to projects focusing on CP or ESC rights; to professional NGOs or social movements; and finally to those addressing problems at home or abroad. These are discussed within the broader concern that the funding of these transnational interventions is largely undemocratic and non-participatory. Younis questions whether a reliance on professional NGOs funded abroad is an appropriate way of achieving social and political change in these communities.

A key question in this book is whether the agenda for change in these communities is set by the INGOs or the communities themselves. In considering this question, Steven Weir shows that Habitat for Humanity began with a very clear moral belief that housing is an important factor in the transformational development of communities. Weir's case studies show how crucial it is for INGOs to work with local communities and to respect local cultures. Nevertheless, Ibhawoh suggests that INGOs need to be more self-critical with respect to their choice of what assistance to provide, to whom and in what way. There are therefore significant challenges when the values or funding requirements of the INGOs do not match those of the communities they are hoping to assist. Coicaud raises this issue briefly in the conclusion and questions whether it is correct to consider gender equality or the treatment of homosexuals when there are perhaps more pressing and basic concerns for local communities such as shelter and food.

The second part of the book, entitled 'INGOs and Governments: The Challenge of Dealing with States that Restrict the Activities of INGOs', examines the challenges confronting INGOs in conflict zones and authoritarian regimes. Lyal S. Sunga examines the strategies to be employed by INGOs when confronted with conditions on providing funding and security in coalition occupied Iraq. He asks whether INGOs providing humanitarian assistance should remain neutral or become involved in the politics of the situation. In a chapter dealing with the support of human rights work in authoritarian countries Birgit Lindsnæs, Hans-Otto Sano and Hatla Thelle identify a range of factors that have resulted in unequal power relations between the Danish Institute for Human Rights (DIHR) and their partners in relation to 'the strength of the power base, political alliances, professional human rights skills, organizational capacity, ability to pursue goals, communication skills, and managing of criticism, conflict and financial resources' (121). Importantly, they suggest that Western INGOs may not always be in a more powerful position. A valuable addition to this section could have been a case study from a 'southern' NGO, which could have shed light on these issues from a 'southern' perspective. The final two chapters in this section deal with China. Sophia Woodman examines the donor programs of bilateral aid from different countries for legal reform and law–related projects in China. Finally Sun Zhe questions whether it is ethical to collaborate with governments who are themselves responsible for violations of human rights and whether it is possible for INGOs to affect real change.

The third section, 'INGOs and Economic Rights: The Challenge of Dealing with Global Poverty' examines the role of INGOs in promoting ESC rights. Kenneth Roth suggests that one of the key problems associated with human rights organisations engaging with economic, social and cultural rights relate to the problem of identifying and dealing with human rights violations. In the context of civil and political rights, Roth argues that identifying the violation, violator and remedy is relatively simple. In the context of ESC rights the situation is less clear, particularly when attempting to identify the violator. Whose responsibility, for example, is it for a substandard public health system—the individual state or the international community? Utilising this methodology, INGOs are restricted to addressing only those issues that are capable of being identified in those terms. Neera Chandoke, however, suggests as an alternative a focus on the non-fulfilment of a right rather than a focus on violations.

The lack of collaboration between the experiences of INGOs and the theorists is discussed by Joseph H Carens in his response to Thomas Pogge's theoretical chapter on the ethical dilemmas confronting INGOs when deciding how to spend the money they have collected. The dialogue between the two contributors and a similar exchange between Roth and Chandoke, are interesting as they highlight differing viewpoints. But it can also be seen as a failure in really getting the theorists and the practitioners to collaborate. It would be interesting to discover whether INGOs would utilise, or have utilised, Pogge's analysis. It is still not clear from the book whether abstract theories about human rights can help guide practitioners.

The concluding chapter addresses the involvement of INGOs in the United Nations (UN) and illustrates the growing power and role of INGOs in wider political and policy debates.

What is the value of this book for lawyers? Does it indicate a need for greater legal accountability of INGOs? The issue for legal practitioners and the international legal community is whether the regulation of INGOs is still adequate.

The book is successful in raising important questions, but it also makes one wonder whether a more radical rethink is required as to how problems of poverty in developing countries are addressed. This is not to sound overly critical of the work currently done by INGOs, but as Plewes and Stuart state, 'eliminating poverty and promoting social justice require more than supporting projects in African countries through voluntary organisations' (25). It would have been useful to determine the focus for the future, which is likely to become more, not less, dominated by INGOs. This book is certainly a good starting point for these important discussions.

Rebecca McKelvie
University of Sussex

Decisions of British Courts During 2009 Involving Questions of Public or Private International Law

A. Public International Law

By Roger O'Keefe*

1. *R (Al-Saadoon) v Secretary of State for Defence*, 21 January 2009, [2009] EWCA Civ 7, [2009] 3 WLR 957, [2010] 1 All ER 271 (CA (Civ Div))

*'Jurisdiction' within meaning of European Convention on Human Rights and Fundamental Freedoms 1950 ('ECHR'), article 1—extraterritorial application of ECHR—Protocol 13 to ECHR, article 1 (abolition of death penalty)—ECHR, article 6 (right to fair trial)—*Soering *jurisprudence—customary international law—regional customary international law—relationship between customary international law and English law—crimes against humanity—torture—inhuman or degrading treatment—*jus cogens*—Iraq—Multi-National Force (MNF)—United Nations Security Council resolution 1790 (2007)—Coalition Provisional Authority Memorandum No. 3 (Revised)—Coalition Provisional Authority Order No. 17 (Revised)—Iraqi High Tribunal—Council of Europe—death penalty—execution by hanging—whether Secretary of State for Defence prevented from ordering transfer to Iraqi High Tribunal of certain detainees held by UK military forces in Iraq*

After the transfer of governmental authority in Iraq from the Coalition Provisional Authority (CPA) to the Interim Government of Iraq on 28 June 2004, UK military forces remained in the country as part of what was known as the Multi-National Force (MNF), at the invitation of the Iraqi government and in accordance with a mandate laid down in relevant United Nations Security Council resolutions. The last such resolution was resolution 1790 (2007),[1] annexed to which was a letter from the Prime Minister of Iraq requesting the extension of the MNF's mandate until 31 December 2008 and which—'in order to strike a balance between, on the one hand, the need to extend, one last time, the mandate of the force and, on the other hand, progress made by Iraq in the area of security'—specified the following 'objective':

* University Senior Lecturer in Law and Deputy Director, Lauterpacht Centre for International Law, University of Cambridge; Fellow and College Lecturer in Law, Magdalene College, Cambridge.

[1] SC res 1790 (2007), 18 December 2007.

The Government of Iraq will be responsible for arrest, detention and imprisonment tasks. When those tasks are carried out by MNF–I, there will be maximum levels of coordination, cooperation and understanding with the Government of Iraq . . .[2]

The Security Council, noting 'that the presence of the multinational force in Iraq [was] at the request of the Government of Iraq', duly extended the MNF's mandate, 'taking into consideration the Iraqi Prime Minister's letter dated 7 December 2007, including all of the objectives highlighted therein'.[3]

In order to give effect after 28 June 2004 to the government of Iraq's responsibility for arrest, detention and imprisonment, as endorsed in resolution 1790 (2007), CPA Memorandum No. 3 (Revised)[4] provided in section 5(1) ("Criminal Detentions") as follows:

A national contingent of the MNF shall have the right to apprehend persons who are suspected of having committed criminal acts and are not considered security internees (hereinafter "criminal detainees") who shall be handed over to Iraqi authorities as soon as reasonably practicable. A national contingent of the MNF may retain criminal detainees in facilities that it maintains at the request of appropriate Iraqi authorities based on security or capacity considerations. . . .

By virtue of CPA Order No. 17 (Revised), extant until midnight on 31 December 2008, premises occupied by MNF contingents were deemed inviolable.[5]

The claimants, apprehended and interned by UK forces originally on security grounds during the period of the UK's belligerent occupation of Basra, were being detained—since 18 May 2006, pursuant to authorization

[2] Ibid, Annex I. 'MNF–I', standing for 'Multi-National Force–Iraq', is simply a fuller name for the MNF.

[3] Ibid, para 1.

[4] Coalition Provisional Authority Memorandum Number 3 (Revised), Criminal Procedures, 27 June 2004, CPA/MEM/27 June 2004/03. Although it is not mentioned in the Court of Appeal's judgment, a Memorandum of Understanding (MoU) was concluded on 8 November 2004 between the UK contingent of the MNF and the Iraqi Ministries of Justice and the Interior respectively, the preamble to which recited in part: 'Whereas Iraq is developing its own custodial capacity with the aim of being able to confine all criminal suspects in its own facilities, it may, in the meantime, request [the UK contingent of the MNF] to confine persons who are suspected of having committed criminal acts in safe and secure detention facilities, subject to security and capacity considerations.' Section 2(1) provided: 'The Interim Iraqi Government (and any successor) has legal authority over all criminal suspects who have been ordered to stand trial and who are awaiting trial in the physical custody of [the UK contingent of the MNF] in accordance with the terms of this Memorandum of Understanding (MoU).' Section 4(1) provided in relevant part: 'In relation to any criminal suspect being held in the physical custody of the [UK contingent of the MNF], the Ministry of Justice will: (a) provide [the UK contingent of the MNF] with a written request for his delivery up to attend a court appearance or for any other purpose connected with the criminal process and will give as much advance notice of the proposed date when the presence of the suspect is required as is practicable.'

[5] Coalition Provisional Authority Order Number 17 (Revised), Status of the Coalition Provisional Authority, MNF-Iraq, Certain Missions and Personnel in Iraq, 27 June 2004, CPA/ORD/27 June 2004/17, s 9(1). Although this too is not made clear in the Court of Appeal's judgment, both CPA Memorandum No. 3 (Revised) and CAP Order No. 17 (Revised) remained in force in Iraq unless and until rescinded by the Interim Government, in accordance with the Law of Administration for the State of Iraq for the Transitional Period, 8 March 2004, art 26(C).

by the Basra Criminal Court—as criminal detainees, within the meaning of CPA Memorandum No. 3 (Revised), in an internment facility on a UK military base at Basra airport on suspicion of having murdered two British servicemen in their custody during the occupation. (The UK contingent of the MNF had referred the case to the Iraqi criminal courts in December 2005.[6]) The Basra Criminal Court, eventually characterizing the alleged conduct as a war crime falling within the jurisdiction of the Iraqi High Tribunal (IHT),[7] transferred the case in 2007 to the Tribunal, which in turn issued a formal request on 27 December 2007 for the transfer of the claimants to its custody from the custody of UK forces. The claimants sought judicial review in the English courts of the Secretary of State's decision to accede to the request for their transfer to the IHT, arguing that section 6 of the Human Rights Act (HRA) prevented him from acting as he did, since there were substantial grounds for believing that, if transferred, they would face a real risk of the death penalty, as outlawed by article 1 of Protocol 13 to the ECHR,[8] and a real risk of an unfair trial, contrary to article 6 of the ECHR. On expedited appeal from the Divisional Court's dismissal of their application,[9] the claimants further submitted before the Court of Appeal that their transfer was unlawful on account of the real risk they would face of a sentence of death by hanging, which they alleged to be in breach of customary international law, which in turn, they argued, was automatically incorporated into English law in such a way as to restrain the Secretary of State.

The Court of Appeal (Civil Division) dismissed the appeal. Laws LJ gave the only substantive judgment, with which Jacob and Waller LJJ agreed.

The threshold question addressed by the Court—which proceeded on the basis that the 'real risk' test was the applicable one[10] in *Soering*[11]-style cases of this kind and that, as held by the Divisional Court, there were substantial grounds for believing that the claimants would indeed face a

[6] The UK had referred the claimants' case to Iraq's Central Criminal Court, but that court had transferred the case to the Basra Criminal Court in April 2006. The claimants had appeared before the Basra court on 18 May 2006 to give evidence in response to the complaint lodged against them by a UK military officer, on which date the court had issued arrest warrants for them and authorized their continued detention by UK forces.

[7] The Tribunal, also known as the Supreme Iraqi Criminal Tribunal, was established pursuant to the Law of the Supreme Iraqi Criminal Tribunal, Law No. (10) 2005, *Official Gazette of the Republic of Iraq*, No. 4006, 18 October 2005, article 13 of which vests it with jurisdiction over a wide range of war crimes.

[8] Protocol No. 13 to the Convention for the Protection of Human Rights and Fundamental Freedoms, concerning the abolition of the death penalty in all circumstances, Vilnius, 3 May 2002, ETS No. 187 ('Protocol 13'). Article 1 provides: 'The death penalty shall be abolished. No one shall be condemned to such penalty or executed.'

[9] See *R (Al-Saadoon) v Secretary of State for Defence* [2008] EWHC 3098 (Admin). The Divisional Court gave its judgment on 19 December 2008. The Court of Appeal heard the case as a matter of extreme urgency on 29 and 30 December 2008, rendering its decision on 30 December and indicating that a full judgment would follow. The Court of Appeal's judgment was handed down on 21 January 2009. The expedited timetable was compelled by the imminent expiration, on 31 December 2008, of the MNF's mandate under Security Council resolution 1790 (2007).

[10] [2009] 3 WLR 957, 966, para 16.

[11] See *Soering v United Kingdom* (1989) 11 EHRR 439.

real risk of the death penalty should they be transferred to the custody of the IHT[12]—was whether the claimants were within the jurisdiction of the UK for the purposes of article 1 of the ECHR. The first relevant consideration in this context was the legal position of the UK forces in Basra prior to the expiration of the MNF's Security Council mandate on 31 December 2008. In this regard, 'the fact of Iraq's sovereignty', the relevant Security Council resolutions (especially resolution 1790 (2007) with annexed letter) and section 5(1) of CPA Memorandum No. 3 (Revised) led Laws LJ to conclude that, 'from at least May 2006 until 31 December 2008, the British forces at Basra were not entitled to carry out any activities on Iraq's territory in relation to criminal detainees save as consented to by Iraq, or otherwise authorised by a binding resolution or resolutions of the Security Council'.[13] 'In these circumstances', his Lordship continued, 'the United Kingdom was not before 31 December 2008 exercising any power or jurisdiction in relation to the claimants other than as agent for the Iraqi court'.[14] That is, '[i]t was not exercising, or purporting to exercise, any autonomous power of its own as a sovereign state'.[15] As for what the situation was after 31 December 2008,[16] when the mandate granted to the MNF at the request of the Iraqi government by Security Council resolution 1790 (2007) expired, his Lordship found it 'wholly inescapable that after that date British forces remaining in Iraq ha[d] done so only by consent of the Iraqi authorities and on such terms as those authorities ha[d] agreed'—and, he added, 'it must have been plain, as soon as it was known when the mandate would come to an end, that this would be the true state of affairs'.[17] Nor was there 'sensible room for doubt but that the terms on which British forces would be permitted to remain in Iraq by the Iraqi authorities would not encompass any role or function which would permit, far less require, British (or any other) forces to continue to hold detainees'.[18] This, too, had come to pass, so that '[a]fter 31 December 2008 British forces enjoyed no legal power to detain any Iraqi'.[19] Turning to apply the relevant authorities to these legal facts, Laws LJ, having earlier reviewed the judgment of the European Court of Human Rights (ECtHR) in *Bankovic*[20] and that of the House of Lords in *Al-Skeini*,[21] stated:

37 It is not easy to identify precisely the scope of the article 1 jurisdiction where it is said to be exercised outside the territory of the impugned state party,

[12] [2009] 3 WLR 957, 968, para 22. [13] Ibid, 977, para 32. [14] Ibid, para 33.
[15] Ibid. [16] Recall that the judgment was handed down on 21 January 2009.
[17] [2009] 3 WLR 957, 977, para 34. [18] Ibid, para 35.
[19] Ibid, 978, para 36.
[20] See ibid, 968–70, paras 24–5, quoting *Bankovic v Belgium* (2001) 11 BHRC 435, paras 57, 59–61, 65, 71 and 80.
[21] See [2009] 3 WLR 957, 970–4, paras 26–7, quoting *R (Al-Skeini) v Secretary of State for Defence* [2007] UKHL 26, [2008] 1 AC 153, 201–2, paras 75–6 and 78–9 (Lord Rodger), 206, para 97 (Lord Carswell), and 208, 214–5 and 215–6, paras 107, 127–9 and 132 (Lord Brown), (2007) 78 *BYIL* 529–46 (HL).

because the learning makes it clear that its scope has no sharp edge; it has to be ascertained from a combination of key ideas which are strategic rather than lexical. Drawing on the judgment in the *Bankovic* case and their Lordships' opinions in the *Al-Skeini* case, I suggest that there are four core propositions, though each needs some explanation. (1) It is an *exceptional* jurisdiction. (2) It is to be ascertained *in harmony* with other applicable norms of international law. (3) It reflects the *regional* nature of the Convention rights. (4) It reflects the *indivisible* nature of the Convention rights. The first and second of these propositions imply (as perhaps does the term *jurisdiction* itself) an exercise of sovereign *legal* authority, not merely de facto power, by one state on the territory of another. That is of itself an exceptional state of affairs, though well recognised in some instances such as that of an embassy. The power must be given by law, since if it were given only by chance or strength its exercise would by no means be harmonious with material norms of international law, but offensive to them; and there would be no principled basis on which the power could be said to be limited, and thus exceptional. As I have said, [counsel for the claimants] submitted that in the *Al-Skeini* case the House of Lords' acceptance of article 1 jurisdiction in Mr Mousa's case was essentially based on de facto control over the territory in question. With respect this was a misconceived reading of their Lordships' decision. It is impossible to reconcile a test of mere factual control with the limiting effect of the first two propositions I have set out, and, indeed, that of the last two, as I shall explain.

38 These first two propositions, understood as I have suggested, condition the others. If a state party is to exercise article 1 jurisdiction outside its own territory, the regional and indivisible nature of the Convention rights requires the existence of a regime in which that state enjoys legal powers wide enough to allow its vindication, consistently with its obligations under international law, of the panoply of Convention rights—rights which may however, in the territory in question, represent an alien political philosophy.

39 The Convention's natural setting is the espace juridique of the states parties; if, exceptionally, its writ is to run elsewhere, this espace juridique must in considerable measure be replicated. In short the state party must have the legal power to fulfil substantial governmental functions as a sovereign state. It may do so within a narrow scope, as in an embassy, consulate, military base or prison; it may, in order to do so, depend on the host state's consent or the mandate of the United Nations; but however precisely exemplified, this is the kind of legal power the state must possess: it must enjoy the discretion to decide questions of a kind which ordinarily fall to a state's executive government. If the article 1 jurisdiction is held to run in other circumstances, the limiting conditions imposed by the four propositions I have set out will be undermined.[22]

[22] [2009] 3 WLR 957, 978–9, citations omitted.

His Lordship concluded:

40 I have held... that before 31 December 2008 the United Kingdom was not exercising any power or jurisdiction in relation to the claimants other than as agent for the Iraqi court. It was not exercising, or purporting to exercise, any autonomous power of its own as a sovereign state. After that date the British forces enjoyed no legal power to detain any Iraqi. Had they taken such action, the Iraqi authorities would have been entitled to enter the premises occupied by the British and recover any such person so detained. In those circumstances, given my approach to article 1 as I have just explained it, it is inevitably my conclusion that the detention of the claimants by the British forces at Basra did not constitute an exercise of article 1 jurisdiction by the United Kingdom, either before or after 31 December 2008. I would accordingly answer the jurisdiction question in favour of the Secretary of State.[23]

This ruling, which contrasted with that of the Divisional Court on the article 1 point, served to dispose of the claim based on the ECHR.

Law LJ nonetheless considered, in case he was wrong on the article 1 point and the UK was indeed obliged to secure to the claimants their Convention rights, whether this obligation was 'modified by an obligation owed to Iraq by the United Kingdom under international law to return the claimants for trial by the IHT'.[24] He referred to the decision of the House of Lords in *Al-Jedda*,[25] which constituted 'recognition that there may be cases where in the same situation a state is obliged both to respect the Convention rights and to make good a separate and potentially inconsistent duty owed under international law'.[26] He also examined closely the judgment in *R (B)*,[27] where the Court of Appeal had held that the ECHR did not require a Contracting State to give refuge to fugitives within consular premises if to do so would violate international law. In this light, his Lordship stated:

48... A state party to the Convention, exercising article 1 jurisdiction in a foreign territory, may certainly owe duties arising under international law to the host state. Article 55 of the Vienna Convention on Consular Relations, referred to in the *R (B)* case, offers an obvious platform for such a potential duty. In this case the United Kingdom was plainly obliged under international law to transfer the claimants pursuant to the IHT's request. In such instances, there may be a conflict between the state party's Convention obligations and its international obligations.

[23] Ibid, 978–9.

[24] Ibid, 979, para 41.

[25] See ibid, 979–80, para 42, quoting *R (Al-Jedda) v Secretary of State for Defence* [2007] UKHL 58, [2008] AC 332, 354–5, para 39 (Lord Bingham), (2007) 78 *BYIL* 564–82 (HL).

[26] [2009] 3 WLR 957, 980, para 43.

[27] See [2009] 3 WLR 957, 980–2, paras 43–4, quoting *R (B) v Secretary of State for Foreign and Commonwealth Affairs* [2004] EWCA Civ 1344, [2005] QB 643, especially 671 and 673–4, paras 84 and 88, (2004) 75 *BYIL* 483–9 (CA (Civ Div)).

49 One solution might have been to hold that the existence of such an international obligation is incompatible with the exercise of article 1 jurisdiction, because it would show that the state party's legal power in the relevant foreign territory lacked the amplitude required to guarantee the Convention rights. In that case there would be no conflict. Such an outcome would of course be no comfort to the claimants—the duty to transfer them would without more negative the Convention jurisdiction, so that they would enjoy no Convention rights. However such an outcome would, I think, have been consistent with the *Bankovic* case; but this is not the direction our courts have taken. Both the *Al-Jedda* case and the *R (B)* case recognise that a state party may be fixed with potentially inconsistent obligations arising under the Convention and international law respectively.

50 With great respect I see no reason to doubt this position. While I have certainly asserted that the scope of the article 1 jurisdiction has to accommodate the pressure on states parties of international obligations apart from the Convention, it by no means follows that the Convention duty must always yield to the other obligation, so that no conflict can arise. No doubt it will be a matter for assessment in any case (where the issue sensibly arises) whether the international law obligations are so pressing, or operate on so wide a front, as in effect to deprive the relevant state party of the espace juridique which the article 1 jurisdiction demands. They may not do so; and where they do not, this court's decision in the *R (B)* case shows the correct juridical approach.

51 I would accordingly answer the conflict question [viz whether the obligation to secure to the claimants their Convention rights was "modified by an obligation owed to Iraq by the United Kingdom under international law to return the claimants for trial by the IHT"] in the affirmative. The court was obliged to have regard to the United Kingdom's obligation, arising under international law, to transfer the claimants to the custody of the IHT in deciding whether to grant relief for the purpose of upholding Convention rights.[28]

In reaching this conclusion, Laws LJ was 'essentially in agreement with the judgment of the Divisional Court on [the same] question'.[29]

On the article 6 point, which again was relevant only if Laws LJ was wrong on the article 1 point, the claimants had submitted, on the basis of the Grand Chamber's judgment in *Öcalan v Turkey*,[30] that, in cases such as theirs where the death penalty was a possibility, claimants were not obliged to show that any breach of the right to fair trial of which there was a real risk would be flagrant. But his Lordship pointed out that *Öcalan* was not a so-called 'foreign' case (that is, a case involving deportation or extradition to another State where the claimant fears treatment which, if meted out by a Contracting State, would amount to a breach of the ECHR) and that, even where the death penalty was a possibility, claimants in 'foreign' cases under article 6 of the Convention had to establish

[28] [2009] 3 WLR 957, 983, citations omitted.
[29] Ibid, 979, para 42. [30] (2005) 41 EHRR 985.

that any violation of that article would be flagrant.[31] As to whether this had been established in the present case, Laws LJ saw no basis for overturning the Divisional Court's conclusion that it had not.[32]

Turning from the claims founded on the ECHR to the claim founded on customary international law, Laws LJ noted that the claimants had in fact made two arguments: first, and primarily, that universal customary international law condemned execution specifically by hanging (whether as a crime against humanity, a form of torture or a form of inhuman or degrading treatment), with the result that the common law, which incorporated customary international law, prohibited the Secretary of State from surrendering the claimants to the IHT; secondly, in the alternative, that a rule of regional customary international law, applicable to member States of the Council of Europe, prohibited the death penalty by any means, with the same result under English law.[33] After citing the selection of English authorities, such as *Trendtex*, relied on by the claimants in seeking to establish that rules of customary international law are automatically incorporated into English law,[34] his Lordship continued:

> So far so good. But the further proposition that the customary rule may be sued on as a cause of action in the English courts is perhaps not so clear cut. It would of course have to be shown that the rule did not conflict with any provision of English domestic law; that creates no difficulty in this case. I apprehend the rule would also have to possess the status of jus cogens erga omnes (a peremptory norm binding on all states). It may be that once the customary rule were shown to exist, this further requirement would not be a step too far.[35]

'Strictly for the purpose of determining this part of the case', his Lordship assumed in the claimants' favour that the further proposition was correct and applied in relation to both of their submissions as to customary international law.[36] As to the alleged rule of regional customary international law prohibiting the death penalty *per se*, his

[31] [2009] 3 WLR 957, 984, para 53, citing *Bader v Sweden* (2005) 46 EHRR 197, para 42.

[32] [2009] 3 WLR 957, 985, para 55.

[33] Ibid, 986, para 57. As also noted by Laws LJ, ibid and 982, para 45, the claimants had made the further argument, this time under the ECHR, that the death penalty specifically by hanging constituted a crime against humanity and that, in *R (B)*, the Court of Appeal had stated obiter as follows, [2005] QB 643, 673–4, para 88: 'Should it be clear, however, that the receiving state intends to subject the fugitive to treatment so harsh as to constitute a crime against humanity, international law must surely permit the officials of the sending state to do all that is reasonably possible, including allowing the fugitive to take refuge in the diplomatic premises, in order to protect him against such treatment. In such circumstances the Convention may well impose a duty on a contracting state to afford diplomatic asylum.' Nothing more came of this submission.

[34] [2009] 3 WLR 957, 986, para 58, citing *Trendtex Trading Corporation v Central Bank of Nigeria* [1977] QB 529, 553, (1976–1977) 48 *BYIL* 353–62 (CA); *J.H. Rayner (Mincing Lane) Ltd v Department of Trade and Industry* [1989] Ch 72, 207, (1988) 59 *BYIL* 267–341 (CA (Civ)); *R (European Roma Rights Centre) v Immigration Officer at Prague Airport* [2004] UKHL 55, [2005] 2 AC 1, (2004) 75 *BYIL* 504–12 (HL); *R v Bow Street Metropolitan Stipendiary Magistrate, Ex parte Pinochet Ugarte* [2000] 1 AC 61, 90 (Lord Berwick), (1999) 70 *BYIL* 277–95 (HL), quoting R Y Jennings & A Watts (eds) *Oppenheim's International Law. Volume I: Peace* (9th edn, Longman, London, 1992) 57.

[35] [2009] 3 WLR 957, 986, para 59. [36] Ibid.

Lordship, although prepared to accept for the purposes of the case that the concept of regional customary international law was a valid one,[37] did not accept that the material sources relied on by the claimants[38] evidenced the rule alleged:

Some of these materials are not sources of law. In my judgment, so far as any of them reveal the law, it is the law established by treaty in the shape of the Convention. The states parties to the Convention, which of course include all the member states of the European Union, are necessarily committed to oppose the death penalty: at least those which have ratified Protocol 13 must be so committed. It is little surprise that this commitment has been expressed in statements and texts other than the Convention and Protocol themselves. These statements cannot in my view suffice to establish a freestanding principle of customary law, effective and enforceable irrespective of the Council of Europe states' adherence to the Convention. It is true (as [counsel for the claimants] asserts) that some of the documents pre-date the adoption of Protocol 13 in July 2003. But the aspiration of states in Europe to achieve a general abolition of the death penalty was fulfilled, not by the emergence of a legal norm from custom and practice, but by the Convention and Protocol. So much is expressly recognised in the very documents on which [counsel] relies: see paras 2 and 3 of the Committee of Ministers' written reply to the Parliamentary Assembly of 23 February 2007 and the Joint European Union/Council of Europe Declaration of 10 October 2008.[39]

As regards the claimants' chief submission under this head of claim, namely that generally-applicable customary international law outlawed execution by hanging, Laws LJ dealt with the Secretary of State's arguments as follows:

65 [Counsel for the Secretary of State] submits that there is no decision of any international court, nor any text from any responsible international organisation, establishing that the imposition of the death penalty generally or by hanging in particular is contrary to customary international law; and the academic literature does not support the suggestion that that position is yet established in customary international law. That is so; but if it were plainly shown that a particular means of execution inflicted so great a degree of pain and suffering that by common

[37] Ibid, 986–7, para 60, citing *Asylum Case (Colombia/Peru)* [1950] ICJ Rep 266, 276–8 and Jennings & Watts, above n 34, 30, as relied on by the claimants. Counsel for the Secretary of State 'did not in terms seek to contradict [the] proposition': [2009] 3 WLR 957, 986, para 60.

[38] As recalled by Laws LJ, [2009] 3 WLR 957, 987, para 61, these included 'article 19 of the Charter of Fundamental Rights of the European Union (OJ 2000 C364, 1) (7 December 2000), guidelines on human rights and the fight against terrorism adopted by the Council of Europe Committee of Ministers, an interpretation by the Committee of Ministers on 23 February 2007 of the principle of non-refoulement in the context of articles 2 and 3 of the Convention, a joint European Union/Council of Europe declaration of 10 October 2008 establishing a European day against the death penalty and referring to the Convention and the Charter of Fundamental Rights of the European Union, and the approval of many European states of a resolution on the moratorium on executions adopted by the General Assembly of the United Nations'.

[39] [2009] 3 WLR 957, 987, para 62.

consensus it would be regarded as a crime against humanity, inhuman or degrading treatment, or a form of torture, I apprehend [counsel for the claimants] might readily establish that it was contrary to a peremptory norm of customary international law notwithstanding that the books had not covered the particular case.

66 [Counsel for the Secretary of State] does not accept that the death penalty (I think he means, however it may be carried out) is within the definition of torture given by article 1 of the United Nations Convention against Torture... But this issue cannot, I think, be made to depend on the niceties of interpretation to which this provision might give rise. As I have indicated, a means of execution might inflict so great a degree of pain and suffering that by common consensus it would be regarded as a crime against humanity, inhuman or degrading treatment, or a form of torture.[40]

He observed that the claimants, on the other hand, had presented 'a good deal of material' in support of at least their argument as to inhuman or degrading treatment and that counsel for the Secretary of State had not sought to challenge this.[41] 'Much, however, depend[ed] on the facts', and this was where the claimants' argument fell down.[42] On the 'very limited' material before the Court, the latter was 'in no position whatever to arrive at any overall conclusion as to the effects of hanging for the purpose of making an assessment of its compatibility or otherwise with norms of customary international law'.[43]

The Court of Appeal's decision and Laws LJ's judgment give plenty of food for thought.

On the vexed article 1 question, his Lordship perhaps loses sight of the wood for the trees. After all, the deceased son of Mr Mousa (the only successful claimant in the *Al-Skeini* litigation)—the application of the ECHR to whom the Secretary of State conceded in that case—had, like the claimants in the present case, been detained on a UK military base in Iraq; as recalled by the Lords in *Al-Skeini* and by the Court of Appeal in *R (B)*, the ECtHR has held the ECHR to apply to diplomatic and consular premises abroad and to ships flying the flag of the State in question, the salient common feature in each instance being the exercise by the relevant State of legal authority and physical control over a self-contained extraterritorial space such that the State is capable of securing to individuals within that space the rights guaranteed by the Convention; and the military base in Iraq on which the claimants in the present case were detained was under the UK's legal authority at the time of the claim, in accordance

[40] Ibid, 988, referring to Convention against Torture and Other Cruel, Inhuman or Degrading Treatment or Punishment, New York, 10 December 1984, 1465 UNTS 112. His Lordship mistakenly dates the Convention '9 December 1975', which is the date of the United Nations Declaration on the Protection of All Persons from Being Subjected to Torture and Other Cruel, Inhuman or Degrading Treatment or Punishment, GA res. 3452 (XXX), 9 December 1975, Annex.

[41] [2009] 3 WLR 957, 988, para 67, quoting one of the authorities cited by the claimants, namely *Fisher v Minister for Public Safety and Immigration* [1998] AC 673, 688 (Lord Steyn) (PC).

[42] [2009] 3 WLR 957, 988, para 68. [43] Ibid, 989, para 70.

with CPA Order No. 17 (Revised), and under its physical control. Just as tellingly for present purposes, as again highlighted in *Al-Skeini*, a UK-run prison in foreign territory was held by the European Commission on Human Rights in *Hess v United Kingdom*[44] to be within the UK's jurisdiction within the meaning of article 1 of the ECHR. All this said, Mr Mousa's son had been detained during the UK's belligerent occupation of Basra, when the international legal regime applicable to detention by UK forces in Iraq was crucially different from that which applied in the present case. In this last light, the Court of Appeal's decision on the article 1 point is by no means manifestly wrong. But it is hard to resist the conclusion that, as the Divisional Court held, the legal authority pursuant to which the UK enjoyed custody over the claimants—as distinct, it might be interpolated, from the legal authority the UK exercised over the base—went to the content of the UK's obligations under the ECHR and Protocol 13, not to the existence of those obligations *in limine*.

The Court's resolution of the *prima facie* conflict between the UK's obligation under article 1 of Protocol 13 to the ECHR and its obligation to surrender the claimants to the IHT, like its resolution in *R (B)* of the *prima facie* conflict between the UK's obligations under articles 3 and 5 of the ECHR and the prohibition on intervention in the affairs of another State, gives implicit effect to the rule of treaty interpretation laid down in article 31(3)(c) of the Vienna Convention on the Law of Treaties, to which the court seems not to have been directed by counsel: where Lord Phillips MR in *R (B)*, quoted and relied on by Laws LJ in the present case,[45] was of the view that 'there must be an implication that obligations under a Convention are to be interpreted, insofar as possible, in a manner that accords with international law',[46] article 31(3)(c) of the Vienna Convention states that there shall be taken into account, when interpreting a treaty, 'any relevant rules of international law applicable in the relations between the parties'. But the difference between the two formulations is the rub: under article 31(3)(c), both States must be parties to the treaty in question before it is permissible to interpret its provisions by reference to other international rules applicable between them; and, of the UK and Iraq, only the former is a Contracting Party to the ECHR. What the present case, like *R (B)* before it, really involves is the application, not interpretation, by a single State of conflicting international obligations owed by it to different parties, a dilemma for which international law still provides no satisfactory substantive resolution, with its lack of a formal hierarchy of norms, leaving aside *jus cogens* and article 103 of the UN Charter. In this light, or darkness, the Court of Appeal's deft and diplomatic solution is arguably as good as, if not better than any other. That said, when it comes to article 1 of Protocol 13, we are talking not about a

[44] (1975) 2 DR 72.
[45] [2009] 3 WLR 957, 981, para 44, quoting [2005] QB 643, 671, para 84.
[46] [2005] QB 643, 671, para 84.

common or garden-variety human rights guarantee but about a non-limitable, non-derogable[47] right.

What is interesting in all of this is that the Secretary of State did not run a variation of the argument that succeeded in *Al-Jedda*. In the present case, the most recent renewal of the MNF's power to detain persons in Iraq—the original source of which was, as in *Al-Jedda*, paragraph 10 of Security Council resolution 1546 (2004),[48] in which the Security Council '[d]ecides that the multinational force shall have the authority to take all necessary measures to contribute to the maintenance of security and stability in Iraq'—was Security Council resolution 1790 (2007). In paragraph 1 of this resolution, it will be recalled, the Council 'reaffirms the authorization for the multinational force as set forth in resolution 1546 (2004) and decides to extend the mandate as set forth in that resolution until 31 December 2008, taking into consideration the Iraqi Prime Minister's letter dated 7 December 2007, including all of the objectives highlighted therein'. In turn, it will further be recalled that one of the 'objectives' highlighted in the Iraqi Prime Minister's letter was that '[t]he Government of Iraq will be responsible for arrest, detention and imprisonment tasks', so that '[w]hen those tasks are carried out by MNF-I, there will be maximum levels of coordination, cooperation and understanding with the Government of Iraq'.[49] The effect, therefore, of paragraph 1 of Security Council resolution 1790 (2007) was to authorize the MNF to detain persons in Iraq subject, arguably, to an obligation to acknowledge the government of Iraq's responsibility for arrest and detention, which in turn involved an obligation to secure 'maximum levels of coordination, cooperation and understanding with the Government of Iraq'. In short, it could be said that the transfer to Iraqi custody, on request, of detainees held by a contributing State to the MNF was rendered obligatory by paragraph 1 of resolution 1790 (2007) and ultimately by article 25 of the UN Charter. Since article 103 of the Charter provides that, in the event of a conflict between the obligations of UN member States under the Charter and their obligations under any other international agreement, their obligations under the Charter shall prevail, the UK's obligation to transfer the claimants to the IHT would prevail over its obligation, by virtue of article 1 of Protocol 13 and the *Soering* line of jurisprudence, not to. That is, the obligation embodied in article 1 of Protocol 13 would, to the extent of its conflict with the obligation to surrender the claimants, be without effect in relation to the UK. And, to round off the *Al-Jedda*-style submission, since the claimants' 'Convention right' for the purposes of section 6 of the HRA was their right under article 1 of Protocol 13 only 'as it has effect for the time being in relation to the United Kingdom',[50] it would not have been unlawful for the Secretary of State to act in a way that was incompatible

[47] See Protocol 13, art 2 ('Prohibition of derogations') and art 3 ('Prohibition of reservations').

[48] SC res 1546 (2004), 8 June 2004.

[49] SC res 1790 (2007), above n 1, Annex I.

[50] HRA, s 21(1).

with it. The weak link in this chain of reasoning is the characterization of the relevant objective in the Iraqi Prime Minister's letter as giving rise, on the basis of the Security Council's merely 'taking [it] into consideration' in resolution 1790 (2007), to a Charter-based obligation on contributing States to the MNF to act in accordance with it, as distinct from an obligation deriving simply from the terms of Iraq's consent to the UK's exercise of police powers in its territory. Nor, however, is this logic palpably specious.

Laws LJ's dicta on the doctrine of incorporation—in the context, ultimately, of the prohibition on inhuman or degrading treatment in customary international human rights law—were, with respect, a little unconsidered, even leaving aside his bizarre requirement that the international rule in question 'possess the status of jus cogens erga omnes'.[51] To the extent that his Lordship entertained for the sake of argument the possibility that a customary international human right could be relied on by way of the common law to restrain executive conduct, he cannot be faulted. The authorities, such as they are, are divided. In dicta in *R v Secretary of State for Foreign and Commonwealth Affairs, ex parte Pirbhai*, Woolf J stated:

> [T]he rule of international law which was being considered in the *Trendtex* case was a rule which had undoubtedly been adopted and incorporated into English law. The principle of sovereign immunity is applied as part of the domestic law. All rules of international law are not so applied. There are rules or principles of international law, for example relating to human rights, which are no part of our domestic law and the domestic courts cannot apply or interpret them in the same way as they apply and interpret domestic law.[52]

Not dissimilarly, Ouseley J remarked in *Chagos Islanders v Attorney General and Her Majesty's British Indian Ocean Territory Commissioner* that '[i]t may be that [counsel for the claimants] has put somewhat too broad an interpretation on *Trendtex* if he regards it as authority for the proposition that international law is enforceable without more by subject against Crown so long as no Act of Parliament is contravened'.[53] On the other hand, in *In re McKerr*, Lord Steyn wondered aloud and wholly obiter whether customary international human rights law might avail an applicant for judicial review of executive conduct:

> [T]here may be an argument that the right to life has long been recognised in customary international law, which in the absence of a contrary statute has been

[51] [2009] 3 WLR 957, 986, para 59. For earlier use of this overheated terminology, see *A v Secretary of State for the Home Department (No. 2)* [2005] UKHL 71, [2006] 2 AC 221, 262, para 34 (Lord Bingham), (2005) 76 *BYIL* 615–26 (HL); *R (Mohamed) v Secretary of State for Foreign and Commonwealth Affairs* [2008] EWHC 2048 (Admin), para 171, (2008) 79 *BYIL* 468–73 (CA (Civ Div)).

[52] 7 September 1984, QBD (Crown Office List), Woolf J, 129 SJ 756, official transcript from LexisNexis® Butterworths.

[53] [2003] EWHC 2222, para 375, (2003) 74 *BYIL* 486–93 (QBD (Admin Ct), Ouseley J).

part of English law since before the 1998 Act came into force.... The point has not been in issue in the present case. It has not been researched, and it was not the subject of adversarial argument. It may have to be considered in a future case.[54]

What is a little surprising, however, is Laws LJ's observation that the requirement that the rule on which the claimant seeks to rely not conflict with any provision of English law 'create[d] no difficulty in this case'.[55] There are certainly constitutional implications. The courts' restraint of Crown conduct by reference to common-law human rights drawn from customary international law would be the judicial coining of an administrative-law action for procuring a breach of public international law by the UK, an action for which the constitutional underpinnings would be highly uncertain. Moreover, there is an argument for saying that the HRA manifests a parliamentary intention to 'cover the field' in relation to human rights—that is, that by providing in domestic law for the enforcement of some international human rights standards binding on the UK as a matter of international law, Parliament has, by implication, excluded the domestic enforcement of others.[56] This is essentially the same reasoning that dissuaded the court in *Viveash v Becker* from giving effect to a customary international rule on consular immunity,[57] although there the original source of the relevant statutory rule was also customary, not conventional; and an analogous argument persuaded Orr and Lawton LJJ in the Court of Appeal and Lord Widgery CJ and May and Bridge JJ in the Divisional Court in *R v Secretary of State for the Home Department, Ex parte Thakrar*.[58] That said, the 'covering the field' logic is not watertight, given that a more than *de minimis* logical distinction can be drawn between those international human rights secured to individuals as a function of treaty-law by the ECHR and those enuring by virtue of customary international law, so that the enactment of the one is not necessarily to be taken as the exclusion of the other. Also on this other side of the equation is, more generally, the courts' traditional role as the safeguard of individual liberty against overweening executive power and today's heightened judicial concern for human rights, the latter manifest in a stricter standard of review when human rights are in play.[59]

The after-life of the present case has been eventful. The Court of Appeal, when dismissing the claimants' appeal from the Divisional Court, denied them leave to appeal to the House of Lords. On 30 December 2008, the same day the Court of Appeal rendered its decision, the ECtHR, with which the claimants/applicants had lodged an urgent application for

[54] [2004] 1 WLR 807, 824, para 52, (2004) 75 *BYIL* 411–9 (HL).
[55] [2009] 3 WLR 957, 986, para 59.
[56] See *Anisminic Ltd v Foreign Compensation Commission* [1969] 1 All ER 208.
[57] See (1814) 3 M & S 284, 298 (Lord Ellenborough CJ).
[58] See [1974] QB 684, 708 (Orr LJ) and 710 (Lawton LJ), (1974–1975) 47 *BYIL* 352–6 (CA); [1974] QB 684, 690–2 (Lord Widgery CJ, with whom May and Bridge JJ agreed).
[59] For a fuller discussion, see R O'Keefe, 'The Doctrine of Incorporation Revisited' (2008) 79 *BYIL* 7, especially 71–3.

interim measures under rule 39 of the Court's rules, informed the UK government that the claimants should not be removed or transferred from the UK's custody until further notice. The claimants were nonetheless transferred to the custody of the Iraqi authorities on 31 December 2008. On 16 February 2009, the Appeal Committee of the House of Lords dismissed their petition for leave to appeal. Their trial before the IHT commenced on 11 May 2009. On 30 June 2009, the ECtHR held their application admissible.[60] On the article 1 point, it stated:

87 During the first months of the applicants' detention, the United Kingdom was an occupying power in Iraq. The two British-run detention facilities in which the applicants were held were established on Iraqi territory through the exercise of military force. The United Kingdom exercised control and authority over the individuals detained in them initially solely as a result of the use or threat of military force. Subsequently, the United Kingdom's de facto control over these premises was reflected in law. In particular, on June 24, 2004, CPA Order No.17 (Revised) provided that all premises currently used by the MNF should be inviolable and subject to the exclusive control and authority of the MNF. This provision remained in force until midnight on December 31, 2008.

88 The Court considers that, given the total and exclusive de facto, and subsequently also de jure, control exercised by the UK authorities over the premises in question, the individuals detained there, including the applicants, were within the United Kingdom's jurisdiction (see Application No.6231/73, *Hess v United Kingdom*, May 28, 1975). This conclusion is, moreover, consistent with the dicta of the House of Lords in *Al-Skeini* and the position adopted by the Government in that case before the Court of Appeal and House of Lords.

89 In the Court's view, the applicants remained within the United Kingdom's jurisdiction until their physical transfer to the custody of the Iraqi authorities on December 31, 2008. The questions whether the United Kingdom was under a legal obligation to transfer the applicants to Iraqi custody and whether, if there were such an obligation, it modified or displaced any obligation owed to the applicants under the Convention, are not material to the preliminary issue of jurisdiction (see, mutatis mutandis, *Bosphorus* (2006) 42 EHRR 1 at [138]) and must instead be considered in relation to the merits of the applicants' complaints.[61]

The ECtHR handed down its judgment on the merits on 2 March 2010,[62] holding that by physically transferring the applicants to the custody of the Iraqi authorities and by referring their case to the Iraqi courts in the first place, having secured in neither case a binding assurance from Iraq that the applicants would not be at risk of the death penalty, the UK had

[60] *Al-Saadoon and Mufdhi v United Kingdom*, Application No. 61498/08, Admissibility, 30 June 2009, (2009) 49 EHRR SE11.

[61] Some citations omitted.

[62] *Al-Saadoon and Mufdhi v United Kingdom*, Application No. 61498/08, Merits, 2 March 2010, (2010) 51 EHRR 9.

violated the applicants' rights under article 3 of the ECHR. The Court did not consider it necessary to decide whether article 2 of the Convention and article 1 of Protocol 13 had also been breached.

2. *R (Mohamed) v Secretary of State for Foreign and Commonwealth Affairs (No 2)*, 4 February 2009, [2009] EWHC 152 (Admin), [2009] 1 WLR 2653 (QBD (Admin Ct), Div Ct)

Prohibition on torture—jus cogens—*whether special status of international prohibition on torture posing absolute bar to redaction of paragraphs of judgment detailing torture*

The factual background to the case has been outlined already in this *Year Book*.[63] At an earlier stage of the proceedings,[64] a Divisional Court of the Administrative Court had ordered the Secretary of State for Foreign and Commonwealth Affairs, subject to any public interest immunity claim by him, to disclose in confidence to the claimant's lawyers certain exculpatory and other relevant documents in his possession. The Court had handed down both open and closed judgments. From the first of these, pending further argument and at the Secretary of State's request, it had redacted seven paragraphs referring to reports by the US government to the UK security and intelligence services detailing the claimant's apparent torture at the hands of US officials, on the basis of which it was arguably evident that the UK security services, which had continued to supply information and questions to the US officials for use in the interrogation of the claimant, had been aware of the latter's treatment by these officials. Although the claimant's lawyers in the US subsequently obtained the information contained in the redacted paragraphs, the claimant sought the paragraphs' restoration to the open judgment. The Secretary of State claimed public interest immunity in order to prevent this. In the course of argument before the Court, it was submitted that the fact that the redacted paragraphs dealt with apparent acts of torture posed an absolute bar to any claim to public interest immunity in respect of them.

The Divisional Court dismissed the claimant's application and, in doing so, rejected the argument founded on the special character of the international prohibition on torture. Thomas LJ handed down the judgment of the Court.

On the torture point, the Court stated:

> It makes no difference, in our view, that the allegations of serious criminality are allegations of torture or cruel, inhuman or degrading treatment or other war crimes. It is clear from the opinions expressed in *A v Secretary of State for the Home Department (No 2)* [2006] 2 AC 221 that although there is an absolute prohibition on the use of evidence obtained by cruel, inhuman or degrading

[63] See *R (Mohamed) v Secretary of State for Foreign and Commonwealth Affairs* [2008] EWHC 2048 (Admin), (2008) 79 *BYIL* 468–73 (QBD (Admin Ct), Div Ct).

[64] See ibid.

treatment or torture against any person, there may be circumstances where the state may have to consider using information obtained in such a way for the protection of its citizens: see para 47 (Lord Bingham), paras 67–69 (Lord Nicholls of Birkenhead) and para 160 (Lord Brown). Furthermore, for reasons which we have set out at length in our first judgment [2009] 1 WLR 2579, we are unable to accept that the particular status of the prohibition on torture in public international law as a rule of *jus cogens* gives rise to an overriding duty to make disclosure of material evidencing such wrongdoing. On the contrary we note that article 72 of the Rome Statute of the International Criminal Court 1998 sets out detailed provisions for dealing with evidence which may prejudice national security, including hearing evidence in camera or refusing disclosure.[65]

'Similarly', the Court continued, 'section 39 of the International Criminal Court Act 2001 expressly provides that nothing in the Act requires the production of documents which would be prejudicial to the security of the United Kingdom'.[66]

As in its first judgment in the same case, the Court's scepticism towards the supposedly miraculous powers of *jus cogens* is, like that of Lords Bingham and Hoffmann in *Jones v Saudi Arabia*,[67] a pleasing counterpoint to more credulous pieties.

3. *RB (Algeria) v Secretary of State for the Home Department; U (Algeria) v Same; Othman (Jordan) v Same*, 18 February 2009, [2009] UKHL 10, [2009] 2 WLR 512 (HL)

*European Convention on Human Rights and Fundamental Freedoms 1950 ('ECHR'), article 3 (freedom from torture and inhuman or degrading treatment or punishment), article 6 (right to fair trial) and article 13 (right to effective remedy for violation of Convention rights)—deportation—*Chahal *jurisprudence—diplomatic assurances—memoranda of understanding—torture—evidence obtained by torture—Human Rights Act 1998—Special Immigration Appeals Commission Act 1997, section 7(1)—Convention relating to the Status of Refugees 1951, article 1F(c)—acts contrary to purposes and principles of United Nations—terrorism—whether question whether conduct in violation of Convention right a 'question of law' for purposes of Special Immigration Appeals Commission Act 1997, section 7(1)—whether possible admission in foreign trial of evidence obtained from others by means of torture by foreign authorities a 'flagrant denial' of fair trial—whether exclusion from refugee status possible for acts contrary to purposes and principles of United Nations committed after recognition as refugee*

The Secretary of State sought to deport the first two appellants to Algeria on the ground that it would be conducive to the public good, each of them

[65] [2009] 1 WLR 2653, 2668, para 30. [66] Ibid.

[67] [2006] UKHL 26, [2007] 1 AC 270, 288–9, para 24 (Lord Bingham) and 292, 293, 294 and 297–8, paras 43, 44, 49 and 63 (Lord Hoffmann).

having been deemed a danger to national security. The UK government sought, and the Algerian government gave, high-level diplomatic assurances that the pair would not be subject on their return to treatment contrary to international human rights standards. Each unsuccessfully contested the lawfulness of his deportation before the Special Immigration Appeals Commission ('SIAC') by arguing, as per *Chahal v United Kingdom*,[68] that there were substantial grounds for believing that he would face a real risk of being subject on his return to treatment which, if meted out by a Contracting State to the ECHR, would be contrary to his rights under article 3 (the freedom from torture and inhuman or degrading treatment or punishment), as secured to him by the HRA. Their challenges to the weight accorded by SIAC to the Algerian government's assurances were dismissed by the Court of Appeal,[69] to which, in accordance with section 7(1) of the Special Immigration Appeals Commission Act 1997 ('SIAC Act'), appeal from SIAC lay only on a point of law and which, as a consequence, held that it had no jurisdiction to entertain the appellants' submissions. They appealed to the House of Lords.

The deportation to Jordan of the third appellant, the tabloid hate-figure better known as Abu Qatada, was sought on the similar ground that, as a threat to national security, his presence in the UK was not conducive to the public good. He had been recognized as a refugee by the UK in 1994 but convicted twice since *in absentia* in Jordan of conspiracy to cause explosions. To facilitate his removal, the UK and Jordan concluded a memorandum of understanding to the effect that he would not be subject on his return, where he would be retried, to torture or other inhuman or degrading treatment or punishment. He unsuccessfully argued before SIAC along *Chahal* lines that his deportation would breach, *inter alia*, article 3 of the ECHR, in that there were substantial grounds for believing that he would face a real risk of torture or inhuman or degrading treatment, as well as article 6 (the right to fair trial), in that there was a real risk that evidence obtained from others by the Jordanian authorities by means of torture would be used against him at his retrial. He also failed to convince SIAC that he did not fall within article 1F(c) of the Convention relating to the Status of Refugees,[70] which provides that the provisions of the Refugee Convention shall not apply to any person with respect to whom there are serious grounds for considering that he has been guilty of acts contrary to the purposes and principles of the United Nations, the acts in this case being terrorist offences. He had argued, in reliance on the Canadian Supreme Court case of *Pushpanathan v Canada (Minister of Citizenship and Immigration)*,[71] that article 1F(c) was limited in its application to cases where the crime in question had been committed prior to the recognition

[68] (1996) 23 EHRR 413.
[69] See *MT (Algeria) v Secretary of State for the Home Department* [2007] EWCA Civ 808, [2008] QB 533, [2008] 2 WLR 159, [2008] 2 All ER 786, (2007) 78 *BYIL* 550–60 (CA (Civ)).
[70] Convention relating to the Status of Refugees, Geneva, 28 July 1951, 189 UNTS 2545.
[71] [1998] 1 SCR 982.

of refugee status. The Court of Appeal[72] upheld his appeal on the article 6 ground, but dismissed it on the remaining grounds. The Secretary of State appealed to the House of Lords, and the third appellant cross-appealed.

The House of Lords unanimously dismissed the first two appellants' appeals, upheld the appeal of the Secretary of State and dismissed the third appellant's cross-appeal.

The first two appellants had argued that the concept of a 'question of law' for the purpose of section 7(1) of the SIAC Act ought to have been construed broadly by the Court of Appeal to encompass the question whether or not the proposed conduct would constitute a violation of a Convention right. Such a construction was said to be required by the object of the HRA, which was to obviate the need for victims to go to Strasbourg to vindicate their Convention rights,[73] the contention being that the Court of Appeal had been obliged in this light to treat an appeal from SIAC in the same manner that the ECtHR would treat a claim of the violation of a Convention right, namely (as per the ECtHR in *Saadi v Italy*) by forming its own view as to whether there would be a violation of the Convention on the basis of all the material before it, both legal and factual, and if necessary on the basis of material obtained *proprio motu*.[74] A broad notion of a 'question of law' was also said to be compelled by, variously, the fact that the Court of Appeal was a public authority bound by section 6 of the HRA from acting in a manner incompatible with Convention rights[75] and the fact that SIAC was so bound, the latter converting SIAC's assessment of whether a violation would occur into a question of law.[76] The House of Lords, however, categorically rejected the overall submission and its various supporting arguments. Neither the ECHR as such nor the HRA had required the Court of Appeal to adopt the approach for which the appellants contended.[77] As to the ECHR, the ECtHR had held that proceedings relating to deportation engaged only the right to an effective remedy under article 13 of the Convention, and this did not imply a need for judicial involvement, let alone a right of appeal to a court on whether a violation of a Convention right would occur.[78] As to the HRA, Lord Phillips stated:

66 By restricting appeals to questions of law Parliament has deliberately circumscribed the review of SIAC's decisions that the Court of Appeal is permitted to undertake, so that it falls well short of the review that will be carried out if the case reaches the European court, as described in *Saadi v Italy*. . . .

[72] See *Othman v Secretary of State for the Home Department* [2008] EWCA Civ 290, [2008] 3 WLR 798.

[73] The appellants cited to this effect *Huang v Secretary of State for the Home Department* [2007] UKHL 11, [2007] 2 AC 167, para 8 (Lord Bingham).

[74] See [2009] 2 WLR 512, 534, para 63 (Lord Phillips), citing (2008) 24 BHRR 123, para 128.

[75] See [2009] 2 WLR 512, 534, para 63 (Lord Phillips) and 574, para 213 (Lord Hope).

[76] See ibid, 568, para 189 (Lord Hoffmann).

[77] Ibid, 534, para 64 (Lord Phillips) and 574, para 214 (Lord Hope).

[78] Ibid, 534–5, paras 64–5 (Lord Phillips) and 568, para 190 (Lord Hoffmann).

67 ... The Court of Appeal is a creature of statute and its powers are those conferred by statute. Section 6(1) cannot be so interpreted as to require public authorities to act beyond their powers.... [79]

Lord Hoffmann added:

It must be remembered that the European court itself is not a court of limited jurisdiction like the Court of Appeal under the 1997 Act. It is not a court of appeal from a national court at all. It decides whether, on its own assessment of the facts, there has been or would be a violation of a Convention right.[80]

Lord Hope was of the same view:

The important point is that the submission for the aliens confuses the jurisdiction that the Strasbourg court exercises under the Convention with that of the appellate courts under the domestic system. How the domestic system may deal with such issues is a matter for Parliament, for whose decisions the United Kingdom must answer if the need arises in Strasbourg. Parliament has entrusted the fact-finding function to SIAC. The counterpart of this arrangement is that the function of the appellate courts is confined to one that is essentially supervisory.[81]

Lord Brown did not mince words:

253 ... The fact that Strasbourg itself might choose to carry out a close factual re-examination of these cases to reach its own decision upon whether expulsion would involve a Convention breach is simply nothing to the point...

254 The most critical question raised in each appeal is whether the proposed deportees would face a real risk of article 3 ill-treatment on return. Par excellence this is a question of fact calling for an evaluation of all the evidence and ultimately a single factual judgment.... [82]

Because the question whether assurances given by the State to which the applicants were to be deported would, where relied on by the deporting State, be sufficient to acquit the latter's obligations under the Convention was one of fact,[83] the Court of Appeal had had no jurisdiction to review SIAC's assessment on this score. The same went for its refusal to second-guess SIAC on whether the third appellant, despite the memorandum of understanding between the UK and Jordan, faced a real risk of being tortured on his return. The only basis on which SIAC's assessment of the risk of torture could be impugned as a question of law was if it were one that no reasonable tribunal, properly directed, could have reached.[84] That

[79] Ibid, 535. See also ibid, 536, para 69 (Lord Phillips) and 574, para 214 (Lord Hope).

[80] Ibid, 568, para 188.

[81] Ibid, 575–6, para 217.

[82] Ibid, 587–8, paras 253–4.

[83] Ibid, 549, para 117 (Lord Phillips), 567–8, paras 184–7 (Lord Hoffmann), 581–2, paras 236 and 238 (Lord Hope), and 588, para 254 (Lord Brown).

[84] Ibid, 568, para 191 (Lord Hoffmann) and 575, para 216 and 582, para 236 (Lord Hope). See, similarly, ibid, 537, para 73 (Lord Phillips).

was not the case here.[85] It was true that the Algerian assurances did not contain express reference to standards of international law as to what counted as torture or inhuman or degrading treatment, but this did not matter, as explained by Lord Hoffmann:

> The arrangements with Algeria were negotiated at the highest level and it was plain to the Algerian authorities that what the United Kingdom required was an assurance which would enable it to comply with its obligations under article 3. On the other hand, the assurances had to be expressed in language which would respect the dignity of a sovereign state. In the cases of [the first two appellants] the assurance therefore said that they would enjoy "the following rights, assurances and guarantees as provided by the Constitution and the national laws currently in force concerning human rights...(h) His human dignity will be respected under all circumstances". The main reason why SIAC thought that this assurance would satisfy article 3 was that it was not in the national interest of the Algerians to fail to comply. In those circumstances, the precise language of the assurance was less important than the effect which both sides knew it was intended to have. So far from being irrational, that seems to me an entirely reasonable conclusion which SIAC was entitled to draw from the basic facts it had found to exist about the situation in Algeria.[86]

Lord Mance agreed.[87]

As for whether the deportation of the third appellant to Jordan would violate the UK's obligations under article 6 of the ECHR, the test was whether there existed a real risk that an alien would, if removed, suffer a flagrant denial of a fair trial in the State of destination; and while authoritative guidance from the ECtHR on what amounted to a flagrant denial of a fair trial was lacking (no Strasbourg applicant ever having successfully resisted deportation or extradition by reference to article 6), Judges Bratza, Bonello and Hedigan, in their joint dissenting opinion in *Mamatkulov and Askarov v Turkey*, had spoken of 'a breach of the principles of fair trial...so fundamental as to amount to a nullification, or destruction of the very essence, of the right guaranteed'.[88] This dictum had been approved by Lord Bingham, in the context of article 8, in *EM (Lebanon)*[89] and applied by both SIAC and the Court of Appeal in the present case. To Lord Phillips' mind, however, it posited 'neither an easy nor an adequate test':[90]

[85] Ibid, 551, para 124 and 551–2, para 126 (Lord Phillips), 569, paras 192–3 (Lord Hoffmann), 583, paras 240–1 (Lord Hope), and 588, para 254 (Lord Brown).

[86] Ibid, 569, para 192.

[87] Ibid, 591, para 265.

[88] Ibid, 554, para 133 (Lord Phillips), 570, para 197 (Lord Hoffmann), and 585, para 244 (Lord Hope), quoting (2005) 41 EHRR 494, para O-III 14.

[89] [2009] 2 WLR 512, 554, para 134 (Lord Phillips), citing *EM (Lebanon) v Secretary of State for the Home Department (AF (A Child) intervening)* [2008] UKHL 64, [2008] 3 WLR 931, 948, para 35, (2008) 79 *BYIL* 473–7 (HL).

[90] [2009] 2 WLR 512, 554, para 136 (Lord Phillips).

137 . . . [T]he fact that the deportee may find himself subject in the receiving country to a legal process that is blatantly unfair cannot, of itself, justify placing an embargo on his deportation. The focus must be not simply on the unfairness of the trial process but on its potential consequences. An unfair trial is likely to lead to the violation of substantive human rights and the extent of that prospective violation must plainly be an important factor in deciding whether deportation is precluded.

138 A conviction that results from a flagrantly unfair trial cannot be relied upon under article 5(1)(a) as justifying detention. . . . Nor can such a conviction justify the imposition and execution of the death penalty. In either case the breach of the procedural rights guaranteed by article 6 will result in a breach of a substantive right. If an alien is to avoid deportation because he faces unfair legal process in the receiving state he must show that there are substantial grounds for believing that there is a real risk not merely that he will suffer a flagrant breach of his article 6 rights, but that the consequence will be a serious violation of a substantive right or rights. . . .[91]

After considering, *inter alia*, *Stoichkov v Bulgaria*, *Tomic v United Kingdom* and *Bader v Sweden*,[92] his Lordship stated:

[T]he Strasbourg jurisprudence, tentative though it is, has led me to these conclusions. Before the deportation of an alien will be capable of violating article 6 there must be substantial grounds for believing that there is a real risk (i) that there will be a fundamental breach of the principles of a fair trial guaranteed by article 6 and (ii) that this failure will lead to a miscarriage of justice that itself constitutes a flagrant violation of the victim's fundamental rights.[93]

Lord Brown agreed that 'only where a prospectively unfair trial would be likely to lead to a serious violation of some substantive human right—for example, an unjust conviction involving grave consequences such as capital punishment or a substantial deprivation of liberty—would article 6 fall for consideration in a foreign case'.[94] Applying these principles to the instant case, Lord Phillips held that the consequences which would follow the conviction of the third appellant, namely life imprisonment for one offence and fifteen years for the other, were 'sufficiently severe to satisfy the second limb of the test'.[95] The 'vital issue' was the first, namely whether the third appellant 'faced a real risk of a fundamental breach of the principles of fair trial as recognised by the Strasbourg court'.[96] For their part, Lords Hoffmann and Hope eschewed the two-stage test posited by Lord Phillips and Brown, focusing instead solely on the requirement of a fundamental breach of the principles of fair trial. Lord Mance

[91] Ibid, 555.

[92] Ibid, 555–6, paras 138 and 140, referring respectively to (2005) 44 EHRR 276, para 51; Application No. 17837/03, Decision on Admissibility, 14 October 2003 (unreported), para 3; and (2005) 46 EHRR 1, para 42.

[93] [2009] 2 WLR 512, 556, para 141.

[94] Ibid, 590, para 259.

[95] Ibid, 556, para 142.

[96] Ibid, 556–7, para 142.

ostensibly agreed with all four of the other Lords' reasoning,[97] chipping in with the following observation:

[A]lthough the European Court of Human Rights' reasoning does not make the connection explicitly, there appears to be a considerable and to my mind unsurprising resemblance, which might in another case be worth exploring further, between the concept of flagrant unfairness adopted by the Court of Human Rights and the concept of denial of justice in public international law generally: see, as to the latter, Paulsson, *Denial of Justice in International Law* (2005). Paulsson states, at pp 60–61: "The modern consensus is clear to the effect that the factual circumstances must be egregious if state responsibility is to arise on grounds of denial of justice", while adding, realistically, that 'the indispensable line between fundamental violations and others' is easy to draw in some instances, but less clear in others.[98]

As to the instant case, insofar as the fundamental breach of the principles of fair trial would, it was alleged, take the form of the admission of evidence obtained from others by the Jordanian authorities by means of torture, Lord Phillips differed from the Court of Appeal in holding that it was not necessary for the UK, in order to satisfy article 6 of the ECHR in the present case, to secure from Jordan 'a high degree of assurance' that evidence obtained by torture would not be used against the third appellant:[99]

[T]he prohibition on receiving evidence obtained by torture is not primarily because such evidence is unreliable or because the reception of the evidence will make the trial unfair. Rather it is because "the state must stand firm against the conduct that has produced the evidence"... That principle applies to the state in which an attempt is made to adduce such evidence. It does not require this state, the United Kingdom, to retain in this country to the detriment of national security a terrorist suspect unless it has a high degree of assurance that evidence obtained by torture will not be adduced against him in Jordan. What is relevant in this appeal is the degree of risk that Mr Othman will suffer a flagrant denial of justice if he is deported to Jordan.[100]

SIAC, after closely considering the law and practice of the Jordanian courts as to the admission of evidence alleged to have been obtained involuntarily, had reasoned that, while the admission of such evidence could not be ruled out, this 'would be the consequence of a judicial decision, within a system at least on its face intended to exclude evidence which was not given voluntarily', and that it could not be said that such a decision 'would probably be wrong, still less that it would be manifestly unreasonable or arbitrary'.[101] In turn, their Lordships all held that

[97] Ibid, 592, para 262.

[98] Ibid, 592, para 262. [99] Ibid, 559–60, para 153. [100] Ibid, 560, para 153.

[101] Quoted at ibid, 558, para 151 (Lord Phillips). See, similarly, the quote from SIAC's decision at ibid, 570–1, para 199 (Lord Hoffmann).

SIAC had been entitled to hold that any deficiencies in Jordanian rules of criminal procedure and evidence did not meet 'the exacting test' of being 'of such significance as fundamentally to destroy the fairness of [the third appellant's] trial or, as SIAC put it, to amount to a total denial of the right to a fair trial'.[102] Lord Hoffmann stated:

> 201 ... [SIAC's] finding was that ... evidence would not be excluded [in the Jordanian courts] only because there was a real risk that it had been obtained by torture. In my opinion it is impossible to say that the application of such a rule would be a "flagrant denial of justice". There is in my opinion no authority for a rule that, in the context of the application of article 6 to a foreign trial, the risk of the use of evidence obtained by torture necessarily amounts to a flagrant denial of justice.
>
> 202 The effect of the decision of the House of Lords in *A v Secretary of State for the Home Department (No 2)* [2006] 2 AC 221 is that a real risk that a statement has been obtained by torture is not enough to make it inadmissible in proceedings before SIAC. The burden is upon the appellant to satisfy SIAC on a balance of probability that the statement was so obtained. Thus the effect of the Court of Appeal's decision is that SIAC ought to have held that the Jordanian court would be perpetrating a flagrant denial of justice if it did not exclude evidence which would have been admissible before SIAC itself. That is too much of a paradox to form part of a rational system of jurisprudence.[103]

The third appellant's appeal under article 6 was therefore dismissed.

In rejecting the third appellant's argument as to article 1F(c) of the Refugee Convention, SIAC had declined to adopt the reasoning of the Canadian Supreme Court in *Pushpanathan* and had applied instead the decision of the Immigration Appeal Tribunal in *KK v Secretary of State for the Home Department*[104] to hold that absence of the words 'prior to his admission to that country', which qualify article 1F(b) of the Refugee Convention, was deliberate and that there was no policy justification for extending them to sub-paragraphs (a) or (c). The law lords were persuaded by this reasoning,[105] with Lord Hoffmann being particularly unimpressed by the third appellant's submission:

> [T]he point seems to me to be hopeless. There is nothing in the language of paragraph (c) to suggest that it is confined to events which happened before refugee status was accorded. By contrast, paragraph (b) refers to the commission of a "serious non-political crime outside the country of refuge prior to his admission to that country as a refugee". If the draftsman of the Convention had

[102] Ibid, 560, para 154 (Lord Phillips). See also ibid, 571, para 201 (Lord Hoffmann), 584 and 586, paras 244 and 249 (Lord Hope), 587 and 590–1, paras 252 and 260 (Lord Brown), and 591–2, para 265 (Lord Mance).

[103] Ibid, 571.

[104] [2004] UKIAT 101, [2004] Imm AR 284.

[105] [2009] 2 WLR 512, 553, para 129 (Lord Phillips), 572, para 206 (Lord Hoffmann), 586, para 250 (Lord Hope), and 592, para 266 (Lord Mance).

wanted to confine paragraph (c) to prior events, appropriate language lay readily to hand.[106]

As it was, according to Lord Phillips and SIAC before him, the point was 'academic', since 'had [the third appellant] been entitled to invoke the provisions of the Refugee Convention in general he would have been prevented from relying upon the prohibition of refoulement imposed by article 33(1) by reason of the proviso in article 33(2)'.[107]

The House of Lords' decision is probably ultimately correct, although two features of the various speeches call for comment.

First, the two-stage test prescribed by Lord Phillips and endorsed by Lord Brown for the application of article 6 of the ECHR in so-called 'foreign' cases is, with respect, nonsense. There is no reason why the court should concern itself for the purposes of article 6 with the consequences of any unfair trial in the State of destination. For a start, the only statement by the ECtHR quoted by Lord Phillips which could possibly be read as supporting his view that an alien must establish a real risk 'not merely that he will suffer a flagrant breach of his article 6 rights, but that the consequence will be a serious violation of a substantive right or rights'[108] is an exceedingly brief allusion in *Tomic*, where the ECtHR did not exclude that an issue might exceptionally arise under article 6 in an expulsion case where the alien risks suffering a flagrant denial of a fair trial 'particularly where there is the risk of execution'.[109] Moreover, this fleeting dictum, if taken to mean what Lord Phillips takes it to mean, is itself plainly illogical. It may well be, as the other ECtHR authorities referred to by Lord Phillips illustrate, that an unfair trial leads in addition to the violation of other rights guaranteed by the Convention or one of its Protocols, but this is immaterial to the question whether article 6 will or will not be violated. As far as the latter is concerned, logically the sole question is whether there exists a real risk of a flagrant denial of the principles of a fair trial, as the straightforward approach adopted by Lords Hoffmann and Hope suggests. Next, even if one were to accept as correct Lord Phillips's twofold test, his second and more formal formulation of the necessary conditions (and the one enshrined in the head-note to the case), namely a real risk '(i) that there will be a fundamental breach of the principles of a fair trial guaranteed by article 6 and (ii) that this failure will lead to a miscarriage of justice that itself constitutes a flagrant violation of the victim's fundamental rights', is impenetrable. The reference

[106] Ibid, 572, para 206.

[107] Article 33(2) of the Refugee Convention provides that the benefit of the protection against *refoulement* afforded by article 33(1) of the Convention may not be claimed 'by a refugee whom there are reasonable grounds for regarding as a danger to the security of the country in which he is, or who, having been convicted by a final judgment of a particularly serious crime, constitutes a danger to the community of that country'.

[108] [2009] 2 WLR 512, 555.

[109] Ibid, para 138 (Lord Phillips), quoting *Tomic v United Kingdom*, Application No. 17837/03, Decision on Admissibility, 14 October 2003 (unreported), para 3.

in the second limb to 'a miscarriage of justice that itself constitutes a flagrant denial of the victim's fundamental rights' is gobbledegook. A flagrant denial of the right not to be executed or not to be tortured is not a 'miscarriage of justice', at least not as the term is ordinarily used. Any 'miscarriage of justice' is the preceding fundamental breach of the principles of a fair trial required under the first limb of the test. Lord Phillips's twofold test is rendered more curious still by the following qualification:

> A different approach will, however, be appropriate in an extradition case. There it is the prospective trial that is relied on to justify the deportation. If there is a real risk that the trial will be flagrantly unfair, that is likely to be enough of itself to prevent extradition regardless of the likely consequences of the unfair trial.[110]

The suggestion that the test to be applied in a 'foreign' case under article 6 depends on whether the alien is deported or extradited is more than passing strange. To top it all off, Lord Phillips appears to modify the second limb of his test in the act of applying it to the facts of the instant case. His Lordship previously demands 'a serious violation of a substantive right or rights'[111] or, synonymously, 'a flagrant violation of a victim's fundamental rights';[112] but he ultimately holds that the prospect of life and fifteen years' imprisonment respectively by way of punishment for the offences for which the third appellant was to be tried—neither of these penalties constituting in itself a violation of a Convention right—is 'sufficiently severe to satisfy the second limb of the test'.[113] (The 'sufficiently severe' standard derives from Lord Phillips's discussion of article 5, where, in perfectly circular fashion, his Lordship defines a 'flagrant breach' of that provision in the context of a 'foreign' case as 'a breach whose consequences are so severe that they override the right of a state to expel an alien from its territory'.[114])

The saving grace of all this is that, *pace* the head-note, there must be doubt as to whether Lord Phillips's twofold test forms part of the ratio of the House's decision. Lords Hoffmann and Hope do not adopt it, and Lord Mance declares himself in agreement with the reasoning specifically in paragraphs 133 to 135 of the speech of the senior law lord, whose twofold test is laid down instead in paragraphs 138 and 141. That said, Lord Mance also allies himself with the observations in paragraphs 158 to 160 of Lord Brown's speech, which include the latter's agreement with Lord Phillips that 'only where a prospectively unfair trial would be likely to lead to a serious violation of some substantive human right... would article 6 fall for consideration in a foreign case'.[115]

[110] [2009] 2 WLR 512, 556, para 139. [111] Ibid, 555, para 138. [112] Ibid, 556, para 141.

[113] Ibid, para 142. See, similarly, Lord Brown's suggestion, ibid, 590, para 259, that 'a substantial deprivation of liberty' would implicate article 6 in a 'foreign' case.

[114] Ibid, 553, para 132. For the link posited by Lord Phillips between the tests under articles 5 and 6 respectively, see ibid, para 133.

[115] Ibid, 590, para 259.

The second aspect of the Lords' judgment which is worthy of note is the peremptoriness of their respective dismissals of the argument under article 1F(c) of the Refugee Convention. The point, which has been discussed at considerable length in an earlier volume of this *Year Book*,[116] is actually far more difficult than their Lordships make out, depending as it does on much more than the superficially persuasive textual contrast between articles 1F(c) and (a) of the Convention, on the one hand, and article 1F(b), on the other. In the final analysis, it is probably only in the light of the recent practice of key Contracting States in the application of article 1F(c)—as reflected in UNHCR's 2003 'Guidelines on International Protection. Application of the Exclusion Clauses: Article 1F of the 1951 Convention relating to the Status of Refugees'[117] and related Background Note,[118] as well as in article 14(3)(a) of Council Directive 2004/83/EC of 29 April 2004[119]—that we can begin to discern weighty support for their Lordships' glib conclusion, although whether this represents the settled view of a sufficient body of the Contracting States to the Refugee Convention remains to be seen.

4. *R (Hassan) v Secretary of State for Defence*, 25 February 2009, [2009] EWHC 309 (Admin), unreported (QBD (Admin Ct), Walker J)

'Jurisdiction' within meaning of ECHR, article 1—extraterritorial application of ECHR—ECHR, article 2 (right to life)—USA-UK-Australia memorandum of understanding on transfer of custody of prisoners of war, civilian internees and civilian detainees taken during operations against Iraq—whether detainees transferred from custody of UK forces in Iraq to US military facility in Iraq pursuant to USA-UK-Australia memorandum of understanding within 'jurisdiction' of UK within meaning of ECHR, article 1

The case was yet another to which the involvement of UK armed forces in Iraq has given rise and, like the others, centred on whether the deceased could be said to have been within the jurisdiction of the UK, within the meaning of article 1 of the ECHR and for the purposes of the HRA, at the time of the alleged breach of his Convention rights. In April 2003, just after the invasion of Iraq, the deceased had been detained by UK troops, who took him to the US military facility at Camp Bucca, where—in a procedure provided for in a Memorandum of Understanding (MoU) between the US, the UK and Australia, applicable 'in the event of the transfer from

[116] See (2007) 78 *BYIL* 554–60.

[117] UNHCR Doc. HCR/GIP/03/05, 4 September 2003. The 2003 Guidelines supersede UNHCR's 1995 Guidelines and 1997 Note on the same topic, and represent a *volte-face* in relation to these and to paragraph 141 of UNHCR, *Handbook on Procedures and Criteria for Determining Refugee Status under the 1951 Convention and the 1967 Protocol relating to the Status of Refugees* (1979, re-edited 1992), UNHCR Doc. HCR/IP/4/Eng/REV.1.

[118] Background Note on the Application of the Exclusion Clauses: Article 1F of the 1951 Convention relating to the Status of Refugees, 4 September 2003.

[119] Council Directive 2004/83/EC of 29 April 2004 on minimum standards for the qualification and status of third country nationals or stateless persons as refugees or as persons who otherwise need international protection and the content of the protection granted, OJ L 304, 30/09/2004, 12–23.

the custody of either the US, UK or Australian forces to the custody of any of the other parties, any Prisoners of War, Civilian Internees, and Civilian Detainees taken during operations against Iraq'[120]—he was issued with a UK Internment Serial Number and guarded by US forces. The claimant, the deceased's brother, asserted and the respondent denied that, at the relevant time, the UK still had an Officer in Command, a Commanding Officer and a senior team at Camp Bucca. The deceased was released the following month. His dead body was found in September 2003 in the countryside, covered in bruises, hands bound with plastic wire and bearing eight gunshot wounds to the chest from a Kalashnikov assault rifle. The claimant sought an independent public inquiry into the death in accordance with article 2 (the right to life) of the ECHR, as secured to the deceased under English law by section 6 of the HRA.[121]

Walker J in the Administrative Court of the Queen's Bench Division dismissed the claim. At the time of his death, the deceased had not been within the jurisdiction of the UK, within the meaning of article 1 of the ECHR.

The claimant had argued that the arrest and detention of an individual, as an exercise of authority and control over that individual, constituted an exercise of jurisdiction for the purposes of article 1 of the ECHR. Walker J held that this was inconsistent with the House of Lords' judgment in *Al-Skeini* and its analysis of the relevant ECtHR case-law,[122] as well as with the observations of Lord Bingham in *Gentle* and of Laws LJ in *Al-Saadoon*.[123] In short, the claim had to fit within the confines of these cases. Insofar, then, as it related to the period before the deceased's detention at Camp Bucca, it plainly could not.[124] Insofar as it related to the period at Camp Bucca, it could succeed only if the camp were treated as akin to an embassy or consulate or ship or other craft, to which, as acknowledged in *Al-Skeini*, the ECHR had been held by the Strasbourg court to apply extraterritorially.[125] But the claimant's alternative submission to precisely this effect was inconsistent with the terms of the MoU.[126] While the MoU stated that the 'Detaining Power' (here, the UK) had sole responsibility for the classification of detainees for the purposes of the Third Geneva Convention, had full rights of access to detainees and could require the 'Accepting Power' (here, the US) immediately to return a detainee,[127]

[120] For the full text of the MoU, see [2009] EWHC 309 (Admin), para 9.

[121] See *R (Amin) v Secretary of State for the Home Department* [2003] UKHL 51, [2004] 1 AC 653, endorsing the relevant Strasbourg jurisprudence.

[122] [2009] EWHC 309 (Admin), para 22 and following paragraphs, referring to *R (Al-Skeini) v Secretary of State for Defence* [2007] UKHL 26, [2008] 1 AC 153, (2007) 78 *BYIL* 529–46 (HL).

[123] [2009] EWHC 309 (Admin), para 29, referring to *R (Gentle) v Prime Minister and others* [2008] UKHL 20, [2008] 1 AC 153, (2008) 79 *BYIL* 422–8 (HL) and *R (Al-Saadoon) v Secretary of State for Defence* [2009] EWCA Civ 7, [2009] 3 WLR 957, above pp 451–66 (CA (Civ Div)).

[124] [2009] EWHC 309 (Admin), para 30.

[125] Ibid.

[126] Ibid.

[127] Ibid, para 31, citing articles 9, 6 and 4 respectively of the MoU and articles 4 and 5 of Convention (III) relative to the Treatment of Prisoners of War, Geneva, 12 August 1949, 75 UNTS 135.

the Accepting Power was responsible under the instrument for maintaining and safeguarding those individuals transferred to its custody and for the 'accurate accountability' of those transferred, and was assigned 'primary jurisdiction' over 'breaches of disciplinary regulations and judicial offenses' committed after transfer.[128] His Lordship continued:

32 It is accepted . . . that the detaining power does not have sole control of the individual in question. To my mind the MOU goes much further than this. It is plain that the detaining power relinquishes, until such time as it requires return of the individual in question, responsibility for maintaining and safeguarding those transferred. Accountability in that regard is the responsibility of the accepting power. As regards adjudications concerning the individual's conduct after transfer to the accepting power the detaining power relinquishes to the accepting power primary jurisdiction. Overall this amounts to a legal regime in which the detaining power has no substantial control over the day to day living conditions of the individual in question.

33 Even if while [the deceased] was at Camp Bucca the UK had there an Officer in Command, a Commanding Officer and a senior team, that would not persuade me that Camp Bucca was a UK military establishment. Under the MOU it remained a US military establishment, and the presence or absence of UK personnel did not affect this. Nor, consistently with *Al-Skeini*, can Camp Bucca be regarded as akin to a UK embassy or ship or aircraft. The defining feature in each case is that the UK is able to impose its own law, and thus to insist on compliance with the ECHR. That feature is not present in Camp Bucca.

The analysis adopted by the House of Lords in *Al-Skeini* had the 'inevitable consequence' that the claim failed.[129]

Walker J's decision is undoubtedly correct, although more for the reasons spelled out in paragraph 33 than in paragraph 32. As the ECtHR's rejection of the Court of Appeal's conclusion on the 'jurisdiction' point in *Al-Saadoon* indicates,[130] the correct focus at the article 1 stage of the analysis in cases such as this is the extent of the respondent State's legal authority and physical control over the extraterritorial premises on which the claimant or deceased was detained, not on the terms of any inter-State bailment, as it were, of the detainee.

5. *Brown (a.k.a. Bajinja) v Government of Rwanda*, 14 April 2009, [2009] EWHC 770 (Admin), unreported (QBD (Admin Ct), Div Ct)

Extradition—Extradition Act 2003, sections 79(1)(b), 81(b), 87(1), 93(4) and 194—Human Rights Act 1998—European Convention on Human

[128] [2009] EWHC 309 (Admin), para 31, citing articles 2, 7 and 12 respectively of the MoU.

[129] [2009] EWHC 309 (Admin), para 35.

[130] See *Al-Saadoon and Mufdhi v United Kingdom*, Application No. 61498/08, Admissibility, 30 June 2009, (2009) 49 EHRR SE11.

Rights and Fundamental Freedoms 1950, article 6 (right to fair trial)—legitimate expectation—International Covenant on Civil and Political Rights 1966, article 14 (right to fair trial)—International Criminal Tribunal for Rwanda (ICTR)—whether extradition of accused génocidaires *to Rwanda barred by fair trial considerations*

The four appellants appealed both a District Judge's decision to send their case to the Secretary of State for the Home Department and the latter's order—pursuant to section 93(4) of the Extradition Act 2003 and four memoranda of understanding in common form ('the MoU') concluded on 14 September 2006 between the UK and Rwanda, one in respect of each appellant—that they be extradited to Rwanda to face charges of genocide in respect of their involvement in the atrocities there in 1994. The fourth appellant additionally sought judicial review of the Secretary of State's order. All four appellants were to be tried by the High Court of Rwanda pursuant to that State's Organic Law of 2007 concerning Transfer of Cases to the Republic of Rwanda from the International Criminal Tribunal for Rwanda and from Other States, article 13 of which secures to transferred defendants a range of fair trial rights analogous to those laid down in the various international human rights law conventions.

The appellants (all of them Hutu, three of them *bourgmestres* in 1994 and the other said to have been a close associate of the assassinated Hutu president Juvénal Habyarimana) argued that they would not receive a fair trial in a Rwanda where the Tutsi government of Paul Kagame held sway. In this regard, section 79(1)(b) of the Extradition Act obliges the judge conducting the extradition hearing to decide whether the person whose extradition to a so-called 'category 2 territory'[131] has been requested is barred by reason of 'extraneous considerations'; and section 81(b) provides that a person's extradition to a category 2 territory is barred by reason of extraneous considerations if it appears that 'if extradited he might be prejudiced at his trial . . . by reason of his race, religion, nationality, gender, sexual orientation or political opinions'. In accordance with section 87(1) of the Act, the judge must further decide whether the per-

[131] Rwanda was rendered the equivalent of a category 2 territory for present purposes by virtue of each MoU and certification by the Secretary of State under section 194 of the Extradition Act. Section 194 reads in relevant part:

> (1) This section applies if the Secretary of State believes that—
> (a) arrangements have been made between the United Kingdom and another territory for the extradition of a person to the territory, and
> (b) the territory is not a category 1 territory or a category 2 territory.
> (2) The Secretary of State may certify that the conditions in paragraphs (a) and (b) of subsection (1) are satisfied in relation to the extradition of the person.
> (3) If the Secretary of State issues a certificate under subsection (2) this Act applies in respect of the person's extradition to the territory as if the territory were a category 2 territory.
> (4) As applied by subsection (3), this Act has effect—
> [...]
> (b) with any other modifications specified in the certificate.
> (5) A certificate under subsection (2) in relation to a person is conclusive evidence that the conditions in paragraphs (a) and (b) of subsection (1) are satisfied in relation to the person's extradition.

son's extradition would be compatible with the Convention rights specified in the HRA, among them the right to a fair trial embodied in article 6 of the ECHR, under which the established test is whether there is a real risk that the person will suffer a flagrant denial of justice. In addition, the fourth appellant, in his application for judicial review, submitted that paragraph 4(d) of the relevant MoU—which specified that extradition would not be granted if the person in question 'would not receive the minimum guarantees in criminal proceedings, as contained in the International Covenant on Civil and Political Rights, article 14'—gave rise to an enforceable legitimate expectation that he would not be extradited if there was a risk that he might not be accorded, in the words of article 14, 'a fair and public hearing by a competent, independent and impartial tribunal established by law'. Moreover, and this was the thrust of the submission, paragraph 4(d) of the MoU did not, it was contended, require that the envisaged denial of fair trial rights be flagrant.

A Divisional Court (Laws and Sullivan LJJ) of the Administrative Court of the Queen's Bench Division allowed the appeals against both the judge's decision and the Secretary of State's order but dismissed the sole application for judicial review of the latter. Laws LJ delivered the judgment of the Court, to which both members had contributed.

Their Lordships prefaced their discussion of the appeals by noting the potential overlap between section 81(b) of the Extradition Act and article 6 of the ECHR, in that '[c]learly the kind of bias contemplated by s. 81(b), at least so far as it affects the trial process, might readily also constitute a denial of the right to "a fair and public hearing within a reasonable time by an independent and impartial tribunal" pursuant to Article 6'.[132] Since the submission based on section 81(b) added nothing to the article 6 claim,[133] they found it convenient to focus on the latter.[134]

Turning to begin with to the fourth appellant's argument that he enjoyed a legitimate expectation, to which paragraph 4(a) of the MoU gave rise, that he would not be extradited from the UK to Rwanda unless the fair trial standards of article 14 of the ICCPR could be assured, the first obstacle identified by the Divisional Court was that the Secretary of State was obliged by section 93(4) of the Extradition Act to order extradition unless she concluded that she was prohibited from doing so under any of the provisions mentioned in section 93(2), 'none of which refers to anything in the nature of a legitimate expectation such as might be generated by the terms of a MoU which constitutes extradition arrangements under s.194(1)(a) [of the Act]'.[135] The obligation under section 93(4) was unqualified, and it was 'elementary that a concrete statutory duty of this kind cannot be overridden by any claim based on legitimate expectation'.[136] Their Lordships continued:

[132] [2009] EWHC 770 (Admin), para 23. [133] Ibid, para 32.
[134] Ibid, para 23. [135] Ibid, para 29. [136] Ibid.

> [Counsel] for the Secretary of State submitted that the MoU constitutes a treaty between sovereign States, regulated by international law, which would not ordinarily give rise to rights enforceable in the domestic courts. However that may be (and given that the MoU, or more accurately these four MoUs, are specifically directed at these appellants, a different rule might apply), the international law context tends in our judgment to support [counsel]'s further submission that the ICCPR is referred to in paragraph 4(d) of the MoU because it is an international measure to which both States Parties to the MoU are signatories. In those circumstances it is not to be supposed that the Secretary of State [when certifying the MoU as a special extradition arrangement within the meaning of s. 194 of the Extradition Act] intended that the MoU would require a different test or standard for the fair trial guarantee than, advisedly, the appellants would enjoy under ECHR Article 6 mediated in this context by s. 87 of the 2003 Act. Had he done so, he would have introduced an appropriate modification pursuant to s. 194(4)(b).[137]

In the event, however, nothing turned on the point, since nothing turned on the adjective 'flagrant' once counsel for the government of Rwanda had conceded that, if the appellants' case was established, the breach of their rights under article 6 of the ECHR could indeed be characterized as such.

In assessing, then, whether there indeed existed a real risk of a flagrant denial of the appellants' right to a fair trial under article 6 of the ECHR, the Divisional Court had recourse to a wide range of materials, prominent among them decisions of the International Criminal Tribunal for Rwanda (ICTR) under rule 11*bis* of its Rules of Procedure and Evidence, to which it 'accord[ed] great respect'.[138] (Rule 11*bis* permits a Trial Chamber to order the transfer of a person indicted by the Tribunal to stand trial in, *inter alia*, the State in whose territory the relevant crime is alleged to have been committed,[139] on the proviso that the Chamber is satisfied that he or she will receive a fair trial.[140]) Starting with the appellants' allegations regarding 'the apprehension that witnesses who could give important evidence for the defence [would] be too afraid of possible reprisals to testify, or too afraid, for like reasons, to travel to Rwanda in order to do so',[141] their Lordships summarized the ICTR cases of *Munyakazi*,[142] *Kanyarukiga*,[143]

[137] Ibid, para 30. [138] Ibid, para 119.

[139] See ICTR Rules of Procedure and Evidence, rule 11*bis*(A)(i).

[140] Ibid, rule 11*bis*(B). The provision continues 'and that the death penalty will not be imposed or carried out'.

[141] [2009] EWHC 770 (Admin), para 37.

[142] *Prosecutor v Munyakazi*, ICTR-97-36-R11*bis*, Trial Chamber, Decision on the Prosecutor's Request for Referral of Case to the Republic of Rwanda: Rule 11*bis* of the Rules of Procedure and Evidence, 28 May 2008 and Appeals Chamber, Decision on Prosecution's Appeal against Decision on Referral under Rule 11*bis*, 8 October 2008.

[143] *Prosecutor v Kanyarukiga*, ICTR-02-78-R11*bis*, Trial Chamber, Decision on Prosecutor's Request for Referral to the Republic of Rwanda, 6 June 2008 and Appeals Chamber, Decision on the Prosecutor's Appeal against Decision on Referral under Rule 11*bis*, 30 October 2008.

Hategekimana,[144] *Gatete*[145] and *Kayishema*[146] by observing that 'the ICTR has not been satisfied that defendants charged with genocide and related offences will be fairly tried in Rwanda, having regard to the apprehension of serious difficulties as regards the availability and presentation of defence testimony' and that '[o]n this ground [the Tribunal] has consistently declined to order referral to Rwanda for trial in such cases under Rule 11 *bis*'.[147] 'In the result', having had regard to numerous other sources of evidence, the Court concluded 'that if they were extradited to face trial in the High Court of Rwanda, the appellants would suffer a real risk of a flagrant denial of justice by reason of their likely inability to adduce the evidence of supporting witnesses'.[148] As for the appellants' contention that the High Court of Rwanda was not an independent and impartial tribunal, as required by article 6 of the ECHR, their Lordships drew attention to the different conclusions reached on this point by the Trial and Appeals Chambers in the only ICTR case to consider the point, namely *Munyakazi*,[149] the Trial Chamber holding that there was a serious risk of governmental interference with the judiciary in Rwanda, the Appeals Chamber the contrary. Their Lordships were at pains to emphasize 'the limited evidential basis for the Appeals Chamber's conclusion in this respect',[150] drawing attention to the fact that it 'was based only on the record before it, and in particular on the failure [of the Trial Chamber] to mention any specific incidents of judicial interference'.[151] The Court, on the other hand, had been presented with what it considered persuasive evidence of at least one 'specific incident of judicial interference that the Appeals Chamber lacked',[152] which, along with other evidence, enabled it to conclude that if the appellants were returned there would be a real risk that they would suffer a flagrant denial of justice.[153]

[144] *Prosecutor v Hategekimana*, ICTR-00-55B-R11*bis*, Trial Chamber, Decision on the Prosecutor's Request for Referral of the Case of Ildephonse Hategekimana to Rwanda: Rule 11*bis* of the Rules of Procedure and Evidence, 19 June 2008 and Appeals Chamber, Decision on the Prosecutor's Appeal against Decision on Referral under Rule 11*bis*, 4 December 2008.

[145] *Prosecutor v Gatete*, ICTR-00-61-R11*bis*, Trial Chamber, Decision on Prosecutor's Request for Referral to the Republic of Rwanda, 17 November 2008.

[146] *Prosecutor v Kayishema (Fulgence)*, ICTR-01-67-R11*bis*, Trial Chamber, Decision on the Prosecutor's Request for Referral of Case to the Republic of Rwanda: Rule 11*bis* of the Rules of Procedure and Evidence, 16 December 2008.

[147] [2009] EWHC 770 (Admin), para 47. The court further noted, ibid: 'Courts in Europe have followed the ICTR. Thus on 23 October 2008 the Toulouse Court of Appeal, in declining to order extradition to Rwanda in *Bivugarabago*, explicitly followed the ICTR in *Munyakazi* and *Kanyarukiga* in relation to the safeguard and protection of defence witnesses. A like decision was arrived at on 3 November 2008 by the Appellate Court of Frankfurt am Main in *Mbarushimana*. There followed *Senyamuhara* in the Mamoudzou Court of Appeal [on Mayotte] on 14 November 2008 and *Kamali* in the Court of Appeal of Paris on 10 December 2008. Even more recently, in *Kamana*, the Lyon Court of Appeal on 9 January 2009 refused to extradite the defendant on like grounds. All these judgments relied heavily on extant decisions of the ICTR.'

[148] [2009] EWHC 770 (Admin), para 66.

[149] Ibid, para 77. [150] Ibid, para 78.

[151] Ibid, para 119. [152] Ibid. [153] Ibid, para 121.

The Divisional Court's judgment is a first in two respects. It is the first time that an English court has refused extradition by reference to article 6 of the ECHR. It is also the first time that an English court has had recourse to the case-law of an international court or tribunal for evidentiary purposes. Such recourse is legitimate, provided the court exercises (as the Divisional Court did here) its own judgment as to the probative value to be accorded the evidence in question, and is on a par with the use to which the International Court of Justice put the judgments of the International Criminal Tribunal for the former Yugoslavia (ICTY) in *Application of the Genocide Convention.*[154] There the Court declared that it 'attache[d] the utmost importance to the factual . . . findings made by the ICTY', and stated that it 'should in principle accept as highly persuasive relevant findings of fact made by the Tribunal at trial, unless of course they have been upset on appeal'.[155] In the present case, the Divisional Court's decision to differ from the conclusion reached by the ICTR Appeals Chamber in *Munyakazi* as to the independence and impartiality of the High Court of Rwanda is rational and defensible.

Their Lordships' ruling on the judicial review point represents the third time now that the superior courts of England and Wales—seemingly constrained by counsel's submissions in each case—have disposed of a *Teoh*-style argument[156] without examining in the first place its soundness in law, despite the fact that in both *Chundawadra*[157] and *Behluli*[158] the Court of Appeal flatly rejected the contention that entry by the executive into a treaty could give rise to a legitimate expectation that the former would act in accordance with the latter. That the ratification of a treaty by the government could, subject to any indications to the contrary, create a legitimate expectation that the treaty's terms would be applied in any governmental dealing with an individual affected by it was at least entertained by two notable members of the Court of Appeal (Lord Woolf MR and Hobhouse LJ) in *Ahmed and Patel*,[159] although no legitimate expectation arose on the facts, having been contraindicated by the clearly stated policy of the Secretary of State. Similarly, in *Lika*, the proposition was neither accepted nor rejected in the abstract by Latham LJ; in either event, however, it was overridden both by the clearly stated policy of the Secretary of State and by the fact that the treaty in question was 'not concerned directly with the provision of rights or entitlements to individual[s]'.[160] Nor did the Privy

[154] *Application of the Genocide Convention (Bosnia and Herzegovina v Serbia and Montenegro), Judgment*, 26 February 2007.

[155] Ibid, paras 403 and 223 respectively.

[156] See *Minister for Immigration and Ethnic Affairs v Teoh*, 104 ILR 460 (High Ct of Australia, 1995), 474 (Mason CJ and Deane J).

[157] *R v Immigration Appeal Tribunal Ex parte Chundawadra* [1988] Imm AR 161.

[158] *R v Secretary of State for the Home Department Ex parte Behluli* [1998] Imm AR 407.

[159] *R v Secretary of State for the Home Department, ex parte Ahmed and Patel* [1998] INLR 570, 583 (Lord Woolf MR) and 592 (Hobhouse LJ), (1998) 69 *BYIL* 330–1 (CA (Civ Div)).

[160] *R (Lika) v Secretary of State for the Home Department* [2002] EWCA Civ 1855, para 26, (2002) 73 *BYIL* 434–9 (CA (Civ Div)).

Council (not, of course, an English court) decide the issue either way in *Thomas v Baptiste*, although it did emphasize, as the High Court of Australia emphasized in *Teoh*, that '[e]ven if a legitimate expectation founded on the provisions of an unincorporated treaty may give procedural protection, it cannot by itself...give substantive protection, for this would be tantamount to the indirect enforcement of the treaty'.[161] 'In this sense', the Board continued, 'legitimate expectations do not create binding rules of law', with the result that 'a decision-maker is free to act inconsistently with the expectation in any particular case provided that he acts fairly towards those likely to be affected'.[162] While the last is patently correct, it can only be hoped that the Supreme Court has the opportunity to rule on the basic principle in the not-too-distant future.[163]

What of the Divisional Court's cryptic aside that, 'given that the MoU, or more accurately [the] four MoUs, are specifically directed at these appellants, a different rule [from that which dictates that a treaty cannot give rise to rights and obligations under English law unless and until Parliament enacts legislation giving effect to it] might apply'[164]? One source of inspiration may have been the most obiter of dicta by Lawrence Collins J in *Lika*, to which Latham LJ's reference to the rights of individuals was seemingly a nod, where his Lordship mused that 'development[s] in the relaxation of the basic rule of United Kingdom constitutional law that an unincorporated treaty cannot confer rights or impose duties in domestic law may yet lead to the creation of an estoppel against the Crown in favour of individuals in the case of unincorporated treaties dealing with human rights which are plainly intended to benefit individuals'.[165] Similarly, in *In re McKerr*, Lord Steyn remarked, to no immediate end (the argument never have been put to the House) and quoting Lawrence Collins J writing in a non-judicial capacity, that maybe 'one day the courts will come to the view that it will not infringe the constitutional principle to create an estoppel against the Crown in favour of individuals in human rights cases'.[166] Lord Steyn's digression was picked up in *Pepushi*, where the Divisional Court, *à propos*

[161] [2000] 1 AC 1, 25. [162] Ibid.

[163] For the position under Scots law, see *Ibrahim v Secretary of State for the Home Department*, 2002 SLT 1150 (OH, Lord Carloway) and *Khairandish v Secretary of State for the Home Department*, 2003 SLT 1358, (2003) 74 *BYIL* 464–71, (OH, Lord Drummond Young). In Australia, the decision in *Teoh* was subsequently overridden by the government: see 'International Treaties and the High Court Decision in *Teoh*', Joint Statement by the Minister for Foreign Affairs, Senator Gareth Evans, and the Attorney-General, Michael Lavarch, 10 May 1995, <http://www.dfat.gov.au/media/releases/foreign/1995/m44.html>, as replaced by 'The Effect of Treaties in Administrative Decision Making', Joint Statement by the Minister for Foreign Affairs (Alexander Downer) and the Attorney-General and Minister for Justice (Daryl Williams), 27 February 1997, <http://www.lib.monash.edu.au/law/teohjs.htm>, both explicitly constituting 'executive indication to the contrary' for the purposes and in the words of *Teoh*. *Teoh* has also been called into question by the High Court of Australia itself in *Re Minister for Immigration and Multicultural Affairs; Ex parte Lam* (2003) 195 ALR 502.

[164] [2009] EWHC 770 (Admin), para 30.

[165] [2002] EWCA Civ 1855, para 31.

[166] [2004] 1 WLR 807, 822, para 49, (2004) 75 *BYIL* 411–9 (HL), quoting L Collins, 'Foreign Relations and the Judiciary' (2002) 51 *International and Comparative Law Quarterly* 485, 497.

once more of nothing (being bound by long-established precedent and in the absence of proper argument on the point), noted 'the cogent arguments advanced that, in the field of human rights treaties, there may be a limitation, whether by estoppel or otherwise, on the ability of the Executive to act against an individual where that action is in breach of the obligations undertaken by the Executive under international human rights treaties'.[167] Four times nothing, however, remains nothing. There is no convincing reason why the separation of powers, which prohibits executive law-making pure and simple, should be swept aside merely because the subject-matter of an unincorporated treaty is the rights of individuals. It is nothing to the point to say that an executive which enters into a treaty conferring individual rights would be fettering only itself. The creation of individual rights under English law is the constitutional province of Parliament and, in constitutionally appropriate areas of the common law, of the courts.

In terms of the decision's practical consequences, the four appellants were set free, since English law as it stood at the time did not permit them to be tried in the English courts on charges of genocide committed in Rwanda in 1994. The Genocide Act 1969, repealed by the International Criminal Court Act 2001, had made no provision for the extraterritorial, let alone universal ambit of the crime of genocide (within the meaning of Article II of the Genocide Convention[168]) established for the purposes of English law by section 1(1) of the Act; and in accordance with the usual canon of construction of the English criminal law, the result was that, in 1994, genocide was a crime under English law only if committed in the UK. The International Criminal Court Act took things further, making genocide and conduct ancillary to genocide crimes under English law also if committed outside the UK by a UK national or UK resident,[169] the latter term being taken to include a person who becomes a UK resident after the commission of the impugned act;[170] but the changes took effect only from 1 September 2001.

On 12 November 2009, however, in response to what critics referred to as an 'impunity gap',[171] Parliament enacted section 70 of the Coroners' and Justice Act 2009, which amends the International Criminal Court Act by inserting a section 65A, which has the effect of making the crimes of genocide and conduct ancillary to it committed outside the UK by a UK national or UK resident (including subsequent resident)—as provided for in Part 5 of the International Criminal Court Act—criminal

[167] *R (Pepushi) v Crown Prosecution Service* [2004] EWHC 798, para 29.

[168] Paris, 9 December 1948, 78 UNTS 277. Genocide was defined in s 1(1) of the Genocide Act by express reference to Article II of the Convention, as scheduled to the Act.

[169] International Criminal Court Act, ss 51(1) and (2)(b) and ss 52(1) and (4)(b) respectively. Sections 51(2)(b) and 52(4)(b) further provide that extraterritorial genocide and conduct ancillary to it is criminal under English law if committed by a person subject to UK service jurisdiction.

[170] Ibid, s 68.

[171] See e.g. African Rights and Redress, Open Letter to UK Government on Rwanda Genocide, London, 8 May 2009.

under English law from 1 January 1991.[172] Section 70 of the Coroners' and Justice Act also expands the meaning to be given to the term 'United Kingdom resident' for the purposes of Part 5 of the International Criminal Court Act[173] to encompass persons who might not as a general rule fall within the legal definition of a UK resident, such as those like three of the four appellants (the other being a naturalized UK national) 'who would be liable to removal or deportation from the United Kingdom but cannot be removed or deported because of section 6 of the Human Rights Act 1998'.[174] In addition, on 11 February 2010, the UK and Rwanda concluded a prisoner transfer agreement[175] which will permit the transfer to Rwanda, at Rwanda's request and without the consent of the sentenced person, of Rwandan nationals sentenced in the UK either before or after the agreement's entry into force. It seems there is more than one way to skin a cat.

6. *Symeou v Public Prosecutor's Office at the Court of Appeals, Patras, Greece*, 1 May 2009, [2009] EWHC 897 (Admin), [2009] 1 WLR 2384 (QBD (Admin Ct), Div Ct)

Extradition—abuse of process—European Council Framework Decision on the European arrest warrant—Extradition Act 2003, Part 1—whether abuse of process jurisdiction of District Judge in extradition hearing extending to alleged abuse by police of requesting State—whether District Judge in extradition hearing pursuant to European arrest warrant permitted to inquire into conformity of foreign domestic warrant with foreign domestic law

The defendant resisted his surrender, under Part I of the Extradition Act 2003 and on the basis of a European arrest warrant,[176] to the Greek prosecuting authorities, arguing, *inter alia*, that the District Judge should exercise his implied jurisdiction—recognized in *R (Bermingham) v Director of the Serious Fraud Office*[177] and *R (United States of America) v Bow Street Magistrates Court*[178] (the 'Tollman case')—to discharge the

[172] Coroners' and Justice Act, ss 70(1) and (3).

[173] See ibid, ss 70(1) and (4), inserting into the International Criminal Court Act a section 67A.

[174] International Criminal Court Act (as amended), s 67A(1)(g).

[175] Agreement between the Government of the United Kingdom of Great Britain and Northern Ireland and the Government of the Republic of Rwanda on the Transfer of Sentenced Persons, Kigali, 11 February 2010, Rwanda No. 1 (2010), Cm 7839 (not yet in force).

[176] See European Council Framework Decision of 13 June 2002 on the European arrest warrant and the surrender procedures between Member States, Decision 2002/584/JHA, OJ 2002 L 190 18.07.2002, 1. Although, as made clear in recital 5 of the preamble, the effect of the Framework Decision is to abolish extradition between Member States and to replace it with a system of surrender between judicial authorities, Part 1 of the Extradition Act 2003 persists in referring to the procedure as 'extradition'. As explained by Lord Hope in *Office of the King's Prosecutor, Brussels v Cando Armas* [2005] UKHL 67, [2005] 3 WLR 1079, 1090, para 21, (2005) 76 *BYIL* 603–15 (HL), the regime provided for in Part 1 'is really just a system of backing of warrants'.

[177] [2006] EWHC 200 (Admin), [2007] QB 727, (2006) 77 *BYIL* 464–9 (QBD (Admin Ct), Div Ct).

[178] [2006] EWHC 2256 (Admin), [2007] 1 WLR 1157, (2006) 77 *BYIL* 520–3 (QBD (Admin Ct), Div Ct).

defendant where the latter's extradition would constitute an abuse of the court's process. The defendant alleged that the Greek police had used violence and intimidation to obtain from two of his friends wrongly incriminating statements, which would be admissible at trial, and that other eyewitness statements incriminating him had been manufactured or manipulated by the Greek police and were demonstrably unreliable. He also argued that the Greek prosecutor knew that the Greek arrest warrant on which the European arrest warrant had been based was invalid on account of its issue in breach of a requirement of the Greek Code of Criminal Procedure enacted for the protection of suspects. In response, the deputy prosecutor of the Patras Court of Appeals challenged the correctness of the defendant's reading of the relevant statutory provision, which he took not to require the procedural safeguard in question in cases such as the defendant's. The District Judge declined to exercise his abuse of process jurisdiction.

On appeal to a Divisional Court (Laws LJ and Ouseley J) of the Administrative Court of the Queen's Bench Division, the Court dismissed the defendant's appeal. Ouseley J delivered the judgment of the Court.

As regards the defendant's reliance on the alleged conduct of the Greek police to ground his argument, Ouseley J stated:

33 In our judgment, the reason why [the police-centred element of] the abuse argument cannot succeed is this. The focus of this implied jurisdiction is the abuse of the requested state's duty to extradite those who are properly requested, and who are unable to raise any of the statutory bars to extradition. The residual abuse jurisdiction identified in *R (Bermingham) v Director of the Serious Fraud Office* and the Tollman case concerns abuse of the extradition process by the prosecuting authority. We emphasise those latter two words. That is the language of those cases. It is the good faith of the requesting authorities which is at issue because it is their request coupled with their perverted intent and purpose which constitutes the abuse. If the authorities of the requesting state seek the extradition of someone for a collateral purpose, or when they know that the trial cannot succeed, they abuse the extradition processes of the requested state.

34 The abuse jurisdiction of the requested state does not extend to considering misconduct or bad faith by the police of the requesting state in the investigation of the case or the preparation of evidence for trial.

35 The reason for the distinction lies in the respective functions of the courts of the requested and requesting state in the European arrest warrant framework. The former are entitled to ensure that their duties and the functions under the Extradition Act 2003 Part I are not being abused. It is the exclusive function of the latter to try the issues relevant to the guilt or otherwise of the individual. This necessarily includes deciding what evidence is admissible, and what weight should be given to particular pieces of evidence having regard to the way in which an investigation was carried out. It is for the trial court in the requesting

state to find the facts about how statements were obtained, which may go to admissibility or weight, both of which are matters for the court conducting the trial. It is the function of that court to decide whether evidence was improperly obtained and if so what the consequences for the trial are. It is for the trial court to decide whether its own procedures have been breached.

36 As those issues are for decision by the trial court in the requesting state, it cannot be an abuse of the extradition process of the requested state for such an issue to be shown to exist and for its resolution to be available only in the courts of the requesting state. The courts of the requested state cannot decide, let alone do so on partial and incomplete evidence, what it is for courts of the requesting state within the European arrest warrant framework to decide about such issues and with what effect on the trial.[179]

The circumstances of the instant case 'illustrate[d] the point':[180]

[The defendant]'s submission would require the Greek authorities, as part of the extradition process, to call evidence before the district judge to show that the statements of the... defendant's friends were not obtained in fact in breach of Greek law, and if they had been, he would also then have to decide whether or not they should be admissible in a Greek court. He would also have to decide whether the way in which the statements of the other five witnesses was taken involved any manipulation of the evidence, an issue which could well be bound up with the reliability of all of the witnesses. He would then have to decide what the Greek court is better placed to decide as part of a trial, on their admissibility or weight. This form of partial second guessing about how the trial court would or should decide issues properly before it, would run clean counter to the intentions of Part I of the Extradition Act 2003.[181]

The Court also dismissed the strand of the argument based on the alleged invalidity of the Greek arrest warrant. In *Cando Armas* and *Dabas*, Lord Hope had made it clear that a District Judge 'need not concern himself' with the criminal law of the requesting State in extradition proceedings pursuant to a European arrest warrant,[182] 'the thrust [being] that he should not do so, except in true abuse of extradition process cases, and should not do so, not as a matter of discretion, but as a matter of jurisdiction'.[183] Such an inquiry was 'simply not his task'.[184] Ouseley J continued:

52 The circumstances of this appeal illustrate the point, and the way in which the contrary view would undermine the legislative intention. The context is an extradition case, pursuant to what is intended to be a simplified decision-making process in an area of mutual recognition of judicial decisions in criminal matters. There is a disagreement among the Greek lawyers about what the Greek Code of

[179] [2009] 1 WLR 2384, 2395–6, citations omitted. [180] Ibid, para 37. [181] Ibid.
[182] Ibid, 2400, quoting *Dabas v High Court of Justice in Madrid, Spain* [2007] UKHL 6, [2007] 2 AC 31, 53–4, para 53 (Lord Hope), (2007) 78 *BYIL* 515–20 (HL), quoting in turn *Office of the King's Prosecutor, Brussel v Cando Armas* [2006] 2 AC 1, 18, para 30 (Lord Hope).
[183] [2009] 1 WLR 2384, 2400, para 51. [184] Ibid.

Criminal Procedure requires. It would be quite extraordinary for the district judge to hear evidence from competing experts on Greek law, including the prosecutor of the requesting state, so as to rule as a matter of fact on what Greek law was, then to find whether in fact the actions of the prosecutor had breached whatever the law was found to be, then to rule on the effect on the validity of the warrant of a breach of its code, each of which might be quite uncertain in Greek law, and then to rule on whether that caused the European arrest warrant to be invalid as a matter of English law implementing the [European Council] Framework Decision [on the European arrest warrant]. And if extradition then ensued, the matter would be dealt with by the Greek courts, who would be unlikely to regard the views of the English courts on Greek law as of more than passing interest. If it did not ensue, the Greek courts would never have the chance to put it right.

53 The district judge, on this basis and he recognised this was probably right, should not have considered evidence about Greek domestic law. If he had ruled that on the facts that there had been a breach of domestic law and that that in Greek law invalidated the domestic warrant, he would have trespassed beyond his functions. . . .[185]

His Lordship recalled that all of this was 'of course subject to the possibility that there ha[d] been an abuse of the extradition process by the prosecutor'; but, given that the prosecutor plainly took the view that Greek law did not require the procedural safeguard referred to by the defendant, the latter had not even begun to prove the requisite bad faith.[186]

The Divisional Court's emphatic view that a District Judge in extradition proceedings pursuant to a European arrest warrant has no business enquiring into the domestic lawfulness of the original, domestic warrant on which the European warrant is based is supported by a consideration of the foreign act of State doctrine, in accordance with which an English court will not enquire into the conformity with national (or international) law of the sovereign acts of a foreign State within its own territory.[187] Indeed, while the context provided by the purpose and preambular recitals of the European Council Framework Decision on the European arrest warrant lend added weight to the argument for deference on the part of the District Judge, the Divisional Court's statements in the present case could be applied, *mutatis mutandis*, to extradition requests proper by non-EU States. While it remains open at all times for the defendant to establish, on the basis of 'very cogent evidence', that the prosecuting authority in the requesting State has 'attempt[ed] to pervert the system to obtain an extradition which could not otherwise have been maintained, or to obtain the return of the defendant for some collateral purpose',[188] the District Judge may not sit in judgment on the domestic lawfulness as such of the conduct of a foreign prosecuting authority within its own territory.

[185] Ibid, 2401. [186] Ibid, para 54.
[187] See *Duke of Brunswick v King of Hanover* (1848) 2 HL Cas 1 and cases since.
[188] [2009] 1 WLR 2384, 2401, para 54.

7. *Wilhelm Finance Inc v Ente Administrador Del Astillero Rio Santiago*, 19 May 2009, [2009] EWHC 1074 (Comm), unreported (QBD (Comm Ct), Teare J)

State immunity—State Immunity Act 1978, section 12 and sections 14(1) and (2)—separate entities—service of process—whether entity a department of government of foreign State or a separate entity within meaning of section 14(1) of Act

Section 14(1) of the State Immunity Act 1978 ('SIA') specifies that the immunities and privileges conferred by Part I of the Act apply to any foreign or commonwealth State other than the UK and that references to a State include references to, *inter alia* and as referred to in subsection (c), any department of the government of that State. Section 14(1) goes on to make clear that references in the Act to a State do not include 'any entity (hereafter referred to as a "separate entity") which is distinct from the executive organs of the government of the State and capable of suing or being sued'. The defendant Argentine shipyard applied to have set aside an order permitting service of proceedings on it, arguing that, as 'a State-owned entity, within the definition of a State for the purposes of the State Immunity Act 1978)',[189] service on it was to be effected in accordance with section 12 of the Act, which stipulates that '[a]ny writ or other document required to be served for instituting proceedings against a State shall be served by being transmitted through the Foreign and Commonwealth Office to the Ministry of Foreign Affairs of the State'. The order had been granted on the basis that the defendant was a separate entity within the meaning of section 14(1) of the Act and not a department of the government of a State within the meaning of section 14(1)(c), and as such did not qualify as a State for the purposes of section 12.

Teare J, in the Commercial Court of the Queen's Bench Division, dismissed the application. The defendant was a separate entity, not a department of the Argentine State, with the consequence that service could be effected in a manner other than that specified in section 12 of the SIA.

His Lordship, after citing the 'two qualities which a separate entity must possess',[190] namely that it be distinct from the executive organs of the government of the State and be capable of suing or being sued, looked to the relevant English authorities for guidance on the matter. He referred to Lord Wilberforce's elaboration of the distinction between *acta jure imperii* and *acta jure gestionis* in *I° Congreso del Partido*; quoted his Lordship's observation that 'state controlled enterprises, with legal personality, ability to trade and to enter into contracts of private law, though wholly subject to the control of their state, [were] a well known feature of the modern commercial scene'; and noted that, in that case, a State trading enterprise was held not to be a department of the Cuban State notwithstanding that it was subject to direction and control by the State,

[189] [2009] EWHC 1074 (Comm), para 1.
[190] Ibid, para 5.

which also provided all the funds necessary for its operation.[191] He continued:

In *Propend Finance v Sing* the Court of Appeal said that the concept of *acta iure imperii* was relevant to a determination of what bodies were part of the "State" and the "government" for the purposes of s.14(1) of the State Immunity Act. "Government" should be given a broad meaning commensurate with the concept of *acta jure imperii*. I therefore approach the phrase "department of government" and the phrase "executive organs of government" in s. 14(1) with that guidance in mind.[192]

His Lordship next recalled the observation of the Court of Appeal in *Trendtex* that 'where an entity has been created by the state the absence of a clear expression of an intent to confer the status of a government department was . . . a pointer to the conclusion that such status was not the intent of the state'.[193] He continued once more:

10 Finally, in *The Altair* [2008] 2 Lloyd's Rep 90 Gross J had to consider whether the Grain Board of Iraq was a department of the Ministry of Trade of the Republic of Iraq or was a separate entity. At paragraph 64 he cited the following principles from *Dick[in]son, Lindsay and Loonam, State Immunity: Selected Materials and Commentary*:

a) The characterisation of a party to proceedings as a department of the government of a foreign sovereign State depends not on any single factor, but on a consideration of all relevant circumstances.

b) The status of the party under the law of its home state is one relevant factor but is not decisive. Nor is the presence of separate legal personality itself decisive against characterising a party as a department of government.

c) A detailed analysis of the constitution, function, powers and activities of the party and of its relationship with the state is likely to be essential. The existence of State control is not, however, a sufficient criterion.

d) The courts are likely to exercise caution before treating a party having separate legal personality as a department of government.

11 Gross J added:

The authors go on to say that there should not be a "judicial no-man's land"; the principles to be applied in determining whether an entity is a "department of government" should mirror those for determining whether the entity is a "separate entity".

[191] Ibid, para 7.
[192] Ibid, para 8, referring to *Propend Finance Pty Ltd v Sing*, 111 ILR 611 (CA, 1997).
[193] [2009] EWHC 1074 (Comm), para 8.

Teare J then considered a range of evidence, including the 1993 decree of the governor of Buenos Aires province which established the defendant 'as a State-Owned Economically Independent Entity'.[194] While the decree did not state expressly whether the entity was capable of suing or being sued, his Lordship, after examining a variety of factors (including the fact that the entity had been sued in two recent cases in Argentina) decided on the balance of probabilities that this was the case.[195] As for whether the entity was distinct from the executive organs of the government of Argentina, his Lordship, after quoting from the speech of Lord Goff in *Kuwait Airways* to support his statement that 'the functions of the Defendant [did] not appear...to fall within Lord Wilberforce's description [in *I° Congreso del Partido*] of sovereign or public acts',[196] addressed an objection to his analysis:

It was submitted on behalf of the Defendant that the commercial nature of the specific transaction between the parties was 'completely irrelevant' because states and state entities engage in commercial activities without altering their status as sovereign entities. However, the nature of the Defendant's functions have to be examined in order to decide whether the Defendant is, within the meaning of s. 14 of the State Immunity Act 1978 as explained by the English authorities to which I have referred, a department of government or an entity distinct from the executive organs of the government of the state.[197]

He continued:

50...I consider, on the balance of probabilities, that it is not a department of government and is an entity distinct from the executive organs of the government of the State, for these reasons:

i) The Defendant was created with the object of managing the shipyard (or more accurately the assets transferred by the national to the provincial state) until the time when the shipyard was privatised.
ii) It determines and carries out the commercial policy of the shipyard (see article 5 of the 1993 decree).
iii) It has power "to act either in the public or private areas" (see article 2 of the 1993 decree) and does so.
iv) The Defendant is...'an organisation aimed at the production of goods and services'.
v) The work the Defendant does is not work of a type associated with the executive organs of government. It is on the contrary work such as a private company might do.

51 I have not overlooked the facts that the Defendant is owned by the state, that the government nominates the board of directors, that the Chief of Cabinet of

[194] Ibid, para 17. [195] Ibid, paras 41 and 42.
[196] Ibid, para 47, quoting *Kuwait Airways Corporation v Iraqi Airways Company* [1995] 1 WLR 1147, 1160 (Lord Goff), (1995) 66 *BYIL* 496–501 (HL).
[197] [2009] EWHC 1074 (Comm), para 49.

the Province of Buenos Aires was assigned the responsibilities of the President of the board, that the Defendant is responsible to the government through the Ministry of Production or that financial support is provided by the government. These factors show that the entity is "of the state" but the English authorities to which I have referred make clear that such characteristics are insufficient to make the Defendant a department of government or an entity which is not distinct from the executive organs of government of the state in circumstances where its functions or activities are those which a private company might have in trade or commerce.

'Having considered,... on the material placed before the court, the constitution, function, powers and activities of the Defendant and of its relationship with the state', Teare J 'concluded that the Defendant [was] a separate entity within the meaning of s. 14 of the State Immunity Act 1978'.[198] It followed that the order for service of proceedings was not contrary to section 12 of the SIA.

Teare J's decision is correct, although his reference to the sovereign or other character of the entity's activities as an index of its status as either a department of the government of a foreign State or a separate entity of that State is an unhelpful gloss on the unvarnished words of section 14(1) of the SIA. To the extent that the Court of Appeal made such reference in *Propend*, it was not in the context of the distinction between departments and separate entities[199] (and, as it was, was somewhat misguided). A legal person having some organizational and/or functional relation to a foreign State is a separate entity of that State within the meaning of section 14(1) of the SIA quite simply as long as, although perhaps entrusted with public functions,[200] it is distinct from the executive organs of the government of that State and is capable of suing and being sued in its own right.[201] In the same way that the characterization of its activities as *jure imperii* or *jure gestionis* is irrelevant to whether the government of a foreign State enjoys that status for the purposes of section 14(1)(b) of the SIA and to whether a department of that government is considered such

[198] Ibid, para 52.

[199] The question in *Propend* was whether an individual police official fell within the definition of a State in SIA, s 14(1). The Court of Appeal noted, 111 ILR 611, 669, that '[t]he concept of a "separate entity" obviously has its place in the overall scheme [of section 14] but has no application in the present case'.

[200] See, in this light, article 27(1) of the European Convention on State Immunity, Basle, 16 May 1972, ETS No 74, to which the concept of a separate entity in section 14(1) of the SIA was intended to give effect.

[201] English private international law dictates that the existence and powers of a body corporate are determined by the law of the State of incorporation or, in the case of public bodies corporate, by the law of the State where the relevant constitutive instrument was promulgated: see L Collins (ed), *Dicey, Morris & Collins on the Conflict of Laws* (14th edn, Sweet & Maxwell, London, 2006) paras 30R-099 and following; A Briggs, *The Conflict of Laws* (2nd edn, Oxford University Press, Oxford, 2008) 265. As such, the question whether an entity enjoys the capacity to sue and be sued and, insofar as it is relevant to whether it is distinct from the executive organs of the relevant foreign State, the question whether an entity enjoys legal personality distinct from those executive organs fall to be determined by reference to the law of the foreign State in question.

for the purposes of section 14(1)(c), so too is it immaterial to whether, under section 14(1), an entity is a separate entity of a State, rather than a department of its government. In the case of a separate entity, the characterization of its acts is relevant only to the subsequent question whether it enjoys immunity from proceedings by virtue of section 14(2) of the SIA, which provides that, although not counting as 'the State' under section 14(1), a separate entity will be immune from the jurisdiction of the courts of the UK if the proceedings relate to anything done by it in the exercise of sovereign authority (that is, if the conduct is *jure imperii*) and if a State would have been immune in the same circumstances (that is, if none of the statutory exceptions to immunity enumerated in sections 2 to 11 of the SIA applies).[202] It is telling in this regard that the passage from Lord Goff's speech in *Kuwait Airways* quoted by Teare J towards the conclusion of his judgment[203] is taken from Lord Goff's discussion of section 14(2), not section 14(1), of the SIA, 'there being no doubt that IAC [was] a separate entity of the State of Iraq'.[204]

8. *R (K) v Her Majesty's Treasury*, 22 May 2009, [2009] EWHC 1643 (Admin), unreported (QBD (Admin Ct), Burton J)

United Nations Security Council resolutions 1267 (1999), 1333 (2000), 1390 (2002) and 1452 (2002)—United Nations Act 1946—Al-Qaida and Taliban (United Nations Measures) Order 2006—asset freezing—humanitarian exemptions—whether requirement in licence granted under Al-Qaida and Taliban (United Nations Measures) Order 2006 to account for all cash expenditure ultra vires *Order*

United Nations Security Council resolutions 1267 (1999) of 15 October 1999, 1333 (2000) of 19 December 2000 and 1390 (2002) of 16 January 2002, adopted under article 41 of the UN Charter, oblige UN Member States to freeze funds and other financial assets and economic resources belonging to Usama bin Laden, to members of the Al-Qaida organization and the Taliban, and to other individuals, groups, undertakings and entities associated with them.[205] The specific persons against whom such

[202] See SIA, s 14(2)(a) and (b) respectively. As to what hangs on the distinction between a State, within the meaning of section 14(1), and a separate entity, not only is there no need, as in the present case, for service on a separate entity to be effected through the procedure spelled out in section 12 of the SIA; more significantly, the property of such an entity—with the express exception, in accordance with SIA, s 14(4), of the property of a State's central bank or other monetary authority, where such bank or authority is considered a separate entity—is not *prima facie* immune from execution pursuant to section 13(2)(b) of the Act, which refers to the property of a State alone. (That said, note SIA, s 13(4), which provides in relevant part that section 14(2)(b) 'does not prevent the issue of any process in respect of property which is for the time being in use or intended for use for commercial purposes'.)

[203] See [2009] EWHC 1074 (Comm), para 47, quoting [1995] 1 WLR 1147, 1160 (Lord Goff).

[204] [1995] 1 WLR 1147, 1158 (Lord Goff).

[205] The regime has evolved over time, via SC res 1452 (2002), 20 December 2002; SC res 1455 (2003), 17 January 2003; SC res 1526 (2004), 30 January 2004; SC res 1617 (2005), 29 July 2005; SC res 1730 (2006), 19 December 2006; SC res 1735 (2006), 22 December 2006; SC res 1822 (2008), 30 June 2008; and SC res 1904 (2009), 17 December 2009.

measures are to be taken are designated by the Committee established under paragraph 6 of resolution 1267 (1999) of 15 October 1999, known as the 'Al-Qaida and Taliban Sanctions Committee', which, on the basis of lists transmitted to it by Member States, adds their names to a Consolidated List kept by it. From the beginning, these measures have been subject to humanitarian exemptions, which were generalised to include all those targeted by the 1267/1333/1390 regime in resolution 1452 (2002) of 20 December 2002, as reaffirmed in subsequent resolutions. The 1267/1333/1390 regime of asset-freezing is given domestic effect in the UK by means of the Al-Qaida and Taliban (United Nations Measures) Order 2006, made under powers conferred by section 1(1) of the United Nations Act 1946.

The claimant's husband was placed on the Consolidated List in 2008, as a result of which his assets were frozen worldwide, including in the UK. The claimant herself, however, was granted a licence under the 2006 Order allowing her to take advantage of the humanitarian exemptions provided for by the sanctions regime. Paragraph 4 of the licence imposed on the claimant and her husband an obligation to report to the Asset Freezing Unit of HM Treasury on or before the twenty-first day of every month to account for all cash expenditure by providing receipts for any cash spent, a bank statement for the previous month in respect of a specially-designated account into which relevant benefits departments were directly to pay, and any other relevant documents. The UK duly notified the Security Council's Al-Qaida and Taliban Sanctions Committee of the licence.

The claimant challenged paragraph 4 of the licence. She argued, *inter alia*, that it was *ultra vires* the 2006 Order in not complying with its 'objectives and purposes',[206] these being the same as those of the Security Council resolutions pursuant to which it was made. There was, the claimant alleged, a 'collateral purpose', within the meaning of the relevant English case-law,[207] for the requirement in paragraph 4 of the licence to account for all cash expenditure, since there was no risk that the money would be spent on terrorist purposes.

Burton J, in the Administrative Court of the Queen's Bench Division, rejected the claimant's submission. It was 'not a question of needing to show a specific risk of use of [the] monies for terrorist purposes':[208]

[206] [2009] EWHC 1643 (Admin), para 41.

[207] See *Galloway v Mayor and Commonalty of London* (1866) LR 1 HL 34, 43: '[It is] a principle well recognized, and founded on the soundest principles of justice... that when persons... have received authority from the Legislature..., the persons so authorized cannot be allowed to exercise the powers conferred on them for any collateral object; that is, for any purposes except those for which the Legislature has invested them with... powers.' See, further, M Sunkin, 'Grounds for Judicial Review: Illegality in the Strict Sense', in D Feldman (ed), *English Public Law* (Oxford University Press, Oxford, 2004), 715, 745–54, paras 14.62–14.79.

[208] [2009] EWHC 1643 (Admin), para 42.

The requirements of the United Nations resolution[s] is that all funds be frozen and the aim is to identify a person who is a risk in the terrorist context and make sure that all his funds are frozen. The words used in resolution 1390 [paragraph] 2(a) are that the Member State is required to freeze without delay the funds and assets of, among others, the claimant's husband and to "ensure that neither these nor any other funds, financial assets or economic resources are made available directly or indirectly for such persons' benefit by their nationals or by any persons within their territory". The purpose is to ensure that the money channelled...through this account is not expended directly or indirectly for his benefit other than on the permitted basic expenses.[209]

'Unless and until some challenge to the entirety of the licence [was] made out', Burton J concluded, 'there [was] no collateral purpose in relation to the existence of paragraph 4, which [was] the monitoring requirement or obligation in respect of a primary obligation that the monies only be spent in accordance with the terms of the licence'.[210]

Subsequent to Burton J's decision in the present case, the sort of challenge to the legality of the licence scheme *per se* alluded to by his Lordship went some way to being made out, on the basis of Community law, in *M v Her Majesty's Treasury*, where the European Court of Justice, on a reference from the House of Lords,[211] held that article 2(2) of Council Regulation (EC) No. 881/2002 of 27 May 2002

must be construed as not applying to the provision by the State of social security or social assistance benefits to the spouse of a person designated by the committee created pursuant to Paragraph 6 of Resolution 1267 (1999) of the Security Council of the United Nations and included in the list in Annex I to that regulation, as amended, on the grounds only that the spouse lives with that person and will or may use some of those payments to pay for goods and services which the designated person also will consume or from which he also will benefit.[212]

The case now returns to the English courts.

9. *EN (Serbia) v Secretary of State for the Home Department; Secretary of State for the Home Department v KC (South Africa)*, 26 June 2009, [2009] EWCA Civ 630, unreported (CA (Civ Div))

Interpretation of treaties—Vienna Convention on the Law of Treaties 1969—relationship between treaty and English law—statutory construction—Convention relating to the Status of Refugees 1951, article 33(2)—Council Directive 2004/83/EC of 29 April 2004 (EU Qualification Directive), article 14(4)—Nationality, Immigration and Asylum Act 2002, section 72—Nationality, Immigration and Asylum Act 2002 (Specification of Particularly Serious Crimes) Order 2004—whether presumption in Nationality, Immigration and

[209] Ibid. [210] Ibid, para 42.

[211] *R (M) v Her Majesty's Treasury* [2008] UKHL 26, [2008] 2 All ER 1097. See also, previously, *M v Her Majesty's Treasury* [2006] EWCH 2328 (Admin) and [2007] EWCA Civ 173.

[212] Case C-340/08, Judgment, 29 April 2010 (ECJ, Fourth Chamber), dispositif.

Asylum Act 2002, section 72(2) as to commission of 'particularly serious crime' rebuttable—whether Nationality, Immigration and Asylum Act 2002 (Specification of Particularly Serious Crimes) Order 2004 ultra vires *Nationality, Immigration and Asylum Act 2002*

The Refugee Convention[213] is given domestic effect in the UK by way of section 2 of the Asylum and Immigration Appeals Act 1993, which provides that nothing in the Immigration Rules enacted under the Immigration Act 1971 shall lay down any practice which would be contrary to the Refugee Convention. Article 33(1) of the Refugee Convention imposes on Contracting States an obligation of *non-refoulement* of refugees.[214] Article 33(2), however, specifies that this obligation does not apply in respect of a refugee 'who, having been convicted by a final judgment of a particularly serious crime, constitutes a danger to the community of that country'.[215] Similarly, the EU Qualification Directive[216]—which is implemented in the UK via the Refugee or Person in Need of International Protection (Qualification) Regulations 2006 and which aims at 'establishing a Common European Asylum System, based on the full and inclusive application of the Geneva Convention relating to the Status of Refugees of 28 July 1951 . . ., thus affirming the principle of non-refoulement'[217]—provides in article 14.4 that 'Member States may revoke, end or refuse to renew the status granted to a refugee by a governmental, administrative, judicial or quasi-judicial body when: . . . (b) he or she, having been convicted by a final judgement of a particularly serious crime, constitutes a danger to the community of that Member State'.[218] (Paragraph 5 of article 14 of the Directive further authorizes a Member State to refuse refugee status to a person to whom paragraph 4 applies.) Section 72(2) of the Nationality, Immigration and Asylum Act 2002, which 'applies for the purpose of the construction and application of Article 33(2) of the Refugee Convention (exclusion from protection)',[219] provides that a person 'shall be presumed to have been convicted by a final judgment of a particularly serious crime and to constitute a danger to the community of the United Kingdom if he is—(a) convicted in the United Kingdom of an offence, and (b) sentenced to a period of imprisonment of at least two years'. Section 72(4)(a) of the

[213] Convention relating to the Status of Refugees, Geneva, 28 July 1951, 189 UNTS 2545.

[214] Section 33(1) reads: 'No Contracting State shall expel or return ('refouler') a refugee in any manner whatsoever to the frontiers of territories where his life or freedom would be threatened on account of his race, religion, nationality, membership of a particular social group or political opinion.'

[215] A refugee may also be subject to refoulement when 'there are reasonable grounds for regarding [him or her] as a danger to the security of the country in which he is'.

[216] Council Directive 2004/83/EC of 29 April 2004 on minimum standards for the qualification and status of third country nationals or stateless persons as refugees or as persons who otherwise need international protection and the content of the protection granted, OJ L 304, 30/09/2004, 0012–0023.

[217] Council Directive 2004/83/EC of 29 April 2004, preamble, recital (2).

[218] Article 14.4(a) permits revocation, by ending of or refusal to renew refugee status when there are reasonable grounds for regarding the refugee as a danger to the security of the Member State in which he or she is present.

[219] Nationality, Immigration and Asylum Act 2002, s 72(1).

Nationality, Immigration and Asylum Act states that a person 'shall be presumed to have been convicted by a final judgment of a particularly serious crime and to constitute a danger to the community of the United Kingdom if ... he is convicted of an offence specified by order of the Secretary of State'. The Nationality, Immigration and Asylum Act 2002 (Specification of Particularly Serious Crimes) Order 2004 specifies a long list of offences for the purpose of section 72(4)(a) of the Act. Section 72(6) of the Act provides that a presumption under subsections 2 to 4 of section 72 that a person constitutes a danger to the community is rebuttable by that person.

The first claimant, a refugee, had been convicted of, *inter alia*, three counts of burglary and one count of possession of an offensive weapon, which were together deemed a particularly serious crime under the 2004 Order,[220] and was sentenced to three concurrent terms of 12 months' detention in a young offenders' institution. He was notified by the Secretary of State that she was ordering his deportation under the Immigration Act 1971 on the ground that it was conducive to the public good. The Immigration Appeals Tribunal (IAT) dismissed his appeal, and his subsequent application for reconsideration of its decision was dismissed on the ground, *inter alia*, that he had been convicted of a crime specified in the 2004 Order as a particularly serious crime for the purposes of article 33(2) of the Refugee Convention. He appealed to the Court of Appeal, arguing, *inter alia*, that the 2004 Order was *ultra vires* the Nationality, Immigration and Asylum Act on account of its deeming as particularly serious crimes for the purposes of article 33(2) of the Refugee Convention crimes that were not particularly serious. The second claimant had been convicted of, *inter alia*, wounding with intent to do grievous bodily harm and, having broken the terms of an initial community rehabilitation order, had been sentenced to three years' imprisonment. His pending application for refugee status was subsequently refused both on its merits and under section 72(2) of the Nationality, Immigration and Asylum Act, and his deportation was ordered. His appeal to the IAT was dismissed at first instance and on reconsideration. He sought permission from the Court of Appeal to appeal, his case turning on, *inter alia*, whether the presumption in section 72(2) of the Nationality, Immigration and Asylum Act that a person had committed a particularly serious crime was rebuttable, a point which turned in turn on section 72(6) of the Act, in accordance with which a presumption under subsections 2 to 4 of section 72 that a person constitutes a danger to the community is rebuttable by that person.

The Court of Appeal (Civil Division) held that the presumption in section 72(2) of the Nationality, Immigration and Asylum Act was

[220] See Nationality, Immigration and Asylum Act 2002 (Specification of Particularly Serious Crimes) Order 2004, Schedule 2 (Theft Act 1968, s 10(1), committing burglary with, *inter alia*, a weapon of offence).

rebuttable and that the Nationality, Immigration and Asylum Act 2002 (Specification of Particularly Serious Crimes) Order 2004 was *ultra vires* the Act. Stanley Burnton LJ gave the leading judgment, with which Hooper and Laws LJJ agreed, the last adding a few words of his own.

Stanley Burnton LJ considered first the terms of article 33(2) of the Refugee Convention. It was common ground that these were to be interpreted in accordance with the rules embodied in the Vienna Convention on the Law of Treaties (VCLT),[221] as made clear by Lord Steyn in *Adan*.[222] On this basis, it was clear to his Lordship that article 33(2) imposed two preconditions to the *refoulement* of a refugee, namely the refugee's conviction by a final judgment of a particularly serious crime and his or her constituting a danger to the community.[223] As to what constituted a 'particularly serious crime' within the meaning of article 33(2), his Lordship explained by way of preface:

> In *Adan* the House of Lords held that Article 1A(2) of the Convention has an autonomous meaning.... I have no doubt that the expression "particularly serious crime", in an international treaty, similarly has an autonomous meaning. This is not to mean, however, that what is a particularly serious crime must be the same in every member state...The criminal laws of member states vary. What are crimes under the laws of one member state are not crimes under the laws of another.... I do not think that the crimes that are particularly serious are a constant, not varying from member state and not varying in time. Rather, the expression 'particularly serious crime' must be applied to what is a crime under the domestic law of the member state when the question of refoulement arises.[224]

The claimants had submitted that the various elements of article 33(2) were to be construed 'narrowly and restrictively',[225] consistent with the provision's character as 'an exception to the general right of international protection created by the Convention',[226] so that, for example, the expression 'danger to the community' was to be read to mean 'very serious danger to the community'.[227] In his Lordship's view, however, this was to 'add an unjustified gloss' to the provision.[228] It was 'to add words that the Member States did not include'—that is, 'to change the meaning of a negotiated settlement',[229] in a manner contrary to the prescriptions of

[221] Vienna, 23 May 1969, 1155 UNTS 331.

[222] *R (Adan and others) v Secretary of State for the Home Department* [2001] 2 AC 477, 516, (2000) 71 *BYIL* 422–6 (HL).

[223] [2009] EWCA Civ 630, para 39.

[224] Ibid, para 40.

[225] Ibid, para 41. The claimants had relied on 'the support of impressive authority' ([2009] EWCA Civ 630, para 41), namely the joint opinion to the UNHCR of Sir Elihu Lauterpacht QC and Daniel Bethlehem QC entitled *The Scope and Content of the Principle of Non-Refoulement* (2001, revised 2003), paras 186 and 191, and J Hathaway, *The Rights of Refugees under International Law* (Cambridge University Press, Cambridge, 2005).

[226] [2009] EWCA Civ 630, para 31(b).

[227] See Lauterpacht & Bethlehem, above n 225, para 191.

[228] [2009] EWCA Civ 630, para 43.

[229] Ibid.

Lord Bingham in *Brown v Stott*[230] (referring to the ECHR) and Lord Brown in *R (Hoxha) v Special Adjudicator*[231] (referring to the Refugee Convention itself), which applied with equal force to the instant case.[232] Laws LJ similarly emphasized 'the need, when the court is engaged upon the interpretation of such a treaty, to bear in mind and respect the limits of what the States Parties were prepared to agree'.[233] His Lordship also quoted from Lord Bingham's speech in *Brown v Stott*[234] before stating:

This passage, with great respect, reflects the importance of the fact that a treaty usually represents a negotiated settlement, a compromise, whose terms will have been carefully chosen so as to identify the limits of what has been agreed. True it is that sometimes the edges are left unclear; that, too, may be deliberate, the parties preferring to leave some matters to the chance of judicial interpretation rather than run the risk of losing the agreement altogether. Overall, however, as Lord Bingham went on to state, any issue of what may be implied into the treaty's express terms has to be approached by the courts with great caution. We are not to overstep what was agreed after painstaking negotiation. I entirely agree with [Stanley Burnton LJ]'s conclusion that this approach applies with undiminished force to the Refugee Convention, and that any gloss on the express words of Article 33(2) is to be avoided.[235]

As it was, Stanley Burnton LJ saw 'no need for any gloss on the express words of Article 33(2)':[236]

The words "particularly serious crime" are clear, and themselves restrict drastically the offences to which the Article applies. So far as "danger to the community" is concerned, the danger must be real, but if a person is convicted of a particularly serious crime, and there is a real risk of its repetition, he is likely to constitute a danger to the community.[237]

230 [2003] 1 AC 681, 703 (PC (Scotland)), quoted by Stanley Burnton LJ at [2009] EWCA Civ 630, para 43.

231 [2005] UKHL 19, [2005] 1 WLR 1063, 1088–9, para 85, quoted by Stanley Burnton LJ at [2009] EWCA Civ 630, para 44.

232 [2009] EWCA Civ 630, para 45.

233 Ibid, para 117.

234 Ibid, quoting [2003] 1 AC 681, 703.

235 Ibid, para 118, reference omitted.

236 Ibid, para 45.

237 Ibid. The claimants had also submitted, ibid, para 46, that article 33(2) required 'that the danger to the community must be causally connected to the particularly serious crime of which the person has been convicted'. To this Stanley Burnton LJ responded, ibid: 'I would accept that normally the danger is demonstrated by proof of the particularly serious offence and the risk of its recurrence, or of the recurrence of a similar offence. I would also accept that the wording of Article 33(2) reflects that expectation. But it does not expressly require a causal connection, and I do not think that one is to be implied. By way of example, I do not see why a person who has been convicted of a particularly serious offence of violence and who the State can establish is a significant drug dealer should not be liable to refouled under Article 33(2). In any event, it seems to me that a disregard for the law, demonstrated by the conviction, would be sufficient to establish a causal connection between the conviction and the danger. If so, the suggested added requirement of a causal connection has little if any practical consequence.'

He added:

> ... I have no doubt that particularly serious crimes are not restricted to offences against the person. Frauds, thefts and offences against property, for example, are capable of being particularly serious crimes, as may drug offences, particularly those involving class A drugs. In addition, matters such as frequent repetition or a sophisticated system or the participation of a number of offenders may aggravate the seriousness of an offence.[238]

Examples of the application of article 33(2) by other Contracting Parties to the Refugee Convention, cited by the Secretary of State in order to demonstrate the compatibility with the Convention of the statutory presumption that a sentence of at least two years' imprisonment indicated a particularly serious crime, were 'not... particularly helpful'.[239] There was 'no uniform interpretation sufficient to establish "a subsequent practice in the application of the treaty which establishes the agreement of the parties regarding its interpretation" within the meaning of Article 31(3)(b) of the Vienna Convention'.[240] Nor, for reasons already highlighted,[241] did his Lordship expect to see uniformity of application.[242] Moreover, without knowing more about the criminal legislation and penal policy of the State concerned, it was not possible to assess the relative seriousness of an offence from its punishment.[243] In this light, his Lordship was content to apply for the purposes of statutory construction—'subject to any applicable mandatory statutory provision'—what he considered to be 'the plain and clear words' of article 33(2) of the Refugee Convention and, with it, of article 14.4(b) of the EU Qualification Directive[244] (the requirements of the latter being the same as those of the former, namely conviction of a particularly serious crime and danger to the community[245]).

Stanley Burnton LJ next considered whether statutory presumptions in respect of the commission of a particularly serious crime, of the sort found in section 72(2) of the Nationality, Immigration and Asylum Act, were compatible with the Refugee Convention and the EU Qualification Directive. The claimants had argued that any statutory presumption of this sort, even if rebuttable, was incompatible with the Convention and Directive in that it imposed a burden of proof on the individual where the Convention and Directive required the State to prove that the individual had been convicted of a particularly serious crime. His Lordship, however, stated:

[238] Ibid, para 47.

[239] Ibid, para 50, referring to the examples cited ibid, paras 48–9.

[240] Ibid, para 50.

[241] See the passage at ibid, para 40 quoted above.

[242] Ibid, para 50.

[243] Ibid.

[244] Ibid, para 51. Counsel for the second claimant had further argued that the Directive was incompatible with the Convention, and was therefore *ultra vires* article 63(1) of the Treaty Establishing the European Community, which provides that the Council shall adopt 'measures on asylum, in accordance with the Geneva Convention of 28 July 1951 and the Protocol of 31 January 1967'. The Court of Appeal held, [2009] EWCA Civ 630, para 64, that it did not have jurisdiction to declare invalid an act of the Community.

[245] Ibid, para 62.

I see no reason why a rebuttable presumption, imposed for the purposes of a decision as to whether removal would be in breach of Article 33(1), should be incompatible with Article 33(2) of the Convention, at least in cases in which it may reasonably be inferred that a conviction gives rise to a reasonable likelihood that a person's conviction is of a particularly serious crime and that he constitutes a danger to the community. The Convention does not prescribe the procedure by which the conditions required by Article 33(2) are to be established; and the creation of a rebuttable presumption is a matter of procedure rather than of substance. I accept that the Convention places an onus on the State of refuge. Under section 72 [of Nationality, Immigration and Asylum Act], it is for the Secretary of State to establish that the person in question has been convicted of a relevant offence. In practice, once the State has established that a person has been convicted of what is on the face of it a particularly serious crime, it will be for him to show either that it was not in fact particularly serious, because of mitigating factors associated with its commission, or that because there is no danger of its repetition he does not constitute a danger to the community.[246]

Nor was the creation of an irrebuttable presumption necessarily incompatible with the two instruments:

I can also conceive of an irrebuttable presumption that would not be incompatible with the Convention, because it was dependent on facts so tightly circumscribed as to lead necessarily to the satisfaction of the Article 33(2) requirements. Those facts would, however, have to include recidivism if both of the requirements were to be satisfied.[247]

But the imposition of certain irrebuttable presumptions would conflict with both the Convention and the Directive:

[W]hat in my judgment is incompatible with the Convention and with the Directive is an irrebuttable presumption that arises from facts that do not necessarily involve the satisfaction of the Article 33(2) requirements but which requires those deciding whether they have been satisfied to determine that they have been satisfied when, untrammelled by the presumption, they would decide that they have not been.[248]

Turning from the abstract to the concrete, his Lordship continued:

I do not think that every crime that is punished with a sentence of 2 years' imprisonment is particularly serious. One only has to appreciate that determinate sentences may be many times longer than 2 years for it to be obvious that a sentence of 2 years' imprisonment is not necessarily indicative of a particularly serious crime. If, therefore, section 72 requires conviction and sentence to 2 years imprisonment to result in irrebuttable presumptions that the requirement of both Article 33(2) of the Convention and of Article 14.4(b) of the Directive of conviction for such a crime have been satisfied, it is incompatible with one or both.[249]

[246] Ibid, para 66. [247] Ibid, para 67. [248] Ibid, para 68. [249] Ibid, para 69.

But, his Lordship concluded, if the presumptions were rebuttable there would be no incompatibility.[250]

His Lordship then came to the crux of the second claimant's case, viz the construction of section 72 of the Nationality, Immigration and Asylum Act, and specifically whether section 72(6)'s express statement as to the rebuttability of the presumption in subsections (2) to (4) that a person constituted a danger to the community was to be taken to indicate *a contrario* that the concomitant presumption that the person had been convicted of a particularly serious crime was irrebuttable. If one applied the 'normal principles of statutory construction' applicable when no question of international obligations arose,[251] the maxim *expressio unius exclusio alterius* would have made it difficult, his Lordship thought, to construe as rebuttable the presumption in section 72(2) that a person had been convicted of a particularly serious crime.[252] But section 72 could not be construed in isolation from the UK's international obligations, as made clear by the Court of Appeal in *Salomon v Customs and Excise Commissioners*.[253] Section 72 of the Act applied expressly for the purpose of the interpretation and application of article 33(2) of the Convention, and it followed that, if there was any ambiguity in section 72, the provision had to be construed so as to accord with the Convention.[254]

The claimants, however, had sought to rely on the Refugee Convention as more than an aid to statutory construction, their premise being that the presumption in favour of conformity with the UK's international obligations was subject always to the unambiguous words of conflicting statute. Citing a statement by Lord Keith, with whom Lords Bridge, Templeman and Griffiths agreed, in *Sivakumaran* (the Refugee Convention having 'for all practical purposes been incorporated into United Kingdom law'),[255] as well as the words of Lord Bingham (the Nationality, Immigration and Asylum Act 1993 having 'strengthen[ed] the mode of incorporation of the Convention') and Lord Steyn (considering it 'clear that the Refugee Convention has been incorporated into our domestic law') in *European Roma Rights*,[256] they had argued that the Convention itself had force of law in England & Wales, with the result that no conflicting statute could override its

[250] Ibid. [251] Ibid, para 71. [252] Ibid, para 72.

[253] Ibid, para 73, quoting [1967] 2 QB 116, 141 (Lord Denning MR) and 143 (Diplock LJ), (1967) 42 *BYIL* 291–3 (CA). See also [2009] EWCA Civ 630, para 74, quoting *Post Office v Estuary Radio* [1968] 2 QB 740, 756 (Diplock LJ), (1967) 42 *BYIL* 295–8 (CA).

[254] [2009] EWCA Civ 630, para 75.

[255] *R v Secretary of State for the Home Department, Ex parte Sivakumaran* [1988] AC 958, 990. The case predates the Asylum and Immigration Appeals Act 1993, Lord Keith's dictum referring to r 16 of the Statement of Changes in Immigration Rules (1983), HC 169, which embodied a somewhat weaker formulation than s 2 of the Asylum and Immigration Appeals Act 1993, viz 'Where a person is a refugee full account is to be taken of the provisions of the Convention and Protocol relating to the Status of Refugees (Cmd 9171 and Cmnd 3906). Nothing in these rules is to be construed as requiring action contrary to the United Kingdom's obligations under these instruments....'

[256] *R (European Roma Rights Centre) v Immigration Officer at Prague Airport* [2004] UKHL 55, [2005] 2 AC 1, 25, para 7 (Lord Bingham) and 45, para 42 (Lord Steyn), (2004) 75 *BYIL* 504–12 (HL).

terms. But Stanley Burnton LJ noted that the authorities cited by the claimants were merely obiter dicta. He also drew attention to the qualification by Lord Bingham, with whom Lords Hope and Carswell agreed, in *R v Asfaw* that, while 'the British regime for handling applications for asylum has been closely assimilated to the [Refugee] Convention model', 'the Convention as a whole has never been formally incorporated or given effect in domestic law'.[257] In this light, Stanley Burnton J continued:

58 I fully accept that the Convention has been incorporated into our law for some purposes. It defines a claim for asylum under our law. It has been given a status superior to the Immigration Rules, but they are not law of the status of a statutory instrument but something rather less: see *R v Home Secretary ex parte Hosenball* [1977] 1 WLR 766, 780–781, 785, 788. But the question arises: for what purposes and to what extent has it been incorporated? The rule that the provisions of a treaty entered into by the executive branch of government are not without more part of our domestic law, save for the purposes of interpretation in the application of the rule enunciated in *Salomon*, reflects the important, indeed basic, constitutional principle that the executive cannot without Parliamentary authority change the law. A change to our law requires Parliamentary authority, i.e., legislation or the conferment of authority by primary legislation to make delegated legislation. So far as the Convention as a whole is concerned, Parliament has legislated in section 2 of the Asylum and Immigration Act 1993, but it did not do so in terms that would give the Convention the force of statute for all purposes. It expressly limited the force given to the Convention to the Immigration Rules. The Convention also affects the lawfulness of administrative practices and procedures, because, as Lord Steyn put it: "It is necessarily implicit in section 2 that no administrative practice or procedure may be adopted which would be contrary to the Convention." But to give the Convention any greater force or status under our law would be to go further than section 2 requires or permits, and in my judgment this is something the court cannot do.

59 It follows that the Convention does not have the force of statute under our law. I reject the Appellants' submission that the Convention has been informally incorporated. It has not. Indeed, I doubt that there can be such a thing as informal incorporation.

Laws LJ shared the same doubts:[258]

A treaty may only be incorporated into the domestic law of the United Kingdom by legislation, and therefore expressly. It is important to remember that under our Constitution, subject to certain arcane exceptions, the Executive is not a source of law save as the maker of subordinate legislation which, however, must be authorised by Act of Parliament. Since treaties are entered into

[257] [2008] UKHL 31, [2008] 1 AC 1061, 1087, para 29, (2008) 79 *BYIL* 440–54 (HL).
[258] [2009] EWCA Civ 630, para 119.

by the Executive, there must be a distinct legislative act if any such measure is to take its place in the body of English law. This is particularly important where the treaty's provisions are sought to be relied on as conferring rights in our courts. The source of the *domestic* law relied on must be clear.[259]

In this light, Stanley Burnton LJ concluded that '[i]f . . . Parliament has enacted a statute that is unambiguously in conflict with the Convention, then subject to any other statutory or equivalent authority the courts must enforce the statute', since, as Diplock LJ had said in *Salomon*, 'the sovereign power of the Queen in Parliament extends to breaking treaties'.[260]

In the event, however, it was not the principle in *Salomon* that the Court of Appeal applied but the principle enunciated by the European Court of Justice in *Marleasing SA v La Comercial Internacional de Alimentación SA*, which, Stanley Burnton LJ explained, imposed a stricter interpretative requirement in respect of EU directives than the common-law requirement in respect of treaties, obliging as it did the court, insofar as it was possible, to interpret legislation, whether adopted before or after the directive, so as to achieve the result required by the directive.[261] If the *Marleasing* principle applied to section 72, his Lordship continued, it was unnecessary to consider what the result would be of applying the *Salomon* principle on its own.[262] The Secretary of State had not denied the application of the *Marleasing* principle to section 72 of the Nationality, Immigration and Asylum Act, and Stanley Burnton J considered her right not to have done so:[263]

It is correct that section 72 refers only to Article 33(2) of the Convention, and does not refer to the Qualification Directive, doubtless because the statute predates the Directive. But Article 14.4 of the Directive and Article 33(2) of the Convention cover the same ground: both define the circumstances in which a refugee may be refouled to a territory where he is at risk of persecution. There is no other national instrument implementing Article 14.4. The Refugee or Person in Need of International Protection (Qualification) Regulations 2006 do not include any relevant provision, and I note that the Explanatory Note to the Regulations stated:

Many parts of the Directive do not require implementation as consistent provision is already made in existing domestic legislation.

If section 72 is not construed compatibly with the Directive, this country would be in breach of its obligation to implement it; if it is applied consistently with the Directive, no question of a breach arises. Hence, the *Marleasing* principle must be applied.[264]

[259] Ibid.

[260] Ibid, para 60, the implied reference being to *Post Office v Estuary Radio* [1968] 2 QB 740, 756, in turn quoting *Ellerman Lines v Murray; White Star Line and US Mail Steamers Oceanic Steam Navigation Co Ltd v Comerford* [1931] AC 126.

[261] [2009] EWCA Civ 630, para 77, quoting [1990] ECR I-4135.

[262] [2009] EWCA Civ 630, para 77. [263] Ibid, para 78. [264] Ibid.

His Lordship then applied the *Marleasing* principle to section 72 of the Act:

> [T]here is in my judgment a sufficient degree of ambiguity . . . Subsection (6) may be regarded as declaratory or emphatic. The conclusion that it is an exclusive statement of what is rebuttable depends on the *expressio unius* rule of interpretation, which is not a particularly strong rule, and itself depends on the assumption that what is expressly stated impliedly excludes what is not mentioned. Subsection (9)(b) does not specify that only one of the presumptions to which it refers is subject to rebuttal, and subsection (10)(b) is in terms that suggest that the appellant is to be given an opportunity to rebut both presumptions.[265]

His Lordship concluded that section 72 of the Act could be and was to be interpreted, in conformity with article 14.4 of the EU Qualification Directive, as creating rebuttable presumptions in relation to both of the requirements specified in article 33(2) of the Refugee Convention—that is, in relation to the seriousness of the crime as much as in relation to the danger to the community.[266] For his part, Laws LJ confessed to having had 'greater difficulty' as to the correct construction of section 72(6) of the Nationality, Immigration and Asylum Act, but declared himself persuaded by Stanley Burnton LJ's reasoning.[267]

As for the first claimant's challenge to the legality of the Nationality, Immigration and Asylum Act 2002 (Specification of Particularly Serious Crimes) Order 2004, Stanley Burnton LJ noted that the Order did indeed include not only offences that could 'sensibly be regarded as particularly serious crimes' but also many that could not.[268] If the presumption that

[265] Ibid, para 79. Subsections (9) and (10) of section 72 of the Act state in relevant part:

> (9) Subsection (10) applies where—
> ···(b) the Secretary of State issues a certificate that presumptions under subsection (2), (3) or (4) apply to the person (subject to rebuttal).
> (10) The Tribunal or Commission hearing the appeal—
> ···(b) if in agreement that presumptions under subsection (2), (3) or (4) apply (having given the appellant an opportunity for rebuttal) must dismiss the appeal in so far as it relies on the ground specified in subsection (9)(a).

[266] [2009] EWCA Civ 630, para 78.

[267] Ibid, para 116.

[268] Ibid, para 81. His Lordship elaborated: 'By way of example only, there are the following: theft, with no qualification as to the nature or value of the item or items stolen (so that theft of a bottle of milk is sufficient); an offence under section 9(1)(a) of the Theft Act 1968 (entering a building as a trespasser, intending to steal, inflict or attempt to inflict grievous bodily harm or rape), which would include someone who enters a building without permission intending to steal a bottle of milk; an offence under section 9(1)(b) of that Act (having entered a building as a trespasser, stealing or attempting to steal or inflicting or attempting to inflict grievous bodily harm), which again would include the offence committed by someone who enters a house without permission and then steals a milk bottle; an offence under section 1(1) of the Criminal Damage Act 1971 (destroying or damaging, without lawful excuse, another's property intending to destroy or damage it or being reckless as to that), which would include the offence committed by someone who scratched the paintwork of another person's car. The offence under section 44 of the Magistrates' Court Act 1980, namely aiding, abetting, counselling or procuring the commission of a summary offence, provided that the offence in question is described in Schedule 1 or 2 to the Order, is specified. It is at best very difficult indeed to see how abetting the commission of a summary offence could be a particularly serious crime.'

an offence listed in a schedule to the 2004 Order was a particularly serious crime had been held to be irrebuttable, the Order would have been 'manifestly irrational'.[269] But even on the basis that the presumption was rebuttable, the Order was 'objectionable'.[270] Although the power conferred on the Secretary of State by section 72(4)(a) of the Nationality, Immigration and Asylum Act was not expressly qualified, it was 'impliedly qualified by its context and purpose':[271]

> It cannot be inferred that Parliament conferred on the Secretary of State the power to specify any offence she or he wanted as one giving rise to the statutory presumptions, irrespective of its seriousness. In my judgment, the power conferred by section 72(4)(a) is restricted to offences that the Secretary of State could reasonably consider as giving rise to the statutory presumptions. The Secretary of State could not reasonably or, I would add, rationally, have considered [a number of the scheduled offences] as an offence that is a particularly serious crime or that gives rise to a presumption that the offender is a danger to the community. . . . I conclude that the Secretary of State misunderstood the extent and purpose of the statutory power when formulating the schedules to the Order, and that in making the Order she exceeded the statutory power.[272]

Since to sever the offending crimes 'would be to assume and to exercise the legislative power that Parliament had conferre[d] on the Secretary of State', it followed that the 2004 Order was *ultra vires* and thus unlawful.[273]

The Court of Appeal's judgment is by and large an excellent one.

In their approach to the interpretation of treaties, their Lordships provide a welcome reminder of the primacy of the text, as emphasized not only by the ICJ[274] but also on numerous occasions in the House of Lords,[275] even if it was overlooked in practice the year before in *Asfaw* by Lord Bingham (*malgré* his own strictures in *Brown v Stott*, *European Roma Rights* and *Asfaw* itself[276]), as well as by Lords Hope and Carswell. That said, as a straightforward matter of construction, one might wonder whether article 33(2) of the Refugee Convention, in permitting the *refoulement* of a refugee 'who, having been convicted by a final judgment of a particularly serious crime, constitutes a danger to the community of that country', really does lay down two distinct criteria, the more natural reading arguably being that a refugee, having been convicted of a particularly

[269] Ibid, para 82. [270] Ibid. [271] Ibid. [272] Ibid. [273] Ibid, para 83.

[274] See *Territorial Dispute (Libyan Arab Jamahiriya/Chad)* [1994] ICJ Rep 6, 22, para 41 ('Interpretation must be based above all on the text of the treaty.')

[275] See e.g. *Adan v Secretary of State for the Home Department* [1999] 1 AC 293, 305 (Lord Lloyd); *Morris v KLM Royal Dutch Airlines* [2002] UKHL 7, [2002] 2 AC 628, 656 (Lord Hope) and 677–8 (Lord Hobhouse), (2002) 73 *BYIL* 389–400 (HL); *R (Hoxha) v Special Adjudicator* [2005] UKHL 19, [2005] 1 WLR 1063, 1088–9, para 85; *Re Deep Vein Thrombosis and Air Travel Group Litigation* [2005] UKHL 72, [2006] 1 AC 495, 508 (Lord Steyn), (2005) 76 *BYIL* 626–30 (HL); *R v Asfaw* [2008] 1 AC 1061, 1103, para 82 (Lord Rodger). See also the statements by Lord Bingham, below n 276.

[276] See, respectively, [2003] 1 AC 681, 703; [2005] 2 AC 1, 31, para 18; [2008] 1 AC 1061, 1079, para 11.

serious crime, is simply deemed to constitute (or, putting it another way, is irrebuttably presumed to constitute) a danger to the community of the country of refuge. But this was not argued by the Secretary of State, on account of the fact that section 72(6) of the Nationality, Immigration and Asylum Act—in what may have been an act of *noblesse oblige* on Parliament's part or else an awareness that such an application of article 33(2) of the Refugee Convention could fall foul of article 6 of the ECHR—provides that a presumption under section 72(2) that a person constitutes a danger to the community is rebuttable; and the Court of Appeal's construction is by no means implausible. If, however, one were to indulge in counsels of perfection, one might wish that the first claimant's reliance on article 31(3)(b) of the VCLT had been knocked more squarely on the head. The question of what can be considered a 'particularly serious crime' within the meaning of article 33(2) of the VCLT is one not of interpretation, the meaning of 'particularly serious crime' being perfectly clear, but simply of application; and the only use to which the subsequent practice of the Contracting Parties to the Refugee Convention in the application of article 33(2) could be put in this context would be as an index of reasonableness by reference to which the UK's good faith in the application of the provision—the customary requirement of treaty law codified in article 26 of the VCLT[277]—could be measured. In the event, by finding contrary to the Convention the creation of an irrebuttable presumption that a crime which is not particularly serious by any reasonable standard is particularly serious for the purpose of article 33(2) of the Convention, what the Court of Appeal is effectively doing is enforcing the requirement of good faith in the application of treaty obligations.

As for the relationship between the Refugee Convention and English law, Lord Bingham redeemed himself in *Asfaw* by rejecting the spurious argument that the Convention had the full force of English law merely because Lord Keith in *Sivakumaran*[278] and Lord Steyn in *Roma Rights*[279] had referred to it in passing, for the limited respective purposes of those cases, as having been 'incorporated'.[280] The Court of Appeal's reiteration of and elaboration upon his Lordship's dismissal of this frankly silly submission, which puts the cart before the horse, is to be commended.

The case would appear to be the first in which the canon of statutory construction familiar from cases such as *Salomon* and *Garland*[281](where

[277] In the words of the ICJ in *Gabčíkovo-Nagymaros Project (Hungary/Slovakia), Judgment* [1997] ICJ Rep 7, 78–9, para 142, article 26 'combines two elements, which are of equal importance', namely fulfilment and good faith, the latter obliging an application of the relevant provision 'in a reasonable way and in such a manner that its purpose can be realized'.

[278] See [1988] AC 958, 990 (the Refugee Convention having 'for all practical purposes been incorporated into United Kingdom law').

[279] See [2005] 2 AC 1, 45, para 42.

[280] [2008] 1 AC 1061, 1087, para 29.

[281] *Garland v British Railway Engineering Ltd* [1983] 2 AC 751, 771 (Lord Diplock), (1982) 53 *BYIL* 291–3 (HL).

the statute is passed to implement the treaty) and *Brind*[282] and *Lyons*[283] (where it is not) has overlapped with the 'strong interpretative obligation',[284] viz to read the statutory provision in conformity with the relevant international instrument insofar as this is possible, laid down in respect of EU directives in *Marleasing*—and in respect of European Council framework decisions in *Pupino*[285] and *Dabas*[286] and in respect of the ECHR in section 3(1) of the HRA.[287] It also illustrates, in deed if not in word, one of the salient differences between the two, which is that, whereas the *Salomon* presumption cannot be brought to bear unless the statutory provision is ambiguous, the *Marleasing* obligation is not so circumscribed. *Pace* Stanley Burnton LJ,[288] section 72 of the Nationality, Immigration and Asylum Act is not ambiguous, at least not self-evidently so. Section 72(6) states that '[a] presumption under subsection (2), (3) or (4) that a person constitutes a danger to the community is rebuttable by that person'; section 72(9) provides that section 72(10) applies where, *inter alia*, 'the Secretary of State issues a certificate that presumptions under subsection (2), (3) or (4) apply to the person (subject to rebuttal)'; and section 72(10) provides that a Tribunal or Commission hearing an appeal against a deportation order, 'if in agreement that presumptions under subsection (2), (3) or (4) apply (having given the appellant an opportunity for rebuttal) must dismiss the appeal'. It is, arguably, tolerably clear from this that the word 'presumptions', in the plural, in section 72(9) and 72(10) refers to the presumption that a person constitutes a danger to the community as it is found in the plurality of subsections represented by subsections (2), (3) and (4), rather than to the two presumptions, namely that a crime is particularly serious and that the person constitutes a danger to the community, found in each of subsections (2), (3) and (4). Now, it is impossible to predict with certainty whether any putative ambiguity would provide enough leeway for the operation of the *Salomon* presumption that Parliament does not intend to legislate in a manner which would place the UK in breach of its treaty obligations. But

[282] *R v Secretary of State for the Home Department, Ex parte Brind* [1991] 1 AC 696, 747–8 (Lord Bridge) and 760–1 (Lord Ackner), (1991) 62 *BYIL* 437–40 (HL).

[283] *R v Lyons* [2002] UKHL 44, [2003] 1 AC 976, 992, paras 27–8 (Lord Hoffmann), (2002) 73 *BYIL* 428–34 (HL).

[284] *R (Hurst) v London Northern District Coroner* [2007] UKHL 13, [2007] AC 189, 216, para 52 (Lord Brown), (2007) 78 *BYIL* 520–7 (HL) and *Dabas v High Court of Justice in Madrid* [2007] UKHL 6, [2007] 2 AC 31, 61, para 79 (Lord Brown), (2007) 78 *BYIL* 515–20 (HL).

[285] *Criminal proceedings against Pupino (Case C-105/03)* [2006] QB 83.

[286] *Dabas v High Court of Justice in Madrid* [2007] 2 AC 31, applying *Pupino* and, [2007] 2 AC 31, 60, para 76 (Lord Brown), characterizing the interpretative obligation laid down therein as the same as that prescribed in respect of directives in *Marleasing*.

[287] Section 3(1) of the HRA states that, so far as it is possible to do so, primary and subordinate legislation must be read and given effect in a way which is compatible with Convention rights. As explained by Lord Steyn in *Ghaidan v Godin-Mendoza* [2004] UKHL 30, [2004] 2 AC 557, 574–5, para 45 and reiterated by Lord Brown in *Dabas v High Court of Justice in Madrid* [2007] 2 AC 31, 60, para 76, the obligation in s 3(1) of the HRA is essentially the same as the obligation laid down, in a different context, in *Marleasing*.

[288] [2009] EWCA Civ 630, para 79.

the point here is that, notwithstanding Stanley Burnton LJ's reference to 'a sufficient degree ambiguity' in section 72,[289] the strong interpretative obligation dictated by *Marleasing* (and by *Pupino/Dabas* and section 3(1) of the HRA) does not depend on the provision's ambiguity.[290] The only limitation is that it not be semantically or syntactically or otherwise logically impossible to construe the statute in the desired fashion. In other words, while a national court is neither compelled nor permitted by Community law to construe national law *contra legem*,[291] the *Marleasing* principle obliges the court to bring the statute into line with the Community obligation even at the expense of Parliament's apparent intention. In this light, there was probably just enough 'wriggle room' in the texts of, and interrelationship among, subsections (2), (6), (9) and (10) of section 72 of the Nationality, Immigration and Asylum Act to enable the Court of Appeal in the present case to construe as rebuttable section 72(2)'s presumption as to the particular seriousness of the crime, without—to borrow Lord Steyn's allusion in respect of section 3(1) of the HRA—crossing the Rubicon.[292]

10. *Republic of Croatia v Republic of Serbia*, 2 July 2009, [2009] EWHC 1559 (Ch), [2010] 2 WLR 555 (Ch D, Briggs J)

Non-justiciability of unincorporated treaties—'Buttes' *non-justiciability—exceptions to non-justiciability—customary international law—relationship between customary international law and English law—dissolution (*dismembratio*) of Socialist Federal Republic of Yugoslavia (SFRY)—Agreement on Succession Issues 2001—Vienna Convention on Succession of States in respect of State Property, Archives and Debts 1983, article 18—whether Croatia having sufficient interest in entry of restrictions in land register in respect of property in London registered in name of SFRY*

In 2001, the five successor States to the defunct Socialist Federal Republic of Yugoslavia (SFRY)—namely Bosnia and Herzegovina, Croatia, Macedonia, Slovenia and the Federal Republic of Yugoslavia (FRY)—concluded an Agreement on Succession Issues (ASI),[293] which came into force on 2 June 2004, by which time the FRY had become the Republic of Serbia and Montenegro, from which in turn Montenegro consensually

[289] Ibid.

[290] As regards s 3(1) of the HRA, see *R (Hurst) v London Northern District Coroner* [2007] AC 189, 215, para 50, where Lord Brown (with whom Lords Bingham, Rodger and Mance agreed to this extent) stated that '[s]ection 3 is only invoked where, to achieve compliance with the Convention, the court must depart from the unambiguous meaning the legislation would otherwise bear'. But *cf R v F* [2007] EWCA Crim 243, [2007] QB 960, 970, para 26, where the Court of Appeal demanded 'absurdity or ambiguity', having at [2007] QB 960, 969–70, paras 23–24 treated as one and the same thing the 'strong interpretative presumption' laid down in s 3 of the HRA and the principle recognized by Diplock LJ in *Salomon*.

[291] *Criminal proceedings against Pupino (Case C-105/03)* [2006] QB 83, 110, para 47, as reiterated in *Dabas v High Court of Justice in Madrid* [2007] 2 AC 31, 40, para 5 (Lord Bingham).

[292] *Ghaidan v Godin-Mendoza* [2004] 2 AC 557, 577, para 49, as echoed in *Dabas v High Court of Justice in Madrid* [2007] 2 AC 31, 61, para 79 (Lord Brown).

[293] 29 June 2001, 2262 UNTS 251.

seceded in 2006, giving rise to the independent States of Montenegro, on the one hand, and Serbia, on the other. The ASI was said in article 7 to represent a final settlement of the mutual rights and obligations of the successor States in respect of the succession issues covered by it. The Agreement provides in Annex B for the distribution in kind of the diplomatic and consular property of the SFRY among the successor States, stipulating that this is to be by agreement and that the total final distribution is to reflect as closely as possible the percentage shares specified in a table in article 3 of Annex B. An appendix to Annex B lists the properties subject to distribution in accordance with that Annex. Article 5 of Annex B creates a Joint Committee composed of an equal number of representatives from each State to ensure the effective implementation of this regime, one of its functions being to verify and as necessary amend the list of properties in the appendix to the Annex. In article 2 of the ASI, each successor State acknowledges that it is obliged to take the necessary measures to prevent loss, damage or destruction to State property of the SFRY in which, in accordance with the Agreement, one or more of the other successors has an interest. Article 4 of the ASI creates a Standing Joint Committee of senior representatives of each successor State (a body distinct from the Joint Committee created in article 5 of Annex B for the implementation of that Annex), the principal tasks of which are to monitor the effective implementation of the agreement and to serve as a forum in which issues arising in the course of this implementation can be discussed. In accordance with Annex F, the division of other rights, interests and liabilities of the SFRY among the successor States is to proceed under the direction of the Standing Joint Committee. Article 5(2) of the ASI provides that where differences over the interpretation and application of the ASI cannot be resolved within a month by discussion among the States concerned, these States are to refer the matter either to an independent person of their choice or to the Standing Joint Committee.

A particular property in London, held on a long leasehold registered in the name of 'the Socialist Federal Republic of Yugoslavia (Ministry of Defence)' and occupied by a certain lieutenant colonel of the Serbian Army who served at the Serbian embassy in London, was not listed in the appendix to Annex B of the ASI as one of the diplomatic or consular properties of the SFRY subject to the distribution arrangements laid down in Annex B to the Agreement. Neither the Joint Committee charged with implementing Annex B nor the Standing Joint Committee charged with directing the distribution of other interests of the SFRY in accordance with Annex F had made a determination as to succession to the property; and despite Croatia's having requested such a determination, none was timetabled. Croatia applied for the entry of restrictions in the land register in respect of the property. In accordance with section 41(1) of the Land Registration Act 2002, where a restriction is entered in the register 'no entry in respect of a disposition to which the restriction applies may be made in the register otherwise than in accordance with the terms of the restriction'. Section 42(1)(c) of the Act states the Land Registry may enter a restriction in the register if it appears that it is necessary or desirable for the purpose of protecting a right or claim in relation to a registered estate. Section 43(1)(c) provides that a person may apply to the register for the entry of a restriction under section 42(1) if he has a sufficient interest in the making of the entry, the concept of sufficient interest being elaborated on in a non-exhaustive fashion in rule 93 of the Land Registration Rules 2003. Serbia objected to the entry of the restrictions requested by Croatia. Croatia argued before the adjudicator to the Land Registry that, under both the ASI and customary international law, the latter being part of the common law of England & Wales, it had a right or claim in relation to the property, within the meaning of section 42(1)(c) of the Land Registration Act, such as to give it a sufficient interest, within the meaning of section 43(1)(c) of the Act, in the making of the entry sought; and that, as a result, the Chief Land Registrar was empowered under section 42(1)(c) of the Act to enter the restrictions, should he consider them necessary or desirable for the purpose of protecting Croatia's right or claim in relation to the property. The adjudicator ruled that Croatia had not established any interest in the property under English law and that he therefore had no jurisdiction to direct the Land Registry to enter the restrictions.

Croatia's appeal to Briggs J, in the Chancery Division of the High Court, was upheld.

His Lordship rejected the argument based on customary international law, which was part of the common law of England & Wales only if it was reflected in a 'general and consistent practice of states'.[294] The question in the present case was whether there was 'sufficiently established consistent practice concerning the succession to the property of a dismembered state, sufficient for it to have become part of English common law'.[295] In this regard, after acknowledging Croatia's argument that article 18 of the Vienna Convention on Succession of States in respect of State Property, Archives and Debts[296] was consonant with customary international law[297] and the International Law Commission's view that what became article 18 reflected what was at the time the current academic opinion,[298] his

[294] [2010] 2 WLR 555, 564, para 33, citing *Sepet v Secretary of State for the Home Department* [2003] UKHL 15, [2003] 1 WLR 856, 876, para 40 (Lord Hoffmann).

[295] [2010] 2 WLR 555, 564.

[296] Vienna, 8 April 1983, UN doc. A/CONF. 117/14 (not in force). Article 18 provides in relevant part:

> 1. When a State dissolves and ceases to exist and the parts of the territory of the predecessor State form two or more successor States, and unless the successor States concerned otherwise agree:
> ...(b) immovable State property of the predecessor State situated outside its territory shall pass to the successor States in equitable proportions...
> 2. The provisions of paragraph 1 are without prejudice to any question of equitable compensation among the successor States that may arise as a result of a succession of States.

[297] [2010] 2 WLR 555, 565, para 34.

[298] Ibid, para 36, referring to *Report of the International Law Commission on the work of its thirty-third session, 4 May-24 July 1981*, reproduced in *Yearbook of the International Law Commission 1981*, vol II(2), 46, para (9).

Lordship concluded that there was 'insufficient evidence to justify a conclusion that a rule as to succession to the property of a dismembered state (however sensible) has yet become a sufficiently general or consistent practice among states to qualify as customary international law for the purposes of recognition by English common law'.[299]

Turning to Croatia's argument based on the ASI, Briggs J first examined whether the question was justiciable. He recalled in this regard the 'long-standing principle of English law, inherent in the very nature of the judicial process', according to Lord Wilberforce in *Buttes Gas & Oil v Hammer (No 3)*, 'that municipal courts do not adjudicate on the transactions of foreign states', so that '[w]here such issues are raised in private litigation, the court exercises judicial restraint and abstains from deciding the issues'.[300] He recalled too the 'closely related principle' that 'the interpretation of treaties to which the United Kingdom is a party, but the terms of which have not either expressly or by reference been incorporated in English domestic law by legislation, is not a matter that falls within the interpretative jurisdiction of an English court of law'.[301] He highlighted, however, that both principles were subject to exception,[302] notably 'where the transactions of the foreign states in question, or the unincorporated treaty, are relevant to the existence or enforcement of private law rights'.[303] His Lordship continued:

> [T]he *AY Bank* case is authority for a further exception to the non-justiciability principle, to the effect that even where the English courts will not adjudicate upon the merits of a dispute between foreign states, they may none the less grant protective measures so as to preserve the status quo pending the outcome of such disputes.[304]

Quoting a passage from *AY Bank*, which similarly centred on the rights of the successor States to the SFRY under the ASI, Briggs J characterized the case as 'implicitly reflect[ing]... acceptance of the principle that, where a decision as to private law rights remains outstanding between foreign states, pursuant to public international law recognised by them, or pursuant to a scheme for determination agreed by them, then the

[299] [2010] 2 WLR 555, 565, para 36.

[300] Ibid, 563, para 27, citing [1982] AC 888, 931–3, (1982) 53 *BYIL* 259–68 (HL).

[301] [2010] 2 WLR 555, 563, para 28, citing *British Airways Board v Laker Airways Ltd* [1985] AC 58, 85–6 (Lord Diplock), (1984) 55 *BYIL* 331–6 (HL).

[302] [2010] 2 WLR 555, 563, para 29, citing *R (Campaign for Nuclear Disarmament) v Prime Minister* [2002] EWHC 2777 (Admin), (2002) 126 ILR 727, 744–5, paras 35–6 (Simon Brown LJ), (2002) 73 *BYIL* 444–52 (QBD (Admin Ct), Div Ct); *J.H. Rayner (Mincing Lane) Ltd v Department of Trade and Industry* [1989] Ch 72, 163–4 (Kerr LJ), (1988) 59 *BYIL* 267–341 (CA), [1990] 2 AC 418, 510–11 (Lord Oliver), (1989) 60 *BYIL* 461–73 (HL).

[303] [2010] 2 WLR 555, 563, para 29, citing *Republic of Ecuador v Occidental Exploration and Production Co* [2005] EWCA Civ 1116, [2006] QB 432, 460, para 37 (Mance LJ), (2005) 76 *BYIL* 585–9 (CA (Civ Div)).

[304] [2010] 2 WLR 555, 564, para 31, citing *In re AY Bank Ltd* [2006] EWHC 830 (Ch), [2006] 2 All ER (Comm) 463, (2006) 77 *BYIL* 489–99 (Ch D (Companies Ct), Sir Andrew Morritt C).

English court may award protective measures designed to preserve the status quo, provided that it does nothing to determine the issue on the merits'.[305]

His Lordship then identified the relevant facts, for which purpose the Court was entitled, 'without infringing the non-justiciability principle, to have regard to the existence of the ASI as a relevant fact, to the extent of any apparent agreement between the parties as to the consequences of the dismemberment of the SFRY, and to the ambit of any dispute between the parties as to those consequences, for the purposes of establishing whether Croatia ha[d] any qualifying claim relating to the registered leasehold interest in the property'.[306] The first relevant fact was that, at the time of concluding the ASI, both Croatia and the FRY (of which Serbia was a part) agreed that the only candidates for succession to the property of the SFRY were the five successor States.[307] Secondly, these States concluded the ASI as a means of finally settling all issues as to succession to, among other things, the property of the SFRY, including in the ASI 'guidelines and machinery designed to lead to a final determination of all succession issues between them'.[308] Thirdly, Croatia and Serbia remained of the view that the only candidates for succession to the property of the SFRY were the successor States.[309] Next, it was agreed that the property at issue in the instant case formed part of the property of the SFRY at the moment of its dismemberment.[310] Finally, while Croatia and Serbia did not agree as to whether the ASI made provision for the determination of the ownership of the property at issue or, if it did, what the relevant provisions of the ASI were and what their effect was, neither disputed that the mechanisms provided for by the ASI had yet to produce a determination as to the ownership of the property and that, if any such determination were to be made, the property could be directed to be distributed to any one of the successor States, so that either Croatia or Serbia could receive the whole or none of the property.[311] His Lordship considered it to follow inevitably from these facts that Croatia (and, indeed, Serbia) had two types of claim in relation to the property, namely a claim, pending any determination as to the distribution of the property pursuant to the ASI, to a beneficial share in the property, which arose from the parties' common understanding that the sole candidates for ownership of the property of the SFRY on its dismemberment were the successor States; and a claim to full beneficial ownership of the property, capable of being pursued by each of the parties pursuant to the ASI, which might or might not have succeeded.[312] In Briggs J's view, it involved 'no breach of the non-justiciability principle . . . to conclude that both th[e]se claims

[305] [2010] 2 WLR 555, 564, para 32, quoting [2006] 2 All ER (Comm) 463, para 54.
[306] [2010] 2 WLR 555, 566, para 40.
[307] Ibid, para 41.
[308] Ibid. [309] Ibid. [310] Ibid, para 42.
[311] Ibid, 566–7, para 42. [312] Ibid, 567, para 43.

satisf[ied] the threshold test of reasonableness, or arguability, such that they ought not to be regarded as fanciful'.[313]

Briggs J next turned to the construction of the Land Registration Act and Rules to ascertain whether Croatia's two arguable claims in relation to the property gave it a 'sufficient interest', within the meaning of section 43(1)(c) of the Act, in obtaining the entry of the restrictions it was seeking. In this regard, the class of persons deemed to have a sufficient interest in the entry of restrictions given by way of example in Rule 93(d)—namely persons with an interest in the due administration of the estate of a deceased person in certain specified circumstances—'afford[ed] a loose parallel or analogy with Croatia's interest (shared with the other successor states) in having the processes of the ASI duly carried into effect'.[314] These processes 'at least arguably include[d] an obligation under article 2 (reinforced by article 7 of Annex B) upon successor states with the power to do so, to take necessary measures to prevent loss, damage or destruction to the property and assets of the SFRY in which, in accordance with the provisions of the ASI, one or more of the successor states have an interest'.[315] This obligation 'would at least arguably require a state such as Serbia in de facto possession of immovable property of the former SFRY, such as the property in the present case, to do nothing to bring about an alienation of that property otherwise than in accordance with the principles and machinery of the ASI'.[316]

[313] Ibid, para 43. As regards Serbia's submission that the omission of the property in question from the list of diplomatic and consular properties of the former SFRY appended to Annex B of the ASI was fatal to Croatia's application, Briggs J found it sufficient to conclude, ibid, para 44, that the contrary was reasonably arguable, 'both because of the obligation of the Joint Committee under article 5(a) of Annex B to verify and if necessary amend the list, and because of the arguably catch-all provisions of Annex F, read in conjunction with article 7 of, and the recitals to, the main agreement'. Serbia had also submitted that the property fell outside the ASI on account of its being military property within the meaning of articles 4 and 5 of Annex A to the Agreement—specifically, property of the former Yugoslav National Army used for civilian purposes, within the meaning of article 4(2). (Article 4 of Annex A to the ASI reads:

> (1) Notwithstanding paragraph (1) of Article 3 of this Annex, tangible movable State property of the SFRY which formed part of the military property of that State shall be the subject of special arrangements to be agreed among the successor States concerned.
> (2) In relation to tangible movable and immovable property of the former Yugoslav National Army used for civilian purposes the arrangements referred to in paragraph (1) of this Article will acknowledge the relevance of Articles 2(1) and 3(1) of this Annex.

Articles 2(1) and 3(a), dealing with property of the SFRY which was located within the territory of the SFRY, are irrelevant for present purposes. Article 5 states in relevant part that '[a] Joint Committee on Succession to Movable and Immovable State Property shall be established by the successor States, which shall ensure the proper implementation of the provisions of this Annex applicable to tangible movable and immovable property (other than military property) and the resolution of any problems which might arise in the course of their application'.) Again, however, while Serbia's arguments might or might not ultimately have prevailed, they came 'nowhere near depriving Croatia's claims of the quality of being reasonably arguable in themselves': [2010] 2 WLR 555, 567, para 44. They were matters to be decided pursuant to the provisions of the ASI and were therefore not justiciable in an English court: [2010] 2 WLR 555, 567, para 44.

[314] Ibid, para 53. [315] Ibid. [316] Ibid.

In sum, then, Croatia had 'a claim to a present interest in the property, a claim to have the property distributed to it *in specie* pursuant to the ASI, and an interest in having the principles and machinery of the ASI carried into effect', the combination of which gave it a sufficient interest, for the purposes of section 43(1)(c) of the Land Registration Act, in the making of the requested entry in the register.[317] This gave the registrar the power, under section 42(1)(a) of the Act, to enter the restrictions sought and the adjudicator, in the event of a dispute, jurisdiction to request him to do so.[318] This conclusion disposed of the case. His Lordship nonetheless emphasized several points:

56 First, it is a weighty consideration against the conclusion which I have reached that the claims of Croatia in relation to the property which I have identified are probably not justiciable by the English court, arising as they do out of the transactions of sovereign states and from an unincorporated treaty to which the United Kingdom is not even a party. I say "probably" because it is unnecessary for me finally to conclude to that effect, and Croatia wishes to keep the position open, in case the ASI procedures ultimately fail to lead to a resolution of the present impasse. I proceed therefore on the assumption that the claims are non-justiciable in England.

57 None the less the claims relate to an interest in or ownership of land situated in England, title to which is identified and guaranteed by the statutory system of land registration, which includes a system of limited protection by restriction designed to assist persons seeking to protect rights or claims in relation to registered estates. This is an equally powerful factor suggesting that arguable (i.e. non-fanciful) claims in relation to the property ought in principle to be capable of being protected by restriction, even if they have to be determined elsewhere than in the English courts.

58 I invited submissions, by way of analogy, in relation to a claim by a spouse in a French divorce to have an English matrimonial home (registered in the other spouse's sole name) transferred to her by way of property adjustment order, and to a claim to an interest in English registered land being pursued in a foreign arbitration. In neither example was any cogent submission made that preservation of the status quo by entry of an appropriate restriction would be unavailable.

59 Secondly, I find it unreal to suppose (as submitted by Serbia) that if for example the workings of the ASI led to a distribution of the property to Croatia or, for that matter, to any other successor state including Serbia itself, the Land Registry would decline to accede to an application to register the successful claimant as proprietor of the property in succession to the SFRY, merely on the ground that the distribution had occurred pursuant to the workings of an unincorporated treaty made between sovereign states. It is noteworthy in that context that Bosnia and Herzegovina (a single successor state) was allocated the London

[317] Ibid, para 55. [318] Ibid, para 54.

Embassy of the former SFRY by article 1 of Annex B to the ASI, and was in fact registered as the freehold proprietor of it, on 11 February 2004, albeit subject to a restriction which prohibits the registration of a disposition otherwise than by an order of the registrar.[319]

He continued:

60 I have already referred to *In re AY Bank Ltd* in which Sir Andrew Morritt C said, in relation to a provision of the ASI which had by the time of the hearing before him determined what were to be the respective interests of the successor states in relevant foreign bank accounts, that the ASI both resolved those matters in a manner capable of being recognised by English law, and formed an essential element in a successor state's proof of title to such property. The same analysis would apply, *a fortiori*, to any decision reached pursuant to the principles and machinery of the ASI in relation to the distribution *in specie* of the property to Croatia, or to any other successor state. That decision would form a part of the successful state's title, or rather, a part of its evidence in seeking to be registered in succession to the SFRY as proprietor of the registered leasehold.

61 For as long as there is a reasonable prospect that the principles and machinery of the ASI may lead to a determination that the property ought to be distributed to Croatia, I see no reason why Croatia's claim to that effect should not be protected by a restriction. In the meantime, for as long as Croatia and Serbia continue to be of the common view (as reflected in the ASI and as stated to Sir Andrew Morritt C in the *AY Bank* case) that the successor states are, between them, entitled to succeed to the property of the former SFRY, I see no reason why Croatia's claim to be, therefore, a joint beneficial owner of the property, pending any determination to the contrary under the ASI, should not also be a claim meriting protection by a restriction, so that Croatia has a sufficient interest in the entry of a suitable restriction for that purpose.[320]

Briggs J added:

Finally, while I recognise that a strict application of the non-justiciability principle, and of the rule that an unincorporated treaty has no consequence in English law, would support Serbia's submissions and the adjudicator's conclusions, it seems to me that English law would fly in the face of reality if it refused to recognise an agreement between successor states as to the devolution among them of property of their dismembered predecessor merely because that agreement was contained in an international treaty, and because the parties to it were sovereign states. Speaking generally, English law readily takes note of any agreement between co-owners of real property as to the amount or proportion of their respective beneficial interest in that property. To apply the non-justiciability principle in a way which would preclude English law from recognising or taking account of such an agreement, whether stated in the ASI or determined as a

[319] Ibid, 569–70. [320] Ibid, 570, citations omitted.

result of the agreed principles and machinery of the ASI, would in my judgment amount to a slavish application of the rule without regard either to its proper purpose, or to the exceptions to it which have been identified, both in *Republic of Ecuador v Occidental Exploration and Production Co* and in *In re AY Bank Ltd*, as I have described.[321]

With that his Lordship allowed the appeal.

Briggs J's subtle judgment is persuasive. In terms of justiciability, there is a world of difference between an English court's not purporting to rule on the disputed content of an unincorporated treaty, including a treaty between third States, and its pretending that the treaty does not give rise to international rights and obligations among the States Parties to it. This was made clear by Lord Oliver in *J.H. Rayner (Mincing Lane)*:

> It must be borne in mind... that the conclusion of an international treaty and its terms are as much matters of fact as any other fact. That a treaty may be referred to where it is necessary to do so as part of the factual background against which a particular issue arises may seem a statement of the obvious. But it is, I think, necessary to stress that the purpose for which such reference can legitimately be made is purely an evidential one. Which states have become parties to a treaty and when and what the terms of the treaty are questions of fact. The legal results which flow from it in international law, whether between the parties *inter se* or between the parties or any of them and outsiders, are not and they are not justiciable by municipal courts.[322]

It was perfectly permissible, therefore, for Briggs J to take account of the uncontested fact that the ASI confers rights under international law on all the successor States to the SFRY and provides for a mechanism by which the precise content of these rights is to be determined. It was similarly correct for his Lordship to characterize as non-justiciable Serbia's argument, opposed by Croatia, that the property at issue in the present case fell outside the ASI on account of its being military property within the meaning of articles 4 and 5 of Annex A to the Agreement.[323] Reaching a decision on the latter point would have necessitated interpretation and application proper, as distinct from taking judicial notice, of the terms of the treaty. It would have required dealing with the treaty as law, rather than fact. As for Briggs J's reading of *AY Bank*, Sir Andrew Morritt C may be surprised to discover that he coined in that case a further exception to the non-justiciability at English law of unincorporated treaties and, more generally, of the transactions of foreign states on the international plane. But there is no reason why the surprise should not be a pleasant one.

[321] Ibid, 570–1, para 62, citations omitted.
[322] *J.H. Rayner (Mincing Lane) Ltd v Department of Trade and Industry* [1990] 2 AC 418, 500–1.
[323] [2010] 2 WLR 555, 567, para 44.

11. *R (Al-Haq) v Secretary of State for Foreign & Commonwealth Affairs*, 27 July 2009, [2009] EWHC 1910 (Admin), unreported (QBD (Admin Ct), Div Ct)

'Buttes' *non-justiciability—non-justiciability of UK government's conduct of foreign affairs—customary international law—relationship between customary international law and English law—International Court of Justice's advisory opinion in* Legal Consequences of the Construction of a Wall in the Occupied Palestinian Territory—*Articles on Responsibility of States for Internationally Wrongful Acts, article 41—European Union-Israel Association Agreement 1995—Fourth Geneva Convention 1949—Occupied Palestinian Territory—whether application to compel UK government not to recognize as lawful conduct of State of Israel and not to render aid or assistance in maintenance of situation created thereby justiciable*

The claimants, a Palestinian non-governmental organization based in the Occupied Palestinian Territory (OPT), sought a declaration that the UK government was responsible for a breach of the UK's international legal obligations, first, not to recognize as lawful the situation created by Israel's conduct of its January 2009 military offensive in the Gaza strip ('Operation Cast Lead') and in its construction of the separation wall in the OPT, including in and around East Jerusalem, and, secondly, not to render aid or assistance in the maintenance of this situation. They also initially sought a mandatory order that the government use its best endeavours to fulfil these obligations through a range of measures, specifically through the public denunciation of Israel's actions in Operation Cast Lead and the construction of the wall; through the suspension of all Standard Individual Export Licences (SIELs) for UK-made military equipment; through the suspension of all UK government financial or ministerial assistance directly given to UK companies exporting military technology or goods to Israel; through a request that the EU suspend the EU-Israel Association Agreement in accordance with article 79(2) of the Agreement and to use its best endeavours to ensure that it was suspended; through the seeking out and suspension of any other financial or military assistance given by the UK government to Israel; and through the calling of a Conference of the High Contracting Parties to the 1949 Geneva Conventions to address Israel's grave breaches of the Fourth Convention.[324] 'Accepting', however, 'that there are limits to the extent to which the courts can direct the UK government how to conduct its foreign relations', the claimants appeared ultimately to seek merely an order mandating the government not to recognize Israel's actions as lawful and not to render aid or assistance in maintaining the situation created

[324] See [2009] EWHC 1910 (Admin), para 8, referring to Euro-Mediterranean Agreement establishing an association between the European Communities and their Member States, of the one part, and the State of Israel, of the other part, Brussels, 20 November 1995, OJ L 147/3, 21.6.2000 and Convention Relative to the Protection of Civilian Persons in Time of War, Geneva, 12 August 1949, 75 UNTS 287.

by them.[325] Precisely what action the government was to take as a consequence of the order sought would be up to it, although any action or inaction would be susceptible to judicial review on the usual grounds.[326] The claimants' argument was that paragraph 159 of the International Court of Justice's advisory opinion in *Legal Consequences of the Construction of a Wall in the Occupied Palestinian Territory* spelled out the UK's customary international obligations in relation to Israel's unlawful conduct in building the separation wall,[327] obligations equally applicable in relation to Israel's serious breaches of peremptory norms of international law in Operation Cast Lead,[328] as indicated in the International Law Commission's Articles on Responsibility of States for Internationally Wrongful Acts;[329] and that the UK's customary international obligations gave rise, via the doctrine of incorporation, to an obligation on the domestic courts to ensure that the government acted to meet the UK's obligations.[330] The application for permission to seek judicial review was referred by Collins J of the Administrative Court of the Queen's Bench Division to a Divisional Court for an answer to three questions, the two of relevance for present purposes being whether a domestic court had jurisdiction to deal with the claim and, if it did, whether it should exercise it.

The Divisional Court (Pill LJ and Cranston J) denied the claimants permission to seek judicial review, holding that it was not arguable that they would obtain the relief sought, for the reason that the subject-matter of the claim was non-justiciable.

Pill LJ stated:

> The subject matter in the present case is, at bottom, the conduct of Israel and whether that state is in breach of its international obligations. . . . For the courts of England and Wales to decide whether Israel is in breach of its international obligations and, if so, the extent and nature of the breach or breaches, is beyond their competence (Lord Wilberforce in *Buttes* . . .).[331]

[325] See [2009] EWHC 1910 (Admin), paras 13 and 25.

[326] See ibid. The claimants suggested, ibid, para 9, that the government might take the following action: 'a. the exercise of universal jurisdiction to prosecute or extradite any individuals involved in grave breaches; b. the enforcement of the system for suppression of such breaches; c. significant diplomatic pressure; d. the introduction of measures to the Security Council under Chapter VII of the UN charter (the Security Council's powers to maintain peace); e. clear public denunciation; f. lawful sanctions; g. application of pressure through withdrawal of preferential trading terms; or h. convening a meeting of the Conference of the Parties.'

[327] Ibid, paras 12 and 57, quoting at para 12 from *Legal Consequences of the Construction of a Wall in the Occupied Palestinian Territory, Advisory Opinion* [2004] ICJ Rep 136, 200, para 159.

[328] [2009] EWHC 1910 (Admin), para 13. For use of the term 'serious breaches of peremptory norms of international law', see ibid, paras 4 and 51; and for reference to the allegedly peremptory character of certain human rights obligations, the right to self-determination and the prohibition on the acquisition of territory by force, see ibid, para 6.

[329] GA res 56/83, 12 December 2001, Annex. The implicit reference in Cranston J's judgment is to article 41.

[330] [2009] EWHC 1910 (Admin), para 40.

[331] Ibid, para 41, referring to *Buttes Gas and Oil Co v Hammer (No 3)* [1982] AC 888, (1982) 53 *BYIL* 259–68 (HL).

Unlike *Kuwait Airways*, this was not a case where the violation of international law was plain and acknowledged or where, as in *Abbasi*, it was clear to the court; rather, the ICJ's opinion in the *Wall* case 'consider[ed] different issues', and there had been 'no authoritative judgment upon Operation Cast Lead as a starting point for the court's consideration of whether to act'.[332] Secondly, the subject-matter was 'one of the forbidden areas' of UK executive conduct, namely 'decisions affecting foreign policy'.[333] The object of the claim was to compel a change in the government's foreign policy, something the courts were not entitled to declare or to direct:[334]

> Constitutionally, the conduct of foreign affairs is exclusively within the sphere of the executive (*Jones, Gentle* in the Court of Appeal, *Abbasi*). While there may, exceptionally, be situations in which the court will intervene in foreign policy issues, this case is far from being one of them.[335]

The government was aware of its international obligations and it was for it, not the courts, to decide what actions were appropriate to comply with those obligations.[336] His Lordship concluded that '[t]he two strands considered, the nature of the underlying claim, that is condemnation of Israel, and the nature of the claim against the Government, that is a direction or declaration as to what foreign policy it should follow, operate[d] together to demonstrate that the court should not be prepared to consider it'.[337]

For his part, Cranston J summarized the claim with dramatic flourish:

> This claim for permission to proceed to judicial review is nothing but bold. As my Lord has explained, what the claimant ultimately wants is for the court to rule that Israel's actions in Gaza are unlawful because they are in serious breach of peremptory norms of international law or constitute war crimes. Once that is done it invites the court to grant a declaration, even give a direction, that United Kingdom foreign policy towards Israel be changed. (One aspect is that the United Kingdom should withdraw from an EU-Israel treaty.) That is because the United Kingdom, in the claimant's contention, is in breach of its international obligations because it does not denounce, and continues to recognise as lawful, situations created by Israel's actions. These international obligations are said to be imposed on the United Kingdom through the application of secondary rules of international law. These are incorporated, in the claimant's contention, into the common law as rules of customary international law.[338]

[332] [2009] EWHC 1910 (Admin), para 42, referring to *Kuwait Airways Corpn v Iraqi Airways Company (Nos 4 and 5)* [2002] UKHL 19, [2002] AC 883, (2002) 73 *BYIL* 400–4 (HL) and *R (Abbasi) v Secretary of State for Foreign and Commonwealth Affairs* [2002] EWCA Civ 1598, 126 ILR 685, (2002) 73 *BYIL* 414–28 (CA (Civ Div)).

[333] [2009] EWHC 1910 (Admin), para 43, citing *R (Abbasi) v Secretary of State for Foreign and Commonwealth Affairs* (2002) 126 ILR 685, 725, para 106(iii).

[334] [2009] EWHC 1910 (Admin), para 44.

[335] Ibid, para 46, referring to *R v Jones (Margaret)* [2006] UKHL 16, [2007] 1 AC 136, (2006) 77 *BYIL* 472–81 (HL) and *R (Gentle) v Prime Minister, Secretary of State for Defence and Attorney-General* [2006] EWCA Civ 1689, [2007] QB 689, (2006) 77 *BYIL* 548–53 (CA (Civ Div)).

[336] [2009] EWHC 1910 (Admin), para 44. [337] Ibid, para 46. [338] Ibid, para 51.

For him too the application was not justiciable. The authorities clearly established that the courts were 'very slow to review the exercise of prerogative powers in relation to the conduct of foreign affairs and the deployment of the armed services, and very slow to adjudicate upon rights arising out of transactions entered into between sovereign states on the plane of international law'.[339] This was not a matter of discretion—that is, it was 'not the case that in the modern administrative State there are no no-go areas for the courts'.[340] The 'non-justiciability of matters of high policy' derived in part from a 'concern about institutional competence'[341] or, putting it another way, from a 'recognition of the limits of judicial expertise'.[342] This 'issue of relative institutional competence' was apparent in the instant case:

56 . . . Were the matter to proceed, Israel's obligations would need to be defined and then breaches identified and proved on the basis of events occurring outside the jurisdiction. Were Israel to appear any justification it advanced, such as proportionality, would need to be explored. Once this was done the claimant's case would turn on an enquiry into breaches by the United Kingdom of its obligations. Those obligations, which the claimant contends derive from customary international law, would need to be defined. Breaches would then need to be proved through a close examination of the conduct of United Kingdom foreign policy. All of this would entail determinations of knotty issues of law and fact. It would be against the backdrop of possibly the most serious, protracted and controversial dispute in international affairs today. And in the evidence of . . . the Deputy Director of the Middle East and North Africa Directorate in the Foreign and Commonwealth Office, compelling the Government to take a public position on the matters in the claim would risk hindering the United Kingdom's engagement with peace efforts in the Middle East. This is not the *CND* case, where the claimant was at pains to emphasise that the issue was purely one of law and there were no disputed issues of fact. Nor is it *Kuwait Airways*, where breaches of international law were plain.

57 Quite apart from the complex factual matters which the present claim would involve, there is an absence of what Lord Wilberforce described as "judicial or manageable" standards: *Buttes Gas and Oil Co v Hammer*. The claimant advances the Advisory Opinion of the International Court of Justice, *Construction of a Wall* as to the obligations of the United Kingdom, coupled with the International

[339] Ibid, para 53, quoting *R v Jones (Margaret)* [2007] 1 AC 136, 162–3, para 30 (Lord Bingham) and citing further [2007] 1 AC 136, 172–3, paras 65–7 (Lord Hoffmann) and *R (Gentle) v Prime Minister* [2008] UKHL 20, [2008] 1 AC 1356, 1367, para 8(2) (Lord Bingham), 1372–3, para 26 (Lord Hope), and 1381, para 58 (Baroness Hale), (2008) 79 *BYIL* 422–8 (HL).

[340] [2009] EWHC 1910 (Admin), para 53.

[341] Ibid, para 55.

[342] Ibid, quoting *R (Campaign for Nuclear Disarmament) v Prime Minister of the United Kingdom* [2002] EWHC 2777 (Admin), 126 ILR 727, 755, para 60 (Richards J), (2002) 73 *BYIL* 444–52 (QBD (Admin Ct), Div Ct).

Law Commission's Articles on Responsibility of States for Internationally Wrongful Acts, 2001. The former is not directly applicable to Gaza, and the latter are, in my judgment, too open-textured to have a great deal of purchase in the present case. It seems to me that much of the ground the claimant seeks to have the court traverse would be more appropriately entrusted to a committee of inquiry, with expertise in diplomacy and international law.[343]

Non-justiciability in cases such as the present involving foreign relations was also justified by comity between States.[344] To the foregoing considerations was to be added the constitutional background, namely that '[c]onstitutionally the overall conduct of foreign policy is entrusted to those with a democratic mandate, the government, in particular the Prime Minister and Foreign Secretary . . . , not to the courts'.[345]

On the doctrine of incorporation, Cranston J offered the following dicta:

The claimant seeks to gain a 'domestic foothold' for the court to review United Kingdom foreign policy through its contention that customary international law is part of English law, so long as there is no constitutional principle or clear statutory authority in contradistinction to it. But Blackstone's view, that the law of nations is adopted in its full extent by the common law (Commentaries, vol IV, ch 5), was penned in an earlier age, on different constitutional and international arrangements. It has not survived as far as the law of treaties is concerned. Under our dualist system these cannot confer rights on individuals, directly enforceable in our courts, without specific transposition into domestic law. In *Jones*, Lord Bingham saw truth in Brierly's contention that international law is not a part, but a source, of our law and agreed that customary international law is applicable by our courts only where the constitution permits. The constitutional principle there was that the power to constitute new crimes is now reserved exclusively to Parliament. The constitutional principle here militating against the incorporation of customary international law is the one I have just mentioned. Whether customary international law should have any purchase in domestic law, without specific transposition, is an issue for another day. Certainly a rule that it does not would be consistent with our dualist system regarding the reception of international law.[346]

Pill LJ was more circumspect, observing simply that '[t]he issue of the incorporation of customary international law into domestic law is not susceptible to a simple or general answer' and that there was 'no need to attempt one' to decide the instant case.[347]

343 Citations omitted, citing [2002] EWHC 2777 (Admin), paras 10 and 22, [2002] AC 883, 903, paras 24–6 (Lord Nicholls), [1982] AC 888, 938 (Lord Wilberforce), and [2004] ICJ Rep 136, 200, para 159.

344 [2009] EWHC 1910 (Admin), para 58, quoting *Buck v Attorney General* [1965] 1 Ch 745, 770 (Diplock LJ) and *Oetjen v Central Leather Co*, 246 US 297, 304 (1918) (Fuller CJ), the latter being approved at [1982] AC 888, 933 (Lord Wilberforce).

345 [2009] EWHC 1910 (Admin), para 59.

346 Ibid, para 60.

347 Ibid, para 40.

The Divisional Court's decision is correct, even if it never quite hits the nail on the head. The most fundamental reason why the application was non-justiciable was that it ultimately sounded in international law alone. As made clear by Lord Hoffmann in *Lyons*, there cannot, by virtue of the doctrine of incorporation, be a secondary obligation at common law for the breach of a primary obligation binding purely as a matter of international law;[348] and the primary rules of customary international law at issue in the present case—the customary international rules of international armed conflict, the right to self-determination, and the prohibition on the acquisition of territory through the use of inter-State force—are structurally unamenable to incorporation into the common law of England and Wales, being rules of a strictly State-to-State or State-to-people character.[349] Moreover, even if these customary international rules were for some reason to be thought at least hypothetically incorporable, the claimants' argument, founded as it was on the law of State responsibility, would need to rely on them *qua* rules of international law, giving rise, in the event of breach, to the responsibility of the State of Israel under international law. In short, the claimants could not possibly hope to construct a case with a foothold in English law, and, without such a foothold, the English courts have no jurisdiction to adjudicate on questions of international law. The words of Simon Brown LJ in *CND* are as apposite to the present case as they were to that one:

> All of the cases . . . in which the court has pronounced upon some issue of international law are cases where it has been necessary to do so in order to determine rights and obligations under domestic law. . . . [But] there is in the present case no point of reference in domestic law to which the international law issue can be said to go; there is nothing here susceptible of challenge in the way of the determination of rights, interests or duties under domestic law to draw the court into the field of international law.[350]

As his Lordship concluded, '[t]he domestic courts are the surety for the lawful exercise of public power only with regard to domestic law; they are not charged with policing the United Kingdom's conduct on the international plain'.[351]

[348] See *R v Lyons* [2002] UKHL 44, [2003] 1 AC 976, 995, para 39, (2002) 73 *BYIL* 428–34 (HL).

[349] See *R v Secretary of State for the Home Department, Ex parte Thakrar* [1974] QB 684, 702 (Lord Denning MR) and 708–9 (Orr LJ), (1974–1975) 47 *BYIL* 352–6 (CA); *J.H. Rayner (Mincing Lane) v Department of Trade and Industry* [1989] Ch 72, 184–5 (Kerr LJ), (1988) 59 *BYIL* 267–341 (CA). Traces of such reasoning, elided with considerations of justiciability, can be found in *West Rand Central Gold Mining Company v The King* [1905] 2 KB 391, 409–12 (Lord Alverstone CJ). Consider also *R (Campaign for Nuclear Disarmament) v Prime Minister of the United Kingdom*, 126 ILR 727, 744–5, para 36, where, by holding without more that the applicant's case did not sound in domestic law, Simon Brown LJ, with whom Maurice Kay and Richards JJ agreed, appeared to give the shortest of shrifts to the argument that the prohibition on the unlawful use of inter-State force, being a rule of customary international law, formed part of the law of England.

[350] 126 ILR 727, 744–5, para 36, quoted by Pill LJ in the present case, [2009] EWHC 1910 (Admin), paras 32–3, when recalling the Secretary of State's submissions.

[351] 126 ILR 727, 745, para 36, quoted [2009] EWHC 1910 (Admin), para 33 (Pill LJ).

12. *R (Kι; brι;s Türk Hava Yollarι;) v Secretary of State for Transport*, 28 July 2009, [2009] EWHC 1918 (Admin), unreported (QBD (Admin Ct), Wyn Williams J)

Statehood—title to territory—sovereignty—effective control over territory—secessionist entity—'Turkish Republic of Northern Cyprus'—Republic of Cyprus—Convention on Civil Aviation 1944 ('Chicago Convention'), articles 1, 2, 5, 6, and 68—interpretation of treaties—Vienna Convention on the Law of Treaties 1969, articles 31 and 32—customary international law—right of government to declare seaports closed—recognition of States—obligation of non-recognition—United Nations Security Council resolutions 541 (1983) and 550 (1984)—effect in English law of non-recognition of statehood by Her Majesty's Government—Civil Aviation Act 1982, section 60—Air Navigation Order 2005, article 138—construction of statutory instrument—non-justiciability—whether Secretary of State for Transport obliged to refuse operating permits for direct flights between UK and Turkish Republic of Northern Cyprus

The Air Navigation Order 2005,[352] enacted pursuant to section 60 ('Power to give effect to Chicago Convention and to regulate air navigation, etc') of the Civil Aviation Act 1982,[353] provides in article 138(1)(a) that no aircraft registered in a Contracting State to the Convention on Civil Aviation 1944 (the 'Chicago Convention'),[354] other than the UK, may take on board or discharge passengers in the UK for valuable consideration without the permission of the Secretary of State for Transport granted under that article. The first claimant, a Turkish airline, held a permit granted under the 2005 Order to operate flights between the UK and Turkey. Some of its flights from the UK to Turkey continued, after stopping, to Ercan airport in the so-called Turkish Republic of Northern Cyprus (TRNC), and some of its flights from Turkey to the UK originated at Ercan. It applied to the Secretary of State to vary the terms of its operating permit to enable it to fly direct from the UK to Ercan and vice versa.[355] At the same time, it and the second claimant, a wholly-owned UK subsidiary which, *inter alia*, organized charter flights to Turkey and the TRNC using aircraft operated by the first claimant, applied under the 2005 Order for an operating permit for specified charter flights on the same route.

[352] SI 2005/1970.

[353] Section 60 of the Civil Aviation Act 1982 reads in relevant part:

(1) ... Her Majesty may by Order in Council under this section (in this Act referred to as 'an Air Navigation Order') make such provision as is authorised by subsections (2) and (3) below or otherwise by this Act or any other enactment.

(2) An Air Navigation Order may contain such provision as appears to Her Majesty in Council to be requisite or expedient—

(a) for carrying out the Chicago Convention...

(b) generally for regulating air navigation.

[354] Chicago, 7 December 1944, 15 UNTS 295.

[355] The first claimant's extant permit in fact authorised it to fly direct between the UK and Ercan, but it prohibited the picking up of passengers in the one for setting down in the other.

The Secretary of State declined to grant either the variation or the permits for the charter flights. While it was the policy of the UK government to support in principle the commencement of direct flights between the UK and northern Cyprus, it would permit such flights only if permission could lawfully be granted, and permitting such flights would not be lawful in the present circumstances. The claimants sought judicial review of the Secretary of State's decision, on the apparent[356] ground of error of law, in that, in the application of the government's policy, the Secretary of State had misdirected himself as to whether granting permission for the claimants' flights would be lawful. The Republic of Cyprus participated in the proceedings as an interested party. The Secretary of State defended his decision on what were really three grounds,[357] all of which asserted the correctness of his understanding of the relevant law. First, article 138 of the 2005 Order was to be interpreted, insofar as it was possible, in such a way that the power it conferred on the Secretary of State to permit flights was not exercised in a manner contrary to the UK's obligations under the Chicago Convention;[358] it followed that, if the grant of the requested permits would place the UK in breach of one or more of its obligations as a Contracting State to the Chicago Convention, the permits could not lawfully be granted;[359] the UK, as a Contracting State to the Convention, was obliged to respect the rights accorded under the Convention to the Republic of Cyprus, another Contracting State; and the grant of the permits would be incompatible with the Republic of Cyprus's rights under the Convention. Secondly, the grant of the permits would amount to implied recognition of the TNRC as a State by the UK, contrary to the UK's obligations under international law. Thirdly, Her Majesty's Government did not recognise the TNRC as a State, recognizing instead a single Republic of Cyprus encompassing the entire territory of the island of Cyprus; to grant the permits would necessarily be to attribute validity to certain acts of the government of the TRNC in the sphere of international civil aviation; and the law of England and Wales did not countenance the attribution of validity to the governmental acts of a State not recognized as such by HMG.

Wyn Williams J, in the Administrative Court of the Queen's Bench Division, dismissed the claims, accepting the Secretary of State's arguments.

[356] The judgment is frustratingly impressionistic regarding the precise basis of the claimants' challenge.

[357] The judgment conflates the second two of these grounds. It is unclear whether the parties did the same.

[358] [2009] EWHC 1918 (Admin), para 36, drawing the relevant proposition, which was not in dispute between the parties, from the wording of section 60(2) of the Civil Aviation Act 1982 and the judgment of Schiemann J in *R v Secretary of State for Transport, ex parte Pegasus Holdings (London) Limited* [1988] 1 WLR 990, 1002–3.

[359] [2009] EWHC 1918 (Admin), para 36.

His Lordship, dealing first with the Secretary of State's reliance on the Chicago Convention, recalled by way of preface (making it clear that his approach to the interpretation of the Convention was to be governed by these principles[360]) both the customary rules of treaty interpretation reflected in articles 31 and 32 of the Vienna Convention on the Law of Treaties (VCLT)[361] and what Lord Steyn had said about them in *Re Deep Vein Thrombosis and Air Travel Group Litigation*, namely that, in accordance with article 31(1), '[t]he primacy of the Treaty language, read in context and purposively, is . . . of critical importance'.[362] He noted, however, that one of the crucial words in the Chicago Convention which fell to be interpreted was 'sovereignty' in article 1 ('Sovereignty over the airspace')—an article which the parties accepted was declaratory of customary international law and which provides that '[t]he contracting States recognise that every State has complete and exclusive sovereignty above its territory'—and that inevitably his interpretation of this word would be influenced by the meaning usually given to it in public international law generally.[363] The Secretary of State and the Republic of Cyprus contended that the meaning to be given to 'sovereignty' in article 1 was the same as that under customary international law;[364] that in this light the word referred to 'the right to exercise the functions of a state to the exclusion of all other states in regard to a certain area of the world';[365] and that, in accordance with this definition, sovereignty continued to subsist even if the State in which it inhered was not in a position to exercise all of the rights that it entailed.[366] The claimants agreed that this was what sovereignty meant as a matter of customary international law and that, for the purposes of customary international law, the Republic of Cyprus retained sovereignty over the whole of the island of Cyprus.[367] They argued, however, that the word was to be given a different meaning in article 1 of the Chicago Convention, a meaning dependent on effective control over the territory in question, with the result that the Republic of Cyprus did not, for the purposes of the Convention, enjoy sovereignty over that part of the island comprising the TRNC.[368] In response to these opposing submissions, Wyn Williams J stated:

[360] Ibid, para 37.
[361] 23 May 1969, 1155 UNTS 331.
[362] [2009] EWHC 1918 (Admin), para 35, quoting [2005] UKHL 72, [2006] 1 AC 495, 508, (2005) 76 *BYIL* 626–30 (HL).
[363] [2009] EWHC 1918 (Admin), para 37. His Lordship further noted that in *Military and Paramilitary Activities in and against Nicaragua (Nicaragua v United States of America), Merits* [1986] ICJ Rep 14, 111, para 212, the ICJ had held article 1 of the Chicago Convention to be consonant with customary international law.
[364] [2009] EWHC 1918 (Admin), para 40.
[365] Ibid, para 38, quoting P Martin *et al.* (eds), *Shawcross & Beaumont, Air Law* (4th edn, Butterworths, London, 1989), no page reference, as relied on by counsel for the Secretary of State.
[366] [2009] EWHC 1918 (Admin), para 38.
[367] Ibid, para 39.
[368] Ibid, para 40.

I am not persuaded that the word sovereignty within the Chicago Convention is to be given a different meaning from its meaning in customary international law. There are a number of reasons why I reach that conclusion. First, nothing in the Treaty itself, its words, aims and objects, suggests that sovereignty is to be understood in any way differently from the way it is normally understood in public international law. Second, as I have said, Article 1 of the Chicago Convention was intended to be and is declaratory of customary international law. In those circumstances it seems very unlikely that the word sovereignty should be given a different meaning from that normally understood in international law. Third, Articles 1 and 2 are drafted in such a way that the meaning to be given to the word sovereignty therein is wholly consistent with the usual meaning attributed to the word sovereignty. It is telling, in my judgment, that the word sovereignty in Article 2 is linked with the words suzerainty, protection and mandate, each of which have settled meanings in international law. No suggestion has been made that these words have a different meaning in the Chicago Convention from their normal meaning. It is hardly to be supposed that these three words are to be given the meaning normally attributable to those words in customary public international law in the context of the Convention, yet sovereignty in that context is to mean something different from its normal meaning. Fourth, it cannot be that the word sovereignty is to be interpreted differently in different Articles of the Convention. Fifth, the Convention is a treaty between contracting states. Most, if not all of the states of the world are signatories. It is acknowledged in public international law that a state may retain sovereignty over territory even though it does not control that territory effectively. Against that background, I can think of no compelling reason why the contracting states to the Chicago Convention should be taken to have intended a different meaning to the word sovereignty in the Convention to its normal meaning in the absence of very clear words to that effect.[369]

His Lordship also drew attention to article 2 of the Convention, which deems the territory of a State, for the purposes of the Convention, 'to be the land areas and territorial waters adjacent thereto under the sovereignty...of such State'.[370] In this light, the territory of the Republic of Cyprus, for the purposes of the Convention, comprised the whole of the island of Cyprus and the territorial waters adjacent thereto, while, conversely, the Republic of Cyprus enjoyed, for the purposes of the Convention, sovereignty to the whole of the island of Cyprus and the territorial waters adjacent thereto.[371]

Turning to whether the grant of the requested permits would place the UK in breach of any of its obligations under the Chicago Convention, and acknowledging that it was common ground '(but if not indisputable in reality)' that the UK was obliged to respect rights enjoyed by the

[369] Ibid, para 41. [370] Ibid, para 42. [371] Ibid, para 43.

Republic of Cyprus under the Convention,[372] Wyn Williams J considered first the question of scheduled flights between the UK and Ercan airport. Article 6 of the Chicago Convention ('Scheduled air services') provides that '[n]o scheduled international air service may be operated over or into the territory of a contracting State, except with the special permission or other authorisation of that State, and in accordance with the terms of such permission or authorisation'. That is, article 6, 'properly interpreted', conferred on the Republic of Cyprus a right, which it had exercised, to refuse permission for scheduled flights by the first claimant to land at Ercan. In this light, were the Secretary of State to grant permission for scheduled flights between the UK and Ercan, it would place the UK in breach of its obligation to respect the Republic of Cyprus's rights under the Convention.[373] As regards charter flights, article 5 ('Right of non-scheduled flight') of the Convention provides that the civil aircraft of one Contracting State, where not engaged in scheduled international air services, have the right to fly into or to transit non-stop across the territory of another Contracting State and to make stops for non-traffic purposes without the need for prior permission from the latter. (Turkey is a Contracting State to the Chicago Convention.) Article 5 continues that such aircraft, if engaged in the carriage of passengers for remuneration or hire on other than scheduled international air services, shall also have the privilege of taking on or discharging passengers, 'subject to the right of any State where such embarkation or discharge takes place to impose such regulations, conditions or limitations as it may consider desirable'. Wyn Williams J noted that the proviso in the second limb of article 5 as to the imposition of such limitations as the Contracting State in whose territory the charter passengers are to be discharged may consider desirable was 'very widely drawn'.[374] In his view, it entitled the Republic of Cyprus to stipulate that charter flights operated by the first claimant not land at Ercan. As a result, were the Secretary of State to grant the claimants the requested permits for charter flights from the UK to Ercan, the UK would stand in breach of its obligation to respect the Republic of Cyprus's right under article 5.[375] Article 10 of the Convention was also relevant, and provides that every aircraft which enters the territory of a Contracting State[376] shall, if the regulations of that State so require, land at an airport, known as a 'customs airport', designated by that State for the purpose of customs and other examination. That is, in his Lordship's formulation, article 10 empowers a Contracting State to make regulations requiring aircraft to land within its territory at a customs airport designated by it.[377] To his Lordship's way of thinking, the Republic of Cyprus was at liberty

[372] Ibid, para 44. [373] Ibid, para 45. [374] Ibid, para 47. [375] Ibid, para 48.

[376] An exception exists in respect of aircraft which, under the terms of the Convention or a special authorization, are permitted to cross the territory of a contracting State without landing.

[377] [2009] EWHC 1918 (Admin), para 49.

under this provision 'to designate airports as "customs airports" in that part of the island of Cyprus which it controls and, further, ... to refuse to designate an airport as a customs airport when that airport lies outside the area of the territory which it controls', since each Contracting State 'has a choice which it, and it alone, is entitled to exercise under Article 10'.[378] As such, given that the Republic of Cyprus had not designated Ercan as a customs airport but had designated as such a number of airports in the territory controlled by it in the southern part of the island of Cyprus, the grant by the Secretary of State of permits for direct flights between the UK and Ercan would place the UK in breach of its obligation to respect the Republic of Cyprus's rights under article 10.[379] The same process of reasoning applied 'with equal force' in respect of article 68 ('Designation of routes and airports') of the Convention,[380] which specifies that each Contracting State 'may ... designate the route to be followed within its territory by any international air service and the airports which any such service may use'. Wyn Williams J observed by way of coda that it was, 'of course', crucial to his reasoning that the rights conferred on the Republic of Cyprus by articles 5, 6, 10 and 68 of the Convention were not dependent on the exercise by its government of effective control over the whole of the territory over which the State enjoyed sovereignty, something which, 'of course', followed from his interpretation of the word 'sovereignty' and of the phrase 'territory of the State' as used in the Convention.[381] Nor did arguments advanced by the claimants by reference to the practice of direct flights between Contracting States to the Chicago Convention and Taiwan[382] serve to challenge his Lordship's conclusions, since his Lordship was 'in no position to deal with whether each direct flight between a state which is a signatory to the Chicago Convention and Taiwan places that state in breach of one or more of its obligations under the Convention'.[383]

[378] Ibid, para 50. [379] Ibid.
[380] Ibid, para 51. [381] Ibid, para 52.
[382] As recalled by his Lordship, ibid, para 55, counsel for the claimants 'placed considerable significance upon the fact of direct flights between contracting states of the Chicago Convention and Taiwan'. 'He pointed out that the territory which comprises Taiwan is under the sovereignty of the People's Republic of China. Despite that, the Government of the People's Republic of China does not exercise effective control over Taiwan. [Counsel] further suggested that the Government of the People's Republic protests vigorously about direct flights from contracting states of the Chicago Convention to Taiwan. Nonetheless such flights take place. Further, they take place to airports which have not been designated as customs airports by the Government of the People's Republic of China.'
[383] Ibid. First, the evidence presented was very limited, so that it would have been 'presumptuous' of Wyn Williams J, 'at the very least', to make assumptions as to the compatibility of direct flights between Contracting States and Taiwan with the obligations of those Contracting States under the Convention. Secondly, there was reason to suppose that there was a 'crucial distinction' between the facts relating to Taiwan '(at least in relation to some flights between contracting states and Taiwan)' and the facts relating to the TRNC, in that, according to other evidence before the Court, 'the People's Republic of China has apparently designated at least one airport in Taiwan as a "customs airport" under Article 10 of the Convention'.

Wyn Williams J then disposed of the claimants' argument that the right to permit the operation of scheduled international flights over or into its territory conferred on a Contracting State by article 6 of the Chicago Convention necessarily implied that the Contracting State enjoyed effective control over that part of the territory in which the airport where the flights were to land was situated, so that as long as the government of that State did not exercise such control the State's right of authorization under article 6 was to be considered suspended,[384] as was the obligation on other Contracting Parties to respect those rights.[385] The argument was based in part on article 61(1) of the VCLT, which provides, *inter alia*, that the temporary impossibility of performing a treaty may be invoked as a ground for suspending the operation of that treaty if the impossibility results from the permanent disappearance or destruction of an object indispensable for the execution of the treaty. His Lordship rejected the submission:

61. I simply do not see how this provision assists the Claimants in their assertion that the rights created by the Chicago Convention have become suspended. The [Republic of Cyprus] has not sought to assert that it regards the Convention as suspended. No other contracting state to the Chicago Convention makes such an assertion . . . Suspension does not occur automatically under Article 61(1). The words of the Article make it clear that the suspension must be invoked. Neither the Claimants nor the government in the TRNC can, conceivably, be entitled to assert that the Chicago Convention or Articles thereof are suspended when none of the contracting states to the Convention make that assertion or seek to rely on temporary impossibility of performance to justify a suspension.

62. There is this further and, in my judgment, insurmountable difficulty for the Claimants. Upon my interpretation of the relevant Articles of the Convention it has not become impossible, even on a temporary basis, for the Interested Party to exercise its rights under the Convention or for the other contracting states to comply with their obligation not to infringe those rights. At the risk of repetition, the rights conferred by Articles 5, 6, 10 and 68 of the Convention are capable of being exercised by the Interested Party for the reasons explained above notwithstanding that it does not have effective control over the TRNC.

Wyn Williams J immediately continued, as regards other submissions to the same end (the precise content of which is not revealed in his Lordship's judgment):

63. This same line of reasoning is fatal to the submissions made on behalf of the Claimants to the effect that the rights conferred upon the Interested Party under Articles 5, 6, 10 and 68 of the Convention have become suspended by virtue of

[384] Ibid, para 57. [385] Ibid, para 58.

other doctrines of law which permit the suspension of rights (or obligations) in defined circumstances. Each of these doctrines has at its heart the notion that events have occurred which prevent the exercise of the rights in question or that events have occurred whereby the legal person subject to an obligation can treat the occurrence of the events as a reason why, at his election, he is absolved from compliance with an obligation. I am not persuaded that any doctrine of public international law exists whereby rights conferred by a treaty are treated as suspended against the will of the legal person upon whom those rights are conferred and in circumstances when the rights can be enjoyed.

The claimants had also relied for support on a rule of customary international law—the existence of which was apparently accepted by his Lordship—to the effect that a State was not entitled to declare closed the seaports in any parts of its territory removed from its government's control, the submission being that there was no principled reason to distinguish between seaports and airports, with the consequence that the right of the Republic of Cyprus to regulate air services to and from Ercan airport was suspended for as long as the territory in which the airport was situated was under the control of the government of the TNRC.[386] This line of reasoning fared no better than the others:

It seems to me that this submission ignores the fact that the Interested Party has rights under the Convention (Articles 5, 6, 10 and 68) which it was capable of exercising regardless of whether it controlled the territory in the north of the island of Cyprus. In my judgment it cannot be that treaty rights relating to international aviation and which are capable of being performed (as I have found them to be) are nonetheless suspended by virtue of a principle of customary international law which has evolved and has been strictly confined hitherto in its application to the closure of seaports.[387]

On this note his Lordship concluded his consideration of the UK's obligation 'to respect and uphold the rights conferred upon the [Republic of Cyprus] by virtue of its status as a contracting state to the Convention', on which ground alone the claim for judicial review was 'doomed to failure'.[388]

Given, however, that the Secretary of State had defended the challenged decision on additional bases, Wyn Williams J decided to address these arguments obiter. He concluded that the Secretary of State was bound to refuse the claimants' application for the operating permits on these grounds too.[389]

The Secretary of State had submitted that granting the operating permits would necessarily imply recognition of the TRNC as a State, in breach of the UK's duty under international law. In contrast, the claimants had contended that the grant of permission for direct flights between

[386] Ibid, para 64. [387] Ibid, para 65.
[388] Ibid, para 66. [389] Ibid, para 91.

the UK and Ercan would amount to no more than an acknowledgment of the undisputed fact that the government of the TRNC was in effective control of the relevant territory.[390] His Lordship rejected the claimants' characterization of the situation, reaching instead the 'clear conclusion' that the grant of the requested permits 'would amount to implied recognition that the Government in control of the TRNC was sovereign over the territory which it effectively controls'.[391] The government of the TRNC had created the organs of a State and was purporting to exercise the rights of the Republic of Cyprus under the Chicago Convention through a range of means detailed by his Lordship, including by establishing an ICAO-compliant aviation authority—which the claimants were inviting the Secretary of State to treat as equivalent to an aviation authority under the Convention[392]—and by designating Ercan as a customs airport.[393] As for whether this would place the UK in breach of international law, the Secretary of State accepted, as the claimants had submitted, that UN Security Council resolution 541 (1983), which called upon all States 'not to recognize any Cypriot State other than the Republic of Cyprus',[394] and Security Council resolution 550 (1984), which reiterated the call 'not to recognise the purported state of the "Turkish Republic of Northern Cyprus" set up by secessionist acts' and 'not to facilitate or in any way assist the aforesaid secessionist entity',[395] did not impose any legally binding obligation on the UK.[396] Equally, however, the claimants accepted, as did Wyn Williams J, the Secretary of State's submission that customary international law obliged the UK 'not to recognise the TRNC as legal or lawful'.[397] In this light, his Lordship concluded 'that the grant of the permits in this case would be a breach of the United Kingdom Government's duty not to recognise the TRNC'.[398]

As for the argument that the Secretary of State 'was obliged as a matter of domestic law to refuse the permits since the grant of such permits would necessarily attribute validity to the acts of the Government of the TRNC (such as designating air routes and designating Ercan Airport as a customs airport)', Wyn Williams J recalled 'the long line of domestic authority which is to the effect that the court cannot take cognizance of a foreign juridical person if to do so would involve the court in acting inconsistently with the foreign policy or diplomatic stance of the

[390] Ibid, para 78. [391] Ibid, para 79.

[392] Ibid, para 80. ICAO, the International Civil Aviation Organization, is established and empowered under Chapter VII of the Chicago Convention.

[393] Ibid, para 81.

[394] SC res 541 (1983), 18 November 1983, para 7.

[395] SC res 550 (1984), 11 May 1984, para 3.

[396] [2009] EWHC 1918 (Admin), para 83.

[397] Ibid, para 84. His Lordship's express acceptance is found ibid, para 90 ('I have reached the conclusion that a legal duty exists whereby the Government of the United Kingdom is obliged not to recognise the TRNC or its Government.')

[398] Ibid, para 90.

Government of this Country in relation to that person'.[399] It was true that this line of authority did not prevent the court from giving effect to 'certain routine acts of administration, if they are unobjectionable',[400] as held by Lord Denning MR in *Hesperides Hotels v Aegean Holidays Ltd*, referring to 'the day to day affairs of the people, such as their marriages, their divorces, their leases, their occupation and so forth',[401] and by Sumner J in *Emin v Yeldag*,[402] relating to a decree of divorce validly granted under the law of the TRNC; and these two English cases were 'consistent with principles of international law'[403] as expounded by the ICJ in *Namibia*[404] and by the ECtHR, in relation to northern Cyprus, in *Loizidou v Turkey*[405] and *Cyprus v Turkey*.[406] But this qualification made no difference to the case before his Lordship:

I cannot accept that I am entitled to give validity to the Acts of the TRNC (as they relate to international aviation)... I accept without hesitation that many of the acts of the Government of the TRNC as they relate to aviation are public and international in character. They are not properly described as laws which regulate the day to day affairs of the people who reside in the TRNC either as described by Lord Denning MR, or Sumner J or in the *Namibia* case. Further, it seems to me that the rationale of the exception to the general principle is the avoidance of serious prejudice to the inhabitants of the area affected. While I do not underestimate the feeling of isolation which the inhabitants of the TRNC may feel and the will which exists in the international community to seek to bring to an end that isolation, I cannot ignore the fact that the population of the TRNC is served by international airports on the island of Cyprus. The evidence seems clear that thousands of people cross the demarcation line between the area controlled by the

[399] Ibid, para 85, citing *Carl Zeiss Stiftung v Rayner and Keeler Ltd (No 2)* [1967] 1 AC 853 and *Gur Corporation v Trust Bank of Africa Ltd* [1987] QB 599, (1986) 57 *BYIL* 405–10 (CA).

[400] [2009] EWHC 1918 (Admin), para 86. His Lordship's explicit acceptance of this position is found ibid, para 90 ('This court is obliged to refuse to give effect to the validity of acts carried out in a territory which is unrecognised unless the acts in question can properly be regarded as regulating the day to day affairs of the people within the territory in question and can properly be regarded as essentially private in character.').

[401] [1978] QB 205, 218, (1978) 49 *BYIL* 259–61 (CA), quoted at [2009] EWHC 1918 (Admin), para 87.

[402] [2002] 1 FLR 956, cited at [2009] EWHC 1918 (Admin), paras 87–8.

[403] [2009] EWHC 1918 (Admin), para 88.

[404] *Legal Consequences for States of the Continued Presence of South Africa in Namibia (South West Africa) notwithstanding Security Council Resolution 276 (1970), Advisory Opinion* [1971] ICJ Rep 16, 56, para 125, quoted at [2009] EWHC 1918 (Admin), para 88 ('In general, the non-recognition of South Africa's administration of the Territory should not result in depriving the people of Namibia of any advantages derived from international co-operation. In particular, while official acts performed by the Government of South Africa on behalf of or concerning Namibia after the termination of the Mandate are illegal and invalid, this invalidity cannot be extended to those acts, such as, for instance, the registration of births, deaths and marriages, the effects of which can be ignored only to the detriment of the inhabitants of the Territory.')

[405] (1997) 23 EHRR 513, cited at [2009] EWHC 1918 (Admin), para 88. The relevant statement in *Loizidou* is at para 45, where the statement of the ICJ in *Namibia*, para 125, is quoted.

[406] (2002) 35 EHRR 731, cited at [2009] EWHC 1918 (Admin), para 88. The relevant passage in *Cyprus v Turkey* is at paras 90–7, where the Grand Chamber discusses the statement of the ICJ in *Namibia*, para 125.

Government of the TRNC and that controlled by the Interested Party on a daily basis. Distances on the island are sufficiently small that the use of airports situated in those areas controlled by the Interested Party is perfectly practicable.[407]

In short, the Secretary of State was obliged by English law to refuse the application for the permits.

Finally, Wyn Williams J recalled that, in the course of oral submissions, counsel for the Republic of Cyprus had raised the issue whether the claim was justiciable. In response, his Lordship simply observed that the Secretary of State had accepted expressly that his decisions to refuse such permits were properly the subject of judicial review and that the Court had proceeded on this basis.[408]

In the context of the arguments put to the court and accepted by the parties, Wyn Williams J's decision is largely a good one, even if his dicta on the second of the Secretary of State's subsidiary submissions are perhaps not watertight. It may well be that the TRNC acts as if it were a Contracting State to the Chicago Convention, but it is self-evidently not, with the result that it does not inexorably follow that the UK's hypothetical grant of operating permits for flights directly into and out of that entity need be premised on its being a State. Presumably, absent the application of the Convention to it, a political-territorial entity need not be a State or derive its authority from a State for it to authorize landing and take-off in and from territory for which, *de jure* or *de facto*, it has the authority to speak. But be that as it may.

Perhaps more to the point, and this is simply a function of how the Secretary of State sought to justify his decision rather than a criticism of his Lordship's reasoning as such, it is not immediately apparent how the TRNC's purporting to authorize flights into and out of the territory under its control and its designation of Ercan as a customs airport entered the equation at all. The Secretary of State was merely being asked to grant permission for, and was capable of granting permission solely for, the UK end of the claimants' operations, viz for flights landing and discharging passengers in the UK from Ercan airport and for flights departing from the UK with a view to landing and discharging passengers at Ercan airport. The realization of the proposed flights remained subject at all times to the grant of permission to the claimant airline by the appropriate authorities at the other end and to the terms of such permission, and it is not obvious why the question by whom this permission was properly to be granted was per force a matter for a UK Secretary of State.[409]

407 [2009] EWHC 1918 (Admin), para 89.

408 Ibid, para 91.

409 *Pace* Wyn Williams J, it is even less clear how, were the Court—and it is to the courts that the prohibition on giving legal effect to the governmental acts of a State not recognized by HMG is in fact directed—to have quashed the Secretary of State's decision, it could have been said to be giving effect under English law to the authorization of flights by the aviation authority of the TRNC or to that authority's designation of Ercan as a customs airport.

This leads in turn to doubts as to the soundness in reality—as distinct from on the basis of the arguments put to the Court—of his Lordship's ruling on the Chicago Convention point, although the *fons et origo* of any dubiousness is again the Secretary of State's defence of his decision and, furthermore, the failure of the claimants adequately to attack this. Rather than running the hopeless argument as to the meaning of 'sovereignty' for the purposes of the Convention, which Wyn Williams J was correct to dismiss, the claimants might have been better off submitting that the identity of the appropriate authorizing body at the Cyprus end of their operations was a matter for them and not for the Secretary of State. It may well be that any permission granted the claimants by the aviation authority of the TRNC would have been invalid for the purposes of the Chicago Convention.[410] It may well be that, by flying into and out of Ercan airport without the consent of the aviation authorities of the Republic of Cyprus, the claimant airline would have violated the aviation law of the Republic of Cyprus,[411] a law likely to have been enacted to give effect to the relevant provisions of the Chicago Convention. But, even if both were true,[412] it is by no means incontestable that the UK, in authorizing flights out of its territory to Ercan and into its territory from Ercan, would have violated any obligation it could be said have owed the Republic of Cyprus under the Convention, since it remained open to the claimants to seek permission from the Republic of Cyprus, not the TRNC, to land and discharge passengers at, and to take on board passengers at and take off from, Ercan. In short, in granting permission for the claimants' flights into and out of its own territory, the UK was not *per se* failing to respect the right of the Republic of Cyprus, as recognized[413] in the Convention, to regulate the occurrence of and conditions imposed on flights into its territory. It is perhaps not irrelevant in this regard that the Secretary of State had been content to renew every six months since 1999 the claimants' extant operating permits in respect of flights to Turkey, even though it had become apparent (if it was not apparent at the time of the original grant in 1999) that the authorized flights to Turkey carried on after stopping, without the permission of the Republic of Cyprus, to the TRNC and that the authorized flights from Turkey originated there, similarly

[410] The claimants could have reserved their position on this.

[411] The claimants could have reserved their position on this as well.

[412] See the two immediately preceding footnotes.

[413] It is more accurate to say that the Chicago Convention recognizes the inherent sovereign right of each Contracting Party to regulate entry into its territory than to say—as does Wyn Williams J, [2009] EWHC 1918 (Admin), paras 45, 52, 58, 62, 63, and 66—that the Convention confers rights on Contracting States in this respect. But the result is the same, given that the canon of statutory construction ultimately relied on by the Secretary of State for the purposes of his English-law argument applies as much in respect of customary international law as it does in respect of treaty: see e.g. *R v Keyn* (1876) 2 Ex D 63, 85 (Sir Robert Phillimore) and 210 (Lord Cockburn CJ) and, more recently, *Salomon v Commissioners of Customs and Excise* [1967] 2 QB 116, 143 (Diplock LJ), (1967) 42 *BYIL* 291–3 (CA) and *Alcom Ltd v Republic of Colombia* [1984] AC 580, 588 (Sir John Donaldson MR), (1983) 54 *BYIL* 285–8 (CA).

without the Republic of Cyprus's consent.[414] None of this is to say that the known facts of the Republic of Cyprus's refusal of consent for direct flights into and out of Ercan and of the claimants' failure since 1999 to seek such permission were not relevant considerations. But the Secretary of State did not defend his decision by arguing that it was rational. He defended it by alleging that he was legally compelled to decide as he did. Nor is it to say that the grant of the permits by the Secretary of State would have squared with the customary obligation on every State, recognized by the ICJ in 1949 in *Corfu Channel*, 'not to allow knowingly its territory to be used for acts contrary to the rights of other states'.[415] But, again, this was not the Secretary of State's argument.[416]

A question left unanswered by the case, given the claimants' acceptance of the Secretary of State's submission to this extent, is whether—insofar as his decision was referable to the Chicago Convention, and assuming for the sake of argument that the UK would indeed have violated its obligations under the Convention had the Secretary of State granted the permits—the Secretary of State was, as he submitted, compelled by English law in this case to act in accordance with the UK's unincorporated treaty obligations. His argument, accepted to this extent by the claimants, was that article 138 of the Air Navigation Order 2005 was to be interpreted, insofar as it was possible, in such a way that the power it conferred on the Secretary of State to permit flights was not exercised in a manner contrary to the UK's obligations under the Convention. That is, the argument was at root one as to statutory interpretation, and was necessarily based on the canon of construction according to which Parliament is presumed not to intend to legislate in a manner contrary to the UK's existing treaty obligations[417]—or, adapting the canon to the subordinate legislation in question, according to which the Queen in Council is presumed not to intend to legislate in a manner contrary to the UK's existing treaty obligations.[418] But it is seriously debateable

[414] Perhaps needless to say, these were not decisions the claimants were likely to impugn.

[415] *Corfu Channel (United Kingdom v Albania), Merits, Judgment*, [1949] ICJ Rep 4, 22. See, similarly, *Trail Smelter Arbitration (USA/Canada)*, 3 RIAA 1905 (1941), 1963.

[416] Moreover, as observed by the arbitral tribunal in *Trail Smelter*, 3 RIAA 1905, 1963, stating the basic rule is one thing, but 'the real difficulty often arises ... when it comes to determine what, *pro subjecta materie* [*sic*], is deemed to constitute an injurious act'.

[417] See e.g. *Garland v British Railway Engineering Ltd* [1983] 2 AC 751, 771 (Lord Diplock), (1982) 53 *BYIL* 291–3 (HL); *R v Secretary of State for the Home Department, Ex parte Brind* [1991] 1 AC 696, 747–8 (Lord Bridge) and 760–1 (Lord Ackner), (1991) 62 *BYIL* 437–40 (HL); *R v Lyons* [2002] UKHL 44, [2003] 1 AC 976, 992, paras 27–8 (Lord Hoffmann), (2002) 73 *BYIL* 428–34 (HL). Note that this was not a situation in which the legislation (here, the subordinate legislation, in the form of article 138 of the Air Navigation Order 2005) was itself promulgated to give effect to the obligations in question. While article 138 of the 2005 Order was enacted by Her Majesty in Council in order, in part, to facilitate the UK's 'carrying out the Chicago Convention', in the words of section 60(2)(a) of the Civil Aviation Act 1982, it did not encompass the UK's obligation to respect the rights of other Contracting States to the Convention, the obligation at issue here.

[418] See, specifically in relation to the Queen in Council, *Post Office v Estuary Radio* [1968] 2 QB 740, 757 (Diplock LJ), (1967) 42 *BYIL* 295–8 (CA); and, in relation to subordinate legislation in general, *R v Secretary of State for the Home Department, Ex parte Brind* [1991] 1 AC 696, 760 (Lord Lowry).

whether there was really an issue of statutory interpretation here at all. Article 138 of the Air Navigation Order 2005 provides in relevant part:

(1) An aircraft registered in a Contracting State other than the United Kingdom, or in a foreign country, shall not take on board or discharge any passengers or cargo in the United Kingdom where valuable consideration is given or promised in respect of the carriage of such persons or cargo unless—

(a) it does so with the permission of the Secretary of State granted under this article to the operator or the charterer of the aircraft or to the Government of the country in which the aircraft is registered, and in accordance with any conditions to which such permission may be subject...

The interpretative presumption in question may be brought to bear only when the legislative text is ambiguous, and there is nothing ambiguous about article 138(1)(a) of the 2005 Order. The Secretary of State is simply given a very wide discretion, a discretion he is perfectly at liberty as a matter of English law to exercise in conformity with or contrary to the UK's unincorporated obligations under the Chicago Convention. The Secretary of State's argument is ultimately no different from the argument put to the House of Lords, and vigorously rejected, in *Brind*, where, framing the application for judicial review in irrationality, counsel for the applicant argued that the Secretary of State was obliged not just to take the unincorporated ECHR into account when taking a decision under section 29(3) of the Broadcasting Act 1981 but to take it into account correctly—in other words, to act in accordance with it. In response, Lord Bridge stated that '[w]here Parliament has conferred on the executive an administrative discretion without indicating the precise limits within which it must be exercised, to presume that it must be exercised within [unincorporated treaty] limits would be to go far beyond the resolution of an ambiguity'.[419] It could perhaps be argued, however, that there is a difference between *Brind* and the present case,[420] in that here the particular provision of primary legislation from which the Queen in Council derives her authority to make an Air Navigation Order, namely section 60 of the Civil Aviation Act 1982, states in subsection (2), after vesting Her Majesty with said authority in subsection (1):

(2) An Air Navigation Order may contain such provision as appears to Her Majesty in Council to be requisite or expedient—

(a) for carrying out the Chicago Convention...

On this basis it could be argued that the clear intention of Parliament in vesting Her Majesty with the power to make an Air Navigation Order—as

[419] Ibid, 748.

[420] The other difference is obviously that, whereas *Brind* concerned a power exercised pursuant to primary legislation, the present case concerns one exercised at one remove, viz pursuant to subordinate legislation.

distinct from the intention of Her Majesty in Council in vesting the Secretary of State, by way of article 138(1)(a) of the 2005 Order, with the power to grant permission to the operator or charterer of an aircraft—is that any such Order made by Her Majesty in Council be in conformity with the Chicago Convention, with the consequence that the scope of the power of the Queen in Council to empower in turn the Secretary of State to grant permission to the operator or charterer of an aircraft is limited to such grants of permission as conform to the Convention. The upshot would be that the Secretary of State's power under article 138(1)(a) of the 2005 Order to grant permission to the operator or charterer of an aircraft is limited to grants which conform to the Convention. Putting it another way, the Secretary of State would be obliged to act in conformity with the Convention. In this regard, it is by no means irrelevant that one of Lord Bridge's reasons for rejecting the applicant's argument in *Brind* was that to accept it 'would be to impute to Parliament an intention . . . that the executive should exercise the discretion in conformity with the [unincorporated treaty]'.[421] No such imputation would be necessary here, since Parliament's intention that the Queen in Council's discretion, and thus ultimately the Secretary of State's, be exercised in conformity with the unincorporated treaty obligation is, the argument goes, made clear in section 60(2)(a) of the Civil Aviation Act 1982. But this complicated argument has its flaws, which probably ought to prove fatal. First, it is arguably too much of a stretch to construe 'carrying out the Chicago Convention', as per section 60(2)(a) of the 1982 Act, to encompass the UK's obligation to respect the rights of other Contracting States to the Convention, the unincorporated treaty obligation at issue here. Secondly, the precise power conferred on Her Majesty in Council by section 60 of the Act is to make, in the words of the chapeau to section 60(2), 'such provision as appears to [her] requisite or expedient' for carrying out the Convention—a notably broader discretion than that on which the argument above is premised. Thirdly, what an Air Navigation Order made by Her Majesty in Council may contain is not limited to what appears to her requisite or expedient for carrying out the Chicago Convention; rather, paragraph (b) of the same provision, again recognizing a broader discretion on the part of Her Majesty in Council than that factored into the argument, provides that such an Order may equally contain what appears to Her Majesty requisite or expedient 'generally for regulating air navigation'. Indeed, it pays to recall that section 60 of the 1982 Act is not entitled 'Power to give effect to Chicago Convention' but 'Power to give effect to Chicago Convention and to regulate air navigation, etc'. In short, it is difficult to conclude that the power vested in Her Majesty in Council by Parliament by way of section 60 of the Civil Aviation Act 1982 is limited to the making of Air Navigation Orders which conform to the UK's obli-

[421] [1991] 1 AC 696, 748.

gation to respect the rights of other Contracting States to the Chicago Convention. In other words, there is no reason to construe the unambiguous and broad terms of article 138 of the 2005 Order in such a way that any grant of permission pursuant to it by the Secretary of State which does not respect the rights of other Contracting States to the Convention would be unlawful.

As to whether, absent the Secretary of State's acknowledgement that his refusal to grant the permits was properly the subject of judicial review, his decision would have been justiciable, the question calls for disaggregation. If what is being asked is whether the separation of powers would have prevented the court from subjecting to scrutiny the exercise by the Secretary of State of the discretion granted him by article 138 of the 2005 Order, the answer is an unambiguous no. This sort of exercise of delegated power by an administrative decision-maker is the bread and butter of judicial review. If, alternatively, the question is whether the court would have been prevented from adjudicating on the Chicago Convention arguments by the non-justiciability, as a general rule, of unincorporated treaties, the answer is still a resounding no. First, the consideration of the Chicago Convention was necessary for the determination of rights and obligations under English law.[422] Secondly, the Secretary of State purported to have taken the challenged decision on the basis, in part, of the Chicago Convention.[423]

Finally, it might seriously be doubted whether the case really had anything to do, as the claimants framed it, with the interpretation of the words 'sovereignty' and 'territory of a State' in articles 1 and 2 respectively of the Chicago Convention. The case is yet another in which questions going to the application of a treaty or even to rules of general international law are characterized as implicating articles 31 and 32 of the VCLT.

13. *Re Barak*, 29 September 2009, unreported (City of Westminster Magistrates' Court, Judge Wickham, Deputy Senior District Judge)

Immunity from jurisdiction—criminal jurisdiction—minister for defence—deputy head of government—special mission immunity—Convention on Special Missions 1969—customary international law—International Court of Justice's decision in Arrest Warrant of 11 April 2000 (Democratic Republic of the Congo v Belgium)*—grave breaches of Geneva Conventions—Fourth Geneva Convention 1949—Geneva Conventions Act 1957—whether*

[422] See e.g. *R (Campaign for Nuclear Disarmament) v Prime Minister* [2002] EWHC 2777 (Admin), paras 36 and 47 (Simon Brown LJ), (2002) 73 *BYIL* 444–52 (QBD (Admin Ct), Div Ct); *Republic of Ecuador v Occidental Exploration and Production Co* [2005] EWCA Civ 1116, [2006] 2 WLR 70, 91–2, para 31 (Mance LJ), (2005) 76 *BYIL* 585–9 (CA (Civ Div)).

[423] See e.g. *R v Secretary of State for the Home Department, ex parte Launder* [1997] 1 WLR 839, 867 (Lord Hope), (1996) 67 *BYIL* 548–51 (HL); *R v Secretary of State for the Home Department, Ex parte Kebilene* [2000] 2 AC 326, 367 (Lord Steyn).

visiting Minister for Defence and Deputy Prime Minister of State of Israel immune from criminal jurisdiction of English courts in respect of allegations of grave breaches of Fourth Geneva Convention

An *ex parte* application was made before Judge Wickham of the City of Westminster Magistrates' Court on behalf of unnamed Palestinian applicants for a warrant for the arrest of the visiting Minister for Defence and Deputy Prime Minister of the State of Israel, Ehud Barak. The crimes alleged were not specified in the transcript of the judgment but are known to have comprised grave breaches of the Fourth Geneva Convention[424] alleged to have been committed by the Israel Defence Forces (IDF) in the course of their offensive operations in the Gaza strip in January 2009 ('Operation Cast Lead'). Mr Barak was present in the UK in order to attend the Labour Party conference and to hold official meetings 'to discuss issues of official high-level engagement between the UK and Israel, including the Middle East Peace Process',[425] with the UK Prime Minister, Secretary of State for Foreign and Commonwealth Affairs and Secretary of State for Defence respectively. The application is reported to have been brought pursuant to the Geneva Conventions Act 1957, which enacts into English law as crimes of universal ambit the various grave breaches of the 1949 Geneva Conventions.[426] Judge Wickham saw her task as being to decide *proprio motu* whether Mr Barak was entitled to immunity from the process of the English criminal courts.

The Court refused the application.

As a procedural matter, Judge Wickham rejected counsel for the applicants' submission that she was first to issue the arrest warrant and to consider Mr Barak's entitlement to immunity only once he was arrested:

> If I go back to apply the *Arrest Warrant* case, there the judgment said [that] the Court was bound to find, given the nature and purpose of the warrant, [that] the mere issue of the warrant violated the immunity of the incumbent Minister for Foreign Affairs.[427]

She turned then to the merits of the application:

> Mr Barak's functions as Israeli Defence Minister and Deputy Prime Minister are equivalent to those exercised by a Minister for Foreign Affairs and I look to the reasoning of the International Court of Justice in the case of *The Democratic*

[424] Convention Relative to the Protection of Civilian Persons in Time of War, Geneva, 12 August 1949, 75 UNTS 287.

[425] Letter from the Treasury Solicitors, instructed by the Secretary of State for Foreign and Commonwealth Affairs, to Deputy Senior District Judge Daphne Wickham (City of Westminster Magistrates' Court), 29 September 2009, quoted in Judgment, first unnumbered paragraph. (A transcript of the unreported judgment, kindly provided by Judge Wickham, is on file with the author.)

[426] Section 1 of the Act reads: 'Any person, whatever his nationality, who, whether in or outside the United Kingdom, commits, or aids, abets or procures the commission by any other person of, a grave breach of any of the scheduled conventions or the first protocol shall be guilty of an offence.'

[427] Judgment, first unnumbered paragraph, referring to *Arrest Warrant of 11 April 2000 (Democratic Republic of the Congo v Belgium)* [2002] ICJ Rep 3.

Republic of Congo v Belgium. I am satisfied that under customary international law Mr Barak has immunity from prosecution *ratione personae* as he would not be able to perform his functions efficiently if he were the subject of criminal process in this jurisdiction.[428]

Judge Wickham continued:

I am satisfied that [Mr Barak] is also entitled to immunity under customary international law as a member of a Special Mission. This immunity is in accordance with article 31 of the Convention on Special Missions of the 8th December 1969 which declares that the representatives of the sending state in the Special Mission and the members of all its diplomatic staff shall enjoy immunity from the criminal jurisdiction of the receiving state. This Convention was adopted by Resolution 2430 of the General Assembly of the United Nations in 1969.[429]

She concluded:

I am therefore satisfied that particularly by virtue of being a member of a Special Mission Mr Barak has immunity [from] prosecution...

On this note, Judge Wickham declined to issue the requested warrant.

Judge Wickham's decision, which is not from a superior court of record and thus has no formal precedential value in the English courts, illustrates once more the effective breadth of the ICJ's judgment in *Arrest Warrant*. Despite its formal caveat, perhaps a shade disingenuous, that it was only the immunity from criminal jurisdiction and the inviolability of a minister for foreign affairs that fell to be considered in that case,[430] the ICJ nowhere stated that absolute immunity *ratione personae* and inviolability were not available to other State officials, and the purposive rationale for its finding as to the immunity and inviolability of a minister for foreign affairs when abroad[431] is equally applicable to a range of other officials—above and beyond diplomats, the head of State and the head of government, treated by the ICJ as archetypal beneficiaries of

[428] Judgment, second unnumbered paragraph. Although the judgment does not make this explicit, Judge Wickham clearly proceeded on the basis that, in the absence of any statutory basis for the immunity in question, the matter was regulated by the common law, which to this extent was consonant with the customary international rules on immunities. The same uncontroversial position was adopted by the Bow Street Magistrates' Court, in relation also to the immunity from criminal jurisdiction of the visiting Minister for Defence of the State of Israel, in *Re Mofaz*, 128 ILR 709, (2004) 75 *BYIL* 408–11, where Judge Pratt, District Judge, recalled the statement by the House of Lords in *R v Bow Street Metropolitan Stipendiary Magistrate, ex parte Pinochet Ugarte (No 3)* [2000] 1 AC 147, (1999) 70 *BYIL* 277–95 (HL) that the English courts would give effect to immunities available under customary international law, subject to statutory requirement not to do so. The Bow Street Magistrates' Court (Judge Workman, Senior District Judge) approached the matter the same way once more, this time in relation to the immunity from criminal jurisdiction of the Minister for Commerce and International Trade of the People's Republic of China, in *Re Bo Xilai*, 128 ILR 713, (2005) 76 *BYIL* 601–3.

[429] Judgment, second unnumbered paragraph, referring to Convention on Special Missions, New York, 8 December 1969, 1400 UNTS 231.

[430] [2002] ICJ Rep 3, 21, para 51.

[431] Ibid, 22, para 52.

such immunity and inviolability[432]—who might be considered to perform, when abroad, a representative function.[433] A minister for defence is a plausible candidate, as the unprecedential decision of the Bow Street Magistrates' Court in *Re Mofaz*,[434] in respect of the then Minister for Defence of the State of Israel, found in 2004. A minister for commerce and international trade was held to be another in *Re Bo Xilai*,[435] an analogous decision of the Bow Street Magistrates' Court in 2005. In this light, especially given the ICJ's explicit and contentious refusal to distinguish between official and private trips abroad,[436] the impact of *Arrest Warrant* on the prosecution of international crimes in the English courts may prove considerable. In this regard, a question left unanswered by Judge Wickham's judgment is whether, had Mr Barak been solely the Deputy Prime Minister of Israel, viz the deputy head of government, he would have been accorded immunity *ratione personae* at common law.

There is no principled reason, however, why an English criminal court, giving effect to the customary international law of jurisdictional immunities via the common law, should embrace the ICJ's reasoning in *Arrest Warrant* to extend the availability of absolute immunity *ratione personae* to those other than its generally accepted beneficiaries. The principles in accordance with which the English courts will seek to ascertain the existence and content of a putative rule of customary international law are the principles applicable under international law itself, as made clear by Lord Bingham in *European Roma Rights Centre*.[437] But as rightly decried by Judge *ad hoc* Van den Wyngaert,[438] the methodology adopted by the Court in *Arrest Warrant* for identifying a rule of customary international law flew in the face of the requirement of State practice and *opinio juris*—of the need for 'a general practice accepted as law', in the words of article 38(1)(b) of the Court's Statute. While it would be a bold domestic court which held, *pace* the ICJ, that a minister for foreign affairs does not in fact enjoy absolute personal immunity from the criminal jurisdiction of a foreign State, there is no good reason why a domestic court should adopt *Arrest Warrant*'s brand of teleological assertion, instead of demanding a widespread and representative practice on the part of States performed in the belief that it comports with a rule of law, when ascertaining whether

[432] See ibid, 21, para 51.

[433] Subsequent to *Arrest Warrant*, the ICJ has clarified that at least certain State officials are not entitled to personal immunity: see *Certain Matters of Mutual Assistance in Criminal Matters (Djibouti v France), Judgment*, 4 June 2008, para 194, in relation to a senior prosecuting magistrate and the head of national security.

[434] See above n 428.

[435] Ibid.

[436] [2002] ICJ Rep 3, para 55. But *cf* ibid, sep. op. Higgins, Kooijmans & Buergenthal, para 84, querying and qualifying the generality of the Court's statement in this regard.

[437] *R (European Roma Rights Centre) v Immigration Officer at Prague Airport* [2004] UKHL 55, [2005] 2 AC 1, 35, para 23, (2004) 75 *BYIL* 504–12 (HL).

[438] [2002] ICJ Rep 3, sep op Van den Wyngaert, 143, para 11.

customary international law affords personal immunity to State officials other than diplomats, heads of State, heads of government and ministers for foreign affairs.

As for article 31 of the Convention on Special Missions, which accords absolute immunity from the criminal jurisdiction of the receiving State, including in respect of measures of execution, to representatives of the sending State in the special mission,[439] it might be queried—*pace* not only Judge Wickham in the present case but also Judge Workman, Senior District Judge, in *Re Bo Xilai*[440]—whether this is consonant with customary international law, since it is difficult to discern a sufficiently widespread and representative body of State practice clearly differentiated from the practice relating to diplomatic, head of State and head of government immunity, on the one hand, and to State immunity, on the other. That said, it is more than likely true, as the United States government put it in 2006 in its Suggestion of Immunity in *Li Weixum v Bo Xilai,* that, while '[t]he full extent of [special mission] immunity may remain unsettled', there is 'widespread consensus that, at a minimum, States are constrained in their ability to exercise jurisdiction... over ministerial-level officials invited on a special diplomatic mission'.[441] Similarly, the Third Criminal Chamber of the German Federal Supreme Court held in the *Tabatabai* case of 1984:

> [T]he question of the customary validity of the Convention, which... is dubious, is not the decisive issue... It is in any case established that... there is a customary rule of international law based on State practice and *opinio juris* which makes it possible for an *ad hoc* envoy, who has been charged with a special political mission by the sending State, to be granted immunity by individual agreement with the host State for that mission and its associated status, and therefore for such envoys to be placed on a par with the members of the permanent missions of States protected by international treaty law.[442]

It is worth noting, however, that the same Court held there to be 'no general rule of international law which effectively guarantees immunity to a special envoy where that immunity does not protect any function and is merely granted *in personam*'.[443] Putting it another way, the individual in respect of whom immunity is claimed must be a *bona fide* part of a *bona*

[439] See Convention on Special Missions, arts 31(1) and (4).

[440] 128 ILR 713, 714.

[441] *Li Weixum v Bo Xilai*, Civ. No. 04–0649 (RJL), Suggestion of Immunity and Statement of Interest of the United States, 24 July 2006, <http://www.state.gov/documents/organization/98832.pdf>, 10. See also *Li Weixum v Bo Xilai*, Civ. No. 04–0649 (RJL), Further Statement of Interest of the United States in Support of the United States' Suggestion of Immunity, 6 December 2006, <http://www.state.gov/documents/organization/98772.pdf>. The US District Court for the District of Columbia deferred to the executive Suggestion of Immunity in *Li Weixum v Bo Xilai*, 568 F Supp 2d 35, 35 (DDC 2008).

[442] 80 ILR 388, 419, para 4. Consider also, in this light, *Kilroy v Charles Windsor, Prince of Wales*, Civ. No. C-78–291 (ND Ohio 1978).

[443] 80 ILR 388, 412, para 1. See also ibid, 420, para 4.

fide special mission agreed between the sending and receiving States,[444] and not simply present in the forum State in what is in reality a private capacity.

As to the procedure by which the present application by private parties came before the Court, while section 1A(3)(a) of the Geneva Conventions Act[445] provides that proceedings for an offence under section 1 of the Act shall not be begun in England and Wales except by, or with the consent of, the Attorney-General, section 25(2)(a) of the Prosecution of Offences Act 1985 provides that the requirement of the Attorney-General's consent shall not prevent the issue of a warrant for the arrest of a person for any offence. The same is the case for a range of other English offences of universal ambit enacted to give effect to serious crimes of international concern. What this means in practice is that private parties, in the exercise of the right to bring private prosecutions preserved by section 6(1) of the Prosecution of Offences Act and on the laying of an information evidencing the essential elements of a *prima facie* case, may be able to secure an arrest warrant for a foreign national for serious crimes of international concern committed abroad even though the case may be brought to an immediate halt by the refusal of the Attorney-General to consent to the initiation of proceedings. This differs from the situation regarding the issue of summonses in respect of the same offences, for which the Attorney-General's prior consent is required.

By way of postscript to the present case, it emerged a few months later that—to the acute embarrassment of the UK government—the Westminster Magistrates' Court had, on the application of private parties, issued a warrant for the arrest of the leader of the Israeli opposition, Tzipi Livni, who had been the Minister for Foreign Affairs of the State of Israel during the IDF's 2009 offensive in Gaza, in respect of whom a *prima facie* case was held to exist in relation to grave breaches of the Fourth Geneva Convention within the meaning of the Geneva Conventions Act 1957, and who was alleged to have been present in the UK—the last allegation proving to be false, leading to the hasty withdrawal of the warrant. The Secretary of State for Foreign & Commonwealth Affairs, Mr David Miliband, immediately issued the following statement:

> Israel is a strategic partner and a close friend of the UK. We are determined to protect and develop these ties. Israeli leaders—like leaders from other countries—must be able to visit and have a proper dialogue with the British Government.

[444] Article 1(a) of the Convention on Special Missions defines a 'special mission' for the purposes of the Convention as 'a temporary mission, representing the State, which is sent by one State to another State with the consent of the latter for the purpose of dealing with it on specific questions or of performing in relation to it a specific task'. This probably accords with customary international law.

[445] Section 1(A)(3)(a) was inserted by way of section 70(2) of the International Criminal Court Act 2001.

The procedure by which arrest warrants can be sought and issued without any prior knowledge or advice by a prosecutor is an unusual feature of the system in England and Wales. The Government is looking urgently at ways in which the UK system might be changed in order to avoid this sort of situation arising again.[446]

In the light of the Livni affair, of the present case and of the issue by the Bow Street Magistrates' Court in 2005 of a warrant for the (unsuccessful) arrest of Doron Almog, former head of the IDF in the Gaza strip, the UK government flagged its intention to enact legislation to amend the Prosecution of Offences Act to remove the capacity for private parties to secure a warrant for the arrest of a foreign national on suspicion of crimes committed abroad. The Secretary of State for Justice and Lord Chancellor, Mr Jack Straw, explained to Parliament:

The Government are concerned about the implications for the United Kingdom's relations with other states of the risk that foreign visitors to this country might be arrested on the application of a private individual, on suspicion of the gravest of offences, on the basis of evidence that might well be insufficient to gain the Attorney-General's consent (which is normally required for offences of this kind to be prosecuted), or to secure a conviction by a jury.

The problem is not hypothetical, as applications for an arrest warrant have been made, on at least two occasions successfully; and there is reason to believe that the risk of arrest may discourage prominent people, with whom HM Government would wish to engage, from visiting this country.[447]

Given opposition to the proposed move within the parliamentary Labour Party[448] and without,[449] the Ministry of Justice engaged in only the briefest and most informal of consultations, publishing a short note on 17 March 2010[450] with annexed draft amending clause[451] and inviting comments by 6 April.[452] The note stated that the UK position in relation to the issue of arrest warrants, while not unique, appeared 'anomalous' and 'unsatisfactory'.[453] It continued:

[446] Foreign & Commonwealth Office, 'Response to UK arrest warrant for Tzipi Livni', 15 December 2009, <http://www.fco.gov.uk/en/news/latest-news/?view=News&id=21448373>.

[447] Hansard, House of Commons, 4 March 2010, cols 117WS-118WS.

[448] See ibid, 28 January 2010, cols 1010–24.

[449] See the views of the non-governmental organization Justice and of the chairman of Lawyers for Palestinian Human Rights quoted in House of Commons Library, 'Private prosecutions', Library Standard Note SN/HA/5281, 26 March 2010, <http://www.parliament.uk/commons/lib/research/briefings/snha-05281.pdf>, 7.

[450] Ministry of Justice, 'Arrest warrants — universal jurisdiction. Note by the Ministry of Justice', 17 March 2010, <http://www.justice.gov.uk/publications/docs/arrests-warrants.pdf>.

[451] <http://www.justice.gov.uk/publications/docs/private-prosecutions-draft-clause.pdf> ('draft clause').

[452] Ministry of Justice, 'Arrest warrants— universal jurisdiction', 5.

[453] Ibid, 3.

The Government remains absolutely committed to upholding the principles of universal jurisdiction, so that there is no impunity for those suspected of grave offences such as those under the Geneva Conventions Act. None of the options discussed... would reduce the scope or effectiveness of universal jurisdiction.

Rather, the approach is to limit the availability of arrest warrants in respect of universal jurisdiction offences. Where applications for such warrants have been made, it has been in respect of war crimes under the Geneva Conventions Act 1957; but as the same mischief would result from arrest warrants being sought in respect of other offences where there is universal jurisdiction, including torture and hostage-taking, any solution would arguably need to extend to those crimes too.[454]

The draft clause ('Prosecution of certain extra-territorial offences: England & Wales') is designed to amend section 25 of the Prosecution of Offences Act so that the existing subsection (2)(a)—which currently permits the issue of an arrest warrant without the Attorney-General's consent in those cases where her consent is required to institute proceedings—'does not authorise the issue of a warrant of arrest (other than pursuant to an information laid by or on behalf of a Law Officer of the Crown or the Director [of Public Prosecutions]) in, or for the purpose of, proceedings to which section 6A... applies'.[455] In turn, the proposed section 6A of the Prosecution of Offences Act, applicable to 'proceedings in respect of a relevant extra-territorial offence which is alleged to have been committed outside the United Kingdom by a person who at the time was not a United Kingdom national' and to the corresponding ancillary offences, lists a range of offences of universal ambit, including piracy, grave breaches of the Geneva Conventions, hostage-taking, hijacking and torture.[456] In short, the effect of the proposed clause will be to remove the ability of private parties to obtain an arrest warrant in England & Wales on the basis of universal jurisdiction, unless the Attorney-General consents to this in advance. The change is supported by the Secretary of State for Foreign & Commonwealth Affairs of the newly elected Conservative-Liberal Democrat government, Mr William Hague, who has announced his 'intention to act speedily' to introduce the necessary legislation, describing 'a position where Israeli politicians feel they cannot visit this country' as 'unsatisfactory' and 'indefensible'.[457]

[454] Ibid, 3.

[455] Draft clause 1(4), inserting a subsection 2A into section 25 of the Prosecution of Offences Act.

[456] Draft clause 1(3), inserting sections 6A(1) and (2) into section 6 of the Prosecution of Offences Act. The term 'United Kingdom national' is deemed in section 6A(5) to include a foreigner subject to UK service law, such as a Nepalese gurkha.

[457] A Hirsch, 'Hague moves quickly to scrap international crimes trials in UK', *Guardian*, 31 May 2010, 12.

14. *Pocket Kings Ltd v Safenames Ltd and Commonwealth of Kentucky*, 16 October 2009, [2009] EWHC 2529 (Ch), unreported (Ch D, Michael Furness QC)

State immunity—constituent territories of federal States—separate entities—service of process—State Immunity Act 1978, sections 12(1), 14(1), 14(2), 14(5), and 14(6)—Commonwealth of Kentucky—United States of America—penal and other public law—whether Commonwealth of Kentucky entitled to State immunity in respect of attempts to enforce its criminal or other public law

The claimant applied for summary judgment in default of acknowledgement of service by the second defendant, the US state of Kentucky, formally styled the Commonwealth of Kentucky. A Kentucky court had served on the first defendant, a UK-based internet domain name registry, a seizure order pursuant to an *in rem* penal forfeiture claim brought in Kentucky by the Commonwealth of Kentucky against the claimant's internet domain name, of which the first defendant was the registrar. The intended forfeiture was by way of enforcement of the criminal and regulatory gaming laws of Kentucky. Before the Chancery Division of the High Court in London, the claimant sought, *inter alia*, a declaration against the Commonwealth of Kentucky that the Court would not recognize or enforce the orders made in the Kentucky proceedings or any subsequent order for the seizure or forfeiture of the claimant's domain name, on the basis that to do so would be to enforce the penal or other public law of a foreign State.[458] The Court granted permission to serve the claim on Kentucky out of the jurisdiction against the US Department of State, in accordance with sections 12(1) and 14(5) of the State Immunity Act 1978 ('SIA'), the latter providing that section 12 of the Act—which in turn provides that service on a foreign State is to be by way of transmission through the Foreign and Commonwealth Office (FCO) to the State's ministry of foreign affairs, such service being deemed to have been effected when the initiating process is received at the ministry—applies to proceedings against the constituent territories of a federal State. The time for acknowledgement of service expired, the claimant made an application for judgment in default, and service of notice of the application was effected. The Commonwealth of Kentucky neither appeared nor made submissions in the eventual proceedings. Nonetheless, in accordance with section 1(2) of the SIA (and without the benefit of adversarial argument[459]), the Court considered *proprio motu* whether Kentucky was to be considered a 'State' within the meaning of

[458] See e.g. *Attorney-General of New Zealand v Ortiz* [1984] AC 1; *Government of Iran v Barakat Galleries Ltd* [2007] EWCA Civ 1374; *Mbasogo v Logo Ltd* [2006] EWCA Civ 1370, [2007] QB 846; *United States Securities and Exchange Commission v Manterfteld* [2009] EWCA Civ 27. See also Collins, above n 201, para 5R-019.

[459] The Court considered this 'regrettable': [2009] EWHC 2529 (Ch), para 7.

the SIA and, if it were not, whether it was nonetheless entitled to state immunity under the Act. It also considered whether, if Kentucky were not a 'State' within the meaning of the Act, it had been properly served with the claim for relief. As to the merits of the claim for relief, the Court addressed whether the Kentucky proceedings were penal or otherwise public in nature.

The Court (Michael Furness QC, sitting as a Deputy Judge of the High Court) held that Kentucky was not a State for the purposes of the SIA, that it was not otherwise entitled to State immunity under the Act and that it had indeed been properly served with the claim for relief.

On the first point, the Court began by succinctly outlining the provisions of Part I of the SIA relevant to what the Act calls the 'constituent territories' (such as Kentucky) of a federal State (such as the United States of America):

> Section 14(1) provides that the immunities and privileges conferred by Part I of the Act apply to a state but not to any entity distinct from the executive organs of the government of the state and capable of suing or being sued ("a separate entity"). Section 14(5) draws a distinction between a constituent territory of a federal state and the state itself. Apart from section 12, the other provisions of Part I of the Act only apply to a constituent territory if an Order in Council so provides. No Order in Council has been made in respect of Kentucky. Section 14(6) provides that a constituent territory in respect of which no Order in Council has been made shall be treated for the purposes of sections 14(2) and (3) as if it were a separate entity.[460]

Furness QC noted that the position under the Act differed from that under the common law, as applied pre-SIA in, for example, *Mellenger v New Brunswick Development Corporation*[461] (where the Court of Appeal held, by reference to the British North America Act 1867, that the several provinces of Canada were States for the purposes of State immunity) and in the era of the SIA in criminal cases, which by virtue of section 16(4) of the SIA are not governed by Part I of the Act.[462] He continued:

> [T]he common law analysis adopted in the *New Brunswick* case is incompatible with the structure of the Act. Section 14 draws a clear distinction between 'the State' and a constituent territory of a federal state. The drafting of section 14 does not make sense if it is possible for an entity to be both a constituent territory of a federal state and a state in its own right. In civil litigation, once the Court

460 Ibid, para 9.

461 Ibid, para 11, citing [1971] 1 WLR 604, (1970–1971) 45 *BYIL* 396–8 (CA).

462 Ibid, citing by way of example *R (Alamieyeseigha) v Crown Prosecution Service* [2005] EWHC (Admin), where a Divisional Court of the Administrative Court distinguished *Mellenger* to hold that the several states of the Federal Republic of Nigeria were not States for State immunity purposes.

> has identified a state, it is impossible for any constituent territory of that state also to qualify as a state. Instead it must be treated as a "separate entity". Granted that Kentucky is, on any view, a constituent territory of a federal state it cannot itself be a state.[463]

In this light, he was compelled to examine whether Kentucky was entitled to State immunity not as a State but, in accordance with section 14(6) of the SIA, as an entity to be treated as if it were a separate entity within the meaning of section 14(2) of the Act.

Section 14(2)(a), the first stage of the two-stage test for the immunity of separate entities provided for in section 14(2), requires that the proceedings relate to anything done by the separate entity 'in the exercise of sovereign authority'. This raised the question, according to Furness QC, 'whether a separate entity such as a constituent territory can have sovereign authority in its own right, or whether the sovereign authority which is referred to in section 14(2)(a) is the sovereign authority of the state itself'.[464] In answer, he quoted, on the one hand, from *Bank of Credit and Commercial (Overseas) Ltd (In Liquidation) v Price Waterhouse (No. 1)*, a case concerning a claim to immunity by the ruler of Abu Dhabi, a constituent state of the United Arab Emirates, where Laddie J in the Chancery Division held that 'the "sovereign authority" in section 14(2)(a) is a reference to the sovereign authority of the recognised state', so that only 'when a constituent territory or other separate entity acts for and on behalf of the recognised State and effectively acts as if it was exercising the State's sovereign authority' can it benefit from 'the immunity that the State would have obtained had it acted on its own behalf'.[465] On the other hand, the Court flagged the counter-argument that 'sovereign authority might lie outside both the recognised state and the separate entity and be shared between them', a 'similar analysis to that adopted in the *Mellenger* case', on which basis 'the separate entity might exercise a sovereign authority which was neither derived from, nor a manifestation of, the sovereign authority of the [recognized] state'.[466] Teasing out this counter-argument, Furness QC drew attention to the Tenth Amendment of the US Constitution, which declares that '[t]he powers not delegated to the United States by the Constitution, nor prohibited by it to the States, are reserved to the States respectively', and noted that among the powers reserved to the respective state governments was, according to expert evidence presented to the Court, the regulation of gambling.[467] Turning to

[463] [2009] EWHC 2529 (Ch), para 12.

[464] Ibid, para 13.

[465] Ibid, quoting [1997] 4 All ER 108, 112, (1997) 68 *BYIL* 318–9 (Ch D, Laddie J). Furness QC noted, [2009] EWHC 2529 (Ch), para 15, that Hazel Fox cites the *BCCI* case in Fox, *The Law of State Immunity* (2nd edn, Oxford University Press, Oxford, 2008), 256, as authority for the proposition that 'the "sovereign authority" referred to in section 14(2)(a) is the sovereign authority of the recognised State'.

[466] [2009] EWHC 2529 (Ch), para 18.

[467] Ibid, para 19.

examine the facts of the instant case, the Court observed that the seizure proceedings in Kentucky had been brought under Kentucky law by a Kentucky public official and not by any federal agency, with the result that it seemed clear on the evidence before the Court that the conduct in respect of which State immunity was sought was the conduct of the Commonwealth of Kentucky, and was not 'the exercise of or manifestation of any sovereign authority of the federal government of the United States'.[468] As such, if the analysis in *BCCI (Overseas) v Price Waterhouse (No. 1)* were correct, State immunity would not be available to Kentucky because the authority by which it regulated gambling within Kentucky was 'an exercise of its own sovereignty, and not the sovereignty of the federal government of the United States of America'.[469] On the same analysis, had the US constitution declared that all sovereign power was vested in the federal government but was delegated in respect of specific subject-matters to the respective constituent states, State immunity would be available to Kentucky, subject to its satisfaction of section 14(2)(b) (the requirement that a State would have been immune in the same circumstances), the second limb of the two-stage test for the immunity of separate entities laid down in section 14(2). By way of aside, Furness QC remarked that '[i]t might be thought surprising that a different result should follow depending on the question whether the federal constitution operates on the basis of delegating sovereignty by the federal states to the federal government or on the basis of delegating sovereign authority from the central government to the federal states'.[470] He continued:

21 However, one has to remember that the evident purpose of the Act was primarily to confer immunity upon states. There is no independent immunity for separate entities or constituent territories; such immunity as they enjoy is parasitic on the immunity conferred on the state. The mere fact that the separate entity performs public functions is clearly not, of itself, sufficient to attract immunity.

22 Furthermore, . . . it has always been the case at common law that for the purpose of state immunity the weight of authority (apart from *Mellenger*) has been decisively in support of the proposition that sovereign authority means the authority of the nation state. Subordinate territories or government agencies do not themselves possess sovereign authority. In particular [counsel] referred me to observations of Lord Wilberforce in *I° Congresso del Partido* [1983] 1 AC 244 at 262C:

> The basis upon which one state is considered to be immune from the territorial jurisdiction of the courts of another state is that of "par in parem" which effectively means that the sovereign or governmental acts of one state are not matters upon which the courts of other states will adjudicate.

468 Ibid, para 20. 469 Ibid. 470 Ibid.

23 [Counsel] also placed reliance on *R v Bow Street Stipendiary Magistrate ex p Pinochet (No. 3)* [2000] 1 AC 147, ... referr[ing] to a passage in Lord Millet's speech at page 268:

> The doctrine of state immunity is the product of the classical theory of international law. This taught that states were the only actors on the international plane, the rights of individuals were not the subject of international law. States were sovereign and equal: it followed that one state could not be impleaded in the national courts of another; par in parem non habet imperium. States were obliged to abstain from interfering in the internal affairs of one another.

As [counsel] points out, the Commonwealth of Kentucky is not an actor on the international plane, and is not a state sovereign and equal to other states. So in the classic theory of public international law it is not a state and it does not, when exercising its own authority, exercise the authority of a sovereign state. This is important because, as Lord Phillips observed *(ibid)* at page 279H, the Act should be interpreted, so far as possible, in a manner which accords with public international law.

24 For the reasons advanced by [counsel] I have come to the conclusion that he is right in saying that "sovereign authority" in section 14(2) refers to the authority of the recognised state. . . .

It followed that Kentucky was not entitled to immunity under the Act 'because it [was] not itself a sovereign state, and it [was] not exercising the sovereign authority of a sovereign state'.[471]

As to whether the claim for relief had been properly served on the Commonwealth of Kentucky, the Court noted several salient facts. A certificate signed by the Pro Consul at the British embassy in Washington, DC certified that copies of the claim for relief had been served on the Department of State, thereby satisfying the requirements of article 12(1) of the SIA.[472] The US Department of State, however, had returned the documents served by the Pro Consul, stating that 'service of proceedings on the Commonwealth of Kentucky must be undertaken in accordance with State's own laws, regulations and procedures'.[473] A letter from the FCO to the claimants' solicitors indicated that the former had never before encountered a refusal by the State Department to accept service of proceedings on behalf of a state of the Union.[474] Furness QC concluded:

It does not seem to me that this unusual development affects the validity of the service effected on the State Department for the purposes of these proceedings. The correct method of service of proceedings before this Court must be determined by the law of England and Wales. As expressed in section 12(1) of the Act

[471] Ibid, para 24. [472] Ibid, para 25.
[473] Ibid. [474] Ibid.

the requirements for service on Kentucky are stated in mandatory terms. It is clear that service in those terms and only in those terms will suffice for the purposes of the Act. I therefore agree with [counsel] that the rejection of service by the State Department in no way impugns the validity of the service of proceedings.[475]

He remarked by way of coda that notice of the application for judgment in default was effected, pursuant to the directions of a judge of the Chancery Division, in accordance with CPR 6.38(1), which also satisfied the requirements for service of proceedings in Kentucky.[476]

When it came to the merits, the Court, having surveyed the relevant case-law,[477] concluded that 'the authorities have in the case of both penal laws and public laws identified the basis of non-enforceability as being that one state does not recognise within its own jurisdiction the penal or public (in the sense of governmental) acts of another sovereign state'.[478] Furness QC continued:

Does that mean, therefore, that my conclusion that in the regulation of gambling Kentucky is exercising its own, non-sovereign authority, and not the authority of the sovereign federal state means that its penal and public laws can be enforced in this jurisdiction? In my view that cannot be right. The authorities were simply not addressing the situation before me, where the penal and public acts in question were undertaken by a government which was a constituent part of a sovereign state, but which did not act by virtue of the authority of that state. If a sovereign state's penal and public acts are not enforceable, the non-enforceability of the penal and public acts of the government of a constituent part of the sovereign state must be an *a fortiori* case.[479]

He concluded that 'the Kentucky proceedings [were] not enforceable in English law as being penal or governmental in nature'.[480]

The Court's judgment is correct on all but the point that mattered. It is self-evident that a constituent territory, such as Kentucky, of a federal State is not a 'State' within the meaning of the relevant provisions of the SIA. It is also uncontentious, on the admittedly curious facts, that the claim for relief was duly served on the Commonwealth of Kentucky. It is furthermore plainer than the Court seems to have thought that, if one accepted that the Kentucky laws in question were penal or otherwise public in character, they were not to be enforced by the English courts by virtue of their being foreign penal or other public laws. As to the crucial question whether the proceedings brought by the claimant related, in the words of section 14(2)(a) of the SIA, to anything done by Kentucky in the exercise of sovereign authority, one might have thought this quite straightforward as well. The enforcement

[475] Ibid, para 26. [476] Ibid, para 27. [477] See above n 458.
[478] [2009] EWHC 2529 (Ch), para 40. [479] Ibid. [480] Ibid.

of law, especially of penal or other public law, by mandated public authorities is an exercise of sovereign authority *par excellence*. It is an act inherently governmental in character, 'as opposed to an act which any private citizen can perform'.[481] And section 14(6)—in accordance with which a constituent territory not the subject of an Order in Council under section 14(5) is treated as if it were a separate entity, with the consequence that, despite not qualifying under section 14(1) as a manifestation of the relevant foreign State, it may nonetheless enjoy State immunity in the circumstances provided for in section 14(2)(a) and (b)[482]—is premised on the assumption that a constituent territory is capable of exercising sovereign authority within the meaning of section 14(a). Looking at it from another angle, the necessary corollary of the Court's reasoning in paragraphs 21 to 23 of the present judgment is that a constituent territory not the subject of an Order in Council under section 14(5) of the Act can never enjoy State immunity, for the sole, syllogistic reason that it is not a State in its own right within the meaning of section 14(1) and public international law. Moreover, applying the Court's logic, a separate entity, by virtue of not qualifying as a manifestation of the State under section 14(1), could never enjoy State immunity either. In short, Furness QC's reasoning renders devoid of effect not only section 14(6) of the Act but also section 14(2). It also treats the relevant House of Lords cases as authority for questions that were not before the House. All of this is a roundabout way of saying that the test whether the relevant acts of a constituent territory (or separate entity, for that matter) are 'done by it in the exercise of sovereign authority' within the meaning of section 14(2) of the SIA is not one of the formal constitutional source of the authority to perform the acts but of the substantive character of those acts. It is a little odd that this did not dawn on Furness QC when he later found himself painted into a corner over the enforceability in the English courts of the penal or other public laws of Kentucky.

[481] See *Kuwait Airways Corporation v Iraqi Airways Company (No 1)* [1995] 1 WLR 1147, 1157 and 1159 (Lord Goff), (1995) 66 *BYIL* 496–501 (HL), quoting *I° Congreso del Partido* [1983] 1 AC 244, 269 (Lord Wilberforce), (1981) 52 *BYIL* 314–9 (HL).

[482] See, analogously, the relationship between article 28 (on the constituent states of a federal State) and article 27 (on separate entities)—the provisions of the former being declared in article 28(1) to be without prejudice to the provisions of the latter—of the European Convention on State Immunity, Basle, 16 May 1972, ETS No. 74, to which the SIA was enacted to give effect. The United Nations Convention on Jurisdictional Immunities of States and Their Property, UN doc. A/RES/59/38, 2 December 2004, Annex, adopts a far more straightforward approach to the availability of State immunity to the constituent territories of federal States. Article 2(1)(b)(ii) of the UN Convention defines the word 'State' to include 'constituent units of a federal State or political subdivisions of the State, which are entitled to perform acts in the exercise of sovereignty authority, and are acting in that capacity'. A constituent unit of a federal State which satisfies the criteria specified in article 2(1)(b)(ii) enjoys State immunity subject to the exceptions enumerated in the Convention, in accordance with article 5.

15. *Republic of Serbia v ImageSat International NV*, 16 November 2009, [2009] EWHC 2853 (Comm), unreported (QBD (Comm Ct), Beatson J)

International legal personality—State succession—State continuity—customary international law—relationship between customary international law and English law—non-justiciability of conduct of foreign affairs—'Buttes' *non-justiciability—doctrine of acquired rights—State Union of Serbia and Montenegro—Republic of Serbia—arbitration—substantive jurisdiction of arbitral tribunal—International Court of Arbitration of International Chamber of Commerce (ICC)—Arbitration Act 1996—whether arbitral tribunal having jurisdiction to determine whether Republic of Serbia continuator or successor* stricto sensu *to State Union of Serbia and Montenegro*

The State Union of Serbia and Montenegro and the respondent company, ImageSat, entered into a contract (termed an 'agreement') in 2005 providing for the purchase of goods and acquisition of rights by the former from the latter. The agreement provided that any dispute or disagreement arising under it was to be settled under and in accordance with the Rules of Arbitration of the International Chamber of Commerce (ICC), with English law as the governing law and England as the default location for the arbitration. The State Union failed to pay sums due under the agreement and, in February 2006, claimed that it was not bound by the agreement. In May 2006, ImageSat forwarded a Request for Arbitration to the ICC's International Court of Arbitration, alleging breach of contract. On 3 June 2006, Montenegro declared itself an independent State, as permitted by the terms of the Constitutional Charter of the State Union of Serbia and Montenegro. The result was two States, the Republic of Montenegro and the Republic of Serbia. On 8 June 2006, ImageSat's Request for Arbitration was sent to the State Union by the ICC. By letter of 12 July 2006, the Public Attorney of Serbia notified the ICC that Serbia agreed to act as respondent to the case, as follows:

> Due to the outcome of [the] referendum . . . [the] State Union of Serbia and Montenegro ceased to exist. Certain rights, obligations and liabilities of the State Union have been undertaken by the Republic of Serbia. Therefore the Republic of Serbia will act as the Respondent in this phase of the procedure . . . [483]

Serbia served its Answer to the Request for Arbitration on 5 September 2006. Following further exchanges of correspondence, the parties and an arbitrator signed Terms of Reference in accordance with which the

[483] [2009] EWHC 2853 (Comm), para 40. The letter added that nothing in what it referred to as Serbia's submission was to be interpreted as its entering into the merits of the case and that it was not to be construed as a waiver of any rights, remedies or claims, 'including [a] plea contesting the jurisdiction of the Arbitration', that it may have had under the ICC Rules and the applicable law.

contractual dispute was submitted to ICC arbitration by a single-member tribunal. The respondent to the case was referred to in the Terms of Reference as 'the Republic of Serbia, as successor to certain rights, obligations and liabilities of the former State Union of Serbia and Montenegro'.[484] On 7 May 2008, the tribunal rendered a Partial Award on the question of the proper parties to the arbitration in which it held that the Republic of Serbia was the continuator State of (viz the same international legal person as) the State Union of Serbia and Montenegro and, as such, was party to and bound by the agreement, including its arbitration clause.

On 2 June 2008, Serbia initiated proceedings in the Commercial Court of the Queen's Bench Division under section 67 of the Arbitration Act 1996, in accordance with which a party to arbitral proceedings may challenge 'any award of the arbitral tribunal as to its substantive jurisdiction' or may seek 'an order declaring an award made by the tribunal on the merits to be of no effect, in whole or in part, because the tribunal did not have substantive jurisdiction'.[485] Its ultimate position was that it, the Republic of Serbia, was a successor State in the strict sense to (viz a different international legal person from) the State Union of Serbia and Montenegro and that, as a successor State proper, it was not bound by the State Union's private-law obligations. It argued in the main, however, that the ICC tribunal had no jurisdiction to determine whether it was the continuator or successor *stricto sensu* to the State Union of Serbia and Montenegro (and hence whether it was a proper party to the arbitration), since, *inter alia*, the reference to the Republic of Serbia in the Terms of Reference as the 'successor' to the State Union was inconsistent with the continuity thesis, with the result that the Terms of Reference could not be interpreted as submission to the tribunal's jurisdiction on any other basis. The same went for the reference in Serbia's letter to the ICC of 12 July 2006, in the context of which the Terms of Reference were to be read, that the State Union had 'ceased to exist'. In addition, Serbia argued that the continuator/successor issue was not justiciable or arbitrable as a matter of English law, the governing law of the arbitration, in that it trespassed on the Crown's prerogative in the conduct of foreign affairs, in particular in the recognition of foreign States; in that there was no settled rule of customary international law on the continuator/successor point such as could be incorporated into the common law, with the consequence that the resolution of the issue would involve a decision by reference solely to public international law; and in that there were no judicial or manageable standards, within the meaning of the doctrine of judicial abstention enunciated by Lord

[484] Ibid, para 47.

[485] Subsequently, on 28 February 2009, the arbitrator rendered a Final Award, in which he held that the contract had been validly entered into by the State Union of Serbia and Montenegro, and had been breached, and in which he awarded ImageSat damages of around 35 million euros plus interest.

Wilberforce in *Buttes Gas & Oil v Hammer (No. 3)*, by which an arbitrator applying English law could reach such a decision.[486]

Beatson J held that the ICC tribunal did enjoy substantive jurisdiction to render the challenged Partial Award. Serbia had submitted to the tribunal's jurisdiction via the Terms of Reference in terms which gave the tribunal substantive jurisdiction to deal with the question whether Serbia was the continuator or successor State *stricto sensu* to the State Union of Serbia and Montenegro.

On whether the use of the term 'successor' in the Terms of Reference indicated that Serbia had submitted to the tribunal's jurisdiction strictly on the basis that it was a different international legal person from the State Union of Serbia and Montenegro, Beatson J reasoned:

> 76.... [A]lthough the primary meaning of "successor" indicates a different legal or juridical entity, in international law the word can relate to the factual position as well as the juridical position and does not necessarily mean that there has been a break of legal personality. For example, Stern (1996) 262 *Recueil des Cours*, 48–49 states that the terms "successor" and "continuator":
>
> > ...are not always used in their strict sense, and both expressions.... are not always clearly distinguished: this is true in the writings (doctrine) as well as in international practice.
>
> 77. Moreover, the use of the term "successor" state does not necessarily involve the extinction of the predecessor and a new legal personality. The terms of Articles 2(1)(b)-(d) of the Vienna Convention on Succession of States in respect of Treaties (1978) show that a "successor" state may become responsible for *part* of the territory of the predecessor State, without the predecessor being extinguished as occurred when Russia sold Alaska to the United States. The case of the Soviet Union and the Russian Federation...also illustrates that political extinction is not equivalent to juridical extinction and must be distinguished from it. While the Soviet Union had become extinct politically, the Russian Federation continued its legal personality: see Crawford, *The Creation of States in International Law*, 676–7....[487]

His Lordship added, referring to Serbia's letter to the ICC of 12 July 2006, that '[a] reference to "ceasing to exist" thus does not necessarily

[486] *Buttes Gas and Oil Co v Hammer (No. 3)* [1982] AC 888, (1982) 53 *BYIL* 259–68 (HL). Note that Beatson J refers throughout his judgment to the report of the case found at [1981] 3 All ER 616.

[487] Original emphasis, citing B Stern, 'La succession d'Etats' (1996) 262 *Recueil des Cours* 9–437 and J Crawford, *The Creation of States in International Law* (2nd edn, Oxford University Press, Oxford, 2006). Beatson J appears to have inserted the parts of this passage dealing with the use of the word 'successor' in the wrong part of his judgment. It is found in a section dealing with Serbia's letter to the ICC of 12 July 2006, but nowhere in this letter, at least as quoted in the judgment, does Serbia use the word 'successor'. Conversely, nowhere in his discussion of the Terms of Reference does his Lordship focus on this word.

mean a break of legal personality'.[488] Beatson J also drew attention to Serbia's statements to various international organizations and to the ICJ at the time of Montenegro's independence:[489]

78. I have referred to the communications between Serbia and the United Nations, the International Court of Justice, and other international organisations at about the same time the Public Attorney of Serbia was corresponding with the ICC Secretariat about ImageSat's Request for Arbitration.... These communications by Serbia reflect the position that being a "successor" state does not necessarily involve a new legal personality. For example, the Serbian Prime Minister stated that the Serbian Parliament would pass a resolution "declaring that Serbia... takes over the state and legal continuity of the State Union"... and the Parliamentary Decision [of the Serbian Parliament of June 2006 entitled "Decision on obligations of state authorities of the Republic of Serbia in exercising competencies of the Republic of Serbia as successor of State Union Serbia and Montenegro"] states that Serbia has "succeeded to its identity within international law... in totality" and "fully inherited its international legal subjectivity" (i.e. legal personality). In its response to the Registrar of the ICJ... Serbia also took the position that "there is continuity between" the State Union and Serbia... But the letter also stated that the State Union has been replaced by two distinct states.

For these and several other reasons, the evidence was insufficient to conclude that Serbia had submitted to the tribunal's jurisdiction solely on the basis that it was a different State in law from the State Union of Serbia and Montenegro.

Serbia's submission to the tribunal's jurisdiction in terms which gave the arbitrator substantive jurisdiction over the continuator/successor issue disposed, in Beatson J's eyes, of objections that the matter was not justiciable before the tribunal. But his Lordship examined obiter the various arguments.

Beatson J considered, first, whether, in the absence of contractual submission, an arbitrator would have been able to deal with an issue that would otherwise be non-justiciable as a matter of English law. It appeared to his Lordship from the Court of Appeal's judgment in *Republic of Ecuador v Occidental Exploration and Production Co*[490] that an arbitrator enjoyed jurisdiction under section 30 of the Arbitration Act[491] to make a

[488] [2009] EWHC 2853 (Comm), para 77.

[489] His Lordship had already reproduced these earlier in his judgment, ibid, paras 22–36.

[490] [2005] EWCA Civ 1116, [2006] QB 432, (2005) 76 *BYIL* 585–9 (CA (Civ Div)).

[491] Section 30 ('Competence of tribunal to rule on its own jurisdiction') reads:

(1) Unless otherwise agreed by the parties, the arbitral tribunal may rule on its own substantive jurisdiction, that is, as to—
(a) whether there is a valid arbitration agreement,
(b) whether the tribunal is properly constituted, and
(c) what matters have been submitted to arbitration in accordance with the arbitration agreement.
(2) Any such ruling may be challenged by any available arbitral process of appeal or review or in accordance with the provisions of this Part.

preliminary determination as to jurisdiction 'even in a case when the determination of that matter involves considering a question which, in another context, would be non-justiciable'.[492] The arbitral tribunal whose decision was at issue in *Occidental* had determined whether the dispute fell outside the categories of claim specified in the relevant bilateral investment treaty, and his Lordship noted that it was never suggested by the Court of Appeal 'that the arbitrators could not deal with Ecuador's objection or should not have dealt with it because the interpretation of the treaty was non-justiciable or non-arbitrable'.[493] Moreover, the Court of Appeal 'appear[ed] to have accepted that "justiciability" in a Court differs from "justiciability" or "arbitrability" before an arbitral tribunal'[494]—and, Beatson J remarked, 'this [was] not surprising', '[g]iven the importance of arbitral tribunals as dispute resolution mechanisms in relation to the commercial transactions of sovereign states, and the unavailability of sovereign immunity or act of state defences to a state which has agreed to submit a dispute to arbitration'.[495] Nor was the situation any different where the jurisdictional issue was whether a person or entity was a party to the underlying contract containing the arbitration clause.[496]

Turning to 'whether, absent the arbitration context, the "continuator"/"successor" issue [would have been] non-justiciable',[497] his Lordship confessed that the answer was 'not straightforward', since the issue was 'not strictly one of recognition of the state which is a matter within the Crown's prerogative relating to the conduct of foreign affairs'.[498] In the event, however, despite Serbia's reference to two US cases in which it was held that issues of State succession were 'solely for determination by the executive branch' and that there were 'no judicially discoverable and manageable standards for a domestic court or arbitrator to resolve questions of succession under international law',[499] various UK cases relied on by ImageSat in which the court had made a determination as to whether a foreign government or a State existed,[500] as well as a further US case in which the court ruled on the question whether a foreign State was

[492] [2009] EWHC 2853 (Comm), para 114.

[493] Ibid.

[494] Ibid, para 120.

[495] Ibid.

[496] Ibid, para 121. See also ibid, paras 122–6.

[497] Ibid, para 127.

[498] Ibid, citing Jennings & Watts, above n 34, 133. Beatson J noted, ibid, that 'Lord Wilberforce, in *Buttes Gas and Oil Co v Hammer* at 632, had regard to United States cases dealing with the principle of non-justiciability despite the difference in the constitutional position and the relationship between the executive and the judicial branches of the State in the two countries'.

[499] [2009] EWHC 2853 (Comm), para 133, recalling the argument made ibid, para 127, citing *Can v United States*, 14 F 3d 160 (2nd Cir. 1994) and *767 Third Avenue Associates v Consulate General of the Socialist Federal Republic of Yugoslavia*, 218 F 3d 152 (2nd Cir. 2000).

[500] See *Luigi Monta v Cechofracht* [1956] 2 QB 552, *Al Fin's Patent* [1971] Ch 160, *Calgar v Billingham* [1996] STC (SCD) 150, *Gerhard Dirks' Applications* (1960) 1 RPC 1, *Korea National Insurance Corporation v Allianz Global Corporate and Specialty AG* [2008] EWCA Civ 1355 and *Republic of Somalia v Woodhouse Drake and Carey* [1993] QB 54, all cited at [2009] EWHC 2853 (Comm), para 128.

a successor State in the strict sense and therefore relieved of prior contractual obligations, persuaded his Lordship that the determination by an English court of the continuator/successor issue would not, at least on these grounds, be barred for non-justiciability.[501] Beatson J next considered the second limb of Serbia's three-pronged argument as to non-justiciability, namely that although '"customary international law is part of the common law" (*ex parte Pinochet (No. 3)* [2001] AC 147, at 276 per Lord Millett)', there was 'no settled principle of customary international law which [was] part of English law on the "continuator"/"successor" issue', with the result that any decision on the point would have to be made solely by reference to public international law.[502] His Lordship observed:

> The fact that the court would have to have regard to public international law principles does not, however, suffice to render the matter nonjusticiable. All depends on context. There are cases, in particular *Ecuador v Occidental*, where the courts have had regard to public international law where this is necessary to determine private law rights. In the present case it was Serbia which raised the issue of its legal identity and the arbitrator had to take account of public international law to deal with that issue.[503]

This second limb of Serbia's argument as to non-justiciability had force, his Lordship thought, only if combined with the third limb (which had already been canvassed to a limited extent), namely that there were no judicial or manageable standards by which a court could decide whether a State was a continuator or successor State 'and there [was] no principle of customary international law on this issue'.[504] After recalling the criteria for the establishment of a rule of customary international law,[505] as well as the arguments of both Serbia (quoting, *inter alia*, Brownlie and Oppenheim)[506] and ImageSat[507] as to whether, as a matter of international law, 'the position... as to the determination of whether a state

[501] Ibid, para 129.
[502] Ibid, para 130.
[503] Ibid.
[504] Ibid.
[505] His Lordship recalled Lord Bingham's speech in *R (European Roma Rights Centre) v Immigration Officer at Prague Airport* [2004] UKHL 55, [2005] 2 AC 1, 35, para 23, (2004) 75 *BYIL* 504–12 (HL), which in turn cited the American Law Institute's *Restatement (Third) of the Law, Foreign Relations Laws of the United States* (1986), para 102(2). He also referred to *North Sea Continental Shelf (Federal Republic of Germany/Denmark; Federal Republic of Germany/Netherlands)* [1969] ICJ Rep 3, 43, para 74.
[506] See [2009] EWHC 2853 (Comm), paras 132 and 133, quoting, para 132, I Brownlie, *Principles of Public International Law* (7th edn, Oxford University Press, Oxford, 2008), 80–1 and Jennings & Watts, above n 34, 207, para 59, including n 8.
[507] See [2009] EWHC 2853 (Comm), para 134, citing Harvard Research Draft on the Law of Treaties (1935) 29 *American Journal of International Law Supplement* 653, the opinion of the UN Assistant Secretary General of Legal Affairs on Pakistan's claim to be a co-continuation of the State of British India, and the *Single German Nationality (Teso) Case*, 91 ILR 211 (German Fed. Const. Ct, 1987).

[was] a continuator or a successor [was] sufficiently clear', Beatson J continued:

The position taken by Serbia in its communications to the UN . . . and the ICJ . . . , and the position taken by those organisations and by the Council of Europe's Committee of Ministers . . . suggest that Serbia and those organisations regarded it as the continuator of the State Union [of Serbia and Montenegro]. The fact that, in some cases, described by [counsel for ImageSat] as exceptional, it has been difficult to determine whether a state is a continuation or successor does not mean that the distinction does not exist or is unworkable. The key is whether there are clear standards of international law from which a domestic court can conclude that there is a principle of customary international law on the matter. The material before me, including the passages from Brownlie and Oppenheim, however, suggests that there are not.[508]

Despite the 'factual indications' in the instant case that Serbia was the continuator of the State Union of Serbia and Montenegro, his Lordship held that, had the context not been that of an arbitration, he would have been unable to conclude that the continuator/successor question was justiciable.[509]

Finally, although such substantive matters did not, in the event, fall for determination, Beatson J addressed obiter whether Serbia was indeed the continuator or successor in the strict sense to the State Union of Serbia and Montenegro and, if it were the latter, whether it was bound by the State Union's contractual obligations nonetheless. As to the first question, his Lordship held that, for contextual reasons, the term 'successor state' in article 60 of the Constitutional Charter of the State Union of Serbia and Montenegro[510] could not be read in the narrow sense and that, rather, there was force to ImageSat's reading of the provision to the effect that, in the event of the secession of one constituent republic of the State Union, the remaining State would 'inherit the legal personality of the State Union and would thus be its continuation'.[511] The position adopted by Serbia vis-à-vis the United Nations, in particular in relation to the ICJ, and vis-à-vis other international organizations, and the position adopted by most of these organizations towards Serbia, were also consistent with the latter's being the continuator State of the State Union of Serbia and Montenegro.[512] Nor, *pace* Serbia, did the ECtHR's decision in *Matijašević v Serbia* lend support to the 'successor' thesis.[513] As to whether, even if it were a successor State proper, Serbia was bound by

[508] [2009] EWHC 2853 (Comm), para 135.
[509] Ibid.
[510] See ibid, para 17.
[511] Ibid, para 137.
[512] Ibid.
[513] Ibid, referring to *Matijašević v Serbia*, Application no. 23037/04, Judgment, 19 December 2006, previously discussed at [2009] EWHC 2853 (Comm), paras 32–5.

the State Union's contractual obligations to ImageSat, ImageSat argued that, by the date of the breakup of the State Union, it had enjoyed an accrued or acquired right under the agreement.[514] But Beatson J indicated that, had a decision on the point been necessary, he would have rejected ImageSat's submission:

> The acquired rights principle is controversial. It appears from the international law materials that there is no extensive and uniform state practice or *opinio juris*... as to the liability of a successor state for its predecessor's private contractual liabilities to a private person or entity. Article 33 of the 1983 Vienna Convention on Succession of States in respect of State Property, Archives and Debts (a) is not in force, and (b) restricts its regime to the predecessor state's obligations to another state, international organisation or subject of international law.[515]

Moreover, even if such a doctrine had existed, such steps as ImageSat had taken were merely preparatory and did not constitute contractual performance.[516]

To the extent that Beatson J's decision on the determinative issue turned on the use of the word 'successor' in the Terms of Reference under which Serbia and ImageSat submitted to the ICC tribunal's jurisdiction, it is perfectly reasonable. It is doubtless true that the terms 'succession' and 'successor' are regularly employed with a degree of laxity to describe situations more accurately legally characterized as State continuity, and Serbia's own statements in a variety of contexts did nothing to suggest that it brought to the second of these words its strictly technical meaning. But whether the finding as to Serbia's submission to the tribunal's jurisdiction disposed at the same time of the non-justiciability point is perhaps a more complex question than his Lordship makes out. If English law was the governing law of the arbitration and if one accepts, as his Lordship does, that 'a principle of non-justiciability "is not one of discretion but is inherent in the very nature of the judicial process"[517] and 'cannot be waived'[518] (or, in the words of the Court of Appeal in *Ecuador v Occidental*, 'cannot, if it applies, be ousted by consent'[519]), one has to work harder to show that Serbia's submission to ICC arbitration in terms which did not exclude consideration of the continuator/successor question

[514] See [2009] EWHC 2853 (Comm), para 138, citing *Certain German Interests in Polish Upper Silesia (Merits)* PCIJ Series A No. 7 (1928).

[515] [2009] EWHC 2853 (Comm), para 139, referring to Vienna Convention on Succession of States in respect of State Property, Archives and Debts, Vienna, 8 April 1983, UN doc. A/CONF. 117/14 (not in force).

[516] [2009] EWHC 2853 (Comm), para 139.

[517] Ibid, para 125, quoting *Buttes Gas and Oil Co v Hammer (No 3)* [1981] 3 All ER 616, 628 (Lord Wilberforce).

[518] [2009] EWHC 2853 (Comm), para 125, citing *Republic of Ecuador v Occidental Exploration and Production Co* [2005] EWCA Civ 1116, [2006] QB 432, 467, para 57, (2005) 76 *BYIL* 585–9 (CA (Civ Div)).

[519] [2006] QB 432, 467, para 57.

could render the latter justiciable (or 'arbitrable', as his Lordship sometimes has it) before the tribunal. What his Lordship might have said is that, just as matters which are non-justiciable before an English court may be justiciable before an arbitral tribunal, so too is the ouster of non-justiciability by consent, impossible before an English court, possible in the arbitral context. As to whether matters which are non-justiciable before an English court may indeed be justiciable before an arbitral tribunal, as Beatson J holds, this would certainly make sense. It is scarcely conceivable that prospective parties to mixed arbitration, by choosing English law as the governing law, intend thereby to import into the arbitral process rules of law specific to the jurisdiction of the English courts. Putting it another way, 'English law', in an arbitration clause, must surely be read as 'English law, *mutatis mutandis*'.

As regards whether, absent the arbitral context, the continuator/successor issue would have been non-justiciable before an English court, there are only two possible reasons why this might have been so, and neither is compelling.

The first, pointed to by Serbia in the instant case, is that any such determination would require the court to rule on matters rightly falling exclusively—the word 'exclusively' being significant—within the executive's prerogative in respect of the conduct of foreign relations. All this means, however, in the UK context, whatever the position in the US, is that a court may not, in relation to the conduct of foreign relations (or any other exercise of the prerogative), make or second-guess what is properly a purely political determination. Whether, for the purposes of English law, a foreign State is a continuator or successor State *stricto sensu*, a mixed question of fact and international law, is not such a determination. This does not mean that the courts may ignore the executive's view in any given case. The self-imposed 'one voice' principle dictates that, as a matter of what might be called constitutional comity or sound policy, the courts may not proceed in a manner which would contradict the position taken by the executive on a 'fact of State'[520] or 'international fact'[521] of this sort (which, like other such mixed questions of fact and international law, would be better termed a 'legal fact of State' or an 'international legal fact'). It is for this reason that, were an English court to seek and receive executive certification as to whether a State is the continuator or successor of another, the view of Her Majesty's Government expressed in the executive certificate, should HMG choose to express any such view, would probably rightly be deemed conclusive of the legal fact to which it relates. But in the absence of executive certification, as in the present case (in which neither party, perhaps insufficiently confident of the document's likely contents, sought the

[520] See F A Mann, *Foreign Affairs in English Courts* (Clarendon Press, Oxford, 1986) 23.
[521] See D P O'Connell, *International Law* (2nd edn, Stevens & Sons, London, 1970) Vol I, 118.

production of an executive certificate from the Foreign & Commonwealth Office[522]), the court may and must, insofar as it is necessary for the disposal of an issue of English law before it, determine the mixed question of fact and international law for itself.[523] In this respect, Beatson J was right to hold, albeit on somewhat flimsy authority, that the absence of executive certification in the present case did not render the question whether Serbia was a proper party to the arbitration non-justiciable on constitutional grounds.[524] He was also right to dismiss the spurious argument that an English court may not have recourse to public international law in its quality as public international law in order to rule on the question.[525] But he was perhaps unwise not to request an executive certificate *proprio motu*.

The second possible and similarly unconvincing reason, also raised by Serbia in the present case, why the continuator/successor question might have been non-justiciable before an English court is on account of the doctrine of judicial restraint enunciated by Lord Wilberforce in *Buttes Gas and Oil Co v Hammer (No. 3)*, where his Lordship stated that the English courts will not adjudicate upon the legality, under either municipal or international law, of 'the transactions of foreign sovereign states'[526] or 'acts done abroad by virtue of sovereign authority',[527] the reason being a lack of 'judicial or manageable standards'[528] by which to judge such issues. It is highly doubtful at the outset whether the legal characterization of a State as either the continuator or successor of another amounts to adjudicating upon a 'transaction' of that State or upon an act done by it abroad by virtue of sovereign authority; but if one accepts that Lord Wilberforce's main concern was the lack of 'judicial or manageable standards', the criticism does not go to the heart of the matter. The real question is whether such judicial or manageable standards exist, and in this regard Beatson J's insistence on the need for clear, *a priori* customary criteria for the determination of the continuator/successor question ('clear standards of international law from which a domestic court can conclude that there is a principle of customary international law on the matter'[529]) is self-defeating. As in other areas of international law where the evidentiary value of recognition weighs heavily in the balance, cogent evidence that the relevant State is viewed by others as either a continuator or successor—the sort of 'factual indications' pointed to by his Lordship in the present case[530]—would suffice to settle the issue. Alternatively, where, as

522 See [2009] EWHC 2853 (Comm), para 125.
523 See O'Connell, above n 521, 119.
524 See [2009] EWHC 2853 (Comm), para 125.
525 See R O'Keefe, 'The Doctrine of Incorporation Revisited' (2008) 79 *BYIL* 7, 10–11.
526 [1982] AC 888, 931.
527 Ibid, 932.
528 Ibid, 938.
529 [2009] EWHC 2853 (Comm), para 135.
530 Ibid.

here, the evidence is somewhat mixed or insufficient, and maybe even where it is not, the more sensible way to proceed would be to request an executive certificate from the FCO and to treat any view expressed by HMG as conclusive of the matter. But if executive certification is not forthcoming or is ambivalent, the court, which is taken to know international law, may not resile from the perhaps difficult task of ascertaining the applicable judicial (viz international legal) standards, abstract or otherwise, and of applying them to dispose of the point of English law before it. It may not render a *non liquet* in the guise of non-justiciability.[531]

16. *R v Horncastle and another; R v Marquis and another*, 9 December 2009, [2009] UKSC 14, [2010] 2 WLR 47 (SC)

Relationship between international law and English law—jurisprudence of European Court of Human Rights—Human Rights Act 1998 ('HRA'), section 2(1)—European Convention on Human Rights and Fundamental Freedoms 1950 ('ECHR'), articles 6(1) (right to fair trial) and 6(3)(d) (right to cross-examine witnesses)—English law on hearsay evidence—whether HRA, section 2(1) obliging English court to follow decision of European Court of Human Rights on precise point before court—whether conviction based solely or to decisive extent on statement of witness whom defence has had no opportunity to cross-examine necessarily infringing ECHR, articles 6(1) and 6(3)

The first two appellants' convictions for causing grievous bodily harm with intent had been based 'to a decisive degree', although not exclusively, on the reading at trial of a witness statement given to the police by the victim, who had died before trial (of other causes) and so had not been cross-examined on his evidence. The statement was admitted pursuant to sections 116(1) and (2)(a) of the Criminal Justice Act 2003 ('CJA 2003'), which render admissible, subject to conditions, the statement of a witness who cannot give evidence because he or she has died.[532] The second two defendants' convictions for kidnapping had been similarly based on, *inter alia*, the reading at trial of a witness statement given to the police by the victim, who had not been cross-examined at trial, having fled out of fear of the consequences of her scheduled oral testimony. Her statement was admitted pursuant to sections 116(1) and (2)(e) of the CJA 2003, which permit the admission into evidence, subject again to conditions, of the

[531] See also Mann, above n 520, 54: 'It is submitted with respect that questions of law, whether municipal or international, can and must be decided by the court which is not entitled to disembarrass itself by describing them as non-justiciable, but if the court can do so at all, it must have exhausted all such help as it may obtain by asking the Foreign and Commonwealth Office for information on facts of State...'.

[532] In accordance with CJA 2003, s 116(1), subparas (a) and (b) respectively, the conditions are that 'oral evidence given in the proceedings by the person who made the statement would be admissible as evidence of that matter' and that 'the person who made the statement... is identified to the court's satisfaction'.

statement of a witness who is unavailable to give evidence on account of fear.[533] A five-strong Court of Appeal[534] had held that these convictions were not based 'to a decisive extent' on the victim's statement, although this finding was challenged before the Supreme Court. All four appellants argued that the admission of the respective statements had violated the rights secured to them, via the HRA, by article 6(1) of the ECHR, the fair trial guarantee, and more specifically by article 6(3)(d), which provides that everyone charged with a criminal offence has the right 'to examine or have examined witnesses against him and to obtain the attendance and examination of witnesses on his behalf under the same conditions as witnesses against him'. They relied before the Supreme Court on the 20 January 2009 decision of the Fourth Section of the ECtHR in *Al-Khawaja and Tahery v United Kingdom*,[535] in which the Strasbourg court found violations of articles 6(1) and 6(3)(d) of the ECHR in circumstances where the statements of witnesses who did not give evidence at trial (one having died and the other being too scared to testify, although not on account of intimidation by the defendants), having been admitted under provisions of the Criminal Justice Act 1988 equivalent to sections 116(2)(a) and 116(2)(e) of the CJA 2003, had formed the sole or at least decisive basis of the applicants' convictions. *Al-Khawaja* was in turn an application of the so-called 'sole or decisive' rule or test posited in the ECtHR's previous case-law, which states that 'where a conviction is based solely or to a decisive degree on depositions that have been made by a person whom the accused has had no opportunity to examine or to have examined, whether during the investigation or at the trial, the rights of the defence are restricted to an extent that is incompatible with the guarantees provided by article 6'.[536] The appellants submitted that the relevant provisions of the CJA 2003 had to be read down so as to preclude the admission of hearsay evidence in circumstances such as theirs or that such evidence was to be excluded under section 78(1) of the Police and Criminal Evidence Act 1984 ('PACE').[537] Section 2(1) of the HRA obliges the English courts to 'take into account' the jurisprudence of the ECtHR; the correct approach to section 2(1) was, it was contended, exemplified by the judgment of the House of Lords in *Secretary of State for the Home Department v AF (No. 3)*,[538] where their Lordships held themselves bound to apply a clear statement of principle by a Grand Chamber

[533] The conditions are those laid down in CJA 2003, s 116(1)(a) and (b).

[534] See *R v Horncastle and another; R v Marquis and another; R v Carter* [2009] EWCA Crim 964, [2010] 2 WLR 47.

[535] (2009) 49 EHRR 1.

[536] *Lucà v Italy* (2001) 36 EHRR 807, para 40.

[537] Article 78(1) of PACE reads: 'In any proceedings the court may refuse to allow evidence on which the prosecution proposes to rely to be given if it appears to the court that, having regard to all the circumstances, including the circumstances in which the evidence was obtained, the admission of the evidence would have such an adverse effect on the fairness of the proceedings that the court ought not to admit it.'

[538] [2009] 3 WLR 74.

of the ECtHR where the latter dealt with precisely the issue before the House; and that *Al-Khawaja* dealt with precisely the issue now before the Supreme Court.

On 16 June 2009, the UK requested the referral of the decision in *Al-Khawaja* to a Grand Chamber of the ECtHR. On 5 June 2009, a five-member panel of the Grand Chamber adjourned consideration of the UK's request pending the outcome of the present case.

The Supreme Court dismissed the appeals, declining to follow the decision of the Fourth Section of the ECtHR in *Al-Khawaja* and holding that a conviction based solely or to a decisive extent on the statement of a witness whom the defence has had no opportunity to cross-examine did not necessarily infringe articles 6(1) and 6(3) of the ECHR. Lord Phillips PSC delivered 'a judgment with which all members of the court agree[d]',[539] Lord Brown JSC adding a few words of his own.

Lord Phillips PSC rejected at the outset the argument that the Supreme Court was, in the application of section 2(1) of the HRA, bound to follow a decision of the ECtHR:

> The requirement to "take into account" the Strasbourg jurisprudence will normally result in the domestic court applying principles that are clearly established by the Strasbourg court. There will, however, be rare occasions where the domestic court has concerns as to whether a decision of the Strasbourg court sufficiently appreciates or accommodates particular aspects of our domestic process. In such circumstances it is open to the domestic court to decline to follow the Strasbourg decision, giving reasons for adopting this course. This is likely to give the Strasbourg court the opportunity to reconsider the particular aspect of the decision that is in issue, so that there takes place what may prove to be a valuable dialogue between the domestic court and the Strasbourg court. This is such a case.[540]

He next summarized, in admirably succinct fashion, why the last was so:

> (1) Long before 1953 when the Convention came into force the common law had, by the hearsay rule, addressed that aspect of a fair trial that article 6(3)(d) [of the ECHR] was designed to ensure. (2) Parliament has since enacted exceptions to the hearsay rule that are required in the interests of justice. Those exceptions are not subject to the sole or decisive rule. The regime enacted by Parliament contains safeguards that render the sole or decisive rule unnecessary. (3) The continental procedure had not addressed that aspect of a fair trial that article 6(3)(d) was designed to ensure. (4) The Strasbourg court has recognised that exceptions to article 6(3)(d) are required in the interests of justice. (5) The manner in which the Strasbourg court has approved those exceptions has resulted in a jurisprudence that lacks clarity. (6) The sole or decisive rule has been introduced into the Strasbourg jurisprudence without discussion of the principle underlying it or full consideration of whether there was justification for imposing the rule as an

[539] [2010] 2 WLR 47, 95. [540] Ibid, 97, para 11.

overriding principle applicable equally to the continental and common law jurisdictions. (7) Although English law does not include the sole or decisive rule it would, in almost all cases, have reached the same result in those cases where the Strasbourg court has invoked the rule. (8) The sole or decisive rule would create severe practical difficulties if applied to English criminal procedure. (9) *Al-Khawaja* does not establish that it is necessary to apply the sole or decisive rule in this jurisdiction.[541]

His Lordship then proceeded to elaborate on this skeleton judgment.

Lord Phillips PSC first outlined the history of the English common-law hearsay rule and the cautious development of statutory exceptions to it, as provided for, in their latest iteration, in the CJA 2003[542] (a history mirrored in other Commonwealth jurisdictions[543]), observing:

The Strasbourg court has accepted that there are circumstances that justify the admission of statements of witnesses who have not been subject to "confrontation" with the defendant. The possibility remains, however, that by propounding the "sole or decisive test" the Strasbourg court has condemned as rendering a trial unfair the admission of hearsay evidence in circumstances where the legislature and courts of this jurisdiction and of other important Commonwealth jurisdictions (Canada, Australia and New Zealand) have determined that the evidence can fairly be received. This is a startling proposition and one that calls for careful analysis of the Strasbourg jurisprudence.[544]

Taking next a brief excursus into the English law on what he saw as the analogous question of the admission of evidence from anonymous witnesses,[545] a practice provided for, subject to strict safeguards, by the Criminal Evidence (Witness Anonymity) Act 2008, his Lordship noted that Parliament had not prohibited the admission of such evidence in circumstances where it was or was likely to be the sole or decisive evidence.[546] After briefly sketching the very different criminal procedure typical of continental civil-law systems,[547] Lord Phillips PSC then subjected to scrutiny the Strasbourg jurisprudence prior to *Al-Khawaja* on the admission of statements by witnesses not called to testify and the admission of the evidence of anonymous witnesses.[548] His Lordship recounted how the ECtHR had accepted that 'some exceptions had to be made to the strict application of article 6(3)(d)' of the Convention,[549] and had on numerous occasions permitted the admission of statements by

[541] Ibid, 97–8, para 14. [542] Ibid, 98–104, paras 15–40.

[543] Ibid, 104, para 41. See also ibid, Annex 1 (prepared by Lord Mance), 124–8.

[544] Ibid, 105, para 46.

[545] Ibid, 108, para 56.

[546] Ibid, 105–8, paras 47–55.

[547] Ibid, 108–9, para 57–62.

[548] Ibid, 110–8, paras 63–86. See also ibid, Annex 2, 128–9, Annex 3, 129–31 and Annex 4 (prepared by Lord Judge CJ), 131–50.

[549] Ibid, 110, para 64.

witnesses whose cross-examination at trial was impossible, including in cases where the witness had died after making the statement and where the witness was too scared to give oral evidence.[550] This authority indicated that 'the fairness of a trial ha[d] to be assessed on a case by case basis, viewing each trial as a whole, and that an inability on the part of a defendant to cross-examine the maker of a statement that is admitted in evidence will not necessarily render the trial unfair'.[551] Turning specifically to the 'sole or decisive' rule, which had entered the Strasbourg jurisprudence in *Doorson v Netherlands*,[552] Lord Phillips PSC observed that the ECtHR in that case had provided no explanation for the rule, which was not relevant on the facts;[553] that in two cases preceding *Doorson*, the ECtHR had found no violation of article 6(1) where there was a justified failure to comply with the strict requirements of article 6(3) in respect of what was, although supported by other evidence, 'the principal evidence' on the basis of which the applicant had been convicted;[554] that in *Ferantelli and Santangelo v Italy*, decided soon after *Doorson*, the 'sole or decisive' test was not mentioned, the Court finding in that case—in which the principal evidence on the basis of which the applicants had been convicted consisted of witness statements read at trial after the suicide of the witness—that articles 6(1) and 6(3) had not been violated, regard being had to the fact that the trial court had subjected the statements to detailed analysis and had found them to be corroborated;[555] and that in *Doorson* itself, which was chiefly an anonymity case, the ECtHR had held 'that it had been acceptable to have regard to a statement of a witness whose attendance could not be procured "especially since it could consider that statement to be corroborated by other evidence before it"'.[556] The decisive factor in the various cases seemed to be the reliability of the evidence.[557] His Lordship next highlighted how the 'sole or decisive' rule would 'give rise to severe practical difficulties', especially under the English system of criminal procedure, with its insistence on trial by jury.[558] Pausing then to assess the situation prior to *Al-Khawaja*, he stated:

> 92 . . . [T]he justification for the sole or decisive test would appear to be that the risk of an unsafe conviction based solely or decisively on anonymous or hearsay evidence is so great that such a conviction can never be permitted. Parliament has concluded that there are alternative ways of protecting against that risk

[550] Ibid, 111–2, paras 66 and 68.

[551] Ibid, 113, para 74.

[552] (1996) 22 EHRR 330.

[553] [2010] 2 WLR 47, 117, para 80.

[554] Ibid, 118, para 83, citing *Asch v Austria* (1991) 15 EHRR 597 and *Artner v Austria*, 25 June 1992, Publications of the European Court of Human Rights, Series A, No. 242-A.

[555] [2010] 2 WLR 47, 118, para 84.

[556] Ibid.

[557] Ibid, para 86. See also ibid, 117, para 83.

[558] Ibid, 118, para 87. See also ibid, 119, paras 88–90.

that are less draconian, as set out in the 1988 and 2003 [Criminal Justice] Acts (and now, with regard to anonymous witnesses, the 2008 [Criminal Evidence (Witness Anonymity)] Act). When the Strasbourg decisions are analysed it is apparent that these alternative safeguards would have precluded convictions in most of the cases where a violation of article 6(1)(3)(d) was found.... Where the witness is unavailable but identified, or present but anonymous, the respective Acts provide the safeguards to which I have referred earlier against the risk that the use of the witness's evidence will render the verdict unsafe and the trial unfair.

...

94 Before *Al-Khawaja*, while the Strasbourg court had repeatedly recited the sole or decisive test, there had... been no case where that test had been applied so as to produce a finding of a violation of article 6(3)(d) in a case where there had been justification for not calling a witness and where the evidence was demonstrably reliable. Nor had the sole or decisive rule ever been applied or cited in an application in relation to the criminal process in this jurisdiction. Thus no consideration had been given as to whether it was necessary or appropriate to apply that rule having regard to the safeguards inherent in our system....[559]

Finally Lord Phillips PSC turned his attention to *Al-Khawaja*, key statements in which were either 'impossible to reconcile... with statements of principle that the Strasbourg court ha[d] regularly made in respect of the interrelationship between articles 6(1) and 6(3)'[560] or were logically uncompelling.[561] Moreover, the ECtHR had recognized in the case that an exception existed where a witness refused to testify through fear induced by the defendant and that 'counterbalancing factors' might exist, even if it held that the protections afforded by the CJA 1988 were insufficient.[562] His Lordship concluded:

105 The sole or decisive rule was first propounded in *Doorson* as an obiter observation, without explanation or qualification. It has since frequently been repeated, usually in circumstances where there has been justification for finding breaches of article 6(1)(3)(d) without reliance on the test. If applied rigorously it will in some cases result in the acquittal, or failure to prosecute, defendants where there is cogent evidence of their guilt. This will be to the detriment of their victims and will result in defendants being left free to add to the number of those victims.

106 The Court of Appeal in this case, comprising five senior judges with great experience of the criminal jurisdiction, referred to the manner in which

559 Ibid, 119–20.
560 Ibid, 121, para 97.
561 See ibid, 122, paras 99–101.
562 Ibid, 123, para 103.

the 2003 Act is working in practice and concluded that provided its provisions are observed there will be no breach of article 6 and, in particular, article 6(3)(d), if a conviction is based solely or decisively on hearsay evidence ... The court thus differed from the doubt expressed in *Al-Khawaja* as to whether there could be any counterbalancing factors sufficient to justify the introduction of an untested statement which was the sole or decisive basis for a conviction.

107 I concur in these conclusions reached by the Court of Appeal and the reasons for those conclusions so clearly and compellingly expressed. The jurisprudence of the Strasbourg court in relation to article 6(3)(d) has developed largely in cases relating to civil law rather than common law jurisdictions and this is particularly true of the sole or decisive rule. ... [The ECtHR's] case law appears to have developed without full consideration of the safeguards against an unfair trial that exist under the common law procedure. Nor, I suspect, can the Strasbourg court have given detailed consideration to the English law of admissibility of evidence, and the changes made to that law, after consideration by the Law Commission, intended to ensure that English law complies with the requirements of article 6(1)(3)(d).

108 In these circumstances I have decided that it would not be right for this court to hold that the sole or decisive test should have been applied rather than the provisions of the 2003 Act, interpreted in accordance with their natural meaning. I believe that those provisions strike the right balance between the imperative that a trial must be fair and the interests of victims in particular and society in general that a criminal should not be immune from conviction where a witness, who has given critical evidence in a statement that can be shown to be reliable, dies or cannot be called to give evidence for some other reason. In so concluding I have taken careful account of the Strasbourg jurisprudence. I hope that in due course the Strasbourg court may also take account of the reasons that have led me not to apply the sole or decisive test in this case.[563]

With this, his Lordship dismissed the appeals.

Lord Brown JSC, after criticizing the substance of the 'sole or decisive' rule for its seeming arbitrariness (permitting one exception but not equivalent others) and impracticability, suggested that the 'better view' could have been 'that no such absolute principle emerges from the Strasbourg court's judgment in *Al-Khawaja*'.[564] He continued:

117 I recognise, however, the distinct possibility that the Strasbourg court in *Al-Khawaja* really did intend to lay down an absolute principle along the lines here contended for and it may be, indeed, that the outcome of that very case itself tends to support such a view. In this event the question then arises: what should this court do? Should we accept and apply this absolute principle with the inevi-

[563] Ibid, 123–4. [564] Ibid, 151, para 116.

table result that these appeals must be allowed or should we instead decline to follow the Strasbourg decision in *Al-Khawaja* and in effect join with the United Kingdom Government in inviting the Grand Chamber to overrule it (the Grand Chamber panel having adjourned the UK's request for such a reference until the pronouncement of our decision on these appeals)?

118 I have not the least doubt that the latter course is to be preferred. This case seems to me a very far cry from *Secretary of State for the Home Department v AF (No 3)* [2009] 3 WLR 74 where the House of Lords was faced with a definitive judgment of the Grand Chamber in *A v United Kingdom* (2009) 49 EHRR 625 on the very point at issue and where each member of the Committee felt no alternative but to apply it. Lord Rodger put it most succinctly, at para 98: "Argentoratum locutum, iudicium finitum—Strasbourg has spoken, the case is closed."

119 Moreover not merely was the Strasbourg ruling in *A* clear and authoritative but, whatever view individual members of the committee may have taken about it (and it is evident that, whilst many agreed with it, others did not), it expressed an entirely coherent view.

120 The contrasts with the present situation are striking. In the first place, we are faced here not with a Grand Chamber decision but rather with the possible need for one. Moreover, not merely is the court's ruling in *Al-Khawaja* not as authoritative as a Grand Chamber decision, but it is altogether less clear than was the decision in *A*. Indeed, as I have already suggested, it is far from certain that *Al-Khawaja* stands for any absolute principle of the sort here contended for. I would reject the appellant's argument that not merely is the court's judgment in *Al-Khawaja* clear but, unlike the position in *A*, it is supported by a whole stream of consistent earlier Strasbourg case law and consequently more, rather than less, authoritative than the ruling in *A*. For the reasons fully elaborated by the Court of Appeal and now by Lord Phillips PSC, I cannot accept that the earlier cases support, still less compel, an absolute principle such as *Al-Khawaja* is now said to stand for.

121 Accordingly, . . . [I] express the hope that the Grand Chamber will clarify the law upon hearsay evidence and recognise that our domestic legislation is compatible with article 6.[565]

In agreement with the Court of Appeal and Lord Phillips PSC, Lord Brown JSC dismissed the appeals.

The gauntlet thrown down by the Supreme Court has been picked up by the ECtHR. On 1 March 2010, *Al-Khawaja and Tahery v United Kingdom* was referred to the Grand Chamber, which heard oral argument on 19 May 2010. Judgment is awaited.

From the perspective of the approach to be taken to the Strasbourg jurisprudence under section 2(1) of the HRA, Lord Scott—who found

[565] Ibid, 151–2.

himself rounded on in the House of Lords only a year before in *Animal Defenders* for having had the temerity to suggest that he might not follow the ECtHR if its case-law 'compelled a conclusion fundamentally at odds with the distribution of powers under the British constitution'[566]—must have chuckled at the breeziness with which Lord Phillips PSC concluded that 'it is open to the domestic court to decline to follow [a] Strasbourg decision' on those 'rare occasions where the domestic court has concerns as to whether a decision of the Strasbourg court sufficiently appreciates or accommodates particular aspects of [the UK's] domestic process'.[567] Baroness Hale JSC—who as Baroness Hale was one of Lord Scott's antagonists in *Animal Defenders* and who agreed with Lord Phillips PSC in the present case—must have breathed a sigh of relief that the former has retired, although her learned friend would no doubt have been too noble to say 'I told you so', even in the more plebeian setting of the new United Kingdom Supreme Court.

[566] *R (Animal Defenders International) v Secretary of State for Culture, Media and Sport* [2008] UKHL 15, [2008] 1 AC 1312, 1352, para 45, (2008) 79 *BYIL* 411–7 (HL).

[567] [2010] 2 WLR 47, 97, para 11.

Decisions of British Courts 2009

B. Private International Law

By Adrian Briggs*

1. *Forum non satis:* finding fault with a foreign court: *Cherney v Deripaska*;[1] *Pacific International Sports Clubs Ltd v Soccer Marketing International Ltd*;[2] *Sharab v Prince Al Waleed Bin Talal Bin Abdal Aziz al Saud*[3]

The cat is well and truly out the bag and is showing signs of making a real nuisance of itself. A claimant resisting a defendant's application for a stay of proceedings is now apparently entitled to make allegations which would tend to show that the foreign court, whether in general or in his specific case, cannot be trusted to do justice according to its law, but may instead prefer to do injustice in spite of the law. Though for decades the courts had been resolute in holding a line which, in effect, prevented such submissions, the breach in the dam, which we noted with some wariness last year,[4] has now been approved by the Court of Appeal. The view taken here is that whether or not one considers this to represent the triumph of transparency and truth, and the only way to ensure that justice for the claimant is not sacrificed on the table of political correctness, for there are some truly terrible parodies of courts out there in the dark, the Court of Appeal has still made a rod for the High Court's back. For even if it said, over and over, that the case before it was a special or an extraordinary one, rare is the claimant who would not say the same of his own case. Whoever prepares this survey in years to come may curse the day the Court of Appeal reverted to an earlier and more judgmental cast of mind, declaring itself open to submissions which impugn the integrity of the courts of a foreign friendly state.

Michael Cherney,[5] a rootless businessman from what was once the Soviet Union, wished to obtain several hundred millions of dollars from Mr Deripaska, a Russian oligarch who had taken care to stay on the right

* St Edmund Hall, Oxford; Professor of Private International Law, Oxford University; Barrister.

[1] [2009] EWCA Civ 849: Waller and Moore-Bick LJJ; Sir John Chadwick (affirming [2008] EWHC 1530 (Comm), [2009] 1 All ER 333; noted this Year Book 79 (2008), 543). The Supreme Court refused permission for a further appeal.

[2] [2009] EWHC 1839 (Ch): Blackburne J.

[3] [2009] EWCA Civ 353, [2009] 2 Lloyd's Rep 160: Arden, Richards and Rimer LJJ.

[4] Year Book 79 (2008), 543.

[5] An Uzbek by birth, who spent a great deal of his working life in Russia, and who in May 2007 was then residing in Israel: see *Cherney v Deripaska* [2007] EWHC 965 (Comm), [2007] 2 All ER (Comm) 785, [1]. A fuller account of his colourful life was given at first instance by Christopher Clarke J: *Cherney v Deripaska* [2008] EWHC 1530 (Comm), [2009] 1 All ER 333, at [46] *et seq.*

side of the law. Cherney did not wish to do so before a Russian court. The reasons for his jurisdictional preference are far too complex and obscure to be gone into here, but in order to bolster his claim to be allowed to haul Deripaska before the English courts, Cherney alleged that he risked being killed by person or persons who would be and remain unknown, or arrested, tried, and convicted on trumped-up charges, the moment he set foot on Russian soil, and that in any event the judiciary of the Russian Federation would not give his claim against Deripaska a fair hearing. So far so predictable: ever since *The Abidin Daver* it had been generally understood that in an extreme case, a stay of English proceedings for a foreign natural forum might not be ordered if there were before the court cogent evidence to support the contention that it would be unjust to consign the claimant to the foreign natural forum. Cases in which claimants had risen to this challenge and hit the target were few and far between. That did not stop the occasional claimant, with everything to lose, from whipping out a tattered pile of newspaper cuttings, surveys of comparative fraudulence and corruption, tables and reports purporting to demonstrate that the only way some judges could afford to eat lunch was to take bribes in the morning, and the odd photograph of someone with spectacles and a prison haircut who fancied himself to have been unjustly done to. The English judge would then be invited to find that justice was not something which the foreign court could be trusted to deliver. On the whole, these claimants failed sufficiently to satisfy the court of what they alleged: 'sufficiently', because even though the court may have been sympathetic, it did not grant the relief which the objector sought. Of course, if the foreign state had itself utterly failed to function—Somalia, Rwanda, Burundi, Congo, Liberia and Sierra Leone in their bad years come to mind[6]—it might be held that there were no courts available in the foreign territory for the trial of the action, so that the question of a stay went no further.[7] After all, if the Foreign and Commonwealth Office says that no-one should set foot in the country in question, no matter the cause, that should be enough to show that its courts are unavailable for litigation; and if a state really has failed, a judicial decision to that effect will cause no offence: no functioning government, no body to be offended. But resistance to a stay, for which the defendant had made a prima facie case, on the ground that the foreign court was no good, was usually futile; and today's Russia is the very antithesis of a failed state.

The novelty in *Cherney v Deripaska* was that it was not a case in which a defendant, served within the jurisdiction, sought a stay of proceedings. Cherney wished to sue in England on the basis of service out of the

[6] The same point extends to make-believe courts in states which are, in effect, thugocracies, such as Burma, North Korea, Equatorial Guinea, and Guinea-Bissau; but the list certainly does not stop there.

[7] For this in relation to the Kolwezi district of the Congo, see 889457 *Alberta Inc v Katanga Mining Ltd* [2008] EWHC 2679 (Comm), [2009] ILPr 675.

jurisdiction, resting on the basis that he had a good arguable case that his claim arose from a contract made within the jurisdiction.[8] To obtain or defend permission to serve, he needed also to show, clearly and distinctly, that England was the most appropriate forum. At first instance it was held that though Russia was the natural forum, England was clearly more appropriate than Russia for the trial of the action. The Court of Appeal agreed with the reasoning and with the result. In effect, worries about the reliability of justice in Russia made England the most appropriate forum, or the proper place for the claim to be brought,[9] even though the case had practically nothing to do with England. The whoops of delight at the Commercial Bar must be audible in caviar canneries the length and breadth of Russia.

The decision brings to the fore the unaddressed tension between the various ways in which Lord Goff's original formulation of the test in *Spiliada Maritime Corp v Cansulex Ltd*[10] was expressed, and the statutory formulation which is associated with it. There are differences, not always easy to measure, between (i) 'the more/most appropriate forum', and (ii) 'the natural forum', and (iii) 'the proper place to bring the claim'. The first of these represents the usage which is probably most faithful to the line of English authority which culminated in *Spiliada*. The second of these is a form of shorthand, almost impossible to avoid using, but which never quite threw off its distinctively Scottish origins, and which English law prior to *Spiliada* went out of its way to shun. Insofar as either was vouched for by statute, it could be seen as the way the House of Lords interpreted the rule that permission to serve would not be given unless it was made sufficiently to appear to the court that the case was a proper one for service out of the jurisdiction.[11] The third of these is the current statutory formulation in the Civil Procedure Rules;[12] its precise relationship to what went before has never been clearly explained.

Assuming[13] for the sake of argument that Cherney were to have a well-founded fear of unjust treatment from the Russian courts, and may have faced a risk of premature death from forces inside Russia, how might this material bear on the question whether service out should be allowed? Granted that it may be said that England is the only plausible forum for the claim, does that make it the most appropriate forum? Or the natural forum? Or the proper place to bring the claim? The answer involves little more than reflection on the use and interpretation of the English language, and cannot be said to be much more than a matter of impression.

[8] The Ground is now to be found in CPR Part 6, Practice Direction B, para 3.1(6).
[9] CPR r 6.37(3).
[10] [1987] AC 460.
[11] RSC Order 11 rule 4(2).
[12] CPR r 6.37(3).
[13] The difficulty inherent in this proposition should not be under-estimated. Whether the facts and matters alleged are probability, possibility or paranoid delusion will often be impossible to say.

The view preferred here is that if a case has, for practical purposes,[14] nothing to do with England, England is neither the most appropriate forum, nor its natural forum, nor the proper place to bring it; but one can still see how a different view may be taken. From the perspective of the claimant, life will seem bitter if he has a well-founded claim and nowhere to go with it; but unless English law is content to adopt a principle that England will provide a forum of necessity to anyone who has an arguable case that his claim can be got within any of the Grounds of the Practice Direction, it may be necessary to say that there are some claims which are just not the business of the English courts, and if that is tough, that is because life is tough.

Even so, none of this will arise unless English courts are prepared to find that a particular foreign court will not, or cannot be sufficiently trusted to, offer a fair trial. By what standards is this to be determined? It can hardly be enough to rely on material put out by bodies which have chosen to give themselves grand-sounding names, such as 'Transparency International'[15] and 'Freedom House'.[16] Neither is the World Bank corruption index any more useful to those who suspect that the organisations most vocal in claiming to be apolitical are frequently the most insidious and secretly-funded. Add to this a collection of newspaper cuttings, and the occasional report from an alleged expert who can be trusted to have been paid for what he says, and the sense that such decisions are in fact founded on little more than tittle-tattle is inescapable. And even if one were to have read all the material which was spilled all over the bench in *Cherney v Deripaska*, so what? None of it came anywhere near establishing that the judge before whom the claim could be brought would be partisan or would be susceptible to being woken in the night by a telephone call whose intent was clear enough, quite apart from whether what it did suggest was advanced on grounds which were credible. But the result was clear enough: the court set aside its usual scheme for taking decisions about service out on the basis of gossip, rumour, whisper, and the slinging of mud. It is not edifying and it is not self-evidently correct. The preferable answer was to say that the claim in question was none of the English courts' business, for the claim had nothing to do with England[17] and everything to do with Russia, and which is where and only where it belonged. If that caused trouble for the parties, well, life's like that: it is a bitter world, and a wholly Russian fight belongs in Russia. It does not belong in the Strand.

In *Pacific International Sports Clubs Ltd v Soccer Marketing International Ltd*, a bitter and acrimonious dispute about the ownership of Dinamo

[14] The fact that it fits within one of the Grounds now listed in para 3.1 of the Practice Direction B to CPR Part 6 does not necessarily mean that there is a substantial connection to England.

[15] Which produces a 'global corruption report'.

[16] Which receives 80% of its funding from the US government.

[17] That proposition is not challenged by the alleged fact that the contract in question was made in a London hotel. But for the significance of this, see the following Note.

Kiev Football Club came before the Chancery Division. The judge was asked to find that the players involved could not get a fair trial in the Ukraine, and to conclude that a stay in favour of the courts of that country, self-evidently the natural forum, should not properly be ordered. It took almost 100 paragraphs of the judgment to arrive at the point where the judge was 'not persuaded that the evidence... quite crosses the threshold of cogency that the jurisprudence requires'.[18] The issue is not whether he was right or wrong. In the context of a stay of proceedings, which had been brought against two defendants who had been properly served within the jurisdiction, one of whom, being domiciled only in Ukraine,[19] was not prevented by *Owusu*[20] from applying for a stay of proceedings, the judge had no choice but consider the evidence put before him; and if it was inescapable in that case, it did no greater harm to assess it in relation to those other defendants who, having been served out of the jurisdiction, applied to have permission and service set aside. Even so, the judge's conclusion, and the manner in which he laboured to arrive at it, will only encourage more of the same.

In *Sharab v Prince Al Waleed Bin Talal Bin Abdal Aziz al Saud*, which is also noted below, it is simply worth observing that the claim was one for permission to serve out of the jurisdiction, and which therefore required the claimant to show that England was the proper place to bring the claim.[21] She sought to do this on the basis that it was, as she saw it, the only place in which she was able to bring the claim: the defendant was not easily or obviously amenable to the jurisdiction of courts overseas. The court seemed to consider that this assisted the claimant in establishing that England was the proper place to bring the claim; when the defendant proffered an undertaking to submit to the courts of Libya, the court rejected it as having been proposed too late in the day, leaving the claimant with England or nowhere at all. This seems to suggest unclarity of thought on the part of those involved, for though an undertaking may be useful in the context of an application for a stay of proceedings, to assist the defendant over the hurdle of showing that there is another court more appropriate than England for the trial of the action,[22] it does not appear to have been useful as part of the exercise of showing that England was the most appropriate forum, unless (as *Cherney* might

[18] At [93].

[19] In fact, one of the defendants was domiciled in England, and the court was therefore pressed with the argument that a stay of proceedings on forum-non-conveniens grounds in favour of a non-Member State was impermissible. But the judge found (at [112]) that the sole English defendant was a relatively minor player in the dispute. He therefore set aside the permission order in respect of the defendant served out of the jurisdiction, and appeared to hope that the claim against the English defendant, about which he could not do anything, would wither on the vine; the judge accepted that a case-management stay might be considered at a later stage if withering did not take place.

[20] C-281/02 *Owusu v Jackson* [2005] ECR I-1383.

[21] CPR r 6.37(3).

[22] Cf *Lubbe v Cape plc* [2001] 1 WLR 1545.

be taken to suggest) England may be the most appropriate forum by default of any other.

One is left with the impression that the common law has allowed itself to be led into something of a muddle. If the lines formerly understood to be clear are fading or being erased, and are to be replaced with a test which asks only whether it is appropriate that the claim be heard in England rather than in a foreign court, or whether England is a proper place for the litigation, this would not necessarily make the law any worse, but it would make it different; and it appears that only the new Supreme Court or legislation can see to it. The correct answers, as deduced from previous case-law, to these three cases would have been to refuse to permit service out in the case of *Cherney v Deripaska*, on the ground that the case was not one for which England was the natural or proper forum; to stay[23] or dismiss[24] the proceedings in *Pacific International Sports Clubs Ltd*, on the footing that Ukraine was the natural forum and that it was, so far as evidence was concerned, not unjust to leave the claimants to go there; and to order service out in *Sharab* on the footing that the claim in question was more closely connected to England than to any other country, ignoring any undertaking from the defendant about the courts of Libya. However, in the two service-out cases, it is possible to read the judgments as saying that if the claim falls within one of the Grounds on which service out may be authorised, that suffices to show that the case is one which an English court may properly be asked and expected to hear. This question is the subject of the next Note.

2. The significance of the grounds for service out of the jurisdiction: *Greene Wood & McLean LLP v Templeton Insurance Ltd;*[25] *Sharab v Prince Al Waleed Bin Talal Bin Abdal Aziz al Saud;*[26] *Novus Aviation Ltd v Onur Air Tasimacilik;*[27] *Cherney v Deripaska*[28]

In *Animal Farm*,[29] some of the older beasts were present when the original Seven Commandments were painted on the wall at the end of the barn. As time goes by, they still believe that they can remember what those commandments were. But their confidence is shaken, and they are increasingly disorientated when, as more time goes by, the text appears to proclaim the very opposite of what they thought they recalled. Something unconsciously similar seems to be happening to the truth, anciently

[23] For the defendant served within the jurisdiction.

[24] For the defendants served out of the jurisdiction with permission.

[25] [2009] EWCA Civ 65, [2009] 1 WLR 2013: Sir Anthony Clarke MR, Longmore and Hooper LJJ.

[26] [2009] EWCA Civ 353, [2009] 2 Lloyd's Rep 160: Arden, Richards and Rimer LJJ.

[27] [2009] EWCA Civ 122, [2009] 1 Lloyd's Rep 576: Sir Mark Potter P, Wilson and Lawrence Collins LJJ.

[28] [2009] EWCA Civ 849: Waller, Moore-Bick LJJ and Sir John Chadwick (affirming [2008] EWHC 1530 (Comm), [2009] 1 All ER 333; noted this Year Book 79 (2008), 543).

[29] George Orwell, (Secker & Warburg, London, 1945).

established by the highest authority, that when an application is made for permission to serve out of the jurisdiction, the claimant must show that his claim falls not only within the wording used in the rule on which he relies, but that it falls within the letter and spirit of it as well;[30] and that when it comes to the construction of these rules, ambiguity is to be resolved in favour of the person out of the jurisdiction, and therefore against service.[31] All this is justified by the fact that 'service out of the jurisdiction is an interference with the sovereignty of other countries [even if] today all countries exercise a degree of jurisdiction over persons abroad'.[32]

A series of cases in the Court of Appeal seem to suggest that such concerns are no longer as inhibiting as they once were, and it is timely to ponder the way in which the law appears to be developing. In *Greene Wood & McLean LLP v Templeton Insurance Ltd* a claim for contribution was advanced by the claimant in circumstances in which there was a insurance contract between the defendant and third parties which should, as the claimants said, have covered the sums which, as they were not paid, the claimants had to pay. Permission to serve out was sought on the basis that the claim was 'in respect of a contract', even though the claimant was not a party to that contract: permission was granted on the basis that the reference to 'a contract' did not necessarily mean 'a contract between the claimant and the defendant'.[33] In *Sharab v Prince Al Waleed Bin Talal Bin Abdal Aziz al Saud* it was alleged that an oral contract was made within the jurisdiction, even though any such agreement was radically altered and overwritten in Libya a couple of years later. The court went out of its way to deny that the claimant had to show that her claim fell within the spirit as well as the letter of the rules, or that a contract whose being once made in London was so incidental and remote as it was in this case, was not within the spirit of the rule relied on as the basis for service out. In *Novus Aviation Ltd v Onur Air Tasimacilik* the court merely observed that what were once the heads of RSC Order 11 were now 'relegated to a Part 6 Practice Direction', in terms which suggested that their importance is less than it used to be. In *Cherney v Deripaska*, the court accepted that as long as the claimant was able to show a good arguable case that he would be entitled as a matter of English domestic law to have the defendant declared to be a constructive trustee of disputed shares, the

[30] *Johnson v Taylor Bros* [1920] AC 144, 153.

[31] *Soc Gen de Paris v Dreyfus Bros* (1885) 29 Ch D 239; (1887) 37 Ch D 215; *The Hagen* [1908] P 189, 201.

[32] Dicey, Morris and Collins, *The Conflict of Laws* (ed Lord Collins of Mapesbury) (Thomson, London, 14th edn, 2006) para 11–148. The significance of this is underlined by Dicey's reference to 'four cardinal points [which] have been emphasised in the decided cases'.

[33] To be fair to the court, its point that the rule ought to be available in connection with claims founded on the Contracts (Rights of Third Parties) Act 1999 is persuasive; but once this step is taken, how many more may follow? What of a tortious claim for damages for wrongful interference with a contract *inter alios*?

claim was one 'in respect of a contract' which related to other property but which had been exchanged for those shares. The fact that there was no contract which related to the property which was claimed in the proceedings was evidently irrelevant to the contention that the claim fell within the contract Ground for service out of the jurisdiction: not much sign of letter and spirit in that, one may think. Indeed, *Cherney* is as remarkable as it is schizophrenic: at the same time as it weakened and extended the material scope of the Ground for service out on which reliance was placed, it diluted the requirement that England be the natural forum for the trial of the action. This does not look like the coherent development of the law.

In none of these cases did the court acknowledge any difficulty when faced with the argument that the contract was *inter alios*, or that the terms of the contract which was to be enforced were agreed in Libya rather than England, or that the contract related to property other than that over which the remedy was sought. It is hard to say that the construction of the rule relied on, which was resolved in favour of the claimant, was the more restrictive of two which were equally tenable. It may well be correct to say, as the court did in *Novus Aviation* that the rules have suffered the indignity of relegation, and to deduce, as the court in that case did not need to do while other courts may yet, that this means that they are to be taken less seriously, and as having less of a controlling influence over the manner in which applications for permission to serve out are disposed of. This is not be a serious problem all the while it is borne in mind that permission to serve out will not be granted unless England is the natural forum, or is the most appropriate place in which to bring the proceedings. But if that requirement is also weakened or diluted, the result may be that service out is permitted even though the claim comes within the letter but not the spirit of the rule, or maybe not even (on one reading of the rule) the letter of the rule; and may be permitted even though the courts—functioning courts, to be sure—of a foreign friendly state represent the natural forum for the claim. It is hard to imagine that this is what Lord Goff had in mind in *Seaconsar Far East Ltd v Bank Markazi Jomhouri Islami Iran*[34] when he observed that it had

> been consistently stated, at least since the judgment of Pearson J in the *Dreyfus*[35] case, that it is a serious question whether the jurisdiction under Order 11 ought to be invoked, to put a person outside the jurisdiction to the "inconvenience and annoyance of being brought to contest his rights in this country".[36] This however is very largely met by the application in this context of the principle of forum conveniens...

For the courts to loosen the requirements imposed by the Grounds on which service out may be permitted, while also diluting the *Spiliada* test

[34] [1994] 1 AC 438, 455. [35] (1885) 29 Ch D 239. [36] At 242–243.

to the point where it simply asks whether England is the proper forum and accepts that this may be so even though the natural forum is elsewhere, is to take several steps in a questionable direction. It is no answer to say, as is sometimes said, that other countries assert jurisdiction over absent defendants, and do not trouble themselves overmuch about whether they are really the natural forum for the litigation of the claim: *tu quoque* is never an attractive component in an argument.[37] But whether or not the law should be as one would gather it from this year's jurisprudence, it is the manner in which the changes have been made without addressing the authority which pointed to another approach which is the real basis for objection. It seems to be getting much easier to persuade a court—if 'persuade' is the right verb, which it probably is not—to allow service to be made out of the jurisdiction, simply by asserting that England is an appropriate place for the claim. That has never been the law.[38]

3. Conflict and confusion in the effect of foreign judgments: *Brunei Investment Agency v Fidelis Nominees Ltd*;[39] *Calyon v Michailidis*;[40] *Re Haji-Ioannou (dec'd), Haji-Ioannou v Frangos*;[41] *D'Hoker v Tritan Enterprises*[42]

The common law on the enforcement of foreign judgments in England is a curious mixture. From some vantage points, principally Canadian,[43] it may appear to be stuck in the late nineteenth century and to be characterised, as the rhetoric has it, by an imperial mistrust of foreign courts and their products. From that same vantage point, it is said that for English private international law to enforce judgments for a fixed sum in money, but to refuse to enforce judgments not of that kind, is wrong: although Dicey Morris & Collins[44] state the law in this form, because as a matter of legal fact the mode of recovery is to bring an action to collect the debt

[37] Even when it characterises a statement in Dicey, Morris and Collins, above n. 32: see para 11–148 fn 94.

[38] It is not otherwise noted, but the decision in *Relfo London (in liq) v Varsani* [2009] EWHC 2297 (Ch) is in the same carelessly slack line. A defendant was out of the country, working in Kenya, but it was held that he had been served with process which had been posted to an address in Edgware. How it can be said that this amounted to service on a person who was not present within the jurisdiction, and certainly not present at the address in Middlesex, is a mystery. But if service were simply understood as made when a document is posted to somewhere within the jurisdiction, this would be sufficient. The trouble is that this is not what service on a defendant has been previously understood to mean. The merits of the case may not have been strong, as the address was occupied by his wife and family, and the defendant, seeking to evade liability in earlier proceedings in Singapore, had deposed to the fact that he was resident in England. But service on a defendant has not been made when the document is sent to one place, and the defendant is in a different continent. The judgment, unexpectedly, did not refer to the equally wrong-headed decision in *Kamali v City & Country Properties Ltd* [2006] EWCA Civ 1879, [2007] 1 WLR 1219 (noted this Year Book, 78 (2007) 600), but it is entirely in line with that unreliable decision as well.

[39] [2008] JRC 152, [2008] Jersey LR 337: Royal Court.

[40] [2009] UKPC 34 (Gib): Lord Rodger of Earlsferry, Lord Browne of Eaton-under-Heywood, Lord Mance, Sir Henry Brooke and Sir Robin Auld.

[41] [2009] EWHC 2310 (QB): Slade J.

[42] [2009] EWHC 949 (QB): Jack J.

[43] See *Morguard Investments Ltd v De Savoye* [1990] 3 SCR 1077.

[44] The Conflict of Laws, Rule 31(1)(a).

created by the judgment, this allows the forms of action to stifle the rational development of the law. Thus it was that the Supreme Court of Canada decided that non-money judgments from American courts could, in principle, be enforced in Canada, and considered that in so doing it was breaking new ground.[45] We shall see about that later.

The Royal Court of Jersey, in *Brunei Investment Agency v Fidelis Nominees Ltd* has now come to the same general conclusion.[46] The law of Jersey on the enforcement of judgments is, subject to a significant exception to be noted below, the same as the common law of England; but the judge seemed to think that it was time for the law of Jersey to strike out in front of the English common law. The issue arose in a factually easy case. Prince Jefri, black sheep of the royal family of Brunei, had been sued in Brunei in respect of various pieces of property alleged to have been misappropriated by him. The proceedings were compromised by way of a settlement agreement and a Tomlin Order. In due course, Jefri failed to comply with the terms of the order, and was sued again in Brunei. This time he was ordered to comply with the terms of the order, included among which was an obligation to hand over shares in two Jersey companies. His appeal to the Privy Council was dismissed in forthright terms;[47] and the claimant then brought proceedings in Jersey to enforce the Brunei judgment. In spite of the fact that the judgment was not a final money judgment, but one decreeing specific performance of the terms of the settlement agreement, the Royal Court held that it was enforceable in Jersey. This was seen as a proper development of the common law, in line with indications from the Supreme Court of Canada. There are two points to be made, each one fairly described as curious.

The first curiosity is that a court in Jersey should allow its law to develop in this way. One of the biggest perceived threats to the activities of the island in the international asset-protection[48] business comes from courts outside Jersey making orders that Jersey trustees disclose information about the assets of a trust, or exercise their powers to make payments out of the trust, or even that the terms of a trust be varied. The Family Division of the English High Court does not usually allow a husband, resisting his former wife's claim for maintenance, to pretend that the assets in a Jersey trust are nothing to do with him, and that as he has barely two halfpennies to rub together, he should not be made to pay anything at all: the courts simply deem the assets to be attributable to the

[45] *Beals v Saldanha* [2003] 3 SCR 416.

[46] It is arguable that Jersey law took this step two decades ago, in *Lane v Lane* [1985–86] Jersey LR 48, but the judgment accepting that an English judgment ordering the defendant to transfer an interest in Jersey land was liable to be enforced, but the Royal Court's judgment was not strongly reasoned.

[47] *HRH Prince Jefri Bolkiah v State of Brunei Darussalam* [2007] UKPC 62 (Brunei).

[48] Some may prefer to read this as 'tax evading and money laundering', but the differences are really of perspective rather than substance.

husband, make their order accordingly, and wait and see.[49] But it is equally clear that they may move more directly against the trust and trustees. In response to this, Jersey law has recently been changed to make such non-Jersey judgments unenforceable in Jersey; and with this alteration safely on the books, it was less of a big deal than it might have been to concede the enforcement of other kinds of non-money judgments.

The second curiosity is more fundamental, for it strikes at the root of the law. What the traditional statement of the common law, in Dicey's Rule 35, fails to say, is that foreign judgments are *never* enforced: only English judgments are enforced in England. With the foreign judgment in his back pocket, a judgment creditor brings proceedings to obtain an English judgment, this usually in the form of an order for the payment of money by way of debt. The path to judgment is usually cut short: it will be pleaded that there is no defence to the claim, and judgment will be entered without looking at the underlying cause of action. Execution then follows in the usual way, but on the English judgment, not the foreign.

Now consider the position of the person who has obtained a judgment for delivery up, or for specific performance of a contractual obligation, or for an injunction. He cannot bring proceedings to recover the debt, for there is none constituted by the foreign judgment. Instead, he takes an initial step back and sues on the original cause of action, but then applies for summary judgment on the ground that there is no defence to the claim, on the ground that the issues of liability are closed to further inspection by the English court by the doctrine of *res judicata*.[50] Liability being incontestable, the English court makes whatever order is appropriate to give effect to the substantive rights which *ex hypothesi* have been determined already. True, this may not be precisely the same as the order made by the original court, but it will be designed to give effect to the rights established as *res judicata* by the judgment of the original court.

It follows that the differences between the treatment of foreign money judgments—said, inaccurately, to be enforceable—and foreign non-money judgments—said, equally inaccurately, to be unenforceable—are much less than is commonly supposed. It does not help matters for Dicey to give the impression that there is a strong distinction, when that is merely an illusion. But equally, for the courts in Canada and Jersey to suppose that they are making a development of the law which English private international law has not been able or willing to make is rather wide of the mark. If the proceedings in *Brunei Investment Agency v Fidelis Nominees Ltd* had been brought in England, the claimant would have brought

[49] For an example, see *Charman v Charman* [2005] EWCA Civ 1606, [2006] 1 WLR 1053 (provision of information); *Charman v Charman* [2007] EWCA Civ 503, [2007] 1 FLR 1246 (financial provision). For another, see *C v C (Ancillary Relief: Nuptial Settlement)* [2004] EWCA Civ 1030, [2005] Fam 250.

[50] Or, to put the matter another way, that the judgment may be recognised even if it may not be enforced.

proceedings to obtain a judgment that the terms of the settlement agreement be carried into effect; would have pleaded that the duty of the prince to do as he had agreed to do was already determined as *res judicata*, and that an English court should therefore make the order that the transfer of shares be executed: in exactly the same way as the Royal Court did. There is no novelty, just the illusion of novelty. It is high time that those who make it their business to state English common law recognised it.

To those who believe that the Brussels I Regulation has made it simple to enforce judgments from the courts of other Member States, the year's crop of cases will come as a terrible embarrassment.[51] They all concerned the effect of Greek judgments in England. One should begin with the judgment of the Privy Council in *Calyon v Michailidis*. To say that it was part of a larger story is a bit like saying that one of the symptoms of malaria is a bit of a headache. The litigation spawned by the life and sudden death of Christo Michailidis, and in particular from the administration of and succession to his intestate estate has been keeping its participants plotting and scheming, and their various lawyers busy and rich, for almost ten years; and the end is nowhere in sight. In this particular round, the target of the proceedings was a collection of furniture which had during his lifetime been in the Kensington house which the deceased, M, had shared with his lifetime partner, S.[52] S had evidently sold the collection and been enriched by the proceeds after their journey had taken them through Liechtenstein, Panama and the British Virgin Islands (for reasons which do not need to be explained here). The collection ended up in Gibraltar, with the local branch of a French bank, Calyon.[53] M's mother and sister took a very dim view of the whole matter. They claimed that they had inherited the assets which, as they said, fell into the estate of M and did not become the property of S. For reasons which are not completely easy to fathom, S launched proceedings in Greece;[54] the mother and sister joined in and counter-claimed against S; S sought to discontinue but was rebuffed; and the Greek court duly issued a declaratory judgment, to the effect that the collection belonged to the mother. The mother then brought proceedings in Gibraltar, against Calyon, alleging that it had wrongfully participated in a breach of trust by S. As part of her claim, the mother needed to establish that she was the owner of the collection; she sought to do this on the sole ground that this had been declared to be so by the Greek courts, which it had, and that the

[51] It is to be noted, though, that the proposals for reform of the Brussels I Regulation have the abolition of the *exequatur* process as a central plank of the programme.

[52] The large problem of ownership and succession seemed to centre on the nature of the partnership between M and S. According to The Times, 15 March 2003, Mr Symes said that the Greek family members were 'acting out of revenge, jealousy and greed. They want to take everything they can from me'.

[53] The corporate and investment banking arm of Crédit Agricole SA, a French bank.

[54] The proceedings which were launched in other jurisdictions are listed in the judgment at [10]–[18].

Greek judgment was entitled to recognition in Gibraltar, which was the issue on which the parties joined. The Privy Council, reversing a rather senior Gibraltar Court of Appeal[55] and restoring the decision below, held that the Greek judgment did not qualify for recognition in Gibraltar. Its reasoning was that the Greek judgment was intended by the Greek court to be a judgment *in rem*; and as a matter of English and Gibraltar law, a judgment *in rem* is recognised as such only if the *res* was within the territorial jurisdiction of the court at the time, which it was not. The judgment could not have been binding on Calyon as a judgment *in personam*, as Calyon was not party to the proceedings in Greece. As a conclusion of common law on the recognition of foreign judgments, it was impeccable. But that is where the problems begin. To judge from the reasons of the Judicial Committee, the case was argued on distinctly odd grounds; certainly something seems to have gone awry.

For Greek judgments, given in civil or commercial matters, take their effect in the legal order of the United Kingdom, which for this purpose includes Gibraltar,[56] according to the terms of the Brussels I Regulation. A cardinal principle of recognition according to the Regulation is that a judgment is to have the effect in the state of recognition that it has in the state of its origin: the Court made this clear long ago,[57] and one may understand easily enough why it should be so. According to Greek law, at least so far as can be deduced from the judgment, the Greek judgment was final and decisive as to the ownership of the collection. And unless there were any more to be said about the matter, that should have been that. The fact that the judgment would not have been recognised (except as operating *in personam* as between the actual parties[58] to the litigation) under the rules of the common law is irrelevant to the recognition required and put in place by Chapter III of the Regulation. There is no obvious distinction drawn within the Regulation scheme between judgments *in personam* and judgments *in rem*:[59] if they satisfy the criteria of being judgments in civil and commercial matters from the courts of a Member State, they are entitled to recognition unless the Regulation itself provides otherwise, and that appears to be that. On that view of the matter, the Greek judgment should have been recognised according to its terms, no matter what the common law might otherwise have said.

Even so, it would still have been striking if a judgment in proceedings to which Calyon had never been, or been intended to have been, a

[55] Stuart-Smith P, Otton and Aldous JJA.

[56] For the Gibraltar court to which the application for registration of a Greek judgment is made, see Annex II of the Regulation.

[57] 144/86 *Hoffmann v Krieg* [1988] ECR 645. To the same effect, C-420/07 *Apostolides v Orams* [2009] ECR I 3571, esp at [63]-[71].

[58] Or, conceivably, also their privies.

[59] A similar distinction, which was proposed to be relevant within the context of the jurisdictional rules of the Brussels scheme, was rejected by the Court as inapplicable to the organisation of what was then the Brussels Convention, in C-406/92 *The Tatry* [1994] ECR I-5436.

party was conclusive as against Calyon; and the Judicial Committee seemed to think that it needed to find a way to give effect to this appreciation of the merits. There were two available, and it chose the wrong one. Basing itself on an evidently-misleading passage in a leading textbook, and a contention by counsel which seemed quite misconceived, it reasoned that recognition involved 'equating the authoritative nature of a foreign judgment with a judgment in the state addressed'.[60] An English[61] judgment in proceedings between those who had been party to the Greek proceedings would not have been binding on Calyon, neither directly (as they were not party to the proceedings, so assumed no obligation to abide by the judgment) nor indirectly (as they were entitled to make their own submissions on the matter);[62] and therefore a Greek judgment would not be any more binding than that. That was not what the Court said in *Hoffmann v Krieg*; and it cannot be correct. There is no reason to suppose that a Greek judgment is 'recognised' by transplanting it into the English legal order and pretending that it is an English judgment. It is and remains, and has to be accepted in spite of the fact that it is, a Greek judgment. The duty of the English court is to give it the effect it has under the law of its state of origin.[63] It is not the duty of the English court to pretend that the judgment had been given in proceedings before an English court, not least because that would involve 'recognising' a non-existent and wholly hypothetical English[64] judgment instead.

There would have been little need to say any more had it not been for a casual and unexplained half-sentence in the recent judgment in *Apostolides v Orams*,[65] where the European Court of Justice said[66] that a recognised foreign judgment should not be given effects which a local judgment would not have had. The reason for that observation is unexplained. It did not appear to be material to the answer given by the Court; and the gymnastics needed if the English court is asked to imagine a hypothetical local judgment are not attractive. Had it been cited to the court, it would have supported the approach which proceeded by imagining that the English court had given a similar kind of judgment, but the decision in *Apostolides* may well have come later than the argument in *Calyon*. At all events, the decision in *Hoffmann* was clear enough, and it is

[60] Layton & Mercer, *European Civil Practice*, (Thomson, London, 2004) para 24.006, cited in the judgment at [22]. Of course, SI 2001/3929, Sch 1 para 2 states that when registered under the Regulation, 'a judgment shall, for the purposes of its enforcement, be of the same force and effect' as if it had been an English judgment. But this does not authorise the argument that, as an English judgment would not be recognised as binding Calyon, the Greek one cannot be recognised against Calyon either.

[61] The reference to 'English' rather than 'Gibraltar' is only for convenience of reference.

[62] *Duchess of Kingston's Case* (1776) 1 Leach 146; *Hollington v F Hewthorn & Co* [1943] KB 587.

[63] 145/86 *Hoffmann v Krieg* [1988] ECR 645.

[64] Or, in this case, Gibraltarian.

[65] C-420/07, [2009] ECR I 3571.

[66] At [66].

hard to believe that its casual knock in *Apostolides* was attributable to anything more than a lack of skill and care.

According to Article 34(2) of the Regulation, a judgment is not to be recognised under the Regulation if it was given in default of appearance, and the defendant was not served in sufficient time to allow his to arrange for his defence. This provision has been held by the European Court to be one of the cornerstones of the Regulation, for it guarantees and reinforces the right to a fair hearing.[67] For this reason it has been held to be applicable even though the court which gave judgment did not consider that it was doing so in default of appearance.[68] Although it has been modified, so that the defendant loses his shield if he fails to bring proceedings to challenge the judgment when he becomes aware of it,[69] the sense of the rule is still clear enough: those who are subjected to the adverse consequences of a judicial order are entitled to a fair hearing of what they themselves have to say before judgment is given against them. Calyon could say, with perfect fairness, that Article 34(2) provided a perfect fit. Not only was Calyon not a party to the Greek proceedings, it was not even told of the proceedings in Greece until after the Greek judgment had been given and appealed.[70] Though the Judicial Committee did not itself say so, it all looks pretty suspicious, and from where Calyon viewed the issues, not unlike a conspiracy. The idea that Calyon should be ordered to deliver up property by reason of a judgment in proceedings in which they had played no part at all, and had been intended to play no part at all, was just as daft as the Judicial Committee considered it to be, but not for the reasons which it advanced.

Indeed, there was even a basis for a submission that, so far as Calyon was concerned, the order of the Greek court was not to be seen as a judgment at all. In *Denilauler v SNC Couchet Frères*[71] the Court explained why a judicial order arresting funds in a bank account as security for a claim was not to be recognised, never mind enforced, against the defendant who had not been notified of the application and of the proceedings: the order was not obtained in adversarial proceedings, or in proceedings which were intended to be adversarial. The party adversely affected had not been summoned to appear, and therefore the order made in those proceedings did not fall within what is now Chapter III of the Brussels I Regulation. As far as Calyon was concerned, it was in pretty much the same position. It had not been notified of the Greek proceedings until far too late; the order had been made and, if it were to be recognised and enforced against Calyon, would have completely undermined its right to speak in its own defence. Either the order was not a judgment so far as its

[67] C-78/95 *Hendrickman v Magenta Druck & Verlag GmbH* [1996] ECR I-4943.
[68] Ibid.
[69] Article 34(2).
[70] See the judgment at [21].
[71] 125/79, [1980] ECR 1553.

recognition against Calyon was concerned, or it was a judgment in default of Calyon's appearance, even if it seems a little odd to speak of default by a party who was never summoned to appear in the first place. The Brussels I Regulation contained all that was needed to produce the decision to which the Judicial Committee was inevitably, and correctly, drawn. It is just a pity that it did not appear to have been shown the true path which should have led it there.

Much the same could be said of the truly weird decision in *Re Haji-Ioannou*. This also represented the latest round in an endless family struggle: this time, by Mr Haji-Ioannou (H) to recover sums advanced to his erstwhile son-in-law (F). It may be that the bitterness of the fight, and the effort put into fighting it, distracted the court and blinded it to the sensible answer. Once again, the problem arose from a judgment obtained from the Greek courts. H had sued F; the Greek courts had ruled that F was indeed indebted to H in the sum of $49 million, plus interest, and ordered F also to pay the costs. As F had no assets in Greece, an application was made on H's behalf to register the judgment for enforcement in England. Everything was therefore going swimmingly, but two days after the application was made, H died, leaving no will. His widow (R) and children had more important things to do than to inform the English court of this development, and they took no step to prevent the application, which was done entirely on the papers and by lawyers in London, from proceeding.[72] The registration was ordered; by a subsequent application, R was substituted as the party obtaining registration of the Greek judgment. When served with the notice of registration, F appealed against the order for registration. This was originally done on several grounds, but in the end F rested on the proposition that at the date of the order for registration, R had no interest in the Greek judgment, and was on that account not entitled to obtain the order for its registration. That being so, said F, the order for registration was a nullity and had to be set aside.[73] The marvel is that the judge agreed, and set aside the order. The simple fact that the application could have been re-made as R left the court, and that there would then have been no obvious answer to it, was neither mentioned nor explained away. It is a judgment which was as careful as it was absurd.

Article 38 of the Regulation provides that 'on the application of any interested party' an order may be made declaring that the judgment is enforceable. As the application was made by or on behalf of the judgment creditor, a literal reading of Article 38 would have confirmed that the application was well made as it was made by H. True, the applicant had died after the application was made, but that fact did not contradict the conclusion that the application had been made by a person entitled to

[72] The irony is that if the conclusion of the judge was right, they had no interest in the judgment, so presumably lacked standing to tell the court anything at all.

[73] Relying on *Bowler v John Mowlem & Co Ltd* [1954] 1 WLR 1445.

make it. This simple answer did not, however, persuade. The court was beguiled to arrive at the conclusion that the registration was a nullity[74] on the ground that R was not a person who had an interest in the judgment at the material time. This was not arrived at by asking what it meant to have an interest in the judgment as a matter of interpretation of this form of words in accordance with European law. Neither was it reached by asking whether the judgment of the Greek court was one in which, as a matter of Greek law, R had an interest.[75] Instead, it was concluded that R would have had an interest in the judgment only if she had inherited the benefit of the judgment by reference to the law which, as a matter of English private international law, determined the succession to H's moveable estate: that is, R had no interest in the judgment unless its benefit had vested in her as a matter of English private international law.

That led to Monegasque domestic law: H had acquired an Monegasque domicile of choice in 1990, and though he had returned to Greece for medical treatment, which eventually failed, this had not been decisive enough to result in the loss of his domicile of choice.[76] The reasoning of the court on this aspect of English private international law was unobjectionable as far as it went. H had, as a matter of English private international law, then died domiciled in Monaco. The private international law of Monaco would have referred the question of succession to English law as (so it was found) the law of the nationality, British law. It would then have interpreted this as meaning the whole of English[77] law, including its rules of private international law; and would have accepted a renvoi from English law back to the domestic law of Monaco. According to the succession law of Monaco, as found by the judge, R inherited the benefit of the judgment only when she formally accepted the inheritance by an *acte de notoriété*, executed a few weeks after the order for registration had been made. As a matter of Monegasque law, the declaration of acceptance of the inheritance related back to the date of the deceased's death; but for the purpose of the analysis accepted by the judge, this was insignificant. At the date on which the English order was made, H was dead, R had not inherited the benefit of the Greek judgment in accordance with Monegasque law, and there was therefore no-one with any interest in it who could have registered the judgment in England; and what happened afterwards was *nihil ad rem*.

This means that whether H's heir could obtain a declaration of enforcement in respect of a Greek judgment was answered by a mixture of English private international law as to succession; the cobwebby antiquity of the common law on retention and abandonment of the domicile of choice; the

[74] Though surely the judge must have meant that it was liable to be set aside.

[75] This conclusion might have been supported by the general principle that the recognition of a judgment means to accord to it the effect it has in the state of its origin: 145/88 *Hoffmann v Krieg* [1988] ECR 645.

[76] At [56].

[77] Sic: there was no reason to suppose that British, to a Monegasque court, meant Scottish or Northern Irish.

private international law of Monaco; and the principles of renvoi of English and Monegasque law. It is possible, one supposes, that such a witches' brew is precisely what those who drafted Article 38 of the Regulation had in mind. But if it is, it will mean that the answer to the question whether R was entitled to obtain an order for enforcement of the judgment, the merits of which were indisputable and beyond question, will vary, and in utterly capricious form, from Member State to Member State. If that is what the free movement of judgments means, it is a marvellous thing to behold. Of course it is true that as a matter of substantive succession, only the person in whom the right to the judgment debt vests will be entitled to enforce it; but there was no doubt that R had succeeded to the estate of H. The answer should have been that the person in whom the benefit of the judgment vests (or, to take the point that the vesting might be defeated by her renunciation of the inheritance, will vest unless renounced) has an interest, and is entitled to register the judgment. After all, the 97 paragraphs of the judgment of Slade J merely meant that a fresh application for registration was bound to succeed; and if ever there was a case for common sense to knock heads together, this was it. That it did not must have been attributable to the persuasive nature of the submissions advanced on behalf of F who, for more than a decade, has left no stone unturned in his attempt to avoid repaying the sums which, according to the only court ever to have investigated the merits of the claim against him, he has no legal right to retain. It is not to their credit that the English courts have aided and abetted him. Greek lawyers, looking at this judgment, and at that in *Calyon v Michailides*, will rub their eyes and wonder what is going on.

One would not normally note the decision in *D'Hoker v Tritan Enterprises*, for Jack J made it clear that he was delivering a short judgment in circumstances of great urgency. But it shows, yet again, how complicated life may get when the implications of the simple proposition that Greek judgments are enforceable when they are registered in England have to be worked out.[78] Spouses to a Greek marriage had fallen out, and matrimonial proceedings were on foot, at least in England where the wife now resided. While all this was going on a company, with which the husband was suspected to be in cahoots, went to the Greek courts and obtained a worldwide Mareva injunction against the wife.[79] The order, remarkably enough, made no provision for her to have access to her bank account even to fund her basic living costs.[80] The order had been registered under Chapter III of the Brussels I Regulation on application *ex parte*, thereby taking effect in England for the purposes of enforcement as though it were the order of an English court. The wife appealed against the order for registration, but by case management it was agreed that she should

[78] Under SI 2001 No 3929, Sch 1, para 2(2).

[79] The suspicion is reported by the judge at [7]. It was striking that, having obtained its order from the Greek courts, it had not commenced substantive proceedings of any kind against the wife.

[80] A fact which came home to her when her debit card was retained by a cash machine.

apply to the Greek court for the variation of the order. This seemed to go awry. The Greek court made a modest variation of its original injunction to allow for living expenses, though at a far leaner level than the wife considered to be appropriate. When the appeal against registration came back before Jack J, he set the registration aside. He observed that although the effect of registration was that the injunction was treated as an English one, it did not appear that this gave the English court any power to vary it, even though that power would have been part and parcel of an original English freezing injunction. As the order as registered was no longer in effect in Greece, and as there was no obvious basis on which the judgment which had been registered could have its material terms rewritten in the records of the High Court,[81] he considered that it would be contrary to public policy to uphold the registration of an injunction which was no longer in force—in the terms made—in the state of its origin.[82] That dealt with the immediate point. But the judge went on to say that the recognition of an order which deprived the wife of the right to instruct and pay for English lawyers to prosecute her appeal and to continue the matrimonial proceedings,[83] and even of the right to buy food, would be contrary to English public policy, at least when made against someone who was resident in England and not in Greece.

The judge must have been right to do as he did, and probably right for the reasons he gave.[84] But the case does raise a really good question about what it means to recognise a judgment from another Member State. Where the original order is one which, by its very nature, is designed to involve a measure of continuous judicial supervision, there is a real risk of incoherence if registration in another Member State takes place. The idea of an English-made freezing injunction, which the court would ordinarily have power to vary but which is ossified by the very act of registration, and by the fact that it is really meant to be the avatar of the Greek judgment, existing alongside the Greek order which only the Greek court had power to vary, is extremely challenging. It may lead one to suppose that the idealistic notion, that Europe is a single legal area throughout which judgments are automatically and freely enforceable, is detached from the practical reality of legal life. It is not clear how the free movement of judgments is to work in this area, but this little case shows that the idea that the English court can simply re-make the foreign order may be far too simplistic to be workable.

[81] This may have been too cautious: it may be that the registration should have been open to amendment as the Greek judgment was amended, but the case was, as the judge said, an urgent one and not the occasion for a reflective analysis of the procedures open to the court.

[82] Article 34(1) of the Regulation.

[83] This last may have been the real point of the antics in the Greek courts.

[84] Saving the possibility that a judgment which has been registered should be liable to amendment as the order made in the state of origin is amended. The judge's further reasons, which addressed Article 34(2) of the Regulation, are not examined here, as the evidence before him of Greek law was too confused to allow him to come to any sensible conclusion.

4. Litigation relating to arbitration in the aftermath of the decision in West Tankers: *West Tankers Inc v Allianz SpA*;[85] *Youell v La Réunion Aerienne*;[86] *National Navigation Co v Endesa Generacion SA, (The 'Wadi Sudr')*[87]

It is not the function of this survey to note the decisions of the European Court of Justice, but the decision in *Allianz Spa v West Tankers Inc* was given in answer to a question referred to that court by the House of Lords, so that is the point of departure. One party to a commercial contract, which contained an agreement to arbitrate, instituted arbitral proceedings in London. The other brought judicial proceedings before the courts of Syracuse, Sicily, for damages in respect of damage done to its property. The first party applied to the English courts for an injunction to restrain the other, as it said, from committing the breach of its contractual agreement to arbitrate; the other objected that this flew in the face of the rule, established by the Court in *Turner v Grovit*,[88] that the principle of mutual trust and confidence in each other's judicial institutions, by which the Member States are bound, prohibits anti-suit injunctions. The view of the House of Lords, as it then was, was that as the entire subject matter of the English judicial proceedings was arbitration, the issues before it fell right outside the material scope of the Brussels I Regulation; the view of the Sicilian court, one may suppose, is that it was dealing with a matter which was well within the material scope of the Regulation,[89] and that the injunction was therefore prohibited. The European Court accepted that the entire subject matter of the English proceedings was arbitration, but denied that this allowed the English court to order an injunction in respect of proceedings before a court in another Member State which were in respect of a civil or commercial matter. It was one of those cases in which each court in each country was perfectly justified in seeing the issues as it did, but where it was also impossible for them to be both completely right at the same time. Though it was greeted with a collective groan of disappointment,[90] the principal objection to the judgment of the European

[85] C-185/07 *Allianz SpA v West Tankers Inc* [2009] ECR I-663. See also the report and note of the case at [2009] *Rev Crit DIP* 373 (note Muir-Watt).

[86] [2009] EWCA Civ 175, [2009] 1 Lloyd's Rep 586: Rix, Jacob and Lawrence Collins LJJ.

[87] [2009] EWCA Civ 1397: Waller, Carnwath and Moore-Bick LJJ, reversing in part [2009] EWHC 196 (Comm), [2009] 1 Lloyd's Rep 666: Gloster J.

[88] C-159/02, [2004] ECR I-3565.

[89] There was no doubt that, if this were so, it had special jurisdiction under Article 5(3) of the Regulation.

[90] An open forum on <http://conflictoflaws.net> made it clear that serious lawyers, across Europe, found the decision an embarrassment. In an unexpected, but delightful, coda, the Cour de Cassation delivered a judgment which, with perfect calm, accepted that an anti-suit injunction delivered by a judge in the Superior Court of Cobb County, Georgia, ordering a French respondent not to bring proceedings in the French courts, was enforceable in France, as it was given by the courts to which the parties had made a contractual agreement to submit: In *Wolberg v In Zone Brands International Inc* (Cass. 1re civ, 14 Oct 2009). The injunction did not deprive the party restrained from access to the courts, as it simply enforced the agreement as to which court; it did not offend public policy for it to be given conclusive effect in France, as the Georgia court gave reasons for the order made, and made orders by way of enforcement of the bargain. The further consequences of this decision remain

Court was the frustrating absence of reasoning in support of its assertion that the injunction could not be justified. After all, its previous jurisprudence had made it clear that a national court was not required to modify its law on a matter excluded from the Regulation just because the Regulation had something to say on a point which was otherwise material: the statement that the Regulation 'shall not apply to' something meant just what it said.[91]

The general view of the arbitration profession was that the removal of a part of its machinery by the Regulation was unjustifiable, for arbitration had been excluded from the Regulation by express words. The arbitration profession does indeed spend much of its time making unilateral declarations of independence from legal systems, except when recourse to a court is useful in making the individual arbitration more effective and therefore arbitration in general more attractive. But the arbitration industry's complaint argues for far too much: the arbitration in *Allianz* was not taking place in Alsatia, but in today's London; and the law of the realm, in London as everywhere else in the United Kingdom, is that judicial injunctions may not be ordered to restrain civil and commercial proceedings in another Member State. Arbitrators may not like it, but they occupy the space which the law of the land allows them, and only that space, because the law of the land permits it. It seems plain that those involved in arbitration cannot ask an English court to do something which the English courts no longer have a legal power to do. For an English judge to grant an injunction and to say that an arbitrator asked him to, or made him, do it would be rather like Adam blaming his transgressions on the beguilement of Eve.

As said above, the European Court accepted that subject-matter of the proceedings before the English court was arbitration, and that the Regulation therefore had no application to them *ratione materiae*.[92] In two cases which came very quickly before the courts, it was necessary to spell out what this meant in rather more detail. In *Youell v La Réunion Aerienne* a French insurer had settled a claim without reference to its English co-insurer. The English insurer therefore brought proceedings for a declaration that it owed no liability to the French insurer, asserting the special jurisdiction of the English court under Article 5(1) of the Regulation to do so. Despite the fact that the proceedings were for negative declaratory

to be worked out, but the proposition that the French courts have now accepted the contractual analysis, and contractual consequences, of an agreement on jurisdiction is undeniable. It is less clear whether they actually accepted that the injunction should be enforced—what would that involve?, one may ask rhetorically—as distinct from recognising as conclusive the decision of the US court to the twin effects that the parties had bound themselves by an agreement not to seise the French courts, and that the contractual agreement should be given effect.

[91] 145/86 *Hoffmann v Krieg* [1988] ECR 645 (a case on personal status). The wording 'shall not apply to' is taken from Article 1(2) of the Regulation.

[92] Judgment, at [23].

relief, the Court of Appeal was bound by its earlier decision[93] that such proceedings were not excluded from Article 5(1).[94]

The real problem in the case was that a claim was being advanced in France, in arbitration and to which the English insurer was objecting, which was the mirror image of what was claimed by the English insurer in the English proceedings.[95] The court had no difficulty in accepting that the matter before the English courts was civil or commercial; that it had as its subject matter the liability (or not) of the English insurer to make a contribution to the French insurer's settlement; and that there was therefore no impediment to its being heard. The French insurer elected not to apply under Arbitration Act 1996, s 9 for a stay of the English proceedings; the fact that there was a prior arbitration in Paris was irrelevant to the English proceedings because the *lis alibi pendens* rule of the Regulation does not take account of arbitrations; and even if the French courts had had power, which they evidently think they do not, to interfere with foreign judicial proceedings which perturb an arbitration, *Allianz* would have prevented its utilisation. In short, the English court was in much the same position as the court in Syracuse; and it got on with the job of adjudicating the contractual matter before it. The decision seems to be a faithful application of the principle in *Allianz*. It runs the risk, of course, that the English judicial and the French arbitral proceedings will run in parallel, and will risk clashing when it comes to enforcement. But that is the result of *Allianz*, as the Advocate-General in that case foresaw; and its solution was not a matter for the Court of Appeal.

In *The 'Wadi Sudr'* a simple enough factual dispute about the sale and sea carriage of coal for use in the generation of electricity, which was delivered short of its destination, spawned a web of bitterly-fought proceedings in Spain and England. Part of these resulted in a Spanish court delivering a judgment which rejected a contention that the parties were bound by an agreement to arbitrate their differences in London. The relief sought in various proceedings in the Commercial Court included a declaration that there was no liability, a declaration that there was an obligation to arbitrate, and an injunction to enforce the agreement to arbitrate. By the time the matter came to judgment, the possibility of granting an injunction had been precluded by *Allianz*. As to the declaration of non-liability, the English court had no jurisdiction under Article 5(1) of

[93] *Boss Group Ltd v Boss France SA* [1997] 1 WLR 351 (CA).

[94] The objection would have been that a matter cannot relate to a contract if the claimant asserts that there is no contract in the first place. But if there is an objection in this, it is not persuasive. For an analogous approach, that a party who denies that he is bound by a contract may still invoke the jurisdiction agreement in the alleged contract which his opponent pleads as binding him, see *Ryanair Ltd v Bravofly* [2009] IEHC 41, [2009] ILPr 701. The judgment was plainly motivated by a need to keep jurisdictional applications as simple as possible, even at the cost of criticism from passing logicians.

[95] Of course, Article 27 had no application as this applies only to parallel judicial proceedings, not to arbitral proceedings.

the Regulation to make the declaration sought, as the only contractual obligation performable in London was to arbitrate, but arbitration fell outside the material scope of the Brussels I Regulation, and the obligation to arbitrate in London therefore conferred no jurisdiction in a claim for a declaration of non-liability.

However, the claim for a declaration that there was an obligation to arbitrate was another matter. Although the English court would ordinarily have had jurisdiction to make such a declaration, the potential obstacle was that the Spanish court had declared, in civil or commercial proceedings, that there was no such obligation and therefore, so the argument ran, Chapter III of the Regulation required the recognition of the Spanish judgment as a complete answer to the claim in the English proceedings. At first instance, the judge found the Spanish judgment to provide no objection. She reasoned that if arbitration falls outside the scope of the Regulation, English proceedings which had arbitration and only arbitration as their subject matter, were not proceedings to which the obligation under Chapter III to recognise a judgment, also given in the matter of arbitration, applied. If she was wrong about this, she would have refused to recognise the Spanish judgment on grounds of public policy.[96] That policy proceeded from the fact that the New York Convention imposed obligations on contracting states to recognise agreements to arbitrate; and the manner in which that obligation had been given effect in England included Civil Jurisdiction & Judgments Act 1982, s 32. This provision required an English court to refuse recognition to a foreign judgment which had, to English eyes incorrectly, held that there was no binding agreement to arbitrate. The entire subject matter of the English proceedings[97] was arbitration, and in those arbitration proceedings there was no obligation on an English court to do otherwise than to apply its own law on arbitration. Part of that law was stated in section 32 of the 1982 Act. The judge did not say—presumably it was not put to her—that the European Court in *Hoffmann v Krieg*[98] explicitly confirmed that the court dealing with a claim in subject matter which falls outside the material scope of the Regulation does not have its wings clipped by an obligation to recognise a judgment in respect of subject matter which falls inside the Regulation. It was a sound piece of legal analysis, which took at face value the legislated rule that the Regulation had no application to proceedings which had arbitration as their subject matter, just as the European Court had confirmed that it did not.

The Court of Appeal, delivering two lengthy judgments, saw it differently. It reversed the judge on the question whether the Spanish

[96] *Philip Alexander Securities and Futures Ltd v Bamberger* [1997] ILPr 73, [111]–[114].

[97] This is correct, for there were in fact two sets of proceedings in England: those for a declaration of non-liability, and those for relief in relation to the agreement to arbitrate. It would have been more complicated if the whole of the relief had been sought in a single set of proceedings, but probably self-contradictory as well.

[98] 145/86, [1988] ECR 645.

judgment was required to be recognised in England as falling within the scope of the Regulation. The court held that it did, on the basis that the Spanish judgment was one given in a civil or commercial matter, and that once that was established, the content of that judgment, and all of it, had to be accepted by an English court, no matter the nature of the proceedings before it. It also rejected the view of the judge that recognition of a Spanish judgment holding that the parties were not bound to arbitrate was, if otherwise within the scope of the Regulation, contrary to public policy.[99] No doubt the decision of the Court of Appeal is tenable, not least because the existence of inconsistent judgments is always an unwelcome spectre in commercial dispute resolution, but it is still unsatisfactory. It regards the Spanish judgment, given to the effect that there was no agreement to arbitrate, as being in a civil or commercial matter, which it obviously was, but not as one having arbitration as its subject matter, but which it also, equally obviously, did have. The correct construction of Article 1 of the Regulation does not ask whether the matter in question is civil or commercial, but whether, if it is civil or commercial, it nevertheless has arbitration as its subject matter. It is very hard to see how the Spanish judicial decision that the parties had not bound themselves to arbitrate did not have arbitration as its subject matter. Indeed, to say as the court did, that because the issue of whether the parties had agreed to arbitrate was part of a civil or commercial dispute, it therefore did not have arbitration as its subject matter, is to denature Article 1(2)(d) of the Regulation. *Allianz* requires no such thing, and it is rather disappointing to see the court take the attitude it did. The decision in *Youell*, which pointed an alternative way ahead, was not referred to in the judgments, which is also very curious.

The trouble obviously originates, as it did in *Allianz* itself, in the fact that the very nature of commercial arbitration is to be commercial and arbitration at the same time. Similar issues, of how to understand that the founder of its faith was 'wholly human and wholly divine', had troubled the early Church, which had required many ecumenical councils and more anathemas to get its version of truth settled and imposed. 'Fully

[99] The Court of Appeal considered that this argument was unavailable on the facts, for if the judgment was required to be recognised, there was no ground of English public policy to trump this. The judgment is, at this point, peculiarly unpersuasive, for it relegates the statutory obligation to uphold an agreement to arbitrate, even in the face of a contradictory foreign judgment, to a rule which yields to a contradictory foreign judgment. At [62], Waller LJ held that an English court was forbidden to examine the facts matters which might be relevant to the application of English public policy. This is to make the same mistake as was suggested by the national court in C-78/95 *Hendrikman v Magenta Druck & Verlag GmbH* [1996] ECR I-4943, and which was put right by the European Court: a national court is obviously entitled to review a foreign judgment where this is required for it to deal with the application of what is now Article 34(1) of the Regulation. But it is not further dealt with here. Moore-Bick LJ preferred to read the provision in Civil Jurisdiction and Judgments Act 1982, s 32 as falling short of the standard set for a matter of public policy by C-7/98 *Krombach v Bamberski* [2000] ECR I-1935. That is a questionable reading of a statutory rule which directs an English court to disregard what a foreign court may have decided on the same point.

commercial and fully arbitration' is more mundane but is no easier to deal with. If, therefore, the Regulation applies its rules to the one and not to the other, it is necessary to divide the indivisible. The court preferred the view that the proceedings[100] with which it was concerned were commercial, and not arbitration, and if it were correct in that, the consequences followed as the court found that they did. One version of pragmatism, no doubt, prefers to recognise judgments to the greatest extent possible, to promote the general public interest in the finality of litigation. A variation on this is sometimes seen in judicial irritation with those parties who resist the accusation that as they have had one bite at the cherry they are now being greedy in demanding another. Even so, the legislative words are plain enough; and the material reasoning of the European Court[101] needs to be examined. The English proceedings undoubtedly had arbitration as their subject matter: they did in *Allianz*, and did in *The 'Wadi Sudr'*. The Spanish judgment was given on the point of arbitration: what else could be needed to demonstrate that the English proceedings did not require recognition of the Spanish judgment? Recall the words of the European Court in *Allianz*:

> In that regard it must be borne in mind that, in order to determine whether a dispute falls within the scope of Regulation 44/2001, reference must be made solely to the subject matter of the proceedings. More specifically, its place in the scope of Regulation 44/2001 is determined by the nature of the rights which the proceedings in question serve to protect. Proceedings, such as those in the main proceedings, which lead to the making of an anti-suit injunction, cannot, therefore, come within the scope of Regulation 44/2001.[102]

That would appear also to mean that the English proceedings which sought a declaration that there was an obligation to arbitrate fell outside the material scope of the Regulation, and that the contradictory Spanish arbitration judgment[103] did likewise. Of course there was a broader commercial dispute, but so what? There was in *Allianz* as well; there always will be in contracts in which the parties have arguably provided for commercial arbitration.

Even if one might not properly say that the answer is clear, the decision in *Hoffmann v Krieg*[104] still supports the contention that judgments on matters which are expressly excluded from the Regulation are excluded for all purposes of the Regulation. The court, however, was not persuaded

[100] It is hard to say whether this should be understood as a reference to the English or to the Spanish proceedings.

[101] By contrast, English decisions handed down before the decision in *Allianz* require much greater care.

[102] [2009] ECR I-663, [22]-[23].

[103] Or part of judgment: a judgment which is entitled to recognition on some points but not on other is liable to severance: Article 48.

[104] 145/86, [1988] ECR 645.

that *Hoffmann*, which dealt with the recognition of a judgment awarding spousal maintenance which was inconsistent with a local judgment dissolving a marriage, applied where the basis for non-recognition was something other than inconsistency with an actual local judgment. But that really will not do: the Court in *Hoffmann* accepted that the foreign judgment fell right outside the material scope of the Regulation; the non-recognition followed from Article 1 just as much as from Article 27(4) of the Convention, which amplified the effect of Article 1 in relation to matters of status. There is no basis for reading *Hoffmann* as dependent on the existence of a Dutch judgment that the parties were no longer married. But the court had evidently made up its mind, and although it went through the motions, it was hearing only one side of the argument.

The principle of the matter is nevertheless clear. Those rules of English law which apply to arbitrations apply to arbitrations, and to judicial proceedings concerned with arbitration. There is a rule of English law that a court may not make an order to restrain or interfere with proceedings in a civil or commercial matter before the courts of another Member State. That rule of English law operates as part of the law applicable in any court which deals with proceedings, whether these have arbitration as their subject matter, or something different as their subject matter. This rule may have been established in *Turner v Grovit* and in *Allianz SpA v West Tankers Inc*, but it is a rule of English law even so. There is another rule of English law, which is tripartite in structure: (i) agreements to arbitrate are upheld and enforced, and that in reasoning such cases, English courts do not defer to what a court in another state may have said on the matter;[105] (ii) the rule under point (i) may be displaced if the issue before the court is in respect of a civil or commercial matter and the Regulation requires that the judgment be recognised;[106] but (iii), the rule under point (i) is not displaced if the subject-matter of the proceedings is arbitration, for the Regulation does not claim to apply in or to arbitration.[107] Point (i) is established by Civil Jurisdiction and Judgments Act 1982, s 32; point (ii) by section 32(4) of the same Act; and point (iii) by *Hoffmann v Krieg*. It makes for a rather untidy outcome; and it may be a good deal untidier still when an English court has to deal with the material inconsistencies in an award and a judgment. But it means that, when she had to decide for herself whether the parties were bound by an agreement to arbitrate, Gloster J was legislatively directed to ignore the Spanish judgment, and she considered that the European Court had not told her otherwise. Her conclusion was unimpeachable; and anything objectionable about it is the fault of the legislation, not of her understanding of it.[108] Although one

[105] Civil Jurisdiction and Judgments Act 1982, s 32(2).

[106] Civil Jurisdiction and Judgments Act 1982, s 32(4).

[107] Brussels I Regulation, Art 1(2)(d).

[108] The ongoing project to reform and repair the Regulation is likely to integrate arbitration more carefully into the system.

may understand the motives which led the Court of Appeal to disagree with her, one cannot approve them. *The Wadi Sudr* is one of those depressing cases which occasionally come along after a judgment from the European Court, in which the English court feels obliged to be as un-English as possible. It takes time for judicial independence to reassert itself.[109] One trusts that there will be a further appeal.

5. The principle of reflexive effect and jurisdiction under the Regulation: *Goshawk Dedicated Ltd v Life Receivables Ireland Ltd*;[110] *Winnetka Trading Corp v Julius Baer International Ltd*;[111] *UBS AG v HSH Nordbank AG*;[112] *Pacific International Sports Clubs Ltd v Soccer Marketing International Ltd*;[113] *Catalyst Investment Group Ltd v Lewinsohn*[114]

One of the great answered questions about the effect of the Brussels I Regulation requires one to puzzle out what account is to be taken of the fact that the parties have agreed upon the jurisdiction of the courts of a non-Member State, or of the fact that the proceedings have as their object legal title to land in (validity of intellectual property rights granted under the law of, validity of the acts of an organ of a company with its seat in) a non-Member State, or the fact that there is a *lis pendens* before the courts of a non-Member State, and so forth. Though the Brussels I Regulation does not state the solution in the form of a legislative rule, for the Regulation cannot require the courts of a non-Member State to exercise jurisdiction, and cannot therefore provide a legally certain answer to the question, the solution is pretty obvious and leaves only details to be worked out. Even Mr Droz, whose contempt for the common law principle of *forum non conveniens* was *plus gaulliste que De Gaulle*,[115] accepted that a court should give 'reflexive effect' to the provisions of what is now the Regulation, treating them as the template for jurisdictional relief actually derived from the court's national procedural law.[116] No sensible person takes issue with this, even though there

[109] While on this point, it is to be noted that the court displayed notable chilliness towards the decision of Burton J in *CMA CGM SA v Hyundai Mipo Dockyard Co Ltd* [2008] EWHC 2791 (Comm), [2009] 1 Lloyd's Rep 213 (noted this Year Book, 79 (2008), 557, 562–64), that as arbitration fell outside the material scope of the Regulation, arbitrators had no obligation to recognise judgments falling under Chapter III of the Regulation: see at [56], [115]–[119].

[110] [2009] IESC 7, [2009] ILPr 435: Supreme Court of Ireland (Denham, Kearns, Macken JJ).

[111] [2008] EWHC 3146 (Ch), [2009] Bus LR 1006: Norris J.

[112] [2009] EWCA Civ 585 [2009] 2 Lloyd's Rep 272: Ward LJ, Lord Collins of Mapesbury, Toulson LJ.

[113] [2009] EWHC 1839 (Ch): Blackburne J.

[114] [2009] EWHC 1964 (Ch) [2010] Ch 218: Barling J.

[115] Even in 1995, Droz said that the doctrine allowed a judge to say: *'votre tête ne me revient pas, votre cause non plus, allez donc vous faire juger ailleurs'. Vous aurez compris que je condamne formellement l'utilisation du forum non conveniens au niveau des compétences raisonnables, au niveau des propre fora*: cited in H van Lith, *International Jurisdiction and Commercial Litigation* (TMC Asser, The Hague, 2009), p 341.

[116] G Droz, *Compétence judiciaire et effets des jugements dans le marché commun* (Dalloz, Paris, 1972): at [164]–[169] (in relation to exclusive jurisdiction regardless of domicile), and [204] (in relation to jurisdiction clauses).

is still room for debate about the detail by which this sensible approach is to be implemented.

Several other things may be observed. First, there is a difference between giving a reflexive effect to an Article of the Regulation, and a remission or renvoi to the national procedural law of the court seised:[117] the difference will determine how closely the court proposing to grant the relief available under its national law must keep to the precise formulation of the Article: must the proceedings have as their object rights *in rem* in or a tenancy of immovable property? Must the agreement on jurisdiction be in writing or evidenced in writing? And so forth. Second, the Court has already said, in the context of a case concerning a jurisdiction agreement for a non-Member State that a court may assess the validity of the agreement in accordance with its own national law.[118] Third, it is plausible that the answers vary across the range of connections as exemplified in Articles 22 (exclusive jurisdiction regardless of domicile), 23 (agreements on jurisdiction), 27 (*lis abili pendens* involving the same parties and the same cause of action), and 28 (*lis abili pendens* in the form of related proceedings).

Yet the English courts sometimes seem reluctant to accept the advice which is proffered.[119] If there is an explanation, it is presumably that they have been traumatised by the recent scornful jurisprudence of the Court,[120] and are profoundly unwilling to be accused of seeking to smuggle the principle of *forum non conveniens* back in under the cloak of reflexive effect. It is obviously correct that national judges apply, faithfully and loyally, the judgments of the European Court on the interpretation of the Brussels I Regulation, because that is what Parliament has told them to do.[121] But it is part of the common law method that where these judgments of the European Court do not apply to the case, a court has to predict where the correct answer will be found, and act as though it had already been laid bare. Unfortunately, a number of strange, almost fearful, judgments suggested that the fear of being accused of *forum conveniens* revanchism had overwhelmed the power of thought. It is right to record at this point, however, that in the next following Note a division of the Court of Appeal with particular expertise in the law of intellectual property has taken a much more stirring view.

A trio of cases examined the proposition that an English court might properly grant relief in circumstances in which the material connection

[117] C-387/98 *Coreck Maritime GmbH v Handelsveem BV* [2000] ECR I-9337 supports the approach of a renvoi to national law, rather than any stricter principle of reflexive effect.

[118] Ibid.

[119] For example, by Dicey, Morris and Collins, above n. 32, para 12-022.

[120] After all, in C-281/02 *Owusu v Jackson* [2005] ECR I-1383 the Court did not even trouble itself to get the principles of *forum non conveniens* right before rejecting any and every case for their use in that case.

[121] European Communities Act 1972, s 2.

was with a non-Member State where it would have been bound to grant relief if the connection had been to a Member State. In *Winnetka Trading Corp v Julius Baer International Ltd*, the judge accepted that the parties to a contract retained their autonomy to decide upon the jurisdiction of a non-Member State, and retained their right to hold the other to it, and did not lose that autonomy if one of them was domiciled in a Member State and was sued there. The judge was therefore willing to give effect to an agreement for the courts of Guernsey, which is in line with the balance of sensible opinion. Less welcome was the decision in *UBS AG v HSH Nordbank AG*. The Court of Appeal concluded that it was not necessary for it to express a view on whether a stay of proceedings for a non-Member State was permissible where the jurisdiction of the English court was founded on Article 23 rather than Article 2 of the Regulation, for it reached the conclusion that the jurisdiction agreement on which the claimant proposed to rely did not apply to the dispute in question, and did not therefore give the English court jurisdiction in the first place. But it is fair to say that the court gave no encouragement to the view that a court which had jurisdiction under the Regulation might ever find reason to not exercise it. Little more can be said of the judgment in *Pacific International Sports Clubs Ltd v Soccer Marketing International Ltd*, where the judge came to the conclusion that whatever was going on before the courts of the Ukraine would not have counted as a *lis alibi pendens* for the purposes of Articles 27 or 28, and that it was therefore not necessary to decide whether it would have been possible to grant jurisdictional relief by analogy with those two Articles.[122] It is equally clear, however, that the tenor of the judgment was not one of great enthusiasm for the idea that such relief was possible; and if this was all there was to say, one would have to concede that what seems clear to writers and commentators, with time on their hands, does not always seem to be as clear to judges who have to deal with jurisdictional applications at some speed and (where possible) in a manner which minimises the opportunity for the disgruntled to appeal.

Help appeared to be at hand, however, from the Irish courts. In *Goshawk Dedicated Ltd v Life Receivables Ireland Ltd* proceedings between the parties had been commenced before the US District Court in Georgia. Some months later the defendant to those US proceedings brought proceedings in Ireland, effectively confecting these as the mirror image of those in the United States. The defendant to the Irish proceedings was Irish, sued in the courts of its domicile. It applied for a stay of proceedings in accordance with ordinary Irish law, contending that as the same cause of action, between the same parties, had already been brought before the courts of

[122] For yet another judgment finding that it was not necessary to answer the question, on the ground that the other forum may have been chosen, but so was the English one, and that the claims of the non-Member State court were not strong enough for a stay to be considered, *Deutsche Bank AG v Sebastian Holdings Inc (No 2)* [2009] EWHC 3069 (Comm), [2010] 1 All ER (Comm) 808): Burton J.

a non-Member State, the Irish courts were entitled to take their lead from Article 27 of the Regulation, and stay the Irish proceedings to wait for the outcome in Georgia. Clarke J[123] had concluded at first instance that he had no power to grant the relief applied for, as to do so would involve the application of the principle of *forum non conveniens*. The Irish Supreme Court, hearing the appeal, ordered a reference to the European Court, taking the view that the answer to the question was not so apparent that it could give it for itself. But by the end of the year, the reference had still not left Dublin for Luxembourg; it is anybody's guess whether it will ever be made.[124]

The Irish Supreme Court was motivated in part by the fact that in *Owusu*, the European Court had refused to answer the second question referred by the English Court of Appeal, which had raised the very issue now before the Supreme Court. It seems that it may have read too much into the Court's evasive irresponsibility, and may not have read enough into the views of those who, from Mr Droz onwards, have reflected on the issue. Even so, there is room for debate, and the Supreme Court was not without justification in making the reference.

No such privilege applied to first instance judges, though.[125] So when the same issue arose before Barling J in *Catalyst Investment Group Ltd v Lewinsohn*, and did need to be ruled on, the judge had to grasp the nettle which others had managed to avoid. Proceedings were commenced before the courts of Utah; six weeks later proceedings, which were rather broader in nature, were commenced before the English courts. The similarity of the proceedings, and their relative timing, prompted the defendant to apply for relief from the English court, on the approximate ground that, if the first set or proceedings had been in a Member State rather than a non-Member State, Articles 27 and 28 would have applied to the English proceedings. The precise submission was sound and orthodox: that Article 27 would have applied by analogy, with the consequence that the court might apply its principles of *forum non conveniens* to justify relief in circumstances defined by Article 27. This contention was not advanced on the basis that as there were proceedings in a non-Member State, the Regulation, in some sense, did not apply. Instead, it was argued that because there were proceedings before the courts of a non-Member State, between the same parties, having the same *objet* and *cause*, and which were definitively pending before the foreign court before proceedings

[123] *Goshawk Dedicated Ltd v Life Receivables Ireland Ltd* [2008] IEHC 90.

[124] One may recall the apocryphal international conference at which a professor of Spanish and a professor of Gaelic were present. The Spaniard asked his colleague whether the Gaelic language had any expression which corresponded to the Spanish 'mañana, mañana'. The professor of Gaelic thought carefully for several minutes and replied that, yes, although his language did have several similar expressions, none of them quite conveyed the sense of urgency of the Spanish.

[125] However, the Treaty of Lisbon, Art 267, which came into effect at the end of 2009, removed the restriction which, by Art 68 of the EC Treaty, had limited the power to make references to a court from the decisions of which there lay no appeal.

were commenced before the English court, jurisdictional relief ought to be granted.[126] Most academic commentary accepts that in such a case, the English court may (rather than must) stay its proceedings to wait for the outcome in the foreign proceedings.

Barling J noted all this but did not agree. His conclusion was that Article 27 could not bear the weight which he considered to be being placed upon it.[127] He took the view (i) that Article 27 did not apply directly, (ii) that the fact that the European Court had refused to answer the second question in *Owusu* was not significant, (iii) that the Advocate General in *Owusu* had not suggested that the principle of reflexive effect might apply to Article 27,[128] (iv) that he had not been shown the original views of Mr Droz, but had only been referred to English material where these were reported,[129] (v) the principle of reflexive effect was not really sound, because the non-Member State court would not determine *its* jurisdiction by reference to Chapter II of the Regulation, but by its own national law which may even contain a principle of *forum non conveniens*,[130] and (vi) if there was to be any mention of *forum non conveniens*, in any case in which the court had jurisdiction according to Article 2, that was absolutely prohibited by *Owusu*.

It is, one has to say, a strange and rather fearful judgment.[131] Given the inevitable absence of decisive words in the Regulation itself, the short and most useful question is whether the policies which inspired the Regulation in the first place, such as the legal protection of persons (in particular, the defendant) established in the EU, are better served by pretending that legal proceedings in an American court are not happening or accepting that they are taking place, one would have thought that the latter had more to be said for it. Assuming[132] that the party domiciled in England had a good cause of action, and a good reason[133] for suing, in the United States, it seems bonkers to contend that the policies underpinning the Regulation require a court in a Member State to pretend that there is absolutely nothing happening before the courts of a non-Member State: *cui bono*? It was not useful for the judge to observe that the Irish Supreme Court had proposed making a reference which had, in the event, not been proceeded with.[134] He had to decide, for good or for ill; he chose ill.

As to the judge's reasons, there is nothing to object to in points (i) and (ii). But point (iii) is without useful substance, as the Advocate General

[126] At [68]. [127] At [69]. [128] At [74]. [129] At [96]. [130] At [102].

[131] The Court of Appeal in the case next noted, *Lucasfilm Ltd v Ainsworth*, did not lend warm support to the answer which Barling J had reached in the case before him: at [134].

[132] If it could be shown that the proceedings were vexatious or oppressive, or utterly opportunistic and brought in bad faith, one assumes that a commercial judge would not find it hard to work out what to do next.

[133] Such as the fact that this was where it needed to be able to enforce the judgment for which it sued.

[134] At [85].

considered the second question referred by the English court in *Owusu* to be inadmissible and therefore, and very deliberately, said nothing about it. Point (iv) is rather unsatisfactory, for if the judge wished to see the originals of Mr Droz's works, he should have told counsel who would, one supposes, have fetched them for him. Point (v) is really rather odd, and leads to the conclusion that not only is there no such principle as reflexive effect, but also that this aspect of the decision in *Coreck* is unreliable: that would follow from the fact, surely true, that the foreign court, nominated by an agreement on jurisdiction, would not determine its jurisdiction by reference to Article 23, Article 23 cannot be applied by analogy either. And in any event, it is clear law that Article 27 applies even where the court first seised first has taken jurisdiction on the basis of its own national law, via the provision on Article 4, and not by reference to the primary rules of the Regulation.[135] The proposition that Article 27 could not apply by analogy because the court in Georgia would not assess its own jurisdiction by reference to the Regulation[136] is plainly bad; though as the correct analysis is not referred to in the judgment, perhaps it was not referred to in submissions. The judge's purported rescue of *Coreck* by asserting that cases of prorogation are just different is not persuasive. And as for point (vi), that as soon as a judge utters the words *forum non conveniens*, he condemns himself out of his own mouth, it is just daft: timid and daft. The result was that a party, established in the European Union, who had instituted proceedings in the United States, in accordance with its law and in circumstances in which no obvious objection could be taken, was liable to be counter-sued in England, and was not entitled even to suggest to the court that it should find this to be objectionable. It is a result which is, with respect to the judge who saw matters differently, intuitively wrong as well as being wrong on closer examination. As it was not a conclusion to which he was bound to come, he should not have allowed himself to be driven towards it. Sooner or later this is going to have to be put right. This may be brought about by legislative amendment of the Regulation itself, which will be both good and bad. It will be good if it removes a needless uncertainty from the law; it will be bad if it means that the unamended Brussels I Regulation is understood to have required formal amendment to permit a court to take proper account of the fact that there are proceedings before the courts of a non-Member State.

6. The impact of the Brussels I Regulation on intellectual property litigation: *Lucasfilm Ltd v Ainsworth*[137]

Last year, the Court of Appeal gave its evaluation of the manner in which the Brussels I Regulation applies to problems of *lis pendens* when

[135] C-351/89, *Overseas Union Insurance Ltd v New Hampshire Insurance Co* [1991] ECR I-3317.
[136] At [72], [102].
[137] [2009] EWCA Civ 1328 [2010] 3 WLR 333: Rix, Jacob and Patten LJJ, on appeal from [2008] EWHC 1878 (Ch), [2009] FSR 103 (noted this Year Book 79 (2008), 537, 540–43).

these arise in the field in intellectual property litigation: gamma plus more or less sums it up, and the mark was that generous only because the court found, in Article 28, a flexibility which was not apparent to others who had read the text of the Article for themselves.[138] The epic facts of *Lucasfilm Ltd v Ainsworth* came back as a sequel, but on this occasion before a division of the court whose collective expertise in intellectual property law meant that the Force was strong with them. Mr Ainsworth, be it remembered, had devised the headgear of the Imperial Stormtroopers in the Star Wars film series. When he, decades later, exploited his design to make an income of a princely $14,000, he was sued by the Lucasfilm Empire for his alleged breach of copyright, in England and in the United States. The US courts awarded 'compensatory' damages of $10 million[139] plus a further $10 million; the question accordingly arose whether this judgment could be enforced in England. The answer was a clear negative: the defendant had not been present within the jurisdiction of the US courts when the American proceedings were begun, and he had not submitted to the jurisdiction of the American courts. As a matter of common law, there was no more to be said. It got Lucasfilm nowhere to contend that Ainsworth had done business in, or had 'traded into' the United States, whether at the time of the proceedings or at all, for none of that could be seen as presence or submission. It got Lucasfilm nowhere, either, to point to the internet as offering some sort of incoherent justification for abandoning the traditional approach to the recognition of foreign judgments in general, and to what amounted to international jurisdiction in particular. A wise court plainly took the view that judicial calm was to be preferred to judicial creativity in the face of new technology, and left the law alone.[140] It is to be applauded, even though this meant that it had no need to consider whether a 'compensatory' award of damages exceeding one hundred fold the profit[141] wrongfully made was fit to be recognised.

Ainsworth was also sued in England for breach of copyright, other claims before Mann J having been abandoned on appeal. Insofar as the copyright asserted was based on English law, Lucasfilm was required to show that the headgear, or the formers on which it was moulded, amounted to 'sculpture'.[142] The judicial survey of the material which led the court to its conclusion that these plastic helmets were not sculpture provides a wonderful diversion, but it is not our concern. Much

[138] *Research in Motion UK Ltd v Visto Corp* [2008] EWCA Civ 153, [2008] ILPr 501.

[139] The Court of Appeal, at [9], was bemused by the arithmetic. They are not alone.

[140] At [193]–[194].

[141] On the footing that the $14,000 sales represented a profit of $7000. If the balance sheet was even less impressive, the point is stronger still.

[142] It had abandoned its previous, hilarious, contention that the headgear constituted art.

more important was the approach taken to the claim based on the infringement of US copyright. As to that, the traditional view of the common law was that the court had no jurisdiction to rule on the validity of (or on claims which would[143] require it to rule on the validity of) a foreign copyright. It was contended that the Brussels I Regulation had swept away that rule, and had replaced it with another, to the effect that where an English defendant was sued before the courts of his domicile, there was no judicial power to refuse to hear the claim on grounds derived from the common law of jurisdiction. This contention was bolstered by reference to *Owusu v Jackson*,[144] and the observation that unless the Brussels I Regulation makes express provision for a court to not exercise a jurisdiction which it has under the Regulation, the court has no power to refuse to hear the case. The court was having none of it. Its complex conclusions may be reduced to three essential points: first, that the common law of jurisdictional exclusivity, which confines the jurisdiction of an English court to claims based on English intellectual property rights, was and remained good law; second, that the private international law of intellectual property[145] was not to be disturbed by a Regulation which did not appear to have been drafted with any of the concerns which animate intellectual property in mind; and third, that the expansion of jurisdiction which may be attributed to *Owusu* is irrational and unprincipled. No punches were pulled. We may take the points in that order.

The view that intellectual property law is more than usually territorial in its concerns was long established. The High Court of Australia was the first to settle the point,[146] aligning the common law of intellectual property with that which had been established by the House of Lords for claims concerning title to foreign land.[147] No-one seriously questioned this understanding until the Court of Appeal, in *Pearce v Ove Arup Partnership Ltd*,[148] took the view that the *Moçambique* rule should not apply to foreign intellectual property rights, and that even if it did, its continued existence was overwritten and countermanded by the Brussels Convention in any case in which personal jurisdiction was claimed against a defendant in accordance with Title II of that Convention. The court in *Lucasfilm* rejected the *Pearce* argument in all its branches. It considered the traditional approach of the common law to be rational and right, for intellectual property disputes will frequently require a court to consider

[143] Or might: the court rejected a proposed distinction between cases in which the infringement claim would or did, and those where it had not appeared, to trigger a defence of invalidity: at [181].

[144] Case C-281/02, [2005] ECR I-1383.

[145] After all, the court found a similar jurisdictional view to be found in the laws of Australia, New Zealand, and the United States: at [157]–[172].

[146] *Potter v Broken Hill Pty Co Ltd* (1906) 3 CLR 479.

[147] *British South Africa Co v Companhia de Moçambique* [1893] AC 603. But for a reinterpretation, see also *Habib v Commonwealth* [2010] FCAFC 12.

[148] [2000] Ch 403 (CA).

economic and policy matters which are so intensely connected to the court for the place of grant or registration that they cannot properly be examined and ruled on elsewhere. And even if there may be some cases in which there would be no real difficulty, there will be others of which that cannot be said; the conclusion had to be that the existence and validity of foreign intellectual property rights is a matter for, and a matter only for, the court of the place of grant or registration. If *Pearce v Ove Arup* stood for a contradictory view, it was wrong, as were cases which had been bound to follow it. On the interpretation of the common law, this seems eminently sensible, and *Pearce* is to be seen as an aberration brought about by excessive zeal for the novelty which was the Brussels Convention.

The common law thus clarified, the court had to address the *Owusu* point: that as the Regulation makes no specific exception for claims based on non-Member State copyright, there is no basis for a court to refuse to exercise jurisdiction over a defendant sued in such matters before the courts for the place where he is domiciled. The court was plainly unimpressed by the suggestion that the intricate landscape of intellectual property law had been reordered by a Regulation which seemed untroubled by the particular issues which underpinned the pre-existing law of jurisdiction in intellectual property disputes. Accordingly, it found that where the English court lacked subject-matter jurisdiction, nothing in the Brussels I Regulation could alter the position. It is submitted, with great respect, that it got rather carried away. For it seemed to reject the idea that the Regulation could[149] give an English court jurisdiction which it could not decline to exercise, over matters which arose in a non-Member State,[150] or over matters which could be litigated before the courts of the non-Member State,[151] or matters which involved no intra-EU interest, however this troublesome idea might be conceived.[152] Unfortunately, such points were canvassed before, and are directly contradicted by, *Owusu* itself. The court also considered it unprincipled to exercise jurisdiction over matters which arose in the United States when the provisions which regulate *lis abili pendens* do not apply in relation to the United States, and when a judgment from the US courts would not be registrable under Chapter III of the Regulation. The court seemed to see jurisdiction and the recognition of judgments as integrated to such an extent that what went on in the United States fell completely outside the economy of the Regulation.[153] Unfortunately, this does not convince, either, not least because it would appear to turn *Owusu* on its head. The court was on far

[149] It referred to Art 65 of the European Treaty, as it then was, to extract a limitation which would have confined the Regulation to cases which bore on the completion of the internal market or the free movement of persons. Nothing wrong with that, except that in *Owusu* the same points were made (albeit in relation to the Brussels Convention) and were specifically rejected.

[150] Or, as the court put it, 'far far away from the EU': at [105].

[151] At [105]. [152] At [105]. [153] At [109].

stronger ground where it observed that if the copyright had been German rather than American, then Article 22(4) would have meant that there was no power to hear the claim in England:[154] it did not use the terminology of reflexive effect, but it could easily, and perhaps should, have done so when it returned to the way the court deals with jurisdiction agreements for non-Member States.[155] And it was also on stronger ground when it distinguished *Owusu*—which might appear to make many of the court's points difficult and dangerous to accept—as a case in which there was no question about the existence of personal as well as subject-matter jurisdiction, though it later reverted to the broad opinion that the Regulation did not set up the courts of the Member States 'as some kind of non-exclusive world tribunals for wrongs done outside the EU by persons who happen to be domiciled in the EU'.[156] That, however, is exactly what the Regulation did, at least where the wrongs are seen as civil or commercial ones. Indeed, some will think that a rule that defendants shall be sued where they are domiciled, no matter where they did that of which complaint is made, is rightly and properly the very foundation of the jurisdictional system put in place by the Regulation. It is submitted that the wider terms in which the justification for the decision that there was no jurisdiction was cast are insupportable: it is not that they were irrational or inconsistent with the text of the Treaty or the Regulation, but that they had been cast aside several years ago by a European Court which had no time for such attention to literal detail: they may have seemed novel to the court in *Lucasfilm*, but they were in fact yesterday's news. The narrow decision, based on the principle of analogy with Article 22(4) or (which in this context is much the same thing), on the absence of subject matter jurisdiction, is much more defensible. The practical reasons for finding that there is no jurisdiction to try cases which have at their core a foreign intellectual property right are wholly persuasive; the only trouble lies in finding the right basis for it.

7. The problem with Article 22(2) of the Brussels I Regulation: *JP Morgan Chase Bank NA v Berliner Verkehrsbetriebe*;[157] *Calyon v Wytwornia Sprzetu Komunikacynego PZL Swidnik SA*;[158] *Choudhary v Bhatter*[159]

Article 22(2) of the Brussels I Regulation provides that for proceedings which have as their object the validity of the constitution of a corporation which has its seat in a Member State, or the validity of the decisions of the organs of such a company, the courts at the seat have exclusive jurisdiction

[154] At [107]. [155] At [133]. [156] At [129].

[157] [2009] EWHC 1627 (Comm), [2010] QB 276: Teare J.

[158] [2009] EWHC 1914 (Comm), [2010] BWLR 138: Field J.

[159] [2009] EWCA Civ 1176, [2010] 1 All ER (Comm) 1031: Ward, Stanley Burnton LJJ; Sir John Chadwick. An earlier application against the defendant B for security for costs was rejected, in part on the ground that if the claimants really wanted to litigate this Indian dispute in London, it was a bit of a cheek to demand that the defendant put up security for the costs of his (as it turned out, successful) appeal: see *Choudhury v Bhatter* [2009] EWCA Civ 510: Longmore LJ.

regardless of domicile. The sense of this is easy enough to grasp, as it combines principle with pragmatism. There are fundamental matters of corporate constitutional law which need to be dealt with by the country whose corporation, and corporations law, they are. The problem comes when a point of corporations law arises, genuinely but not immediately, in the context of a commercial dispute. For example, a company may enter into a commercial contract, but when called upon to perform, point to some defect within the company's own decision-taking structure or authorisation mechanisms, and assert that the decision to enter into the contract was not binding on the company because the act did not have the prior approval of the board, or was outside the authority of the officer who purported to bind the company to it, and so forth. It is a common enough problem when times are troubled and companies search for ways to avoid financial obligations which have turned sour. Such cases involve commercial claims to which an issue of company law arises by way of defence; and there is no easy way to pretend the difficulty away. In both the cases under consideration, the company sued on an obligation arising from a commercial contract raised, among other things, a company law defence.[160] In *JP Morgan Chase Bank NA v Berliner Verkehrsbetriebe*, it was alleged that the contract was *ultra vires* the company, though the expert evidence revealed a fundamental disagreement as to whether German company law contained a doctrine of *ultra vires* at all.[161] In *Calyon v Wytwornia Sprzetu Komunikacynego PZL Swidnik SA*, it was that the officer who purported to bind the company to the contract did not have authority to do so. Both cases involved contracts with English governing law clauses, and agreements for the jurisdiction of the English courts. As a result, the reference to Article 22(2) represented the only way for the defendant entities to remove themselves from the jurisdiction to which they could be said to have agreed.

As to the proper interpretation of Article 22(2), two models are available to form answers. In relation to Article 22(1), it has been held that unless the issue of rights *in rem* in immovable property is the principal concern of the action, the proceedings do not have rights *in rem* as their object. This has allowed the Court to find that complaints arising from disappointing package holidays and disastrous time-share contracts do not have as their object rights *in rem* or tenancies, as the case may be, for

[160] For another example, but which did not trigger Article 22 because the corporation was Taiwanese, see *Deutsche Bank AG v Asia Pacific Broadband Wireless Communications Inc* [2008] EWCA Civ 1091, [2008] 2 Lloyd's Rep 619 (noted this Year Book 79 (2008), 557).

[161] See also *Haugesund Kommune v Depfa ACS Bank* [2010] EWCA Civ 579, which deals with an analogous issue in relation to transactions alleged to be *ultra vires* a Norwegian municipality, and in relation to which it was unclear whether Norwegian law had a doctrine of *ultra vires*. It was eventually held that the loans were void as *ultra vires* the municipality, but that a restitutionary claim lay for the sums advanced insofar as the law of restitution provided no defence of change of position or the like. The loan contracts were expressed to be governed by English law; it appears to have been accepted without argument that the restitutionary claim was governed by English law, too.

the land-rights component may be only an element within the package holiday package,[162] or the right to occupy a particular apartment a financially rather minor part of the rights of membership of a time-share club.[163] In relation to Article 22(4), by contrast, it has been held that whenever the issue of validity or invalidity of a patent is raised as a defence to an infringement action, the court hearing the claim for infringement has no authority to determine the question of validity, which is, by contrast, within the exclusive jurisdiction of the Member State in which the intellectual property right in question was created. There is no room for the argument that the proceedings are not principally concerned with validity; no room for the argument that the court seised of the infringement claim may determine the issue of validity as between the parties and for the purpose of the infringement claim alone, this having no broader or *in rem* effect;[164] and no room for the argument that the operation of Article 22 is undertaken by reference to the claim alone, rather than by reference to the combination of claim-plus-defence. It was not put in these precise terms, but the question for the judge in each case was whether to regard Article 22(2) as following the pattern of Article 22(1) or Article 22(4).

One possible way out turned out to lead up a blind alley. The English-language versions of Article 22 draw an apparent distinction between 'proceedings which have as their object' rights *in rem* in immovable property, and 'proceedings concerned with the registration or validity of patents'. Taken at face value, these suggest the possibility that Article 22(1) applies only where *the* object of the proceedings is legal title to land, but that Article 22(4) is engaged whenever there is an issue concerning the validity of patents, no matter the context in which it arises. That would give Article 22(4) a wider scope than Article 22(1). However, other language versions neither reflect nor support such a distinction, and in *JP Morgan Chase Bank NA v Berliner Verkehrsbetriebe*, the judge declined to be drawn by it.[165] Instead, he exercised a choice, or judgment, to align Article 22(2) with Article 22(1) and to mark its separateness from Article 22(4). He was right to do so.

Laddie J, who knew these things like the back of his hand, was once reported to have said that 'we have always taken the view that you cannot infringe an invalid patent'.[166] That seems right, and it explains why, when the issue of validity of a patent is properly raised by way of defence to a

[162] C-289/90 *Hacker v Euro-Relais GmbH* [1992] ECR I-1111.

[163] C-73/04 *Klein v Rhodos Management Ltd* [2005] ECR I-8667, where the Court, rather improbably, assessed the apartment-occupation part of the time-share club membership as representing only 15% of the overall fee charged: at [18]–[19].

[164] C-4/03 *Gesellschaft für Antriebstechnik mbh & Co KG v Lamellen und Kupplungsbau Beteiligungs* KG [2006] ECR I-6509.

[165] At [13].

[166] *Coin Controls Ltd v Suzo International (UK) Ltd* [1999] Ch 33, 51; cited by the judge in *JP Morgan* at [36].

claim, the provision for exclusive jurisdiction will assert itself, no matter that the claim had not done so. But if one were to try saying: 'we have always taken the view that you cannot enforce an unauthorised contract', one would be simply and plainly wrong. An agent who lacks actual authority may still make a contract by which his principal is bound; a company which makes a contract but without the prior and proper approval (say) of the board makes a contract which may be enforced against it. For a century and more those who deal with companies have had the comfort of legal doctrines which provide, in various ways, that a contract which was, on the company's part, not properly authorised may still be enforced against the company, and that the person dealing with the company is entitled to assume that the indoor management of the company has been properly undertaken.[167] The result is that a contract which, from one perspective, a company did not properly make becomes binding on and enforceable against it notwithstanding the defect in contracting. Seen in that sense, the contention that the particular corporate officer had not done all he needed to do to equip himself with authority to bind the company does not lead to the contract's becoming unenforceable; and in this sense, then, it does not fit within Laddie J's wisdom about invalid patents. It should therefore have been easy to accept that an action to enforce a contract, over which the court had jurisdiction by virtue of an agreement on jurisdiction, should not have been liable to defeat by the defendant company pointing to some internal imperfection, or procedural defect, prior to the making of the contract.

Several other factors, no doubt, pointed to the conclusion which the cases arrived at: four may be mentioned. First, to have allowed the company to rely on internal irregularity to impugn the agreement on jurisdiction was not comfortably consistent with the dogma that an agreement on jurisdiction may be valid and binding even where the substantive contract with which it is associated is invalid.[168] It was one thing to foresee that the company may attempt to rely on internal irregularity to evade liability under the substantive contract, but it would rub salt in the wound if it were able to avoid the agreement on jurisdiction as well. Second, the Court has recently made it clear that Article 22(2) was to be given a restrictive interpretation, on the ground that it derogated from the usual rules of the Regulation, denying the jurisdiction of both the courts of the defendant's domicile and of the court upon the jurisdiction of which the parties had agreed.[169] Although so general a statement is not really very

[167] *Mahony v East Holyford Mining Co* (1875) LR 7 HL 869, approving the effect of *Royal British Bank v Turquand* (1856) 6 E&B 327; see further, Companies Act 1985, s 35A, and now Companies Act 2006, s 40.

[168] The closest authority to this point is English: *Deutsche Bank AG v Asia Pacific Broadband Wireless Communications Inc* [2008] EWCA Civ 1091, [2008] 2 Lloyd's Rep 619 (noted this Year Book 79 (2008), 557). The European Court's decision in C-269/95 *Benincasa v Dentalkit srl* [1997] ECR I-3767 does not go this far.

[169] C-327/07 *Hassett v South Eastern Health Board* [2008] ECR I-7403.

helpful when it comes to the task of specifying exactly what the provision in question means, it does encourage a court to prefer the narrower of two tenable meanings, just because it is the narrower one. Third, English private international law draws a reasonably clear distinction between the question whether an agent had authority to bind his principal to a contract, and the question whether the contract is binding on the principal if the agent did not. Absence of authority is not a complete answer to a claim to enforce a contract unless the law which governs the contract accepts that it is.[170] And fourth, it was at least arguable that the real meat of the substantive dispute was to be the effect, as a matter of English law as *lex contractus*, of the fact that one of the parties to the contract did not go through the proper decision-taking mechanism, or maybe had no capacity to make the particular contract. That does not raise a question of company law properly so called, or of corporate constitutional law, but a question of the contract law consequences of a corporate law fact. If, then, part of the justification for Article 22 is that matters of land law, housing law, company constitutional law, *et cetera*, ought to be dealt with by the court for which they are local law, there was no reason to consider that the issues which arose when the two claimant banks sued their two corporate customers under contracts governed by English law ought to be resolved in Germany or in Poland.

The result of the cases was correct, even though it still looks a little odd, for it may well mean that an English court has to determine whether the entity which runs the public transportation system in Berlin had the right in law to enter into interest rate swap agreements, and whether a Polish aircraft manufacturer could be legally bound to foreign exchange derivative transactions by the word of a member of its management board. Those issues are issues which look to German and Polish company law. But they do so in order to determine a preliminary question, and to provide data for the principal question, namely the enforceability of a contract governed by English law; and that is why Article 22(2) properly had no application to them.

A curious but small point on the application of Article 22(2) arose in *Choudhary v Bhatter*, in which various persons, all Indian and involved in the affairs of a company carrying on the whole of its business in the jute industry in India but in dire financial straits, found themselves in litigation in London. The cause for complaint lay in various allegations against B, a director and manager of the company. In consequence of this, various orders were sought appointing and removing members of the company's governing structures, cancelling the issue of shares and so forth, together with an order that B pay compensation under Companies Act 1985, s 92, and otherwise be restrained from acting.

The matter was before the English courts because the company was incorporated in England. To be sure, nothing ever happened in England

[170] Dicey, Morris and Collins, above n. 32, Rule 228.

save that an annual report was received at Companies House and a registered office was maintained in England. But this was sufficient to establish that the seat of the company was in England for the purposes of Article 22(2), and that the English courts therefore had exclusive jurisdiction over the company in respect of those matters stated in the Article. B, however, was domiciled in India, and did not wish to be made to answer in England. He therefore challenged the jurisdiction. The jurisdictional point taken against him was two-fold: that as Article 22(2) was expressed to operate regardless of domicile, it therefore gave the court personal jurisdiction over B, wherever he was domiciled; and insofar as B contended that jurisdiction over him, as an Indian domiciliary, was based on Article 4, Article 4 made an express reservation for the superior role of Article 22. The Court of Appeal disagreed, finding that to read the expression 'regardless of domicile' in that way was to take them out of their context, and would lead to an assertion of jurisdiction over B which was not warranted by the overall scheme of the Regulation. It came to the right conclusion, but not for a good reason.

The allegations against B were that he had done various things for which compensation should be ordered. It was not alleged that any of the things done by him had been void of effect. Given that the validity of the acts of B, who might be regarded as an organ of the company, was not in dispute, and the claim against B should have fallen outside Article 22(2) *ratione materiae*. The court did reach this conclusion as well,[171] but only after it had found that Article 22(2) did not apply to persons not domiciled in a Member State. It is a pity that this prior conclusion was quite wrong. For Article 22(2) means what it says; and it says the same throughout Article 22. In proceedings which have as their object rights *in rem* in immovable property in a Member State, the courts of that state have exclusive jurisdiction, regardless of domicile, whether the defendant is domiciled in a Member State or not. Suppose a claim against a defendant which has as its object rights *in rem* in French land, but that the defendant is domiciled in New York and not in any Member State. If one asks whether the English courts would be entitled to exercise jurisdiction under Article 4, notwithstanding that the land was in a Member State, the answer would certainly be not. Article 22 may operate, and may establish exclusive jurisdiction over a defendant, wherever that defendant is domiciled. Elsewhere in Article 22 the same is true. If a claim concerns the execution of a Member State judgment against a defendant domiciled in a non-Member State, the courts for the place of execution have exclusive jurisdiction under Article 22(5), no matter where the defendant is domiciled—local Member State, other Member State, non-Member State. The consequence should have been that Article 22(2) applied to impose exclusive jurisdiction no matter the domicile of the defendant—just as it said it did; but only insofar as the claim fell within the material

[171] At [47].

scope of the rule. But as to that, it had no application to a claim against a director that he pay compensation for an act done by him which was not void. The claim against B should have fallen outside Article 22(2) *ratione materiae*, but not *ratione personae*. This is not to say that proceedings against a corporate officer may not fall within Article 22(2), just that the complaint against B did not. Had the material claim against B fallen within Article 22(2), neither Article 4 nor his Indian domicile could have been relied on to allow him to escape from the exclusive jurisdiction of the English courts.

As to the claims made against the company, it was clear to the court that they fell plumb within Article 22(2); but the company did not seek to challenge the jurisdiction. It is no answer to say that the claim against B should be joined with them, however, for Article 22(2) does not provide the anchor for accessory jurisdiction over another, albeit related, defendant, or related claim. As to the question whether, if the court did have jurisdiction over B on the basis of Article 22(2), it could have stayed it for the courts of India—a multiply hypothetical question if ever one was—the court chose to say nothing.[172] In the circumstances, that was just as well.

8. Pinpointing where economic loss or damage occurs: *Maple Leaf Macro Volatility Master Fund v Rouvroy*;[173] *Dolphin Maritime & Aviation Services Ltd v Sveriges Angfartygs Assurans Forening*[174]

The Brussels I Regulation gives special jurisdiction, in matters relating to tort and delict, to the courts for the place where the damage occurred. This is to be distinguished from the place of the event which gave rise to the damage, but also from the place where damage, which had occurred originally and somewhere else, was suffered.[175] Conceptually this is easy enough to understand where there has been physical damage followed by economic consequences, and not too difficult to apply where there has been an interference with tangible things which has resulted in economic loss. But its application is not confined to cases in which economic loss is the consequence of earlier loss; it applies just as much to cases of damage to reputation,[176] and to loss which is purely economic.[177] It will be no surprise that the principle is harder to apply where there is no physical damage or loss of property; and a first instance judge must do what he can.

In *Maple Leaf Macro Volatility Master Fund v Rouvroy* the claimant advanced, among several other things, a claim based on deceit. It was, as

[172] At [54].

[173] [2009] EWHC 257 (Comm), [2009] 1 Lloyd's Rep 333: Andrew Smith J.

[174] [2009] EWHC 716 (Comm): Christopher Clarke J.

[175] For this, see C-220/88 *Dumez France SA v Hessische Landesbank* [1990] ECR I-49; C-364/93; *Marinari v Lloyd's Bank plc* [1995] ECR I-2719.

[176] C-68/93 *Shevill v Presse Alliance SA* [1995] ECR I-415.

[177] C-18/02 *DFDS Torline A/S v SEKO* [2004] ECR I-1417; C-168/02 *Kronhofer v Maier* [2004] ECR I-6009.

it said, tricked into entering into a 'Funding Agreement' by fraudulent misrepresentation, as a result of which it sustained financial loss. In the case itself, as will frequently be the way these things happen, the transaction was completed by a process which involved the several parties to it sending messages by e-mail; and the flows of money which resulted from this, and which led to the claimant's loss, were far harder to pin down to a single geographical location. But the judge adopted a satisfyingly clear approach. He said that the claimant suffered[178] its damage when, and therefore where, it committed itself to accepting the proposed contractual deal and sent the subscription form. At that point the opportunity to avoid the loss, if any were to materialise, had been put beyond its control: it handed over the keys to its safe, and any damage was done. How much damage, if indeed there was any, remained to be revealed, but the computation of how much damage was a second order task as far as special jurisdiction was concerned. *Dolphin Maritime & Aviation Services Ltd v Sveriges Angfartygs Assurans Forening* concerned a claim alleging a tortious procuring of a breach of contract, and a conspiracy to injure by unlawful means. The judge held that for the purpose of Article 5(3), as the contract in question had required payment to be made in London, London was the place where the damage occurred. Loss or damage taking the form of non-payment of sums due and expected occurred where the contract provided that the payment should be made, in the same way that loss or damage in the form of the non-delivery of goods at their port of destination takes place at the destination port.[179]

Prior to *Maple Leaf*, there had been some reason to think that the place where loss occurred might be that from which the claimant's money departed. The troubles with that were two: a potential claimant might be able, by judicious selection from among his many bank accounts, to choose where the loss was to occur, and as a result exercise an improper influence over the question of which court had special jurisdiction under Article 5(3). This, though, is surely a red herring: the proposition that the victim of fraud, still unknowing of the malpractice, makes a self-serving choice of paying from a bank account in France in order to be able to sue in France if and when it becomes apparent that he was the victim of fraud is pretty fanciful. The second objection might be that it may not be quite so easy to locate where the money was lost, not least because there must be a place of notional departure and a place of notional arrival; and because there is usually no transfer of actual notes and coins, there is some artificiality in the idea that the loss occurs at the place at which the money is lost. The instinct of the judge in *Maple Leaf*, which was surely correct, was that the loss occurred when the claimant

[178] This, it is suggested, might not be the most apt of expressions, if a distinction of importance separates where damage *occurs* and where it is *suffered*.

[179] Judgment at [60], referring to C-51/97 *Réunion Européenne SA v Spliethoff's Bevrachtingskantoor BV* [1998] ECR I-6511.

became legally bound to the transaction of which complaint was made.[180] If that was *when* the loss occurred, the material jurisdictional question was 'where did it occur'. This is fair to the claimant, who can hardly deny that if (as in the case of misrepresentation, it always is) the actual loss is the becoming bound to a contract, it takes place where the commitment to that contract was actually made; it is fair to the defendant who knows or ought to know that this will have been the time and place at which unilateral control over part of the claimant's patrimony passed over to him.[181]

The judge, in coming to his conclusion, was not as much assisted by the jurisprudence of the European Court as he may have hoped to have been. The latter has tended to answer all questions concerning the 'place of the damage' sub-rule of Article 5(3) by forcing the facts into the mould of primary-damage, secondary-damage, and regarding this as a complete answer.[182] In *Kronhofer v Maier*,[183] for example, an Austrian investor had been induced into the making of unwise investments. He had transferred money from his Austrian bank account to a German account, from where funds had been abstracted by the defendant to make useless investments. It followed, said the Court, that the jurisdictionally-significant loss occurred in Germany. This makes sense if it was in Germany that control over the funds irreversibly passed from claimant control; but as the referring court had not invited the European Court to find that the place of the damage was the Austrian bank account from which the funds had originally passed, the authority of the judgment is impaired. The other case was *DFDS Torline A/S* v *SEKO*,[184] which arose from the campaign of economic warfare organised by certain trade unions against companies carrying on business in international passenger shipping. In the case itself, an order that the claimants' sea ferry, the *Tor Caledonia*, be 'blacked' was issued by the trade union from Sweden.[185] The result was that the claimants, a Danish company, had to hire another vessel to ply its route between Sweden and the United Kingdom. The loss of which the claimant complained took the form of money spent in making a contract for the hire of a vessel which would not otherwise have needed to be made. As to the question where that damage, which was really loss, occurred, the Court observed that

[180] The fact, if it was a fact, that the transaction gives rise to a right to sue, which would reverse the loss, is obviously irrelevant.

[181] True, there may be tricky cases, such as where the commitment takes the form of typing and sending an e-mail. But the difficulty of some imagined cases does not call into question the soundness of the principle.

[182] It originates in C-220/88 *Dumez France SA v Hessische Landesbank* [1990] ECR I-49 (a case on secondary victims) and C-364/93 *Marinari v Lloyd's Bank plc* [1995] ECR I-2719 (a case on the financial consequences of physical loss by confiscation), and therefore only by analogy applies to the present circumstances.

[183] C-168/02, [2004] ECR I-6009.

[184] C–18/02 [2004] ECR I-1417.

[185] This was therefore the place of the event which gave rise to the loss or damage.

the damage allegedly caused to DFDS by SEKO consisted in financial loss arising from the withdrawal of the *Tor Caledonia* from its normal route and the hire of another ship to serve the same route. It is for the national court to inquire whether such financial loss may be regarded as having arisen at the place where [the claimant] is established.[186]

That instruction does not seem to advance matters very far. If it were to be contended that the loss arose in Denmark, on the footing that the *Tor Caledonia* was flagged in Denmark, the Court took the view that this would not satisfy the rule unless the national court found that the loss arose on the *Tor Caledonia* itself.[187] If the case is seen as one, like *Marinari*, in which the economic loss is simply the consequence of the imprisoning of the claimant's property, this is probably correct, if a little forced.

The place where the commitment was made, however, seems to work well in the case of loss resulting from misrepresentation. It does not focus on the dodgy assets acquired by the victim, referring to these only for the purpose of quantification of the loss which occurred, or arose, where the commitment was made. It will not work in cases in which the financial loss is not in the form of a contractual commitment, but is instead a non-receipt of that which was expected to be received; as to this, see further, below.

The cases also dealt with a number of other points of some importance, which are mentioned here for the sake of completeness. In *Maple Leaf*, the judge found that the English court had jurisdiction on the basis of Article 24, on the ground that there had been submission to the jurisdiction by appearance. The defendant had originally indicated that he would be contesting the jurisdiction of the court, but then did nothing overt to make that challenge; the judge interpreted this, also quite correctly, as the abandoning of the jurisdictional challenge. It is therefore clear that to forestall the application of Article 24, not only must the challenge to the jurisdiction be made at the first opportunity, it must also be prosecuted.[188] And on the question whether the contract in question was a consumer contract, the judge expressed some reservation about the rightness of the decision in *Standard Bank London Ltd v Apostolakis*.[189] But as he found that the defendants made the contract as part of their own trade or business, the contract was not one made by a consumer for the purposes of the Regulation, and there was no more to be said about it.

9. Direct claims against insurers: jurisdiction and choice of law: *Maher v Groupama Est*[190]

When the victim of a traffic accident makes a direct claim against the insurer of the wrongdoer, questions of jurisdiction and choice of law are liable to

[186] At [42]–[43]. [187] At [44].

[188] Cf *Starlight International Inc v Bruce* [2002] EWHC 374 (Ch), [2002] ILPr 617.

[189] [2001] 1 Lloyd's Rep Bank 240, doubted on this point in A Briggs & P Rees, *Civil Jurisdiction and Judgments* (Informa, London, 5th edn, 2009), para 2.94.

[190] [2009] EWCA Civ 1191, [2010] 1 WLR 1564: Mummery, Moore-Bick, Etherton LJJ.

arise. Sorting them out is not always straightforward (though they would make for a marvellous examination question), especially if the rules for choice of law are less than ideal. So it turned out when M brought proceedings in England against G, the French insurer of K, who was also French and who had injured M, and had killed himself, in a road accident in France. M was entitled to sue G in England by reason of Articles 11(2) and 9(1) of the Brussels I Regulation. France was the place where the claimant was when he sustained his injury, and it was common ground that, insofar as choice of law for the tort committed by K was or would have been in issue, the Private International Law (Miscellaneous Provisions) Act 1995, s 11, pointed to French law. But this did not necessarily compel the conclusion that every aspect of the case was governed by French law. Neither the quantum of damages, liability for which M sought to lay at the door of the insurer, nor the question of whether and at what rate interest was recoverable, was agreed. G contended that the claim against it was contractual, on the theory that M was a third party beneficiary of the contract of insurance who sued as such; and that as any claim against K was one which would have had to have been brought in France, the limit of G's liability under the insurance, and therefore under the direct claim, was the sum which could have been recovered by M had K been sued in France. The Court of Appeal did not agree. It concluded that (i) it would have been lawful for K to have been sued in England, with the consequence that the principal premise on which G's contentions were based fell away; (ii) the direct claim was to be characterised as a claim in tort so that the substance of the claim was governed by French law; but (iii) the quantification of loss and damage was determined by English law as *lex fori*; and (iv) the awarding of interest was a procedural matter governed by English law.

The question of jurisdiction over K was hypothetical, as neither K nor his estate was sued. The curiosity of Section 3 of Title II of the Regulation was that although Article 11(1) allows an insurer to be joined as a party to a claim against the insured in a court which had jurisdiction over the insured, and although Article 11(3) appeared to allow for the insurer, so sued, to join the insured as a party to the action, it did not on its face allow the claimant to join the insured as co-defendant to a claim against the insurer in a court with jurisdiction only against the insurer. Moore-Bick LJ was prepared to find that, had it been sought, K could have been joined to the proceedings against G, as co-defendant. It is hard to see how that this is correct. The broad justification, that it would be desirable for the Regulation to allow the joinder, the better to avoid the possibility of irreconcilable judgments resulting from trials in different courts, should have prompted the answer that, yes, indeed, the Regulation should provide for it. But it seems that it does not. At one level, the jurisprudence is ambivalent. Some authority applies the provisions of Section 3 according to their letter with the result that irreconcilable verdicts may ensue,[191] whereas

[191] *Jordan Grand Prix Ltd v Baltic Insurance Group* [1999] 2 AC 127.

others are prepared to bend the text of the legislation to produce a more sensible answer than a literal reading might offer;[192] but the proposition that a tortfeasor could be joined to proceedings outside the Member State of his domicile just because a direct claim is also brought against his insurer is much less persuasive. It is the insurer who may be expected to bear the inconvenience of defending away from home. Whatever economic and social justification may be offered for that, it does not translate to the insured tortfeasor; and to extend the jurisdictional scheme of Section 3 to widen jurisdiction against an insured tortfeasor beyond that which is expressly provided for is wrong. Efficiency of litigation will not always overcome the basic rule that defendants should be sued in the courts of their domicile.

Be that as it may, K had not been sued; and the decisive question for the court was to locate the principles by which the extent of G's liability was to be assessed.[193] The contention that the direct claim against G was contractual in nature was rejected, partly because the assertion that this was how the matter was characterised in French law was unsupported by evidence,[194] and partly because the court preferred the view that the matter was tortious in any event. This was because the claim against the insurer was consequential on the claim against the insured, which was tortious.[195] No real reasons were given; but the matter really is one of impression or of point of view, and the conclusion is right enough. For the claim is not 'for whatever the contract of insurance says the insurer would have paid to the insured', but 'in respect of such damage as was sustained by the claimant as victim of the tortfeasor': the claim is more tort than contract. Such questions are always tricky. Another may be seen when choosing the law for contribution claims between tortfeasors: as individuals viewed from the perspective of the victim, they are all tortfeasors. But it does not follow that their relationship to each other is also a matter of tort.[196] It depends on one's point of view, and the court's was not wrong.

So the material question was what was recoverable as a result of the tortiously-caused accident, as a matter of English private international law. As to that, though the substance of a claim in tort was governed by French law, its quantification was a matter for English law as procedural *lex fori*. As Moore Bick LJ put it, 'the only question that matters is how English law

[192] Case C-463/06 *FBTO Schadeverzekeringen NV v Odenbreit* [2007] ECR I-11321.

[193] In this respect, the question whether the insured could have been sued in England may be disregarded, by (loose) analogy with the law of contribution: *RA Lister Ltd v Thomson (Shipping) Ltd* [1987] 1 WLR 1614 (noted Jolowicz [1988] CLJ 32); *The Kapetan Georgis* [1988] 1 Lloyd's Rep 352.

[194] At [12].

[195] At [22].

[196] Indeed, Dicey, Morris and Collins, above n 32, para 34–051, expresses the view that the claim for contribution is not governed by the Private International Law (Miscellaneous Provisions) Act 1995, but by the law with which the obligation to make contribution is most closely connected, unless the Civil Liability (Contribution) Act 1978 applies as an overriding provision of the law of the forum: cf *Arab Monetary Fund v Hashim (No 9)*, The Times, 11th Oct 1994 (noted [1995] LMCLQ 437).

characterises the particular issue that arises for determination, namely how much should Mr and Mrs Maher receive to compensate them for the injuries that they have suffered'.[197] Put in those terms, the law seems to have reverted to something which Lord Guest would have recognised. In *Boys v Chaplin*,[198] he said that: 'these elements comprise the head of damage due to an injured person by English law. It would not be correct, in my view, to talk of compensation for pain and suffering as a head of damage apart from patrimonial loss. It is merely an element in the quantification of the total compensation.' That our private international law should have regressed to the point where a speech which nobody ever attempted to defend is to be regarded as accurate and reliable is, of course, the consequence of *Harding v Wealands*[199] and its bizarre conclusion that the quantification of damages was and must forever be, as a matter of English private international law, a procedural question. But *Harding v Wealands* stands for the proposition that if the question is 'how much is the injury worth in damages?' the answer is 'whatever English domestic law would say it was worth'. The Court of Appeal had no choice to do other than it did. At least no-one suggested that the case was one in which the court was called upon to do the impossible and to quantify the damages for heads of damage alien to English domestic law, though perhaps that will come.

And interest? It is at this point that the attempt to apply the law in *Harding v Wealands* becomes truly surreal. It led Moore-Bick LJ to conclude that the question whether there was a right to recover interest was a substantive issue,[200] governed by French law (which did not deny it *in limine*), but that the quantification of that interest would be a procedural question, governed by English law as *lex fori*.[201] This conclusion was taken to be reinforced by the observation that the Senior Courts Act 1981,[202] s 35A, gave the court a statutory discretion to award interest: a statutory rule which, by virtue of its discretionary character, could not be seen as substantive in nature. But in the exercise of that statutory, or remedial, or procedural, discretion, an English court might have regard to provisions of French law as to the

197 At [22]. 198 [1971] AC 356, at 382.

199 [2006] UKHL 32, [2007] 2 AC 1; noted this Year Book, 77 (2006), 565.

200 Likewise, the right to recover damages for late payment, in circumstances where this may be seen as a surrogate for interest, is governed by the lex causae. In *Karafarin Bank v Mansoury Dara* [2009] EWHC 3265 (Comm), Iranian law, which governed the contractual relationship between a bank and its customer in respect of a dishonoured cheque or other bill of exchange, did not provide for the payment of interest, but did allow a claim for damages for late payment of a commercial debt. Blair J held that a claim based on this provision of Iranian law allowed the recovery of such damages as part of the substantive right relied on; the judgment deliberately said nothing about the availability of damages on the judgment debt. An earlier judgment in the same proceedings, *Karafarin Bank v Mansoury Dara* [2009] EWHC 1217 (Comm), concerned Civil Jurisdiction and Judgments Act 1982 s 34, holding that where a judgment from an Iranian court could not be recognised in England for want of personal jurisdiction over the defendant, there was no objection to the bringing of fresh proceedings in England on the same cause of action, whether by reference to Section 34 or to the principles of abuse of process.

201 At [33].

202 As the Supreme Court Act 1981 is now renamed (Constitutional Reform Act 2005, s 59).

recovery of interest. The result was that interest was recoverable in principle if French law allowed the recovery of interest, but if it did, the question of how much to award was a matter for the exercise of discretion according to English principles, unhampered by any rule of foreign law.

One may ask how much of this makes sense. Of course, if the quantification of damages and the currency of their award is governed by English law, it makes sense that English law be permitted to award the interest which correlates to its award of damages. The rate of interest appropriate to be awarded where damages are ordered in sterling may, at least in principle, differ from the rate appropriate if the damages were to be assessed in a hard currency. The interest is probably so tied up with the currency of the award, and therefore with its quantification, that it should be seen as part and parcel of the law by which the quantification is done. If quantification is governed by English law, interest needs also to be. But if this were correct, it may have been better to see the statutory power to award interest as an overriding rule of the forum. In the end, it is hard to avoid the sense that only when choice of law for non-contractual obligations is governed by the Rome II Regulation[203] will English courts finally be able to get away from *Harding v Wealands* and apply a coherent set of rules for choice of law.

10. The role of comity in common law jurisdiction: *Masri v Consolidated Contractors International Co SAL*;[204] *United States Securities & Exchange Commission v Manterfield*;[205] *Harms Offshore AHT 'Taurus' GmbH & Co KG v Bloom*;[206] *Deutsche Bank AG v Highland Crusader Offshore Partners LP*[207]

In the transcript of oral argument before the High Court of Australia in *Dow Jones & Co Inc v Gutnick*,[208] the following exchange is recorded:

GAUDRON J: That is a policy decision. You make that argument by reference to policy rather than by reference to legal principle?
MR ROBERTSON: By reference to policy and to comity.
GAUDRON J: Comity is a funny word.
MR ROBERTSON: It is.
GAUDRON J: I mean, really, we know that judges of various countries use it when they want to.
HAYNE J: Before they apply the law of the forum.

[203] Regulation (EC) 593/2008.
[204] [2009] UKHL 43, [2010] 1 AC 90, [2009] Bus LR 1269: Lord Scott of Foscote, Lord Rodger of Earlsferry, Lord Walker of Gestingthorpe, Lord Brown of Eaton-under-Heywood, and Lord Mance, reversing [2008] EWCA Civ 876, [2009] QB 699: Sir Anthony Clarke MR, Longmore and Lawrence Collins LJJ (noted this Year Book, 79 (2008), 522).
[205] [2009] EWCA Civ 27, [2010] 1 WLR 172: Waller, Moses and Hackett LJJ.
[206] [2009] EWCA Civ 632, [2010] 2 WLR 349: Ward, Stanley Burnton LJJ and Sir John Chadwick.
[207] [2009] EWCA Civ 725, [2010] 1 WLR 1023: Carnwath, Toulson and Goldring LJJ. The House of Lords gave permission to appeal to the Supreme Court of the United Kingdom.
[208] [2002] HCA Trans 253 (28 May 2002). I am happily indebted to Dr Bell, SC, of the NSW Bar, for reminding me of this little exchange.

This caustic irruption from Hayne J succeeds very well in conveying the sense that appeals to comity in private international law are, as often as not, no more than cover for a decision which is not otherwise quite so easy to arrive at or justify. In this context, recourse to comity has tended to be negative: the decision to enforce an agreement on choice of court, or for arbitration, by injunction to restrain a breach is said not to infringe comity, on the ground that the efficient reinforcement of a contractual agreement assists, rather than interferes with, the administration of justice, and therefore does not offend against comity. Likewise, an injunction ordered to restrain proceedings wrongfully brought overseas does not offend against comity if the intervention is confined to cases in which the natural forum for the resolution of the dispute is England, and so forth. This year has been quite significant, though, for the way in which the courts have asserted the principle of comity as the measuring-stick for the limits of their power. It is hard to avoid the conclusion that there really is nothing in the point, and that comity is, if anything, a secondary concern, adding nothing of measurable value to a judgment deduced from primary legal rules. But as a rhetorical device, it still finds a role.

In *Masri v Consolidated Contractors International Co SAL* the defendant company had submitted to the jurisdiction and had gone down to judgment in a substantial commercial action. Its stance led Masri to believe, perfectly plausibly, that the defendant would never, ever, part with a penny piece, no matter what any court told it to do. So Masri applied for orders,[209] under CPR Part 71, against K, an individual who was the Chairman, the General Manager, and a director of the defendant company, requiring him to come to court and give evidence as to the whereabouts of the company's assets. K[210] was not willing, and disputed the authority of the English court to demand his attendance and to threaten him with imprisonment for contempt if he did not. His objections

[209] For some of the other orders applied for, namely the anti-suit injunction and the appointment of a receiver by way of equitable execution, see the judgments of the Court of Appeal reported as *Masri v Consolidated Contractors International Co SAL (No 2)* [2008] EWCA Civ 303, [2009] QB 450 (receivership), and *Masri v Consolidated Contractors International Co SAL (No 3)* [2008] EWCA Civ 625, [2009] QB 503, both of which were noted in this Year Book, 79 (2008), 522. The general theme of the judgments was that as the defendant had submitted to the jurisdiction of the English court for the trial of the claim on its merits, its submission, and the court's power to make orders against it, was untrammelled by the jurisdictional rules of the Brussels I Regulation, save only that an injunction to restrain the judgment debtor from bringing proceedings before the courts of another Member State was precluded by C-159/02 *Turner v Grovit* [2004] ECR I-3565. As the appeal to the House of Lords in the matter under review was disposed of as a matter of English procedural law, the fact that the Court of Appeal had relied on the same general justification, that the judgment debtor had submitted and had therefore licensed the court to make such orders as it considered necessary, is probably not impaired. However, the House of Lords had indicated that, had it not interpreted the material provisions of English law in the manner it did, it would have made a reference to the European Court for a preliminary ruling. It is therefore proper to acknowledge that the rightness of the reasoning in the decisions of the Court of Appeal which were not appealed is open to technical question. The position taken here, however, is that the Court of Appeal was absolutely correct, and that any objection on purported grounds of European law would have been unfounded.

[210] The power to make the order against officers is expressly conferred by CPR r 71.2(1)(b).

were that English law did not allow the order that he attend to be issued and served on him, as he was out of the jurisdiction. Quite separately and distinctly, he contended that European law did not allow him to be summoned to give evidence either. As he was domiciled in Greece he was, as he said, protected by the Brussels I Regulation from being sued in England; alternatively, the procedure under CPR Part 71 was a procedure for the taking of evidence, and the mechanism of its implementation was the Taking of Evidence Regulation,[211] which had not been relied on or complied with by the claimant.

A notably strong Court of Appeal,[212] resolutely in favour of making judgments effective, held that as the defendant company had submitted to the jurisdiction, the English court had, as far as European law was concerned, full power to make any and all such orders against the company as were necessary or desirable to do justice according to the law. That extended, so the judgment ran, to ordering the defendant company's officials, or at least its high officers, to come and give evidence of the whereabouts of the company's assets. The view was put forward in this Year Book last year that the real question posed for the court was whether officers (as distinct from shareholders, proprietors) were sufficiently involved with, or sufficiently identified with the company for this summoning to be within the scope of the 'full powers' which the defendant company's submission conferred on the English court. After all, if there is a general principle that individuals may lend themselves to what goes on in certain jurisdictions—if you make a commercial contract with an Australian corporation, you cannot really complain if the corporation's insolvency is administered according to Aussie rules;[213] if you take shares in a company which then goes and does something daft like submitting to the jurisdiction of a foreign court, you may find that your interest in it is placed in jeopardy,[214] and so on—the real question is whether persons holding high office in a defendant corporation may be considered to be in a similar position. There is room for a proper debate about that:[215] after all, it is not being supposed that they may be placed under some personal financial liability, only that they may be required to give such evidence as they may about the affairs of the company in which they hold office (and if they worry that they may incriminate themselves, they can argue the law).

The House of Lords did not hear argument on the European law point, but ruled that as a matter of English procedural law, the power to order a corporate director under CPR Part 71 was territorially limited to those

[211] Council Regulation (EC) 1206/2001, [2001] OJ L174/1.

[212] Sir Anthony Clarke MR; Lawrence Collins LJ (both shortly thereafter appointed to the House of Lords and now Justices of the Supreme Court) and Longmore LJ.

[213] *Re HIH Casualty and General Insurance Ltd, McGrath v Riddell* [2008] UKHL 21, [2008] 1 WLR 852 ((2008) 79 *BYIL* 501).

[214] *Cambridge Gas Transport Corp v Official Committee of Unsecured Creditors of Navigator Holdings plc* [2006] UKPC 26, [2007] 1 AC 508 ((2006) 77 *BYIL* 575).

[215] See further below.

persons who were physically present within the jurisdiction when the order was applied for or made. This conclusion was derived from their interpretation of the procedural rule which governed the matter. Rather disappointingly, it purported to be reinforced by the slight difficulty in identifying the mechanism, in the CPR Part 6 as it then stood, by which such an order could actually be served on a person out of the jurisdiction, though the sense that this would be a copybook example of tails wagging dogs, and of bigger questions being ducked, is very hard to put from one's mind.[216] Not only that: it appears that the procedural rule which is now made as CPR r 6.39[217] meets the service need precisely, at least if what is served is the application notice, rather than the order itself, for it provides for the service of an application notice on a non-party out of the jurisdiction, and extends to such person the right to dispute the jurisdiction under CPR Part 11. But it will now not be any use, as the House of Lords has emasculated CPR Part 71. It was a shame that the House of Lords should go out, as far as private international law is concerned, not with a bang but with a whimper.[218]

A startling submission, that the Rules Committee had had no power under the Civil Procedure Act 1997 to make rules which might apply to persons out of the jurisdiction unless there was primary legislation dealing with the specific matter in hand, was rejected, as it should have been. But on the principal question, the view of Lord Mance was that 'in the light of the accepted practice of nations and comity in the field of international law and relations, eyebrows might be raised' at the proposition that the English courts had power to summon any officer to give evidence as to the defendant's assets;[219] and that in fact they had, or had been given, no such power. The conclusion was bolstered by the rhetorical question why, if a court has no power to compel witnesses to come from overseas to give evidence at a trial, where their absence may have a catastrophic

[216] It was argued that service might be made by virtue of CPR r 6.30(2). Tomlinson J had been sceptical of this in *Vitol AS v Capri Marine Ltd* [2008] EWHC 378 (Comm), [2009] Bus LR 271, but the Court of Appeal in *Masri* did not share his doubts. The House of Lords has rehabilitated the decision in *Vitol*. The miserable irony is that the express power to serve an application notice on a non-party out of the jurisdiction is now found as CPR r. 6.39, but this was not mentioned in the decision even though the perceived difficulty with service was considered to bolster it.

[217] The Court of Appeal had considered that what is now CPR r 6.39(2) permitted service of the order made *ex parte*, which is a separate point.

[218] The House of Lords was abolished as a judicial tribunal by the Constitutional Reform Act 2005, and replaced from 1 October 2009 by the Supreme Court of the United Kingdom.

[219] The quotation is actually from Dillon LJ in *re Tucker (RC) (A Bankrupt)* [1990] Ch 148, where it was used in relation to the power to summon a person who might be able to give evidence about a bankrupt under Bankruptcy Act 1914, s 25. The quotation appears in *Masri* at [19], and was adopted in relation to CPR Part 71 at [24]. It is far from obvious that this should convince. The person proposed to be summoned was the brother of the bankrupt who could, by no stretch of the reasonable imagination, be said to have lent himself to the jurisdiction of the English bankruptcy jurisdiction: he was not, to put it a little crudely, a voluntary participant in his brother's affairs. The position of a person who elects to hold office in a company—perhaps even to act as its head and hands—is very different, and certainly more different that Lord Mance suggests at [23].

effect on the court's ability to get at the truth, the court should have considerably greater powers to summon those who may be able to give evidence about assets during the procedure for the enforcing a judgment.[220] There are several answers to that, many of them good.

As a judgment, it was less of a last hurrah, and more of a damp squib. The wording of CPR Part 71 did not require the limitation which the House of Lords placed upon it, as Lord Mance admitted. It is a blessing that such timidity did not stifle Lord Denning, or we would never have seen the *Mareva* injunction, for example. And if people were to raise their eyebrows, so what? The courts administer justice according to the law, not justice according to the facial expression of foreigners. As to the case of K, no-one forced him to hold office in the defendant company. Lord Mance was rather dismissive about the possibility of office-holders within the jurisdiction making themselves scarce in order to avoid the very possibility of being summoned, which as a prediction of actual human movements may be fair enough. But K had resigned from his office shortly before the appeal to the Court of Appeal, which does rather suggest that he was prepared to leave few stones unturned in his efforts to avoid compliance,[221] while still enjoying the benefit of representation by Messrs Olswang, Mr Layton QC, and Mr Raphael.[222] Perhaps comity really was implicated, but without any comparative analysis in the judgment which would tend to show that, so far as the *ius gentium* was concerned, an assertion of jurisdiction of this kind of thing was unprecedented, it is a little hard to see in comity any more than a self-justifying assertion of a conclusion already arrived at.

A perfectly good argument was available, which would have asked whether the corporate officers against whom the order was sought had volunteered to put themselves in a position in which this exposure to the English courts could be properly taken to have been inflicted on them by act of the company or, to put it another way, had put themselves at risk by taking office in the company. The Court of Appeal seemed to think that it had, and many will agree with them. As said above, the company had submitted, and when a company does that, its act may alter the legal position of others involved in it. As a matter of instinct and impression, the idea that the individual who held office as chairman, general manager, and director of the company could shrug and say 'nothing to do with me,

[220] At [23], [26].

[221] And by curious chance, in *Vitol AS v Capri Marine Ltd* [2008] EWHC 378 (Comm), [2009] Bus LR 271, the director, Kalogiratos, against whom the same order was sought did exactly the same: see at [20]–[23]. It appears that Greek company directors whose family names begin with the letter 'K' are prepared to resign at the drop of a hat if they think it will fend off an application under CPR Part 71. Tomlinson J was 'sceptical about the circumstances' of the resignation: see at [23]. It is a thousand pities that the House of Lords neither shared the scepticism nor saw the need to look past it.

[222] Judgment at [7]. One supposes that this professional representation did not come cheaply. Not only that: the company was put into judicial administration in Lebanon (see at [7]), and the suspicion that this was motivated by a desire to keep Masri out of his money is just as hard to put out of one's mind.

guv', and find a unanimous House of Lords nodding in agreement with him, is surprising. On the other hand, the difference between shareholders and office-holders and employees, may be more of a gulf than a matter of detail. The former own the company, and should not be heard to complain when the thing which they own affects their legal position. The latter do not own, but serve, the company. The proposition that they are similarly affected when the company goes and participates in overseas litigation is not so obvious. There was, as is suggested here, a substantial debate to be had about the nature and consequences of acts undertaken by a company for those persons who are, in a loose sense, of or associated with the company. It may be that the correct answer lay in an analysis of 'sufficient identity of interest' with the company. But the analysis in the House of Lords, at least so far as one can deduce it from the judgment, shunned this question. The issue is one of principle; it deserved a proper debate. The decision of the court to set aside the order may have been correct, but the reasons given for it were not what they might have been.

More satisfactory was the approach and the decision of the Court of Appeal in *United States Securities & Exchange Commission v Manterfield*. Freezing injunctions were sought against a person who was being sued as a fraudster in the US courts, and against whom remedies by way of disgorgement and restitution for the benefit those who had been defrauded were sought: the victims were primarily Taiwanese. Jurisdiction to make such orders in England was to be found in Civil Jurisdiction and Judgments Act 1982, s 25; the only conceivable objection to the orders lay in the contention that they were sought to assist the enforcement of a foreign penal, revenue, or analogous public law which, as Dicey's Rule 3 makes clear, may not be enforced in an English court. The Court of Appeal reached the conclusion, easily enough, that even though the American proceedings were being brought by a public authority, the obligation sought to be enforced against the defendant, and in that sense the right relied on in the proceedings, was an ordinary civil obligation: in the first place, not to defraud in the first place, and in the second place, to recompense those whom one has defrauded. Given the uncertainty as to which of the defrauded investors had lost exactly what, and given the uncertain quantum of actual recovery, the American legislation provided, rationally, enough, for a central authority to bring collective proceedings, and for a plan of distribution to be proposed to and approved by the court. One would have thought that this made it as plain as it could possibly be that the proceedings were not founded on a sovereign right, but on a civil liability, and that this and this alone exempted them from the scope of Dicey's Rule 3.

Much the same issue had been settled by the New South Wales Court of Appeal in *Robb Evans v European Bank Ltd*.[223] Although the Australian

[223] (2004) 61 NSWLR 75. The commentary on the case at [2004] LMCLQ 313 was, perhaps unfortunately, not shown to the court.

interpretation of Dicey's Rule 3 is a little different from that which has, so far at least,[224] been accepted by English courts,[225] there was no reason to suppose that the careful and rigorous judgment of the New South Wales Court of Appeal would be anything less than conclusive in England. In a complex world, the mark of a successful fraud is that it makes it difficult for the victims to sue when they discover what has happened. In *Robb Evans,* those who had their credit card details stolen and their cards debited for apparent downloading of pornography may well have thought twice about identifying themselves as victims; in *Manterfield* the victims may have felt that they would lose face from admitting to their credulousness, even if they had been left with enough money to be able to fund litigation. To guard against such modern wickedness, states have put in place various schemes for collective or organised redress, and in some cases, an official of or recognised by the state is given the power and the duty to bring the proceedings. Even if it were alleged that the very particular right by which it does so is given to it alone, the liability of the defendant which is asserted in the proceedings is as straightforward a civil liability as can be imagined. It is ancient law that thieves are to be hated[226] and punished, but it is also the law that they can be sued. It was the second response which was in issue in *Manterfield*, and for the court to have gone looking for objections to the order which it had power to grant would have been quite wrong. The difficulties which may have arisen if the proceedings in the United States had had a clear, additional, and discrete penal financial component were not before the court, any more than they were in *Robb Evans* or will ever be, for by the time the police arrive, the fraudster has usually parted with most of the proceeds of the fraud, and the prospect of there being any surplus out of which to pay a penalty, especially after the professionals have taken their cut, is unreal.[227]

The decision of the court did not overtly invoke the principle of comity, but it did proceed on the very clear footing that assisting the judicial process of a foreign friendly state was the right thing to do. Judicial co-operation, when the co-operation is requested from overseas, ought to be very hard to refuse. When the co-operation is not requested, it is a different thing altogether. The ever-developing law of anti-suit injunctions tests the principle that it may not be consistent with inter-curial comity for an English court to order a respondent over whom it has personal jurisdiction to refrain from bringing proceedings before the courts of another state. Pendulums, as is their nature, swing to and fro. In 2009, it swung in favour and against intervention in the form of injunctions,

[224] See *Equatorial Guinea v Royal Bank of Scotland International* [2006] UKPC 7 (Guernsey); *Mbasogo v Logo Ltd* [2006] EWCA Civ 1370, [2007] QB 846 (noted this Year Book, 77 (2006), 554).

[225] See *A-G v Heinemann Publishers Australia Pty Ltd* (1988) 165 CLR 30.

[226] *Odio furti* was said to be the explanation for the cumulation of actions, not all of them logical, which lay against thieves in Roman law: Gaius *Institutes* IV.4.

[227] For further analysis of this point, see [2004] LMCLQ 313.

referring to the principle and limitations imposed by comity as part of the reasoning. The references to comity were, one has to say, not terribly useful. In *Harms Offshore AHT 'Taurus' GmbH & Co KG v Bloom*, an injunction was granted 'notwithstanding comity'.[228] An English company had been put into administration with a view to its being sold as a going concern. Shortly thereafter, certain German creditors obtained an order attaching its property in the United States, *ex parte* and without disclosing to the American court that the company was in administration. In due course the Administrators, still in ignorance of the order of attachment which had not been served on them, transferred $3m-odd to a US bank to settle the account of a post-administration supplier, at which point the funds were attached. Despite the fact that there was no provision of English insolvency law which applied directly to parties who, outside the jurisdiction,[229] took steps to improve on what the English rules on insolvency or administration would get them, administrators are charged with an obligation to take control of all of the company's property, wherever situated.[230] Any right which the court has to prevent a creditor taking steps overseas was founded on the *in personam* jurisdiction and the right and duty to restrain wrongdoing. Although considerations of comity might require each court—English and American—to get on with managing their own business, the conduct of a particular creditor may make the case an exceptional one, and justify the court in acting to protect its administration by preventing wrongdoing. For this to be described as a power 'tempered by considerations of comity'[231] was, with respect, not very illuminating. Sir John Chadwick described the acts of the respondents as being designed to 'set a trap for the administrators;'[232] and such wrongful behaviour took the case outside the ordinary.

The result is right: for the English administration to be undermined in this way was intolerable. But the proposition that the considerations of comity which are owed to another court can be overridden by the identification of wrongdoing done to a litigant is a rather troubling one, at least if comity is thought to have any meaning. It suggests that comity is an aspiration rather than a pledge; the idea that it works only in the quiet times when no-one does anything wrong which might attract judicial intervention in the first place, is odd. The impression with which one is left is that a wrongdoer, for some reason subject to the jurisdiction, was liable to be restrained. References to comity may have dressed the window, but that is all they did.

228 At [29].

229 Service of the application notice on the respondents will presumably have been made, with leave, under Insolvency Rules 1986, SI 1986/1925 (as amended), Rule 12.12(3). At any rate, no point on jurisdiction was taken by the respondents.

230 At [23], referring to Insolvency Act 1986, s 436, and Schedule B1 para 67.

231 At [25].

232 At [32].

But odder by far was the analysis thrown up by *Deutsche Bank AG v Highland Crusader Offshore Partners LP*, which arose out of a financial arrangement which went wrong. It began straightforwardly enough: the material documentation contained a clause which, in material part, read as follows:

This Agreement shall be governed by and construed in accordance with the laws of England. Buyer and Seller hereby irrevocably submit for all purposes of or in connection with this Agreement and each Transaction to the jurisdiction of the Courts of England... Nothing in this paragraph shall limit the right of any party to take proceedings in the courts of any other country of competent jurisdiction.

Proceedings were commenced in Texas, by Highland against the Bank, alleging fraud and other forms of disreputable practice. Three weeks later the Bank brought proceedings in England for the sums due under the agreement. Meanwhile the Bank contested the jurisdiction of the court in Texas, but its motion for dismissal of the proceedings was denied by Judge Molberg in laconic fashion:[233]

This is fascinating. I understand the competing interests, and I am particularly swayed in many personal respects by what [counsel for the Bank] has just said [about the Texas court not wanting to be known for allowing international forum shopping]. Given that, I'm denying the [Bank's] motions.

And one month later, Burton J granted an anti-suit injunction. He accepted that the jurisdiction clause was not one which purported to confer exclusive jurisdiction on the English courts, but considered that where there were proceedings in the courts which had been designated with non-exclusive jurisdiction, it was ordinarily wrongful to prosecute proceedings, in parallel, in another jurisdiction. He saw nothing in the principles of comity to prevent the granting of the injunction which was applied for. The sum and substance of his judgment was that there was a contractual agreement for the English courts which, on a true construction, made it wrongful to sue in the courts of another country. He dismissed the express words which provided that neither party was to be limited by the agreement and prevented from suing elsewhere as 'simply spell[ing] out what is otherwise shorthand in the words "non-exclusive jurisdiction"'.[234] At this point his judgment surely fell into error, for his conclusion that the words of the agreement, however they were construed, *did* have an adverse impact on where the bank could be sued, was plainly untenable: on any fair view, his construction of the agreement was wrong. But in a one-day hearing, with judgment the next day, mistakes will happen.

The Court of Appeal was not convinced. Toulson LJ delivered a lengthy judgment, but with respect, there was rather little said in it which

[233] At [22]. [234] [2009] EWHC 730 (Comm), [21].

needed saying to put matters right. The true bargain struck by the parties was to the effect that either party could sue wherever it could find a judge; it was explicit that parallel proceedings were, as far as it was up to the parties to decide the matter, entirely permissible; and for the judge to interpret the *clause* as though it removed the right of Highland to sue where it chose to sue had been wrong. Another way to make the same point might be that the very terms of the contract served to estop either party to the agreement from complaining about the bringing of proceedings in a court which had jurisdiction to hear them. With these conclusions there could be no quarrel. An argument to the contrary, in support of the judge, seemed misconceived form the start. In *Sabah Shipyard (Pakistan) Ltd v Islamic Republic of Pakistan*[235] the Court of Appeal had accepted that a jurisdiction agreement for the English courts was not exclusive in nature, but that the manoeuvrings of the Pakistan government to undermine it, by bringing proceedings in Pakistan in which an anti-suit injunction was applied for, was wrongful and liable to restraint. The decision is manifestly correct, and makes the simple enough point that a jurisdiction clause, like any other contractual term, needs to be read carefully to see what it really means, to see what the parties really bound themselves, as between themselves, to accept. The court in *Sabah Shipyard* construed the clause as one which required the government of Pakistan not to impede the bringing of proceedings in the nominated court, on the footing that this was exactly what they had promised. The court did not say that an injunction would go to reinforce any jurisdiction agreement, exclusive or non-exclusive, but it denied, absolutely correctly, that an injunction could never be the proper response to proceedings brought outside a contractual but non-exclusive, forum. Despite the clarity and sense of this, some people have claimed to make the strange deduction that because the injunction was ordered in *Sabah Shipyard* there is no real difference between exclusive and non-exclusive jurisdiction agreements. It takes little time to show how inane such a reading of an intelligent judgment is.[236] Toulson LJ appeared to think that *Sabah Shipyard* needed 'to be seen in the context of its own particular facts',[237] but as the case turned, as all jurisdiction clause and injunction cases always turn, on the construction of the agreement and the behaviour of the contracting parties in relation to their assumed obligations, any implication that *Sabah Shipyard* is suspect is quite unwarranted.

The parties to the contract in *Highland Crusader* had made an express agreement, which the judge below had distorted and denatured, that parallel proceedings were not to be objected to. The real question for the Court of Appeal, therefore, should have been whether it was a matter for the parties, or for the court, to decide whether parallel litigation was to

[235] [2002] EWCA Civ 1643, [2003] 2 Lloyd's Rep 571.
[236] See the judgment at [85]–[87], and the material there cited.
[237] At [112].

be permitted when, contrary to the agreement of the parties, objection was taken.[238] The judgment is, at this point, very short. The analysis was that where the parties have made this agreement, they will be held to it, even though parallel litigation will result, unless the case is an exceptional one. For those who believe that the interpretation and operation of jurisdiction clauses ought to be seen as a straightforward matter of holding parties to their agreement, because *pacta sunt servanda*, this is a good decision. All the same, the view of the judge below was that a contradictory perception of the public interest might override what the parties had agreed or had purported to agree; and with this there can be no quarrel, either.

It was a pity that this aspect of the question was touched on so lightly. Toulson LJ set out a list of what he called 'key principles'[239] on the law of injunctions in respect of jurisdiction agreements. These made several references to comity as a restraining influence. He appears to have understood this as meaning that, in principle, a judge should decide for himself whether the proceedings in his own court should be allowed to proceed, and that it will generally not be consistent with comity for a foreign court, whether English or otherwise, to look beyond the seas and intervene. This suggests that the principles of comity speak to judges, and not to parties. It suggests that the restraint called for by comity is a judicial self-restraint. Indeed, comity was mentioned, over and over again, as a reason for not interfering so far as there were proceedings before another court. In this respect, if in this respect only, the approach of the court appears to reflect the principle of mutual trust and confidence which the Member States observe in relation to each other. In the context of the Brussels I Regulation, however, the non-interference is accompanied by a strict rule which prohibits[240] or restricts[241] parallel litigation of claims; it is not so obvious that the principle of non-interference is equally justified in a context where there is no separate, independent, mechanism to prevent parallel

[238] In two cases the High Court held, clearly and deliberately, that where the parties had made an agreement on jurisdiction, and where if an injunction were granted to restrain a party to that agreement from bringing proceedings in breach of it, the result would be that other entities which had a claim would continue in their preferred forum, the fracturing of the overall process of dispute resolution was not a matter of which complaint could be made. The injunctions applied for were therefore granted. Complaint by the respondent as to the effect of such an order would be attributable to the limited personal scope of the agreement on jurisdiction; the party who complained about the fracturing of a complex dispute would have only himself (or his lack of foresight) to blame: *Morgan Stanley & Co International plc v China Haisheng Juice Holdings Co Ltd* [2009] EWHC 2419 (Comm), [2010] 1 Lloyd's Rep 265; *Skype Technologies SA v Joltid Ltd* [2009] EWHC 2783 (Ch). It is evident that there is choice between the upholding of an agreement on jurisdiction, and securing the orderly resolution of complex disputes. *Donohue v Armco Inc* [2001] UKHL 64, [2002] 1 Lloyd's Rep 425 was distinguished on the ground that in the two cases before the High Court, the dispute resolution was bound to be fractured in any case (just as would have been the case if the agreement in question had been for arbitration), and therefore the policy of upholding and enforcing agreements prevailed.

[239] At [50].

[240] Article 27 (same cause of action and same parties).

[241] Article 28 (related proceedings).

litigation.[242] In the context of the Regulation, the fact that the parties may have provided for the possibility by express agreement will make no difference. It may be that the common law takes a diametrically different view of the matter, but though the facts of *Highland Crusader* presented the opportunity for a discussion of this important question, the submissions to the court—one side behaving as though part of the express wording of the clause was not there, the other saying that the contract provided precisely for and permitted what was taking place and that this is all that one needed to know—seem to have blinded the court to an issue which could and probably should have been dealt with as discrete. Those who have proposed that agreements on jurisdiction should be interpreted and enforced according to their terms may consider that we have had something of a vindication, but on this occasion there is more than trace of missed opportunity about it.[243]

11. Freezing orders made against foreigners mixed up in another's fraud: *Belletti v Morici*[244]

When proceedings are brought in England against a fraudster, and it is alleged that some of the assets against which execution of the judgment should be made have been put into the hands of another, to defeat the enforcement, the English courts are able to assert jurisdiction over, and make freezing orders against, the recipient or custodian, up to the value of the assets or the judgment, whichever is the smaller.[245] Matters are inevitably more complicated where the substantive proceedings against the fraudster are before the courts of another Member State, the recipient of the assets and intended respondent is domiciled and resident in another

[242] See *Airbus Industrie GIE v Patel* [1999] 2 AC 119. It is not clear how Toulson LJ would have seen the role of comity if the clause had been exclusive and had made it plain that to sue in a non-designated court was a breach of contract. The policy of non-intervention, which comity was thought to underpin, and the enforcement of the contract, which Toulson LJ seemed to consider was the start and the end of the analysis, would then be in opposition. Given this, it is far from obvious that comity has anything of value to contribute to the analysis, save for the appearance of support for whatever the judge has otherwise decided to do.

[243] Something similar may be said of the decision of the Supreme Court of New South Wales in *Ace Insurance Ltd v Moose Enterprise Pty Ltd* [2009] NSWSC 724. The court ordered an anti-suit injunction on the basis that an agreement on jurisdiction was exclusive in nature, and that the overseas proceedings were therefore vexatious or oppressive; it did not accept that an agreement on choice of law, at least one in plain vanilla form, would give rise to promissory obligations. If defensible as a matter of general law, it is still a truly odd decision when one reads the actual contract. It provided that '[s]hould any dispute arise concerning this policy, the dispute will be determined in accordance with the law of Australia and the States and Territories thereof. In relation to any such dispute the parties agree to submit to the jurisdiction of any competent court in a State or Territory of Australia'. It can easily be seen that (i) the reference to choice of court is not, on the face of it, drafted in exclusive terms; and (ii) that the reference to the applicable law is *not* a statement of the law which is to govern the policy of insurance, *but* a statement of the law which will be applied in dispute resolution. Some will conclude that the judge may well have misread, and therefore have misrepresented, the nature of the promises to which the parties had actually subscribed. The argument is now out in the open, but it will require a better judgment than this to get to grips with it.

[244] [2009] EWHC 2316 (Comm), [2009] ILPr 960: Flaux J.

[245] See, for example, *C Inc plc v L* [2001] 2 Lloyd's Rep 459.

Member State, the assets are in a non-Member state, and the recipient has made it perfectly clear that it will disregard any order which the English court may make. If the English court is nevertheless to make an order, this time in aid of the foreign proceedings or the judgment which has already been given in them, it has to consider whether it has jurisdiction *in personam* over those whom it is asked to restrain, whether it is entitled to make the order if it does have that jurisdiction, whether it should make the order if it is entitled, and how to deal with the defiance of the person to be restrained. All this and more[246] was analysed in *Belletti v Morici*, and the judgment represents a textbook account of how to disentangle threads in the context of a case in which the inventiveness of counsel made life challenging for the judge.

To a substantial extent, the path to the answer had been mapped in *Motorola Credit Corp v Uzan (No 2)*.[247] To begin with, the fact that intended respondents were foreigners who had made it clear that they were not prepared to comply with orders made by the English court, and who had so far refused to comply with orders which had been made, and who were therefore in contempt, did not serve to preclude their arguing why the orders should not be made. If they were right in their contentions that the court lacked personal jurisdiction over them, with the consequence that the orders made without notice to them were to be set aside, their contempt would dissolve. Whilst no-one was going to applaud their behaviour, a refusal to comply with orders which the court may conclude should not have been made, and which it sees fit to set aside, is hardly high treason. *Motorola* had accepted the reality, but also the logic, of the position of the indignant absentee, and the judge was right to do likewise.

The individuals concerned were Italian domiciled and resident. With the issue of contempt cleared out of the way, the next question was therefore how to serve them with process in the application for a freezing injunction. The judge correctly saw that the answer was pursuant to Ground (5),[248] which allows for service out where the claim is for an interim remedy under Civil Jurisdiction and Judgments Act 1982, s 25. The alternative contention, that service could be made on the basis that the respondents were necessary or proper parties to a claim against the defendant,[249] or that they were properly sued as co-defendants to a claim brought against a defendant before the courts for the place of his domicile,[250] were rejected on the footing, surely correct, that these jurisdictional rules applied to substantive claims against the person to be served,

[246] In particular, those parts of the judgment which deal with allegations of material non-disclosure in the obtaining of an order without notice are not commented on here.

[247] [2003] EWCA Civ 752, [2004] 1 WLR 113.

[248] Paragraph 3.1 of Practice Direction B to CPR Part 6.

[249] Ground (3) of Paragraph 3.1.

[250] By reference to Article 6(1) of the Brussels I Regulation.

and not to claims for interim relief. Had the claimants made allegations that the respondents were constructive trustees, dishonest assisters, knowing receivers, conspirators, or some such allegation, it might have been possible to found substantive jurisdiction on some other basis, with the result that jurisdiction to make other orders would have been unrestricted,[251] but no such allegations were made against them, and these grounds for such an assertion of merits jurisdiction were plainly not available. The relief sought against them was interim relief and only interim relief, and jurisdiction was therefore governed by the combination of section 25 and Ground (5).

As to that, the limitations were European and national. The national limitation was that if the substantive liability was not being determined by an English court, an order for interim relief was not to be made if that fact made it inexpedient for the court to act. The European limitation was that the English court was empowered by Article 31, in the sense that Article 31 allowed it to overcome the respondents' presumptive immunity from the jurisdiction of the courts of a Member State in which they were not domiciled and were not being sued, if there was a real connecting link between the assets and the order proposed to be made.[252] The assessment of expediency is a complex matter, but the elements which demonstrated the inexpediency of making the order included the complete absence of any residential or asset-presence connection with England;[253] quite apart from the fact that if the intended respondents were bent on disregarding the order in any event, it was hard to see that there was a sensible point in making it. That made it unnecessary to enquire into whether the test of 'a real connecting link', prescribed by the European Court, to allow Article 31 to be relied on, was present. But it seems plain that the two requirements march hand in hand. The intended respondents had no residential connecting link to England; and the absence of assets means that they did not demonstrate such a link either. Even allowing for the fact that the 'real connecting link' test is of uncertain application where the court is asked to make what looks very much like an asset-freezing order but which has no effect on the assets as such, as is the case with the freezing injunction, it was simply none of the English court's business to tell the intended respondents what they were required to do with or to the assets. The Italian courts were possessed of jurisdiction over the substance of the claim, and the intended respondents were Italian residents. Given those facts, there was little or no connecting link, never mind a real connecting link, to England; and the absence of

[251] *Masri v Consolidated Contractors International Co SAL (No 2)* [2008] EWCA Civ 303, [2009] QB 450; *Masri v Consolidated Contractors International Co SAL (No 3)* [2008] EWCA Civ 625, [2009] QB 503: both noted in this Year Book, 79 (2008), 522–28.

[252] C-391/95 *Van Uden Maritime BV v Deco-Line* [1998] ECR I-7091.

[253] *Banco Nacional de Comercio Exterior SNC v Empresa de Telecomunicaciones de Cuba SA* [2007] EWCA Civ 662, [2008] 1 WLR 1936; *Mobil Cerro Negro Ltd v Petroleos de Venezuela SA* [2008] EWHC 532 (Comm), [2008] 1 Lloyd's Rep 684.

merits jurisdiction meant that it was not expedient to make the order. It may be that divergences will yet be seen to separate the requirement in *Van Uden* that there be a real connecting link with the court asked to make the order, and the requirement that it not be inexpedient to make the order asked for, but this decision brings the two requirements into close alignment, and this can only be for the benefit of the law.

12. Pragmatism in the identification of the lex contractus: *Pablo Star Ltd v Emirates Integrated Telecommunications Co PJSC*,[254] *FR Lurssen Werft GmbH & Co KG v Halle*,[255] *Accentuate Ltd v Asigra Inc*[256]

After a period during which it seemed possible that the choice of law provisions of the Rome Convention on the law applicable to contractual obligations might unsettle the expectation of sensible commercial people, a series of decisions allows it to be said that common sense has, for the time being, asserted itself. The primary area of concern lay with those cases in which the parties had not made a choice of law, with the consequence that the governing law fell to be identified by Article 4 of the Rome Convention, which in general terms subjects the contract to the law of the *country*, as distinct from the system of law, with which it is most closely connected. In many cases this is not problematic: indeed, it may make sense. But there will be cases in which a contract may appear to be more closely connected to country A, when this closeness of connection is measured in factual and geographical terms, but more closely connected to the law of B than to any other law, when this closeness of connection is measured by reference to the law which the terms of the contract exude. The English response has tended to be that Article 4(5) of the Rome Convention can rescue a contract from the application of a law which would be inappropriate; the year's jurisprudence is not hostile to that general approach. At least, it seems so. It has to be admitted that the cases which vouch for this submission tend to arise on jurisdictional applications, in the circumstances of which it may be required only that the contention as to governing law be shown to meet the standard of a good arguable case. In *Pablo Star Ltd v Emirates Integrated Telecommunications Co PJSC*, for example, an application for permission to serve out was resisted on the basis that the contract in respect of which the claim was made was on terms which the defendant had proposed to the claimant, and which provided for the law of Dubai to govern. Had that contention succeeded, service out under Ground 6(c),[257] which allows service out if the contract in question is governed by English law, would not have been permissible. The case was of the common type in which the negotiators each acted as though they wished their own terms, each referring to their own law, to apply to the

[254] [2009] EWCA Civ 1044: Waller, Ward, Wall LJJ.
[255] [2009] EWHC 2607 (Comm), [2010] 2 Lloyd's Rep 20: Simon J.
[256] [2009] EWHC 2655 (QB), [2009] 2 Lloyd's Rep 599: Tugendhat J.
[257] Paragraph 3.1 of Practice Direction B to CPR Part 6.

eventual contract.[258] In such cases, the temptation may be to find that the party seeking to uphold the jurisdiction has done enough to show that a reference to English law was included into the contract. This was all the more so in *Pablo Star*, in which the Court of Appeal took a very dim view of the stance of the defendant in resisting jurisdiction where the claimant sought to recover only £50,000. As to which law governed the contract, the initial steps in the legal reasoning were as follows: (i) as a matter of fact, the defendant's standard terms were not agreed to: this conclusion does not appear to depend on anything other than a standard English analysis of the battle of the forms; (ii) there was therefore no choice and expression of law on the terms proposed by the defendant and defined in its standard terms; (c) it followed that according to Article 4(2) of the Rome Convention, the contract was governed by the law of the country with which it was most closely connected, but that this was presumed to be the law of the claimant, whose performance was characteristic of the contract. That yielded English law: so far, so predictable. But the defendant contended that it could rebut the presumption that English law governed by showing, in accordance with Article 4(5), that the contract was more closely connected with Dubai. It sought to do so by showing that though the factual connections and obligations of the defendant were with Dubai, and that although the project for which the claimant was engaged, was to encourage people in Dubai to shop in Dubai, the claimant was at liberty to perform its duties under the alleged contract wherever in the world it chose. That it chose to do so in England was of no significance for the purpose of the enquiry under Article 4(5) of the Rome Convention. The court disagreed, almost entirely without giving reasons: Waller LJ stated that[259]

> [i]t seems to me that Pablo Star have the better of the argument as to whether EITC are able to rebut the presumption and that they have much the better of the argument that the law with which any contract that Pablo Star establish has its closest connection is English.

He offered no more, and neither did anyone else. As an example of judicial reasoning, it is hard to recall anything thinner, though as the court was plainly cross with the defendant,[260] it was perhaps no surprise that it did not condescend to give lengthy reasons: the less said, the less can what is said be complained about on appeal. But the very capacity for flexibility suggested by Article 4(5) meant that the way was open for the court to reach whichever outcome it felt like. Even though the result was that Article 4(5) did not disturb the conclusion derived from Article 4(2), it is no wonder that the courts of other jurisdictions have gone on the record

[258] The chronology of the inter-party communication is set out at [8]. For another illustration of the problems which arise when the parties do not pay close enough attention to the dispute resolution issue in the negotiation phase, see *Africa Express Line Ltd v Socofi SA* [2009] EWHC 3223 (Comm), [2010] 2 Lloyd's Rep 181, a case on competing choice of court.

[259] At [18]. [260] At [6].

as wishing to restrict Article 4(5) to the point where it is practically impossible to satisfy.[261] It was also notable that the court seemed to attach no significance to the point, which seemed not to be contradicted, that the claimant had chosen to do the work in England which it could, so far as the obligations were spelled out in detail in the contract, have done anywhere. It is a shame that this was not properly analysed. For the significance of the fact that a contracting party *chose* to perform in a particular place, though was not *required* by the contract to undertake the performance in that place, has been held to make the permitted and actual, as distinct from required and contractual place, of performance relevant for the purposes of Article 4(2) of the Rome Convention,[262] irrelevant for the purposes of Article 4(2) of the Rome Convention,[263] and irrelevant for the purposes of Article 5(1) of the Brussels I Regulation.[264] There was room for debate whether the fact that the claimant chose to perform in England could properly prevent the defendant making his case that the contract was more closely connected to Dubai. But the Court of Appeal evidently did not encourage lengthy submission on the point.

It is convenient to make reference at this point to the decision of the European Court in *Intercontainer Interfrigo SC v Balkenende Oosthuizen BV*[265] which was the first occasion for the European Court to give a ruling on the interpretation of the Rome Convention. In a case referred by the Dutch Supreme Court and which called for a decision on, among other things, how strong a case needed to be before a court was entitled to use Article 4(5) to find the contract to be governed by a law other than that otherwise identified by the earlier paragraphs of the Article, the Court simply observed that when the contract was more closely connected to a country than it was to the country identified by the earlier paragraphs of Article 4, it was for the court 'to refrain from applying Article 4(2) to (4).[266] The Court specifically rejected the Dutch contention that Article 4(5) was not to be invoked unless the indicators identified by Articles 4(2)–(4) 'do not have any genuine connecting value'.[267] In other words, Article 4(5) means what it says: that if the contract is more closely connected to a country other than that identified by means of Article 4(2)–(4), then it is to be applied. The flexible, pragmatic, and English[268] approach

[261] The approach taken in the Netherlands is the most extreme in this respect: *Soc Nouvelle des Papeteries de l'Aa v BV Machinefabriek BOA* [1992] NJ 750, noted [1996] LMCLQ 18, though Scotland (*Caledonia Subsea Ltd v Microperi srl* 2002 SLT 1022) runs it close.

[262] *Iran Continental Shelf Oil Co v IRI International Corp* [2002] EWCA Civ 1024.

[263] *Ennstone Building Products Ltd v Stanger Ltd* [2002] EWCA Civ 916, [2002] 1 WLR 3059. Both cases are noted in this Year Book, 73 (2002) 473.

[264] Most recently in *Grand Marine & Energy Ltd v Lloyd Tunnicliffe* [2009] EWHC 2388 (Comm).

[265] Case C-133/08, [2010] 3 WLR 24.

[266] At [63].

[267] At [61].

[268] See, for example, *Samcrete Egypt Engineers and Contractors SAE v Land Rover Exports Ltd* [2002] EWCA Civ 2019, [2002] CLC 533; *Ennstone Building Products Ltd v Stanger Ltd* [2002] EWCA Civ 916, [2002] 1 WLR 3059.

has been confirmed. It is probably fair to say that this will have been as much of a surprise in London as it was in Amsterdam. No doubt when in due course a contract is litigated which falls within the temporal scope of the Rome I Regulation,[269] the Dutch Supreme Court will try again, contending that the revised version of Article 4 is something completely different. In the meantime, the flexible and pragmatic approach to Article 4(5) has prevailed. None of which, however, justifies the judgment in *Pablo Star*.

One would have thought that where the parties have not made and expressed a choice, Article 4 is the mechanism by which the governing law is identified. But there is also support for the view that, in some such cases, Article 3 may still apply, on the ground that a choice of law may still be demonstrated with reasonable certainty. In *FR Lurssen Werft GmbH & Co KG v Halle* it was held that although the contract in question did not contain an expression of choice of law, a choice could still be ascertained on the basis that if the 'other' contract, with which it was closely connected, contained an express choice of English law, a choice of English law for the contract which expressed no such choice, could still be demonstrated from the circumstances, or (as the judge said,[270] perhaps unhelpfully) inferred. A ship construction contract contained an express choice of English law; an associated commission agreement was held to be governed also by English law, but on the basis of unexpressed choice. Perhaps the judge was aware that if the conclusion could not be derived from Article 3, it might be more difficult to get it from Article 4, which places its focus on connections to countries rather than to laws; but the decision, for all that it reaches a pragmatic solution, represents a rather surprising illustration of choice of law.

An express choice of law is, according to the Rome Convention, overridden in only very limited circumstances. Indeed, it can been argued that in those few cases where the chosen law is not dominant, such as where the certain mandatory or protective laws are superimposed, they simply add to the totality of the applicable law. But legal sources outside the Rome Convention may override a choice of law (and of jurisdiction, for the matter of that) contained in a contract and validated by the Rome Convention. Or so it was held in *Accentuate Ltd v Asigra Inc*, in which Reg 19 of the Commercial Agents' (Council Directive) Regulations[271] was held to annul a choice of law for Ontario, and an arbitration agreement for a tribunal in Ontario, to which exception could not otherwise have been taken. The reasoning of the judge was that the Directive, which had been transposed into English law, required him to annul any contractual provision which would have resulted in the non-application

[269] Regulation 593/2008, [2008] OJ L177/6, applicable to contracts concluded after 17 December 2009 (see Corrigendum of 19 October 2009).

[270] At [33].

[271] SI 1993/3053, implementing the Commercial Agents' Directive: Directive 86/653/EEC.

of the substantive rules for compensation set out in Article 17 of the Directive to a commercial agency agreement which otherwise fell within its terms. This had the effect of elevating the Regulations to the status of a mandatory law of the forum, a conclusion which was confirmed and required by *Ingmar GB Ltd v Eaton Leonard Technologies Ltd*,[272] though it is far from clear that the same result would have been reached if the European Court had not already confirmed the mandatory force of the Agents' Directive. Indeed, so mandatory was it that the arbitration agreement was to be regarded as null and void, inoperative, or incapable of being performed,[273] even though the effectiveness of an arbitration agreement was legislatively established pursuant to an international convention, and the Rome Convention[274] does not apply to arbitration agreements. That the agreement on choice of law was likewise annulled was, in the circumstances, predictable. But having annulled the arbitration and choice of law clauses, the judge still had to decide which law governed the contract-minus-these-two-clauses. Whether it was open to him to find that Ontario law still governed was not considered. He simply found that English law, and Article 17, applied by default. In a matter with different facts, there may be more to this past point than there was in the instant case.

13. The meaning of the *lex situs*: renvoi and title to moveable property: *Dornoch Ltd v Westminster International BV (No 1)*;[275] *Dornoch Ltd v Westminster International BV (No 2)*[276]

The issue of how the principle of renvoi affects the rule that questions concerning title to chattels, including questions of priority between claimants, are determined by the *lex situs*, arose twice in the context of an otherwise-impenetrable dispute about marine insurance. A 'mega-size trailer hopper dredger', originally flagged in the Netherlands, had been fatally injured in a collision off the China Sea, and had been towed to a Thai naval dockyard, in all probability to avoid Chinese jurisdiction.[277] The various interested parties seemed to be consumed by intense mutual suspicion, and various manoeuvres were executed, including the sale of the vessel without notice to the underwriters, the further detail of which need not concern us. The eventual litigation required the determination, among other things, of the law which governed the proprietary consequences of the material transactions, in particular the sale while the vessel was in Thailand. The contending laws were Dutch law as the law of the original

[272] Case C-381/98, [2000] ECR I-9305.
[273] Arbitration Act 1996, s 9(4).
[274] Including, therefore, its mechanism for the identification and application of mandatory laws.
[275] [2009] EWHC 889 (Admlty), [2009] 2 Lloyd's Rep 191 (*sub nom The WD Fairway (No 2)*): Tomlinson J.
[276] [2009] EWHC 1782 (Admlty); [2009] 2 Lloyd's Rep 420 (*sub nom The WD Fairway (No 3)*): Tomlinson J.
[277] [2009] EWHC 1782 (Admlty), [2009] 2 Lloyd's Rep 420, [138]: the salvors had been Chinese.

registration of the vessel,[278] Thai domestic law as the local law of the place where the vessel was at the material time, and such law as a Thai court would look to if the question of title were before it for determination. Cometh the hour, cometh the judge: Tomlinson J delivered two magnificent judgments[279] which examined the *lex situs* rule at it applied to property of this enormous, shipwrecked, kind. In the end, the analysis was defeated by the absence of material evidence, but the reasoning of the judge provides a splendid opportunity to reflect on choice of law for tangible moveable property, and an elegantly lethal insight into the process by which evidence of foreign law arrives before the courts.

The first judgment dealt with a number of purely legal issues. They included the question of the law to which an English court would look if it had to decide ownership, or the priority between competing claims to ownership, of the vessel. Even though the dispute arose in the broader context of a battle between insurers and the owner, there was no basis for looking to the law which governed the insurance. That left the *lex situs* to be applied as Dutch law, or Thai domestic law, or the result of the application of Thai rules for choice of law. The judge rejected the claim of the place of registration, influenced in part by the fact that the vessel had been de-registered, which served to point up one of the differences between a share register and a ship register, but also by the fact that, as successive judges and commentators have observed, the more the exceptions to the rule that one looks to the *lex situs*, the less certain the law, which will do no-one any good. It would have been an utter fiction to say that the *situs* of the vessel was in Holland when it was filling up most of a Thai dockyard. For the law to develop by adding to its stock of fictions is not very sensible; and it is all the more so where the place of registration may be concerned with legal title but not with lesser interests. In short and in sum, the ship was in Thailand and not in Holland, and the choice was therefore between the two possible senses of Thai law.

As to these, the authorities allowed the judge a pretty free hand. Until the peculiar decision of Eady J in *Islamic Republic of Iran v Berend*[280] there had probably been a slight preference for the view that if renvoi was part of the choice of law rule for the *lex situs* when the property was immovable, it probably was—though the need for it to be so understood was appreciably less compelling—where the property was a tangible moveable: probably, because although the court of the *situs* may still have control of the thing, the principal characteristic of moveables is, as Mr Carter[281]

[278] But the vessel was de-registered a few days before the sale; it was unregistered at the date of the sale.

[279] The first on various issues determined as 'Phase I' on the basis of an agreed set of facts; the second required more facts to be found, but opened with a re-examination of the question of renvoi.

[280] [2007] EWHC 132 (QB), [2007] 2 All ER (Comm) 132 ((2007) 78 *BYIL* 626).

[281] QC; Fellow of Wadham College, Oxford; Compiler of this Annual Survey until 1994.

gravely informed a generation of BCL students, that they move. But even if Eady J had recoiled from the very idea of renvoi being used to fine-tune the question of which law governed title to moveable property which had turned up in an auction room, there was still a perfectly good reason for the court to open its mind to the possibility that 'Thai law' should mean 'the law which a Thai judge would apply to the issue'. This was because, as the High Court of Australia had made clear in *Neilson v Overseas Projects Corp of Victoria Ltd*,[282] the real function of the principle of renvoi is to allow a court to refine its choice of law rule, the more faithfully to promote the objectives which underpin the choice of law rule in the first place. For the High Court, this meant that for the purpose of the Australian choice of law rule for torts, the *lex loci delicti* meant the *lex* that a court at the *locus delicti* would have applied to the case. As Australian law is still in a state of denial about the utility of the principle of *forum non conveniens*, as *Neilson* took for granted, the next best way to ensure that cases are dealt with as they would have been dealt with if litigated in their natural forum is to deal with them in Australia as they would have been dealt with in their natural forum. If that is correct, then the *lex loci delicti* is the law which a judge at the place of commission of the tort would apply.

But in order to have made this analysis work at all one needed, as the judge made clear, to know what a Thai judge would have done, to which law he would have looked, on the question of priority of title to the vessel. On the first hearing there was no such evidence, with the result that the foundation for the application of a renvoi to such law as the Thai judge would have referred to was absent. The judge therefore left the question open, though adding the observation that to find that there was a role to the principle of renvoi would involve his 'rowing against a strong tide'.[283] But where the judge saw a tide, others might have recognised flotsam. The fact that Lord Diplock saw renvoi as playing no part in the private international law of contract,[284] and that the various legislators who settled the terms of the Private International Law (Miscellaneous Provisions) Act 1995, and the Rome I and Rome II Regulations, excluded renvoi from their instruments, really should not have had any impact on the question which was before the judge, which was a proprietary one of pure common law. For all that, if one is to undertake the kind of investigation proposed by the High Court of Australia, there needs to be an evidential foundation for it.

When the case came back for the taking of evidence, and trial, the judge first had to deal with the loose end left over from the renvoi debate. It took him no time at all. There was evidently nothing in Thai law to suggest that anything other than Thai domestic law would be applied to the

[282] [2005] HCA 54, (2005) 223 CLR 331.

[283] At [87]. Even so, as the only actual decision against renvoi as part of the *lex situs* for moveable property was that of Eady J in *Iran v Berend*, the tide may not have been as strong as all that.

[284] *Amin Rasheed Corp v Kuwait Insurance Co Ltd* [1984] AC 50.

question of title. There was therefore nothing to be done except to interpret the *lex situs* as a reference to Thai domestic law.[285] That concluded the interpretation of Thai law; it also leaves the English authorities a little less open to the application of renvoi in this area than they were before the judgment. But in giving the only answer which was open to him, the judge also shone a light onto the process by which evidence of Thai law was before the court.

It appeared that the claimants' expert, the hapless Mr Wutipong, had originally stated that a Thai court would apply Thai domestic law, but had then 'attempted to resile from his earlier views... in his subsequent oral evidence he attempted to maintain this line, but unconvincingly'. In stating that he preferred the evidence of the defendants' Thai expert, the judge evaluated 'Mr Wutipong's evidence as confused and unconvincing. Indeed, I am constrained to agree with Mr Gaisman that Mr Wutipong's second thoughts on this issue born an uncanny resemblance to the unorthodox submissions made by Mr Milligan at the hearing as to the approach of English private international law to the overlap between contractual and proprietary issues'.[286] No doubt this was entirely correct, and all Mr Wutipong had done was to try and fail[287] to understand a script which had been written for him by others. If this were to be at all representative of the way foreign law is proved in the common law, it is pretty damning: it is one thing to organise the evidence of witnesses of fact into coherent form for it to be given in a witness statement, but it is quite another to write an expert's report so as to put words into his uncomprehending mouth. It does also tend to suggest that if Thai law is going to be applied, it is better done by a Thai court than by Tomlinson J, especially when what may be material provisions of Thai law are agreed on all sides to be impenetrable.[288] The judge may also have reflected to himself that, if he had been asked to make a finding about Thai principles of private international law, it may not have been a completely straightforward exercise. It was quite complicated enough, as the bulk of the second judgment amply demonstrated, to have to decide whether the claimants acquired a proprietary interest in the vessel according to Thai domestic law.

The final question of interest from the perspective of the conflict of laws was whether the English court had any power under the Insolvency Act 1986, ss 423–425, which allows the court to order property which was transferred in fraud of creditors to be re-transferred. It is not, as the judge observed, a provision which is confined in its operation to cases in which there has been a formal insolvency.[289] It is also notorious that the statutory jurisdiction has no express territorial limitation, at least, none which is

285 At [4].
286 At [7]. Further evaluation, at [49], and [150], was no more kind.
287 At [49].
288 At [150].
289 At [126]; see also *IRC v Hashmi* [2002] EWCA Civ 981, [2002] 2 BCLC 489.

expressed in the legislative words,[290] with the consequence that a judge is not obviously precluded from making an order under the Act even though many of the parties were overseas companies and the property was in a Thai naval dockyard. The judge took the view that as the insurance in question was governed by English law, and provided for the exclusive jurisdiction of the English courts, there was sufficient connection to England for sections 423–425 of the Act to be applicable. Indeed, according to the judge, the manner in which non-English connections were contrived by the seller, in order to create difficulties, just went to show how important it was to allow the Act its application. The dispute was, in essence, a dispute arising from a policy of marine insurance, governed by England law and bound to be litigated only in England. As between the parties to the insurance, it was of secondary importance where the thing insured actually was. The connections with England were closer than those which connected the insurance dispute to any other country, with the result that it was uncontroversial that the 1986 Act should apply. It was the correct answer to a question which, when properly exposed in the manner in which the judge did it, was not as complicated as it seemed.

14. The law to be evaded as the proper law of a trust: *Martin v Secretary of State for Work and Pensions*[291]

M, domiciled in England, claimed income support on the ground that he was unfit for work. He neglected to tell the relevant department, the DSS, that there was a house in Brittany of which he was registered as proprietor; and when asked, he denied it.[292] But when the truth came to light, and repayment of income support was demanded, M contended that though the house was in his name, it was beneficially owned by V, also domiciled in England and with whom he lived, on the ground that she alone had financed the purchase. On the question whether the capital value of house was attributable to M, the DSS took the view that it was. M contended that, as a matter of English law, there was an implied, resulting, or constructive trust in favour of V, and that the value represented by the equity in the house was hers but not his. However, French law would, as it was found, have regarded M as absolute owner, having nothing like the implied, resulting or constructive trust of English property law.

This is not the place to get to the bottom of whether the social security legislation relied on did properly mean that the equity in the house was attributable to M if it were not held on trust, but was not attributable to M if there were a trust in favour of v The court was prepared to proceed on that basis, but it does not feel wholly persuasive. For even if there were held to be no trust of the land in France, M would presumably owe a personal obligation to V to reverse his unintended and unjust enrichment; if

290 *Re Paramount Airways* [1993] Ch 223.
291 [2009] EWCA Civ 1289: Mummery, Arden and Elias LJJ.
292 It is hard to avoid the feeling that this did him no end of harm.

there were no intention to gift the house to him, it will have remained ungifted and, one would have thought, no part of his estate. However, the court preferred to pose the question whether the house was held by M on trust for V; and to answer that question by recourse to the law which was 'applicable to the relationship between the people concerned and their property arrangements'.[293] That was held to be French law, according to which M was absolute owner and the value in the house attributable to him. The demand for repayment of income support was therefore sustained, principally because M and V had not obtained the legal advice on which professional tax avoiders, as distinct from those on income support, would have had. The judgment gives off an unattractive smell.

As said, the court approached the question of which law to apply by enquiring as to the law which was 'applicable to the relationship between the people concerned and their property arrangements'. As to the relationship between the parties, it was self-evidently connected most closely to England and to English law. It was asserted or admitted, however, that the house was registered in M's name to prevent its devolving, when V died, to children of hers from an earlier marriage. That single fact, said the court, meant that the reaction against French succession law was 'the dominating presence from the start and permeated the arrangement'.[294] That meant that whether the parties had created a trust of the French land was determined by looking to French law.

Well, maybe. The case was one in which two English people acquired property overseas, as a holiday or rental house; and dealt with the question of whose name should go onto the register of title by asking which would be the best outcome when it came to succession. If the decision is taken at face value, the question whether there was a trust of the property bought will be answered by asking whether the registration was done to reflect the incidents of the parties' relationship, or to produce a particular outcome under the law of the situs. Such a question is as incomprehensible as it is unanswerable. It appears to mean that the question of which law is looked to to determine how property is owned will depend on the motivation for (and on the location of the motivation for) the particular form of ownership.

The court referred to *Lightning v Lightning*,[295] but did not follow its guidance. That case had approved the application of the law 'applicable to the relationship between the parties before [the court] in the absence of any event governed by the *lex situs* destructive of the equitable interest being asserted'. In *Martin*, the relationship between the two English parties was plainly governed by English law, according to which V was beneficiary of a trust of the land, and M had bare legal title. If, however, that beneficial interest was impossibly contrary to French law, the *lex situs*, the

[293] At [29], referring to *Lightning v Lightning Electrical Contractors Ltd*, 23 April 1998.

[294] At [32].

[295] 23 April 1998.

consequence might have been that there was no trust after all, there being an 'event' under the *lex situs* which negated the possibility of the supposed trust.[296] There could be no complaint at that conclusion, though the personal liability of M to V would still remain as a liability on his balance sheet. But the proposition that the French law was applicable 'as France was the country with which the parties' arrangements had the closest connection'[297] is simply not credible, at least unless the word 'arrangements' bears a very peculiar meaning.

One might think that the proposition for which the case appears to stand, that whether there was a trust was governed by French law because the parties made the arrangement to avoid a rule of French law, will cause alarm in the offshore tax evasion industry. These arrangements, which noisily proclaim themselves trusts,[298] are designed to avoid English law: laws on the payment of taxes, laws which make financial provision for a former spouse, and other civilised prescriptions which are so disliked by those whose wealth is surpassed only by their selfishness. The idea that these edifices might therefore be governed by English law might alarm those who had assumed that their structures were governed by the protective *lex portus*: Bahamas, Cayman, British Virgin Islands, Jersey, and all the other tax havens and money laundries. From that point of view, the decision in *Martin* would not be wholly unwelcome. However, in tax havening there will usually be an express choice of law to make sure that the court looks no further to work out who really owns what. By contrast, M and his partner were evidently not the kind of people to take the professional advice which would have guaranteed that the ownership which they intended was given effect in law. *Martin v Secretary of State for Work and Pensions* conforms to the old view that there is one law for the rich and another for the benefit claimant.

15. Prenuptial agreements and financial provision: *Radmacher v Granatino*[299]

A cardinal rule of English family law is that a prenuptial[300] contract made between the parties is, formally at least, without effect as being contrary to public policy. English law has its own statutory mechanisms for dealing with the financial aftermath of divorce, and these do not include giving effect to a pre- or post-nuptial agreement. The reasons are obvious enough, if not especially convincing. Numbered among them are: the fact that, whatever the parties may have thought, the law of maintenance exists to prevent former spouses being a burden on the state;[301] the ineradicable possibility

[296] That being accepted as the effect of French law.

[297] At [30].

[298] The irony of this nomenclature should not go unremarked: the whole point of the enterprise is the mistrust by the tax dodger of everyone other than himself.

[299] [2009] EWCA Civ 649, [2009] 2 FCR 645: Thorpe, Rix, Wilson LJJ. The Supreme Court granted permission for a further appeal.

[300] The same is true for post-nuptial.

[301] *Hyman v Hyman* [1929] AC 601, esp at 614, 629.

that the agreement was infected by a lack of full disclosure and absence of free consent; a slight distaste at the whole idea that those who marry should prepare for divorce: *si vis ducem, para bellum*, may be a motto for our times, but that is a comment about the times; a greater distaste for the blatant demonstration of wealth and selfishness; and the basic truth that whatever the circumstances were when the agreement was made, they may not be the same now. Commercial contracts are one thing; agreements made between spouses or civil partners are quite another. Whether it is the presumption against legal relations, or the fear of undue influence, it is all the same thing: holding parties to such agreements is, in the end, contrary to public policy. In *MacLeod v MacLeod*[302] the Privy Council confirmed that this was still the law, and that it was for Parliament to alter it if it saw fit.

It is also true that other laws see matters differently. The law of Florida regards them as valid, as the Privy Council recorded.[303] And Florida will not be alone. Closer to home, as we must now accept, the laws of many European systems treat such agreements as valid according to their terms. Among other things, this divergence of view encouraged the European Union to see whether it could propose a draft Regulation to harmonise the law, the better to encourage citizens to exercise their right of free movement for something other than forum shopping. And so far, it has failed. The first eleven paragraphs of *Radmacher v Granatino* tell the tale perfectly well. A European Green Paper was produced,[304] but as the United Kingdom, having sounded out those with an interest in the matter, was evidently quite unable to give a coherent response to it, the idea that the 27 Member States might come to terms on which they all agreed was and is fantastical. The project remains mired.

It is further true that the public policy strikes only against the contention by one of the parties that the agreement should or must be enforced as a contract. There is and can be no public policy to prohibit the making of such agreements: they are not unlawful, wicked, or *malum in se*. And if they are made, they form part of the data by which the English court, choosing to apply the *lex fori*, will have before it when determining, in accordance with Matrimonial Causes Act 1973, ss 23–25, what should be ordered. The very broad statutory direction to have regard to 'all the circumstances of the case'[305] certainly allows a judge to receive evidence of an agreement which the parties made. So it is that the Family Division and the Court of Appeal have been increasingly willing to look at the agreements.[306] The proposition that the court should be even more willing where the contract and the marriage and the maintenance have little

[302] [2008] UKPC 64, [2009] 1 All ER 851 (IoM)

[303] At [7], referring to *Posner v Posner* 233 S 2d 381 (Fla 1970).

[304] On July 17, 2006: COM (2006) 400 (final). The intention was that there be a Regulation to be designated 'Brussels III'. In the meantime, the text of a proposed 'Brussels IV Regulation', covering wills and succession, was released on 14 October 2009: COM (2009) 154.

[305] Matrimonial Causes Act 1973, s 25(1).

[306] See, for example, *Crossley v Crossley* [2007] EWCA Civ 1491, [2008] 1 FLR 1467.

to do with England, so lowering the level of engagement of English public policy, is almost inescapable.

So it was when the Court of Appeal had to decide *Radmacher v Granatino*. W, the wealthy German daughter of an even wealthier family, proposed to marry H, a French national whose career path as an international banker had appeared to be pretty stellar.[307] At the ostensible behest of her father, who was said to be threatening to disinherit W if H did not agree to be bound, though also in accordance with the unexpressed[308] wish of W herself, that H do this to prove that he was marrying for love of her rather than for love of her money, H signed a prenuptial agreement, expressed to be governed by German law. This provided for separation of property, and pretty much excluded any right of recourse of either against the assets of the other in the event of divorce. As a matter of German law, and (so far as one can tell) French law, such an agreement would be valid and binding according to its terms. The parties stayed married for only seven years, W then bringing divorce proceedings in London. As a choice of forum, that was pretty astonishing,[309] even though that was where they were then living, as it threatened to have a severe impact on W's ability to hold and limit H to the terms of daddy's prenuptial agreement. The substantial question for the Court of Appeal was whether the traditional view of English law, as the Privy Council had just re-stated it, was one which they would adhere to, in spite of the fact that French and German law would regard this as a valid agreement. Rather surprisingly, perhaps, they declined to accept the guidance the Privy Council had given. Instead, they took the view that while it was not open to W to demand the simple enforcement of the contract, the court would pay close attention to its content in determining what relief to order.

In doing so, the court seemed to be struck by the oddness of the proposition that an agreement made between intelligent adults, both of whom came from countries whose legal systems regarded prenuptial agreements as ordinary and straightforward, and would regard this one as valid, should be set at naught simply because the English courts were seised first[310] and do not regard such agreements as decisive. The Court of Appeal seemed drawn to the position that the old approach was no longer tenable, at least in the light of overseas developments which suggest that the position of the United Kingdom was out of line. If one took the view that the ease of establishing matrimonial jurisdiction should not entail

[307] At least, until he fell back to earth by deciding to go back to university.

[308] It was not suggested that this amounted to a form of non-disclosure which affected the validity of the agreement, for the decision of the court did not, formally at least, depend on the agreement being valid.

[309] Thorpe LJ characterised it as 'seemingly bizarre': at [11].

[310] They were the only courts seised, as it happened. But Thorpe LJ, at [11] was making a more general point about the Brussels II*bis* Regulation and the manner in which it applies a first seised rule to the determination of applications for maintenance. The instrument which will replace it, Council Regulation 4/2009, [2009] OJ L7/1, will have effect in the United Kingdom.

the consequence that all reference to foreign law was then cast aside in favour of the English *lex fori*, then it was necessary to revisit the English hostility to prenuptial agreements. And that is just what the court did.

The broad conclusion was that the contents of the matrimonial contract should be taken very seriously: not taken as conclusive, for the general[311] contract law of vitiating factors would still tend to apply, and the power of the judge to do his duty under Matrimonial Causes Act 1973, s 25 would entail the duty to overlook manifestly unfair contractual provisions. The broader reason was that adults should not be treated like children, and that English law should not estrange itself from Europe *and* (which was the larger surprise) the wider common law world. Waiting for Parliament to sort itself out and then sort out the law of financial provision seemed like a very bad idea.[312]

The difficulty lay in mapping with any precision exactly where the agreement should be allowed to stand. It was not made clear whether its effect depended on whether the parties (either or both) were domiciled in, or had married in, or were now resident in, a country whose law gave effect to matrimonial contracts. It was perfectly plausible that the approach taken to the agreement between H and W would differ from that applied to two English people who had contracted marriage or civil partnership in England, perhaps under the impression that such agreements were not regarded by English law as binding on them.[313] Thorpe LJ was certainly sensitive to such issues, observing that if one were simply to apply foreign law, the unacceptable face of muslim sharia law would not take long to show itself, and that was not the path to fairness.[314] Wilson LJ considered whether the better advice was that the judge may take a 'sideways look' at the law of the country with which the parties[315] had a primary connection:[316] where the parties had made an express choice of law, to disregard

[311] It was not made clear whether this should be understood as a reference to domestic law or to private international law.

[312] As a matter of historical record, at the point when the matter was before the Court of Appeal, April-July 2009, Parliament was paralysed by the exposure of its members' dishonourable misuse of expense accounts. It is small wonder that Thorpe LJ did not seem to think that waiting for legislation was much of an option. In this respect, the political background to *Radmacher v Granatino* was far distant from that in *MacLeod v MacLeod*: Tynwald, the Manx Parliament, must have seemed a reliable and trustworthy body, on whose decision whether to amend the Manx Matrimonial Proceedings Act 2003 it was perfectly sensible to wait.

[313] Rix LJ, at [70], considered that such a distinction in treatment might be justified. He also considered the possibility that if the parties married young, it was simply unreal to treat that agreement as an informed agreement about future circumstances of which neither may have had the slightest inkling.

[314] He could have put it more strongly if he had wanted. The alien nature of muslim family law, and its mistreatment of women (to say nothing of its view of civil partnership) was the principal reason why the government of Sweden, standing alone (to the shame of others) for the decent and humane values of the enlightenment, defended Europe from the proposed Brussels III Regulation. This proposed Regulation might have had the effect of requiring courts in Member States to apply laws which were and are incompatible with civilised values.

[315] Perhaps it is significant that he did not say 'the marriage'.

[316] At [147], and in the cases there cited.

the contents of that law 'would border on the absurd'.[317] The remainder of the judgments were given to the translation of these principles into actual figures.

The outcome is hard to capture with precision; but it is clear that though the *lex causae* for financial provision remains the *lex fori*, the English *lex fori* will not now disregard a pre- or post-nuptial agreement. The question is what regard it will give, and to which agreements. On one view of the matter,[318] there may be two parts to the enquiry. If it is argued that the pre-nuptial agreement is to be given effect, it may first be established that the agreement is valid and binding according to the law under which it derives any authority which it has: it must be intrinsically valid. If Rix LJ was right, and these agreements are in some sense to be treated as being rather closer to commercial contracts than hitherto, then their validity needs to be assessed by reference to a law or laws. The obvious contenders are the law chosen and expressed, where there is one, and the law with which the marriage originally had its closest connection, where no law was expressed as chosen.[319] This would exclude a formal role the law of the place where the parties married, and would similarly exclude the law of the parties' ante-nuptial domiciles.[320] Even so, the private international law of contract contains a wealth of detail concerning the troubles which arise when the contract is impugned, and a law has to be chosen, and one party denies that it is right to refer to a law whose status derives from the existence of the contract which, *ex hypothesi*, one party denies. If the intrinsic validity of the agreement is established, then there will be a second question, which is the extent to which it should be given effect in England, as part of the material to which the court has regard in exercising its broad statutory discretion. The judgments in *Radmacher v Granatino* address the second point, but not the first, for there was no suggestion in the case that the agreement was invalid as a matter of French or German law. Cases in which the agreement is not alleged to be inherently invalid are, from this point of view, easier to deal with, even though the justification for not according them conclusive effect is, for the same reason, harder. And blinkered recourse to the *lex contractus* may not be desirable in cases in which that law makes rather less—or perhaps rather more—of what English law would regard as vitiating factors. It is difficult to commit to a position which would prevent an English court taking a second look at the validity of the agreement by reference to its own sense of what is fair.

On the other hand, if English parties contract a marriage or civil partnership in England, and make such an agreement; and if it is taken that as

[317] At [147].

[318] Though not the view preferred here.

[319] This is broadly consistent with the approach to the effect of marriage on property rights, in Dicey, Morris and Collins, above n. 32, ch 28.

[320] Unless, of course, that same law qualifies for adoption for some other reason.

a matter of English domestic law these agreements are invalid as sources of strict legal obligation, can it really be correct that they are then ignored? Suppose the parties make such an agreement, and that it is governed by the law of the Isle of Man, under the law of which the agreement is, as the Privy Council said, simply void and contrary to public policy. Is it really correct that the agreement will have no impact at all in the English proceedings? It is hard to accept that this should be so, for even if it is not intrinsically valid, that does not mean that it did not happen as a fact. If the agreement is not going to be decisive in the assessment of financial provision, it is not so clear that it needs to be legally valid and binding in the first place: it may be sufficient that it was agreed to, no matter the finer legal consequences. Thorpe LJ may have been right—indeed, it seems quite likely that he was—when he suggested that the judge should give 'due weight' to the agreement, with the clear hint that there is nothing to be gained from asking for particulars of 'due'. After all, if the contract is not to be enforced as such, the case for assessing its validity as though it were to be enforced in a commercial action is considerably weaker. One wonders whether choice of law is the answer to this. A better analogy, given the complex interplay of competing social values, may be to proceed as some cases have done when asking whether an equitable cause of action is available against a person who has done some or all of what is complained about overseas. According to one strand of argument, the correct approach is to apply English equitable principles, but in doing so, to take account of the foreign law, as data, in helping demonstrate whether the conscience of the respondent is affected.[321] In the present context, the choice of law is for the *lex fori*, but in the course of applying it, proper account may be taken of factors which include the parties' intentions as disclosed by a pre- or post-nuptial agreement.

Quite by chance, the Singapore Court of Appeal was confronted by almost the same problem, and in a very substantial judgment in *TQ v TR*,[322] handed down several months before *Radmacher v Granatino* reached the Court of Appeal, came to almost exactly the same conclusion: that though the statutory instruction to the courts when dealing with financial provision did not deal expressly with pre- and post-nuptial contracts, they should be given a great deal of weight where they were governed by a foreign law and were valid according to that law; that notice may still be taken of them even if there is a basis for their invalidity under the *lex contractus*, for not all invalidities are alike; and that it would not be just and equitable for one spouse to ask the court to disregard the terms of an agreement to which substantive objection could not otherwise be taken. In this, the two Courts of Appeal have arrived at much the same point: agreements, and especially foreign agreements, will be taken

[321] See *Kuwait Oil Tanker SAK v Al Bader* [2000] 2 All ER (Comm) 271; *Grupo Torras SA v Al Sabah* [2001] CLC 221.

[322] [2009] 2 Sing LR 961 (noted Leong [2009] Sing LJS 211).

seriously, but the overriding statutory discretion of the court means that the court's hands are not tied. In the Singapore context, as the state provides little or nothing by way of social security, the objections put forward in *Hyman v Hyman* in an English context should perhaps cut less ice. It may also be that, in a contemporary Singapore idiom, one may describe these agreements as an aspiration rather than a pledge. But however it is approached these two cases show the basic instinct of the common law to take account, but not too much account, of an agreement which the parties made. It is, one has to say, the best and fairest outcome to a problem which does not lend itself to a more precise regime for choice of law. No wonder the European Commission is finding this topic more of a challenge than those it usually encounters.

16. Jurisdiction in matters of parental responsibility: *Re I (A Child)*[323]

The Supreme Court of the United Kingdom made its debut in matter of private international law in a case concerning jurisdiction to make orders concerning parental responsibility. It did a very thorough job; the surprising length of the judgments may have been a reaction to its having decided to reverse an experienced Court of Appeal. The parents, M and F, were United Kingdom nationals resident in England but hailing from the Indian sub-continent. When they divorced, the Family Court granted F a residence order which permitted him to take the child of the marriage, Q, to live with him in Pakistan.[324] Three years later, M applied to the High Court for a contact order, by which time F had returned to England, but without Q who remained with his paternal grandparents in Pakistan. In proceedings in which both parents were initially acting in person, the court ordered F to return Q to England to facilitate the contact order. F applied to have the order set aside, but did not challenge the jurisdiction of the court to have made the order in the first place. But as the proceedings ground on, and the parties acquired legal representation, a judge raised the question whether the High Court had ever had jurisdiction to make the order in respect of a child who was then habitually, and perfectly properly,[325] resident in Pakistan. That issue was ordered to be tried. At first instance the jurisdictional issue was argued on the basis of Family Law Act 1986, according to which the court had no jurisdiction to make the order. When the case reached the Court of Appeal, M raised, for the first time, the possibility that the Brussels II*bis* Regulation[326] gave the court jurisdiction; the court held that it did not do so, going on to

[323] [2009] UKSC 10, [2010] AC 319: Lord Hope, Lady Hale, Lord Collins, Lord Kerr and Lord Clarke JJSC; reversing [2009] EWCA Civ 965. The principal judgment was given by Lady Hale, with whose judgment there was agreement even from those Justices who delivered judgments of their own.

[324] The order was made by Hedley J in 2004, pursuant to Children Act 1989, s 13.

[325] That is, not by reason of parental abduction.

[326] Regulation (EC) 2201/2003: [2003] OJ L338/1.

express satisfaction that the outcome, as it saw it, was the same as that resulting from the Family Law Act.[327] On further appeal to the Supreme Court, however, it was held that the English courts had jurisdiction by reason of Article 12 of the Regulation, on the grounds that (i) at the material time, (ii) the parties had accepted the jurisdiction of the English court, (iii) in a matter concerning a child properly resident in a non-Member State (iv) in which the exercise of that jurisdiction would be in the best interests of the child. We may examine the decision under these three heads, starting with the second.

The scheme of this part of the Brussels II*bis* Regulation, so far as it relates to child responsibility, is a rational one. If the court is exercising matrimonial jurisdiction, and the parents accept, expressly or otherwise unequivocally, the jurisdiction of the court in relation to an issue of parental responsibility, the court has jurisdiction under Article 12(1). That jurisdiction comes to an end, however, once the matrimonial issue has been determined, as it had in the instant case, for the claim for contact was instituted after the conclusion of the divorce proceedings. However, Article 12(3) then had the potential to apply, because M and F were both habitually resident in England. All depended on whether the jurisdiction of the court had been accepted by both parents; and it had been. M had invoked the jurisdiction; and although F had opposed and appealed against the contact order, he had not taken any jurisdictional point, which had instead been raised, of its own motion, by the court. This introduces into Article 12 a principle similar to that which operates in civil and commercial matters, according to which initial appearance not preceded, or at least accompanied, by a challenge to the jurisdiction amounts to prorogation by agreement.

However, the jurisdiction of the court had to be so accepted 'at the time the court was seised'. Before the Supreme Court the parties, and then the Justices, managed to make an issue out of the meaning of this expression. All members of the court reached the welcome conclusion that, whatever the expression meant, it had been satisfied on the facts. If it required the parties to have accepted the jurisdiction when the document instituting proceedings was issued,[328] then they had done, because neither[329] had shown any sign of objecting before the court was seised, and neither challenged the jurisdiction of the court after service was made.[330] If it was instead to be no more than an adjectival reference to those persons who had accepted the jurisdiction, then all concerned had done.[331] Indeed,

[327] See at [12].

[328] Article 16(a); cf Article 30 of the Brussels I Regulation.

[329] More particularly, the respondent.

[330] Lord Collins specifically rejected a construction of Article 12 which would have required the acceptance to have taken place, or at least to have been demonstrated, before the court was seised: at [59]. Lord Clarke was not so sure: at [89].

[331] The writer confesses that he does not really understand how such a construction is tenable at all.

though the court was prepared to accept that there was room for disagreement, and that on another day it may appropriate to make a reference to the European Court for a preliminary ruling, it is hard to see why that really is.[332] The principle of Article 12(3)(b) is surely plain for all to see: if the jurisdiction is agreed to by the parents,[333] in the sense that it is not objected to, it may be exercised; if that is not so, then it may not be. It is not obviously necessary to look further into the complexities than that.

A question of scope *ratione personae*, however, looked to be more challenging. Q was, from every perspective, habitually and lawfully resident in Pakistan. It was not obvious that the Brussels II*bis* Regulation applied or ought to apply where the child was lawfully and habitually resident in a non-Member State: such cases might, abduction aside, be thought to better belong before the child's home court. But the Supreme Court thought otherwise. They interpreted the reference in Article 12(3) to a child which had its habitual residence in a 'third state' as extending to a non-Member State; and bolstered that conclusion, primarily justified by *a contrario* reasoning from the other provisions of Article 12, also by recourse to secondary materials.[334] And, one supposes, the perception that the jurisdictional control of the Regulation should not be so easy to side-step. At first sight it may seem tantamount to treating the child as an asset, and jurisdiction rules as being written solely in terms of the parents, the principal jurisdictional rule of Article 12(3), but the requirement that those concerned must have accepted the jurisdiction of the court makes such concerns merely marginal. For the court will not accept jurisdiction in relation to an absent child against the jurisdictional wishes of one of the parents, but only when it has been or is agreed that the court have jurisdiction in matters of parental responsibility. If that is taken as given, the residence of the child in a non-Member State does not seem to impose a necessary jurisdictional barrier; the point is better dealt with under the rubric of whether the exercise of that jurisdiction, in relation to a child habitually resident elsewhere, is in the best interests of the child.

So it was necessary to establish, according to Article 12(3)(b), that the exercise of jurisdiction to determine whether to order contact in favour of M was in the best interests of the child. As to that, the court seems to have proceeded that the natural forum to decide whether M, resident in England, should or should not have contact with a child habitually resident in Pakistan, was England. From the perspective of one with no prior expertise in matter of domestic child law, it is very hard to assess whether this was a compelling approach to the best interests point. It would be quite wrong to suppose that the court harboured a preference for England

[332] Indeed, at [31], Lady Hale came very close to regarding the point as one of little practical importance. It is submitted that at this point, she was absolutely right.

[333] Assuming for the sake of writing that the parents are the only parties involved.

[334] Especially Rauscher, The European Legal Forum, 2005-I, 37–46.

over Pakistan which was based on apprehensions about the approach which might be taken by a Pakistani court, but stranger things have happened at sea; and the speculation[335] that the Pakistani courts might be 'grateful' for the assessment of the English courts on the question of contact with a parent who had been, in the past, the subject of suspicion,[336] was unpersuasive. The question whether a child habitually resident in Pakistan should have contact with a parent resident in England is not, one would have thought, a matter on which the English courts are clearly more appropriate than the courts of Pakistan: one does not need to be a professional sceptic to wonder whether, if the boot were on the other foot and the child habitually resident in England, it would have been considered natural for access to be determined by the Pakistani court of one parent's residence. However, as Pakistan was not a party to the 1996 Hague Convention,[337] Article 12(4) did direct the court to the conclusion that proceedings in England rather than in Pakistan were in the best interests of the child. The conclusion was probably correct, but it may be that the nature of child cases is such that the reasoning in favour of one court rather than another is rarely completely persuasive.

17. Financial provision after overseas divorce: *Agbaje v Agbaje*[338]

The Matrimonial and Family Proceedings Act 1984, Part III, allows a court to grant financial relief after a foreign divorce, and expressly extends that power to cases in which the foreign court has made an order of its own. The safeguards which serve to prevent misuse of the legislation are threefold: an applicant must first obtain the leave of the court;[339] the jurisdiction of the court is defined in terms of prior domicile or habitual residence;[340] and the court is required to consider whether it is appropriate as venue for the application.[341] Unfortunately, those safeguards give litigants—who by this stage are likely to be particularly embittered—plenty apart from the merits to argue about, as *Agbaje v Agbaje* amply demonstrated.[342]

The spouses were Nigerians of retirement age. H was a barrister who had been called in England but who returned to Nigeria in the seventies

335 At [43].

336 At [3], where it was reported that one reason why F had originally been awarded custody had been that injuries to Q had been inflicted, non-accidentally, by M.

337 On jurisdiction, applicable law, recognition, enforcement and cooperation in respect of parental responsibility and measures for the protection of children, of 19th October 1996.

338 [2009] EWCA Civ 1, [2009] 1 FLR 987: Ward, Longmore and Jackson LJJ. Permission to appeal to the Supreme Court of the United Kingdom was given by the House of Lords and the decision of the Court of Appeal was reversed by the Supreme Court: [2010] UKSC 13, [2010] 2 WLR 709.

339 Matrimonial and Family Proceedings Act, section 13.

340 Ibid, section 15.

341 Ibid, section 16. The wording, and the omission of a definite or indefinite article, is deliberate.

342 The court was bothered by the evidently substantial expense: see Ward LJ at [32], [64]; Longmore LJ at [68]. Similar judicial exasperation may be seen in *Cook v Plummer* [2008] EWCA Civ 484, [2008] 2 FLR 1437, [13]. But it may just be that this goes to show how much the issue of jurisdiction matters: at least one of the parties must have thought that the expense would be justified, and this may sometimes be a result of financial judgment rather than the wish to destroy a former spouse.

to establish a practice there; W went with him. Two of the four children of the marriage were educated in England, and a couple of houses were acquired in England to provide a base. But for all practical purposes, the family home and business was in Nigeria until the turn of the century, when the marriage failed. W came to England, the precise date being unclear; H petitioned for divorce in Nigeria; W cross-petitioned in Nigeria; and in due course the Nigerian court dissolved the marriage and made its own order for financial provision. There was no trace of suggestion that it did anything other than justice according to its own law, but W felt that the provision made for her was insufficient for her wants or needs. She therefore sought leave to bring proceedings under the 1984 Act, satisfying the jurisdictional criteria of section 13. H challenged the grant of permission, at which point the case fell into a procedural labyrinth in which both parties seemed happy to allow it to wander. Eventually the case came before a Court of Appeal which was unimpressed with the time- and cost-wasting and which, in a pretty short judgment, held that though the Nigerian order for relief might have been a bit mean, the Nigerian court had not so failed to do justice that it could, in effect, be upset by a further English order for relief. The judge below had said that the case was an exceptional one, in which W could be allowed a second bite at the cherry, but he had not said why, at least in sufficient detail; and the court thought that was reason enough to reverse him.

When the 1984 Act was passed, the mischief at which it was principally aimed was the previous rule which confined the power to order relief to the court which dissolved the marriage. A string of cases on the recognition or non-recognition of foreign judgments had been motivated by the fact that if recognition could be refused, the court could grant a decree of its own, with financial relief to follow. All such shadow boxing came to an end when the court was given power to order relief despite the validity of the foreign divorce. And it must have seemed right that if the court should have power to act even though the parties were divorced, it should also have power to act even though some order for financial provision had been made or not made: there will be some systems in which the approach to financial relief is so far adrift from what English law would consider appropriate that there has to be a power to act.[343]

The principal control mechanism, aside from the duty to apply for leave to make the application, is that the court must consider whether it is appropriate for the order to be made by a court in England. The wording is opaque on the point at which it needed to be clear. The wife in *Agbaje* was living in England, and had been for some time. If there was a court to which it made sense, or would have made sense, for her to look, it was the High Court. But she had participated and claimed in the Nigerian proceedings, and had sought and obtained relief. An unsophisticated

[343] See, for example, *Jordan v Jordan* [1999] 2 FLR 1069, 1080.

version of common sense would suggest that she had chosen her court, and had to live with it. After all, in the commercial sphere, Civil Jurisdiction and Judgments Act 1982, s 34 prevents a party having a second bite at the cherry unless the judgment in their favour but with which they find fault is not entitled to recognition in England. If one adapted that to the context of *Agbaje*, the answer would be that W had brought a claim in the Nigerian proceedings; that there was nothing wrong with the Nigerian judgment which might prevent its recognition in England; and that there was therefore no cause to allow the cherry to bitten at again. The Court of Appeal did not put it in quite those terms, but its cast of mind was clear enough. The marriage was more Nigerian than English; and if one asked whether the Nigerian court had treated her unjustly, the answer seemed to be that it had not. It had been the appropriate court to deal with the matter, by reason of objective connection and by virtue of submission, and that was enough.

The court was aware that if it was not careful, there would be more to the proposition that London had become the divorce capital of the world, but for wives, than tabloid headlines.[344] It is hard to see much wrong with the proposition that the application of the ordinary principles of *forum conveniens* would have pointed to the conclusion that England was not an appropriate place for the application because Nigeria was. The court seemed perfectly content, rightly as it is supposed, to accept that if Nigeria was the natural forum, England was not going to be an appropriate forum: an altogether prefereable approach to that taken by the court in *Cherney v Deripaska*.[345] No doubt there will be some cases—where the foreign court which represents the natural forum would apply some ghastly principles which require the wife to go homeless and penniless and to risk being beaten if she appeared on the streets to beg— in which an exception ought to be made; but in these the intervention of the court will be justified by reference to the wife who will have to satisfy the jurisdictional requirements of section 15.

The court made references to the principles of comity, effectively to bolster its refusal to tread on the toes of the Nigerian judge. This was right enough, though it is hard to see that it added anything of measurable quality to the judgment. The unwillingness of the court to encourage wives to arrive in London for a further bite at the husband's assets was plain enough. It was capable of being defended in English terms, without saying, in effect, that it was all done out of respect for the Nigerian court (and if you don't like the result, don't blame us). The proper question for the court was, given that Parliament had given them the power, whether they should exercise it. The conclusion that they should not in *Agbaje* was sufficiently justified by the fact that the parties had fought this particular battle before the Nigerian courts; that the Nigerian judgment would have

[344] At [52].

[345] See the first of the Notes in this Survey.

met any criteria for recognition which might have been applied to it; and that the general policy of the law ought to be that parties do not get second bites at cherries, especially where there are no issues of child maintenance[346] to bear in mind. There was really no more to be said about it than that. It will be interesting to see whether the Supreme Court wishes to make it any more complicated.[347]

18. The impact of insolvency on arbitration proceedings: *Syska v Vivendi Universal SA*[348]

What happens when an arbitration proceeding is underway in London, the defendant to the claim goes into insolvent administration in Poland, and Polish law provides that on the opening of bankruptcy proceedings, the arbitration clause is annulled and pending proceedings shall be discontinued? That was the issue before the Court of Appeal in *Syska v Vivendi Universal SA*. The answer was to be found in the Insolvency Regulation[349] and the decision of the court was that English law, rather than Polish law, determined the consequence for the pending arbitration of the defendant's insolvency. The case needs only an abbreviated mention because the way the case presented the issues meant that the answer was so clear that it was surprising that the judge gave permission to appeal to the Court of Appeal at all.

A basic division of responsibility is put in place by the Insolvency Regulation. The effect of opening insolvency proceedings, in particular on events which might take place after that opening, is governed by the law of the place where the insolvency is opened.[350] But the effect of the insolvency on legal and arbitral proceedings pending at the time of the opening of the insolvency is a matter for the law which governs those legal or arbitral proceedings.[351] The effect, therefore, was that the impact of the Polish insolvency on the English arbitration proceedings was a matter for English, not for Polish, law.

This result followed, almost inevitably, from the wording of the Regulation. Longmore LJ, in a judgment of exemplary clarity, considered that it followed as a matter of commercial common sense as well: it would strike most people as daft that pending proceedings, designed to ascertain whether the claimant has a right against the defendant (now the insolvent defendant) that he may enforce (now that he may introduce in the insolvency) should, as the judge put it, 'come to a shuddering halt'. If the Regulation had provided otherwise, it would have come as a very great surprise; and it did not. There was therefore no place in the analysis for

[346] Which might fairly be thought to override the strictly inter-spousal issues.

[347] See n 338, above.

[348] [2009] EWCA Civ 677, [2009] Bus LR 1494: Mummery, Longmore and Patten LJJ. The Supreme Court refused to grant permission for a further appeal.

[349] Council Regulation (EC) 1346/2000.

[350] Article 4.

[351] Articles 4(2)(f), which excludes this from the material scope of Article 4, and Article 15.

the rather extraordinary rule of Polish insolvency law, and it was therefore ignored.

However, this regards the Polish rule as one about insolvency proceedings, or about the legal enforceability of agreements to arbitrate. There is, surely, another way to look at the rule of Polish law. It could just as easily be read as a rule which denied, or withdrew, capacity to make an agreement to arbitrate. The proposition that a legal entity has power to do some things and not to do others is a basic and commonplace one; and it would not have been difficult to read the Polish rule as one which removed the capacity of the company to bind itself to an agreement to arbitrate. It said: 'Any arbitration clause concluded by the bankrupt shall lose its legal effect as at the date bankruptcy is declared and any pending arbitration proceedings shall be discontinued'. It does not appear to have been put to the court that the effect of the Polish law was to incapacitate the Polish company, and to deny its capacity to arbitrate. Indeed, this conclusion appears to have been arrived at by the Swiss Federal Tribunal in proceedings before it arising from an ICC arbitration in Geneva.[352] It is not clear that this is correct, for in the end the answer presumably depends on knowing the correct characterisation and legal impact of the Polish law. For the English court to deal with the question without seemingly being asked to consider whether the Polish company had been incapacitated by its own law was not altogether satisfactory, but as the material required to discuss the issue properly is not to be found in the judgment, there is no more to be said.

[352] *Vivendi SA v Deutsche Telekom AG*: 4A_428/2008, 31 March 2009.

United Kingdom Materials on International Law 2009

Compiled by Kaiyan Kaikobad,[1] Jacques Hartmann,[2] Sangheeta Shah[3] and Colin Warbrick[4]

1. This selection of UK materials on international law (UKMIL) is made from published sources. It does not purport to include everything that could be of interest to an international lawyer but it is not wholly restricted to materials that could be called 'state practice' in the strictest sense: some context is provided.

   We have to make very considerable exclusions of material that we know would be of interest to some international lawyers. We bear in mind first, the need to avoid the purely ephemeral, and second, to exclude materials that are concerned mainly with the UK's implementation of the international law of co-operation, particularly at the general level. We are very sparing with matters of EU law, though we report some EU positions on questions of international law with which the UK is associated.

   There is only limited material on UK treaties because the texts and explanatory memoranda are readily available on the web: <www.fco.gov.uk/treaties>.

   Extracts are generally reproduced in their original form, which leads to inconsistencies, e.g. in spelling ('judgement'/'judgment') or capitalisation 'UN charter' or designation ('Chapter Seven'/'Chapter VII'/' Chapter 7').

   We have inserted a small amount of editorial material in the form '[...Ed.]' where it appears to be helpful to do so.

   Cross-references to the present edition of UKMIL are written 'See **16/14**' and to previous editions of UKMIL are written, 'See **UKMIL [2008] 16/1**'.

2. Hansard references are to the Web version. There may be minor discrepancies between the column references in the Web edition and the bound volumes.

[1] Brunel Law School.
[2] Lauterpacht Centre for International Law, Cambridge.
[3] School of Law, Nottingham University.
[4] The Birmingham Law School.

References to Hansard are given in the following forms:

Commons—HC Deb 13 November 2001 Vol 374 c345 or c134W or c101WH or c1WS, where W, WH and WS stand for Written Answers, Westminster Hall and Written Statements;

Lords—HL Deb 8 October 2002 Vol 639 or 16 October 2003 Vol 653 cWA125, where WA stands for Written Answer or HL Deb 29 January 2003 Vol 643 cGC170 where GC stands for Grand Committee.

3. The texts of Statutes and Statutory Instruments (SIs) are not normally reproduced, though references will be given to those which are of international law interest. Occasionally, the full text of SIs will be included.

4. Some sources are given as <www.fco.gov.uk>. These are references to Press Releases or Speeches on the FCO website: search for the date given for the item in the text.

5. From its start in 1978 and up to and including 1996 the materials in UKMIL were classified on the basis of the Model Plan for the Classification of Documents concerning State Practice in the Field of Public International Law adopted by the Committee of Ministers of the Council of Europe in its Resolution (68) 17 of 28 June 1968. The Committee of Ministers considered that developments in public international law since 1968 made it necessary to amend the Model Plan. Accordingly, by Recommendation (97) 11 of 12 June 1997, it adopted an Amended Model Plan as a contribution by the Council of Europe towards implementing General Assembly Resolution 2099 (XX) on technical assistance to promote the teaching, study, dissemination and wider understanding of international law. The present issue of UKMIL is based on the 1997 Amended Model Plan.

6. We are glad to acknowledge the assistance of Joanna Foakes and Diana Brookes and their colleagues in the Legal Adviser's Department of the Foreign & Commonwealth Office.

7. We are grateful for financial assistance in the preparation of UKMIL to the Whittuck Trust.

INDEX

C. Types of States
   1. Unitary States, federal States and confederations
   2. Personal and real unions
   3. Protected States
D. Formation, continuity, extinction and succession of States
   1. Conditions for statehood
   2. Formation
   3. Identity and continuity
   4. Extinction
   5. Succession
      (a) Cases of State succession
         (i) Union with or without the demise of the predecessor State
         (ii) Dismemberment
         (iii) Separation
         (iv) Newly independent States
      (b) Effects of State succession
         (i) Territory and other areas under national jurisdiction
         (ii) Nationality
         (iii) Succession in respect of treaties
         (iv) Archives
         (v) Debts
         (vi) Property
         (vii) Responsibility
         (viii) Other rights and obligations
E. Self-determination

II. International organizations
   A. In general
      1. Status and powers
         (a) Personality
         (b) Privileges and immunities of the organization
         (c) Power, including treaty-making power
      2. Participation of states in international organizations and in their activities
         (a) Admission
         (b) Suspension, withdrawal, expulsion
         (c) Obligations of membership
         (d) Representation of States, including privileges and immunities
      3. Legal effect of the acts of international organizations
      4. Personnel of international organizations

PART EIGHTEEN: NEUTRALITY AND NON-BELLIGERENCY

PART NINETEEN: LEGAL ASPECTS OF INTERNATIONAL RELATIONS AND CO-OPERATION IN PARTICULAR MATTERS 931

Part One: International Law in General

Part One: I.A. *International Law in General—Nature, basis, purpose—In general*

1/1

The Foreign Secretary replied to the Foreign Affairs Committee's (FAC) Report on 'Global Security: Non-Proliferation'. The FAC had written:

The rules-based approach: 63. We conclude that the rules-based approach to counter-proliferation taken by the Government has been moderately successful thus far and has greater prospects of being so than any alternative approach. However, we further conclude that more priority must be given to the enforcement of rules-based regimes. We recommend that the Government should continue to press for national implementation of treaty obligations, and strongly support verification mechanisms. We further recommend that the Government should advocate the inclusion in future international agreements of a defined set of 'disagreeable consequences' that would act as a deterrent to states flouting their commitments or withdrawing. (Paragraph 358)

The Government said that:

[it] agrees with the Committee on the critical importance of strengthening existing verification regimes and enforcement mechanisms to ensure compliance with non-proliferation obligations and effective and credible international rules-based non-proliferation architecture. In his speech on 17 March, the Prime Minister set out the Government's view that the international community should ensure that there are appropriate mechanisms preventing proliferation with clear, tough and immediate sanctions for those who break the rules. We therefore consider the unanimous condemnation of a nuclear test by the DPRK and the adoption of another set of targeted sanctions by the UN Security Council in its Resolution 1874 as encouraging. The Government will continue to work with the P5, EU, UN Security Council and other international partners to sustain pressure on countries of concern, including by the adoption of additional sanctions. The Government also shares the Committee's view that there might be value in considering innovative proposals to deal preventively with non-compliance and withdrawal, with a view to deterring states' flouting their non-proliferation commitments and withdrawing from the Treaty. This is the objective of the proposal put forward in a working paper by the European Union at the 2007 NPT Preparatory Committee, referenced above. The Government will continue to engage with partners on this and other proposals in the run-up to the 2010 NPT Review Conference. While giving due account to the UN Security Council's primary responsibility for tackling threats to international peace and security, we will also give consideration to other proposals and ideas to deter non-compliance, including the Committee's recommendation to advocate the inclusion of a defined set of "disagreeable consequences" in any future international agreement.

(Fourth Report from the Foreign Affairs Committee, 2008–2009, Global Security: Non-Proliferation, Response of the Secretary of State for Foreign and Commonwealth Affairs, Cm 7692)

1/2

The FAC put questions to an FCO Minister about the Government's 'rule-based' approach to proliferation and disarmament matters. The Minister said:

[The policy] has had some considerable success, but the scale of the threat and the challenge is enormous. Just a few years before the establishment of the nuclear non-proliferation treaty in 1968, President Kennedy had said that by the 1970s we would have in excess of 20 nuclear weapon states—that was not the reality. In that sense, the NPT has worked. We need stronger verification mechanisms and greater universality, but it has worked. If you look at the chemical weapons convention, you will see that we are making progress towards the eradication of stockpiles, and there are similar moves under the biological and toxins weapons convention.

Given where we started, again going back to the NPT, our track record, and that of the US—50% down on its arsenals from the height of the cold war—progress has been made. But bluntly, given the scale and the seriousness of the challenge, we must do more, and that is why we want a re-invigorated NPT to come out next year, a comprehensive test ban treaty and an urgent start to negotiations on fissile material cut-off. (Q. 216)

The Minister was asked about the enforcement of non-proliferation and disarmament treaties. He said:

Specifically on the NPT, in the review conference next year, we must generate political commitment to re-invigorate the bargain that is at the heart of the NPT—so, while the nuclear weapons states continue to make real progress on multilateral disarmament, we rein in rogue states that are seeking to get around the treaty. We need a stronger International Atomic Energy Agency and a number of different initiatives to try to get greater adherence.

But the blunt reality is, yes, you can establish an international treaty, have sanctions—which is part of the debate that we are looking at—and have activity at the level of the UN Security Council to focus on states of concern, but you still run the risk that some people will try to get around it, and that is what we have to ward against. (Q. 217)

It was put to the Minister that 'a more holistic approach' to disarmament and arms control would be better than concentrate on individual weapons systems. The Minister said:

[I]f you want real focus on the issues, you have to look at them in their own right. Although there are ongoing, significant challenges, the track record of the NPT is relatively good. If you look at chemical weapons, leading up to the 2012 deadline, you see that real progress is being made there. So I think that merit of a rules-based approach, but one that focuses specifically on the different types of disarmament that is needed, is the right one. (Q. 218)

(FAC, Fourth Report: Global Security: Non-Proliferation, HC222 (2009))

1/3

The Government were asked whether adherence to the international rule of law and to the United Kingdom's obligations to the United Nations would remain paramount in their future policy towards Iran. An FCO Minister wrote:

As a matter of absolute principle, UK policy is made in accordance with international law, and we take our obligations to the UN very seriously.

We also expect Iran to abide by its own international obligations, including by respecting the international human rights commitments to which it is signed up, and abiding by the five UN Security Council resolutions passed since 31 July 2006.

(HL Deb 24 February 2009 Vol 708 cWA55)

Part One: I.C. *International Law in General—Nature, basis, purpose—Soft law*

1/4

The Foreign Secretary replied to the FAC's Report on 'Global Security: Non-Proliferation'. The FAC had written:

Action against ballistic missile proliferation

37. We conclude that the proliferation of ballistic missile technology is a significant security concern. We further conclude that the Government is correct to acknowledge that stronger action is required to curb the international transfer of ballistic missile technology. We recommend that in its response to this Report, the Government should set out specific steps which it plans to take to this end. (Paragraph 228)

The Government replied:

The transfer of missile technology is covered by the Missile Technology Control Regime (MTCR) which is a voluntary association of countries which share the goal of non-proliferation of unmanned delivery systems through the use of export controls. The UK is an active member and has contributed ideas to the intercessional meeting of the MTCR on how to improve the regime. This included ideas on facilitating the way partners work together outside of the annual meetings and improvements to the electronic secretariat and related documentation. The UK has also worked on amendments to the technology annex to make sure it keeps pace with current developments in missile technology, and we are currently working with specific countries on ways to improve export controls.

The UK is one of the original subscribing states of the Hague Code of Conduct [for text, see <www.armscontrol.org/documents/icoc>, Ed.] which seeks to limit ballistic missile proliferation. The Code consists of a set of general principles and limited confidence building measures (CBM's), including annual declarations by each subscribing state on its space and ballistic missile policies and pre-launch notifications. The UK fulfils its obligations with regard to the CBM's and has participated in a working group meeting to look at ways of improving the

Code. This has led to a planned EU outreach project to non subscribing states to explain the benefits of membership.

(Fourth Report from the Foreign Affairs Committee, 2008–2009, Global Security: Non-Proliferation, Response of the Secretary of State for Foreign and Commonwealth Affairs, Cm 7692)

1/5

The UK representative said in the debate in the Sixth Committee of the General Assembly on the Report of the ILC (A/64/10) on the question of the protection of persons in the event of disasters:

Turning first to Chapter VII of the Report of the International Law Commission on the protection of persons in the event of disasters, the United Kingdom welcomes the careful consideration given by the Commission to this topic and notes that the Commission has now embarked upon the task of producing draft articles. We also thank the Special Rapporteur, Mr. Valencia-Ospina, for his continued work on this topic.

The United Kingdom would like to reiterate the importance of this work fitting with the work of the 30th International Conference of the Red Cross and Red Crescent, which adopted *Guidelines for the Domestic Facilitation and Regulation of International Disaster Relief and Initial Recovery Assistance* [http://ocha.unog.ch/drptoolkit/PreparednessTools/IL%20Frameworks/IDRL%20guidelines%20-%20en.pdf, Ed.] The United Kingdom supports the Guidelines and greatly values the efforts of The International Federation of Red Cross and Red Crescent Societies. We would urge the Commission to avoid duplicating this work; it is unclear at present how it is envisaged that the two will interact.

The United Kingdom agrees that the primary focus of the work on this topic should be on States, whilst acknowledging that there is a role for other actors. The United Kingdom agrees with the view expressed by some members that the Commission should proceed on the basis that the notion of a right to humanitarian assistance does not imply a right to impose assistance on a State that does not want it. Further, we would welcome a needs-based, rather than a rights-based approach. This would have the additional benefit of consistency with the aforementioned Guidelines.

The United Kingdom agrees with the suggestion that a draft article on objectives be prepared, separate to that on scope. We further suggest that "adequate and effective" in article 1 be replace with "timely and effective". It may be helpful if the terminology of the "protection" of persons was revised to refer to assistance and relief. The United Kingdom would welcome further work to consider whether or not this topic should cover all stages of disasters, and on the definition of disaster, which is currently very wide. Such work should have due regard to existing definitions. The United Kingdom notes that the draft articles clearly remove international humanitarian law from the scope of this work, and we would welcome further work on the delimitation of the topic, including avoiding any duplication with the Responsibility to Protect principles (perhaps by excluding this from the definition of disaster) and, for the avoidance of doubt, clarification that consular assistance is also a separate area. Considerations such as the scope, definition of disaster, and scope of the duty of cooperation will need to be revisited once the text is complete. The United Kingdom therefore suggests that all three draft articles be considered in more detail, as and when the Commission has a better idea as to the scope and direction that the work on this topic will take. Finally, regarding the form of the Commission's work, the United Kingdom believes that the codification or progressive development of comprehensive and detailed rules is likely to be unsuitable for this topic. In our view, the development of non-binding guidelines or a framework of principles for States and others engaged in disaster relief is more likely to be of practical value and enjoy widespread support and acceptance. The United Kingdom welcomes further discussion on the proposed future areas of work on this topic.

(Sixth Committee 64th Session of the United Nations General Assembly 29 October 2009. Text supplied by FCO)

Part Two: Sources and Codification of International Law

Part Two: II. *Sources and Codification of International Law—Codification and progressive development of international law*

2/1

The FCO Legal Adviser said in the debate in the Sixth Committee of the General Assembly on the Report of the ILC (A/64/10) on the issues facing the ILC:

I would like to make some introductory remarks about wider issues facing the Commission. In respect of the Commission's long term programme of work, there has been a sense for some time that the Commission may be running out of core topics of international law. We were therefore pleased to note that the Working Group on the Long-term Programme of Work, under the chairmanship of Mr Enrique Candioti, continues to be active and to study ideas for new topics. It is crucial that decisions on whether a new topic should be embarked upon are taken after careful consideration within the Commission, preferably after States have had an opportunity to offer comments in the Sixth Committee. Such debate within the Commission is necessary if new subjects are to be chosen that will result in work of practical use. The United Kingdom welcomes the Commission's decision to devote at least one meeting at its sixty-second session to a discussion on "Settlement of disputes clauses", and that in this respect the Secretariat has been requested to prepare a note on the history and best practice of the Commission in relation to such clauses, taking into account recent practice of the General Assembly. As we reflect on the work of the Commission, a key question is whether the outcome of the work of the Commission ought in all cases to lead to a codifying treaty text. This has very properly been the norm over the past 60 years of the Commission's work. As the Commission explores new topics, however, it may be that new forms of work would be appropriate. The United Kingdom would encourage the Commission to be flexible on the final form of its work. Draft articles with a view to a treaty or convention may not be right for all subjects. Some topics are not yet ready for codification or progressive development in the traditional sense and may benefit from more non-traditional outcomes; perhaps in the form of studies.

The United Kingdom welcomes the decision, on a pilot basis, to place the edited summary records of the work of the Commission up to 2004 on the Commission's website. In the past the publication of the summary records has taken up to 10 years; the United Kingdom agrees with the Commission that there is a need to expedite publication of the summary records of the Commission, and hopes that even more progress can be made in this regard. Is there any reason why the provisional records cannot be placed on the website within a few weeks?

(Sixth Committee 64th Session of the United Nations General Assembly 27 October 2009. Text supplied by FCO)

2/2

The UK representative said in the debate in the Sixth Committee of the General Assembly on the Report of the ILC (A/64/10) on the question of shared natural resources:

The United Kingdom would like to recall its statement to this Committee last year expressing our serious doubts about the usefulness of the Commission seeking to codify or develop a set of draft articles or guidelines relating to the oil and gas aspects of the topic shared natural resources. As we observed on that occasion, our experience of negotiating agreements in this area is that, whilst States should be encouraged to cooperate with each other on these matters, the content of such arrangements and the solutions reached are largely the result of practical considerations based on technical information, which are bound to differ in accordance with the specificities of each case. We recall that other States with practical experience in this field made similar observations. Therefore, whilst we would be willing to answer the Commission's questionnaire, the clear view of my Government is that the work and expertise of the Commission would be better directed towards projects which are likely to yield results of real utility to States.

(Sixth Committee 64th Session of the United Nations General Assembly 29 October 2009. Text supplied by FCO)

2/3

The UK representative said in the debate in the Sixth Committee of the General Assembly on the Report of the ILC (A/64/10) on the question of treaties over time:

On treaties over time, the United Kingdom feels that the Study Group Chairman should be guided by a narrower approach to this issue, focusing on subsequent practice and agreement, rather than attempting a broader view taking into account all the possible factors that might affect the operation of a treaty over the span of its existence. In practice, issues such as spent treaties, supervening impossibility of performance, dispute resolution, interpretation, termination or withdrawal are all dealt with to a greater or lesser extent by reference to the original treaty provisions, or with reference to the residual rules of the Vienna Convention on the Law of Treaties and parallel rules of customary international law. It is not clear to us that it will be either practical or possible to devise guidelines or draft articles that go much further than the existing articles of the VCLT. However, if the work of the ILC identifies any significant lack of practice, jurisprudence or guidance in this area, then this would be useful and merit further consideration. We look forward to Mr Nolte's report in due course.

(Sixth Committee, 64th Session of the United Nations General Assembly, 2 November 2009. Text provided by FCO)

Part Three: The Law of Treaties

Part Three: I.C. *The Law of Treaties—Definition, conclusion, and entry into force—Reservations, declarations, and objections*

3/1

The instrument of ratification of the undermentioned Agreement by the Russian Federation was accompanied by a statement, an English translation of which reads as follows:

In order to implement the Agreement among the States Parties to the North Atlantic Treaty and the Other States Participating in the Partnership for Peace Regarding the Status of Their Forces, signed June 19, 1995, the Russian Federation proceeds from the following understanding of the provisions of the Agreement among the Parties to the North Atlantic Treaty Regarding the Status of Their Forces, of June 19, 1951 (hereinafter the Agreement): 1) the provision of Article III (4) of the Agreement, which obligates the authorities of the sending State to immediately inform the authorities of the receiving State of cases where a member of a force or of a civilian component fails to return to his country after being separated from the service, shall also apply to cases where those persons absent themselves without authorization from the site of deployment of the force of the sending State and are carrying weapons; 2) on the basis of reciprocity, the Russian Federation will understand the words 'possess arms' used in Article VI of the Agreement to mean the application and use of weapons, and the words 'shall give sympathetic consideration to requests from the receiving State' to mean the obligation of the authorities of the sending State to consider the receiving State's requests concerning the shipment, transportation, use, and application of weapons; 3) the list of offenses set forth in subparagraph c of Article VII (2) is not exhaustive and, for the Russian Federation, includes, apart from those enumerated, other offenses that are directed against the foundations of its constitutional system and security and that are covered by the Russian Federation Criminal Code; 4) pursuant to Article VII (4) of the Agreement, the Russian Federation presumes that the authorities of the sending State have the right to exercise their jurisdiction in the event that at sites where the sending State's force is deployed, unidentified persons commit offenses against that state, members of its force, and members of its civilian component, or their family members. When a person who committed an offense is identified, the procedure established by the Agreement takes effect; 5) the assistance mentioned in subparagraph a of Article VII (6) of the Agreement is provided in conformity with the legislation of the requested State. In providing legal assistance, the competent authorities of the States Parties to the Agreement interact directly, and if necessary, through the appropriate higher authorities; 6) the Russian Federation allows importation of the goods and vehicles mentioned in Article XI (2), (5) and (6) of the Agreement, and the equipment and items mentioned in Article XI (4) of the Agreement which are intended for the needs of the force, in accordance with the terms of the customs regime for temporary importation that were established by the customs legislation of the Russian Federation. In this connection, such importation is carried out with full exemption from payment of customs duties, taxes, and fees, except for customs fees for storage, customs processing of goods, and similar services outside of the designated places or hours of operation of the customs authorities, and for the periods provided for in the Agreement if such periods are expressly stipulated in the Agreement. The Russian Federation presumes that the procedure and terms for importation of the goods mentioned in Article XI (4) of the Agreement and intended for the needs of the force will be governed by separate agreements on the sending and receiving of forces between the Russian Federation and the sending State. None of the provisions of Article XI, including paras. 3 and 8, restrict the right of Russian Federation customs authorities to take all necessary steps to monitor compliance with the terms for importation of goods and vehicles provided for by Article XI of the Agreement, if such measures are necessary under Russian Federation customs legislation. The Russian Federation presumes that the sending State will send confirmation to the Russian Federation customs authorities that all goods and vehicles imported into the Russian Federation in accordance with the provisions of Article XI of the Agreement and with separate arrangements on the sending and receiving of forces between the Russian Federation and the sending State may be used solely for the purposes for which they were imported. In the event they are used for other purposes, all customs payments stipulated by Russian Federation legislation must be made for such goods and vehicles, and the other requirements set by Russian Federation legislation must also be fulfilled. Transit of the aforesaid goods and vehicles shall be carried out in accordance with Russian Federation customs legislation. Pursuant to Article XI (11), the Russian Federation declares that it permits the importation into the customs territory of the Russian Federation of petroleum products intended for use in the process of operating official vehicles, aircraft, and vessels belonging to the forces or the civilian component, with exemption from the payment of customs duties and taxes in accordance with the requirements and restrictions established by Russian Federation legislation. The Russian Federation permits the importation of the vehicles that are mentioned in Article XI (2), (5) and (6) of the Agreement and intended for personal use by members of the civilian component and their family members under the terms of temporary importation that are established by Russian Federation legislation. The Russian Federation presumes that customs processing of goods imported (exported) by members of the civilian component and their family members and intended solely for their personal use, including goods for initially setting up a household, shall be carried out without the exacting of customs payments, except for customs fees for storage, customs processing of goods, and similar services outside the designated places or hours of operation of the customs authorities. 7) The Russian Federation also presumes that documents and materials appended to them that are sent to its competent authorities within the framework of the Agreement will be accompanied by duly certified translations thereof into the Russian language.

The UK lodged the following objections with the United States, as depositary, to the statements made by Russia on ratifying the Agreement:

The United Kingdom has the honour to refer to the statements made by the Russian Federation upon its ratification of the Agreement amongst the States Parties to the North Atlantic Treaty and Other States Participating in the Partnership for Peace Regarding the Status of Their Forces, signed on June 19, 1995 ("the Partnership for Peace Agreement") and the Additional Protocol thereto. In connection with its implementation of the Partnership for Peace Agreement, the Russian Federation has made these statements with respect to certain provisions of the Agreement among the Parties to the North Atlantic Treaty Regarding the Status of Their Forces, signed on June 19, 1951 ("the NATO SOFA").

The provisions of the NATO SOFA apply by virtue of Article I of the Partnership for Peace Agreement to the Parties to the Partnership for Peace Agreement as if they were Parties to the NATO SOFA, except as otherwise provided for in the Partnership for Peace Agreement and any Additional Protocol thereto.

Article III(4) NATO SOFA. The United Kingdom considers that the Russian statement purports to modify the legal effect of the Partnership for Peace Agreement in its application to the Russian Federation in respect of Article III(4) of the NATO SOFA which applies by virtue of Article I of the Partnership for Peace Agreement and is accordingly a reservation. The United Kingdom objects to this reservation because it seeks to create a new obligation for Parties to the Partnership for Peace Agreement.

Article VI NATO SOFA. The United Kingdom considers that the Russian statement purports to modify the legal effect of the Partnership for Peace Agreement in its application to the Russian Federation in respect of Article VI of the NATO SOFA which applies to the Russian Federation by virtue of Article I of the Partnership for Peace Agreement and is accordingly a reservation. This seeks to create a new obligation for Parties to the Partnership for Peace Agreement, on the basis of reciprocity. The United Kingdom objects to this reservation and does not accept that it would be applied on a reciprocal basis between itself and the Russian Federation.

Article VII (2c) NATO SOFA. The United Kingdom is concerned by the breadth of the Russian statement in respect of Article VII(2c) NATO SOFA. To the extent that any offences directed against the foundations of the Russian constitutional system and security go wider than those which can be considered to fall within Article VII (2c), the United Kingdom considers that the statement modifies the legal effect of the Partnership for Peace Agreement in its application to the Russian Federation in respect of Article VII(2c) of the NATO SOFA which applies to the Russian Federation by virtue of Article I of the Partnership for Peace Agreement and amounts to a reservation. The United Kingdom objects to the statement on the basis that it appears very wide in scope and does not clearly define for the other Parties to the Partnership for Peace Agreement the scope of the list of offences applying in the case of the Russian Federation.

Article VII(4) NATO SOFA. The United Kingdom considers that the Russian statement purports to modify the legal effect of the Partnership for Peace Agreement in its application to the Russian Federation in respect of Article VII(4) of the NATO SOFA which applies to the Russian Federation by virtue of Article I of the Partnership for Peace Agreement. It is accordingly a reservation.

The United Kingdom objects because it purports to create a new right for the Russian Federation under the Partnership for Peace Agreement.

Article VII (6a) NATO SOFA. The United Kingdom considers that the Russian statement purports to modify the legal effect of the Partnership for Peace Agreement in its application to the Russian Federation in respect of Article VII (6a) of the NATO SOFA which applies to the Russian Federation by virtue of Article I of the Partnership for Peace Agreement. It is accordingly a reservation. The United Kingdom objects to this reservation because it seeks to create a new right for the Russian Federation in the event that the Russian Federation is the requested State and a corresponding obligation for the other Parties when they are the requesting State.

Article XI NATO SOFA. The United Kingdom considers the Russian statements purport to modify the legal effect of the Partnership for Peace Agreement in its application to the Russian Federation in respect of Article XI of the NATO SOFA which applies to the Russian Federation by virtue of Article I of the Partnership for Peace Agreement. They are accordingly reservations. The United Kingdom is particularly concerned by the numerous references to national legislation, the intention not to treat official documents under official seal as inviolable and the purported creation of new obligations for the other Parties to the Partnership for Peace Agreement. It accordingly objects to these reservations.

Certified Translations. The Russian statement would create an additional obligation for the other Parties to the Partnership for Peace Agreement without their consent in respect of the application of the NATO SOFA which applies to the Russian Federation by virtue of Article I of the Partnership for Peace Agreement. The United Kingdom accordingly considers that this statement purports to modify the legal effect of the Partnership for Peace Agreement. It is therefore a reservation. The United Kingdom objects to it on the basis that it purports to create an obligation for the other Parties to the Partnership for Peace Agreement.

The United Kingdom is of the view that the cumulative effect of the reservations is to undermine the integrity of the Partnership for Peace Agreement and also the NATO SOFA as it is applied by virtue of Article I of the Partnership for Peace Agreement. The United Kingdom considers that the entry into force of the Partnership for Peace Agreement between itself and the Russian Federation is precluded. Accordingly the Partnership for Peace Agreement does not apply between the United Kingdom and the Russian Federation.

(Agreement among the States Parties to the North Atlantic Treaty and the Other States Participating in the Partnership for Peace regarding the Status of Their Forces Brussels 19 June, 1995, (2000) UKTS No 49, Cm 4701. Treaty Series No. 17 (2008), Fourth Supplementary List of Ratifications etc for 2008, Cm 7699)

3/2

On 18 November 2008, the Secretary–General of the United Nations, as depositary, received from the government of United Kingdom a notification, as follows:

[T]he Government of the United Kingdom withdraws the following reservations, made at the time of ratification of the Convention [on the Rights of the Child]:

The United Kingdom reserves the right to apply such legislation, in so far as it relates to the entry into, stay in and departure from the United Kingdom of those who do not have the right under the law of the United Kingdom to enter and remain in the United Kingdom, and to the acquisition and possession of citizenship, as it may deem necessary from time to time.

And

Where at any time there is a lack of suitable accommodation or adequate facilities for a particular individual in any institution in which young offenders are detained or where the mixing of adults and children is deemed to be mutually beneficial, the United Kingdom reserves the right not to apply article 37 (c) in so far as those provisions require children who are detained to be accommodated separately from adults.

The withdrawal of these reservations in respect of the territory of the United Kingdom is without prejudice to the continued applicability of the reservation and declarations made by the United Kingdom in respect of its dependent territories.

[The notification took effect on 18 November 2008 in accordance with article 51 (3), Ed.].

(Treaty Series No. 17 (2008), Fourth Supplementary List of Ratifications etc for 2008, Cm 7699)

3/3
The Justice Secretary was asked what the status was of the UK's reservation to Articles 9 and 10 of the European Convention on the Legal Status of Children Born out of Wedlock in respect of matters relating to succession to the Crown and what attempts had been made to renew the reservation in or prior to September 2007. He wrote:

The reservation referred to is in fact a declaration. When renewing other UK reservations to this Convention, we have also taken the opportunity to reaffirm our understanding of the meaning of Articles 9 and 10. The UK reservations to the Convention were originally made in 1981, and were renewed in 1986, 1994, 1991 and 2002.

(HC Deb 12 February 2009 Vol 487 c2230W)

3/4
The Government were asked why they had not ratified the Fourth Protocol to the ECHR with reservations similar to those which they attached to their ratification of the ICCPR. A Minister wrote:

Article 57 of the European Convention on Human Rights does not permit reservations of a general character, and Article 19 of the Vienna Convention on the Law of Treaties does not permit reservations which are incompatible with the object and purpose of the treaty in question. The Fourth Protocol to the European Convention on Human Rights has a much more specific focus than the UN International Covenant on Civil and Political Rights. Ratification of the Fourth Protocol would require significant reservations to two of its four substantive articles. The Government do not consider it appropriate to ratify the Fourth Protocol with such significant reservations to such a large proportion of its substantive provisions. However, the Government will continue to keep this position under review.

(HL Deb 18 March 2009 Vol 709 cWA46)

3/5 (See also **6/65, 66**)
During a debate on the Convention on the Rights of Persons with Disabilities. A Minister said:

[W]e entered a reservation with regard to mental capacity issues. We did that because, although we have a system in place where people can be supported and appointed to receive benefits on behalf of others, we do not have a formal review procedure. We need to do that to be compliant with the convention but, as we have stated and made clear, we intend to introduce that system. Regrettably, it cannot be done overnight because a number of people are involved with this; it could take some two years. However, we are intent on removing the reservation as quickly as we can.

He further stated:

I am not sure that I agree with the characterisation of the justification as thin. We have certainly said that we would review the liberty of movement reservations within 12 months. The noble Lord will be aware that we debated the reservation in respect of the Armed Forces recently. That reservation is necessary because in our other domestic legislation the Armed Forces are not subject to the employment conditions of the Disability Discrimination Act. For as long as that remains the position, it is absolutely technically right that a reservation is maintained in respect of the convention. Otherwise, there would be a mismatch between the convention and our domestic legislation.

The declaration and reservation on education will always be kept under review, but for as long as there is the assumption-if that is what it is-that the convention would prohibit special schools, there will be the need to maintain an interpretive declaration. Our system of education recognises the importance of mainstream schools, but also that there should be an element of choice and special schools for those who need them.

(HL 2 Deb July 2009 c325–327)

3/6
The UK representative said in the debate in the Sixth Committee of the General Assembly on the Report of the ILC (A/64/10) on the question of reservations to treaties:

On reservations to treaties, the United Kingdom would firstly like to extend its appreciation to Mr Pellet, the Special Rapporteur for his Fourteenth report. In Chapter III of the ILC's 2008 Report on this question, the Commission posed four specific questions on the invalidity of reservations and the effects thereof (for example, on the effect of silence as a response to an interpretative declaration, and the consequences of an interpretative declaration for its author, an approving State, or an opposing State), and invited comments accordingly. We felt that this was a particularly useful initiative, which encouraged clear responses and helped to focus the attention of participating States on specific issues. Continuing this approach with subsequent reports would have similar advantages, and enable all States to contribute in a meaningful way to this process.

We have some concern that use of the word "permissibility" in the ILC's 2009 Report may be capable of misinterpretation. In our view, there are three possible interpretations which arise from this, as follows: 1) the procedure for formulating reservations or objections; 2) the substantive requirements for validity for the reservations or objections, for example that are not contrary to its object and purpose or *jus cogens*, or 3) the legal effects that reservations or interpretative declarations may have, together with the reactions to them, such as opposition, approval or "recharacterisation". We would urge the Commission to provide greater clarity on the use of the term "permissibility".

Although the ILC did not invite further comment on the draft guidelines on reservations to treaties sent to the Drafting Committee in the 61st session, we would nevertheless like to address ourselves to those guidelines dealing with what is described as the permissibility of reactions to reservations (including conditions for permissibility of objections with intermediate effect), and on the permissibility of interpretative declarations and reactions thereto. Accordingly, the United Kingdom would like to place on record that it finds the following Guidelines acceptable as they stand; 3.41, 3.42, 3.5, 3.51 and 3.6. However, we do not find Guideline 3.52 acceptable as presently drafted, on account of our view that conditional interpretative declarations are not comparable to reservations. Further, we do not accept Guideline 3.53 for the reason that monitoring bodies may not be best equipped to adjudicate on the matter of validity of reservations. We would also like to comment on the competence of treaty monitoring bodies, as set out in the draft Guidelines 3.2.1 to 3.2.5 [Competence of treaty monitoring bodies and effects of their decisions, Ed.] and provisionally adopted by the Drafting Committee (on 5, 6, 18, 19, 27, 28 and 29 May 2009). We believe that any role performed by a treaty monitoring body to assess the validity of reservations (or any other role) should derive principally from the legally-binding provisions of any given treaty; and that these same provisions are the product of free negotiation between States and other subjects of international law. We would question the wisdom of attempting to create a very high-level permissive framework for such activity when it is best left to the negotiating States to decide what powers should be assigned to any treaty monitoring body on a case-by-case basis. Similarly, the legal effect of any assessment of the validity of reservations made by a monitoring body should be determined by reference to the functions it derives under the treaty articles. Regarding Guideline 3.2.2 [Specification of the competence of treaty monitoring bodies to assess the permissibility of reservations, Ed.], we consider that where there is an express intention on behalf of negotiating States to endow a treaty monitoring body with such a role, they will act appropriately to ensure treaty provisions reflect this. The absence of any specific reference in treaty provisions to powers to assess the validity of reservations should not under any circumstances be interpreted as permitting a legally-binding role in this respect. Turning to Guideline 3.2.3 [Cooperation of States and international organisations with treaty monitoring bodies, Ed.], the requirement to "cooperate" with a treaty monitoring body, and to give "full consideration to that body's assessment of the validity of reservations that they have formulated" does not specify the extent or limits of such cooperation or consideration. It is open to question therefore, to what extent this requirement could be deemed to be satisfied under this Guideline. We agree with draft Guideline 3.2.4 [Bodies competent to assess the permissibility of reservations in the event of the establishment of a treaty monitoring body, Ed.]. And we agree with Guideline 3.2.5 [Competence of dispute settlement bodies to assess the permissibility of reservations, Ed.] on the basis that both parties in a dispute have accepted (or not reserved their position in respect of) the power of the dispute settlement body to adopt legally-binding decisions. On the *form of interpretative declarations*, as discussed at the 61st Session, the United Kingdom agrees that there should be no binding conditions or requirements on States to provide reasons for the making of interpretative declarations, nor should the making of interpretative declarations be restricted to a specific time scale. There should be no pre-determined conditions for the validity of such statements, beyond the fact that they should not frustrate the object and purpose of a treaty or contravene *jus cogens*. In a similar fashion, there should be no binding conditions or requirements on States exercising the right to react to interpretative declarations (approval, opposition or recharacterisation), beyond those related to frustrating the object and purpose of a treaty or contravention of *jus cogens*. As such, we agree with draft Guideline 2.9.4 [Freedom to formulate approval, opposition or recharacterisation (to an interpretative declaration), Ed.] in particular.

(Sixth Committee 64th Session of the United Nations General Assembly 28 October 2009. Text supplied by FCO)

Part Four: Relationship between International Law and Internal Law

Part Four: II. *Relationship between International Law and Internal Law—Application and implementation of international law in internal law*

4/1

The Government were asked what assistance they or the European Union were providing to the Government of Iraq to recover items looted from Iraq's museums, libraries and archives during the invasion in April 2003. A Minister wrote:

In 2003 the UK introduced the Iraq (United Nations) Sanctions Order in response to the United Nations Security Council Resolution 1483. The order makes it an offence to deal in an item of Iraqi cultural property, if it was illegally removed from Iraq after 6 August 1990. The UK is also a signatory to the 1970 UNESCO Convention on the Means of Prohibiting and Preventing the Illicit Import, Export and Transfer of Ownership of Cultural Property. This places an obligation on the UK to prevent the import of items looted from Iraq's museums and assist the Government of Iraq to secure their return. The Dealing in Cultural Objects (Offences) Act 2003 also helps strengthen the law in this respect as it makes it an offence to deal in tainted cultural objects.

In addition, the Government have secured the assistance of the UK art trade in locating and identifying material looted from Iraq. My department has also provided funding to the Museums, Libraries and Archives Council for the creation of a website offering advice to anyone wishing to purchase art and antiquities, to help them avoid purchasing illegally traded cultural property: <www.culturalpropertyadvice.gov.uk>. In September 2006, the Metropolitan Police formally returned to the Iraqi Government an 11th century manuscript and an ancient Aramaic incantation bowl, confiscated from illegal traders in 2003. The British Museum and others are working with museum colleagues and the British Army in Iraq on the protection of archaeological and other heritage sites and has, in the past, offered practical advice and assistance on the damage and scale of looting at the Iraqi Museum. The British Museum is also working with the British Army on its Operation Heritage Initiative which offers assistance to the Iraqis on the protection of cultural heritage.

(HL Deb 12 January 2009 Vol 706 cWA112)

4/2

The Government were asked whether, in accordance with the duty imposed by Article 46 of the European Convention on Human Rights to abide by judgments of the European Court of Human Rights, they would introduce legislation to enable United Kingdom courts, below the level of the House of Lords, to depart from decisions of the House of Lords which were incompatible with the Convention rights as interpreted by the European Court of Human Rights in their binding judgments. A Minister wrote:

No. This issue was carefully considered by the Judicial Committee of the House of Lords in the cases of *Kay and others v London Borough of Lambeth and others* and *Leeds City Council v Price and others* [2006] UKHL 10 and in *R (on the application of RJM) v Secretary of State for Work and Pensions* [2008] UKHL 63. Their conclusion was that the doctrine of precedent should not be altered.

(HL Deb 10 March 2009 Vol708 cWA231)

4/3

Release of Abdelbaset Ali Mohmed al-Megrahi (See also **19/21, 22**)

[On 20 August 2009, the Scottish Justice Minister decided to allow the return to Libya of Abdelbasset Ali Mohmed al-Megrahi, a Libyan national, the only person convicted of involvement in the bombing of PanAm flight 103 which was blown up over Scotland in 1988. The reason given for the decision was that al-Megrahi was in the final stages of a terminal illness—he was released according to Scots law and practice on 'compassionate grounds'. Al Megrahi abandoned his appeal against conviction in Scotland and the Scottish Crown Office withdrew its appeal against his sentence. There were suggestions that the case might have been affected by the UK-Libya treaty on prisoner transfer, about the ratification of which there had been some controversy. Condemnation of the decision to allow the return from some quarters, including the US government, was intense. These materials relate to the treaty, about which the Joint Committee on Human Rights (JCHR) had concerns not directly related to the Al Megrahi case, and to the decision to allow al Megrahi to return to Libya, Ed.]

The JCHR reported on the Prisoner Transfer Treaty with Libya. It wrote:

1. A treaty between the UK and Libya on the transfer of prisoners was signed on 17 November 2008 and laid before Parliament on 27 January 2009.[5] We decided that it potentially raised human rights concerns and wrote to the Secretary of State for Justice on 3 March indicating that we intended to scrutinise the treaty and requesting that ratification be delayed until the end of April, so that we could publish a substantive report.[6] The Secretary of State replied on 12 March to say that he would delay ratification only until the Easter recess because "a delay beyond early April is likely to lead to serious questions on the part of Libya in regards to our willingness to conclude [this and three other judicial cooperation] agreements".[7] 2. We sent questions about the treaty to the Secretary of State on 17 March and he replied on 27 March.[8] Our correspondence is published with this report. We are grateful for the speed with which the Secretary of State replied but regret that we have been unable to publish a substantive report on the treaty before Easter and, therefore, before ratification. We note that the Secretary of State cited exceptional reasons why ratification of the treaty could not be delayed until we had been able fully to scrutinise the treaty. In our view, when a select committee states that it intends to scrutinise a treaty, ratification should be delayed until the committee's inquiry has concluded. We make some further comments about parliamentary scrutiny of treaties in our second report on the UN Convention on the Rights of Persons with Disabilities.[9] 3. Although we have been unable to publish a substantive report on the treaty before ratification, we draw the Government's attention to an error in the Secretary of State's letter to us of 27 March. In his answer to our question six, Mr Straw states that a deportation order for a prisoner being transferred to Libya "would be subject to appeal in the normal way". This is incorrect: although judicial review is available, there is no right of appeal against such orders by foreign prisoners.[10]

Correspondence between the Committee and the Justice Minster was attached to the Report:

[Page 5, Ed.] (a) Letter from the Chairman to Rt Hon Jack Straw MP, Secretary of State for Justice, dated 3 March 2009 We recently received a copy of the treaty between UK and Libya signed on 17 November 2008 concerning the transfer of sentenced prisoners (Cm 7540) and the associated explanatory memorandum, signed by Rt Hon David Hanson MP. The explanatory memorandum is dated 17 January and, as I understand it, ratification may occur any time after 5 March once the period for parliamentary scrutiny under the Ponsonby Rule has elapsed. My Committee discussed the treaty at its meeting last week and intends to send you some specific questions about human rights safeguards. I hope we will be in a position to send these questions next week. Depending on your reply, we may wish to publish the correspondence or publish a short report. Either way, we should be in a position to conclude our scrutiny of the treaty by the end of April.

[5] Cm 7540. [6] Page 5 [of this Report, for text see below, Ed.].

[7] Page 6 [of this Report, for text see below, Ed.].

[8] Page 6 [of this Report, for text, see below, Ed.].

[9] Twelfth Report, 2008–09, UN Convention on the Rights of Persons with Disabilities, HL Paper 71, HC 398 [sc HL paper 70, HC 397, Ed.], paragraphs 14–18.

[10] Section 35 of the UK Borders Act 2007.

I would be grateful if you could delay ratification of the treaty until that time, to enable us to conclude our work.

(b) Letter from Rt Hon Jack Straw MP to the Chairman, dated 12 March 2009
Thank you for your letter of 3 March in which you sought an extension of the time allowed under the Ponsonby Rule for consideration of the UK/Libya Prisoner Transfer Agreement. I am keen to facilitate further discussion by the Joint Committee on Human Rights but I am unable to consent to the full extension requested. I am however, willing to delay ratification until the House rises for the Easter recess. This will give the Committee an additional 16 sitting days to consider the Treaty further. I have not reached this decision lightly but the delay that you request would mean delaying ratification of the agreement until the end of April or possibly even later. Ratification of the agreement by the United Kingdom has already been delayed by six days due to the February recess and delaying it further would take us well into the second quarter of the calendar year. Furthermore, delays in the ratification of this Treaty would have an impact on three other treaties in the field of judicial cooperation which are due to be ratified this month. Both the Foreign Secretary and I believe that, in the interests of our judicial and wider bilateral relations with Libya, it is important to ratify all four as far as possible at the same time. In May 2007, the then Prime Minister signed a Memorandum of Understanding with Libya in which he committed the United Kingdom to concluding with Libya a prisoner transfer agreement, an extradition agreement, and agreements on mutual legal assistance and civil and commercial law. As you have noted, all four agreements were signed in London on 17 November 2008. These four agreements form a package of legal instruments in the field of judicial co-operation. It had been our intention to exchange Instruments of Ratification on each element of the package before the end of March. It is on this basis that both the UK and [Page 6, Ed.] Libya have been proceeding. Libya has already completed its integral procedures and is ready to ratify. A delay beyond early April is likely to lead to serious questions on the part of Libya in regards to our willingness to conclude these agreements. The UK-Libya relationship is one of great importance. It has been transformed since Libya's voluntary renunciation of Weapons of Mass Destruction in 2003. The agreements are part of the UK Government's continuing effort to work with Libya to engage constructively with the international community. I note your intention to provide me with questions by the Committee this week. If you are able to do so this will help me to ensure that you receive a full response to your questions at the earliest opportunity.

(c) Letter from the Chairman to Rt Hon Jack Straw MP, dated 17 March 2009
Thank you for your letter of 12 March in which you indicated that you are willing to delay ratification of this Treaty until the House rises for the Easter recess and that you will endeavour to ensure answers to my Committee's questions at the earliest opportunity. My Committee's main concerns about the Treaty relate to the lack of human rights safeguards in the Treaty itself, the value of such safeguards in any event in relation to Libya, and the limited opportunity to challenge on human rights grounds a decision to transfer. As you will be aware, the Memorandum of Understanding between the UK and Libya dated 18 October 2005 [See UKMIL (2005) **6/24**] concerning the provision of assurances in respect of persons subject to deportation contains a number of detailed assurances concerning the protection of the human rights of the deported person, including, for example, that they will be afforded adequate accommodation, nourishment and medical treatment, and treated in a humane and proper manner in accordance with internationally accepted standards.

The MOU also provides for an independent monitoring body to monitor implementation of the assurances. In *AS and another (Libya) v Secretary of State for the Home Department* [[2007] UKSIAC 42/2005, Ed.] the Special Immigration Appeals Commission (SIAC) considered the reliability of these assurances and concluded that there was a real risk that the individuals who were to be deported in that case, on the ground that they were a threat to national security, would be treated in a way which breached Article 3 ECHR notwithstanding the assurances contained in the MOU. SIAC concluded, at para. 371 of its decision:

"...we think that there is a real risk that that would happen. The need in this case to make a large allowance for the unpredictable reaction, which in the short term or occasionally diverges from the pragmatic path upon which the Libyans are set means that we cannot eliminate the real risk which we have identified. The fact that the direction of Libyan foreign relations would largely remain the same does not remove the risk. There are no domestic changes, institutions or considerations which would assist. Above all the risk is not reduced sufficiently by the monitoring system because it is at these times that its limitations would be most evident and felt. We have to bear in mind that the monitoring system is intended to deter and check on potential breaches which can occur quite quickly, and to alert the UK's diplomats to the problem rapidly. [Page 7, Ed.] The diplomatic pressure which the UK could bring to bear and the responses adverse to Libya's interests which it could deploy, would not be engaged if the monitoring were ineffective to report on possible abuse. We do not therefore have the confidence which we need to have, for the return of the Appellants not to breach the UK's international obligations. In short there is too much scope for something to go wrong, and too little in place to deter ill-treatment or to bring breaches of the MOU to the UK's attention."

The Court of Appeal upheld SIAC's decision ([2008] EWCA Civ 289) and we understand that the Government has not appealed against the Court of Appeal's decision.

The Treaty on the Transfer of Prisoners does not contain even those human rights safeguards contained in the MOU which the UK courts have found to be insufficient to remove the real risk of torture of those it was sought to deport on national security grounds. We are also concerned about the adequacy of the recourse to a court for a prisoner who wishes to challenge on human rights grounds the decision to transfer them. A prisoner who a court recommends for deportation at the time of sentencing has a right of appeal against the recommendation for deportation. However, a prisoner who the Secretary of State subsequently decides to deport, while they are serving their sentence, has no right of appeal against that decision, only the right to apply for judicial review. Although the judicial scrutiny given to decisions which affect human rights on judicial review is more intensive under the Human Rights Act, it is still inferior to a full right of appeal on the merits of the decision to deport, to an appellate court, with full fact finding powers and the power to substitute its own decision on the merits if it disagrees with the Secretary of State's decision. There is also no right of appeal against a decision of the Secretary of State to transfer a prisoner to Libya under the Treaty, only a right to challenge that decision by way of judicial review. In the light of the above, we would be grateful to receive your answers to the following questions: Q1: How many Libyan nationals are currently detained in UK prisons? Q2: How many of those have been convicted of terrorism-related offences? Q3: What do you consider to be the relevance of the judgments of SIAC and the Court of Appeal that the assurances contained in the MOU with Libya did not remove the real risk that the deportees in that case would be subjected to treatment contrary to Article 3 ECHR? Q4: Why does the Treaty on Prisoner Transfer not include any human rights safeguards concerning matters such as treatment, conditions and independent monitoring? Q5: What is the justification for not providing a full right of appeal on human rights grounds to a prisoner whom the Secretary of State decides to transfer under the Treaty? [Page 8, Ed.] Q6: Why do the conditions for transfer in Article 3 of the Treaty not include that "they would otherwise be deported at the end of their sentence", which is one of the preconditions of transfer without consent under Article 3 of the Additional Protocol to the European Convention on the Transfer of Sentenced Persons? I would be grateful if you could respond at the earliest opportunity in order to enable us to report to Parliament prior to ratification if we think it appropriate.

(d) Letter from Rt Hon Jack Straw MP to the Chairman, dated 27 March 2009
Thank you for your letter of 17 March in relation to the Prisoner Transfer Agreement (PTA) which has been signed between the United Kingdom and Libya. The letter contains a number of specific questions in relation to the PTA, principally concerned with the issue of safeguards for transferred prisoners. I address those questions below but it may help if, perhaps, at the outset, I state that the UK Government is mindful of its human rights obligations and we would not proceed with the compulsory transfer of any serving prisoner unless we were satisfied that such a transfer would be compliant with our obligations such as under Articles 3 and 8 of the European Convention on Human Rights (ECHR). As your Committee is aware, the Police and Justice Act 2006 removed the requirement in the Repatriation of Prisoners Act 1984 for the consent of a prisoner to transfer in each case. The Government has made it clear, including in answers to parliamentary questions, that, wherever possible, it will seek to negotiate bilateral prisoner transfer arrangements on this basis. The PTA with Libya will be the first "no consent" PTA to be ratified. Active negotiation of the PTA commenced in June 2007 and the initial text was based closely on the model agreement used for previous prisoner transfer agreements; which was in turn drawn from the European Convention for the Transfer of Sentenced Persons of 1983. Only slight amendments were made to the text to remove the requirement for prisoner consent. Since that time, a new model agreement has been developed which takes more explicit account of the different nature of "no consent" transfers. It is our intention that, if any compulsory transfer of prisoners are sought under this PTA, the safeguards spelled out in the new model will be applied. In any event, the UK's obligations under the European Convention on Human Rights and the Human Rights Act will of course apply in relation to any transfer under this PTA. Under all existing prisoner transfer agreements to which the UK is party, applications for transfer are considered on a case-by-case basis. This principle will continue under the PTA with Libya, but in addition to the normal procedures there will also be an assessment of compatibility of transfer with Article 3 of the ECHR which will include seeking advice as to the current state of Libyan prisons. A prisoner would be advised of the Government's intention to transfer and would be invited to make written representations. These representations would be taken into account when determining whether or not transfers should proceed. Any decision to proceed would have to be compatible with the Government's obligations under the

Human Rights Act and with ECHR and would be subject to judicial review. Moving on to the Committee's specific questions: [Page 9, Ed.] Q1: How many Libyan nationals are currently detained in UK prisons? As at 31/12/08 there were 26 Libyans in UK prisons, of whom 25 were in England and Wales and one in Scotland. Q2: How many of those have been convicted of terrorism-related offences? One prisoner only has been convicted of a terrorism-related offence. Q3: What do you consider to be the relevance of the judgments of SIAC and the Court of Appeal that the assurances contained in the MOU with Libya did not remove the real risk that the deportees in that case would be subjected to treatment contrary to Article 3 ECHR? The judgments in question reflected the particular circumstances of the individuals concerned who were found to be threats to Libya's national security. The decision has no direct relevance to prisoner transfers. Decisions to transfer a particular prisoner under this PTA will likewise fall to be decided on the basis of the particular circumstances of the proposed transfer. In proposing the transfer of any prisoner under this PTA HMG shall of course act consistently with its obligations under ECHR and the Human Rights Act. Q4: Why does the Treaty on Prisoner Transfer not include any human rights safeguards concerning matters such as treatment, conditions and independent monitoring? Although this PTA provides for transfer without the prisoner's consent it does not require either party to seek or agree to the transfer of any particular individual prisoner. As outlined above, any compulsory transfer of a prisoner under this PTA would be subject to an Article 3 ECHR assessment and would have to be compatible with our international obligations. Where it is thought appropriate and necessary in any individual case, the Government will seek assurances about the conditions and treatment that the prisoner will receive in Libya and if satisfactory assurances cannot be reached, the Government will not proceed with the transfer. Q5: What is the justification for not providing a full right of appeal on human rights grounds to a prisoner whom the Secretary of State decides to transfer under the Treaty? Where transfer is sought on a compulsory basis a prisoner will be able to seek judicial review of the decision made by the Secretary of State or the Scottish Ministers. Such a review would have regard to the prisoner's human rights and the weight given to them by the decision maker. Given that prisoners already have the right to seek judicial review a formal appeal proves is not considered necessary. Q6: Why do the conditions for transfer in Article 3 of the Treaty not include that "they would otherwise be deported at the end of their sentence," which is one of the preconditions of transfer without consent under Article 3 of the Additional Protocol to the European Convention on the Transfer of Sentenced Persons?

As outlined above, the text of this first "no consent" PTA was drawn from the standard model previously used for voluntary transfers. The UK Government would not consider for compulsory transfer under this PTA any prisoner who would not be subject to [Page 10, Ed.] deportation at the end of their sentence. Indeed it will be part of the process of transferring the prisoner to seek a deportation order if one is not already in place prior to the consideration of transfer. This order would be subject to appeal in the normal way.

(Joint Committee on Human Rights, Thirteenth Report, Prisoner Transfer Treaty with Libya, HL71/HC398 (2009))

4/4

The Justice Secretary wrote to the JCHR after the publication of its Report on 30 June 2009:

Thank you for your Committee's Report "Prisoner Transfer Treaty with Libya" published on 15 April 2009.

I note the Committee's view that when a committee states that it intends to scrutinise a treaty, ratification should be delayed until the committee's inquiry has concluded. The Government recognises and supports the valuable work undertaken by parliamentary committees in scrutinising treaties. This is an important part of our constitutional arrangements. When a committee seeks additional time to scrutinise a treaty the Government would aim to respond positively to such requests provided circumstances permit and cases are justified, in accordance with the undertaking given to the House of Commons Procedure Committee in October 2000. Wherever possible the Government would prefer to delay ratification of a treaty until the relevant committee's inquiries are complete. However, the circumstances of each case must be considered and this may not always be possible. I want to assure you and your committee that I considered your request for an extension of the time allowed under the Ponsonby Rule to consider the prisoner transfer agreement with Libya very carefully. The decision not to grant the full extension requested and to proceed with ratification was not taken lightly. However, given the circumstances outlined to you in my letter of 12 March, I felt that we went as far as was feasible in granting additional time to the Committee and ensuring a prompt response to the questions set out in your letter of 17 March. The Committees second point relates to whether or not prisoners subject to deportation have a right of appeal. Foreign nationals subject to a decision to make a deportation order do have a statutory right of appeal against that immigration decision (s82 (2) (j) and s82 (3A) of the Nationality, Immigration and Asylum Act 2002). The exercise of that appeal suspends deportation (i.e. the appeal is "in country") unless it is an appeal against a decision to make a deportation order in accordance with s32 (5) of the UK Borders Act 2007 (i.e. the "automatic deportation provisions" that apply to foreign criminals sentenced to a period of imprisonment of at least 12 months). Under the automatic deportation provisions, there is an appeal against the application of s32 (5) but it would ordinarily only be exercised after deportation (s92 (2) of the 2002 Act). Also, even where an individual is being deported under the automatic deportation provisions, an appeal from within the UK still lies when the individual has made an asylum or human rights claim while in the UK by virtue of s92(4)(a) of the 2002 Act. Once domestic appeals are determined, judicial reviews are sometimes applied for in relation to further representations when they are not considered "fresh claims" or when claims are certified for being unfounded or for being raised too late. Judicial Review may also be brought in relation to the actual removal directions that are set after the deportation order is made.

(Joint Committee on Human Rights, Twenty-first Report, Legislative Scrutiny... Government's Response to the Committee's Thirteenth Report of Session 2008–09, HL142/HC918)

4/5
The Scottish Justice Secretary made the following statement on 20 August 2009:

A prisoner transfer application has been submitted by the Government of Libya seeking the transfer of Mr Abdelbaset Ali Mohmed Al-Megrahi, the man convicted of the Pan Am bombing in the Scottish courts. He has also now sought to be released on compassionate grounds due to his prostate cancer that is terminal...

Let me be absolutely clear. As Cabinet Secretary for Justice in Scotland it is my responsibility to decide upon these two applications. These are my decisions and my decisions alone. In considering these applications I have strictly followed due process, including the procedures laid down in the Prisoner Transfer Agreement and in the Scottish Prison Service guidance on compassionate release. I have listened to many representations and received substantial submissions. Let me be quite clear on matters on which I am certain. The Scottish police and prosecution service undertook a detailed and comprehensive investigation with the assistance of the US and other authorities. I pay tribute to them for the exceptional manner in which they operated in dealing with both the aftermath of the atrocity and the complexity of a world-wide investigation. They are to be commended for their tenacity and skill. When Mr Al-Megrahi was brought to justice, it was before a Scottish court sitting in the Netherlands. And I pay tribute to our Judges who presided and acted justly. Mr Al-Megrahi was sentenced to life imprisonment for the murder of 270 people. He was given a life sentence and a punishment part of 27 years was fixed. When such an appalling crime is perpetrated it is appropriate that a severe sentence be imposed. Mr Al-Megrahi has since withdrawn his appeal against both conviction and sentence. As I have said consistently throughout, that is a matter for him and the courts. That was his decision. My decisions are predicated on the fact that he was properly investigated, a lawful conviction passed and a life sentence imposed. I realise that the abandonment of the appeal has caused concern to many. I have indicated that I am grateful to and proud of those who have served in whatever capacity in bringing this case to justice. I accept the conviction and sentence imposed. However, there remain concerns to some on the wider issues of the Lockerbie atrocity. This is a global issue, and international in its nature. The questions to be asked and answered are beyond the jurisdiction of Scots law and the restricted remit of the Scottish Government. If a further inquiry were felt to be appropriate then it should be initiated by those with the required power and authority. The Scottish Government would be happy to fully co-operate in such an inquiry. I now turn to the matters before me that I require to address. An application under the Prisoner Transfer Agreement and an application for compassionate release have been made. I now deal with them in turn. **Prisoner Transfer** Firstly, the prisoner transfer agreement. The Libyan Government applied on 5 May 2009 for the transfer of Mr Al-Megrahi. Prisoner Transfer Agreements are negotiated by the United Kingdom Government. Throughout the negotiations and at the time of the signing of the PTA with Libya, the Scottish Government's opposition was made clear. It was pointed out that the Scottish Prison Service had only one Libyan prisoner in custody. Notwithstanding that, the UK Government failed to secure, as requested by the Scottish Government, an exclusion from the PTA for anyone involved in the Lockerbie Air Disaster. As a consequence Mr Al-Megrahi is eligible for consideration for transfer in terms of the agreement entered into by the Governments of the United Kingdom and Libya. I received numerous letters and representations, and recognised that a decision on transfer would be of personal significance to those whose lives have been affected. Accordingly, I decided to meet with groups and individuals with a relevant interest. I met with the families of victims: those from the United Kingdom who had relatives on board the flight, as well as those whose kinfolk were murdered in their homes in Lockerbie; a lady from Spain whose sister was a member of the cabin crew; and I held a video conference with families from the United States. I am grateful to each and every one of them for their fortitude on a matter which I know is still a source of great pain. I also spoke to the United States Secretary of State Hillary Clinton and the United States Attorney General, Eric Holder. I met Minister Alobidi and his delegation from the Libyan Government to hear their reasons for applying for transfer, and to present to them the objections that had been raised to their application. I have noted and considered all the points presented, and also relevant written representations I received. Prior to ratification of the Prisoner Transfer Agreement, it was scrutinised by the Westminster Joint Committee on Human Rights [see above **4/3**], to which Jack Straw, UK Secretary of State for Justice, gave a commitment that in cases where applications were not submitted personally by the prisoner, the prisoner must be given the opportunity to make representations. Mr Al-Megrahi had the opportunity to make representations, and he chose to do so in person. Therefore I was duty bound to receive his representations. I accordingly met him. It was clear that both the United States Government and the American families objected to a prisoner transfer. They did so on the basis of agreements they said had been made, prior to trial, regarding the place of imprisonment of anyone convicted. The United States Attorney General, Eric Holder, was in fact deputy Attorney General to Janet Reno at the time of the pre-trial negotiations. He was adamant that assurances had been given to the United States Government that any person convicted would serve his sentence in Scotland. Many of the American families spoke of the comfort that they placed upon these assurances over the past ten years. That clear understanding was reiterated to me, by the US Secretary of State Hillary Clinton.

I sought the views of the United Kingdom Government. I offered them the right to make representations or provide information. They declined to do so. They simply informed me that they saw no legal barrier to transfer and that they gave no assurances to the US Government at the time. They have declined to offer a full explanation as to what was discussed during this time, or to provide any information to substantiate their view. I find that highly regrettable. I therefore do not know what the exact nature of those discussions was, nor what may have been agreed between Governments. However, I am certain of the clear understanding of the American families and the American Government. Therefore it appears to me that the American families and Government either had an expectation, or were led to believe, that there would be no prisoner transfer and the sentence would be served in Scotland. It is for that reason that the Libyan Government's application for prisoner transfer for Abdelbasit Ali Mohmed Al-Megrahi I accordingly reject. Compassionate Release [This is a matter of Scots law. The Minister was satisfied that the conditions for compassionate release were made out, Ed.] Conclusion . . . Our justice system demands that judgment be imposed but compassion be available. Our beliefs dictate that justice be served, but mercy be shown. Compassion and mercy are about upholding the beliefs that we seek to live by, remaining true to our values as a people. No matter the severity of the provocation or the atrocity perpetrated.

For these reasons - and these reasons alone - it is my decision that Mr Abdelbaset Ali Mohmed Al-Megrahi, convicted in 2001 for the Lockerbie bombing, now terminally ill with prostate cancer, be released on compassionate grounds and allowed to return to Libya to die.

(<www.scotland.gov.uk/News/This-Week/Speeches/Safer-and-Stronger/lockerbiedecision>)

4/6

The FCO issued the following statement on 1 September 2009:

Along with the Ministry of Justice (MoJ), we have released on 1 September our correspondence with the Scottish Executive on the transfer of Abdelbasset Al-Megrahi from Scotland to Libya...The correspondence shows that, throughout, we have made clear that the transfer of Al-Megrahi was a decision for Scottish Ministers. The 3 July letter makes clear that "the decision in relation to such a request is a matter for Scottish Ministers". The correspondence also makes clear that no attempt was made to steer the Scottish Executive in any direction. The 3 August letter makes clear that FCO officials were "not making representations on whether Mr Megrahi ought to be transferred to Libya". In both his statements of 19 June and 24 June, the Scottish Justice Secretary confirmed that the final decision was his alone. These letters were written in response to requests by the Scottish Executive for advice by the Foreign Office on whether there were any international legal reasons why Megrahi might not be transferred under the Prisoner Transfer Agreement, should Scottish Ministers decide to do so. This request and the responses were entirely normal practice in view of the FCO's responsibility for the UK's foreign policy. The Foreign Office provided an authoritative view that there was no international legal bar to transfer *should* the Scottish Executive decide to approve a request. The redactions in the letters relate solely to US views expressed through confidential diplomatic exchanges and have been made in consultation with the US Government. The name of a Foreign Office official has also been removed.

(<www.fco.gov.uk/news>, 1 September 2009) [The FCO correspondence is at <www.fco.gov.uk/en/news/latest-news/?view=news&id=20789408>; the Ministry of Justice correspondence is at <www.justice.gov.uk/news/announcement010909a.htm>; and the Scottish government correspondence is at <www.scotland.gov.uk/Topics/Justice/legal/lockerbie/correspondence>, Ed.]

Part Four: III. *Relationship between International Law and Internal Law—Remedies under internal law for violations of international law*

4/7

The Government were asked what progress the Attorney General was making in investigating possible criminal wrongdoing by British and United States security services in the case of Mr Binyam Mohamed Al-Habashi; whether they would publish a report or make an announcement on the matter; and, if so, when. The Attorney-General wrote:

The Home Secretary referred the question of possible wrongdoing by intelligence and security personnel in the Binyam Mohamed case to me on 23 October 2008. I was provided with the open and closed judgments of the Divisional Court in the case [*Mohamed, R (on the application of) v Secretary of State for Foreign & Commonwealth Affairs (3)* [2008] EWHC 2519 (Admin), Ed.]; transcripts of all the evidence given by witness B; the other evidence and submissions made to the court; and the Foreign Secretary's PII (public interest immunity) certificates, together with their sensitive schedules and associated documents. I have also received material from third parties about the case. After undertaking a preliminary review of this material I took the view that I should seek advice from the Director of Public Prosecutions. All the material provided to me has been made available to the DPP. At this stage no decision has been reached and it would be premature to speculate as to the outcome of this consideration. In performing this function as Attorney-General, I act wholly independently of government and in the public interest. Similarly the DPP acts as an independent prosecuting authority, subject to my statutory superintendence. You will understand it is not possible to give a precise timescale. There is a substantial quantity of material to consider. Some of it is very highly classified and must be handled under the most secure conditions. It is being considered by specialist prosecutors within the CPS who are progressing this important work as quickly as possible. I would intend to report to Parliament on my assessment. But you will understand that what can be said publicly at any given stage may depend on a variety of factors, including whether any police investigation is to follow (and the need to avoid prejudicing any such investigation and potential prosecution), and the need to protect national security.

[No report to Parliament had been made by December 2009, Ed.]

(HL Deb 4 March 2009 Vol 708 cWA160)

4/8 (See also **6/113–121**)
The Prime Minister said:

Let me say right at the outset that this Government unreservedly condemn the use of torture. Under no circumstances will we participate in, encourage or condone the use of torture for any purpose. Where allegations are made about torture, I have instructed that they must be properly examined—including, if necessary, by the courts. The Attorney-General is looking at the very specific allegations in this case. If there is evidence, it will be referred to the police, who will conduct a criminal inquiry. At the moment, the matter is with the Attorney-General, who is looking at all the evidence. As I say, I have instructed that whenever allegations are made, they are properly investigated... The Home Secretary, in her role as an adviser to Government, referred the question of possible criminal wrongdoing to the Attorney-General. She is consulting others, as is necessary, about what needs to be done. It is obviously for her to decide how she is likely to proceed. The court that heard Binyam Mohamed's judicial review case has made it clear that it thinks this is the right way to proceed. I hope the right hon. Gentleman will allow the inquiries taking place to proceed. On the general issues he raised, Britain, because of our defence of freedom and liberty, of course wishes to be seen to be doing everything in our power to deal with questions that arise about the use of torture or rendition. I believe that, at this stage, the best way to proceed is with the Intelligence and Security Committee, but let us hear the report of the Attorney-General.

(HC Deb 11 March 2009 Vol 489 cs289–290)

Part Five: Subjects of International law

Part Five: I.A.1. *Subjects of International Law—States—Status and powers—Personality*

5/1
The UK submitted a written intervention in the *Accordance with International Law of the Unilateral Declaration of Independence by the Provisional Institutions of Self-Government of Kosovo (Request for Advisory Opinion)* made by the General Assembly to the International Court of Justice (ICJ).

[The followings extracts refer to points on the applicability of international law to the general question of the creation of States. The whole submission is at <www.icj-cij.org/docket/files/141/15638.pdf>, Ed.]

CHAPTER 5 THE CREATION OF STATES: GENERAL ISSUES

1. Introduction

5.1 Before turning to the question asked of the Court, some general issues concerning the creation of States should be touched on. These constitute the legal landscape against the background of which the question posed falls to be considered.[11]

Six such general issues will be discussed, as follows:

• the relevance or otherwise of issues of legality under internal law, in particular the constitutional law of the predecessor State;• the operation of the principle of territorial integrity;• the legality or otherwise of secession under general international law;• the practice of coordinated non-recognition in cases where fundamental norms of international law are engaged;• the relevance or otherwise of recognition by the predecessor State and third States in other cases;• the relevance or otherwise of membership in the United Nations.

[11] There is a substantial literature on secession, but it is variable in quality. Particular reference is made to the various expert opinions tendered to the Canadian Supreme Court, reprinted in Anne Bayefsky, Self- Determination in International Law. Quebec and Lessons Learned (Kluwer, The Hague, 2000). None of the experts engaged in that case supported the view that secession is per se unlawful under international law: J Crawford, "Response to Experts Reports of the Amicus Curiae", para.9, p.159, para.13, p.160; Thomas M Franck, "Opinion Directed at Question 2 of the Reference", para.2.9, p.78, "Opinion Directed at Response of Professor Crawford and Wildhaber", paras.3–4, pp.179–180, para.8, p.181; Alain Pellet, "Legal Opinion on Certain Questions of International Law Raised by the Reference", para.44, p.122, "Legal Opinion on Certain Questions of International Law Raised by the Reference", p.212; Malcolm Shaw, "Re: Order in Council PC 1996–1497 of 30 September 1996", para.43, p.136, "Observations Upon the Response of Professor Crawford to the Amicus Curiae's Expert Reports", para.24, p.221.

2. Irrelevance of internal law

5.2 As a general matter, the domestic legality or illegality of an act does not determine whether it is in accordance with international law or is capable of producing effects under international law. International law is a distinct legal order with its own criteria of legality and validity and its own autonomous standards for determining the legal effects of conduct of public authorities. **5.3** This principle is reflected across the whole of international law. For example, Article 4 of the Articles on State Responsibility, adopted by the International Law Commission and appended to General Assembly resolution 56/83 of 14 December 2001, establishes that: "The characterization of an act of a State as internationally wrongful is governed by international law. Such characterization is not affected by the characterization of the same act as lawful by internal law." **5.4** Similarly, Article 43, dealing with the consequences of an internationally wrongful act, provides:"The responsible State may not rely on the provisions of its internal law as justification for failure to comply with its obligations under this Part." **5.5** Consistent with this general approach, international law has not treated the legality of the act of secession under the internal law of the predecessor State as determining the effect of that act on the international plane. In most cases of secession, of course, the predecessor State's law will *not* have been complied with: that is true almost as a matter of definition.[12]

5.6 Nor is compliance with the law of the predecessor State a condition for the declaration of independence to be recognised by third States, if other conditions for recognition are fulfilled. The conditions do not include compliance with the internal legal requirements of the predecessor State. Otherwise the international legality of a secession would be predetermined by the very system of internal law called in question by the circumstances in which the secession is occurring. **5.7** For the same reason, the constitutional authority of the seceding entity to proclaim independence within the predecessor State is not determinative as a matter of international law. In most if not all cases, provincial or regional authorities will lack the constitutional authority to secede. The act of secession is not thereby excluded. Moreover, representative institutions may legitimately act, and seek to reflect the views of their constituents, beyond the scope of already conferred power

3. The principle of territorial integrity

5.8 By contrast with the internal law of the predecessor State—which has no special status in international law—the principle of territorial integrity of States is a principle of international law. It is reflected in particular in Article 2(4) of the UN Charter: "The Organization and its Members, in pursuit of the Purposes stated in Article 1, shall act in accordance with the following Principles . . . 4. All Members shall refrain in their international relations from the threat or use of

[12] On the few occasions (including the SFRY itself) where the constitution of the predecessor State expressly made provision for separation or secession, its provisions have not in fact been followed.

force against the territorial integrity or political independence of any State, or in any other manner inconsistent with the Purposes of the United Nations." **5.9** The protection of the territorial integrity of States is a protection in "international relations". It is not a guarantee of the permanence of a State as it exists at any given time. Nor does it apply to secessionist movements within the territory of a State. Generally speaking, international law does not prohibit the separation of part of the territory of a State arising from internal processes.[13]

5.10 To put the same proposition in other terms, although a State's territorial integrity is protected under international law, as a general matter this protection has been extended only insofar as the use of force and intervention by third States are concerned. It has not been extended to the point of providing a guarantee of the integrity of a State's territory against internal developments which may lead over time to the dissolution or reconfiguration of the State. **5.11** This is not to say that international law *favours* the dismemberment of a State's territory, nor, in particular, that it favours secessionist claims. Rather, international law favours the territorial integrity of States in the interests of stability and the peaceful settlement of disputes, including disputes arising within a State. Under international law, secessionist movements—or the populations they claim to represent—have no legal right to independence, outside the special context of colonial self-determination. International law seeks to avoid the dissolution or dismemberment of its subjects, but not to the point of guaranteeing that these situations can never occur.

4. Secession is not as such contrary to international law

5.12 Secession involves the unilateral, non-consensual separation of part of the territory of a State for the constitution of a new State. The claim is normally presented in declarations adopted by the leaders of the seceding entity, i.e., by way of a "unilateral declaration of independence".[14] Historically, secession has been an often-used method for the creation of new States. It was, without doubt, the most important method up to the First World War, and it has gained relevance again after 1989.

5.13 It is not surprising that existing States have generally felt an aversion to secession. This aversion has sometimes led them to adopt language suggesting the unlawfulness of secession as a matter of international law. Of course attempts at secession may well—as already noted—be contrary to the municipal law of the State concerned. The Declaration of Independence of 4 July 1776 was (at the time) considered an act of treason under British law. But, from the standpoint of international law there was, and is, no prohibition *per se* of secession. 217 As noted in Chapter 1 above, the phrase "unilateral" in these cases adds little. Declarations of independence are by definition unilateral acts.

[13] In certain cases specific guarantees against separation of parts of a State may be established: see e.g., concerning Cyprus, the Treaty of Guarantee, London, 16 August 1960, UKTS 1961 No. 5; 382 UNTS 3.

[14] As noted in Chapter 1 above, the phrase "unilateral" in these cases adds little. Declarations of independence are by definition unilateral acts.

4.1 *Secession before 1945*

5.14 It is hardly necessary to recall, in the period after 1776, such events as the dissolution of the Spanish and Portuguese Empires in Central and South America and the separations of Greece and Belgium. The establishment of these new States was generally achieved through wars of independence, which made recognition of the seceding entities by third States particularly relevant. **5.15** That international law accepted these factual situations did not mean that international law gave the emerging entities a "right" to statehood. This was made clear by the Committee of Jurists appointed by the League of Nations to determine whether the Aaland Islands claim to independence fell within the domestic jurisdiction of Finland. In its Report of 1920, the Committee said that: "Positive international law does not recognize the right of national groups, as such, to separate themselves from the State of which they form part by the simple expression of a wish, any more than it recognizes the rights of other States to claim such a separation. Generally speaking, the grant or the refusal of such a right to a portion of its population of determining its own political fate by plebiscite or by some other method, is, exclusively, an attribute of the sovereignty of every State which is definitely constituted."[15]

5.16 The Commission of Rapporteurs subsequently advised that:"To concede to minorities, either of language or religion, or to any fractions of a population the right of withdrawing from the community to which they belong, because it is their wish or their good pleasure, would be to destroy order and stability within States and to inaugurate anarchy in international life; it would be to uphold a theory incompatible with the very idea of the State as a territorial and political unity".[16]

5.17 But it is one thing to say that there is no right to secede in international law and another to say that secession is *contrary* to international law or that it is legally impossible. Seceding entities did not rely on international law as giving them a right to independence. International law, however, was flexible enough to acknowledge these situations, once they had achieved the necessary stability and effectiveness, so that a successful reassertion of sovereignty by the former State was practically excluded.

4.2 *The relevance of the United Nations Charter*

5.18 Article 1(2) of the UN Charter provides that it is a purpose of the Organization: "To develop friendly relations among nations based on respect for the principle of equal rights and self-determination of peoples, and to take other appropriate measures to strengthen universal peace." **5.19** Article 55 provides that: "With a view to the creation of conditions of stability and well-being which are necessary for peaceful and friendly relations among nations based on respect for the principle of equal rights and self-determination of peoples, the United

[15] Report of the Committee of Jurists, LNOJ, Special Supplement No. 3 (1920), pp. 5–6.

[16] Report of the Commission of Rapporteurs, 16 April 1921: LN Council Doc.B7/21/68/106[VII], pp.27–28.

Nations shall promote: a. higher standards of living, full employment, and conditions of economic and social progress and development; b. solutions of international economic, social, health, and related problems; and international cultural and educational co-operation; and c. universal respect for, and observance of, human rights and fundamental freedoms for all without distinction as to race, sex, language, or religion." **5.20** Article 80 of the Charter states that Mandated territories and peoples were to preserve all their previous rights pending agreement on their final status or their transfer to the Trusteeship system. **5.21** The principle of self-determination was articulated as a right of all colonial countries and peoples by General Assembly resolution 1514 (XV).[17]

5.22 The scope of the principle of colonial self-determination was not simply equated with independence. In Resolution 1541, the General Assembly indicated the possible outcomes from the application of the principle: "(a) Emergence as a sovereign independent State; (b) Free association with an independent State; or (c) Integration with an independent State."[18]

5.23 Similarly, the Declaration on Friendly Relations spoke of "any political status" which represented the free will of the people concerned.[19] In practice, independence was the normal outcome of the process of self-determination.

5.24 Under the United Nations Charter the process of decolonization was carried out and virtually completed, resulting in the creation of over 100 States. The principle of self-determination, now developed into a legal principle, played an important role in this process, as the Court noted in the *Namibia Opinion*: "In the domain to which the present proceedings relate, the last fifty years, as indicated above, have brought important developments. These developments leave little doubt that the ultimate objective of the sacred trust was the self-determination and independence of the peoples concerned."[20]

5.25 It is not necessary to trace the steps by which the principle of self-determination developed through the institutions of the Mandate and Trusteeship systems as well as in the practice of the United Nations under Chapter XI of the Charter. The Court itself has dealt with certain of these developments on a number of occasions, and has attached legal significance to them. In *Western Sahara*, the Court defined the principle of self-determination in terms of "the need to pay regard to the freely expressed will of peoples".[21] In *East Timor* it held that it was "irreproachable" to maintain that "the right of peoples to self-determination, as it evolved from the Charter and United Nations practice, has an *erga omnes* character".[22] This was further reaffirmed in the Court's advisory opinion on the *Legal Consequences* of *the Construction of a Wall in the Occupied Palestinian Territory*.[23]

5.26 But the processes of decolonization which were variously at stake in those cases left open the possibility, which existed under previous law and practice, of

[17] A/RES/1514 (XV), 14 December 1960.

[18] A/RES/1541 (XV), 15 December 1960, Principle VI.

[19] A/RES/2625 (XXV), 24 October 1970.

[20] Legal Consequences for States of the Continued Presence of South Africa in Namibia (South West Africa) notwithstanding Security Council Resolution 276 (1970), ICJ Rep 1971, p.16, at p.31, para.53.

[21] Western Sahara Advisory Opinion, ICJ Rep 1975, p.12, at p.33, para.59.

[22] East Timor (Portugal v Australia), ICJ Rep 1995, p.90, p.102, para.29.

[23] Legal Consequences of the Construction of a Wall in the Occupied Palestinian Territory, ICJ Rep 2004, p.136, at p.199, paras.155–156.

secession occurring, in special circumstances, in independent States and independently of the application of Chapters XI and XII of the Charter. More than 20 new States have come into existence since 1945 outside the colonial context, some of them by secession. **5.27** The language used by States in condemning particular cases of secession does not imply the existence of a *general* prohibition under international law. Security Council resolution 169 (1961), adopted in reaction to the purported declaration of independence of Katanga from the Congo, "strongly deprecat[ed]" the secession and declared that:

"all secessionist activities against the Republic of the Congo are contrary to the *Loi fondamentale* and Security Council decisions and specifically demands that such activities which are now taking place in Katanga shall cease forthwith."[24]

5.28 In the case of Southern Rhodesia, the Security Council adopted several resolutions condemning the Smith regime, an "illegal racist minority regime"[26] that had "usurped power".[25] The Council held the unilateral declaration of independence to have "no legal validity", as it was considered by the United Kingdom, the colonial power, as an "act of rebellion".[27]

5.29 No *general* rule of international law prohibiting secession may be implied from this language. These resolutions did not articulate such a general rule but were concerned with specific features of those cases, which will be discussed in more detail shortly. Furthermore, to maintain that a seceding entity is acting unlawfully under international law is to recognize some form of international subjectivity to the entity, precisely when the objective of such condemnations—in the cases referred to—is the denial of any status whatever.

4.3 "Remedial self-determination"

5.30 General Assembly resolution 2625 (XXV), the Friendly Relations Declaration, included in paragraph 7 of principle 5, the following statement:"Nothing in the foregoing paragraphs shall be construed as authorizing or encouraging any action which would dismember or impair, totally or in part, the territorial integrity or political unity of sovereign and independent States conducting themselves in compliance with the principle of equal rights and self-determination of peoples as described above and thus possessed of a government representing the whole people belonging to the territory without distinction as to race, creed, or colour." **5.31** This clause was reaffirmed in the Vienna Declaration of 1993, adopted during the United Nations World Conference on Human Rights. The Declaration establishes that:"In accordance with the Declaration on Principles of International Law concerning Friendly Relations and Cooperation Among States in accordance with the Charter of the United Nations, this shall not be construed as authorizing or encouraging any action which would dismember or impair, totally or in part, the territorial integrity or political unity of sovereign and independent States

[24] S/RES/169 (1961), 24 November 1961, para.8.
[25] S/RES/216 (1965), 12 November 1965, para.2.
[26] S/RES/217 (1965), 20 November 1965, para.3.
[27] Ibid., preamble.

conducting themselves in compliance with the principle of equal rights and self-determination of peoples and thus possessed of a Government representing the whole people belonging to the territory without distinction of any kind."[28]

5.32 The Supreme Court of Canada in the *Quebec Secession Reference*, after referring to these declarations, noted that: "A number of commentators have further asserted that the right to self-determination may ground a right to unilateral secession in a third circumstance. Although this third circumstance has been described in several ways, the underlying proposition is that, when a people is blocked from the meaningful exercise of its right to self-determination internally, it is entitled, as a last resort, to exercise it by secession... While it remains unclear whether this third proposition actually reflects an established international law standard, it is unnecessary for present purposes to make that determination. Even assuming that the third circumstance is sufficient to create a right to unilateral secession under international law, the current Quebec context cannot be said to approach such a threshold."[29]

4.4 Conclusion

5.33 To summarise, international law favours the territorial integrity of States. Outside the context of self-determination, normally limited to situations of colonial type or those involving foreign occupation, it does not confer any "right to secede". But neither, in general, does it prohibit secession or separation, or guarantee the unity of predecessor States against internal movements leading to separation or independence with the support of the peoples concerned.

5. Relevance of coordinated practice of non-recognition in certain cases

5.34 The statement which concluded the previous paragraph was qualified by the phrase "in general". This is because there can be cases where separation or secession from a State raises issues of illegality under international law; indeed such cases can involve issues of fundamental concern. They may involve external aggression or intervention, or widespread violation of basic human rights. In the Charter period, the response to such cases has involved general non-recognition—concerted and in some cases mandated by the Security Council acting under Chapters VI or VII of the Charter. Collective non-recognition in these cases is a means of preventing the development and consolidation of situations which are unlawful under international law,

[28] United Nations World Conference on Human Rights, Vienna Declaration and Programme of Action, 25 June 1993, 32 ILM 1661 (1993), p.1665.

[29] Reference re Secession of Quebec, [1998] 2 S.C.R. 217, paras.134–135.

including situations involving secession or otherwise affecting the status of territory. **5.35** The practice of the Security Council and the General Assembly has been to call on States not to recognize territorial situations raising fundamental questions of illegality under international law. But in no case has the Security Council or the General Assembly acted on the basis that secession is *per se* unlawful under international law. In each case, the unlawfulness—and consequent non-recognition—flowed from an assessment of the gravity of the particular circumstances and the threat they presented to international peace and security, in light of applicable fundamental principles. This can be demonstrated from the following brief review. [The submission referred to the cases of Katanga, Southern Rhodesia, the South African Bantustans, Namibia, the Turkish Republic of Northern Cyprus and Iraq's invasion of Kuwait. The analysis of the practice is not reproduced, Ed.]

6. Relevance of recognition by the predecessor State and third States

5.51 The practice of collective non-recognition is only applied in very limited cases and only for good, evident reasons. Its rationale is to prevent the consolidation of status that general recognition, and concomitant participation in international relations, brings in cases where fundamental values or norms of international law are at stake. By contrast, in the absence of collective action by the international community, individual States are left to an appreciation of the position, the consequences of which are reflected in the practice of each State in dealing with the new entity on a State-to-State basis, in opening diplomatic relations and/or in extending formal recognition. **5.52** When secession occurs, there will be a range of matters that the seceding State and the predecessor State need to regularize. Secession usually implies a series of claims and counterclaims on issues of property, succession, etc. The existence of such outstanding issues cannot be taken to preclude recognition by third States when it becomes clear that the independence of the new State is the only way forward. **5.53** The practice of recognition in the case of Yugoslavia provides a good example. The situation was seen initially as one concerning the unilateral declarations of independence by some of the constituent republics of the SFRY. But when it became apparent that the Federation was dissolving, many third States extended recognition to the constituent republics that had declared their independence. Third parties, and eventually, all parties concerned, came to the conclusion that the dissolution of the SFRY was a fact, and acted accordingly. This characterization, for a considerable time unaccepted by Belgrade, influenced the handling of the situation from that point onwards. **5.54** To summarise, just as collective non-recognition has legal significance in denying status to the entity in question, so widespread recognition is significant in confirming status. Since it is usually accorded piece-meal, recognition by all or virtually all States may take a considerable period to be achieved. By contrast there can be no mistaking—in cases such as those reviewed above—the practice of collective non-recognition, which has been maintained and been effective, even to the point of unanimity, over considerable periods of time.

7. Membership in the United Nations is not a pre-requisite for statehood

5.55 Article 4 of the United Nations Charter provides that: "1. Membership in the United Nations is open to all other peace-loving States which accept the obligations contained in the present Charter and, in the judgment of the Organization, are able and willing to carry out these obligations. 2. The admission of any such State to membership in the United Nations will be effected by a decision of the General Assembly upon the recommendation of the Security Council." **5.56** For an entity to be qualified for admission to the United Nations it must be a State and be judged to fulfil the other requirements of Article 4. That decision is made by the General Assembly on the recommendation of the Security Council. **5.57** United Nations membership is not a condition for statehood; rather the reverse. As the Court said in the advisory opinion on *Admission of a State to the United Nations*:

"The requisite conditions are five in number: to be admitted to membership in the United Nations, an applicant must (1) be a State; (2) be peace-loving; (3) accept the obligations of the Charter; (4) be able to carry out these obligations; and (5) be willing to do so."[30]

5.58 Neither is the act of admission to the United Nations equivalent to recognition by individual States. A General Assembly resolution admitting a State to the United Nations is an act of the Organization. By contrast, recognition is a unilateral act by which a State recognizes that an entity has fulfilled the requirements of statehood. **5.59** During the San Francisco Conference the Norwegian delegation proposed an amendment of the Dumbarton Oaks text to the effect that the new Organization would be empowered to recommend collective recognition: but the proposal was not adopted.[31] In 1950 the Secretary-General maintained that: "... the United Nations does not possess any authority to recognize either a new State or a new Government of an existing State. To establish the rule of collective recognition by the United Nations, would require either an amendment to the Charter or a treaty to which all members would adhere".[32]

5.60 Membership of the United Nations is thus *evidence* that the Member is a State. But it is not constitutive.

8. Conclusion

5.61 To summarise, international law does not accord to entities within a State any *right* to separate, whether by way of a declaration of independence or otherwise. But neither does it guarantee the territorial integrity of the State against

[30] Admission of a State to the United Nations (Charter, Art. 4), ICJ Rep 1948, p.57 at p.62.

[31] United Nations Conference on International Organization, Amendments and Observations on the Dumbarton Oaks Proposals, submitted by the Norwegian Delegation, 4 May 1945, Doc. 2, G/7, n.(1), pp.2–3.

[32] Memorandum on the Legal Aspects of the Problem of Representation in the United Nations, UN Doc. S/1466, 9 March 1950.

internal developments which may lead to separation or even dissolution. In the absence of some pronounced international illegality leading to collective non-recognition, international law neither authorises nor prohibits secession. [The submission applied these general considerations to the situation in Kosovo and concluded:] **6.64** The question asked of the Court is whether the unilateral declaration of independence by the Provisional Institutions of Self-Government of Kosovo is in accordance with international law. **6.65** It would be a complete and sufficient answer to the question for the Court to state that international law does not address the legality of declarations of independence *per se* and that, accordingly, the Declaration of Independence by Kosovo is not incompatible with international law. As noted previously in chapters 1 and 4, the Institutions were representative of the people of Kosovo as a whole. International law did not prevent them acting as they did. **6.66** If the Court construes the question to focus on whether the Declaration of Independence is in accordance with a wider range of factors, the conclusion is no different. The following points are stressed by way of conclusion. **6.67** Unlike previous measures, Resolution 1244 (1999) specified a full-scale international interim administration for Kosovo. It did not, however, predetermine the final status of Kosovo. The operative provisions of Resolution 1244 (1999), which referred to Kosovo enjoying substantial autonomy "within" Yugoslavia (para.10 and Annex 2, para. 5), concerned only the interim administration that commenced in 1999. Those provisions did not constrain or predetermine the form or substance of the final settlement. Taking account of Resolution 1244 (1999) as a whole, it is clear that the resolution neither required that Kosovo remain within Yugoslavia nor precluded its independence as a final status. Resolution 1244 (1999) did not prohibit or preclude the independence of Kosovo. Nor did it grant Serbia a veto over proposals for a final settlement.

(*Accordance with International Law of the Unilateral Declaration of Independence by the Provisional Institutions of Self-Government of Kosovo (Request for Advisory Opinion)* ICJ, UK written submission, <www.icj.-cij.org/docket/files/141/15638.pdf>)

Part Five: I.A.2. *Subjects of International Law—States—Status and powers—Sovereignty and independence*

5/2
Bahrain

The Foreign Secretary was asked if he would make representations to the Government of the Islamic Republic of Iran on the sovereignty and independence of the Kingdom of Bahrain. An FCO Minister wrote:

The Foreign and Commonwealth Office (FCO) noted recent media reports that an adviser to the Supreme Leader in Iran had claimed Iranian sovereignty over the Kingdom of Bahrain. The FCO welcomes the fact that the Iranian Foreign Ministry has made clear this is not the view of the Iranian government. The UK's view is clear and firm, and we made this public in a press statement at the time: the Kingdom of Bahrain is a sovereign and independent state and a member of the UN. We refute any suggestion to the contrary.

(HC Deb 16 March 2009 Vol 489 c847W)

5/3
Kosovo, South Ossetia, Abkhazia

The Foreign Secretary was asked what assessment he had made of the merits of *(a)* the claim for independence of Kosovo from Serbia and *(b)* the claims of independence of South Ossetia and Abkhazia from Georgia. An FCO Minister wrote:

Kosovo's independence was the culmination of a UN-led political process, envisaged in UN Security Council Resolution 1244 (99), to determine its final status. This process exhausted all avenues to negotiate a solution between the parties and in the UN Security Council. In declaring independence, Kosovo explicitly undertook to implement the UN Special Envoy's Comprehensive Settlement proposals, including the provisions on minority and community rights. It has adopted a constitution and legislative framework which give effect to this undertaking. The UK recognised Kosovo on 18 February 2008. Kosovo has been recognised by a total of 54 states, has diplomatic missions accredited to 10 states and has applied for membership of the International Monetary Fund and other international organisations. Russia recognised Abkhazia and South Ossetia immediately following Russia's military action against Georgia. This occurred without any process of negotiation to seek a durable solution. Russia's use of disproportionate force and its violation of Georgia's sovereignty and territorial integrity had no justification. Russia's actions were in defiance of successive UN Security Council Resolutions, most recently UNSCR 1808 (2008), which Russia had supported. Russia's recognition of the separatist regions, and its use of disproportionate force to achieve its objectives undermine the principles of multilateralism and Russia's own reputation as a reliable member of the international community and the United Nations. Russia has isolated itself on this issue. Only Russia and Nicaragua have recognised these entities. The general criteria that we apply for recognition of an independent state remain as described in the written answer dated 16 November 1989, *Official Report*, column 494, by then Parliamentary Under-Secretary of State for Foreign and Commonwealth Affairs... We consider that Kosovo has met these criteria, but that South Ossetia and Abkhazia have not.

(HC Deb 2 February 2009 Vol 487 c891W)

5/4

The Foreign Secretary commented on the first anniversary of Kosovan independence on Tuesday 17 February 2009. He said:

Kosovo is consolidating its place as a sovereign international actor. Fifty-five states have recognised Kosovo and this number continues to grow steadily.

... I want to reassure the Serbian government that we recognise their continuing legitimate interest in the welfare of the Kosovo Serb community, and I urge the government to redouble its efforts to win the confidence of all communities.

(<www.fco.gov.uk/en/newsroom/)

5/5

The Defence Secretary wrote:

The Supreme Allied Commander Europe has decided that the specific capability, currently provided by the UK to the NATO force in Kosovo, is no longer required. Our current force of 167 personnel will draw-down to a small number of posts between the end of March 2009 and 1 September 2009. Our draw-down reflects the changed circumstances in Kosovo, in particular the improved security situation. The key milestones in Kosovo's independence have passed without major incident and the security situation in Kosovo is generally calm. The EU rule of law mission has recently rolled out across Kosovo. Against this backdrop, and with over 14,000 personnel still in theatre, NATO remains well placed to deal with any potential security incidents.

(HC Deb 4 March 2009 Vol 488 c54WS)

Part Five: I.A.3. *Subjects of International Law—States—Status and powers—Domestic jurisdiction*

5/6
Iraq
An FCO Minister wrote:

We have been aware for some time of Iranian interference in Iraq and in particular Iran's provision of lethal aid to Iraqi militia groups. We have evidence to suggest that a significant proportion of the equipment and armaments used by insurgents against our forces in Iraq was of Iranian origin, or had been transited through Iran. As Iraq's neighbour Iran should have an important role in helping to build a stable and secure Iraq, but instead Iran is undermining stability by supplying weapons, funding and training to militia groups and through political interference and bribery. This action only serves to undermine security in Iraq and should not be tolerated. Both the Government and the Iraqi Government have raised Iranian interference in Iraq with the Iranian authorities on many occasions. We and the Government of Iraq will continue to send strong messages that it is not in Iran's interest to destabilise southern Iraq.

(HC Deb 9 March 2009 Vol 489 c51W)

5/7 (See also **5/13–16**)
Somalia

Answering questions about the conflict in Somalia, an FCO Minister said:

[T]he Djibouti process led to the expansion of the Somali Parliament and its selection of a new President. The formation of a more broadly based Government provides the best opportunity to create a lasting peace and reconciliation necessary for tackling the ongoing humanitarian crisis. Although that Government are battling an assault by the armed insurgency, they must continue to strive for further reconciliation with those outside the political process.…there is pretty strong evidence of Eritrean collusion in the upsurge of violence against the Government and of possible arms resupply to the rebels by the Eritreans. They were condemned in a Security Council presidential statement at the end of last week and have furiously denied the charges, but frankly that does not give me much confidence—it does not mean that the charges are not true. There is also a real risk of this situation escalating; there have been reports, again denied, of Ethiopian troops returning into Somalia. This is an enormously serious challenge to the Government and we all have reason to be very concerned to support and reinforce them over the coming weeks.

The Minister was asked about the recognition of Somaliland. He said:

[T]his is one of those perennial issues which, quite rightly, come up every time that Somalia lurches back into crisis... our position is that we try to give Somaliland support but we think that its status and potential independence must be dealt with through African forums: first, through talks between the two sides in Somalia and, subsequently, through the AU. We do not think that British recognition of Somaliland would help its goal of independence.

(HL Deb 21 May 2009 Vol 710 cs1432–1433)

5/8
Zimbabwe

The International Development Secretary was asked what steps his Department was taking to provide food aid to the people of Zimbabwe. A Minister wrote: The Department for International Development's (DFID) programme in Zimbabwe is focused on providing immediate humanitarian support and broader livelihoods assistance to meet the essential needs of the people of Zimbabwe. This year we have provided: £9 million to the World Food programme for food aid; £10 million to support the growing season; and £10 million to HIV/AIDS prevention and treatment. We also recently made £10 million available to tackle the cholera outbreak and support life-saving essential health systems. We anticipate a total spend of £49 million this financial year across these vital areas of support. Our aid is channelled through the UN and NGOs and not the Government of Zimbabwe. We anticipate the need for sustained large-scale humanitarian support from the international community for the foreseeable future and we are monitoring the situation very closely. However, a sustainable and credible political solution is required to fully address Zimbabwe's problems. In principle, we are ready to support economic and social recovery in Zimbabwe but this will depend on the new Government's commitment to reform, including a clear commitment to macroeconomic stabilisation and sound economic management; restoration of the rule of law; commitment to democracy; respect for human rights, and the guarantee of full humanitarian access.

(HC Deb 13 March 2009 Vol 489 c792W)

Part Five: I.B.1. *Subjects of International Law—States—Recognition of states*

5/9
An FCO Minister wrote:

As a matter of foreign policy, the Government do not take a view as to whether an area is a country. The term "country" has no specific meaning under international law unlike the term "state". The issue is really whether an area or a country can be recognised as a state. The normal criteria which the Government would apply for the recognition of a state remain those that are set out in the Written Answer dated 16 November 1989 (*Official Report*, col. 494) by the then Parliamentary Under-Secretary of State for Foreign and Commonwealth Affairs. They are that "it should have, and seem likely to continue to have, a clearly defined territory with a population, a Government who are themselves able to exercise effective control of that territory, and independence in their external relations. Other factors, including some United Nations resolutions, may also be relevant".

(HL Deb 9 November 2009 Vol 714 cWA113)

5/10
Israel/Palestine

The Government were asked what was their approach to the Middle East peace process should a two-state solution be unattainable. A Minister said:

...we continue to consider that a two-state solution is the only realistic way to achieve sustainable peace in the Middle East. Our vision is of two democratic states—Israel and Palestine—living side by side in peace with secure and recognised boundaries... It is also a vision shared by a majority of Palestinians, Israelis and a number of members of the international community.

He said further:

It is clear that settlements remain illegal. They are in violation of international law. Therefore, the UK and international position remains the same—to tell the Israeli authorities, both privately and in public, that they should be dismantled.

(HL Deb 16 June 2009 Vol 711 cs945–946)

5/11
An FCO Minister wrote:

We welcome the fact that the Palestinian Authority recognises the state of Israel and is prepared to negotiate a peace deal with it. The nature of the state of Israel, and the role that religion plays, is a matter for Israelis, although we would expect Israel to respect the rights of minorities as undertaken in Israel's declaration of independence and basic laws. We welcome the fact that the Israeli Government has not said that Palestinian recognition of Israel as a Jewish state should be a precondition for entering negotiations with the Palestinians. The UK position is clear that a comprehensive peace should be based on two states, living side by side within secure and agreed borders based on those of 1967, with Jerusalem as the capital for both states. Such a solution is the only way to do justice to the national aspirations of the Jewish people and of the Palestinians. The two-state solution was envisioned in UN Security Council resolution (UNSCR) 1850 of 16 December 2008, which the UK supported, and reaffirmed by the UK-led UNSCR 1860 of 8 January 2009. The UK will continue to make this position clear in future UN discussions.

(HC Deb 21 July 2009 Vol 496 c1258–1259W)

5/12
Kosovo

An FCO Minister wrote:

56 states have now recognised Kosovo as an independent sovereign state, including the UK and 21 other EU member states. Discussions in the EU around the

time of independence concluded that the decision to recognise Kosovo's independence is one for individual states to make, not the EU as a whole. Therefore, there have been no recent discussions on Kosovo's political status.

(HC Deb 31 March 2009 Vol 490 c1118W)

5/13 (See also 5/7) Somalia/Somaliland

An FCO Minister said about the recognition of Somaliland:

[I] t has been a continuing feature of the situation [in Somalia] that Somaliland has been a relative haven of stability, although it too has been subject to tragic terrorist attack recently. The British Government's position has always been to be sympathetic to Somaliland's demand for independence but we feel, first and foremost, that this is a matter for the different components of Somalia to negotiate between themselves; and, secondly, that it is for the AU, which has shown a deep suspicion of any redrawing of African boundaries, to move on this and that any overt British support for this goal would actually set it back. We have to let Africa sort out this problem.

(HL Deb 14 January 2009 Vol 706 c1223)

5/14

An FCO Minister said:

We have had contact with the President of Somaliland, and the Foreign Secretary will meet him. Our position remains the same: first and foremost, the leaders of Somalia and Somaliland must sit down to try to resolve their differences. Beyond that, it is for Africa to take the lead in any change of status that might follow. We certainly cannot overlook the fact that Somaliland is the one part of broader Somalia where there is, at the moment, some reasonable government and development progress. Indeed, some 60 per cent of our development assistance is applied to Somaliland because of the success that is possible there.

(HL Deb 5 March 2009 Vol 708 c907)

5/15

The Government were asked why they do not recognise Somaliland as an independent state. An FCO Minister wrote:

The UK has signed up to an EU common position and endorsed many UN Security Council resolutions that refer to the territorial integrity and unity of Somalia. We believe that, through dialogue between the Somaliland authorities and the Transitional Federal Government of Somalia, the Somali people themselves should determine the most appropriate future arrangements. Beyond that we believe that any process of international recognition must begin in Africa and countries in the region should take the lead in recognising any new arrangements. We acknowledge that Somaliland has achieved relative peace and stability. Nevertheless, we continue to apply the recognition criteria specified in the Written Answer of 16 November 1989 (*Official Report*, col. 494). These criteria are more likely to be met if countries in the region themselves recognise Somaliland. We remain committed to supporting development in Somaliland and continue to engage with its authorities in a range of areas.

(HL Deb 11 June 2009 Vol 711 cWA163)

5/16
The Government were asked about the criteria for recognising Somaliland and independent State and whether they would raise the matter in the European Union with a view to gaining agreement on the recognition of Somaliland's independence. An FCO Minister wrote:

The general criteria that we apply for recognition of an independent state remain as described in the Written Answer dated 16 November 1989 (Official Report, col. 494) by the then Parliamentary Under-Secretary of State for Foreign and Commonwealth Affairs. The UK has signed up to an EU common position, and to many UN Security Council resolutions, which refer to the territorial integrity and unity of Somalia. The Government do not propose to raise this issue in the EU.

(HC Deb 2 February 2009 Vol 487 c891)

Part Five: I.B.2. *Subjects of International Law—States—Recognition of governments*

5/17
Afghanistan

A Downing Street spokesman said:The Prime Minister has spoken to President Karzai to congratulate him on his re-election as president of Afghanistan.

... during the phone call Mr Brown also welcomed President Karzai's statesmanlike handling of events in recent days. [President Karzai was re-elected following an election of highly disputed legitimacy and his rival withdrew from the run-off process, Ed.]

(<www.number10.gov.uk>, 2 November 2009)

5/18 (See also **5/49**)
Fiji

After Interim Fijian Prime Minister Frank Bainimarama held a press conference on 3 November 2009 announcing his intention to expel the Australian High Commissioner and the New Zealand Deputy High Commissioner with 24 hours notice and recalling the Fiji High Commissioner to Australia, a Foreign Office Minister said:

I am deeply disappointed that the regime in Fiji has expelled the Australian High Commissioner and the New Zealand Deputy High Commissioner. This is a backward step which will isolate Fiji further from the international community. The people of Fiji need their government to be engaging with their neighbours, and diplomatic channels must be kept open. The UK government maintains its strong opposition to the regime in Fiji and again urges a swift return to democracy, freedom of expression and the rule of law.

(<www.fco.gov.uk/news>, 3 November 2009)

5/19
Gaza

In the course of answering a question about the exploitation of natural gas resources off Gaza, a Minister wrote:

The UK does not recognise the legitimacy of the current authorities in Gaza [viz the Hamas authority in Gaza, Ed.]

(HL Deb 17 March 2009 Vol 709 cWA25)

5/20
Guinea-Bissau

An FCO Minister wrote:

A spokesman for the interim government of Guinea-Bissau has confirmed that President Viera was assassinated on 2 March 2009. The Government have expressed their condolences to the people of Guinea-Bissau and have urged that those responsible be brought to justice. The UN Security Council has issued a statement which condemned the assassinations in the strongest terms. The Government support the Guinea-Bissau interim government's call for elections to take place within 60 days as specified in the constitution.

(HC Deb 18 March 2009 Vol 489 c1187W)

5/21
Honduras

An FCO Minister condemned the expulsion of President Zelaya of Honduras and called for the restoration of democratic, constitutional government in the region. He said:

The UK condemns the expulsion of President Zelaya and calls for the restoration of democratic, constitutional government in Honduras. We support the Organisation of American States' call supporting the rule of law and are deeply concerned about the deployment of military personnel onto the streets of Tegucigalpa.

(<www.fco.gov.uk/news>, 28 June 2009)

5/22
A Minister said:

We made it clear before the elections that we believed that President Zelaya should not have been removed from power, and that if the elections were to be valid, they had to be engaged in under President Zelaya. Without his return before the end of his term, which is at the end of January, it will be impossible to believe that those were proper elections. However, we recognise and welcome the fact that the elections that did take place did so in a peaceful situation.

(HC Deb 1 December 2009 Vol 501 c973)

5/23

The EU issued a statement about the violation of the constitutional order in Honduras by the events of 28 June 2009, when President Zelaya was forced into exile. [He had subsequently returned clandestinely to Honduras and was in the Brazilian Embassy in Tegucigalpa. He left Honduras for exile in the Dominican Republic in January 2010, following the election of a new president, Ed.]:

The European Union reiterates its condemnation. The European Union has since the beginning of the crisis called for a peaceful negotiated solution to the political crisis and has taken steps with other international partners to bring this about. The European Union regrets that the Tegucigalpa/San José Accord has not been fully implemented ahead of the elections on 29 November, leading to an electoral process under abnormal circumstances. However, the European Union sees the elections as a significant step forward in solving the crisis in Honduras. In this regard, the European Union awaits the outcome of the deliberations of the Honduran Congress scheduled for 2 December 2009. The EU calls upon all actors to seek a dialogue in order to reach national reconciliation and to re-establish constitutional and democratic order in the country, and expects them to assume their full responsibility in this regard. Furthermore, the European Union demands that all actors promote and respect the rule of law, good governance and human rights.

(<www.fco.gov.uk>, 2 December 2009)

5/24
Mauritania

In reply to a question about the UK's relations with Mauritania, an FCO Minister wrote:

We regularly assess our relationship with Mauritania, and the political situation in the country, following the 2008 coup. We remain concerned that there has been little progress towards the restoration of democracy, despite increasing international pressure. We, in line with international partners like the EU, US, North Atlantic Treaty Organisation and the African Union, maintain working level contact with Mauritanian officials.

The UK continues to fully support the EU in its efforts to restore democracy through the provisions of the Cotonou Agreement.

(HC Deb 19 May 2009 Vol 492 c1326W)

5/25

An FCO Minister welcomed signature of an agreement between the Mauritanian political parties establishing a multiparty interim government and a timetable for democratic elections. The agreement follows months of concerted international pressure to reverse the August 2008 military coup. He said:

I welcome the agreement signed today between the Mauritanian political parties establishing a clear timetable for free and fair elections and the restoration of constitutional government.

The agreement follows months of concerted and co-ordinated international action by the African Union, the UN, the EU, including the UK, and the United States to reverse the August 2008 military coup. The agreement will ensure the release of all political prisoners in Mauritania and the resignation of the coup leader General Abdelaziz.

He added:

[I]t is now vital that the parties implement this agreement fully and now move swiftly to hold free and fair elections in Mauritania.

An addition to the statement said:

Agreement on the formation of an interim government and a timetable for free elections was agreed in Dakar, Senegal on 2 June following the concerted efforts of the International Contact Group on Mauritania. The agreement will then be formally signed by the political leaders on 4 June in Nouakchott, Mauritania.

The EU suspended development assistance to the Mauritanian military junta in August 2008 and worked, with UK support, for a peaceful return to constitutional rule. The Junta have undertaken to release all political prisoners as part of the transition.

(<www.fco.gov.uk>, 5 June 2009)

5/26
Northern Cyprus

After a meeting, which took place in the House of Commons on 4 December 2009, the Prime Minister said:

I was pleased to welcome Mehmet Ali Talat, the Turkish Cypriot leader, to London today and to have the opportunity to discuss the Cyprus settlement talks with him. This is a critical time for the talks. Having striven for a settlement for many years, Mehmet Ali Talat knows well how vital a solution in Cyprus is for all Cypriots as well as for the region and for Europe. I commend both leaders for the perseverance and resolve they have displayed in their search for a settlement. The two Cypriot leaders have shown enormous courage and determination to get this far. I know that both leaders are fully committed to finding a solution and I hope that the negotiations can be intensified so the two leaders can fully exploit the opportunity that now exists to resolve the issue to the benefit of all Cypriots. The UK continues to support these efforts and welcomes the good progress made so far. We hope to see further progress over the coming months. With political courage and compromise on both sides, these talks have every chance of success.

(<www.number10.gov.uk/page21612>, 4 December 2009)

5/27
Zimbabwe

The Government were asked what representations they would make to the Government of Zimbabwe concerning recent death threats to opposition members of the joint Government. An FCO Minister said:

We remain deeply concerned about human rights abuses in Zimbabwe—harassment of human rights defenders, arbitrary arrests and intimidation, repressive legislation and the lack of press freedom. The inclusive Government have, in the global political agreement, committed to ending human rights abuses and violence and to restoring the rule of law. We and the international community continue to urge the inclusive Government to respect these commitments and adhere to international standards.

(HL Deb 11 June 2009 Vol 711 c742)

Part Five: I.B.6 *Subjects of International Law—States—Recognition—Acts of recognition—Non-recognition and its effects*

5/28

Cyprus (See also **6/7**)

In a reply to a question about the case of *Apostolides v Orams* [2008] EUECJ C-420/07 (the 'Orams' case), an FCO Minister wrote:

The European Court of Justice judgment in case C-420/07 concerns the interpretation of certain aspects of Council Regulation (EC) No.44/2001 of 22 December 2000 on jurisdiction and the recognition and enforcement of judgments in civil and commercial matters. The ruling confirmed the applicability of the regulation to judgments of the courts of the Republic of Cyprus given in respect of property in northern Cyprus. The regulation is therefore potentially applicable in relation to other judgments made by those courts against citizens of all EU member states, whether those judgments relate to property in the north or south of the island.

(HL Deb 20 May 2009 Vol 710 cWA315)

Part Five: I.E. *Subjects of International Law—States—Self-determination*

5/29 (See also **5/61**)

Falkland Islands

A Minister said:

The Government have no doubt about their sovereignty of the Falkland Islands. The principle of self-determination underlies that. Nevertheless, Argentina unfortunately continues to make regular representations on its supposed claim to sovereignty.

(HC Deb 1 December 2009 Vol c961)

5/30

Israel and Palestine

In answering questions about the situation between Israel and Palestine, an FCO Minister wrote:

We welcomed US support in December for UN Security Council Resolution 1850 which set out the vision of a two-state solution. We will work closely with the Obama Administration, including at the UN, to work to create an independent Palestinian state living alongside a secure Israel. We do not believe it is productive to talk to Hamas directly until it makes significant movement towards the quartet principles of rejecting violence, accepting Israel's right to exist and recognising previous agreements. The Arab League has mandated Egypt to communicate with Hamas. We are in regular contact with both the Arab League and Egypt.

(HL Deb 24 February 2009 Vol 708 cWA58)

5/31
In answer to a question about East Jerusalem, an FCO Minister wrote:

We have made clear our position that we believe that a lasting peace between Palestinians and Israelis will mean, among other things, the creation of a Palestinian state based on 1967 borders and with East Jerusalem as its capital. We are strongly opposed to any attempts to change the facts on the ground in East Jerusalem by excluding Palestinians from the city and by increasing the number of settlers living there. Such acts raise tensions and undermine prospects for peace. We have made these concerns known to the Israelis both in private and in public, most recently in the form of statements by the EU on the threat of house demolitions in Silwan village and house evictions in the Sheikh Jarrah neighbourhood.

(HC Deb 27 March 2009 Vol 490 c813W)

5/32
Overseas Territories

The Foreign Secretary was asked what steps his Department had taken to monitor the implementation of UN General Assembly Resolution 63/110 on Granting of Independence to Colonial Countries and Peoples. An FCO Minister wrote:

This is a twofold process: The UK carefully examines the UN Secretariat's reports to the General Assembly's Fourth Committee. The UK also continues to fulfil its obligations to the Overseas Territories under the UN Charter. The UK's relationship with its Overseas Territories is a modern one based on partnership. The UK is committed to the future development and continued security of the Overseas Territories for as long as the Territories choose to retain their link to the UK. The UK has no intention of imposing independence against the will of the peoples concerned, whilst the established policy of successive Governments has been to give every help and encouragement to those Territories which wished to proceed to independence, where it is an option.

(HC Deb 27 February 2009 Vol 488 cs1194–1195W)

5/33
Western Sahara

The Foreign Secretary was asked what guidance his Department had issued to firms about trade with Morocco where such trade drew upon the resources of the Non Self-Governing Territory of Western Sahara. An FCO Minister wrote:

Commercial deals are a matter for the companies concerned. However, the Government work to ensure that companies are aware of the undetermined status of the non self-governing territory of Western Sahara when trading with Morocco. The UK supports UN efforts to resolve the conflict and urge all parties to achieve a mutually acceptable solution that provides the people of the Western Sahara with an opportunity to exercise their right of self-determination.

(HC Deb 5 February 2009 Vol 487 c1411W)

5/34
The Environment Secretary was asked about plans for UK vessels to fish in the waters of Western Sahara. A Minister wrote:

The UK has two vessels operating in Moroccan waters under the EU/Morocco Fisheries Agreement. They have fished in the waters of Western Sahara in previous years and it is likely that they will do so again during the course of 2009.

(HC Deb 11 February 2009 Vol 487 c2027W)

5/35
Answering questions about Western Sahara, an FCO Minister wrote:

The Government continue to believe that progress towards a negotiated solution to the dispute in Western Sahara which provides for the self-determination of the people of Western Sahara is best achieved under the auspices of the United Nations. We continue to support the efforts of the UN Secretary-General and his staff to secure agreement between the parties on the future status of Western Sahara. The date and terms of any eventual referendum should be agreed by all parties to the dispute. In this respect the Government welcome the appointment of the UN Secretary-General's new personal envoy to Western Sahara, Christopher Ross, and encourages all the parties to the dispute to enter into renewed negotiations in a spirit of realism and compromise.... The Government are aware, through press releases and media reports, that representatives of the Polisario have declared, on behalf of the Saharawi Arab Democratic Republic, an offshore exclusive economic zone in the waters off the coast of Western Sahara. The status of Western Sahara remains unresolved pending the efforts of the UN Secretary-General and his staff to achieve a negotiated, lasting solution between the parties to the dispute, providing for the self-determination of the people of Western Sahara.

(HC Deb 12 February 2009 Vol 487 c2205W)

5/36
The Foreign Secretary was asked what assessment he had made of the compatibility of the EU-Morocco Fisheries Agreement with international law in respect of its application to waters off Western Sahara. An FCO Minister wrote:

The EU-Morocco Fisheries agreement sets fishing priorities for EU Community vessels in the Moroccan fishing zone or, as defined in article 2 of the agreement, "in the waters over which the Kingdom of Morocco has sovereignty or jurisdiction". This approach is in conformity with international law and with the legal opinion of the UN as of 29 January 2002 [Letter dated 29 January 2002 from the Under-Secretary-General for Legal Affairs, the Legal Counsel, addressed to the President of the Security Council S/2002/161, Ed.] Morocco is the administrative authority of Western Sahara and it is the obligation of the Moroccan side to assure the full application of the Fisheries Partnership Agreement in accordance with its obligations under international law. There are no references to the Western Sahara in the agreement and this was already the case in the previous agreement between the EC and Morocco.

(HC Deb 10 March 2009 Vol 489 c228W)

5/37

The Foreign Secretary was asked what requests the United Nations had made to the power which had responsibility for the administration of the Western Sahara under Article 73 of the UN Charter for the transmission of information under the provisions of that article. An FCO Minister wrote:

On 26 February 1976, Spain informed the UN Secretary-General that as of that date it had terminated its presence in Western Sahara and relinquished its responsibilities over the territory, thus leaving it under the administration of both Morocco and Mauritania in their respective controlled areas. Mauritania withdrew from the Territory in 1979 and since then Morocco has administered a substantial part of the territory of Western Sahara alone. Morocco however, is not listed as the administering power of the territory in the UN list of non-self-governing territories, and has therefore not transmitted, or been asked to transmit, information on the territory in accordance with Article 73E of the Charter of the UN.

(HC Deb 18 March 2009 Vol 489 c1190W)

5/38

The Foreign Secretary was asked what representations the Government had made to the Moroccan government to ensure that the indigenous people of Western Sahara received licensing revenues or aid derived from the EU-Morocco Fisheries Agreement as a result of the fishing activity of UK trawlers in the waters of the occupied Western Sahara. An FCO Minister wrote:

The Government maintain the position that the Government of Morocco—as the de facto administering power of Western Sahara—are obliged under international law to ensure that economic activities under administration, including the extraction and exportation of phosphates, do not adversely affect the interests of the people of Western Sahara. Our officials in Rabat discuss a range of issues relating to the Western Sahara with their Moroccan counterparts, including when appropriate the issue of fishing revenues.

There are currently only two UK vessels operating in the waters off Western Sahara under the EU—Morocco Fisheries Agreement. All the fish caught are landed in Dakhla, Western Sahara and sold through the local markets or processed in a local factory.

(HC Deb 23 March 2009 Vol 490 c32W)

5/39
An FCO Minister wrote:

The UK maintains its position that Morocco, as the de facto administering power of Western Sahara, is obliged under international law to ensure that economic activities under administration—including the extraction and exportation of phosphates—do not adversely affect the interests of the people in Western Sahara. The UK has not recently raised this issue with the Moroccan authorities. However, the Government firmly support the principles of transparency and good governance with regards to the extractive industries generally. In November 2008, the Extractive Industry Transparency Initiative (EITI) held a roundtable meeting in Tunis, which included Morocco. Participants discussed the opportunities and challenges which implementing the EITI can bring for the north African region and for further enhancing resource management and economic growth. [For details on EITI, see <www.eiti.org>, Ed.]

(HC Deb 23 March 2009 Vol 490 c32W)

5/40
A Minister wrote:

The Government believe that progress towards a negotiated solution to the dispute in Western Sahara, providing for the self-determination of the people of Western Sahara, is best achieved under the auspices of the UN. In accordance with UN Security Resolution 1871 of 30 April 2009, the UK fully supports the efforts of the UN Secretary General and his Personal Envoy, Christopher Ross, to facilitate a negotiated solution to the conflict.

The UK maintains its position that Morocco, as the de facto administering power of Western Sahara, is obliged under international law to ensure that economic activities under administration—including the extraction and exportation of natural resources—do not adversely affect the interests of the people in Western Sahara.

(HC Deb 14 July 2009 Vol 496 c336W)

5/41
A Minister wrote:

The UK does not regard any country as administering de facto that part of the territory of Western Sahara not under Moroccan control.

While Morocco has administered most of the territory of Western Sahara since 1976, the UK regards the status of the whole of Western Sahara as undetermined pending UN led efforts to achieve a just, lasting and mutually acceptable political solution to the conflict, which will provide for the self-determination of the people of Western Sahara. The UK Government fully support the efforts of the UN Secretary-General and his Personal Envoy Christopher Ross in this regard.

(HC Deb 1 December 2009 Vol 500 c637W)

5/42
A Minister wrote:

When considering their policy on the extraction of resources in the disputed territory of Western Sahara, the Government took into account the opinion set out by the UN Legal Counsel, then Hans Correll, in his letter to the President of the Security Council of 29 January 2002 [Letter dated 29 January 2002 from the Under-Secretary-General for Legal Affairs, the Legal Counsel, addressed to the President of the Security Council S/2002/161, Ed.]. On this basis, the UK's position remains that Morocco, as the de facto administering power of Western Sahara, is obliged under international law to ensure that economic activities under administration—including the extraction and exportation of natural resources—do not adversely affect the interests of the people in Western Sahara.

(HC Deb 3 December 2009 Vol 501 c881W)

Part Five: II.A.1.(b). *Subjects of International Law—International organisations—General—Status and powers—Privileges and immunities of the organisation*

5/43
A Minister wrote:

There are 11 organisations of the European Union with facilities in the UK that are entitled to certain privileges and immunities. They are: European Commission; European Investment Bank; European Centre for the Development of Vocational Training; European Maritime Safety Agency; European Medicines Agency; European Molecular Biology Laboratory; European Network and Information Security Agency; European Parliament; European Patent Office; European Police School; andEuropean School.

The Foreign and Commonwealth Office (FCO) has been notified of 2,282 staff and their dependants at the above listed organisations that may be entitled to some form of privileges and immunities. The extent of the privileges and immunities accorded varies between the different organisations, such as immunity from jurisdiction and legal process and exemption or relief from certain taxes.

(HC Deb 9 July 2009 Vol 712 WA165)

Part Five: II.A.1.(c). *Subjects of International Law—International organisations—General—Status and powers—Powers, including treaty-making power*

5/44
A Minister wrote:

The principle of subsidiarity is not a mechanism for "returning powers" to the member states, but for determining whether or not Community action should be set in motion. The member states, through the EU treaties, set the EU certain tasks and give it the powers to achieve those tasks. Article 5 of the treaty establishing the European Community states that, in areas which do not fall within its exclusive competence, the Community shall take action, in accordance with the principle of subsidiarity, only if and in so far as the objectives of the proposed action cannot be sufficiently achieved by the member states and can therefore, by reason of the scale or effects of the proposed action, be better achieved by the Community. Further guidelines for assessing whether these requirements are met are laid down by the Protocol on the application of the principles of subsidiarity and proportionality. The Protocol also requires the Commission to justify the relevance of any of its legislative proposals with regard to the principle of subsidiarity.

The Lisbon treaty would strengthen the role of national Parliaments in EU decision-making, so that for the first time national parliaments could challenge draft EU legislation on subsidiarity grounds. It is for Parliament to decide how to exercise its rights under these procedures.

(HC Deb 22 October 2009 Vol 497 c616W)

5/45
In answering a question about EU action relying on Article 308, EU Treaty, an FCO Minister wrote:

In assessing the legal basis of proposals brought forward by the Commission, the Government apply criteria laid down by the Court of Justice in case law dating back to the 1980s and consider each proposal as a whole, and in particular its aim and content. Article 308 requires that a proposal be necessary for the attainment of a Community objective, and that the Council must act unanimously. The Government have given an undertaking that where the Commission puts forward a legislative proposal citing Article 308 as its legal base, the Commission's justification of its choice of legal base will be provided to the Scrutiny Committee.

(HL Deb 12 November Vol. 714 WA208)

5/46
An FCO Minister wrote:

The EU has only the competences that have been conferred on it by member states. Competences not conferred on the EU through the treaties remain the exclusive competence of the member states. The Union may act only within the limits of the competences conferred on it. The fact that the Union is given competence in relation to a specific area does not mean that it can act on any aspect of that area, nor that it can act in any way it chooses. The Union can only exercise the powers it has been given by the member states for the purposes for which they were given and in accordance with the principles laid down in Articles 2 to 6 of the Treaty on the Functioning of the European Union, as amended.

(HL Deb 12 Nov Vol. 714 WA237)

Part Five: II.A.2.(a). *Subjects of International Law—International organisations—General—Participation of states and international organisations in international organisations and in their activities—Admission*

5/47

Asked about Rwanda joining the Commonwealth, the FCO Minister wrote:

Rwanda first applied to join the Commonwealth in the mid-1990s, and was considered in the run-up to the 1997 Commonwealth Heads of Government Meeting (CHOGM) in Edinburgh in 1997. At that stage, the UK supported the then criteria, which included the need for a constitutional link with an existing Commonwealth member. As such, Rwanda would not have been eligible to join. The 2007 CHOGM in Kampala saw a review of the membership criteria and the condition of a constitutional link was replaced by a close link to an existing Commonwealth member state. The UK has supported Rwanda's bid to join the Commonwealth from this time onwards. This matter has been discussed publicly since this time. However, it is not the practice to ratify such decisions made by the Commonwealth or member states in national parliaments–including that of the UK.

The decision on new applications to join is taken by all the Commonwealth Heads of Government. Commonwealth Heads of Government voted unanimously to allow Rwanda to join the organisation in Trinidad in November.

(HL Deb 14 December 2009 Vol. 715 cWA175)

5/48
Taiwan

An FCO Minister welcomed the news that Taiwan has been invited to participate in the World Health Assembly. He said:

I welcome the news that Taiwan will be invited to participate in the World Health Assembly as an observer. It is important that Taiwan can meaningfully participate in the global health safety net. The fact that the rapid spread of diseases is again high in the news emphasises the importance of this decision.

We hope that both sides of the Taiwan Strait will continue to engage in direct dialogue to resolve differences and strengthen cross-Strait stability.

(<www.fco.gov.uk/news> 29 April 2009)

Part Five: II.A.2.(b). *Subjects of International Law—International organisations—General—Participation of states and international organisations in international organisations and in their activities—Suspension, withdrawal, expulsion and deportation*

5/49 (See also **5/18** and **6/71**)
Fiji

An FCO Minister said:

Following a significant deterioration in the situation in Fiji, and the expiry of the 1 September 2009 deadline for a commitment to 2010 elections set by the

Commonwealth Ministerial Action Group (CMAG), the Commonwealth Secretariat have confirmed to us that Fiji is suspended from the Commonwealth with immediate effect. [The military regime took over in Fiji in a coup in 2006. Following more than two years of discussions and negotiations with the military regime, CMAG set a deadline for a commitment to 2010 elections at its meeting on 31 July 09, Ed.].

The Minister said:

It is absolutely right to suspend Fiji from the Commonwealth. The events of April this year showed shocking disregard for Commonwealth principles, with the regime effectively suspending the constitution and invoking 'Public Emergency Regulations' which include restrictions on gatherings of more than three people, restrictions on the opening hours of businesses, and measures to control the press. All Commonwealth member states must adhere to the principles laid out in the Harare Declaration, including respect for democracy, the rule of law, the independence of the judiciary, and fundamental human rights. CMAG rightly demanded that the regime commit to resuming the independent and inclusive President's Political Dialogue Forum process, supported by the Commonwealth and the UN, which would lead to credible elections by 2010. Despite numerous opportunities, the Interim Government in Fiji has consistently failed to meet CMAG's 1-September deadline for such a commitment. As a consequence, Fiji has been suspended with immediate effect. We welcome the visit of the delegation of Sir Paul Reeves to Fiji from 9–11 September. I hope his visit will lead to the Interim Government to take steps towards Fiji's return to democracy and the eventual return to the Commonwealth Family. The door is open to a Fijian government that respects the principles on which the Commonwealth is founded.

[For the Commonwealth statement, see <www.thecommonwealth.org/press/31555/34582/213087/010909.htm>, Ed.]

(<www.fco.gov.uk/news>, 1 September 2009)

Part Five: II.A.2. (c). *Subjects of International Law—International organisations—General—Participation of states and international organisations in international organisations and in their activities—Obligations of membership*

5/50
British Overseas Territories

A Minister wrote:

The British Overseas Territories do not contribute to the UK's subscriptions to international organisations. Some territories make their own contributions to certain international organisations. For example, Bermuda, the British Virgin Islands, the Turks and Caicos Islands and St Helena pay their subscriptions to the International Commission for the Conservation of Atlantic Tuna (ICCAT).

None of the overseas territories contributes to the UK's bilateral and multilateral aid expenditure. Bermuda runs a small-scale aid programme to fund a number of projects chosen by Bermuda. Recent examples have been assistance to a South African township and to hurricane relief in the Caribbean.

(HL Deb 6 July 2009 Vol. 712 cWA97)

Part Five: II.A.5. *Subjects of international law—International organisations—General—Responsibility of international organisations* (see also Part Thirteen:II.A.2.(a).)

5/51

The FCO Legal Adviser said in the debate in the Sixth Committee of the General Assembly on the Report of the ILC (A/64/10) on the question of the responsibility of international organisations:

I turn now to the statement of the United Kingdom on chapter IV of the International Law Commission's Report, dealing with the topic of responsibility of international organisations. The United Kingdom welcomes the significant progress made by the Commission during its 61st Session on this important and complex topic. We extend our gratitude to the Special Rapporteur, Mr Giorgio Gaja, for his seventh report and thank him, together with the Drafting Committee, for reflecting upon the comments provided previously by States and international organisations. The provisional adoption on first reading of the draft articles is an important step. It presents States with the first opportunity to consider the Commission's work on this topic as a whole. After further study, the United Kingdom will provide fuller written comments and observations to the Secretary-General by 1 January 2011, as requested by the Commission, and will also submit responses to the specific questions posed by the Commission in its Report. I will begin with some general comments. Since the ILC decided to include the topic of responsibility of international organisations in its programme of work, the United Kingdom has consistently cautioned against the wholesale application of the articles on State responsibility to international organisations, without giving proper consideration to the differences between States and international organisations. In particular, it must be recalled that, unlike international organisations, States enjoy full sovereignty under international law and have the complete range of powers to carry out their international obligations. It is also necessary to take account of the diversity of the types of international organisations. We agree that the articles on State responsibility provide a valuable starting point, but further consideration should be given to whether such rules may be sensibly extended to international organisations or whether distinct rules for international organisations have been or should be developed. We suggest that the Commission focus its attention on the specific issues raised by the contemporary practice of international organisations and urge caution in extending the analogy of State responsibility beyond well-established rules. The United Kingdom appreciates that these matters have been given considerable attention by the Special Rapporteur and the Commission. However, in our view it remains unclear how and whether a number of the draft articles will ever be capable of application to international organisations—for example, draft articles 20, 23 and 24 on self-defence, distress and necessity, respectively. We commend the Commission for its analysis of the available practice of international organisations, and appreciate its candid assessment that, in many cases, a material body of practice is lacking. While we recognise the necessity for the draft articles to be expressed at a level of generality, and appreciate their articulation of principles, it must be acknowledged that their utility in providing clear and practical guidance to States and international organisation is lessened wherever they are relatively unsupported by significant practice (such as draft articles 13–15 concerning aid and assistance, direction and control, and coercion). Accordingly, we would encourage the Commission to continue its endeavour to identify and analyse the practice of States and international organisations and to proceed cautiously in its absence. We also note, perhaps as a consequence of the lack of relevant practice, that a number of the draft articles use terminology and refer to concepts that are vaguely drawn or have unsettled meaning in the context of the responsibility of international organisations (for example, acts that would "circumvent an international obligation" of an international organisation (draft article 16), the safeguarding of "an essential interest of the international community as a whole" (draft article 24), "serious breach" and the "gross or systematic failure" to fulfil obligations (draft article 40), and references to "the international community as a whole" (in draft articles 42 and 48)). The United Kingdom would suggest that further work by the Commission is necessary to refine or review the use of such terms and concepts in the present context. I will now offer some comments on the draft articles. Concerning draft article 2, the United Kingdom agrees that the scope of the draft articles should include international organisations whose membership includes a mix of States and other entities, but at the same time be limited to international organisations with separate legal personality. This best reflects reality and the accepted legal character of international organisations. Similarly, we agree with the inclusive definition of "rules of the organisation" in draft article 2(b). However, further explanation about what constitutes "established practice" and when such "established practice" of an international organisation amounts to a "rule" would be helpful. We understand the Special Rapporteur considers the term "vague" but "indispensable". We share that concern and wonder whether "established practice" is best considered a means for interpreting the rules of an international organisation, rather than constituting a rule in itself. Further elaboration by the Commission would assist. Turning to questions of attribution, the United Kingdom has previously indicated that the attempt in draft article 5 to describe the conduct of both organs and agents of international organisations by reference to "conduct in the performance of functions" has resulted in a lack of clarity. As before, the United Kingdom would suggest that, in relation to agents, describing acts as taken in "his or her official capacity" may well provide a clear basis for attribution. The Special Rapporteur, at paragraph 22 of his Report, recognises that the formulation "in the performance of functions" implies that the organ or agent is acting in an official capacity. However, no such acknowledgment is made in the commentary to draft article 5. The United Kingdom considers that it would be useful to include such an acknowledgement. The United Kingdom is concerned that the use of "effective control" as a test for attribution of conduct to an international organisation in draft article 6 may not be capable of application across the range of factual circumstances and in light of the diversity in the kinds of relationships and co-operation that exist between international organisations and their members States. Much of the commentary and practice relied upon by the Commission is drawn from member States' participation in military operations mandated by international organisations. We question whether a general rule can or should be extrapolated from this particular context, and would certainly question an interpretation of "effective control" that was inflexibly applied. The cases of *Behrami* and *Saramati* [(2007) ECtHR's Nos 71412/01, 78166/01 (dec), Ed.] before the European Court of Human Rights illustrate the complexity of this issue. In its judgment, the Court cited the "effective control" criterion adopted by the ILC with apparent approval. However, the Court went on to decide that conduct was attributable to the United Nations, not its members States, because "the United Nations Security Council retained ultimate authority and control so that operation command only was delegated". The term "effectiveness" was used by the Court to describe the operational control exercised by NATO. We note the Special Rapporteur's view that, in the absence of judicial criticism in the *Behrami* and *Saramati* case, no change is required to draft article 6. Yet at the same time, the Special Rapporteur states that the Court "applied a different criterion for attribution and ... reached a conclusion that differed from the one that would have been reached on the basis of [draft] article [6]". In our view, this perhaps illustrates the limitations of "effective control" as a universal rule of attribution. What must be recognised is that the Court placed considerable weight on the practice of the United Nations in lawfully delegating and authorising the use of force by member States. More importantly, the United Kingdom is concerned that, in its discussion of *Behrami* and *Saramati*, the Commission may be understood to have proposed an "effective control" test that could be interpreted to undermine the general principle that when member States act pursuant to the authority and carry out the delegated functions of an international organisation their acts are attributable to the international organisation. The United Kingdom agrees that "control" of the conduct of a member State contingent by an international organisation would not be "effective" if that contingent sought and obtained orders from its State authorities before executing the orders issued by the central command, or if it operated totally outside the structure of the command and control of the international organisation. In this regard, it is important to consider the specificity of the delegation and the objectives of the conduct to be undertaken. The retention of some discretion by member States as to operational matters or implementation is not sufficient to detach their conduct from the delegated functions or mandate of the international organisation. The United Kingdom agrees with the Commission that it is relevant to compare the degree of control exercised by the lending State and the international organisation. However, we remain concerned that an interpretation of "effective control" in this context that emphasises operational control, as opposed to ultimate authority and control, suggests that the Commission may be imposing a general rule at the cost of considering the full factual picture and particular context in which international organisations and their members operate. Turning to draft article 9, the United Kingdom agrees with the Commission that it is not possible or desirable to establish a general rule to determine which rules of an international organisation constitute an obligation under international law. It is unsurprising that there is some divergence of view on this issue given the range of international organisations, some of which have developed and elaborate internal legal orders. In the circumstances, it is far better, in our view, to refrain from attempting to define which rules amount to international obligations (for example, by drawing distinctions between the source and subject matter of rules) and instead apply the draft article to rules of international organisations to the extent that those rules constitute obligations under international law. This leaves the issue to be resolved in a particular case. The United

Kingdom supports the policy rationale behind draft article 16—an international organisation should not be allowed to circumvent its international obligations by taking advantage of its separate legal personality and outsourcing conduct in breach of its obligations to its members. But it does not necessarily follow that the draft article should use the term "circumvention". That term lacks clarity, and it is difficult to see what it adds to paragraph 1. Although the commentary suggests that "paragraph 1 assumes that compliance with the binding decision of the international organisation necessarily entails circumvention of one of its intentional obligations", that is not evident from the drafting of the draft article, which seems to impose "circumvention" as an additional condition for responsibility under paragraph 1. We would suggest the ILC revisit this draft article to provide greater clarity. Moreover, in draft article 16 the Commission draws a distinction between binding decisions of an international organisation on the one hand, and recommendations and authorisations on the other. However, the quantity and consistency of practice of international organisations is arguably insufficient to support the use of these categorisations. For example, in the practice of some international organisations authorisations may produce binding legal effects whereas recommendations may not. And it is evident from the *Bosphorus* case [*Bosphorus Hava Yollari v Ireland*, ECHR, 30.6.05 Application No. 45036/98 Ed.] that the characterisation of a decision by an international organisation as a binding decision, authorisation or recommendation, and whether it in fact permits discretion by members in complying with or implementing the decision, is a difficult task. The United Kingdom would be wary of adopting the approach to responsibility set out in draft article 16 in circumstances where it is untested and its consequences hard to foresee. Regarding Chapter V on circumstances precluding wrongfulness, the United Kingdom appreciates the Commission's acknowledgement in the commentary that "available practice relating to international organisations is limited" in this area. Moreover, we agree with the Commission that there should not be "a presumption that the conditions under which an organisation may invoke a certain circumstance precluding wrongfulness are the same as those applicable to States". Yet, despite that conclusion, the Commission has largely transposed the circumstances precluding wrongfulness found in the articles on State responsibility. We suggest that the Commission revisit its approach. Of particular concern is the adoption of draft article 20 on self defence. We note the initial proposal of the Special Rapporteur to withdraw the draft article, and the careful reconsideration of the issue by the Drafting Committee. It must be recalled that article 51 of the Charter of the United Nations applies only to States whereas the application of self defence to international organisations remains unclear and the scope of existing practice is narrow. The practice highlighted by the ILC in its commentary is limited to the conduct of international organisations in peacekeeping operations. But it is not clear how the concept of self-defence would apply in light of the particular terms of a specific mandate pursuant to which an international organisation might deploy armed force or administer territory. It is hard to see how such specific mandates can give rise to a general right of international organisations to have recourse to self defence. In practice, only a few international organisations are ever likely to be in a position where they would need to exercise self defence, and the draft article offers no guidance on the conditions upon which self defence could be exercised by such them. Regarding draft article 22 on *force majeure*, the United Kingdom recalls its general comments that supporting practice is lacking. In that regard, we are somewhat surprised that the

Commission considers it "immaterial" that the available practice of international organisations invoking *force majeure* are limited to a dispute between an organisation and one of its employees and an express provision in an agreement between two international organisations. In our view, this is not practice from which to draw general rules and principles. Turning to draft article 24, the United Kingdom recognises the efforts of the Commission to reach a compromise between the various views of States on the applicability of necessity to international organisations. However, we remain concerned that the pre-conditions and parameters of necessity as set out in draft article 24 are vague. Although necessity is limited to the protection of the "essential interests of the international community" to prevent the abuse of the doctrine, the boundaries of such a concept are uncertain. Who or what constitutes the international community in this context? In what circumstances would it be within the "functions" of the international organisation to protect such an interest? Moreover, it is not evident why such an interest is more worthy of protection than the essential interests of the international organisation itself, or even a common essential interest of its members. We would encourage the Commission to provide further clarification. Without such refinement, the United Kingdom finds it difficult to judge whether it would ever be appropriate for international organisations to invoke necessity as a circumstance precluding wrongfulness.

Turning to the content of international responsibility of international organisations, draft articles 27–30 reflect the equivalent provisions of the articles on States responsibility. Subject to what I will say in a moment regarding *lex specialis*, the United Kingdom agrees that, given their general character, these provisions are appropriate in the context of international organisations. However, draft article 31 requires closer consideration. The rule it sets out is based on article 32 of the articles on State responsibility, which provides that a State may not invoke its internal rules as a justification for breaching its international obligations. These situations are not identical. First, the internal rules of an international organisation may affect the responsibility of the organisation towards its members. Accordingly, the United Kingdom agrees with the Commission that such a situation should remain unaffected by the draft article. Second, and more fundamentally, States enjoy complete sovereignty under international law, whereas international organisations have only those powers conferred upon them by their member States and organisation through their constituent instruments. This may leave States and international organisations in an unequal position to fulfil their international obligations. Although this may not pose any difficulty in fulfilling treaty obligations, where international organisations may be assumed to have the competence to comply with those treaties they enter into, difficulties may be encountered in relation to obligations arising from other sources of international law. In our view, the lack of practice in this context makes it hard to assess whether the draft article offers assistance to States in their relations with international organisations. Regarding reparation for injury, I need only address some comments to draft article 39 on "ensuring the effective performance of the obligation of reparation". The United Kingdom is pleased to note that the Commission has confirmed in the commentary that draft article 39 does not "envisage any further instance in which States and international organisations would be held internationally responsible for the act of the organisation of which they are members". Similarly, we appreciate the clarification, in accordance with the view of the majority of the members of the Commission, that "no subsidiary obligation of members towards the injured party is considered to arise when the responsible organisation is not in a position to make reparation", and thus "the injured party would have to rely on the fulfilment by the international organisation of its obligations" to make reparations. The United Kingdom fully subscribes to this view. However, the United Kingdom is disappointed that the text of the draft article does not appear to adequately reflect these points. Although the draft article addresses the central issue—that "appropriate measures" be taken "in accordance with the rules of the organisation"—it does not make clear to whom the obligation to take appropriate measures is owed. Is the obligation owed only to other member States as a function of the rules of the organisation, or is the obligation also owed to non-member States? Unfortunately, it appears to us that the draft article leaves unresolved the relationship between the proposed requirement to take appropriate measures and the rules of the international organisation in determining what role member States might have in ensuring the organisation can meet its obligations to make reparations. We would be grateful if the Commission could consider whether greater clarity could be brought to this question. As the United Kingdom has previously noted, debate continues regarding which norms may be classified as "peremptory" and what constitutes a "serious breach" or a "gross and systematic failure" to fulfil an obligation. Draft article 40 must be seen in the context of that debate and, consequently, the lack of clarity regarding the meaning of those terms will inevitably affect the utility of the draft article. Nevertheless, the United Kingdom accepts that in some circumstances States should cooperate to bring an end to certain breaches. We agree with the Commission that "it cannot be entirely ruled out" that such a breach may be committed by an international organisation. However, it must equally be recognised that international organisations are not ordinarily in a position to breach peremptory norms as such conduct would almost certainly be *ultra vires* the constituent instruments and rules of the organisation. We welcome the Commission's observation that the draft article is not intended to vest an international organisation with functions that it would not otherwise have. We would also welcome clarification by the Commission, perhaps in the commentary, that not all States would be equally affected by a serious breach of a peremptory norm, nor, more importantly, would they necessarily be in an equal position to take steps to bring about the cessation of such conduct. As presently drafted, the draft articles impose a single rule for all States without qualification. The United Kingdom notes that the draft articles and their commentary do not define the concept of the "invocation of responsibility", which is referred to repeatedly in draft articles 42–49. The Commission states in the commentary that invocation of responsibility "implies the entitlement to claim from the responsible international organisation compliance with the obligations in 3 of the draft articles", but no further guidance is provided. In our view, it would be helpful if the Commission made clear that informally calling upon an international organisation to abide by its obligations, or initiating investigations or dispute settlement procedures that do not entail a binding decision, do not constitute the invocation of responsibility and, hence, would not be subject to the limits set out in the draft articles. We invite the Commission to consider providing a definition or further elaboration. Regarding draft articles 42 and 48, the United Kingdom reiterates that, in light of the diversity of functions, nature and membership of international organisations, it is not evident that international organisations are in the same position as States to protect the interests underlying obligations owed to "the international community as a whole" and, accordingly, we doubt whether international organisation should be able to invoke responsibility for their breach. On the question of the entitlement of a State to invoke the responsibility of an international organisation, this may depend on whether the State is a member of the organisation and whether it is permitted by the rules of that organisation. Accordingly, there may be inconsistencies between the rules of an organisation and the provisions of draft articles 42 and 48. Is an obligation that is owed to all member States under the constituent instruments of an international organisation owed "individually" to each Member State? If not, it may be that responsibility could be invoked in accordance with draft article 48, paragraph 1, where the obligation is "established for the protection of a collective interest" of the members. In the commentary to draft article 48, the Commission notes that "obligations that an international organisation may have towards it members under its internal rules do not necessarily fall within this category". Consequently, the draft articles do not appear to provide clarity on how their provisions interact with any rules of an international organisation concerning the invocation of responsibility by members for the breach of an obligation owed under the organisation's constituent instruments. The United Kingdom notes that practice regarding invocation in circumstances where there is a plurality of responsible States and international organisations is very limited. This makes it difficult to assess the provisions of draft article 47 and, in particular, whether the so-called "subsidiary responsibility" of member States and organisations can be invoked only after attempts to seek reparation from the primarily responsible State or organisation have failed. Accordingly, the United Kingdom would urge caution here. Similarly, practice is limited regarding the invocation of responsibility for a breach by an international organisation of an obligation owed to the international community as a whole, and particularly invocation of such responsibility by an international organisation. In principle, the United Kingdom welcomes that limitation in paragraph 3 of draft article 47 that an international organisation may only invoke such responsibility when "safeguarding the interest of the international community underlying the obligation breached is included among the functions of the [organisation]". Such a limitation ensures that the draft article does not expand the powers or functions of the international organisation. The entitlement of international organisations and its members to take countermeasures against each other is a difficult and sensitive matter. The United Kingdom appreciates the care with which the Special Rapporteur and the Drafting Committee have addressed draft articles 21 and 50–56 on this issue. As we have expressed on previous occasions, the United Kingdom is not convinced that, among all the circumstances precluding wrongfulness, countermeasures requires the detailed elaboration provided in Part IV, Chapter II, particularly given that practice is scarce and the legal regime uncertain. The United Kingdom agrees that any right of international organisations to take countermeasures should be subject to applicable rules of the organisation, as set out by the Commission in draft article 21, paragraph 2(a) and draft article 51, paragraph (a). Members must be entitled to limit the conduct of the organisation in this regard. The more difficult question is whether, absent any applicable rules, an international organisation may take countermeasures against a member State or organisation. In general terms, the United Kingdom is uncomfortable with the notion that countermeasures should play a role in relations between an international organisation and its members. As expressed on previous occasions, the United Kingdom remains concerned that draft articles 57–59 largely duplicate the corresponding provisions of the articles on State responsibility, and without significant State practice, the commentary is unable to provide concrete examples of when and how the draft articles would apply. As the Commission recognises, the practice cited in the commentary to draft article 57 in fact provides an example of a breach of a primary rule of international law, not a State incurring responsibility for aiding and assisting an international organisation. More importantly, we appreciate the recognition by the Commission that mere participation in the decision-making process of an international organisation does not constitute aiding or assisting. But this does not provide a clear distinction between the ordinary incidence of membership and participation in an international organisation and what may be considered "aiding and assisting" by a member State. We would also urge the Commission to give further consideration to the circumstances in which a State might "direct and control" or "coerce" an international organisation. Turning to draft article 60, the United Kingdom supports the general principle that a State should not be able to avoid responsibility for breaching an international obligation by transferring competence to an international organisation of which it is a member and taking advantage of its separate legal personality. We commend the Commission for its willingness to take a novel approach to this issue. However, we remain concerned by the breadth of responsibility envisaged under draft article 60 and the uncertainty of its operation. We note that the Commission has given careful consideration to the suggestions made by States that the scope of responsibility be narrowed by the requirement of some element of bad faith, misuse or particular intent. We do not necessarily disagree with the Special Rapporteur that such a subjective requirement could make the draft article difficult to apply. However, such difficulties do not appear to be alleviated by the formulation in draft article 60 that a State "seeks to avoid compliance" with one of its international obligations by "taking advantage" of the organisation's competence and thereby "prompting" the organisation to act in its place. The scope and meaning of these terms are by no means settled. We would also suggest that the Commission give further thought to paragraph 2 of draft article 60 and the suggestions made by others that the scope of responsibility be limited to circumstances in which a member State and the international organisation do not share the same or an equivalent obligation. The United Kingdom notes the statement by the Commission in the commentary that draft article 61 "implies" that "membership does not as such entail for member States international responsibility when the organisation commits an internationally wrongful act". The United Kingdom agrees. Such a conclusion arises from the separate legal personality of international organisations and is amply supported by the jurisprudence cited by Commission in its commentary. However, we wonder whether it would offer greater clarity for this rule to be stated in the draft articles themselves. Given the broad recognition of the rule of separate legal personality, one must be slow to infer exceptions. The United Kingdom is concerned that the interpretation of draft article 61 is uncertain, particularly regarding the circumstances in which an injured party may be entitled to rely on the responsibility of a member. It remains unclear how the rules of the international organisation affect the acceptance of responsibility by a member State or the entitlement of an injured party to rely on such responsibility. Accordingly, we would suggest that the Commission revisit the draft article. The new General Provisions concluding the current set of draft articles are a sensible addition. We agree that the general rules of international law should continue to govern questions of responsibility not addressed by the present draft articles, as provided in draft article 64. This also acknowledges the possibility of further developments in international law relating to the responsibility of international organisations. Similarly, we welcome the inclusion of draft articles 65 and 66 that ensure the draft articles do not prejudice or any question of individual responsibility arising out of the conduct of international organisations or the Charter of the United Nations. Let me conclude my comments on this topic by welcoming the inclusion of draft article 63 on *lex specialis*. The United Kingdom agrees with the Special Rapporteur that the wide variety of international organisations makes it essential to recognise the existence of special rules. Such rules ought to be able to qualify, supplement or even replace the general rules set out in the draft articles, as provided by draft article 63. In our view, the Commission is also right to highlight the rules of international organisations as special rules that are relevant throughout the draft articles wherever they concern the relationship between international organisations and their members. We note with interest the suggestion considered by the Drafting Committee that a provision requiring the special characteristics of a particular organisation to be taken into account in applying the draft articles also be included, in addition to the *lex specialis* provision. The United Kingdom is attracted by such a suggestion, which would go some way to ensuring that the draft articles are applied in a flexible manner that allowed appropriate and important distinctions to be drawn between the various international organisations. We do not see any real risk that such a provision would allow international organisations to seek to escape their responsibility. In fact, the contrary may be true—such a provision could assist in holding a particular international organisation responsible where a strict application of the draft articles may not have. We would urge the Commission to reconsider including such a provision.

(Sixth Committee 64th Session of the United Nations General Assembly 27 October 2009. Text supplied by FCO)

Part Five: II.B.1. *Subjects of International Law—International organisations—Particular types of organisation—Universal organisations*

5/52

The Foreign Secretary was asked what representations he had received from the Government of Iraq on *(a)* the return of monies held in escrow under the UN oil-for-food programme and not yet received and *(b)* the disbursement of international commitments for development aid; what estimate he had made of the sums due to the Iraqi Government in each case. An FCO Minister wrote:

The Government have not received any specific representations from the Government of Iraq (GoI) on the oil-for-food programme. However, the GoI has asked us to help it resolve outstanding UN resolutions relating to Iraq. We support the review of those UN Security Council Resolutions that are still in effect as part of the process to help Iraq normalise its relationship with the international community. We will continue to work with other members of the UN Security Council to resolve outstanding issues on the oil-for-food programme so that it can be concluded with the mutual agreement of all parties, including the Iraqi Government. We have not received any representations from the GoI on the disbursement of international development commitments. Any outstanding commitments from the international community regarding the disbursement of development funds are a matter for the GoI to address directly with donors.

(HC Deb 19 May 2009 Vol 492 c1325W)

Part Five: II.B.2. *Subjects of International Law—International organisations—Particular types of organisation—Regional organisations*

5/53 (See also **7/5**)
Iran

Hossein Rassam, an Iranian national who was a political advisor at the British Embassy in Tehran, was arrested following the disputed presidential elections in Iran in June 2009, convicted at a trial the British government regarded as being in breach of his human rights and given a 4-year sentence. A British government statement said:

Reports that Hossein Rassam has been sentenced to four years in prison are deeply concerning. Such a decision is wholly unjustified and represents further harassment of Embassy staff for going about their normal and legitimate duties. Our Ambassador in Tehran has spoken to the Deputy Foreign Minister to express our concerns and our acting Permanent Under Secretary has called in the Iranian Ambassador in London.

We understand the sentence can be appealed. I urge the authorities to conduct this quickly and overturn this harsh sentence. We are in close touch with EU and other international partners, who continue to show solidarity in the face of this unacceptable Iranian action. This will be seen as an attack against the entire diplomatic community in Iran and important principles are at stake.

The French Foreign Ministry have also condemned the sentencing. A spokesperson said:

We note with great concern the sentencing of Hossein Rassam, an employee of the British Embassy in Tehran and we express our full solidarity with the UK. We consider any action taken against a member state of the EU, whether a citizen or employee, to be an action against the EU as a whole.

France considers the sentencing of Hossein Rassam to be unjustified. France strongly recommends that appeals to this sentence should be considered without delay in order that the sentence be changed. Furthermore, France expects the Iranian justice system to confirm the innocence of Clotilde Reisse, along with the other locally employed staff of the French and British embassies.

An EU Presidency statement also expressed 'deep concern' for Hossein Rassam and said the sentence was 'unjustified and harsh'.

(<www.fco.gov.uk/news>, 28 October 2009)

Part Five: IV.B. *Subjects of international law—International organisations—Entities and groups other than states and international organisations—Dependencies*

5/54
British Overseas Territories

An FCO Minister said:

I welcome the new Constitution for St Helena, Ascension and Tristan da Cunha (The St Helena, Ascension and Tristan da Cunha Constitution Order 2009 No. 1751, Ed.). I am pleased to see that there has been so much public discussion about the Constitution over a number of years. The UK and the Councils on the three islands have worked together openly and constructively to ensure that the new Constitution will serve those islands well in the future.

The previous Constitution from 1988 reflects a very different world. The new Constitution, on the other hand, is one fit for the 21st Century. For the first time it includes a Bill of Rights; it is also clearer on the role of the Governor, introducing a number of important limits on Governor's powers; and there will be separate chapters for each of the three islands allowing for institutions that really suit the islands they serve. It represents the kind of modern partnership that we aim for with all of our Overseas Territories.

This is good news for all those who live on St Helena, Ascension and Tristan da Cunha, and I look forward to working with them under these new arrangements.

Notes appended to the statement said:

The St Helena, Ascension and Tristan da Cunha Constitution Order 2009 was made on 8 July by Her Majesty and the Privy Council. It is expected to come into operation in the autumn.

The 1999 White Paper on the Overseas Territories (OTs) committed the UK to review constitutional frameworks for the territories to ensure consistency with the principles that underlie the modern partnerships between Britain and the OTs. Intensive consultation on a new Constitution on St Helena began in 2003 and a number of rounds of negotiations and public consultations have taken place since then. The Ascension and Tristan Councils wrote in support of the new Constitution at the end of June 2009; and the majority of the St Helena Legislative Councillors have expressed their support for it.

The new Constitution replaces a 1988 Order which no longer serves the needs of those living on the three islands well in the 21st century. For example, it gives some very broad powers to the Governor and has no bill of rights. It is also confusing in the way it sets out what provisions relate to St Helena, to Ascension and Tristan da Cunha. The new Constitution makes changes in all of these respects, it recognises legal change that has gone on on the islands and elsewhere since, and reflects the reality of changes that have taken place in practice. A bill of rights will mean that individuals wanting to make a complaint will now be able to do so in the local courts, and not have to go to Strasbourg. The Constitution also establishes true independence for the judiciary and the public service and a new set of provisions on financial issues will ensure greater transparency, accountability, and independent audit.

(<www.fco.gov.uk/news>, 9 July 2009)

5/55
The FCO Minister of State wrote:

The Overseas Territories are responsible for their own public finances. The Foreign and Commonwealth Office does not accept any legal liability for borrowing undertaken by the Overseas Territories. However, we continue to seek involvement in Overseas Territories Governments' borrowing decisions in order to ensure the good governance of the territories. Explicit permission is required for borrowing when certain public finance guidelines have been breached. These guidelines relate to levels of debt and cash reserves.

(HL Deb 28 October 2009 Vol 713 cWA148)

5/56
The Foreign Secretary was asked what recent assessment his Department has made of the merits of granting full independence to *(a)* the British Virgin Islands, *(b)* Bermuda, *(c)* the Turks and Caicos Islands, *(d)* Anguilla and *(e)* the Cayman Islands. An FCO Minister wrote:

The 1999 White Paper on the Overseas Territories (Partnership for Progress and Prosperity) [Cm4264, Ed.] made clear that it is for the citizens of each territory to determine whether they wish to stay linked to Britain or not. Our policy remains to give every help and encouragement to those territories that wish to proceed to independence, where it is an option. Since the White Paper, no territory has opted for independence, we have therefore not made a recent assessment of the merits of granting independence to any overseas territory.

(HC Deb 2 February 2009 Vol 487 c881W)

5/57
An FCO Minister wrote:

British and Mauritian Government officials met in London on Wednesday 14 January 2009. The purpose of the meeting was to establish a dialogue between the UK and Mauritius on the British Indian Ocean Territory (BIOT) as agreed by the Prime Minister and the Mauritian Prime Minister, Dr Navinchandra Ramgoolam.

Officials discussed the latest legal and policy developments relating to BIOT. British officials set out the view of the UK on sovereignty and how the United Kingdom had to bear in mind its treaty obligations with the USA. Mauritian officials set out the view of Mauritius on sovereignty. There were discussions on fishing rights, environmental concerns, the continental shelf, future visits to the territory by the Chagossians and respective policies towards resettlement.

(HL Deb 24 February 2009 Vol 708 cWA35)

5/58
Bermuda

The Foreign Secretary was asked several questions about the transfer of four Chinese ethnic Uighurs from Guantanamo to Bermuda. He said:

The Government of Bermuda began discussions with the US Administration on or about 20 May 2009. The FCO received notification from the Governor of Bermuda on 11 June 2009 that the Government of Bermuda had been in discussion with the US on the transfer of four former detainees from Guantanamo Bay. The Government of Bermuda acted outside their competence.

The four former detainees arrived in Bermuda early on 11 June 2009. The Government of Bermuda notified the Governor a few hours earlier that some Muslim Uighur refugees were on their way, without mention of the United States or Guantanamo Bay.

We are working with the Government of Bermuda and the US to ensure that the security assessment will be completed as soon as possible.

We are not reviewing the Bermuda constitution, but in light of this case we are reviewing the operation of the General Entrustment which is the agreement that delegates to the Government of Bermuda the authority to conduct external negotiations in specified areas. We expect to complete this by the end of July 2009.

An FCO Minister added:

There were no discussions between the Foreign Secretary and his US counterpart on the transfer of four detainees from Guantanamo Bay to Bermuda before the transfer took place.

(HC Debs 22 June 2009 Vol 494 c630–631W)

5/59
Later, the Foreign Secretary said, answering a question about the competence of the Governor and Government of Bermuda in Foreign Affairs:

The Governor has responsibility for the conduct of any business of the Bermuda Government with respect to the external affairs of Bermuda in accordance with section 62 of the Bermuda Constitution. The Government of Bermuda have been delegated, subject to certain conditions, authority under a 1968 General Entrustment to negotiate and conclude agreements in certain specified areas with other countries. Other entrustments have also been issued at various times authorising specific negotiations.

[Bermuda Constitution, Section 62: Governor's special responsibilities

1. The Governor, acting in his discretion, shall be responsible for the conduct (subject to the provisions of this Constitution and of any other law) of any business of the Government, including the administration of any department of government, with respect to the following matters -a. external affairs . . . Ed.]

(HC Debs 6 July Vol 495 c545–546W)

5/60
Cayman Islands

An FCO Minister wrote:

The International Union for Conservation of Nature has identified the species listed in the following table, which are found in the Cayman Islands, as endangered species. The management and protection of the environment has been devolved to the individual Overseas Territories. However, we recognise that there are capacity limitations in the Overseas Territories and that they need help to address conservation issues. The Government support the Overseas Territories by providing funding through the Overseas Territories Environment Programme, a joint Foreign and Commonwealth Office and Department for International Development funded programme, and through the Darwin Initiative, a Department for Environment, Food and Rural Affairs funded programme, to encourage the conservation and preservation of biodiversity in the Cayman Islands.[There follows a list of the designated species, Ed.]

(HC Deb 9 March 2009 Vol 489 c44W)

5/61 (See also **5/29**) **Falkland Islands**

An FCO Minister answered several questions about the Falkland Islands Dependencies. She wrote:

Fishery protection and management are the responsibility of the government of South Georgia and the South Sandwich Islands which uses a range of measures including a strict licensing regime, fisheries protection vessels, at sea inspections, satellite-based vessel monitoring systems and the deployment of observers.

The Foreign and Commonwealth Office represents UK interests at the Commission for the Conservation of Antarctic Marine Living Resources (CCAMLR). A key UK objective at CCAMLR is to defend the integrity and economic viability of the South Georgia fishery. This is achieved by obtaining consensus on total allowable catch (TAC) limits which are agreed on the basis of robust scientific evidence. The UK strives to ensure that CCAMLR adopts effective conservation measures to curb illegal, unregulated and unreported fishing across the Southern Ocean as a whole. The government of South Georgia and the South Sandwich Islands (GSGSSI), the Foreign and Commonwealth Office and the British Antarctic Survey work collaboratively to protect wildlife on South Georgia. The Government works closely with the Commission of the Conservation of Antarctic Marine Living Resources (CCAMLR) and the international Agreement on the Conservation of Albatrosses and Petrels to conserve most of South Georgia's breeding populations. In addition the GSGSSI has a number of polices in place to protect life in both the marine and terrestrial environment, these include the designation of specially protected areas, specially protected species as well as prohibitions on disturbing, killing, capturing or exporting native fauna. These are set out in South Georgia's Plan for Progress—Managing the Environment 2006–2010. The Foreign and Commonwealth Office, (FCO) the British Antarctic Survey (BAS) and the government of South Georgia and the South Sandwich Islands (GSGSSI) work collaboratively to investigate and protect biodiversity and ensure the conservation of endangered species at South Georgia. The BAS have a long-term monitoring and survey programme which monitors seabird and seal population dynamics, feeding ecology and reproductive performance. The GSGSSI has strict procedures in place to prevent the introduction or transfer of alien species and in support of this the FCO is part-funding the development of a biosecurity store to be built at South Georgia to safeguard native species and control invasive species.

(HC Deb 2 February 2009 Vol 487 c884W-886W)

5/62 (See also **11/2–4**)
Gibraltar

The Government were asked whether they would support Gibraltar's application to the European Court of Justice which challenges the habitat environmental directives which give Spain rights over British waters around Gibraltar on environmental issues. A Minister wrote:

As the UK is the only member state competent to propose a site covering British Gibraltar Territorial Waters (BGTW), we do not recognise the validity of the site in question. We therefore do not consider that the decision allows Spain any rights in BGTW. We are aware that the Government of Gibraltar have applied to the Court of First Instance to challenge the listing of Estrecho Oriental under Commission Decision 2009/95/EC. This is a matter which we take very seriously and we are examining Gibraltar's case in detail to determine what action we might take.

(HL Deb 16 June 2009 Vol 711 cWA201)

5/63
Sark

The Government were asked what was the constitutional and fiscal relationship between the United Kingdom and Sark. A Minister said:

Sark is an island of the Bailiwick of Guernsey—a self-governing Crown dependency. The Crown is responsible for its good governance. The States of Guernsey legislates for Sark in certain matters, but generally not without Sark's consent. Sark has its own legislature with the power to reform its constitutional system. Sark has an independent relationship with the UK through the Lieutenant Governor of Guernsey, and legislation made by Sark must be assented to by Her Majesty on the advice of her Privy Council. Sark does not have a fiscal relationship with the UK.

(HL Deb 16 June 2009 Vol 711 c947)

Part Six: The Individual (including the Corporation) in International Law

Part Six: I. *The Individual (including the Corporation) in International Law—Nationality*

6/1
The Borders, Citizenship and Immigration Act 2009, SS.39–49, make provision for certain means of acquiring British citizenship, including by naturalisation and registration.

6/2

The Government were asked which categories of British nationals currently enjoyed a right to a United Kingdom passport; and what were the circumstances in which that right might be revoked. A Minister wrote:

All categories of British nationals, i.e. British citizens, British Overseas Territories citizens, British Overseas citizens, British subjects, British Nationals (Overseas) and British Protected Persons, are eligible for United Kingdom passports. Passports are currently issued at the discretion of the Secretary of State in exercise of the royal prerogative, but in practice once nationality and identity have been established, passports may be refused or withdrawn only in the limited circumstances that have been notified to Parliament. In addition eligibility for a United Kingdom passport could be revoked in certain circumstances by deprivation of citizenship. Section 40 of the British Nationality Act 1981 enables the Secretary of State to deprive a person of their citizenship status, if acquired as a result of naturalisation or registration, if that status was obtained by fraud, false representation or concealment of material fact. The Secretary of State may also deprive of citizenship status on conduciveness grounds—for example, in cases where an individual has committed serious criminality following their acquisition of that British citizenship status. Deprivation of citizenship status would mean the UK passport held by the individual would subsequently be revoked by the Secretary of State under the royal prerogative powers.

(HL Deb 2 February 2009 Vol 707 cWA97)

6/3

The Government were asked whether the Borders, Citizenship and Immigration Bill would redress any racially discriminatory impacts of United Kingdom nationality law arising from the distinction between British citizens and other categories of British national with more limited rights of entry to the United Kingdom. A Minister wrote:

We are not proposing to make any changes in relation to the status of British nationals within the Borders, Citizenship and Immigration Bill. We have already made provision for those holding other forms of British nationality to register as British citizens. If a person lives in the United Kingdom for a period of five years, and meets certain residence requirements, he or she can apply for registration under Section 4(2) of the British Nationality Act 1981. Since April 2003, British overseas citizens, British subjects and British protected persons have been able to apply for registration under Section 4B of that Act if they do not have any other nationality. The British Nationality Hong Kong Act 1997 also provides for the registration of those who would otherwise be stateless and are ordinarily resident in Hong Kong. In his citizenship review Lord Goldsmith noted that there are particular legal reasons why we need to retain the category of British National (Overseas) with links to Hong Kong, because of our treaty commitments. He also acknowledged that the status of British overseas territories citizen needs to continue in order to recognise connections to a particular overseas territory as well as to Britain. He therefore proposed a change to end the separate statuses of British overseas citizen, British subject and British protected person [Lord Goldsmith, "Citizenship: Our Commoin Bond (2008), Ch,4, Ed.].

We are of the view, however, that any changes to the status of those in these three groups at this time would still leave complications in the overall nationality framework, and that our earlier reforms and the passage of time will have the combined effect of reducing any current anomalies.

(HL Deb 12 February 2009 Vol 707 cWA215)

6/4

The Government were asked whether the Borders, Citizenship and Immigration Bill was compatible with Protocol 4 to the European Convention of Human Rights which guaranteed the right of nationals to enter their country of nationality. A Minister wrote:

The right of British Nationals to enter the UK and any compatible rights under Protocol 4 to the European Convention of Human Rights is not an issue that is covered by the Borders, Citizenship and Immigration Bill. Only persons with the right of abode in the UK under Section 2 of the Immigration Act 1971, being British citizens and certain Commonwealth citizens, are free to enter and remain in the UK without being subject to immigration control. British nationals without the right of abode do not enjoy a right as set out in the Protocol 4 of the European Convention on Human Rights. This is because the UK has signed but not ratified Article 3 of Protocol 4 to the European Convention on Human Rights. The protocol was signed in 1963 but not subsequently ratified because of the potential conflict with our domestic law in relation to the issue of British passports and the acquisition of a right of abode by categories of British nationals who do not currently have that right. British nationals continue to be admitted freely to the United Kingdom on production of a United Kingdom passport issued in the United Kingdom and Islands or the Republic of Ireland prior to 1 January 1973, unless their passport has been endorsed to show that they are subject to immigration control. British nationals may also naturalise or register as a British citizen under the British Nationality Act 1981 and therefore acquire the right of abode in the UK under the Immigration Act 1971.

(HL Deb 2 March 2009 Vol 708 cWA123)

6/5

A Minister wrote:

The UK has always maintained the position that all countries are under an obligation to readmit their own nationals who are removed from another country, independently of readmission agreements. The UK wants to build international alliances to help deliver our policies. A key element of this is to co-operate on migration through bilateral and multilateral relationships with other countries. To this end the UK has formal agreements and informal arrangements with various countries to readmit their nationals. Only where there is a specific need does the UK seek to negotiate readmission agreements. There is a bilateral readmission agreement in force with Switzerland, signed on 16 December 2005, and we also have another with Algeria which was signed on 11 July 2006. There are currently no negotiations being undertaken for a bilateral readmission agreement with any third country. The UK also works closely with our European partners in the area of returns. The European Union has its own framework of agreements called European Community Readmission Agreements (ECRA). These are negotiated and signed by the European Commission on behalf of the member states and Ministers decide on the UK's opt-in position to these agreements.

There are 11 European Community readmission agreements which have been signed and are now in force as follows:

Hong Kong signed on—27 November 2002 Macao signed on—13 October 2003 Sri Lanka signed on—4 June 2004 Albania signed on—14 April 2005 Russia signed on—25 May 2006 Ukraine signed on—18 June 2007 Former Yugoslav Republic of Macedonia signed on—18 September 2007 Serbia signed on—18 September 2007 Montenegro signed on—18 September 2007 Bosnia Herzegovina signed on—18 September 2007 Moldova signed on—10 October 2007

There are also open ECRA mandates with the following countries, but these are at various stages of negotiation and agreements have yet to be signed: China, Pakistan, Algeria, Morocco, Turkey and Georgia. The UK has opted into all ECRAs negotiated so far, and to all negotiating mandates proposed to date.

(HC Deb 4 March 2009 Vol 488 c1637W-1638W)

6/6
On naturalisation, a Minister wrote:

The qualifying period of residence for naturalisation may begin as soon as the refugee presents him/herself to the authorities. There is an additional requirement for naturalisation that the applicant should not have been in breach of immigration law during the qualifying period. However, those who present themselves to the authorities immediately upon arrival in the United Kingdom will not be considered to be in breach of immigration law during the period in which their asylum claim is under consideration.

(HL Deb 11 March 2009 Vol 708 cWA248)

Part Six: II. *The Individual (including the Corporation) in International Law—Diplomatic and consular protection* **(see also 13/2)**

6/7
The Government were asked what advice they were offering to United Kingdom citizens who had bought property in Cyprus but had not received their title deeds. An FCO Minister wrote:

The Foreign and Commonwealth Office (FCO) travel advice for Cyprus, available on the FCO website, advises British citizens who encounter difficulties as a result of purchasing property in Cyprus to seek qualified legal advice on their rights and methods of redress. This would include difficulties in obtaining deeds to property to which the purchaser is entitled. Although the Government are unable to become involved with individual cases, our High Commission in Cyprus does support community associations in Cyprus that are dedicated to resolving the problems of property buyers, and gives details of those associations on its website, accessible via the Cyprus travel advice . . . Our High Commissioner in Cyprus recently raised the issue of title deeds not being supplied to purchasers on completion of a property purchase in Cyprus with the Republic of Cyprus Ministry of the Interior, and received assurances that the Cypriot Government intend to introduce a Bill to address this issue. The Government recognise that this issue has the potential to affect a large number of British citizens who have purchased property in Cyprus, and will continue to take a close interest in the measures by which the Cypriot Government attempt to resolve this problem.

(HL Deb 12 January 2009 Vol 706 cWA93)

6/8

The FAC had concluded in its Report on the Human Rights Report 2008:

11. We conclude that the Government's intention to establish the same standards for dual and mono British nationals in relation to consular access is to be welcomed. We recommend that this change should be brought into effect as soon as possible, and that in its response to this Report the Government sets out a timetable for this to be achieved. We further recommend that all British nationals should be offered consular advice as soon as the Government is aware of their detention, and certainly before they are interrogated by any foreign intelligence service. (Paragraph 57)

The FCO replied:

32. The Government welcomes the Committee's conclusions on the importance of consular access and assistance. Consular staff aim to contact British nationals detained overseas within 24 hours of being told about their arrest or detention. If the detainee so wishes, consular staff will then seek access in order to visit them as soon as possible. How soon a consular visit takes place will depend on the detaining authorities and on the practicalities of access to the place of detention. 33. We would not normally offer consular assistance to a dual British national in the state of their other nationality. However, as the Foreign Secretary indicated when giving evidence to the FAC in June, we may make an exception to this if we consider that there is a special humanitarian reason to do so. Current consular guidance makes clear that such reasons would include situations where we have reason to believe there is the possibility of mistreatment or torture. It specifies that in all cases of alleged mistreatment of a dual national in the country of their other nationality, consular staff should record the allegation and follow the same procedures as for a mono British national. The Guidance goes on to say that in a country where there are general concerns about mistreatment of certain detainees, such as those held in relation to terrorist or political offences, consular staff should try to contact any dual national held in relation to such offences, regardless of whether specific concerns have been raised. These guidelines are already in operation. 34. At the moment, the Government do not propose to make a more general change to the policy of not seeking access to dual nationals in the country of their other nationality where there are no concerns over mistreatment or other special humanitarian considerations. 35. In the Government's response to the Committee's report last year we stated that we were aware of eight cases of British or dual British/Pakistani nationals having been detained on suspicion of terrorist offences in Pakistan since 2000. A recent Joint Committee on Human Rights report raised a discrepancy between this figure and 11 cases mentioned in a footnote to their report. As the Committee is aware we reviewed

our files in light of this and confirmed that we were aware of 11 individuals. Of the three individuals not referred to in our response last year, one was a mono British national, and the other two were dual nationals. Consular officials were aware of all at the time of their detention. Consular access was sought in all cases but only provided in one. Consular records indicate that allegations of mistreatment were made in one case. None of these three individuals are still detained in Pakistan. 36. Consular records are designed to allow us to manage and record individual case work. The records are therefore designed to be searched primarily by individual case. At the moment there are limits on how easily the records can be searched by thematic criteria. In response to recent parliamentary and public interest in allegations of mistreatment of those detained overseas, we are putting in place systems for certain categories of case to be recorded separately in future in order to make retrieval easier. In addition, we are not always informed by the local authorities when a British national is detained, particularly in the case of dual nationals in their country of other nationality. Any number of cases we give therefore cannot be definitive and may be subject to change.

(Seventh Report from the Foreign Affairs Committee, Annual Report on Human Rights 2008: Response of the Secretary of State for Foreign and Commonwealth Affairs Cm 7723 (2009))

6/9

An FCO Minister said in a debate about UK national prisoners in custody abroad:

I will begin by briefly setting out the kind of support that consular staff can provide to British prisoners in foreign jails, before speaking in more detail about Mr. Campbell's case. Our consular staff aim to contact all British nationals detained overseas within 24 hours of being told about their detention. They will then aim to visit the detainee as soon as possible, if he or she wishes. Consular staff keep in regular contact with prisoners, either by visiting personally or by telephone or letter. How often they visit will depend on local conditions and the prisoner's circumstances. In France, consular staff will visit once every 12 months when a detainee is on remand. After sentencing, consular staff in France would aim to visit a detainee once in prison to establish what prison conditions are like. Further visits could be arranged if particular circumstances made them necessary. As my right hon. Friend made clear, the Foreign and Commonwealth Office does not take any view about the guilt or innocence of any British nationals detained overseas; that is a matter for the detaining state. Our role is primarily one of welfare—to ensure that prisoners are treated fairly and in accordance with international standards. When that is not the case, we can, with the individual's permission, take up any justified complaints about ill treatment, personal safety or discrimination with the relevant authorities. However, we cannot obtain special treatment for British nationals. Our staff help to ensure that the detainee has legal representation. They can provide a list of local lawyers who speak English and provide detainees with information on the prison and on local judicial systems. They will also try to ensure that, if necessary, the detainee receives adequate medical attention. If the detainee asks for their family to be informed of their situation, consular staff will arrange for this to be done. Consular staff can help with the transfer of money from the family to the detainee for additional comforts to those provided by the prison, and they can help families to arrange visits. Consular staff will also tell detainees and their families about the charity Prisoners Abroad and how it can help them. Foreign and Commonwealth Office staff work closely with that charity. We provide it with some funding, and we will continue to do so in future…

In respect of a specific prisoner [Alistair Iain Campbell] who had been extradited to France, the Minister said:

[O]ur consular staff provided him with information on the prison and on the local judicial system and gave advice on how his family could send money and clothing to him. Once permission was obtained from the French prison authorities, consular staff visited Mr. Campbell in prison to check on his welfare. At that time, the only complaint that Mr. Campbell raised was that he was unable to appeal the court's sentence, and he was advised to write to his lawyer to explore any possible avenue to appeal. Consular staff continue to keep in touch with Mr. Campbell and with his family in the UK….the question of how Mr. Campbell's pre-extradition detention will impact on his final sentence is a matter for his legal representation to take forward with the relevant authorities in France. A pack of general information was provided to Mr. Campbell on 7 March 2008. That pack included information on the services that consular staff can offer, as well as general details on what assistance is available through local legal systems, such as obtaining legal aid. The information pack also included general guidance on the French judicial system, on how families can arrange visits and financial assistance, and on how detainees can arrange appointments with prison health workers…Mr. Campbell's lawyer is currently attempting to arrange an appeal and until that is settled, the transfer back to the UK under the prisoner transfer agreement cannot take place. If the appeal goes forward and is successful, I will look [at the possibility of] the arrangements that would fall into place if a transfer was possible under that scheme. Since Mr. Campbell's imprisonment, consular staff have monitored his situation and they have been in contact with prison medical staff to ensure that he knows how he can arrange visits with the prison doctor and social workers. Consular staff have spoken to prison staff to satisfy themselves that health workers speak English to ensure that Mr. Campbell has no linguistic problems. Again, if there is any evidence to the contrary, I would be happy to double check with consular staff that that is still the case. Consular staff also took up Mr. Campbell's concerns with prison officials once the appropriate permissions had been obtained from Mr. Campbell. We note his complaints about the conditions in the prison. However, consular staff have informed me that the prison came into service in 1991 and that it is regarded as a modern facility. Clearly, there is a large gulf in opinion on this matter, but having been built in 1991 it is obviously not a particularly old building. If we can bring ourselves closer together on that issue, I am sure that it would help everybody concerned…As I stated earlier, our policy in western Europe is to visit once after sentencing and then only if there is a real need. Consular officers provide prisoners with the contact details of the consulate and details of whom to contact if a problem arises. Prisoners are able to write to or telephone the consulate with any concerns that they have. As I said, consular staff will decide how best to address those concerns and whether a visit is needed. As I mentioned earlier, we work collaboratively with Prisoners Abroad and greatly value the work that it does. It is an independent charity funded from a number of sources including the Foreign and Commonwealth Office, other

Whitehall Departments and private donations. The FCO's current funding commitment to it runs until the end of the 2009–10 financial year.

[Campbell had been implicated by a fellow lorry driver, who had been convicted in France of drug smuggling, of being involved in smuggling cocaine in 2000. He was convicted in his absence in 2002 and returned voluntarily to France in 2008 after the issue of a European Arrest Warrant. Campbell's complaints were directed principally to the conditions in which he was being held, Ed.]

(HC Deb 25 February 2009 Vol 488 cs343–345)

6/10
A Ministerial statement about British nationals in Zimbabwe said:

There are an estimated 3,000 British citizens and British nationals in Zimbabwe with the right of abode in the UK who are 70 or over or who are vulnerable because of their care needs or medical conditions. The Government's advice to vulnerable British people and their families has been that if they are concerned about the situation in Zimbabwe they should consider their need to remain. This advice has been unchanged since 2007 and still stands. But the Government are concerned about older and vulnerable British people who may be increasingly unable to support themselves in Zimbabwe and who are unable to return to the UK without assistance. We recognise that a power-sharing accord has now been agreed and that Morgan Tsvangirai was sworn in as Prime Minister on 11 February. However, some British people have been badly affected by the collapse of Zimbabwean infrastructure and we cannot expect this to be put right overnight. They are facing severe difficulties getting access to the food, medicines and care they need. The Government are therefore ready to offer assistance in resettling in the UK to those older and vulnerable British people who are unable to make their own arrangements to leave and unable to support themselves financially in Britain. The Government are making arrangements to receive, assess needs of and support those eligible British citizens and British nationals with the right of abode who wish to resettle in the UK, including through early access to benefits . . . We are informing older and vulnerable British people in Zimbabwe of the assistance available through the British Embassy in Harare. It is difficult to anticipate the extent of interest in this offer, but we estimate that up to 750 people may wish to come to the UK over 18 months. The British Embassy is not advising British people to leave Zimbabwe and continues to provide a full range of consular services to those who remain.

(HC Deb 23 February 2009 Vol 488 c3WS)

6/11 (See also **13/2**)
The Foreign Secretary was asked what factors his Department took into account when making decisions on requests formally to espouse a legal claim of torture. An FCO Minister wrote:

Where the Government consider that another Government is responsible under international law for an injury to a UK national, it may in certain circumstances take over and formally espouse a claim against that Government. Before that stage is reached the claimants should have made all possible effort to secure settlement of the claim through local or other legal remedies, if such remedies exist. Any individual request would be considered on a case by case basis. On receipt of such a request, the Government would consider what factors may be relevant at that time.

(HC Deb 2 March 2009 Vol 488 c1251W)

6/12

An FCO Minister wrote:

On 4 May 2009 the Government filed an amicus curiae brief with the US Fifth Circuit Court of Appeals, the court currently considering the case of Ms Linda Carty, a British national sentenced to death in Houston, Texas. The brief focused on two related issues: the lack of consular notification in Ms Carty's case, and ineffective assistance of counsel. The fifth circuit has yet to rule on Ms Carty's outstanding appeal or comment on the contents of the brief. [Extracts from the brief are below, Ed.]

(HL Deb 30 June 2009 Vol 712 cWA36)

Amicus Curiae Brief

This case is before the Court on appeal from the District Court's denial of Ms. Carty's petition for habeas corpus, by which she challenges her conviction for capital murder and death sentence based in part on the violation of her right to effective assistance of counsel at the trial and sentencing. Among the failures of Ms. Carty's trial counsel was his failure to notify or seek assistance from the British Consulate-General in Houston, Texas. By a bilateral treaty duly ratified by both parties, the United States has undertaken an obligation to the United Kingdom to notify the appropriate British consular officials whenever a British national is detained in the United States. [Convention on Consular Officers, U.S.-U.K., art. 16(1), June 6, 1951, 3 U.S.T. 3426 [hereinafter Bilateral Consular Convention]]. By the same treaty, the United Kingdom has undertaken a reciprocal obligation to notify American consular officials whenever an American national is detained in the United Kingdom. [*Id.*] Under the plain terms of the Convention, the detainee's wishes as to notification have no bearing on the detaining state's obligation to notify the consulate. The right of consular notification in multilateral and bilateral consular treaties is accepted as a necessary element to an individual's fair trial when tried abroad, and the concern that that right be respected is at its highest in capital cases for the straightforward reason that the State's objective to protect its nationals abroad is at its most compelling when a national's life is at risk. In Ms. Carty's case, Texas authorities failed to comply with the obligation to notify British consular authorities of her detention, and Ms. Carty's trial counsel made no attempt to correct that failure. The United Kingdom raises the United States's breach of the Convention at this stage because it may not have a further opportunity to seek a remedy for the breach. Specifically, the United Kingdom submits this brief *amicus curiae* to provide the Court with an understanding of the rights and interests of the United Kingdom and of its national, Ms. Carty, in regard to the obligation of consular notification. The brief addresses the importance of consular assistance to foreign nationals, the rights and obligations of the United States and the United Kingdom under the Bilateral Consular Convention, and how consular involvement would have helped to ensure the fairness of Ms. Carty's trial. It is a fundamental principle of international law that "[a] State responsible for an internationally wrongful act is under an obligation to make restitution, that is, to re-establish the situation which existed before the wrongful act was committed . . . " [United Nations International Law Commission, Draft Articles on Responsibility of States for Internationally Wrongful Acts, G.A. Res. 56/83, Annex art. 35, U.N. Doc. A/RES/56/83 (Dec. 12, 2001)]. As a matter of international law, then, the clear breach of the Bilateral Consular Convention requires that this Court provide a remedy that will ensure that any consular assistance that the United Kingdom could have provided in the case of Ms. Carty be brought to bear on her trial and sentencing. Like the United States, the United Kingdom is committed to the rule of law. Hence, in light of the material assistance that could have been rendered in Ms. Carty's case, the United Kingdom calls upon this Court to reverse the District Court's decision and grant the writ of habeas corpus.

SUMMARY OF ARGUMENT

Consular assistance has been internationally recognized as both an essential element of due process and an indispensable guarantee of other due process rights—most importantly, of the fundamental right to an effective defense. The United States and the United Kingdom concluded the Bilateral Consular Convention in recognition of the invaluable nature of the assistance that consular officials can provide. That Convention imposes a mandatory obligation on the receiving state to notify the consular officials of the foreign national's arrest, irrespective of the national's wishes. Detained foreign nationals suffer from discrete and particular vulnerabilities that consular assistance seeks to redress, and the mandatory notification requirement enables consular officials to provide support to the detained national from the earliest phase of the proceedings. Consular officers act as a cultural bridge between the national and counsel, thus enabling the national to communicate openly, helping counsel to be fully aware of circumstances that warrant further investigation. Consular officers can also act to facilitate access to legal and investigative assistance. In capital trials, counsel has an obligation to conduct a thorough investigation into the accused's prior life experiences, character, and mental state, in order to present compelling evidence in the defense of that individual—both during trial and sentencing. In the case of a foreign national, such investigations are often only possible with the logistical and political support of consular officials. Failure to take advantage of such assistance where available is inconsistent with fundamental principles of effective assistance of counsel. British consular officers provide support in pre-trial proceedings in capital cases; it is common practice for them to facilitate the involvement of dedicated legal and investigative experts to take all appropriate steps to amass evidence and ensure that the national has the means to offer an adequate defense at trial and sentencing. At the time Ms. Carty was arrested, it was the practice of British consular officials to collaborate in the provision of this assistance with Reprieve, an organization providing substantial legal and investigative support to British nationals facing the death penalty. With the support of British consular officials and Reprieve, Ms. Carty's *pro bono* counsel Baker Botts LLP gathered forceful mitigating evidence, including affidavits from top officials in St. Kitts attesting to Ms. Carty's good character and a clinical psychiatric assessment showing a disturbing history of abuse and trauma leading up to the crime at issue. Had trial counsel sought the Consulate's assistance in time, this crucial evidence, which was directly responsive to the prosecution's characterization of Ms. Carty at trial and sentencing, could have been presented to the jury. [The detail of the argument is omitted, Ed.]

CONCLUSION

For the reasons stated above, *amicus curiae* the Government of the United Kingdom of Great Britain and Northern Ireland respectfully urges the Court to reverse the judgment below and grant Ms. Carty a new trial, new sentencing or other appropriate relief.

(*Linda Anita Carty v Nathaniel Quarterman, Director, Texas Department of Criminal Justice, Correctional Institutions Division:* Brief of the Government of Great Britain and Northern Ireland as amicus curiae in support of Petitioner-Appellant and Reversal [for full text, see www.reprieve.org.uk/static/downloads/2009_05_04_Carty_UK_Govt_Amicus_ Brief.pdf, Ed.])

6/13

The Secretary of State for Foreign and Commonwealth Affairs was asked what contacts his Department's officials have had with *(a)* Linda Carty and *(b)* her legal team on her sentence. In reply, a Minister wrote:

Since we became aware of Ms Carty's case in 2002 we have maintained regular contact with her and her legal team. Consular staff keep in touch with her by letter and telephone and make prison visits. We last spoke to Ms Carty on 9 September 2009 and visited on 25 June 2009. Consular staff maintain regular contact with Ms Carty's US legal representatives, whom we last met on 29 September 2009, and with the UK non-governmental organisation Reprieve, with whom we work closely on death penalty cases. We have also submitted two Amicus Curiae briefs to the US courts in relation to the case, the first in May 2006 and the second on 4 May 2009.

The Government are strongly opposed to the death penalty. We express our opposition to its use on British nationals at whatever stage and level is judged appropriate from the moment when the imposition of a death sentence becomes a possibility. We have made a number of representations to the US Government on this case concerning our view on the death penalty, and will continue to do so.

(HC Deb 12 October 2009 Vol 497 c45W)

6/14

A Minister wrote:

From consular records we are aware of one case since 2000 of a British national who has been detained by the Egyptian authorities in which suspicion of terrorist activities has been given as the reason. We are aware of no cases in this period of British nationals having been charged in Egypt with terrorist activities. We are also aware of a case of a British national who was detained on suspicion of involvement in extremist-related activity. There were three cases of British nationals who were detained and found guilty of their involvement with an organisation which is illegal in Egypt. A fourth British national was briefly held and released on the same grounds. Additionally, there were a small number of British nationals during this period who were detained on arrival at Cairo airport and returned to the UK, with no formal reason given. Consular officials find out about the detention of British nationals overseas in various ways. The local authorities should inform us when they detain a British national. However, this does not always happen, particularly in the case of dual nationals in their country of other nationality. In many cases, consular officials will find out about a detention from the family, friends or the media. For these reasons, our records of detentions may not be definitive. We do not provide consular assistance to non-national UK residents, and would not expect to be notified by the Egyptian authorities of their arrest. We cannot therefore give a figure for the number of British residents arrested on suspicion or charge of terrorist activities during this period.

(HC Deb 7 July Vol 495 2009 c628W)

6/15

A Minister wrote:

From our consular records we are aware of four British nationals who have been arrested or detained in Eritrea since 2004. In one case we were informed of the detention only after the individual had been released. In the other three cases we contacted the authorities to clarify the situation and requested consular access.

Of those three cases, two were subsequently released. We have been unable to confirm the release of the other individual, as the Eritrean authorities do not acknowledge the UK's interest in the person concerned (a dual British-Eritrean national resident in Eritrea) as a British national, and will not discuss the case with consular staff, despite representations.

(HC Deb 15 July Vol 496 2009 c453W)

6/16

An FCO Press Statement said about UK yachtsmen who had been taken into custody by Iran:

On 25 November, a racing yacht owned by Sail Bahrain and crewed by five British nationals, was stopped by Iranian naval vessels. The yacht was on its way from Bahrain to Dubai and may have strayed inadvertently into Iranian waters. The five crew members are still in Iran. All are understood to be safe and well and their families have been informed. During interviews . . . on Tuesday 1 December, the Foreign Secretary . . . provided an update on the diplomatic efforts that have been made through-out the day. He said: 'There's been an intensification of contact in the course of the day. I've tonight spoken with the Iranian Foreign Minister and the Iranian Ambassador has had talks in London. We've been making a very simple point which is that this is a consular case; here are five young British people, they're passionate about yachting, they've got nothing to do with politics. The Iranian investigation of the incident can take place quickly and then they should get home. We explained to the Ambassador tonight that we believe that there may have been some inadvertent straying in to Iranian waters, that we expect this to be treated in a professional and clear way that befits a consular case. Obviously we understand that there was the Eid holiday in Iran over the weekend, but now that the Iranian system is back fully functioning we look forward to this being sorted out as soon as possible. Initially responding to the news on Monday 30th November, the Foreign Secretary said: FCO officials immediately contacted the Iranian authorities in London and in Tehran on the evening of 25 November, both to seek clarification and to try and resolve the matter swiftly. Our Ambassador in Tehran has raised the issue with the Iranian Foreign Ministry and we have discussed the matter with the Iranian Embassy in London. I hope this issue will soon be resolved. The Foreign Secretary commented in more detail on the situation during an interview . . . on Tuesday 1 December. He pointed out that the five British people currently being held in Iran are civilians and not military personal, unlike UK Navy personal held by Iranian authorities in 2007. As such the diplomatic handling of the current situation would be different.

He said:

I think that this is an important consular matter for the five individuals. I think it's important to say that these are civilians and not Royal Naval personnel. It's worth making the point that while you made the comparison with the Royal Navy personnel who were on active duty on the Iraq/Iran border, these are five civilians, they're yachtsmen, they were going about their sport and it seems they may have strayed inadvertently into Iranian waters. We look forward to the Iranian government dealing with this promptly and clearly. The Ministry of Foreign Affairs in Tehran have said that they'll be making a statement later today, and it's obviously also important to point out that over the weekend it's been the Eid holiday in Iran and elsewhere in the Muslim world, and that perhaps explains some of the delay since 25 November. But we look forward to the statement today, and, from our point of view, this is a purely consular matter involving five civilians, and we look forward to it being treated as such.

Elaborating on the nature of negotiations and the timescale of the British citizens' release, the Foreign Secretary said:

There's certainly no confrontation or argument. As far as we're aware, these people are being well treated, which is right and what we would expect from a country like Iran. We understand that the Iranian government are investigating the incident, which is perfectly reasonable, and then we look forward to it being promptly sorted out. I think it will be sorted out. Of course, foreign ministers talk to each other about these issues as well but our officials in London and in Tehran have been in touch with their Iranian counterparts. They've had perfectly good discussions about it. The Iranian government have explained, or the Ministry of Foreign Affairs have explained, the difficulties created by the fact that the Eid holiday meant that large parts of the Iranian government were on holiday over the weekend. But, as I say, our ambassador was in the Ministry of Foreign Affairs in Tehran last night; he explained the civilian nature of this work; he asked the Ministry of Foreign Affairs to look into it as promptly as possible, and I've had a message this morning that there should be a statement later today from the Ministry of Foreign Affairs in Tehran.'

(<www.fco.gov.uk/news>, 1 December 2009)

6/17

The Foreign Secretary commented on the positive outcome of this situation... on Wednesday 2 December. He said:

I was obviously very pleased to hear earlier this morning that the five young yachtsmen have indeed been released. I've had confirmation that they're now heading towards international waters on their way to Dubai. I welcome the fact that this has been dealt with in a professional and straightforward way by the Iranian authorities. As I said yesterday this is a purely consular case. Obviously there's been a real ordeal for the young men and for their families and I'm really delighted that it's over for them and that we can call the matter closed. I think that the Iranian authorities gave us every indication that they wanted to deal with this in a straightforward, consular way. It was never a political matter and I welcome the fact that they've dealt with it in this professional way. In answer to a question about whether this incident will have affected Iran's standing in the international community the Foreign Secretary said:I think that this is just a straightforward matter. It's not a political matter. I don't believe there's any wider significance on it. It shows that diplomacy can work. As far as we know the young men have been treated perfectly well. We'll obviously be able to hear from them relatively soon. But they have now departed the island of Siri. They're on their way to international waters...

(<www.fco.gov.uk>, 2 December 2009)

Part Six: IV. *The Individual (including the Corporation) in International Law—Members of minorities*

6/18

The FAC had concluded in its Report on the Human Rights Report 2008:

34. We reiterate the conclusions of our 2008 Report on *Global Security: Japan and Korea* that China is in breach of its obligations under the 1951 Refugee Convention as regards its treatment of North Korean migrants. We remain particularly exercised by China's continuing failure to allow the UN High Commission on Refugees access to its border region with North Korea, and by its practice of forcible repatriation of North Koreans who have not had access to a determination-of-status process. We recommend that the Government should urge the UN High Commissioner on Refugees to give a high priority to the issue of the treatment of North Korean migrants in China. We further recommend that the Government works internationally and more actively to encourage China to find ways of fulfilling its international obligations on this issue as part of the process of becoming a responsible global power. (Paragraph 184)

The FCO replied:

73. The Government agrees with the Committee's assessment. We continue to urge China to observe its obligations under the 1951 convention on the status of refugees and to allow the UN High Commissioner for Refugees access to the China/Democratic People's Republic of Korea (DPRK) border region. This subject was raised with the Chinese at the UK-China Human Rights Dialogue in January 2009. We urged China not to return those people crossing the border

from DPRK to China. China continues to maintain the position that cases are dealt with in line with domestic and international law. At our request, the issue was included in the UN Human Rights Council resolution on DPRK at the 10th session of the Human Rights Council on 27 March. We will continue to work with international partners to make sure that they do not lose sight of this issue. The UNHCR share our view of the seriousness of the issue of North Korean migrants in China but we will continue to encourage them to maintain this as a high priority. [An FCO Minister] lobbied the Chinese on this point during his visit to Beijing in early September 2009.

(Response of the Secretary of State for Foreign and Commonwealth Affairs Foreign Affairs Committee Session 2008–09, Annual Report on Human Rights 2008, Cm 7723)

6/19 (See also **6/103**)
With reference to the Republic of Peru, the Government were asked about the definition of indigenous people. A Minister wrote:

The Government make reference to the definition of indigenous people given in Article 1a of ILO International Labour Organisation (ILO) Indigenous and Tribal Peoples Convention 1989, 169 Article 1, which stipulates that the International Labour Standards Convention applies to:
"tribal peoples in independent countries whose social, cultural and economic conditions distinguish them from other sections of the national community, and whose status is regulated wholly or partially by their own customs or traditions or by special laws or regulations".

The Government are not a party to this Convention.

The Government recognise that indigenous individuals are entitled to the full protection of their human rights and fundamental freedoms in international law, on an equal basis to all other individuals. Human rights are universal and equal to all.

(HL Deb 5 Nov Vol 714 cWA83)

Part Six: VI. *The Individual (including the Corporation) in International Law—Refugees*

6/20 (See also **15/15**)
The Foreign Secretary was asked whether he had held discussions with the government of Thailand regarding the treatment of Burmese boat people near the Andaman Islands. An FCO Minister wrote:

We are deeply concerned by allegations that refugees from Burma were abandoned at sea by the Thai navy. We have raised the issue with the Thai authorities and welcome Prime Minister Abhisit's assurances of an investigation into the matter. Working with EU partners, and in close consultation with the UN High Commissioner for Refugees, we will continue to press the Thai authorities to establish the facts and take appropriate action.

(HC Deb 26 January 2009 Vol 487 c126W)

Part Six: VII.A. *The Individual (including the Corporation) in International Law—Immigration and emigration, extradition, expulsion, asylum—Immigration and emigration*

6/21
A Home Office Minister made the following statement:

The Government are today announcing the conclusion of an agreement between the United Kingdom and the Government of Belarus in respect of the travel of children affected by the Chernobyl incident to the United Kingdom on charity-sponsored respite visits. On 13 October 2008 President Lukashenko of Belarus issued a decree which suspended permission for children affected by the Chernobyl incident to travel abroad for respite visits. Since this date the UK Border Agency and the British ambassador in Minsk have been in close contact with the Belarusian Government to negotiate an agreement to see this ban lifted in respect of children travelling to the United Kingdom. The Belarus request that the United Kingdom should enter into such a written agreement was not related to any specific concerns in relation to previous United Kingdom visits. The agreement, which entered into force on 22 May, allows for the immediate resumption of visits by Belarusian children under the age of 14. It will remain in force for the next five years and will be automatically extended by five-year periods thereafter. The agreement will enable the highly worthwhile work by UK charities in this area to continue and for many thousands more children to visit the United Kingdom in the years to come and to receive the benefits of a temporary period of rest and recuperation.

(HC Deb 11 June 2009 Vol 493 c48WS)

Part Six: VII. B. *The Individual (including the Corporation) in International Law—Immigration and emigration, extradition, expulsion, asylum—Extradition*

6/22 [See **UKMIL [2008] 6/22–30**]
Extraordinary rendition

In answer to a question about extraordinary rendition, an FCO Minister wrote:

There is no universally accepted understanding of the meaning of the term "rendition". Accordingly the need for, and extent of, any action to determine the extent of post-rendition practices can not be assessed at a generic level. In recent years public debate has focused on the term "extraordinary rendition". The Intelligence and Security Committee has defined this as the extra judicial transfer of persons between jurisdictions for the purposes of detention and interrogation outside the normal legal system, where there is a real risk of torture or cruel, inhuman or degrading treatment. The Government unreservedly condemn any "extraordinary rendition" to torture. With regard to the identification and prosecution of crimes, these are a matter for the relevant authorities. Where there is sufficient evidence of unlawful activity on board an aircraft, or anywhere else, in UK territory or airspace, be it a rendition operation or otherwise, this would be investigated by the UK authorities. Where appropriate, the UK law enforcement authorities work with colleagues abroad in this respect. With regard to the prevention of future rendition flights, our international partners are aware that we would grant permission for a rendition flight to pass through UK territory or airspace only if we were satisfied that it would accord with our domestic law and international obligations. We expect all states to abide by their international obligations.

(HL Deb 18 March 2009 Vol 709 cWA39)

6/23

In its reply to the Report of the FAC on Human Rights Report 2008, the FCO wrote about rendition through Diego Garcia:

8. The law applied by the courts of the Territory of Diego Garcia consists, first, of those Acts of Parliament and Orders in Council, etc, that apply (or have been applied) to the Territory; second, the Ordinances that have been enacted by the Commissioner (under the usual power to make laws "for the peace, order and good government of the Territory") and the subordinate legislation made under such Ordinances; and third and always subject to any such "specific law", the law of England as from time to time in force in England. 9. We consider that the US Government should have sought permission from the UK before undertaking rendition operations through Diego Garcia. The US Government has since underlined the firm US understanding that there will be no rendition through the UK, UK airspace or Overseas Territories without express British Government permission. The US have also stated that, should there be any doubt as to whether an operation falls inside or outside the Exchange of Notes that govern the use of Diego Garcia, then the US Government would consult the UK Government.

(FAC, Annual Report on Human Rights 2008, Reply of the Secretary of State for Foreign and Commonwealth Affairs, Cm7723 (2009))

Part Six: VII.C. *The Individual (including the Corporation) in international law—Immigration and emigration, extradition, expulsion, asylum—Expulsion*

6/24

Diplomatic Assurances [See **UKMIL [2008] 6/38–42**]

The Foreign Secretary was asked with which countries the United Kingdom had signed memorandums of understanding to ensure that any deported terrorism suspects would not face torture or ill-treatment on their return; and with which countries similar memoranda were currently being negotiated. An FCO Minister wrote:

We have secured framework arrangements on assurances with Jordan, Lebanon, Libya, Algeria and Ethiopia. The Government are pursuing possible arrangements with other countries, but it would not be appropriate to identify them until negotiations have been concluded.

(HC Deb 10 March 2009 Vol 489 c220W)

6/25

The Foreign Secretary was asked whether he had made any representations to the Algerian government on the welfare of the six individuals deported to that country since 2006 on national security grounds; and whether he planned to make representations on the welfare of those individuals. An FCO Minister wrote:

Eight Algerian nationals have returned to Algeria voluntarily under the terms of the exchange of letters signed by the Prime Minister and President Bouteflika in 2006. The exchange of letters allows for individuals deported or voluntarily returned under its terms (and their families) to maintain contact with our embassy in Algiers. Our embassy initiated contact with the individuals proactively immediately following their return to Algeria. In 2007 our ambassador wrote to the Algerian authorities regarding four returnees who had been detained. The returnees and their families retain the right to contact our embassy at any time. None has done so recently. Further contact with the Algerian authorities will be on a case by case basis.

(HC Deb 12 March 2009 Vol 489 c616W)

6/26
Exceptional leave to remain

The following information covers situations where there was a policy to suspend enforced returns and situations where there was a policy to grant Exceptional Leave to Remain (ELR) to all nationals of a particular country, or part of it, who did not qualify for asylum.

There was an effective suspension of enforced returns to all of Iraq from before 2000 until October 2000. From October 2000 until February 2003 returns to central and southern Iraq were suspended. From February 2003 enforced returns to all of Iraq were again suspended. On 24 February 2004 the Home Secretary announced that enforced returns to Iraq were to resume. There was an effective suspension of enforced returns to the whole of Somalia since before 2000 until July 2001. From July 2001 until October 2002 the policy was varied enabling return of those from the Somaliland and Puntland regions of Somalia. There has been no suspension of enforced returns to any part of Somalia since 7 October 2002. Enforced returns to Eritrea have not been suspended in this period. Enforced returns to the Democratic Republic of Congo were suspended from 23 August 2007 until 3 December 2008 pending the outcome of litigation. There was an effective suspension of enforced returns to Afghanistan from before 2000 until 11 July 2002. There has been no suspension of enforced returns since that date.

Enforced returns to Iran have not been suspended in this period.

(HC Deb 3 November 2009 Vol 498 c849W)

6/27
Expulsion of aliens

The UK representative said in the debate in the Sixth Committee of the General Assembly on the Report of the ILC (A/64/10) on the question of expulsion of aliens:

Turning to the topic of expulsion of aliens, as we explained in our statement last year, this raises difficult and complex issues which intrude directly into the domestic sphere of States. We remain of the view that it is a problematic topic for the ILC to address. We do not believe that it is a suitable topic for codification or consolidation at the present time. [See **UKMIL (2008) 6/32**]

(Sixth Committee 64th Session of the United Nations General Assembly 28 October 2009. Text supplied by FCO)

6/28
Sri Lanka

The Home Secretary was asked what assurances her Department had sought from the Sri Lankan Government regarding the safety of Tamils deported from the UK. A Minister wrote:

All asylum claims including those from Sri Lankan Tamils are considered on their individual merits in accordance with our obligations under the Refugee Convention and the European Convention on Human Rights. Those identified by the decision making process and the independent appeals process not to be in need of international protection are expected to leave the UK voluntarily. Failed asylum seekers can and do voluntarily return to Sri Lanka. Those who do not leave voluntarily may have their return enforced. Provision is made for post arrival assistance of all failed asylum seekers we remove to Sri Lanka. We have not sought assurances from the Sri Lankan government regarding the safety of returnees but we do closely monitor the respect for human rights in all countries that we return to. We do not routinely monitor foreign nationals who do not need our protection in their own country, but if specific allegations are made that any returnee has experienced ill-treatment on return from the UK, then these will be followed up through our High Commission in Colombo.

(HC Deb 12 February 2009 Vol 487 c2208W)

6/29
A Minister wrote:

The UK Border Agency expects those with no right to remain in the United Kingdom to return home voluntarily; if they choose not to, we will enforce their removal. Where an individual, through not fault of their own, cannot be removed we will provide support to prevent destitution. This form of support is called section 4 support [Immigration and Asylum Act 1999, Ed.] and is intended as a limited and temporary form of support. Section 4 support is currently administered through a voucher system. I have approved plans to introduce a plastic payment card system for the administration of section 4 support, personalised for each applicant. This will enable the UK Border Agency to cut down on the abuse of asylum support and provide a more efficient system.

(HC Deb 19 March 2009 Vol 489 c69WS)

6/30
The Home Secretary was asked to which countries her Department could not return unsuccessful asylum seekers on humanitarian grounds. A Minister wrote:

There are no countries to which there is a blanket approach of not returning failed asylum seekers on humanitarian grounds. The Government believe that the right approach is to consider the protection needs of individuals on an individual basis. Each asylum and human rights claim is considered on its individual merits in accordance with our international obligations and taking full account of conditions in the country concerned as they impact on the individual. Those found to be in need of international protection are provided with it. Failed asylum seekers of all nationalities who have been found by the Home Office and the appeals process not to be in need of international protection and have no legal basis of stay in the UK are expected to return to their country of origin and may have their removal enforced.

(HC Deb 30 March 2009 Vol 490 c940W)

6/31

A Minister wrote:

The UK Border Agency only deports foreign national offenders who meet the following criteria for deportation:

A court recommendation. For non-European economic area nationals-a custodial sentence of 12 months or more either in one sentence, or as an aggregate of two or three sentences over a period of five years or a custodial sentence of any length for a drug offence (an offence other than possession only). For EEA nationals-a custodial sentence of 12 months or more for an offence involving drugs, violent or sexual crimes or a custodial sentence of 24 months or more for other offences.

At the point where no barriers to removal exist, the UK Border Agency will set a direction to remove. According to provisional management information, as at 20 November, approximately 125 foreign nationals who met the relevant deportation criteria had removal directions set against them.

Of these, around one third had also submitted a claim for asylum at some stage prior to the removal direction being set.

(HC Deb 30 November 2009 Vol.501 474W)

6/32
France

A Minister wrote:

The United Kingdom (UK) continues to work with France—one of our closest European partners—in fighting illegal migration. Our shared determination has already created one of the toughest border crossings in the world at Calais. As part of this co-operation, the UK and France are assessing the feasibility of joint return flights to fly back to their country of origin potential illegal entrants who have no lawful basis with which to be in either country.

The UK Border Agency does not disclose information in advance about the dates or destinations of charter flights in order to ensure the safety and security of our own staff, our contractors, and those we are seeking to return. Additionally, the government of the country of origin may request that we do not publicise our operation as a condition of granting clearance for the flight. As there are currently no firm arrangements in place for the UK and France to operate a joint flight, there has been no agreement about cost allocation or whether any payment to returnees is appropriate. Any details about costs or breakdown of costs to an airline contracted for the purpose of a joint flight would be regarded as commercially confidential.

(HL Deb 15 July 2009 Vol 496 c407W)

6/33
Iraq

A Minister wrote:

Iraqi asylum seekers who are found not to need international protection and who have no legal basis of stay in the UK are expected to leave. We prefer that they do so voluntarily but where they do not, we will seek to enforce their removal.

Removal may be to any part of Iraq. Enforced removals have taken place to the Kurdish Regional Government controlled area of northern Iraq and to Baghdad.

(HL Deb 10 November 2009 Vol 714 cWA144)

6/34
Zimbabwe

The Government were asked what was their response to the recommendation of the Independent Asylum Commission that destitute Zimbabweans should be allowed a temporary and revocable permit to work in the United Kingdom. A Minister wrote:

Our asylum system provides protection to individuals where it is needed in the form of leave to remain in the United Kingdom. Asylum seekers who need support to avoid destitution are given it from the time they arrive in the UK until their claim is fully determined. Any failed asylum seeker who is unable to return home through no fault of their own can apply for support. It is not government policy to grant failed asylum seekers permission to work. As the UK Border Agency noted in response to the Commissioners' findings, the Government believe that managed economic migration is a valuable source of skills and labour for the UK economy, and maintains recognised routes into the UK for those seeking to work. It is important to maintain the distinction between economic migration and asylum. Allowing failed asylum seekers to work would be likely to encourage asylum applications from those without a well founded fear of persecution, thus slowing down the processing of applications made by genuine refugees and compromising the integrity of our asylum system.

(HL Deb 2 February 2009 Vol 707 cWA99)

6/35
The Government were asked why they were deporting Zimbabwe citizens to Malawi, in view of the possibility that they might be immediately sent on to Zimbabwe; and what discussions the government had had with

the Government of Malawi concerning Zimbabwean asylum applicants whom they wish to send to Malawi; and whether they had received any assurances from Malawi. A Minister wrote:

Unsuccessful asylum claimants are returned to Malawi only if they are entitled to reside there, and only when the decision-making and independent appeals system have found that this would be consistent with our obligations under the refugee convention and the European Convention on Human Rights. Among many other factors, decision-makers and the courts take full account of any risk that the claimant would be removed from Malawi to another country where they could be at risk.

The nationality or entitlement of an applicant to reside in a country is determined by looking at and weighing up all of the available documentary and oral evidence. Where a person holds a genuine and legally obtained Malawian passport or other identity document issued by the Malawian authorities, that would normally be enough to show that the holder is entitled to reside in Malawi. As an additional safeguard in the case of those who claim connections to Zimbabwe, the British High Commission in Lilongwe has obtained from the Malawian immigration authorities confirmation that they would not deport an individual who has Malawian nationality or the right to reside in Malawi, regardless of ancestral nationality or previous residence in a third country.

(HL Deb 2 February 2009 Vol 707 cWA100)

6/36

The Minister for Borders and Immigration made the following announcement:

I am announcing today our intention to make changes over time to our returns policy to Zimbabwe, recognising the different categories of people currently living in the UK. This reflects developments in Zimbabwe following the formation of the inclusive Government led by Prime Minister Tsvangirai.

As Prime Minister Tsvangirai has set out, including during his visit to the UK in June, there have been some positive changes in the situation in Zimbabwe over the past six months. While a great deal remains to be done to institute the political and other reforms set out in the global political agreement, the indiscriminate violence which marred the elections of 2008 has abated. And the formation of the inclusive Government has led to improvements in the economy, schools and the availability of basic commodities. In response to this changed situation some Zimbabweans in the UK are considering returning home to help rebuild their country. I consider we should be doing more to help them. On 1 February we announced enhancements to the assisted voluntary return (AVR) package for Zimbabweans. AVR packages are available for individuals of all nationalities who are within the asylum system. The standard package provides support to help them reintegrate into their home country, including £4,000 for vocational training, assistance in setting up a business and a flight home. Since February the package for Zimbabweans has been supplemented with an extra £2,000 of reintegration assistance. This includes an additional £500 cash on departure, an extra £1,000 "in kind" assistance for business set up, a £500 basic subsistence package and cholera prevention kits. We are today changing the way we deliver our supplementary package for Zimbabweans such that the total value remains the same but, instead of providing the assistance "in kind", cash payments will now be phased in over a six-month period through the IOM office in Harare. Making cash available to those who go home will support economic reform in Zimbabwe - enabling people to return voluntarily and use their skills to support change and help rebuild Zimbabwe with capital behind them. The scheme will also be extended until 31 December and will be reviewed at that point. Alongside these changes to our voluntary returns package we have also considered carefully our position on enforced returns to Zimbabwe. We have kept this issue under review since the Home Office first deferred enforced returns to Zimbabwe in September 2006 and the courts have found that not all Zimbabweans are in need of international protection. The UK Border Agency will therefore be starting work over the autumn on a process aimed at normalising our returns policy to Zimbabwe, moving towards resuming enforced returns progressively as and when the political situation develops.

The agency takes its obligations under the 1951 Refugee Convention seriously. We will continue to consider each case on its individual merits and where someone needs protection it will be granted. However, we have always expected those found not to be in need of protection to return home. We prefer these individuals to return voluntarily and the enhancements to the AVR scheme will support this, but where they choose not to do so we are bound to take steps, over time, to enforce the law.

(HC Deb 29 October 2009 Vol 498 c24W-25W)

Part Six: VII. D. *The Individual (including the Corporation) in International Law—Immigration and emigration, extradition, expulsion, asylum—Asylum*

6/37

Speaking about social benefits for non-British citizens, a Minister said:

Asylum seekers . . . are subject to immigration control and have no recourse to social security benefits until they have been granted leave to remain in the UK. However, those who are destitute and have children—I will come to this later—can apply through the UK Border Agency for both financial support and help with accommodation. The level of support reflects its temporary nature and the fact that supported asylum seekers do not pay council tax or utility bills . . . Last year, we extended support to cover facilitation of travel to medical appointments, the nutritional needs of pregnant mothers and young children, and clothing for children. [I was asked] several questions, particularly about asylum seeker applications and the average times taken for decisions on asylum claims. We are making decisions quicker than before and beat our target of concluding 40 per cent of cases within six months by the end of last year. Indeed, we are on track to conclude the majority of cases within six months by the end of December 2008. We aim to conclude 90 per cent of cases within six months by 2011 . . . I should like to make it clear that we do not provide routine free healthcare for unregulated illegal migrants or other visitors who may come seeking free healthcare. However, it is important to state that urgent treatment should never be denied to, or delayed for, any person, irrespective of their legal status or financial position. They should be charged subsequently for their care and we take reasonable steps to recover the cost. Our regulations are designed to protect the NHS, a free service established primarily for British residents, from inappropriate access by overseas visitors, while providing appropriate entitlements to EEA citizens and other current residents... Asylum seekers awaiting a formal decision on their claim are eligible for both primary and secondary NHS medical treatment free of charge; and the basic humanitarian needs of unsuccessful asylum seekers continue to be met. The Department of Health and the Home Office are currently undertaking a review of the rules governing immigrant access to healthcare.... reference [was made] to the JCHR's criticism of our treatment of asylum seekers. Of course, the Government responded to the Committee's 17th report on 5 July 2007. We believe that our asylum support system is fair and properly balanced. There are safeguards for supporting unsuccessful asylum seekers who are vulnerable; for example, families with minor dependents and those who have a genuine reason for why they cannot return home. The UK Border Agency is committed to working with stakeholders to continue to improve the asylum system and the treatment of asylum seekers.

(HL Deb 3 February 2009 Vol 707 cs629–632)

6/38 (See also **6/90–96, 17/6–9**)
The Government were asked about Camp Ashraf, Iraq, and whether the people there might be given political asylum. A Minister said:

...the UK Government have no locus in Iraq in relation to these people. The discussions have been held internationally through the United States, which had control prior to the ending of the Geneva Convention status. That status was given in the first place only because the Americans chose to accept and adopt it, rather than because there was any international obligation. It is clear that there is no nation - alas, it might be said - for these individuals outside the country that they are in, albeit that they are very reluctantly accepted; no other country is prepared to give residence status to them.

(HL Deb 23 November 2009 Vol 715 c133)

6/39
A Minister wrote:

It is the Government's policy that all claims for asylum, including those from Pakistani nationals, are considered on their individual merits in accordance with the 1951 United Nations Convention Relating to the Status of Refugees and the European Convention on Human Rights, against the background of the latest accurate, objective, sourced and up-to-date information on asylum seekers' countries of origin produced by the UK Border Agency country of origin information service.

(HL Deb 10 December 2009 Vol 715 cWA161-WA162)

Part Six: VIII. *The Individual (including the Corporation) in International Law—Human rights and fundamental freedoms*

[The following items dealing with representations on human rights matters to individual States are only a selection of the many examples when the UK brings human rights questions to the attention of other States. For more practice, see Human Rights Report 2009, 78–173, <http://centralcontent.fco.gov.uk/resources/en/pdf/human-rights-report/human-rights-report2009>. For a statement of policy about when to make such representations, see **6/97**, Ed.]

6/40
Afghanistan

Answering a question about Afghanistan's proposed Personal Status Law, the Foreign Secretary wrote:

We continue to urge the Afghan Government to uphold the Afghan Constitution, which demands equal treatment of men and women, and to adhere to Afghanistan's international legal obligations under the human rights conventions it has signed up to, including the Convention on the Elimination of Discrimination Against Women.

...the Afghans obviously have the right to write their own laws. However, we were dismayed that some reported provisions of the Bill as it was drafted ran counter to Afghanistan's international human rights obligations. This Bill, if it had become law as drafted, would have had a significantly detrimental impact on the rights of women.... the Prime Minister raised our concerns about the law with President Karzai. We welcome President Karzai's decision to ask the Minister of Justice to review the legislation in question, and his announcement on 27 April 2009 that the law would be changed to bring it in line with the constitution, and the international treaties to which Afghanistan is a party. We will continue to follow the progress of this issue closely.

(HC Deb 21 May 2009 Vol 492 c1497W)

6/41
A Minister wrote:

We are aware that attacks against female journalists have taken place, for example the attack on Zakia Zaki, who ran the private radio station Peace Radio. She was killed by multiple gunmen in her home north of Kabul, in the central province of Parwan, on 5 June 2007. We deplore attacks on any journalist—male or female—and supported the joint EU-Norway declaration on freedom of expression made on 16 April 2009:www.delafg.ec.europa.eu/en/downloadable_documents/Nov_2008/Press_Release/DFE_16apr09.pdf We welcome the huge growth in independent Afghan media since 2001, but, as the declaration states, we are concerned about evidence of a gradual deterioration of the situation regarding freedom of expression, including the growing intimidation and violence targeting Afghan journalists, and challenges to the independence of the media. If the Afghan Government were to enact the new Media Law, already passed by the Lower House of the Afghan Parliament, it would do much to help ensure respect for freedom of expression, particularly in the run-up to the elections this August... the Prime Minister has raised this issue with President Karzai and we will continue to lobby the Afghan Government to pass the law. Strengthening the rule of law is also essential to protecting individuals, including journalists, from violence and intimidation. But the challenges are long-term and significant. We continue to support the Afghan authorities in developing an effective police force, improving access to justice and strengthening the formal justice system's ability to prosecute offenders and tackle corruption. In 2008–09, the UK allocated £29 million to strengthen Afghan interdiction and law enforcement capacity.

(HC Deb 2 July 2009 Vol 495 c384W)

6/42

A Minister wrote:

We share the . . . concern about the continuing imprisonment of journalism student Sayed Pervez Kambakhsh. We urge the Afghan state to honour the Afghan Constitution and comply with the international human rights standards, to which it is a party, including the right to a fair trial and freedom of expression. We opposed the death sentence imposed upon Mr. Kambakhsh at his initial trial in January 2008 after his imprisonment in October 2007. While it is positive that he no longer faces the death penalty, we are disappointed by the 20 year prison sentence he received on the 21 October 2008, a decision sadly upheld by the Afghan Supreme Court in early February. We have serious concerns about the fairness of his trials. In April 2009, as part of the EU, we asked President Karzai to carefully consider the legitimacy of Mr. Kambakhsh's trial. We continue to follow Mr. Kambakhsh's case closely and, in conjunction with our international partners, will continue to raise it with the relevant Afghan authorities, wherever appropriate.

(HC Deb 4 July 2009 Vol 496 c318W)

6/43 (See also 6/58)

The Secretary of State for Defence was asked for the names of two persons detained by the UK, handed over to the US in Iraq and then transferred to Afghanistan. A Minister wrote:

It is not the practice of this Department to release personal information, such as the names of these two individuals. The individuals were initially held at a US detention facility in Baghdad before they were transferred to US detention facilities at Bagram Air Base in Afghanistan. As my predecessor made clear in his statement, when this information came to light officials immediately engaged with their US counterparts and were assured that the individuals are held in a humane, safe and secure environment that meets international standards that are consistent with applicable cultural and religious norms. I am satisfied that these assurances are reliable; although there is no formal legal power for the UK to demand access to the individuals, close relationships with the US satisfy me that this is not required. After 31 December 2008 the UK has no power of detention in Iraq so demanding the return of these two individuals would not be practical nor possible. The review examined the available historical records, which suggest that British officials became aware of an intention to transfer in March 2004, although this was some days after the initial capture had occurred. British officials had learned by mid-June 2004 that the individuals had been transferred to Afghanistan. What particular international law provisions apply will depend on the operational theatre and the circumstances; I am not in a position to make general statements on what legal provisions may apply as each operational theatre is different.

(HC Deb 6 July 2009 Vol 495 c549W)

6/44
Anti-Semitism

A Minister wrote:

The Government are committed to tackling anti-Semitism. We condemn all instances of persecution and discrimination against individuals and groups wherever they occur. The recommendations of the London Declaration [<www.fco.gov.uk/en/news/latest-news/?view=PressS&id=13819255>, Ed.] have informed activity both within cross-Government hate crime programmes and in our international work, particularly within the Organisation for Security and Cooperation in Europe (OSCE). The Prime Minister became the first world leader to sign the London Declaration on Combating Anti-Semitism on 25 February 2009 and on signing the declaration he said "So many of the principles it enshrines are already things we are doing here in Britain and while I'm proud of the bold action Britain has taken to combat anti-Semitism such as improved reporting, prosecutions for anti-Semitic internet hate and the funding of Holocaust Education in schools, there is no room for complacency." The Cross-Government Hate Crime Action Plan includes activity in support of the declaration and was launched on 14 September. It can be viewed at:www.homeoffice.gov.uk/documents/hate-crime-action-planMore recently in December the OSCE Ministerial Council agreed a Decision on Combating Hate Crimes. It contains helpful UK-inspired language on addressing "the increasing use of the Internet to advocate views constituting an incitement to bias-motivated violence including hate crimes". It also encourages OSCE participating states to seek opportunities to co-operate and tasks the OSCE's Office of Democratic Institutions and Human Rights to undertake some exploratory work.

(HC Deb 16 December 2009 Vol 502 cs1223W-1224W)

6/45
Belarus (Death Penalty)

A Minister wrote:

The EU raised [a capital sentence case] with the Belarusian authorities on 8 July 2009. We are disappointed that the death penalty was imposed following earlier efforts by the Belarusian authorities to reduce its use. Belarus is the last country in Europe to use the death penalty; its abolition would be an important step in improving EU—Belarus relations. The Parliamentary Assembly of the Council of Europe passed a resolution on 23 June 2009 supporting the lifting of the suspension of Belarus' special guest status after a moratorium on the execution of death penalties.

(HC Deb 15 July 2009 Vol 496 cs450W-451W)

6/46

A Minister wrote:

Vasily Yuzepchuk and Andrei Zhuk have been sentenced to death in Belarus this year. We, and EU partners, have raised their cases with the Belarusian authorities on a number of occasions. We also took part in a European Commission press conference on 12 October 2009 to mark World Day Against the Death Penalty. EU member states are working with local and international non-governmental organisations to promote public debate, and publicise EU views on the death penalty. We continue to urge Belarus to abolish the death penalty or, as an initial measure, to introduce a moratorium. A moratorium would be beneficial for the development of EU-Belarus relations, and is a pre-requisite for enhanced relations with the Council of Europe. We have agreed with Spain that the death penalty will be one of four priority areas when the UK holds the local presidency on behalf of Spain in the first half of 2010.

(HC Deb 23 November 2009 Vol 501 cs7W-8W)

6/47
Burma

An FCO minister answered a number of questions about the human rights situation in Burma. He wrote:

We regularly discuss Burma with members of the UN Security Council, as well as those countries participating in the UN Secretary-General's Group of Friends. We use this frequent dialogue to reinforce our deep concern at the political and human rights situation in Burma, and urge those with influence on the military government to help the UN Good Offices Mission deliver tangible progress on the ground. The UN Security Council will continue to seek a briefing from the Secretary-General and his representatives on the outcome of their interaction with Burma...

Our embassy in Rangoon has discussed the effectiveness of the supplementary understanding on forced labour with the office of the executive director of the International Labour Organisation (ILO). Our assessment is that the mechanism is continuing to produce results. Of 80 complaints referred to the Burmese authorities over the last year, all but eight have seen some action to resolve them. The military government has shown signs of genuine co-operation with the ILO. However, the problem of forced labour remains widespread and we are particularly concerned by the failure of the authorities to publicly condemn the practice and address its use by the military. We will continue to support the work of the ILO in Burma.

(HC Deb 24 March 2009 Vol 490 c188W)

6/48
A Minister wrote:

...the Prime Minister has expressed UK's deep concern over the arrest and trial of Aung San Suu Kyi, commenting that it shows the Burmese regime is intent on finding any pretext to extend her unlawful detention. He released a statement on the morning of her arrest on 14 May 2009 condemning the actions of the regime. On receiving news of her arrest, our embassy in Rangoon also immediately registered its concern with the Burmese authorities. Our ambassador contacted them again on 18 May 2009 and the following days to seek access to her trial. Former Foreign and Commonwealth Office Minister...raised the arrest and trial of Aung San Suu Kyi, the detention of over 2,100 political prisoners and the implications for a genuine transition to democracy in Burma with EU and Asian partners at the EU-Association of South East Asian Nations (ASEAN) Summit and Asia-Europe Meeting in the region at the end of May. He spoke directly to Burmese Ministers to express the UK's outrage at their actions. Most recently, the Prime Minister issued a statement on Aung San Suu Kyi's birthday, 19 June 2009, reiterating his call for her release. Our embassy in Rangoon transmitted a message from the Government to the Burmese Ministry of Foreign Affairs early on 1 July 2009 expressing our continued concern about Aung San Suu Kyi's trial and urging the regime to co-operate with the UN General Secretary upon his visit.

(HC Deb 6 July 2009 Vol 495 c545W)

6/49
Convention for the Protection of All Persons from Enforced Disappearance

A Minister wrote:

The Government support the International Convention and believe that it will have an important role in preventing enforced disappearance and secret detention in the future. The UK played an active part in the negotiations prior to the drafting of the convention and supported its adoption in 2008 at the UN Human Rights Council and the UN General Assembly. The UK is prepared to give its signature to treaties only when it has a clear intention to ratify within a reasonable timescale. The Government are conscious of the potentially significant impact of the convention in the domestic context, and we are therefore continuing our detailed assessment of the provisions of the convention and their effect across all areas of UK law and policy. In particular, we are analysing the extent to which common law provisions may need to be replicated in statute law; whether any new criminal offences would need to be introduced; and whether the UK would enter any reservations or declarations on ratification. Ratification will require primary legislation to facilitate changes to domestic law and the introduction of such primary legislation will depend on securing parliamentary time. The complexity of the issues still under consideration means that we are not setting a deadline for completion of our analysis, but work is being progressed as rapidly as possible.

(HC De 19 October 2009 Vol 497 c1231W-1232W)

6/50
Convention on the Rights of the Child: Optional Protocol

A Minister wrote:

There are no plans to review the operation of the interpretative declaration on article 1 of the Optional Protocol to the UN Convention on the Rights of the Child on the Involvement of Children in Armed Conflict. Government policy is that Service Personnel under the age of 18 are not routinely deployed on operations outside the UK. The exception to this is where the operation does not involve personnel becoming engaged in or exposed to hostilities, such as disaster relief. The MOD believes that its policies on under 18s are robust and compliant with national and international law. We remain fully committed to meeting our obligations under the United Nations Convention on the Rights of the Child on the Involvement of Children in Armed Conflict.

(HC Deb 13 October 2009 Vol 497 c795W)

6/51
Death Penalty

An FCO Minister wrote:

The UK opposes the death penalty in all circumstances as a matter of principle. We continue to make our position on capital punishment clear to the Iraqi government at every opportunity both bilaterally and with the support of our EU partners. As recently as 8 March 2009 the UK joined other EU member states in supporting a démarche, delivered by the current Czech EU presidency to Iraqi vice-President Tareeq al-Hashemi and to the head of the Iraqi prime minister's office on the proposed resumption of executions in Iraq. We strongly supported the resolutions adopted by the UN General Assembly in December 2007 (A/Res/62/149) and November 2008 (A/Res/63/168) which called upon all states that maintain the death penalty to establish a moratorium on executions with a view to abolition. The resolutions expressed the conviction of the majority of UN members that the use of the death penalty undermines human dignity; recalled that there is no conclusive evidence of its deterrent value; and noted that any miscarriage or failure of justice in the implementation of the death penalty is irreversible and irreparable... Following reports of an imminent move to carry out the death sentences of 117 individuals on death row at Kadhamiyah-Max Prison in Iraq, the UK joined other EU member states in supporting a démarche against the sentences delivered on 8 March 2009 by the Czech EU presidency to Iraqi vice-president Tareeq al-Hashemi and to the head of the Iraqi Prime Minister's office. Vice-president al-Hashemi said he had no information about the enforcement of these sentences which had been passed by the courts in full compliance with Iraqi law and the Iraqi Constitution. We will continue to pursue the Iraqi government on this matter, including making clear our position on the death penalty...The UK joined other EU member states in supporting a demarche against the death sentences against 117 people which was delivered on 8 March 2009 by the Czech EU presidency to Iraqi Vice President Tareeq al-Hashemi and to the Head of the Iraqi Prime Minister's Office. We are asking the Iraqi Government for further information about these sentences and regularly make clear our opposition to the death penalty.

(HC Deb 23 March 2009 Vol 490 c30W)

6/52
Death Penalty (Iran: Children)

A Foreign Office Minister attended the launch of a new report by the *Foreign Policy Centre* and organisation *Stop Child Executions* on juvenile executions in Iran [<www.ohchr.org/EN/HRBodies/UPR%5CPAGES%5CIRSession7.aspx>, Ed]. Speaking about the execution of children in Iran, the Minister said:

Such acts are simply wrong. They are also in clear violation of internationally accepted norms and legal standards. The Iranian government must know this, not least because it has ratified the International Covenant on Civil and Political Rights and actively participated in the drafting of the Convention on the Rights of the Child. Both unequivocally prohibit the use of the death penalty against people convicted of crimes committed under the age of 18.

The Iranian government has committed themselves to protecting and enshrining the rights contained within. They have also agreed to hold themselves accountable before the international community. The UK Government is determined to help that happen. Alongside our EU partners we are committed to speaking out publicly against the death penalty wherever it is applied, and make representations on behalf of each and every juvenile at risk of execution.

Over the last eighteen months we, alongside our EU partners, have made direct representations to the Iranian authorities on behalf of juveniles facing the noose. And international pressure has made a difference. In many cases they have been issued a stay of execution. Yet this is not enough. Words are not enough. And the present situation has made it even harder for us to get our message across. The international community and civil society has a role to play. We are strongest when we work together. That is why the work of organisations such as Stop Child Executions is so important. Not only do they provide valuable information for the outside world, they provide hope and support to the victims and their families, and also to millions of Iranians who are campaigning for their government to abolish juvenile executions for good. I am extremely encouraged by the publication of this comprehensive report. It provides irrefutable evidence as to the situation on the ground and makes many excellent recommendations for both Iran and the international community to take forward. Importantly, the report highlights the many legal inconsistencies in Iran's judiciary and stark contradictions between its actions and its human rights commitments. Reports such as this are particularly important as Iran prepares to stand before the UN's Universal Periodic Review in 2010. The UN's "UPR" [Universal Periodic Review] process is an increasingly effective mechanism used to examine member States' human rights records. The UK government is committed to engaging with the process and hope we can work together with organisations such as SCE and the Foreign Policy Centre to make that happen.

Publications and events like this serve to remind the Iranian authorities that the eyes of the world are on them. Their actions do not go unnoticed. In conclusion, I want to thank the authors of this report for doing just that. And for reminding us all here tonight just how far Iran really is from implementing its freely undertaken human rights commitments, and why we must all continue to work together to fight for the rights of those who are denied a voice.

(<www.fco.gov.uk/speeches>, 1 July 2009)

6/53

A Minister wrote:

We were appalled to learn of the execution of Delara Darabi on 1 May 2009 for a crime she had allegedly committed at the age of 17. The EU, with strong UK support, issued a declaration on 2 May 2009 condemning her execution and urging the

Iranian authorities to eliminate the death penalty for juveniles from its penal code. In a press release issued on 7 May 2009 my predecessor, now the Minister for Armed Forces ... echoed these sentiments and expressed our deep sorrow at the news.

My hon. Friend also summoned the Iranian ambassador to the Foreign and Commonwealth Office to condemn Ms Darabi's execution and the continued practice of executing juvenile offenders. He expressed concern at Iran's continued disregard for international human rights law; and reminded Iran of their freely undertaken obligations. Iran is signatory to the International Covenant on Civil and Political Rights and the Convention on the Rights of the Child, both of which unequivocally prohibit the use of the death penalty for crimes committed by those under the age of 18.

(HC Deb 1 July 2009 Vol 495 cs282W-283W)

6/54
Death Penalty (China)

The UK condemned the execution of Akmal Shaikh in China on 29 December 2009. Echoing the Prime Minister's sentiments the Foreign Secretary said:

I condemn in the strongest terms the execution of the British national Akmal Shaikh. I join the Prime Minister in expressing my deepest condolences to Mr Shaikh's family and friends. The UK is completely opposed to the use of the death penalty in all circumstances. However I also deeply regret the fact that our specific concerns about the individual in this case were not taken into consideration despite repeated calls by the Prime Minister, Ministerial colleagues and me. These included mental health issues, and inadequate professional interpretation during the trial. The European Union also repeatedly raised the same concerns. This is not about how much we hate the drug trade. Britain as well as China are completely committed to take it on. The issue is whether Mr Shaikh has become an additional victim of it.

6/55
An FCO Minister also commented on the execution of Akmal Shaikh during interviews with BBC Radio. He said:

As the Prime Minister and Foreign Secretary have said, it's a deeply depressing day for anyone with a modicum of compassion or commitment to justice in Britain and throughout the world. Our thoughts are with Mr Shaikh's family at this dreadful time. It's true he was found guilty of a serious crime but it's equally clear that he had serious mental health problems, and the unwillingness of the Chinese courts to take account of this and request a proper medical assessment is reprehensible.

(<www.fco.gov.uk/news>, 29 December 2009)

6/56
Democratic Republic of Congo

A Minister wrote:

According to a recent report by the UN Secretary General, 226,000 people have been displaced in the Democratic Republic of Congo (DRC) as a result of the activities of the Lord's Resistance Army since the beginning of 2009. We are aware that many displaced people from the DRC have moved to South Sudan. We are also aware that some refugees may have fled to Uganda and the Central African Republic. We strongly condemn the atrocities committed by the Lord's Resistance Army in the northern DRC and throughout the Great Lakes Region of Africa. They have committed appalling human rights abuses against the civilian population, including mass executions and abductions. The UN Mission to the DRC, MONUC, has increased its presence in the north of the country, after being urged to do so by the UK and other governments. MONUC is providing logistical support to humanitarian organisations, which are providing relief to the civilian population. We also strongly urge co-ordination between the different peacekeeping missions in that region of Africa.

(HC Deb 22 October 2009 Vol 497 c1614W)

6/57
Detention

MEMORANDUM OF UNDERSTANDING BETWEEN THE UNITED KINGDOM OF GREAT BRITAIN AND NORTHERN IRELAND CONTINGENT OF MULTINATIONAL FORCES-IRAQ AND THE MINISTRIES OF JUSTICE AND INTERIOR OF IRAQ (together hereinafter referred to as the Participants) REGARDING CRIMINAL SUSPECTS

Whereas the mandate for the Multinational Force Iraq (MNF-I) set out in United Nations Security Council Resolution 1546 (2004) authorises MNF-I to take all necessary measures to provide security in Iraq,

Whereas in accordance with that mandate, the UK national contingent, of the MNF-i is authorised to intern persons for imperative reasons of security ("security internees"),

Whereas in accordance with Coalition Provisional Authority Memorandum Number 3 (Revised), the national contingents of MNF-I may apprehend persons who are suspected of committing criminal acts,

Whereas although Iraq is developing its custodial capacity with the aim of being able to confine all criminal suspects in its own facilities, it may, in the mean time, request the MNF-I to confine persons who are suspected of having committed criminal acts in safe and secure detention facilities, subject to security and capacity considerations,

Now, therefore, the Participants have decided to apply the following arrangements:

Section 1 Purpose and Scope

This Memorandum of Understanding (MOU) sets out the authorities and responsibilities in relation to criminal suspects. For the purpose of this MOU, "criminal suspects" are:

(a) individuals who are apprehended by the UK contingent of the MNF-I ("UK MNF-I") and who aresuspected of having committed criminal acts; (b) security internees who are in the physical custody of the UK MNF-I and who are also suspected of having committed criminal acts for which they may be tried in an Iraqi court of competent jurisdiction; and (c) individuals who are suspected of having committed criminal acts who are held at the request of the Iraqi authorities.

Section 2 Authorities and Responsibilities Generally

1.The Interim Iraqi Government (and any successor) has legal authority over all criminal suspects who have been ordered to stand trial and who are awaiting trial in the physical custody of UK MNF-I in accordance with the terms of this Memorandum of Understanding (MOU).

2. The UK MNF-I has a discretion whether to accept any particular criminal suspect into its physical custody and whether to continue to provide custody for a suspect who is in its custody at the time this MOLT comes into operation or who, at any time in the future, comes into its custody,

3. The Ministry of Justice of Iraq ("MOJ"), and where appropriate the Ministry of Interior (MOI), will: (a) inform UK MNF-I of any support requirements under Iraqi law or which it believes are appropriate for UK MNF-I to provide in respect of criminal suspects; (b) provide a liaison officer to UK MNF-I to ensure continuous co-ordination on any issues concerning criminal suspects; (c) ensure that investigations of criminal suspects and any criminal proceedings commenced against criminal suspects progress without undue delay; and (d) provide the guards, escorts, security and transportation that UK MNF-I requests within its means and capabilities.

Section 3 Authorities and Responsibilities in relation to individual criminal suspects

1. In relation to any criminal suspect being held in the physical custody of the UK MNF-1, the MOJ will: (a) provide UK MNF-I with a written request for his delivery up to attend a court appearance or for any other purpose connected with the criminal process and give as much advance notice of the proposed date when the presence of the suspect is required as is practicable; (b) ensure that all documents requested by UK MNF-I relating to the suspect, such as a valid warrant by a competent judicial authority, are provided as soon as practicable; (c) advise UK MNF-I of any court orders relating to the suspect and give UK MNF4 prompt notice of any change in his status; and (d) ensure that any criminal proceedings commenced against a criminal suspect progress without undue delay.

2. In relation to any criminal suspect being held in the physical custody of UK MNF-I, the UK MNF-I: (a) will provide humane treatment and will not subject any criminal suspect to torture or to cruel, inhuman or degrading treatment or punishment; (b) will provide custodial support for the suspect, including but not limited to housing, feeding clothing guarding and health care; (c) will take appropriate steps to ensure the conditions of custody meet the standards set out in CPA Memoranda Nos 2 and 3; (d) will adhere to the requirements of CPA Orders with respect to co-operation with, and the reasonable access to be provided to, the Iraqi Ombudsman for Penal and Detention Matters and the International Committee of the Red Cross; (e) will have exclusive discretion regarding all matters of security and force protection for all criminal suspects in its custody; (f) will take appropriate steps to ensure that criminal suspects who have invoked

their right to counsel are not questioned without their counsel being present; (g) will take appropriate steps to ensure that criminal suspects are able to meet with their counsel, with court investigators arid the investigative judge as needed, subject to the notice requirements of sub-section 1(a) above.

3. In relation to any criminal suspect apprehended by the UK MNF-I and handed over to the Iraqi authorities as soon as reasonably practicable, in accordance with section 5 of Coalition Provisional Authority Memorandum Number 3 (Revised), the MOJ and the MOI, as the case may be:(a) will provide humane treatment and will not subject any criminal suspect to torture or to cruel, inhuman or degrading treatment or punishment; and(b) hold the criminal suspect in accordance with Iraqi law.

4. In relation to any criminal suspect transferred to the MOI or the MOJ by UK MNF-I from its detention facilities, the MOJ and the MOJ, as the case may be, will:(a) inform UK MNF-I before releasing any individual and will comply with any request by UK MNF-I that UK MNF-I should reassume custody if, (i) the individual is wanted for prosecution by any state that has contributed forces to the MNF for breaches of the laws and customs of war, or (ii) the internment of the individual is necessary for imperative reasons of security,in which case UK MNF-I will assume custody of that individual after consultation between the Participants to reach an agreed solution; (b) provide facilities, if requested, for a member or representative of UK MNF-I to accompany any suspect during his court appearance, or during any questioning by Iraqi authorities or during any other time when he is outside the UK MNF-I detention facility; and (c) provide an assurance that during any temporary periods when a suspect is in the hands of the Iraqi authorities whether at the UK MNF-I's detention facility or elsewhere and at any time following the transfer of a suspect to Iraqi facilities, (i) the suspect will be treated humanely and will not be subject to torture or to cruel, inhuman or degrading treatment or punishment; and (ii) the requirements of CPA Orders with respect to co-operation with and reasonable access to be provided to the Iraqi Ombudsman for Penal and Detention Matters and the International Committee of the Red Cross will be adhered to.

5. If UK MNF-I decides that it is no longer prepared to provide custody facilities for a particular suspect, it shall give notice of this decision to the MOJ as soon as possible to enable the MOJ to make other arrangements for the custody of that suspect if it so wishes. The MOJ will then notify the UK MNF-I of the arrangements it has made or alternatively will indicate that the suspect should be released. UK MNF-I will then use its best endeavours to enable any such alternative arrangements to be put in place.

Section Four Disputes

Any difference in the interpretation or execution of this MOU will be resolved exclusively by negotiation between the Participants.

Section Five Amendment and Effective Period

1. This MOU may be amended at any time with the written consent of the Participants.
2. This MOU will come into effect on the signature of the Participants and will remain in effect until terminated by any of the Participants giving a month's written notice to the other Participants.

(FAC, Global Security, Evidence, <www.publications.parliament.uk/pa/cm200809/cmselect/cmfaff/memo/globalsecu/ucgsir20.htm>)

6/58 (See also **6/43**)
The FAC had concluded in its Report on the Human Rights Report 2008:

Transfers of detainees. We conclude that it is a matter of concern that the Government has not provided details of the fate of individuals detained by US forces in Iraq as a result of operations by UK forces, or those captured by UK forces and detained by US forces. We recommend that, in its response to this Report, the Government informs us of the number of such detainees, relevant details of the circumstances of their capture and the degree of involvement of UK forces, and any assurances it has received from the US authorities about their treatment and whereabouts, on an individual basis. We further recommend that the Government, in its response, provides us with a full statement of its record-keeping practice in respect of persons captured by UK forces in Iraq and Afghanistan, whether or not UK forces make the eventual detention. (Paragraph 90)

The FCO responded:

50. The Government does not agree with the Committee's conclusion. As the previous Secretary of State for Defence... reported to the House of Commons on 26 February 2009, [See **6/60**] a comprehensive review of detention was conducted following unsubstantiated allegations by a former serviceman (Ben Griffin). The review concluded that UK Forces had exercised appropriately their responsibilities towards all captured personnel handed to US custody and it uncovered no evidence of mistreatment. [The Defence Secretary] informed the House that the Ministry of Defence had completed a detailed review of records of detention in Iraq and Afghanistan since the start of each campaign, and that he was placing in the Library details of all detentions in southern Iraq in each year since 2003. Where UK Forces have captured individuals who were subsequently held in US detention this was governed by an MOU which covered arrangements for the treatment and transfer of detainees. Given the sensitive nature of these operations it is not the practice of this Government to comment further upon them.

The FAC wrote further: 21. We conclude that the Government should have waited for the European Court of Human Rights to rule on whether the transfer of Faisal Attiyah Nassar Al-Saadoon and Khalaf Hussain Mufdhi to the Iraqi authorities in December 2008 was consistent with its obligations under the European Convention on Human Rights before proceeding with the transfer. We further conclude that explicit assurances that the death penalty would not be used in the event of a conviction in these cases should have been obtained in writing from the Iraqi authorities at the highest level. We recommend that in future the Government obtains such explicit assurances in writing from any national authority to which it transfers a detainee. (Paragraph 95) [*Al-Saadoon and Mufdhi v the United Kingdom* ECtHR's (2009) No.61498/08 (dec); Id (2010), finding violations of Articles 3, 13 and 34, Ed.]

The FCO replied:

51. The Government notes the Committee's view. However, as we made clear at the time of transfer, after 31 December 2008 the UK had no legal power to

detain any individuals in Iraq and continued detention would have been a breach of the UK's international law obligations. Compliance with Rule 39 indications would normally be a matter of course but these are exceptional circumstances. The only lawful action open to the UK was to transfer these individuals to the Iraqi authorities. The European Court of Human Rights at Strasbourg asked the UK to retain custody in Iraq of Mr Al Saadoon and Mr Mufdhi when we had no legal power to do so. This case is still before the European Court at Strasbourg.
52. The Government's stance against the death penalty is clear and well known to the Iraqi authorities. Before the transfer to the Iraqis took place, we received assurances from the Iraqi Government, which the UK courts found to be sufficient to enable us to discharge our legal obligations, that the two detainees would be treated humanely and we made clear that the death penalty should not be applied in the case. The government thanks the Committee for the recommendation that in future written assurances that the death penalty will not be used should be obtained ahead of any detainee transfer. The Government will always endeavour to seek assurances about the death penalty ahead of any detainee transfer to a country that retains capital punishment. [The ECtHRs was not satisfied with the assurances obtained by the UK, above, paras 141–143, Ed.]

(Response of the Secretary of State for Foreign and Commonwealth Affairs Foreign Affairs Committee Session 2008–09, Annual Report on Human Rights 2008, Cm 7723 (2009))

6/59

The FAC had concluded in its Report on the Human Rights Report 2008:

22. We conclude that the onward transfer to Afghanistan of two Pakistani men transferred from UK to US custody in Iraq in 2004 is of great concern. We do not regard the stated reason for this transfer, that US forces did not have sufficient linguists available in Iraq, as being convincing. We further conclude that it is not acceptable that the Government is unable to identify these detainees, or to provide assurances about their subsequent treatment. We recommend that the Government, in its response to this Report, identifies these men, and inform us of what steps it has taken to discover whether they have been treated in an acceptable way since being transferred to US forces. We conclude that the allegation by Reprieve that these two cases were not, as the Government asserts, isolated ones, gives cause for concern. We recommend that the Government investigates in detail any specific allegations put before it by Reprieve and reports to us the outcome of those investigations. (Paragraph 101)

The Government responded:

53. The Government agrees with the Committee that the transfer of these two individuals by the US to Afghanistan should not have taken place. We have discussed options with the US Government for these individuals, including the possibility of return to their country of origin or country of detention. We have been informed that—according to the findings of the US military 6-monthly 'Enemy Combatants Review Board' assessments—they continue to represent significant security concerns. We have sought and received assurances about their welfare and treatment. The US has assured us that the detainees are held in a humane, safe and secure environment that meets international

standards that are consistent with cultural and religious norms. The ICRC has had access to these individuals. A due diligence search by US officials of the list of all those individuals captured by UK Forces and transferred to US detention facilities in Iraq has confirmed that we have no reason to believe that this was anything other than an isolated incident. We would, of course, carefully consider any further credible information. We have nothing to add to previous statements on the issue of the identities of these two individuals. The Government has received a letter from Leigh Day, on behalf of Reprieve, on this issue and will respond in due course. A copy of the response will be passed to the FAC.

The FAC wrote further:

23. We conclude that the potential treatment of detainees transferred by UK forces to the Afghan authorities gives cause for concern, given that there is credible evidence that torture and other abuses occur within the Afghan criminal justice system. We recommend that the Government institutes a more rigorous system for checking on the welfare of transferees in Afghanistan, on an individual basis, and that in its response to this Report, it informs us of the steps proposes to take to achieve this end. (Paragraph 105)

The FCO replied:

54. The Government notes the Committee's conclusion. Whilst HMG does not have any legal obligation to monitor UK captured individuals once they have been transferred to the custody of another state, there are procedures in place to monitor the subsequent treatment of detainees transferred from British Forces to other nations. These visits take place further to the undertakings given in the Memorandum of Understanding (MOU) between the UK and Afghan Governments, which commits all participants to proper treatment of prisoners. The Memorandum of Understanding also provides for the International Committee of the Red Cross (ICRC) and the Afghan Independent Human Rights Commission (AIHRC) to visit and report on what they find. All allegations of abuse are taken very seriously and HMG takes steps to ensure that they are duly investigated. [See **6/43**]

(Response of the Secretary of State for Foreign and Commonwealth Affairs Foreign Affairs Committee Session 2008–09, Annual Report on Human Rights 2008, Cm 7723 (2009))

6/60

The Government were asked whether they had received representations from the government of Afghanistan or from Afghan non-governmental organisations about those people detained without trial at Bagram Air Base and other detention centres, including those at Khost, Kandahar and Jalalabad; whether the International Committee of the Red Cross was allowed full access to all detainees; and, if not, what action they would take. A Minister wrote:

The UK has not received representations from either the Afghan Government or from Afghan non-governmental organisations regarding detention facilities at Bagram airbase, Khost, Kandahar or Jalalabad. Access by the International

Committee of the Red Cross (ICRC) to detainees held by US authorities is a matter for the ICRC and the US. Whenever UK forces detain an individual in Afghanistan, the ICRC is informed and has full access to these persons when in UK custody. The UK has an agreement with the Afghan Government that any person detained by UK forces and transferred to Afghan custody will be accessible to the ICRC and the Afghan Independent Human Rights Commission.

(HL Deb 11 February 2009 Vol 707 cWA185)

6/61

The Defence Secretary made a statement about security detentions made by British forces in Iraq and Afghanistan. He said:

I wish to make a statement on the results of a recent Ministry of Defence review of records of detention resulting from security operations carried out by UK armed forces in Iraq and Afghanistan. It is, I believe, essential that our armed forces are able to detain people who pose a real threat to our troops, our allies or the local population whom we are seeking to protect. These operations are conducted by our forces with courage, integrity and professionalism. In undertaking them, we take fully into account our obligations under international law. In February last year, allegations were made that persons captured by UK forces in Iraq were transferred to US detention facilities and were mistreated and removed unlawfully from Iraq. My predecessor... rightly launched a review, and much of the work was led personally by a very senior British Army general. [He] was right to satisfy himself that appropriate procedures were in place to ensure that persons captured by UK forces and transferred to US detention in Iraq were treated in accordance with UK policy and legal requirements. Separately, he also set in hand work to examine all available documentary material relating to detention operations in Iraq and Afghanistan, and to review the parliamentary record. The Ministry of Defence has now completed a detailed review of records of detention in Iraq and Afghanistan since the start of each campaign. I am today placing in the Library details of all detentions in southern Iraq in each year since 2003.

In Iraq, we have reviewed the record of detainee numbers listing all individuals held in UK detention facilities, first at the Shaibah logistics base and subsequently at the contingency operating base at Basra. In December 2003, when the facility at Shaibah was first opened, records show that 105 internees captured by UK forces were transferred into it from US custody at Camp Bucca. A further 19 were released at that stage. After December 2003, an additional 546 individuals were interned in these facilities. The majority, 491, were released once it was judged that they no longer represented an imperative threat to security, while 141 were transferred to the Iraqi authorities. A further 12 escaped, six were transferred to US detention facilities and... one sadly died in custody. In conducting this review, it became apparent that, in three parliamentary answers since February 2007, Ministers had overstated by approximately 1,000 the numbers of detainees held by UK forces in the period since January 2004. Nine further answers contained minor inaccuracies... We have also reviewed our records of detentions in the period from March to December 2003, when large numbers of individuals were captured by UK forces during the initial, high-intensity combat phase of the operation. Many of them were held for very short periods or were transferred to the US facility at Umm Qasr and then released. This facility was run by the UK from late March to mid-April 2003, at which point it was transferred to US control. Given the circumstances in which the database was compiled, we cannot be confident that the data that we hold today are entirely complete. On a small number of occasions, answers or statements provided by my Department have included figures relating to the position in 2003 that indicated that we initially held up to 5,000 Iraqi prisoners during that period. However, a significant number of these were held on behalf of other coalition forces. We now believe that UK forces transferred around 3,000 individuals to the detention facility at Umm Qasr between March and December 2003, but I would ask the House to treat this figure as a best estimate. In areas outside multinational division south east, UK forces have undertaken operations to capture individuals who were subsequently detained by the United States. These individuals do not feature in the data that I have set out today, but I want to reassure the House that the review has concluded that UK forces have exercised appropriately their responsibilities towards all captured personnel handed to US custody, whether in Multi-national Division (South-East) or elsewhere, and that it has uncovered no evidence of mistreatment. During the final stages of the review of records of detentions, we found information about one case relating to a security operation conducted in February 2004...that that period saw an increased level of insurgent activity as the transfer to Iraqi sovereignty drew closer. During the operation, two individuals were captured by UK forces in and around Baghdad. They were transferred to US detention, in accordance with normal practice, and subsequently moved to a US detention facility in Afghanistan.

This information was brought to my attention on 1 December 2008, and I instructed officials to investigate the case thoroughly and quickly so that I could bring a full account to Parliament. Following consultations with US authorities, we confirmed that they transferred the two individuals from Iraq to Afghanistan in 2004 and they remain in custody there today. I regret that it is now clear that inaccurate information on this particular issue has been given to the House by my Department. However, I want to stress that that was based upon the information available to Ministers and those who were briefing them at that time. My predecessors as Secretaries of State for Defence have confirmed to me that they had no knowledge of these events. The individuals transferred to Afghanistan are members of Lashkar-e-Taiba, a proscribed organisation with links to al-Qaeda. The US Government have explained to us that those individuals were moved to Afghanistan because of a lack of relevant linguists to interrogate them effectively in Iraq. The US has categorised them as unlawful enemy combatants and continues to review their status on a regular basis. We have been assured that the detainees are held in a humane, safe and secure environment that meets international standards that are consistent with cultural and religious norms. The International Committee of the Red Cross has had regular access to the detainees.

A due diligence search by US officials of the list of all those individuals captured by UK forces and transferred to US detention facilities in Iraq has confirmed that this was the only case in which individuals were subsequently transferred outside Iraq. This review has established that officials were aware of the transfer in early 2004. It has also shown that brief references to this case were included in lengthy papers that went to the then Foreign Secretary and the

Home Secretary in April 2006. It is clear that the context provided did not highlight its significance at that point to [them]. In retrospect, it is clear to me that the transfer to Afghanistan of these two individuals should have been questioned at the time. We have discussed the issues surrounding this case with the US Government. They have reassured us about their treatment but confirmed that, as the individuals continue to represent significant security concerns, it is neither possible nor desirable to transfer them to either their country of detention or their country of origin. The UK no longer has power to detain suspects in Iraq, and only limited powers of detention in Afghanistan. For Afghanistan, robust checks have confirmed that we have detailed and precise numbers of all those detained by UK forces since we deployed Task Force Helmand in July 2006. As of 31 December 2008, our database holds the capture details of 479 individuals, including 254 who were subsequently transferred to the authority of the Government of Afghanistan, 217 who were released, and eight who died as a result of injuries sustained on the battlefield. We hold capture details relating to a total of a further seven individuals detained by UK forces between 2001 and April 2006, and I believe that this represents a complete record. I am also placing the complete details of the detainee numbers for Afghanistan in the Library of the House. Our detention operations in Iraq and Afghanistan are underpinned by arrangements with our international partners. We have a memorandum of understanding in place with the Government of Afghanistan, signed on 23 April 2006, covering the treatment of individuals detained by UK forces and transferred to Afghan custody. We also have a memorandum of understanding with Iraq, agreed on 8 November 2004, on the treatment of detainees transferred to Iraqi custody. Iraqi Interior, Justice and Defence Ministers have confirmed to us that Iraqi detention procedures remain consistent with the principles set out in that memorandum of understanding. For the initial stages of the campaign in Iraq, we also had in place a memorandum of understanding with the US and Australian Governments covering arrangements for the treatment and transfer of detainees. We worked on the mutual understanding that the key provisions of the memorandum of understanding continued to apply until it was replaced last year by a further memorandum of understanding with the US. We have also confirmed with the US that the provisions on arrangements for the treatment and transfer of captured prisoners remain under the new legal framework in Iraq and that no person captured with assistance from UK forces will be removed from the territory of Iraq without prior consultation with the UK. Let me make a final observation. We ask our armed forces to operate in highly dangerous environments, where there is often a limit to the capacity of local agencies to enforce security and the rule of law. In those circumstances, it is essential that we provide our forces with the authority and capabilities to deal effectively with individuals who represent a serious threat to our troops or those they are there to protect; the two detainees to whom I referred earlier fall into that category. We recognise the sensitivity of detention operations. We have put in place rigorous safeguards to ensure that detainees are treated properly. We will continue to carry out detention operations in accordance with our legal and policy obligations, in concert with the US and other allies. This is, and will remain, absolutely central to the way our armed forces conduct these vital operations.

(HC Deb 26 Feb 2009 Vol 488 cs394–397)

6/62

The Defence Secretary was asked what steps his Department was taking to ensure that detention facilities run by international military forces in Afghanistan meet the standards required under international law in the treatment of women and children. A Minister wrote:

The Ministry of Defence can only answer this question in respect of UK run facilities. The UK takes its human rights obligations very seriously and has policy and procedures in place regarding the standards within military detention facilities. All our facilities are regularly inspected to ensure that they meet our obligations under international law. The ICRC and the Afghan Independent Human Rights Commission have access to all the UK's operational detention facilities in Afghanistan. When any females or juveniles are detained they are separated from male prisoners and/or adult prisoners, unless they are housed with family members. All persons, especially those under 18 are only detained if absolutely essential and in Afghanistan, detainees are held for a maximum of 96 hours before being released or transferred to the Afghan authorities.

(HC Deb 18 May 2009 Vol 492 c1166W)

6/63

The Secretary of State for Defence issued the following Ministerial Statement:

UK forces in Afghanistan form part of the NATO-led International Security Assistance Force (ISAF) and contribute to the efforts of the international community to assist the Government of Afghanistan to expand security and build the rule of law.

The Taliban insurgents are ruthless and indiscriminate in their attempts to kill and maim our troops and the Afghan people. In his statement on the 26 February 2009, *Official Report*, column 394 on the detention and transfer of persons captured by UK forces in Iraq and Afghanistan [the then Defence Secretary] set out the value of detention operations to our campaign in Afghanistan. Detention operations by UK forces are conducted in accordance with, and the holding of detainees in UK facilities meets, the standards required by, the relevant provisions of international law. In the light of the evolving threat to our forces, we have continued to keep our approach to these operations under review. Under NATO guidelines individuals detained by ISAF are either transferred to the Afghan authorities within 96 hours for further action through the Afghan judicial process or released. And in the majority of cases, the UK forces will operate in this manner. However, in exceptional circumstances, detaining individuals beyond 96 hours can yield vital intelligence that would help protect our forces and the local population-potentially saving lives, particularly when detainees are suspected of holding information on the placement of improvised explosive devices.

(HL Deb 9 November 2009 Vol 714 c5WS)

6/64

The FCO Minister wrote:

The issue of detainees at Bagram is a matter for the US and Afghan Governments as the Bagram facility is a US facility. Detentions operations are absolutely vital when conducting counter-insurgency campaigns. The ability to detain suspect insurgents is essential for operational effectiveness in Afghanistan. Counter-insurgency work is vital to international efforts to bring stability to Afghanistan. The US plays a key role in this work. In the case of UK detention operations in Afghanistan, detainees are held in accordance with ISAF guidelines for a maximum of 96 hours and then transferred to the Afghan authorities or released. In exceptional circumstances, and with ministerial authorisation, detention can be extended to allow for gathering intelligence that is vital for the protection of UK forces and Afghan nationals. The UK is clear that all detainees should be treated humanely.

(HL Deb 6 December 2009 Vol 715 cWA225)

6/65 (See also **3/5**)
Disabilities Convention

A Minister wrote:

I am pleased to announce that the Explanatory Memorandum and Command Paper for ratification of the UN Convention on the "Rights of Persons with Disabilities" will be laid before Parliament later today (Cm7564). In taking this important step, the Government have confirmed their commitment both to this Convention, and to the principle that it enshrines that disabled people have, and should be able to enjoy, the same human rights as other people. In working towards this point, Government Departments and the devolved Administrations have been checking their legislation, policies, practices and procedures against the convention's provisions. The UK does not ratify any international treaty until it is in a position to ensure that it can implement the provisions and therefore comply with its obligations. The Explanatory Memorandum which has been laid explains the basis on which the Government proposes the UK should now ratify the Convention, and the handful of reservations and interpretative declarations that are required in order that we may do so. A reservation is proposed in respect of service in the armed forces to preserve the position already reflected in the Disability Discrimination Act 1995 as amended (DDA). Service in the armed forces is exempt from the employment provisions of the DDA. This approach is entirely consistent with EU Council Directive 2000/78/EC establishing a general framework for equal treatment in employment and occupation. Service in any of the naval, military or air forces of the Crown are excluded from the DDA's employment provisions to preserve their combat effectiveness. The Government decided to exclude members of the armed forces in the DDA because armed forces personnel need to be combat effective in order to meet a world wide liability to deploy, and to ensure that military health and fitness remain matters for Ministry of Defence Ministers based on military advice, not for the courts. An interpretative declaration is proposed to make clear that the UK general education system includes both mainstream and special schools, thereby clarifying how the UK Government interpret the Convention. This will make it clear that special schools are considered part of the UK's general education system and that parents have the right to express a preference for a special school. A reservation is proposed to allow for circumstances where disabled children's needs may be best met through specialist provision, which may be some way from their home—so they will need to be educated outside their local community. This also maintains parental choice for schools outside the local community. A general reservation is proposed in order to retain the right to apply immigration rules and to retain the right to introduce wider health screening for applicants entering or seeking to remain in the UK, particularly in the event of a global health emergency, if this is considered necessary to protect public health. This clarifies the Government's understanding that the convention does not create new or additional rights for non-UK national disabled people relating to the entry into, stay in and departure from the United Kingdom. This reservation will be subject to review 12 months after the UK has ratified the Convention in order to assess whether there is a continued need for it in practice. A reservation is proposed in respect of article 12.4, which concerns safeguards for the exercise of substituted decision-making and includes a requirement for "regular review" by a competent, independent and impartial authority or judicial body. There is currently no review system for Department for Work and Pensions (DWP) appointees; that is, people who are appointed to claim and collect benefits on behalf of another person due to that person's lack of physical or mental capacity. Those appointee arrangements are not at present subject to the safeguard of regular review, as the Government believe this article requires. DWP is therefore actively working towards a proportionate system of review to address this issue. Moving towards ratification is a major achievement. I believe that this step will be welcomed, along with the signing of the Optional Protocol to the UN Convention last week (Cm7644). Together, these two actions send out a very strong signal—the Government are serious about achieving equality of human rights for disabled people and are making real progress towards their goal of disability equality by 2025.

(HC Deb 3 March 2009 Vol 488 cs51WS-52WS)

6/66
The Government were asked what their assessment was of the practical benefits to the people of the United Kingdom of allowing the right of individual petition under the Optional Protocol to the United Nations Convention on the Rights of Persons with Disabilities. A Minister wrote:

Assessment of the benefits will come in the light of the outcome of any applications that follow ratification. The Government will keep under review the applications that are made under this Protocol, including how they are handled by the relevant committees at the United Nations, and whether the outcomes demonstrate significant additional benefits to people in the United Kingdom.

(HL Deb 6 July 2009 Vol 712 cWA110)

6/67
Discrimination

The Government were asked whether there was a gap between the protection given by the general right to equality without discrimination by article 26 of the United Nations International Covenant on Civil and Political Rights and the protection given in United Kingdom human rights and discrimination law; and, if so, what was the nature of that gap; and whether they had had regard to the way in which the United Nations

Human Rights Committee has handled individual applications under the Optional Protocol to the International Covenant on Civil and Political Rights; and, if so, what was their assessment of the substantive benefits to those who have had recourse to that mechanism. A Minister wrote:

Article 26 of the International Covenant on Civil and Political Rights (ICCPR) differs from UK human rights and discrimination law both in nature and in scope. However in the Government's view this does not mean that in practice there is any gap in protection. In light of the protections in domestic law that I outlined in my previous Answer (col. *WA 58*, 28 January 2009), the mechanisms that already exist in international law for regular periodic examination of the UK's compliance with the ICCPR, and the findings of the review of our experience of individual petition under the Optional Protocol to the Convention for the Elimination of All Form of Discrimination Against Women—CEDAW (col. 11WS, 4 December 2008), the Government do not consider there is sufficient evidence that additional practical benefit would be provided by accepting the right of individual petition in respect of complaints under the ICCPR.

The Government do not consider it necessary to undertake a further evaluation in respect of the handling of individual petitions by the UN Human Rights Committee because of the nature of the UN monitoring committee processes (that they cannot, for example, give legal rulings) and because of the conclusions of the review on the CEDAW experiment.

(HL Deb 12 February 2009 Vol 707 cWA228)

6/68 (See also 5/54)

The Secretary of State for Foreign and Commonwealth Affairs was asked how many recently amended constitutions of Overseas Territories do not prohibit discrimination on the grounds of sexual orientation. A Minister wrote:

Since 2006, the Government have agreed new constitutions with five Overseas Territories and implemented them by Order in Council: the British Virgin Islands, the Falkland Islands, Gibraltar, the Turks and Caicos Islands and the Cayman Islands (not yet in force). Only the Falkland Islands' constitution specifically mentions sexual orientation as a ground on which discrimination is prohibited. The new St. Helena, Ascension and Tristan da Cuhna Constitution, which has been agreed and will be submitted to Her Majesty the Queen in the Privy Council on 8 July 2009, also specifically mentions sexual orientation as a ground on which discrimination is prohibited. The Government take the protection of human rights very seriously. Even though there may not be specific provision within a constitution for non-discrimination on the grounds of sexual orientation, we do ensure that all constitutions contain a Bill of Rights that reflects at a minimum the European Convention of Human Rights (ECHR) and the International Covenant on Civil and Political Rights. The effect is that all groups, whether or not specifically mentioned in the Bill of Rights have at least the same degree of protection under the constitution as people in the UK have under the ECHR and the Human Rights Act.

(HC Deb 8 July 2009 Vol 495 c854W)

6/69
A Minister wrote:

We condemn all instances of violence and discrimination against individuals and groups because of their faith or belief, wherever they happen or whatever the religion of the individual or group concerned. The Government continue to be extremely concerned about continuing reports of serious, widespread, and systematic human rights abuses in North Korea, including the suppression of religious freedoms. We raise these concerns with the North Korean authorities at every appropriate opportunity, most recently in February 2009, urging them to engage with the international community, particularly the UN Special Rapporteur on North Korea Human Rights. They continue to refuse to engage on this issue. We are also working with non-governmental organisations, including Christian Solidarity Worldwide, as we prepare for the Universal Periodic Review (UPR) of North Korea's human rights record at the UN Human Rights Council in December 2009. The human rights situation in Saudi Arabia remains poor. We particularly oppose the lack of freedom of expression and religion. Saudi Arabia is a Muslim country which does not allow the practice of other religions. We continue to urge the Saudis to respect freedom of religion and to honour article 18 of the Universal Declaration of Human Rights. This is done at ministerial, ambassadorial and official level. In February 2009 the UN UPR reviewed human rights in Saudi Arabia. The UK made a number of recommendations. On 26 March 2009 the Foreign and Commonwealth Office's 2008 Annual Human Rights report was launched by the Foreign Secretary. In the report we highlighted that "the public practice of any religion other than Islam remains banned. Renouncing religious belief in Islam is an offence punishable by death". Our embassy last raised Freedom of Expression with the Saudi Government in Riyadh on 13 July 2009. We will continue to lobby on this and other important issues. The security situation in Iraq shows continued signs of improvement, but violence does continue to affect many people, including Christians. The UK continues to encourage the Government of Iraq to protect all communities and to take tough action against those responsible for any acts of violence and intimidation regardless of political, ethnic or religious affiliation. Promoting human rights is integral to building a stable democracy in Afghanistan. But after 30 years of conflict Afghanistan is starting from a low base. Poverty and weak state institutions are big contributors to human rights violations. Conservative cultural values often exacerbate the severe hardships many still face. We condemn all instances where individuals, including Christians, are persecuted because of their faith or belief and take every opportunity to urge Afghanistan to implement laws and practices which foster tolerance and mutual respect. This includes full implementation of those norms laid out in the 1981 UN Declaration on the Elimination of all Forms of Intolerance and of Discrimination Based on Religion or Belief. Our embassy in Kabul continues to follow the human rights situation on the ground closely and raise matters of concern with the Afghan Government. We recognise that the human rights situation in Somalia has been appalling for a very long time. The ongoing civil conflict has impacted adversely on all sections of society, but particularly on vulnerable ethnic and religious minorities including the small community of Christians. We continue to urge the Transitional Federal Government to combat human rights abuses as an important component of the Djibouti Process to restore peace and stability to the country. We support the mandate of the UN Independent Expert on Human Rights in Somalia and the work of human rights organisations to gather accurate information and evidence about the situation on the ground.

(HC Deb 20 July 2009 Vol 496 c954W-955W)

6/70 (See also **14/4**)
European Convention on Human Rights

A Minister wrote:

The majority of the rights protected by the European Convention on Human Rights are not absolute. Most rights are qualified, which means that interference with a right is permitted where that is in accordance with the law, proportionate to a certain specified aim, and/or necessary to protect the rights and freedoms of others. For example, it is sometimes necessary to balance the right of the media to freedom of expression with the right of individuals to respect for their private life. Many areas of Government policy involve making these difficult decisions on a daily basis and it is not possible to list them exhaustively. It is also possible for states party to make reservations to some rights or to derogate from some articles of the Convention in times of emergency. However, the UK currently has no derogations to the Convention.

(HC Deb 24 November 2009 Vol 501 c84W)

6/71 (See also **5/49)**
Fiji

A Minister wrote:

I remain extremely concerned over the human rights situation in Fiji, particularly since the abrogation of the constitution in April this year. Through our High Commission in Suva, among other sources, we continue to watch events closely. These include the cancellation of the Methodist Church annual meeting in July and the arrest and detention of church leaders. We have made our concerns at these and other developments clear to the military regime in Fiji, and have drawn them to the attention of international partners, including the EU. Fiji was suspended from the Commonwealth on 1 September following meetings of the Commonwealth Ministerial Action Group, of which the UK is a member. The UK most recently raised its concerns on human rights in Fiji in a statement to the UN Human Rights Council in Geneva in September.

(HC Deb 12 October 2009 Vol 497 c41W)

6/72
Guantanamo Bay (See also **5/58, UKMIL [2008] 6/59–62**)

The Foreign Secretary was asked what recent discussions he had had with the United States administration on allegations of torture at Guantanamo Bay. An FCO Minister wrote:

The Foreign and Commonwealth Office maintains an active bilateral dialogue on a range of human rights and international legal issues with the US Government, including on the prohibition of the use of torture. We have raised with the US allegations of mistreatment put to us by our nationals or residents currently or formerly detained at Guantanamo Bay. In the last year we have asked the US Administration to investigate allegations of mistreatment raised by UK residents Omar Deghayes, Abdennour Sameur and Binyam Mohamed including in relation to periods of detention prior to their transfer to Guantanamo Bay.

(HC Deb 23 February 2009 Vol 488 c362W)

6/73 (See also **6/115**)
The Foreign Secretary made a statement about the release of Binyam Mohamed from Guantanamo. He wrote:

Mr. Binyam Mohamed returned to the UK yesterday, 23 February, following his release from Guantanamo Bay. A team of Foreign and Commonwealth Office (FCO) officials, including a doctor, met with Mr. Mohamed on 14 February and confirmed there were no immediate medical concerns that would prevent him from travelling to the UK. The same team, along with officers of the Metropolitan Police Service, accompanied Mr. Mohamed on his return to the UK. The FCO was in close contact with Mr. Mohamed's family and legal representatives to inform them of his return. This is the direct result of our request for his release and return, and follows intensive negotiations with the US Government over the past 18 months, since my request to Secretary of State Condoleezza Rice on 7 August 2007. These negotiations included pressing for and securing the disclosure by the US to Mr. Mohamed's lawyers of the 42 documents, which were the subject of a judicial review in the English courts, that could be used for Mr. Mohamed's defence. Further public disclosure of these documents remains a matter for the US Administration. In this regard we welcome the US Attorney General's order for a review of all the assertions of the state secrets privilege in the US Courts. The Government abhor torture and do not order or condone it. We have raised with the US allegations of mistreatment put to us by UK nationals or residents currently or formerly detained at Guantanamo Bay, including Mr. Mohamed. The question of possible criminal wrongdoing that arose in Mr. Mohamed's case was referred by the Home Secretary to the Attorney General for her to consider. This was, as the court acknowledged, the proper legal process. Mr. Mohamed's return does not constitute a commitment by the Home Secretary that he may remain permanently in the UK. His immigration status is being reviewed following his return. As always, the Government's top priority is national security, and should any steps be necessary, we will take them. Mr. Mohamed is the first Guantanamo detainee to be released under President Obama's Administration. We have welcomed, and strongly support, the Obama Administration's aim to close Guantanamo. Our request for Shaker Aamer's return to the UK remains and we stand ready to share our experience in receiving former detainees with European member states, and others, as they consider how they can assist towards closure.

(HC Deb 24 February 2009 Vol 488 cs18WS-19WS)

6/74
The Foreign Secretary was asked whether he had *(a)* received representations from and *(b)* had held discussions with the Government of Ethiopia on the Guantanamo detainee Mr Binyam Mohamed. He wrote:

We have not received any representations from the Government of Ethiopia on Mr. Binyam Mohamed's case. We informed the Government of Ethiopia in August 2007 of our decision to seek Mr. Mohamed's release and return to the UK. We have sought to keep the Government of Ethiopia informed on developments in his case.

(HC Deb 9 March 2009 Vol 489 c50W)

6/75
The Government were asked whether they have agreed to offer Great Britain as a place of humanitarian protection for detainees released from Guantanamo Bay. An FCO Minister wrote:

We have already secured the release and return of 14 individuals from Guantanamo Bay. The decision to request release and return is restricted to UK nationals and those previously legally resident in the UK. The US Government have not agreed our request for the release and return of Mr Shaker Aamer to the UK but we have made clear to the US that our request still stands should its position change. There are no plans to make representations on behalf of any other detainees. However, we will continue to share our experience in accepting the transfer of former Guantanamo detainees with our European partners and others to help support the closure of the detention facility.

(HL Deb 30 March 2009 Vol 709 cWA187)

6/76
A Minister made a written statement about the meeting of the European Council (Justice and Home Affairs), 4/5 June 2009:

Ministers adopted conclusions on a co-ordinated EU approach to the closing of the Guantanamo Bay detention centre. The conclusions put in place a framework for information sharing to facilitate member states' acceptance of former detainees from Guantanamo Bay. The conclusions also outline that it is for individual member states to decide whether they accept ex-detainees. The Council noted that primary responsibility for the closure of Guantanamo rests with the US, but the EU should do its part to assist this process. The UK supported the conclusions, highlighting that closure of Guantanamo was a key issue not only for transatlantic relations but also for the radicalisation and recruitment of potential terrorists. Getting the message right was important in adding to the safety and security of citizens by countering extremism and the conclusions were a step forward in that regard. [The text of the statement appears below, Ed.]

(HL Deb 11 June 2009 Vol 711 cWS45)

6/77
Conclusions of the Council and of the representatives of the Governments of the Member States on the closure of the Guantanamo Bay Detention Centre:

The Council of the European Union and the representatives of the Governments of the Member StatesWishing to foster closer transatlantic cooperation with the United States of America in the area of Freedom, Security and Justice based on shared values, in particular on respect for the rights of individuals and for the rule of law, principles resulting from the constitutional traditions of the United States and the EU Member States, and on mutual respect, common interests and reciprocity,Considering that the European Union and the United States of America share the common objectives of fighting terrorism while upholding the rule of law and observing and promoting respect for international law, human rights and fundamental freedoms,Welcoming the decision of the President of the United States of America to close the Guantanamo Bay Detention Centre and to order a review of detention, trial, transfer and interrogation policies in the fight against terrorism,Taking note of the request made by the Government of the United States to assist it in finding residence for those persons "cleared for release", who for compelling reasons cannot return to their countries of origin, but have expressed the wish to be received by one or other EU Member State or Schengen associated country, Reaffirming that the primary responsibility for closing Guantanamo and finding residence for the former detainees rests with the United States,Taking note that the United States recognises its responsibility in accepting certain former detainees who indicate a desire to be admitted to the United States,

Wishing to lend its support to this process against the background of a thorough review of US counter-terrorism policies consistent with the rule of law and international law in the expectation that the underlying policy issues would be addressed, Recognising that decisions on the reception of former detainees and the determination of their legal status fall within the sole responsibility and competence of a receiving Member State or Schengen associated country, Considering that as a rule third country nationals legally residing within one Member State or Schengen associated country have the right to move freely within the territories of the other Member States or Schengen associated countries, under conditions set by the provisions of Schengen acquis, Recognising that as a result of the abolition of controls at internal borders within the Schengen area, a decision to accept a former detainee by one Member State would be relevant for other Member States and Schengen associated countries including in regard to internal security, and that therefore consultation and thorough information-sharing is important both before and after decisions to receive former detainees are taken including information on a change of residence of former detainees, in order to give all Member States and Schengen associated countries the opportunity to share relevant information and to take appropriate measures including measures that may temporarily affect freedom of movement if necessary, in accordance with the Schengen acquis and national law,

Stressing the importance of involving Schengen associated countries in information-sharing among the Member States as described in the annex to these Conclusions,Wishing to contribute to creating conditions which may help those Member States that are willing to receive former detainees to cooperate with the United States Government in finding residence for those former detainees who are "cleared for release" and who the US administration does not wish to prosecute, and who for compelling reasons cannot return to their home countries of origin and who want to be transferred to a Member State or Schengen associated country, Call upon the Member States who are willing to receive former detainees to consider accepting only those former detainees, who fall into the category defined above,Call upon the receiving Member States to take into account the public order and security concerns including those of other Member States so as to avoid former detainees compromising the public order or internal security of the Member States and Schengen associated countries and also call upon the receiving Member States, without prejudice to possible support from United States, to promote integration of the persons concerned through appropriate measures, while fully respecting their human rights and fundamental freedoms,

Agree that information sharing through existing channels among all Member States and Schengen associated countries is equally important both before and after decisions to receive former detainees are taken, Agree herewith on the mechanism for the exchange of information concerning former detainees of Guantanamo as described in the annex to these Conclusions,Take note of the full support for these Conclusions on the part of the Schengen associated countries.

Reaffirm that nothing in these Conclusions should be interpreted as an invitation to those Member States or Schengen associated countries which do not intend to receive former detainees to do so.

(Council of the European Union (Justice and Home Affairs), 4 June 2009, 10523/2/09 Rev 2)

6/78
The Government were asked what was the status of the two former British residents held at Guantanamo Bay; how long they had been held; and what action they would take to secure their release. An FCO Minister wrote:

The Government's decision to seek the release and return of former residents was limited to those who were lawfully resident in the UK prior to their detention. Following the safe return of five former legal residents to the UK, only one individual with this status, Shaker Aamer, is at Guantanamo Bay, where he has been held since February 2002. We requested his release and return to the UK in August 2007. The US has so far declined our request, owing to security concerns. We continue to make clear that our request stands for his release and return. We maintain an ongoing dialogue with the US regarding Mr Aamer's welfare, and are in frequent contact with his family and legal representatives.

(HL Deb 30 June 2009 Vol 712 cWA34)

6/79
A Minister wrote:

We have sought the release and return of Shaker Aamer, a Saudi national formerly lawfully resident in the UK, from Guantanamo Bay since August 2007. The US has not so far agreed to his release and return to the UK in the light of security concerns in his case. We have made clear to both the current and previous US Administrations that our request for Mr. Aamer's release and return to the UK stands. My right hon. Friend the Foreign Secretary has reiterated this position to Secretary of State Hillary Clinton. Other Ministers and senior officials across Government have raised Mr. Aamer's case with their counterparts in the US State Department, the Department of Defense, the Department of Justice and the National Security Council.

(HC Deb 12 October 2009 Vol 497 c34W)

6/80 (See also 5/21–23)
Honduras

A Minister wrote:

We are concerned about reports of human rights violations in the Honduras since the political crisis began in June-in particular the growing restrictions imposed on the Honduran population since President Zelaya's return to Tegucigalpa on 21 September 2009 We continue to monitor the situation through discussions with those EU Partners who have embassies in Tegucigalpa and with UK-based non-governmental organisations operating in Honduras. UK officials from our embassy in Guatemala City have visited Tegucigalpa periodically since the crisis began, most recently between 21 September and 2 October 2009. A Mission representing the Organisation of American States Inter-American Commission on Human Rights visited Honduras last month. We await the report of their visit. We hope that the signing, by representatives of President Zelaya and the de facto government, of an accord on 30 October will lead to the establishment of a power sharing government, and a return to full democratic, constitutional order and respect for human rights in the country.

(HC Deb 9 November 2009 Vol 499 c159W)

6/81
Iran

The Foreign Secretary was asked what the Government's policy towards the People's Mujaheddin Organisation of Iran was in the light of the recent judgment by the European Court of First Instance [*People's Mojahedin Organisation of Iran v Council* EUECJ T-284/08, Ed.]. A Minister wrote:

On 26 January 2009, taking account of the judgment by the Court of First Instance on 4 December 2008, the General Affairs and External Relations Council adopted a list which did not include the MeK (Mujaheddin-e-Khalq, also known as the People's Mojaheddin of Iran). However, we remain mindful of the MeK's history as an organisation responsible for a number of serious terrorist attacks—it claimed responsibility for large numbers of violent attacks inside Iran for a number of years, including 96 in a three-month period in early 2001. We do not agree with its claim that it represents a credible democratic opposition in exile.

(HC Deb 10 February 2009 Vol 487 c1846W)

6/82
The Foreign Secretary was asked what representations he had made to the Iranian authorities on the detention without charge of Maryam Rostampour and Marzieh Amirizadeh in Evin Prison in Iran. An FCO Minister wrote:

We have received worrying reports that Maryam Rostampour and Marzieh Amirizadeh are being held in Evin prison following their arrest by Iranian security officers on 5 March 2009. The women are known to be practising Christians. Reports suggest that neither have been charged with any crime defined under Iranian or international legislation, nor have they been permitted access to lawyers. The UK has genuine concerns for their safety and well-being, which are heightened by the fact that the Iranian Parliament is currently debating a draft Bill which could codify life imprisonment for female apostates. We have made clear to the Iranian authorities on many occasions that we believe persecution of individuals on the grounds of their ethnicity or religious beliefs is unacceptable, and will continue to do so through the EU and bilaterally. We will continue to press the Iranian authorities to take seriously their international human rights obligations and uphold the right to freedom of religion and belief as described in Article 18 of the International Covenant on Civil and Political Rights (to which Iran is a state party). [The women are Iranian Christians who were detained in March 2009 and released in November 2009, Ed.]

(HC Deb 19 May 2009 Vol 492 c1325W)

6/83

During a debate in the House of Commons, the Prime Minister was asked about seven Baha'i leaders facing trial in Iran. He said:

I am sure that the whole House will share my deep disappointment at the recent behaviour of the Iranian regime: disappointment at the manner in which legitimate demonstrations have been suppressed; disappointment at the restrictions that [the previous speaker, Ed] has mentioned on the freedoms of the Iranian people, with people due to stand before a closed court on 11 July; and disappointment that the Iranian Government have expelled two of our diplomats and detained several of our embassy staff. This action is unjustified and unacceptable. Some people in Iran are seeking to use Britain as an explanation for the legitimate Iranian voices calling for greater openness and democracy. However, we will continue, with our international partners, to raise our concerns with Iran, including on the issue that the hon. Gentleman raised.

(HC Deb 1 July 2009 Vol 495 c300)

6/84

A Minister wrote:

We have serious concerns about the situation of religious and ethnic minorities in Iran. The Iranian authorities continue to prohibit the use of minority languages in schools, and ethnic groups such as Ahwazi Arabs, Azeris, Baluchis, Kurds and Turkmen face persecution and arbitrary arrest for campaigning for their basic rights. Many activists remain in detention on charges of endangering national security. Iran's religious minorities continue to suffer gross human rights violations, including extra-judicial killings, detention without charge, confiscation of property, and denial of education. Such events appear to be increasingly commonplace, and are cause for serious concern. Alongside our EU partners we have made clear to the Iranian authorities that the persecution of individuals on the grounds of religion, belief or ethnicity is unacceptable. We have expressed concern about the persecution of ethnic minorities and, in a declaration of 25 May 2009, called on the Iranian authorities to uphold their international legal undertakings to safeguard religious freedom and to stop their persecution of legitimate religious activities.

(HC Deb 3 July 2009 Vol 495 c472W-473W)

6/85
A Minister wrote:

We are extremely concerned by reports that the Iranian Government have set up special courts to deal with those arrested [in demonstrations after the election] and have threatened harsh sentences. Ayatollah Khatami's comments are absolutely unacceptable and we urge the Iranian authorities to guarantee the lives and rights of those arrested in the post-election violence. These individuals must be protected from torture or ill-treatment, allowed access to their families, lawyers and any necessary medical treatment. Along with our EU partners, we have strongly supported UN statements voicing grave concern about the use of excessive police force, arbitrary arrests and killings in the Islamic Republic of Iran and urging the Government fully to guarantee freedom of expression and assembly throughout the country.

(HL Deb 9 July 2009 Vol 712 cWA168)

6/86 (See also **7/4**)
Hossein Rassam, an Iranian national who was a political advisor at the British Embassy in Tehran, was arrested following the disputed Presidential elections in Iran in June 2009 and later convicted at a trial the British government regarded as being in breach of his human rights. In a statement, the Foreign Secretary said:

Reports that Hossein Rassam has been sentenced to four years in prison are deeply concerning. Such a decision is wholly unjustified and represents further harassment of Embassy staff for going about their normal and legitimate duties. Our Ambassador in Tehran has spoken to the Deputy Foreign Minister to express our concerns and our acting Permanent Under Secretary has called in the Iranian Ambassador in London.

We understand the sentence can be appealed. I urge the authorities to conduct this quickly and overturn this harsh sentence. We are in close touch with EU and other international partners, who continue to show solidarity in the face of this unacceptable Iranian action. This will be seen as an attack against the entire diplomatic community in Iran and important principles are at stake.

(<www.fco.gov.uk/news>, 28 October 2009)

6/87
A Minister wrote:

The UK has ongoing concerns about the number of executions in Iran and in particular its use against juvenile offenders. We are committed to speaking out publicly against the death penalty and frequently make representations on behalf of individuals at risk of execution. We have done so on over twenty occasions in 2009. In October . . . the Foreign Secretary condemned the execution of Behnood Shojaee for a crime he committed at the age of 17, and expressed grave concern for Safar Angoti, a juvenile facing imminent execution. Most recently, on 20 November 2009, the Swedish Government, as president of the EU, summoned the Iranian ambassador in Stockholm to condemn a spate of executions, including that of Kurdish activist Ehsan Fattahian. They expressed concern that a high number of Kurds faced a similar fate and called for clemency. The presidency also expressed concern that at least five persons have been sentenced to death as a result of mass trials following the disputed election result. We are concerned that the accused had not been given the right to fair trial in accordance with standards laid down in international law.

(HC Deb 1 December 2009 Vol 501 c629W)

6/88
An FCO Minister said:

I am deeply concerned by reports that Mohammad Reza Haddadi is to be executed in Iran on 9 December. Mr Haddadi was sentenced to death for a crime committed at the age of 15. This is the fourth time Mr Haddadi's execution has been scheduled, and I echo the concerns expressed by the European Union to the Government of Iran on a number of occasions, most recently in a statement of 2 December. I urge Iran to show clemency in the case of Mr Haddadi and to commute his sentence. Mohammad Reza Haddadi was sentenced to death in 2004 for a murder he allegedly committed when he was 15. His death sentence was confirmed by the Supreme Court in July 2005. He was first scheduled for execution in October 2008, but it was stayed on the order of the Head of the Judiciary. His execution was then scheduled again on 27 May 2009 and 16 July 2009. The EU, with strong UK support, has intervened on all prior occasions to try and halt this execution.

(<www.fco.gov.uk/news>, 8 December 2009)

6/89
Iraq

An FCO Minister wrote:

The Government of Iraq took a significant step in 2008 to address the slow processing of cases by implementing the Iraqi Amnesty Law which has since helped enable around 12,700 releases. Iraqi security operations throughout 2008 meant an understandable increase in numbers held and it is estimated that approx 26,000 remain in Iraqi detention awaiting processing or trial.

The Ministry of Justice has pledged to make detention centres more efficient by speeding up paperwork, introducing rehabilitation and vocational training and addressing overcrowding. Arrangements for US-held detainees are covered separately under the Iraqi/US Status of Forces Agreement under which the relevant Iraqi authorities may request assistance from the US forces in detaining or arresting wanted individuals. There are currently around 15,000 in US detention but it is expected that the number of US-held detainees should be reduced under this agreement. The Government recognise that the current levels of detainees needs to be greatly reduced and we will continue to closely monitor the situation, making representations as necessary. We shall also continue to assist the Iraqi authorities where possible to implement effectively the amnesty law and required judicial processes.

(HL Deb 2 February 2009 Vol 707 WA92)

6/90 (See also **6/38, 17/6–9**)
In answering a question about 'Ashraf City' in Iraq, an FCO Minister wrote:

[Ashraf City is a camp for Iranian expatriate dissidents in Iraq, established for some years, about which concerns had been expressed concerning conditions there and risks that the residents might be returned to Iran. Some residents in the camp were associated with the MEK (Mujahedin-e Khalq), Ed.] I should clarify that it was the US, not the UK, who had sole responsibility for the security and administration of the camp. The responsibility for the camp was handed to the Iraqi authorities from 1 January 2009 by the US... Whilst residents of the camp were treated as "protected persons", this was exercised at the good will of the US authorities in charge and was not granted through any legal obligation under international law.

(HC Deb 12 February 2009 Vol 487 c2200W)

6/91
In a debate on the conditions in 'Ashraf City' in Iraq, an FCO Minister said:

The legal position was [raised]. As I understand it, the US Government's position is that members of the MEK in Camp Ashraf are to be treated as protected persons for the purposes of the fourth Geneva Convention. The UK position has been that as the fourth Geneva Convention ceased to apply in Iraq after 28 June 2004, the designation of "protected persons" under that particular convention could no longer be applicable as 28 June 2004 signified the end of the occupation. However, that does not mean that the residents in the camp are entitled to no protection under Iraqi or international law. Our view is that we stopped being the occupiers under the Geneva Convention after 28 June 2004. Our obligations as occupiers continued for one year only after the occupation... The year starts after 28 June 2004. I will come on to how we are trying to carry out our responsibilities notwithstanding the fact that we are now dealing with a sovereign state and a democratic country that has its own rights and responsibilities. Inevitably, in those circumstances, our relationship will be different from the one in which we are the occupier. It has always been clear that, with the expiry at the end of 2008 of the UN Security Council resolution mandate for the coalition forces in Iraq, responsibility for the security and administration of the camp and its residents would have to pass from the US to the Government of Iraq. That transfer was carried out in phases and was completed on 1 January 2009. At that time, we understand that some 3,000 members of the MEK were present at the camp. Throughout its discussions with the Government of Iraq on the modalities of the transfer, the US rightly sought assurances that the Camp Ashraf residents would continue to be treated humanely, that their fundamental human rights would be maintained, and that they would be treated in accordance with the constitution of Iraq, in accordance with Iraqi law, and in accordance with Iraq's international obligations. Such assurances were readily provided by the Iraqi authorities to the satisfaction of the US authorities. Moreover, the Iraqi authorities agreed to allow access to the camp by appropriate international organisations to assist the camp residents in securing a safe future. In that regard, we are comforted in the knowledge that the International Committee of the Red Cross continues to visit the camp on a regular basis. It follows developments closely and we very much welcome its involvement. In parallel, the Iraqi Ministry of Human Rights regularly visits the camp and has given assurances to a representative body of the residents. Plans were made to conduct a survey, through interviews with residents of the camp, in an effort to establish whether they wished to be voluntarily repatriated to Iran, or to seek residency in a third country. That survey would also enable the Ministry of Human Rights to verify the details of those currently residing in the camp. [My office was contacted] last week concerning recent developments at the camp...we understood that the MEK had seized back a building that had been designated for the purpose of those interviews. We are unclear as to their motives for taking that action. We are also aware that the Iraqi security forces had taken measures to restrict visitors into the camp out of concern that they would not be permitted by the MEK to leave. Notwithstanding the action, we believe that residents remain free to meet family members and other visitors outside the camp. The Red Cross is rightly monitoring such visits, and we are told that UN officials have also visited the camp as recently as 19 March this year. All of that is welcome. However, the British embassy in Baghdad is pursuing the possibility of a visit by a consular official to Camp Ashraf to confirm whether any of its residents are entitled to UK consular assistance. Importantly, that will also allow us to remind the Iraqi Government further of their earlier assurances regarding Camp Ashraf residents and of the amount of interest in the issue within the United Kingdom.... I can say that the Iraqi Government have repeatedly maintained assurances to respect the human rights of Camp Ashraf residents. We shall certainly remind them of that obligation as we pursue the consular visit. [The de-proscription of People's Mujahideen of Iran (POMI) has been mentioned] There have been two court cases: the UK court case in respect of de-proscription of the MEK and the decision in the European Court of First Instance [See **UKMIL [2008] 6/75**]. Government—rightly, in my view, whatever opinion we might have of the MEK—sought to uphold the rule of law; certainly in the European Union case, we were instrumental in ensuring that. However, I agree...that upholding de-proscription is not the same as saying that the MEK best represents the interests and views of the Iranian people. We certainly have reservations about the MEK's assertion that it represents a democratic opposition in exile. We see no evidence of popular support for the MEK in Iran, partly because of its responsibility for terrorist attacks resulting in the deaths of many Iranian citizens and partly because it fought alongside Iraqi forces against Iran in the Iran-Iraq war. Nevertheless—this is the important point that cuts to the heart of the concerns expressed—the Government of Iraq have stated that no residents of Camp Ashraf will be forcibly transferred to a country where they have reason to fear persecution based on their political opinions or religious beliefs, or where there are substantial grounds for believing that they would be tortured. We are satisfied that the Iraqi Government are working with international organisations, including the United Nations High Commissioner for Refugees, to ensure a humanitarian solution that will allow camp residents either to return home or to be resettled, if they choose, in third countries. We will do everything in our power, consistent with the recognition that Iraq is now a sovereign democratic state, to encourage that process.

(HC Deb 25 March 2009 Vol 490 cs89WH-92WH)

6/92
A Minister wrote:

Camp Ashraf is in a sovereign and democratic Iraq and the camp residents subject to its laws. The UK is of the view that the residents of Camp Ashraf, as with all people in Iraq, enjoy rights and protections under the Iraqi constitution and applicable international obligations to which Iraq is a signatory. We do not consider that they have 'protected persons' status.

(HC Deb 25 November 2009 Vol 501 cs163W-164W)

6/93
Israel

A Minister wrote:

The administrative detention and treatment of Palestinian prisoners, especially Palestinian teenagers, in Israeli Prison Service facilities is a serious concern. We have called on the Israeli Government to take immediate action to ensure all cases are reviewed by a court in accordance with fair procedures, and that their rights, particularly the rights to a fair trial and family visitation, are upheld. We made our concerns clear during Israel's Universal Periodic Review (UPR) in the Human Rights Council in December 2008 and also in the Foreign and Commonwealth Office's 2008 Human Rights Report. We will continue to raise this with Israeli officials.

(HC Deb 1 July 2009 Vol 495 c288W)

6/94
The Government were asked what representations they have made to the Government of Israel concerning elected Palestinian parliamentarians held in Israeli prisons. The FCO Minister wrote:

We remain concerned by the administrative detention of a significant number of Palestinians, including parliamentarians, in Israeli prisons. We continue to call for all elected Palestinian Legislative Council members detained by Israel to be either released or subject to due legal process. We made this explicitly clear in our 2008 Human Rights Report, published in March this year.

(HL Deb 19 October 2009 Vol 713 cWA47)

6/95
An FCO Minister wrote:

We are extremely concerned by aspects of the Israeli military justice and detention system, including allegations of Palestinian children being detained and interrogated without access to a lawyer or to visits by family members; and allegations that they are subjected to treatment that breaches the UN Convention Against Torture and other Cruel, Inhuman, and Degrading Treatment or Punishment of 1984, in order to obtain confessions. The Government expressed their concern about this issue at the Human Rights Council in November 2008. It was also one of several concerns highlighted in a report, published in May 2009, by the UN Committee Against Torture. Israel is a state party to both the UN Convention on the Rights of the Child of 1989 and the UN Convention against Torture of 1984. Israel has also stated it takes seriously its periodic reports before the treaty bodies, using them as an opportunity for in-depth self-examination. We strongly urge Israel to abide by its obligations in the UN conventions and other relevant rules of international law.

(HL Deb 12 November 2009 Vol 714 csWA211-WA212)

6/96
Kenya

An FCO Minister wrote:

The UK and Kenya have entered into a framework Memorandum of Understanding for the transfer of suspect pirates. This affirms that the suspects will be treated in accordance with international human rights law standards, including the right to a fair trial. The UK Government have worked with the European Commission and United Nations Office on Drugs and Crime to complete reviews of the legal framework in Kenya, to assess the adequacy of the Kenyan judicial, legal and prison systems for prosecuting pirates in accordance with international standards, and to provide assistance where appropriate. This assistance has included supporting prosecutors through ensuring evidence handover protocols are in and training in the law of the sea. The UK Government hope that in addition to strengthening Kenya's legal capacities, this support will provide impetus to faster implementation of Kenya's judicial reform programme, in line with the recommendations set out by Kenya's judicial reform task force.

(HL Deb 1 December 2009 Vol 715 cWA29)

6/97
Monitoring

The Government were asked by what standards they decided whether to monitor a country's human right abuses; and how often those standards were reconsidered. An FCO Minister wrote:

Our diplomatic missions overseas report events, activities and other information relevant to our policy goals back to the Foreign and Commonwealth Office (FCO) and to other government departments. This includes information on the human rights and democracy situation in countries.

An important factor in deciding how to deploy our finite resources is the state's own capacity to address human rights concerns, as well as access to regional mechanisms, for example the European Court of Human Rights. The level of monitoring or reporting also depends on the seriousness of the human rights situation as assessed by our diplomats on the ground, FCO and other relevant officials, and their relevance to the Government's policy goals.

Human rights are essential to the delivery of our strategic goals whether in combating the global scourge of terrorism and its causes; preventing conflict and fostering its resolution; promoting a high-growth, low-carbon global economy; or strengthening institutions such as the UN, EU and the Commonwealth. We do not therefore have discrete criteria for monitoring human rights abuses as we do not see human rights and democracy issues as separated from our broader international interests.

(HL Deb 15 June 2009 Vol 711 cWA182)

6/98
Nepal

An FCO Minister wrote:

The UK strongly supports the right to freedom of religion or belief. We are disappointed that the interim constitution of Nepal does not guarantee a person's right to choose or change their religion. We will, however, urge the Government of Nepal to ensure that the new constitution provides this right. We are providing technical and financial assistance to the Constituent Assembly to assist it in the drafting of the new constitution. This includes raising its awareness of Nepal's obligations under international treaties such as the International Covenant on Civil and Political Rights to protect human rights, including the freedom of religion.

(HL Deb 7 December 2009 Vol 715 cWA93)

6/99
North Korea

A Minister wrote:

The Government take the human rights situation in North Korea extremely seriously. We are deeply concerned by continuing reports of serious, widespread and systematic human rights abuses there. We raise this issue with the North Korean Government at every appropriate opportunity. Our ambassador in Pyongyang raised our concerns most recently in February 2009 during the visit to North Korea by Lord Alton and Baroness Cox with the Vice-Minister of Foreign Affairs and Speaker of the North Korean Parliament. He emphasised the importance of dialogue on human rights and urged North Korea to accept a visit by the UN Special Rapporteur. However the North Korean Government refuse to engage. With EU Partners we sponsored annual resolutions on North Korea human rights at the UN General Assembly (in December 2008), and at the UN Human Rights Council (in March 2009). The latter includes the mandate for the UN Special Rapporteur on North Korea Human Rights, whose work in evidence gathering we strongly support. We have worked closely with a number of non-governmental organisations (NGOs) over the past year. We sponsored an NGO report on children's rights in North Korea ahead of the February 2009 periodic report by the UN Committee on the Rights of Child on North Korea. We also supported the participation of a leading UK NGO at an international conference on North Korean Human Rights in Canberra in March. We are now working with NGOs and international partners to prepare for the Universal Periodic Review of North Korea's human rights record which is scheduled to take place at the UN Human Rights Council session in December 2009. Locally, our embassy in Pyongyang has given support to the project work of Handicap International in the DPRK which is designed to help improve the rights of the disabled there, and is looking at ways to increase that activity.

(HC Deb 7 July 2009 Vol 495 c631W)

6/100
A Minister wrote:

As set out in the Foreign and Commonwealth Office's (FCO) Annual Human Rights Report, the Government continues to be deeply concerned by the reports of serious, widespread, and systematic human rights violations in North Korea. We raise these issues with the North Korean authorities at every appropriate opportunity. However, the North Korean government refuses to engage. Our ambassador in Pyongyang raised our concerns with the Vice-Minister of Foreign Affairs and Speaker of the North Korean parliament in February 2009 during the visit to North Korea by [two members of the House of Lords]. He emphasised the importance of dialogue on human rights and urged North Korea to accept a visit by the UN Special Rapporteur. The Government have also continued to look for opportunities to engage on the issue of North Korean refugees. We urge China to observe its obligations under the 1951 convention on the status of refugees and to allow the UN High Commissioner for Refugees access to the China-Democratic People's Republic of Korea (DPRK) border region. This subject was raised with the Chinese at the UK-China Human Rights Dialogue in January 2009. We urged China not to return those people crossing the border from DPRK to China. At our request, the issue of North Korean refugees was included in the UN Human Rights Council resolution on DPRK which was agreed on at the 10th session of the Human Rights Council which was concluded on 27 March 2009.

(HC Deb 12 October 2009 Vol 497 c46W)

6/101
Pakistan

A Minister wrote:

The UK, together with our EU partners, condemned the murder of five women in Baluchistan in July 2008, and called on the Government of Pakistan to bring those responsible to justice. We welcomed the resolution adopted by Pakistan's Senate for strong action to be taken against the perpetrators. Through both multilateral and bilateral representation, we continue to encourage the Government of Pakistan to promote and protect women's rights in accordance with international standards such as the International Convention on the Elimination of All Forms of Discrimination Against Women which Pakistan has signed. The UK delegation to the UN Human Rights Council also raised this during the Universal Periodic Review of Pakistan's human rights record in May 2008. Through our High Commission in Islamabad we support projects which promote women's rights and help obtain better access to justice, for example by supporting community-based lawyer-activists who represent women in cases of forced marriage, domestic violence and other crimes; encouraging the creation of a lawyers' network of human rights advocates with prominent women advocates; improving investigative journalism in Pakistan to encourage impartial reporting on political, electoral and human rights issues; and raising awareness and teaching of human rights, including women's rights, in schools.

(HC Deb 8 July 2009 Vol 495 c860W)

6/102
A Minister wrote:

We are concerned about reports that members of the Christian community in Bahmari Wala, Pakistan have been attacked. The UK supports freedom of religion and condemns persecution because of faith or beliefs. Incidents such as the attack in Bahmari Wala are an example of the discrimination and violent extremism faced by religious minorities in Pakistan. We regularly raise our concerns with the government of Pakistan about the situation of religious minorities, both with our EU partners and bilaterally in London and through our High Commission in Islamabad, and will continue to do so. The most recent EU démarche called upon the government of Pakistan to promote tolerance, to effectively protect freedom of belief and freedom of expression and to reform discriminatory legislation in particular blasphemy laws. With regard to the latest incident officials from the High Commission in Islamabad are monitoring developments closely. We note that a compensation package that has been announced for those affected by the attack.

(HC Deb 9 September 2009 Vol 496 c1964W)

6/103
Racism

The UK representative to the Durban Review Conference of the World Conference against Racism announced the following interpretative statement to the Outcome Document on 4 April 2008. [<www.un.org/WCAR/durban.pdf>, Ed.]:

The United Kingdom welcomes adoption by consensus of the Outcome Document of the Durban Review Conference. We were pleased to join that consensus. And in that regard, I would like to make the following precisions about my Government's understanding of the commitments it has undertaken in agreeing to the Outcome Document. At the outset, my Government would like to make two general points. Firstly, it reaffirms the precisions contained in the statement delivered by Belgium, on behalf of the European Union, during the 20th plenary meeting of the World Conference Against Racism on 8 September 2001, following adoption of the Durban Declaration and Programme of Action. Secondly, the UK's support for the outcome document of the Review Conference is on the clear understanding that it is a generic document and does not single out any particular country or region for consideration. It applies equally to all states. I would also like to make the following points about specific issues addressed in the Outcome Document. The fight against racism, discrimination and intolerance is a priority for the UK. Crimes motivated by racial, religious, or other forms of hatred are not just attacks on the individual, they are attacks on the whole of society. We therefore have strong and effective laws against racially and religiously motivated violence and incitement to racial and religious hatred. Our judges can impose higher penalties where the crime is motivated by hatred of the person's sexual orientation or disability. Our laws are underpinned by strong policies and programmes to promote equality, understanding and good relations between different groups. The UK also has a long tradition of freedom of expression, which allows individuals and organisations to hold and express views that may be offensive or distasteful to the majority. We believe that such people have their right to express those views, however abhorrent, so long as they are not expressed violently or incite violence or hatred. The UK therefore maintains its interpretation of Article 4 of the International Convention for the Elimination of all forms of Racial Discrimination, stated on signature of the Convention in 1966, that article 4 requires a party to the Convention to adopt further legislative measures in the fields covered by sub-paragraphs (a) (b) and (c) only if it considers - with due regard to the principles embodied in the Universal Declaration of Human Rights and the rights expressly set forth in article 5 of the Convention (in particular the right to freedom of opinion and expression and the right to freedom of peaceful assembly and association)—that any additional legislation or variation of existing law and practice is necessary to meet those ends. The UK's understanding of the treatment of these issues by the Review Conference Outcome Document is therefore subject to that same interpretation. We condemn all individuals and organisations that promote racism, anti-Semitism or religious and other forms of intolerance. They, and their message of division and fear, must be condemned marginalised. The UK's combination of legislative, judicial and policy measures to tackle does just that. We believe that positive action can be a powerful to tool tackle inequality, when carefully targeted at groups that experience particular disadvantage. We note that paragraph 72 cites two particular groups, but interpret those as examples, which may vary from country to country. The Outcome Document makes a number of references to indigenous people. The UK would like to reiterate that it does not recognise the concept of collective human rights in international law, with the exception of the right of self-determination. As explained in our interpretative statement made on 29 June 2006 at the adoption of the United Nations Declaration on the Rights of Indigenous Peoples, the UK considers that indigenous individuals are entitled to the full protection of their human rights and fundamental freedoms in international law, on an equal basis to all other individuals, as human rights are universal and equal to all. However, the UK does not accept that some groups in society should benefit from human rights that are not available to others. This is a long-standing and well-established position of the UK. It is one we consider to be important in ensuring that individuals within groups are not left vulnerable or unprotected by allowing rights of the group to supersede the human rights of the individual. This is without prejudice to the UK's recognition of the fact that the governments of many States with indigenous populations have granted them various collective rights in their constitutions, national laws and agreements. Our support for the Outcome Document as a whole does not change in any way our general position on collective rights, which remains as set out in our interpretative statement made at the adoption of the UN Declaration on the Rights of Indigenous Peoples on 29 June 2006 [See **UKMIL [2006] 5/62**]. Finally, Mr

Chairman, the UK would like especially to endorse the references in the Outcome Document to multiple discrimination. In the UK, our laws protect people from discrimination on grounds of race, gender, disability, sexual orientation, religion or belief and age. There must be no hierarchy of discrimination. It is no more acceptable to discriminate against a person because of their sexual orientation than it is to discriminate against a person because of their racial or ethnic origin. Disapproval of a person's beliefs, sexual orientation or personal characteristics can never justify violence or hatred. Victims of such crimes, including lesbian, gay, bisexual and transsexual people, deserve the full protection of the law. I request that this statement be reflected verbatim in the report of the Conference.

(Text supplied by FCO)

6/104

The Foreign Secretary made the following statement at the conclusion of the Durban Review Conference:

I would like to update the House on the UN Durban Review Conference, the follow-up to the 2001 UN World Conference Against Racism, Racial Discrimination, Xenophobia and Related Intolerance which took place in Geneva from 20 to 24 April. The Government are firmly committed to the elimination of all forms of racism and intolerance. We engaged in this conference because we share its goal of fighting racism.

The UK's engagement in the review process has always come with clear red lines that, if breached, would have led to our withdrawal. We made clear in particular that we would not accept a repeat of the appalling anti-Semitism seen at the first Durban conference in 2001. And the outcome text would need to meet a number of explicit conditions.

In the event, we negotiated a text that did meet those conditions. In particular, we resisted attempts for language calling for restrictions to the right of freedom of expression, including through the concept of "defamation of religions". We secured language on Holocaust remembrance (to which Iran objected but then, in a minority of one, agreed) and the fight against anti-Semitism, and successfully rebutted attempts to single out any country for criticism in the outcome document. We also ensured the text included references to multiple forms of discrimination—which we interpret to cover also the rights of lesbian, gay, bisexual and transgender people—and the importance of the right to freedom of expression in combating racism.

Given that the UK and its partners were successful in achieving our red lines in the outcome document, we decided that the UK should participate in the conference. But we shared the concerns of those who feared the misuse of this conference for intolerant ends and worked hard to avoid such a scenario. I wrote to the UN High Commissioner for Human Rights on 17 April making it clear that we would not accept intolerant behaviour in the conference.

On 20 April, on the first day of the conference, President Ahmadinejad of Iran delivered a statement to the conference, in which he made unacceptable comments describing Israel as a "racist Government" established on the "pretext of

Jewish suffering". The Government deemed these comments offensive, inflammatory and utterly unacceptable. That such remarks were made at the UN's anti-racism conference was all the more shocking and outrageous. On instructions agreed between several like-minded countries, the UK delegation—along with a number of others—left the hall in protest and in solidarity with those targeted by the Iranian President. The delegation returned to the hall once the Iranian President had finished speaking.

The British ambassador to the United Nations in Geneva, Peter Gooderham, delivered a statement on 22 April condemning the Iranian President's speech, but also making it clear that we did not want to leave the stage only to those, like President Ahmadinejad, who would take global efforts against racism backwards. We remained in the UN conference because we wanted an outcome that advanced global efforts against racism. The UN Secretary-General, Ban Ki-moon, and High Commissioner for Human Rights, Navi Pillay, also condemned the President's interventions, as did many other speakers.

The UK delegation kept in close touch with UK-based non-governmental organisation stakeholders throughout the conference.

The fight against racism remains a global struggle. Victims of racism deserve better than political squabbling and intolerant polemics. I believe that the Government did the right thing by remaining in the conference, having our voices heard, and ensuring an acceptable outcome document.

(HC Deb 28 April 2009 Vol 491 cs41WS-42WS)

6/105
Religious Freedom

An FCO minister replied to a motion on the human right to freedom of religious belief. He said:

[T]here has been a bipartisan commitment over many years that this Government seek to pursue the promotion of religious freedom and belief—or the right not to believe, as we heard earlier—with all the tools that we have. This includes both our bilateral activities and our efforts to ensure that religion and belief remain high on multilateral agendas. As Ministers, we raise the issue when we travel to countries of concern and with visitors from those countries when they see us here. That includes, for example, the many countries which still penalise blasphemy and use that offence to harass religious minorities; in some jurisdictions, the punishment for it still involves corporal punishment or even the death penalty. That can never be condoned. The Foreign Office is producing guidelines for our posts on how to promote freedom of religion or belief, and to combat violations of it. Those will be published in March. Multilaterally—and I stress that it is so often multilateral channels that offer us a much more forceful way to make our case—we, together with our EU partners, are making full use of the new universal periodic review mechanism at the Human Rights Council in Geneva to raise the issues of religious freedom. That is one of the few public fora where we can engage with countries that otherwise are reluctant to engage. So, when the DPRK is examined in December, we will raise those issues. In that case, we have concerning evidence about the persecution of believers in those Potemkin-like churches in Pyongyang. We also maintain regular dialogue with representatives of religious groups whose members frequently suffer violations of their rights, such as the Baha'is, the Ahmadiyyas, the Jehovah's Witnesses and other Christian groups. We encourage NGOs and others to draw violations to our attention, and we have a stakeholder group on freedom of religion that meets FCO officials to enhance co-operation in this work. I turn to the points that have been raised tonight. Apostasy is a difficult issue, especially when it concerns Islam, as several Islamic countries prohibit and punish apostasy. In some countries, it is even punishable by death. In others, apostates are charged with other offences such as blasphemy, defaming Islam or insulting their country. However, this does not deter us from making representations to promote the freedom of individuals to change their religion, nor from promoting Article 18 of the Universal Declaration of Human Rights, which has been quoted tonight and is a formidable article of an extraordinary document. We strongly believe that people have the right to practise their beliefs as well as to change their religion if they so wish. Some of the countries in which we have made this case are Eritrea, China, Mauritania, Lebanon, Egypt, Syria, Jordan, Libya, Afghanistan, Bangladesh, Iran, Malaysia, Nigeria and Pakistan, among others.... In Nigeria's recent universal periodic review, the UK raised the issue of economic, social and cultural rights. We also recommended that Nigeria should take further steps to address discrimination against minority and vulnerable groups. Last week, I met a remarkable Muslim leader from northern Nigeria, the Sultan of Sokoto, who agreed with me, and indeed volunteered the point, that those who are responsible for the intercommunal violence last year needed to be held to account and brought to justice, and that only if that sort of impunity was brought to an end would these problems be resolved.... our ambassador in Rangoon frequently presses the Burmese authorities to end human rights abuses. We condemn the marginalisation or persecution of any community based on its religious beliefs. Although it makes the abuses no less serious, the persecution of religious minority groups by the Burmese authorities is often based in reality on their ethnicity and a perceived threat to security rather than solely on their faith. Sudan was also mentioned. We have reminded the Government of Sudan of their responsibility to maintain order, to protect the deployment of UNAMID, which is so important in Darfur, and to allow full access for humanitarian assistance. More critically, we must ensure the effective implementation of the north-south agreement, the CPA, because it was from that agreement that the release of those in the south from the violent persecution of those in the north finally came. Ensuring that the steps laid out in that agreement are fully honoured and lead to elections and a referendum that allows the people of the south to choose whether they wish to remain in Sudan is the critical political track to solving this issue. As to India... that through the EU delegation, which visited Orissa state in December, and through the EU-India human rights dialogue, which will take place later this month, we will continue to press our concerns about what happened in Orissa. I have raised this issue directly with the high commissioner here and with officials in India. Equally, in the case of Egypt, a former Minister raised the issue of religious freedom directly with the Speaker of the Egyptian Parliament about a year ago. On 11 March last year, our embassy in Cairo met the Egyptian Deputy Minister for Human Rights, and again there was a discussion of the freedom of religion and Egypt's wider commitment under these conventions. As regards the DPRK, North Korea, there is no freedom of religion. While I am delighted to hear perhaps the first green shoot—a term that a politician uses carefully—of some freedom, when it comes to the orthodox church, our view remains that those churches are primarily limited showcases for outsiders and that nothing close to freedom of religion is operating across the country as a whole. We will work closely with NGOs, including Christian NGOs, in the run-up to the Human Rights Council review of the DPRK this year. . . . we perhaps do not lobby as specifically on religious persecution as we should. Our main concerns have been the use of labour camps, torture, the absence of any freedom of speech and certainly the absence of any right to organise or to come together as groups of any kind in North Korea. I acknowledge that the 2008 EU-sponsored UN General Assembly resolution on human rights specifically mentioned freedom of religion. Recently, we lobbied on human rights more generally when the director of our Asia-specific department met a delegation here of the Workers' Party of Korea. We raised religious freedoms during the visit of that delegation. On China and returnees to North Korea, we are as concerned as the noble Lord about the status of North Korean border crossers to China. We raised that issue most recently at the UK-China human rights dialogue in January of this year. We are all aware that the defamation of religions, which has come up in several forms, is difficult. We have to find our way, because, as we saw just recently with the visit of the Dutch MP, who has been referred to, we must protect a person's right to criticise the religion of other people, but we have to take care when it crosses the barrier, not any more into freedom of speech, but to incitement of violence and a potential racial prejudice. Since July 2005, 270 people have been excluded from entering the UK on the suspicion of being a threat to national security or of fostering extremism. There is a clear test—the incitement test—which the Home Secretary uses in making that determination. It is notable that a Dutch court has recently ordered that Mr Wilders should be prosecuted for making statements about Muslims. In closing, perhaps I may say that the duty of this Chamber and the role that this Chamber can play goes much broader than the UK alone. A debate like this is heard everywhere around the world by those religious minorities who feel oppressed and feel that their case has been forgotten. To everyone who has participated tonight, let us hope that we have lit one more candle in this long quest for religious freedom for all.

(HL Deb 24 February 2009 Vol 708 cs192–194)

6/106
Responsibility to Protect

The Government were asked steps they were taking to give effect to the United Nations doctrine of Responsibility to Protect ['R2P']. An FCO Minister said:

My interest in R2P is personal. I was in Rwanda and what was then Zaire in 1994 during the immediate aftermath of the genocide. The memory of those days will stay with me all my life. I have also been to Darfur, to Chad, to south Sudan on a number of occasions, and to the eastern Congo. All the suffering I have seen testifies to the need for us to undertake the shared responsibility, the binding commitment to tackle the structural causes of conflict which include social and economic inequalities, impunity-something that really has not been mentioned-and injustice. I can confirm that the UK Government are fully engaged and indeed were in the vanguard of efforts to ensure that the world summit agreement reached in 2005 included a clear and ground-breaking commitment to R2P. But while we have the tools and the instruments needed to fulfil the responsibility to protect... the biggest challenge that remains is how we can make it all work. First, it is clear that we must strive to create a culture of the responsibility to protect, a culture that is accepted across the world. This is work in progress for our Governments. We have to build confidence in the principle that states have a fundamental responsibility to protect their own populations, and indeed we have to bring clarity and acceptability at the United Nations and European Union level to the concept of the responsibility to protect. Secondly, R2P must be a holistic concept in its development and in its application. Many noble Lords have spoken about the four R2P crimes; those crimes of genocide, war crimes, crimes against humanity and ethnic cleansing. But R2P must not just be about responding to such atrocities. It must relate to conflict prevention, mediation and peace-building. It must include efforts to increase awareness of potential tension... and listening and then acting when the alarm bells ring. Thirdly, we must tackle the misconception that R2P is somehow an initiative of the developed world, one that is being imposed on the south. The concept of non-indifference to crimes, which has been mentioned, was actually in the Constitutive Act of the African Union 2000, long before the UN adopted the responsibility to protect. It was the African Union that took an early lead in responding to the violence in Kenya last year when an estimated 600,000 people were displaced. We must also tackle the misconception that R2P is somehow a justification for military intervention. It is not about imposing solutions on countries from outside. It is about encouraging world leaders, politicians and representatives of civil society to play their own parts. It is as much about responsible sovereignty as it is about intervention. That is what I mean when I talk about the culture of R2P. The Government continue to follow closely developments at both the EU and the UN levels in the run-up to the UN General Assembly debate, which I understand is to take place on 20 July. The UK has welcomed the reaffirmed commitment to R2P in the December report on the implementation of the European Security Strategy and the 2007 EU Consensus on Humanitarian Aid. R2P is a priority for the General Assembly, and I am glad to say that the member states of the European Union have confirmed this. Further to those actions, the Government continue to explore how we can ensure that awareness of R2P informs all our work on conflict, on development and on human rights at the domestic level, at the regional level and globally. We will therefore continue to work to secure better and more effective responses to the four R2P crimes and we will support the building of better early warning systems-which is essential-more deployable military and civilian capacity, and more effective regional reaction, particularly from the African Union and from the European Union. All experience tells us that international diplomacy and mediation, and being prepared to use all the tools at our disposal, is how we should proceed. The Government have welcomed the UN Secretary-General's report, which is generally well balanced and shows a determination to change those words into deeds. We are particularly focused on the UN General Assembly and the resulting opportunity to build a real consensus on the 2005 agreement and secure practical measures related to the implementation of the Secretary-General's report. This task will involve a high level of political commitment for the foreseeable future. The Government understand that and are committed to fulfilling that aim.... R2P is not a legal obligation. That is a very important point for us to realise in this debate. It is a moral and a political commitment that we have made. When you use the term "R2P" people often become very defensive in situations of tension. Quite often you can move things forward more effectively if you do not use that vocabulary. It is very important for us to say that the suspicion about R2P, to which some noble Lords have referred, is something we need to be aware of, conscious of, and respond to appropriately. It is also important to mention that action can be taken, including that in Chapter 7 at UN level, if military intervention is considered to be appropriate and necessary; that is something that we would be looking at. [See **UKMIL [2007] 6/13, 6/68**]

(HL Deb 30 June 2009 Vol 712 cs203–206)

6/107
An FCO Minister said:

I close with a word on the responsibility to protect. Although it is a controversial concept in Africa and things such as the ICC indictment only increase the suspicion of it among many African and other Governments, nevertheless we press ahead because it is an absolutely indispensable concept in today's world. In that sense, the UN report prepared by the Special Adviser to the UN Secretary-General and published recently in New York, "Integrated and coordinated implementation of and follow-up to the outcomes of the major United Nations conferences and summits in the economic, social and related fields" [Follow-up to the outcome of the Millennium Summit Implementing the responsibility to protect, Report of the Secretary-General, A/63/677, Ed.] stresses, we think sensibly, that the responsibility to protect is not just about military intervention: it is more about upstream interventions intended to pre-empt conflict before it occurs—such as Kofi Annan's mediation in Kenya before the situation there turned to wider violence.

(HL Deb 5 March 2009 Vol 708 c908)

6/108
Russia

The Foreign Secretary wrote:

We regularly raise our concerns regarding the case of Mikhail Khodorkovsky [who was a Russian "oligarch" and political opponent of the then President of Russia, and was jailed on a series of charges relating to his business interests in Russia, Ed.], bilaterally and through the EU. The issue was raised bilaterally at the UK/Russia human rights consultations in January in Moscow. Our concerns include the arbitrary application of the rule of law, due process and fair treatment of Khodorkovsky and others who have been arrested or prosecuted in the Yukos Affair, access to lawyers and medical care, conditions of detention and the alleged harassment of defence teams and witnesses.... the Prime Minister did not specifically raise Mr. Khodorkovsky's situation during his bilateral with President Medvedev at the G20 summit. However, during their bilateral the Prime Minister and President Medvedev agreed that both governments should continue to work together to resolve the areas on which the UK and Russia differ. The Government will continue to raise specific human rights cases, not only through the bilateral human rights consultations. The UK is participating in trial monitoring with EU partners and the US. We will continue to follow developments in Mr. Khodorkovsky's case.

(HC Deb 21 May 2009 Vol 492 c1498W)

6/109
Sri Lanka (See also **19/6**)

The International Development Secretary was asked a number of questions about the aftermath of the armed conflict in Sri Lanka. A Minister wrote:

Security screening for civilians escaping the conflict zone initially takes place in an area of the Vanni to which no international humanitarian agencies have access. Secondary screening takes place at Omantai checkpoint where the United Nations High Commissioner for Refugees has only limited access to observe the screening process. There is no established security screening process in the IDP camps and there are reports of people being removed for questioning and detention. This lack of international observation continues to cause concern and the UK Government have repeatedly called for full access for international humanitarian agencies to assist and protect all displaced people on their journey to the camps.... The United Nations High Commissioner for Refugees (UNHCR) has not had a permanent presence in the Vanni since September 2008 when the Government of Sri Lanka required all UN agencies and NGOs to leave. Until January 2009 there were occasional visits of UNHCR personnel aboard humanitarian convoys into the Vanni. But since January there has been no UNHCR access to the Vanni except restricted access to the IDP security screening centre at Omantai checkpoint. The UK Government have repeatedly called for full UN access to the conflict zone, and for a UN team to be allowed to make a full humanitarian assessment of the needs there. The UN Secretary General's Chief of Staff, Vijay Nambiar, went to Sri Lanka on 15 May to press for full humanitarian access and respect for international humanitarian standards....Only a few hundred people have been able to return to their homes in Mannar district—formerly longer term residents of two small camps which pre-date the present exodus of civilians. The UK Government have consistently pressed the Government of Sri Lanka to abide by its commitment to return 80 per cent. of the new displaced population by the end of the year.... The only deliveries of aid to the conflict zone since February have been made by sea, all under the auspices of the International Committee of the Red Cross (ICRC). Recently, only very small consignments of 25 tonnes at a time have been possible. The overwhelming constraint is the reluctance of both parties to allow humanitarian access and permit the ICRC ships to enter the zone and unload supplies safely. The UK Government have continually pressed the Government of Sri Lanka to allow full humanitarian access to the conflict zone, including guaranteeing safe passage for a 1,000 tonne vessel which has not been able to return since last unloading on 8 April.... As at 12 May 194,303 people have been registered in more than 40 camps for displaced persons. More than 173,000 of these are in Vavuniya, most of them in three very large camps at Menik Farm. The conditions are far from ideal but starting slowly to improve. There are no reliable data available for deaths in the camps or to what extent those could be attributable to the conditions there. By far the greatest concern is the terrible loss of life in the conflict zone and in hospitals overwhelmed with sick and wounded patients....

In terms of international standards for assistance such as shelter, water and sanitation, food, health and education, the camps started from a very low standard but are gradually improving. Large influxes such as more than 113,000 people in one week made camp conditions very difficult to manage, particularly their sanitation. The UK Government have repeatedly pressed the Government of Sri Lanka to abide by international humanitarian standards and to work with humanitarian agencies to improve both protection and assistance, with a view to meeting their commitment of early return of at least 80 per cent. of the displaced population before the end of the year.... Department for International Development (DFID) assistance is provided directly only to United Nations and independent humanitarian organisations such as the International Committee of the Red Cross, International Organisation for Migration and reputable international and national NGOs. DFID follows rigorous grant management procedures. Its humanitarian staff in Sri Lanka and London monitor and evaluate its programmes. No DFID humanitarian funding is transferred to the Government of Sri Lanka or any other governmental organisation in Sri Lanka.... We have no firm figure. Access to Government of Sri Lanka controlled camps was a serious concern earlier this year, especially with regard to non-governmental organisations (NGOs). United Nations (UN) agencies, the International Committee of the Red Cross (ICRC) and the International Organisation of Migration (IOM) generally had better access to the camps. The UK Government repeatedly pressed the Government of Sri Lanka for greatly increased access to the camps, especially for NGOs.... Although the situation is far from ideal the 194,303 internally displaced people registered in camps in Vavuniya, Jaffna and Mannar do have access to humanitarian assistance. The situation is improving slowly. However, the population trapped in the conflict zone in Mullaitivu district is almost entirely isolated from any humanitarian assistance. Only the International Committee of the Red Cross (ICRC) has any kind of access and is able only to deliver 25 tonnes of food and other emergency items three times a week to a population of at least 50,000—barely three days of food each week. The UK Government repeatedly press at the highest level for an immediate humanitarian ceasefire to enable the ICRC to evacuate the sick and wounded and to deliver sufficient humanitarian aid.

(HC Deb 18 May 2009 Vol 492 cs1186–1190W)

6/110

The Foreign Secretary made a statement on the conclusion of the armed conflict in Sri Lanka. He wrote:

On 19 May, the Sri Lankan President formally announced that on 18 May military forces had retaken all the territory once held by the Liberation Tigers of Tamil Eelam (LTTE) and that they had captured or killed the senior leadership of that organisation. Many Sri Lankans of all communities, Sinhalese, Tamil and Muslim, will be relieved that the long and brutal conflict may at last be over. Sri Lanka has before it an historic opportunity to resolve the underlying causes of the conflict and ensure a lasting peace. We must continue to work with Sri Lanka's Government and all their communities to ensure that this opportunity is taken and that it leads to a sustainable end to the conflict. Our concern has never been whether it was right to defeat the LTTE. The issue has been the price in lives and the future in terms of reconciliation. We may never know exact numbers but thousands of innocent civilians have died, hundreds of thousands made homeless and confined to camps, caught up in a system which continues to restrict access to the international humanitarian agencies. For many, many people, the misery continues. Our primary concern remains the immediate humanitarian crisis and the long-term political and economic peace and stability of Sri Lanka. We have continued to work with international partners in the EU, UN, and G8 to urge the Government of Sri Lanka to do all that they could to protect their citizens, minimise the risk of casualties and allow the UN and other international agencies access to the conflict area to oversee the possible surrender of the LTTE and the evacuation of the civilians. We also called on the LTTE to lay down their weapons and release the civilians. Tragically, these calls did not prevent the loss of many lives. I welcome the assurance given to me by Foreign Minister Bogollogama yesterday that the UN and non-governmental organisations will now be able to enter the former conflict zone to provide whatever support is still needed. I would like to pay tribute to the courage of the staff of the International Committee of the Red Cross and others who continued to try and deliver food, water and medical supplies into the conflict zone at enormous risk to themselves. Undoubtedly, their bravery in the face of great danger saved the death toll from being higher. Although the territorial conflict seems to be over, the grave humanitarian crisis continues to unfold. Some 250,000 civilians who have fled the fighting are either being processed by the Government of Sri Lanka to ensure that they are not escaping LTTE members, or are being held in camps. The Government does not have the resources to cope, but they have not yet offered international aid agencies unrestricted access to the camps. This risks exacerbating the humanitarian crisis and fuelling the resentment of the internally displaced people (IDPs). We urge the Government of Sri Lanka to allow full and unhindered access to the camps where the IDPs remain in urgent need of shelter, food, water, and medicine. The Government of Sri Lanka has also already committed to resettle 80 per cent. of IDPs before the end of this year. This will be a difficult task. We and others in the international community stand ready to assist the Government of Sri Lanka to meet these humanitarian challenges. The Department for International Development has recently announced an additional £5 million of humanitarian funding for Sri Lanka, bringing our total contribution to the humanitarian relief effort to £12.5 million since September 2008. We will channel this funding through the UN and other humanitarian agencies. We urge the Government of Sri Lanka to use the opportunity of the visits by the UN Secretary General's Chief of Staff Vijay Nambiar and the UN Secretary General himself later this week, to recognise that the UN has a central role to play, both in the delivery of humanitarian aid and in encouraging the process of political reconciliation that must be an integral part of rebuilding Sri Lanka's civil society. Lasting peace can only come when all communities in Sri Lanka believe that they are accepted and valued members of society. We recognise that the process of political reconciliation will not be easy. There are many entrenched attitudes and resentments. Sri Lankan people from all communities, working on the basis of mutual respect and equality, need to agree the way forward. On 18 May . . . the Prime Minister urged President Rajapakse to be magnanimous in victory. I repeated the message to the Sri Lankan Foreign Minister the same day, saying that whatever process emerged, it needed to be inclusive and based on equality. We welcome the President's statement to the Sri Lankan Parliament on 19 May that he will embark on an inclusive political process involving all communities on the basis of equality and absence of fear. I endorse the conclusions reached at the European Council on 18 May calling for alleged violations of international humanitarian and human rights law to be investigated through an independent inquiry and for those accountable to be brought to justice. This could play an important role in the post-conflict reconciliation process.

(HC Deb 19 May 2009 Vol 492 cs73WS-75WS)

6/111
A Minister wrote:

At the UN Human Rights Council Special Session on 26–27 May 2009, we raised our concerns about the human rights and humanitarian situation in Sri Lanka. We condemned the killing of civilians in the conflict and expressed concern for the many thousands displaced from their homes. We also used the opportunity to draw attention to the worrying reports of extra-judicial killings, politically motivated disappearances and attacks on the media. A copy of the UK's full statement can be found here: (http://ukungeneva.fco.gov.uk/resources/en/pdf/pdf1/hrc-sri-lanka-statement-26052009).

(HC Deb 13 July 2009 Vol 496 c112W)

6/112
The Foreign Secretary made the following Ministerial Statement:

Human Rights The wider human rights situation in Sri Lanka remains very worrying following the end of the conflict. Although reduced, reports of extra-judicial killings, abductions, disappearances and intimidation have continued. Media and civil society organisations who are critical of the Government remain at particular risk and continue to be the victims of anonymous death threats and, in some cases, violent attack. The recent sentencing of a journalist, Tissainayagam, to 20 years imprisonment sent a very negative message about media freedom in Sri Lanka. A culture of impunity continues, with no progress towards identifying the individuals behind recent high profile human rights abuses, such as the murder in January of Lasantha Wickrematunge, a leading newspaper editor. We welcome the fact that in two recent cases, the alleged abduction of a university student and the killing of two youths in southern Sri Lanka, the Government have ordered investigations into alleged police involvement and action is being taken through the Sri Lankan courts. The Sri Lankan Government continue to retain extraordinary emergency powers which limit the fundamental democratic freedoms of its citizens. With the LTTE defeated and a substantially reduced terrorist threat we hope to see the Emergency Regulations lifted soon. In our bilateral contacts we have encouraged the Government of Sri Lanka to tackle the culture of impunity in Sri Lanka. In this light we welcome the investigations and subsequent legal action against police officers involved in alleged abuses and encourage the Government to take similar action in all cases where such allegations are made. We have also been active in working with the EU to call for an improvement in human rights in Sri Lanka. An improvement is important too in the context of the investigation by the EU Commission looking at whether Sri Lanka should continue to benefit from the EU trade scheme, GSP+ which is dependent on the implementation of a number of human rights-related conventions. We have consistently encouraged the Sri Lankan Government to engage constructively with the Commission.

(HL Deb 13 October 2009 Vol 713 c18WS)

6/113 (See also **4/8**)
Torture

In its Report on Torture, the JCHR wrote:

17. It is not alleged that the UK Government or its agents have themselves engaged in torture, or directly authorised torture. The essence of the allegations which we have summarised in chapter 2 above is that the UK Government and its agents have been complicit in the use of torture by others. The alleged complicity is said to have taken a number of different forms, including (but not necessarily confined to) the following: requests by UK agents to foreign intelligence services, known for their systematic use of torture, to detain and question a terrorism suspect; the provision of information by UK agents to such foreign intelligence services enabling them to apprehend a terrorism suspect or facilitate their extraordinary rendition; the provision of questions by UK agents to such foreign intelligence services to be put to a detainee who has been, is being, or is likely to be tortured; the sending of UK interrogators to question a detainee who is, or should have been, known to have been tortured by those detaining and interrogating them; the presence of UK intelligence personnel at interviews with detainees being held in a place where it is known, or should be known, that they are being tortured; the lack of any apparent action taken by the UK personnel to establish whether torture was occurring and to prevent it from continuing the systematic receipt by UK agents of information known or thought likely to have been obtained from detainees subjected to torture, without apparent comment on, concern about or action to establish its provenance. 18. Each of these, it is alleged, amounts to complicity in torture by the various UK agents concerned, which is in direct breach of the UK's human rights obligations. Moreover, it is alleged that the UK Government's practice in these various respects amounts to a policy of complicity in torture, which has ministerial authorisation, and which is also in breach of the UK's human rights obligations. 19. The allegations raise a number of detailed factual questions, to which we return below. Which facts are relevant, however, is determined by a number of prior legal questions. First, is complicity in torture unlawful? Second, if it is, what does "complicity" mean in this context? What are the facts which would need to be proved in order to demonstrate that individual agents have been complicit in torture, or that a Government policy of complicity existed? Is complicity in torture unlawful? UNCAT 20. UNCAT expressly prohibits complicity in torture as well as torture itself. Article 4(1) provides: "1. Each State Party shall ensure that all acts of torture are offences under its criminal law. The same shall apply to an attempt to commit torture and to an act by any person which constitutes complicity or participation in torture." 21. Article 6 of UNCAT also requires the UK to take into custody any person present in the UK who is alleged to have committed an act constituting complicity or participation in torture if satisfied, after an examination of information available, that the circumstances so warrant, and it must then immediately make a preliminary inquiry into the facts. 22. The UK is therefore under a positive obligation under UNCAT, both to make it a criminal offence in UK law for any person to commit an act which constitutes complicity or participation in torture, and to investigate credible allegations of complicity or participation in torture, including by detaining any person present in the UK who is alleged to have committed any such act.

ECHR 23. There is no equivalent to Article 4 of UNCAT in the ECHR, but the European Court of Human Rights has long recognised that the deportation or extradition of a person to another State where he is likely to suffer inhuman or degrading treatment or punishment constitutes a breach, by the removing State, of the prohibition of such treatment contained in Article 3 ECHR.[33] This well established line of Strasbourg case-law can be seen as recognition by that Court of a form of complicity in torture or inhuman or degrading treatment, in the shape of the facilitation by States of torture or inhuman or degrading treatment even where they do not themselves carry out the treatment in question.

GENERAL PRINCIPLES OF STATE RESPONSIBILITY

24. Complicity in torture conducted by other States or their agents is also recognised to be unlawful under general international law principles of State Responsibility for internationally wrongful acts. Torture is recognised to be an internationally wrongful act, under the Universal Declaration on Human Rights, the International Covenant on Civil and Political Rights, regional human rights treaties such as the European Convention on Human Rights, UNCAT and as part of customary international law. The prohibition against torture is recognised as what international lawyers call a "peremptory norm of general international law", that is, one which is "accepted and recognized by the international community of States as a whole as a norm from which no derogation is permitted and which can be modified only by a subsequent norm of general international law having the same character."[34] The status of the prohibition against torture as a peremptory norm of international law has been recognised by UK courts on a number of occasions.[35]

25. The general principles of state responsibility in international law are now conveniently set out in the International Law Commission's Articles on the Responsibility of States for Internationally Wrongful Acts, which were approved by the UN's General Assembly on 12 December 2001.[36] They recognise that internationally wrongful conduct often results from the collaboration of more than one State rather than one State acting alone. Article 16 deals with the situation where one State provides aid or assistance to another with a view to facilitating the commission of an internationally wrongful act by the latter. It provides:

ARTICLE 16 Aid or assistance in the commission of an internationally wrongful act A State which aids or assists another State in the commission of an internationally wrongful act by the latter is internationally responsible for doing so if: (a) that State does so with knowledge of the circumstances of the internationally wrongful act; and (b) the act would be internationally wrongful if committed by

[33] Soering v UK (1989) 11 EHRR 439 at paras 33–36; Cruz Varas v Sweden (1991) 14 EHRR 1 at paras 69–70; Vilvarajah v UK (1991) 14 EHRR 248 at paras 115–116.

[34] Vienna Convention on the Law of Treaties 1969, Article 53.

[35] See, for example, the Court of Appeal in *Al Adsani v Government of Kuwait* (1996) 107 ILR 536 at 540–1; and the House of Lords in *R v Bow Street Metropolitan Magistrate, ex p Pinochet Ugarte* (No. 3) (1999) 2 WLR 827 at 841, 881 and *A and others v Secretary of State for the Home Department* (No. 2) [2005] UKHL 71, [2006] 2 AC 221 at para. 33.

[36] The Articles on State Responsibility are annexed to United Nations Resolution 56/83 adopted by the General Assembly on 12 December 2001. The Articles are recognised as an authoritative statement of the principles of State responsibility in international law: see, for example, the reference to them by the House of Lords in R v Lyons [2002] UKHL 44, [2003] 1 AC 976 at para. 36.

that State. 26. In international law, particular consequences also flow from "serious breaches" of obligations under peremptory norms of international law.[37] A breach of such an obligation is "serious" if it involves "a gross or systematic failure by the responsible State to fulfil the obligation."[38] States are under a positive obligation to co-operate to bring such serious breaches to an end,[39] and are required not to recognise as lawful a situation created by such serious breaches, nor to render aid or assistance in maintaining that situation.[40] So, for example, where a State systematically tortures terrorism suspects, other States are under a duty to co-operate to bring such a serious breach of the prohibition against torture to an end, and are required not to recognise the practice as lawful nor to give any aid or assistance to it continuing. We are concerned that these positive obligations in relation to torture, not to acquiesce in torture or to validate the results of it, are not fully appreciated by the Government, which often gives the impression that it is only under a negative obligation not to torture: see, for example, the statement by the Prime Minister in his letter of 18 June 2009 that 'neither the UN Convention Against Torture nor the European Convention on Human Rights...include a positive legal obligation to report or seek to prevent acts of torture carried out by other states abroad'.[41]

27. There is therefore no room for doubt, in our view, that complicity in torture would be a direct breach of the UK's international human rights obligations, under UNCAT, under customary international law, and according to the general principles of State Responsibility for internationally wrongful acts. 28. If complicity in torture is unlawful, the remaining legal question is what, exactly, does "complicity" mean? What does "complicity" mean? 29. Although UNCAT refers expressly to "complicity or participation in torture", and imposes obligations on states to criminalise it and to investigate credible allegations of it, the Treaty does not define the terms "complicity" or "participation". 30. We took evidence on this question from Professor Philippe Sands QC, Professor of International Law at University College, London and an acknowledged expert on the application of UNCAT.[42] Professor Sands's evidence attempted to shed some light on the meaning of "complicity" in Article 4(1) UNCAT by reference to a number of different sources, including its drafting history, its interpretation by the UN Committee Against Torture (the treaty body charged with overseeing the implementation of UNCAT), and the interpretation by the International Criminal Tribunal for the Former Yugoslavia ("ICTY") of the meaning of "aiding and abetting" in Article 7(1) of the ICTY Statute.

31. We noted, however, that these sources appeared to differ slightly as to the precise ingredients of "complicity" and therefore as to the scope of that concept. According to the judicial interpretation of the concept by ICTY, in the context of a criminal trial for aiding and abetting torture, three elements must be established in order for the offence of complicity to have been committed:[43] (1) knowledge

[37] Articles on State Responsibility, Articles 40 and 41.
[38] Article 40(2). [39] Article 41(1). [40] Article 41(2). [41] p. 53.
[42] Ev 60–79 and Qq155–196.
[43] Prosecutor v Anto Furundzija (Case No. IT-95-17/1-T 1988). Article 7(1) of the ICTY Statute provides for individual criminal responsibility: "7(1) A person who planned, instigated, ordered, committed or otherwise aided and abetted in the planning, preparation or execution of a crime referred to in articles 2 to 5 of the present Statute, shall be individually responsible for the crime."

that torture is taking place; (2) a contribution by way of assistance, which (3) has a substantial effect on the perpetration of the crime of torture itself.

32. The UN Committee Against Torture, on the other hand, appears to have adopted a wider definition of complicity, which includes "tacit consent" and "acquiescence", and includes constructive as well as actual knowledge that torture was taking place (i.e. it is enough if the party who is alleged to be complicit should have known that it was taking place). The UN Committee also appears less concerned with the requirement that the assistance must have had a substantial effect on the perpetration of the crime of torture itself. So for example, the Committee Against Torture has made clear that the involvement of doctors is to be treated as a form of participation, even if only for the purpose of ensuring that the victim of torture does not die or suffer physical injuries during interrogation.[44]

33. Professor Sands addressed this apparent difference of approach in his Additional Note of Evidence submitted after we had heard oral evidence.[45] Any difference of approach between the UNCAT Committee and the ICTY, he said, was to be explained by the fact that they were interpreting different texts. "Complicity or participation" in Article 4 of UNCAT has a wider meaning than "aiding and abetting" in Article 7(1) of the ICTY Statute. Complicity or participation includes "aiding and abetting", but is not limited to that narrower concept. In Professor Sands's view, "complicity" in UNCAT would encompass tacit consent that falls short of the contribution by way of assistance that ICTY required, as well as a failure to take steps to prevent abuse in circumstances in which it is known to be occurring.

34. We are grateful to Professor Sands for his assistance in helping us to understand the meaning of complicity. In our view, it is necessary to distinguish between complicity for the purposes of individual criminal responsibility and complicity for the purposes of State responsibility. We consider that a narrower meaning is likely to be adopted in the context of individual criminal responsibility, but principles of state responsibility more readily recognise positive obligations on states (as opposed to individuals) to take action to prevent torture from occurring or continuing. Complicity may therefore be given a wider meaning for the purposes of deciding whether the State is responsible for particular acts which have the effect of allowing torture to occur or continue. 35. We therefore conclude that complicity has different meanings depending on whether the context is individual criminal responsibility or State responsibility:

for the purposes of individual criminal responsibility for complicity in torture, "complicity" requires proof of three elements: (1) knowledge that torture is taking place, (2) a direct contribution by way of assistance that (3) has a substantial effect on the perpetration of the crime; or the purposes of State responsibility for complicity in torture, however, "complicity" means simply one State giving assistance to another State in the commission of torture, or acquiescing in such torture, in the knowledge, including constructive knowledge, of the circumstances of the torture which is or has been taking place. Would the allegations, if

[44] CAT/C/SR.105 at para. 5.
[45] Ev 78.

proved, amount to complicity? 36. As we noted above, the allegations which have been made are that complicity in torture has taken place in a variety of forms. Assuming complicity in torture to be unlawful, and complicity to mean what we have defined it to mean above, would any of those allegations, if proved, amount to complicity in torture on the part of the UK state, or criminally culpable complicity by individual agents? 37. We are in no doubt that requests to foreign agencies to arrest and detain an individual, the provision of information enabling their arrest, the provision of questions for their interrogation, the sending of interrogators to question a suspect who is being tortured and of observers to sit in on interrogations, are all forms of assistance and facilitation capable of amounting to complicity in torture by the State concerned when those things are done in the knowledge that the person concerned is being, has been or will be tortured by the State which is detaining him, or where that ought to be obvious to the State providing the assistance. Although it may be harder to prove, we are also in no doubt that in principle each of those forms of aiding and abetting torture is capable of making a sufficient contribution by way of assistance to amount to the crime of complicity in torture by individual agents where the other ingredients of the offence are made out. 38. We have found it more difficult to decide whether the passive receipt of information which has or may have been obtained under torture amounts to complicity in torture in the sense we have described above. The House of Lords in A and others v Home Secretary, whilst deciding that evidence obtained under torture is not admissible in legal proceedings, nevertheless made clear that in certain circumstances information obtained under torture can be used by the Secretary of State to take action to save life. This is the point made by the FCO in its annual report for 2008, quoted above, where the Government effectively reserves the right to consider and even act on intelligence which is possibly derived from torture where that intelligence bears on threats to life. The passive receipt of information is also not obviously a form of "assistance" or facilitation, because it seems likely that the torture will continue to take place anyway whether the information is received or not by the other State. This would not apply, however, to circumstances where the receipt of such information (that it is reasonable to suspect is produced as a result of torture) is so regular that it becomes an expectation, or where it is part of a reciprocal arrangement (regardless of whether the arrangement is formal or explicit), or where the information is received over a long period with no apparent concern being raised about its provenance. 39. In our 2006 Report on UNCAT we acknowledged that the "one-off" use of information obtained by torture might be justified in a genuine case of necessity to protect life, but pointed out that "care must be taken to ensure that the use of such information [which might have been obtained under torture], and in particular any repeated or regular use of such information, especially from the same sources, does not render the UK authorities complicit in torture by lending tacit support or agreement to the use of torture or inhuman treatment as a means of obtaining information which might be useful to the UK in preventing terrorist attacks."[46]

40. We remain of the view that whether such passive receipt is capable of amounting to complicity in torture depends on whether there is systematic reliance on such information, or whether the circumstances set out at the end of paragraph 38

[46] UNCAT Report, above, n.1, at para. 55.

above exist. As Professor Sands said in evidence, "there is a world of difference between the one-off receipt of information that comes into your mailbox and a relationship that is premised on regular, systematic, continual reliance against the background of a broader relationship between two sovereign entities."[47]

41. The question is, at what point does the systematic receipt of such information cross the line into complicity?[48] We agree with Professor Sands's view, that if the Government engaged in an arrangement with a country that was known to torture in a widespread way and turned a blind eye to what was going on, systematically receiving and/or relying on the information but not physically participating in the torture, that might well cross the line into complicity.

42. Systematic, regular receipt of information obtained under torture is in our view capable of amounting to "aid or assistance" in maintaining the situation created by other States' serious breaches of the peremptory norm prohibiting torture. As a number of witnesses to our inquiry put it, the practice creates a market for the information produced by torture.[49] As such, it encourages States which systematically torture to continue to do so. We therefore consider that, if the UK is demonstrated to have a general practice of passively receiving intelligence information which has or may have been obtained under torture, that practice is likely to be in breach of the UK's international law obligation[50] not to render aid or assistance to other States which are in serious breach of their obligation not to torture.

43. It follows from the above that, in our view, the following situations would all amount to complicity in torture, for which the State would be responsible, if the relevant facts were proved: A request to a foreign intelligence service, known for its systemic use of torture, to detain and question a terrorism suspect. The provision of information to such a foreign intelligence service enabling them to apprehend a terrorism suspect. The provision of questions to such a foreign intelligence service to be put to a detainee who has been, is being, or is likely to be tortured. The sending of interrogators to question a detainee who is known to have been tortured by those detaining and interrogating them. The presence of intelligence personnel at an interview with a detainee being held in a place where he is, or might be, being tortured. The systematic receipt of information known or thought likely to have been obtained from detainees subjected to torture. 44. We also draw attention to the fact that our views on what sorts of assistance are likely to constitute complicity are shared by the UN Special Rapporteur on the promotion and protection of human rights and fundamental freedoms while countering terrorism, Professor Martin Scheinin, in his recent report to the Human Rights Council of the UN.[51]

[47] Q162. [48] Q155.

[49] See, to the same effect, the Report of the Eminent Jurists Panel on Terrorism, Counter-Terrorism and Human Rights, Assessing Damage, Urging Action (International Commission of Jurists, 2009) at p. 85: "States have publicly claimed that they are entitled to rely on information that has been derived from the illegal practices of others; in so doing they become 'consumers' of torture and implicitly legitimise, and indeed encourage, such practices, by creating a 'market' for the resultant intelligence. In the language of criminal law, States are 'aiding and abetting' serious human rights violations by others."

[50] Recognised by Article 41(2) of the Articles on State Responsibility.

[51] Report of the Special Rapporteur on the promotion and protection of human rights and fundamental freedoms while countering terrorism, A/HRC/10/3 (4 February 2009).

45. The Special Rapporteur expressed his concern about the participation of foreign agents in the interrogation of people held in situations that violate international human rights standards: The active participation through the sending of interrogators or questions, or even the mere presence of intelligence personnel at an interview with a person who is being held in places where his rights are violated, can be reasonably understood as implicitly condoning such practices. The continuous engagement and presence of foreign officials has in some instances constituted a form of encouragement or even support. This is particularly the case if - as alleged in Pakistan - persons are held at the request and with the approval of foreign agents.... [T]he active or passive participation by States in the interrogation of persons held by another State constitutes an internationally wrongful act if the State knew or ought to have known that the person was facing a real risk of torture. 46. The Special Rapporteur was also concerned about the sending and receiving of intelligence for operational use. Taking advantage of the coercive environment by receiving intelligence would constitute a violation of human rights law: States which know or ought to know that they are receiving intelligence from torture or other inhuman treatment...and are either creating a demand for such information or elevating its operational use to a policy, are complicit in the human rights violations in question....The Special Rapporteur is equally concerned about the supply of information to foreign intelligence services, when there are no adequate safeguards attached to the further distribution of such information among other governmental agencies in the receiving state.

(Joint Committee on Human Rights, Twenty-third Report: Allegations of UK complicity in Torture, (2009) HL 152/HC 230)

6/114

The Government were asked for their reaction to a report by REDRESS, 'The United Kingdom, Torture and Anti-Terrorism: Where the Problems Lie'. An FCO Minister wrote:

(a) Rendition, Guantanamo Bay and "legal black holes"The UK's position on rendition and Guantanamo Bay is clear. We do not render people in breach of our legal obligations and unreservedly condemn any practice of "extraordinary rendition to torture". We have repeatedly called for the closure of the detention facility at Guantanamo Bay and we welcome the steps President Obama is now taking to close it. The Government oppose any form of deprivation of liberty that amounts to placing a detained person outside the protection of the law. The UK supports the rule of law, and our policy remains that individuals suspected of involvement in terrorism should be brought to justice whenever possible. (b) US assurancesThe US is our closest bilateral partner, and we cannot proceed with them on the basis of mistrust or a presumption of deceit. Notwithstanding the new information which emerged in Feb 2008 concerning two cases of rendition through Diego Garcia in 2002, we fully accept that the US gave its earlier assurances in good faith. We have worked closely with the US to ensure that the renewed assurances they have given us are correct and that we are providing accurate information to Parliament. (c) DeportationThe Government will not deport someone where there are substantial reasons for believing that there is a real risk of torture or other inhuman or degrading treatment, or where the death penalty will apply. We can only deport someone if their removal is compatible with our international commitments, including our obligations under the

European Convention on Human Rights. Accordingly, we have secured arrangements on deportation with assurances with certain countries so that we can satisfy ourselves that a particular removal is compatible with those obligations.

We firmly believe that, in seeking assurances from countries to which we wish to deport foreign nationals who pose a threat to our security, we are both safeguarding their rights and protecting the public. The Government are satisfied that diplomatic assurances can provide effective safeguards for the proper treatment of individuals being returned and can ensure that their rights will be respected. (d) Public inquiry into whether UK agents have acted unlawfully. If there were any question of anyone acting in an official capacity being engaged in an unlawful act, then this would be a matter for the police. Where allegations of mistreatment have been made to us by British nationals or residents whilst in Guantanamo Bay or following their release, and where we have been asked to do so by the individual concerned, we have raised those allegations with the US authorities.

If individuals believe that their human rights have been infringed as a result of actions carried out by or on behalf of any of the UK intelligence agencies, then they may take their case to the Investigatory Powers Tribunal. (e) Compensation for those tortured. The Government take all allegations of torture very seriously indeed. Where allegations of torture of British nationals overseas are made, we are able to make consular representations on behalf of the individuals concerned. We may also occasionally make representations on humanitarian grounds on behalf of non-British nationals. The question of compensation is one for the individuals concerned and their lawyers.

(HL Deb 5 February 2009 Vol 707 csWA151-WA152)

6/115 (See also **6/73–74**)

As part of his statement about the case of Binyam Mohamed, the Foreign Secretary said:

The fundamentals of the case are as follows. Mr. Binyam Mohamed, an Ethiopian national formerly resident in the UK, was arrested in Pakistan in 2002. In 2004 he was transferred to Guantanamo Bay. Until August 2007, the Government had taken responsibility for the release and return of British nationals from Guantanamo Bay. In August 2007, my right hon. Friend the Home Secretary and I wrote to then US Secretary of State to seek Mr. Mohamed's release from Guantanamo Bay and his return to the United Kingdom, along with four other former UK residents. Over the past 18 months, we have mounted what the Court has called a strenuous effort to achieve that objective. We have throughout kept Mr. Mohamed's family and lawyers informed of his situation and our efforts to resolve it. The United States brought terrorist charges against Mr. Mohamed in May last year before a military commission. Mr. Mohamed subsequently brought proceedings against the British Government in an effort to secure the disclosure to his legal counsel of any material held by the British Government that might assist the defence of his case before the military commission. Having looked through all the material that we held across government, we provided through the appropriate legal and statutory mechanisms a great deal of both classified and unclassified UK information. Among the information we held, however, we identified some highly classified US intelligence material. We took the view that the material was potentially exculpatory and ought to be disclosed to Mr. Mohamed's legal counsel. As this was sensitive US Government material, we informed the relevant US authorities of our view; we also informed Mr. Mohamed's counsel. We have worked since then to ensure that all the material was, indeed, made available to Mr. Mohamed's legal counsel by the US Government through their own procedures. Across the four judgments handed down by the High Court since last August, the Court has explicitly recognised the efforts of the Government both to secure Mr. Mohamed's release and return, and to ensure that the material that we considered ought to be disclosed to him was, indeed, disclosed. The latter objective was achieved some time ago, when the US Department of Justice disclosed the material to Mr. Mohamed's counsel in the course of proceedings in the US federal courts. At the heart of Mr. Mohamed's case have been allegations that he was tortured by foreign Government officials in a number of locations. It is the long-standing policy of this Government that we never condone, authorise or co-operate in torture. I repeat that commitment today. We also take very seriously all allegations of torture and investigate them fully. Allegations have been made in the course of these legal proceedings that the UK is in some way complicit in the alleged mistreatment of Mr. Mohamed. Following the Court's judgment of 22 October, on 23 October last year my right hon. Friend the Home Secretary referred the question of possible criminal wrongdoing to the Attorney-General. That question is now being considered by the Attorney-General. That is, as the Court acknowledged yesterday, the proper democratic and legal process. [The Foreign Secretary went on to say that the litigation in the UK had not been about the substance of the torture allegations or any involvement by the UK in them but about the confidentiality of intelligence information supplied by the US to the UK, to which the Foreign Secretary attached great priority. See *Mohamed, R (on the application of) v Secretary of State for Foreign & Commonwealth Affairs* [2010] EWCA Civ 65 and at para 7 for the earlier judgments, Ed.]

(HC Deb 5 February 2009 Vol487 c989)

6/116

The FAC had concluded in its Report on the Human Rights Report 2008:

16. We conclude that it is essential that the UK maintains effective intelligence relationships with other countries, and we note that these countries may include ones, such as Pakistan, where there are most serious concerns about human rights abuses of detainees. We further conclude that the Government is correct to base decisions about intelligence co-operation on an assessment of the risk of mistreatment of detainees, and we are heartened to learn that there have been cases in which on this basis co-operation had not taken place. We further conclude that it is essential that the Government emphasise to its foreign counterparts that torture is unacceptable, and that it should work pro-actively to persuade other states to renounce the use of torture against all detainees, whatever their nationality. (Paragraph 74)

The FCO replied:

45. The Government agrees with the Committee's conclusion. Intelligence from overseas is critical to our success in stopping terrorism. All the most serious plots and attacks in the UK itself in this decade have had significant links abroad. Our agencies must work with their equivalents overseas. Many other

countries have different legal obligations and different standards to our own in the way they detain people and treat those they have detained. That cannot stop us from working with them where it is necessary to do so to protect our country and our citizens. But it does mean we have to work hard both to ensure we do not cooperate or collude in torture or mistreatment, and to seek to reduce and eradicate it. When working with partners overseas, the intelligence and security Agencies operate to strict guidelines, including about their duties and responsibilities regarding human rights. The Prime Minister has made a commitment to publish this guidance, once it has been consolidated and reviewed by the ISC.

The FAC wrote:

17. We conclude that the use by the UK Government of intelligence information which may serve to avert a potentially catastrophic terrorist attack, but which is supplied by foreign states and which may have been obtained through torture, raises profoundly difficult moral questions. We further conclude that the Government has a duty to use information that comes into its possession, from whatever source and however obtained, if it believes this will avert the loss of life. At the same time, we strongly recommend that the Government should continue to exert as much persuasion and pressure as possible to try to ensure world-wide that torture is not employed as a method of interrogation. (Paragraph 79)

The FCO replied:

46. The Government agrees with the Committee's conclusion. The suggestion from some quarters that the Government has a policy of accepting intelligence gained through torture is misleading. The reality of the situation is that the precise provenance of intelligence received from overseas is often unclear. However, we ensure that our partners are well aware that we find the use of torture or cruel, inhuman or degrading treatment unacceptable. All intelligence received is carefully evaluated, particularly where it is clear that it has been obtained from individuals in detention. 47. This position is in line with the House of Lords' 2005 Judgement in *A and Others v the Secretary of State for the Home Department* [[2005] UKHL 71, Ed.]. In that judgement Lord Brown said: 'Generally speaking it is accepted that the executive may make use of all information it acquires: both coerced statements and whatever fruits they are found to bear. Not merely, indeed, is the executive entitled to make use of this information; to my mind it is bound to do so. It has a prime responsibility to safeguard the security of the state and would be failing in its duty if it ignores whatever it may learn or fails to follow it up.' [para 161].

The FAC wrote:

18. We conclude that it is imperative that the UK fulfils its legal obligations in respect of the prevention of torture, including any duty to act positively to prevent it, investigate allegations that it has taken place, and expose it. We further conclude that there is a risk that use of evidence which may have been obtained under torture on a regular basis, especially where it is not clear that protestations about mistreatment have elicited any change in behaviour by foreign intelligence services, could be construed as complicity in such behaviour. (Paragraph 83)

The FCO replied:

48. The Government is in agreement with the Committee concerning the importance of fulfilling our legal obligations in respect of the prevention of torture. The Government's position is that the receipt of intelligence should not occur where it is known or believed that receipt would amount to encouragement to the intelligence services of other States to commit torture.

(Seventh Report from the Foreign Affairs Committee Session 2008–09: Annual Report on Human Rights 2008, Response of the Secretary of State for Foreign and Commonwealth Affairs, Cm 7723 (2009))

6/117

The Government were asked whether they would request each foreign Government with whom they had a memorandum of understanding concerning extradition or deportation to ratify the United Nations Convention Against Torture and its Optional Protocol. An FCO Minister wrote:

The UK regularly lobbies foreign Governments who have not ratified the United Nations Convention Against Torture (UNCAT) and the Optional Protocol to the Convention Against Torture (OPCAT) to take steps towards doing so. Our recent efforts have included, where relevant, lobbying in the countries with which we have memoranda of understanding regarding deportations with assurances, and countries with which we have extradition arrangements. Lebanon, with which the UK has a memorandum of understanding on deportation with assurances, ratified the optional protocol in December 2008.

(HL Deb 24 February 2009 Vol 708 cWA50)

6/118

The Prime Minister wrote:

Our security and intelligence services and armed forces do an outstanding job. They take significant personal risks to make Britain more secure and operate across the world in circumstances they do not control. I have seen for myself their success in preventing terrorist attacks. We are all safer today because of the work they do with integrity and bravery. In the last months, the involvement of the security services and armed forces in detention activities has been under intense scrutiny while they have been unable to reply. Britain condemns without reservation the use of torture for any purpose. Torture has no place in a modern democratic society. We will not condone it. Nor will we ever ask others to do it on our behalf. It is to protect the reputation of our security and intelligence services and to reassure ourselves that everything has been done to ensure that our practices are in line with United Kingdom and international law that we will do four things:

we will publish our guidance to intelligence officers and service personnel about the standards that we apply during the detention and interviewing of detainees overseas once it has been consolidated and reviewed by the Intelligence and Security Committee. It is right that Parliament and the public should know what those involved in interviewing detainees can and cannot do. This will put beyond doubt the terms under which our agencies and service personnel operate. Once published, copies will be placed in the Libraries of both Houses;we will invite Sir Peter Gibson who is the former Lord Justice of Appeal and current Intelligence Services Commissioner to monitor compliance with the guidance and report to the Prime Minister annually;in order to ensure that our systems are robust and to be certain that any lessons have been understood, I have asked the Intelligence and Security Committee to consider any new developments and relevant information, since its 2005 report on detention (cm 6469) and its 2007 report on rendition (cm 7171), building on the follow-up work that they have already undertaken;wherever allegations of wrongdoing are made, they are taken seriously. Some detainees have already put their allegations before the civil courts, where they can and should be tested. If any cases of potential criminal wrongdoing come to light, the Government will refer them to the Attorney-General to consider whether there is a basis for inviting the police to conduct a criminal investigation. Any decisions on prosecutions will be reached only after such an investigation.

We are fortunate to have the best security and intelligence services and armed forces in the world. They are highly effective, widely respected and operate unselfishly on our behalf. It is vital that we allow them to act to protect our country. But we must do so in a way that is consistent with our unequivocal commitment to human rights. I am confident that this is the case.

(HC Deb 18 March 2009 Vol 489 c55WS)

6/119

The Foreign Secretary was asked how many UK nationals had claimed to his Department's staff in the last three years that they had been tortured overseas; and how many such cases have been investigated. An FCO Minister wrote:

The UK is opposed to torture and is one of the most active countries in the world in the fight to eradicate it. Ensuring the welfare of British nationals detained abroad is one of the Foreign and Commonwealth Office's highest consular priorities, and any allegation of abuse or torture is taken particularly seriously. Since 1 April 2005 we have collated statistics on the number of cases where we have, with the permission of the British national concerned, raised concerns with the detaining authorities over allegations of torture or abuse. These are as follows:

	Number of allegations raised
April-December 2005	39
January-December 2006	69
January-December 2007	75
January 2008-March 2009	60

Our case files also record all instances where UK nationals have approached departmental staff overseas claiming to have been mistreated overseas. Until this month we did not centrally collate these records, and to extract this information would incur a disproportionate cost. However, since May 2009 we have introduced a new system to record the total number of cases of mistreatment raised with us anywhere in the world, and we expect the first data to be available in

October 2009. While we cannot conduct investigations in another sovereign country ourselves, the objective of our representations to foreign Governments is to end any ongoing mistreatment, and have the incident investigated and the perpetrators of any abuse brought to justice.

(HC Deb 15 May 2009 Vol 492 c1072W)

6/120

The Foreign Secretary wrote to the FAC on 15 July 2009 about counter-terrorism policy in which he touched on questions related to the UK's attitude to torture:

The Government has been absolutely clear that the UK stands firmly against torture and cruel, inhuman and degrading treatment or punishment. There is strong cross-party support for this. It is a fundamental principle guiding our approach and that of those who work to protect us. That is not just a question of our obligations under domestic and international law - including under the Human Rights Act and the UN Convention Against Torture. It is also a question of our values as a nation.

It is for this reason that this Government, and the Foreign Office in particular, have over the last twelve years sought to take a lead on international efforts to eradicate torture, including through support to international mechanisms against torture, and capacity building work overseas to foster a law enforcement environment in which torture is simply not considered an option.

This is also the approach and ethos set out in our counter-terrorism strategy, CONTEST. As that strategy makes clear, our work to reduce the threat of terrorism is based on a set of core principles and values including respect for human rights and the rule of law. The Government has been absolutely clear that the UK abhors torture and that is an inviolable principle underpinning our approach.

When detainees are in our custody, we can be sure of how they are treated, and ensure we meet our obligations and standards. When they are not, we cannot have the same degree of assurance. Yet we cannot act in isolation in order to protect British citizens. UK terror networks nearly always have overseas links which must be investigated if attacks in the UK are to be stopped. We therefore need to work in cooperation with partners all over the world. Some other countries have different legal obligations - and different standards - to our own in the way they detain people and treat those they have detained. That cannot stop us from working with them, where we can, in order to protect this country's national security, but it does mean we have to work hard to ensure we do not cooperate or collude in torture, and to seek to reduce and eradicate it.

In enabling the detention of individuals who pose a threat to our national security, in passing questions to them, or participating in interviews of them, we must seek to minimise the risk that the individual in question is mistreated by the detaining authority. Enormous effort, within the Agencies and Armed Forces, goes into carefully assessing the risks in each case. Ministers consider carefully each case that is put to them. As the ISC has reported, operations have been blocked on the grounds that the risk of mistreatment is too high. Equally, it is not always possible to eradicate the risk of mistreatment. A judgement needs to be made.

Our guidance to Agency staff (which will be reviewed by the Intelligence and Security Committee, and is in the process of being consolidated) makes clear the careful and considered way we go about making the choices that we face. That guidance reflects the best thinking and advice that we are able to provide to those who act in the name of the United Kingdom. Through this guidance, the Agencies, and the Government more generally, set parameters for the conduct of their officers. The guidance is designed to ensure that anyone following it is acting within the law. In accordance with our obligations under the Convention Against Torture we keep it under review. The steps outlined by the Prime Minister on 18 March 2009, including on publication of this guidance, are part of the process of setting out for the British public the choices we face and the careful, considered way we all go about making them.

Accountability is a vital part of our system. But by definition the work of the Agencies requires a different set of checks and balances than the work of any other part of government. The first responsibility is for Ministers and Agency Heads to uphold our law and our values. The law is available to provide recourse to those who feel their rights have been abused. As you know, 12 civil claims are currently in the court system, including the Binyam Mohammed case. It is right too that the Intelligence and Security Committee should have an important role. The Committee is a creation of Parliament, not the Executive, with the avowed purpose of squaring the circle between secrecy and accountability. The Committee - and the Intelligence and Interception Commissioners - are an invaluable part of our constitutional checks and balances. As the High Court recently said, the ISC "is a very significant means of democratic accountability". These bodies have the access to the sensitive intelligence material they need to discharge their duties fully and effectively. But to ensure operational effectiveness is also properly protected, the individuals involved are notified under the Official Secrets Act and their official reports are published with appropriate redactions, though each and every redaction is explained and debated in detail with the reports' authors before publication.

Together with the Investigatory Powers Tribunal, which investigates complaints by individuals about the Agencies' conduct towards them, these bodies provide comprehensive oversight of the Agencies. That is their role. However, I also want to emphasize that, although there are good reasons for the limits on what we can say in public on some of these issues, I welcome your Committee's interest in them. You play an essential role in scrutinizing Government and stimulating public debate.

(HR 183: Letter to the Chairman of the Committee from the Secretary of State for Foreign and Commonwealth Affairs, Foreign and Commonwealth Office, Human Rights Report 557-ii (2009))

6/121
An FCO Minister said:

I want to place it on record that the Government's policy is that torture is an abhorrent crime and we are fundamentally opposed to it. That principle guides all of the Government's work, including that of the intelligence agencies and armed forces.... International action against torture has been a priority for the Government since the launch of the United Kingdom initiative in 1998. This includes efforts to support wider ratification and implementation of the United Nations convention against torture and the optional protocol to the convention against torture through a combination of bilateral lobbying campaigns, multilateral engagement in the European Union and UN and project work. For the period 2008–2011, the UK has allocated £5.5 million for overseas criminal justice, prison reform and torture prevention projects. The UK also supports strongly the work of the Association for the Prevention of Torture, the leading non-governmental organisation, which advocated the adoption of the Optional Protocol to the Convention against Torture and continues to campaign for its ratification. My point is that the Government have taken a proactive approach to the work internationally against torture. If that is the case, how is that consistent with the right hon. Gentleman's accusation that the UK Government have colluded in the use of torture? I say with respect to him that the two do not coincide, and that this is not a consistent statement of the facts. I also say . . . that ensuring the welfare of detained British nationals is a priority in the Foreign and Commonwealth Office's consular work. Any allegation of abuse is treated very seriously. All consular staff receive training which covers prisoner issues, including what to do when they have concerns over torture or mistreatment. When we have permission from the individual concerned, we can raise concerns with the relevant authorities with a view to ending the mistreatment and, when possible, have the incident investigated and the perpetrators brought to justice. In exceptional circumstances, we now consider raising concerns even without an individual's express consent. Even when an individual does not want us to take up their case specifically, our knowledge of it may enable us to lobby far more effectively for improvements in the way in which detainees are treated in general. In many countries we also raise far more general concerns about the treatment of detainees as part of our wider human rights dialogue.

(HC Deb 7 July 2009 Vol 495 c944–945)

6/122 (See also **19/16–18**)
Trafficking

In a statement on human trafficking, a Minister wrote:

The Government are investing a further £3.7 million over the next two years into the POPPY project to help vulnerable victims of human trafficking. The POPPY project, managed by Eaves Housing for Women, has provided refuge to hundreds of victims of human trafficking since 2003, backed by £5.8 million Government support. This new investment will help meet the commitments of the Council of Europe convention on action against human trafficking which the UK ratified in December 2008, coming into force in April. It is part of a wider package for victims, with the introduction of a 45 day extendable recovery and reflection period; new temporary residence permits for those participating in a criminal investigation; and a more co-ordinated and multi-agency way of identifying and referring victims into support. The new resources will see:

an expansion of supported accommodation with refuge places for victims of trafficking for sexual exploitation and domestic servitude in London, Sheffield and Cardiff; an increase in advocacy workers to provide one-to-one tailored support to victims;

facilitating their access to services and helping them through the criminal justice process; the continuation of the community outreach team; link workers based within the UK Human Trafficking Centre to work in partnership with the police, UK Border Agency and other partners to help with victim identification and onward referral into support; and a new national co-ordinator to help set consistent standards of care, capacity build and raise awareness with local agencies and funders.

Victims are often subjected to multiple crimes including rape, physical violence, kidnapping and threats. The Government are committed to making the United Kingdom a hostile environment for traffickers and protecting victims. We published a comprehensive UK action plan in March 2007 which was updated on 2nd July 2008. We will continue to work internationally and in this country to combat these crimes. [The POPPY Project was set up in 2003. It is funded by the Office for Criminal Justice Reform (reporting to the Ministry of Justice) to provide accommodation and support to women who have been trafficked into prostitution or domestic servitude, Ed.]

(HC Deb 24 March 2009 Vol 490 c10WS)

6/123
UN Human Rights Council

The Government were asked whether they would consult the former President of the Czech Republic, Vaclav Havel, before voting in elections for membership of the United Nations Human Rights Council; and whether they had proposals for reforming the Council. An FCO Minister replied:

We did not consult the former President of the Czech Republic, Vaclav Havel, before voting in the UN Human Rights Council elections which took place on Tuesday 12 May 2009. As is usual in elections to UN bodies, the ballot was secret and details of voting are not made public. The UK is firmly committed to the UN Human Rights Council and to working to make it the most effective body possible for the promotion and protection of all human rights. We are devoting our efforts to making mechanisms of the council, such as the universal periodic review, effective and have no reform proposals at this stage.

(HL Deb 19 May 2009 Vol 710 cWA306)

6/124
Vietnam

The FCO Minister wrote:

The Government are concerned about the severe prison sentences given to nine Vietnamese citizens between 6 and 9 October for conducting propaganda against the state. We believe that all nine were peacefully expressing their right to freedom of expression in line with Article 19 of the International Covenant on Civil and Political Rights to which Vietnam is a party. As with previous cases of this nature, the Vietnamese Government maintain that these nine individuals have broken the law and must be punished accordingly. Our British embassy in Hanoi and our EU partners sent representatives to witness three of the trials. Following the trials we raised our concerns with the Vietnamese Government about the grounds for the convictions and the severity of the sentences. We regularly highlight to the Vietnamese Government the importance of the free flow of ideas, analysis and debate to Vietnam's long-term sustainable development. We will continue to press the Vietnamese Government to adhere to their international human rights obligations.

(HL Deb 9 November 2009 Vol 714 cWA154)

6/125
Women

An FCO Minister wrote:

The Foreign and Commonwealth Office (FCO) has taken several positive steps toward supporting moves to implement the objectives of the UNSCR, including:

Supporting the development and strengthening of the capacities of national institutions, in particular judicial and health systems and local civil society networks in the Democratic Republic of Congo and Afghanistan, in order to provide assistance to victims of sexual violence. Working to mainstream the provisions of UNSCR 1820 into the mandates of UN peacekeeping missions, such as UNSCR 1861 for Chad/Central African Republic, and highlighting the importance of gender considerations in the training that peacekeepers receive, including from UK supported training. Working for greater levels of representation of women in the mediation services provided by the UN and among deployed peacekeeping troop contingents. Highlighting the importance of conduct and discipline of peacekeepers in committees such as the C-34 Special Committee on Peacekeeping Operations and the UN Security Council, including the provision of UK funding to the UN Conduct and Discipline unit.

We are looking forward to the UN Secretary-General's report on the implementation of this resolution on 30 June 2009 and the recommendations it contains. We will consider them carefully in relation to our own National Action Plan on UNSCR 1325.

(HC Deb 26 March 2009 Vol 490 c609W)

6/126
Zimbabwe

With regard to the UN Special Rapporteur on torture, Mr Nowak, having been denied entry into Zimbabwe, a Minister said:

. . . those who listened to the rapporteur's interview on Radio 4 will have no doubt how badly he was treated in contravention of international law and in contravention to the invitation already issued. In that sense, we are totally supportive that international law has to be applied. We have heard nothing since from the UN about how the rapporteur will take that forward, but clearly it will be an issue and not one on which we are likely to find ourselves in sympathy with the Zimbabwean Government.

(HC Deb 2 November 2009 Vol 714 c10)

Part Six: IX. *The Position of the Individual (including the Corporation) in International Law—Crimes under international law*

6/127
Amnesties

The Government were asked whether it regarded amnesties as a barrier to making conduct retrospectively criminal in UK law. A Minister replied:

We certainly do not say that the UK is bound by previous amnesties, but we certainly need to consider them and bear them in mind. I think it would be fair to say that, whilst the Government's view is that individuals should not escape justice for these types of crimes, incredibly serious crimes, we would not want to pursue an avenue which risks increasing tensions and perhaps even rekindling armed conflict simply because we have something in place but we are not actually able to make some flexibility on a case-by-case basis. [Q. 73] [See also the evidence of the ex-DPP Sir Ken Macdonald, Qs 18 and 19, Evidence of 19 May 2009, in the same Report.]

An official added:

...[an amnesty] would not automatically act as a bar to a prosecution being brought if such an amnesty existed and there was retrospective application. Inevitably, any decision to prosecute would be a matter for the CPS to pursue and the Attorney General to consent to and, inevitably, the existence of an amnesty would be one highly relevant factor, among many others, to take into account. [Q.74]

And the Minister said:

Perhaps I should reiterate it then: that essentially [amnesties] are not a bar; they are something we need to bear in mind—in a process that allows the CPS, and possibly the Attorney General, to consider the case-by-case basis. [Q.78]

(Joint Committee on Human Rights, Twenty-fourth Report: Closing the Impunity Gap: UK law on genocide (and related crimes) and redress for torture victims, (2009) HL 153/HC 553)

6/128
Burma

The Government were asked what assessment they had made of evidence presented to them of alleged abuses of human rights, crimes against humanity and genocidal acts committed by the Burmese military regime; and in what circumstances they would submit such evidence to the United

Nations Security Council requesting referral to the International Criminal Court. An FCO Minister said:

We remain deeply concerned at the human rights situation in Burma. Over 2,100 political prisoners, including Aung San Suu Kyi, continue to be detained. Political freedoms are completely absent and any dissent is brutally crushed. Treatment of Burma's ethnic groups is of particular concern. Appalling human rights abuses are undoubtedly happening in Burma. However, as Burma is not a state party to the Rome Statute, it would require a Chapter VII UN Security Council resolution to refer the situation in the country to the prosecutor at the International Criminal Court. In the past two years our efforts have helped to secure unprecedented Security Council action on Burma, in the form of two strongly worded presidential statements. It is, however, highly unlikely that the Council would agree to pass a binding resolution on this issue. Our efforts to secure a non-binding resolution on Burma in 2007 were blocked by other members. We regularly test the degree of consensus as we seek Security Council action and strong resolutions in the Human Rights Council and General Assembly.

(HL Deb 30 June 2009 Vol 712 cWA31)

6/129
Democratic Republic of Congo

A Minister wrote:

Our ambassador in Kinshasa has repeatedly called for members of the armed forces guilty of human rights abuses to be brought to justice. The UN Security Council, including the UK permanent representative, raised this issue in May with Democratic Republic of Congo (DRC) President Kabila and DRC Prime Minister Muzito. Kabila gave a speech to the nation on Independence Day in June this year, promising renewed efforts to ensure "total security" for the population, including ending sexual and gender-based violence. Military courts in Rutshuru have since prosecuted several cases against some Congolese national army (FARDC) officers for crimes including rape. The UK continues to push for legal action against five senior FARDC commanders accused of committing sexual violence, named by the UN Security Council during their visit. We will continue to stress the importance of ensuring the implementation of the UN Mission to the DRC (MONUC)'s policy of withdrawing support from FARDC units implicated in serious human rights abuses.

(HL Deb 22 October 2009 Vol 716 c1613W)

6/130
Gaza

It was put to a Minister with respect to the conduct of operations in Gaza that:

...now the International Criminal Court has for the first time issued a warrant against a serving head of state, in the case of Sudan, and that a number of Governments in the Arab world and Africa, including the Saudis, are saying that this is a perfect example of the way in which the West uses international law against the developing world but does not apply standards against its own friends and allies participating in conflict, is it not important that we are all seen to judge actions not only of other Governments but also of our own Government against the standards of international law that we wish to insist on?

The Minister said:

...of course, that is an unimpeachable principle, but the noble Lord will also recognise the fact that these are very different circumstances in which conflict occurs. Of course, there are higher priorities than these issues, important though they are. The world is mostly interested in securing a fair and peaceful arrangement for the development of the relationships between Israel and the people of Palestine and Gaza. Those matters need to be taken into account. It is not always the case that a threatening challenge to those who have been responsible for reprehensible conduct is necessarily the next stage forward in advancing the cause of peace.

(HL Deb 18 March 2009 Vol 709 c224)

6/131
Crimes under International Law (See also **8/3–4**)

The Secretary of State for Justice said:

I told the House on 5 May 2009, *Official Report*, column 19 that I had met representatives from the all party parliamentary group for genocide prevention, and they had made a very powerful case for the inclusion of genocide as an extraterritorial offence within our law. Since then I have consulted widely with colleagues about the best way to proceed. Serious crimes of this nature are best dealt with in the country where the crimes took place. That is where the evidence will be most easily accessible, and where witnesses will be easier to contact. It is also the best solution because witnesses and survivors can see justice being done. Failing that, these crimes should be dealt with by international courts or tribunals where they exist. However, there may be circumstances where these options are not available. We have therefore decided that we should strengthen domestic law in this area. We propose that, as far is permissible under the legal principles applicable to retrospection, we should seek to cover the categories of crime of genocide, war crimes and crimes against humanity from 1 January 1991. It is that date from which the International Criminal Tribunal for the former Yugoslavia had jurisdiction to try offences under the tribunal's statute adopted by the United Nations Security Council. Making these changes will be quite complex. The offence of genocide, along with offences of war crimes and crimes against humanity, is contained in the International Criminal Court Act 2001. From 2001, we have jurisdiction to try those crimes in the UK if committed by a UK national or resident wherever they took place. The 2001 Act is based on the Rome Statute of 1998 establishing the International Criminal Court. While international law existed in respect of all these areas earlier, the offences in the 2001 Act may be wider than those recognised before the Rome Statute and any change will need to take account of this. We propose no change to the categories of people covered by the legislation, which should remain UK nationals and residents (including those who commit crimes, and subsequently become resident). However we are exploring the possibility of providing more certainty as to who may (or may not) be considered to be a UK resident. We intend to introduce these changes by bringing forward amendments to the Coroners and Justice Bill at report stage in the House of Lords in the autumn.

(HC Deb 7 July 2009 Vol 495 c41WS-42WS)

6/132
In a press statement, the Ministry of Justice wrote:

The government proposes that, as far is permissible under the legal principles applicable to retrospection, we should seek to cover the categories of crime of genocide, war crimes and crimes against humanity from 1 January 1991. It is that date from which the International Criminal Tribunal for the former Yugoslavia had jurisdiction to try offences under the Tribunal's Statute adopted by the United Nations Security Council. The offence of genocide, along with offences of war crimes and crimes against humanity, is contained in the International Criminal Court Act 2001. From 2001, we have jurisdiction to try those crimes in the UK if committed by a UK national or resident wherever they took place. The most serious types of war crimes committed in international armed conflicts, namely grave breaches of the Geneva Conventions, have been covered in UK law since 1957 under the Geneva Conventions Act 1957. The 2001 Act is based on the Rome Statute of 1998 establishing the International Criminal Court. While international law existed in respect of all these areas earlier, the offences in the 2001 Act may be wider than those recognised before the Rome Statute and any change will need to take account of this... Going back to 1991 would cover, for example, the period of the Rwanda genocide and the conflict in the former Yugoslavia.

(Ministry of Justice statement 7 July 2009, <www.justice.gov.uk/news/newsrelease070709b.htm>)

6/133

The Coroners and Justice Act 2009, s.70 provides for certain limited retrospective jurisdiction over the crimes of genocide, crimes against humanity and war crimes as they appear in the International Criminal Court Act 2001. The Act also provides an extensive definition of 'residence' for the purpose of jurisdiction over these crimes. These sections came into force on 6 April 2010, The Coroners and Justice Act 2009.

[Coroners and Justice Act 2009 (Commencement No.4, (Transitional and Saving Provisions) Order 2010, SI No.816/2010), Ed.]

6/134
Kenya

A Minister wrote:

The UK is concerned that no action has been taken on bringing to justice those accused of orchestrating Kenya's post-election violence in 2007, neither by a special tribunal nor referral to the International Criminal Court (ICC). With our EU partners and other like-minded countries we are continuing to make clear that credible action is necessary. The Foreign Secretary encouraged Kenya's reform process, including tackling impunity and post-election violence, during his meeting with Prime Minister Odinga in London last July. Since then, the Prime Minister, the Secretary of State for International Development and the former Minister of State for Africa have also encouraged the Kenyan Government to establish a credible tribunal to investigate and prosecute those responsible.

The Government support the role being played by Kofi Annan and endorses his proposal that the ICC continue its discussions with the Kenyan Government to achieve justice. We continue to believe action on impunity is needed to prevent future violence and to send a strong message that Kenyans will not tolerate violence.

(HL Deb 22 October 2009 Vol 713 c619W)

6/135
Pakistan

The Government were asked whether they would consider prosecuting those accused of torture of British citizens in Pakistan. The FCO Minister wrote:

Torture is prohibited under UK and international law and perpetrators can be prosecuted in the UK regardless of where the crime was committed. This is in accordance with the UK's obligations under the UN Convention Against Torture and enacted through Section 134 of the Criminal Justice Act 1988. Any decision to bring prosecutions against those accused of torture in Pakistan is a matter for the Crown Prosecution Service and requires the Attorney General's consent.

(HL Deb 7 December 2009 Vol 715 cWA94)

6/136
Serbia

An FCO Minister wrote:

Our assessment is that the Serbian government is working actively to secure the arrest and transfer of the remaining International Criminal Tribunal for the former Yugoslavia (ICTY) indictees, including Ratko Mladic, to The Hague. We continue to urge the Serbian authorities to make every effort to ensure that the arrest and transfer of the remaining indictees take place as soon as possible.

(HC Deb 26 March 2009 Vol 490 c602W)

Part Seven: The State and its Organs

Part Seven: III. *The State and its Organs—Other organs of the state*

7/1
The Government were asked why it did not support an exception to the rules of state immunity in actions for torture. A Minister said:

Because it is a general principle of international law that one state is not subject to the jurisdiction of another, except in certain circumstances. Therefore we have not taken that position, simply to unilaterally assume jurisdiction over this area. [Q.107] ... when the UN adopted [United Nations Convention on Jurisdictional Immunities of States and their Property], it considered whether or not jurisdiction should be on criminal grounds or on civil. My understanding is that it determined that criminal, yes, but not to extend it to civil. [Q. 110] And as far as States were concerned that had taken a different position, the Minister said: They have decided to [limit immunity in criminal and civil actions for torture, Ed.]. That is not in the normal round of what is done within the international community. [Qs. 111–113]

(Joint Committee on Human Rights, Twenty-fourth Report: Closing the Impunity Gap: UK law on genocide (and related crimes) and redress for torture victims, (2009) HL 153/HC 553)

7/2
The Department of Justice wrote to the Joint Committee on Human Rights about a proposal to limit State immunity in civil cases alleging extraterritorial torture.

21. A unilateral assumption of civil jurisdiction, as provided for by the Bill, would place the UK in breach of our obligations under international law. The exercise of such extra-territorial jurisdiction, even where States and State officials are not involved, remains a difficult and highly controversial area. When the United Nations Convention Against Torture was negotiated, the option of creating an international civil cause of action was, accordingly, not pursued. Furthermore, the United Nations adopted in 2004 the Convention on Jurisdictional Immunities of State and Their Property, after a period of prolonged negotiation. The United Kingdom signed the Convention in 2005. The Convention makes no exception in respect of civil actions in respect of personal injury or death that is alleged to have occurred outside the territory of a State.... 23. The Government is also concerned that while the Bill could make it possible for those who claim to have suffered torture to seek an award of damages, it would remain essentially impossible to enforce any such judgment against a foreign State. Any attempt to seize the property or assets of a State would be particularly controversial, and liable to lead to retaliatory action against United Kingdom interests.

(Joint Committee on Human Rights, Twenty-fourth Report: Closing the Impunity Gap: UK law on genocide (and related crimes) and redress for torture victims, (2009)HL 153/HC 553)

Part Seven: IV. *The State and its Organs—Diplomatic missions and their members*

7/3
The FAC had recommended in its Report on the Human Rights Report 2008:

27. We recommend that, in its response to this Report, the Government gives us full particulars of the individual members of staff [of Private Military Security

Companies, Ed.] who enjoy diplomatic immunity, and the grounds on which this has been justified, and that it supplies us with a full statement of its policy on the provision of diplomatic immunity to staff who are not directly employed by the Government. (Paragraph 138)

The Government replied:

61. It is the Government's policy to comply strictly with the provisions of the Vienna Convention on Diplomatic Relations. Members of staff of PMSCs who provide security services for a diplomatic mission may be performing administrative and technical functions for that mission, even if they are not employees of the State concerned. Accordingly, such persons may properly be notified as members of the administrative and technical staff of the mission, and will therefore be afforded privileges and immunities by the receiving State including immunity from jurisdiction in accordance with Article 37 of the Vienna Convention.

(Response of the Secretary of State for Foreign and Commonwealth Affairs Foreign Affairs Committee Session 2008–09, Annual Report on Human Rights 2008, Cm 7723)

7/4
The Foreign Secretary was asked in what ways the Iranian authorities had obstructed the activities of staff at the British Embassy in Tehran and what activities had been obstructed. He wrote:

The Iranian authorities have obstructed the activities of our embassy in Tehran in numerous ways, including: by placing restrictions on vehicle access to the embassy compounds for embassy staff and visitors, harassing embassy staff, guests, and contractors carrying out work on our compounds (including security work recommended by the Iranian authorities), and failing to provide airside access for the collection of diplomatic bags. Additionally the British Council was forced to suspend its operation in Iran earlier this year, because of unacceptable pressure put on its staff by the Iranian Government.

We have raised these issues with the Iranian authorities on numerous occasions and reminded them of their obligations under the Vienna Convention on Diplomatic Relations.

(HC Deb 30 March 2009 Vol 490 c858W)

7/5 (See also **5/53**)
An FCO press statement said:

EU Foreign Ministers have condemned the continued arrest and detention of peaceful demonstrators in Iran, and have called for the immediate release of Iranian staff working at the British Embassy in Tehran:

The Foreign Ministers of the European Union remain seriously concerned about events in Iran. They condemn the continued arrest and detention of peaceful demonstrators and journalists, and the increasing restrictions on both the domestic and foreign media. EU Foreign Ministers condemn the unjustified expulsion of two UK Diplomats and the detention of several Iranian staff working at the British Embassy in Tehran.

They call on the Iranian authorities to release these Embassy staff immediately and to offer full protection of all staff working in EU Embassies in Tehran in accordance with the Vienna convention and Diplomatic norms. They make clear to the Iranian authorities that harassment or intimidation of foreign or Iranian staff working in Embassies will be met with a strong and collective EU response.

Commenting on the situation in Tehran the Foreign Secretary said:

The United Kingdom is deeply concerned at the arrest and, in some cases, continued detention of some of our hard-working locally-engaged staff in Tehran. This is harassment and intimidation of a kind which is quite unacceptable. These are hard-working diplomatic staff.

The idea that the British Embassy is somehow behind the demonstrations and protests that have been taking place in Tehran in recent weeks is wholly without foundation. We have protested in strong terms, directly to the Iranian authorities, about the arrests that took place yesterday.

I think it is very important that I discuss this with my EU colleagues later on this afternoon. All European countries have made clear that they want to stand together in standing up for the diplomatic principles that are important for our diplomatic activity all over the world. At the moment our top priority is the position of our locally-engaged staff who we want to see released unharmed and back to work.

(<www.fco.gov.uk>, 28 June 2009)

7/6

The Foreign Secretary was asked how many locally employed British Embassy staff in Iran have immunity from jurisdiction under Article 38.1 of the Vienna Convention on Diplomatic Relations 1961. A Minister wrote:

No locally employed members of staff at British Embassy in Tehran have immunity under Article 38 (1) of the Vienna Convention on Diplomatic Relations 1961.

(HC Deb 20 July 2009 Vol 946 c961W)

7/7

The Foreign Secretary was asked what assessment he had made of the merits of conferring diplomatic status on non-Diplomatic Service staff employed by the British Embassy in Iran in accordance with the Diplomatic Service Regulations 2006. A Minister wrote:

Staff are appointed under article 7 of the Vienna Convention on Diplomatic Relations 1961, according to the functions they perform at the mission. In practice, the privileges and immunities staff enjoy stem from the receiving state's recognition that they have been appropriately classified, in line with their functions. The diplomatic service regulations do not apply to locally engaged staff who are employed on local terms and conditions, governed by local law and practice.

(HC Deb 20 July 2009 Vol 946 c961W)

Part Eight: Jurisdiction of the State

Part Eight:I.D. *Jurisdiction of the State—Bases of jurisdiction—Universality*

8/1
Universal Jurisdiction—General

The UK representative made the following statement in the Sixth Committee of the General Assembly in a debate on Universal Jurisdiction:

The scope and application of universal jurisdiction Fighting impunity is a common goal among member States of the United Nations and universal jurisdiction is one of the essential mechanisms established by the international community to help ensure that those who commit some of the most serious international crimes are brought to justice. The principle of universal jurisdiction—that is to say, the ability of a State to prosecute crimes in its domestic courts in the absence of any link to the prosecuting State—has its origins in customary law and was first accepted in a treaty in the Four Geneva Conventions of 1949. The scope of the principle has since been extended, but even today, universal jurisdiction applies only to a limited range of crimes, in recognition of their exceptional gravity in the eyes of the world community. The Geneva Conventions themselves have gained universal participation, illustrating the very wide-spread acceptance among States of the principle of universal jurisdiction... Universal jurisdiction is an important complement to, but is distinct from, the jurisdiction of international judicial mechanisms, including under the Rome Statute of the International Criminal Court. International justice mechanisms were never designed, and can never aspire, to prosecute all cases of crimes within their jurisdiction. Such courts and tribunals will only ever address a small number of the most serious cases. Prosecutions at the domestic level will therefore continue to be a vital component in the pursuit of justice for the victims of international crimes. And the possibility of domestic prosecution in a third State helps ensure that perpetrators cannot evade justice... Universal jurisdiction should of course be exercised by States only in appropriate cases, in accordance with international law. In the United Kingdom, universal jurisdiction is provided for in national legislation where it is necessary to comply with international obligations and safeguards exist to ensure that it is exercised responsibly. For example, in England and Wales, senior level consent from the Attorney General must be obtained before a prosecution for most international crimes can proceed. Different States and legal systems will have other solutions to the issues which may arise when cases are brought based on universal jurisdiction, especially when there are competing jurisdictions involved. But if disputes occur between States, established mechanisms exist under international law to enable them to be resolved...

The evidence shows that prosecutions based on universal jurisdiction occur rarely in practice. And the reality is that such prosecutions are unlikely ever to become commonplace in national jurisdictions. The practical difficulties of prosecuting complex cases in circumstances when the witnesses and evidence may be thousands of miles away will see to that. But even if it is used rarely, it is vital that universal jurisdiction remains available to States as a weapon in the fight against impunity for the most serious international crimes.

(Text supplied by FCO)

8/2
Enforcement of Universal Jurisdiction—Tzipi Livni

Following media reports that an arrest warrant for ex-Israel Foreign Secretary, Tzipi Livni on war crimes charged had been issued in London (and then withdrawn when it was established that Livni was not in the UK), the Foreign Secretary said that Israeli leaders, like leaders from other countries, must be able to visit and have a proper dialogue with the British Government. He went on:

[T]he Government is looking urgently at ways in which the UK system might be changed in order to avoid this sort of situation arising again.

Israel is a strategic partner and a close friend of the UK. We are determined to protect and develop these ties. Israeli leaders—like leaders from other countries—must be able to visit and have a proper dialogue with the British Government.

The procedure by which arrest warrants can be sought and issued without any prior knowledge or advice by a prosecutor is an unusual feature of the system in England and Wales. The Government is looking urgently at ways in which the UK system might be changed in order to avoid this sort of situation arising again.

(<www.fco.gov.uk/news>, 15 December 2009)

8/3
(See **also 6/131–133**) **International Crimes**

The Government were asked by the JCHR why it should be possible for someone to be prosecuted for torture committed in Rwanda, but not for genocide committed at the same time and place. A Minister replied:

... it is important first of all to look at the fact that the legislation which Parliament passed in 2001 [The International Criminal Court Act 2001, Ed.] allowed them to look at this issue and to consider whether or not they should take a much greater jurisdiction—and certainly in respect of Rwanda—to go back, to be retrospective on that. They considered that and decided that they did not wish to do so. The difference essentially between the legislation around torture and the legislation as it stands around genocide is that the international community has decided collectively what it wishes to allow that position to be. That is not the case in respect of universal jurisdiction around genocide. [Q. 59]

The Minister was then asked why the UK could not extend its jurisdiction to extraterritorial genocide, even in the absence of an international obligation to do so, given that other, common law States had done so.

The Minister said:

There are considerable difficulties with extending jurisdiction and essentially taking jurisdiction. If it is not something that internationally has been accepted for a unilateral position in a state to do so [*Sc* If it is not something that internationally has been accepted, it is not for state to take a unilateral position, Ed.]. Where it has been done it has been done in discussions and in cooperation internationally, hence the position that we are currently in with torture. That is why it is a much more difficult position to do so for other offences. I think from the UK's point of view we would be seen, if we simply took the jurisdiction without that international agreement, as simply being a policeman of the world and not getting agreement to do so. [Q. 60]

The Minister went on:

We are looking at all these difficulties and we are sympathetic to the issues that have been raised. We understand that there are these problems around the pre-2001 period. As I say, it is not a simple issue on which to proceed. I would not say that we should look too easily towards other countries to be able to solve that problem either. My understanding is that where universal jurisdiction has been in place with other countries, for example Belgium, they have stood back from this, my understanding is that Spain is already considering whether or not they should do so too. So there may not be that as a simple option. The first port of call clearly must be to look at whether or not the countries of origin, where these allegations of criminal activity may have taken place, are in a position to be able to conduct a prosecution, or, indeed, a third country may be in a position to do so. Those have to be the first ports of call. [Q. 62]... In the case of Rwanda, clearly one of the things that we are doing as a Government is doing what we can to support the Rwandan system of justice, to try and ensure that it is up to the full standards we talked about. The difficulty... is that those four alleged genocidaires from Rwanda are not in a position to be deported either. [*Brown (aka Vincent Bajinja) & Ors v Government of Rwanda & Ors* [2009] EWHC 770 (Admin), Ed.] [Q. 63]

The Government were asked specifically about retrospectivity: should not the principle be that, wherever legally possible, the UK should have jurisdiction to prosecute? Did the Minister disagree that international law permitted jurisdiction dates before the coming into force of the 2001 Act?

The Minister said:

...it is not simply a matter of reflecting the 2001 Act backwards to an earlier date. In respect of genocide, genocide has already been recognised for a considerable number of years as a crime internationally. Therefore, reflecting it back perhaps to cover the period of the early 1990s for Rwanda, and indeed the former Yugoslavia, may be an issue; but how far back would one want to go? If you look at war crimes or crimes against humanity, there are details of those crimes which it may not simply be possible to be reflected backward from the 2001 Act, because those details may not actually have existed in international criminal law at the time—trying to reflect backwards. So it is not as simple as saying, "Let's take the legislation and make it retrospective to 1990/1991". These are difficult issues. I would say to the Committee that we are aware of those difficulties. We are aware of the issues that are being raised, and the Justice Secretary has met with the All-Party Parliamentary Group [on Genocide Prevention]; they have made very strong representations on these issues; and it is something that we are looking at... [Q. 66]

It was put to the Minister that there were dates by which certain conduct constituted offences by international law: 1948 for genocide; 1991 for crimes against humanity; and 1957 for war crimes. Could legislation not be made retrospective to those dates?

The Minister said:

[There were difficulties of presentation because the dates of international criminality were not uniform for the various offences.] My understanding is that, for example, somebody may well be alleged to have committed genocide. The [international criminality of] genocide . . . may go back to 1948. However, if the allegations and the prosecution were to fall short of genocide, they [viz. the defendants] could well be liable for prosecution on crimes against humanity or war crimes; but the dates for those could not go back quite so far. Therefore, while there has been some debate about whether or not prosecutors would be confused by the dates . . . there is an issue about how it is perceived and how victims would perceive it, and the ability perhaps not quite to meet the threshold of genocide, maybe meet the threshold for another crime, but not being able to prosecute it because the dates were not the same. [Q. 67]

The Government were asked why mere presence was sufficient to found jurisdiction for extraterritorial torture but that it was necessary to establish residence for jurisdiction over genocide.

The Minister said:

Essentially, it is because the international community has allowed for that level of jurisdiction around torture but not in respect of genocide. That is what Parliament decided in 2001. We certainly recognise that there is an issue about the clarity of the term “resident”. It is considered by the courts on a case-by-case basis as a matter of fact. One of the issues that we are taking into consideration at the moment is whether or not we can give greater clarity in the legislation for the courts, still allowing the courts to be able to have discretion but perhaps a little more clarity around those difficult issues which you mention. [Q. 83] . . . it is about whether or not we are providing a safe haven for people to come to the UK. We make it quite clear that people who are coming to the UK, who are transitory in one form or another, are not simply seeking a safe haven. Those who are resident in the UK—a matter of fact about whether or not they are resident, determined by the court—are seeking a safe haven. That is essentially the distinction, on the basis of presence or residence. [Q. 87]

The Minister continued:

We are also looking at the practical issues of being able to enforce these matters. We are also looking at the impact that this will have in terms of our having to deal with other countries. We have to ensure that there is some agreement on how these things are worked. If you look at other countries, how many of those have successfully taken those prosecutions? As I have said before, it is okay to put this legislation onto statute but you have to be able to ensure that it is going to work and it is going to be able to work practically. [Q. 91]

And, asked about the jurisdictional claims of Spain and Belgium, the Minister said:

It might be worth considering the fact that the two countries that I understand did have that level of jurisdiction—Belgium has already rolled back from it and Spain are in the process of considering doing so. Therefore, that might actually suggest that there are a lot of difficulties with having that high level of jurisdiction. I think that we also need to bear in mind how that would be seen internationally, as the UK as the policeman of the world. We may have very strong views on this issue but this has been written into statute since 2001. [Q. 92]

The Minister was asked about the role of the Attorney-General in relation to international crimes. It was the issue of separation of powers. Was it right that someone who was sitting in Parliament and sitting in Government should have the decision-making over whether the prosecution may take place or not? Would it not be better to leave this to the Director of Public Prosecutions? The Minister said:

I think the level of crimes we are talking about are such serious and significant crimes that they also in most cases will have some impact upon our international relations and, potentially, the UK's security. Therefore, it is important that not only the DPP has a view on this but that the Attorney General is in a position to take account... [An intervention asked: Are you really saying that political considerations apply when somebody is potentially guilty of the most horrendous war crimes and crimes against humanity?]. The Minister continued:

I think that it is not simply about political considerations; it is about public policy considerations and about taking into account the overview of the situation, which I think the Attorney General is in a position to do. [Qs. 95, 96]

She continued:

In normal circumstances, the decision by the Crown Prosecution Service to prosecute, at whatever level, will also take into account whether it is in the public interest. I believe, and the Government believes, that—certainly in crimes such as this and the impact that this may have upon international relations, potentially on UK security—these are issues that are of such a high level that, yes, they should be considered by the Attorney General, who will consider whether or not it is in the public interest to prosecute. [Q. 97]

(Joint Committee on Human Rights, Twenty-fourth Report: Closing the Impunity Gap: UK law on genocide (and related crimes) and redress for torture victims, (2009) HL 153/HC 553)

8/4

The Ministry of Justice wrote to the Joint Committee on Human Rights about jurisdiction over international crimes.

Memorandum submitted by the Ministry of Justice

OFFENCES OF GENOCIDE, TORTURE AND RELATED OFFENCES

10. Any exercise of universal jurisdiction carries with it the risk of infringing the sovereignty of another State, and it is not something that the UK does lightly. In general, we would only do so when required to by an international convention or agreement, where the international community as a whole has agreed that the

crimes are such as to warrant, and even require, universal jurisdiction. They do so ordinarily in order to give effect to an "extradite or prosecute" obligation. There are such conventions covering torture and hostage taking, and the UK has signed and ratified them. We therefore have legislation which enables us to fulfil our international obligations. There is no such requirement or agreement covering war crimes, genocide or crimes against humanity. 11. In the case of war crimes, genocide and crimes against humanity, these offences are also triable by the International Criminal Court, where the international community rather than the UK can see justice done. The 2001 Act also made these crimes extraditable. Although it is only possible for the court to deal with the most serious cases, where the acts in question occurred after 1 September 2001, other cases should, in the interests of justice, be dealt with in the country where the offence or offences took place. We therefore believe it is more important that we help to build up the capacity of those countries to deal with cases effectively, than that we take jurisdiction over crimes in which the UK may have no direct involvement. 12 Offences of war crimes, genocide and crimes against humanity can be prosecuted wherever they were committed. But Parliament agreed to restrict the offences to UK nationals and UK residents. The term "resident" is flexible. It would not cover, for example, short-term visitors or students. But it is for practical reasons unlikely that we would be able to mount a successful prosecution in a short time against someone who is here temporarily. Such a person should stand trial in the country where their offence took place, or their country of permanent residence if that is different. This is because it is important that justice is seen to be done locally, and because local justice is less likely to encounter the practical problems detailed in paragraph 5. 13. If a person is here for a longer period, they may become resident and be able to stand trial here for their crimes. We have no evidence that the term "resident" as opposed to "present" represents any practical gap in UK law. The UK Government takes seriously its international obligations to ensure that the UK does not provide a safe haven for suspected war criminals. A suspect who is here temporarily cannot be said to have a "safe haven" since that person cannot remain any length of time in the UK and cannot become resident here without risking prosecution. The International Criminal Court Act 2001 allows for the prosecution of a person who commits a crime and subsequently becomes resident, so the law does not depend on the nationality or residence of the suspect at the time of the alleged crime.

In relation to making the existing substantive provisions of the International Criminal Court Act 2001 retrospective, the Minister said:

The practical effect of any proposed retrospection will depend in part on the date from which the offences would apply. If there is no time limit, that will mean any crime could be investigated and tried if the suspected perpetrator is or may be still alive. In order to meet the principle that there should be no punishment without law, it is important that any retrospective effect should date from a time when the offences were clearly recognised under international law. In the case of the International Criminal Court Act the statute on which the crimes are based is not retrospective, so it is not necessarily evident that all elements of those crimes were recognised in international law prior to 2001.

(Joint Committee on Human Rights, Twenty-fourth Report: Closing the Impunity Gap: UK law on genocide (and related crimes) and redress for torture victims, (2009) HL 153/HC 553)

8/5 (See 11/10)
Piracy

The UK representative in the Security Council in a debate on piracy off the coast of Somalia on 18 November 2009 said:

The United Kingdom also welcomes the achievements of the Contact Group on Piracy off the Coast of Somalia [set up in 2009 following SC resolution 1851, consisting of States with an interest in the suppression of piracy and convened by the UK, Ed.] in coordinating the efforts of the international community to address piracy in the region and the constructive contribution being made to these efforts by the Transitional Federal Government and the regional authorities of Somalia. We are pleased to lead work in the Contact Group on operational coordination and regional capacity development. The level of coordination being achieved in the region by naval forces from a wide range of States is unprecedented and impressive. Close cooperation between these forces, in particular the establishment of patrolling of the Internationally Recommended Transit Corridor in the Gulf of Aden, has managed to ensure that only one ship following this route and adhering to agreed best practice has been hijacked in the Gulf since December 2008. The statistics in the Secretary-General's report on the protection of World Food Programme aid and AMISOM [African Union Mission in Somalia, Ed.] supplies underline a successful role of the military operations in safeguarding essential shipping.

But we cannot underestimate the significant challenge that we face. Even though the proportion of successful attacks continues to fall, the overall number of pirate attacks continues to increase and currently 11 ships and 254 crew members are currently hijacked. Pirates are now willing to venture further out to sea in search of targets and to counter this we need a different type of military response, led by intelligence. The Military Commanders know what they need in terms of military capability, and the international community must help to deliver this. But one message from the Military Commanders remains consistent. They are shocked by the lack of adherence by sectors of merchant shipping community to the guidance which is given by the International Maritime Organisation and industry bodies. Estimates suggest that a quarter of merchant shipping fails to follow this guidance. This failure makes them much easier targets. We have joined other major Flag States in signing the New York Declaration on Best Management Practice to avoid and deter acts of piracy and are pressing all United Kingdom ships to adopt these practices when in the region and we urge all Flag States to do the same. [For text of the New York Declaration, see <www.fco.gov.uk/resources/en/pdf/3849543/ny-declaration.pdf>, Ed.] The release of the Spanish fishing boat Alakrana earlier this week is obviously a welcome development and we hope that all other hostages will soon be free, including the British Nationals, Paul and Rachel Chandler, who were seized from their yacht on 23 October . . . We pay tribute to Kenya for its leadership within the region in taking forward the detention and prosecution of pirates. The UK also welcomes the agreement by the Republic of Seychelles to accept pirate suspects for trial and detention. We stand ready with other partners to provide assistance to signatories of the Djibouti Code of Conduct who have undertaken to enact national legislation to enable the prosecution of pirates. [For text of the Djibouti Code of Conduct, see <www.fco.gov.uk/

resources/en/pdf/pdf9/piracy-djibouti-meeting>, Ed.] We strongly support the work being taken forward by the UN Office of Drugs and Crime to help the Transitional Federal Government and regional authorities of Puntland and Somaliland to deal with suspects within Somalia.... the Secretary-General's report clearly highlights the need to address the situation on land in Somalia. The Contact Group decided on a number of measures at the meeting of its Working Group in London this week. Donors now need to commit themselves to providing financial and technical support to Somalia and to States throughout the region—including work on governance, rule of law, justice, alternative livelihoods and strategic communications. The implementation of the Djibouti Code of Conduct remains at the heart of regional capability development, transforming regional political will into action.... piracy is only one of the symptoms of instability in Somalia and, as the Special Representative has said, we must also address the root causes of that instability. I pay tribute to the efforts led by the SRSG to support the Transitional Federal Government of Somalia in developing effective political and security structures. And I should like to thank AMISOM and Uganda and Burundi in particular, its two troop contributing countries, for their outstanding efforts to support the Government against insurgents. I hope that others will join them to bring the mission up to full strength. The international community has shown unity and resolve in taking action to contain the threat of piracy. But we now need to show more of the same determination and unity on shore if we are to address its roots causes.

(S/PV.6221, 18 November 2009) [See also SC resolution 1846 and <www.fco.gov.uk/en/global-issues/conflcit-prevention/piracy/>, Ed.]

Part Eight: II.B. *Jurisdiction of the State—Types of jurisdiction—Adjudicative*

8/6 (See also **15/17**)

The Justice Secretary was asked what consents were required for the prosecution of an alleged offence relating to war crimes committed overseas following a citizen's arrest in the UK. A Minister wrote:

The Attorney-General's consent is required for the prosecution of war crimes under the War Crimes Act 1991 or the International Criminal Court Act 2001. The Attorney-General's consent is also required for the prosecution of offences under the Geneva Conventions Act 1957.

(HC Deb 10 February 2009 Vol 487 c1917)

Part Eight: III.A. *Jurisdiction of the State—Extra-territorial exercises of jurisdiction—General*

8/7

The Government were asked (1) what powers the Financial Services Authority (FSA) had to investigate the operations of subsidiaries of British-based banks operating in the United States; and what reports had been received from the FSA on the implications for the United Kingdom banking sector of the operations of UK banking subsidiaries in the United States sub-prime mortgage market (2) what reports had been received from the FSA on its communication with the United States Securities and Exchange Commission on its inquiries into the practices of subsidiaries of British banks operating in the United States securitization of mortgages market.

A Minister wrote:

Firms carrying on a regulated activity, by way of business, within the UK, are required to be authorised with the Financial Services Authority (FSA) and are subject to FSA regulation, unless they benefit from a statutory exemption. To the extent that an overseas subsidiary of a British-based bank's activities take place entirely outside the UK and do not involve services to UK firms or individuals, those activities are likely to be outside the scope of UK financial services regulation and not subject to FSA authorisation requirements...

(HC Deb 9 March 2009 Vol 489 c101W)

Part Nine: State Territory

Part Nine: I.A.1. *State Territory—Territory—Elements of territory—Land, international waters, rivers, lakes and land-locked seas* (see also parts ten and eleven)

9/1 (See also **11/9**)
An FCO Minister wrote:

The island of Rockall is UK sovereign territory, as provided for in the Island of Rockall Act 1972, which incorporated the island "into that part of the United Kingdom known as Scotland", and made provision for the law of Scotland to apply to it. UK sovereignty extends to the 12 nautical mile territorial sea around Rockall, under the provisions of the UN Convention on the Law of the Sea.

(HL Deb 12 March 2009 Vol 708 cWA279)

Part Eleven: Seas and Vessels

Part Eleven: I. *Seas and Vessels—Internal waters, including ports and harbours*

11/1
A Minister wrote about Climate Change and the Arctic:

[The Department of Energy and Climate Change] funds the Met Office Hadley Centre (MOHC), through its Integrated Climate Programme with joint funding from the MOD and DEFRA, to monitor, understand and predict climate change; this research includes incorporating sea ice into global climate models to ensure best possible predictions on melting of Arctic sea ice. We also liaise with other research groups in the U.K. and internationally on this topic. The Northwest Passage temporarily became fully open and navigable in summer 2007, for first time in recorded history, due to the record low extent (September average area: 4.28 million sq km) of Arctic sea ice melt. The same situation occurred in summer 2008, when the sea ice area (4.67 million sq km) was at its second lowest on record. Satellite monitoring data since 1979, available from the US National Snow and ice Data Centre (NSIDC) shows there has been a long-term decline in the extent of summer Arctic sea ice and that this decline has accelerated over the last decade; the long-term downward trend of around 10 per cent. per decade can be linked to human emissions of greenhouse gases and aerosols. It is not yet clear if the much larger summer ice melt in the last two years is an acceleration of this long term trend or a short term variation around it. Recent analysis by the MOHC suggests that changes as large as the observed record low in 2007 can indeed result from natural year-to-year variability around the longer term downward trend; this provides confidence in the ability of the MOHC's climate model to simulate changes in the area of Arctic sea ice and its continuing decline. However, it is evident that climate models show a wide range of future predicted rates of sea ice decline. Whilst the IPCC's Fourth Assessment Report suggested the Arctic would be largely free of summer ice by 2100, many more recent models predict this will happen much sooner—by the middle of this century or even earlier; several experts suggest there may possibly be no summer sea ice by the mid 2010s. Satellite and other records also show a long-term decline in the average thickness and age of Arctic sea ice over recent decades. For example, scientists from University College London recently reported that the thickness of the ice was significantly lower (by an average of 10 per cent.) during the winter of 2007–08 than during the previous five winters, indicating that the total volume of sea ice has decreased significantly. Though based only on satellite data (which are not ideal for measuring sea ice thickness), this result confirms previous evidence of decreasing sea ice thickness over the past three decades from US and UK submarine sonar measurements. The retreat of Arctic sea ice has geo-political implications, with the Northwest Passage becoming increasingly ice free and fully open to shipping. There are other important implications; by reducing the reflectivity (albedo) of the Earth's surface, it increases the amount of solar radiation that the surface absorbs, thereby accelerating warming. Temperatures have already risen almost twice as quickly in the Arctic as in the rest of the world over the past 100 years. Sea ice retreat also has significant impacts on Arctic ecosystems, as many organisms (including certain species of fish) depend on its presence for survival. DECC is continuing to seek updated assessments of Arctic sea ice conditions and impacts from UK and international experts.

(HC Deb 23 February 2009 Vol 488 c293W)

Part Eleven: II. *Seas and Vessels—Territorial sea, including overflight*

11/2 (See also **5/62**)
Gibraltar

In reply to a question about the territorial waters of Gibraltar, an FCO Minister wrote:

There have been no recent talks between the UK and either Spain or Gibraltar on the sovereignty of territorial waters. The Government are fully confident of its sovereignty over British Gibraltar Territorial Waters (BGTW) and continues to make this clear to Spain whenever appropriate. However, the UK has made written and oral representations to Spain regarding European Commission Decision 2009/95/EC. Under the decision, Spain has put forward a site of community importance under the Habitats Directive which encompasses BGTW, including an existing site designated by the UK under the same directive. As the UK is the only member state competent to propose a site covering BGTW, we do not recognise the validity of the adopted site. The UK is deeply concerned that Spain should seek to designate an area of BGTW and that this designation should have been approved.

(HC Deb 19 May 2009 Vol 492 c1328W)

11/3

The Government were asked whether progress has been made to annul European Commission Decision 2009/95/EC which designated British Gibraltar territorial waters as being under the control of Spain; whether they have made representations to the Kingdom of Spain and to the European Commission; and, if so, what has been the response in each case. The Minister for Europe wrote:

European Commission Decision 2009/95/EC did not designate British Gibraltar territorial waters (BGTW) as being under the control of Spain. Rather, Spain proposed an area, which included BGTW, to the Commission as a site of community importance (SCI) and the decision confirmed the listing of this site. We have clearly stated that we do not recognise the listing as the United Kingdom is the only state competent to include a site within BGTW on a list of SCIs submitted to the Commission.

We are deeply concerned that Spain should seek to have an area of BGTW listed and that this listing should have been approved. We have made representations to both the European Commission and Spain on this matter and will continue to do so in order to redress this issue. In the mean time, we have placed on record that the UK does not recognise the validity of the Spanish listing.

Separately we are aware that the Government of Gibraltar have commenced an action against the European Commission in the European Court of First Instance seeking annulment of the relevant listing. At the end of 2008 Spain put forward a "Site of Community Importance" (SCI) under the habitats directive which encompasses British Gibraltar Territorial Waters (BGTW). As the Commission only consulted each state bilaterally on the sites it put forward, the UK discussed only our own proposed sites (including two in Gibraltar) with the Commission. We therefore discovered the existence of the Spanish site in BGTW only after the complete list of sites across the EU was published in February 2009.

The Government have however, within the time allowed, requested permission to intervene in support of the Government of Gibraltar legal case against the European Commission relating to a Site of Community Interest (SCI) proposed by Spain which overlaps with British Gibraltar Territorial Waters (BGTW) (case T-176/09). We await a response from the court to our request.

The case does not concern a Spanish claim to BGTW. In fact the case involves an Article 230 application before the Court of First Instance by the Government of Gibraltar for annulment of Commission Decision 2009/95/EC, made under the habitats directive, to the extent that the listing of the Spanish SCI, Estrecho Oriental, includes British Gibraltar Territorial Waters (BGTW) and an area of the high seas beyond BGTW.

On 7 August 2009 the Government requested permission from the Court of First Instance to intervene in support of the Government of Gibraltar (GoG) against the European Commission seeking annulment of Commission Decision 2009/95/EC in so far as it includes a Site of Community Interest (SCI) proposed by Spain which overlaps with British Gibraltar Territorial Waters (BGTW) (case T-176/09). It should be noted that at this stage, in requesting permission from the court to intervene, we have not submitted our substantive written intervention. We are currently awaiting a response from the court to our request.

The UK is the only state competent to include a site within BGTW on a list of SCIs submitted to the Commission. We have placed on record that the UK does not recognise the validity of the Spanish listing.

(HC Deb 12 October 2009 Vol 497 c41W)

11/4

An FCO Minister wrote:

On Monday 7 December 2009, officers from a Spanish Civil Guard patrol boat chased another vessel into British Gibraltar territorial waters and then ashore in Gibraltar. We consider that their actions exceeded their jurisdiction and failed to respect the UK's sovereignty, and we have formally protested. Spanish authorities have apologised for the error and stressed there was no political motive. We welcome this. Officials from the UK, Spain and Gibraltar are committed to working together through the Trilateral Forum to improve law enforcement co-operation, and we welcome ongoing co-operation between police services from Gibraltar and Spain.

(HL Deb 15 December 2009 cWA211)

11/5

Maritime and Coastal Access Bill

In a debate on the Maritime and Coastal Access Bill, a Minister said:

In this opening debate, I stress that IFCAs [In-shore Fishery and Conservation Areas] will be different from sea fisheries committees in a number of ways. As we have discussed, the membership will be different. We are also introducing a clear duty on inshore fisheries and conservation authorities to ensure that the exploitation of sea fisheries resources is undertaken sustainably. That duty includes the need to protect the marine environment from the impact of fishing activity. This is at the heart of the model for inshore fisheries and conservation authorities. . . . [I was asked] about the limit of six nautical miles. IFCAs will be responsible for the enforcement of legislation regulating inshore fisheries out to six nautical miles; that is the same as sea fisheries committees now, with the addition of marine species management in estuaries. This will bring together responsibility for inshore fisheries management into one organisation, thereby streamlining the delivery landscape and ensuring efficient use of resources.

We have heard already that between six and 12 nautical miles, access rights for certain member states are set out in the common fisheries policy. Limiting IFC districts to six nautical miles avoids the need for IFCAs to submit all their by-laws to the European Commission and affected member states for approval. We have the option, in the light of circumstances and if we feel it necessary, to extend the seaward jurisdiction of IFCAs out to a maximum of 12 nautical miles. That provision gives us the required flexibility.

(HL Deb 16 March 2009 Vol 709 c21)

11/6
Northern Ireland

The Government were asked (a) what was the extent of the United Kingdom's territorial seas adjacent to Northern Ireland; (b) what part of the sea within the British fishery limits would be lost if Northern Ireland were no longer in the United Kingdom; and (c) what part of the sea would be shared by the remainder of the United Kingdom and the former Northern Ireland if Northern Ireland was no longer in the United Kingdom. A Minister wrote:

(a) The territorial sea limit adjacent to Northern Ireland is 12 nautical miles, calculated from a normal baseline, except where the coasts of Northern Ireland and Scotland are less than 24 nautical miles apart, where a median line is the limit. The approximate area is 1,380 square nautical miles. Regarding parts (b) and (c), there are two small areas of British fishery limits adjacent to Northern Ireland. The area to the north off County Londonderry is approximately 75 square nautical miles and the area to the south off County Down is approximately 439 square nautical miles. It is not possible to say what the position would be in the hypothetical circumstance suggested by the question. The Belfast Agreement and the Northern Ireland Act 1998 make clear that Northern Ireland in its entirety remains part of the UK and shall not cease to do so without the consent of a majority of the people of Northern Ireland.

(HL Deb 5 February 2009 Vol 707 cWA143)

11/7
Somalia

The Foreign Secretary wrote:

The international community, including the UK, is keen to ensure that illegal fishing does not occur in Somali territorial waters, and to this end is seeking to help Somalia regularise its maritime claims and laws relating to maritime security. This would be the essential first step towards establishing what fishing activity could be regarded as illegal, as well as towards credible and effective fisheries licensing and enforcement.

We recognise the concerns of the Transitional Federal Government of Somalia (TFG) and the Somali population about illegal fishing. The international community, including the EU, is engaging with the TFG on this issue both on the UN Security Council and in the Contact Group on Piracy off the Coast of Somalia.

(HC Deb 30 November 2009 Vol 501 c431W)

Part Eleven: VI. *Seas and Vessels—Exclusive economic zone, exclusive or preferential fisheries zone*

11/8

The Marine and Coastal Access Act 2009 provides in s.41 for an Exclusive Economic Zone for the UK, subject to action by the devolved authorities as appropriate. S.42 provides for a 'UK Marine Area', as defined in detail in the section. S.110 makes provision for criminal jurisdiction over offences, *inter alia*, committed in the Exclusive Economic Zone and the Maritime Area.

[These sections were brought into force from 12 January 2010 by The Marine and Coastal Access Act 2009 (Commencement No.1 and Transitional Provisions) Order 2009, SI No.3345/2009 for the UK area and the Welsh zone, Ed.]

11/9 (See also **9/1**)

The FCO replied to a Freedom-of-Information request:

The island of Rockall was annexed to the Crown by proclamation in 1955, and was incorporated into Scotland by the Island of Rockall Act 1972. The rock had no bearing in the designation of the UK continental shelf, but we did claim a 200 mile Fisheries Zone drawn from the rock until our ratification of UNCLOS in 1997, when we relinquished this zone. Rockall comes under article 121.3 of UNCLOS, which states that "Rocks which cannot sustain human habitation or economic life of their own shall have no exclusive economic zone or continental shelf." Rockall does have a 12 mile territorial sea limit, to which UK sovereignty extends under the provisions of UNCLOS. The rock has no bearing on any claim to extended continental shelf and, apart from its 12 mile territorial sea limit, does not play any part in fisheries zones. There has been no conference between the UK, Denmark, Iceland and Ireland to discuss either Rockall, or the question of exclusive economic zones. Perhaps you are thinking of an informal meeting held between officials of those four governments, who met in Torshavn in June 2009, to discuss issues relating to the continental shelf in the Hatton Rockall area of the north-east Atlantic. This was the latest in a series of such meetings, and the officials agreed to meet again in Dublin in the first half of 2010. The United Kingdom and Ireland have both made submissions to the UN Commission on the Limits of the Continental Shelf in respect of the seabed in the Hatton Rockall Area. Details of these submissions, and the responses made by Denmark and by Iceland, can be found at the following link: www.un.org/depts/los/clcs_new/commission_submissions.htm

(Freedom of Information request 0814–09, 9 October 2009, <www.foi.fco.gov.uk>)

Part Eleven: VII. *Seas and Vessels—Continental shelf*

11/10

The Foreign Secretary was asked in which areas of the world the UK was making territorial claims. An FCO Minister wrote:

The UK is not making any territorial claims as such. In relation to the continental shelf, where as a coastal state the UK would have limited rights to explore and exploit the natural resources of the seabed and subsoil, the UK has, to date, made two submissions to the UN Commission on the Limits of the Continental Shelf. These relate to the continental shelf beyond 200nm in the Bay of Biscay (jointly with France, Ireland and Spain), and around Ascension Island. This has been done in accordance with Article 76 of the UN Convention on the Law of the Sea.

(HC Deb 18 March 2009 Vol 489 c1186W)

11/11

The Government submitted the following claims to the outer continental shelf:

Submission in respect of the Falkland Islands, and of South Georgia and the South Sandwich Islands Executive Summary

1 Introduction This submission to the Commission on the Limits of the Continental Shelf is made by the United Kingdom of Great Britain and Northern Ireland (UK) pursuant to Article 76, paragraph 8 of the Convention jointly on behalf of the UK Overseas Territory of the Falkland Islands, and the UK Overseas Territory of South Georgia and the South Sandwich Islands and in support of the establishment of the outer limit of the continental shelf in the area around those Territories.

The Falkland Islands The Falkland Islands are a UK Overseas Territory of around 700 islands in the South Atlantic, the largest being East Falkland and West Falkland. They are situated about 770 km (480 nautical miles) north-east of Cape Horn and 480 km (300 nautical miles) from the nearest point on the South American mainland.

Supreme authority is vested in HM The Queen and exercised by a Governor, resident on the Falkland Islands, on her behalf, advised by the Falkland Islands Executive and Legislative Assembly, and in accordance with the Falkland Islands Constitution.

South Georgia and the South Sandwich Islands South Georgia and the South Sandwich Islands are a UK Overseas Territory and lie south of the Southern Ocean Convergence. South Georgia is a crescentshaped island about 185 km (100 nautical miles) long and between 1.85 and 45 km (1 to 24 nautical miles) wide. South Georgia lies between 53°56' and 54°55'S, and is situated 1,370 km (740 nautical miles) east-south-east of the Falkland Islands and 4,815 km (2,600 nautical miles) from South Africa. The South Sandwich Islands lie in an arc some 740 km (400 nautical miles) further south-east and consist of a chain of 11 volcanic islands approximately 400 km (215 nautical miles) in length.

Supreme authority is vested in HM The Queen and exercised by a Commissioner, resident on the Falkland Islands, on her behalf in accordance with the constitution of South Georgia and the South Sandwich Islands. Two Government Officers live on South Georgia at King Edward Point but the majority of administration is carried out from Stanley by officers of the Government of South Georgia and the South Sandwich Islands.

2 Outer limit of the continental shelf in the region of the Falkland Islands, and of South Georgia and the South Sandwich Islands The present submission deals only with the outer limit of the continental shelf in the region of the Falkland Islands, and of South Georgia and the South Sandwich Islands region, and is thus a partial submission of the UK.

3 Provisions of Article 76 invoked The outer limits contained in this submission are based on the provisions of Article 76, paragraphs 4 (a) (ii), 4 (b), 5 and 7.

4 Names of any Commission members who provided advice during the preparation of the submission No advice was provided by any member of the Commission.

5 Other Potential Overlapping Submissions In accordance with Article 76 paragraph 10 and Article 9 of Annex II of the Convention, and paragraph 2(a) of Annex 1 to the Commission's Rules of Procedure (CLCS/40/Rev.1), the UK wishes to inform the Commission that the subject of this partial submission is also the subject of a submission by Argentina.

In accordance with paragraph 2(b) of Annex I to the Commission's Rules of Procedure, the UK wishes to inform the Commission that, in its view, this partial submission and the recommendations of the Commission made in respect of it will not prejudice matters relating to the delimitation of boundaries between the UK and any other State.

The United Kingdom has no doubt about its sovereignty over the Falkland Islands, South Georgia and the South Sandwich Islands and the surrounding maritime areas.

Figure 1: [Not reproduced, Ed.] Outer limit of the continental shelf beyond 200M for the Falkland Islands, South Georgia and the South Sandwich Islands region. In accordance with the UK's Note No. 168/08 of 9 May 2008, this submission does not include areas of continental shelf appurtenant to Antarctica.

(<http://www.un.org/Depts/los/clcs_new/commission_submissions.htm/>)

A note added:

Commission on the Limits of the Continental Shelf (CLCS), Outer limits of the continental shelf beyond 200 nautical miles from the baselines:

Submissions to the Commission: Submission by the United Kingdom of Great Britain and Northern Ireland

On 11 May 2009, United Kingdom of Great Britain and Northern Ireland submitted to the Commission on the Limits of the Continental Shelf, in accordance with Article 76, paragraph 8, of the United Nations Convention on the Law of the Sea, information on the limits of the continental shelf beyond 200 nautical miles from the baselines from which the breadth of the territorial sea is measured in respect of the Falkland Islands, and of South Georgia and the South Sandwich Islands.

It is noted that the Convention entered into force for the United Kingdom of Great Britain and Northern Ireland on 24 August 1997.

According to the submitting State, "this represents the final partial submission to the Commission which the United Kingdom will make to the Commission, prior to the deadline of 13 May 2009."

In accordance with the Rules of Procedure of the Commission, a communication is being circulated to all Member States of the United Nations, as well as States Parties to the Convention, in order to make public the executive summary of the partial submission, including all charts and coordinates contained in that summary. The consideration of the partial submission made by the United Kingdom of Great Britain and Northern Ireland will be included in the provisional agenda of the twenty-fifth session of the Commission to be held in New York in March-April 2010.

Upon completion of the consideration of the submission, the Commission will make recommendations pursuant to Article 76 of the Convention.

(<www.un.org/Depts/los/clcs_new/submissions_files/submission_gbr_45_2009.htm>)

Part Eleven: VIII.A. *Seas and Vessels—High seas—Freedom of high seas, including overflight*

11/12 (See also **15/14**)
The Foreign Secretary replied to the FAC's Report on 'Global Security: Non-Proliferation'. The FAC had written:

Restricting the resources required for proliferation2. We conclude that the UK's failure so far to ratify the 2005 Protocol to the 1988 Convention for the Suppression of Unlawful Acts Against the Safety of Maritime Navigation is regrettable, given the way in which the Protocol will strengthen the UK's ability to impede the trafficking by sea of WMD-related materials. We further conclude that the provisions of the planned Transport Security Bill which will facilitate UK ratification are to be welcomed, and look forward to their early passage. We recommend that the Government should work actively to secure ratifications of the Protocol by other states so that it may rapidly enter into force. (Paragraph 33)

The Government wrote:

The UK Government welcomes the Committee's interest in the SUA Protocols and agrees with their assessment that they will strengthen the UK's ability to impede the trafficking by sea of WMD-related materials. There are now legal questions which need to be clarified before the relevant legislation can be brought before Parliament, to facilitate UK ratification of the SUA Protocols. The Foreign and Commonwealth Office is working with other relevant Government Departments to resolve the legal issues as soon as possible but it is unlikely that such a Bill will be included in the 09/10 Parliamentary session. Despite this regrettable handicap, the Government will continue to encourage other states to ratify the SUA Protocols.

(Fourth Report from the Foreign Affairs Committee, 2008–2009, Global Security: Non-Proliferation, Response of the Secretary of State for Foreign and Commonwealth Affairs, Cm 7692)

Part Eleven: VIII.D. *Seas and Vessels—High seas—Piracy*

11/13 (See also **8/5**)
The Defence Secretary was asked what progress had been made towards reaching an international agreement on a legal framework for the detention and trial of pirates. A Defence Minister wrote:

Piracy is a crime of universal jurisdiction which any state is entitled, as a matter of international law, to prosecute. However it remains for individual countries to ensure legislation or suitable arrangement are in place for the detention and trial of pirates. In line with UN Security Council Resolution 1851, the inauguration of the International Contact Group on Piracy off the Coast of Somalia took place on 14 January to discuss an international response to piracy. The Contact Group was attended by 24 countries and five organisations, including UK representatives. One of the key focus areas is strengthening judicial frameworks for arrest, prosecution and detention of pirates, exploring regional arrangements, bilateral arrangements, and international judicial systems. A working group is taking forward discussions on this important issue.

(HC Deb 26 January 2009 Vol 487 c39W)

11/14
The Transport Secretary was asked he will hold discussions with his European and US counterparts on counter-piracy and counter-terrorism measures aboard passenger cruise ships. A Minister wrote:

Currently there are no plans for Department for Transport Ministers to hold discussions with European or US counterparts on improving counter-piracy and counter-terrorism measures on board passenger cruise ships. The Government work with international partners, including the International Maritime Organization, to ensure UK registered cruise ships are given the best advice available to prevent acts of piracy and terrorism. We undertake a programme of inspection to check that our ships are complying with their on board counter-terrorism security plans. Such plans are approved by the Department for Transport as meeting the relevant provisions of the Safety of Life at Sea Convention, the International Ship and Port Facility Code and European Regulation. Our advice on preventing pirate attacks, including the measures that can be taken on board ships, is contained in Marine Guidance Note 298.

(HC Deb 5 February 2009 Vol 487 c1388W)

11/15
A Minister wrote about aspects of the control of operations against piracy off Somalia:

The Council of Ministers agreed in a Joint Action at the General Affairs and External Relations Council on 10 November 2008 to establish operation Atalanta and that it should be launched in December 2008. A draft of the Joint Action was cleared in advance by the European Scrutiny Committee on 22 October 2008. The final version of the Joint Action was submitted to the European Scrutiny Committee by the Foreign Office on 10 November 2008... In his role as EU Operation Commander for operation Atalanta, Rear Admiral Philip Jones is accountable to the Political and Security Committee, a Council body in which ambassadors from each of the EU member states exercise political control and strategic direction over the operation, on instructions from national authorities.

The Political and Security Committee reports regularly on the progress of the operation to the Council of Ministers, which comprises national Ministers from each of the EU member states... Ships made available voluntarily by countries to participate in EU-led military operations come under the command of the relevant Operation Commander. An Operation Commander is appointed for each EU-led military operation by the Council of Ministers of the European Union. Ships participating in Operation Atalanta, for example, come under the command of the Operation Commander Rear Admiral Philip Jones RN based in his operation headquarters at Northwood. The Operation Commander for each EU-led military operation reports to the Political and Security Committee...

(HC Deb 9 March 2009 Vol 489 c178W)

11/16

Answering questions on piracy an FCO Minister wrote:

The last pirates detained by the Royal Navy were those captured by HMS "Cumberland" in the Gulf of Aden on 11 November 2008. As piracy is a crime of universal jurisdiction, they were transferred to Kenya for investigation. They have been charged with piracy offences under Kenyan law and are currently being prosecuted in Kenya. The Piracy Act 1837 deals with piracy with violence; the punishment for piracy is life imprisonment. In addition, the United Nations Convention on the Law of the Sea 1982, which defines piracy, was incorporated into UK law by the Merchant Shipping and Maritime Security Act 1997, Section 26 and Schedule 5.

(HL Deb 9 March 2009 Vol 708 cWA211)

11/17

The Government were asked by the House of Lords Committee on European Scrutiny, Sub-Committee C, what were the arrangements for dealing with pirates once they had been captured in the EU operation; how arrangements differed between different Member States; what legal protections and guarantees were in place to ensure their rights were respected and upheld; and what monitoring mechanisms were in place to ensure that countries which had agreed to receive and prosecute pirates implement their commitments on human rights. The Government were asked, further, how far the protection of human rights of the pirates obstructed the operation and prevented its effectiveness. An FCO Minister said:

On the latter point, much of what is behind that question lies this controversy at the beginning where we were extremely reluctant to bring pirates back to the United Kingdom for trial for fear that they would then try to claim refugee status. I, on behalf of the Foreign Office, approached the Kenyan Foreign Minister to secure his agreement to trials in Kenya. We are very clear; our policy is that we will not allow transfer to third States for prosecution unless we are satisfied that they will not be subject to cruel treatment, death penalty or face a trial which is grossly unfair. In November 2008 HMS Cumberland captured eight pirates and in the absence of a MoU, were transferred to Kenya authorities on an exchange of notes. However in December our MoU with the Kenyans was signed by [a Home Office Minister] in Kenya. The HMS Cumberland trial began in January and is currently underway. Our legal advisers are completely satisfied that we have got suitable guarantees on the standard of prisoner handling and sentencing. Since then, the Europeans have said they would not mind having one of those agreements too, so they have now negotiated basically the same MoU with the Kenyans. [The UK-Kenya MoU is not publicly available but see EU-Kenya MoU OJ L 79/49, which the UK MoU is believed to closely resemble, Ed.] That, of course, has raised understandably on the Kenyan side an alarm that they are going to get their whole court system clogged up with pirates which, given these numbers, would not be the case. Therefore, the EU is now trying to negotiate a similar agreement with Tanzania so there are at least two choices of where pirates might be taken. I might add that the MoU specifically includes provision in it enabling access by international organisations to monitor prisoner conditions.

The Minister continued:

...I do not think the pirates relish the prospect of a Kenyan jail sentence - they would probably prefer a British prison - so we are meeting that. We will need to see what the sentences are at the end of this current trial. I think that will give us a yardstick going forward. [Qs 62, 63]

[Eight pirates captured by HMS Cumberland were convicted in Kenya and sentenced to twenty years in jail (<www.ukun.fco.gov.uk/en/news/?view=News&id21878552>, 12 March 2010). Kenya later said that it was refusing to take any more pirate suspects (it held more than 100 in custody) and was reconsidering its MoU with the EU, <http://bbc.co.news/2/hi/8599347.stm>, 1 April 2010, Ed.]

The Minister told the Sub-Committee:

The handling of hostage situations is a national responsibility. It is a curious, you might argue, anomaly of international law that paying a ransom is not illegal. Ship owners say that the ability to pay ransom is absolutely critical to saving the lives of their crews and are universally in favour of it, despite the fact that it, of course, amounts to both an incentive for further hostage taking and a huge tax on their operations. We are very clear that while we recognise this practice goes on, we will not be a party to it. We do not endorse or condone it, we do not participate in it, but it is a reality of this situation. Perhaps the other bit I should say...is that more broadly on land-based operations, not so much the hostage end of it, but the United Nations Security Council Resolution 1851 adopted last December does authorise military operations against pirate bases on land in Somalia. While this authority has not been used at this point, it is very much something that is there in reserve and obviously I do not want to comment on it too much because of the operational sensitivity, but it should give pirates pause for thought because it means we can pursue them on land now. [Q. 79]

(European Union Select Committee, Sub-Committee C: Foreign Affairs, Defence and Development Policy (Lords), 19 March 2009)

11/18
The Defence Secretary was asked what protocols governed the seizure of suspected pirate ships and their equipment by British armed forces. A Minister wrote:

Royal Navy vessels participating in counter-piracy operations are provided with detailed rules of engagement (ROE) setting out the measures they may take in relation to pirate vessels, including the seizure of suspected pirate vessels and equipment. These ROE are in accordance with international law, including the United Nations convention on the law of the sea (UNCLOS), and are kept under regular review. I am withholding details of ROE as their release would be likely to prejudice the capability, effectiveness or security of our armed forces.

(HC Deb 30 March 2009 Vol 490 c894W)

11/19
The Defence Secretary was asked what seized property had been transferred to the Kenyan authorities by the EU-led naval force under the Provisions of Transfer of Suspected Pirates and Seized Property published in the Official Journal of the European Union of 25 March 2009. A Defence Minister wrote:

Operation Atalanta is an EU led operation and the operational detail requested is held by the EU Operation Commander for Atalanta, who reports to EU member states sitting in the Political and Security Committee in Brussels. The EU-led naval force (EUNAVFOR), Operation Atalanta, where practicable, has handed over seized property such as skiffs (small boats) and other pirate related paraphernalia such as ladders, buoys and weapons. In some cases the skiffs and weaponry have been destroyed by the detaining ship for navigational and safety of life reasons. All of the incidents in which suspected pirates have been detained by EUNAVFOR are currently being prosecuted by the Kenyan authorities and therefore a more specific answer is not possible without jeopardising the court proceedings.

(HC Deb 18 May 2009 Vol 492 c1172W)

11/20
A Minister wrote:

In the last 12 months, the Royal Navy has seized weapons from suspected pirates in accordance with the United Nations Convention on the Law of the Sea (UNCLOS) Article 105.

(HC Deb 20 July 2009 Vol 496 c889W)

11/21

A Minister wrote:

The Government are taking a comprehensive approach to piracy off the coast of Somalia. This involves close co-ordination among all relevant government departments, the UK shipping industry, the International Maritime Organisation and the wider international community. The aim is to reduce the risk to vessels transiting the seas off the Horn of Africa while tackling piracy at its root—instability in Somalia—through the provision of humanitarian and development assistance. UN Security Council Resolution 1851 established a Contact Group on Piracy off the Coast of Somalia (CGPCS) whose work is taken forward by four working groups. The UK chairs Working Group 1 on operational co-ordination and regional capacity development. The Royal Navy is actively countering piracy around the Horn of Africa and is playing a leading role in international efforts to do so. The UK is at the forefront of the European mission, Operation ATALANTA, providing the operation commander and the operation headquarters at Northwood. The UK commands the Standing NATO Maritime Group (SNMG), which has a counter-piracy mandate, from HMS "Cornwall". We are also providing ships to the Combined Maritime Forces (CMF), which conduct maritime security operations in the region. Operation ATALANTA is achieving positive results in providing protection to World Food Programme (WFP), AMISOM reinforcements and other vulnerable shipping. ATALANTA has delivered a significant reduction in the number of successful attacks in the internationally recognised transit corridor in the strategically critical Gulf of Aden through close co-operation with the international shipping industry. Thirty-six shipments of WFP shipping have been escorted, which equates to 243,179 metric tonnes of food. This is an important first step in a comprehensive approach to tackling the problem of piracy on land. ATALANTA has warships from 10 European countries, including Norway, on patrol in the Gulf of Aden and the Somali Basin. The Maritime Security Centre (Horn of Africa) has been established at Northwood and is a world-leading example of military co-ordination and co-operation with industry, set up by the UK-led European operation. ATALANTA is also leading the way in encouraging the Somali authorities to take ownership of the problem and is working in support of the European Commission—a good example of military-civil-diplomatic co-operation. The UK and EU are at the forefront of the international response to piracy, whether it is through legal arrangements for the prosecution of detainees in Kenya and other regional nations, involvement in the Contact Group on Piracy off the Coast of Somalia (CGCPS) or co-chairmanship of the military co-ordination mechanism known as the shared awareness and deconfliction meeting (SHADE), which brings together EU, NATO, CMF with China, Russia, Japan and India, among others. More than 80 suspected pirates have been apprehended by UK and EU warships in the past few months and they are currently being processed through the Kenyan legal system. The warships and maritime patrol aircraft are fully engaged in protecting merchant ships, disrupting pirate activity, pursuing suspects and helping regional nations improve their own capacity to deal with the problem.

(HL Deb 12 October 2009 Vol 713 cWA18)

11/22

A Minister wrote:

Although this year has seen an increase in the number of attempted pirate attacks (156 attacks from January-September 2009, compared to 111 attacks from January-September 2008), the number of successful attacks has reduced significantly, especially in the critical Gulf of Aden transit artery. According to International Maritime Bureau statistics the actual rate of successful hijacking against attacks has reduced from one in three in December 2008 to one in 11 in June 2009. Up to 30 September 2009 the EU Naval Force had successfully escorted 44 World Food Programme (WFP) vessels, providing 220,880 tons of aid to Somalia, which the WFP would otherwise not have been able to send. Furthermore international efforts to tackle piracy off the coast of Somalia have achieved unprecedented levels of naval coordination with international partners including India and China coordinating their efforts with EU, North Atlantic Treaty Organisation and coalition forces through a Shared Awareness and Deconfliction forum. The Contact Group of Piracy off the Coast of Somalia (CGPCS) represents 53 nations. The CGPCS also established the New York Declaration (to which the UK is a signatory) that strengthens best management practices in dealing with piracy as well as supporting regional capabilities to tackle piracy. The international community in conjunction with the International Maritime Organisation have also established a code of best practice for industry while travelling off the coast of Somalia. Between December 2008 and October 2009 there has only been one successful attack on a ship complying with best management practices while transiting the Gulf of Aden. Agreements have been initiated with Kenya and the Seychelles to allow pirates apprehended in the region to be prosecuted there. Collectively, these measures are improving the effectiveness of the international community's efforts to tackle piracy off the coast of Somalia, but in the long term the solution has to be found on land. To this end Working Group 1 (chaired by the Foreign and Commonwealth Office) led a regional needs assessment to the Horn of Africa in September 2009, which provided a clear map on how regional states can be assisted in addressing piracy on land as well as at sea.

(HC Deb 2 November 2009 Vol 498 c666W)

11/23

A Minister wrote:

Royal Navy vessels participating in counterpiracy operations are provided with the required rules of engagement to conduct deterrence and disruption operations. The Royal Navy can seize and dispose of suspected piratical equipment. If it is considered that there is sufficient evidence on which to charge suspected pirates they will be detained and transferred to a regional state for prosecution. The UK has a transfer arrangement with the Kenyan and Seychellois Governments. The guidance given to ships draws on UK and international law, including the United Nations Convention on the Law of the Sea.

(HL Deb 12 November 2009 Vol 714 cWA229)

11/24

The Secretary of State for Defence was asked what steps his Department has taken to contribute to measures to deter piracy in the Gulf of Aden in the last five years; what contribution his Department has received from the governments of *(a)* Kenya and *(b)* the Seychelles in such effects; and what steps are available to armed forces personnel upon detection of an act of piracy on the Gulf of Aden. A Minister wrote:

We are taking the situation off the coast of Somalia very seriously and have played an important role in developing the military response to pirate activity. We have key command roles within all of the international task forces and continue to develop our strategies in line with changing operational and political requirements. Piracy is a symptom of wider instability in Somalia and the MOD continues to work comprehensively with other Government Departments and the International community as part of a coherent strategy to address the root causes of piracy. The UK is providing a sizeable contribution to the military effort in the region and has a leading role in countering pirate activity off the coast of Somalia: MOD has been at the forefront of the European Union mission-Operation Atalanta-since it was introduced in December 2008, providing the Operation Commander, the Operation HQ at Northwood, and a frigate for the first period of the operation. The Royal Navy has a long standing commitment of frigates and a tanker to the Combined Maritime Force conducting maritime security operations in the region. The Royal Navy is a contributor to the Standing NATO Maritime Groups, which at present are rotationally undertaking NATO's counter piracy mission-Operation Ocean Shield. The UK currently has command of Standing NATO Maritime Group 2. The Royal Navy manned UK Maritime Trade Organisation has been supporting Merchant Vessels transiting through the region since 2001. The UK has a bilateral arrangement with the Kenyan and Seychellois Governments which allows the transfer of suspected pirates for prosecution. Kenya is currently prosecuting eight suspected pirates detained by a Royal Navy vessel. We are very grateful for their ongoing support. Royal Navy vessels and coalition forces in the region seek to deter and disrupt pirate activity. Specifically, Royal Navy vessels can actively search for suspected pirate vessels. The Royal Navy can also take robust action to come to the aid of a victim vessel under attack by pirates in international waters. This can again range from deterring and disrupting the attack to the use of reasonable force to defend the victims. However, the safety of any hostages involved remains paramount. If suspected pirates are encountered, a decision will be made by the UK Maritime Component Commander, based on legal advice, on whether or not they could be transferred to a regional state for prosecution. If there is insufficient evidence to be confident of a successful prosecution, they will be released. Any piracy equipment found, such as ladders and weapons will be seized and disposed of accordingly.

(HC Deb 2 December 2009 Vol 501 c728W)

Part Eleven: VIII.E. *Seas and vessels—High seas—Conservation of living resources*

11/25

The Government were asked a number of questions about hunting whales for purposes of scientific research and the 'Chairs' suggestions on the Future of Whaling'. A Minister wrote:

Under the terms of Article VIII of the International Convention on the Regulation of Whaling, Japan's lethal research takes of minke whales in the Southern Ocean and of minke, Bryde's, sei and sperm whales in the North Pacific are, regrettably, quite legal. Any decision by the International Whaling Commission (IWC) to set quotas for North Pacific whale species (whether for highly localised use by the people of coastal communities in Japan who have a tradition of whaling, or for wider commercial use) would require to be framed as amendments to the schedule to the International Convention on the Regulation of Whaling, and could be brought into force only by a three-quarter majority vote of those present and voting at a recognised meeting of the IWC. The intersessional IWC meeting which will take place in Rome from 9 to 11 March has no power to make such decisions... The right of any contracting Government to the International Whaling Commission (IWC) to issue special permits and to conduct lethal research whaling is enshrined in Article VIII of the International Convention on the Regulation of Whaling (ICRW). The Chairs' suggestions do not include any proposal to amend Article VIII. The extent to which current so-called scientific whaling may or may not be curtailed as a result of pursuing any of the options advanced in the Chairs' paper will depend on the willingness of those Governments currently pursuing such operations to scale them back voluntarily, in exchange for other possible concessions. There would be no legal recourse for the IWC if such voluntary action were ever discontinued... Trade matters are within the competence of the Convention on International Trade in Endangered Species and outside that of the International Convention on the Regulation of Whaling... Save through an amendment to Article VIII of the International Convention on the Regulation of Whaling (which would probably require the convening of a formal diplomatic conference to adopt it and subsequent ratification by all parties to bring it into effect), the International Whaling Commission has no power to alter the legal status of whaling under special permit. The UK could agree to the legalisation of other forms of whaling only if it was convinced that by doing so it would bring about a significant improvement of whale conservation in the long term.

(HL Deb 4 March 2009 Vol 708 cWA164-WA165)

11/26

The Government were asked if they would support measures at the IWC meeting which sought to end imports of whale meat by Japan from Norway and Iceland. A Minister wrote:

Trade matters are within the competence of the Convention on International Trade in Endangered Species (CITES) and outside that of the International Convention on the Regulation of Whaling (ICRW), the parent treaty of the International Whaling Commission (IWC). The UK Government firmly support the CITES ban on the international trade in whale meat and whale products. We are increasingly concerned about the trade in whale products between countries holding reservations to the CITES appendix I listing, or to countries which have not joined CITES. To eliminate the unacceptable risk of market-driven whaling in the future, we believe that contracting Governments to the IWC should lift all CITES reservations to cetacean species in order to aid negotiations on the future of the IWC.

(HL Deb 12 March 2009 Vol 708 cWA274)

11/27
A Minister for the Environment, Food and Rural Affairs said:

On 20 October, British officials met the Japanese Government and expressed continued concern about Japanese dolphin hunts, among other things. I wrote personally to the Japanese Fisheries Minister last week on a range of issues, including whaling, and expressed the British public's concern about the hunting of dolphins, urging Japan to prohibit the killing and capture of dolphins and other small cetaceans. We also welcome the reports that Taiji in Japan, which is at the centre of "The Cove"-the file and the film [the film is a dramatic documentary report on the slaughter of dolphins in confined, shallow water, Ed.]-is trialling a no-kill bottlenose dolphin policy.

(HC Deb 29 October 2009 Vol 498 c432)

11/28
A Minister wrote:

On 24 October I wrote to the Japanese Fisheries Minister expressing the UK's continued opposition to the killing of whales in the southern and northwest Pacific oceans and to the hunting of small cetaceans in Japanese coastal waters. At this year's International Whaling Commission meeting in June, I raised concerns over the animal welfare implications of small cetacean hunts. The UK also highlighted the plight of the Dall's porpoise in Japan and the high levels of toxic chemicals found in cetacean meat.

The UK Government will continue to make our position known to Japan at every appropriate opportunity and argue that Japanese whaling operations undermine the credibility of the IWC as an effective organisation for the conservation of cetacean stocks world-wide.

(HC Deb 30 November 2009 Vol 498 c383W)

11/29
A Minister wrote:

I wrote to the Japanese Minister of Fisheries on 24 October expressing the UK's continued opposition to the killing of whales in the Southern Ocean and the North west Pacific and to the hunting of small cetaceans in Japanese coastal waters. On 2 October, the UK took part in a strong diplomatic protest (démarche) to Iceland expressing our extreme disappointment with the killing of almost 200 minke and fin whales this year and called upon the Icelandic Government to review Iceland's Whaling policy. Before the next annual meeting of the IWC Foreign and Commonwealth Office posts will again lobby countries in support of the UK's position, seeking to encourage new anti-whaling nations to join the IWC and endeavouring to change the opinion of Governments which currently support whaling.

(HC Deb 16 December 2009 Vol 502 c1145W)

Part Eleven: XIII. *Seas and Vessels—Protection of the marine environment*

11/30

A Minister wrote:

The Oslo and Paris (OSPAR) Convention has a litter programme which looks at the problem of litter in the north-east Atlantic and is currently investigating how it might be addressed.

Litter has been set out as one of the 11 descriptors of good environmental status (GES) under the EU marine strategy framework directive (MSFD). Member states will be required to assess whether properties and quantities of marine litter are causing harm to the coastal and marine environment and to introduce measures where relevant. No decision has yet been taken on whether a Marine Protected Area will be established in the British Indian Ocean Territory (BIOT). A decision will be taken following the public consultation which is at present underway. The geographic extent of protection will depend on which, if any, of the options for the fisheries is decided upon. The maximum limit of any Marine Protected Area in the BIOT would be within the 200 nautical miles radius of the Environmental Preservation and Protection Zone of the BIOT. This zone was established by formal Proclamation No. 1 of 17 September 2003 and issued by the Commissioner for BIOT. A copy of the Proclamation, together with copies of the relevant charts and co-ordinates was deposited with the UN on 12 March 2004 in accordance with Article 75, paragraph 2 of the Convention on the Law of the Sea, and can be viewed at the following link: www.un.org/Depts/los/LEGISLATIONAND TREATIES/STATEFILES/GBR.htm

(HL Deb 1 December 2009 Vol 715 cWA28)

Part Twelve: Airspace, Outer Space and Antarctica

Part Twelve: I.A. *Airspace, Outer Space and Antarctica—Airspace—Status*

12/1

The Defence Committee recommended to the Government that:

Russia's unauthorised flights into international airspace, including the UK's flight information region, do not pose a direct security threat to NATO or the UK; nevertheless, they are not the actions of a friendly nation and risk escalating tension. A further issue is that Russia's actions threaten the safety of civil flights and risk leading to serious accidents; Russia should not be making such flights without informing the appropriate authorities. The Government should take a more robust approach in making clear to Russia that its continued secret incursions by military aircraft into international airspace near to the UK is not acceptable behaviour. The Government should call on NATO to ensure that it monitors and assesses the threat posed by unauthorised Russian military flights into NATO and international airspace near to NATO's territorial perimeter. (Paragraph 49)

The Government replied that it:

...agrees with the Committee's conclusion that the Russian military flights do not pose a direct security threat to NATO or the UK, but that they risk escalating tension. They are not, however, 'unauthorised': these flights exercising Russian military capability take place in international airspace. As was stated during the evidence sessions, [Defence Committee: Russia: a new confrontation? HC454 (2009), Evidence 21 April 2009, Qs.254–263, Ed.] some flight safety issues have resulted from Russian military aircraft not adhering to International Civil Aviation Organisation regulations. These issues have been mitigated by close liaison between UK Air Defence and Air Traffic Control units and, where necessary, by the launch of UK Quick Reaction Alert aircraft. That said, the safety of civilian flights is an issue that is addressed by the Department of Transport in conjunction with the Civil Aviation Authority. NATO already assesses the threat posed by Russian military flights in NATO and international airspace near its territorial perimeter continuously. We are content that appropriate arrangements are in place in NATO for the surveillance, command and control, and interception of unidentified aircraft under the Allied Command air policing task. (para 49)

(Defence Committee, Sixth Special Report: Russia: a new confrontation? Government Response to the Committee's Tenth Report 2008–2009, HC987 (2008))

12/2

The Defence Secretary wrote:

The Ministry of Defence has a system in place that requires all countries to seek clearance for aircraft registered as military or state aircraft that wish to enter, fly over or depart from UK airspace or for civilian aircraft wishing to land at a military base. All other types of aircraft are subject to the requirements of the Civil Aviation Authority. A request for clearance from the MOD includes the final destination of the flight and details of dangerous cargo that may be in transit. I can confirm that we have had no such requests from the US with regards to flights to Israel through UK airspace in the last six months.

(HC Deb 4 March 2009 Vol 488 c1597W)

Part Twelve: I.B. *Airspace, Outer Space and Antarctica—Airspace—Uses*

12/3

The Foreign Secretary was asked what agreements there were affecting the use of British military airbases for the transfer of weapons from the United States to Israel; and whether the terms of such agreements had been invoked in the last two months. A Minister wrote:

The Ministry of Defence has a system in place that requires all countries to seek clearance for all aircraft registered as military or state aircraft that wish to enter, fly over or depart from UK airspace or for civilian aircraft wishing to land at military bases. All other types of aircraft are subject to the requirements of the Civil Aviation Authority. A request for MOD clearance includes the final destination of the flight and details of any dangerous cargo that may be in transit. I can confirm that we have had no such requests for clearance from the US with regards to flights on to Israel in the last two months.

(HC Deb 5 February 2009 Vol 487 1410W)

Part Twelve: III.B. *Airspace, Outer Space and Antarctica—Antarctica—Uses*

12/4

The Environment Secretary was asked what progress had been made under the Agreement on the Conservation of Albatrosses and Petrels to help reduce the numbers of seabird deaths caused by longline fishing in the British Antarctic Territory; and whether the treaty covered other British Overseas Territories in the region. A Minister wrote:

The waters around the British Antarctic Territory are wholly within the area covered by the Convention on the Conservation of Antarctic Marine Living Resources (CCAMLR). It is mandatory for all long-line fishing vessels to undertake measures to minimise seabird by-catch and to deploy an international scientific observer to monitor compliance with these requirements. In recent years, there has been no by-catch of seabirds in legal fisheries in these waters. There has thus been no need for the Agreement on the Conservation of Albatrosses and Petrels (ACAP) to work to reduce by-catch in these waters and it has instead focused its efforts on by-catch reduction in other parts of the oceans. In those areas the Parties to the Agreement have begun to work with regional fisheries management organisations to advance the use of mitigation technologies as well as to improve by-catch monitoring and have agreed a strategy to take this forward.

The UK's ratification of ACAP includes all UK Overseas Territories in the range of the albatrosses and petrels covered by ACAP, for example, the Falkland Islands, Tristan da Cunha, South Georgia and South Sandwich Islands and British Antarctic Territory.

(HC Deb 19 January 2009 Vol 486 c1011W)

12/5

Asked about what international laws governed drilling and mineral extraction rights in Antarctica, an FCO Minister wrote:

The Protocol on Environmental Protection to the Antarctic Treaty sets out a comprehensive regime for the protection of the Antarctic environment and prohibits any activity relating to mineral resources, other than scientific research. We have received no reports on attempted oil exploration or research in the Antarctic by other countries.

(HC Deb 2 February 2009 Vol 487 c879W)

Part Thirteen: International Responsibility

Part Thirteen: II.C.2. *International Responsibility—General issues of international responsibility—Procedure—Consular Protection*

13/1 (See also **17/31**)
A Minister wrote:

I can confirm the Israeli navy boarded the vessel "Spirit of Humanity" on 30 June 2009. The Israeli navy took control of the vessel and diverted it to Ashdod port in Israel, where all those on board, including six British nationals, were handed over to Israeli immigration officials. British consular officials have had good access to the British detainees and confirm that they are in good health and being treated well. When…the Foreign Secretary spoke to his Israeli counterpart Avigdor Lieberman on 1 July 2009, he raised the issue with him and asked for clarification of whether the "Spirit of Humanity" was intercepted in international waters. We will continue to press the Israeli Government for clarification.

(HC Deb 7 July 2009 Vol 495 c633W)

13/2 (See also **6/11**)
The Foreign Secretary wrote:

Consular staff are specifically trained on what action to take in response to any allegation of mistreatment, and there is clear guidance for such cases. This guidance includes the identification of possible signs of torture and mistreatment, as well as the procedures to be adopted in such circumstances. The first step when a British national is detained overseas is to seek and secure access by our consular staff. Our staff are instructed to ask our nationals whether they have suffered abuse or mistreatment, and to look out for signs of mistreatment even where an individual does not raise it. They are required to follow up all reports of mistreatment whether they come from the individual themselves, from their friends, family or representatives, or from other sources. What form this follow up action will take will depend on the individual circumstances of the case. Most obviously, we can raise our concerns with the relevant authorities. Whatever action we take the objective remains the same: to end the mistreatment, and have the incident investigated and the perpetrators of any abuse brought to justice. In many countries we also raise more general concerns around the mistreatment and abuse of detainees as part of our wider human rights dialogue.

(HC Deb 16 September 2009 Vol 496 cs2231W-2232W)

Part Thirteen: III.A *International responsibility—Responsible entities—States*

13/3
The Government were asked about the implications of non-implementation in Crown Dependencies and British Overseas Territories of international conventions and treaties which the United Kingdom has ratified. A Minister wrote:

If a treaty to which the United Kingdom is a party has been extended to one or more Crown Dependency or Overseas Territory and the Crown Dependency or

Overseas Territory fails to implement the treaty, putting the United Kingdom in breach of its obligations under the treaty, then the United Kingdom is ultimately responsible under international law.

(HL Deb 14 July 2009 Vol 712 cWA197)

13/4
The Foreign Secretary was asked for his assessment of the role of the Iranian Qods force in terrorist activity in the Middle East. He wrote:

The Qods Force (QF) is a branch of the Iranian Revolutionary Guards Force (IRGC). We have previously expressed concern that the IRGC and the IRGC-QF are involved in training, equipping and supplying, to varying degrees, Iraqi armed militia groups, the Taliban, Hezbollah, Hamas and other Palestinian Rejectionist Groups. This further undermines international confidence in the Iranian regime's intentions, and is at odds with the regime's claims to the international community and its own people to want to work for stability, security and prosperity.

(HC 16 December 2009 Vol 502 c1229W)

Part Thirteen: III.C. *International Responsibility—Responsible entities—Entities other than states and international organisations*

13/5
The Government were asked about their policy on meetings with representatives of Hamas. A Minister wrote:

The UK position is clear: we do not believe it is productive to talk to Hamas directly. The military wing of Hamas is proscribed in the UK as a terrorist organisation: they fire rockets at innocent civilians and put ordinary Palestinians in harm's way. We believe that to talk to Hamas directly at this time would simply undermine those Palestinians who are committed to peace. The Arab League has mandated Egypt to communicate with Hamas. We are in regular contact with both the Arab League and Egypt.

(HC 20 July 2009 Vol 496 cs953W-954W)

Part Fourteen: Peaceful Settlement of Disputes

Part Fourteen: II.B. *Peaceful settlement of disputes—Means of settlement—Good offices*

14/1
During a debate in the House of Lords, an FCO Minister said:

[T]he presidents of Armenia and Azerbaijan have met six times during 2009 to take forward negotiations on the Nagorno-Karabakh conflict, including most recently on 22 November. These meetings have been constructive but many issues remain unresolved. We fully support the Minsk process and we have encouraged both sides to continue working towards a peaceful settlement to provide a stable, secure and prosperous future for the people of the region . . .

She continued:

[T]he UK strongly supports the OSCE Minsk process but of course understands the limitations of what has been achieved to date . . . the UK supports the independence, sovereignty and territorial integrity of Azerbaijan in accordance with UN Charter and OSCE principles. We encourage the parties to reach a negotiated settlement, which could include the International Court of Justice. Under the UN Charter, rulings of the ICJ are binding on the parties concerned.

(HL Deb 10 December 2009 Vol 715 cs1143-c1144)

Part Fourteen: II.D. *Peaceful settlement of disputes—Means of settlement—Mediation*

14/2
A Minister wrote:

The UK strongly supports the African Union/UN political process for Darfur led by Joint Chief Mediator Bassole and welcomes also Qatar's important contribution. We have committed £1 million to support the process. We welcomed the signing in Doha on 17 February 2009 of an initial agreement by the Government of Sudan and the Justice and Equality Movement (JEM). We have urged the parties to fully implement the commitments they made. We support the mediators' intention to engage other Darfur leaders and also civil society in further discussions. The UK Special Representative for Sudan, together with his P5 and EU counterparts, reaffirmed their support for the Darfur political process in a meeting in Qatar on 27 May 2009. They jointly urged the Government of Sudan and JEM to show flexibility, stressed the need for input from all sectors of Darfuri society, and reiterated calls for all parties to urgently accept the invitation extended by the mediators. We continue to maintain contact with the government of Sudan and other parties to the conflict to urge them to take concrete steps to find a just and lasting solution to the problems of Darfur.

(HC Deb 1 July 2009 Vol 495 cs289W-290W)

Part Fourteen:II.G.1. *Peaceful settlement of disputes—Means of settlement—Judicial settlement—International Court of Justice*

14/3
The Foreign Secretary was asked what assessment he had made of the implications for UK policy of the Advisory Opinion of the ICJ in the 'Wall case'. An FCO Minister wrote:

The Government agree with the conclusion of the International Court of Justice (ICJ) that the construction of the barrier along the chosen route, and its associated regime, is unlawful under international law. The Government have consistently made this position clear and supported the UN General Assembly Resolution which acknowledged the ICJ advisory opinion on the legal consequences of the construction of the barrier in the Occupied Palestinian Territory. While the advisory opinions of the ICJ are not legally binding, and the UK is not obliged under international law to take such diplomatic action, we continue to lobby the Government of Israel to ensure that any Israeli barrier is routed within Green Line Israel.

(HC Deb 27 February 2009 Vol 488 c1206W)

Part Fourteen: II.G.2. *Peaceful settlement of disputes—Means of settlement—Judicial Settlement—Courts and tribunals other than the International Court of Justice*

14/4 (See also **6/70**)
European Convention on Human Rights

The Government were asked what were the obligations of the United Kingdom under Article 34 of the European Convention on Human Rights where the European Court of Human Rights issues an interim measure under Rule 39 of the Rules of Court. An FCO Minister wrote:

The Government have undertaken, in Article 34 of the European Convention on Human Rights, not to hinder in any way the effective exercise of the right of individual application to the court. The failure of a contracting state to comply with a measure indicated under Rule 39 may entail a breach of Article 34 of the convention. It is the Government's policy to comply with Rule 39 measures indicated by the European Court of Human Rights as a matter of course where it is able to do so. The Government were asked further on how many occasions they had not complied with a decision on interim measures handed down by the European Court of Human Rights.

The Minister wrote: It is the Government's policy to comply with Rule 39 measures indicated by the European Court of Human Rights as a matter of course where it is able to do so. The Foreign and Commonwealth Office is aware of two occasions since February 2005 on which the UK has failed to comply with Rule 39 measures indicated by the court. On the first occasion, in May 2008, the measure (requiring the Government not to remove an individual to China) was communicated to the Government less than half an hour before the plane upon which the applicant was to be removed was due to take off and there was insufficient time to give effect to the measure. The second occasion occurred on 31 December 2008, when the Government took the view that, exceptionally, they could not comply with the measure indicated by the court (not to remove or transfer two individuals in Iraq from the custody of the UK Government). In the wholly exceptional circumstances of that case, and in particular given that continued detention of the individuals would have been unlawful, the Government took the view there was no lawful option other than transfer to the Iraqi authorities. [See **6/57**.]

(HL Deb 2 February 2009 Vol 707 cWA89-WA90)

14/5
The International Criminal Court

The following Statutory Instrument was laid before Parliament on 19 March 2009:

The International Criminal Court (Darfur) Order 2009

In consequence of the referral of the situation in Darfur since 1 July 2002 to the Prosecutor of the International Criminal Court by the United Nations Security Council by Resolution 1593 (2005), it is expedient to make the provision set out in this Order. Her Majesty, by and with the advice of Her Council, in exercise of the powers conferred by section 1 of the United Nations Act 1946(1), as extended by section 23(5) of the International Criminal Court Act 2001(2), makes the following Order in Council–1. This Order may be cited as the International Criminal Court (Darfur) Order 2009.2.–(1) Any state or diplomatic immunity attaching to a person does not prevent proceedings under Part 2 of the International Criminal Court Act 2001 in relation to that person. (2) Paragraph (1) applies to proceedings in relation to a person alleged to have committed an ICC crime, or to have been convicted by the ICC, as a result of the referral of the situation in Darfur since 1 July 2002 to the Prosecutor of the International Criminal Court by the United Nations Security Council by Resolution 1593 (2005). (3) The Secretary of State may in any particular case, after consultation with the ICC and the State concerned, direct that proceedings (or further proceedings) under Part 2 of the International Criminal Court Act 2001 which, but for paragraph (1), would be prevented by state or diplomatic immunity attaching to a person shall not be taken against that person. (4) In this Article, "the ICC" and "ICC crime" have the same meaning as in section 1(1) of the International Criminal Court Act 2001, and "state or diplomatic immunity" has the same meaning as in section 23(6) of that Act.

EXPLANATORY NOTE (This note is not part of the Order)

This Order makes provision so that proceedings under Part 2 of the International Criminal Court Act may be taken against a person who would otherwise enjoy state or diplomatic immunity. It only applies where the person is charged or convicted by the ICC as a result of the referral of the situation in Darfur by the United Nations Security Council.

(The International Criminal Court (Darfur) Order 2009, No. 699/2009)

14/6
The Foreign Secretary gave the following response to the FAC:

The International Criminal Court (ICC) issued its arrest warrant for President Bashir on 3 March 2009 shortly before the publication of the FCO Annual Report on Human Rights. Since the issuing of the arrest warrant, the call for its deferral under Article 16 of the Rome Statute has intensified. We share Human Rights Watch's concern at the subsequent intensification of the campaign and we have made clear that Article 16 is intended for exceptional circumstances only. We would not consider it unless [the Government of Sudan] engaged with the ICC and took bold, concrete action for peace in Darfur, reflected in real change on the ground.

(Response of the Secretary of State for Foreign and Commonwealth Affairs Seventh Report from the Foreign Affairs Committee Session 2008–09, Annual Report on Human Rights 2008, Cm 7723)

14/7
The Foreign Secretary was asked about his assessment of the arrest warrant issued by the International Criminal Court of Sudan's President al-Bashir. A Minister wrote:

We have a long-standing position of support for the work of the International Criminal Court (ICC) as an independent judicial body, and also of not commenting substantively on its decisions. We have consistently urged the Government of Sudan to co-operate with the Court, and reiterated our support for peace in Sudan. We continue to monitor the situation closely, and to make clear our expectation that all countries should cooperate with the ICC investigation, in accordance with UN Security Council Resolution 1593 of 2005, and the particular legal obligations of States Party to the ICC.

(HC Deb 16 December 2009 Vol 502 c1232W)

14/8
Permanent Court of Arbitration

During a debate in the House of Lords, a Minister said:

...we welcome the public commitment made by both parties (viz the government of Sudan and the leaders of the administration in southern Sudan) to abide by the decision of the Permanent Court of Arbitration on the Abyei boundary. The UK urges both parties to ensure that the decision is fully implemented in a timely manner and in a way that does not escalate tensions or cause conflict. This was reiterated by the UN Security Council on 17 July.

(HL Deb 20 July 2009 Vol 712 c1378)

14/9
A Minister wrote:

The UK welcomes progress that has been made in recent months towards implementation of the Comprehensive Peace Agreement (CPA). This includes acceptance by both the Sudanese People's Liberation Movement (SPLM) and the National Congress Party (NCP) of the ruling of the Permanent Court of Arbitration in relation to the Abyei area and both parties' commitment to implement the decision.

The UK also welcomes the signing by the SPLM and NCP under the facilitation of US Envoy General Gration, of the "Points of Agreement" document on the outstanding CPA milestones. We are concerned however that further progress is required on several critical issues, including agreement of the census results, preparations for the elections in April 2010 and for the referendum on self-determination for South Sudan in 2011. The UK is working closely with both parties and with international partners to press for implementation of the outstanding issues.

(HC Deb 16 September 2009 Vol 496 c2235W)

Part Fourteen: II.I. *Peaceful Settlement of Disputes—Means of settlement—Other means of settlement*

14/10
A Minister wrote:

The Government remain to be convinced of the added practical value to people in the United Kingdom of rights of individual petition to the United Nations. The experiment with the CEDAW Optional Protocol did not provide sufficient empirical evidence to decide either way on the value of other individual complaint mechanisms. We will need further evidence, over a longer period, to establish whether there are practical benefits. We hope that ratification of the Optional Protocol to the Convention on the Rights of Persons with Disabilities will assist in providing us with the evidence we seek.

(HC Deb 21 July 2009 Vol 712 cWA345)

Part Fifteen: Coercive Measures short of the Use of Force

Part Fifteen: I.B. *Coercive Measures short of the Use of Force—Unilateral measures—Counter-measures*

15/1 (See also **11/12**)
The Foreign Secretary replied to the FAC's Report on 'Global Security: Non-Proliferation'. The FAC had written:

11. We conclude that the Government is correct to identify a need to strengthen generic enforcement mechanisms for the Nuclear Non-Proliferation Treaty (NPT), in the face of states which violate and/or withdraw from it. However, we note that the Minister told us that this objective was unachievable at present. We recommend that in its response to this Report, the Government should set out the specific legal and institutional mechanisms for strengthened NPT enforcement which it will be advocating at the 2010 NPT Review Conference. In particular, we recommend that the Government should outline how it envisages that pre-announced penalties for NPT withdrawal might be strengthened. (Paragraph 89)

The Government replied:

[It] believes that the primary objective of an effective nuclear non-proliferation regime must be to prevent non-compliance. Where non-compliance has occurred, we must ensure early detection and certainty of serious consequences for the party responsible. The Government's proposals for strengthening enforcement mechanisms for the Non-Proliferation Treaty (NPT) are set out in chapter six "International governance and the IAEA" of the "Road to 2010 Plan (sections 6.13 to 6.14) [see <www.cabinetoffice.gov.uk/media/224864/roadto2010.pdf>,

Ed.]. We will engage intensively to raise awareness in the broader international community of the dangers to both regional and global security posed by nuclear proliferation and of the imperative to take firm action to prevent it. We believe it is particularly important to clarify the legal requirements set out in Article X of the NPT and the consequences of attempting to withdraw from the Treaty. Where such action could constitute a threat to international peace and security, there should be a much higher cost to the party responsible. The Government fully supports the detailed proposals put forward by the European Union at the 2007 NPT Preparatory Committee, which are available on the official United Nations website at: http://daccessdds.un.org/doc/UNDOC/GEN/N07/330/32/PDF/N0733032.pdf?OpenElement.

(Fourth Report from the Foreign Affairs Committee, 2008–2009, Global Security: Non-Proliferation, Response of the Secretary of State for Foreign and Commonwealth Affairs, Cm 7692)

Part Fifteen: II.A. *Coercive measures short of the Use of Force—Collective measures—United Nations*

15/2
Counter-terrorism

The Exchequer Secretary to the Treasury issued the Ministerial Statements in accordance with a previous written ministerial statement on 10 October 2006, in which the then Economic Secretary undertook to report to Parliament on a quarterly basis on the operation of the UK's counter-terrorism asset-freezing regime. The recent Statements are at: HC Deb 23 February 2009 Vol 488 c3WS; HC Deb 19 May 2009 Vol 492 c11WS; HC Deb 15 July 2009 Vol 496 cs18WS-19WS; HC Deb 30 November 2009 Vol 501 cs105WS-106WS.

15/3

The Exchequer Secretary to the Treasury issued the following Ministerial Statement:

The Government are strongly committed to tackling terrorist finance. Just as there should be no hiding place for those who perpetrate terrorism, so there should be no hiding place for those who finance terrorism. Global measures to freeze the assets of those suspected of involvement in terrorism are an important tool in suppressing terrorist finance. The global framework for freezing terrorist assets was established by United Nations Security Council Resolution 1373, adopted unanimously on 28 September 2001. It is also set out in Special Recommendation III of the Financial Action Task Force, the international standard setting body for anti-money laundering and counter terrorist finance. The United Kingdom gives effect to its international obligations to freeze terrorist assets through Orders in Council under the United Nations Act 1946. The Government report quarterly to Parliament on the operation of the UK's terrorist asset freezing regime. Consistent with our international obligations, the Government have put in place a robust and effective terrorist asset freezing regime. As set out in today's quarterly report to Parliament, as of the end of June 2009, a total of 237 accounts containing £607,661 of suspected terrorist funds were frozen in the UK. As our quarterly reports set out, the UK has an active approach to reviewing cases and to granting exemptions licences to ensure that the asset freezing regime operates in a fair and proportionate way that is consistent with human rights. The Financial Action Task Force reviewed the UK's terrorist asset freezing regime in 2007 and concluded that the UK was fully compliant with international standards, the first country to be awarded the fully compliant rating. The Government keep the asset freezing regime under review to ensure that it remains operationally effective, fair and proportionate. Today the Treasury is laying before Parliament the Terrorism (United Nations Measures) Order 2009. This Order in Council updates the UK's domestic framework for freezing the assets of suspected terrorists.

The overall objective of the changes is to tailor asset freezing restrictions to ensure that the prohibitions are focused more closely on areas of genuine operational concern, in particular the access to, control and use of funds by designated persons; and to strengthen and make more explicit safeguards in how the regime is operated where this can be done without compromising its effectiveness. The main changes set out in the new Order in Council are:

Formally reflecting the Court of Appeal judgment in October last year which struck out the grounds for the Treasury to designate a person when the Treasury has reasonable grounds to suspect that they may be (as opposed to are) involved in terrorism. The introduction of a further safeguard that designations must be necessary for public protection.

Setting a renewable 12-month time limit on designations. Modifying the prohibitions on making funds, economic resources and financial services available for the benefit of a designation person so that they only apply if the designated person obtains, or is able to obtain, a significant financial benefit. The prohibitions on making funds, economic resources and financial available directly to a designated person remain unchanged and are a blanket prohibition. Modifying the prohibition on making economic resources available to a designated person by providing a defence for a person if they did not know and had no reasonable cause to suspect that economic resources which they provided to a designated person would be likely to be exchanged or used in exchange for funds, goods or services. Modifying reporting provisions to bring obligations on money service businesses into line with other financial institutions.

Clarifying and expanding information gathering powers to ensure that the Treasury is able to request information from designated persons in all cases where this is necessary to ensure effective implementation of and compliance with the asset freeze.

Overall, these changes will improve the operation of the asset freezing regime, ensure that it remains fair and proportionate and help facilitate effective compliance by ensuring that prohibitions are more tailored and clearer in how they apply. The Terrorism (United Nations Measures) Order will come into effect on 10 August 2009.

(HC Deb 15 July 2009 Vol 496 cs19WS-20WS)

15/4

The representative of the UK made the following statement in the Security Council in the open debate on the Resolution 1267, 1373 and 1540 Committees. [The Committees are concerned with Al-Qaeda related terrorism, international terrorism generally and nuclear non-proliferation, Ed.]

International terrorism remains one of the principal threats of our time. The appalling attack on UN personnel in Kabul on 28 October was a tragic reminder of the threat faced daily around the world by the UN and its personnel. We offer our condolences to their families and friends... The current stocktaking exercise is an opportunity for dialogue with states whose implementation of Resolution 1373 is inadequate. This is not just a bureaucratic exercise. It should be used to focus on specific challenges identified by CTED [Counter-Terrorism Committee Executive Directorate]. Linked to this, preliminary implementation assessments should be made more user-friendly, so that they can better focus technical assistance. We are pleased that "focused visits" have given CTED greater flexibility and allowed them to conduct more and better targeted visits, focusing on the main issues of concern. This has allowed CTED to draw out examples of good practice to share more widely. We also welcome the strengthening of CTED-CTAG [Counter-Terrorism Action Group] relations, including through more focused local donor meetings... We welcome the Committee's work on the Comprehensive Review of Resolution 1540. It was useful to hear views from the wide range of states and international organisations at the Review's open meeting. And we look forward to its final outcome document, which should contain practical recommendations for improving implementation. We want to see the emphasis now shift further towards effective implementation in those states with more serious deficiencies. Improving the delivery of assistance will be critical. We were pleased that the first meeting of the working group on assistance took place earlier this month, and hope that this will create momentum for a more effective 1540 assistance strategy. The effective organisation of the Comprehensive Review, and the improving work on delivering assistance, show the benefits of the new 1540 Committee Working Group structure. Through the United Kingdom's Global Threat Reduction Programme, we have committed up to $750m towards countering the spread of Weapons of Mass Destruction, supporting the objectives of Resolution 1540. We have undertaken work in 18 countries on projects covering physical protection work, improving the security of materials, contributing to the reduction in chemical weapons stocks, and supporting sustainable employment for former weapons scientists. The UK also continues to support the IAEA Nuclear Security Fund, and doubled our 2009 contribution to $6m... We welcome the substantial advances which Resolution 1822 made to the 1267 Al Qaeda/Taliban sanctions regime. The Committee continues to work hard to ensure that the Resolution is implemented efficiently and effectively... But the Committee has more to do to help make the regime more robust and sustainable. In particular, we need to safeguard the fundamental rights of those designated, and work on improving the credibility of the overall list. As you pointed out in your report, Mr President, the key to this is the delisting procedure. We must be able to demonstrate that it is possible for those designated to come off the list when they no longer pose a threat to international peace and security. That process needs to be more transparent and merit-based. Individuals should be provided with clear, reasoned and timely responses to delisting requests. The United Kingdom remains committed to working with our Security Council partners on the forthcoming Resolution to address these issues and we hope to see a stronger and more effective sanctions regime as a result.

(SC/PV.6217, 13 November 2009)

15/5

The Minister for Europe issued the following Ministerial Statement:

The Government are committed to keeping Parliament informed of the sanctions regimes which the UK implements. Currently the UK implements United Nations sanctions in relation to Al Qaida and the Taliban, Côte d'Ivoire, the Democratic Republic of the Congo, Democratic Peoples' Republic of Korea, Iran, Iraq, Lebanon, Liberia, Sierra Leone, Somalia, Sudan and in relation to terrorism as laid out in UN Security Council Resolution 1373.

The UK also implements sanctions regimes imposed autonomously by the EU in relation to Belarus, Burma, China, the former Federal Republic of Yugoslavia (in connection with individuals indicted by the International Criminal Tribunal for the former Yugoslavia or responsible for certain acts of violence at Mostar), Guinea, the Transnistrian region of Moldova, and Zimbabwe. In accordance with a decision of the Organisation for Security and Co-operation in Europe, the UK implements arms embargoes on Armenia and Azerbaijan. The Government also take full account of the economic community of West African states moratorium on certain exports of small arms and light weapons to economic community of West African states members. A document listing the sanctions regimes and restrictive measures implemented by the UK is being laid in the Libraries of both Houses. It is also published on the Foreign and Commonwealth Office website at: www.fco. gov.uk/en/about-us/what-we-do/services-we-deliver/business-services/export-controls-sanctions/. This document outlines the restrictive measures in place and includes objectives and lift criteria for each regime.

(HC Deb 24 November 2009 Vol 501 c50WS)

15/6
Iran

An FCO Minister wrote:

We have serious concerns about Iranian support for Hezbollah. Iran provides Hezbollah with significant financial resources, military equipment and training. Many of the most lethal and sophisticated weapons that Hezbollah used during the Israel/Lebanon conflict were of Iranian manufacture or procured from Iran. Such support is unacceptable and only serves to undermine regional security.

Arms supplies to Hezbollah are contrary to the arms embargo established by UN Security Council Resolution (UNSCR) 1701. We also have long-standing concerns about the support that Iran provides in the form of funding, arms and training to Palestinian Rejectionist Groups including Hamas, which are undermining peace in the middle east through violence. We hope that Iran will give political and diplomatic support to the Palestinian Authority in its attempts to build institutions and improve security. We understand that Iran continues to hold some al-Qaeda (AQ) members in custody, but that members of AQ and affiliated groups have used, and possibly continue to use, Iran as a base, transit route and refuge. We have urged Iran to act against this and to co-operate fully with the rest of the international community against terrorism, as required by UNSCR 1373. The UK would like to see Iran making a positive contribution to creating a secure, stable and prosperous middle east. But its current behaviour is a cause for serious concern for us and others. Iran needs to work with the international community and its regional neighbours to restore confidence in its intentions.

(HC Deb 2 February 2009 Vol 487 c889W)

15/7

The Foreign Secretary was asked about breaches of the prohibition against the sale, transfer or supply of arms from Iran in Security Council Resolution 1747. He wrote:

I am aware of reports that Iran has breached UN Security Council Resolution 1747 by attempting to transfer arms-related material via the MV Monchegorsk, a Cypriot-flagged vessel. We understand that the MV Monchegorsk was ordered into Limassol harbour by the Government of Cyprus in late January, where it now remains. Cypriot Foreign Minister Marcos Kyprianou has said that the Monchegorsk was in "clear" breach of UN sanctions banning Iran from exporting arms and related material. Cyprus has dealt with the situation effectively and entirely in line with UN and EU requirements. We continue to urge Iran to comply with international law. It is unacceptable that Iran acts in breach of UN Resolutions and such action only serves to further undermine international confidence in Iran.

(HC Deb 13 March 2009 Vol 489 c779W)

15/8

The Foreign Secretary was asked what the Government's policy was on the application of financial sanctions against *(a)* individuals, *(b)* entities and *(c)* organisations involved in Iran's nuclear and ballistic missile programme. He wrote:

The Government fully support the application of financial and other sanctions against individuals, entities and organisations that are involved with, or support, Iran's nuclear and ballistic missile programmes. Five UN Security Council resolutions (UNSCRs) require Iran to suspend enrichment related activities, three of which impose sanctions. The UNSCRs require states to freeze assets owned or controlled by individuals, entities and organisations involved with, or supporting, nuclear activities in Iran. They must also exercise vigilance over Iranian banks.

The Government also strongly support the Common Position and Council Regulation adopted by the EU which implemented UNSCR 1803 in full. Indeed, the EU went beyond the UN by extending financial vigilance against Iran, including a further autonomous asset freeze on individuals and entities involved in Iran's nuclear and ballistic missile programmes, but not specifically listed by the UN.

(HC Deb 16 March 2009 Vol 489 c848W)

15/9 (See also **16/18**)
A Minister wrote:

The Government fully support UN Security Council Resolution (UNSCR) 1747, paragraph five of which calls upon Iran not to supply, sell or transfer directly or indirectly from its territory any arms or related materiel, as well as other relevant UNSCRs including 1701 and 1860. Following a number of interdicted shipments, we assess that Iran continues to act in breach of that Resolution by its ongoing supplying of weapons and funding to militia in Iraq, the Taliban in Afghanistan, Hamas and Hezbollah. This is unacceptable and further undermines international confidence in Iran. We will continue to work through the UN and with international partners to urge Iran to comply with its UN obligations.

(HC Deb 2 November 2009 Vol 498 c662W)

15/10
A Minister wrote:

We have no plans to take specific actions at the UN at this time. However, the UK led the way at the UN to achieve UN Security Council Resolution 1860 which makes clear the need to combat the smuggling of weapons through the tunnels into Gaza. We continue to push for full implementation of this resolution. We have serious concerns about Iranian support for Hezbollah. Iran provides Hezbollah with significant financial resources, military equipment and training. Arms supplies to Hezbollah are contrary to the arms embargo established by UN Security Council Resolution 1701.

We have long-standing concerns about the support that Iran provides in the form of funding, arms and training to Palestinian Rejectionist Groups, including Hamas. These groups undermine peace in the Middle East through violence. We hope that Iran will instead give political and diplomatic support to the Palestinian Authority in its attempts to build institutions and improve security. We understand that members of al-Qaeda and affiliated groups have used, and possibly continue to use, Iran as a transit route for arms smuggling. We have urged Iran to act against this and co-operate fully with the international community against terrorism, as required by UN Security Council Resolution 1373. The UK would like to see Iran making a positive contribution to creating a secure, stable and prosperous Middle East, free from violence. But its current behaviour is a cause for serious concern for us and others. Iran needs to work with the international community and its regional neighbours to restore confidence in its intentions.

(HC Deb 9 July 2009 Vol 495 cs950–951W)

15/11
Lebanon

A Minister wrote:

UN Security Council Resolution (UNSCR) 1701 establishes an area in southern Lebanon free from armed personnel, assets and weapons other than those of the Government of Lebanon and of the UN Interim Force in Lebanon (UNIFIL). The UK believes that UNSCR 1701 is the best way of achieving lasting stability in Lebanon. We are deeply concerned that Hizballah maintains a substantial military capacity. This is a destabilising factor for the whole region. We strongly condemn all violations of UNSCR 1701 and urge its full implementation. We fully support the work of UNIFIL and its continued role in Lebanon.

(HC Deb 9 September 2009 c1963W)

15/12
North Korea

The Government were asked whether British naval vessels have been given authority to compel North Korean ships to dock at foreign ports in support of paragraph 13 of United Nations Security Council Resolution 1874. A Minister wrote:

United Nations Security Council Resolution 1874 does not provide the UK with legal authority to compel North Korean ships to dock at foreign ports. Consequently, Royal Naval ships have not been directed to do so.

(HL Deb 6 July 2009 Vol 712 cWA111)

15/13
Non-proliferation—High Seas Inspections

A Minister wrote:

UNSCR 1874 does not authorise use of force to compel a ship's Master to submit to an inspection either with or without flag state permission. A warship can conduct a hail and query interception-to ask questions or even make assertions. However we do not currently intend to use British naval assets to conduct interdiction on the high seas in support of United Nations Security Council Resolution 1874 and although we will continue to keep the situation under review we have made no assessment of availability at this stage.

(HL Deb 7 July 2009 Vol 712 cWA143)

15/14
Peacekeeping

The Government were asked whether progress had been made in implementing United Nations Security Resolution 1325 on Women, Peace and Security. An FCO Minister wrote:

The implementation of UN Security Council Resolution (UNSCR) 1325 is a global challenge and it is not possible to provide an exhaustive list of progress made. Nationally, the UK's national action plan on UNSCR 1325 provides the framework for domestic activity and gives impetus to our global efforts that include:Increased representation of women at decision-making levels in conflict institutions—the UK has called for progress in the process of appointing women to senior posts in the UN. The UN Secretary-General now routinely insists that there are female candidates on every shortlist for senior appointments in UN peacekeeping missions and headquarters roles. Gender perspectives included as part of peacekeeping operations—the UK consistently requests that women's protection issues and their role in conflict resolution is addressed in mandates for UN peacekeeping missions. Gender advisers or gender focal points are now present in UN-led peacekeeping missions. Training on protection, rights and needs of women in conflict—the UK has run training and awareness raising events for its conflict prevention officers, strategy managers and staff in its UN mission in New York. The UK provides peace support operations (PSO) training to peacekeepers and includes aspects of UNSCR 1325, as they are covered in UK PSO doctrine and training. Protection of women in conflict-affected areas—the adoption of UNSCR 1820 in June 2008 was a significant step forward in strengthening previous calls to address the scourge of widespread sexual violence in conflict-affected situations. The UK was a key driver behind the design and passage of this resolution. The Government also work on the ground in conflict and post-conflict areas to further the aims of UNSCR 1325.

(HL Deb 18 March 2009 Vol 709 cWA60-WA62)

Part Fifteen: II.B. *Coercive measures short of the use of force—Collective measures—Outside the United Nations*

15/15
Burma (See also **6/20**)

A Minister wrote:

Following the sentence imposed on Aung San Suu Kyi on 11 August 2009, the EU put in place further sanctions intended to specifically target the Burmese regime's economic interests, as well as imposing a travel ban on those members of the judiciary responsible for the verdict. These measures came into force on 14 August 2009. The fact that new EU trade and investment is negligible is an indication of the success of this policy. Moreover, these sanctions leave the regime in no doubt about our determination to see real democracy established and human rights respected in Burma. Their objective is to target those individuals and entities that are most closely linked to the regime's misrule, rather than punishing the Burmese population as a whole.

(HC Deb 22 October 2009 Vol 497 c1608W)

15/16
Guinea

The Government were asked about exports to Guinea. A Minister wrote:

All export licence applications are assessed on a case-by-case basis against the National and EU Arms Export Licensing Criteria, taking into account the circumstances prevailing at the time. Licences will not be issued where there is a clear risk that the goods might be used for internal repression or if we assess that goods might be diverted from their stated end use. The UK has not licensed any exports of military equipment to the Government of Guinea since 2000. Following the arms embargo imposed on Guinea by the EU on 27 October 2009, we will not licence any equipment that would be deemed incompatible with our international commitments under the embargo. We are constantly monitoring the situation in Guinea and will continue to take into account any changes in circumstances during our assessment of future applications.

(HC Deb 2 November 2009 Vol 498 c657W)

15/17
Iran (See also **15/3, 16/18**)

A Minister replied to a debate on the settlement by Lloyds TSB of a criminal case in the US involving violations of the sanctions against Iran. He said:

I want first to explain a little more of the facts of the US case; secondly, to explain how the case fits into UK law and international best practice at that time... thirdly, to explain more generally the actions that we have taken to improve the transparency of inter-bank payments and to deal with the financial threats posed by Iran. The US Department of Justice's statement of 9 January 2009 set out that Lloyds TSB committed a violation of the US International Emergency Economic Powers Act—legislation under which the US Executive are able to prohibit transactions in response to an "extraordinary threat" arising outside the United States. Of course, the US has had sanctions in place against Iran since 1979, so now for 30 years. They have been progressively tightened since then due to growing concerns about the Iranian regime's sponsorship of terrorism... and, more recently, its nuclear programme. However, until November last year, US financial sanctions against Iran included a special licensing arrangement... known as the U-turn exception, which allowed some US dollar transactions that involved Iran to be processed through US dollar clearing in New York. Those transactions were allowed if, first, they were sent between two non-US banks; and secondly, if the transactions did not require the debiting or crediting of an account of an Iranian individual or entity managed on the books of a US bank... My understanding is that that was a general licence that could be exercised if those two conditions were met. In other words, the exception applied if the Iranian link to the transaction did not touch the US or a US bank directly. It was designed to prevent US sanctions completely shutting off Iranian access to the dollar, given that oil transactions are globally denominated in US dollars. There was quite a wide interest in Iranian oil sales having such access. The point that I want to underline is that the general licence allowed banks to conduct such transactions with Iran in those circumstances. The US Department of Justice's statement sets out that, between 1995 and 2007, Lloyds TSB, in both the UK and Dubai, made changes to SWIFT messages—messages on the international worldwide funds transfer network, which are known in the US as wire transfers—worth more than US$350 million that involved principally Iran, but also Sudan... and, I understand, Libya as well. That involved removing payment originator information from some inter-bank payment instructions, so that payments would not be identified by US correspondent banks as originating from countries subject to US sanctions. The infringement related to removing originator information, rather than to the transactions themselves. That is quite an important point. The infringement had to do with the removal of that information. I understand that Lloyds TSB ceased removing payment originator information from Iranian transactions in 2003... It is perhaps worth noting that the US banks did process the payments, even though the SWIFT messages did not contain originator information... There is at least a question that ought to be raised about how the transactions were processed by the US banks, even though the messages did not contain originator information. As we have heard, as a result of the breaches of US law, Lloyds has agreed to pay a fine of $350 million. Lloyds has notified the markets of that, and made provisions in its accounts last year for the payment of the penalty. Given its hedging arrangements, the £180 million provision in place in its accounts will, I understand, cover the full size of the penalty. It is important to stress that the US investigation is specific to breaches of US sanctions law... The US investigation does not allege that Lloyds TSB breached international sanctions, or that it facilitated terrorist finance, proliferation finance or money laundering. Indeed, the deferred prosecution agreement between the US authorities and Lloyds records that subsequent screening of the payments routed through the US between August 2002 and the time when the accounts were closed found no matches with names on the US terrorist or weapons of mass destruction watch lists. The US Department of Justice has acknowledged that Lloyds' co-operation with it has provided substantial assistance to the New York District Attorney and the Department of Justice.[I was asked] why no one has been prosecuted in the UK over the issue... the answer is: it is that we can prosecute only for breaches of UK law, and not for breaches of US law. As I have set out, the US case against Lloyds TSB concerns breaches of US sanctions. I certainly have not seen evidence of breaches of UK law in this case. I have seen no evidence of breaches of international sanctions, money laundering rules or terrorist finance rules. That is consistent with the findings in the US case, which is specific to breaches of US sanctions. It is worth noting that the US imposed comprehensive financial sanctions on Iran after the Iranian revolution in 1979; we remember some of the circumstances. However, United Nations and European Union sanctions against Iran have been much more recent, and more targeted. Given the history of relations between the US and Iran, it is not a surprise that breaches of US-Iran sanctions did not necessarily amount to breaches of UK or European Union law.... I shall say a little more about how international banking practice relating to the transparency of inter-bank payments has developed. Decisions on what payment information should be included in SWIFT messages has, in the past, been regarded as a commercial matter for the banks. The decision was dependent mainly on what was required, technically, to allow the SWIFT messaging system to be used successfully. However, new international standards for measures to counter illicit financing were introduced following the 11 September terrorist attacks. The Financial Action Task Force... made nine special recommendations on terrorist financing in 2001, one of which—special recommendation VII—covers wire transfers. It aimed to correct the lack of transparency in inter-bank payments, which was recognised as a potential weakness in the system. Special recommendation VII calls on countries to"take measures to require financial institutions, including money remitters, to include accurate and meaningful originator information... on funds transfers and related messages". That recommendation was agreed in 2001, and was followed up by technical work on how it should be implemented, which continued until 2005. Once the technical work was complete, the European Union decided to implement special recommendation VII at the Community level. That was done through the Transfer of Funds (Information on the Payer) Regulations 2007, known as the wire transfer regulation, which was taken forward during the UK presidency of the EU in 2005. Following an agreement by the Council of Finance Ministers in, I think, November 2006, the regulation came into effect in January 2007. The EU wire transfer regulation requires payments to contain complete information—name, address and account number—on the payer. To remove payment information... is not permitted under the regulation. Until the regulation took effect in January 2007, there was no requirement in UK or EU law for banks to provide full payer information. So the actions of Lloyds TSB involving transactions before January 2007 do not constitute breaches of UK or EU law. And, as I pointed out, Lloyds stopped removing payment information from Iran transactions in 2003, well before 2007 when the legal obligation to do so under UK law and EU law came into effect. Actions to tighten the law have been complemented by efforts by the banking organisations to raise standards of best practice. The Wolfsberg group of international banks has set out what it calls messaging practice standards to ensure that the payment system is not abused. Wolfsberg also acted to encourage SWIFT to make technical changes to the messaging system that will increase the amount of data that accompanies certain kinds of payment. Those changes are expected to come into effect at the end of 2009. In addition, the Basel committee on banking supervision has been considering the issue at the request of the international regulatory community, and will shortly publish its own statement on the steps that banks should take to increase transparency in international payments. Let me conclude by setting out the Government's approach to financial restrictions against Iran. We have been at the forefront of international efforts, in the Financial Action Task Force and the European Union, to strengthen controls on terrorist finance and to improve the transparency of inter-bank payments.... The FATF special recommendation to which I referred was agreed in October 2001, but the specific requirements on banks were not clarified until the Financial Action Task Force agreed an interpretive note in the middle of 2005. [I was asked] why it took so long. That is a fair question. That was the period that the FATF took to achieve and agree that interpretive note. The European Union then acted quite promptly and a proposal was made in July 2005. As I have said, ECOFIN approved the regulation in November 2006, and the regulation took effect on 1 January 2007. I shall set out a little bit more information on UK policy. We have been at the forefront of international efforts, including action to deal with the threats posed by Iran's nuclear programme and by its weak anti-money laundering and terrorist finance controls. We continue to work closely with the US and other international partners to utilise a dual-track strategy towards Iran of pressure and engagement. We have taken a leading role in negotiating international financial measures to maintain pressure on the Iranian Government and to protect our financial systems from abuse. Key measures that we have taken in the past few years include negotiating an international asset freeze against two Iranian banks—bank Melli and bank Sepah—negotiating FATF statements calling on states to protect their financial systems from money laundering and terrorist finance risks emanating from Iran, negotiating an EC regulation requiring banks to undertake enhanced due diligence on Iranian transactions and adopting new domestic powers in the Counter-Terrorism Act 2008 to allow us to impose financial restrictions in response to external money laundering, terrorist finance or weapons of mass destruction proliferation risks. Taken together, those measures and others constitute a robust package of measures to protect our financial sector, which places the UK at the forefront of international action to tackle the threats posed by illicit financing linked to Iran.

(HC Deb 12 February 2009 Vol487 c1577–1581)

15/18
Non-Proliferation

The Foreign Secretary replied to the FAC's Report on 'Global Security: Non-Proliferation':

The FAC had written:

4. We conclude that restricting the finance available to those intending to proliferate nuclear, chemical or biological weapons and their delivery systems is a potentially effective mechanism to achieve non-proliferation aims. We recommend that the Government should consider how this can be done as quickly as possible when proliferation risks are identified. We further recommend that in its response to this Report, or earlier if possible, the Government should send us a copy of the imminent report of the international Financial Action Task Force, with an accompanying memorandum indicating whether, when and how it will implement its recommendations. (Paragraph 39)

The Government replied:

We agree with the Committee that working to restrict the finance available to proliferators is a potentially effective mechanism to achieve non-proliferation aims. HM Treasury are working with colleagues across other government departments to consider how this can be done as quickly as possible when proliferation risks are identified. As noted in 'The Road to 2010', [<www.cabinetoffice.gov.uk/media/224864/roadto2010.pdf> Ed.] at the end of last year, the Counter-Terrorism Act 2008 gave the Treasury new powers to respond when the development of nuclear weapons overseas poses a risk to the UK. The Treasury can now impose financial safeguards including reporting requirements, additional due diligence, or can require the cessation of business, with entities posing a threat of proliferation. The report of the Financial Action Task Force (FATF) on Proliferation Financing will not be completed until later this year. HM Treasury will reply separately to the committee with a copy of the FATF report and accompanying memorandum. In the interim, the following is a link to the FATF's 2008 report on the typologies of proliferation financing: www.fatf-gafi.org/dataoecd/14/21/41146580.pdf.

(Fourth Report from the Foreign Affairs Committee, 2008–2009, Global Security: Non-Proliferation, Response of the Secretary of State for Foreign and Commonwealth Affairs, Cm 7692)

15/19
Uzbekistan

The Foreign Secretary was asked what assessment he had made of the efficacy of EU sanctions on Uzbekistan. An FCO Minister wrote:

The UK has consistently argued that sanctions have been an important factor in bringing about positive, albeit limited, progress in the human rights situation in Uzbekistan. While serious concerns persist about the overall human rights situation, recent developments include:

the release of five human rights defenders, including Mutabar Tojibayeva, the most egregious of the Uzbek human rights cases of concern to the EU; the resumption of prison visits by the International Committee of the Red Cross; the entry into force of the abolition of the death penalty, and the introduction of a limited form of habeas corpus.

(HC Deb 23 March 2009 Vol 490 c39W)

15/20
Zimbabwe

An FCO Minister wrote about Zimbabwe sanctions:

The EU has maintained an embargo on arms and related material entering Zimbabwe since 2002. The EU has also prohibited the provision of any technical assistance relating to military activities and has imposed a ban on the supply of any equipment that might be used for internal repression. The EU has further imposed targeted financial and travel restrictions on 203 individuals and 40 entities who supported the government of Zimbabwe or were associated with its violence and human rights abuses prior to Morgan Tsvangirai's inauguration as the Zimbabwean Prime Minister. There are no comprehensive trade sanctions in place . . . 54 accounts belonging to individuals subject to targeted financial and travel restrictions on Zimbabwe have been frozen in the UK. The list of those subject to these EU sanctions include members and former members of the government of Zimbabwe, business people and others associated with the violence and human rights abuses of the regime as constituted prior to the inauguration of Morgan Tsvangirai as the Zimbabwean Prime Minister.

(HC Deb 27 March 2009 Vol 490 c818W)

Part Sixteen: Use of Force

Part Sixteen: I. *Use of Force—Prohibition of the use of force*

16/1
Iran

Answering questions about missile development by Iran, the Defence Secretary said:

We routinely assess the military capabilities of other nations' armed forces, including those of Iran. Iran is attempting to improve its ballistic missile capabilities; we continue to monitor these developments very carefully indeed.... Iran should stop meddling in the affairs of the Middle East. That is what it should do. The supply of armaments to Hamas in Gaza is profoundly unwelcome and must stop. We have made an offer to try to help the interdiction of those missile supplies and we stand ready to do that. We have no information to suggest that the capabilities that the Iranians are seeking to acquire pose a threat to UK forces, but Iran's growing interest in developing ballistic missile technology goes far beyond what is and can ever be justified in terms of Iranian self-defence, so we are entitled, along with our allies, to keep a very close eye on the continuing malign influence that Iran is playing in the middle east.... It is quite clear that Iran is continuing to take steps to seek to acquire a nuclear weapons programme. We must do everything we possibly can, with our international allies, to ensure that that never happens.... I do not think that there is any doubt that, in recent years, the Iranians have been assisting various groups in Iraq to attack British forces. That is totally unacceptable. Iran should keep its nose out of Iraq and other countries. Iran has a legitimate set of interests in the middle east, but it has no right whatever to involve itself in the internal security situation of other countries. Its role in assisting those groups to kill British forces is one that we will never forget.

(HC Deb 23 February 2009 Vol 488 cs11–12)

16/2
Russia

The Defence Committee recommended to the Government that:

We welcome the EU's investigation into the causes of the Georgian-Russian conflict. Understanding the history and causes of the conflict is a prerequisite to achieving peace in the region. While awaiting the EU's forthcoming report that should provide a more detailed assessment of the causes of the conflict, we conclude that: Responsibility for the conflict was shared, in differing measures, by all parties. Both Russia and Georgia share responsibility for the humanitarian consequences of the conflict that have left hundreds dead and thousands displaced from their homes. Russia provoked Georgia through its actions over many years. Russian provocation included fuelling separatism in the region through the distribution of passports in the breakaway Georgian territories, building up its military forces in the region and through its recognition of the separatist territories in Spring 2008.

President Saakashvili's decision to launch an offensive on 7 August was politically reckless. Russia reacted swiftly to remove Georgian forces from South Ossetia. Russia also acted with disproportionate and illegal use of force by encroaching deep into Georgian territory, far beyond the conflict area.

The Government replied:

We too look forward to the publication of the report by Ambassador Tagliavini, now scheduled for the end of September. [Independent International Fact-finding Mission on the Conflict in Georgia, <http://91.121.127.28/ceiig/Report.html>, Ed.] We share the Committee's hope that it will provide a clearer picture of events and their aftermath than has previously existed, which will aid our understanding of the causes of the conflict. As well as a focus on the origins of the war, we look forward to the mission's findings on humanitarian and human rights issues. We are also clear that, whatever the report's conclusions, we will need to manage any increased tensions between Georgia and Russia that arise from their attempts to apportion blame on each other. We agree that both Russia and Georgia must accept responsibility for the events of August 2008. Tensions between Russia and Georgia date back to post-independence conflicts in the 1990s. They rose significantly in the months before the war when Russia issued a decree in Spring 2008 establishing closer legal relations with the separatist territories. In April 2008, a Russian fighter shot down a Georgian UAV over Abkhazia and sent troops and military equipment into the region in breach of their commitments under the 1993 Moscow Agreement, which provided for a CIS peacekeeping Force in Georgia. Russia also admitted publicly that its aircraft had overflown South Ossetia. We share the Committee's assessment that Georgia's decision to try to take and hold Tskhinvali was ill-advised and reckless. But Russia's use of disproportionate force, which extended the geographical range of the conflict and the scale of fighting, had no justification and was rightly condemned by the international community. Nor is Russia's continuing violation of Georgian sovereignty and territorial integrity justified, and this continues with Russia's occupation of Georgian territory.

Given the horrific legacy of the conflict, we continue to stress to all parties their duty to allow unhindered access for humanitarian assistance in areas they control and to recall their obligation to protect human rights. We take any substantive allegations of war crimes and human rights abuses very seriously and it is important that the perpetrators of such abuses are held to account. Despite the demise of the OSCE and UN missions, we will continue to call on Russia and the separatist de facto authorities to permit access to the separatist regions for humanitarian assistance. (para 74)

(Defence Committee, Sixth Special Report: Russia: a new confrontation? Government Response to the Committee's Tenth Report 2008–2009, HC987 (2008))

16/3

The Defence Committee recommended in a report on Russia that, because Russia is failing to honour its ceasefire commitments under the agreements of 12 August and 8 September 2008, [w]e recommend that the UK Government send a strong message to Russia that it needs to withdraw its military forces to its pre-conflict positions as previously agreed. (para 81). The Government replied:

We share the Committee's view that Russia has not complied fully with the 12 August and 8 September agreements. Russia has not withdrawn its troops to their pre-conflict positions. Russia has continued to militarise the separatist regions and in recent months deployed FSB Border Guards to patrol the Administrative Border Line with South Ossetia and Abkhazia under "border management agreements" signed on 30 April with the separatist regions. These actions add to tension. We, and our EU partners, continue to press Russia at every opportunity to comply fully with the 12 August and 8 September agreements. The Foreign Secretary has raised Georgia with Russian Foreign Minister Sergei Lavrov and others on many occasions to encourage Russian co-operation. (para 81)

(Defence Committee, Sixth Special Report: Russia: a new confrontation? Government Response to the Committee's Tenth Report 2008–2009, HC987 (2008))

16/4

The Defence Committee wrote in a report on Russia:

Russia has breached internationally accepted principles of sovereignty and territorial integrity by unilaterally recognising the independence of South Ossetia and Abkhazia. The prospect of South Ossetia and Abkhazia returning under the sovereign control of Georgia in the near future appears slight while the Russian military presence remains in these territories. It is vital for international security that NATO, EU and the UK Government remain resolute in their commitment to Georgia's sovereignty and international law. The international community has a vital role in securing stability and peace in the region. UK Ministers should press for the EU, UN and OSCE to secure a lasting peace settlement in the disputed territories. (Paragraph 93)

The Government replied:

Despite the demise of UNOMIG and the OSCE monitoring mission, we remain committed to keeping an effective international presence on the ground, and to maintaining the EU Monitoring Mission in Georgia, adapting its activities if necessary to the changed political landscape in Georgia. We are exploring options with our partners in New York that might ensure a continued UN presence, not least to cover the continuing humanitarian needs in UNOMIG's former field of operations and in Vienna on the future shape of OSCE involvement. We have been clear in our support for Georgia's territorial integrity. [An FCO Minister] stressed this during her visit to Georgia in June 2009. Meanwhile, we have also encouraged the Georgian authorities to look at increased dialogue with the separatist regions, which remains the only way that a comprehensive and durable settlement can be achieved. This will be a lengthy process, but the UK Government will support Georgia in pursuit of this goal. We also continue to encourage Georgia to pursue internal reforms which will bring the country closer to achieving the criteria necessary for future EU and NATO membership. These aspirations are a powerful driver to lever reform. A democratic, prosperous Georgia, with a free media, strong civil society and trusted judiciary, will also provide an effective tool to increase the chances of rapprochement between Georgia and its separatist regions. (para 93)

(Defence Committee, Sixth Special Report: Russia: a new confrontation? Government response to the Committee's Tenth Report 2008–2009, HC987 (2008))

16/5

The Defence Committee wrote in a report on Russia:

If NATO does grant Georgia membership it should do so to the whole of Georgia's sovereign territory, including Abkhazia and South Ossetia. To do otherwise would be to recognise Russia's actions in those parts of Georgia as having some legitimacy. This is a very serious issue to which we do not have an answer (Paragraph 128)

The Government replied that:

it remains committed to the sovereignty and territorial integrity of Georgia. The 2009 Summit Declaration repeated NATO's condemnation of Russia's recognition of South Ossetia and Abkhazia as independent states and called on Moscow to reverse the decision. The UK and NATO allies continue to press Georgia and Russia to use the forum of the Geneva talks to work towards a comprehensive peace that addresses the status of Georgia's separatist regions. (para 128)

(Defence Committee, Sixth Special Report: Russia: a new confrontation? Government response to the Committee's Tenth Report 2008–2009, HC987 (2008))

16/6
The Foreign Secretary was asked about his assessment of the compliance by Russia of the agreements of August and September 2008 on Georgia. He wrote:

On 12 August 2008, the EU and Organisation for Security and Co-operation in Europe (OSCE) brokered a ceasefire between the parties. These points were supplemented by an implementation plan, again brokered by the EU and OSCE, and agreed on 8 September 2008. Russia has met a number, though not all, of its commitments under the 8 August and 12 September 2008 plans. Though Russia withdrew from most of the areas adjacent to South Ossetia and Abkhazia within 10 days of the deployment of an EU Mission to Georgia, it retains a checkpoint at Perevi, which is in the rest of Georgia outside South Ossetia. And within South Ossetia and Abkhazia it has failed to withdraw to its pre-conflict positions: Russian forces are now stationed in the Upper Kodori Valley in Abkhazia and the Akhalgori region of South Ossetia. Neither area was under Russian control before hostilities began. Along with our partners, we continue to call on Russia to meet its commitments to the international community in full.

(HC Deb 12 February 2009 Vol 487 c2202W)

16/7
In answering a question about relations with Russia, an FCO Minister wrote:

[S]ignificant differences remain. In our bilateral relationship, we have outstanding issues over the refusal of Russia to provide real co-operation with the investigation into the murder of Alexander Litvinenko and over the closure of British Council offices in St Petersburg and Ekaterinburg. Internationally we remain deeply concerned by Russia's breach of its international obligations in Georgia. We will continue to press Russia to resolve these issues.

(HL Deb 24 February 2009 Vol 708 cWA73)

Part Sixteen: II.A. *Use of Force—Legitimate use of force—Self—defence*

16/8
Afghanistan

During a debate in the House of Commons, the Foreign Secretary said:

The defining mission in Afghanistan is simply stated: to ensure that, with al-Qaeda having been driven out of Afghanistan, it cannot come back under the safe umbrella of renewed Taliban rule. The Prime Minister set out this mission in this House in December 2007 and in April 2009. It is the mission agreed by all NATO countries, which made this vow at the Bucharest summit last year: "Neither we nor our Afghan partners will allow extremists and terrorists... to regain control of Afghanistan or use it as a base for terror". The mission is also at the heart of the US strategy document published in February. In President Obama's words:

"And if the Afghan government falls to the Taliban—or allows al Qaeda to go unchallenged—that country will again be a base for terrorists who want to kill as many of our people as they possibly can." The purpose of rehearsing this unity of mission is twofold—first, to underline the self-interest as well as the realism of our objectives and, secondly, to emphasise that this is a shared operation.

He continued:

As the Foreign Secretary has said, we are operating in Afghanistan to protect our national security. We are fighting the Taliban to prevent al-Qaeda, and the terrorists whom they bring, from returning to Afghanistan and threatening us directly. For Britain to be secure, Afghanistan needs to be secure. This is not just about the UK's national security; 42 nations are taking part in one of the widest ever international coalitions, and it is about their national security too. The international community has a joint strategy for success, not just a military strategy but a comprehensive strategy for governance, development and reconstruction.

(HC Deb 16 July 2009 Vol 496 c487 and 549)

16/9
Democratic Republic of Congo

The Foreign Secretary was asked about his recent assessment of the effectiveness of Operation Kimia II against the Democratic Forces for the Liberation of Rwanda rebels in eastern Democratic Republic of Congo. An FCO Minister wrote:

The success of Operation Kimia II has been mixed so far. The Democratic Forces for the Liberation of Rwanda (FDLR) militia continues to carry out attacks against the civilian population and the Democratic Republic of Congo armed forces in north and south Kivu provinces. However, the military effort against the FDLR in north Kivu has maintained pressure on the group. We understand that in some areas the FDLR has been forced to withdraw from ground it had held. The operation extended into south Kivu only recently. It is too early to assess its impact there but we continue to urge the UN peacekeeping mission to the Democratic Republic of Congo and the Congolese armed forces to do all it can to protect civilians. While it remains our view that military pressure is necessary to weaken the FDLR, a lasting solution to the problems posed by the militia requires a political settlement.

(HC Deb 3 July 2009 Vol 495 c470W)

16/10
Iran

The Defence Secretary was asked what the Government's policy was on a ballistic missile defence shield in Europe to provide security against Iran. He wrote:

The Government see ballistic missile defence as an important defensive capability which could contribute to the defence of the UK and our NATO Allies against potential future ballistic missile threats.

(HC Deb 25 March 2009 Vol 490 c436W)

16/11
Israel

An FCO Minister wrote:

The UK agrees with the International Court of Justice (ICJ) broad conclusions that building a barrier along the current route, on occupied land, is a clear violation of international law. The Government therefore supported UN General Assembly resolution (ES-10/15) that acknowledged the ICJ's advisory opinion on the legal consequences of the barrier in occupied Palestinian territory. While we recognise fully Israel's right to self-defence and agree that if it decides to build a barrier it should be able to do that, we will continue to make clear to Israel, both in private in and in public, that the barrier must be built either on or behind the Green Line.

(HC Deb 9 September 2009 Vol 496 cs1961–1962W)

Part Sixteen: II.B.1. *Use of Force—Legitimate use of force—Collective measures—United Nations*

16/12
Introducing a debate on the situation in Afghanistan and Pakistan, the Foreign Secretary said:

The subject of this debate is the challenge posed by Afghanistan and Pakistan together; the two countries need to be seen together. A mix of violent extremist groups poison the tribal belt on both sides of the Durand line. There are intimate connections between the insurgency in Helmand and that in Waziristan, and between the criminals, spoilers and terrorists who operate in Kandahar and Quetta, Peshawar and Nangahar. A combined and comprehensive approach is needed. However, the responses in each country have to be different. In Afghanistan, a UN-mandated, NATO and EU-supported international effort—military and civilian—helps the Government. In Pakistan, the international community must play a different role in supporting the new, democratic Government in their response to violent extremism. It is clear from my experience, and that of everyone I have talked to, that the withdrawal of British and other international forces would lead to the collapse of Afghanistan's first democratic Government and to the overwhelming of the Afghan state, with very serious consequences. After all, Afghanistan is the incubator of choice for al-Qaeda. For that reason, we have a central national interest in sustaining the ability of the democratic Government in Afghanistan to defend themselves. The critical point, as I shall try to explain, is that we are not in Afghanistan to create a new colony; we are there to enable the Afghan people, the Afghan Government and the Afghan state to defend themselves. Our strategy is to help the Afghan Government divide the insurgency, and co-opt those who are prepared to renounce al-Qaeda, obey the laws and accept the principles of the Afghan constitution. Equipping the Afghan authorities with the means and the authority to conduct such reconciliation activity both nationally and—critically, in my view, locally—is key to the future. Thirdly, there is military force. By pressurising those who refuse to co-operate with the Afghan state, and protecting those who do, it can directly support political reconciliation. By enabling the Afghans to secure and stabilise their territory, then delivering aid and promoting development, the military show not only that the insurgents can be defeated, but what is possible once they have gone. There is no purely military solution to the problems of insurgency and disorder in Helmand or across Afghanistan generally. However, equally, there is no non-military solution. That is why our approach—creating a combined civil-military mission in Helmand, staffed by some 65 civilians and some 55 military officers, and led by a civilian—has been so important, and, I believe, right. It is also why, when I say that Britain is in Afghanistan as part of an international effort, I refer not only to the NATO-led military force of some 41 nations, but the civil alliance, which encompasses some 60 nations and international organisations.

(HC Deb 5 February 2009 Vol 487 c1032)

16/13

An FCO Minister wrote:

UK forces, along with 41 other contributing nations, participate in the North Atlantic Treaty Organisation's International Security Assistance Force (ISAF) in Afghanistan at the invitation of the democratically elected Afghan Government and at the request of the UN. The objective of the international community's involvement in Afghanistan is to establish the right security environment in which accountable and effective institutions can develop and Afghan-led reconstruction and development can be established. Gaining and securing the confidence of the Afghan population is critical to achieving our objectives. The newly appointed commander of ISAF, General Stanley McChrystal, is currently conducting a review of ISAF operations. We await its recommendations. We welcome General McChrystal's recent statements emphasising ISAF's determination to protect the Afghan population from the insurgents and to seek to minimise the effect of ISAF operations on the population. The UK will continue to support ISAF and the Government of Afghanistan in their efforts to do this. ISAF and the wider international community working in Afghanistan, including the UN Assistance Mission in Afghanistan, will continue to work closely with the Government of Afghanistan and the Afghan National Security Forces in pursuit of their objectives on behalf of the people of Afghanistan.

(HL Deb 9 July 2009 Vol 712 cWA161)

16/14
The Prime Minister said in a speech on 16 November 2009:

So tonight I want to leave you with a clear summary of Britain's case, and that of the coalition as a whole. We are in Afghanistan because we judge that if the Taleban regained power al Qaeda and other terrorist groups would once more have an environment in which they could operate. We are there because action in Afghanistan is not an alternative to action in Pakistan, but an inseparable support to it. As I have shown, the world has succeeded in closing down much of the space in which al Qaeda can operate, and we must not allow this process to be reversed by retreat or irresolution.

(<www.number10.gov.uk/Page21339>)

Part Sixteen: II.B.2. *Use of Force—Legitimate Use of Force—Collective Measures—Outside the United Nations*

16/15
The Defence Committee wrote in a report on Russia:

NATO needs to ensure that a continued commitment to mutual protection—Article 5—is at the heart of the new NATO Strategic Concept. NATO's global role is vital, given the shared challenges its Member States face. Yet this should not come at the expense of the Alliance's commitment towards mutual defence.

The Government replied:

We agree. As the Declaration on Alliance Security (Strasbourg/Kehl Summit, April 2009) states, "Article 5 of the Washington Treaty and collective defence, based on the indivisibility of Allied security are, and will remain, the cornerstone of our Alliance". That will not change. But the Strategic Concept will also need to underscore the Alliance's determination to work together to address the full range of challenges to its security, wherever these occur. It is not, and cannot be, a question of one or the other. The two are tightly linked: the out-of-area operation in Afghanistan emanates from our Article 5 commitment, and indeed, the capabilities that NATO needs for Article 5 collective defence and for crisis response operations beyond the transatlantic area are pretty much one and the same. We need an Alliance that is flexible and capable enough to respond to every eventuality it faces. (para 133)

(Defence Committee, Sixth Special Report: Russia: a new confrontation? Government Response to the Committee's Tenth Report 2008–2009, HC987 (2008))

Part Sixteen: II.C. *Use of force—Legitimate use of force—Others*

16/16 [See **UKMIL [1992] p.824; UKMIL [1997] p.629; UKMIL [1999] pp.563–567]**

The Ministry of Defence submitted the following document on the Iraq 'No Fly' Zones to the Iraq Inquiry (Chilcot):

Iraq: No Fly Zones Background - The Gulf War 1. On 2 August 1990, Iraq invaded Kuwait, prompting the UN Security Council to pass Resolution 660 the same day demanding 'that Iraq withdraw immediately and unconditionally all its forces'. 2. Iraq's failure to comply led to Resolution 661, adopted on 6 August 1990, which called for the restoration of the 'sovereignty, independence and territorial integrity of Kuwait' and imposed wide-ranging economic sanctions against Iraq. 3. The US and the UK began deployments of troops to the region soon afterwards (Op DESERT SHIELD), with the initial aim of deterring further Iraqi aggression against Saudi Arabia which was threatened by large numbers of Iraqi forces on its border. 4. On 29 November 1990, the Security Council passed Resolution 678 which authorised Member States "to use all necessary means to uphold and implement resolution 660 (1990)..." unless Iraq withdrew from Kuwait on or before 15 January 1991. 5. Iraq's failure to meet the UN deadline led to the coalition war against Iraq, Operation DESERT STORM, which began on 16 January 1991 and continued until Iraqi forces were driven from Kuwait on 28 February, when hostilities were suspended. 6. Saddam's defeat gave hope to his opponents inside Iraq and there were two separate but parallel attempts to overthrow his regime. On 1 March 1991, spontaneous demonstrations in Basra and Najaf developed into battles between Shia fighters and Saddam's security forces and within days the unrest had spread to all the main Shia cities in southern Iraq. Similarly, Kurdish forces saw an opportunity to seize control of northern Iraq. Beginning on 4 March, they had, by 20 March, captured every city in the North, including Kirkuk. Saddam's forces responded with brutal, indiscriminate force, using helicopter gunships and artillery to crush the resistance. Thousands of Shia and Kurds were killed and many more fled their homes, particularly in the North. Fearing an even greater massacre, US commanders warned that they would shoot down any Iraqi aircraft flying over the country; two Iraq Su-22 aircraft were subsequently shot down, one on 15 and one on 22 March. 7. By the end of March, Saddam had reasserted his control over the South and the Northern areas were also back under control in early April. On 5 April, Iraq's ruling Revolutionary Command Council announced "the complete crushing of acts of sedition, sabotage, and rioting in all towns of Iraq". 8. The same day, the UN Security Council passed Resolution 688, which "condemns the repression of the Iraqi civilian population in many parts of Iraq...demands that Iraq...immediately end this repression...requests the Secretary-General to pursue his humanitarian efforts in Iraq...appeals to all Member States...to contribute to these humanitarian relief efforts". The No Fly Zones—Summary 9. The Iraqi no-fly-zones were established in April 1991 (north) and August 1992 (south) as a coalition (US, UK and France) initiative in support of UNSCR 688 demanding an immediate end to Saddam's brutal repression of Kurds in north and Shias in south. 10. Iraqi aircraft were forbidden from flying inside the zones. This was enforced by US, UK and French[52] aircraft patrols.

11. Saddam's internal security organisations continued to persecute all opponents of the regime on the ground but coalition aircraft helped to protect the interests of these minorities by ensuring he could not use his airforce to mount all-out assaults. While supervising the no-fly zones, coalition aircraft also col-

[52] France withdrew in 1996

lected tactical reconnaissance to help monitor Saddam's compliance with UNSCR 688. 12. On 16–19 December 1998, the US and UK took military action against Iraq under Operation Desert Fox on the basis of Iraq's non-compliance with UNSCOM and the growing concern that Iraq was continuing to develop its chemical and biological weapons capability. From that point on, Iraq no longer recognised the no-fly zones and attacks on coalition aircraft became a common occurrence, although no coalition aircraft were ever shot down by Iraqi forces. Coalition aircraft responded by targeted attacks on elements of Iraq's Integrated Air Defence System. No-fly zone operations ceased in March 2003. The No Fly Zones - detail Northern No Fly Zone 13. On 6 April 1991, US-led Operation Provide Comfort began to bring humanitarian relief to the Kurds in the North and a no-fly zone was established north of the 36th parallel, enforced by US, UK and French aircraft based at Incirlik in Turkey. The UK contribution was called Op HAVEN and involved 3 Commando Brigade as well as RAF aircraft. 14. In a Parliamentary Statement on 15 April, the then Foreign Secretary explained that the aim was 'to create places and conditions in which refugees can feel secure . . . We support the territorial integrity of Iraq'. 15. On 7 June 1991, relief operations were handed over to the UNHCR and by mid-July almost all the 400,000 Kurdish refugees who had fled into the mountains on the Iraq-Turkey border region had returned back to their homes or to the camps constructed for them by coalition forces. On 24 July 1991, Op Provide Comfort (and the UK Op HAVEN) ended and was replaced by Op Provide Comfort II. The UK contribution was called Op WARDEN. Its primary aims were to prevent Saddam from attacking the Kurds from the air by maintaining the no-fly zone and to monitor that Saddam was complying with UNSCR 688. There was also a limited humanitarian element to the mission, with the continued distribution of supplies to Kurds and other minorities in the region. In October 1995, the UN assumed full responsibility for the humanitarian elements and on 27 December 1996, France announced that because of the lack of a direct humanitarian element, it would not participate in the successor to the operation. On 31 December 1996, Op Provide Comfort II formally ended. On 1 January 1997 Op Northern Watch began as a successor to Op Provide Comfort II with just US and UK aircraft taking part. The Southern No Fly Zone 16. In 1992, concern mounted about Saddam's continued persecution of the Shia in the South, including his draining of the Arab marshland and forced relocation of the local population. The forced resettlement programme in the marshes was accompanied by a counterinsurgency campaign that included indiscriminate attacks by artillery, helicopter gunships and fixed-wing aircraft on villages. On 11 August 1992, the UN special rapporteur on Iraq set out his concerns directly to the UN Security Council. On August 27, in response to these concerns, US, UK, and French forces launched Operation Southern Watch, imposing an "air-exclusion" zone south of the 32nd parallel using aircraft based in Saudi Arabia. The UK contribution was known as Op JURAL. 17. The first two years involved relatively routine patrolling of the no-fly zone, although two Iraqi fighters were shot down and elements of Iraq's ground based air defence system posing a threat were attacked in three incidents in December 1992 and January 1993. In October 1994, there was an increase in tension after Saddam deployed a large number of ground troops south of the 32nd parallel. The coalition responded by deploying additional forces to the Gulf (the UK deployed six additional Tornado GR1s and sixteen extra crews, plus 45 Commando Group under Op DRIVER), following which Iraqi forces were withdrawn north of the 32nd parallel. In August 1996, after a period of inter-Kurd conflict in northern Iraq between the Kurdish Democratic party (KDP) and the Patriotic Union of Kurdistan (PUK), Saddam allied himself with the KDP and at their request intervened militarily, providing 15,000 troops to help them re-occupy Irbil and take Sulaymaniyah from the PUK. Concerned at the possibility of Saddam reasserting control in the north under the cover of inter-Kurdish fighting, planning began for a possible coalition response (Op Desert Strike). In the UK this was known as Op LANCASTER. RAF aircraft were placed on standby to reinforce the detachments at Incirlik and Dhahran but, in the event, military action was confined to US Tomahawk cruise missiles, launched in two attacks on 3rd and 4th September and Iraq was informed that the no-fly zone had been extended northwards to the 33rd parallel (French aircraft only continued to participate in patrols up to the 32nd parallel). Iraqi forces then withdrew from Kurdish controlled northern Iraq. 1997–98 crisis 18. Patrolling the (extended) southern no-fly zone continued as normal until mid-1997, when Iraq resumed its blocking of some UNSCOM operations. On 29 September 1997, Iran attacked Iranian terrorist camps in Iraq. The Iraqi response was to launch aircraft to defend their airspace, violating both no-fly zones but particularly the southern no-fly zone. Violations continued for around 5 weeks before ceasing in response to intensified coalition patrols. In the UK, plans were drawn up and refined throughout October for possible coalition response to further Iraqi violations of the no-fly zones and in response to their lack of cooperation with UNSCOM. On 13 November 1997, following a demand that US personnel working for UNSCOM leave Iraq immediately, UNSCOM decide to withdraw temporarily from Iraq. On 14 November, the UK initiated Op BOLTON and HMS INVINCIBLE was ordered to sail from the Caribbean to Gibraltar in preparation for a possible deployment to the Gulf, and duly embarked RAF Harriers. Op BOLTON formally took over the southern no-fly zone operations previously conducted under Op JURAL. 19. Despite intense diplomatic activity, from mid-December to mid January 1998, UNSCOM continued to report Iraqi non-compliance with their inspectors. On 16 January, the UK authorised an aircraft carrier to sail for the Gulf and on 6 February it was decided to deploy Tornado GR1 aircraft to Kuwait. Discussions between the UN and Iraq continued in a similar vein throughout 1998. Although the UN Secretary General appeared to have brokered an agreement in late-February 1998, the UK decided to retain forces in the Gulf until it was clearer whether Iraq would actually resume cooperation with UNSCOM. In late March, following improved Iraqi behaviour, UK forces began an incremental re-posturing, withdrawing the aircraft carrier but deploying additional Tornado aircraft to Kuwait. 20. On 5 August 1998, Iraq declared that it was halting cooperation with UNSCOM and the IAEA pending the oil embargo being lifted and UNSCOM being reorganised. On 9 September, the UN Security Council passed Resolution 1194 condemning Iraq's decision. Following further diplomatic activity, on 31 October Iraq announced that it would cease all forms of interaction with UNSCOM. On 5 November, the UN Security Council passed resolution 1205 condemning Iraq's actions and calling for it to rescind its decisions of 5 August and 31 October. UNSCOM withdrew all its personnel from Iraq on 11 November 1998. 21. On 12 November 1998, the US and the UK warned Iraq that it would face a substantial military strike if it did not return to full compliance with UN Resolutions. On 14 November the US and the UK authorised the launch of an initial wave of strike aircraft. Two hours before the first air strikes were due to take place, Iraq indicated that it was willing to comply with UN demands. The UK and the US suspended military action on the basis that Iraq had agreed to 'unconditional resumption of co-operation'. UNSCOM inspectors returned to Iraq on 17 November. Iraqi co-operation was short-lived and on 15 December 1998 the Executive Chairman of UNSCOM, Richard Butler, wrote to the UN Secretary General to update him on Iraqi compliance since November, concluding that 'Iraq's conduct ensured that no progress was able to be made in either the fields of disarmament or accounting for its prohibited weapons programmes'. The same day, France announced that it was suspending its involvement in the southern no-fly zone. Operation Desert Fox and its aftermath 22. On 16 December 1998, military action against Iraq was initiated by US and UK forces under Operation DESERT FOX. This was on the basis of Iraq's non-compliance with UNSCOM and the growing concern that Iraq was continuing to develop its chemical and biological weapons capability. 23. The legal basis for DESERT FOX was not the same as for the establishment of the No Fly Zones. The UK relied on UN Security Council Resolution 1154 (under which Iraq was required to accord immediate and unrestricted access to UNSCOM and IAEA inspectors and warned that failure to do so would have 'the severest consequence for Iraq') and Resolution 1205 (condemning the decision to stop co-operation with UNSCOM and demanding rescission of that decision). This, the UK argued, had revived the authority to use military force under Resolution 678. 24. The objective of the operation was "to reduce substantially Saddam's ability to threaten his neighbours and international security, in particular by degrading his weapons of mass destruction capability, including control and delivery systems, and his wider military capability". 25. US and UK forces used over 400 cruise missiles (more than in the 1991 Gulf Conflict), and 218 tactical bomber sorties to attack 100 targets including: • sites identified as being involved in Iraq's weapons of mass destruction programmes; • command and control facilities through which Saddam controlled military and internal security forces; • the Iraqi Republican Guard; • the Iraqi air defence system; • airfields, including those associated with helicopter forces used for internal repression. 26. The operation ended on 19 December. UK forces participated in 32 bomber sorties (15 per cent of the total missions) involving Tornado GR1 aircraft based in Kuwait. 27. All no-fly zone patrols were suspended during Operation Desert Fox, but resumed (by US and UK aircraft only) in the southern no-fly-zone on 22 December 1998, and in the northern no-fly-zone on 28 December. 28. After December 1998, Iraq no longer recognised the no-fly zones and attacks on coalition aircraft became a common occurrence. Coalition aircraft were fired at by Iraqi surface-to-air missiles and anti-aircraft artillery or targeted by fire control radars. In responding to this threat, coalition aircraft targeted a variety of different elements of Iraq's Integrated Air Defence System, such as radar sites and associated communications and control networks, surface-to-air missile batteries, and anti-aircraft artillery positions. RAF Jaguars flying reconnaissance operations in the northern no-fly zone did not carry or drop air-to-ground ordnance, but RAF Tornado aircraft did so in the southern no-fly zone on numerous occasions. The end of the No Fly Zones 29. Operations in both no-fly zones ceased in March 2003 with the start of Op Iraqi Liberation (later called Op Iraqi Freedom). They were stood-down formally on 1 May 2003. Legal basis for the No Fly Zones 30. Generally speaking there are only two bases for using force: a. if it is in exercise of the right of individual or collective self defence under customary international law, which allows the use of force to defend against an actual or imminent armed attack using force that is necessary (i.e. the only effective means of dealing with the threat) and proportionate (no more than reasonably necessary to deal with the threat); b. if it is authorised by the UN Security Council under Chapter VII of the UN Charter. 31. The No Fly Zones were not themselves justified on the grounds of self defence—there was no evidence of the threat of an imminent attack. (There were separate issues about targeting which are dealt with further below). Nor were the No Fly Zones explicitly authorised by the Security Council. 32. UN Security Council Resolution 688 did however demand an end to the repression of the Shia and Kurd peoples. This is often cited as the legal base for the No Fly Zones, but that is not the whole picture. The relevance of UNSCR 688 was that the NFZs were consistent with its purpose, but as UNSCR 688 was not made under Chapter VII it could not authorise the use of military force. 33. In answer to a Parliamentary Question in 1998[53], Baroness Symons, answering a question about the use of force in Kosovo, made reference to the Government's position in respect of Northern Iraq. She said that, while there is no general doctrine of humanitarian necessity in international law, cases have nevertheless arisen (as in Northern Iraq in 1991) when, in light of all the circumstances, a limited use of force was justifiable in support of the purposes laid down by the Security Council but without the Council's express authorisation, when that was the only means to avert an immediate and overwhelming humanitarian catastrophe. Such cases would be exceptional, and would depend on an objective assessment of the factual circumstances at the time and the terms of the relevant Security Council decision.

34. The Secretary of State for Defence explained the legal justification for the NFZs to the House of Commons Select Committee on Defence in 2000 (Thirteenth Report, para 30). He justified it as: "essentially based on the overwhelming humanitarian necessity of protecting people on the ground, combined with the need to monitor the effect of UNSCR 688; so it is the two taken in combination that provide the legal justification.". 35. Similarly, in the House of Commons (Hansard, 26 February 2001), the Secretary of State for Defence, Geoff Hoon, explained[54]: "The legal justification for the patrolling of the no-fly zones does not rest on Security Council Resolution 688. That has not been the government's position. In terms of humanitarian justification, we are entitled to patrol the no-fly zones to prevent a grave humanitarian crisis. That is the legal justification in international law. It does not rest on Resolution 688, although that Resolution supports the position we have adopted.".

36. In relation to the Northern No Fly Zone, the government's position then was that the measure was necessary to save lives—those of the Kurds - threatened on a massive scale. This would justify the deployment of civilian personnel, along with their necessary military protection. There were, it was recognised, no clear precedents for this, and it was seen as an emergency measure. 37. With regard to the Southern No Fly Zone, the Government was satisfied that it would be legally defensible on the basis that the humanitarian need,

[53] HL Deb 16 November 1998 Hansard vol 594 cc 139–40
[54] HC Deb 26 February 2001 vol 363 cc 620–34

while not sufficiently extreme to justify offensive action, nevertheless was serious and was likely to deteriorate if no action was taken. 38. The US/UK patrols of the NFZ were therefore in the government's view based on humanitarian necessity and the need to uphold Resolution 688. 39. This remained the consistent position until Operation Telic was authorised in March 2003. Legal basis for defending the No Fly Zones 40. As to targeting of assets within the No Fly Zones, it remained the UK's position that it was engaged in a lawful activity in monitoring the NFZs and if coalition forces were attacked or under imminent threat of attack, they were entitled to defend themselves. So UK forces participating in the No Fly Zones were permitted to attack targets which were or contributed to actual or imminent threat of attack. This was based on the inherent right of self defence. 41. The need to defend the No Fly Zones was particularly acute following DESERT FOX, after which Iraqi activity and attacks on coalition forces increased significantly. 42. The Prime Minister in a statement following events in 2001, when US and UK aircraft attacked a number of targets, noted that the action was for the sole purpose of defending the pilots and aircrew patrolling the no-fly zones. The Ministry of Defence said that the mission was conducted in self defence in response to repeated Iraqi threats to coalition aircraft carrying out routine patrols of the Southern no-fly zone.

(<www.iraqinquiry.org.uk/media/38010/mod-no-fly-zone-r1.pdf>)

Part Sixteen: III. *Use of Force—Disarmament and arms control*

16/17
Ballistic Missiles

During a debate, a Minister said:

Other than the US, the UK and France, about 20 countries possess ballistic missiles. In 2007, there were 100 non-US ballistic missile launches around the world, which is 30 per cent. more than in 2006 and slightly fewer than in 2008. Those figures reflect the determination of many countries to acquire a ballistic missile capability. Although many countries possess only short-range weapons that do not threaten the UK mainland, we remain concerned by missile development in countries such as Iran and North Korea. We recognise that neither of those countries has a confirmed long-range ballistic missile capability, but Iran does possess a medium range missile, the Shahab 3, that could reach Turkey and much of the middle east. The recent test firings of those missiles and the accompanying rhetoric is a worrying development. Reports suggest that Iran is developing longer-range missiles that in time could pose a greater threat to the UK and our European allies. Tehran has acknowledged that it is pursuing a space launch capability. The successful launch of the Safir rocket, which put a small satellite into orbit earlier this year, is testament to the growing Iranian mastery of rocket and missile technologies. As we have seen recently, North Korea continues to develop and test its missile capabilities, and shows gradual improvement in its understanding of missile and rocket systems. It continues to develop the Taepodong-2 missile, and earlier this year attempted to use Taepodong-type technology to place a satellite into Earth's orbit. That vehicle failed to reach orbit, but the North Koreans' intention to develop long-range rocket technology cannot be ignored. Both Iran and North Korea claim that their developments are designed for civilian applications and are meant to allow them to join the ranks of peaceful space-faring nations. However, the technologies could equally be used to develop missile systems capable of delivering military payloads over intercontinental distances. Those payloads could include chemical, biological or nuclear weapons that are capable of killing many people and inflicting massive damage with a single missile. We assess—this is the nub of the challenge—that within the next 10 years, both North Korea and Iran could have the capability to target the UK with ballistic missiles if they so wished. Of course, the development of technological and technical capability is only one facet of the threat; the other is the intent to use missiles. We can monitor the development and proliferation of ballistic missiles and the associated technology, and we can prepare to defeat them, but it is more difficult to know with any certainty when, or even if, intent changes. At the moment, the Government assess that there is no ballistic missile threat to the UK homeland, but if we look to future trends, that could change. Let me address some of the questions that my hon. Friend has asked. First, I shall respond to his underlying challenge about what we as a country, and particularly as a Government, want to do about the threat of nuclear proliferation and the challenge of nuclear weapons. We are very clear that we want to work towards a world free of nuclear weapons—that is our absolute intent. Of the existing nuclear weapon states, under the auspices of the non-proliferation treaty, we have the best and most forward-leaning record on disarmament. That has been attested by independent observers and is borne out by the fact that in the past decade we have reduced the explosive capability of our nuclear arsenal by 75 per cent. We want to go through further multilateral negotiations, and that is why we are emphatically committed to, and have signed up to, a comprehensive test ban treaty. That is also why we want a fissile material cut-off treaty. My hon. Friend referred to the START 2 process, involving the United States and Russia. One of the most encouraging aspects of the current debate about nuclear weapons is the impetus and vigour that President Obama has brought to discussions. He is considering taking a comprehensive test ban treaty to Congress, which would be a very positive step forward, and he is committed to bringing about further multilateral nuclear weapons reductions through the START 2 process. I think we should support that approach.... Let me deal with that point directly. We have always been clear that we want Israel to sign up to the NPT as a non-nuclear weapons state, and we are committed to having a middle east that is free from nuclear weapons. It is right that we should make that position as clear as we make our concerns about Iran. Nevertheless, our concerns about Iran are real. I welcome President Obama's commitment to engage with the Iranian regime, but that regime must understand that it has a choice to make about engaging with the international community and reassuring us about its nuclear weapons intentions. The alternative is a much tougher regime of sanctions and pressure.... One thing that is certain is that any future plans will include greater engagement with Russia, which the Government strongly welcome and will support. As we all know, Russia has consistently and incorrectly claimed that US proposals to place 10 ballistic missile interceptors in Poland and a radar in the Czech Republic is aimed at reducing the effectiveness of Russia's strategic missile forces. Emphatically, that is not the case. The proposals are designed to defend against a limited threat from states of concern, rather than from countries with large arsenals of sophisticated weapons. None of us should forget that Russia understands missile defence. It has had a BMD system protecting Moscow since the cold war, and—this is the key point—it knows that 10 US interceptors would have little impact on the many long and medium-range missiles that it possesses. The Russians are fully aware of the capabilities and limitations of the proposed US system, and are aware that Russia's security should not, and could not, be threatened by that system. Indeed, they have acknowledged that privately. Given the dialogue that has taken place with Russia, and the fact that the United States is reviewing these issues, I think that there is a way forward that addresses the concerns that my hon. Friend has raised, working with Russia to establish a collective BMD system so that it is clear that that is a defensive, rather than aggressive, posture. In those circumstances, we should support that process. I genuinely want to get to a situation in which we live in a world that is free of nuclear weapons. The Government are leading the process multilaterally to try to achieve that state of affairs, and we should all strongly support that approach. I do not believe that a defensive BMD capability system is in contravention of that. If we get things right and work with our partners, that could give us greater security.

(HC Deb 7 July 2009 Vol 495 cs250WH-254WH)

1.6/18 (See also **15/9**)
Counter-terrorism

The Exchequer Secretary to the Treasury issued the following Ministerial Statement:

The Government have today laid before the House a statutory instrument under the Counter-terrorism Act 2008 containing a direction requiring the UK financial services sector to cease all business with the Iranian Bank Mellat and the Islamic Republic of Iran Shipping Lines. This means that from today, financial and credit institutions will no longer be able to enter into new transactions or business relationships with these entities nor to continue with existing transactions or business relationships unless they are licensed by HM Treasury. Consistent with the commitment provided to the House during the passage of the Act, I would like to set out the reasons behind our decision. The Treasury is satisfied, as required by the Act, that activity in Iran that facilitates the development or production of nuclear weapons poses a significant risk to the national interests of the UK. Iran continues to fail to meet its international obligations. Most notably, its nuclear programme presents an immediate challenge to the global non-proliferation regime. The International Atomic Energy Agency (IAEA—the UN body charged with monitoring Iran's activities and ensuring that no nuclear material is being diverted to non-civilian applications) is being refused the access it seeks by Iran, which also declines to answer questions put to it by the agency's staff about alleged studies suggesting a military aspect to Iran's programme. As a result, the IAEA director general has stated that he is unable to verify Iran's nuclear programme is for exclusively peaceful purposes. Iran's ongoing improvement of its ballistic missile capabilities also continues to cause international concern. Its failure to answer questions from the IAEA about possible military dimensions to its nuclear programme increase concerns that its ballistic missile programme represents a potential nuclear delivery system.

The UK has for many years been clear that we would prefer a more productive relationship with Iran, and for Iran to take its place as a responsible member of the international community. We continue to work through the E3+3 [UK, US, China, France, Germany and Russia, Ed.] and urge Iran to accept our, and US, offers of engagement in order to achieve a diplomatic resolution of the nuclear issue. The Government welcome the talks recently held between the E3+3 and Iran. However, Iran continues to pursue its proliferation sensitive nuclear and ballistic missile activities in defiance of five UN Security Council Resolutions.

We cannot and will not ignore specific activities undertaken by Iranian companies which we know to be facilitating activity identified by the UN as being of concern, particularly where such activities have the potential to affect the UK's interests. On the particular entities in question, vessels of the Islamic Republic of Iran Shipping Lines (IRISL) have transported goods for both Iran's ballistic missile and nuclear programmes. Similarly, Bank Mellat has provided banking services to a UN listed organisation connected to Iran's proliferation sensitive activities, and been involved in transactions related to financing Iran's nuclear and ballistic missile programme. The direction to cease business will therefore reduce the risk of the UK financial sector being used, unknowingly or otherwise, to facilitate Iran's proliferation sensitive activities.

(HC Deb 12 October 2009 Vol 497 c1WS-2WS)

16/19
Iran

During a debate, a Minster said:

Any positive progress on the nuclear issue is likely to come through tough diplomacy, which can only proceed if Iran is prepared to accept, clearly and unequivocally, its international obligations. The UK and the wider international community remain deeply concerned about the Iranian nuclear programme. Five United Nations Security Council resolutions require Iran to suspend enrichment, co-operate fully with the International Atomic Energy Agency, and answer outstanding questions about the nature of its programme. The Prime Minister made it clear on 17 March that Iran has a right to civil nuclear power, but to claim what is rightfully available to it, Iran must recognise and act on the obligations to which it has committed itself under the non-proliferation treaty. However, Iran continues to refuse to meet those obligations and is ignoring the Security Council.... it is abundantly clear that Iran is not meeting its obligations, and the latest report from the director general of the IAEA also makes that clear. Iran is still not co-operating fully with the agency or granting the access that it seeks and is required. The IAEA made it clear that Iran is increasing its enrichment capabilities, which is totally contrary to the Security Council's requirements, and confirmed that Iran has still not answered questions about the possible military dimensions of its programme. We simply cannot have confidence in the intentions of a country that acts in that way.... I emphasise three points. First, the onus is on Iran and now is the time to take positive steps towards taking up the E3 plus 3's offer. The E3 plus 3 have reaffirmed their commitment to the diplomatic process; the US has made it clear that it will play a full role in talks; and the international community has fully recognised Iran's right to civil nuclear power. We cannot and should not allow Iran to make the same old arguments to delay talks. Those historic arguments are simply no longer valid. Secondly, the offer to negotiate will not be on the table indefinitely. The US has made it clear that the hand will not be outstretched for ever. We should not be prepared to wait and wait for an answer from Iran while it advances its nuclear plans. That is not acceptable. Thirdly, Iran cannot expect a decision not to respond positively to the E3 plus 3 to be cost free. The implications of recent events for progress on the nuclear issue are not yet clear, but it is clear that we must see positive steps from Iran very soon. It is also clear that hard-headed diplomacy may be needed to reach the destination to which we remain 100 per cent. committed—a diplomatic resolution to the issue that assures us of Iran's intentions in its nuclear programme.

(HC Deb 9 July 2009 Vol 495 c357WH-358WH)

16/20

The Foreign Secretary wrote:

We remain extremely concerned about Iran's nuclear programme. In August the IAEA Director General reported that Iran had not suspended its enrichment activities contrary to the requirements of five UNSCRs and still refuses to answer questions about studies with a possible military dimension. The fact that Iran has been covertly developing an enrichment facility near Qom, in breach of UN and IAEA obligations, casts further doubt on their peaceful intentions.

(HC 22 October 2009 Vol 497 c1618W)

16/21

The Foreign Secretary wrote:

The measures taken by the Treasury under the Counter Terrorism Act 2008 against Bank Mellat and the Islamic Republic of Iran Shipping Lines was used specifically to mitigate the risks posed to the UK national interest by activity in Iran that facilitates the development or production of nuclear weapons. Where the Government identify such activities, they are committed to acting to curtail them.

We are clear that if Iran does not engage seriously in negotiations to restore the international community's confidence in its nuclear programme, multilateral sanctions will be required. We are working closely with other EU member states to ensure that the EU is in a position to enact measures if this should prove necessary. At the present, the content of this work must remain confidential, but I will inform the House when it is possible to discuss these measures in more detail.

(HC 22 October 2009 Vol 497 c1618W)

16/22
A Minister said:

First, we should not be distracted by the announcement made this week. [Iran announced that it intended to build another 10 uranium enrichment plants, Ed.] The issue is that after six years of engagement and five UN Security Council resolutions Iran has still refused to comply with its responsibilities under international law. What has been agreed by the international community is that there will be a meeting of officials of the E3 plus 3 this month, an assessment will be made of the engagement strategy so far, and at that time an appropriate judgment will be made about the next stage. What is clear is that the international community will not tolerate Iran developing nuclear weapons. Not only is that a threat to the stability of the middle east, but it would also trigger an arms race in that region, which would have no limit.

(HC Deb 1 December 2009 Vol 501 c964)

16/23
Israel

A Minister wrote:

We are clear in our call, both privately and publicly, on Israel to accede to the Nuclear Non-Proliferation Treaty as a non-nuclear weapon state. We also call on Israel to ratify the Comprehensive Test Ban Treaty. The Foreign and Commonwealth Office Permanent Under Secretary, Peter Ricketts, emphasised our commitment to a Middle East free of weapons of mass destruction in meetings during his visit to Israel earlier this month.

(HC Deb 27 October 2009 Vol 498 c256)

16/24
The Foreign Secretary was asked for his assessment of the provenance and destination of a shipment of arms seized by the Israeli navy off the coast of Cyprus in November 2009. He wrote:

The information provided by the Government of Israel to the UN Security Council in early November alleging that it had intercepted an arms shipment (on the Francop ship) from Iran to Syria potentially indicates a serious breach of both UN Security Council Resolutions 1737 and 1701. It also appears to be part of a pattern of arms shipments from Iran. If that is the case, it is deeply irresponsible. We will work in New York to ensure that the Iran Sanctions Committee pursues this matter thoroughly and urgently.

(HC Deb 30 November 2009 Vol 501 c425W)

16/25
Non-Proliferation

The Foreign Secretary replied to the FAC's Report on 'Global Security: Non-Proliferation'. The FAC had written:

13. We welcome India's granting of greater international access to its civilian nuclear facilities. However, we reiterate our 2006 conclusion that the US-India civil nuclear cooperation agreement undermines one of the central bargains of

the international non-proliferation regime, namely that access to nuclear power for civil purposes is due only to states which do not develop nuclear weapons and place all their declared nuclear facilities under international safeguards. We conclude that, given its stated commitment to the international non-proliferation regime, the Government's support for the US-India deal is thus regrettable. We recommend that in its response to this Report, the Government should set out how it foresees the US-India agreement being used to secure further disarmament and non-proliferation steps by India, such as ratification of the Comprehensive Nuclear Test Ban Treaty. (Paragraph 99)

The Government replied:

We believe that the US-India nuclear deal, along with the IAEA safeguards agreement and the Nuclear Suppliers Group (NSG) exemption that allowed it to take effect, will bring India closer to the nonproliferation mainstream, including adherence to the principles underpinning the Non-Proliferation Treaty. The deal gives us the opportunity to engage in a constructive non-proliferation dialogue with India, including continuing to encourage them to ratify the CTBT. We expect them to fulfil their nonproliferation commitments under the deal, including separation of their civil and military nuclear programmes, to work towards the conclusion of a Fissile Material Cut-Off Treaty, and to continue their unilateral moratorium on nuclear testing. It also gives us the opportunity to discuss nuclear security issues with India. The Government's stance on the UN General Assembly resolution on this issue was laid out in the 'Explanation of Vote' that was issued at the time. [SC Res 1803, S/PV.5848, 12–14, Ed.]

(Fourth Report from the Foreign Affairs Committee, 2008–2009, Global Security: Non-Proliferation, Response of the Secretary of State for Foreign and Commonwealth Affairs, Cm 7692)

16/26

The Foreign Secretary was asked what the Government's policy was on the entry into force of the Central Asian nuclear-free zone. An FCO Minister wrote:

The UK supports the principle of a Central Asia Nuclear Weapon-Free Zone and welcomes Kazakhstan's recent ratification of the treaty of Semipalatinsk [Treaty on a Nuclear-Weapon-Free Zone in Central Asia, signed at Semipalatinsk: 8 September 2006, entered into force: 21 March 2009, Ed.]. The Government believe this gives the central Asian states the opportunity to amend articles IV and XII, the provisions of which pertaining to transit arrangements and the primacy of previous security arrangements are not in our view compatible with a nuclear weapon-free zone. Acceptable amendments to these provisions will enable the UK to ratify the protocol to the treaty.

[Article IV: Foreign Ships, Aircraft, and Ground Transportation Without prejudice to the purposes and objectives of this Treaty, each Party, in the exercise of its sovereign rights, is free to resolve issues related to transit through its territory by air, land or water, including visits by foreign ships to its ports and landing of foreign aircraft at its airfields. Article XII: Other Agreements This Treaty does not affect the rights and obligations of the Parties under other international treaties which they may have concluded prior to the date of the entry into force of this Treaty. The Parties shall take all necessary measures for effective implementation of the purposes and objectives of this Treaty in accordance with the main principles contained therein. Ed.]

(HC Deb 12 February 2009 Vol 487 c2198W)

16/27

The Defence Secretary was asked if he would assure the House of Commons that there would be no expenditure on developing a new warhead [for the successor system to Trident, Ed]. without the specific approval of the House of Commons, and that he was satisfied that the development of a whole new warhead system was legal within the terms of the nuclear non-proliferation treaty, which would come up for review in 2010. The Defence Secretary said:

Yes, I believe that it certainly would be within the framework of the non-proliferation treaty. The NPT did not require unilateral disarmament on the part of the United Kingdom, and we are able to maintain very properly within the terms of the NPT our minimum nuclear deterrent; and, yes, I believe that there should be a vote in this House before such a decision was taken.

(HC Deb 30 March 2009 Vol 490 c651)

16/28

A Minister wrote:

The Government are committed to retaining only the minimum credible nuclear deterrent capability. We regularly review the number of warheads in the UK stockpile in that light. The UK technical capability to disassemble warheads is exercised and maintained at a level appropriate to enable effective warhead surveillance, essential stockpile maintenance and the timely disassembly of the stockpile should the need arise.

We do not rely on US capabilities to dismantle UK warheads. However, the UK has regular specialist technical exchanges with the US through the 1958 Mutual Defence Agreement. These exchanges include warhead disassembly, to share best practice and experience.

(HC Deb 21 October 2009 Vol 497 c1469W)

16/29

The Foreign Secretary said:

[W]e have voted consistently for the aspiration of a nuclear-free middle east as part of a drive for nuclear disarmament around the world. However, I think that it is important to bear in mind that although it is right to acknowledge that Iran is a signatory to the NPT-and that is welcome-signing is only the first step. Obeying the treaty's injunctions and following its requirements should go with that signature. I hope that my hon. Friend will join me in sending a united message from this House that Iran has the hand of engagement outstretched towards it and that it will be treated as a normal country, not least in respect of civilian nuclear power, but that it must behave as a normal country would in its relations with the IAEA and the rest of the international community.

(HC Deb 20 October 2009 Vol 497 c757)

16/30 North Korea

An FCO Minister said:

Everybody in this country and the rest of the world who has seen the news about North Korea this year is concerned about the situation there. With a second nuclear explosion in May, North Korea has shown open defiance of its obligations. I am glad that the United Nations moved swiftly, and the Security Council provided an unambiguous response. Similarly, Iran continues to enrich uranium in open defiance of numerous Security Council resolutions. Let me make it absolutely plain that we as a country and a Government want further cuts in stockpiles in all countries that retain nuclear weapons. The world community is presented with a significant new problem, or challenge, by the expansion of nuclear energy. We need to make sure that there is security in the production of fissile material, and that countries moving towards nuclear energy options—often in response to rightful climate change concerns—are doing so for peaceful ends. There are key issues that we need to address. First, we want a strengthening of the mechanisms and institutions that surrounded the issue of non-proliferation. We want to make sure that there is early and absolutely certain detection of clandestine activity in countries around the world. If we had been able to detect that more certainly in the case of Iran, we might have been able to provide a far clearer and far earlier response from the international community, but we also point out that Iran has no opportunity to move beyond its obligations, and the international community stands firm in response to what Iran has been doing. We need to strengthen enforcement, because where there is early cognisance of clandestine activity that could be used to move towards producing nuclear weaponry, there should be robust sanctions, as there have been in the cases of North Korea and Iran. There should be tough consequences for those who seek to withdraw from the non-proliferation treaty, and we want to clarify article X of that treaty. We are interested in the proposals that have come from the European Union, and we want to make sure that the clarification goes ahead; we will work with our allies to make sure that it does. It is clearly important that we secure fissile material. One of the greatest dangers to security around the world is the possibility of rogue states or rogue organisations gaining access to fissile material. For that reason, we have doubled our contribution to the funding of the International Atomic Energy Agency nuclear security fund. The Government believe that the prospects for the comprehensive test ban treaty—an issue raised by my right hon. Friend the Member for Edinburgh, East—and, for that matter, a fissile material cut-off treaty, are brighter than they have been for a good many years. We will continue to make a powerful case for all states to sign up to, and ratify, the comprehensive test ban treaty. We also want talks on a treaty to cap the production of fissile material for explosive military purposes to be under way by early next year. Nationally, we will continue our groundbreaking work with Norway and the non-governmental organisation VERTIC—the Verification Research, Training and Information Centre—on the science of verifying warhead reduction. We will host a conference for the nuclear weapon states on confidence-building measures, including the verification of disarmament, later this year, in September.

(HC Deb 9 July 2009 Vol 495 cs1227–1228)

16/31
An FCO Minister said:

By conducting a nuclear test, North Korea contravened its international legal obligations under the NPT, and its ballistic missile launches are a clear breach of UN Security Council resolutions. Those provocative actions undermine regional security.

(HC Deb 11 November 2009 Vol 499 cs104WH-105WH)

Part Seventeen: The Law of Armed Conflict and International Humanitarian Law

Part Seventeen: I.B.6. *The Law of Armed Conflict and International Humanitarian Law—International armed conflict—The law of international armed conflict—Distinction between combatants and non-combatants*

17/1
A Minister wrote:

We regret incidents where civilians are accidentally killed as a result of actions by international forces. Procedures are in place, and constantly updated in the light of experience, both to minimise the risk of these casualties occurring and to investigate any incidents that do happen. UK personnel operate at all times under rules of engagement which ensure that force is used in accordance with international humanitarian law. This ensures that civilian casualties and damage to civilian infrastructure are minimised. Wherever possible, local populations are warned of impending operations. We should remember the insurgents are the real threat to the safety and security of the Afghan people by their indiscriminate use of violence. ISAF forces are not present on a permanent basis in many parts of Afghanistan, which makes it difficult to monitor atrocities against the civilian population by the Taliban. The UK Government do not collate or publish figures for civilian casualties in Afghanistan because of the immense difficulty and risks of collecting robust data, including the nature of any munitions involved.

All reports of civilian casualties are investigated promptly and thoroughly, in co-ordination with the Afghan authorities.

(HC Deb 14 July 2009 Vol 496 c264W)

17/2
A Minister wrote:

UK forces thoroughly investigate all reports of civilian casualties in Afghanistan, regardless of their potential cause. We regret incidents where civilians are accidentally killed as a result of actions by UK armed forces. In addition to investigating all reports of civilian casualties, procedures are in place, and being constantly updated in the light of experience, to minimise the risk of these casualties occurring.

(HC Deb 20 July 2009 Vol 496 c864W)

Part Seventeen: I.B.7. *The Law of Armed Conflict and International Humanitarian Law—International armed conflict—The law of international armed conflict—International humanitarian law*

17/3
International humanitarian law—General

The Council of the European Union issued the following conclusions:

Council conclusions on promoting compliance with international humanitarian law

The Council adopted the following conclusions:1. In the year of the 60th anniversary of the Geneva Conventions, the Council reaffirms its strong support for the promotion and protection of international humanitarian law (IHL). To this end, the Council has adopted an updated version of the EU guidelines on IHL. It reaffirms its commitment to ensuring their implementation and the importance of continuing to improve the mainstreaming of IHL throughout the external action of the European Union. The Council will continue to give priority to efforts to improve compliance with international humanitarian law by third states and non-state actors in armed conflicts, and to ensure the protection of civilians, who are the most frequent victims of serious violations of IHL. 2. The Council affirms its strong opposition to impunity for serious violations of international humanitarian law and human rights law. The Council confirms that the primary responsibility to investigate and prosecute such violations rests with the parties to an armed conflict or the state party concerned. The Council underlines the important role the International Criminal Court can play in cases where the State or States in question are unable or unwilling to exercise their jurisdiction. The Council emphasizes the importance of dealing effectively with the legacy of serious violations of international humanitarian and human rights law by supporting appropriate accountability mechanisms. 3. The Council underlines the close link between European Union action under the Guidelines on IHL and the EU Guidelines on human rights, including those on children and armed conflict, on violence against women and on torture. In order to strengthen the impact of the European Union's action in support of IHL and human rights, further efforts will be made to ensure coordinated action in selected countries on the basis of all relevant guidelines. 4. The Council reaffirms its intention to improve coherence, complementarity and coordination between the various policies and actions targeting the respect for IHL and the situation of civilians and others affected by armed conflict in the various policy areas, including CFSP/CSDP (Common Foreign and Security Policy / Common Security and Defence Policy), development cooperation and humanitarian aid. The need for respect for international humanitarian law should be raised in all relevant political dialogues with third countries. 5. The Council reiterates the importance of integrating respect for IHL in the full range of EU crisis management efforts, from decision-making to the training of personnel. 6. The Council expresses its intention to redouble the efforts to implement the IHL guidelines in all relevant decision-making instances, in civilian and military missions, in other relevant offices and agencies, and by the special and personal representatives of the High Representative, as appropriate. It invites other EU institutions to do the same. 7. The Council recognizes the importance of strengthening the mandates of the European Union Special Representatives by the inclusion of IHL references, where relevant. 8. The Council recognizes the key role of the Commission in promoting compliance with IHL, inter alia under the various financial instruments for external assistance. 9. The Council reaffirms that EU action should support and complement the work of the United Nations, including the implementation of UN Security Council resolutions 1325, 1612, 1820, 1882 and 1888 on children affected by armed conflict and women, peace and security and welcomes Security Council Resolution 1894 on protection of civilians in situations of armed conflict. The Council undertakes to further integrate the protection of civilians in its CSDP missions. 10. The Council calls on states to consider accepting the competence of the International Humanitarian Fact-Finding Commission under Article 90 of Protocol I Additional to the Geneva Conventions of 1949. The Council recalls the role of the International Committee of the Red Cross as guardian of international humanitarian law. 11. The Council underlines that international law, including international humanitarian law, is one of the strongest tools the international community has to ensure the protection and dignity of all persons. The European Union recalls the commitment to respect and ensure respect of the Geneva Conventions in all circumstances. The European Union will continue to do its utmost to promote an international order where no state or individual is above the law and no person is outside the protection of the law.

(2985th [EU] Foreign Affairs Council meeting Brussels, 8 December 2009)

17/4
Afghanistan

A Minister wrote:

ISAF forces in Afghanistan continue to work hard, in conjunction with the Afghan National Security Forces, to afford all Afghan nationals, both men, women and children, a safe and secure environment in which to go about their daily lives. Afghan cultural awareness training is provided to all UK personnel deploying to Afghanistan which includes cultural differences when interacting with Afghan women. UK personnel operate at all times under rules of engagement which ensure that force is used in accordance with international humanitarian law. This ensures that civilian casualties and damage to civilian infrastructure are minimised.

(HC Deb 3 December 2009 Vol 501 c910W)

17/5
Armenia

A Minister wrote:
We are aware that both Armenia and Azerbaijan report incidents in which their servicemen have been held by the other side.

We encourage both sides to work towards a peaceful, negotiated settlement and to explore the possibilities for confidence-building measures to reduce tension along the line of contact and international border between the two countries. We expect all countries to respect international humanitarian and human rights law in dealing with captured soldiers and civilians.

(HL Deb 2 July 2009 Vol 712 cWA66)

17/6 (See also **6/38, 90–96**)
Camp Ashraf

During a debate in the House of Lords, the Government were asked whether they had made representations to the governments of the United States and Iraq concerning the current threats to the inhabitants of Camp Ashraf in Northern Iraq. A Minister said:

[T]he UK ambassador to Baghdad called on the Iraqi Human Rights Minister, Widjan Salim, on 13 April this year to raise the issue of Camp Ashraf, and to remind her of the early assurances made by the Iraqi Government about the humane treatment of its residents. Officials at the British embassy in Baghdad continue to discuss Camp Ashraf with staff at the US embassy; the most recent discussion took place on 10 June 2009.... the UK Government remain concerned that the fundamental human rights of all the residents of Camp Ashraf are fully observed. We particularly sought assurances from the Iraqi Government, who have given them-I now give the assurance that the noble Lord seeks-that no Ashraf residents will be forcibly transferred to a country where they have reason to fear persecution or where substantial grounds exist to believe that they would be tortured. We continue, as the noble Lord rightly says, to have no direct interest or control in this camp, but we continue to liaise with our colleagues in the United States, who are monitoring events with the Iraqi Government....the United Kingdom view is that the residents of Ashraf are not protected persons under the status provided by the fourth Geneva Convention. That ceased to apply in Iraq after 24 June 2004, the date of the end of hostilities and occupation. The United States Government have continued to grant protected persons status as a good-will gesture, but this is not granted through any legal obligation under international law, and the UN High Commissioner for Refugees has previously determined that Camp Ashraf residents do not qualify as refugees. However, the United Kingdom continues to take an interest to ensure that human rights are protected, as does the United States.

(HL Deb 1 July 2009 Vol 712 c220–221)

17/7
A Minister wrote:

Our ambassador in Iraq has written to the Iraqi authorities to ask for a review into the recent events at the camp [sc., Camp Ashraf]. Officials from our embassy in Baghdad are continuing to follow developments, and will shortly undertake a further visit to the camp. Our view remains that the residents of Camp Ashraf are not entitled to 'protected persons' status as the Fourth Geneva Convention ceased to apply in Iraq after 28 June 2004, following the end of active hostilities and occupation.

(HC Deb 9 September 2009 Vol 496 c1961W)

17/8
During a debate in the House of Lords, a Minister said:

Alas, it is not the case that people in Camp Ashraf have protected person status under the Fourth Geneva Convention. That has ceased to apply. That view is shared by the United Nations, the Government of Iraq, the United States and us. It is a mistake to believe that there is international protection for these individuals. However, that does not mean that we should abandon them to be subject to inhuman treatment or to be transferred to regimes in countries where their lives would be in danger.

(HL Deb 23 November 2009 Vol 715 c133)

17/9

The Government were asked whether they classify the residents in Camp Ashraf as not being 'protected persons' under the Fourth Geneva Convention; whether that classification takes account of their international obligations; what assessment they have made of the Spanish Central Investigative Court ruling that the residents of Camp Ashraf are 'protected persons' under the Fourth Geneva Convention; and whether they recognise the right of that court to investigate the alleged attacks in July by Iraqi forces on the residents of the Camp. A Minister wrote:

The Government view is that, with the formal end of hostilities in Iraq and the transfer of responsibility for the camp to the Iraqi authorities, any claim to protected person status has ceased to apply. This is a view also shared by the US. The decisions of the Spanish National High Court are a domestic matter for Spain. It is for the Spanish to judge how they interpret their adherence to the international treaties and conventions to which they are signatories, including any investigations they may commission or carry out.

(HL Deb 16 December 2009 Vol 715 cWA247)

17/10
Democratic Republic of Congo

A Minister wrote:

The UK has stressed on various occasions to the UN that the UN Mission in the Democratic of Congo (DRC) (MONUC) should not provide such support, including to operations which involve Bosco Ntaganda, an International Criminal Court indictee. MONUC has assured the international community that it takes every effort to avoid doing so.

The UK continues to push for implementation of this policy. DRC President Kabila recently announced a policy of "Zero Tolerance" for abuses, including those committed by the security forces. We continue to urge the DRC Government to fully implement this policy.

(HC Deb 26 October 2009 Vol 498 c67W)

17/11
Fourth Geneva Convention

A Minister wrote:

The UK has fully implemented the Geneva Conventions through the Geneva Conventions Act of 1957, which includes all the necessary legal provisions to ensure the UK's compliance with the Conventions, including the fourth. It is for individuals to decide what legal action they wish to take in accordance with UK law, and it is not for the Government to comment on such action.

(HC Deb 9 September 2009 Vol 496 c1959W)

17/12
Gaza

The Foreign Secretary made a statement and answered questions about the conflict in Gaza. He said:

The United Nations resolution [1860] is clear, but so was the response. The passage of the resolution on Thursday night, New York time, was followed within hours by its rejection by both sides to the conflict. The resolution calls on all states in the region to support peace efforts. The Prime Minister and I have been in close touch with the Israeli Government since the onset of the crisis. The Israeli Prime Minister, Foreign Minister and Defence Minister argued strongly against any UN resolution. Their argument is that there can be no equivalence between a democratic state and a terrorist organisation.

There is and can be no equivalence. Hamas has shown itself over a number of years ready to be murderous in word and deed. Its motif is "resistance" and its method includes terrorism. Israel is, meanwhile, a thriving, democratic state with an independent judiciary. However, one consequence of the distinction between a democratic Government and a terrorist organisation is that democratic Governments are held to significantly higher standards, notably by their own people. That is one reason why we supported resolution 1860—to uphold the standards on which Israel and the rest of us depend. As a beacon of democracy in the middle east, Israel's best defence is to show leadership in finding a political solution to the crisis and comply with the standards of international humanitarian law.

(HC Deb 12 January 2009 Vol 486 c23)

17/13
Answering a question about the Inquiry under Judge Goldstone into allegations of war crimes in Gaza, an FCO Minister said:

[W] e urge both Israel and Hamas to co-operate with that mission and will consider carefully any report it produces. We have consistently said that all credible allegations of breaches of international humanitarian law during the military operation, by either side, should be properly investigated.

(HL Deb 21 May 2009 Vol 710 c1430)

17/14
Asked for the Government's response to Amnesty International's report 'Operation "Cast Lead": 22 Days of Death and Destruction', on the conflict in Gaza, an FCO Minister said:

[W]e are concerned by the findings of the recent Amnesty report. We take seriously any allegations of violations of international humanitarian law made by credible organisations during the Gaza conflict. We have consistently stated that they should be properly investigated. In that regard, we urge all parties involved to co-operate with the Human Rights Council fact-finding mission led by Justice Richard Goldstone, and will carefully consider the findings of that report once released.

(HL Deb 7 July 2009 Vol 712 c566)

17/15
The Foreign Secretary was asked for his assessment of the allegations of war crimes made in respect of each party to the recent conflict in Gaza. A Minister wrote:

There are allegations of serious concern which cannot be ignored. Rocket attacks by Palestinian militants targeted at innocent civilians in southern Israel constitute a breach of international humanitarian law. There are also serious allegations about Israeli conduct and we urge the Israeli Government to carry out full, credible and impartial investigations.

(HC Deb 29 October 2009 Vol 498 cs506W-507W)

17/16
A Minister said:

[T]he report to which the noble Baroness refers ['Goldstone Report', Report of the United Nations Fact Finding Mission on the Gaza Conflict, A/HRC/12/48, Ed.] is due to be debated in the United Nations on 4 November, which I believe is the earliest opportunity. That debate will reveal the arguments and why nations support or do not support the Goldstone report. It made broad interpretations of international law with which we did not agree, which will become evident when we make our views known on that occasion. It does not allow us to resile from our obligations to have an independent and thorough investigation into the Israeli defence forces. It has happened in respect of previous conflicts and Israel can be proud of those reports because they have hidden nothing and revealed everything. That will help everyone involved in the peace process.

(HL Deb 2 November 2009 Vol 714 cs6–7)

17/17
A Minister wrote:

As our ambassador made clear to the Human Rights Council, the UN fact finding mission on Gaza has its flaws: not adequately recognising Israel's right to protect its citizens or paying sufficient attention to Hamas's actions; making broad assertions about detailed interpretation of international law with which we differ; and (because Israel did not cooperate) lacking an authoritative Israeli perspective so crucial to determining the legality of actions. However, the report raises very important issues that are of serious concern and that we want to see addressed. Rocket attacks by Palestinian militants targeted at innocent civilians in southern Israel constitute a breach of international humanitarian law. The report also makes serious allegations about Israeli conduct and we urge the Israeli Government to carry out full, credible and impartial investigations into the concerns raised by the report. The full text of our intervention can be found at: www.fco.gov.uk/resources/en/press-statement/11644804/ 21015315/goldstone-161009

(HC Deb 2 November 2009 Vol 498 c664W)

17/18
A Minister wrote:

There have been various reports conducted into the Gaza conflict, some by human rights organisations such as Human Rights Watch and Amnesty International. However, the specific issue of directions given to civilians in Gaza by Palestinian armed groups is documented in the Government of Israel's July 2009 report "The Operation in Gaza: Factual and Legal Aspects" (paragraphs 186 to 189) and the UN Fact Finding Mission on Gaza Report.

Copies of these reports can be found at:

www.mfa.gov.il/MFA/Terrorism+Obstacle+to+Peace/Hamas+war+against+Israel/Operation_in_Gaza-Factual_and_Legal_Aspects.htm

and

www2.ohchr.org/english/bodies/hrcouncil/docs/l2session/A-HRC-12–48.pdf

. . . the Foreign Secretary has been clear from the beginning of the Gaza conflict that all allegations of violations of international humanitarian law committed by anyone during the conflict should be properly investigated.

(HC Deb 16 December 2009 Vol 502 c1227W)

17/19
Israel

A Minister said:

Any decision on the release of prisoners is a matter for the Israeli Government and has to be a case for negotiation between the Israelis and the Palestinians. In the context of that debate, we strongly urge Hamas immediately to release Gilad Shalit [an Israeli soldier who was abducted on 25 June 2009, Ed.], who was illegally detained against international law.

(HC Deb 1 December Vol 501 c972)

17/20
Military training

A Minister wrote:

All members of the armed forces receive training on the Law of Armed Conflict (LOAC) shortly after joining and regularly throughout their careers.

The UK armed forces do not routinely train all personnel on the Optional Protocol [on Children in Armed Conflicts, Protocol to the Convention on the

Right of the Child, Ed.] specifically, but personnel involved in handling prisoners of war, internees and detainees receive training which addresses the handling of juveniles and children.

(HC Deb 14 October 2009 Vol 497 c795W)

17/21

A Minister wrote:

Aspects of the Geneva Convention are applied throughout military training and will be bolstered before deployment to an operational theatre by further mandatory training, common across all the Services. Irrespective of the theatre to which a person is deploying, specific training based on the Geneva Convention as applied to UK law must be fulfilled. This training includes: compliance with operational law, such as the legal basis for operations, the law of armed conflict, the application of the rules of engagement, the use of force, prisoner handling, understanding the powers of stop and search and the powers of arrest; culture and language training, including cultural awareness; firepower training, including identifying and engaging targets and reacting to fire control orders; and protection training, including procedures for challenging and reaction to direct and indirect attack.

All deployed personnel are issued a rules of engagement card, which specifies exactly the aspects of the law that allows them to conduct operations and react to hostile action.

Role specific training that covers the pertinent application of the Geneva Convention is also undertaken. For example, dedicated prisoner handling teams and medics are briefed in depth of their responsibilities that may be in addition to those usually held.

Trained and qualified lawyers are deployed on all standing operations and are an integral part of the targeting process, are consulted on all forms of the conduct of operations and are available for specialist queries if doubt exists.

(HC Deb 2 December 2009 Vol 501 c727W)

17/22

Protection of Cultural Property

A Minister wrote:

The Government intend to introduce the Cultural Property (Armed Conflicts) Bill, which will enable the UK to ratify the Hague Convention, as soon as parliamentary time allows.[See (2008) UKMIL **17/11**]

(HC Deb 30 March 2009 Vol 490 c934W)

17/23

The Defence Secretary wrote:

There are no plans to appoint specialist staff to protect ancient monuments and works of art in locations where British troops are operating. However, operations are always conducted with due regard to the obligations contained within the

Hague Convention for the Protection of Cultural Property in the Event of Armed Conflict of 1954.

(HL Deb 5 October 2009 Vol 712 cWA434)

17/24
Sri Lanka

The Foreign Secretary made a written statement about the situation in Sri Lanka. He said:

The UK has consistently maintained that one of the prerequisites for lasting peace in Sri Lanka is a political settlement that fully takes into account the legitimate grievances and aspirations of all communities. When . . . the Prime Minister spoke to President Rajapakse on 18 May he urged him to be magnanimous in victory. On the same day I pressed Foreign Minister Bogollagama to seize the historic opportunity-and duty-to lay the foundations for the peaceful, secure and prosperous Sri Lanka that we all want to see. Despite some recent welcome developments the Government need to show greater urgency in making clear their plans for future political reforms if they are serious about wanting to win the confidence of Tamils, Muslims and other communities in Sri Lanka. We hope to see an inclusive, genuine political process initiated as soon as possible.

We have consistently called for a credible process of accountability, most recently during the visit to the UK of the Sri Lankan Attorney-General and Justice Permanent Secretary in early October and the visit of the Sri Lankan Justice Minister in September. Addressing accountability could play an integral role in the process of reconciliation and will be essential in creating conditions for a sustainable end to the conflict. The recent broadcast of mobile phone footage purporting to show members of the Sri Lankan military summarily executing Tamils underlines the importance of lifting the fog of uncertainty surrounding events of the final months of fighting when independent observers had no access to the conflict zone.

The Government remain actively involved in working for a peaceful Sri Lanka. We have urged the Sri Lankan Government, in a number of direct contacts, to make greater progress on improving conditions inside the camps, on returning IDPs to their homes and on working for reconciliation. We urge that freedom of movement be returned to IDPs, and highlight the urgency of doing so before the monsoon. We also encourage swifter progress on the development of an inclusive political process to address minority concerns and for an improvement in the rule of law, including accountability for possible violations of international humanitarian law, as both would be essential for a sustainable end to the conflict.

(HL Deb 13 October 2009 Vol 713 c19WS)

17/25
White Phosphorus

The Defence Secretary wrote:

In Afghanistan, white phosphorus munitions are routinely used to protect troops on operations by producing a smoke screen to provide cover. Records show white phosphorus munitions were last used for the same purpose in Iraq in 2005. In accordance with the UN third convention on conventional weapons, UK training in the use of white phosphorus emphasises that it should be used solely for its intended purpose and not as an anti-personnel weapon.

(HC Deb 23 February 2009 Vol 488 c18W)

17/26
The Foreign Secretary was asked about the use of white phosphorus by Israeli forces in Gaza. A Minister wrote:

We are very concerned about reports of white phosphorus ammunition being used by the Israeli defence force in Gaza. We have made this clear directly to both the Foreign Ministry and Defence Ministry in Tel Aviv. I have also made clear to the House that Gaza is an exceptionally densely populated area where white phosphorus used as an air burst is liable to cause particularly horrific injuries to non-combatants. We consider such use in these circumstances unacceptable.

(HC Deb 26 February 2009 Vol 488 c951W)

17/27
A Minister wrote:

White phosphorus munitions are only used by UK forces to protect troops on operations by producing a smoke screen to provide cover in accordance with the Third Protocol of the UN Convention on Prohibitions or Restrictions on the use of Certain Conventional Weapons, ratified by the UK in 1995, when it became illegal to use white phosphorus as a primary incendiary weapon under UK law. Training of UK forces in the use of white phosphorus emphasises that it should only be used for its intended purpose; as an obscurant and not as an anti-personnel weapon. The Government do not collate figures for civilian casualties in Afghanistan, Iraq or on other operations. Every effort is made to avoid civilian casualties in all theatres, and any that are the result of action by UK armed forces are always a matter of profound regret.

(HC Deb 6 July 2009 Vol 495 c560W)

Part Seventeen: I.B.8. *The Law of Armed Conflict and International Humanitarian Law - International armed conflict—The law of international armed conflict—Belligerent occupation*

17/28
An FCO Minister wrote about the status of Gaza:

We, along with the EU presidency, are concerned with the serious humanitarian situation in Gaza and consider the restrictions of Gaza's borders to the passage of relief supplies a disproportionate and inappropriate response to the security threat.

Although there is no permanent physical Israeli presence in Gaza, given the significant control that Israel has over Gaza's borders, airspace and territorial waters, Israel retains obligations under the Fourth Geneva Convention as an occupying power. The Fourth Geneva Convention is clear that an occupying power must co-operate in allowing the passage and distribution of relief consignments.

We will continue to urge the Israeli Government to ease the restrictions on the Gaza border and permit the flow of essential supplies.

(HL Deb 26 January 2009 Vol 707 cWA8)

17/29
The Foreign Secretary was asked what recent reports he had received on access by Gazan fishermen to *(a)* Gazan and *(b)* international waters. An FCO Minister wrote:

Gazan fishermen are prevented by the Israeli navy from entering international waters. The Israeli navy also severely limits their access to Gaza's own territorial waters. We believe that the current limit is enforced at around three miles from the shore. Many Gazan fishing boats were also destroyed or damaged during Operation Cast Lead. The Israeli authorities say that they are enforcing these limits to prevent the smuggling of weapons into Gaza.

(HC Deb 23 March 2009 Vol 490 c34W)

17/30
The Government were asked what remedy existed under international law to remove any illegal settlements in the West Bank. An FCO Minister wrote:

In its Advisory Opinion on the Legal Consequences of the Construction of a Wall in the Occupied Palestinian Territory (2004), the International Court of Justice concluded that,

"the Israeli settlements in the Occupied Palestinian Territory (including East Jerusalem) have been established in breach of international law",

and the UN Security Council has also taken that position (for example, UN Security Council Resolution 446 [1980]). International law requires Israel to cease settlement activity that is in breach of international law and to make reparation. Israeli settlement activity is also in contravention of Israel's obligations under the road map agreement of April 2003. It clearly sets out the steps the Palestinian Authority and Israel need to implement to achieve a negotiated settlement. Both sides have accepted the road map. The Government have raised the issue with the Israeli Government on many occasions. My right honourable friend the Foreign Secretary voiced strong opposition to illegal Israeli settlements during his visit to the region on 16 to 19 November 2008.

(HL Deb 30 March 2009 Vol 489 cWA216)

17/31 (See also **13/1**)
The Government were asked:

The information that the Israeli Government have given to me is that they intercepted the 'Spirit of Humanity' [a ship claiming to be importing humanitarian aid into Gaza] in Gazan waters, not in international waters, so does Israel have the right to intercept vessels in that location?

An FCO Minister said:

As far as I am aware, although there may be a debate about whether that is appropriate, it is not in itself a breach of international law. The accusation that is being made about this intervention is that it in some way contravened international law. If the vessel was in Gazan waters, people may have a political debate about whether that action was appropriate, but it would not have breached international law.

(HC Deb 13 July 2009 Vol 496 c134)]

17/32
A Minister said:

I have made it clear that we expect individuals and organisations who seek to get aid to Gaza to do so in consultation with the appropriate authorities. We advise that that is the best way to proceed if organisations and individuals genuinely want to get humanitarian aid through to the people of Gaza. I will not give a running commentary on what the United Kingdom may do in circumstances that may prevail at some stage in future; that would not be appropriate in this debate. I shall make some progress now. We are very concerned about the humanitarian situation in Gaza. We know that the conflict earlier this year intensified an already difficult situation. It is true that the pace of deterioration has slowed since the ceasefire in January, but it is evident that the humanitarian situation remains extremely serious. The strict border restrictions, including on legitimate aid, reconstruction materials, trade goods and the movement of people, are having a major impact on the lives of ordinary Gazans, who suffer serious hardship. Approximately 90 per cent. of Gazans depend partly on food aid. During May, according to the UN Office for the Co-ordination of Humanitarian Affairs, the number of truckloads of goods allowed entry into Gaza was approximately 2,960.

However, that is not enough; it represents less than a quarter of the monthly average of truckloads that entered Gaza in the first five months of 2007, before the tightening of the border restrictions in June of that year. We are concerned that those restrictions, and Hamas's control of the economy and the smuggling tunnels, mean that the people of Gaza are being denied hope, access to the means to rebuild their lives, and the chance of economic growth and education. Although there is no permanent, physical Israeli presence in Gaza, Israel retains significant control over Gaza's borders, airspace, and territorial waters. It therefore retains obligations under the fourth Geneva Convention. The convention is clear that an occupying power must co-operate in allowing the passage and distribution of relief consignments. It is therefore essential that the Government of Israel ease the restrictions on the Gaza border and allow an immediate increase in the flow of essential aid and reconstruction materials into Gaza, as well as the legitimate flow of trade, goods and people. My right hon. Friend the Foreign Secretary raised the United Kingdom's concerns on that general issue in his meeting with the Israeli Defence Minister, Ehud Barak, on 6 July, and in his conversations with the Israeli Foreign Minister—I referred to one of those conversations—which took place on 13 May and 1 July. Together with the European Union, the United States, and the wider international community, we will continue to press the Israeli Government at the highest levels to reduce the restrictions, but Israel is not the only party that should move. Hamas must renounce violence, recognise Israel, accept previous agreements, and work with the Palestinian Authority towards a positive outcome in the current national dialogue negotiations presided over by Egypt. Hamas must also release Gilad Shalit, whom it kidnapped and has held illegally for more than three years without contact with his family, or access for the Red Cross. As my right hon. Friend the Foreign Secretary stated on the third anniversary of Gilad Shalit's abduction on 25 June, we call on Hamas for his immediate, unconditional and safe release. We share the Shalit family's dismay at Hamas's refusal to allow the International Committee of the Red Cross access to Gilad.

(HC Deb 13 July 2009 Vol 496 c135–136)

17/33
A Minister wrote in reply to a question about the activities of the British Gas Group ['BG Group'] regarding the natural gas resources off the coast of Gaza:

Our consulate-general in Jerusalem and our embassy in Tel Aviv have been in regular contact with British Gas Group regarding the natural gas resources off the coast of Gaza since British Gas Group first began exploration in 1999. Discussions have also taken place in the past year with the Cabinet Office and UK Trade and Investment. The most recent meeting on this matter was between the head of UK Trade and Investment at the British consulate-general in Jerusalem and representatives of British Gas Group in December 2008.

In the last meeting BCG [British Coal Gasification, Ed.] had with BG Group, discussion centred on BG's negotiations with Israel Electricity Company (IEC) concerning buying Gaza gas.

(HL Deb 17 March 2009 Vol 709 cWA24)

17/34
Israel

A Minister wrote:

We have not received any reports outlining the number of settlements removed by the Israeli Government since 1997.

We consider all Israeli settlement activity to be illegal and in contravention of international law. Settlement activity remains one of the major obstacles towards achieving a peaceful solution in the Middle East. My right hon. Friend the Foreign Secretary made this clear during his recent meeting with the Israeli Defence Minister. We will continue to raise this issue both in public and private.

(HC Deb 13 July 2009 Vol 496 c110W)

17/35
In response to Israel's announcement of a ten-month freeze on building Jewish settlements in the occupied West Bank, the Foreign Secretary said:

Britain has strongly and consistently supported the vision of two states living side by side in peace and security, based on 1967 borders, with Jerusalem as a shared capital, and a fair settlement for refugees. Britain wants today's announcement by Israel to become a step towards resuming meaningful negotiations to achieve this vision. Britain continues to call for a full settlement freeze in the West Bank and East Jerusalem, including so-called 'natural growth', in accordance with the responsibilities set for both sides in the 2003 Roadmap. Settlements are illegal. Britain will do all it can to support US efforts to relaunch negotiations. Negotiations are the only way for the Israelis and Palestinians to achieve a comprehensive, just, and secure peace.

(<www.fco.gov.uk/news>, 25 November 2009)

17/36
Palestine

In answer to a question about Israeli settlements in Palestinian areas, an FCO Minister wrote:

The International Court of Justice expressed the following opinion in its Advisory Opinion on the *Legal Consequences of the Construction of a Wall in the Occupied Palestinian Territory* of 9 July 2004: "The court concludes that the Israeli settlements in the Occupied Palestinian Territory (including East Jerusalem) have been established in breach of international law". In its Resolution 446 (1979) of 22 March 1979 the UN Security Council determined that:"the policies and practices of Israel in establishing settlements in the Palestinian and other Arab territories occupied since 1967 have no legal validity and constitute a serious obstruction to achieving a comprehensive, just and lasting peace in the Middle East".

(HL Deb 10 March 2009 Vol 708 cWA253)

17/37
A Minister wrote:

We are extremely concerned by the continued eviction notices served on Palestinian families in East Jerusalem and have pressed the Israeli Government to suspend these eviction notices immediately. We have supported an EU presidency statement expressing the EU's deep concern about the issue of eviction notices to the al-Rawi and Hanoun families in East Jerusalem and calling for the al-Kurd family to be allowed to return to their home. Additionally... the Foreign Secretary made the UK's concerns clear in his statement to the UN Security Council on 11 May 2009 and it was also discussed during the EU Foreign Ministers' meeting on 15 June 2009. The UK will continue to raise this with Israeli officials both in public and in private.

(HC Deb 6 July 2009 Vol 495 c548W)

17/38
A Minister wrote:

The demolition of houses in East Jerusalem is, with very few exceptions, illegal under international law. It also threatens the viability of a comprehensive, just and lasting settlement in the Middle East.... the Foreign Secretary made clear the UK's concerns about the demolition of Palestinian buildings in East Jerusalem during his statement to the UN Security Council on 11 May 2009 and it was also raised during the EU Foreign Ministers' meeting on 15 June 2009. The Foreign Secretary also continues to call on Israel to freeze settlement construction, including in East Jerusalem. We will continue to raise these issues as a high priority with Israel both privately and publicly; the Foreign Secretary last did so in his conversation with the Israeli Foreign Minister on 1 July 2009.

(HC Deb 7 July 2009 Vol 495 c632W)

17/39

The Foreign Secretary was asked what representations he had made to the Israeli government on its decision to expand the settlement east of Jerusalem at Ma'ale Adumim. A Minister wrote:

The UK's position is clear: all settlements in the Occupied Palestinian territories, including the west bank and east Jerusalem, are a clear violation of international law. This includes the settlement of Ma'ale Adumim. We will continue to press Israel to adhere to its 2003 Road Map commitments, including to freeze immediately all settlement activity and remove all outposts erected since 2001. We regard a freeze on the expansion of settlements as a key element in restarting peace talks.

(HC Deb 12 October 2009 Vol 497 c46–7W)

17/40

The Trade Secretary issued the following Ministerial Statement:

Defra has today issued advice to retailers and importers who wish to respond to consumer demand for information about the origin of food that has been produced in the Occupied Palestinian Territories (OPT). Importers, retailers, NGOs and consumers have asked the Government for clarity over the precise origin of products from the Occupied Palestinian Territories (OPTs). The label "West Bank" does not allow consumers to distinguish between goods originating from Palestinian producers and goods originating from illegal Israeli settlements. Rules on the labelling of produce are set by the European Union and require that the place of origin or provenance should be supplied on foodstuffs where omission of such information might materially mislead the consumer about true origin or provenance of the foodstuff. Since the "West Bank" is a recognised geographical area within the OPTs, labelling produce with the "West Bank" does not infringe EU labelling rules. However, retailers have informed us of consumer demand for more detailed information. Therefore, in March, the Government arranged a roundtable discussion between interested parties to look at how retailers could make labelling clearer for consumers. We have taken these views into account, and have today issued advice to retailers and importers. This will help them consider how best to respond to consumer demand for information about the origin of food that has been produced in the OPT. The Government will keep its policy on labelling food imports from the OPTs under review, in conjunction with the European Commission and other EU Member States, and in the light of developments in the Middle East Peace Process. The Government believes that that existence, and continued growth, of Israeli settlements poses a significant obstacle to peace in the Middle East. At the same time, the clear position of the Government is that we are opposed to boycotts of Israel or Israeli goods. We do not believe that boycotts help engage or influence Israel, or lead to progress in the Middle East Peace Process.

(HL Deb 10 December 2009 Vol 715 c28WS)

Part Seventeen: I.B.9. *The Law of Armed Conflict and International Humanitarian Law—International armed conflict—The law of international armed conflict—Conventional, nuclear, bacteriological and chemical weapons*

17/41
Biological, Chemical and Toxin Weapons

The Foreign Secretary replied to the FAC's Report on 'Global Security: Non-Proliferation'. The FAC had written:

36. We recommend that in its response to this Report the Government should set out its view on non-lethal agents such as herbicides, defoliants and incapacitating biochemical weapons and the status of such agents under the Biological and Toxin Weapons Convention and Chemical Weapons Convention. We conclude that there is a case for certain biological and chemical agents which are non-lethal or which target plants, including crops and vegetation, to be prohibited from use as weapons for the purposes of these Conventions. We further recommend that the Government should press for negotiations on an unambiguous prohibition of their use as weapons to commence at the next Review Conferences. (Paragraph 218)

The Government replied:

Herbicides and defoliants are not covered by the CWC and we see no need to amend the Convention accordingly. The 1977 Environmental Modification Treaty however does prohibit the hostile use of such materials where they would have widespread, long-lasting or severe effects as the means of destruction, damage or injury to any other State Party. Their position under the BTWC is more complex. Herbicides and defoliants are generally held to be chemicals, but such agents could be based on chemicals derived from natural sources—such as hormones—a fact which would make their development, production, stockpiling, acquisition or retention for hostile purposes or in armed conflict a breach of the BTWC. Anti-crop biological agents are already prohibited if held contrary to the provisions of the BTWC's Article I. The Sixth Review Conference Final Declaration made clear that the Convention's Article I prohibitions apply to human, animal and plant agents Development, production, retention, acquisition or use of "Incapacitating biochemical weapons" are prohibited by both Conventions. Use of the word "weapons" here is crucial. We must recall that although there is no express prohibition on use in the BTWC, the Fourth Review Conference in 1996 reaffirmed that the use in any way and under any circumstances of microbial or other biological agents or toxins that is not consistent with prophylactic, protective or other peaceful purposes, is effectively a violation of Article I of the Convention. This point was reiterated at the Sixth Review Conference in 2006. There is less clarity under the CWC in relation to chemicals that have an incapacitating effect and are also intended for use for law enforcement purposes.

However it is important to note that the rules of the general purpose criterion apply—namely that as long as the types and quantities are consistent with a permitted purpose, then there is no problem in terms of compliance with the Convention. We believe that in the long run greater clarity may be required on how incapacitating chemicals used for law enforcement purposes are to be treated under the Convention particularly in terms of increasing transparency about States Parties' activities involving these chemicals We see no need for any negotiations to commence at the next Review Conference on an unambiguous prohibition of the use of certain biological and chemical agents, which are non-lethal or which target plants, including crops and vegetation. As noted above, the BTWC Fourth and Sixth Review Conferences affirmed that any use (i.e. against humans, animals or plants) inconsistent with permitted purposes would be an effective violation of the Convention.

(Fourth Report from the Foreign Affairs Committee, 2008–2009, Global Security: Non-Proliferation, Response of the Secretary of State for Foreign and Commonwealth Affairs, Cm 7692)

17/42
A Defence Minister wrote:

The UK's chemical protection programme is designed to protect against the use of chemical weapons. Such a programme is permitted by the Chemical Weapons Convention, with which the United Kingdom is fully compliant. Under the terms of the Convention, we are required to provide information annually to the Organisation for the Prohibition of Chemical Weapons (OPCW).

(HC Deb 12 March 2009 Vol 489 c23WS)

17/43
Cluster Munitions

Answering questions about Cluster Munitions, a Defence Minister wrote:

We will have eight years, from entry into force of the Convention on Cluster Munitions for the UK, to destroy all cluster munition stockpiles under UK jurisdiction and control. [An FCO Minister] said in another place on 3 June 2008 that it was his expectation

"that there will be no such weapons on British Territory at the end of the eight year period".

Concerning any cluster munitions stored on UK territory but under United States control, we are engaged with the United States in order to meet the eight year deadline. All UK cluster munition types have been withdrawn from service. A progressive UK cluster munition disposal programme has begun, with some munitions already destroyed. We expect that all UK stockpiles will be destroyed by 2013 which we anticipate will be four or five years ahead of the deadline.... All UK cluster munitions, prohibited once the Cluster Munition Convention enters into force, were withdrawn from operational service on 30 May 2008, when the Convention was adopted. All were immediately segregated for disposal to prevent use and transfer and some have already been destroyed. Those that are awaiting disposal are stored in a number of secure licensed munitions storage locations and, as such, all cluster munitions are fully accounted for at all times. The MOD has contractual control and oversight over all disposal contracts and disposal certificates are issued when each cluster munition has been destroyed. The MOD carries out checks on contractors to ensure compliance. There is no scope in the disposal contracts for a disposal contractor to do anything other than destroy the munitions. Furthermore, cluster munitions are recorded on the Department's inventory and explosives safety management IT systems, which means that they can be tracked and prevented from being inadvertently issued for either operational or training purposes. In withdrawing these munitions from service on 30 May 2008, the UK complied with the spirit of the Convention immediately and well ahead of ratification at which point the provisions of the Convention will become a legal requirement.

(HC Deb 23 February 2009 Vol 488 c25W)

17/44
In reply to a question about the implementation by the UK of the Oslo Convention on Cluster Munitions, a Minister wrote:

The Ministry of Defence immediately withdrew service cluster munitions prohibited by the convention from operational service following the adoption of the text of the convention on cluster munitions on 30 May 2008 and before its signature on 3 December 2008. Further, the MOD has already started a destruction programme that aims to destroy these munitions ahead of the deadline set out in the convention of eight years after its entry into force.

(HC Deb 30 March 2009 Vol 490 C887W)

17/45
A Minister wrote:

It is the Government's intention to ratify the Convention as soon as possible. In accordance with Article 9 of the Convention of Cluster Munitions, the criminal offences to enforce the Convention's prohibitions on use, development, production, stockpiling, retention and transfer of cluster munitions need to be in place before ratification. A Cluster Munitions Prohibitions Bill which will create the necessary criminal offences has a place in the Government's Draft Legislative Programme that was published on 29 June 2009.

(HL Deb 13 July 2009 Vol 712 c928)

17/46
A Minister said:

Article 9 of the [Cluster Munitions] Convention stipulates that states parties are required to prevent prohibited activities from taking place both on their territory and being engaged in by persons under their jurisdiction or control.... However, I reiterate that under no circumstances will any UK national ever use or produce cluster munitions. Furthermore, I can reassure the House that, in compliance with the Convention, no UK national will request the use of cluster munitions when the decision to do so is within their exclusive control.... Under Article 3 of the Convention we have an obligation to destroy the UK's stockpiles of cluster munitions. This is being taken forward. On 30 May, on the eve of adopting the Convention, the MoD proactively withdrew all its cluster munitions from service and began a destruction programme. Destruction of UK stocks is now well underway, with one third of total stocks already destroyed . . . this is an enormous task and should not be underestimated. There were in the region of 38 million submunitions held in UK stocks; to date we have destroyed nearly 13 million. We intend that the considerable majority, if not all, of our stocks will be destroyed by 2013. This will be well before the eight-year deadline that the states parties will have under the Convention. I am aware that there has been speculation about the fate of the stockpiles of cluster munitions that other countries may have on UK territory. Last June, [an FCO Minister] told the House that it was his expectation that there would be no permanent stockpiles of cluster munitions on UK territory at the end of the eight-year convention deadline. This is also my firm expectation.

Once it comes into force, the Convention will establish an effective framework for international co-operation on the clearance of cluster munitions' remnants and support for victims of cluster munitions. The Convention obliges states parties to support other states parties that are affected by cluster munitions. . . . The Convention obliges states parties to discourage the use of cluster munitions and encourage others to join, with the ultimate goal of universal global adherence. The Government are fully committed to a global convention and we are playing our part in supporting this important effort. At the Commonwealth Heads of Government Meeting, I was able to speak to a number of Commonwealth Ministers as part of our efforts to achieve this goal. Forty-seven of the 53 Commonwealth states have signed the Ottawa Convention [on Land Mines], but so far only 26 have signed the Convention on Cluster Munitions. We want to change that. At CHOGM, we co-sponsored with Australia a declaration inviting non-signatories to commit to signing the convention. Several countries associated themselves with the declaration, which is a useful step in advancing adherence to the convention within the Commonwealth. I shall write to all Commonwealth Foreign Ministers, represented in London by their High Commissioners, urging them to add their signatures to the Convention as quickly as possible. We intend to continue working closely with these countries to assist their signature and ratification. I have met representatives from Landmine Action and the Cluster Munition Coalition, who have agreed to support these efforts. To date, 103 countries have signed and 24 have ratified, but we know that there is a long road ahead . . . some of the major users and producers of cluster munitions have not yet joined the Convention. The Government will continue vigorously to promote the convention with those states whenever it is practical. . . . I should like to clarify what is required under the Convention on Cluster Munitions with regard to stockpiles. The Convention states:

"States Parties are required to destroy all stockpiles of cluster munitions under their "jurisdiction and control" ".

While US stockpiles on UK territory are under UK jurisdiction, they are not under our control. Notwithstanding that, there have been discussions with the United States on this matter . . . In July 2008, the US announced its new policy on cluster munitions that after 2018 the US will employ only cluster munitions containing submunitions, which after arming do not result in more than 1 per cent unexploded ordnance. As a result of this policy on cluster munitions and unintended harm to civilians, signed on 19 June 2008, our understanding is that the US has identified the cluster munitions on UK territory as exceeding operational planning requirements. These cluster munitions will be removed from sites in the UK in 2010 and from all UK territories by 2013.... On the timing of transparency, under the convention we will be required to submit a transparency report within 180 days of the convention entering into force. Thereafter, we will be obliged to present an annual report.

(HL Deb 8 December 2009 Vol 715 c994)

17/47
Landmines

In answer to a question about de-mining operations in the Falklands, a Minister wrote:

Immediately following the conflict, approximately 1,855 mines were removed and destroyed. In total, the 117 mined areas that remain cover just over 13 sq km and contain an estimated 20,000 land mines. Clearing these mined areas presents significant technical and environmental challenges, covering as they do a wide range of terrain including sand dunes, rock screes and peat. Under the Convention on the Prohibition of the Use, Stockpiling, Production and Transfer of Anti-personnel Mines and on their Destruction (Ottawa Convention), the UK has an obligation to clear these mined areas by March 2019. A Feasibility Study on the clearance of landmines in the Falkland Islands was completed in October 2007. In November 2008, the Government announced their decision to proceed with the clearance of selected mined areas. The Foreign and Commonwealth Office is now taking forward the procurement process to carry out this de-mining, and has established a National Mine Action Authority (which includes representatives from the Falkland Islands Government) to oversee this. The Foreign and Commonwealth Office issued a Prior Information Notice on 20 February 2009 for the contract which we will put out to tender. In the meantime, in full compliance with the Ottawa Convention, the mined areas are clearly marked, fenced and regularly monitored... Since the end of the conflict in 1982 there have been no deaths involving land mines in the Falkland Islands... No funding has been provided to the Falkland Islands for the purposes of de-mining. As the state party to the Ottawa Convention it is the responsibility of the Government to clear the mined areas in the Falkland Islands. There is a Ministry of Defence funded Joint Explosive Ordnance Disposal Detachment permanently based in the Falkland Islands that regular monitors the mined areas and disposes of mines that surface.

(HC Deb 27 March 2009 Vol 490 c810W)

17/48
Nuclear Weapons

The FAC asked about the use of nuclear weapons against a terrorist threat to use nuclear weapons against a UK target. An FCO official said:

I was . . . just going to remind the Committee of what was said about Trident in the 2006 White Paper, because it is sometimes misquoted or misinterpreted. What the Government said then about the rationale for wanting to retain the nuclear deterrent was that terrorists have an aspiration to get their hands on nuclear materials. The only route by which they would acquire that capability would be via proliferation from a state, and what we would be holding to account would be the state that might be tempted in the direction of that sort of proliferation. The Government have never said that they intended to direct nuclear weapons against a terrorist; they were simply setting out a wide range of ways in which they might want to retain a nuclear deterrent against the possibility of a nuclear state misusing its own nuclear weapons. (Q. 267)

(FAC, Fourth Report: Global Security: Non-Proliferation, HC222 (2009))

Part Seventeen: II. *The Law of Armed Conflict and International Humanitarian Law—Non-international armed conflict*

17/49
The Foreign Secretary was asked what account UK forces in Afghanistan had taken of the concerns about Afghan civilian casualties expressed by the Secretary General of the United Nations; and what steps are being taken to minimise such casualties. A Minister wrote:

We share the Secretary-General's concerns about civilian casualties, the vast majority of which are caused by the insurgency. We do everything we can to avoid civilian casualties but, despite our efforts to specifically target the insurgents, there are times when the ordinary people of Afghanistan are harmed by the conflict. We are deeply saddened by any civilian deaths in Afghanistan. We particularly regret incidents where civilians are killed as a result of actions by international forces. We continue to take incidents of civilian casualties very seriously. They present a real risk to the North Atlantic Treaty Organisation's International Security Assistance Force (ISAF) and international forces' presence and support in Afghanistan. ISAF has made strenuous efforts to reduce incidents. The UK welcomes the recent Tactical directive from the commander of ISAF which further tightens the rules of engagement in Afghanistan to cut civilian casualties. The new rules stress the need for proportionate use of force and for Afghan forces to take the lead in searching Afghan homes and religious sites unless a clear danger is identified.

(HC Deb 27 February 2009 Vol 488 c1192W)

17/50
The Defence Secretary was asked Secretary of State for Defence what steps his Department was taking to afford special protection from military action for Afghan citizens, with particular reference to women and children, as required under international humanitarian law. A Minister wrote:

UK personnel operate at all times under rules of engagement which ensure that force is used in accordance with international humanitarian law. This ensures that civilian casualties and damage to civilian infrastructure are minimised. This does not, however, restrict the inherent right of self defence that enables our military personnel to defend themselves. The rules of engagement are reviewed regularly to ensure that they remain effective and compliant with international law.

(HC Deb 19 May 2009 Vol 492 c1273W)

17/51
The Foreign Secretary was asked about discussions he had had with the Government of Sri Lanka about civilian deaths in the conflict there. An FCO Minister wrote:

[W]e are appalled at the recent reports of heavy fighting and civilian casualties. We condemn the killing of civilians in the strongest possible terms. During his recent visit to Sri Lanka with French Foreign Minister Kouchner, the Foreign Secretary made clear to the Sri Lankan Government that the safety of civilians must be paramount and that hostilities must end immediately. Most recently, the Foreign Secretary spoke to Sri Lankan Foreign Minister Bogollogama on 10,11 and 13 May 2009 to express our grave concern over the continued reports of heavy fighting and civilian casualties and to underline the urgent need for a pause in fighting to allow civilians to leave the conflict area safely.

(HC Deb 21 May 2009 Vol 492 c1499W)

Part Nineteen: Legal aspects of international relations and co-operation in particular matters

Part Nineteen: I.A. *Legal Aspects of International Relations and Co-operation in Particular matters - General economic and financial Matters—Trade*

19/1 (See also **5/33, 17/40**)
The Foreign Secretary was asked what the Government's policy was on the labelling of produce originating from territories occupied by *(a)* Morocco and *(b)* Israel. An FCO Minister wrote:

On the labelling of produce originating from territories occupied by Israel, various Government departments such as the Department for Business, Enterprise and Regulatory Reform, The Department for the Environment, Food and Rural Affairs, and the Food Standards Agency are working together to provide retailers with clearer voluntary guidance on labelling best practice for produce sourced from the occupied Palestinian territories, that comply with our European Commission and World Trade Organisation obligations. There are no comparable guidelines in place for commercial products originating from the disputed territory of Western Sahara. The Government, however, maintain the position that the Government of Morocco, as the 'de facto' administering power of Western Sahara, is obliged under international law to ensure that economic activities carried out under their administration do not adversely affect the interests of the people of Western Sahara.

(HC Deb 16 March 2009 Vol 489 c849W)

19/2

The Foreign Secretary was asked to confirm that the UK will push for and support the suspension of the generalized system of preference (GSP) plus trade benefits that Sri Lanka currently enjoys, and argue for that across the EU. He said:

I repeat that the European Commission has produced what is called a pre-report on GSP plus, and that our position is absolutely clear: Sri Lanka must respect its international human rights obligations to continue to benefit from GSP plus... when the Commission finally publishes its report, as opposed to its pre-report, there will be a maximum of two months before a final decision is taken. We will play a full part in ensuring respect for that principle....

Our position on the human rights aspect is that there are 27 international agreements that countries wishing to benefit from GSP plus need to adhere to, including on critical issues to do with children's rights, torture and so on. They must be adhered to for GSP plus to continue.

(HC Deb 20 October 2009 Vol 497 c767–768)

19/3

The UK representative said in the debate in the Sixth Committee of the General Assembly on the Report of the ILC (A/64/10) on the question of most favoured nation clauses:

The United Kingdom welcomes the work of the Study Group in seeking to clarify the scope of MFN clauses and to evaluate the extent to which the 1978 Draft Articles remain applicable today. As the Study Group notes, a substantial volume of jurisprudence has been generated since 1978 both within the World Trade Organisation and by tribunals in investment treaty arbitration. In addition, the United Kingdom is conscious that detailed studies on the interpretation and scope of MFN clauses have been undertaken by other international bodies, in particular the United Nations Conference on Trade and Development, and the Organisation for Economic Cooperation and Development, in the fields of trade and investment respectively. The United Kingdom is therefore concerned that the Working Group should avoid replication of this existing body of work. The United Kingdom believes that the Working Group should consider identifying whether outside of the economic sphere (trade and investment) MFN clauses have any relevance and if so whether, based on the existing research, any broad principles can be drawn in relation to the scope and application of MFN clauses. This would assist the Working Group in its assessment of the continuing relevance of the 1978 Draft Articles, the subject of proposed paper (ii). Such broad conclusions may of course be difficult to draw. As the United Kingdom noted in its statement at the 63rd Session [UKMIL 2008, **19/7**], the interpretation of MFN clauses by tribunals has been heavily dependent on the particular wording of the clause in question, and it is for this reason that the United Kingdom continues to have doubts as to whether the interpretation of such clauses is ultimately an area of law that is suitable for codification. Furthermore, the United Kingdom questions whether there is merit in the Working Group conducting the proposed analysis of the relationship between MFN and National Treatment, which is the subject of proposed paper (iii). The United Kingdom considers that the relationship between MFN and national treatment clauses must be considered in the specific contexts in which they arise (for example within the context of the WTO agreements or bilateral investment treaties) and that it would be difficult for the Working Group to draw any principles of general application.

(Sixth Committee, 64th Session of the United Nations General Assembly, 2 November 2009. Text provided by FCO)

19/4
A Minister said:

Reference was made to the international arms trade treaty, and it is important to recognise the important role that it will play in taking Government policy forward. We are playing a leading role in working towards a globally agreed, robust arms trade treaty. Since introducing the initial resolution at the United Nations back in December 2006, in which we called for work on such a treaty, we have worked closely with international partners, civil society and the defence industry. On 30 October, UN member states voted overwhelmingly in favour of an arms trade treaty, and that vote mandates preparatory committee meetings in 2010 and 2011 to work towards a UN conference in 2012, when the text of an arms trade treaty will be finalised. Clearly, a lot of work must be done in those committees to make the treaty a reality, but as . . . the Foreign Secretary said:

This groundbreaking achievement is a defining point in the work that has been led by a global coalition including the United Kingdom over the last three years towards a treaty that will save lives, safeguard human rights and support development across the world.

(HC Deb 5 November 2009 Vol 498 c344WH)

19/5
A Minister wrote:

The European Commission is pushing forward with negotiations towards a Multi-Party Trade Agreement with Colombia on behalf of the EU. The UK is leading efforts within the EU to ensure that any agreement with Colombia is linked to a robust human rights clause. This clause will enable us to suspend the agreement if it is breached, and will act as a catalyst for frank dialogue with Colombia on this issue. We believe that free trade agreements can help to create the right circumstances for improved stability, where human rights stand a better chance of flourishing. Denying Colombia access to the economic opportunities presented by the Multi-Party Trade Agreement would undermine this prospect.

(HC Deb 26 November 2009 Vol 501 c302W)

Part Nineteen: I.B. *Legal Aspects of International Relations and Co-operation in Particular Matters - General economic and financial matters—Loans*

19/6 (See also **6/109–112**)
The Foreign Secretary wrote the following in a Ministerial Statement on Sri Lanka:

At the International Monetary Fund (IMF), the UK took the decision in July not to support the stand-by arrangement for Sri Lanka. While we acknowledged the need to help Sri Lanka avoid a damaging balance of payments crisis that would have disproportionately affected the poorest and most vulnerable members of society, we judged that the risks of a default had diminished and that the humanitarian and political situations posed risks to implementation of the programme. The programme was passed by the IMF board and we will now turn our attention to monitoring the programme's implementation through a robust review process.

(HC Deb 13 October 2009 Vol 497 c18WS)

Part Nineteen: I.F. *Legal Aspects of International Relations and Co-operation in Particular Matters - General economic and financial matters—Development*

19/7
The Secretary of State for International Development wrote:

The Government remain committed to delivering 0.7 per cent. of GNI as official development assistance by 2013. We have recently announced plans to introduce legislation to ensure the commitment is met. In 2008 UK official development assistance stood at 0.43 per cent. of GNI in line with the trajectory set out in the 2007 comprehensive spending review and will reach at least 0.56 per cent. by 2010–11.

(HC Deb 21 October 2009 Vol 497 c1493W)

Part Nineteen: III. *Legal Aspects of International Relations and Co-operation in Particular Matters—Environment*

19/8
The Minister of State, Department of Energy and Climate Change wrote:

We closely follow the impact of policy announcements by the United States and other major countries on plans to mitigate their greenhouse gas (GHG) emissions in line with their legal obligations under the United Nations Framework Convention on Climate Change (UNFCCC). Under the Convention, parties are required periodically to report their climate policies and emissions inventories to the UNFCCC secretariat. We take a strong interest in these reports, and use the data presented to inform our understanding of countries' progress in reducing emissions through existing policies, and the further actions that will be required from countries in order to avoid dangerous climate change. The Government are also monitoring unilateral announcements by major countries on the mitigation actions that they expect to undertake in future. Current negotiations on the overall shape of a future international climate change agreement foresee the adoption at Copenhagen later this year of new, improved international rules for measuring, reporting and verifying the impact of countries' emissions reduction policies. We also actively monitor the longer term impact of mitigation actions on global concentrations of carbon dioxide and other GHGs in the atmosphere, including through research conducted by the Meteorological Office Hadley Centre. However, we would expect a lag of several years between any significant changes in greenhouse gas emissions and the measurable atmospheric effects that would result from this, due to inertia in the global climate system.

(HL Deb 2 July 2009 Vol 712 cWA67)

19/9
The Prime Minister said:

We have met the Kyoto targets. We have got the first climate change Act of any country in the world. We have committed ourselves to very radical cuts in emissions not only in the long term, but in the short term. We are fighting hardest to get an agreement in Copenhagen. I have said that I will go to Copenhagen; I want there to be an agreement in Copenhagen. It is based first on us agreeing a political understanding about how the treaty will be developed. We then need to agree on the intermediate targets. I think all countries will have to accept that they have got to make commitments, and we need to have a financial proposal such as the one that we have put forward. This will be discussed at the European Council this week, and I believe that the European Council will want to make progress. I believe Europe will have a position, which can then be put to Copenhagen.

(HC Deb 28 October 2009 Vol 498 c281)

19/10
A Minister wrote:

The Adaptation Fund was established under the Kyoto Protocol of the UNFCCC and launched at COP-7 in Marrakech, in 2001. Its aim was to finance concrete adaptation projects and programmes in vulnerable developing countries. The Board of the Adaptation Fund was then established in 2008. The Fund is expected to become operational before the climate change conference in Copenhagen at the end of this year. The Adaptation Fund has a unique mechanism for financing, which is not dependent on contributions from specific countries. Instead, it is financed by a market-based source of funding-a 2 per cent. levy on the proceeds of the Clean Development Mechanism (CDM), which was also established under the Kyoto Protocol. Nevertheless, the UK has been supporting the design and implementation of the Adaptation Fund both as a board member and through provision of £0.5 million start-up funding.

(HC Deb 2 November 2009 Vol 498 c755W)

Part Nineteen: V. *Legal Aspects of International Relations and Co-operation in Particular Matters—Technology*

19/11

An FCO Minister spoke about relations with Iran. He said:

So far, the fist [of Iran—President Obama had said that he would present an open hand to Iran, Ed.] has remained clenched, but there is still time for Iran to change its approach. Iran could, and should, choose to transform its relationship with the international community. Such a decision would benefit Iran and its people and the whole international community. However, to take advantage of the opportunities that would flow from such a change, Iran must face up to its responsibilities, many of which it currently chooses to ignore. We touched on the nuclear issue. Iran ignores its obligations to the UN and the International Atomic Energy Agency. It chooses to defy the will of both by continuing to enrich uranium, and refusing the IAEA the access that it seeks. Iran disregards its responsibilities; it supports terrorism and chooses to undermine stability and security in its own neighbourhood. Inside its borders, Iran pays no heed to the commitment that it has freely undertaken to its people to uphold international standards of human rights. The point is that Iran has choices to make and the opportunity to change course. On the nuclear file, Iran can suspend enrichment, take up the E3 plus 3 [UK, US, China, France, Germany and Russia, Ed] offer and enjoy the many benefits that will come from co-operating with the international community, rather than standing toe to toe with us and seeking further confrontation and isolation. Iran could pursue its legitimate interests in the region through legitimate means, and play a constructive rather than destructive role. On human rights, Iran could take steps to recover the prestige it claims for itself by guaranteeing the rights of its people. Our position is clear; we would like to have the opportunity of engaging in a positive and constructive relationship with Iran. We share interests across a wide range of issues, including promoting stability, security and economic development in Iraq and Afghanistan. If Iran took the opportunity and changed course, we could work together constructively. However, Iran's behaviour undermines our confidence, and makes a mockery of the claims that it makes for itself. Until Iran changes course, we will be uncompromising in calling on it to meet its obligations.

(HC Deb 4 March 2009 Vol 488 c274WH)

Part Nineteen: VIII. *Legal Aspects of International Relations and Co-operation in Particular Matters—Legal matters (for example judicial assistance, crime control, etc.)*

19/12

Arms Exports (See also **1/4**)

In a debate on arms export controls, a Minister said:

[W]e are coming to the end of the post-implementation review of the controls introduced in 2004. We are grateful for the input of the Committees, NGOs and industry stakeholders. All parties were struck by the collaboration that we managed to achieve together, and I look forward to that continuing. We will soon have completed implementation of most of the changes coming out of the review. We have taken significant steps to strengthen export controls where there has been concern, and to fulfil commitments and our responses to the public consultation. Hon. Members will be aware that we have introduced controls on sting sticks, and fully extended extraterritorial controls to UK persons anywhere in the world trading in small arms and man-portable air defence systems—MANPADS. We changed the controls on cluster munitions, subjecting them to the strictest controls, and we have controlled both extraterritorial trading by United Kingdom persons and trading within the United Kingdom, in addition to the full range of support activities. On 6 April, legislation will come into force to extend the fully extraterritorial trade controls to light weapons and to tighten controls on the transport of those weapons and similar goods of heightened concern between overseas destinations, and controls on their transit or transhipment via the UK. Officials have started work on pursuing our commitments on torture and military end-use controls at European level. Thanks to the positive and constructive engagement of our stakeholders, we have a strong package that will significantly enhance our controls where concerns have been expressed for a considerable time. I want to refer to some significant successes over the past year or so, and to respond fully to the many points that have been made during this debate. I was pleased that when I appeared before the Committee, I was able to announce that we were proceeding with plans for the introduction of civil penalties. I am firmly convinced of their value, and hope that we can obtain the necessary consensus in government so that the process of introducing a regime can begin in earnest. We have also introduced procedures for companies or individuals to have their registration for open general export licences withdrawn if they have a poor compliance record, or for other appropriate reasons, such as being convicted of export control-related offences. There have been two major successful prosecutions... John Knight... was convicted of transferring machine guns between Iran and Kuwait, and sentenced to four years' imprisonment with a confiscation order of £53,000. Mehrdad Salashoor was convicted of illegally exporting to Iran navigation equipment that could be adapted for use in missile guidance systems. He was sentenced to 18 months' imprisonment with a confiscation order of £433,000. On enforcement activity, we have increased the number of awareness events by 10 per cent. and the number of company training visits by 80 per cent. We are developing, and are about to launch, an online searchable database to improve access to publicly available licensing information. The industry and NGOs have been involved in the development and testing of the database, and we have offered to organise a demonstration for the Committees.... a directive to simplify the terms and conditions for the transfer of defence-related products in the EU was adopted by the European Parliament on 16 December. It will now be considered for adoption by the Council of Ministers. Due to the efforts of the UK delegation, which included the Export Control Organisation, and representatives negotiating the directive, the Government believe that there will be few practical implications for the UK export licensing system, which remains robust.... the important issue of end-use monitoring [was raised]. Our position remains that the best means of ensuring that goods are not diverted is to conduct a rigorous assessment at the licence application stage. That includes careful examination of the information on the proposed end use and end user of the goods... UK diplomatic posts are regularly asked to check the accuracy of the information in the end-user documentation submitted in support of an application. Should that assessment identify an unacceptable risk, the application will not be approved. The primary purpose of any monitoring of equipment once it has left the UK is to generate information to assist the risk assessment of other current or future applications that are similar. The Government believe that we already have adequate systems in place to do that. The use of military equipment in destinations of concern is monitored by UK overseas posts using a variety of information, including from the media, NGOs and intelligence reports. Those posts have standing instructions to report misuse of UK-origin defence equipment. Given that the ECO issues about 10,000 individual export licences a year and that, in addition, a substantial volume of exports are made under cover of the open individual and open general export licences, the Government do not have the resources to monitor routinely end use overseas. It simply would not be practical for every export to have a British civil servant attached to it or to have a British person in post, meeting it at the border... I wish to discuss briefly the no re-export clauses, a subject that was raised by several Members and mentioned during my appearance before the Committees. The Government remain unconvinced that it is necessary or feasible to require overseas entities to seek permission from the UK authorities in order to re-export items that are already outside the UK. Such a system would be onerous to operate and extremely difficult to enforce outside the UK's legal jurisdiction. In reality, re-export clauses would not increase our real-world powers; and we factor the risk of diversion or re-export to undesirable end users into our risk assessment at the application stage. We would not license the export unless it was consistent with the consolidated criteria. When applying for a seal, all exporters have to provide an undertaking from the end user that the goods will be used for the purposes stated in the undertaking. If the export is going to a consignee who intends to hold the goods in stock against future orders, he must state whether the goods will be re-exported from their original destination. In the latter case, that is factored into the licensing risk assessment.

(HC Deb 26 March 2009 Vol 490 cs165WH-170WH)

19/13
Drug-trafficking

The Foreign Secretary was asked what action had been taken to tackle drug-trafficking and to minimise money-laundering in the British Overseas Territories of Anguilla, Montserrat and the Turks and Caicos Islands. A Minister wrote:

Through the Governors of the respective Territories we work closely with the local police forces to help them develop and implement strategies to counter drug trafficking. Where appropriate we have provided financial support for these strategies, for example by providing co-funding for three retired UK police officers to establish the Drugs and Crime Task Force in Anguilla. We also support initiatives for cross territory and wider regional collaboration. My officials are working with regulators, police investigators and prosecutors in the Overseas Territories (OT) and have drawn up action plans tailored to each of the OT, which include projects to strengthen regulatory systems, laws and expertise. They also take into account independent evaluations of anti-money laundering and counter terrorist financing systems by the Caribbean Financial Action Task Force (CFATF). Departmental funding has been used to strengthen the Financial Crime Unit in the Turks and Caicos Islands (TCI) and to update the proceeds of crime law. Similar projects are underway in Anguilla and Montserrat. In addition, the Department is part-funding the new head of the Anguilla Financial Intelligence Unit, which has brought about increases in the reporting and investigation of suspected financial crimes. Training for financial investigators from Anguilla and Montserrat has been arranged and external consultants are helping to boost supervisory practice in these Territories. We are also working with the authorities in TCI to help them to respond to the recommendations in the November 2008 CFATF mutual evaluation report. We are working with Anguilla and Montserrat to help them prepare for their CFATF evaluations later this year.

(HC Deb 27 February 2009 Vol 488 cs1193W-1194W)

19/14
Extradite or Prosecute

The UK representative said in the debate in the Sixth Committee of the General Assembly on the Report of the ILC (A/64/10) on the question of the obligation to extradite or prosecute:

As stated on previous occasions, the United Kingdom's position continues to be that the obligation to extradite or prosecute arises as a result of a treaty obligation. We do not consider that we have yet reached the stage at which the obligation can be regarded as a rule or principle of customary international law. In view of the United Kingdom's position that any obligation to extradite or prosecute arises under the terms of international agreements, we consider that those terms must govern both the crimes in respect of which the obligation arises and the question of whether the custodial State has discretion as to whether to extradite or prosecute.

We continue to be of the view that further consideration by the International Law Commission of this area of law should begin with a systematic review of relevant international treaty provisions, domestic legislation and judicial decisions. We would support further work based on an analysis along these lines. We welcome the establishment of the open-ended Working Group to take forward the issues that may need to be addressed in the future work of the Special Rapporteur.

(Sixth Committee, 64th Session of the United Nations General Assembly, 2 November 2009. Text provided by FCO)

19/15
Georgia

The Minister for Europe wrote:

The UN Observer Mission in Georgia (UNOMIG) ceased all mandated activity on 16 June 2009. There are now no international military monitors operating in Abkhazia. The EU Monitoring Mission is mandated to operate in the whole of Georgia, but in practice has never had proper access to the separatist regions. We continue to press for this. The UK and partners are exploring options to strengthen the international presence in Abkhazia. The closure of UNOMIG has had no effect on the status of other UN agencies, such as the UN Children's Fund (UNICEF) and the UN High Commissioner for Refugees (UNHCR), who continue to operate in Abkhazia. Our embassy officials in Georgia have visited Abkhazia since the war, most recently in May 2009. We have supported the role of international monitors in investigating-where they can-allegations of human rights violations. This is especially relevant in the case of the increasingly exposed ethnic Georgian population in Abkhazia. We will continue to remind all parties of their obligations to protect human rights and to allow unhindered humanitarian access in areas they control as enshrined in the Sarkozy-Medvedev agreement. We will push them to deliver on this. The Organisation for Security and Co-operation in Europe (OSCE) military monitoring operation is due to close on 30 June 2009. The monitors currently operate in Georgian-controlled territory adjacent to South Ossetia. Prior to August 2008 they had access to South Ossetia, but they have never had access to Abkhazia. We continue to press Russia to re-engage on the Greek chairman's proposals regarding the OSCE Monitoring Mission in Georgia, which would allow OSCE monitors to work in South Ossetia. We are concurrently looking at options for an alternative OSCE presence working in Georgia on specific issues, not necessarily related to conflict.

(HL Deb 2 July 2009 Vol 712 cWA76)

19/16
Human Trafficking (See also **6/122**)

The Home Secretary was asked under what protocols her Department operated when managing people deemed to have been trafficked. A Minister wrote:

On 17 December 2008 we ratified the Council of Europe convention on action against trafficking in human beings. By April 2009 at the latest we will introduce a reflection period of 45 days and a renewable one year residence permit for identified victims of human trafficking. Additionally we are introducing formal identification measures under a national referral mechanism by which victims are systematically identified by a competent authority and referred to appropriate support. This will further strengthen our existing collaborative way of identifying, referring and supporting victims.

(HC Deb 26 January 2009 Vol 487 c94W)

19/17
A Justice Minister wrote:

The Government fund the Poppy project to provide specialist support to adult victims of human trafficking. Victims are provided with unconditional intensive support for an initial four-week period, with longer-term term services provided in return for co-operation with a criminal investigation. Victims are offered support with resettlement and have access to compensation through the courts and the Criminal Injuries Compensation Scheme. It is also open to victims to apply for protection through existing humanitarian and immigration routes. Eligibility for non-third sector public services is in line with existing immigration policy. The Government have ratified the Council of Europe Convention Action against Trafficking in Human Beings. This will enhance our existing measures by extending the reflection-period to a minimum of 45 days and introducing new renewable one-year residence permits for those co-operating with the authorities.

The temporary residence permits will allow recourse to public funds. It will also remain open to victims to apply to stay using the existing human rights and immigration protection routes.

(HC Deb 26 January 2009 Vol 487 c193W)

19/18

Replying to a debate on Human Trafficking, a Minister said:

This is an opportunity for me to set out what work the Government have done on the issue. The implementation of the Council of Europe Convention [Council of Europe Convention against Trafficking in Human Beings, No.197, 2005, Ed.] plays a crucial role in our overall strategy. Clearly, human trafficking is an important crime. It is important that we create an environment hostile to it in the UK, identify victims and take action as appropriate. We unveiled an action plan in March 2007...and updated it in July last year. [The Action Plan was further revised in October 2009, <www.crimereduction.homeoffice.gov.uk/humantraffickng.004.pdf>, Ed.] Ratification of the Council of Europe Convention is the first of 85 specific actions laid out in the plan. As part of our efforts to ratify and implement the Convention, we have made some significant decisions, including the granting to victims of the 45-day reflection period, but longer if necessary. [I was asked] how we would decide whether it should be longer. The answer is that it depends on individual circumstances, and that is why we need to rely on the expertise of the UK Human Trafficking Centre...We also offer one-year temporary residence permits in certain circumstances. Both measures go further than the minimum standards outlined in the convention, which are for 30 days and six months. We have therefore already set the bar higher, and I hope that European colleagues will learn from that. We are also setting up a national referral mechanism. It will be a nationwide system that will enable the proper and consistent identification of victims to ensure that they receive the necessary care and support. That applies to all victims of all ages—children as well as those over the age of 18...We will be making announcements in the near future about how that will work. We are working out the full details, but we will work collaboratively with all key external organisations, including non-governmental ones, whose expertise...has proved invaluable throughout, whether on the action plan, Pentameter or the Convention. We have made an announcement on the competent authority function. There has been some concern about having a single competent authority, but we are considering something that is multi-agency and we are working closely with other partners. It is important that we set off with a body that can do the job well and effectively, but, once things have been going for a while, we can always look at how it is working...it is important that we start as we mean to go on, with an organisation that can do the job effectively, identify victims and provide support. Several organisations can refer to it. If the police find someone, they can work with a local non-governmental organisation, and that body can refer to the UK centre. It is important that we get that right. The competent authority will be based at the Human Trafficking Centre, and that will be the key, central point of contact. The UK Border Agency is a separate but linked competent authority. The link with immigration is important, because trafficking is often raised during an asylum claim. It would be foolish to decouple the two issues. Immigration is not always an issue, but that is a sensible approach, and in my work on immigration, the issue often arises. We are applying the rules of the Convention. It would not be our intention to deport anyone who was identified as a victim, but I can obtain further clarification, if necessary. I think it is clear, however, that if somebody is identified as a victim, we would not intend to deport them. Many victims choose to return voluntarily, and we have assisted voluntary packages to help those young women—they are mostly young women—to return to their families, which is actually where they want to go. It is important to differentiate between deportation and removal, and voluntary removal is often beneficial for the victim.

(HC Deb 3 February 2009 Vo9l487 csWH176-WH178)

19/19
Iraq

The Defence Secretary was asked what factors he would take into account when making decisions on the number of troops to be deployed in Iraq. He wrote:

As the Prime Minister set out on 18 December 2008, *Official Report*, columns 1233–1235, we will complete our remaining military tasks in Iraq by 31 May 2009 and move to a normal bilateral defence relationship. As part of the future relationship, the government of Iraq have indicated that they would like the UK to continue to provide military training and education. The precise scope of this training and education will inform decisions on the number of UK service personnel in Iraq after 31 July. Decisions will also be based on advice from our military commanders and conditions on the ground. On the basis of our discussions with the Iraqi government to date, I anticipate that this future activity would involve no more than around 400 UK service personnel, which military commanders judge should be sufficient to support the delivery of these tasks safely and effectively.

(HC Deb 2 February 2009 Vol 487 c877W)

19/20
The Minister for Defence issued the following Ministerial Statement:

I am making a statement on the UK's bilateral agreement with the Government of Iraq on defence training and maritime support . . . The House will be aware that the UK concluded combat operations in Iraq on 30 April, and that our combat forces were withdrawn by the end of July in accordance with our previous arrangement with the Government of Iraq. As the Prime Minister announced on 18 December last year, the Iraqi Government have requested our continued military assistance, particularly in officer training, naval training and maritime support. The two Governments therefore concluded an agreement concerning naval training and maritime support to Iraqi forces in June. Since then, the agreement has been considered by the Iraqi Council of Representatives and received its Third Reading on 13 October. The agreement will now enter into force once both parties have completed their parliamentary procedures and exchanged diplomatic notes. . . . the Defence Secretary wrote to Opposition spokesmen and the Chair of the House of Commons Defence Committee last month to explain our intention to bring the agreement into force as soon as the Iraqi Government are ready. Training of the Iraqi Navy has been paused since June, and it is important to resume this activity as soon as possible to ensure that they quickly develop the capacity to protect their own territorial waters and the offshore oil platforms which are so vital to Iraq's economic revival. A prompt resumption of training would allow our Royal Navy trainers, who have been held at readiness since June, to return to the task that they are so adept at delivering. The agreement was published as a Command Paper and laid before both Houses on 25 September. However, due to our summer recess, it will not now be possible to allow the agreement to lay for the full 21 sitting day period before exchanging diplomatic notes. Since it is agreed that our training activity should resume as soon as possible, and having kept Parliament informed of progress throughout the recess, the Government intend to notify the Iraqi Government within the next few days that the UK is ready to bring this agreement into force. [The agreement referred to is Agreement concerning the Training and Maritime Support to the Iraqi Forces by and between the Government of the United Kingdom of Great Britain and Northern Ireland and the Government of the Republic of Iraq, Cm 7707, for coming into force see Article 11. Ed.]

(HC Deb 22 October 2009 Vol 497 c68WS)

19/21
Libya (See also **4/3**)

The Minister for Europe wrote:

Throughout the 1980s and 1990s, the Libyan Government were linked to a number of terrorist organisations, including the Provisional IRA. Libya's support for international terrorism defined its relations with the western world. As honourable and right honourable Members will recall, WPC Yvonne Fletcher's murder in April 1984 led us to cut off diplomatic relations. The bombing of a nightclub in West Berlin in 1986 was followed by US air strikes on Tripoli and Benghazi. When evidence emerged supporting allegations that Libyan intelligence officers had been involved in the bombing of Pan Am flight 103 over Lockerbie in December 1988, the UN Security Council demanded that Libya hand over the accused and imposed sanctions when it failed to comply. During the 1990s, there was evidence from a range of sources that the Libyans were also actively pursuing a range of nuclear, chemical and biological weapons programmes as well as the development of ballistic missiles. Libya was a pariah state whose activities posed a clear and unambiguous threat to international peace and stability and to our own security in this country. The story of the past decade has been very different. Libya has abandoned its support for international terrorism and stopped its pursuit of WMDs in a series of events that merit the term "unforeseeable". In 1998, the US and UK Governments put forward a detailed joint proposal for the trial of the two accused of the Lockerbie atrocity. Our joint commitment to close and transparent working in all matters has continued throughout this case. We reported our proposal to the United Nations Secretary-General, gained the support of the United Nations Security Council and, in 1999, persuaded the Libyans to surrender the two accused to a specially constituted court in the Netherlands where a Scottish panel of judges, without a jury, would try the accused under Scots law. Libya also agreed to pay $10 million compensation to each of the families of the victims, whatever their nationality, if the defendants were convicted. Megrahi was found guilty under Scottish law by the court in 2001, and his conviction was upheld on appeal in 2002. Against this background and, as I will explain later, in particular after the Libyan admission of responsibility for WPC Fletcher's murder, the UK restored diplomatic relations in July 1999. The long-term aim was clear: the normalisation of relations with Libya. On 19 December 2003, following months of secret discussions with the UK and the US, the Libyans announced that they would eliminate their weapons of mass destruction and nuclear weapon programmes and restrict the range of their missiles. They also agreed to immediate international inspections and to be bound by all the relevant international agreements, which they now are....

The UK had a model agreement, based on Council of Europe arrangements, which was the starting point for negotiation on our prisoner transfer agreements with any country, and which provided the starting point for negotiations with the Libyans. Four points are relevant. First, a PTA provides for a prisoner transfer, not prisoner release. Secondly, it provides a framework for transfer, not a right to transfer. Thirdly, it cannot be used when appeals, including by the prosecuting authority, are outstanding, as in this case. Fourthly, Ministers in the sentencing jurisdiction, in this case Scotland, have an absolute right to veto any transfer. This standard draft has no provision for any carve-out for any named prisoner. However, the Scottish Executive made strong representations for us to seek to alter the standard PTA so as specifically to exclude Mr Megrahi. The UK negotiating team, led by the Ministry of Justice, sought in good faith to achieve this goal. The Libyans insisted that the only PTA that they would sign was a PTA without any exclusions. So the Government had a clear choice: we could agree to a standard PTA with no exclusions, retaining for Scottish Ministers an absolute veto over any request for prisoner transfer in the case of Megrahi—a veto which they used in August this year—or we could have ended the negotiations to prevent an application for prisoner transfer. This would have set back our wider national and commercial interests that flowed from normalised relations, as the Justice Secretary has made clear. Since the PTA involved no prejudice to the rights of the Scottish Executive, nor pressure on the Scottish Executive, the Government decided that it was right to go ahead. The PTA took effect in April 2009.

(HL Deb 12 October 2009 Vol 713 cs37–38)

19/22
The Secretary of State for Justice wrote:

The prisoner transfer agreement between the United Kingdom and Libya was one of four agreements in the field of judicial cooperation signed by the United Kingdom and Libya on 17 November 2008. Signature of these agreements is a tangible sign of the normalisation of the relationship between Libya and the United Kingdom and between Libya and the wider international community following its renunciation of international terrorism and weapons of mass destruction. In negotiating the prisoner transfer agreement account was taken of the impact of the agreement across a range of issues, including trade. However, there was no deal between the UK and Libya to secure the transfer of any individual in return for commercial contracts, or otherwise.

(HC Deb 2 November 2009 Vol 498 c742W)

19/23
Mutual Legal Assistance

A Minister wrote:

Parts of the 1959 [European] Convention [on Mutual Assistance in Criminal Matters] undertake to give the widest measure of mutual assistance possible within domestic law. The MLA [Mutual Legal Assistance] process relies on good faith, mutual trust and a common interest in fighting crime. MLA arrangements between the UK and countries designated in this order have been good and ratification of the second additional protocol should only strengthen those relations. If any problem arises in relation to the MLA, the aim will be to deal with these problems at official level and to escalate them to a ministerial level if necessary. If that does not prove to be successful were there to be a problem, there is a provision in the second additional protocol, Article 29, to support the friendly settlement of any problem arising out of the application of the convention and its protocols through the European Committee on Crime Problems of the Council of Europe.... Ratification of the second additional protocol is necessary for the UK to be able to access the full range of mutual legal assistance available under it. It provides a framework for a broad range of mutual legal assistance and is specifically available to states that have ratified it. This includes assistance in relation to joint investigation teams, covert investigations and controlled deliveries. The protocol also provides a number of operational benefits. By requiring process to be sent directly to individuals and by allowing direct transmission of mutual legal assistance requests by prosecutors, bureaucracy is reduced and the entire mutual legal assistance process expedited. It is important for the UK to show its commitment to MLA internationally and the importance that it attaches to it as a tool in the fight against international crime.

(HL Deb 9 December 2009 Vol 715 cGC67)

19/24
NATO

The Minister for Defence wrote:

Collective defence and deterrence remain NATO's core purpose. Under Article V of the Washington treaty, an armed attack against any ally is considered an attack against all 28. Threat assessments and the requirement for contingency planning are reviewed as required, and are routinely considered in the North Atlantic Council, NATO's Military Committee and Allied Command Operations. With regard to the Baltic, NATO allies continue to conduct air policing in the region, with quick reaction alert aircraft operating out of Lithuania. As part of a UK initiative, Defence Ministers agreed in June that the NATO Response Force should be given an overt Article V territorial defence role including in the three Baltic states. In this capacity, the UK would support the NATO Response Force exercising in the Baltic region.

(HL Deb 12 November 2009 Vol 714 cWA222)

19/25
A Minister said:

[I]t is clear that Article 5 of the treaty, as affirmed by the Declaration on Alliance Security at the Strasbourg summit, will remain the core purpose of NATO, binding us to defend any nation within NATO which is under attack. That does not gainsay the fact that new forms of terrorism mean not only that we can have a defensive role but that we should be able to go on deployable operations. It is not a choice of one or the other. Threats to our security are continually evolving and are likely to become increasingly complex. NATO must be willing and able respond to these threats whenever possible.

(HL Deb 25 November 2009 Vol 715 c362)

19/26
UK/US Extradition agreement

During a debate on the operation of the 2003 Extradition Act, a Minister said:

I disagree profoundly about there being an absence of any safeguards, but I shall come on to that shortly, and I certainly reject the suggestion that the extradition arrangements between the UK and the US, as set out in the 2003 Act and in the treaty, are somehow unbalanced. That argument has traditionally been made on the following basis. First, it is argued that the evidential requirement placed on US authorities seeking to extradite people from the UK is somehow less burdensome than the evidence that the UK is expected to produce to extradite people from the US. Historically, all requests by countries to extradite people from the UK had to provide prima facie evidence.... prima facie evidence is evidence that if taken at face value would be enough to convict someone. This was a much stronger requirement than some other nations demanded for UK extradition requests. The requirement was dropped for all EU member states, signatories to the 1957 European Convention on Extradition and other trusted international partners with mature judicial systems such as Canada, New Zealand and Australia. UK courts instead asked for "reasonable suspicion"—in other words, the same level of evidence required by the magistrates court to issue an arrest warrant in the UK. Following the introduction of the 2003 Act, the relaxation of the evidence requirement was extended to cover other trusted extradition partners including, but not limited to, the US. That is hugely significant, because it means that the UK and the US now demand of each other essentially the same level of evidence. The imbalance was prior to the change, not after it.... The US and the UK have different legal systems. I am sure that there are no hon. Members who think that we could put the two legal systems together and—hey presto!—get similar definitions. However, what we ask for in demonstrating reasonable suspicion is as follows: the "circumstances of the case being such that a reasonable man"—this language is not gender-friendly—"acting without passion or prejudice would fairly have suspected the person of having committed the offence". That is what we in this country apply. The US asks in its legal terminology for "probable cause"—this dates back to the Constitution, so it has always been the case and was not developed as part of the treaty—which is defined as "facts and circumstances which are sufficient to warrant a prudent person to believe a suspect has committed, is committing, or is about to commit a crime". Those two definitions are about as close as they can be in any two different legal systems.... The Home Secretary is then legally obliged to order that person's extradition, except in three specific circumstances set out in law: where it is possible that the person who is to be extradited could be sentenced to death if convicted; where there are inadequate arrangements in place in that country to prevent someone's being also charged with an offence that was committed prior to extradition and not included in the request that led to their extradition; and where the person who is to be extradited was previously extradited to the UK from another country and that country has not consented to any further extradition. If none of these circumstances apply, the Home Secretary must order extradition.... The individual can then appeal against the decision of the magistrates court and the Home Secretary in the High Court. If their appeal fails, they can appeal it in the other place. If that fails, there is then a legal duty on the UK Government to extradite the individual within 28 days. But within that time, the person in question can also refer their case to the European Court of Human Rights, which will look at whether the extradition would breach that person's human rights. If the court rules that an extradition would not breach their rights, the UK is legally obliged to continue with the extradition. So there are safeguards at every single stage.

Following these failed appeals, only if powerful and compelling evidence comes to light that demonstrates clearly that the extradition would breach our obligations under the European Convention on Human Rights—for example, a life-threatening illness—can the Home Secretary halt the extradition. In doing so, he or she must apply strict legal tests to determine whether the new information about the subject's mental or physical health would mean that their human rights would be breached should the extradition continue. If the case does not meet that test, they cannot halt the extradition, although their decision not to do so can be challenged in the courts.

(HC Deb 15 July 2009 Vol 496 c330–335)

19/27
Peacekeeping

The Foreign Secretary was asked when the Armstrong Formula was introduced in relation to peacekeeping costs; and when and for what reasons its usage was withdrawn. The Foreign Secretary wrote:

The Armstrong formula was introduced in 1984 during a period of relative stability in UN peacekeeping. Vote responsibility for all peacekeeping operations rested with the Foreign and Commonwealth Office (FCO) and money was annually allocated to the FCO in the public expenditure survey to meet these costs. Under the Armstrong formula, in the event of an unforeseen increase that could not be met in-year from within existing funds, and subject to Treasury agreement, the FCO had recourse to Treasury's central contingency reserve. Peacekeeping activities increased sharply in the early and mid 1990s, and peace support operations became more complex, requiring a broader range of political, military, development and economic activities. In 2001 two new tri-departmental Conflict Prevention Pools (the Africa and Global Conflict Prevention Pools) were established with strands for both peacekeeping and programme activity. Under current arrangements, the first £374 million of assessed contributions are met by

HM Treasury and costs above that are borne by FCO, the Ministry of Defence and the Department for International Development from the Conflict Pools and/or from within departmental expenditure limits.

(HC Deb 16 December 2009 Vol 502 c1230W-1231W)

19/28
Piracy (See also **11/10–11, 16–24**)

A Minister wrote:

The UK armed forces have provided a colonel to the UN political office in Somalia. We have also provided staff officers on request for short periods of time to support the AU Mission in Somalia (AMISOM), and we provide training assistance to AMISOM forces before deployment. The UK is also carrying out training and support activity with countries in the region in order to reduce the threat of terrorist activity. We are providing considerable support to counter-piracy operations off the coast of Somalia. The Royal Navy is contributing two frigates and a support tanker, as well as sizeable contributions to all of the operation headquarters. Some 320 members of the armed forces are specifically engaged in countering piracy as part of the EU operation ATALANTA and NATO Operation OCEAN SHIELD. A further 560 are contributing to maritime security in the region within NATO and the combined maritime forces, including countering smuggling and piracy. MOD is looking to enhance international operations underway in and around Somalia, and is working with our international colleagues on the best way in which we can support security sector development for the Somali Transitional Federal Government. These considerations include manpower enhancements in niche capacities where UK expertise can make a difference.

(HC Deb 29 October Vol 498 2009 c499W)

19/29
Russia

The Government were asked whether they have made an assessment of the military exercises held in western Russia and Belarus during October. The Minister for Defence wrote:

The military exercises held during the period 18 to 29 September in western Russia and Belarus involved troops from the Russian Federation and Belarus. Belarus notified this exercise to the OSCE, as required by the terms of the Vienna Document 1999, and invited observers from neighbouring countries and diplomatic representatives based in Belarus to attend. No UK observer attended this year. Exercises of this nature are routinely assessed by the MoD.

(HC Deb 12 November 2009 Vol 714 cWA233)

19/30
Status of Forces Agreement

The Defence Secretary was asked a number of questions about US use of the base at Menwith Hill and the facilities at Fylingdales. A Minister wrote:

The use of RAF Menwith Hill by the United States Visiting Force and US Agencies is governed by the terms of the NATO Status of Forces Agreement of 1951 and other confidential arrangements between the UK and US.... The Space-Based Infrared Red System (SBIRS) facilities at RAF Menwith Hill are ready for operation. The operational date for SBIRS is a matter for the United States, but is unlikely to be before 2010.

In support of the US missile defence system, the UK provides missile early warning information from the radar at RAF Fylingdales, and allows the US to route early warning satellite data via a satellite downlink at RAF Menwith Hill.

(HC Deb 30 March 2009 Vol 490 c894W)

TABLE OF CASES

INDEX

The manufacturer's authorised representative in the EU for product safety is Oxford University Press España S.A. of el Parque Empresarial San Fernando de Henares, Avenida de Castilla, 2 – 28830 Madrid (www.oup.es/en or product.safety@oup.com). OUP España S.A. also acts as importer into Spain of products made by the manufacturer.

www.ingramcontent.com/pod-product-compliance
Ingram Content Group UK Ltd.
Pitfield, Milton Keynes, MK11 3LW, UK
UKHW021500220926
475862UK00003B/61
* 9 7 8 0 1 9 9 5 9 7 0 2 4 *